Wine

André Dominé

Wine

Photographs
Armin Faber
Thomas Pothmann

Authors
Eckhard Supp
David Schwarzwälder
Anthony Rose
Dunja Ulbricht
Hélène Jaeger
Ulrich Sautter
Joachim Krieger
Patrick Fiévez
Sabine Rumrich
Wolfgang Faßbender
Steffen Maus
Beate Berkelmann-Löhnertz
Michael Ben-Joseph
Klaus Feiten
Hartwig Holst

BARNES & NOBLE BOOKS

NEW YORK

Endpaper:
Detail from a Roman mosaic
Vine in a crater
Archeological Museum, El Djem, Tunisia
© A.K.G./Photo: Erich Lessing

Frontispiece:
Juan de Espinosa, *Still life with grapes,*
Oil on canvas, 83 × 62 cm,
Musée du Louvre, Paris
© A.K.G., Berlin/Photo: Gilles Mermet

Notes on abbreviations used in the entries on
Select Producers

→　　　= Specially recommended
*–**** = Grading system for wines

The standard unit of volume in this book is the U.S. gallon
which is the equivalent of 128 fl. oz.

© 2004 KÖNEMANN*, an imprint of Tandem Verlag GmbH, Königswinter

This edition published by Barnes & Noble, Inc., by arrangement with KÖNEMANN*

2004 Barnes & Noble Books

M 10 9 8 7 6 5 4 3 2 1

ISBN 0-7607-6154-X

Creative and Publishing Director: Peter Feierabend
Art Direction: Sabine Vonderstein
Project Management: Sabine Baumgartner
Editorial Team: Uta Büxel, Kordula Esser, Ulla Wöhrle
Specialist Advisor: Dr. Christa Hanten
Indexes: Christoph Eiden
Cartography: Studio für Landkartentechnik, Detlef Maiwald

Original Title: Wein

For the English edition:
Translation from German: Paul Aston, Helen Atkins, Peter Barton, Anthea Bell, Susan Cox, Richard Elliott, Harriet Horsfield,
Susan James, Eithne McCarthy, Michele McMeekin, Martin Pearce, Michael Scuffil, Christine Smith, and Anthony Vivis in
association with Cambridge Publishing Management, Cambridge, U.K.
Editorial Team: Catherine Hurley, Annie Jackson, and Emma Johnson-Gilbert in association with Cambridge Publishing Management
Typesetting: Sheila Kirby for Cambridge Publishing Management
Project Management: Jackie Dobbyne and Sheila Hardie for Cambridge Publishing Management
Project Coordinator: Nadja Bremse-Koob

For the new, updated edition:
Translation from German: Susan James, Eileen Martin in association with Cambridge Publishing Management
Proofreading: Tammi Reichel for A-P-E International; Alison Kelt and Kevin Parnell for Cambridge Publishing Management
Typesetting: Paul Queripel for Cambridge Publishing Management
Project Management: Karen Beaulah and Mine Ali for Cambridge Publishing Management

*KÖNEMANN is a registered trademark of Tandem Verlag GmbH

Printed in Germany

CONTENTS

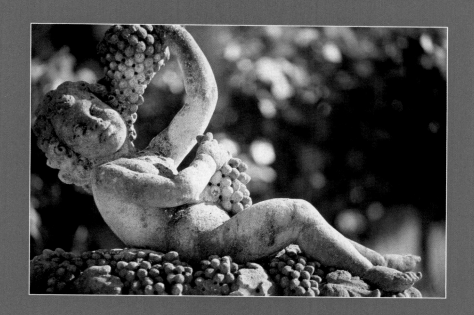

André Dominé, Eckhard Supp, Dunja Ulbricht

A HISTORY OF
ENJOYING WINE

The Many Pleasures of Wine

As increasing numbers of people in an ever-growing number of countries are becoming interested in wine, the drink has taken on a new role. Sharing a bottle with friends, colleagues or relatives is no longer simply a pleasant way of creating a congenial and relaxed atmosphere: wine itself is becoming a source of encounters with new people and new experiences.

Today, wine is part of enjoying life – for women and men, and all classes of society.

The times when good wine was the preserve of a social elite are, thankfully, well and truly past. Nowadays, all wines are accessible to everyone, at least in principle, as even the most exclusive vintages can be sampled by anyone who is so inclined, either at one of the increasingly common tasting events, in one of the many tasting clubs that have been set up, or by buying a bottle with like-minded friends to discover together what the quality and character of a famous wine is all about.

Wine—both a cult and a cultural drink—has also become more egalitarian in that never before in its history has such a huge, high-quality range been available to so many people. The sheer number of different wines from which to choose offers consumers an interesting point for comparison. A semi-luxury item, wine differs from all other agricultural products in that its infinite varieties far outnumber even those of cheese.

Whether you simply follow your nose or are guided by information and advice received, you may well find that you have questions about wine and would like to know more. This book deals in detail with all aspects of the subject, including the best way to drink a particular bottle, its potential for cellaring, grape varieties and vineyards, harvesting and fermentation, methods of production and maturation, and the origins of wine, as well as individual countries and regions.

Knowing what you are drinking enhances the pleasure, and every wine has its own story. With simple table wines, this is usually limited to the grape variety and region of origin. In the case of a great wine, however, it leads us to a specific vineyard and a tradition that often will have been followed for generations. With manually produced wines from regions whose potential has only been demonstrated in recent years or decades, the story may lie with the wine producer personally. Wine is increasingly cited as a reason for visiting a specific location, be it a traditional vine-growing area with historic estates or a region that is only just beginning to achieve recognition, giving rise to personal encounters with other peoples, landscapes, and cultures.

The New Age of Wine

The euphoria that has gripped the world of wine is the result of developments that began in the 1950s. Until then, wine, whether a glorious

The strictest hygiene in the winery is essential for the development of wine as a popular consumer product.

Many wine producers in the famous village of Hautvillers near Épernay adorn their houses with signs reflecting an aspect of their work.

vintage or a crude, low-quality variety, was seen simply as an intoxicant or as one more part of the diet, depending on social circumstance.

The wine producers' situation became particularly desperate from the end of the 19th century to the middle of the 20th century. A series of infections, culminating in the catastrophic phylloxera epidemic, decimated almost every vineyard. Then, just when the replanted vines were producing their first good yields, economic crises and war brought about a serious slump in sales. Against such a background, the desire for a secure income and an effective means of protection against pests and diseases was entirely understandable. Indeed, these became the recurring themes of agriculture in general after 1945, and are scarcely less influential today. Once the use of artificial fertilizers, chemical agents and productive clones had enabled growers to achieve the necessary yields, attention turned primarily to the cellars where the wine was produced, and undoubted progress was made in terms of hygiene and temperature control.

Nevertheless, the wines from the famous estates and younger wines from a select few producers who followed their own tradition and philosophy continued to serve as a yardstick. In the 1970s, however, a new way of thinking began to gain acceptance, recognizing that high quality could only be achieved by reducing

yields and concentrating on the optimal ripeness of the grape—an endeavor in which modern technology would play only an incidental role. Aided by favorable economic conditions, this brought about a fundamental change in the entire world of wine. In the classic wine-producing regions it was most readily evident in completely renovated and redesigned cellars, whereas in the countries of the New World, it led to a rise in new estates and cellars being established. This dynamism continued during the 1980s and 1990s. As a result, increasingly convincing wines gradually began to appear on the market, where they were greeted ever more enthusiastically by the consumer. Not only did demand for top-quality wines rise, but the quality of the simpler wines also continued to improve. A new genre of publishing sprang up, providing an ever-growing number of interested consumers with increasingly detailed information.

In a parallel development, the trend spread to what had been less well known or little recognized winemaking countries and regions, whose native growers or foreign investors were keen to show that great wines could be produced there.

Even though the results are frequently as disappointing as ever, more and more of today's wines are being tailored to the general market, industrially produced using all the technological, enological and economic means available. This often gives rise to perfectly pleasant bulk-productions, which are enhanced using all sorts of tricks, both permitted and otherwise. Here we see the dividing line running through the world of wine, although the boundary is somewhat fluid: on one side are the industrially produced wines, and on the other those produced by manual methods which, increasingly, are based on an awareness of environmental issues. Only the latter guarantee the diversity and richness of enjoyment and experience that an interest in wine has to offer. It is to these wines and their producers, and to the wine lovers that seek them out, that this book is dedicated.

A Long History: Wine in Antiquity

The development of viticulture is inextricably linked with the birth of European civilization and culture, particularly in the Mediterranean region. It is likely that nomadic peoples were fermenting wild grapes and berries into wine as early as 6,000–7,000 years ago. With the transition to a settled existence, grapevines, along with olives and figs, became the first wild fruits to be cultivated by man. Although the existence of vinifera plantations can be conclusively proved only from the 4th millennium BC in Egypt and Mesopotamia and from around 2500 BC in the Aegean, there are indications that there were rudimentary vineyards in the Near East as early as the 6th millennium BC. The oldest known tools and vessels which may have been used for producing wine were made in the 5th and 6th millennia BC in the region north of the Caucasus (present-day Georgia and Armenia), and in the 4th millennium BC in Persia.

The origin of the word "wine" is not absolutely clear. Its derivation can be traced back to the Latin *vinum*, which itself comes from the Greek *oinos* or *woinos*, but that is the extent of linguistic evidence. What is certain, however, is that the cradle of viticulture was the eastern Mediterranean or the Caucasus, and that it first began to flourish in Pharaonic Egypt. Under the Pharaohs, knowledge of viticulture and winemaking was meticulously expanded, and the

Egyptian mural from the tomb of Nakht at Thebes. 15th century BC.

Ancient Egyptian depictions of grapes and viticulture reveal the importance of wine during the age of the Pharaohs. Relief fragment, Amarna period, about 1350 BC (found at Hermopolis)

Egyptians began to extract the precious grape juice using pressing methods that remained unchanged for thousands of years.

From Egypt to Greece

The Nile Delta also witnessed the first flowering of the wine trade. Long caravans and fast ships brought their liquid cargo to the most important trading centers of the Mediterranean. There is a (not uncommon) view among historians that the foundations of our modern economy—its money, contracts, payment systems, courts, accounting procedures and commercial professions, even our way of counting and measuring time—were developed as a result of the wine trade from Pharaonic Egypt.

Ancient Greece was the next stage in the vine's conquest of the ancient world. The Minoans on Crete had close cultural and economic ties with the Egyptians, and probably forged the first link between Egypt and Greece. It is also possible, however, that viticultural knowledge reached Greece via Asia Minor or Thrace. Whatever the case, we know that wine became an important part of Greek culture in the second half of the 2nd millennium BC. Vines were planted throughout ancient Greece, and the islands of the Aegean were famous for the resulting produce both within the country and beyond. Chios, the Bordeaux of the ancient world, sent exports as far as Egypt and present-day Russia, and the wines of Thasos, Lesbos, and Rhodes also enjoyed a good reputation. Wines from Lesbos were matured under a thin layer of FLOR YEAST, in a similar fashion to sherry, but in other parts of the country it was usual to improve the smell and taste of wine with spices, honey, resin, and other fragrant substances. The Greek philosopher and scientist Theophrastus (4th century BC) recognized the important interrelation between grape variety, mesoclimate, and soil quality, and even the Romans, centuries later, were aware that Greek grape varieties were synonymous with low yields and thus higher quality wines.

Wine was so important to the Greeks that they declared it a divine gift: Dionysus, or Bakchos (the Roman Bacchus), a popular deity from Asia Minor, was supposed to have created the vine and used his divine power to make wine, milk, and honey flow from the ground. It was said that he freed man from his day-to-day worries with this lush vegetation—thanks in no small part to the intoxicating effects of wine.

The Early Wine Trade Shapes the Economy

Following their decisive conquest of territories throughout the Mediterranean region during the first half of the 1st millennium BC, the Greeks

Amphora by the Amasis painter from Athens. Around 530 BC. Antiquities collection of the University of Würzburg Martin von Wagner Museum.

introduced viticulture to their new colonies: Sicily, southern Italy and the south of France saw the development of new European vines. Southern Italy rose to the status of OINOTRIA or "wine land" for the Greeks, a designation that became *Enotria* under the Romans, who planted vines throughout Italy as early as the 3rd century BC. The Romans not only turned viticulture into a fully developed branch of trade managed according to economic criteria, but also brought it to central Europe.

The most important center of the wine trade in Italy had long been Pompeii, from where wines were exported even to the far-off Bordeaux region. When the city was destroyed by the volcanic eruption of 79 BC, the Romans made great efforts to develop viticulture in all parts of the Empire, to such an extent that in the Roman heartland, modern day Lazio, almost all cultivable land was stocked with vines. This prompted the Emperor Domitian to forbid the planting of any further vineyards—an edict that remained in force for almost two hundred years.

From the Roman Wine Empire to Plutocratic Florence

Marcus Aurelius Probus was the first to lift Domitian's ban in order to ensure his troops in the northern and eastern provinces were supplied with wine. He ordered intensive viticulture along the Mosel and the Danube, paving the way for the modern vine-growing regions of Germany and Austria. Trier and Bordeaux, already important export centers for the Empire's more northerly colonies, now became centers of viticulture in their own right, which made the task of supplying Imperial outposts with wine significantly easier, both in financial and logistical terms.

In Spain, the south of France, and along the Rhône, the Romans were able to build on the work already done by the Phocaeans, a Greek people who founded the city of Marseille (Massilia). As they consolidated their Empire, repelling or subjugating Gauls, Celts, and Teutons, the Romans planted large areas with vines almost everywhere they went. They imported new varieties of vine or improved what was already in place, spreading their knowledge of winemaking and its associated paraphernalia, such as the press, the amphora, and even the wooden barrel. However, neither the wines from Marseille, nor the majority of

Left
Fresco from Herculaneum depicting a banquet. National Museum, Naples

Right
This fresco of Bacchus, covered with grapes, standing in front of Vesuvius, and also showing a snake in front of an altar, is from the House of the Centenary in Pompeii, 1st century AD (in the National Museum in Naples).

the Spanish wines, had a particularly good reputation, and only Rhône wines, plus a few from Andalusia and other provinces of the Iberian peninsula, were traded in Rome, the center of power.

Toward the end of the Roman era, the Wachau, Mosel Valley, Rheingau, Pfalz, Burgundy, Bordeaux (although not the present-day Gironde area, but rather the regions lying further inland, such as Bergerac), Rhône Valley, and La Rioja wine regions all became centers of the European wine industry, and largely remain so today. However, this coincided with the "migration of the peoples," a troubled period of social and military upheaval in most of the colonies during which the decadent pleasures of the declining Roman Empire no longer seemed to have their place.

The disintegration of Roman power brought stagnation to almost all of Europe's wine-producing regions. Viticulture, too, survived some difficult times of its own: the long Arab rule in Spain, which proved surprisingly tolerant regarding the ban on alcohol that is one of the most important tenets of the Islamic faith; and the sacking and pillaging of Bordeaux in 870, the climax of a series of conquests by Gascons, Saracens, Ostrogoths, Visigoths, and eventually even Vikings. Nevertheless, it was not until the 7th and 8th centuries, in the north—in Germany, and above all France—that the continent really began to see an upturn in the wine trade. In the south—Italy and Spain—it took a little longer.

Decay and High Finance

The consequences of the fall of the Roman Empire were demonstrated most dramatically in Italy itself. The collapse of centralized political control, only gradually replaced by the Catholic Church, created a power vacuum in the country. Time and again, foreign peoples were able to invade: Rome was conquered by the Ostrogoths, the Visigoths, and in 455 by the Vandals, and large areas of the country were devastated and plundered. Moreover, the established economic and social mechanisms lost their status and their role. Although viticulture did not disappear completely from the lives of the Italians, it went from being a flourishing branch of the national economy to a purely subsistence farming activity for people living in rural areas.

Not until the development of the coastal cities of Genoa and Venice, which profited from the Crusades, and the emergence of Florence as a European capital of finance in the 13th and 14th centuries, did the wine trade began to revive. It was in Florence of this period that some of today's most renowned Italian wine producers first began making a name for themselves, including the Antinoris and the Frescobaldis. These families had both made their fortunes in other fields or in the financial trade between the Vatican and England, but their experience and contacts convinced them that there was money to be made from wine.

Their trade was not primarily concerned with Tuscan wines, however, but rather, and particularly in the case of the Frescobaldis, with the wines from the dynamically evolving French Bordeaux region, which found great favor at the royal court in England.

Even so, viticulture in the financiers' Tuscan homeland was not entirely unaffected. Although it was to be centuries before the Italian wine industry recovered and subsequently surpassed its former glory, wine, both for everyday drinking and for trade, gradually became a more profitable agricultural commodity again, aided by the practice of sharecropping.

Silenus giving drink to two satyrs, with a drunken Dionysius in Ariadne's lap; a detail from a fresco in the Villa dei Misteri in Pompeii, about 50 BC.

lished in Piedmont, the first cooperatives came into being in Tuscany, and a viticultural institute was founded at San Michele in the Trentino.

Wine Improves its Character

The Right Choice

Everyone has their own taste in wine—we can accept that. But where quality is concerned, it is not a question of preference. Wine is perhaps the most varied and innovative consumable item we can buy ready-made—but it is not easy to know what we are buying. We cannot tell from the label whether the winemaker has exploited the full potential of a particular location and grape variety. We cannot tell whether he or she has used the most "natural" methods in the vineyard and the winery, and translated them into wine of the quality that is a prerequisite for real enjoyment. Even so-called "organic" wine offers no real guarantee in this respect.

Nowhere in the world has legislation caught up with the use of chemicals and technology in the wine industry. Indeed, it lags further behind than ever before. So far, law-making bodies have reacted slowly, if at all, to new developments, with the result that in many wineries worldwide, anything goes. Wine producers experiment with anything that is not expressly forbidden—and sometimes even if it is. In most countries, none of this needs to be declared on the label.

More so than with many other items of food or drink, therefore, we as consumers need to acquire some knowledge, sharpen our senses, and be fully aware of the wine we are drinking. An important aspect of this is the effect a wine has on the body. If only moderate consumption of a particular wine causes stomach problems and headaches, then it has probably been manipulated by some chemical and/or technological means. To deserve the designation "quality wine," it should not only taste good, but contribute to a person's physical wellbeing as well.

The Diversity of Wine

Traditional views as to what wine is all about have their origins in the 19th century, and are based on assumptions that are fundamentally different than those facing the 21st-century consumer. In the first place, the range of wines offered then was much more limited. The wine trade was basically confined to the large châteaux and merchant-houses of Bordeaux and Burgundy, a few German vintners, and the odd specialty wine such as Tokay or port. Wines sold by the makers themselves were largely destined for the local and regional market, and thus easier to overlook than their equivalent today.

Nowadays, however, the world of wine is significantly larger and rather more diverse. Professional wine industries now operate in countries where, even a few decades ago, vineyards were primarily a source of table grapes. Improved transport has made it easier to import specialty wines from all over the world. Never before, moreover, have such large numbers of consumers been prepared to risk trying something new, thereby creating a market for wines that is very different than the traditional wine trade, not only because it is so varied, but also because of the speed at which it changes.

The globalized world of the third millennium is no longer a place for the romanticized notions of previous centuries with regard to wine—the appeal of which was, in any case, reserved for a social elite. Wine's appeal now encompasses all sections of the population. It has become a mass-produced article across much of the world, and thus increasingly an industrial product as well. The range of wines offered is almost incomprehensibly vast, even for a connoisseur. In very general terms, the current wine market can be divided into four main categories.

Part Industry, Part Craft

The biggest group on the market by far continues to be the wines that reach, at best, a minimum technical standard, have probably been produced industrially, and are sold at the lowest prices in the shops. They generally come from a commercial bottling line, and their origins are obscured with an imaginative brand name or by identifying on the label only the larger zone of vineyards from which the grapes came. These simple wines, which have disproportionately high sums spent on packaging and advertising, are estimated to form three-quarters of the present world market for wine.

A second, rapidly growing group of modern wines are now being produced, which are squarely aimed at the more sophisticated, brand-conscious consumer, but necessarily follow a standardized, international model that is subject to the fast-moving dictates of fashion. These wines justify their prestige factor and by no means low prices with their method of production, which makes use of every technological, physical, and chemical means available.

The third category, "traditional" wines in the best sense of the term, is experiencing a real renaissance with an increasingly knowledgeable section of consumers. These estate-bottled wines are produced with a craftsman's care and a sense of responsibility, using "natural" methods in both vineyard and winery. They reflect the regional grape varieties from which they are made, and are thus the real representatives of variety within the world of wine. Their main advantages are that they are "easy drinking," and that the price/enjoyment ratio is readily understood by the consumer.

The fourth category comprises the truly great wines—vintages that do not simply give the illusion of fine quality. This group is naturally small, and their production demands the highest levels of skill, enthusiasm, and boldness. Wines in this category are distinguished by a complexity and intensity of AROMA and flavor, and are balanced, without excessive TANNIN or fruit. They reflect not only the grape variety, but also the soil and the particular vintage, that is to say the *terroir*. Their multi-layered bouquet is demanding and can be enigmatic, meaning that these wines are sometimes "difficult." In principle, all of the world's wine regions are capable of producing such wines, and the traditional, prestige regions and their renowned winemakers do not, on average, provide any more of them than some of the newer regions. Prices range from moderate, for wines that are not of great value to collectors, to completely over inflated prices for bottles that the market has found to be a very good investment commodity.

Anybody who is healthy and whose senses of taste and smell are not impaired, has all the basic equipment necessary not only for drinking wine, but for appreciating its quality as well. This is what separates the consumer from the connoisseur; for the latter, wine is not simply a means to an end. A connoisseur wishes to understand the wine he or she is drinking, so as to experience its aromas and flavors in all their dimensions. To this end, it is hoped that the following pages dealing with the smell, taste and color of wine will enhance your enjoyment of drinking it.

Variety is the key to the range of wines available today. The classic regions may still be dominant, but wines from all countries are finding a place in the wine racks.

The Color of Wine

The color of a wine plays a less significant role in our enjoyment because, objectively, it has no influence on the flavor. At a tasting, however, it is an important and underestimated indicator of quality, because the development, extraction, and maturation of a wine's aroma compounds and its pigments are closely linked. The color can give clues as to how good the vintage was, the grape variety, intensity of flavor, method of production, and maturity. This assumes, however, that the color is natural, i.e. that it has not been artificially boosted with additives or enzymes. Using such practices, even a medium quality red wine can now be given a very dark, if not almost black, color relatively cheaply.

When winemaking only involved chemicals that were already naturally present in the grapes, color was an entirely reliable indicator of quality. Generally speaking, the deeper and darker a wine's red coloring was, the greater the amount of tannins and other substances in its extractions. The acidity and maturity of a wine could also be accurately estimated from the presence of blue or brown tinges respectively.

Assessing the color on anything other than aesthetic principles, however, requires extensive knowledge of the chemistry of wine. For a long time, therefore, although color continued to be judged at tastings, it was seldom regarded as a reflection of quality. It was not until very dark, almost black, red wines became fashionable, that more serious attention was again given to how a wine looked. Since dark reds achieved greater market success, some winemakers started to give nature a helping hand. Consumer ignorance of the technological and chemical methods of manipulation that had become available meant that color was overestimated as a sign of quality.

All red wine grapes, and to a limited degree all white wine grapes, contain natural pigments. Depending on the grape variety, these can be paler, darker, or more concentrated in the skins of the fruit. Consequently, a wine's potential color is decided in the vineyard, and starts with the genetic code of the particular grape variety. This does not mean, however, that all Pinot Noir or all Cabernet is the same, since the most commonly cultivated grape varieties exist in numerous versions. Selective cloning of plants that produce small or large fruits, or low or high yields, has laid the foundations for improvements in terms of quality and quantity. Beyond this, pruning, canopy management, and the application of fertilizer affect the quality of a wine in general, and its color in particular. Then the winemaking process itself must make full use of the grapes' potential for producing a good color (and with it a good aroma). Finally, the duration and method of maturation will leave their mark on a wine's appearance, and here again, changes in color are bound up with the evolution of its taste and smell.

The Subtle Palette of White Wines

White wine is often described as colorless, since the grape juice usually has no SKIN CONTACT during VINIFICATION. This perception is not entirely accurate, however. The colors found in white wine range from pale green through to golden yellow, but are more difficult for the human eye to perceive, simply because they largely occupy the ultraviolet region of the spectrum. A mixture of green and yellow plant pigments (PHENOLICS) are present in the flesh as

well as the skins of pale-colored grapes, which is why even white wine, which is not fermented along with the skins, contains a certain amount of pigment.

Grapes with a slight purple or grayish-pink tinge have the most potential for producing a good color. In other varieties, anomalies in the chemical structure of the pigments can lead to greenish tinges in the wine or a tendency to turn into a brownish color.

Dark, Mysterious Wines

Red wine contains on average ten times more color compounds than white wine. These anthocyanins are only found in the skins of the grapes, and are produced by the action of direct sunlight as the fruits ripen. The thicker and riper the skins, therefore, and the less juice the grapes contain, the greater the potential for producing wine of a good color. In addition, tannins have a stabilizing effect on the pigments, which is why wines that are rich in tannins have a deeper color. Thick-skinned grape varieties such as Cabernet Sauvignon and Syrah naturally deliver dark red wines, while the color from thin-skinned varieties will not be as intense. Nevertheless, assuming optimal conditions in the vineyard, even a thin-skinned grape variety can produce wines with a deep color, if the yield is kept low and the canopy is adequately managed. In the winery, the extraction of color will largely depend on how long and at what temperature the grape juice remains in contact with the skins. When fermentation starts, the color compounds are subjected to physical, chemical and biological influences which leave greater or lesser traces in the wine. It is easy to overdo this, however, and rob the wine of any elegance. Consequently, the most intensely-colored wines are not always the best. Even so, only in exceptionally rare cases will a pale, watery appearance be concealing a great wine.

Every wine has its own particular color, which can provide information about type and age.

From the left: young, fresh white; older, possibly *barrique*-aged white; the ruby color of a mature, relatively light-bodied red; the blackish red of a concentrated red wine; the delicate effervescence of a young champagne; the fascinating golden color of a mature dessert wine.

HANDLING WINE: A QUESTION OF AGE

Even for the poet Horace, who was enjoying wine with discretion and moderation in Roman times and wrote 16 poems on the subject, great wine was always old wine—provided that the fermented grape juice had sufficient substance to withstand years of storage in earthenware amphorae. Less sophisticated wine, by contrast, was simply the produce of the most recent harvest. The position has altered little since that time. Today, 2,000 years after Horace, connoisseurs still find old wine irresistibly attractive. Every year, record sums are paid at auction for aged rarities. Whether the contents of such finds are worth the price is entirely questionable, of course. First, very few wines actually have the capacity to be kept for several decades, and second, the maturation process is terribly susceptible to a wide variety of hazards.

AGING POTENTIAL

When laying down a wine, it is important to differentiate between the length of time a wine can be cellared before it "dies," and the time it needs to reach its peak. Although scientists from different disciplines have repeatedly studied wine from their respective angles, there are no technical standards from which to gauge the aging potential of fermented grape must—we can only give a rough prediction.

Few wines have the capacity to last for centuries, as this legendary bottle from 1787, once owned by the American President Thomas Jefferson, has done.

The life expectancy of most wines is only a few years. Even if a wine is suitable for aging, however, a lot will also depend on the external storage conditions. Generally speaking, sweet wines will keep for longer than dry ones.

If anything, it has become even more difficult to estimate how long a wine will keep, given that advances in the modern wine industry have brought a rapid increase in the number of methods of physical and chemical manipulation. With many of today's wines, whose basic structure may have been altered, we have absolutely no experience to inform our assessment.

The practice of buying a significant stock of expensive bottles, possibly *en primeur* (i.e. long before the wine is delivered and can be tasted), is never advisable, therefore, unless you have reliable information regarding the development of the wine in question. Even a famous name and a cult status are no longer any guarantee that the contents will have a long life.

RED WINE

The backbone of a red wine, and the factor that largely determines its capacity for aging, is tannin—a chemical substance with preservative properties. It dissolves into the wine from the skins, seeds, and sometimes also the stems of the grapes during the winemaking process, and also from the wooden barrel during maturation. The quality and quantity of tannins in red wine vary. Quantity depends partly on the grape: thicker-skinned varieties such as Cabernet Sauvignon and Syrah contain more of these preservatives, and thus have a greater capacity for aging. The vintage (a dry summer produces thicker skins and correspondingly more tannins) and the work of the winemaker also play a role, however, because low yields, long skin-contact times and barrel-aging enable larger amounts of the compounds to be extracted. At least as important for the development of a wine's flavor is the quality of the tannins. Only tannins that were fully ripe when the grapes were harvested will integrate harmoniously into the overall taste of a wine after years in the bottle. What is often described as the maturation of the tannins during bottle-aging is in essence a gradual reduction in the number of such compounds in the wine: polymerization alters the structure of the tannins, which form bigger and more complex molecules and eventually precipitate as SEDIMENT. Wines that taste excessively raw, ASTRINGENT, and bitter in their youth will still do so when they have been aged; indeed, they may seem even less harmonious, since older tannins of this sort often make the mouth seem dry.

The widespread belief among wine collectors that a harsh, unbalanced red need only be kept for long enough to become a great wine is, therefore, a fallacy. Similarly erroneous is the assumption that a young wine that is already pleasantly drinkable is not a good candidate for aging.

The constituents of a great red wine generally begin to weave themselves into a harmonious whole around three to four years after bottling. Reacting with the little oxygen it contains, a wine with a suitable extract will gradually start to develop a bouquet—its originally fruity fragrance will be enriched with spicy, leathery, and earthy nuances. The interactions of alcohols, aldehydes, and acids initially produce a beneficial change, but eventually lead to the impoverishment of both the taste and the smell of the wine. Tartaric acid, which is the most stable component of the wine, scarcely decreases at all, and will become the dominant aroma.

Visually, the progress of the aging process can be gauged from the color of the wine. In a young red (and depending on grape variety), it should be as intense, dark, and purple-tinted as possible. As the pigments oxidize, they are precipitated along with the tannins. As a consequence, the color of the wine loses its blue tinge and becomes first a glowing red, then gradually brownish. The chemical deterioration that occurs in wine at the end of the aging process is reflected in a parallel loss of color. Depending on the grape variety, method of production, and storage conditions, this can occur after anything from a few years to (ideally) several decades, and leaves the wine looking extremely faded—a sure sign that its aroma has reached the end of the road.

WHITE WINE

Long-term cellaring of white wines is a considerably more risky venture than laying down reds. Except for dessert wines, their aging potential is far smaller, because they are largely lacking in antioxidant tannins. The role played by the various acids in determining the lifespan of white wine has yet to be sufficiently explained by science to allow us to make reliable predictions. In the end, any such forecasts can only rely on past experience, and experience tells us that, irrespective of grape variety, the greater the amount of tartaric acid and extract in a white wine, the longer it can be kept in the bottle. As a general rule, wines that had significant contact with oxygen before being bottled, such as those matured in wooden barrels, are considerably more stable than those

The color of a wine is a clear indicator of its age.

that were largely protected from the air during the production process. The likely importance of "good" oxidation in relation to longevity is also indicated by the fact that white wines that are made from botrytized grapes invariably age well in the bottle.

DESSERT WINES

Wines containing residual sugar tend to be better suited to long-term cellaring than dry ones. The longer you wish to keep a wine, the higher the amount of sugar should be. Whites with only a little residual sugar can be allowed to develop for up to a decade, provided that they have sufficient extract capable of the task. Really great dessert wines, such as certain Sauternes, Tokaji Aszú, and those made from the Chenin Blanc grape variety (which has particularly good aging potential), can last for generations. Even after decades in the bottle, they are usually still bursting with fragrances and aromas.

WINE AND ENTERTAINMENT

According to received wisdom, there is a strict set of rules for drinking wine with food: whites go with fish, reds with meat, dry wines should be served before sweet, young before old, no wine with salad, champagne with caviar, and so on. In no other area of life are rules passed on to successive generations as unquestioningly as with food and drink, even though the type of food we eat, and the ways we cook and serve it, have seen a number of fundamental changes in the past 50 years, as has the wine industry.

Progress in enology and a number of improved techniques, machines, and chemical agents triggered a revolution in the wine industry from around the middle of the 20th century. We began to intervene in, and increasingly tighten our control over, the winemaking process using stainless steel tanks, temperature control systems, fermentation enzymes, cultured yeasts, and aroma additives, and thus it is no longer the vagaries of nature that decide what the alcohol content, levels of tannin and acidity, and aromas in a wine will be. Almost every aspect of the taste of a wine can now be manipulated. Moreover, wine has become subject to the dictates of fashion, and this has fundamentally altered our long-established perceptions of how wine should taste. There is a wealth of luxurious, full-bodied, wood-flavored whites on the market today, for example, which have nothing in common with the classic acidic "fish wine"

except color—and often not even that. Many of the world's great reds, moreover, can be soft and mellow even when they are young, and no longer have to be matured for years before they are ready to drink.

The only rule which is valid today is that there really are no rules any more. Modern wines are aromatically too complex to have overly simple dictums applied to them. Not only are there hundreds of different grape varieties worldwide, which are bottled in an infinite number of blends, but also carefully produced hand-made wines which reflect the part played by the soil and climate of their respective vineyards, and by the individual winemaker.

If wine and food are to be matched so that they do not interfere with, but instead complement or even emphasize each other's flavors, then the most suitable place for a particular wine within a menu must really be assessed on an individual basis.

WHICH WINE FOR WHICH GUESTS?

There are a number of aspects to consider when planning a menu comprising a series of courses and wines. The first thing to bear in mind is the occasion. Are you planning a light-hearted garden party in high, midsummer temperatures, or a contemplative evening with other wine lovers? If you provide an unsuitable bottle at

Left
A light bistro wine with jumbo shrimp (prawns).

Right
The ideal combination: game with red wine.

the wrong time, there is a risk that both a good wine, and also the event itself, will be badly served. It is not a sign of meanness, therefore, to refrain from offering a great Bordeaux at an afternoon barbecue; its astringent, bitter heaviness would not go at all well with a highly seasoned sausage. A fruity red with a fresh acidity would be much more enjoyable, especially since the complex aromas of the Bordeaux would quickly evaporate with the high air temperature.

You should not ask too much or too little of your guests. People who rarely drink wine find an elegant, top-quality white just too demanding—it often seems rather thin. Similarly, a great red comes across as unpleasantly astringent and heavy. A wine that is well-made and easy to drink, on the other hand, would be enjoyed by all. As a rule, novices prefer light-colored (i.e. white and rosé) wines, and find inky, super-concentrated reds largely inaccessible.

At a garden party, a wine buff is likely to find a luscious, fruity Californian Zinfandel more of a pleasant surprise than any rosé wine. Committed Burgundy drinkers will be put off by a powerful Australian Shiraz, but a good Pinot Noir from a different country may gently lead them to explore new territory. It is easy to impress (and possibly even convert) fans of Bordeaux with an excellent New World Cabernet or Merlot. If you have an open-minded wine lover as a guest, he or she will hardly be overjoyed if you proffer a simple, albeit perfectly creditable *vin de pays* and rave about its value for money, when a quality wine from an unknown region would always be a pleasure, and need not cost a fortune.

Unique fine wines should always be reserved for a special occasion, not merely out of respect for their high quality, their origins, and the knowledge of the winemaker who produced them, but also in order that they can be enjoyed with deliberate awareness of the unusual pleasures they afford. Wines like these are satisfying in their own right, and so it is not vital that they accompany and complement good food.

If your cellar houses any such rare, character-laden bottles, then a visit from friends who know something about wine is an opportunity not to be missed. For it is only when these liquid treasures are shared in like-minded company that they will fulfil their real purpose and provide some unforgettable moments.

Bottles should be matched not only to the food, but also to the occasion. A relaxed gathering of friends would enjoy a cheerful, uncomplicated wine, for example, while a stylish party requires stylish wines.

FULL-BODIED, WOOD-AGED WHITES

White wines that have been matured in wooden barrels are frequently reminiscent of great reds, both in their alcohol content, which is often as high as 13 or 14% vol, and their opulence. The distinct tannic dimension to their structure is a further link with red wine, although in this case the tannins come from the wood of the barrels rather than from the grapes themselves.

The acidity of such wines is generally reduced to moderate levels by malolactic fermentation, and is further masked by the inherent sweetness of the alcohol. They tend to seem astonishingly full-bodied, even when young, and have good potential for bottle aging. Their aromas can be vaguely reminiscent of exotic fruits like papaya, guava, and mango. Wines made from the Chardonnay grape frequently have distinct hints of pineapple.

TEMPERAMENTAL STARS

Although very popular, the combination of "white" taste and "red" texture makes this group the wine waiter's biggest headache, for they do not take at all well to being accompanied by unsuitable foods.

The first consideration when looking for the right match should be the full-bodied nature of these wines. Alcohol is largely perceived as texture in the mouth: the wine seems more viscous and leaves behind a sensation of warmth. Contrary to established practice, therefore, these wines are not generally suitable accompaniments for fish dishes. Their high alcohol content makes the fish taste oily and old. Conversely, the slightly sour sauce often served with poached fish makes the wine seem a little sweet and flabby. Moreover, the tannins resulting from barrel maturation produce a fairly unpleasant taste when combined with fish oil. Only shellfish, which are naturally slightly sweet, can adequately counter the heaviness of wood-matured whites.

The alcohol content of these wines means that they are an unsuitable accompaniment to salty foods, because salt combined with alcohol produces a bitter taste. Particular care needs to be taken with cheese, therefore, especially blue varieties. Very spicy foods are also best avoided, as they intensity the effect of the alcohol, and vice versa.

Despite these restrictions, Meursault and similar wines can accompany food in a number of excellent combinations.

BETTER WITH CREAM

Dishes prepared with reasonable amounts of cream and butter are almost always the perfect choice, because they can hold their own against the wine's creamy texture and the initial impression of subtle sweetness it produces in the mouth. In addition, the fat content of the food will lessen the astringency of the tannins in the wine, while the tannins, for their part, prevent the dishes from seeming overly rich. Stylish combinations of food and wine can be created, therefore, if the basic tastes work well together, the textures are similar, and consideration is given to the aromas. Whether the wine has the sumptuous pineapple fragrance of wood-matured Californian Chardonnay, the exotic aromas of Australian or New Zealand Sauvignon, the powerful elegance of a German, Italian, or Austrian Grauburgunder, or the highly individual hints of smoked bacon fat and

honey in the best wood-matured Bergerac Sec, it can be integrated into the meal with success if you ensure that the aromas in the food are, as far as possible, an identical match. A simple trick is to include roasted nuts in the meal, because their smell carries the wine's finish through into the food. Tarragon, honey, or a touch of vanilla acts in a similar way: a sauce flavored with any of these, accompanying white meat or poultry, sets off perfectly the aromas of nuts, cream, and often freshly-made toast in these wines.

A great oak-fermented Chardonnay really comes into its own alongside delicate poultry with a cream sauce and walnuts.

Typical grape varieties: Chardonnay, Sauvignon Blanc, Semillon, Pinot Blanc, Pinot Gris, Grenache Blanc.

Typical wines: Corton Charlemagne, Meursault, Puligny-Montrachet, Graves, Limoux, and numerous New World wines.

Elegant, Spicy, Silky Reds

Red wines made from grape varieties with relatively thin skins are naturally pale in color. Thus, their tannin content is lower than in thick-skinned varieties such as Cabernet Sauvignon or Syrah. In the right location, however, Pinot Noir, Sangiovese and the like can produce wines that rank among the greatest in the world. Although heavy and concentrated, such wines are also characterized by finesse: the transparency of their color matches their silky texture, and their soft tannins should not be too obtrusive. In addition, delicate acidity is perfectly balanced by an equally delicate sweetness. The particular appeal of these wines is their bouquet which, depending on grape variety and maturation method, can include aromas ranging from raspberries, violets, wild cherries, plums, blackberries, and numerous spices, to smoke, soil, oak, and liquorice.

The finely-tuned balance of acidity, sweetness, and tannins in these wines is the essence of their charm, and requires special consideration when choosing food to accompany them. It is all too easy to ruin the taste of a Gevrey-Chambertin or Brunello. Their delicate taste, which in some cases can seem almost fragile, should not be paired with very sumptuous dishes. The nature of the sauce is the deciding factor here. If it is excessively concentrated, creamy in texture, and has a very full flavor, it will make an elegant wine appear thin and bland. Sauces made with butter, cream, or egg yolks also pose a danger: the coating they give the tongue is so long-lasting that the papillae can hardly detect a delicate wine at all. The ideal partner for younger wines in this group are dishes with the fine, distinct aromas of young spring vegetables and fresh herbs, accompanying preferably lean meat, and underscored with a light sauce. Silkier, more mature wines, on the other hand, are better suited to autumnal dishes and the earthy, smoky aromas of freshly picked wild mushrooms. Aggressively fruity Pinot Noir wines are among the few reds that can cope with Asian-inspired cuisine, provided the spices in the food are not too strong. Pinot Noir and ginger, in particular, can make an amazingly harmonious combination.

Straightforward Sangiovese wines often work best with a rustic style of cooking, which favors fresh herbs rather than finicky seasonings. Concentrated Chianti and Brunello wines, which are often improved with a touch of

Cabernet Sauvignon and matured in small wooden barrels, smell strongly of cherries. They frequently reveal a delicate scent of orange peel as well, however, which makes them the perfect choice with mildly orange-flavored sauces.

Grape varieties such as Grenache and Pinotage can also be included in this category, even though they can seem rather powerful in their youth—as is the case, for example, with Châteauneuf-du-Pape and other Grenache-based wines from the southern Rhône region. The fruity sweetness present even in dry wines of this type makes them the ideal accompaniment for dishes that taste of dark fruits such as prunes.

Left page, large picture
This kind of wine has a particular affinity with mushrooms. The newest of reds are especially suited to champignons.

Left page, center
More mature reds are served with boletus mushrooms—Sangiovese wines are preferred in particular.

Left page, bottom
The earthy note of chanterelles combines exceptionally well with Pinot Noir.

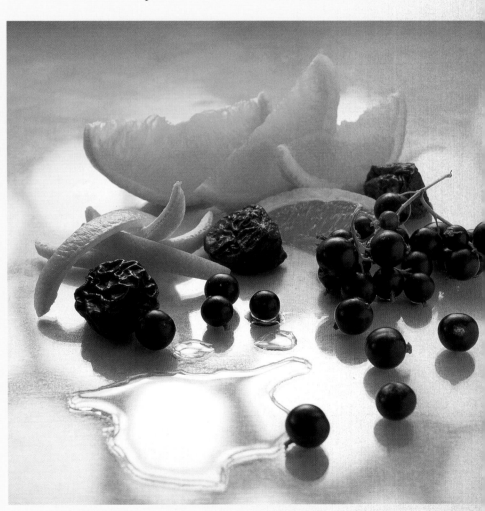

Typical grape varieties: Pinot Noir, Sangiovese, Grenache, Pinotage.

Typical wines: red Bourgogne, Brunello di Montalcino, Chianti Classico.

This piquant, fruity mix requires a sweeter wine, such as a spicy Pinotage.

Luxurious Velvety Reds

The plump wines made from grape varieties such as Merlot or Zinfandel make particularly pleasant accompaniments to a meal. There are relatively few problems combining them with food; they can be served within a succession of other wines, and are appropriate for almost every occasion and time of year. In their youth, such wines are characterized by a luxurious fruitiness that covers the entire palette of reddish-black berries, from blackberries, through black-currants, to cranberries. They normally mature more quickly than tannic reds; with every year they remain in the bottle, their intense fruitiness gives way a little more to the aromas of chocolate, cocoa, coffee, cedar, toast, and smoke. In the mouth, these wines feel full, velvety, and soft. Since they are made from grape varieties with skins of medium thickness, the tannin content is usually less than in wines made from Cabernet Sauvignon or Syrah, for example, and generally integrates to good effect in the overall package. In addition, the level of acidity tends to be low, except in bad vintages or where the yield has been too high. If the grapes are ripe when harvested, these wines have a good alcohol content, which

The taste of charbroiled meat is robust enough to cope with an equally intense wine, such as a smoky, mouth-filling Zinfandel.

also makes them glossy and lends a certain sweetness. They make for agreeable, easy drinking.

The sweet fruitiness of these wines, alongside their soft, sleek texture and opulent range of aromas, always goes well with similarly structured dishes that are not overly heavy. Our first impression is that sweetness, bitterness, and acidity are well balanced, and this harmony should be reflected in the food. Merlot, for example, makes a good partner for braised meat dishes, which if cooked carefully, develop a strong, full, slightly bitter-sweet flavor. A touch of acidity can always be provided by the sauce, perhaps using fruit, tomatoes, or balsamic vinegar.

Zinfandel wines are frequently reminiscent of jam, and can cope with a fair degree of seasoning in the accompanying food. Even salty or somewhat spicy foods—rarely a good idea with other wines—are permissible, thanks to Zinfandel's lavish fruitiness. It is advisable to be careful, however, with chilies or cayenne pepper if the wine, however fruity, has a high alcohol content. Hot spices together with a high percentage of alcohol by volume will really set your tongue on fire.

The compatible nature of soft, velvety reds makes devising combinations with food a largely straightforward affair. We therefore have a great deal of room for maneuver with regard to matching the more volatile aromas. Herbs such as rosemary, thyme, mint and bayleaf, and seasonings such as cinnamon,

cloves, black pepper, juniper berries, and fennel seeds are the best way of linking the flavors on the plate with those in the glass.

Wines on which the wooden barrel has left its mark are good with well seared or broiled fish, poultry, and vegetables: the caramelized proteins and sugar on the food bear an astonishing resemblance to the aromas that toasted barrels impart to the wine.

Typical grape varieties: Merlot, Zinfandel, Blauer Zweigelt, St. Laurent.

Typical wines: Pomerol, Saint-Émilion, and numerous New World wines.

The ideal accompaniment to char-grilled meats is a full bodied, *barrique*-matured red wine.

Dessert Wines

Wines containing residual sugar lead an unjustly shadowy existence when it comes to serving them with food, for included amongst their ranks are some of the greatest wines in the world. On many menus, dessert wines either find no place at all, or are simply served alongside *foie gras* or the sweet course without any real thought. Only in exceptional cases, however, does the simple motto "sweet with sweet" lead to a satisfactory combination. Usually, neither the food nor the wine is really experienced to its best advantage.

The dominant sweetness of these wines is partly the result of unfermented grape sugar, the proportion of which varies from around $1/4$ to 2 ounces or more per pint (20 to 100 grams or more per liter). Among the other sweet substances contained in the wines is alcohol, which not only tastes sweet itself, but also reinforces the sweetness of the sugar. Acidity is the next strongest taste component, and also needs to be taken into account when deciding what food to serve. Sweetness deadens the taste buds even at a relatively low intensity, making anything that is less sweet seem dull and bland. To a certain extent, however, acidity and sweetness can neutralize each other.

In contrast to almost all other wines, the flavors and aromas of a dessert wine play only a secondary role in planning a successful meal combination. The most important consideration is that the sweetness of the wine should have a complement in the dish served with it. This certainly does not mean, however, that it must always be balanced by sugar in the food. Salt, in particular, often makes an excellent contrast to sugar, which is why most cheeses (as long as they are rich and strong smelling) work much better with sweetish whites than with reds—witness the classic combination of port and Stilton.

A medium dry, aromatic white can also go perfectly with Asian cuisine, whose spiciness should not be coupled with acidic wines. A further possibility is to counter the sweetness in the wine with fat, as in the combination of *foie gras* with Sauternes.

Almost as important as balancing the sweetness, the second factor to be considered when matching dessert wines with food is their texture. The degree of viscosity, which is largely determined by the wine's sugar, glycerin, and alcohol content, must be suited to the dish concerned. The more delicate the consistency of a wine, the lighter the food should be; oilier wines should be served with correspondingly creamier dishes. A Riesling TROCKENBEERENAUSLESE, for example, is excellent with a warm apple tart made with shortcrust pastry, while a Sauternes is an excellent accompaniment for puff pastries filled with confectioner's custard.

Combining dessert wines and food becomes a real challenge if you try to take the varied aromas into account as well as the basic tastes and the texture. Depending on their grape variety, method of production, and age, dessert wines release fragrances ranging from orange peel, mangoes, and apricots, through quince, figs, and raisins, to honey and caramel. A good tip with young dessert wines, which at this stage have an acidic structure, is to serve fruity sauces that create an aromatic bridge between the wine and the food. High-quality dessert wines should never be served too cold, since this can easily make them seem unbalanced. In the event that a particular wine is too sweet for the chosen dish, however, cooling the wine can restore a degree of harmony again.

Combining it with a
dessert wine often adds an
entire new dimension of
enjoyment to a fine dessert.

Left page
Almond biscuits are a suitable base for enjoying
dessert wines.

Hélène Jaeger

IN VINEYARD AND WINERY

Destroyed at the Root?
Mechanization in the Vineyard

Every day at first light he would walk to the vineyard, a heavy tool on his shoulder. He would eat lunch with his neighbors in a simple stone or wooden hut; all the hard labor was done by hand, or where feasible, with horses or oxen.

Talk to a winegrower over 60 and you might hear an account like this. Does he regret that those days are gone? A little, perhaps—village life may have been better back then. But mechanization has made his work significantly easier over the last 50 years.

Tractors first appeared in vineyards in the 1950s. Their function, and consequently their appearance, has evolved and changed with time, and from region to region. Small vineyard tractors that drive between rows are used where the vines are sufficiently spaced; they are common in Germany, the south of France, California, and Chile, for example. If the vines are planted closer together, as they are in Burgundy or Champagne, so-called straddle-tractors which span one or two rows are used, although their

One of the biggest problems in modern viticulture is compaction of the soil caused by heavy machinery. Ideally, vineyards should be worked with horses or mules, as shown here, plowing on the Los Boldos estate in Chile.

extremely high center of gravity can make the use of these machines precarious: where the slopes become steeper, they can lose their grip and tip over. Manufacturers are attempting to overcome these difficulties and improve stability by shifting or if necessary reducing the weight.

Little by little growers have been forced to adapt their vineyards for mechanization, by planting the vines in rows and as far as possible training the curtain of foliage along wire frames, so that machinery can pass in between. In vineyards that are laid out in terraces, however, such as in Portugal's Douro valley, in Germany along the Mosel and in the Wachau, in France in the north of the Côtes du Rhône, or in any mountainous wine region of the world, it is impossible to mechanize viticulture. Here, the work is done manually, just as it always has been, although helicopters are used in some areas for spraying the vines.

The difficulty of mechanizing production is often one of the reasons used to justify

In Burgundy, around 100 of the top estates jointly produce compost, which this specially designed spreader then applies in the vineyards.

In densely planted vineyards, straddle-tractors can negotiate the narrow rows to carry out tasks such as spraying and canopy pruning.

This harrow with sturdy claws is popular in eco-friendly viticulture, because it loosens and aerates the soil without turning it.

The weight of small caterpillar tractors is distributed more evenly. Consequently, they cause less soil compaction than tractors with tires.

elevated prices in industrialized nations, where it is more cost effective, once wages and employer's social security contributions are taken into account, for the work to be done mechanically rather than by hand. Elsewhere in the world—in South America, for example—labor is still very cheap, and wine producers are largely turning back to human workers.

Although many tasks are done by specialized machines nowadays, including pest control, soil cultivation, foliage trimming, and to a certain extent, grape picking, one task that has proved difficult to mechanize is the pruning of the vines.

Soil compaction

The use of ever heavier machines in vineyards compacts soil to a depth of 12 inches (30 cm), compressing the pore spaces within it. As a result, the soil is not adequately aerated. Such damage can be avoided, however, or at least reduced. The first step is to restrict the driving of machinery through vineyards to the bare minimum, only spraying crops, for example, if absolutely necessary.

The second step is to buy lighter vehicles and equipment. Inflating the tires to a lower pressure can also help, because it increases the

area of the tire in contact with the ground, thereby reducing the weight pressing down on the soil at any particular point. Caterpillar vehicles cause little soil compaction, because their weight is equally distributed over a larger contact area, and they have the advantage of being able to cope with steep slopes.

Soils that have been compacted by heavy machinery are not well aerated.

VINE PESTS AND DISEASES

Viruses, bacteria, phytoplasma, fungi, mites, insects, and nematodes—the vine has many enemies. Fortunately, they are rarely found in the same place simultaneously. Some diseases and pests are more common in some wine regions than others.

DISEASES

Of the 40 or so known vine viruses, those involved in the complex of diseases known as fanleaf degeneration occur most frequently. These viruses are spread by threadworms (nematodes), and infected vines may suffer extremely reduced yields. Fanleaf degeneration is combated by only planting healthy vines (following strategies similar to those used in tree nurseries), and by allowing cleared vineyards to lie fallow for a period before they are replanted. Care must be taken to remove as much root material as possible, so that the nematodes have nothing to live on and die of starvation. Treating the soil with agents to kill nematodes is harmful to the environment, and so the practice is banned in some countries (Germany and Switzerland, for example), whilst other countries (such as France) impose tight controls.

Two significant vine diseases are caused by phytoplasma, organisms similar to bacteria: Pierce's disease, which causes a great deal of damage in the U.S.A.; and *flavescence dorée*, which mainly occurs in the south of France.

Certain harmful fungi attack the trunk of the vine and can cause it to die, while others damage the green parts of the vine (leaves, shoots, and grapes). The first group includes the diseases eutypa dieback and esca. To limit their spread the grower must prune the vines without creating large wounds through which the fungi can enter. It is essential that dead rootstocks are burned, otherwise they can become new sources of infection.

Of the second group of fungi, three are particularly widespread: downy mildew (*Plasmopara*), powdery mildew (*Oidium*), and gray rot (*Botrytis*). Downy mildew primarily attacks the leaves, and to such an extent that the vine sheds them before time. This severely affects photosynthesis, reduces the concentration of fructose in the grapes, and alters the composition of the nutrient reserves in the roots of the vine. Copper is an important active ingredient for controlling downy mildew. Commonly used preparations are copper oxychloride and Bordeaux mixture (copper neutralized with lime).

Powdery mildew can colonize foliage and grapes, causing a reduction in quality or even the loss of the crop. Not all vine varieties are equally susceptible: some, such as Carignan, are very prone to infection; others, such as Syrah or Pinot Noir, less so. Once the fungus has taken hold, however, it is very difficult to treat, and so preventative measures are essential. *Oidium* control is generally undertaken using preparations containing sulfur. Organically-based products are also available, and should be deployed only once or twice a year, to prevent the appearance of resistant strains of fungus.

Powdery mildew: individual berries have split open.

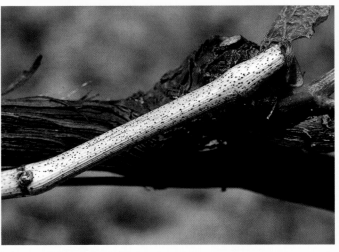

Phomopsis infection: pycnidia (the spore receptacles) on winter wood.

The third great enemy of the vine is *Botrytis*, or gray rot, which can affect both the quantity and the quality of the yield. It is best combated through the use of preventative strategies that promote the vitality of the vine and ensure good ventilation in the canopy. This necessitates reducing the amount of nitrogen added to the soil, training the vines so that they have adequate space, and undertaking work on the canopy (removing the secondary shoots; thinning out the foliage) in good time.

Organic substances used to control fungal diseases can be divided into three categories: products that work on the contact principle, and thus only protect the organs to which they are applied (contact fungicides); products that penetrate the treated organs and stop the attack within the plant (locally systemic fungicides); and products that penetrate and spread throughout the vine (systemic fungicides).

PESTS

The two types of grape berry moth, cochylis (*Eupoecilia ambiguella*) and eudemis (*Lobesia botrana*), are significant vine pests. They produce two or three generations every summer, and their various larval stages damage the buds, the immature flowers, and the maturing grapes.

The chosen methods of control must be appropriate for the particular stage of development (eggs or larvae), and be deployed at the right time. The less harmful the products are to the environment, vineyard-workers, and beneficial insects, the more precisely an optimal treatment date must be determined; in some cases, one or two days can make a great deal of difference.

Spraying the vines with pesticide.

Eutypa dieback: cross-section through a trunk.

Methods of treatment

Treatment should be targeted specifically at the areas damaged by the pest or disease, such as the foliage (as with mildew) or the grapes (e.g. grape berry moth). Good coverage of the affected parts is vital to the success of the treatment, as is the choice of agent, time of deployment, use of the correct nozzle setting on the spraying equipment, and the speed at which the machinery is driven through the vineyard. Incorrect settings on the spraying equipment and too much speed can lead to unnecessary pollution of the environment (such as increased drift).

The Working Year in the Vineyard: Care of the Soil—and More

Planting new vines is the most time-consuming job in the vineyard—and the most satisfying when the young plants thrive.

Weed Control

Grapevines demand constant and careful attention. The work carried out on both the soil and the plants is crucial for the quality of that season's wine, but also lays the foundations for the following year. The techniques used to cultivate the soil depend on the grower's chosen methodology. Chemical weed-killing employs herbicides that reduce the need for manual or mechanical soil cultivation. However, the soil is generally cultivated once or twice a year to loosen and aerate it. This can be done in the fall, or in spring, or in both seasons. Another

The leaves of the vines grow so thickly, especially in the damper wine-growing regions, that they have to be pruned to let light and air get to the vine stocks.

possibility is to target the use of herbicides only along the rows of vines. Following this, the ground in between the rows is either cultivated or planted with a grass cover crop.

The most promising course of action combines various methods of cultivation: piling up earth around the trunks of the vines and tilling, leveling, or hoeing the soil in between, as necessary. The layer of earth around the graft zone serves to protect the vine from the effects of very cold spells in winter. The piles of earth must be removed in the spring to prevent the scion from growing under the soil and putting down unwanted roots.

The frequency of weeding will depend on the extent of the weed population. Following rain, it can sometimes be difficult to drive tractors across the plots. If the grass is to be a permanent feature, it will have to be mown several times per season. To reduce competition during the growth period, however, some growers prefer temporary coverage: the grass is destroyed at the end of the winter, either by mechanical soil cultivation or with herbicides.

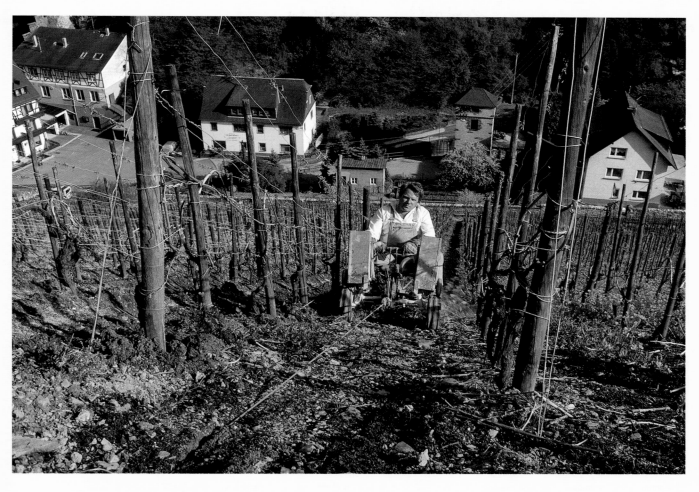

Once again, however, there is no solution that can be applied in all situations. The soil's properties, access to the plot, the problems of erosion, spring frosts, competition for water, and operating costs all have to be taken into account. Sowing grasses is an interesting strategy that looks after the structure of the soil and the creatures living in it, but it is not suitable for steep slopes, because the tractor tires cannot get a grip on such a surface. Neither is it recommended in areas where there is a risk of late frosts: the cover crop raises the moisture content of the soil, thereby increasing the danger of frost damage in spring.

MAINTAINING AND TRAINING THE VINES

There is also a series of tasks to be undertaken to look after the vine. The best time to repair trellises, stakes, and wires is during the winter, usually after pruning. If the cane pruning method has been used, the cane is fastened to the wire of the trellis. As soon as growth has begun, superfluous shoots are removed to aid ventilation in the canopy and make pruning easier the following winter. The WATER SHOOTS (i.e. shoots growing directly from the trunk)

should also be removed, either at the same time or later on.

If the vineyard uses a cordon training system, the shoots must be tied up with trellis wire as soon as they are long enough, and fastened along the wires between the stakes. This work has to be done manually, and the canopy should be trimmed at the same time.

In cooler regions, growers may decide to remove a certain number of bunches per vine around midsummer (i.e. just before veraison), to ensure a high-quality crop. This practice is mainly used with red grape varieties to increase the concentration of color compounds, and is known as "crop thinning" or *vendange verte*. If it is carried out early enough, the vine compensates for the loss with the remaining bunches.

In spectacular hillside positions such as these along the Mosel, the winegrowers use ropes to move ploughs and other equipment. The best sites cannot be maintained without using such aids.

Nowadays we know that care of the leaves is extremely important for better wine quality. If all shoots that do not support fruit are removed, the grapes are improved in flavor.

Noble and Mass-produced Wines

To make a good wine, you need good grapes. This ought to be the principle guiding every winemaker. From a practical point of view, it is much easier to make wine using healthy, ripe grapes than ones that are damaged and not ripe enough. Consequently, wine production really begins in the vineyard. One of the keys to obtaining a quality crop is to ensure that the grape

production, namely VINIFICATION, maturation, and bottling. Better hygiene, for example, prevents a vinegary edge developing. It is increasingly rare for wines to turn to vinegar. Another significant improvement has been the use of temperature regulation during wine production, which has made it possible to control the FERMENTATION process.

In order to emphasize the character of small estates and support the *terroir*, the appropriate small fermentation barrels are required.

variety, the rootstock, and the soil are well matched. The winemaker's preferred methods of cultivation—as regards vine density, pruning, canopy management, soil cultivation, and the age of the vines, for example—also influence the end result, as do the changing climatic conditions and the presence or absence of pests and diseases that make each vintage a new challenge.

Advances in ENOLOGY have contributed to a better understanding—and therefore greater mastery—of the three main stages of wine

Nowadays, winemakers also have the knowledge and the means to compensate for any deficiencies in the grapes. With experience, they can produce good wine even in difficult vintages. Nevertheless, all these positive developments can just as easily be a step in the wrong direction if they lead to vinification being seen as an industrial process. Each country takes a different view of such matters, and procedures that are allowed in some countries (such as aromatizing the wine with oak shavings) are prohibited in others.

Agreement also needs to be reached over what constitutes a wine, a good wine, and a great wine. According to the European Union definition, wine is a product "obtained exclusively by alcoholic fermentation, wholly or partially, of raw grapes, whether crushed or not, or of their must." In some parts of the world, however, drinks made from other fruits may also be called "wine."

Beyond this, a distinction can be made between mass-produced wines and noble wines. The former are required only to fulfil the basic criteria and industry norms—in a word, to be

speaking, we drink less, but better wine. Such wines must display all the usual qualities, but also reflect their region of origin, grape variety, and VINTAGE. Given the right climatic conditions, a good wine can sometimes become an excellent one. The goal of every good winemaker is to exploit fully all the advantages of the grapes while at the same time allowing their natural character to come through. One of the greatest dangers of modern enology is the standardization of wines as a result of overly systematic interventions and adjustments. In some cases, the methods of vinification and the

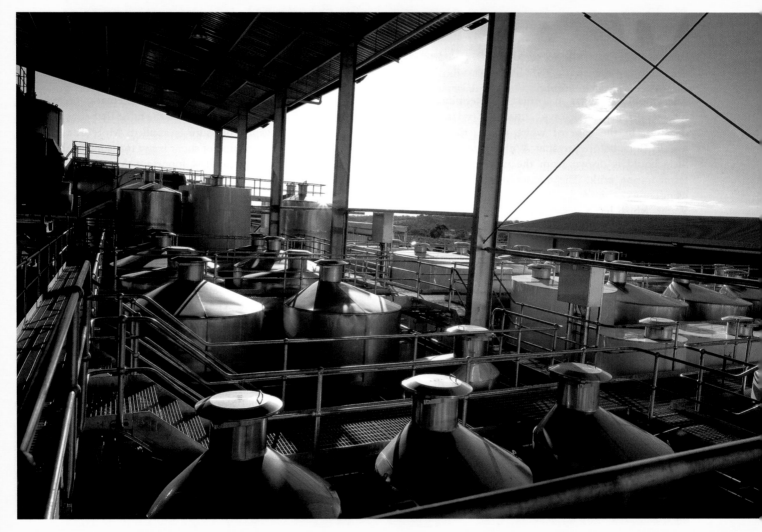

"drinkable." Consumers expect a standardized quality, and this is delivered using high-yielding vines planted in fertile soil. These everyday wines are primarily intended for sale in their country of origin, and are increasingly being rejected in favor of finer wines. As late as the 1960s, and especially in France, this type of wine was watered down and used as a thirst quencher and daily accompaniment to meals.

Today, however, consumer interest is moving toward wines of higher quality. Generally

techniques of the enologist or winemaker can be more evident in a wine than the TERROIR. Each winemaker has his or her own way of doing things, and the acceptability of the resulting wines will depend entirely on enlightened consumers choosing to buy them.

Large wineries make use of the latest technology to produce large volumes of wine, maintaining as far as possible the same quality from year to year.

TRADITIONAL RED WINE PRODUCTION IN BURGUNDY

The great red wines of Burgundy are made exclusively from Pinot Noir, which is a challenging grape variety, particularly as regards extracting the color. From the harvest onwards, therefore, producers try to avoid oxidation. The grapes are picked by hand, and usually transported in crates. Unwanted matter is then removed on the sorting table, or *table de tri*. The next step is the total or partial destemming of the grapes, depending on the grade of the *appellation*, the condition of the stalks, and the style of the winemaker.

In years when ripening the grapes has been difficult and the stalks are still green, they can all be removed. Some producers would rather destem the entire crop and have longer maceration times. Others prefer to leave the stalks on a proportion of the grapes, particularly when producing wines for aging. There are advantages and disadvantages to both methods.

One of the golden rules is to minimize the use of pumps to move the grapes around, because they crush the stalks and seeds, which can give the wine a herbaceous edge and harsh, ASTRINGENT tannins. Conveyor belts have proved to be a good way of transporting the grapes to the destemming machine or filling the fermentation tank. Sulfur is usually added at this point. An initial "pumping over" takes place, for the purposes of homogenization, and the levels of sugar and acid are measured for the first time.

The alcoholic fermentation then gets under way, with *pigeage* and *remontage* operations

Opposite
Pinot grapes are crushed underfoot—the traditional method and the gentlest. Once fermentation has begun during this gentlest of all pressing methods, the cap of skins is broken up and submerged in the must—a process known as *pigeage*.

carried out every day. Once fermentation is complete, a few more days' maceration may be allowed. Carbon dioxide is no longer being produced, and so the cap gradually sinks. Caution is required if open tanks are being used, because there is a danger of a vinegary edge developing once fermentation is complete.

Emptying the tank starts with the wine being run off. The pomace is then pressed, and the free-run wine blended with some or all of the press wine. Next, the wine is clarified and transferred to barrels, where, sooner or later (depending on the vintage), MALOLACTIC FERMENTATION begins. With a particularly acidic vintage, for example, this may not begin until spring.

Once the malolactic fermentation is finished, the first RACKING is carried out. The clear wine is separated from the sediment that has settled at the bottom of the barrel. The wine is exposed to the air during this process, to allow some of the carbonic acid with which it is saturated to be given off as carbon dioxide gas.

The wine is then transferred to another barrel for a period of maturation. Further racking may become necessary during this time, using either an oxidative or protective method, depending on the results of a tasting.

Malolactic fermentation

This second fermentation converts malic acid to lactic acid with the aid of lactic bacteria, which may be naturally present in the winery or artificially added. As with alcoholic fermentation, the reaction is accompanied by the release of carbon dioxide, but in much smaller quantities. Malolactic fermentation alters the taste of the wine, and so is deliberately encouraged or specifically avoided. It reduces the wine's ACID content, improves its aromas, and sometimes leads to a slight increase in volatile acids. The wine is made more stable, because there is no longer a danger that this second fermentation will take place in the bottle.

The lactic bacteria can also cause a decrease in other components of the wine besides malic acid. If they affect the sugars, for example, the taste may develop a lactic acid edge.

Naturally present or artificially added lactic bacteria alter the taste of wine.

Consequently, it is vital that all the sugar is broken down during the alcoholic fermentation. Sulfur dioxide added after pressing or to the tanks or barrels can render the bacteria inactive, without overly impairing the yeasts.

Most red wines undergo malolactic fermentation. Its use with whites and rosés depends on the region and the style of the wine. In regions with a Mediterranean-type climate, where the wines are often lacking in acidity, this second fermentation is avoided. In cooler regions, the wines tend to contain more acid, and so malolactic fermentation is often employed, provided that dry wines are being produced. If a wine contains RESIDUAL SUGAR, chemical de-acidification is used in preference to malolactic fermentation. In countries where there is no great tradition of producing sweet wines, this tends to be the practice with dry whites as well.

French Oak Forests

Since the 1990s, the demand for BARRIQUES—small oak barrels traditionally used in Bordeaux, usually with a 59-gallon (225-liter) capacity—has risen in leaps and bounds. In all the world's wine-producing countries, an ever-growing number of winemakers are choosing them as the vessels in which to vinify special white wines or mature their best reds. Oak from a number of countries is used to make *barriques*, but French oak is generally considered to be the finest raw material.

An oak tree takes 150 to 230 years to reach maturity and the stage when it can be used for timber. Consequently, sustainable, high-quality production can only be achieved by managing forests for the long term. Controls on logging were imposed in France as early as the middle of the 17th century, in order to end the unregulated exploitation of the forests and guarantee a high-quality supply for future generations. As a result, France's oak forests are probably the finest in Europe today. The pedunculate oak (*Quercus robur*) and the sessile oak (*Quercus petraea*) account for more than one-third of France's 34 million acres (14 million hectares) of woodland, and only a small proportion of this is allowed to be used for COOPERAGE.

For a French oak, the route from the forest to the winery is a long one. The owner of the forest generally sells his trees to a forester before they have been cut down, and the forester then sees to the felling and commercial exploitation of the entire tree. The bark-covered stemwood used in the production of barrels is usually entrusted to a specialist timber merchant, the *merrandier*, who cuts it into *merrains*, the long lengths of wood from which the staves of the barrel are fashioned.

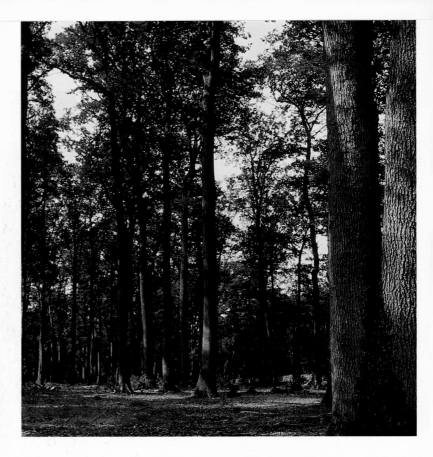

The finest oak forests in France have been managed by the State since the time of Louis XIV. The trees used for the highly prized small wooden barrels are over 200 years old.

The timber supplied to the cooper is generally this stave wood, but sometimes the middleman is cut out and the cooper begins his task by preparing the bark-covered stemwood himself.

The production of stave wood requires a trunk that is free of defects, more than 16 inches (40 cm) in diameter, and can be divided into lengths of 43 inches (1.10 m)—the length of a stave. A forester's idea of a splendid oak, therefore, may not be the same as that of someone out for a stroll among the trees.

Of the 11 million acres (4.5 million hectares) of oak woods in France, 4.5 million acres (1.85 million hectares) are in public ownership (as national forests or communal woodland) and are administered by the National Forestry Office (*Office National des Forêts*). The rest is privately owned. Most of the finest forests are managed by the state, as it is not easy for private individuals to bear the costs involved in exploiting them, because their capital is tied up for a very long period of time.

The quality of the timber depends principally on the forestry practices employed. A stand of trees managed as a high forest can usually regenerate itself naturally with the seedlings produced when the acorns drop. Sometimes, however, plantings are needed to supplement this process. With a coppice system, regeneration is provided by the shoots growing from the stumps of the trees. In a coppice-with-standards, both forms of regeneration occur side by side. Today, most managed woodland is operated as high forest.

The trees in the overstory of a high forest stand are almost all the same age. Improvement

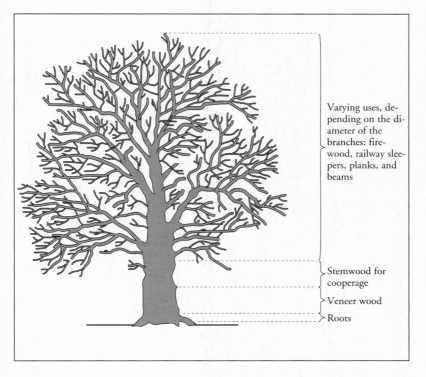

Varying uses, depending on the diameter of the branches: firewood, railway sleepers, planks, and beams

Stemwood for cooperage

Veneer wood

Roots

work is carried out as they grow, which involves selecting the best trees to become the overstory and felling the remainder. When a forest plantation reaches full maturity after about 200 years, only around 40 of the original 20,000 trees per acre (100 out of the original 50,000 per hectare) will still be standing. There are a number of factors to be taken into consideration. If, for example, thinning out allows too much light to penetrate the canopy, it may stimulate the growth of the lower branches and decrease the value of the timber. Once maturity is reached, the stand is felled progressively over a period of around 15 years. The canopy is thus opened up evenly, improving the growth prospects of the seedlings and next generation of trees.

The best wood is obtained from mature high forest trees. Younger oaks in a high forest often have defects, and tend to produce shorter logs. This kind of understory tree accounts for 90 percent of French oaks. Fully mature high forest timber is still relatively rare, and commands correspondingly high prices on the market.

The oaks in the understory of high forest stands are usually complemented by hornbeam and beech trees. This understory is completely cleared during the inspections carried out every 25 years or so, and a selection process among the overstory trees removes those that are mature, dying, or in the way. Thinning out yields a large amount of hard-to-sell firewood.

Each year, the Forestry Office publishes a detailed list of the sections that have been released for sale in each forest, and marks the relevant trees. The lots are always sold as a complete unit. The coopers or their buyers inspect the area to be felled with all due care, and discuss things with the foresters. They assess each part of the trees and indicate whether they are interested in buying. Some coopers also make the actual purchase themselves. The lots are sold in September and October at auctions with decreasing bids: a series of prices is announced, starting at a level suggested by the Forestry Office, and the first person to interrupt the bidding is awarded the lot.

If the purpose of the auction is to sell standing trees, the forester will fell them during the winter. Should a tree damage another as it falls, the forester has to pay the owner compensation. The wood is taken away as soon as it is dry enough, to avoid damaging seedlings, paths, and ditches. In the forests of eastern France, the trees are usually sold "at the wayside," meaning that they have already been felled.

The level of attendance at an auction will depend on the reputation that wood from a particular forest enjoys among winemakers. The sale in Tronçais, near Nevers in central France, is one of the more important dates on the calendar, as many coopers must have wood from this forest in stock if they wish to satisfy their customers. To secure their supply, they will often act directly as buyers.

Fully mature oaks from high forests provide the best wood for cooperage. The timber is cut to the required dimensions *in situ*.

Barrel Making

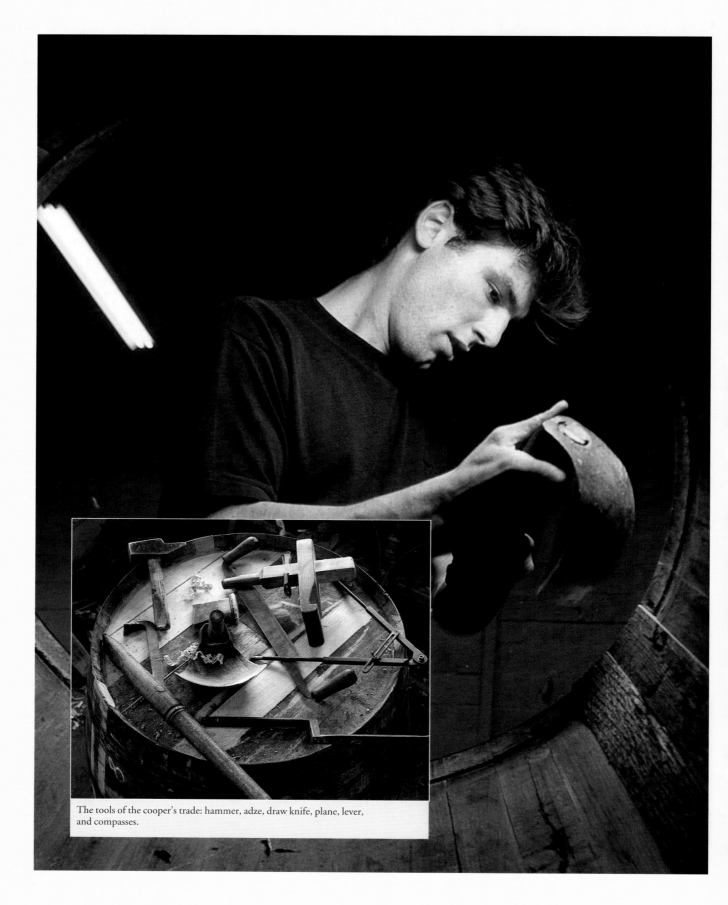

The tools of the cooper's trade: hammer, adze, draw knife, plane, lever, and compasses.

The split wood is passed through a bandsaw so that the staves are equal in both length and width from the outset.

The cooper uses a metal ring to hold the tapered staves as he begins to assemble the barrel.

When the circle is complete, the cooper secures it by hammering a second and then a third hoop around the barrel.

The staves are still splayed out at the other end of the barrel, and are heated over an open fire so that they can be bent to shape.

The intensity of this toasting is crucial in determining the aromas the finished barrel will impart to the wine.

The cooper places a metal cable around the barrel and uses leverage to draw it progressively tighter, whilst also dampening the outside of the staves.

The staves at the other end eventually form a perfect closed circle that can be secured with a hoop.

The barrel still has no opening in the side, and so the cooper bores a bung-hole into the oak, which he then enlarges to a prescribed size.

The outside of the barrel is given its final planing before the bottom and lid are fitted.

Barrel
Maturation

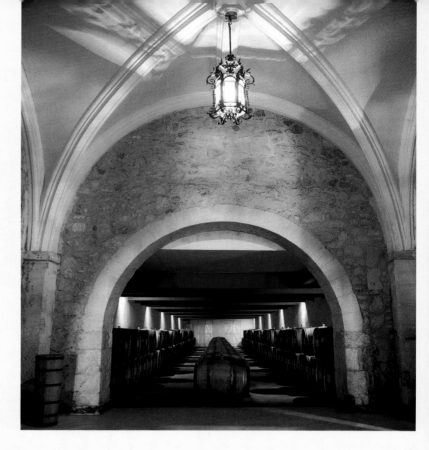

There is no instant recipe for success in the art of turning grapes into wine, and the same is true of maturing the wine in barrels. The first decision each winemaker must make is the extent to which barrels should be used. In some cases, a proportion of the wine may be finished off in barrels, and the rest in tanks; the two are reintegrated directly before bottling to homogenize the blend. For wine matured in barrels, especially new *barriques*, the origin of the wood, and the degree of toasting can emphasize particular characteristics in the wine that have been determined by the grape variety, weather conditions, and soil properties.

As a rule of thumb, the more "structure" a wine has, the better it will withstand barrel aging. If a light wine is matured in a wooden barrel, all the care and effort that has been put into it up to that point can quickly be wasted. As well as adding certain aromatic compounds, barrel aging allows slow oxidation, which encourages maturation. The various components of the wine combine with each other, making the wine more harmonious. At the same time, this controlled development makes the wine less perishable and more resistant to future oxidation—in short, it gives it greater

Many influential estates have made architectural attractions of their cellars.

Tartrates and fine deposits are removed from the barrels using water pressure.

aging potential. The additional oak tannins refine the tannins already present in red wine, and give whites a sophisticated tannic element that they previously did not possess.

Winemakers agree that the best way to achieve an appealing but integrated note of wood and more body in a white wine is to carry out the fermentation process in the barrel and then allow a period of maturation with the wine in contact with the lees. In this case, the must is transferred to the barrels after clarification. Once the alcoholic fermentation is complete, the barrel is topped up and the bung-hole sealed. The lees—the deposit left after fermentation—are stirred up periodically, a process known as BÂTONNAGE. This ensures that the oxygen introduced into the barrel is carried right to the bottom, preventing the development of any faults in the aroma of the finished wine. How often the lees are stirred depends on the wine and the style of the winemaker. Initially, it may happen twice a week, then gradually be reduced to once every two weeks. Whatever the frequency, it is generally continued for three months. After this time, the wine is either left on the lees or racked off. In the latter case, it may be transferred directly to another barrel, or the winemaker may use the opportunity to blend the wine (the process of ASSEMBLAGE) before returning it to tanks or barrels.

Alcoholic fermentation in small barrels is out of the question with red wines, because it takes place in contact with the skins, seeds, and possibly the stalks. It would be difficult to

The pipette, used to take samples from the barrels, is the winemaker's most important tool.

Samples are taken regularly to check the progress of the wine by tasting or analysis.

Pneumatic pressure makes for especially gentle rakking of the wine.

transfer all this into a barrel, and even more difficult to get it out again. After the wine is drawn off from the tank and pressing has taken place, it can be returned to the tank or to barrels for the process of malolactic fermentation. Barrels seem to produce more convincing results in this regard, because the tannins are blended more smoothly.

All barrels "drink" the wine, particularly new ones: the loss is estimated to amount to three to five percent. This means about 3 US gallons (11 liters) will disappear from a Bordeaux *barrique* with a 59-gallon (225-liter) capacity. The barrels cannot be left with an empty space inside, because a vinegary edge may develop in the wine. Consequently, they must regularly be topped up, a procedure known in French as *ouillage*. This occurs weekly at the beginning of the maturation period, and then at increasing intervals. In the Gironde, it is common to see barrels oriented so that their bung-holes are on the side, to reduce both evaporation and the amount of air getting in—and thus minimize the need for topping up. Thanks to new, airtight stoppers made of silicon, however, barrels can continue to be positioned with the bung-holes

Oak slats can be suspended in a tank to give the wine attractive and desirable oak aromas without incurring the expense of barrel maturation. The method is principally practiced in New World countries.

facing upwards, which makes it much easier to carry out the various tasks needed to monitor the progress of the wine.

The duration of barrel aging varies from three to more than 18 months, and will depend on the type of wine being matured and the amount of volatile acid that forms in the barrel. If the level becomes too high, the period of barrel maturation is shortened. This decision is usually made by a taster, who is able to assess the general balance of the wine. A frequent mistake is to end barrel maturation too early, because the woody aromas that are often very prominent at the beginning need time to become smoother.

Barrel maturation, whether of red or white wine, is more labor intensive than aging the same volume in a tank. Add to this the cost of purchasing the barrels into the equation, and it is easy to see why it is so much more expensive. In deciding to use barrels, therefore, winemakers take into account not only the type of wine being produced, but also the final price. Only high-quality wine is worth carefully MATURING in wood, to give it a harmony and complexity that it could never attain in a more neutral container.

Truth and illusion

Although aromatic compounds are absorbed during maturation in oak barrels, this is not "aromatizing" the wine in the true sense. Adding wood chips or installing wooden slats in stainless steel tanks is a different matter, however, because they have only one purpose: to impart aromas to the wine in the same way that seasonings are used with food. The positive secondary effects of barrel maturation, deriving from beneficial oxidation or contact with the lees, are not achieved with artificial additives.

The controversial use of wooden chips or slats in tanks is officially still banned in Europe, but properly registered experiments are permitted, and laboratories are already carrying out research and tests.

Some producers try to simulate the aromas produced by barrel maturation by steeping oak shavings in the wine, teabag-style.

Elsewhere in the world, this form of additive is widely used, and wines treated in such a way have long been sold across the globe. There is a problem with this winery practice: European legislation requires that any product labeled as wine is made entirely from grapes, a regulation that emphasizes the traditional precepts of purity. In an apparent effort to tailor products to the demands of the market, however, modern winemaking practice is resorting to a wide range of additional substances and aromatic compounds, even going as far as using specially manipulated cultured yeasts and a variety of enzymes. Should the consumer not claim the right to be informed about these additives, just as they are with other food and drink products?

Bottle Manufacture

The main raw material for the production of glass bottles is silicic acid (silicon dioxide, 70 percent), which occurs in nature primarily in the form of quartz sand. It is possible to make glass purely out of sand, but this requires temperatures in excess of 3,272°F (1,800°C). Consequently, an alkali is added (soda or potash, around 15 percent), which lowers the melting point to 2,732°F (1,500°C). Quicklime (10 percent) prevents the glass from crystallizing as it cools. The remaining 5 percent is mostly aluminum oxide, magnesium, or iron oxide, which primarily help to determine color and viscosity. Scrap glass (from manufacturing remnants or bottles collected for recycling) is also added. The amount of each ingredient is measured using electronic precision balances.

The mixture is melted down in a furnace at around 2,822°F (1,550°C). Bubbles of gas form in the molten glass at this stage, which rise to the surface and burst during the fining process. The now homogenous mass flows into channels which feed the molding machines. A plunger pushes the molten glass through a calibrated orifice at regular intervals. This produces a series of gobs of glass, which are cut off with automatic shears. Their weight, and hence the rhythm of the plunger, is determined by the amount of molten glass needed for the particular article being made. The temperature, now between 2,012° and 2,372°F (1,100° and 1,300°C), is constantly monitored, because a sudden sharp drop would cause the glass to lose its viscosity.

The molding process can now begin (see diagram, opposite). Each gob of molten glass drops into a parison mold. The lower part of this mold is a ring that shapes the upper part of the bottle neck. A plunger punches through the molten glass via the ring, and compressed air is blown in through the hole this creates, forming a hollow body from the gob.

This parison is transferred into a finishing mold, and compressed air is again introduced to give the bottle its final shape. This method of manufacture is known as the blow-and-blow technique. In the press-and-blow technique, the first blow molding operation is replaced by a pressing operation. Some machines can produce up to 700 bottles a minute.

Once molding is complete, the glass still has a temperature of 1,202°F (650°C). The external walls tend to cool off quickly, whilst the temperature inside the cavity drops much more slowly. If the bottles were allowed to cool naturally, the glass could develop cracks and easily break. For this reason, they are put through another furnace on a conveyor belt, so that they can cool off very gradually from around 1,022°F (550°C).

The bottles then have to undergo one final process to remove microscopic flaws on the surface of the glass. One method involves spraying the bottles with metal oxide vapors, which act on the surface of the glass, and this is carried out during the heating phase between molding and cooling. Alternatively, a protective film of polyethylene is applied to the surface of the glass once cooling is complete.

At the end of the production process, the size, shape, capacity, and technical properties of the bottle are checked. They are then piled in several layers on pallets to be dispatched. The pallets are usually tightly wrapped in plastic film so that no dust, small insects, or other pollutants can get in.

Although the true raw material for glass making is quartz sand, recycled glass has become very important for bottle manufacture.

Manufacturing bottles using the
blow-and-blow process

The molten gob of glass is dropped into the parison mold.

The lower part shapes the neck of the bottle.

Compressed air is forced in through a jet and blows the glass into shape.

The parison is transferred to a finishing mold, and another burst of compressed air forms the final bottle shape.

The bottles are put back into a furnace so that both the interior and the exterior reach the same temperature and can then cool off evenly.

Metal oxide vapors are sprayed onto the surface of the glass to remove any flaws.

A number of checks are carried out on the finished bottles.

André Dominé

WINES OF THE WORLD

THE WORLD OF WINE: A SURVEY

A glance at the distribution of wine-growing regions on our planet shows at once that vines will grow only in certain conditions. The most important factor for viticulture is climate, and above all, temperature. Here there is a striking difference between the northern and southern hemispheres. In the southern hemisphere, the 59°F (15°C) line during the winter month of July describes an almost straight course, running between about 60 and 50 degrees latitude south,

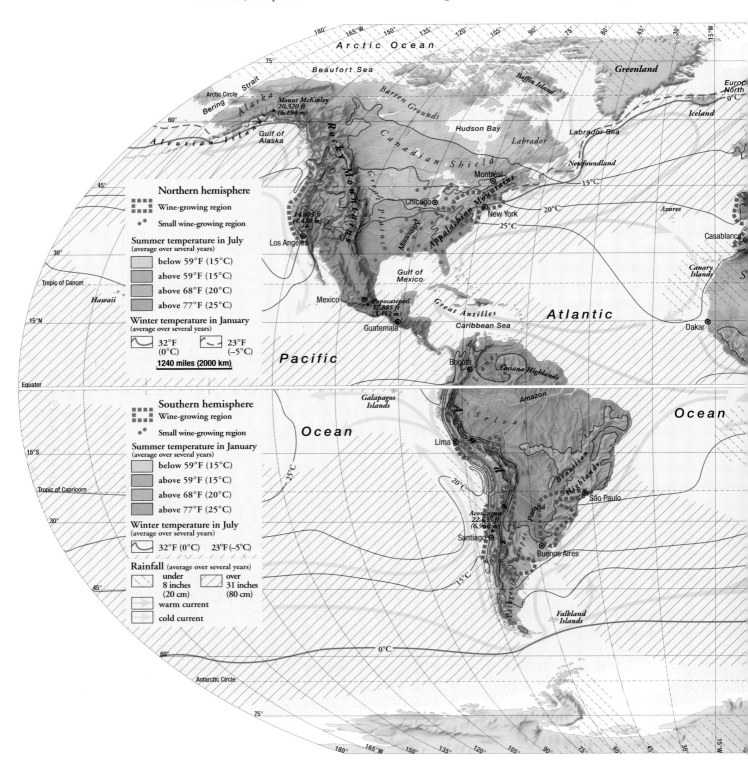

missing land entirely. Whereas in the northern hemisphere, where the considerably larger land masses receive more warmth in summer—and where warm water currents such as the Gulf Stream are a contributory factor—the 32°F (0°C) line passes through a number of major wine-growing areas. However, the map also shows that vines clearly prefer moderate conditions. They seldom thrive where temperatures rise above 77°F (25°C) in the summer months of July and January in the northern and southern hemispheres respectively. Rainfall and drought also play an important part. It is almost impossible to grow wine with less than 8 inches (200 mm) of rain a year; on the other hand, too much rain also makes it difficult to cultivate grapes. All over the world, however, wine growers have found ways of adapting to natural conditions, and they have been particularly resourceful in borderline areas.

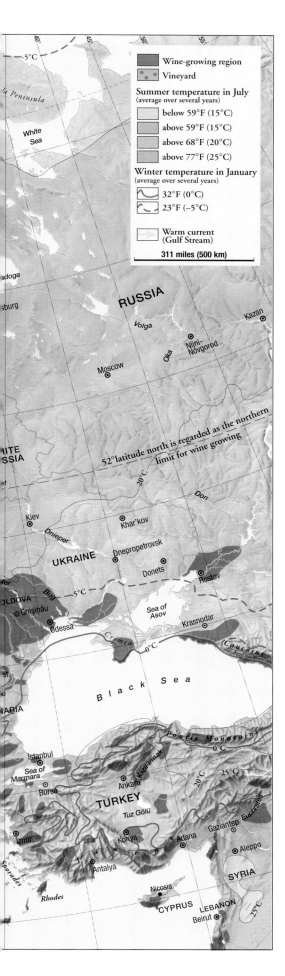

VITICULTURE IN EUROPE

As noted on the map, 52 degrees latitude north can usually be regarded as the northern limit for wine growing. However, several British winegrowers, in a very sportsmanlike manner, seem to have ignored this "rule." The further north viticulture extends, so the average temperatures will be cooler, and the amount of rainfall to which the vines are exposed will increase. While cool temperatures inhibit the ripening process, too much moisture can threaten the health of vines and grapes alike, and at the same time thin the MUST. The more extreme the temperatures and the rainfall, the more the vine's photosynthesis is impaired, and with it the formation of glucose; as a result, it is impossible to grow grapes for winemaking north of 54 degrees latitude.

The close connection between rivers and wine-growing areas, especially in the north, center, and east of Europe, is also obvious. The Loire and the Garonne, the Rhine and the Rhône, the Danube and the Dniester are all lifelines to important viticultural areas, where they moderate any extremes of climate.

In a large part of western Europe, average July temperatures vary between 59 and 68°F (15 and 20°C), and it is in this zone that the majority of Europe's classic viticultural regions lie. A moderate climate, with adequate to relatively high rainfall, provides ideal conditions for producing both fragrant white wines with a good structure of acidity, and well-balanced red wines with good potential for MATURING.

Even in the relatively small area of Spain, the south of France, and Italy a remarkable number of interlocking temperature zones occur. However, two elements clearly distinguish the Mediterranean south from the north of Europe: these are distinctly higher temperatures and much stronger sunshine. These factors contribute to the optimum ripening of the grapes from appropriate vine varieties, and the result is a completely different type of wine, full and velvety.

In eastern Europe, where the weather is often hot, with summer temperatures of over 68°F (20°C), hard frosts can also occur. During the course of the year these can give rise to extremes of temperature from which the rest of Europe is largely spared. Great fluctuations between day and night temperatures, however, tend to improve the quality of the wine. The supreme product of such conditions is Tokaji, in which fullness and freshness are united in timeless grandeur.

North America and South America

The U.S.A. is almost bisected by the 32°F (0°C) line. South of it—apart from the Pacific seaboard—temperatures of over 77°F (25°C) predominate, and as such the land is unsuitable for wine growing. Meso- or microclimates may offer limited opportunities, but two other extremes complicate matters: drought or almost tropical humidity. In the northeast, rain and cold restrict the chances of wine growing. Only on the west coast, thanks to the moderating influence of the Pacific, do certain areas provide ideal conditions for making outstanding red wines in particular.

Wine-growing region

Vineyard

Summer temperature in July
(average over several years)

below 59°F (15°C)

above 59°F (15°C)

above 68°F (20°C)

above 77°F (25°C)

Winter temperature in January
(average over several years)

32°F (0°C)

23°F (−5°C)

Warm current

Cold current

621 miles (1,000 km)

In the South American continent, only a few exceptional districts offer the conditions necessary for making good wine. The best of these are in the Andes where, even in the dry regions, rivers provide the irrigation without which viticulture here would be impossible.

On the Argentinian side of the Andes the altitude—and there are vineyards at up to and even above 6,500 ft (2,000 m)—often moderates the prevailing heat, and well-balanced wines can be made. In Chile, on the other hand, the influence of the Pacific Ocean provides a temperate climate, in fact one of the best in the world for wine growing. On the Atlantic coast conditions are considerably less favorable, as the wine-growing regions shown on the map suggest, although Uruguay is something of an exception. In sub-tropical climates the temperature often makes it impossible to produce wines of quality. In addition, the heat and humidity can encourage diseases to which only the hybrid vine varieties are resistant.

Wine-growing region

Summer temperature in January
(average over several years)

below 59°F (15°C)
above 59°F (15°C)
above 68°F (20°C)
above 77°F (25°C)

Winter temperature in July
(average over several years)

32°F (0°C)

Warm current

Cold current

621 miles (1,000 km)

Grape-growing Areas and Wine Production

The vine gives us two kinds of fruits. Some taste delicious as they are, and take their place on the table as dessert grapes or raisins. The others usually have too thick a skin to be eaten as raw fruit, and are therefore used to make wine. The reason for this difference lies in a process of the selection of varieties that can be traced back over thousands of years. It is unusual to find grapes that are good both for eating as fruit and for making wine. As the statistics of grape-growing areas illustrate, some countries grow vines for dessert grapes or raisins over very large areas, far outstripping the planted areas of wine-producing countries. This is why Turkey comes fourth in the overall table, because it is the world's leading producer of dessert grapes and raisins. Although in 1998 the official statistics of the *Office International de la Vigne et du Vin*

The Spätburgunder grape, with its small berries, is used for making wine, but in many parts of the world vines are cultivated principally or exclusively for the production of dessert grapes.

(OIV)—the international wine bureau based in Paris—ranked Iran in sixth place with 270,000 hectares growing vines, and China was placed tenth, it appears that countries which mainly produce dessert grapes and raisins are no longer listed in the tables. This is probably also due to a lack of up-to-date information. The fact remains that quite a number of Asian and North African countries have extensive vine-growing areas but do not use them—or use only a small part of them—for wine production.

Little has changed at the top of the wine production table. Italy and France compete for the top listing as far as production is concerned, and often change place, depending on the climate of a particular year. Spain, which still has the largest grape-growing area of all, continues in third place for wine production. Considerably more interesting is the lower end of the list. Portugal, which was for a short time pushed out of the ten most important wine-producing countries, has been able to consolidate its production. It has today almost tripled its production compared to the end of the 1970s, when it made 96 million gallons (3.65 million hectoliters). Chile has overcome the crisis which led to a drastic slump in production between 1986 and 1990, and is now producing increasingly large amounts of wine, growing grape varieties that are in international demand in restructured vineyards. In Argentina, production has been falling for more than 25 years, and the decline continues. What the figures do not show is the increase in the production of high-quality wines.

Areas planted in 1000s of acres (hectares)		Source: O.I.V. 2000
Country	Area planted	World percentage of areas planted
Spain	2,901 (1,174)	14.9
France	2,266 (917)	11.6
Italy	2,244 (908)	11.5
Turkey	1,436 (581)	7.4
USA (California)	1,021 (413)	5.2
Portugal	645 (261)	3.3
Romania	613 (248)	3.1
Argentina	516 (209)	2.7
Chile	430 (174)	2.1
Australia	346 (140)	1.8
10 countries in total	12,462 (5,025)	63.6
The world in total	19,485 (7,885)	100

Wine production in millions of gallons (1,000 hectoliters) Source: O.I.V. 2000			
Country	Wine production 2001	Wine production 1990	Percentage of change
France	1,538 (58,240)	1,730 (65,529)	−12.2
Italy	1,354 (51,300)	1,448 (54,866)	−6.5
Spain	822 (31,130)	1,021 (38,658)	−19.5
USA	628 (23,800)	419 (15,852)	+50.1
Argentina	321 (12,150)	371 (14,036)	−13.4
Australia	284 (10,770)	117 (4,446)	+142.2
Germany	255 (9,660)	225 (8,514)	+13.5
South Africa	197 (7,470)	237 (8,998)	−16.9
Portugal	185 (7,010)	300 (11,372)	−38.4
Chile	159 (6,000)	105 (3,978)	+50.8
10 countries in total	5,743 (217,530)	5,973 (226,239)	−3.8
The world in total	7,284 (275,892)	7,468 (282,897)	−2.5

WINE CONSUMPTION

France is the leader in wine consumption per country—at 1,439 million gallons (34.5 million hectoliters), beating Italy at 814 gallons (30.8 million hl) (the trend is moving downward). The U.S.A. follows with 550 million gallons (21.2 million hectoliters), then Germany at 518 million gallons (19.6 million hl), Spain at 365 million (13.8 hl) and Argentina at 327 million (12.4 hl). Other wine-growing countries consume less than 265 million gallons (10 million hectoliters) a year.

THE EXTREME REGIONS OF AFRICA

The only wine growing worth mentioning in Africa is in the extreme regions. In the North African countries of the Maghreb only mountain slopes provide conditions suitable for viticulture. In the very south—therefore below the equator—the Benguela Current from the Antarctic moderates temperatures. In practice, however, only the Cape area offers the conditions for viticulture in southern Africa.

André Dominé, Eckhard Supp, Ulrich Sautter, Wolfgang Fassbender

FRANCE

THE FRENCH WINE REGIONS

Geological and climatic diversity combine to make France one of the most richly diverse wine countries in the world. Under differing natural conditions, the vine varieties have acclimatized over the centuries, and diverse methods of cultivation have developed.

Champagne, France's northernmost wine region, borders the area where average temperatures are not sufficiently high to ripen grapes. Toward the Atlantic coast, rainfall is too high for growing vines. The acidic character of Champagne is determined by this border climate.

Alsace enjoys a particularly favorable climate, and the Vosges mountains to the west form a superb natural border to the wine-growing district. Here, on sloping sites facing the sun, the grapes become overripe, and the moisture rising from the fluvial plain encourages the development of the NOBLE ROT fungus, which is responsible for the greatest wines of the region.

In the northern part of Burgundy, which has the best-known *appellation* of Chablis, the winegrowers must take frost protection measures to prevent some of the best Chardonnay locations from freezing. The Chardonnay grape, which has spread all around the world, develops incomparable mineral expression here on the soil, which is a mix of marine limestone and

Historic estates, surrounded by vines, are a frequent sight not only in Beaujolais but all over France.

clay. Here, as in other Burgundy *appellations*, it generally rains so much that growers use a particularly high planting density to control the growth of the vines. This also applies to Beaujolais. Between the broad valley of the Saône and the Monts du Beaujolais, the Gamay grape finds its ideal *terroir* on the granitic or marl soil, but the winegrowers have to prune the vines in a completely different way to that used by their neighbors in Burgundy for the Pinot Noir vines.

The far eastern French wine regions of Jura and Savoie are characterized by their situation in the mountains. Beside the cultivation of some unique grape varieties, the Jura region is also home to *vin jaune*, a wine kept for six years under a film-forming yeast.

At its estuary, the Loire is a climatically mild and very damp area, because of the influence of the warm Gulf Stream. Thus in the Muscadet region, near the mouth of the Loire, the grapes must often be brought in early. Up river, the continental influences increase, so that great dry and sweet white wines as well as excellent reds thrive here. The Cabernet Franc grape is being increasingly propagated now, as it yields better results than Cabernet Sauvignon in the earlier cool temperatures.

The Bordeaux region, in particular the Médoc, is the stronghold between the Gironde river and the Atlantic Ocean, where a temperate climate

1   Details of the country of origin
2   Name of the wine estate or wine merchant
3   Coat of arms or logo of the producer
4   Vintage
5   Wine region and name of the appellation
6   Wine designation: statutory guarantee of controlled appellation
7   Here: fermented in oak barrels (*elevé en fût de chêne*), or often here, the name of the *cuvée*
8   Bottled at the property where it is made
9   Name of the winegrower or the property
10 Name of the owner-manager (or name of the firm)
11 Address of the business
12 Alcoholic strength (often rounded to the nearest 0.5%, rarely an exact figure)
13 Nominal volume of the bottle

accommodates late ripening, and good, porous, gravel beds prevent frequent rainfalls from thinning the vines. In the Southwest it is often warmer and the mountains have greater influence.

WHERE THE MEDITERRANEAN RULES

The influence of the Atlantic extends amazingly far to the east and, in the cultivated areas of the Southeast, three factors above all influence vine cultivation: warmth, wind, and aridity. These are at their most temperate in the northern Rhône, where they lend superb balance to both red and white wines. Here, and throughout the Midi, is the realm of the Syrah grape, while further south—at their stronghold of Châteauneuf-du-Pape—the Grenache and Mourvèdre grape varieties dominate. In Provence—the epitome of Mediterranean life—the proximity of the Alps to the north affects the wines as much as the Mediterranean Sea does to the south. Accordingly, there is a great range of grape varieties and wine styles. Corsica, meanwhile, is not only geographically closer to the Italian coast, but its typical grape varieties are Italian and are best suited to the Mediterranean climate.

The Languedoc-Roussillon region overlooks the Golfe du Lion and is one of the largest wine regions in the world. This region receives the greatest number of sunshine hours and also shares raging northwesterly winds with Provence, which guarantee the best health for the grapes. These wines reach their optimum concentration in reduced yields.

CHAMPAGNE—HOME OF A NOBLE AND HISTORIC DRINK

Champagne is an invigorating and often even erotic bubbly, the legendary drink of the elite, the undisputed quality sparkling wine. From the Sun King Louis XV to the czars, from Winston Churchill to the English royal family, Formula One winners to stock market flotations—the sparkling wine from the northernmost wine region of France is always present. Unlike any other wine, it has established its *appellation* as a brand name with which the greatest prestige—and the highest prices!—are inextricably linked. Even though there is increasing competition, which must be taken seriously, from Spanish Cava and Italian Franciacorta, as well as Californian and Australian products, the world's premier *appellation*, which specializes exclusively in the production of sparkling wine fermented in the bottle, is the undisputed holder of pole position in the world, even though today it produces less than ten percent of wine in this category.

The name of the wine region which lies northeast of the French capital—in the Middle

A great champagne has tremendous aging potential.

Were it not for Dom Pérignon, champagne would not be what it is today.

Ages, it also included today's Île de France and Paris—comes from the Latin word *campus* and refers to the vineyards and countryside along the Marne valley, known as *Champagne viticole*. The region's geographical extent was strictly defined and delimited by a decree of the Institut National des Appellations d'Origine in 1927. The region is centered around the towns of Reims and Épernay and, from its earliest history, it has been at the crossroads of the major north–south and east–west trade routes. An area blessed with great prosperity, its wine history can be traced back to the 5th century, although it did not specialize in sparkling wines until considerably later.

DOM PÉRIGNON AND HIS LEGACY

A generic *vin de Champagne*, which was predominately still and only foamed occasionally in the bottle, has existed since the 17th century, when these slightly pinkish still wines, made chiefly from the Pinot Noir grape, enjoyed a certain popularity in the salons of London café society. From the second half of the 17th century onwards, this *vin de Champagne* underwent the radical changes which made it the sparkling product, fermented in the bottle, which we know today.

The cornerstone of this development was laid by the monk, Dom Pérignon, the famous cellarmaster of the Abbey of Hautvillers. He did not, as is often believed, invent champagne in its present form, but he was revolutionary in his choice of grape varieties, his vineyard techniques, and his blending of *cuvées* from different varieties and vineyards. He was also the first to

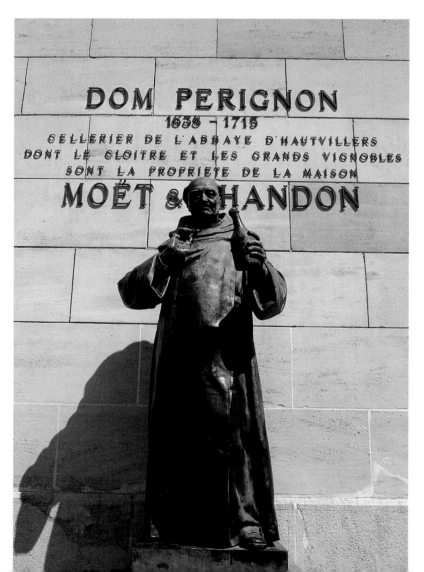

ferment an adequate red wine, and the first to press true white wines from black grapes. He initiated the use of stronger bottles with corks tied down with string, which could withstand greater pressure, thus making it possible to supply and export sparkling wines.

Until the 19th century, production of this sparkling champagne amounted to little more than a few thousand bottles. It was the cellar-master of the famous Veuve (widow) Clicquot who first invented the RIDDLING process called REMUAGE and the exact dose of BOTTLING LIQUOR *liqueur de tirage* for the second fermentation, which advanced production to industrial levels. Commercial success arrived in the middle of the 19th century with a group of young Germans by the names of Krug, Bollinger, Roederer, and Deutz—names which are still the elite of the champagne industry today. They quickly ousted the majority of the local merchants from the market and took up the reins in Reims and its environs.

This success outlived world wars and changes of ownership—today almost every fourth bottle of champagne comes from the cellars of the Louis Vuitton Moët Hennessy (L.V.M.H.) group which owns famous brands such as Veuve-Clicquot-Ponsardin, Krug, Pommery, Ruinart, Moët et Chandon, and Canard-Duchène—and culminated in the sale of 300 million bottles of champagne in the millennium year. That such an unprecedented development was possible is based not only on a unique combination of climate, soil, and grape varieties, but also on the champagne trade's far sightedness and discipline which, over the centuries, has helped it build up the most homogenous *appellation* in the world.

The most visible expression of this unity has been the long-established pricing system used to pay growers for the grapes supplied by them to the champagne houses, which formerly owned very few vineyards. Each year, these prices are established in negotiations and then fixed as standard for the whole region. This pricing committee was established after the collapse of the market in the 1920s and early 1930s. In addition, a number of winegrowers took the CHAMPAGNE METHOD into their own hands and until 1990 ensured relative market stability for the growers and winemakers. Since then, however, not even champagne has been exempt from the ups and downs of the market and the economy.

In damp cellars, labels may rot, but not the champagne.

Chalk is doubly important in Champagne. It not only affects the soil in which the vines grow, but it also provides endless cellars that maintain an ideal temperature and in which wines can survive for over 100 years.

Hautvillers is worth a detour for the growers' signs alone.

ACIDITY AND SUGAR FOR GOOD CHAMPAGNE

The majority of planted vines, and all the classified vineyards of Champagne, lie on the deep, chalkly soil of the slopes of the hills. These provide both good humidity and excellent drainage and their high pH values are responsible for the high acidity levels of the grapes. The slopes also offer the essential requirement—sufficient warmth—since, in what is for vineyards a very northerly location, champagne can hardly guarantee a surfeit of warmth and light for the grapes. Furthermore, the weather, which is affected by maritime changeability, means a longer growing season, which contributes to increased acidity even in ripe grapes—one of the most important factors for sparkling wines. Big, structured white or red wines are never produced in the Champagne region. Despite the original existence of many different grape varieties, in the vineyards between Reims and Épernay only three grapes have been successful, Chardonnay, Pinot Noir, and Pinot Meunier. This may be because of their proximity to Burgundy—two of these vine varieties are also used to make great white wines in Chablis and the Côte d'Or—or because these grapes are well adapted for ripening in cooler climates.

In the region as a whole, more than 35 percent of the whole area given over to vineyards is planted with the simple base variety, Pinot Meunier. Pinot Noir occupies a good third and Chardonnay just over a quarter of the area. However, in the top communes where the base wines for *cuvées de prestige* are made, the reverse is the case, with Chardonnay in the lead at over two fifths. Although almost all champagne is white, it is no contradiction that the black grape varieties dominate in the vineyards. However, when these black grapes are picked, they must be pressed rapidly, using a specific procedure, to prevent the color running from the grape skins. This is the main reason mechanical harvesters are banned in Champagne, since they crush the grapes and the start of the MACERATION process is then inevitable.

Champagne is not exempt from another problem in post-war European wine cultivation: the trend toward attaining ever bigger yields per acre. Between 1940 and 1980, yields increased threefold in the region and, despite an increase in permitted grape quantities—from 330 to 350 pounds for $26\frac{1}{2}$ gallons (150 to 160 kg for 100 liters) of MUST—this led to thinner and thinner base wines, with the final result being that up to 3.5% vol of the actual alcohol was no longer made from the sugars in the grape juice but from CHAPTALIZATION.

Who has actually bottled your wine?

Beside technical details (see illustration), a champagne label often bears a number in very small print which is usually preceded by two letters: these refer to the type of bottler of the champagne concerned, as follows.

N.M.: *Négociant-manipulant*—these merchants or houses harvest or buy grapes, must, or base wines which they then process in their own cellars.

R.M.: *Récoltant-manipulant*—this winegrower makes his own champagne in his own cellars from his own grapes.

R.C.: *Récoltant-coopérateur*—this winegrower is a member of a cooperative, and he sells the wine made by the cooperative to his own customers.

C.M.: *Coopérative de manipulation*—wine cooperative which makes and matures champagne in its own cellars from its members' grapes.

S.R.: *Société de récoltants*—an organization of independent winegrowers which makes and bottles champagne from the harvests of its members.

N.D.: *Négociant distributeur*—wine merchant or company which buys champagne which has already been bottled and then provides the label.

R.: *Récoltant*—this winegrower allows his grapes to be made into wine by a *négociant-manipulant* and receives back the champagne in bottles.

M.A.: *Marque auxiliaire*—literally, additional brand: this is the reseller's own brand shown on the label.

Information on a champagne label:

Champagne House	MOËT et CHANDON
Place	Épernay
Year established	Fondée en 1743
Appellation	Champagne
Cuvée	Cuvée Dom Pérignon
Alcoholic strength	12.5%
Nominal volume	750 ml
Type of dosage	Brut
Registered no. and type of bottler	élaboré par
Firm, place, country	MOËT et CHANDON ÉPERNAY/FRANCE
Registered trademark and design	Muselet EPARNIX
Vintage	Millésime 1990

Champagne consumption

Champagne is always something special and it should be treated as such, so that it can meet all expectations. The level of care required begins when you buy it. Basically, there is an appropriate champagne for every occasion and every dish—it just has to be the right one. Almost no other wine has such a broad range. By mixing grape varieties, wines from different vineyards, and different vintages, as well as altering DOSAGES, each champagne producer has the opportunity to bestow each CUVÉE with its own personal character. Thus there are slim and corpulent, fruity and flowery, fresh and mature, sweet and very dry, young and mature champagnes. And of course, there are good and bad, fine and ordinary, harmonious and coarse, expensive and cheap ones. Even in the case of the most popular type of champagne— non-vintage BRUT—there are big differences. In such cases, the advice of a SOMMELIER, a specialist in the trade, an expert wine merchant, a serious wine guide, or one's own experience is helpful.

Champagne makes a wonderful aperitif, provided it is lively, fresh, and dry, as are the majority of non-vintage *bruts* and young Blanc de Blancs. Blanc de Blancs wines are a superb accompaniment to oysters and shellfish. For caviar and lobster, a more powerful *brut* is preferable. Many fish dishes are ideally accompanied by a *brut* or Blanc de Blancs. However, if the taste, consistency, or sauce of a dish are stronger, then the champagne should also have more structure and complexity, and so a vintage or rosé wine would be recommended. The rare *cuvées de prestige* require careful matching. A powerful, dry champagne can be good with cheese, while for desserts—if possible not too sweet—*sec* and *demi-sec* champagnes are recommended.

The best temperature at which to serve champagne is between 43°F and 48°F (6°C and 9°C), at which temperature the wine should be gently chilled. Ideally, once open, the bottle should be kept in a bucket filled with ice and water. You should not serve champagne in flat champagne glasses, but instead in clear, slender, tulip-shaped, crystal glasses with a stem long enough to ensure that the body heat of the hand is not transmitted to the bowl.

The Communes and Wine Villages

The unique character of Champagne and its wines lies in the fact that, over the last two centuries, its protagonists have built up a tremendously strong corporate identity from an *appellation*, a method—BOTTLE FERMENTATION—and a product conceived like a brand. There are no fluctuations between locations and vintages, and those wine-specific attributes such as origin, grape variety, producer, and VINTAGE do not apply.

Champagne is first and foremost a landscape, a geographical area, and a designated *appellation*—the only significant French wine region which has a single, albeit tremendously popular and strong *appellation*. As in all top French wine regions, Champagne has its own specific, classified *terroirs* and *crus*. Although the majority of its bottled products come from blends of different wines and different vintages, such classification details are only very rarely listed on the labels. What is relevant, however, is how prices are set for grapes from the different areas and communes in the wine region, the best prices being paid for grapes from the *grands crus* and then for those from the *premiers crus*.

This is based on the subdivision of the entire *Champagne viticole* into five natural areas with different conditions, each of which favors different grape varieties, namely: the Montagne de Reims, the Marne Valley, the Côte des Blancs, the Côte de Sézanne and the Côte des Bar in the Aube. The vineyards on the northern and eastern slopes of the Montagne de Reims are chiefly planted on sandy, clayey soil on chalk cliffs, sandstone, and

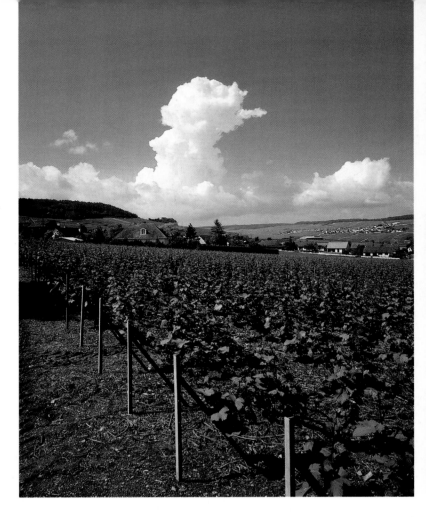

In Cuis, one of the Côte des Blancs villages, the champagnes are made exclusively from the white Chardonnay grape and are noted for their striking freshness.

The house of the champagne producer is evidence of its glorious past.

marl. Marl and sandy clay form the topsoil in the Marne Valley, while on the Côte des Blancs, sand and clay on chalk cliffs predominate. On the Côte de Sézanne, marl, clay and sand lie on chalk, while in the Aube, gravelly limestone soil is dominant.

Grands and Premiers Crus

The vineyards of 17 communes in total—Montagne de Reims (nine), the Côte des Blancs (four) and the Marne Valley (four)—have *grand cru* status and growers in these communes are paid 100 percent of the agreed prices for their grapes.

There are a further 38 communes, amounting to just 12,000 acres (5,000 hectares), whose vineyards have *premier cru* status and growers in these communes receive between 90 and 99 percent of the full price for their grapes. Very few of the communes are known to the consumer or even feature on the labels (for example, the Clos des Goisses of the Philipponnat house). One of the most famous examples is the Clos du Mesnil vineyard belonging to the Krug house, which produces a champagne made solely from Chardonnay grapes from the house's own vineyard in Le Mesnil-sur-Oger, which grows only this variety. In the higher areas of this location, the grapes make particularly dense, aromatic

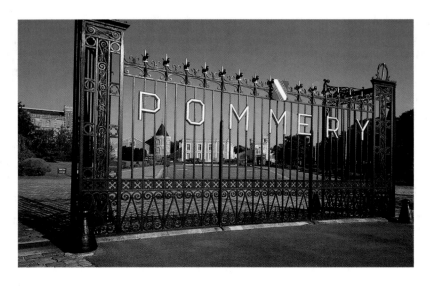

champagne, full of finesse. The person who discovered their qualities was Eugène-Aimé Salon, the founder of the house of the same name, which today still produces one of the best champagnes in the area from local grapes.

Similar (almost) pure Chardonnay champagne is also produced in other communes in the Côte des Blancs, where famous Champagne houses such as Veuve Clicquot-Ponsardin, Moët et Chandon, Mumm, Perrier-Jouët, Heidsieck Monopole, Pommery & Greno, Pol Roger, and Taittinger all have their own vineyards, but where the wines are seldom bottled as single-varietal or from a single village. By far the most popular are the *cuvées de prestige*, which are made almost exclusively from grapes from *grand cru* communes, but in which grapes are also used from communes where Pinot Noir is the dominant variety at over 80 percent. Examples of such *cuvées de prestige* are Bollinger's R.D., Laurent-Perrier's Cuvée Grand Siècle, Roederer's Cristal, Ruinart's Dom Ruinart, Moët et Chandon's Dom Pérignon, Deutz's Cuvée William Deutz, and Pol Roger's Winston Churchill. Made from particularly high-value wines, often fermented or stored in wooden barrels, which mature over many months on the lees, and whose structure and balance also imply great aging potential, such *cuvées de prestige* represent the very best champagnes— rare and costly, but also expensive jewels for special celebrations.

Chalk Cellars and Millions of Bottles

Unlike any other wine region, in Champagne the name of the product is linked with a specific production process—in this case, bottle fermentation, which is also known as the champagne method or *méthode champenoise*. With its numerous, strictly regulated procedures, the production of champagne is one of the most complex in the wine world.

The rules with which growers must comply begin in the vineyard itself. The maximum yield is 89 to 98 pounds per acre (100 to 110 kg per hectare), and this limit may be increased by the regulatory authorities in specific years—although many critics feel it is too high to be able to guarantee base wines that are both concentrated and structured. The must yield in PRESSING is also regulated, to prevent any undesired color or taste transferring from the grapes to the must by overly-strong pressing.

Grapes must be harvested by hand. Mechanical harvesters are forbidden in order to prevent

For the most famous Champagnes, the base wines are stored in wooden barrels and so some houses still employ their own coopers.

premature crushing and fermenting of the grapes, and to keep both the astringency and color of the must to a minimum. The harvested grapes are taken as quickly as possible to one of the many pressing centers belonging to the big champagne houses and cooperatives. The traditional round, very flat wicker winepresses, which still take precedence over modern pneumatic presses, can hold 8,818 pounds (4,000 kg) of grapes, (a quantity known as a MARC). The first and best must extracted from the grapes is known as the *cuvée*—this is mostly used to make the highest value wines. The rules state that a maximum of 26½ gallons (100 liters) of juice can be made from 350 pounds (160 kg) of grapes and thus, from the 8,818 pounds (4,000 kg) in a press, 660 gallons (2,500 liters) of wine may be made, the *cuvée* accounting for four-fifths of this. The next amount of the juice extracted from the marc is known as the *première taille*, followed by the *deuxième taille*. These pressings show higher pH and TANNIN levels and are only used in ordinary champagne brands.

MÉTHODE CHAMPENOISE

After pressing, the must is purified, sulfurized, occasionally also clarified and afterwards fermented, by which time almost all base wines will have undergone MALOLACTIC FERMENTATION. FERMENTATION takes place mostly in temperature-controlled stainless steel vats. Only at the famous brands of Krug, Alfred Gratien, and Bollinger are the once-common wooden casks still used systematically. A number of wine growers who have only a limited variety of different *terroir* characteristics available, can still give their wines some complexity by aging them partly in wood. This will provide some oxygenation to the wine, which assists in harmonizing flavor, but under no circumstances does it involve imparting the vanilla or smoky notes of barrel-fermented Chardonnay.

After a certain amount of aging, there follows one of the most important stages in making champagne, the ASSEMBLAGE process, which is the true art of the cellar-master and the closely guarded secret of each champagne house or grower. The base wines from Chardonnay, Pinot Noir, and Pinot Meunier grapes are blended, and wines from different vineyards and even from different vintages are also used, unless a VINTAGE (*millésimé*) champagne is involved.

The aim is to produce, every year, a champagne which matches the brand as closely as

Left
At Ruinart in Reims, a model shows how the cellar was originally arranged.

Right
The champagnes develop their special finish in almost endless chalk cellars.

possible. It is primarily through the addition of wines from earlier vintages, the *vins de réserve* (reserve wines), that balanced, complex end-products are achieved.

The wine which is the result of the *assemblage* process is then put into bottles with a mixture of wine, YEAST, and sugar, known as the bottling liquor or *liqueur de tirage*, and the bottles are capped with a crown cork. The sugar added at this stage is not for sweetening purposes—this comes later—but is used solely to feed the yeast, to ensure complete fermentation of the base wine. Approximately 1.5 percent vol of additional alcoholic strength may result from the second fermentation which takes place completely in the bottle, the real crux of the *méthode champenoise*, whereby the internal pressure of the bottle reaches four to six atmospheres through the carbon dioxide building up, at the same time as the alcohol.

The second fermentation ideally takes place at very cold, stable temperatures—conditions which are especially found in the chalk cellars used by some houses such as Charles Heidsieck. Some of these tunnels are occasionally open to visitors, and with their white walls, against which hundreds of thousands of bottles are stacked carefully waiting for the completion of their yeast fermentation, cellars are a spectacular sight.

In addition to the production of alcohol, the yeast also has an important function in contributing to taste. After complete fermentation, the yeast slowly begins to decompose—a process known as yeast autolysis—and forms a series of

Champagne has always had a luxurious ambience—and this also applies in its homeland.

always lie steeply in the rack. Today, machines are used for this purpose and complete the same work in a shorter time and without requiring the same level of technical input from specialists. Some houses still have at least their *cuvées de prestige* riddled by hand, although there is no conclusive evidence that machine *remuage* results in a reduction in quality.

Ordinary brand champagnes are then made ready for sale, while the better *cuvées* remain for a certain time, sometimes several years *sur pointe* while the wine matures further. The last step in creating champagne is the process known as DISGORGEMENT (*dégorgement*), which was previously done by hand (*à la volée*) but is mostly done by machine today. This removes the yeast deposits that have collected in the neck of the bottle during the riddling process. The neck of the bottle, containing the yeast deposit, is frozen in a liquid coolant (salt solution) and the bottle is then opened. The pressure in the bottle shoots out the sediment.

To top up the wine lost in the disgorgement process, a *liqueur d'expédition* or dosage is added to the wine, which also serves to balance the sweetness of the finished wine. Mostly this dosage is a mixture of the base wine and sugar syrup, the amount of additional sugar used determining the sweetness (*brut, sec, doux,* etc.) of the wine. After corking and attaching the metal cap and wire muzzle, labeling and packing, the champagne is finally ready for that special party, glittering ball, celebration of success at work, wedding, anniversary, or special birthday.

fragrant and flavorsome substances which enrich and round off the champagne. At the same time, the carbon dioxide created during the second fermentation gets better and finer in the wine, so a particularly long storage time leads to the finest and longest-lasting fizziness in the glass.

"LIQUEUR" IN WINE?

When the sparkling wine has almost reached its desired maturity, the yeast deposit, which over the months has dropped to the bottom of the bottle, is carefully moved to its neck. This process of riddling or *remuage* was once done manually, with the bottles placed head down in special riddling racks (*pupitres*) and turned slightly every two days, so that one part would

---

Types of champagne

Extra-brut: also known as *brut non dosé, brut nature, ultra-brut, brut zéro, brut intégral:* this is a champagne made with no dosage, which naturally has less than 0.04 ounces per pint (2 g per liter) of RESIDUAL SUGAR.

Brut: this dry champagne has a low dosage, up to a maximum permitted level of $^1/_4$ ounce per pint (15 g per liter) of additional sugar.

Sec: although the name means dry, the *liqueur d'expédition* in this case gives it a sugar content of just over $^1/_4$ to $^1/_2$ ounce per pint (17–35 g per liter).

Demi-sec: primarily designed as a dessert wine, the sugar content of this sweet wine is $^1/_2$ to 1 ounce per pint (35–50 g per liter).

Doux: the sugar content of this rare, very sweet champagne is anything over 1 ounce per pint (50 g per liter).

Brut sans millésime: this bone-dry, non-vintage is the signature of each brand of champagne, because it represents 80 percent of total turnover. Varies widely.

Blanc de Blancs: made exclusively from white Chardonnay grapes, as a rule this is fresh and lively and a good aperitif.

Blanc de Noirs: made exclusively from black Pinot Noir or Pinot Meunier grapes, this has stronger structure and fruitiness.

Crémant: champagne which is semi-sparkling and more winey; that from Cramant is the most sought after, not to be confused with *crémants* from other regions.

Rosé: or pink champagne is seldom made from black grapes with some skin contact, but is more often a mixture of red and white wine; often more powerful and fruitier than white, it is good with food.

Millésimé: vintage champagnes come only from years in which conditions have been particularly good. They are aged for three and often six years, have more volume and body, and mature well for several more years in the bottle.

Cuvée de Prestige, etc.: these are the deluxe wines of the champagne houses. For the most part, they are long matured wines from an outstanding vintage—some of which have legendary reputations—and naturally, prices to match.

Ruinart—light, nervy, refreshing

Deutz—lively, nervy, good with seafood

De Venoge—fruity tones, pleasant aperitif

Lanson—citrus notes, crisp

Pommery—winey, harmonious, and fresh

Veuve Clicquot Ponsardin—aromatic, fine fruit

Laurent Perrier—complex, fruity tones, lively

Pol Roger—harmony, elegance, complex aroma

Piper Heidsieck—classic, balanced

Jacquard—complex bouquet and good length

Krug Grand Cuvée—a wine full of finesse

Louis Roederer—fine fruit, balanced, and elegant

Moët et Chandon—straight, consistent

Ayala Brut—delicate bouquet, good fizz

Taittinger—fruity, good mouthfeel

limits, or adopt ideas from other regions of France. Thus red wine has made its debut over the last few years. While Pinot Noir was already cultivated here, it was almost always made into a hybrid between rosé and red wine, which would be served chilled. Now a number of winegrowers are trying to produce real reds, and are experimenting with longer must fermentation and storage in barrels. Maturation in BARRIQUES, which imparts various degrees of oak flavor to the wine, has also become fashionable over the last few years. Several of the Pinot Noir wines matured in this way are a match for the great red Burgundies. Many winegrowers are also turning their attention to white wines fermented in *barriques*—here and there the visitor to Alsace is likely to come across Pinot Gris or Sylvaner wines that have spent a few months in barrels of this sort. Pinot Noir is also being commercially produced in small quantities as a white Blanc de Noirs.

RENAISSANCE OF THE SPARKLING WINES

The specialty sweet wines, the *vendanges tardives* (late-harvested wines) and *sélections de grains nobles* (produced from even riper grapes), have experienced an upswing over the last few years. Another innovation in wine production in Alsace, at least as successful, is the Crémant d'Alsace sparkling wine. Although it was produced in a few small areas by the end of the 19th century, official recognition only dates from 1976. *Crémants* are produced using the classic bottle fermentation process exclusively, spend at least nine months on their yeast, and consist primarily of the Pinot Blanc, Pinot Gris, and Sylvaner grape varieties, and occasionally Chardonnay (which is permitted to be used only in the production of sparkling wine in Alsace). Riesling is seldom used. Within a few

Rodern, one of the most beautiful wine villages, revealing the checkerboard pattern of its vineyards.

years, Crémant d'Alsace has developed into a winner both in France and as an export, and 14 percent of all Alsace wines are now sparkling.

However, another category of wines with a rich tradition is currently in free fall. The Edelzwicker which, in the early 20th century, was a high-quality *cuvée* or blend of noble grape varieties, is of little consequence now. In winemaking of the last few decades, this wine has mutated into the "garbage can" of the Alsace winegrowers. Only a few demanding producers (e.g. Hugel) offer Edelzwicker today, and those who do often use the French name Gentil, which has not yet become debased.

THE SEVEN GRAPES OF ALSACE

Nearly all still Alsace wines are single-varietal wines. In general, reference is made to just seven Alsace grape varieties: Riesling, Gewürztraminer, Muscat, Pinot Gris, Sylvaner, Pinot Blanc, and Pinot Noir, the sole red variety. But others, whose names can be read on labels from time to time, do exist. Chasselas used to be widespread, but today only covers a few acres. It usually produces a neutral everyday wine and can therefore be ranked alongside Sylvaner and Pinot Blanc. Very seldom do these three grape varieties attract the sort of attention given to the noble Riesling, Gewürztraminer, Muscat, and Pinot Gris varieties. The latter was once known exclusively as Tokay d'Alsace, although it is not related to its Hungarian namesake. The term Tokay may now be used only to designate Pinot Gris wines, and from 2006 on, it will have disappeared for good.

The name Muscat actually embraces two different varieties: Muscat Blanc à Petits Grains and Muscat Ottonel, which are almost always blended together. The same is true of Pinot

Blanc: true Pinot Blanc and Auxerrois are usually blended and only occasionally drawn off independently to produce single-varietal wines. Production of Klevener de Heiligenstein, a less flowery relative of Gewürztraminer, is permitted only within the limits of the Heiligenstein commune. The name Klevner, on the other hand (without the second e) is commonly used as a synonym for Pinot Blanc.

SWEET OR DRY?

Whether an Alsace wine is dry or sweet is not stated on the label. While Sylvaner and Pinot Blanc wines are almost always thoroughly fermented, and most Muscats also reach the bottle without any great degree of sweetness, this is not true of the Riesling, Pinot Gris, and Gewürztraminer varieties. A few growers (e.g. Trimbach) are known for their consistently dry style, but many *grand cru* wines have a distinct residual sweetness that balances out the alcohol levels of 13 or 14 percent.

Alsace has a long tradition of very sweet wines, made from ripe and very ripe grapes and were already produced hundreds of years ago. However, growers have been producing them on a large scale for only a few years. In 1984 the French authority in charge of the *appellation* system, the I.N.A.O., laid down official requirements for them. For the *vendange tardive* or late-harvested wines, they stipulate a specific must gravity of at least 95° on the OECHSLE scale. *Sélection de grains nobles* wines, produced from even riper grapes, can only be produced using grapes that reach a minimum of 110°. Growers with a greater commitment to quality, however, frequently exceed the official SPECIFIC GRAVITY levels by considerable amounts.

Hand-picking.

Left
Pinot Gris grapes affected by noble rot.

Right
Ripe Gewürztraminer grapes.

The addition of sugar to either class of sweet wine is forbidden, even though this is a perfectly legal and customary practice for all other Alsace wines. Compared to the world-famous German *Beerenauslese* and *Trockenbeerenauslese* wines, the sweet wines of Alsace usually have rather less residual sugar and therefore more alcohol. In this respect they have a greater resemblance to their counterparts from Sauternes.

Vin de paille (traditionally made from grapes dried on beds of straw) and *vin de glace* (made from grapes naturally frozen on the vine) are very rarely encountered in Alsace: only a handful of dedicated wine producers are bold enough to experiment with these particular sweet specialties.

GRANDS CRUS AND OTHER NAMED VINEYARD WINES

Up to now, only the four noble grape varieties (Riesling, Gewürztraminer, Muscat, and Pinot Gris), and only three percent of all the region's wines, have been permitted to use the *grand cru* designation. However, discussions over the classification of the top vineyards, which began in 1975, continue to this day. It is said that many of them have become too large, and that other vineyards widely recognized as being among the best were not even included in the classification. Thus the renowned Kaefferkopf in Ammerschwihr has still not been made a *grand cru*—the reason for this being the lack of uniformity of the vineyard, which comprises various soil types. Other vineyards have failed to win a classification because they are all owned by the same grower.

Generally speaking, however, the Alsace *grand cru* classification is a useful tool in the identification of top wines. Other named vineyard wines have managed to get established in its wake, and there are many above-average wines in the ranks of these *lieux-dits* or named locality wines that offer significantly better value than a *grand cru*.

The 50 *grands crus* of Alsace

Vineyard and locality	Geological characteristics
Altenberg de Bergbieten	clay marl containing natural gypsum
Altenberg de Bergheim	limestone marl
Altenberg de Wolxheim	limestone marl
Brand (Turckheim)	granite
Bruderthal (Molsheim)	limestone marl
Eichberg (Eguisheim)	limestone marl
Engelberg (Dahlenheim and Scharrachbergheim)	limestone marl
Florimont (Ingersheim and Katzenthal)	limestone marl
Frankstein (Dambach-la-Ville)	granite
Froehn (Zellenberg)	clay marl
Furstentum (Kientzheim and Sigolsheim)	limestone
Geisberg (Ribeauvillé)	limestone marl and sand
Gloeckelberg (Rodern and Saint-Hippolyte)	granite and clay
Goldert (Gueberschwihr)	limestone marl
Hatschbourg (Voegtlinshoffen and Hattstatt)	limestone marl and loess
Hengst (Wintzenheim)	limestone marl and sandstone
Kanzlerberg (Bergheim)	clay marl containing natural gypsum
Kastelberg (Andlau)	slate
Kessler (Guebwiller)	sand with clay
Kirchberg de Barr	limestone marl
Kirchberg de Ribeauvillé	limestone marl and sandstone
Kitterlé (Guebwiller)	volcanic sandstone
Mambourg (Sigolsheim)	limestone marl
Mandelberg (Mittelwihr and Beblenheim)	limestone marl
Marckrain (Bennwihr and Sigolsheim)	limestone marl
Moenchberg (Andlau and Eichhoffen)	limestone marl and alluvium
Muenchberg (Nothalten)	stony volcanic sandstone
Ollwiller (Wuenheim)	sand with clay
Osterberg (Ribeauvillé)	marl
Pfersigberg (Eguisheim and Wettolsheim)	chalky sandstone
Pfingstberg (Orschwihr)	limestone marl and sandstone
Praelatenberg (Kintzheim)	granite and gneiss
Rangen (Thann and Vieux-Thann)	volcanic
Rosacker (Hunawihr)	dolomite limestone
Saering (Guebwiller)	limestone marl and sandstone
Schlossberg (Kientzheim)	granite
Schoenenbourg (Riquewihr and Zellenberg)	marl containing sand and gypsum
Sommerberg (Niedermorschwihr und Katzenthal)	granite
Sonnenglanz (Beblenheim)	limestone marl
Spiegel (Bergholtz and Guebwiller)	clay marl and sandstone
Sporen (Riquewihr)	stony clay marl
Steinert (Pfaffenheim and Westhalten)	limestone
Steingrubler (Wettolsheim)	limestone marl and sandstone
Steinklotz (Marlenheim)	limestone
Vorbourg (Rouffach und Westhalten)	limestone and sandstone
Wiebelsberg (Andlau)	quartz and sandstone
Wineck-Schlossberg (Katzenthal and Ammerschwihr)	granite
Winzenberg (Blienschwiller)	granite
Zinnkoepflé (Soultzmatt and Westhalten)	limestone and sandstone
Zotzenberg (Mittelbergheim)	limestone marl

SELECT PRODUCERS IN ALSACE

ALBERT BOXLER****—****
NIEDERMORSCHWIHR
25 acres (10 ha); 55,000 bottles • Wines include:
→ *Riesling Sommerberg, Riesling Brand, Riesling
Vieilles Vignes, Gewürztraminer Brand, Pinot Gris,
Muscat,* → *Vendanges Tardives*
Although this estate in remote Niedermorschwihr is not
in the best position, it has long outgrown its status as a
hot tip. Jean-Marc Boxler's concentrated and juicy
Rieslings are among the longest-lived in Alsace.

ERNEST BURN****—****
GUEBERSCHWIHR
*25 acres (10 ha); 60,000 bottles • Wines include:
Gewürztraminer Clos Saint-Imer, Pinot Gris Clos Saint-
Imer,* → *Muscat Clos Saint-Imer,* → *Cuvées La Chapelle*
An unusual estate with unusual wines: opulent,
concentrated, and juicy. Additionally, the top-quality
cuvées from the Clos Saint-Imer plot (which is part of
the Goldert *grand cru*) are marketed under the La
Chapelle label.

CAVE DE PFAFFENHEIM**—****
PFAFFENHEIM
*593 acres (240 ha); 2,000,000 bottles • Wines include:
Gewürztraminer Zinnkoepflé, Gewürztraminer
Steinert, Muscat Goldert, Pinot, Vendanges Tardives*
Founded in 1957, this is the most committed of the
Alsace wine cooperatives, and regularly sweeps the
board in competitions. It produces elegant wines in
a modern winery.

MARCEL DEISS*****
BERGHEIM
*49 acres (20 ha); 120,000 bottles • Wines include:
Riesling Altenberg,* → *Gewürztraminer Altenberg,
Riesling Schoenenbourg,* → *Grand Vin d'Altenberg,
Pinot Burlenberg Vieilles Vignes*
Jean-Michel Deiss is most at home in the vineyard, and
this is the basis of his leading position among Alsace
winegrowers. Yields are minimal and the wines
uniquely concentrated. Even the simplest Sylvaners
show finesse, and the rare and expensive Grand Vin, a
cuvée or blend of Gewürztraminer, Riesling, and Pinot
Gris, even more so.

DIRLER-CADÉ****
BERGHOLTZ
*138 acres (17 ha); 100,000 bottles • Wines include:
Sylvaner Vieilles Vignes, Gentil, Muscat Spiegel,
Gewürztraminer Kessler, Gewürztraminer Saering,
Gewürztraminer Spiegel*
Jean-Pierre Dirler's undisputed specialty is the
Gewürztraminer. Here in the south of the Alsace wine
route, it is particularly full-bodied and spicy. On this
estate, cultivated according to biodynamic principles,
the Sylvaner produced from old vines demonstrates this
variety's potential.

DOMAINE BARMÈS-BUECHER***—****
WETTOLSHEIM
*40 acres (16 ha); 90,000 bottles • Wines include: Riesling
Hengst, Gewürztraminer Steingrubler, Pinot Gris
Rosenberg;* → *Pinot Vieilles Vignes, Vendanges Tardives,
Sélections de Grains Nobles, Crémant d'Alsace*
François Barmès convinces with a style of wine that is
unmistakable: natural fermentation with wild yeasts,
crystal clear fruit, aging in steel tanks, and late bottling.
The Vendanges Tardives always have a specific must
gravity above the official minimum, and the Pinot,
matured in *barriques*, is one of the region's great red wines.

DOMAINE PAUL BLANCK***—*****
KIENTZHEIM
86 acres (35 ha); 220,000 bottles • Wines include:
→ *Riesling Schlossberg,* → *Riesling Furstentum, Pinot
Gris Furstentum, Gewürztraminer Furstentum,*
→ *Vendanges Tardives, Sélections de Grains Nobles,*
→ *Pinot "F", Sylvaner*
The slender bottles used by this grower seldom contain
anything but top-flight wine. Frédéric and Philippe
Blanck age their dense Rieslings and Gewürztraminers
in steel tanks. An exception is their red wine, which is
matured in *barriques*.

DOMAINE JULIEN MEYER**—****
NOTHALTEN
20 acres (8 ha); 60,000 bottles • Wines include:
→ *Riesling Muenchberg, Gewürztraminer Cuvée des
Pucelles,* → *Sylvaner Zellberg, Pinot, Crémant*
Patrick Meyer experiments with malolactic fermentation,
and storage in *barriques*, and even dispenses with filtration.

DOMAINE SCHOFFIT***—*****
COLMAR
37 acres (15 ha); 120,000 bottles • Wines include:
→ *Riesling Clos Saint-Théobald,* → *Gewürztraminer Clos
Saint Théobald, Muscat,* → *Chasselas Vieilles Vignes*
Bernard Schoffit owns a parcel of land (Clos Saint-
Théobald) in the Rangen vineyard, the southernmost
and most famous of the *grand crus*. This winegrower
benefits from the volcanic rock to make incredibly
elegant and concentrated wines that are left to mature
for a long time on the lees.

DOMAINE WEINBACH****—*****
KAYSERSBERG
*64 acres (26 ha); 130,000 bottles • Wines include:
Gewürztraminer Furstentum, Riesling Schlossberg,
Gewürztraminer Altenbourg, Riesling Cuvée Theo,*
→ *Riesling Sélection de Grain Nobles,* → *Riesling
Quintessence*
Colette Faller and her daughters run this imposing
estate with great dedication. The Clos des Capuchins
has been in the family since 1898. The name
Quintessence, not officially classified, was introduced
by the Fallers to denote outstanding sweet wines.

PIERRE FRICK***—****
PFAFFENHEIM
*30 acres (12 ha); 80,000 bottles • Wines include:
Sylvaner, Pinot Blanc, Muscat,* → *Riesling Steinert,*
→ *Pinot Gris S.G.N.,* → *Gewürztraminer S.G.N.*
In 1981 this producer switched from organic to
biodynamic methods, wholeheartedly supported by
Pierre and Chantal Frick. Their wines, to which no extra
sugar is added, disclose their grape variety and *terroir*
with uncompromising clarity.

HUGEL****
RIQUEWIHR
*61 acres (25 ha); bought-in grapes; 1,300,000 bottles
• Wines include:* → *Riesling Jubilée, Gewürztraminer
Jubilée, Pinot Gris Jubilée, Muscat Tradition* → *Gentil,*
→ *Vendanges Tardives,* → *Sélections de Grains Nobles,
Pinot Jubilée*
The firm of Hugel, stretching back 360 years, was one of
the driving forces behind the *grand cru* system, but it no
longer uses vineyard names on its wines today as it
believes the classification to have been overly generous.
The best wines, therefore, are called Jubilée, while the
second best are known as Tradition. Gentil is the name
given to one of the best Alsace Edelzwickers.

JOSMEYER**–****
WINTZENHEIM
*61 acres (25 ha); bought-in grapes; 240,000 bottles
• Wines include: Riesling Brand, 'Riesling Hengst, Riesling Le Kottabe 'Auxerrois "H", Pinot Blanc Mise du Printemps*
One of Jean Meyer's specialties is his Auxerrois, an unusually concentrated example of this grape variety, which grows in the Hengst vineyard (hence the "H").

ANDRÉ KIENTZLER***–****
RIBEAUVILLÉ
*28 acres (11 ha); 80,000 bottles • Wines include:
→Riesling Greisberg, →Riesling Osterberg, Muscat Kirchberg, Pinot Gris Kirchberg, →Chasselas*
André Kientzler produces concentrated, minerally wines in his modern winery buildings between Ribeauvillé and Bergheim. The long-lived Chasselas is one of the region's few successful wines to be made from this grape variety.

MARC KREYDENWEISS***–****
ANDLAU
*30 acres (12 ha); 60,000 bottles • Wines include:
→Riesling Wiebelsberg, Pinot Gris Moenchberg, Gewürztraminer Kritt, →Riesling Kastelberg →Clos du Val d'Eléon, →Klevner Kritt, Pinot Blanc Kritt*
Marc Kreydenweiss is completely committed to biodynamic wine production. His concentrated Rieslings, and rarities such as the Clos du Val d'Eléon (a blend of Riesling and Pinot Gris), or the mature Kritt Klevner (a pure variety of Auxerrois), are as remarkable as his modern tasting room.

SEPPI LANDMANN***–****
SOULTZMATT
*21 acres (8.5 ha); 65,000 bottles • Wines include:
→Riesling Zinnkoepflé, →Gewürztraminer Zinnkoepflé, Pinot Gris Vallée Noble*
Seppi Landmann's Vendanges Tardives and S.G.N. Zinnkoepflé Gewürztraminer are even more eloquent than he is, but even the simpler Rieslings, Pinot Gris, and Sylvaners reflect the vitality of this particular winegrower.

MEYER-FONNÉ***–*****
KATZENTHAL
*25 acres (10 ha); 75,000 bottles • Wines include:
Gewürztraminer Kaefferkopf, Gewürztraminer Wineck-Schlossberg, Riesling Kaefferkopf, Riesling Wineck-Schlossberg, →Pinot Gris Hinterburg, →Muscat Tiré sur Lie, Pinot Noir*
This estate, run by Félix Meyer, is still a well-kept secret, but his simultaneously dense and elegant Rieslings, Gewürztraminers, and Pinot Gris are extremely good value.

FRÉDÉRIC MOCHEL**–****
TRAENHEIM
81 acres (10 ha); 75,000 bottles • Wines include Pinot Blanc, Muscat, Riesling Altenberg de Bergbieten, →Riesling Cuvée Henriette
Frédéric Mochel and his son Guillaume have worked their way up ever so quietly to join the elite of Alsace Riesling producers. Mineral, dry, complex—all these virtues mean that the Cuvée Henriette in particular sets the standard.

RENÉ MURÉ***–****
ROUFFACH
*70 acres (29 ha); 330,000 bottles • Wines include:
Gewürztraminer Clos Saint-Landelin, Riesling Clos Saint-Landelin, Muscat, →Pinot, Vendanges Tardives, →Sylvaner "Cuvée Oscar"*
A top-flight, carefully worked vineyard (part of the Vorbourg *grand cru*) and long storage on the lees—little

Marc Kreydenweiss, biodynamic winegrower.

else is needed by René Muré for the production of elegant, dense wines that include a very fine Sylvaner.

ANDRÉ OSTERTAG***–*****
EPFIG
*45 acres (18 ha); 100,000 bottles • Wines include:
→Riesling Muenchberg, Pinot, Pinot Gris Zellberg, Pinot Gris Muenchberg, Vendages Tardives, Sélections de Grains Nobles*
Ostertag, when he took over this estate in 1985, introduced aging in *barriques*, malolactic fermentation for white wines as well as reds, and the use of wild yeasts. He has divided his wines into three very different categories: *vins de fruit* (displaying the character of the grape variety), *vins de pierre* (showing the character of the vineyard) and *vin de temps* (made from grapes that are overripe or affected by noble rot).

JEAN-PAUL SCHMITT**–***
SCHERWILLER
*65 acres (8 ha); 45,000 bottles. • Wines include:
Riesling Rittersberg, Gewürztraminer Rittersberg, Vendanges Tardives*
First of all, you have to find Jean-Paul Schmitt and his estate in the Huhnelmühle. The isolated position and the lack of *grand cru* vineyards have not discouraged this young winemaker. The Riesling, as well as the Gewürztraminer and Pinot Gris, are extremely elegant, upright wines.

TRIMBACH**–****
RIBEAUVILLÉ
*80 acres (33 ha); bought-in grapes; 1,000,000 bottles
• Wines include: Riesling Frédéric Émile, Gewürztraminer Seigneurs de Ribeaupierre, Pinot Gris, →Riesling Clos Sainte-Hune*
The wines of this merchant are almost always dry and in great demand with restaurants. The Riesling from the three-acre (1.2-ha) fully-owned vineyard Clos Sainte-Hune is a legend.

ZIND-HUMBRECHT****–*****
TURCKHEIM
*99 acres (40 ha); 160,000 bottles • Wines include:
→Riesling Clos Saint-Urbain, →Riesling Pinot Gris Clos Jebsal, Riesling Clos Windsbuhl, Riesling Herrenweg, Muscat*
Léonard Humbrecht and his son Olivier produce exceptional wines in the cellar of their modern winery. The concentrated Rieslings, Pinot Gris, and Gewürztraminers from the Clos Saint-Urbain enclave are some of the truly great wines of this region.

JURA

The wines of the Jura are seldom named in any discussion of France's greatest wines, with one exception: the legendary *vin jaune* that was prized at the French court as far back as the Middle Ages and is still valued as a rarity today. With only around 4,448 acres (1,800 ha) of vineyards (before the (Reblaus) catastrophe at the end of the 19th century it was almost 49,420 acres (20,000 ha)) and just 2,906,000 gallons (110,000 hl) of wine production, the Jura is one of the smaller wine-producing areas. The center of production is the small medieval town of Arbois, where the French chemist, Louis Pasteur, discovered the causes of alcoholic fermentation.

A Harsh Region

The Jura, situated between Burgundy and Switzerland, has a harsh climate, and is dominated by limestone mountains. Growing between 820 and 1,640 feet (250 and 500 m), the grapes make use of every sheltered spot they can find. The vineyards face west, southwest and to a certain extent south, and the soil consists overwhelmingly of blue, red, and black marl, and,

In the Jura, cask-aging is a quite particular skill, since it cultivates and accentuates the unmistakable character of the region's dry white wines.

to the north, partly of limestone scree and slate as well.

The climate is full of contrasts: cold winters and hot summers are followed by generally sunny autumns. The indigenous grape varieties are best adapted to these conditions. For white wines and *vin jaune* the Savagnin plays the leading role. According to many experts, this variety, also known as Naturé, is related to the Traminer; it accounts for 15% of the planting area and results in low yields of between 320 and 375 gallons per acre (30 and 35 hl/ha). Picking often continues into November and occasionally into December. Light red wines are traditionally obtained from the Poulsard grape. This variety, also known as Ploussard, was previously only capable of producing a light and sweet pale red, but there are now Poulsards that mature into proper red wines as a result of several days of must fermentation. More intensely colored reds, however, have always been made from the Trousseau grape. Chardonnay (also called Melon d'Arbois here) and Pinot Noir, both imported from Burgundy, are grown to produce single-varietal wines or *cuvées* in a blend with indigenous varieties.

Wines with their own Unique Style

Over the last few decades, more and more independent wine producers have emerged from the shadow cast by the cooperatives and the enormous company Henri Maire—who dominates a large proportion of wine production in the

Jura—to make a mark for themselves. Today's white wines are clearer in terms of fruit, and the red wines have become more elegant. Yet the region's wines have been able to retain their unmistakable style: a nutty spiciness, honey perfume, or overtones of dried fruit predominate in the Savagnin white wines or Chardonnay and Savagnin blends, while a charming blackcurrant or cherry fruit along with discreet animal notes can be detected in the red wines. The Crémant du Jura has rapidly developed into one of the region's major successes and Macvin has also become an increasingly hot tip. This *vin de liqueur* is a mixture of fermented grape juice and *marc* brandy, from which it takes its name. Whereas Macvins and *vins de paille* (made from grapes dried—traditionally on straw—after picking) are served at a maximum temperature of 50°F (10°C), Savignins and *vins jaunes* are customarily served at between 57° and 61°F (14° to 16°C) in order to bring out their richness of taste in full. Likewise, most red wines should not be served at more than 61°F (16°C).

Vin jaune, the most famous of all the yellow wines, comes from the picturesque Château-Challon.

The Jura *appellations*

Arbois

Arbois is not just a picturesque medieval town and the Jura's main center of wine production, but also the name of an *appellation*, which was recognized as France's first *Appellation d'Origine Contrôlée* in 1936. The vineyards, covering 2,100 acres (850 ha) are spread over 12 communes. Only one locality, Pupillin, known for its good Poulsard, is entitled to put its name on its labels. The *appellation* currently offers red and white wines, *vins de paille*, *vins jaunes*, and sparkling wines.

Château-Chalon

The birthplace of *vin jaune* is the only *appellation* dedicated exclusively to this type of wine and covers a total of four communes. The producers, whose vineyards total a mere 124 acres (50 ha), have banded together to form a committee that every year checks the grapes for ripeness and condition before harvesting, and sets the permitted yields. In bad years—such as 1984, for example—the Château-Chalon *appellation* is not awarded.

L'Étoile

This tiny *appellation* with a planting area of just 198 acres (80 ha) is reserved for white wines: still, sparkling, *vin jaune*, and *vin de paille*. The vineyards are spread over three communes whose slopes have the best possible orientation. The marl soil is studded with minute, star-shaped fossils that give the village of L'Étoile and the *appellation* their name.

Côtes du Jura

Around 60 wine-growing communes, cultivating approximately 1,530 acres (620 ha), make up this general *appellation*, which covers the whole wine region. Among the best-known localities are Poligny, Voiteur, Arlay, Le Vernois, Grevingey, and Rotalier. Both red and white wines are recognized by the Côtes du Jura *appellation*; rosé, sparkling wine, *vin jaune*, and *vin de paille* are allowed to be sold under the designation as well.

Crémant du Jura

In 1995 the legal foundations were laid for the Crémant du Jura, and within a short while this sparkling wine became a winner. Sparkling wines had been produced in the region for two centuries, but only in the last few years have producers properly understood what lies at the heart of the Jura Crémant's charm: freshness. As is the case with champagne, the second fermentation takes place in the bottle. Both red and white grapes are used in the production of the basic wine. Frequently producers blend Pinot Noir (pressed white), Chardonnay, and also Trousseau and Savagnin, but some single-variety sparkling wines do exist. Compared to champagne, the Jura Crémant is usually more sparkling, has an aroma of green apples or pears, and is only seldom characterized by yeasty overtones. Its success has been astonishing: over a sixth of the entire production of the Jura is today sold as Crémant. And at a reasonable price, too!

Macvin du Jura

This *vin de liqueur* is the Jura equivalent of Pineau des Charentes (in the Cognac region) or Floc de Gascogne (in Armagnac). The *appellation* has been in existence only since 1991, but growers have been producing Macvin for centuries. Made from a combination of red or white must that has undergone its preliminary fermentation and *marc* brandy, it retains a considerable amount of residual sugar. An 18-month period of barrel-aging is stipulated for this refined specialty.

BURGUNDY

Burgundy and its wines are legendary in the wine world. Many a connoisseur will confidently declare that no other red wine in the world can beat the complexity, fullness, and style of a great Pinot Noir from the Côte de Nuits. The great Chardonnays from Chablis and the Côte de Beaune have also retained their originality and perfection, despite the worldwide love affair with Chardonnay. Yet, wherever there is light, there are shadows too. The region is highly fragmented and standards of quality can be extremely erratic, even in the higher price categories. Those purchasing at random run the risk of disappointment even more than in other regions.

HISTORY

The earliest evidence of wine growing in Burgundy dates back to the 2nd century AD. However, it is possible that the Celts were cultivating vines and pressing wine even before the Romans arrived. The history of Burgundian wine growing during the Middle Ages is of great importance to the whole of Europe.

The tradition of wine growing in the monasteries began with donations to the abbey of St. Benignus in 587 and the monastery at Bèze near Gevrey in 630. In 910 Cluny was founded in the Mâconnais. In the centuries that followed,

the abbey not only grew into a center of clerical power, but it also procured important real estate in the wine-growing communities of the Côte d'Or.

The Cistercian Order founded in 1098 in Citeaux near Nuits-St.-Georges systematically promoted the culture of wine growing in the monasteries. The Clos de Vougeot was used by the monks to explore different aspects of wine growing, which then quickly spread throughout Europe as the Order grew in size.

Two events that took place in the late Middle Ages have a bearing on the wine industry today. A decree issued by Philip the Bold in 1395 was to drive the Gamay variety out of Burgundy, paving the way for Pinot Noir's domination of quality wine production. In 1443 the Chancellor of Philip the Good, Nicolas Rolin, donated the Hospices de Beaune, whose annual wine auction is still regarded today as the most important measure of the wine market in Burgundy.

Following the French Revolution, the Napoleonic law of inheritance provided the basis for the social and land ownership structure that still prevails in Burgundy today. Since that time, property has been divided equally between all the children of a family, which has meant that the parcels held by individual landowners have tended to get smaller and smaller. In 1851 came the opening of the rail link

La Tâche, monopoly of the *domaine* of the Romanée-Conti and their most powerful *grand cru*.

LA TACHE

between Dijon and Paris, which provided access to a vast market and increased the demand for cheap wines, usually produced from the Gamay variety. However, the first attempt to classify superior wines dates back to the same period, coming in 1861. Following the PHYLLOXERA attack of the 1870s, resistance to grafted vines was greater in Burgundy than anywhere else. Nevertheless, the crisis had generally eased by the start of the 20th century. The creation of the A.O.C. system in the 1930s, along with gradual moves toward bottling wines at the property where they are made, prepared the ground for present-day Burgundy.

GEOLOGY, TOPOGRAPHY, AND CLIMATE

Burgundy's leitmotif is the *terroir*. What this signifies is the whole of the natural environment in which a vineyard is located, in other words, the combination of soil, topographical, and climatic features. In Burgundy the famous *terroirs* are, without exception, characterized by limestone. Chablis, with its limy, chalky soil, offers ideal conditions for Chardonnay. The limy, loamy, and marly soils of the Côte d'Or were created by the erosion of the high plateau of Jura limestone rising above the Côte d'Or, as strata broke off and fell into the valley. This explains why, within a very small area, a variety of *terroirs* are to be found with characteristic properties that are reflected in the flavor of the wines. In the Côte Chalonnaise and the Mâconnais limestone deposits are more sporadic and mixed with more loamy, sandy soils. Of great importance to all Burgundy's *terroirs* is the interaction between good drainage in rocky areas and the water retention of the loamy, clay, or marly substrata.

The topography of Burgundy's vineyards is far less spectacular than elsewhere. The steepness of the land and its south-facing orientation are less dominant factors here, with most of the *grands crus* in the Côte d'Or, for instance, facing due east on only a slight incline. The elevations vary between around 650 and 1,300 feet (200 and 400 m), with lighter wines tending to come from higher vineyards.

The climate is neither particularly warm nor especially dry. Winters are cold and can return with late frosts well into spring, particularly in Chablis. High summer temperatures reflect the continental influence, but are far less consistent than in the more southerly wine-growing areas. Precipitation is a particular threat, and the risk-taking yield discipline of the winegrower,

The château belonging to Bouchard Père et Fils is situated in the old part of the town of Beaune.

resulting from hard pruning, takes on the greatest importance. Seasonal fluctuations are greater here than in regions with a more moderate climate. On the other hand, in the Burgundian climate, the Pinot Noir can take on a mixture of finesse and robustness, elegance and strength almost unparalleled anywhere in the world.

OUTLOOK

Apart from the legendary wine-producing areas of Chablis and the Côte d'Or, recent years have seen the arrival of an ever-increasing number of supposedly secondary areas too. In the Mâconnais, on the Côte Chalonnaise and the Hautes Côtes enthusiastic winegrowers are producing wines well above the average. In the meantime, however, they have become just as rare and almost as expensive as their big brothers next door. When one considers that the total wine-growing area of Burgundy is just over 61,500 acres (25,000 ha), it is clear that at present the region as a whole is far from exhausting its potential for producing top-quality wines.

THE GEOGRAPHY OF THE WINES OF BURGUNDY

The northerly outposts of Burgundy are the wine-growing enclaves around Chablis and Auxerre in the department of Yonne (13,100 acres/5,300 ha). Chablis has become a symbol of quality thanks to its vigorous, elegant Chardonnay and has top-quality *grand cru* and *premier cru* locations. From the Côtes d'Auxerre come light, white and red wines, among which the fragrant, dry reds from Irancy, in particular, have acquired a degree of prominence. On the same degree of latitude, but some 25 miles (40 km) to the east, is the small wine-growing area of

Châtillonais, which belongs to the department of the Côte d'Or, yet only produces simple wines with the A.O.C. Bourgogne, except for a few interesting *crémants*. About 60 miles (100 km) southeast of Chablis begins the Côte d'Or itself (23,000 acres/9,300 ha), the heart of Burgundy. Almost all of Burgundy's *grands crus* and *premiers crus* are found within the confines of this wine-growing area that stretches for some 30 miles (50 km). Its northern part, the Côtes de Nuits, produces complex Pinot Noir wines with plenty of finesse, but virtually no white wines. The Pinot Noir produced on the Côte de Beaune is more solid and robust. The great wines come from Chardonnay. Above all, the combination of mellowness, fruit, and mineral characteristics make it unique. In the hinterland of the Côte d'Or communes is the Hautes Côtes region. These wines are referred to as Hautes Côtes de Nuits or Hautes Côtes de Beaune, depending on their geographical location. They generally tend to be somewhat lighter, and above all, harder structured than wines from the lower regions.

The southern end of the Côte de Beaune forms the boundary with the department of Saône-et-Loire (25,450 acres/10,300 ha). The best wines (both reds and whites), from the Côte Chalonnaise, which abuts the Côte de Beaune are extremely reasonably-priced alternatives to those from the Côte d'Or. Although there are no *grands crus* here, a number of truly noteworthy *premiers crus* are evidence of the region's pretensions. One of the area's curiosities is the town of Bouzeron, which focuses solely on Aligoté. A small region to the west of the Côte Chalonnaise, the Couchois, produces mainly simple wines. A few miles to the east begins the Mâconnais, a district that occasionally produces somewhat rustic Chardonnays, although the good examples are pleasant and absolutely typical of this variety. Wines of above-average character and aspiration come from the village of Pouilly-Fuissé and its surrounding area. The red wines are usually light blends of Pinot Noir and Gamay. The Mâconnais extends southward into the Rhône department and with it the Beaujolais region.

THE A.O.C. SYSTEM AND THE QUALITY PYRAMID IN BURGUNDY

The reputation of Burgundy's classification system vies with that of Bordelais for being exemplary in the French understanding of wine.

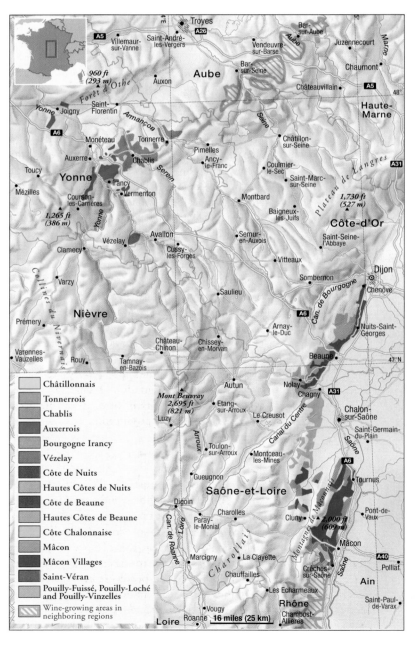

Map legend:
- Châtillonnais
- Tonnerrois
- Chablis
- Auxerrois
- Bourgogne Irancy
- Vézelay
- Côte de Nuits
- Hautes Côtes de Nuits
- Côte de Beaune
- Hautes Côtes de Beaune
- Côte Chalonnaise
- Mâcon
- Mâcon Villages
- Saint-Véran
- Pouilly-Fuissé, Pouilly-Loché and Pouilly-Vinzelles
- Wine-growing areas in neighboring regions

Immediately following the foundation of the I.N.A.O. (*Institut National des Appellations d'Origine*) in 1935, the legislators defined all the important indications of origin for Burgundy in the years that followed, incorporating the classifications that had already been established in the mid-19th century. The *Appellation d'Origine Contrôlée* (A.O.C.) covers the following elements: the variety of grape(s), traditional wine-growing techniques, the wine's minimum and maximum alcohol content and its typical style.

THE GEOGRAPHICAL ORIGIN

The A.O.C.s are structured according to quality grades like the layers of an onion. Regional, communal, and *grand cru appellations* are graded according to the regard in which they are held and, within the regional and communal A.O.C.s, there are in turn more refined classifications. The simplest regional A.O.C. is Bourgogne. Any white or red wines produced from grapes harvested in Burgundy are entitled to use this *appellation*, as are Gamay reds from the ten cru communes in Beaujolais, for the sake of honor to some extent. The Bourgogne A.O.C. may be supplemented by other *appellations* associated with additional official requirements. For example, Bourgogne Aligoté is a white wine that must be produced purely from the Aligoté grape variety. "Bourgogne passe-tout-grains" is a wine produced from no more than two-thirds Gamay and no less than one-third Pinot Noir, which have been pressed together. Other additions restrict the regional origin. Around 54 percent of all Burgundian wines carry a regional A.O.C. on the

This is Burgundy—three adjacent plots with widely divergent natural conditions in relation to aspect, slope, and height. With the same grape variety but separate production processes, the result is three wines with a completely different bouquet.

There are hundreds of small winegrowers in Burgundy who welcome visitors and who sell their wines to them direct.

label. Apart from the different A.O.C.s beginning with "Bourgogne," the "Mâcon" and "Mâcon supérieur" *appellations* also belong in this group.

Communal (*villages*) A.O.C.s stand for a type of wine introduced and associated with a particular wine-producing commune. If the name of an individual location is also mentioned, the wine concerned must come from there. *Villages* wines account for some 34 percent of Burgundy's wine production, *premiers crus* for around 10 percent. The *grand cru* A.O.C. is still reserved for the 32 best locations on the Côte d'Or and seven in Chablis. In 1861 Dr Jules Lavalle devised the first systematic classification, which was officially sanctioned by the agricultural authorities in Beaune. The *grands crus* incorporated in the A.O.C. statute in the 1930s largely reflect the classification at the time. The most rigid upper yield limits apply to *grands crus* and they tend to assume primary responsibility for upholding Burgundy's reputation. They account for barely two percent of the total amount of Burgundy produced.

THE UPPER YIELD LIMITS

This is the foremost quality criterion in Burgundy. The climatic conditions and capriciousness of the Pinot Noir, in particular, require modesty if great wines are to be made. The regulations laid down by the A.O.C. system do, however, leave scope for casual interpretations, which do nothing to promote the reputation of Burgundy. In reality, an ever increasing number of *premier* and *grand cru* wines are appearing on the market, which really are quite thin.

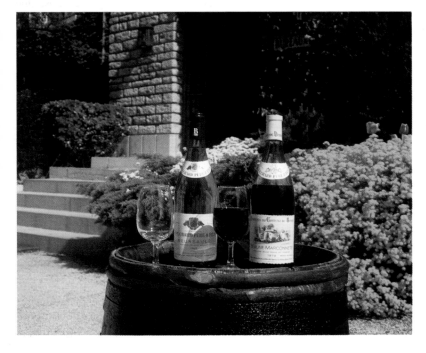

The Grape Varieties

Burgundy is a region *par excellence* when it comes to single-grape wines. The Burgundian palate strives to achieve the greatest complexity by probing the full diversity of a grape variety. Ideally, the *terroir* should be reflected in the wine. Burgundy's two leading grape varieties, in particular, are especially sensitive not only to the soil and microclimate, but also to man's cultural achievements.

Pinot Noir

The Pinot Noir variety is hard to cultivate, difficult to press, and maturing the wine calls for real flair and sensitivity. Pinot Noir wines could certainly not be described as straightforward. The origin of the variety is uncertain; in Burgundy it can be traced back as far as 4 BC. The large number of sub-varieties is evidence that man has worked intensively with this family of grapes for many centuries.

The vines put out shoots early in the spring, making them susceptible to late frosts. If they are to ripen evenly and develop an intensive aroma, the grapes requires a long, equable growing season, during which heat can be just as damaging as moisture.

The small, compact grapes are not only at great risk from BOTRYTIS, but also from viruses: genuine and bogus mildew give the winegrower cause for concern. Although vine cultivation has created a number of less sensitive Pinot Noir clones, it is often the more sensitive varieties that produce the highest-quality wines. In

In autumn the Pinot Noir displays its magical colors.

Left and right
The Chardonnay vine is easy to cultivate, but only produces outstanding wines when grown on a particular type of terrain.

Burgundy approximately 50 highly selected clones are approved. Producers with a strong sense of tradition rely on what is known as *sélection massale* either entirely or as an addition to these "official" clones. This procedure involves reproducing certain vines that have proved themselves in terms of health and ripening characteristics.

The Pinot Noir requires extreme care from the vineyard staff. Many of the Burgundian winegrowers attempt to limit the vigorous growth and high yields of the individual vines. Cutting back the fruit cane hard is intended to achieve this goal. The foliage also requires a good deal of care and attention. This is important because there must be enough healthy foliage for photosynthesis, but at the same time foliage must be deliberately removed to allow air to reach the grapes.

Old vines *(vieilles vignes)* promise particularly high-quality wine, because their roots are deep and well spread out, and they have an inherently lower yield. The Pinot is also no easy partner during winemaking, even in the best vintage years. Virtually no other variety of grape makes it so difficult to achieve the desired color and tannin content. At the lower end of the scale, the grape produces light-colored wines low on structure, while excessively long and intensive maceration, extremely low fermenting temperatures, or the exaggerated use of pressed wine may produce more color, but can also bring green fermenting substances and hints of bitterness to the wine. Little wonder that the waves of contradictory winemaking philosophies are so powerful when it comes to Pinot Noir. While some vineyards use automatic rotofermenters, others stick to the manual immersion of the cap of skins. Some producers swear by cold-maceration prior to the start of alcoholic fermentation, to obtain color and particularly elegant tannins; some let maceration take place in the wine at the end of fermentation in warm temperatures. Others, however, use a combination of the two techniques. The least controversial issue remains the use of wooden casks. The traditional Burgundian *pièce*, capable of holding 60 gallons (228 l), is the barrel of choice for any serious Pinot. There is plenty of scope for individuality here too, ranging from the correct type of wood to be used and the degree of roasting to the proportion of new wood. The types of wine produced from the Pinot Noir are as numerous as the *terroirs* and the people who work them.

CHARDONNAY

It is debatable whether Burgundy is the home of Chardonnay. There is a village of the same name in the Mâconnais, yet it would appear that the village was named after the grape, rather than the other way round. Although the Austrian enologist, Ferdinand Regner, identified a certain genetic similarity between Chardonnay and the Burgundy family, there is no evidence of a direct affiliation. It may be that Chardonnay did not reach Burgundy until the 16th century; what is certain, however, is that it did not take over from the Aligoté in terms of large-scale cultivation until the mid-19th century.

Unlike Burgundy's main red grape variety, the Chardonnay is very easy to cultivate. In contrast to the Pinot Noir, it is less susceptible to viruses and fungus, but its early shoot development can leave it vulnerable to late frosts. It can tolerate relatively high yields without a complete breakdown in quality, it ripens uniformly and delivers constantly high volumes of must. A very important element is choosing the right time to harvest. If allowed to over-ripen, Chardonnay will tend to lose its acidity, producing excessively broad, plump wines.

Enologists enthuse over the versatility of Chardonnay. Relatively simple provenances can produce fresh, fruity whites with the help of modern, reductive wine processing.

Traditional types of wine, whether aged in wooden casks or not, are golden, fruity, and expansive. Almost all top-quality wines are fermented in the *pièce*, where after the first RACKING they are molded through repeated, week-long agitation of the fine yeast (so-called *tonnage*), into sparkling, full, strong wines that combine fruit and nerve, wood, and yeast influences in a complex yet multifaceted unit.

GAMAY

In Burgundy the rivalry between Gamay and Pinot Noir dates back to the 14th century. Because Gamay produces high yields, its grapes are bigger than those of the Pinot, their flesh juicy, and skins thin, it usually goes to produce mass-consumption wines with little structure. In the *cru* communes of Beaujolais, however, where there are low yields, it is still able to demonstrate the potential of the *terroir* type. In the rest of Burgundy, it is now only used in the Mâconnais and on the Côte Chalonnaise for blending with Pinot Noir.

ALIGOTÉ

In centuries gone by, the Aligoté—probably an indigenous Burgundian variety—was an important ingredient in the blend of white grapes used to produce white Burgundy. This high-yield variety has a tendency to dry acidity, but can develop a remarkable fruitiness in good locations and ripe years. Simpler, somewhat lean Aligoté wines are ideal for the production of *crémant* and the typical Kir (an aperitif made with *crème de cassis*). The town of Bouzeron on the Côte Chalonnaise has the only communal A.O.C. for Aligoté.

Whenever a vineyard in Burgundy is surrounded by a wall, it is entitled to call itself a *clos*.

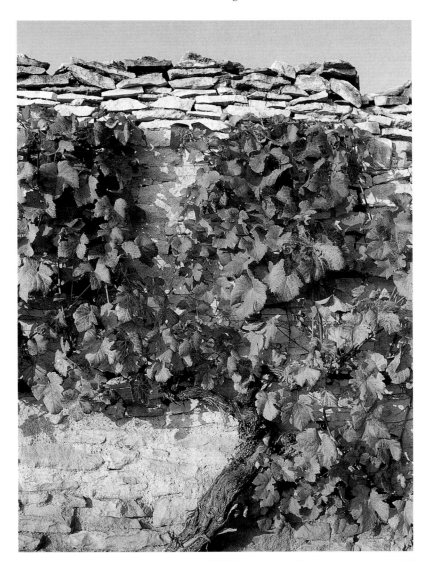

A National Shrine:
The Domaine de la Romanée-Conti

The Domaine de la Romanée-Conti, referred to simply as D.R.C., enjoys a cult status even greater than that of Pétrus or Mouton in the Bordeaux region. No other estate in one of the traditional wine regions so symbolizes its commitment to quality as does the D.R.C. to Bourgogne. It is the only *domaine* in Burgundy with more than one vineyard that manages exclusively to produce *grands crus*. The D.R.C. does not rack grapes harvested from its less illustrious parcels of land.

Historically, the D.R.C. had its origins with the monks from the monastery of Saint-Vivant, who claimed for their own five outstanding locations in Vosne and Flagey. In 1584 the monks sold this estate under the name of Le Cros de Cloux. It was only in 1651, after Roman ruins were found close by, that Burgundy's most prestigious vineyard was renamed Romanée. In 1760 the *domaine* finally fell into the ownership of Prince von Conti. However, the name Romanée-Conti only became established following the French Revolution, when the expropriated estate was first referred to by this name at auction in 1794.

The estate's present structure was essentially created by Jacques-Marie Duvault-Blochet during the last thirty years of the 19th century, when he bought additional parcels of land in Richebourg, Echézeaux, Grand Echézeaux and part of La Tâche. He bequeathed the *domaine* to the Villaine family, who have run it since 1911.

Aubert de Villaine is fully aware of the cultural and historical importance of the Domaine de la Romanée-Conti

The Clos de Vougeot is at the root of Burgundy's wine hierarchy. Today the historic buildings under the management of the La Confrèrie des Tastevins wine fraternity are used to hold many events.

In the 1930s the estate was able to acquire the missing part of La Tâche. The first of three parcels of Montrachet followed in 1963 and in 1988 there was an opportunity to take over parts of Romanée-Saint-Vivant that had been rented hitherto. In 1942 Edmond Guidon de Villaine gave his friend, the wine merchant Henri Leroy, the opportunity of becoming an equal partner in the D.R.C., thereby obtaining strong practical and financial support in the management of the highly renowned estate. At the same time Leroy acquired sole marketing rights to the wines, everywhere except the U.K. and the U.S.A., something that led to repeated quarrels with the De Villaines. From 1975 on the D.R.C. was jointly managed by Lalou Bize-Leroy and Aubert de Villaine, until Lalou Bize was replaced by Charles Roch, son of her sister Pauline, in 1993 and, following his death in an accident, by his brother Henri.

The soil at Romanée-Conti is only about 24 inches (60 cm) deep and is interspersed with a good deal of limestone and 45 to 50 percent clay. What is particularly unique about the soil is its ability to provide the right amount of drainage, thanks to the limestone; and water retention, thanks to the clay. However, in the upper part of Romanée-Conti there is a severe risk of erosion, as there is also in the lower parcels of La Tâche. Prince Conti had fresh loam brought to the estate from the meadows of the Saône valley as early as 1886/87. No fewer than 800 wagon loads were deposited.

Soil management is one of the central themes of the *domaine*. In the final analysis, perfectionist vine cultivation, the lowest yields (roughly 6.5 gallons/120 sq. yds, 25 liters/100 sq. m as a long-term average), and attention to detail in vinification are treated as a matter of course in a *domaine* of this size. The crux remains the retention of the irreplaceable natural conditions. For this reason, organic cultivation methods were introduced as early as the 1980s, and these have been consistently developed to the present day.

The cultural and historical heritage is treated with the greatest reverence and respect. This consistently conservative approach was exemplified by the fact that only when the battle against phylloxera finally proved hopeless in 1945 were the own-rooted vines of the Romanée-Conti uprooted, and La Tâche restocked with the grafted scions.

THE CLOS DE VOUGEOT: A MICROCOSM OF CATHOLIC BURGUNDY

125 acres (50 ha) within a half-mile long wall make the Clos de Vougeot the largest *grand cru* in Burgundy and a wine of special symbolic significance. It reflects both the history and present of Burgundy in all its facets. The Cistercians received some land near Vougeot in 1110 and created this *cru* as the first of their major feats in wine growing. Parcel by parcel, donation by donation, they added to the land, uprooted and planted, set up a cellar right in the middle of the vineyard and around 1330 they built the wall.

The Clos de Vougeot became the first experimental vineyard known to man. The monks studied the microclimate and growth conditions, varieties of Pinot, and soil types. If the origin of the concept of *terroir* can be in any way pinned down, then it must be to here. According to legend, the monks are said to have quite literally tasted the soil to learn as much as possible about the differences.

The Clos de Vougeot is unique in its variety. Every few yards the ground changes. The ratio of clay to limestone, the depth, local climatic conditions, all these factors that are largely uniform within most other *grand cru* locations are subject to great diversity here. The only definable trend is that in the upper section, particularly where the château has been standing since 1551, the soil is particularly scant and rich in limestone. Lower down, alongside the main highway, the less valued loamy, heavy soils susceptible to waterlogging predominate. But there too are veins of limestone that make it impossible to generalize.

This mosaic of locations was helpful to the Cistercians in their research. Even their wine, which must have been a blend of grapes from all the different parcels, does not seem to have come to any harm from it.

Secularization cast a new light on the patchwork quilt of the Clos de Vougeot.

Today between 65 and 82 owners share the vineyard's parcels of land. Accurate records of ownership are hard to keep due to the notorious disputes on inheritance. It is clear that in view of this widely dispersed ownership, it is now virtually impossible to produce a Clos de Vougeot in the manner envisaged by the founders of this vineyard—a wine that acquires its complexity from the blending of all or at least some clearly distinct *climats*. (*Climat* in Burgundy refers to a vineyard's mesoclimate

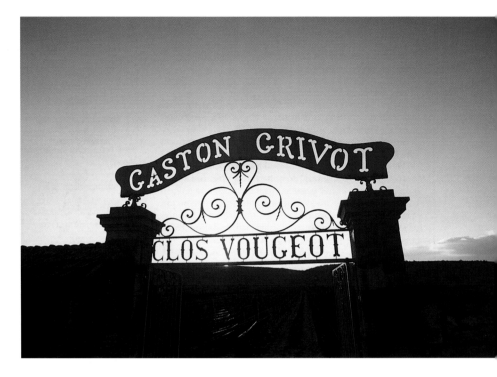

In area, the Clos de Vougeot is the largest *grand cru*, but between 65 and 82 owners divide up the area among them, which is typical of the way in which vineyard ownership in Burgundy has been split up into ever smaller properties.

Richebourg is one of the leading *grands crus* of the Vosne-Romanée commune, producing wonderfully rich, powerful, long-lasting reds.

and its soil.) Most pressings today come from individual parcels of varying size. Each year roughly 40 different wines come onto the market with "Clos de Vougeot" on their label. Little wonder that many of these wines do not merit the *grand cru* classification. Today the Clos de Vougeot is not only a microcosm of natural growth conditions, as it has always been, but it also offers a social and economic image of Burgundy in all its variety—both good and bad.

A good Clos de Vougeot, however, is a *grand cru* through and through. Although it does not develop the exotic spice of the neighboring Grands-Echézeaux and does not sparkle through the fineness of nearby Musigny, it has a special stature and density, which gives the Pinot Noir variety with all its complexity its own expression.

What is typical of the *terroir* of the Clos de Vougeot is not the marked refinement of an individual outstanding feature, but the fact that this wine depicts the entire image on an exceptional level. This also explains why the vineyard continues to merit its special status, even nine hundred years after its foundation.

Not Just Poor Relations: Wines of the Mâconnais

Barrels of different sizes and ages are used to fine-tune the character of the wine.

It is in the Mâconnais that Burgundy begins its transition into southern French culture. In an area measuring 30 × 9 miles (50 × 15 km), the vineyards lie between meadows and arable land, spread across limestone hills. Climatically, the Mâconnais has more sun and fewer worries over frost and hail than most other parts of Burgundy. Consequently, historically speaking, vine cultivation has had a rural orientation and been rather lacking in ambition.

The north of the region, in particular, is dominated by mixed agriculture and organization into cooperatives (some 70 percent of all wines in the Mâconnais are produced by cooperatives), while in the south there are a greater number of professional winegrowers and private estates. The spectacular rock formations of Solutré and Vergisson are made from the same Jura limestone that characterizes the Côte d'Or and have become the symbol of wine growing in the Mâconnais. Not far from these particularly privileged Chardonnay locations, there is also granite soil like that in Beaujolais. The transition between the two is in many respects smooth. The Chardonnays from Saint-Amour, a Beaujolais-Cru commune, for instance, have a claim to the communal Mâconnais A.O.C. St-Véran. Red Mâcon, on the other hand, is mainly Gamay or with the emphasis on Gamay, although it is rarely of good caliber. Roughly two-thirds of the Mâconnais vine-cultivation area is stocked with Chardonnay. There are no *premiers* or *grands crus*, the quality pyramid being limited to regional and communal A.O.C.s. There is no doubt that a few producers from certain

Right page
The rock of Solutré dominates the Pouilly-Fuisse region—the underground prehistoric museum is worth a visit. It has exhibits from the Old Stone Age period—the Solutrean—from which the rock derives its name.

communes have been consistently producing outstanding Chardonnays that are being sold below-value in view of the current regulations, at least in terms of their classification.

The region suffers from a misrepresentation of its producing capability. Due to a lack of prestige, up to three-quarters of Mâconnais whites have in recent years been sold under the A.O.C. Bourgogne. An important reason for this is that the cooperatives themselves have largely left the marketing of their wines to the wine trade, who, unlike the cooperatives, have no interest in consumers linking these reliable Chardonnays to the name Mâcon. Even today, only about half the wines from the Mâconnais carry the name of their own area. Nevertheless, in recent years a few cooperatives have started to market relatively large quantities of their wines themselves.

The Mâconnais is about to enter a period of expansion—not so much in terms of quantity, but rather quality and attitude. The wines of the A.O.C. Pouilly-Fuissé have rapidly won international prestige and appreciation. Even Saint-Véran, until recently the only other communal A.O.C. of any importance, has benefited from the boom on the Burgundy market. The 1999 vintage saw the establishment of the third communal A.O.C. of "Viré-Clessé."

There are gratifying signs that producers are becoming bolder when it comes to working to improve the quality of their wines, for example, in the conflict over the sweet wines of Jean Thévenets (which were finally denied the A.O.C.). It is to be hoped, therefore, that in addition to the highly mechanized production of balanced, value-for-money Chardonnays, the regional A.O.C.s of Mâcon and Mâcon-Villages will find a suitable place on the market for more demanding types of Mâconnais wine.

Appellations

Mâcon/Pinot-Chardonnay Mâcon: 171 acres (69 ha); Only Mâcon is now used as a declassification A.O.C.
Mâcon Supérieur: 2,175 acres (880 ha); higher alcohol potential required than for Mâcon.
Mâcon Villages or Mâcon followed by the name of the commune: 7,532 acres (3,048 ha) in 43 locations. The name "Villages" can be used only with white wines. Upper yield limits (basic): 14 gallons/120 sq. yds (55 l/100 sq. m) for rosé and red wines,

16 gallons/120 sq. yds (60 l/100 sq. m) for Chardonnay.
Viré-Clessé: For the first time with sales of the 1999 vintage.
Pouilly-Fuissé 1843 acres (746 ha), **Pouilly-Louché** 72 acres (29 ha), **Puilly-Vinzelles** 124 acres (50 ha): Chardonnay with nutty overtones and a lovely smoothness, maximum yield 11 gallons/120 sq. yds (50 l/100 sq. m).
St-Véran: 1,379 acres (558 ha); maximum yield (basic) 12 gallons/120 sq. yds (55 l/100 sq. m).

the once famous Poitou has managed to salvage a small wine industry over the centuries.

As varied as the wines of the Loire are, freshness and finesse are their common denominators. They owe these to the natural acidity that remains preserved in the grapes on the northern climatic limit even when they are completely ripe physiologically. Yet the Loire has the right wine for every occasion: white, rosé, and red wines are produced here as well as sparkling wines and *pétillants*. The rosé palette ranges from the simple to the elegant, the reds from the light and fruity to multifaceted wines with aging ability, the whites from the superficial to the easy-drinking or opulent and sometimes incredibly complex sweet wines, the fizz from uncomplicated *pétillants* to quite exquisite sparkling wines.

If no Loire vineyard can compete with the famous labels of Burgundy, Champagne, or Bordeaux, we can confidently blame the Parisians. There is scarcely a bistro, brasserie, or restaurant in the capital that does not have one of the agreeable, inexpensive Loire tipples on its wine list—a Muscadet or Sauvignon, Cabernet or Gamay. The wines are easy to sell, and as is always the case in the wine world everywhere, this does not encourage growers to go for quality. Even so, the region has unique wines to offer us today, and three grape varieties are principally responsible for this.

The *caves* of Vouvray served as accommodation and perfect wine cellars.

Opposite
Although the Loire has its venerable *crus*, it has never in its history produced as many outstanding wines as it does today.

THREE UNRECOGNIZED GENIUSES

The top variety is the highly versatile Chenin or Chenin Blanc, which is also called Pineau de la Loire here. Almost every conceivable variety of wine is made from it, ranging from light dry wines to heavy dessert wines or even fortified liqueur wines. In France, Chenin is not very common outside the Loire region, but it is intensively cultivated in South Africa (where it is called Steen), California, and South America. The Loire dessert wines made from Chenin are notable for their capacity to improve with age. Vintage 1874 or 1893 Vouvray or Coteaux du Layon still arouse enthusiasm.

Cabernet Franc—often mocked in the Bordeaux region as Cabernet Sauvignon's little brother—provides single-variety Loire red wines that are multifaceted, elegant, and that will keep. Though lighter than in Bordeaux, they can be as good.

It would be unforgivable not to mention the Sauvignon Blanc, which occupies a special position. Particularly in the Sancerre and Pouilly area, wines of enormous spirit and finesse are made, which stand out most agreeably from the often very superficial Sauvignon-based Bordeaux white wines.

Pearls of Sweet Wine
in Rosé Country

When you travel upriver from the Pays Nantais, you reach the Anjou and Saumur region, whose 37,100 acres (15,000 hectares) planted to vines produce a wide range of wines. Anjou, the western part of this region around the city of Angers, is a well-established concept, especially in the French market, with its cheap, medium-dry rosés, though they are markedly losing ground these days. Until the phylloxera disaster, the region was planted almost exclusively with white wine varieties. Afterward, they returned to a mere 20 percent of the area planted, and have only recently become more common again.

Rosé d'Anjou is an unpretentious-to-weak wine produced from the native Grolleau or Groslot variety that is still cultivated on about 9,880 acres (4,000 ha) but is increasingly being ousted by Cabernet Franc or Gamay. The Cabernet Franc especially, which now covers almost a third of the red wine areas in Anjou, has made a lot of friends, with its Cabernet d'Anjou, a rosé with a more decidedly acidic quality that is rarely sweet. But the grape also

The wine region of the Loire provides endless fascination, with its ancient walls and Romantic scenery.

produces some of the best reds of the region, and under the Anjou-Villages label, an *appellation* allocated the *terroirs* southeast of Angers, achieves remarkable strength and structure.

The real specialty of Anjou are of course the whites made from Chenin Blanc. The vines grow mainly on the south-facing schist slopes near Angers, which once produced mainly sweet Savennières but are now developed mostly as dry wines. Its two single-site labels Coulée de Serrant—a 17-acre (7-ha) monopoly—and La Roche-aux-Moines, which have separate *appellation* statuses, are the outstanding bases for wonderfully intense, complex growths that improve with age and are reckoned among the best white wines in the world. However, Chenin is most suited to the production of sweet wines, to which four Anjou *appellations* are dedicated. In the same district on the left bank of the Loire where Anjou-Villages is made, mellow dessert wines are produced under the Coteaux de l'Aubance label, with a dry counterpart bottled as Anjou Blanc. But the most important and largest sweet-wine area is the Coteaux du Layon, on the steep slopes of the Loire tributary of the same name, running 30 miles (50 km) southward from Rochefort-sur-Loire. In recent years, talented growers have invested enormously to create wines under the Chaume and Villages *appellations*, which can bear comparison with the more famous growths of the *grand cru* areas of Bonnezeaux and Quarts de Chaume, which in turn are embedded in the Coteaux du Layon.

Things are quite different in the Saumurois, the eastern part of the region. Instead of schist, the character of the wines is determined by the white chalky tuff. Here, red and white grapes are in balance, though the red wines, especially the Saumur-Champigny Rouge *appellation* made from Cabernet Franc, are not only the best known but, with their aromas of red fruits, harmony, and elegance, are also are the best. The whites—the dry wines are marketed as Saumur Blanc or Saumur Champigny, the sweet ones as Coteaux de Saumur—are made mainly from Chenin Blanc, and display a fine touch of acidity and very good aging ability. In marketing terms, of course, the leading role in the region is played neither by white nor red but by sparkling wines called Saumur Mousseux, made from Chenin, Chardonnay, and occasionally Sauvignon Blanc.

HEAVENLY TIPPLE

Some of the best sweet wines in the world come from Anjou-Saumur. Although celebrated since the 15th century and further developed by the Dutch in the 16th and 17th centuries, in recent decades they were unrecognized classics and largely ignored. This is changing due partly to the re-awakened interest in sweet wines and partly to the re-awakened quality consciousness of the growers, who are now ready to take the risks always associated with producing sweet wines. The basic material of the sweet Loire wines is the Chenin Blanc, which despite its alternative name Pineau de la Loire is not related to the Pinot varieties of Burgundy. It is native to the Loire itself and was already cultivated in Anjou in the 9th century. Chenin can be

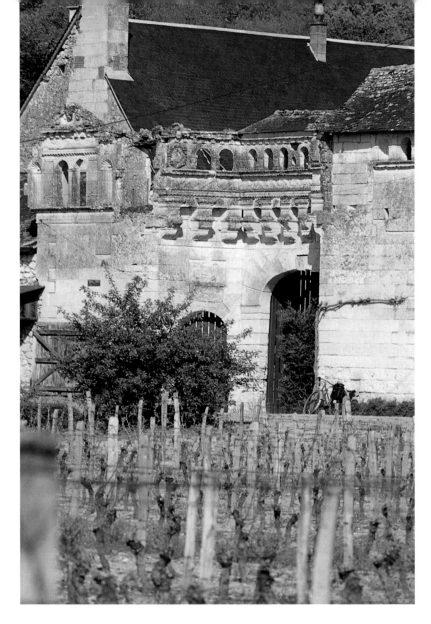

turned into a wide range of different wines depending on the degree of ripeness. In worse years, the grapes cannot produce more than 6 oz (170 g) of sugar or about 10 percent abv (alcohol by volume), in which case they are suitable only for dry whites and sparkling wines. If weather conditions are more favorable and help the grapes reach a sugar content of 7 oz–9 oz (190–260 g), at least some finish up as medium-dry or sweet wines.

In exceptional years, however, when the sugar content can reach 17.5 oz (500g), almost exclusively sweet wines are made from the grapes. Their potential alcohol content is then up to

In almost no other region is the architecture as sophisticated as it is along the Loire, where even the wine cellars have often been designed and built with great creativity and skill.

Haut Poitou

In the Middle Ages, the wines of Poitou, the region around the city of Poitiers, were better known than the growths of Bordeaux. They were shipped via the port of La Rochelle mainly to England, until in the 13th century the city fell into French hands and English merchant ships could no longer enter the port. These days Haut-Poitou, a 1,730-acre (700-ha) area south of Saumur, is a V.D.Q.S. label found on bottles of all kinds of grape—Sauvignon Blanc, Gamay, Cabernet and others. The renaissance the region has seen in recent years is founded above all on the quality of its white wines made from Sauvignon Blanc. The best and most dynamic producer in the district is the cooperative in Neuville.

FLINT AND GOOSEBERRIES

The upper Loire is a stronghold of Sauvignon, in fact the true, genuine thing—Sauvignon Blanc. Not the Sauvignon Gris, or the Sauvignon Violet, or the Sauvignon Jaune or even the Sauvignonasse or Sauvignon Vert, a relative of the Tocai Friulano, which is still sold in South America under the name of Sauvignon. As most members of this extensive family of grape varieties are of little or no importance, the *blanc* is often omitted. In the 1970s and 1980s Sauvignon in the form of Sancerre—the major *appellation* in this area—was one of the most popular white wines in almost the whole world, comparable with the Pinot Grigio, which was also fashionable at the time. Not much of this craze for white Sancerre is left now, but the grape itself continued its triumphal march across the wine-growing countries of the world. In terms of white wines, it is a march outshone only by that of the Chardonnay grape. Sauvignon Blanc is now found not only in the Loire and Bordeaux but also in Styria (Austria), Friuli (Italy), California, Australia, South America (though with the above caveat!), and South Africa.

Sauvignon has an uncommonly intense aroma. When young or harvested too soon, it manifests its typical grassy vegetational character.

In the upper Loire, in the vineyards around Sancerre and Pouilly-Fumé, Menetou-Salon and Reuilly, Sauvignon can unfurl a complex intensity and finesse—even without being blended with other varieties—such as is rarely found elsewhere.

SANCERRE AND POUILLY

Sancerre, a charming old wine-growing area, whose houses straddle a hilltop above the Loire, is the best known of the four names. The town itself and 14 of its neighboring villages constitute the 4,940-acre (2,000-ha) Sancerre cultivation area. Until the phylloxera disaster in the late 19th century, Pinot Noir and Gamay were the principal grapes. Afterwards, whites were given preference, and the light, fruity red wines made from Pinot fell out of favor, and today make only a third of the output.

Sancerre provides Sauvignon with three separate *terroirs*, though most wines are blended from grapes of different localities. In the extreme west, clay soils and chalk marls are predominant, and produce the strongest wines. Around the town itself you find the famous flint, the aroma of which is reminiscent of newly struck matches. Between the two zones the most delicate wines of the *appellation* thrive on gravel and limestone. Aging is usually done in steel tanks, as best suits the fruity, direct character of Sauvignon, and barrels are rarely used. Not so well known as its popular neighbor but more highly regarded by connoisseurs are the Sauvignon wines from Pouilly-sur-Loire, on the other bank of the Loire.

Pouilly-Fumé is the *appellation*, applied solely to white wines made from Sauvignon Blanc. The name is the source of some confusion with the

Few top localities are so easily overviewed as Clos de la Poussie near Sancerre.

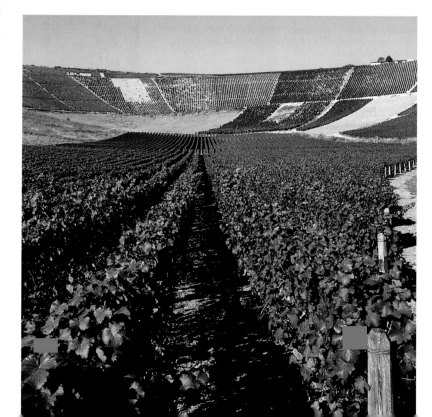

village of Pouilly-Fuissé in the Mâconnais in Burgundy, where the wines are of course made from Chardonnay. In Pouilly, not only are the hills softer than in Sancerre, the wines too are more rounded, softer and somewhat less emphatically aromatic. The best Pouillys, which are occasionally aged in wood, are, however, more complex and longer-lived than the Sancerre drinker will be used to.

The western neighbors of Sancerre have also specialized in Sauvignon. Menetou-Salon, and even more Quincy and Reuilly, lie in the great arc of the Loire so far from the river that one often ascribes them to another unspecified center. About half-way between Sancerre and Bourges is the Menetou-Salon district which, like Sancerre, produces red and white wines. Here the Sauvignon Blanc is often just as good as the more famous district directly on the Loire, only much cheaper.

Somewhat more rustic are the wines of the twin *appellations* Quincy and Reuilly, which are produced beyond Bourges along the central reach of the Cher. Sauvignon is cultivated on

about 247 acres (100 ha) of Quincy. In Reuilly, vines are planted in almost equal measure in red and white varieties. The Gamay harvested here is not an *appellation* wine but instead is sold as *vin de pays*.

SELECT PRODUCERS ON THE UPPER LOIRE

CHÂTEAU DU NOZET – LADOUCETTE***–****
POUILLY-SUR-LOIRE
257 acres (104 ha); 1,200,000 bottles • Wines include: Pouilly-Fumé: Baron de L, Sancerre Comte Lafon Grand Cuvée
Ladoucette is symbolic of Pouilly and Sancerre in general. Whenever Sauvignon is discussed worldwide, you hear this name mentioned.

DOMAINE HENRI BOURGEOIS**–****
CHAVIGNOL
148 acres (60 ha); 500,000 bottles • Wines include: Pouilly-Fumé Sancerre: Grande Réserve, Les Baronnes, La Chapelle des Augustins, Jadis
A family-run estate producing clean, clearly defined Sancerres and Pouillys with the latest winery technology.

DOMAINE PASCAL COTAT****
SANCERRE
4.5 acres (1.9 ha); 14,000 bottles • Wines: Sancerre: Chavignol La Grand Côte, Cuvée Spéciale, Les Mont Damnés
Pascal Cotat's wines are among the best Sancerre has to offer; sold in advance.

DOMAINE DIDIER DAGUENEAU*****
SAINT-ANDELAN
27 acres (11 ha); 50,000 bottles • Wines: Pouilly-Fumé: Silex, En Chailloux, Pur-Sang
Dagueneau's reputation is based on the extraordinary Sauvignon-Cuvées Silex and Pur Sang, which are known throughout the world as model wines of this grape variety.

DOMAINE MASSON-BLONDELET***
POUILLY-SUR-LOIRE
44.5 acres (18 ha); 100,000 bottles • Wines: Pouilly-Fumé: Les Angelots, Villa Paulus, Tradition Cullus, Sancerre
Jean-Michel Masson's wines manifest clear Sauvignon fruit and solid qualities.

DOMAINE LA MOUSSIÈRE***–*****
SANCERRE
119 acres (48 ha); 275,000 bottles • Wines include: Sancerre: Blanc, Rouge: La Moussière, →Ceneration XIX; →Edmond
Alphonse Mellot and his son Alphonse have gone back to the best of craftsmanship, and use only their own grapes. With new inspiration and modern technology, they create outstanding wines.

DOMAINE HENRY PELLÉ**–****
MOROGUES
131 acres (53 ha); 500,000 bottles • Wines include: Menetou-Salon: Morogues, Clos des Blanchais; Sancerre La Croix au Garde
Henry Pellé's Clos des Blanchais has proved for years that Sauvignon Blanc from Menetou is no poor relative of a Sancerre.

DOMAINE VINCENT PINARD***–****
BUÉ
37.1 acres (15 ha); 100,000 bottles • Wines: Sancerre Blanc: Florès, Nuance, Harmonie; Sancerre Rouge and Charlouise
Whether fermented in tanks or barrels, Vincent Pinard's white and red wines possess great intensity and splendid ripe fruit. The Cuvée Charlouise has proved itself one of the best red wines of this *appellation*.

SILICES DE QUINCY***–****
QUINCY
17.3 acres (7 ha); 12,000 bottles • Wines: →Silice de Quincy, VdT: Silice Millénium, Silicette Millénium
Jacques Sallé, the wine journalist and former "Vintage International" publisher, has been involved as a winegrower in his home region since 1995. Using biodynamic cultivation methods and barrel fermentation, he gets a great deal of character and body out of his Sauvignon vines, some of which are very old indeed.

BORDEAUX: MAKING A CAREER OF AN EMPORIUM

Bordeaux is more than just a famous wine-growing area. It is a symbol for great wine in general, a model for the whole world of wine. Bordeaux is the largest and most successful *appellation* in France and the world, producing over 100 million gallons (four million hecto-liters (660 million bottles) of wine a year from more than 247,000 acres (100,000 ha) of vines, or as much as the whole of Germany. The elite wines, which have established the fame of the region in modern times, constitute a modest five percent of this, of course, but their aura is so strong that it is not just the local wine industry that benefits. The whole wine industry from

Italy to California, Australia to Austria, and Chile to Germany is orientated to Bordeaux style and quality and takes it as a benchmark.

Viticulture is documented in the Dordogne by the Roman poet Ausonius, who settled in what is now the Saint-Émilion region in the 4th century AD and made his own wine. It is not clear whether there had been vine cultivation in the Landes around Burdigala, now Bordeaux, even earlier. At any rate, as neither Pliny the Elder nor Strabo mention it, historians assume that the vine arrived much later, after it had already become established in Provence and the Rhône Valley. The Romans treated Bordeaux as just a trading center for exporting their wines to England.

Even the assumption that Roman legionaries brought the main grape variety of the region from what is now Albania seems questionable in the light of recent research. As we now know that Cabernet Sauvignon contains genetic material from Cabernet Franc and Sauvignon Blanc, it is more likely that it came about much later as a cross or spontaneous mutation of these two varieties. Another untenable theory is that it is the old Biturica grape, named for the Gaulish tribe of Bituricans, a name that mutated over time by folk etymology to Vidure (*vigne dure*) meaning "hard vine wood" and is still current in the Graves region.

Early medieval sources relating to the history of regional viticulture are likewise meager. A series of successive conquests of Bordeaux by various peoples—Gascons, Saracens, Vandals, and Visigoths—is documented, as is the total destruction of the city by Vikings in 870, but wine growing never succumbed. However, the true success story of the vine began only in 1152, when Eleanor of Aquitaine married the duke of Normandy, Henry Plantagenet, who later became King Henry II of England. With the aid of generous excise privileges, Gascony became the most important supplier of the English court and London society, so that when the rival exporting port of La Rochelle was taken over by the French, Bordeaux retained its pre-eminent position in the English wine trade.

The expanse of the Gironde seen from Château Latour in Pauillac.

The Development of Modern Bordeaux

At that time, the wines did not come from the Médoc, the modern heart of the region—it was fenland until the 17th century and at best suitable for plowing—but from the gravelly soils of Graves and the upriver territories of Gaillac and Bergerac. They were not in the least comparable with the vigorous, dark, and ageable reds of our day, but light and thin (hence "claret" as they became known in England, from the Latin *vinum clarum*). Until the 14th century, almost all wine drunk in England came from Gascony. The end of the Hundred Years' War in 1453 put an end to this export splendor, when Gascony was annexed by France. Although trading links with England were not severed entirely, other markets gained in importance until Holland became a world power during the 17th century, and took over England's place in Bordeaux's trading affections.

With their huge fleet, the Dutch controlled the greater part of world trade and imported wine from all areas under cultivation, but especially Portugal and Bordeaux. At the beginning of the 17th century they also drained the marshes of the Médoc with an ingenious canal system, and introduced sulfurization as a way of conserving wine. This created the basis for the great wines of later centuries. It was also the time when the great châteaux such as Haut-Brion, Latour, Lafite, and Margaux were first established.

Bordeaux's reputation is based on the aging potential of its wines.

But Dutch control of the seas did not last long. By the 18th century the English were back in Bordeaux, founding trading companies such as Barton & Guestier, which until very recently controlled the fate of the wine industry in the region. Soon after, this successful approach was taken up by a series of German immigrants.

The trading firms and their traveling buyers, the *courtiers*, made the first attempts to classify individual châteaux in the early 19th century. This was intended to bring stability to a very unstable market, which always tended to fluctuate between overheating and crisis. The result of these endeavors, which focused solely on the Médoc region and Sauternes, was the classification of 1855 and triumphal presentation of the châteaux at the Paris Exposition in the same year. The golden age of Bordeaux had begun.

Turbulence in the 20th Century

Despite the enormous prestige that Bordeaux wines have enjoyed since then and have managed to further enhance, the 20th century was a period of crisis. It began with the phylloxera catastrophe, which wiped out virtually the entire stock of vines. After a brief period of recovery, during which exports to Germany, England, and Belgium picked up again, and laws for the protection of labels of origins were worked out, the First World War and economic crisis led to the collapse of important foreign markets such as Russia and the U.S.A.

Only in the 1950s did the sales graphs begin to point steadily upwards. It was the heyday of the Médoc's neighboring regions. In 1953 and 1955 respectively the wines of Graves and Saint-Émilion were classified—only Pomerol still has no official hierarchy even today—and the best wines of the region reached a dizzying price level as a result of sharply increased demand. The ensuing shortage of wine was to some extent compensated for by one or two shippers adding wines from other areas. The fraud was discovered in 1973, to great scandal, and prices tumbled again.

At the same time, the Bordeaux region was increasingly exposed to competition from the New World. Californian or Australian growths triumphed over Bordeaux's best in top-ranking competitions. They included wines such as the Australian Grange Hermitage or those of California's Clos du Val estate, run by natives of Bordeaux. The international competitors trumped Bordeaux with wines that had the same strength and density as the great

The vine varieties of Bordeaux

For all the differences between the *terroirs* in the various areas of Bordeaux, the wines have a common basis: a small number of grape varieties used in proportions that vary according to the *terroir* or fashion. Red has priority, and occupies a good 85 percent of the area under cultivation, and this proportion has risen in the last 15 years.

RED WINE VARIETIES
Cabernet Sauvignon—one of the best red wine grapes in the world and the star of the Bordeaux region, it probably developed from Cabernet Franc and Sauvignon Blanc. Its special qualities reside in its concentration of PHENOLICS, without the fruit being wholly masked by the tannins thereby. Cabernet wines are dark red, smell of cedar and blackcurrant, and manifest much strength and structure on the palate. When immature or with excessive yields, the aroma changes in the direction of green paprika pods.

Cabernet Franc/Bouchet/Breton—the grape was long considered the junior brother of Cabernet Sauvignon, but recent discoveries show Franc as the parent. Its wines have a fine berry fruitiness, and are slimmer than Cabernet Sauvignon and have more discreet tannins, but may therefore also be more acidic.

Merlot (Noir)—the grape ripens early and has a high yield, and is therefore well-suited to both aging on its own and blending with stronger wines of greater tannin content. In the Bordeaux region, its best results are in the Saint-Émilion and Pomerol *appellations*. Its wines are fruity and velvety, and it matures more quickly than Cabernet.

Petit Verdot—a late-ripening variety and therefore difficult in the aging, it produces wines that have intense color and high tannin content. Small quantities of the grape go into Médoc wines.

Malbec/Cot/Auxerrois/Pressac—a red wine variety that was once very widespread in the Bordeaux region. It was replaced there by Merlot, but is still cultivated in Cahors. The wines have a rustic character, but are very well suited to blending with other varieties.

WHITE WINE VARIETIES
Sémillon—with a tendency to noble rot, the grape is the basis for the great sweet wines of the Bordeaux region. The best dry growths are found in Pessac-Léognan. Sémillon wines have good aging ability, and then develop aromas of honey, candied fruits, and chocolates while often retaining a fresh lemony tang.

Sauvignon Blanc—when young or harvested too soon, the grapes manifest their typical grassy-vegetal aromas. Good Sauvignon wines develop an aroma of blackcurrants or gooseberries and are fruity with good acidity. When fully ripe or over-ripe, they become more complex, developing ripe fruit, and can even come to resemble highly ripe Rieslings. In the last century the French considered Riesling as just a variety of Sauvignon. The Sauvignon family also has rare red varieties.

---

growths of the Gironde region but were much more accessible.

This new style of wine was so successfully promoted and insisted upon by the American specialist in Bordeaux, Robert Parker Jr., the wine king of the 1980 and 1990s, that it became a standard for the whole international market. To keep pace with the new requirements, the estates of Médoc, Graves, Saint-Émilion, or Pomerol looked primarily to re-equipping their wineries. Vinification had changed both in respect of tannin structure and the make-up of grape varieties, in which Merlot became increasingly prominent. Bordeaux became a hotbed of technical innovation. Such modern techniques as concentrators—appliances for REVERSE OSMOSIS—and vacuum evaporizers are now used in the wineries of the most celebrated châteaux. Many estate managers even resorted to methods for which they had long criticized the New World, such as using wood chips instead of aging in expensive wooden casks.

Left
Typical gravelly soil in the Médoc area.

Right
Château Mouton-Rothschild, one of the most famous wine-growing estates in the world.

IDEAL TERROIR

Not only does the Gironde make the Médoc climate more temperate and favor wine growing, it also offers splendid opportunities for relaxation along its banks.

Even though the Dutch had to drain a large part of the territory—later the most successful part—before vines could be planted, Bordeaux had nonetheless the best possible natural conditions for great wines. Lying exactly half-way between the Equator and the North Pole, it enjoys a particularly balanced climate that is ideal for wines with strength and structure on the one hand and finesse and elegance on the other. The proximity of the Atlantic with the warm Gulf Stream ensures mild conditions and prevents extreme variations of temperature. The extensive forests of the coast of Aquitaine offer additional protection against storms from the sea. Frost risk—the grower's great enemy in Champagne or Burgundy—hardly exists here, if we disregard the exceptional year of 1991. However, June can be very unstable, which causes problems when the vines flower. Long, dry hot summers and an often variable autumn make the harvest a lottery in bad years.

In respect of soil conditions, three zones should be distinguished within the huge Bordeaux area, each of which forms an independent entity. Bordeaux is not a wine-growing area with a single, homogeneous *appellation* but a complicated, hierarchically subdivided network of 54 *appellations* in all, some of which date back to the first days of A.C. legislation, others to recent decades. A law passed in 1911 protecting French *appellations* specified that only wines from the Gironde department

could be sold as Bordeaux wines—a regulation intended to put a stop to the hitherto frequent blending with other more stronger provenances, although this could still occur, as the scandal of 1973 showed.

A large proportion of the wines—40 percent of the total output, and up to 70 percent of the whites—are marketed under the regional *appellations* Bordeaux, Bordeaux Supérieur, or Bordeaux Crémant. These labels indicate wines from areas for which no higher grade or more closely defined indication of origin is provided, or those grown in *appellation* vineyards that do not come under the *appellation*.

TWO SEAS AND THEIR VINEYARDS

The remaining A.C.s are generally divided into three zones. The first lies on the left bank of the Garonne and Gironde, and is a strip of sandy, gravelly soils (*graves*) north and south of the city of Bordeaux washed down from the Pyrenees, Limousin, and the western Massif Central. This zone is subdivided into the Médoc *appellation* north of Bordeaux, on whose thin, well-drained sand and gravel soils virtually only red grapes are grown, and Graves proper in the west and south, which incorporates the sweet wine areas of Sauternes. The latter's alluvial soils are well suited to both delicate, aromatic reds and dry whites, as well as sweet specialties.

Between the Garonne and Dordogne rivers is the Entre-Deux-Mers district, the area "between two rivers," a plateau of the Tertiary period with heavy clay and gravel soils. Its wines range from aromatic, lively, and even mellow wines to sometimes very full-bodied reds in which Merlot dominates. Lastly, on the right bank of the Dordogne, we find a number of wholly independent areas of very varying quality. The soils are similar to those of Entre-deux-Mers. Different wines grow on the gravel soils of Pomerol to those growing on the clayey chalk of the Fronsadais or in Saint-Émilion.

The three zones mentioned are heavily subdivided, with the subdivision system varying considerably from zone to zone. The best arranged is that of the Médoc, which is divided into Haut-Médoc and Médoc proper. The former, closer to Bordeaux, contains the highly prestigious communal *appellations* Margaux, Listrac, Moulis, Saint-Julien, Pauillac, and Saint-Estèphe. The Graves area has no such

Médoc

- Médoc
- Saint-Estèphe
- Pauillac
- Saint-Julien
- Haut-Médoc
- Listrac-Médoc
- Moulis-en-Médoc
- Margaux
- Côtes et Premières Côtes de Blaye
- Côtes de Bourg
- Bordeaux and Bordeaux Supérieur

- Fronsac
- Canon-Fronsac
- Pomerol
- Lalande-de-Pomerol

Saint-Émilion

- Saint-Émilion
- Lussac-Saint-Émilion
- Montagne-Saint-Émilion
- Saint-Georges-Saint-Émilion
- Puisseguin-Saint-Émilion
- Bordeaux-Côtes de Francs
- Côtes de Castillon

- Premières Côtes de Bordeaux
- Entre-Deux-Mers
  Bordeaux et Bordeaux Supérieur
- Graves-de-Vayres
- Sainte-Foy-Bordeaux
  Bordeaux and Bordeaux Supérieur
- Cadillac et
  Premières Côtes de Bordeaux
- Bordeaux et
  Entre-Deux-Mers-Haut-Benauge
- Côtes de Bordeaux-
  Sainte-Macaire
- Pessac-Léognan
- Graves
- Sweet Bordeaux
- Cérons
- Barsac
- Loupiac
- Sainte-Croix-du-Mont
- Sauternes
- Wine-growing areas in neighboring regions
- ···· Limit of Bordeaux A.C.

6 miles
(10 km)

hierarchical arrangement. Instead, a higher—quality *appellation* of Pessac-Léognan has been created for the northern end-as an equivalent of the communal A.C.s of the Médoc—and the Sauternes label at the southern end.

The structure is similar in Entre-Deux-Mers. The *rive droite*, or right bank, of the Dordogne is more complicated. It comprises a row of individual *appellations* that do not constitute part of any official hierarchical arrangement with each other, even though their prestige varies widely. In the northwest are the vineyards of Bourg and Blaye, in the southeast Fronsac with Canon-Fronsac and the Libournais, which is subdivided into Pomerol and Saint-Émilion and a series of satellites—the areas are so labeled

that the name of the more prestigious A.C. forms part of their own *appellation*, like Lalande-de-Pomerol or Puisseguin-Saint-Émilion. The final label in the east is the Côtes-de-Castillon.

Hierarchical Relationships

unchanged—only Château Mouton-Rothschild was added in 1973 as a fifth member to the illustrious family of *premiers crus* first nominated by Jefferson. Overall, 87 châteaux are included in this classification.

Château Haut-Brion is the only representative of Graves in the *premier cru*. Sixty Médoc *domaines* are ranked (including four *premiers*, 14 *deuxièmes*, 14 *troisièmes*, 10 *quatrièmes*, and 18 *cinquièmes*) and 26 châteaux of Sauternes and Barsac, with only the Sauternes Château Yquem given the top title of Premier Cru Supérieur. Below these *crus classés*, the Crus Bourgeois, a further classification of 444 wines in the Médoc, was worked out in the 1930s. Updated and officially sanctioned in 1972, 322 châteaux belong to this group today, still representing almost 50 percent of the total Médoc output.

Setting an Example

Of course, the success of Médoc, the classification of which had been one of the triggers of a huge commercial success, attracted jealousy. However, it would take until 1936—and the crises that the French wine industry had undergone in the previous 150 years were certainly in part to blame—before a similar venture was undertaken in Saint-Émilion on the right bank of the Dordogne. It became reality only after the Second World War, in 1954–55. The classification was much simpler here than in the Médoc. In the first place, a distinction was made between the *appellations* Saint-Émilion and Saint-Émilion Grand Cru, with only the latter having the right to further subclassification. Overall, 75 châteaux in this group are labeled once again as *grands crus classés*, and 11 of them are graded one rank higher, as *premiers grands crus classés*.

The real top rank of the *appellation* is occupied by only two estates, Château Cheval Blanc and Château Ausone, which form an A group within the *premiers grands crus*, while the other nine have to make do with B-group membership. Apart from being somewhat simpler, the Saint-Émilion system has a further substantial advantage. Whereas the Médoc classification does not in principle allow for modification— this being one reason why Mouton took decades to be acknowledged as *premier cru classé* despite the obvious quality of its wines—

One of the milestones in the success story of Bordeaux wines was the classification of the various *crus*, first officially undertaken in 1855. Thomas Jefferson had made a previous attempt with the Médocs *crus* during his visit in 1787, with the names of Latour, Lafite, Margaux, and Haut-Brion—still dominant today—top of the list. However, another half-century was to pass before the world exposition of 1855 in Paris provided the occasion to designate the best châteaux officially as such. The Bordeaux chamber of commerce—the Libournais did not belong to it and therefore did not participate in the classification exercise—was asked to draw up lists. This was done with the help of *courtiers* from the Bordeaux exchange, who had long operated on the basis of such classifications for their own purposes. In contrast to Burgundy, where the monasteries especially had been practicing the art of classifying individual vineyards for centuries, the *courtiers* allowed not only for the factor of the *terroir* but also for the human achievement involved—more precisely, the reputation of the châteaux and the average prices that their wines had commanded in the markets over a long period. Their scheme distinguished five classes, ranging from the *premier* to the *cinquième grand cru classé*, the first to the fifth growth. However difficult as such an exercise appears, the *courtiers* carried out their work in such model fashion that their assessments have remained in forced virtually

The barrels of the Château Lafite-Rothschild are stored in the cellars under the vineyard.

Every year since 1945, a different well-known artist has been commissioned to design the label for the Premier Grand Cru Classé Château Mouton-Rothschild.

One of the vital features of each classification in France is, beside the *terroir* designation, the limit of the maximum permitted yield per hectare for each *appellation*. Depending on the prestige of the given *appellation*, these permitted maximum yields are specified more or less liberally.

For the regional *appellation* Bordeaux it is 55 or 65 hl/ha, for Bordeaux Supérieur

50 hl/ha. For years, however, the possibility has existed of moving this limit upwards, as a result of which it can reach 68 or 78 hl/ha for Bordeaux Rouge and Blanc and 66 for Bordeaux Supérieur.

The base and highest values for the most important *appellations* are set as follows: Médoc 50/66, Haut-Médoc 48/66, communal *appellations* (Pauillac etc.) 47/66, Graves 50,

Pessac-Léognan 45 (red) and 48 (white) / 66, Sauternes, Barsac 25/28, Entre-deux-Mers 60/75, Premières Côtes de Bordeaux 50/66 (red) and 50/55 (white), Pomerol 42/60, Fronsac 47/65, Côtes de Bourg 50/60 (red) and 60/75 (white).

*1 ha = 2.47 acres; 1 hl = 26.42 U.S. gallons

such revision is prescribed in Saint-Émilion every ten years. This periodic check offers a real incentive to growers to keep the quality of their work and their products at a level that matches their grading. Such motivation is alas lacking in the Médoc, if we judge only by the downright lamentable image that some classified *crus* present time and again.

producers more freedom of movement here, in 1989 an additional category of *cru artisan* was introduced. This offers connoisseurs the opportunity to buy really top wines at very favorable prices, which is hardly possible any more within the classified growths.

CRUS ARTISANS: TIPS FOR CONNOISSEURS

Particularly in the Médoc, it often happens that wines only labeled as *cru bourgeois*, if we just follow the hierarchical system, are markedly better presented than many a fifth or even fourth growth, and occasionally better even than châteaux ranked still higher. To allow

MÉDOC
37 million bottles, 127 crus bourgeois, 113 crus artisans, 5 caves coopératives
A broad range of red wines, many of which are lighter and therefore more accessible in character, while others are rounder and take more time in the bottle; often Merlot provides a certain softness and harmony.

SAINT-ESTÈPHE
8.3 million bottles, 5 crus classés, 43 crus bourgeois, 25 crus artisans and others, 1 cave coopérative
They are known for marked and spirited tannins which, mingling with the often present acidity of the wines, guarantee long aging. They then manifest characterful, often earthy tones.

PAUILLAC
8.1 million bottles, 18 crus classés, 16 crus bourgeois, 7 crus artisans and others, 1 cave coopérative
Wines with body and structure which contain powerful tannins and age magnificently to reveal their second character trait—elegance and finesse.

SAINT-JULIEN
6 million bottles, 11 crus classés, 8 crus bourgeois, 11 crus artisans and others
Much harmony and finesse, both in the bouquet and on the palate, but with firm

tannins and a good structure that often confer great potential.

LISTRAC-MÉDOC
4.8 million bottles, 29 crus bourgeois, 12 crus artisans and others, 1 cave coopérative
Often very inaccessible when young, these wines are solid and rich in tannins, but their usually relatively high Merlot content gives them a full, velvety character when mature.

MOULIS-EN-MÉDOC
4 million bottles, 31 crus bourgeois, 13 crus artisans and others
The wines of Moulis are as varied as the soils, with a broad range from soft to full and more tannin-rich growths that reach their peak after about a decade.

MARGAUX
9 million bottles, 21 crus classés, 25 crus bourgeois, 38 crus artisans and others
Elegance is the key concept of Margaux, combined with delicious fruit when young. The subtle tannins hold firm during long aging, leading, in the case of the greatest wines, to fantastic refinement.

HAUT-MÉDOC
30 million bottles, 5 crus classés, 140 crus bourgeois, 116 crus artisans and other crus, 5 caves coopératives

Comprises the famous crus, and its wines often show strength and solidity with strongly marked Cabernet Sauvignon, usually intense aromas and after some years of aging a complex bouquet and balance.

PESSAC-LÉOGNAN
9 million bottles, 15 crus classés: 6 for red and white wines, 7 only for red, 2 only for white wine; another 41 châteaux
Four-fifths red wines with elegant character, intense, sometimes floral aromas and an occasional special smoky overtone, fleshy, well-structured and with great aging ability. A fifth is dry, very aromatic white wines with astonishing durability and a remarkable roundness and finish.

GRAVES
About 24 million bottles, 400 producers
The red wines have pleasant aromas of ripe red berries, a good fullness and juiciness, and with aging, finesse and harmony. About an eighth of the production constitutes intensely perfumed white wines. They are characterized by good *nervosité* and at the same time typical roundness, which improves with aging in the bottle.

Médoc: A Sea of Vines in Two Parts

The Médoc, a coastal strip no more than 6 miles (10 km) wide on the left bank of the Gironde, that stretches almost 50 miles (80 km) from Bordeaux almost to the Atlantic, is far better known than its neighbors and rivals, and its classified *crus* account for a large part of the prestige of the region. About 37,100 acres (15,000 ha) planted to vines produce on average 18,500,000 gallons (700,000 hl) of wine per annum.

Prior to the 17th century, the region was so marshy that large parts of it could only be reached by boat. With the arrival of the Dutch—experts in drainage—the nobility of the Bordelais region began to use the overwhelmingly flat landscape with its gravel soils for wine. The division into a northern part, the Médoc *appellation* proper, and the southern half or Haut-Médoc, established itself quickly and is still valid. The Haut-Médoc in particular, where numerous châteaux and mansions have documented the wealth of their owners since the 18th century, has proved an outstanding area to produce top wines.

Only about a third of the total Médoc production comes from the northern part. The vineyard holdings here are divided among over 650 owners, of whom almost a third market their own wines. There are no *crus classés* here, but about 130 châteaux, who account for more than half of the production, belong to the group of *crus bourgeois*. For all the variety of the *terroirs*, Médoc wines are not so firmly structured nor so complex and ageable as those of the Haut Médoc, but they often display great charm and are drinkable young.

The situation is quite different further upriver in Haut-Médoc, home of the most famous *crus classés* and the prestigious communal *appellations* Saint-Estèphe, Pauillac, Saint-Julien, Listrac, Moulis, and Margaux. Though this part of the overall region includes two-thirds of the cultivated area, because of the special situation of the localities mentioned, only something over 9,880 acres (4,000 ha) are classed as Haut-Médoc proper, which produce on average 5,020,000 gallons (190,000 hl) of wine. The Haut-Médoc *appellation* also possesses only a small number of classified estates, which account for a mere 8 percent of the total production, whereas the 140 *crus bourgeois* make up 70 percent.

The Realm of Cabernet

Médoc, Haut-Médoc, and the communal *appellations* are the real home of the most famous red wine grape of Bordeaux, the Cabernet Sauvignon. A late-ripening variety that easily

Château Comtesse de Lalande in Pauillac.

Key/Legend:

- Médoc
- Saint-Estèphe
  - 1 Cos d'Estournel
  - 2 Haut-Marbuzet
  - 3 Montrose
- Pauillac
  - 4 Lafite-Rothschild
  - 5 Latour
  - 6 Mouton-Rothschild
  - 7 Grand-Puy-Lacoste
  - 8 Lynch Bages
  - 9 Pichon Longueville-Baron
  - 10 Pichon Longueville Comtesse de Lalande
- Saint-Julien
  - 11 Léoville-Las-Cases
  - 12 Ducru-Beaucaillon
  - 13 Gruaud-Larose
  - 14 Léoville Barton
  - 15 Léoville Poyferré
  - 16 Beycheville
- Listrac-Médoc
  - 17 Mayne Lalande
- Moulis-en-Médoc
  - 18 Poujeaux
- Margaux
  - 19 Margaux
  - 20 Palmer
  - 21 Monbrison
  - 22 Siran
- Haut-Médoc
  - 23 Sociando-Mallet
  - 24 Cantemerle
  - 25 Citran
  - 26 Maucamps
- Côtes and Premières Côtes de Blaye
- Côtes de Bourg
- Bordeaux and Bordeaux Supérieur
- •••• Limit of Bordeaux A.C.s

adapts to the most wide-ranging climatic and geological conditions, it makes wines of unequaled greatness and complexity on the gravel soils of the Gironde, which allow its roots to explore to great depths.

Of course, the otherwise really quite hardy Cabernet needs a lot of sun, or its wines manifest the grassy, unpleasant flavor of green paprika pods and hard, bitter tannins that do not become more harmonious during aging. The enormous concentration of tannin in the wine derives from the small berries with their thick skins, which requires much skill from the vintner in balancing the *cuvées*. For this, the growers and winemakers of the Médoc have four other varieties of grape available: Merlot, Cabernet Franc, Malbec, and Petit Verdot. They are used in a wide range of quantities and ratios, though the lively but (from a grower's point of view) rather troublesome Petit Verdot, is cultivated less and less. Of course,

wines with a high Cabernet Sauvignon content need long maturing to establish a balance and allow the bouquet to unfold. Changing consumer patterns and the trend to quicker, early-maturing wines has also changed the structure of Médoc wines to some extent. This has meant a higher proportion of Merlot, especially in *appellations* with lighter, simpler wines.

In the best-known châteaux of the Médoc, Cabernet Sauvignon continues to reign supreme, and is allowed to unfurl its great glories. There was such a run on the great names of Médoc viticulture, particularly during the 1990s, that prices reached astronomical levels once again. It is a situation not without risk for the châteaux, especially if the trade profits more than they do.

Bourgeois, artisans, and paysans

Although everyone seems to talk only about the *crus classés*, the real development of recent decades has been in the *crus bourgeois*, and to a lesser extent in the *crus artisans* and *paysans* as well. While the *crus classés* represent only 23 percent of total production, the *bourgeois* make almost 50 percent, the *artisans* and *paysans* about 11 percent. The remaining production is processed by the cooperatives.

Although the term *cru bourgeois* is probably much older, it was first used commercially in the Bordeaux region in the 19th century. The same *courtiers* who had drawn up the 1855 classification also classified all the wines in the area into various types: *paysans*, *artisans*, *artisans supérieurs*, *premiers artisans*, *bourgeois*, *premiers bourgeois*, and *bourgeois supérieurs*, with the famous *crus classés* really being just the top end of the *bourgeois*, or *crus bourgeois classés*, to be precise.

That social classifications were used to describe a wine hierarchy has historic reasons. An observer had already

noted in the 18th century that given two plots of land, one belonging to a leading personality, the other to a peasant, the wines of the former always obtained better prices.

The economic crises of the 1920s and 1930s and a series of bad harvests prompted the gradation of 444 (now 322) châteaux as *crus bourgeois*, of which 99 were classed as *supérieurs* and 6 as *supérieurs exceptionnels*. The labeling within the category was modified again in 1962. The *supérieurs* became *grand crus bourgeois* and the *exceptionnels* turned into *crus grands bourgeois exceptionnels*, but like the distinction of the 1930s this was not backed by legal recognition. Only in recent years has the community of the *crus bourgeois* come to an understanding about working out a formal hierarchical classification of member châteaux and getting it officially recognized.

A Class of its Own

Château Pichon
Longueville-Baron and its
avantgarde winery.

One of the continuing strengths of the Bordeaux region lies in the classification of its vineyards and its wines that the growers and the trade carried out themselves. In contrast to many other areas, where jealousy and misconstrued egalitarianism do not permit such hierarchical gradations, here they dared to assess which wines were the best, and also used this as a prime marketing instrument for the whole region. Ultimately, Bordeaux became the most famous wine-growing district in the world because of the enormous prestige of the *crus classés*, and the whole industry, whether classified or not, benefited from it.

On the occasion of the 1855 exposition in Paris, Napoleon III asked the Bordeaux region chamber of commerce to undertake a selection of the best wine-growing estates to represent the region in Paris. The job was passed to the syndicate of wine-brokers (*courtiers*), who had long worked with such classifications, albeit unofficially. The basis of their system was the prices that could be achieved by the various growths. With the exception of the Château Haut-Brion from Graves, the system applied only to the Médoc and the sweet wines of Sauternes and Barsac. The wines of the right bank of the Dordogne were not included because their areas of cultivation came under the auspices of the Libourne Chamber of Commerce, whose reputation would develop only later anyway.

Attempts at classification had begun much earlier. Even in 1730 brokers on the Quai des Chartrons in Bordeaux, where the best-known shippers had their offices, were already working with lists of this sort. Of course, at this date the lists had little relevance for the consumer as the wines were exported in barrels, blended in London and reached the end consumer as anonymous products. Somewhat earlier, at the end of the 17th century, Arnaud de Pontac, owner of the Château Haut-Brion, had gone directly to the English market, dissatisfied with the prices he was getting from the system, and had begun to sell the wines under the name of the *domaine*. Haut-Brion soon became the most sought-after and expensive wine of its day.

Spurred on by this success, the interest of the Bordelais families was now directed at sites whose wines displayed similar potential that could be turned into hard cash. Their eye fell on the flat hilltops of the Médoc, where the Margaux, Lafite, and Latour estates looked particularly promising. Margaux belonged to the Lestonnac family, who had allied themselves at the time with the Pontacs by intermarriage, and in the early 18th century Margaux became the second Bordeaux estate to cause a stir in London. Only a few years later, Lafite and Latour followed suit. Thus today's ruling elite of the Bordeaux wine industry were firmly established three hundred years ago.

A Solid System to Stand the Test of Time

During the 18th century, the other Médoc *domaines* developed that were classified later. The first more or less reliable ratings began to circulate, including that by Thomas Jefferson, who had unerringly picked out the above four châteaux as the absolute top *crus*. The ratings only became obligatory, however, with the official classification of 1855, which was backed by statute. The amazing thing about it is that it has remained virtually unchanged to this day. Although time and again various *domaines* were merged or others were split up, although the owners and the winemakers changed and some names disappeared altogether, the 1855 list is still valid today.

Countless attempts have been made to amend, abolish, or replace the original classifications with alternative ratings, but in vain. This is not to overlook the disadvantages that the Bordeaux classification system had (and still has), even if you ignore the confusion sown in the consumer's mind by the co-existence of such widely differing schemes in the Médoc, Saint-Émilion, and Graves. However, the greatest handicap of the Médoc list lies rather in the very result that its enormous success first made possible—its permanence and stability. It took decades of lobbying for a top château like Mouton to be admitted to the illustrious elite of the *premiers crus classés*. On the other hand, even the prolonged crisis at many Margaux *domaines* in the 1970s did not pose a threat to their membership for a single moment. Regular revision of the ratings, say many critics of the Médoc system, would not only give consumers better quality and more up-to-date information, but also motivate the estates not to rest on their laurels. They would have to keep their quality standards up.

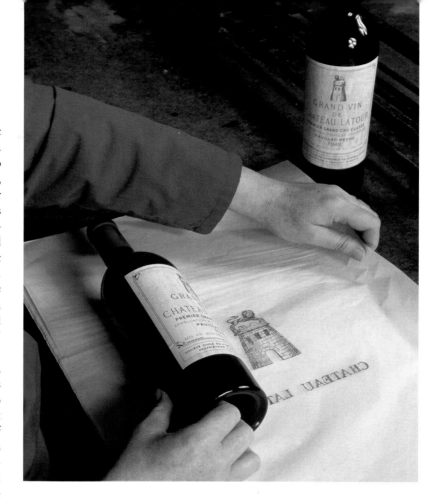

Great wines deserve great respect even in packing.

The châteaux keep bottles from every vintage as a reference.

Even a standardization of the various classification systems, and their extension to as yet unclassified *appellations* such as Pomerol, would certainly be considered progress by many consumers. This would make the *premiers crus* of individual areas comparable with each other—an idea that the Bordelais folk fear like the Devil fears holy water. Their argument is that wines of different *appellations* cannot be assessed in confrontation: they are not better or worse, just different. It is a fig leaf whose logic makes an absurdity of the whole classification to which the Bordelais have become so attached. After all, it was they who with their system of hierarchically graded *appellations*—Pauillac ranks higher than Haut-Médoc, which ranks higher than Bordeaux, even if the wines all come from one and the same parish—that made such comparisons the basis of their wine legislation in the first place.

CONCENTRATED STRENGTH IN A TRIO

In contrast to the southern part of the Médoc, where lavishly constructed châteaux and wine-growing estates were created in the 18th and 19th centuries, the northern half of the Haut-Médoc cannot offer massive splendor. Instead, this area shines with a unique concentration of great wines—34 of the 60 classified growths of the Médoc: 18 in the Pauillac area alone, 11 in Saint-Julien, and five in Saint-Estèphe.

In the days when large parts of the marshy Médoc were inaccessible by land, the harbors of Saint-Estèphe—the Port de la Chapelle—and Pauillac played a key role as the only points of access. Particularly in times of crisis, Pauillac offered a good alternative facility in maritime trade for ships that could not berth in Bordeaux.

Saint-Estèphe—which was called Saint-Estèphe de Calon until the 18th century, *calon* meaning "wood," and occurring also in the name of the famous Calon-Ségur estate, for example—is the most northerly of the trio. Wine was produced here even in Roman days, and the industry developed enormously in the 13th century. Prestigious *premiers crus classés* are, however, not to be found. All the *crus classés* together account for only about 20 percent of the output by volume, which is the lowest proportion for all communal *appellations* of the Médoc. This compares with 54 percent for the *crus bourgeois*, including some outstanding names such

Château Ducru-Beaucailloux, a *deuxième grand cru classé* in Saint-Julien, stands on a gently rounded hill rising directly from the bank of the Gironde.

The large bottles of the best *grands crus* of the Médoc, which come on to the market in very limited numbers, are coveted collectors' items.

as Phélan-Ségur, Ormes des Pez, Lilian Ladouys, Tour de Pez, or even Pez.

CHARACTER NEEDS AGE

In comparison with its more southerly neighbors, Saint-Estèphe suffers from spread: the best localities of the over 3,060 acres (1,240 ha) under vine are distributed over three rather widely separated areas: the Cos d'Estournel area in the south, the area around Montrose in the east and the sites around Château Calon-Ségur in the north. The soils consist primarily of gravel and sand with silicate elements, though the ferrous or chalky substrata are responsible for the differing characters of the wines.

The intense color of the Saint-Estèphe wines is considered a strong *terroir* feature. The wines often seem somewhat heavier than those of Pauillac or Saint-Julien, their strong tannins being very challenging, and when young they can seem very austere, to which their marked acidity contributes. This is offset by a higher proportion of Merlot compared with Pauillac or Saint-Julien.

Although the area under vine in Pauillac, the southern neighbor of Saint-Estèphe, is somewhat smaller with 2,970 acres (1,200 ha), the *appellation* has incomparably greater prestige, above all because its wines exude pure *noblesse*. The only village in the region with a promenade along the Gironde embankment has been systematically involved in viticulture only since Louis XV's day, but even so is home to three of the five *premiers crus classés* (the classic Lafite and Latour plus the "newcomer" Mouton) and 15 other classified *crus*. In its total number of *crus* it is surpassed only by Margaux.

BLACKCURRANT, MINT, AND CEDARWOOD

A good 84 percent of Pauillac's annual output comes from the famous châteaux—only in Saint-Julien is the proportion still higher. The rest is divided among 16 *crus bourgeois* and seven *artisans*. Like Saint-Estèphe, Pauillac also has varying soil formations, which can, for example, lead to wines from Château Lafite revealing a finesse untypical of Pauillac and being compared more often with Margaux *crus*. Certainly this is one of the limitations of the *appellation* system, which is ultimately directed at administrative parish boundaries that do not always reflect real *terroir* borders. It is one reason why Château Lafite has special permission to run vineyards in the neighboring Saint-Estèphe area.

Overall the soils of Pauillac are very barren but deep, and consist of predominantly iron-bearing gravels. The best growths are on two flat hilltops called *plateaux*, with Latour and the two Pichon-Lalandes in the Saint-Lambert part that once belonged to Saint-Julien, and Mouton and Lafite on Le Pouyalet in the north. In the distribution of grape varieties, Pauillac has the highest Cabernet Sauvignon proportion of any Bordeaux wine. It is normally between 60 and 80 percent, and only falls below 50 percent in a few cases, such as Pichon Comtesse.

Cabernet Franc and Merlot share a rather meager proportion of the area under vine, while Petit Verdot is unusually strongly represented and sometimes can make 10 percent of the blend. The special combination of varieties is what ensures the specially firm, well-structured, and powerful wines of Pauillac, whose rich bouquet manifests the typical Cabernet aromas of blackcurrant, mint, and cedarwood, and which possess great aging ability.

Not so forceful, but possessing unsurpassed harmony and balance, are the wines of Pauillac's southern neighbor Saint-Julien, which with only 2,220 acres (900 ha) is the smallest of the three northern *appellations*. Fruit and juice on the one hand, and structure and tannins on the other, make up perhaps the most modern wines of the Médoc.

Balanced in Every Respect

Although the village of Saint-Julien-Beychevelle can offer no *premier cru*, it does have five seconds, two thirds and four fourth growths. These 11 produce a noteworthy 85 percent of total production, which is a record for the region. As the other châteaux grow virtually only good *bourgeois* and *artisans*, you can buy wines from Saint-Julien really almost blindly.

Like in Pauillac, the best vineyard localities are on two hilltops, with that of the village itself including the three Léovilles *appellations* and Talbot, while the other, called Beychevelle, including Ducru-Beaucaillou, Gruaud-Larose, and Beychevelle itself. These hilltops are separated from each other by small water courses and drainage ditches. As everywhere in the Médoc, the best wines are in the direct vicinity of these ditches and channels.

On the large estates of Saint-Julien the Cabernet Sauvignon proportion is between 65 percent and 70 percent, 25 to 30 percent is Merlot, leaving only a small proportion of Cabernet Franc.

In the damp cellars of Bordeaux, wines often keep for decades.

In the circular cellar of Lafite-Rothschild all the barrels are about the same distance from the middle.

PURE FINESSE

Château Palmer has equipped itself with thoroughly modern winery technology.

In contrast to Graves, where the vineyards still extend almost into the center of Bordeaux, there is in the north a relatively broad strip between the city and the Margaux district and its neighboring parishes.

Margaux, Listrac, and Moulis are the three communal *appellations* of this southernmost part of Haut-Médoc. The natural conditions are not markedly different from those of Pauillac, Saint-Julien, or Saint-Estèphe. The typical sandy, pebbly Graves gravels with limestone subsoils are the characteristic soil structure, and in terms of climate the proximity to the Gironde plays the same stabilizing role as in the more northerly districts. Here, too, small rounded hillocks, called *croupes* or *plateaux*, on which the soils are well drained and the gravel layers particularly deep, offer the best conditions for the vines.

On the western edge of this half of the Haut-Médoc are the two territories of Moulis-en-Médoc and Listrac-Médoc. Neither has a *cru classé*, but they do have a large number of good to very good *bourgeois*. In Listrac, the more northerly of the two areas with about 1,730 acres (700 ha) of vineyards, three zones are particularly suited to viticulture—Fonréaud in the south and Fourcas in the north of the commune, and finally Listrac itself—and at up to 400 feet (122 m) high are some of the highest sites in the whole of the Médoc.

A LOT OF MERLOT IN MÉDOC

The soils of these areas, despite the common features, are very different in detail. Fourcas, whose *crus* are the best of the *appellation*, has silicate-rich sandy soils on which Cabernet

Left
Château Lascombes in Margaux is an architectural gem but in wine terms it is still searching for an individual style.

Right
Under young Claire Villars, Château Chasse-Spleen is making a name as one of the best Moulis.

ripens well and gives the wine strength, whereas Merlot turns out better on the limestone formations in the other areas. Generally, Cabernet and Merlot are planted in a ratio of 2:1 or 1:1, with a slightly rising trend in the Merlot, which yields soft, fruity wines.

Still smaller than Listrac is Moulis, adjoining in the southeast, where there is a similar spectrum of grape varieties: Cabernet ranges from 50–70 percent, Merlot from 20–50 percent. The vineyards are split up and scattered all over the parish territory, though some of the dominant *crus bourgeois* here—especially Poujeaux and Chasse-Spleen—display a level of quality that can bear comparison with that of many *crus classés* of neighboring parishes.

Vines that grow on sandier soils tend to resemble those of Margaux, those on limestone soils Pauillac. Undoubtedly the greatest prestige name of the southern Haut-Médoc is the Margaux *appellation*, which includes the villages of Arsac, Labarde, Cantenac, Issan, and Soussans. With 3,210 acres (1,300 ha) planted to vine, this is the largest of the Médoc individual areas, and also includes the most *crus classés*. The wines of Margaux may be 60–75 percent Cabernet Sauvignon, but they are considered to have more finesse and a stronger bouquet than the other *appellations*, and to be unsurpassed in elegance, almost like burgundies from Bordeaux, as they are often apostrophized. This particular quality resides in a combination of the particularly sheltered climate of the zone and the extremely barren gravel soils on top of limestone or marls. The characteristic climate is brought about by the long islands in the Gironde opposite the district, which keep off the cold north winds that occasionally blow up from the estuary.

Even the incomparable prestige of the *appellation* could not save it from a profound crisis that struck in the 1970s. The general tendency in the European wine industry to go for quantity instead of quality, in combination with the great scandal of the adulterated Médoc wines and the preceding overheating of market prices, led to a collapse in the market. After some very modest vintages, the wines of the area have now regained their position.

Select Producers in Listrac, Moulis, and Margaux

Listrac

Château Clarke***–****
Listrac-Médoc
173 acres (70 ha); 350,000 bottles • Wines: Listrac Cru Bougeois, Le Merle Blanc
Baron Edmond de Rothschild has built up this estate from scratch since 1973. Wine was first produced in the newly constructed cellar in 1978. Today the vines have reached an age that ensures better quality, and Clarke has risen to become one of the best Listrac producers.

Château Fourcas-Hosten***–****
Listrac
116 acres (47 ha); 320,000 bottles • Wines: Listrac Cru Bougeois, Les Cèdres d'Hosten
The best of the four Fourcas châteaux, belonging to Peter Sichel, Bertrand de Rivoyre and Patrice Pagès. In good years, the wine carries clear aromas of berries and vanilla, but can also turn out very cedary and rather austere.

Château Mayne Lalande***–****
Listrac
49.5 acres (20 ha); 100,000 bottles • Wines: Listrac Cru Bougeois, Château Malbec Lartigue, Château Myon de l'Enclos, La Grande Réserve du Château Mayne Lalande
Bernard Lartigue has built up this *domaine* from scratch since 1991. In the marvelous modern *barrique-chai* fine cedary wines are produced with a lot of fruit.

Margaux

Château Brane-Cantenac****
Margaux
210 acres (85 ha); 140,000 bottles • Wines: Margaux Deuxième Cru Classé
Rising to ever higher standards since 1996.

Château Dauzac***–****
Margaux
111 acres (45 ha); 280,000 bottles • Wines: Margaux Cinquième Cru Classé, La Bastide Dauzac, Haut-Médoc Château Labarde
Another remolded Margaux given luster and harmony by its high Merlot content. Dauzac belongs to the M.A.I.F. insurance group, but is run by the Lurton family from Entre-deux-Mers.

Château Kirwan****
Margaux
86.5 acres (35 ha); 170,000 bottles • Wines: Margaux Troisième Cru Classé, Les Charmes de Kirwan
Under the guidance of enologist Michel Rolland, this Margaux *cru* has undergone a renaissance.

Château Margaux*****
Margaux
245 acres (99 ha); 390,000 bottles • Wines: Margaux Premier Cru Classé, Margaux Pavillon Rouge, Pavillon Blanc
The only *premier cru* of the *appellation*. Since the 1980s, the fate of the house has been in the hands of Paul Pontallier, one of the best enologists in France. The wines have since re-discovered their unique elegance and character.

Château Palmer****–*****
Margaux
126 acres (51 ha); 240,000 bottles • Wines: Margaux Troisième Cru Classé, Alter Ego
Palmer has been esteemed for decades because of its consistent quality and velvetiness. Since 1998 it has offered serious competition to the *premier cru* on its northern borders.

Château Rauzan-Ségla****
Margaux
124 acres (50 ha); 200,000 bottles • Wines: Margaux Deuxième Cru Classé, Ségla
The Rauzan estate, well-known since the 17th century, is now in the hands of the Wertheimer family, who own Chanel. It displays its highly elegant style in a masterly fashion.

Château Siran***–****
Margaux
99 acres (40 ha); 160,000 bottles • Wines: Margaux Cru Bougeois
A bourgeois that can hold its own among so many *crus classés* of its *appellation*. Siran is unusually firmly structured for Margaux, which is due both to the relatively high Petit Verdot content and the *terroir*.

Moulis

Château Chasse-Spleen****
Moulis-en-Médoc
210 acres (85 ha); 600,000 bottles • Wines: Moulis Cru Bougeois, Haut-Médoc L'Ermitage de Chasse-Spleen, Bordeaux Blanc
The better known of the two top Moulis *crus* is 75 percent Cabernet Sauvignon, and in good years manifests an extract density without equal in the *appellation*.

Château Poujeaux***–****
Moulis-en-Médoc
124 acres (50 ha); 240,000 bottles • Wines: Moulis Cru Bougeois, Château La Salle de Poujeaux
The *grand vin* of Poujeaux consists only half of Cabernet. The wine is harmonious and more accessible, but no longer has the density and depth of earlier years.

GRAVELLY GRAVES

The oldest vineyards of the Bordeaux area were planted in the direct vicinity of the trading center of Burdigala—the region that now belongs viticulturally to the Graves region. Geographically the famous alluvial gravels of the left banks of the Garonne and Gironde are also Graves (gravels), but for wine purposes only the vineyards adjacent to the city and up the Garonne carry the name as a designation of origin. The Graves district, which stretches for about 30 miles (50 km) from Bordeaux in a southerly direction, is planted to vines over about 12,400 acres (5,000 ha), and is therefore one of the smaller zones of the Bordelais area, which overall covers a good 247,000 acres (100,000 ha). Two thirds of the Graves area is planted to red varieties, one third to white, and the region is the only one which can boast of outstanding reds and superb whites as well as overwhelming sweet wines. Geographically, the district is divided up much more simply than Médoc, north of the city. Here there is only one large *appellation* of Graves (around 7,410 acres/3,000 ha), which incorporates the small *appellation* Cérons and—in the extreme north—the still very young district of Pessac-Léognan. In the south, Graves encompasses the sweet wine districts of Sauternes and Barsac (4,940 acres /2,000 ha).

Whereas the Graves *appellation* is now reserved for dry whites, the Graves Supérieur label is for dessert wines that do not come from the Sauternes-Barsac or Cérons *appellations*, while Pessac-Léognan provides excellent whites and reds alike. The reason for this is not so much the pebbly, gravelly soils, which are comparable to those of the Médoc, but the more prominent landscape relief compared with its northern neighbor, which is responsible for a series of differing microclimates. The best vineyards in the region are scattered in the higher wooded areas as small or even extensive clearings, or surrounded by the relentlessly expanding sprawl of Bordeaux. At the end of the 19th century, Graves still covered about 247,000 acres (100,000 ha), but urbanization has reduced this to little more than 12,400 (5,000 ha). The red wines are made from the Cabernet Sauvignon, Cabernet Franc and Merlot grape varieties that predominate in the Médoc as well, and bear a strong resemblance to Médoc wines. But the real stars of this part of the Bordelais region are Sémillon and Sauvignon Blanc, which make the dry whites, the dessert wines of Cérons and the sumptuous sweet Sauternes and Barsacs. A strong

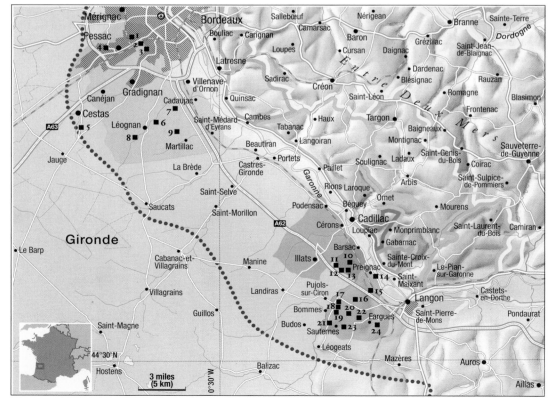

SELECT PRODUCERS IN THE GRAVES REGION

CHÂTEAU D'ARDENNES***–****
ILLATS
153 acres (62 ha); 350,000 bottles • Wines: Graves Blanc, Graves Rouge
François Dubrey produces white and red Graves that are among the most elegant in the region and are also excellent value for money.

CHÂTEAU DE CHANTEGRIVE**–****
PODENSAC
217 acres (88 ha); 560,000 bottles • Wines: Graves Blanc, Graves Rouge, Graves Blanc Caroline, Cérons
Famous for many years for its white wines, and in particular for its Cuvée Caroline, fermented in the barrel, this estate's reds have now made considerable progress and display good concentration and ripe fruit.

CHÂTEAU RESPIDE MÉDEVILLE***–****
TOULENNE
30 acres (12 ha); 70,000 bottles • Wines: Graves Blanc, Graves Rouge
The region around Langon is better known for its Sauternes, but Respide Médeville proves that good reds can be grown here too. Cabernet Sauvignon and Merlot are used in a 60:40 ratio. In the estate's whites, a relatively high proportion of Muscadelle is introduced.

CLOS FLORIDÈNE****
PUJOL-SUR-CIRON
47 acres (19 ha); 100,000 bottles • Wines: Graves
Denis Dubourdieu is professor of enology at the University of Bordeaux and runs not only the Château Reynon in the Premières Côtes but also this Graves estate, whose modern whites and reds with their consistent quality are on a par with many a Pessac-Léognan.

VIEUX CHÂTEAU GAUBERT***
PORTETS
34.5 acres (14 ha); 120,000 bottles • Wines: Graves Blanc, Graves Rouge
Good whites, mainly made of Sémillon and fermented in the barrel, are the ace products of the Haverlan family's estate.

VILLA BEL AIR***
SAINT-MORILLON
114 acres (46 ha); 280,000 bottles • Wines: Graves Blanc, Graves Rouge
Jean-Michel Cazes of Château Lynch-Bages founded the estate in 1990, and has since then convinced with his round, fruity reds, which consist about half and half of Cabernet and Merlot.

proportion of Sauvignon Blanc is often found in the more emphatically fruity whites. When young or picked early, the variety shows its customary grassy, vegetal aromas, and only acquires its more complex, riper fruity overtones when fully ripe or over-ripe.

Some of the classified growths contain up to 50 percent Sémillon. This is considered one of the world's great grape varieties not only because of its tendency to botrytization (which makes it pre-eminent for producing the great sweet wines of the Sauternes area), but also because of its legendary aging ability. The wine styles of the individual white wine *appellations* and the châteaux themselves are distinct not only in the way they combine the varieties, but also in the use of different aging techniques. The use of new barrels is not unchallenged because individual growths can become coarse, thereby losing their finesse. On the other hand, the better *barrique* whites are certainly of higher quality than the superficial fruity representatives of the variety from steel tanks, whose youthful charm is often quickly dissipated.

Going from Bordeaux in a southerly direction, the proportion of Sémillon in the vineyards increases, as does the residue sugar content of the white wines. Far removed from the sweet power packs of Sauternes but still clearly mellow or even sweet are the wines of Cérons, a small *appellation* in the south of the Grave region. Though red wines are indeed also produced in the villages of Podensac, Illats, and Cérons, the whites are more important, the medium-dry output being bottled as Bordeaux Supérieur, the sweet wines as Cérons.

Left
Classiness is in the detail—spittoon at Château La-Mission Haut-Brion.

Right
Château Haut-Brion is the oldest wine estate of Bordeaux to have made an individual name for itself.

A Rising Star: Pessac-Léognan

A cathedral of wine—the winery of the Domaine de Chevalier.

this legendary birthplace of wine in the Bordelais region. The numerical decline was of course more than offset by the qualitative improvement in the *appellation*, which has two Bordelais standard bearers in Haut-Brion and Pape Clément and whose other *crus*, classified in 1959, are of rare consistency and high quality.

Red-White Alliance

Pessac-Léognan is also the only top wine-growing area in the Bordeaux that produces outstanding whites as well as reds. The quickly established prestige and consequent rising revenues have ensured that the retreat of the planted area has been stopped and in individual cases even reversed. The fast-improving image results from the inclusion of all wines in the new A.C. that were first ennobled as Graves Crus Classés only in 1959. This is incidentally also why the classified growths of Pessac-Léognan continue to be labeled as *crus* of Graves, i.e. they now effectively carry a double A.C.

Only in 1987 did Pessac-Léognan become the most important *appellation* of the Graves region, occupying the northern third of it closest to the city of Bordeaux. Basically, this independence was established much too late. The number of wine-growing estates, particularly in the areas closest to the city, has fallen drastically since the mid-19th century. In Mérignac, the number dropped from 22 to only one, in Pessac from 12 to four, in Talence from 19 to three, and viticulture threatened to vanish altogether from

The classification of the area applies of course equally to red and white wines. The châteaux that dance at both weddings include Bouscaut, Carbonnieux, Domaine de Chevalier, Malartic-Lagravière, Olivier, and La Tour Martillac. For Couhins, Couhins-Lurton, and Laville Haut-Brion only the whites, for Fieuzal, Haut-Bailly, Haut-Brion, La Mission Haut-Brion, Pape

The oldest châteaux in the Bordelais region

When Bertrand de Goth, youngest son of a rich noble family, was appointed Archbishop of Bordeaux in 1299, his elder brother presented him with a wine estate in Pessac, now within the city borders. Only six years later he was elected Pope, upon which he named the estate Pape Clément, thus establishing the name of the oldest extant wine estate in the region. Although its existence was threatened more than once in the course of its history (notably by the French Revolution and 20th-century urbanization), wine has been produced uninterruptedly at Pape Clément ever since. With less than 74 acres (30 ha) planted to vines, 90 percent of them red varieties—60 percent Cabernet Sauvignon, 40 percent Merlot—Pape Clément is certainly no giant, and until recently certain other *crus* had a better reputation for quality. Nonetheless, in recent years the quality has stabilized and in the 1990s reached a level that is surpassed by few Graves reds.

The wines of the second historic estate, Château Haut-Brion, a few miles closer to the city, have always been at this level. Since its early days in the 17th century, Haut-Brion has been among the small group of elite Bordelais *crus*, and has never disappointed. It was the only Graves *premier cru classé* château in the Médoc classification in the 1855 listing and again in the 1973 revision. The peculiar situation of the vineyards, surrounded by outlying districts of the city of Bordeaux, has a positive effect climatically. In order to be able to maintain constant top quality, in recent years the winery of the estate has been updated with the very latest technology.

Haut-Brion's neighbor La Mission Haut-Brion also benefits from the special climatic situation and soils of Haut-Brion, where a second wine (La Tour Haut-Brion) and a white wine (Laville Haut-Brion) are also made. As the estate has belonged to the

Château La Mission Haut Brion in Pessac-Léognan is the sister of Haut Brion opposite it.

owners of Haut-Brion for nearly 20 years, the wines are now produced by the same team with the same perfection.

Clément, Smith-Haut Lafite, and La Tour Haut-Brion only the reds were classified, while the non-classified wines of these châteaux are labeled Graves sec. About 3,210 acres (1,300 ha) of the communities of Cadaujac, Canéjan, Gradignan, Léognan, Martillac, Mérignac, Pessac, Saint-Médard-d'Eyrans, Talence, and Villeneuve-D'Ornon are planted three-quarters to red and only a quarter to white varieties of grape, though Cabernet Sauvignon scarcely exceeds 60 percent among the reds. In some cases, it is only marginally present in the make-up of the wines. With Les Carmes de Haut-Brion for example, it only accounts for 10 percent of the mix, with Cabernet Franc making 40 percent and Merlot up to half the grape total.

SELECT PRODUCERS IN PESSAC-LÉOGNAN

CHÂTEAU CARBONNIEUX***–****
LÉOGNAN
222 acres (90 ha); 540,000 bottles • Wines: Pessac-Léognan Cru Classé Blanc, Le Sartre Rouge; La Tour Léognan
In terms of area, one of the largest estates in Graves, with both its reds and whites classified. Although the whites with their strong Sauvignon content must be considered the better-known Carbonnieux wines, the reds also attain the same standard.

CHÂTEAU DE FRANCE***–****
LÉOGNAN
84 acres (34 ha); 190,000 bottles • Wines: Pessac-Léognan Blanc, Rouge
Château de France is a splendidly situated *domaine*, whose commercial buildings reflect a piece of Bordeaux history. Under the young Arnaud Thomassin, white and red wines have gained in clarity and character.

CHÂTEAU HAUT-BAILLY****
LÉOGNAN
69 acres (28 ha); 120,000 bottles • Wines: Pessac-Léognan Cru Classé
Consistent qualities at a very high level are the trademark of Haut-Bailly, whose exclusive red traditionally belongs among the best Léognans and is 65 percent Cabernet Sauvignon.

CHÂTEAU HAUT-BRION*****
PESSAC
114 acres (46 ha); 270,000 bottles • Wines: Pessac-Léognan Rouge Premier Cru Classé, Pessac-Léognan Blanc, Bahans Haut-Brion, Les Plantiers du Haut-Brion
One of the best wine-growing estates of the whole Bordeaux region, whose whites and reds are equally convincing (see page 252).

CHÂTEAU LA LOUVIÈRE***–****
LÉOGNAN
119 acres (48 ha); 250,000 bottles • Wines: Pessac-Léognan Blanc, Rouge, Pessac-Léognan L de Louvière Blanc, Rouge, Bordeaux Rosé L de Louvière, Pessac-Léognan Le Louvetier Blanc, Rouge
This holding, part of André Lurton's empire, produces equally good whites and reds that are excellent value for money.

CHÂTEAU MALARTIC-LAGRAVIÈRE****
LÉOGNAN
104 acres (42 ha); 150,000 bottles • Wines: Pessac-Léognan Cru Classé
Pierre de Malartic bought the estate known as Lagravière in 1803. Since the 1998 change of

ownership, this estate has woken up out of its long sleep and its wines, both white and red, display a notable finesse and polish.

CHÂTEAU LA MISSION HAUT-BRION***–*****
PESSAC
52 acres (21 ha); 100,000 bottles • Wines: Pessac-Léognan Cru Classé, La Chapelle de la Mission
An eternal rival of Haut-Brion, La Mission—separated from its more famous neighbor only by a road—is now under the same ownership and has achieved almost the same quality.

CHÂTEAU OLIVIER***
LÉOGNAN
111 acres (45 ha); 230,000 bottles • Wines: Pessac-Léognan Cru Classé Blanc, Rouge
A most fascinating castle and house set in a lovely park. The Olivier wines—both white and red are classified—are less rounded and have less depth than the other *crus classés*, but age well and develop in harmonious fashion.

CHÂTEAU PAPE CLÉMENT****–*****
PESSAC
80 acres (32.5 ha); 160,000 bottles • Wines: Pessac-Léognan Cru Classé
The oldest wine-growing estate of Bordeaux brought forth a very convincing series of red wines in the second half of the 1990s. The whites, in which Sémillon and Sauvignon are about equal, also reach very high levels.

CHÂTEAU SMITH HAUT-LAFITTE****
LA BRÈDE
136 acres (55 ha); 200,000 bottles • Wines: Pessac-Léognan Cru Classé
Château Smith Haut-Lafite is no longer satisfied just with turning out excellent whites and reds. In recent times, a luxury hotel complex has grown up alongside the architecturally notable château, where treatments based on wine and grape products are offered.

DOMAINE DE CHEVALIER****
LÉOGNAN
84 acres (34 ha); 140,000 bottles • Wines: Pessac-Léognan Cru Classé Blanc, Rouge; L'Esprit de Chevalier Blanc, Rouge
The former Chibaley was already an established leading light in Léognan in the 18th century. Under Olivier Bernard, not only the famous whites, but now also the red wines are once again among the best in this *appellation*.

The Sweet Desserts of Château d'Yquem and its Neighbors

pigments in the skin—can in the case of whites produce golden, honeyed wines that have almost unlimited aging ability and seem made for eternity. The Sémillon grape in particular finds the pebbly soil with a clayey, chalky subsoil the ideal *terroir* to attain the necessary over-ripeness without which the botrytis fungus cannot develop.

The first lovers of the Sauternes area crus were the Dutch shippers on the Quai des Chartrons in Bordeaux, who launched these wines on an unparalleled career. The crises of the late 19th and first half of the 20th centuries brought a decline of the sweet *crus*, of course, which was stopped only by the growth of a new generation of wine-lovers, combined with a series of great vintages in the 1980s.

Incomparable Effort

Even with the best climatic conditions, the producers of great sweet wines must work in the vineyards with a rigor unnecessary for any other kind of wine. The major requirement is a strict limitation of yields—at best, only one or two glasses of wine can be pressed from each vine—to provide the necessary ripeness and concentration. The weather in the harvesting period must also help, otherwise all the effort would be wasted. At Château d'Yquem, 280 feet (86 m) above sea level and the highest part of the *appellation*, Comte Alexandre de Lur Saluces has presided since 1968, showing how legendary qualities are to be attained. The château employs

Probably like no other wine-growing area in the world—an exception in the last two decades is the Seewinkel in Austria's Burgenland—the hilly landscape north of the small town of Langon on the Garonne has concentrated on producing sweet white wines. Unlike, for example, the Rhein and Moselle, these are not marginal quantities that put a dot on the "i" of production but are the main and often the only product the châteaux in the region have to offer.

In the 18th and 19th centuries, the sweet wines were the real stars of the Bordeaux region, and this was probably why, unlike all the other *appellations*, they were classified at the same time as the Médoc *crus*. Top of the list is a *premier cru supérieur*, Château d'Yquem, which thus occupies a unique position compared with all other *premiers crus*. Behind it, nine other Sauternes were selected for the *premiers crus* grading and seven *deuxièmes crus*. In addition, neighboring Barsac registered two *premiers* and seven *deuxièmes crus*.

The basis for the rare specialization of the area is the interplay of early morning mists and warm afternoon sunshine, which at the confluence of the cold Cirons with the warmer Garonne, offers ideal climatic conditions for the development of *Botrytis cinerea*, a sporal fungus. This pierces the skin of the berries, which leads to the water evaporating and consequently to enormous concentrations of sugar, acids and extracts. A situation to be feared in the case of red grapes—the fungus destroys the

The vineyards of Sauternes are close to the villages of Barsac and Sauternes.

Opposite
A Sauternes grower who sticks to tradition.

Without the early morning mist there would be no noble rot wines at the Château d'Yquem.

put overnight in refrigerated chambers, where they freeze depending on their sugar concentration. When pressed, only the juice of the ripe unfrozen berries is released—a tiny quantity of thick, uncommonly extract-rich must. Of course, wines of this sort are not really of the same sweet quality as the real thing. They resemble more closely the EISWEIN product of Canada or California. What they chiefly lack are all the typical taste-forming trace elements that only botrytization can give—for example the exotic aroma overtones or extreme glycerine content—which surface fully only after long aging. Such wines using the most modern technology can be very pleasant to drink when young, with their strong emphasis on fruit, but they virtually never attain the greatness of mature, naturally produced *crus*.

50 people all year in the 250 or so acres (100 ha) of vineyard, for a yield of less than 20 gallons per acre. No pesticides are used here, and manuring is done at most every three or four years with horse manure. Instead, plowing is carried out, the plants are hugely cut back in winter, and in summer the leaves are removed from around the grapes, to permit maximum sunlight to reach the grapes. At harvesting, up to 120 seasonal workers are employed, who over three or more weeks effect up to ten or eleven gleanings—in years when botrytization develops quickly and evenly it can be fewer—to pick only botrytized berries. The must is pressed in three stages, fermented in new oak barrels and left to age in them for up to three years, with racking and transferring to another barrel every three months. In bad years there is no Yquem, as last happened in 1992. In good years, the nectar produced is incredibly intense, with a bouquet of honey, nuts, sultanas, apricots, and candied oranges, together with enormous strength, fullness, sweetness, and spice on the palate.

Not all wine estates in Sauternes—and still fewer in the other sweet wine *appellations*—can afford or want to incur such expense, or risk not producing any wine at all. For this reason, many businesses have been content in botrytis-less years to harvest over-ripe but non-botrytized grapes. The wines from them—although established at the same high price levels as the botrytized *crus*—achieved a quality that sometimes rated no higher than high-grade *sélections* and at an international level scarcely reached the standard of German or Austrian Auslese wines. For this reason, in the last decade the technique of CRYOEXTRACTION has been increasingly used, borrowed from the New World. The grapes are

These wooden blocks are used to close the barrels.

Opposite, above
Botrytized grapes for Sauternes.

The grapes are picked in several stages, with only the botrytized grapes being selected. The rest are given further time to become over-ripe.

Select Producers in Sauternes

Château Clos Haut-Peyraguey****
Bommes
42 acres (17 ha); 37,000 bottles • Wines: Sauternes Premier Cru Classé, Sauternes Château Haut-Bommes
The vines of Jacques Pauly grow in the immediate vicinity of Yquem. His wines of the 1990s display remarkable concentration, but take a long time to unfold their charms.

Château De Fargues****–*****
Fargues-de-Langon
37 acres (15 ha); 12,000 bottles • Wines: Sauternes
The wines that Alexandre de Lur-Saluces produces on his small private estate are scarcely below those of Yquem in quality, and the yields are hardly any higher.

Château Gilette****–*****
Preignac
11 acres (4.5 ha); 7,000 bottles • Wines: Sauternes
This small estate produces sumptuous wines with marked, fruity and exotic bouquets that are of consistent quality year after year.

Château Guiraud***–****
Sauternes
247 acres (100 ha); 100,000 bottles • Wines: Sauternes Premier Cru Classé, Bordeaux Blanc Sec
With approximately 270 acres (100 ha), Guiraud is one of the very large estates of the Sauternes region. Despite excellent growth in good years, the quality of the wine is subject to a degree of fluctuation.

Château Lafaurie-Peyraguey***–*****
Bommes
99 acres (40 ha); 75,000 bottles • Wines: Sauternes Premier Cru Classé
The château below Yquem dates to the 17th century. Virtually all the somewhat scattered vineyard areas are planted to Sémillon.

Château Raymond-Lafon****–*****
Sauternes
44.5 acres (18 ha); 20,000 bottles • Wine: Sauternes
This unclassified estate in the Yquem neighborhood was taken over by Pierre and Francine Meslier in 1972. Since then, it has gained a place alongside the *crus classés* purely through the outstanding quality of its wines. Today, it is managed by the next generation but in the same spirit.

Château Rieussec****–*****
Fargues-de-Langon
185 acres (75 ha); 90,000 bottles • Wines: Sauternes Premier Cru Classé, Sauternes Clos Labère, Bordeaux Blanc R. de Rieussec
Rieussec is one of the best-known names of Sauternes, which is undoubtedly due to the successful marketing of the dry R. de Rieussec whites. The estate belongs to the empire of the Baron de Rothschild (Lafite) *domaines.*

Château Sigalas Rabaud****–*****
Bommes
34.5 acres (14 ha); 30,000 bottles • Wines: Sauternes Premier Cru Classé
Conditions at the highly-esteemed Sigalas Rabaud are virtually as ideal for the development of botrytis as in Yquem. The 17th-century estate now belongs to the Cordier wine firm and is considered one of the best in the area.

Château Suduiraut****
Preignac
217 acres (88 ha); 130,000 bottles • Wines: Sauternes Premier Cru Classé
The wines of Suduiraut stand out more for finesse than for body and strength, which is in part due to the subtle touch of acidity. The bouquet often displays overtones of exotic fruits and figs.

Château La Tour Blanche****
Bommes
104 acres (42 ha); 60,000 bottles • Wines: Sauternes Premier Grand Cru Classé, Sauternes Les Charmilles de Tour Blanche, Bordeaux Blanc Sec Isis, Bordeaux Blanc Osiris, Bordeaux Rouge Cru du Cinquet
The wines of La Tour Blanche have joined the top ranks of the region only since the end of the 1980s.

Château d'Yquem*****
Yquem
255 acres (103 ha); 95,000 bottles • Wines: Sauternes Premier Cru Supérieur Classé, Ygrec
Château Yquem belonged to the Lur-Saluces family from 1785, but the family is now only a minority shareholder. However, Comte Alexandre continues to guarantee the legendary quality of the wines by his personal management.

Sweet, Sweeter ...

Although Sauternes is a symbol for the prestige of all the sweet wines of the Bordelais region in general and of Graves in particular, it is not the only *appellation* under which semi-sweet or sweet wines are produced. Barsac, for example, is a region adjacent to Sauternes in the north, whose yields can be bottled under its own A.C. or that of its better known neighbor. Château Coutet is one example of such a wine. This rule only applies in one direction, and it probably wouldn't make much sense the other way around. Additional areas that generate sweet wines include Cérons on the left bank of the Garonne, and Loupiac, Cadillac and Sainte-Croix-du-Monde on the right.

Barsac, which under English rule had been the leading village in the area and was its principal port (Sauternes was also shipped from here) produced the best-known wines of the southern Graves district at the time. Nowadays its name is overshadowed by that of its neighbor, even though the A.C. specifications are virtually identical and ten Barsac châteaux were included in the 1855 classification of Sauternes, including the Climens and Coutet *premiers crus*. The *crus classés* today still account for 30 percent of production by volume, and Barsac's wines are considered by many observers just as good, even if they are occasionally somewhat lighter than the best Sauternes.

North of Barsac is the district of Cérons, where two different sweet wine types are made:

Château d'Yquem has occupied a special position for over 150 years because of the quality of its wine.

If the sun smiles on the grapes in late autumn, a great vintage is imminent.

on the one hand a kind of medium sweet *sélections*, which are mostly marketed as Graves Supérieurs by the trade; on the other sweet and dessert wines marketed as Cérons. The latter *appellation* is scarcely known even to avowed wine specialists, so it is not surprising that only 20 percent of the wines of the area carry the label, and Cérons as a sweet-wine *appellation* is becoming increasingly sidelined by Sauternes and Barsac. Dry whites and red wines are also grown here and labeled Graves, while the small quantities of dry whites from Sauternes and Barsac are sold under these labels themselves.

Right of the Garonne

A series of villages along the right bank of the Garonne at the same height as Sauternes and Barsac have also specialized in sweet wines. To some extent, they benefit from similar climatic conditions as those on the opposite bank, but the landscape is quite distinct from that in Sauternes and surroundings. The relief is livelier, and more recent alluvial soils alternate with limestone plateaus of maritime origin, on whose slopes the vineyards can be pitched very steeply. The best-known of the *appellations* here is probably Loupiac, on whose 988 acres (400 ha) the vines are planted mainly on south-facing sites with good conditions for over-ripeness and botrytization. The high Sémillon content in the vineyards, which can reach 70–80 percent, would seem natural terrain for good sweet wines, yet the style of the wine tends to resemble fruity *sélections*, and is quite distinct in concentration and structure from Barsac or Sauternes. Cadillac, an *appellation* of a series of villages around the town of that name (founded by the

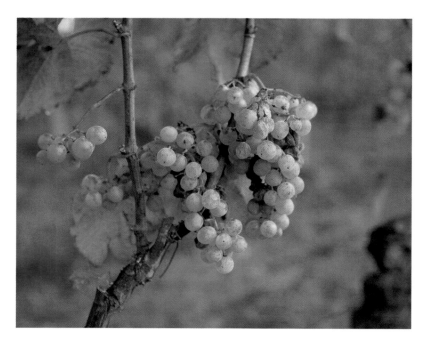

English in the 13th century) produces mostly light, at best aromatic and decidedly fruity wines, though they are rarely really expressive. As part of the Premières Côtes de Bordeaux—a designation of origin that is only used for dry *crus*, the name Cadillac being reserved exceptionally for the sweet wines—the area would basically not have merited any *appellation* at all, but in 1973 the legislation was of a different view. In terms of potential, the best sweet wines of the right bank of the Garonne comes from the 1,480-acre (600-ha) *appellation* of Sainte-Croix-du-Mont, which lies directly opposite Sauternes and Barsac and the Cirons tributary.

Though the sometimes very steep slopes of the vineyards are clearly geographically different from those in Sauternes, the wines reflect a markedly higher incidence of botrytization than is the case in Loupiac or Cadillac. In alcohol content and sweetness, they are on a par with their famous counterparts, even if they are relatively deficient in structure and aging ability. Here too, dry whites and reds of the district are generally bottled as Bordeaux or Bordeaux Supérieur.

SELECT PRODUCERS IN BARSAC, LOUPIAC, AND SAINT-CROIX-DU-MONT

CHÂTEAU CAILLOU***–****
BARSAC
44.5 acres (18 ha); 30,000 bottles • Wines: Barsac Cru Classé
Though a neighbor of the great Climens, Caillou used to be different in the style of its wines, which were much less sumptuous; they are now much more concentrated.

CHÂTEAU CLIMENS*****
BARSAC
71 acres (29 ha); 40,000 bottles • Wines: Barsac Premier Cru Classé, Cyprès de Climens
Climens is the Yquem of Barsac. Sometimes the *premier cru* of less famous *appellation* is ranked higher than that of the illustrious Sauternes château. The wines from the higher sites develop an uncommonly rich exotic and fruity bouquet as they age.

CHÂTEAU CLOSIOT**–****
BARSAC
19.8 acres (8 ha); 18,000 bottles • Wines: Barsac: Château Closiot, Passion de Closiot, Château Camperos
Françoise Sirot and her husband Bernard, a popular Belgian wine journalist, offer a finely graded range of sweet wines, from the rich and refined to the fruity and delicate. They belong to the circle of new Sauternes producers who dare to experiment with different balance of wine.

CHÂTEAU COUTET****–*****
BARSAC
95 acres (38.5 ha); 60,000 bottles. Wine: Barsac Premier Cru Classé
One of the Barsac estates which markets its wines under the more prestigious neighboring *appellation*. Despite fairly high yields compared to the most famous names in the regions, the wines nonetheless have great aromatic finesse and are long-lasting.

CHÂTEAU DOISY DAËNE***–****
BARSAC
37 acres (15 ha); 40,000 bottles • Wines: Sauternes Cru Classé
The wines of this estate were once made entirely from Sémillon, but today 20 percent Sauvignon Blanc is part of

the *cuvée*. They are vinified by Denis Dubourdieu, son of the owner, who prefers a very aromatic style.

CHÂTEAU LOUBENS***–****
SAINTE-CROIX-DU-MONT
57 acres (23 ha); 80,000 bottles • Wines: Sainte-Croix-du-Mont
In good years, the sweet wines of Loubens can easily outdo many a Barsac or even a Sauternes in quality.

CHÂTEAU DE MYRAT***–****
BARSAC
54.5 acres (22 ha); 40,000 bottles • Wines: Barsac Cru Classé
Following a period of difficulty, Myrat was able to recover its previous high quality only in the second half of the 1990s.

CHÂTEAU LA RAME***–****
SAINTE-CROIX DU-MONDE
49.4 acres (20 ha); 100,000 bottles • Wine Sainte-Croix-du-Mont
Yves Armand knows how to give his Réserve du Château sweet wines a sweetness and complexity in good years that can stand any comparison. In lighter years, the Cuvée Tradition enchants wine drinkers with its clear aromatics and balance.

CRU BARREJATS****
PUJOLS-SUR-CIRON
12.3 acres (5 ha); 6,000 bottles • Wine: Sauternes
In ten years, Mireille Daret and Philippe Anurand have shown what can be achieved with passion and skilled work. Their wines are full of refinement and brilliant character. They belong to the number of young wine-makers who are breaking new ground for Sauternes and Barsac.

DOMAINE DU NOBLE****
LOUPIAC
37 acres (15 ha); 55,000 bottles • Wines: Loupiac
Pleasing fruit aromas and great aromatic elegance are the well-known and esteemed trademarks of Loupiac wines, even though they are lacking the sumptuousness and full sweetness of the great Sauternes. In their style, the wines of the Domaine du Noble attain a standard of excellence, and must be considered a bargain at their price.

RIVE DROITE

In the Bordelais region, the *rive droite* (right bank) is the whole area north of the Dordogne, one of the two great rivers that run together as the Gironde not far downriver of Bordeaux.

Just as the Graves district on the left bank of the Garonne is divided into the zones of the Médoc and the Graves proper, so the right bank is also divided into two zones with distinctive characters. One is the Libournais with the Fronsadais on the Garonne in the southeast, the other the area of Bourg and Blaye in the northwest, which lies partly on the Gironde, directly opposite Margaux. Altogether, about a quarter of the total area planted to vine of the whole wine-growing region belongs to this part of the Bordelais area, with the Libournais 32,100 acres (13,000 hectares) getting the lion's share.

Viticulture was certainly carried on here in Roman times. In the 4th century, the poet Ausonius, for whom one of the most famous châteaux in France is named, boasted that his wine was drunk even in the Eternal City. Some centuries later Charlemagne stayed in Fronsac, and in the Middle Ages Pomerol and Saint-Émilion were celebrated stopping places on the pilgrim route to Santiago de Compostela. After the Hundred Years' War between England and France the wine trade developed on this side of the Gironde as well, and the Dordogne served

The vineyards of the Côte de Bourg lie on the right bank of the Gironde.

as a transport route along which the red wines of Bergerac could be carried to England.

The rise of the wine industry in the 17th and 18th centuries was nevertheless much less pronounced than in the Médoc. The classification of 1855 also passed the Libournais by, and it took till the middle of the 20th century for Saint-Émilion to get a classification of its own, while Pomerol, the second famous *appellation* of the region, still has none.

An unequal couple—Merlot and Cabernet Franc

The diversity of the wines of Saint-Émilion and Pomerol and those of the individual châteaux within the two *appellations* is primarily attributable to differences in the *terroirs*—Pétrus for example has very chalky soils—and microclimatic zones. Further variety, however, comes from the different mix of grape varieties—in contrast to the Médoc-Cabernet Sauvignon, which requires the warmest of sites to be able to ripen fully, is only a very small component in the blends.

The difference in the ripening patterns of the varieties means that in the Saint-Émilion district Merlot constitutes 50–70 percent (and in exceptional cases such as at Château Troplong Mondot even 80 percent) of the content, with Cabernet Franc making the other 20–50 percent, whereas in the best Pomerol *crus* the Merlot proportion tends to be even higher. The art of *assemblage*, or blending, begins therefore not in the winery or *cuvier* but in the vineyard, where the grower has to plant the most suitable varieties of vine. While

Old Merlot vine stock.

Cabernet Franc achieves remarkable results on pebbly or sandy soils, Merlot benefits more from loamier soils.

The differing responses to the given *terroir* explains at least in part the considerable differences in the ratios of grape varieties within individual *appellations*. In Saint-Émilion, for example, there are châteaux such

as Ausone and Canon La Gaffellière that grow half and half Cabernet Franc and Merlot, whereas at others (e.g. Cheval Blanc) Cabernet Franc predominates, with up to 60 percent. In the Pomerol area, the Merlot proportion can vary from over 90 percent, such as at Trotanoy and Pétrus, for example (observers even believe that in recent years the latter has consisted entirely of Merlot), to just 65–70 percent, only marginally above Saint-Émilion, as at La Conseillante, L'Evangile, or Nenin.

In order to find the perfect ratio of the two varieties for the given vintage, the grapes from the individual parcels of land are initially vinified and aged separately in the cellar. This allows the vintner the opportunity to react to the moods of nature. Independently of conditions in the vineyard, he can increase the proportion of early ripening Merlot in the finished wine in bad years, or after very hot autumn days step up the proportion of later ripening Cabernet.

THE RED WINE COUNTRY OF LIBOURNE

Whereas both red and white wines are grown in the more northerly Bourgais, the Libournais is almost exclusively red-wine country. In contrast to Médoc and Graves, where Cabernet Sauvignon rules supreme, here it is Cabernet Franc (alias Bouchet) and Merlot that dominate. The way they are put together during blending—along with the influences of differing *terroirs*—distinguishes the individual *appellations*, which are grouped in a semi-circle around Libourne. In the immediate vicinity of the town itself, in its northeastern suburbs, are the vineyards of Pomerol, which cover a total area of under 1,980 acres (800 ha) divided among 180 or so châteaux.

In the southeast of Libourne, but already a certain distance away from the town center, is Saint-Émilion, where wine was grown even in Roman times. With almost 13,600 acres (5,500 ha) between them, the two *appellations*, Saint-Émilion and Saint-Émilion Grand Cru, cover the greatest area and, because of their classification system, are the best known. The next circle of viticulture, often only a few paces from this center of prestige, is constituted by the "satellites" of these *appellations*, Lalande-de-Pomerol (Pomerol) and Montagne, Lussac, Saint-Georges, and Puisseguin (Saint-Émilion), whose *appellations* include the cognomen Saint-

Émilion as well. The eastern and southeastern end of the Libournais is formed by two relatively unknown cultivation districts, Côtes de Castillon and Côtes de Francs. They form the border of the Gironde department toward the Dordogne and comprise a total of somewhat over 7,410 acres (3,000 ha) of vineyards.

Castillon-La-Bataille, the main commune in Côtes de Castillon, has important historical associations for the Bordelais region, if not for the whole of France. At the confluence of the Lidoire and Dordogne, the decisive battle that ended the Hundred Years' War in the French king's favor took place, bringing to an end the English domination of Gascony.

Both *appellations* are the most recent in Bordeaux: Francs was made a separate A.C. in 1967, Castillon only in 1989. Côtes de Francs also produces a small quantity (less than 1 percent of the total production) of white or sweet wines from the usual varieties of Bordeaux, the only area anywhere in the Libournais area to do so.

The real strength of the two areas is of course in their reds, which turn out much more complex and structured than the products sold under the regional Bordeaux label, but at the same time are much better value for money than the other much better-known communes of the Libournais district.

THE CAPITAL OF MERLOT: SAINT-ÉMILION

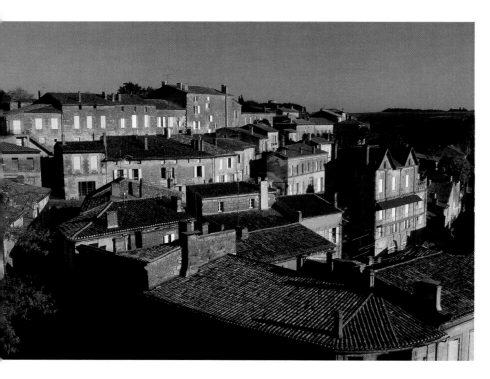

Saint-Émilion with its stately old houses has been designated a cultural monument. It stands on a limestone hill whose cellar galleries are as legendary as the wines that are aged in them.

Every wine pilgrimage in the Bordelais region has one not-to-be-missed destination—the lovely little town of Saint-Émilion, which clings to the slopes of the Dordogne Valley less than 25 miles (40 km) east of Bordeaux. Narrow alleys wind between old stone houses up to the plateau where the imposing parish church towers over all the surrounding vineyards. Although elsewhere the name Saint-Émilion is synonymous with the white Ugni Blanc grape variety, the town on the Dordogne is—like almost all the Libournais—a purely red wine district, and moreover one of the best in the region.

Though the circumference of the area is scarcely 30 miles, virtually the entire 13,600-acre (5,500 ha) wine-growing area is completely covered with rows of vines, making this one of the most intensive monocultures of the entire Bordelais region. There are around 1,000 wine-making businesses making a living from it, of which over 400 are only mini-estates just growing grapes. Four or five sub-areas are usually distinguished, though some experts identify up to 17 *terroirs*, each of which has its own soil formation and individual wine types. The most important *terroir* of the *appellation* is certainly the "plateau" with its limestone formations, on top of which are flatter layers of argillocalcite or sandy clay. The second area is the *Côtes*, the slopes off this plateau. Their soils

developed by erosion from the first area, and differ less in their composition than in the angle and direction of the slope. The third major zone is defined as the Graves (pebbly and gravelly soils) in the northwest, on the border with Pomerol, while the fourth is the Sables, the sandy plateaus west and east of the town. The last area is that of the alluvial gravels of the Dordogne plain directly below the town.

HISTORIC LOCALITIES WITH RECENT PRESTIGE

Wine has been produced in this part of the Bordelais since the 3rd century, and thus has perhaps the most longstanding tradition in the whole wine-growing area. A start was made by Roman legionaries, who cleared the Saint-Émilion plateau and neighboring Pomerol. Not far from the present town the poet Ausonius cultivated his own grapes and made the first documented record of viticulture in the area.

In the 8th century, a Breton hermit called Emilion settled in a cave near the old villa, and the town took its name from him. His spiritual aura attracted numerous believers, who in the centuries that followed extended the grotto into a monolithic rock church, which is impressive even today for its dimensions and atmosphere. The limestone from the countless caves that arose at that time and served as wine cellars with their ideal climate were used by the residents of the village to build their houses, whose pale yellowy white tones lend the place a great deal of its fascination today.

At the end of the 12th century, King John of England, son of Henry II and brother of Richard the Lionheart, gave the town a charter, which meant it could elect its own council, the *jurade*, which still exists. Even though this no longer functions as a town council but more as a kind of wine fraternity, it is more than just another piece of folklore. It acted and still acts as an important supervisory body for the wine industry in Saint-Émilion, and in earlier days branded barrels that in its judgment contained high-quality wine with a *marque du vinetier*. Wines that did not carry this seal of quality had to be destroyed.

The later history of the town was notable more for its wars than its wines. During the Hundred Years' War and the French Revolution it was repeatedly the object of military conflict, perhaps one reason why Saint-Émilion took a long time to catch up with the prestige of the Médoc and Graves.

COMPLEX CLASSIFICATION

Although a wine syndicate was established back in 1884 and the district was declared an *appellation d'origine* in 1936, it took until the 1950s before the best *crus* were classified here. In 1951, the *jurade* introduced a new quality control of wines which in 1954—almost 100 years later than in the Médoc—led to a separate rating system. Its classification would be revised every ten years, unlike in its long-established neighbor. The new system provided for five grades overall, for which two separate *appellations* were set up: Saint-Émilion and Saint-Émilion Grand Cru. Astonishingly, the latter more prestigious label produces somewhat over 3 million gallons (130,000 hl), i.e. a good third more wine than the basic *appellation*. The *grands crus* themselves were subdivided into four classes: plain *grand crus*, *grands crus classés* and finally the small group of *premiers grands crus classés*, which in turn were subdivided into A and B. Whereas only two châteaux were admitted to this top A group

of *premiers grands crus* (Ausone and Cheval-Blanc), the B group includes 11 names: L'Angélus, Beau-Séjour-Bécot, Beauséjour, Belair, Canon, Figeac, Clos Fourtet, La Gaffelière, Magdelaine, Pavie, and Trottevieille.

Their wines are distinctive not only because of the differing soils on which the vines grow but also because of the greatly differing proportions of the three main grape varieties used in the blending, though the precise ratios are not always explicable directly in terms of geographical situation. Thus the top estates both on the plateau and on the Côtes have examples of balanced Merlot-Cabernet proportions, and also of wines where the Merlot is clearly more prominent. On the boundary with Pomerol, where the Merlot content is in general much higher than in Saint-Émilion, paradoxically the Cabernet proportion rises, such as Cheval-Blanc, for example, where Cabernet Franc makes 60 percent. In turn, Cabernet Sauvignon is unusually high both on the *côte* near Pavie and on the Pomerol boundary at Figeac.

Château Canon La Gaffelière, an estate of almost 50 acres (20 ha) at the foot of Saint-Émilion, has come along amazingly under Stephan von Neipperg, and now produces one of the best wines of the famous *appellation* year after year.

THE SOUTHWEST:
IN THE SHADOW OF MIGHTY BORDEAUX

To define southwest France precisely in wine-growing terms is a matter that requires instinctive feeling. Geographically, after all, Bordeaux also belongs to the Southwest, but there they do not want to be too closely associated with the "poor neighbor," and insist on their status as an independent wine region. The winegrowers of Bergerac or Cahors do just the same, being unwilling to have their *appellations* identified with the Southwest. But such local sensibilities can be overlooked, because geography provides a ready orientation.

HISTORIC TRADING CENTER

In viticultural terms, the *Sud-Ouest* is a wine region like Loire, Bordeaux, or Rhone. Historically there is much more to it: it comprises the whole territory upriver from Bordeaux to the edge of the Pyrenees and the distant Massif Central. Earlier, the whole region whose wines had to be transported on the Garonne or Dordogne to the sea, to be shipped to ports in England or Holland, was known as the *Haut-Pays*, an expression that now refers only to the northern hinterland of Agen and Toulouse around Gaillac and Cahors.

Winemaking started much earlier in the Haut-Pays than along the Gironde, but suffered terrible setbacks, first when the port of La Rochelle was closed to ships from northern

Opposite
The Dordogne region with its rivers, villages, and vineyards is one of the most romantic landscapes of France.

Below
Bergerac could never hold its own against Bordeaux as a trading center, but its wine association, based in the historic town center, is providing fresh impulses.

Europe, and subsequently as the Bordelais region began to develop its own wines, boosted by numerous tax and excise privileges from the English crown.

Bordeaux had functioned as the main trading center for the wines of the region ever since Roman times. Unfortunately, in the course of time the harbor proved to be more of an obstacle for the hinterland than a gateway to the world. Time and again the burghers of the city managed to ship their own wines in their entirety before the other regions had a look in. By the time its turn finally arrived in the spring, many an Haut-Pays wine had already turned to vinegar.

UP AND DOWN IN HISTORY

Nonetheless, the winegrowers of Bergerac or Cahors, Gascony, and Gaillac managed again and again to find a market for their products. In the Middle Ages, the monasteries had done much to promote wine growing in the area. In the 17th century, the Dutch began to take an interest in the *crus*. What they chiefly wanted was thin brandywines or intense sweet wines. Bergerac decided to go for it, thus creating the basis for Monbazillac, which developed a great reputation in the 18th century.

Though the trade restrictions that Bordeaux set up like a fortified wall around itself have long gone, the region around the Gironde established such supremacy in the markets of the world that all other wine-growing areas of the hinterland were bound to get a raw deal. In the 1940s, a handful of pioneers sought to plant out new areas and construct a modest image, such as for example the Vignerons de Buzet. But only in the last decade or two has the region—especially individual growers in the areas nearer Bordeaux—begun not just to catch up but also to produce some outstanding *crus* that have caught the attention of wine lovers everywhere. For the latter, the southwest of France has, meantime, become a treasure trove of good-quality wines of high standard.

like the best Côtes de Bergerac, are aged in the barrel and require a degree of maturing in the bottle before their pronounced tannins become soft and the bouquet becomes complex and elegant.

Sweet Wines with Fruit and Elegance

Unlike the eastern part of the Bergeracois, where red wines dominate the scene, the three *appellations* of Montravel apply only to wines from white grapes. Under the plain Montravel designation, which covers the southern half of this district, fruity, fresh wines are made principally from Sauvignon grapes. On the other hand, Côtes de Montravel, the northern half, produces mellow wines in which Sémillon plays an important part. Haut-Montravel, the smallest and most easterly of Montravel's subdivisions—where the chalky soil helps the Sémillon to higher concentrations, but the wines always appear remarkably balanced because of the ever present acidity—gets the third independent *appellation*.

The sweet wines, which were already famous in the heyday of the Dutch, deserve mention as a specialty of the region. While the small Rosette district to the northwest of the town of Bergerac is almost totally forgotten, Monbazillac and Saussignac enjoy a certain celebrity. After a long crisis, Monbazillac has for some time been at pains to re-establish its former renown. Sémillon is the lead grape in this, and the vineyards profit from the special climatic conditions at the confluence of two rivers, the Gardonette and the Dordogne. However, botrytization is less common here than in the Sauternes district, and the wines are consequently somewhat lighter but perhaps more elegant.

The Bordure Aquitaine

The western parts of the Bordure Aquitaine are even closer to the Bordelais region than are the Bergeracois. To be more precise, the Côtes du Marmande are simply a continuation of Graves in the south and Entre-deux-Mers in the north. Its 4,450 or so acres (1,800 ha) are given over to producing full-bodied, balanced red wines and rosés, with the palette of grape varieties including not only the usual Bordeaux crop but also Fer, Gamay, Syrah, Malbec, and the native Abouriou. Only a small area is planted to white-wine varieties corresponding to those of Graves.

However, Buzet, an *appellation* established in 1973, lies somewhat further up the left bank of the Garonne, and in the south spills over into the production area of Armagnac brandy. Its loamy, partly gravelly soils produce mostly red wines. These are made mainly from the Bordelais varieties, with Merlot playing a predominant role. Great efforts have been made in recent years by the Vignerons du Buzet cooperative, which vinifies a wide range of different *cuvées* and ages them in barrels.

The last zone of cultivation in this area is squeezed between the Côtes du Marmandais in the south and Bergerac in the north. Like the Marmandais, it borders the Gironde in the west, and here too Bordelais varieties are grown. In the past, Sémillon used to dominate, from which mainly mellow wines were made. Nowadays production has largely gone over to producing white wines from the more aromatic Sauvignon. The red wines from the two Cabernets, Merlot and some Malbec—here called Cot—are often aged separately per variety, and they range from the light, uncomplicated bistro wines to the stronger, tannin-rich crus aged in the barrel.

In the Shadow of the Pyrenees

acreage had shrunk to 124 (50 ha), even though Madiran had been recognized as an *appellation* only two years previously. However, the low point prompted rethinking. New *domaines* were established, whose wines revealed good qualities. Even so, Madiran was on the verge of losing its soul. The state viticultural office I.N.A.O. set a limit of only 40–60 percent on the prescribed proportion of the native, tannin-rich Tannat grape variety and recommended the addition of the more popular Cabernets or Fer Servadou to the wines.

This was the last straw for the winegrowers. Young Alain Brumont, a grower's son who had taken over the rundown Château Montus, spearheaded the revolution, stocking the excellent gravelly soils of the estate with the now unfavored Tannat. Adopting greatly limited yields, three weeks of mash fermentation, long aging in new barrels and frequent racking of the wines in the cellar, he succeeded in taming the Tannat. When he first aged the varieties separately in 1985, a new star appeared in the wine firmament. The *prestige-cuvée* at Montus beat even the best-known Bordeaux in blind tastings, and opened the market to Madiran wines.

New Methods for Aging

Since then, numerous growers have followed his example. However, not everyone was satisfied with the traditional methods of aging difficult varieties. Among those seeking a new approach was Patrick Ducourneau, inventor of MICRO-OXYGENATION. In this, the wines are given a carefully judged dose of oxygen even before malolactic acid conversion, using a

The countryside between the Garonne and the Pyrenees is probably better known for Armagnac, or for its culinary specialties than for its wines, but the latter do have something to offer. A range of *appellations* stretch from Agen in the northeast to Pau in the southwest that are among the best in the Southwest.

The first among equals is the Madiran cultivation area. Vines here date back to Roman times. From the 12th century, when Gascony belonged to the English crown, it quickly prospered, and the wines were shipped via the Adour and Bayonne to northern Europe.

In the 19th century, the area was still planted to vines on 3,460 acres (1,400 ha). By 1950, the

The vineyards of the Domaine Brana near Saint-Jean-Pied-de-Ports—one of the most spectacular sites in the Irouléguy *appellation*.

Charles Hours at Clos Uroulat, and Henri Ramonteu—two musketeers of Jurançon.

ceramic probe in the tank. This rounds off the tannins more quickly and makes the wine drinkable at an earlier stage. Critics see it as a manipulation of the wine that diminishes its aging potential. However, this has had no effect on the success of the method, which is used today in thousands of wineries in countries all over the world.

The dynamism that had seized the Madiran area was bound to awaken the sleeping beauty of the area—the Pacherenc du Vic-Bilh. This is made from a range of grape varieties that include Manseng, Courbu, Sauvignon, and Sémillon as well as the native Arrufiac. The dry whites are unusually aromatic, but the grapes for the best products—golden yellow, dense sweet whites which need not stand in awe even of Jurançons and Sauternes—are harvested between October and the New Year.

A neighbor of Madiran is the red or white Côtes de Saint-Mont, made of regional varieties of grape. It is not only the spicy, often more lightly structured reds, but above all the highly aromatic whites that display interesting qualities. Almost the entire output is marketed by a single high-quality cooperative. Much less well known is a wine that grows not far from here, the Tursan, which also exists in white and red versions.

In the hilly region south of Mont-de-Marsan, the hardy Baroque variety has been cultivated ever since the phylloxera disaster, a white-wine variety that produces rustic, dry, strongly alcoholic wines. With Manseng and Sauvignon, these are acquiring much more freshness and complexity than before, and enjoy even greater popularity.

BÉARNAIS: NOT JUST A SAUCE

Apart from the world-famous *béarnaise* sauce, the hills between Gascony and the Pyrenean massif also have excellent wines to offer. Béarn itself has lent its name to an *appellation* on whose 395 acres (160 ha) of vines—90 percent of them lie on the secluded slopes of Bellocq parish—both strong rosés and red wines are made from Tannat and marketed under the Béarn label, like the lighter Cabernet Franc, which is bottled under the double label of Béarn-Bellocq. However, the only really important wine in Béarn is, of course, Jurançon.

In the undulating hills of the Béarnais area, vines are planted at heights of up to 1,000–1,300 feet (300–400 m) exclusively on south-facing slopes. Even though it can be cold and rainy here in spring, the area enjoys long, sunny autumns. This is when a warmer

southerly wind blows over the Pyrenees, which allows growers to wait to the end of November, sometimes even into December, before harvesting. Only at this point does the showy Petit Manseng variety display its true grandeur. The small, airily dangling grapes get darker, their skins begin to wrinkle and the berries dry out. Under the influence of hot days and cool night, the next stage is the *passerillage*, a kind of exaggerated over-ripeness.

The must of these grapes makes great sweet wines, which have precisely the right amount of fine, fresh acidity to give them spirit and balance. Of course, this quality is obtained only at the price of very low yields—yields that in bad times would not give growers a living. For this reason, they prefer to plant the plumper sibling of the Manseng, the Gros Manseng, and to a lesser extent Courbu as well. However, since neither of these reaches full maturity in lesser years, the idea arose of also making a dry Jurançon, which in 1975 was allowed a separate *appellation*, Jurançon *sec*.

The last French wine-growing area in the direction of the mountains and Spain is the other side of Pau, close to the peaks of the Basque country. This is the home of Irouléguy, planted to vines on a little over 494 acres (200 ha) on the slopes of the Tize and Arradoy valleys, where elegant reds, scented rosés, and very interesting whites are made.

Alain Brumont's massive new tower house at Château Bouscassé has become a symbol for the new Madiran. Thanks to a group of committed growers and winemakers, this tannin-rich red wine once again enjoys a high reputation.

The Rhône Valley and the Savoie

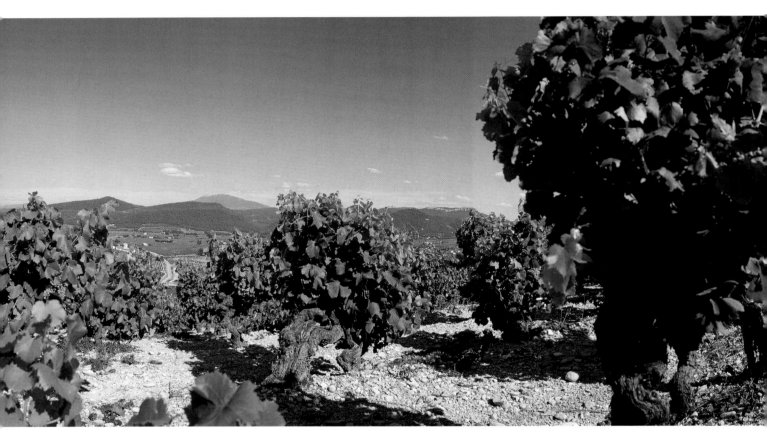

Wine of Two Worlds

Few regions of France can boast of a wine-growing tradition as ancient as that of the Rhône Valley. The Phocaeans, Greek settlers from the city of Phocaea in Asia Minor who founded Marseille in 600 BC, already knew that the region was particularly suitable for viticulture, and they planted vines. Under the rule of the Romans, who are supposed to have learned the art of improvement from the Gauls, viticulture then spread to the central and northern part of the valley, where Gaulish tribes were certainly cultivating vines by 71 AD in the Côtes Rôtie and Hermitage areas.

However, the career of Côte du Rhône wines was checked by the powerful Duchy of Burgundy, which wanted to supply its own wines to the most important markets of London and Paris. They therefore imposed high transit duties on Rhône growths or banned their transport down the only route available at the time, the Saône, as was the position from the 14th to the 16th centuries. Only in the 17th century, when conditions for overland transport improved, and still more in the 19th century when the first railways were built, did Rhône wines become popular in Paris.

Rasteau is known not only for its full reds but also its fortified *vin doux naturel*.

The period after the Second World War brought a dramatic loss of image. The cheap sources of wines in the former French colonies of North Africa, used as blending wines to provide color and alcoholic strength, dried up, prompting many a Bordeaux château—quite illegally, of course—to try Rhône wines instead. Slack sales in the barreled wine market did not exactly motivate growers in the Valley to develop their own qualities. What reached consumers under the Côtes du Rhône label were at best simple but palatable reds in the lowest price brackets. It was only in the 1980s that growers of the region realized the size of the potential available to them thanks to their unique *terroir* and still better grape varieties.

Northern and Southern Climate

Along with the Rhine, Danube, Loire, Douro, Garonne, and Moselle, the Rhône is one of the most important wine rivers in the world. Even in its uppermost reaches in Valais, in Switzerland, there is an extensive wine industry with splendid products. In the main part of the French section, from Lyons, the broad river valley runs almost dead straight southwards for almost 125 miles (200 km), with the foothills of the Alps on one side and the Massif Central on the other side. For almost the entire stretch, the valley is covered with steep vineyards and large fields of vines, which between Vienne in the north and Avignon in the south constitutes one of the most varied vine-growing regions in the country. Around 124,000 acres (50,000 ha) are planted with vines in six departments and 163 localities; the region also boasts the most-produced red-wine *appellation* (Côtes du Rhône rouge) in France. The Rhône in a wider sense also includes a series of fringe areas such as Diois, Côtes du Ventoux, Coteaux du Tricastin, Costières du Gard, and the Muscat de Lunel region, with the two last-named constituting a transition to Languedoc-Roussillon.

The diversity of the wines is due principally to a special geographical constellation. In the northern part of the Rhône Valley, where vines are planted mainly on the terraces of steep granite slopes, a markedly cooler continental climate prevails than in the southern part with its broad alluvial and sandy plains, where it can be very hot in the summer and remains pleasantly mild in winter. These climatic differences are also the reason the northern sites produce single-variety wines, as is the case in most northern wine-growing regions of Europe, while in the south *cuvées* predominate.

The greatest resource of the region is its white and red grape varieties which—although largely ignored, especially in France itself—are among the best in the world and have long produced splendid wines outside their region of origin. The

Syrah (left) is the star variety of Rhône red wines, while Marsanne, Rousanne, and Viognier (right) go into the white specialties.

pride and joy is the blue Syrah, which in recent years has developed into a sort of designer grape. As far back as the Romans, the dark grapes with their small berries were known to have a special quality. In the best conditions for ripening, the dark and at the same time fruity, tannin-rich wines can prove very complex and extremely ageable, and they accord with the image of firm and yet harmonious wines such as are popular with modern consumers. Pure Syrah wines are produced under the Côte Rôtie, Hermitage, Saint-Joseph, or Crozes-Hermitage *appellations* of the northern Rhône, but they are being planted more and more often in the vineyards of the south as well.

Séguret, one of the loveliest villages of France and home of one of the best Rhône red wines.

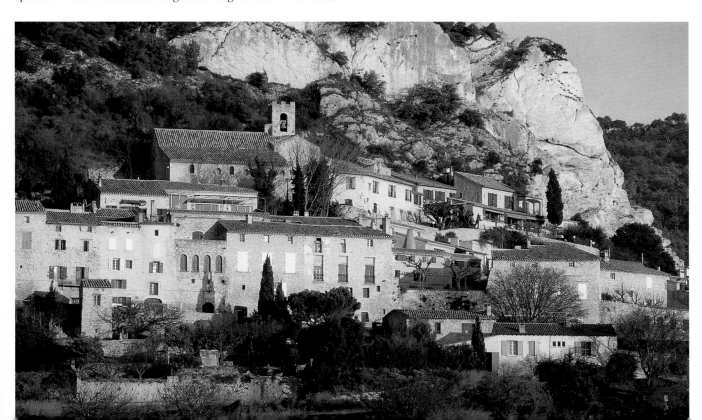

RHÔNE VARIETIES IN THE NEW WORLD

Even before the French became aware of the real qualities of the variety, the Australians made it their showpiece variety under the name Shiraz, gaining their greatest and most important successes with it in international markets in the 1970s and 1980s. The top Australian cult wine of all, Penfolds' Grange, was once made solely from Syrah, and even today contains only small quantities of Cabernet Sauvignon. How conscious the Australians were of the origin of their favorite is evident from the fact that the strong reds made from the Rhône grape were long sold as Hermitage. The success of the Australians inspired not only the Rhône growers. In the last two decades, numerous vineyards in California and South Africa have also been planted with Syrah, while in France itself the grape has conquered many vineyards in the Languedoc.

The second important red-wine variety, the high-yield Grenache, also had to adopt an Australian-Californian accent. Unlike Syrah, this came not from the Rhône itself but from Aragón, spreading along the Mediterranean coast and into the southern reaches of the Rhône. Anyone who hastily dismisses it as a characterless mass-market variety forgets that some of the finest reds from Châteauneuf-du-Pape and the Villages *appellations* are made from Grenache vines where the yield is kept low. How full, dense, and full-bodied these wines can be has recently been demonstrated by the Spanish Priorat area.

Mourvèdre too, a late-ripening variety that needs a lot of warmth, whereupon it produces wines with a lot of tannin, has become more and more popular in the southern Rhône as well as in the hotter areas of the New World.

Together with the above varieties and the soft, fruity Cinsault or the deep red, strongly alcoholic Carignan, it forms the basis of practically all the red wines of the southern Rhône. In the white wines, on the other hand, the most interesting varieties come undoubtedly from the north. Wines sold under the Condrieu A.C. made from 100 percent Viognier grapes stand out particularly, with their dense, intense aromas of honey, apricots, and peaches.

In recent years, the white Marsanne and Roussanne varieties have become popular in the New World and won a real fan club among growers and winemakers, whose members like to call themselves Rhône Rangers. On the

Left
Syrah is allowed to attain its most profound eloquence in the vineyards of the Hermitage.

Right
At Chapoutier in Tain-l'Hermitage, the *pigeage* is carried out in the traditional way.

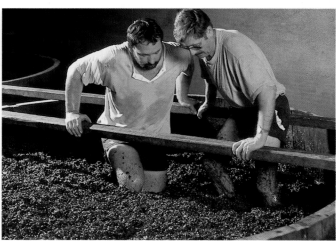

Rhône itself, these two varieties are responsible for the great wines of the Hermitage, but together with Clairette, Grenache Blanc, Counoise, Bourboulenc, and others also form the basis for the white Villages wines and crus on the southern reaches of the river.

VILLAGES, CRUS, AND RÉGIONAUX

One of the strengths of the Rhône wine industry is at the same time one of its weaknesses, namely the ingenious *appellation* system. At the base of this quality pyramid you find the mainly red wines of the regional Côtes du Rhône *appellation*, which is produced principally in the lower reaches of the river. A step above this are wines labeled Côtes du Rhône Villages. Products of a total of 95 communes in the departments of Drôme, Gard, and Vaucluse belong to this group, with 16 communes of the A.C. designation being able to add their own village names to this. At the top are the *crus*, geographically demarcated *appellations* such as Gigondas or Côte Rôtie, whose labels no longer bear any reference to their belonging to the Rhône family.

IN THE REALM OF SYRAH AND VIOGNIER

Founded as a Roman garrison town in 121, and with a now picturesquely ruined Roman amphitheater that still offers views over the Rhône Valley, Vienne is the northernmost point of the Côtes du Rhône *appellation*. In the mostly rather narrow valley, the vines clamber up steep granite slopes. This is an area with a largely continental climate and warm summers, in which the sunlight is exploited to the full by terraced vineyards but the heat is tempered by a permanent wind. Winters are unusually cold for the latitude. The northern part of the Rhône, in which mainly single-variety wines are grown, constitutes the southern boundary of the viticultural regions of France where chaptalization is carried out. Heat and coolness together give the wines their rich aromatic character and elegant structure.

The production of this part of the overall *appellation* is bottled almost exclusively under the name of the local *appellations* of the more prestigious *crus*, of which the area has eight. (The south has only five.) Labels of the Côtes-du Rhône regional *appellation* are practically non-existent here. The best-known *crus* also include the most northerly quality wines of the Rhône, apart from a small table-wine output in the direct vicinity of the town of Vienne. This is the Côte Rôtie, home of wonderful Syrah

Marcel Guigal can well smile—his cellar in Ampuis is full of liquid treasure.

wines, in which up to 20 percent of the white Viognier is officially permitted but rarely effected by growers.

Although wine growing here dates back to Roman times and perhaps even a few centuries earlier, the name of the *appellation*, which means "scorched slope," only goes back to the 19th century. Until the 1950s the wine had virtually no reputation, and the area planted out even in past centuries rarely exceeded the current 494 acres (200 ha). A specialty of the growing area is cultivation on pyramidal stilts, which appears to be the only sensible arrangement on the narrow terraces.

THE CRUS OF THE NORTH

Directly south of the Côte Rôtie is the small white wine district of Condrieu, in which Viognier is the star. The name of the administrative and commercial town with its distinctive Rhône bridge means *coin du rieux*, or "stream place." Chalky soils on rock, with schist and mica in the upper strata provide a basis for subtle, multi-layered Viognier wines. The constant ventilation of the steep slopes is of great benefit, because the variety is prone to rot. Although some Condrieu wines from good vintages are wholly suited to aging, it is best to drink them young, when aroma and fruit in the nose are still accompanied by sumptuous juiciness on the palate. The largest *appellation* in the north territorially is Saint-Joseph, with almost 2,220 acres (900 ha) planted to vines, scattered over a riverine strip almost 30 miles (50 km) long. It is also the first in which both reds and whites are made, with Marsanne and Roussanne taking the place of Viognier. Dense, fruity red wines—the whites are less interesting—are found more and more often, and at very reasonable prices. In the area around the town of Tain l'Hermitage the vineyards move to the left bank. This is where the 331 acres (134 ha) of the Hermitage hills are, the famous *appellation* which has lent its name to many an overseas Syrah wine, and the less famous Crozes-Hermitage, with more than 2,970 acres (1,200 ha) planted to vines producing both 100 percent Syrah reds and white wines blended from Marsanne and Rousanne. While the granite-based, south-facing slopes of the Hermitage generate firm, dense, and ageable growths, the Crozes wines grown on flatter gravels or loess sites are much lighter.

The last of the northern Rhône districts are the Cornas and Saint-Péray *appellations*, both directly opposite Valence on the right bank of

In his own steep vineyards at Les Ruchets, enologist Jean-Luc Colombo has created a paradigm of a modern northern Rhône wine, which is particularly convincing even in lesser years.

the Rhône. Saint-Péray used to be known exclusively for simple sparkling wines, but in recent years has forged a reputation for good still whites, although the total acreage is only a little over 148 (60 ha), hardly enough to establish a real market presence.

Cornas is not much larger. It also used to produce whites, but now makes only reds from Syrah. The wines are somewhat lighter than the Côte Rôtie, but can have a lot of character.

Select Producers from the Northern Rhône

Thierry Allemand****
Cornas
9 acres (3.5 ha); 12,000 bottles • Wine: Cornas: →Chaillot
Allemand's Cornas wines have strong character, excellent structure and firm tannins. Only after a few years' maturing in the bottle do they display their aromatic variety.

Bernard Burgaud****
Ampuis
10 acres (4 ha); 15,000 bottles • Wine: Côte Rôtie
A deep color and concentrated, clear Syrah fruit notes are the trademark of Bernard Burgaud's wines.

M. Chapoutier***–*****
Tain L'Hermitage
395 acres (160 ha); 3,000,000 bottles • Wines include: Condrieu, →Hermitage Blanc De Lorée, Côte Rôtie de la Mordorée, Hermitage: Le Pavillon, →Monier de la Sizeranne, Crozes-Hermitage, Châteauneuf-du-Pape La Bernardine
Ever-busy Michel Chapoutier makes some of the best Hermitage and Côte Rôtie wines. He also produces wines from the southern Rhône *appellations* and even Australia.

Jean-Louis Chave***–****
Mauves
37 acres (15 ha); 48,000 bottles • Wines: Hermitage →Blanc, Rouge; E. Catelain, →Vin de Paille
This old master of Hermitage is one of the largest vineyard owners of this prestigious *cru*. The white Hermitage combines an elegant honey, vanilla and flower bouquet with a rich, fresh structure in the mouth, and the red is in no way inferior.

Yann Chave***–****
Mercurol
41 acres (16.5 ha); 80,000 bottles • Wines: Crozes-Hermitage Blanc: Cuvée, →Le Rouvre; Rouge: Tradition, →Tête de Cuvée, Hermitage

In 2001, Yann Chave took over the estate which his parents Bernard and Nicole had founded in 1970. The main wine produced is the red Crozes, and the Tête de Cuvée is excellent. The quality of the wines has been rising recently. A new cellar was ready for use in 2003.

Louis Chèze***–****
Limony
49 acres (20 ha); 80,000 bottles • Wines include: →Condrieu; Saint-Joseph: Blanc, Rouge, →Cuvée des Anges
The reserved Louis Chèze produces delightful Condrieus and better and better Saint-Josephs.

A. Clape****
Cornas
15 acres (6 ha); 25,000 bottles • Wines: →Cornas, Saint-Péray, Côtes du Rhône
Auguste Clape runs his 15-acre (6-ha) estate in Cornas, with the help of his son Pierre Marie. Some of his wine stocks are well over 60 years old.

Jean-Luc Colombo****–*****
Cornas
Acres: not recorded; 300,000 bottles • Wines include: Cornas: Les Ruchets, Saint-Péray, Côtes du Rhône; Hermitage, Saint-Joseph; →Coteaux d'Aix-en-Provence Domaine de la Côte Bleue, Coteaux du Languedoc Domaine de la Salente, →Côtes du Roussillon Domaine Saint-Luc
Colombo is to the Rhône what Rolland is for Bordeaux: the most inspiring of wine experts. At the same time, he is an excellent winemaker based in Cornas and now also in the Gulf of Marseille. His company offers carefully selected *appellations*.

Laurent & Dominique Courbis***–****
Châteaubourg
64 acres (26 ha); 120,000 bottles • Wines include: Cornas: Eygats, →La Sabarotte, →Champelrose, Saint-Joseph

Laurent Courbis is considered the best wine-maker in the community. His Cornas Cuvées display a dense color, a many-layered bouquet and plenty of body and fine tannins.

YVES CUILLERON***–*****
CHAVANAY
76.5 acres (31 ha); 150,000 bottles • Wines include: Condrieu: →Chaillets, Vertige, Ayguets; Saint-Joseph Blanc: Lyceras, Saint-Pierre; rouge: L'Amarybelle, →Les Sérines; Côte Rôtie: Bassenon, →Terres sombres
You may become enthusiastic about the very ripe Viogniers, but the red Saint-Josephs show increasing potential, as do the first-class Côtes Rôties.

DELAS***–*****
SAINT-JEAN DE MUZOLS
30 acres (12 ha); 1,500,000 bottles • Wines include: Condrieu: →Clos Bucher, → Vin de Pays Viognier; Côte Rôtie: →Seigneur de Maugiron; Hermitage: →Marquise de la Tourette; Crozes-Hermitage: →Tour d'Albon; Saint-Joseph
Founded in 1835, Delas rather missed the boat in the 1980s, when it was owned by Champagne Deutz. Since 1993 it has belonged to Roederer, and the general manager Fabrice Rosset has made considerable investments. In Jacques Grange, a former Colombo employee, he has gained an outstanding winery manager. Since 1999, Delas has once again assumed its rightful place alongside Chapoutier and Jaboulet with excellent red wines.

DOMAINE COMBIER***–****
PONT DE L'ISÈRE
34.5 acres (14 ha); 50,000 bottles • Wines: Crozes-Hermitage: Blanc, Rouge, →Clos de Grives
The Clos is a masterpiece of density and harmony, not least because of many years of organic cultivation.

DOMAINE ALAIN GRAILLOT****
PONT DE L'ISÈRE
49 acres (20 ha); 100,000 bottles • Wines: Crozes-Hermitage: Blanc, Rouge, La Guirade
A master of Syrah, which has a unique clear fruit at Graillot.

DOMAINE ROCHEPERTUIS—JEAN LIONNET***
CORNAS
37 acres (15 ha); 35,000 bottles • Wines: St. Péray, Cornas
Lionnet produces superb Cornas—the top selection is Rochepertuis—and a white wine with 50% new wood fermentation.

PIERRE GAILLARD***–****
MALLEVAL
39.5 acres (16 ha); 100,000 bottles • Wines include: Jean Elise, Condrieu: →Côte Rôtie; Rose Pourpre, →Côte Brune et Blonde, Saint-Joseph; Les Pierres, Clos de Cuminaille
For many years, Pierre Gaillard was *chef de culture* in the vineyards of Guigal, and he thoroughly mastered his trade there. He uses cold maceration before fermentation, subsequently fermenting at 90°F (32°C) with frequent punchdown. His rich, sweet Condrieu Jeanne Elise reaches the highest level.

YVES GANGLOFF****
CONDRIEU
7.5 acres (3 ha); 15,000 bottles • Wines: →Côte Rôtie La Barbarine, Condrieu
Yves Gangloff has 5 acres (2 ha) for Côte Rôtie and 2.5 acres (1 ha) for Condrieu—and a rare obsession with quality.

JEAN-MICHEL GÉRIN***–*****
AMPUIS
12 acres (5 ha); 40,000 bottles • Wines include: Condrieu, →Côte Rôtie: Les Grandes Places, →Champin Le Seigneur, Ladone

Grandes Places is the gem of the Gérin family, who have been producing wine in Ampuis for five generations. With La Landone, they have now added another splendid example.

E. GUIGAL***–*****
AMPUIS
160.5 acres (65 ha); 5,500,000 bottles • Wines include: Condrieu, Hermitage: Blanc, Rouge, Côte Rôtie: Château d'Ampuis, → La Landonne, Côte Brune La Turque, →Côte Blonde La Mouline, →Saint-Joseph Vignes de l'Hospice, Côtes du Rhône, →Gigondas, Tavel, Châteauneuf-du-Pape
The great magician, undisputed best vinifier and *négociant* of the northern Rhône, has recently fitted out his business as one of the most modern in France. In 2001, Guigal took over two other estates with an excellent reputation: that of Jean-Louis Grippat and the Domaine de Vallouit.

PAUL JABOULET AÎNÉ***–*****
TAIN DE L'HERMITAGE
247 acres (100 ha); 200,000 bottles • Wines include: Hermitage: →Blanc Chevalier de Sterimberg, La Chapelle, Crozes-Hermitage, Côtes Rôtie Les Jumelles, Cornas, Saint-Joseph, Châteauneuf-du-Pape, Gigondas, Vacqueyras, Côtes du Rhône, Tavel
The Hermitage La Chapelle of this venerable winery is still one of the greatest and most consistent elite wines of France. In 2001, the winery opened a spectacular cellar for aging in a quarry dating back to Roman times.

JEAN-PAUL & JEAN-LUC JAMET***–****
AMPUIS
17 acres (7 ha); 20,000 bottles • Wine: Côte Rôtie, Côte Rôtie Côte Brune
Jean-Paul and Jean-Luc Jamet cultivate only Syrah on the edge of the high plateau behind Ampuis and make excellent Côte Rôtie from it. The wines are aged for 20 months in small oak barrels.

ANDRÉ PERRET***–****
CHAVANNAY
27 acres (11 ha); 50,000 bottles • Wines: Condrieu, →Clos Chanson Coteau Chéry, Saint-Joseph: Les Grisières
Although the Condrieu is considered Perret's showpiece wine, the Saint-Joseph has remarkable fruit and structure.

GEORGES VERNAY****
CONDRIEU
39 acres (16 ha); 100,000 bottles • Wines include: →Condrieu: Coteau de Vernon, Les Chaillés d'Enfer; Côte Rôtie
One of the Condrieu classics with various *cuvées* of very consistent quality.

FRANÇOIS VILLARD****–*****
SAINT-MICHEL-SUR-RHÔNE
25 acres (10 ha); 45,000 bottles • Wines: →Condrieu: →Grand Vallou, →Deponcius; Côte Rôtie, →Saint-Joseph Le Reflet
In only a few years, this young ex-chef has turned out to be a driving force on the northern Rhône. White and red wines of the highest standard.

LES VINS DE VIENNE****
SEYSSUEL
25 acres (10 ha); 200,000 bottles • Wines include: → Vin de Pays des Collines Rhodanéenes: Sotanum, →Taburnum; Côtes du Rhône and Villages, Condrieu, Côte Rôtie, Hermitage, Cornas, Vacqueyras, Gigondas
The three friends Yves Cuilleron, Pierre Gaillard and François Villard have helped the historic location of Seyssuel near Vienne to achieve a comeback. They have also created a small trading company and, with an unmistakable trained nose, have been maturing and bottling small quantities of excellent wines.

GATEWAY TO THE SOUTH

As you travel southward, it becomes markedly hotter between Valence and Montélimar and the landscape and towns take on a more Mediterranean appearance. The Tricastin area, the gateway to Provence, is firmly in the truffle, fruit, and lavender-growing businesses, and instead of the steep terraces of the north, the grapes are cultivated here in great fields on a landscape that is slightly undulating at most. The larger part of the planted area of this southern half of the Rhône Valley, which accounts for at least 95 percent of the total production, is marketable only under the regional *appellation* Côtes du Rhône. Despite the generally hot, dry climate with optimum ripening conditions for the grapes, the weather also has its latent risks—for example in the

If the Brunel ancestors knew what class their Château La Gardine had attained today…!

form of the often unpredictable, and even violent Mistral wind.

Traditionally 13 different red and white varieties of grape are grown that go into the wines in greater or lesser ratios, with white wine grapes occasionally finding use in red wines. The area is of course mainly planted to red varieties, with Grenache, Mourvèdre, and Syrah making at least 70 percent of the total. The whites must be made at least 80 percent from Grenache Blanc, Clairette, Marsanne, Roussanne, Bourboulenc, and Viognier. Unlike in the Bordeaux area, where blending of different grape varieties takes place only after the completion of fermentation, wines here in the southern Rhône Valley are fermented together whenever the *vendange* (harvest) permits. In the reds of the regional *appellation*, carbonic maceration has been increasingly used in recent years. One of the characteristics of the district is the key position of the viticultural cooperatives, apart from that in the prestige *appellations* such as Châteauneuf-du-Pape, while a *négoce* of the reputation of the great houses in the northern Rhône could not develop here.

THE COMPLETE HIERARCHY

Besides the huge regional *appellation*, the south also has five *crus*, plus more than 14,800 acres (6,000 ha) classified as Côtes du Rhône Villages. Unlike in the north, there are no exclusively white *crus*—only Châteauneuf-du-Pape, Lirac, and Vacqueyras have a smallish white wine production. More significant is the position of the rosés, which are bottled under the designations Gigondas, Lirac, Vacqueyras, and Tavel (the latter exclusively for rosés). Gigondas, at the foot of the climbers' paradise of the Dentelles du Montmirail, is, after Châteauneuf-du-Pape, the best known of the southern *appellations*. Because of the differences in the *terroirs* within the 2,970 acres (1,200 ha) of the parish—the higher, warmer sites are chalky and sandy, the lower ones are loamy and pebbly—the wines turn out very differently. The best growths are deep in color, emphatically fruity, strongly alcoholic, and powerful, without being overfull of tannins.

A similar division occurs in neighboring Vacqueyras, which is almost the same size, where the soils contain both loam and chalk and pebbly gravel. The wines here are somewhat less massive, show more finesse than

---

Sweet wines from the Rhône

A specialty and rarity of the southern Rhône are the two fortified *vins doux naturels* (V.D.N.s) Muscat Beaumes-de-Venise and Rasteau, which are produced only here and in Languedoc-Roussillon. The name (natural sweet wines) is misleading, as the residual sweetness arises not from a natural end of fermentation but as a result of the conversion of sugar into alcohol being artificially terminated. If the two sweet wines of the famous *villages* parishes of Beaumes-de-Venise and Rasteau share a

sweet taste and winery technique, however, they are distinct in one key point: the Muscat de Beaumes-de-Venise is produced from Muscat Blanc à Petits Grains, a variety of grape introduced to southern France by the popes in the 14th century that displays typical Muscat aromas. The Rasteau on the other hand is mainly the product of the classic red wine varieties of the *appellation*, and is more like a very thick red or brown port.

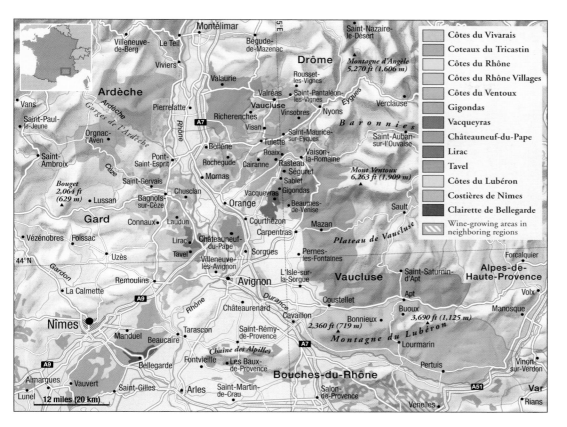

strength and are thus as clearly distinct from the growths of Gigondas as those of nearby Châteauneuf-du-Pape.

The two remaining *crus* lie on the right bank of the Rhône. Here, the hilly limestone formations come much closer to the river, offering the grapes optimum conditions with their good drainage. The historical roots of viticulture here go back at least as far as they do on the eastern bank of the Rhône, but Lirac and Tavel first enjoyed a cautious upturn only after the Second World War. Lirac was one of the first districts of France infected by phylloxera (in 1863), as a château owner had imported seedlings from America and with them the destructive pest. Although under wine legislation they do not belong to the Rhône *appellations* proper, there are a series of peripheral cultivation areas attached to the region. The most northerly of these is Diois, where the Crémant de Die is found—once called Clairette de Die and produced from the Clairette grape—and a sparkling wine produced from Muscat with a single fermentation, an approach described as *méthode ancestrale*. Not far from this are the Coteaux du Tricastin, where the wine industry has developed at breakneck speed in recent years. Here mainly red wines from the usual southern Rhône varieties are grown that are pleasantly fruity and seem soft enough, but rarely show much character. On the southern flank of Mont Ventoux is the cultivation area called Côtes du Ventoux, which has had a separate *appellation* since 1973 and with a total of 51 communes in all is one of the most extensive in the Rhône. The area produces white wines, rosés, and reds, with the ratios of varieties in the blending slightly differing from the neighboring villages on the west flank of Ventoux.

The hierarchy of *appellations* in the Rhône Valley

r = red wine, rs = rosé, w = white wine

A—Côtes du Rhône (r, rs, w)

B—Côtes du Rhône Villages (r, rs, w) without mention of the commune (wines from a total of 95 communes in the departments of Drôme, Gard, and Vaucluse)

C—Côtes du Rhône Villages with the name of the commune added (16 communes in the departments of Drôme, Gard, and Vaucluse. They are: Cusclan (r, rs), Laudun (r, rs, w), and St.-Gervais (r, rs, w), in Gard, Rochegude (r, rs, w), St.-Maurice (r, rs, w), St.-Pantaléon-les-Vignes (r, rs, w), Roussets-les-Vignes (r, rs, w) and Vinsobres (r, rs, w) in Drôme, Beaumes-de-Venise (r, rs, w), Cairanne (r, rs, w), Rasteau (r, rs, w), Roaix (r, rs, w), Sablet (r, rs, w), Séguret (r, rs, w), Valréas (r, rs, w) and Visan (r, rs, w) in Vaucluse.)

D—13 *crus* (geographically localized *appellations*) of the northern and southern Rhône that no longer contain any reference to Côtes du Rhône in the name. They are the Côte Rôtie (r), Condrieu (w), Château Grillet (w), Saint-Joseph (r, w), Crozes Hermitage (r, w), Hermitage (r, w), Cornas (r) and St-Péray (w, sparkling wine) in the north, Châteauneuf-du-Pape (r, w), Gigondas (r, rs), Vacqueyras (r, rs, w), Lirac (r, rs, w), Tavel (rs) in the south.

VILLAGES WITH CHARACTER

Cairanne is among the Rhône villages that has established a position at the top of the *appellation* thanks to the qualities of its *terroir* and skills of its growers.

The greatest development in the Rhône wine industry has been the progress in the *villages appellations* in the southern part of the region, with around 15,300 acres (6,200 ha) planted to vines. Amazing quality was produced mainly in the parishes that were granted the right to use their own names on the label together with the *appellation*, which applies to 16 out of the 95, though they in fact have more than half the total acreage.

Even more than in the case of the *crus*, the *villages* parishes are largely on the left bank of the Rhône, where the hills are quite gentle and rise toward the Alps quite slowly, and a total of 13 of the small cultivation areas are situated. The remaining three *villages appellations* are in the hills and on the high plateau on the right bank of the Rhône.

Whereas the permitted yield is 548 gallons per acre (52 hl/ha) for the regional *appellation* and 476 gallons per acre (45 hl/ha) for the simple *villages* labels, for the *villages* labels with the parish name as well the limit is only 440 gallons (42 hl/ha). The grape variety ratios in the reds must contain at least 50 percent Grenache and at least 20 percent Syrah or Mourvèdre, while with whites a minimum proportion of 80 percent of the principal varieties such as Clairette, Viognier, Bourboulenc, Marsanne, Roussanne, and Grenache Blanc is specified. Unlike in many wine-producing areas in the rest of Europe, the rosés can include up to 20 percent of white grape varieties, and with the exception of Chusclan, white, red and rosé wines can all carry the *villages appellations* in all the *villages* parishes.

The least-known *villages* lie on the right bank of the Rhône in the area of Bagnols-sur-Cèze. They are Laudun, Chusclan, and Saint-Gervais, with Laudun alone comprising almost two-thirds of the 1,560 acres (630 ha) under cultivation. The preponderantly dry, sandy and gravelly soil—only in Saint-Gervais do you find limestone with layers of loess and clay—produce fine, elegant wines that are largely made and sold by cooperatives.

There are, of course, also a number of splendidly functioning estates in the districts selling their own wines, but they often sell their products under the simple *villages appellation* or even the regional Côtes du Rhône label.

THE LEFT BANK

The concentration of the prestige *villages* labels bearing parish name is on the left bank, and the parishes lie in the departments of Drôme and Vaucluse. The most northerly group, which includes Rousset-les-Vignes, Saint-Pantaléon-les-Vignes, Valréas, Vinsobres, Visan, and Saint-Maurice, lies well within the foothills of the Alps and here the landscape provides the best scenery in the whole region.

For their part, the best wines undoubtedly come from Vinsobres, a small parish on the edge of the former papal enclave around Valréas—and also the largest *villages* parish, where notably very fruity reds with low tannin content are made. Its hilly vineyards on clay and limestone-bearing soils turn out dense wines with a fine balance between fruit and tannins. The "three Vs"—Valréas, Vinsobres, and neighboring Visan—are also the best-known *appellations* of the zone, while Saint-Pantaléon and Rousset have a rather low profile. In the central area of the region are the four parishes of Cairanne, Roaix, Rasteau, and Rochegude.

Cairanne and Rochegude have come up with some very good wines in recent years, and have produced perhaps the most consistent *villages* products anywhere. Both are located on the last undulations of the Alpine foothills towards the Rhône Valley before the backdrop of the Dentelles du Montmirail and Mont Ventoux. The best reds are made just along the boundary between the two parishes, whose loamy soils are excellently suited to the production of dense, tannin-rich reds that need not fear competition from much more prestigious *crus* in the area.

In the immediate vicinity of this *cru*, right on the slopes of the Dentelles du Montmirail, are the last three *villages* parishes: Séguret, Sablet, north of Gigondas, and Beaumes-de-Venise, south of Vacqueyras. The hill of Sablet is a particularly remarkable phenomenon, with entirely sandy soils in part. Some of the vineyards look as if the vines had been planted on the beach, and the hill itself is riddled with grottoes buried beneath the compacted masses of sand. The wines here turn out much softer and finer, which the growers to some extent offset by increasing the proportion of Mourvèdre.

Séguret too, the old romantic neighboring village built into the slope and protected as a conservation area, produces very soft wines, though they do not always have the expressiveness and character of the wines of Sablet. The absolute star of the *villages appellations* is Beaumes-de-Venise, though it is better known

Sablet [*sable* = sand] did not acquire its name by accident, because both the hill and the vineyard soils are made of sand.

In Gigondas, the growers are proud of the sturdy character of their *grand cru*.

for its Muscat than the splendid red wines produced here.

In good years, the local cooperative, which is considered the best of the *villages* cooperatives, produces *cuvées* and prestige bottlings of a standard well up to that of the best wines of the neighboring *crus* of Vacqueyras, and they can vie even with good Gigondas.

Select Producers in the Southern Rhône

Cave Coopérative Cairanne**–****
CAIRANNE
2,964 acres (1,200 ha); 3,700,000 bottles • Wines include:
Côtes du Rhône: Les Grandes Vignes; Côtes du Rhône
Villages Cairanne: →*Cuvée Antique, Cuvée des Voconnes,*
→*Temptation; Cairanne Blanc:* →*Grande Réserve,*
→*Cuvée Passion; Vin de Pays de la Principauté d'Orange*
The top *cuvée* of this cooperative is the Antique, and a
very high quality wine it is. Alongside this, the firm sells
a wide range of good to very good wines.

Château d'Aquéria***–****
TAVEL
161 acres (65 ha); 400,000 bottles • Wines: Lirac Blanc,
Rosé, Rouge; l'Héritage, Tavel
Known as the best producer of the strongest Rhône
rosé, the estate also endeavors to shine with its reds.
The Cuvée l'Héritage is excellent.

Château de la Canorgue***
BONNIEUX
74 acres (30 ha); 100,000 bottles • Wines: Côtes du
Lubéron →Blanc, Rosé, →*Rouge and Cuvée Vendange*
de Nathalie
Jean-Pierre Margan is one of the pioneers of organic
wine growing in the South. His wines are unusually
consistent in quality. The reds age superbly.

Château Signac***–****
BAGNOLS-SUR-CÈZE
94 acres (38 ha); 200,000 bottles • Wines include: Côtes
Rhône Villages: →*Come d'Enfer,* →*Terra Amata*
Alain Dugas, owner of La Nerthe in Châteauneuf,
bought the rather rundown estate some years ago and
has rebuilt its reputation. Already the wines are of the
high quality associated with La Nerthe.

Château du Trignon***–****
GIGONDAS
161 acres (65 ha); 250,000 bottles • Wines include:
Côtes du Rhône, →*Cuvée Bois des Dames,* →*Gigondas,*
→*Sablet,* →*Rasteau*
Few other growers in the area can boast of Gigondas,
Sablet and Rasteau of such consistent quality, and the
Côtes du Rhône Cuvée Bois des Dames is also excellent.

Clos du Joncuas—F. Chastan***–****
GIGONDAS
71 acres (29 ha); 125,000 bottles • Wines include:
Gigondas: rosé, →*Clos Joncuas,* →*Vacqueyras La Font*
de Papier, →*Séguret Domaine de la Garancière*
Dany Chastan, who runs this organically cultivated estate
together with her father Fernand, proves with her wines—
regularly among the best of the three *appellations*—that
organic estates can turn out excellent products and that
she is among the best winemakers of the Côtes du Rhône.

Domaine Brusset****
CAIRANNE
215 acres (87 ha); 400,000 bottles • Wines include:
Côtes du Rhône Villages Cairanne: Coteaux des Travers,
→*Vendange Chabrille,* →*Cuvée Hommage; Gigondas: Le*
Grand and →*Le Hauts de Montmirail; Côtes du Ventoux*
The wines of this important estate, especially the
Gigondas, have reached a very high standard.

Domaine de Cabasse***–****
SÉGURET
49.5 acres (20 ha); 80,000 bottles • Wines include: Sablet
Les Deux Anges, Séguret Rosé, Séguret Rouge, Cuvée
Garnacho, Cuvée de la Casa Bassa, Les Deux, Gigondas

Swiss grower Alfred Haeni bought the estate and soon
made it one of the best in the *appellation*. He grafted
Syrah on Cinsault rootstocks by the row, and is still
experimenting both in the vineyard and the winery.

Domaine Didier Charavin**–****
RASTEAU
133 acres (54 ha); 80,000 bottles • Wines include: Côtes
du Rhône Blanc, Rosé, Rouge; Côtes du Rhône Villages
Rasteau: Cuvée Prestige, →*Cuvée de Parpaioune,*
Rasteux Vin Doux Naturel: Doré, Rouge
Originally founded as the Domaine Papillon, the firm
shines today with its dense, firm Rasteau reds, whose
star number is the Cuvée de Parpaioune.

Domaine les Goubert**–****
GIGONDAS
57 acres (23 ha); 90,000 bottles • Wines include:
Gigondas: Cuvée Florence, Sablet, Beaumes-de-
Venise, Séguret
Jean-Pierre Cartier manages 40 different plots in
Gigondas, Séguret, Beaumes and Sablet. His best wine,
the Cuvée Florence, is made from Grenache and Syrah
vines. Half of this wine is aged for a year in new wood
and blended before bottling with the other half from
the tanks.

Domaine Gourt de Mautens****–*****
RASTEAU
35 acres (14 ha); 30,000 bottles • Wines: Côtes du
Rhône Villages Blanc, Rouge
In only a few years Jérome Bressy has joined the elite
of the Rhône valley. His secret is passion, unremitting
discipline and a great talent.

Domaine de l'Oratoire Saint Martin****
CAIRANNE
57 acres (23 ha); 120,000 bottles • Wines include: Côtes
du Rhône Blanc, Rosé, Rouge, Côtes du Rhône Villages
Cairanne Haut-Coustias, →*Cairanne: Réserve des*
Seigneurs, →*Cuvée Prestige, Haut-Coustias*
The Alary family has been growing wine in Cairanne
for 300 years. Frédéric and Françoise Alary offer quality
products of very consistent standards, particularly in the
red *cuvées*.

Domaine de Piaugier***–****
SABLET
64 acres (26 ha); 110,000 bottles • Wines include: Côtes
du Rhône Villages Blanc, Rouge, Sablet Montmartel
Solid, vigorously structured wines that need a few years
to age in the bottle.

Domaine de la Réméjean***–*****
SABRAN
86.5 acres (35 ha); 150,000 bottles • Wines: Côtes du
Rhône: Arbousiers, Chèvrefeuilles; Côtes du Rhône
Villages: Églantiers, Genévriers
Set apart from the well-known *appellations*, Ouahi and
Rémy Klein—he is from Alsace, she is from Morocco—
make outstanding *cuvées* under the regional and generic
villages appellation. The Églantiers is on a par with the
best representatives of the prestigious *crus*.

Domaine Marcel Richaud****
CAIRANNE
99 acres (40 ha); 120,000 bottles • Wines include:
Côtes du Rhône Villages Cairanne: Blanc, Rouge,
→*L'Esbrescade*
Marcel Richaud sets the example for optimum ripeness
and thus produces wines of great roundness and finesse.

DOMAINE DOMINIQUE ROCHER***–****
CAIRANNE
37 acres (15 ha); 75,000 bottles • Wines include: Côtes du Rhône Villages, Cairanne, Monsieur Paul
This still very young estate produces most modern wines of the *appellation*. The Cuvée Monsieur Paul is superb.

DOMAINE SAINTE-ANNE***–****
SAINT-GERVAIS
76.5 acres (31 ha); 125,000 bottles • Wines include: Côtes du Rhône, Côtes du Rhône Villages and Saint-Gervais
This estate was the first to show the heights that Côtes du Rhône Villages from the right bank can reach.

DOMAINE DE LA SOUMADE***–*****
RASTEAU
66.5 acres (27 ha); 170,000 bottles • Wines: Côtes du Rhône Villages Rasteau: Cuvée Confiance, Prestige, → Rasteau Vin Doux Naturel: Rouge, Doré
The Roméros' two top red *cuvées* and the red Vin Doux have long been among the best of the southern Rhône area. The Cuvée Confiance especially is in no way second to the *crus* of the north in terms of elegance.

DOMAINE VIRET***–*****
SAINT-MAURICE-SUR-EYGES
74 acres (30 ha); 110,000 bottles • Wines include: Côtes du Rhône Villages Saint-Maurice: → Maréotis, Colonnades, → Emergence, → La TriLoGie
Philippe Viret and his father André have created a spectacular *domaine* in only a short time. They use biodynamic methods.

MAS DE LIBIAN**–****
SAINT-MARCEL-D'ARDÈCHE
42 acres (17 ha); bottles not recorded • Wines include: Côtes du Rhône Blanc, Rouge; Côtes du Rhône Villages Rouge, → La Calade

On this charming estate on the right bank of the Rhône, the young winemaking couple Hélène Thibon and Alain Macagno produce high quality wines with their own distinctive style.

MONTIRUS**–****
SARRIANS
133 acres (54 ha); 220,000 bottles • Wines include: Vacqueyras Blanc, Rosé, Rouge; Montirius; Clos Montirius; Gigondas
Christine and Eric Saurel have converted the old family estate to biodynamic cultivation and now produce finely fruity, balanced wines of great depth in their own winery.

TARDIEU-LAURENT****–******
LOURMARIN
90,000 bottles • Wines include: Côtes du Rhône, Côtes du Lubéron, Côtes du Rhône Villages Rasteau, Gigondas, Châteauneuf-du-Pape, Condrieu, Hermitage, Côte Rôtie
As wine dealers, Michel Tardieu and Dominique Laurent set the standard. Their selection from the Rhône valley is of the very highest quality.

LES VIGNERONS BEAUMES-DE-VENISE*–****
BEAUMES-DE-VENISE
2,970 acres (1,200 ha); 6,000,000 bottles • Wines include: Muscat de Beaumes-de-Venise: Carte Or, Bois Doré; Vacqueyras, Côtes du Rhône Villages; Beaumes-de-Venise: Terroir du Trias, → Carte Noire; Notre Dame d'Aubune Blanc, Rosé, Rouge; Côtes du Rhône: Cuvée des Tocques; Côtes du Ventoux: Cuvée Spéciale, Cuvée des Tocques
The most celebrated cooperative of the southernmost Rhône stands out particularly for its red Beaumes-de-Venise *cuvées* and of course for its Muscat.

Papal Wines: Châteauneuf-du-Pape

By far the best-known, largest, and highly regarded single *appellation* in the Rhône Valley is Châteauneuf-du-Pape, which has over 7,410 acres (3,000 ha) planted to vines in only five localities (Châteauneuf, Courthézon, Bédarrides, Orange, and Sorgues), where predominantly red wine varieties are grown. In 1157, the Templars settled on the site of the ancient decisive battle (in 121 BC) between the Romans, led by Quintus Fabius Maximus, and the Gaulish tribe of the Allobroges. They named the place Castrum Novum. Pope John XXII, who is believed to have encouraged viticulture, had a castle built on the Templars' former property in 1323. The castle was used mainly as a papal summer residence. The present name is 19th-century. Despite the long history, the reputation of the *appellation* is of recent date, because up to the Second World War the wines were mostly sold in Burgundy.

Châteauneuf is an exception in every respect. Lying on a rocky hill visible from a great distance, the town clings picturesquely to its sandy clay slopes surrounded by a plain densely overlaid with a deposit of reddish pebbles, a relic of the Rhône glacier. There are also sandy and loamy soils, and the fragmentation of vineyard ownership in most *domaines* means that the majority of *cuvées* are blends of wines from a great variety of *terroirs*, which engenders balance and at the same time helps to minimize the risks associated with ripening.

Overall, 13 varieties of grape are permitted in the *appellation*, of which Grenache, Cinsault, Mourvèdre, Syrah, Muscardin, Counoise, Clairette, and Bourboulenc are those mainly used. Many of the top growers consider Grenache as the most complex variety, while Mourvèdre, which is hard when young and inclined to reduction, gives the wines aging ability. In recent years, more Syrah has been planted, but in the hot southerly climate it does not display much of the subtlety and complexity it reveals in the northern Rhône. Much has also changed in recent decades during the winemaking. Whereas the reds used to be left on the mash for two or three months and then aged for five to ten years in the barrel, the equivalent periods now are two weeks and two years respectively. Experiments were also made with carbonic maceration, but this does not make much sense with a wine whose typical features are great strength and density.

Unusual Reds

The most unconventional way of making red wine is probably that found at the famous Domaine Beaucastel, located on a site dominated by giant red pebbles. On the Perrin brothers' estate they follow an old family recipe in which the mash is heated to 176°F (80°C) immediately after leaving the wine press, in order to improve the extraction of tannins. In good vintages, these wines are among the most characterful in the *appellation*, but in lesser years they can seem over-extracted and over-structured. The changing style of Beaucastel wines, however, suggests that the mash is not being heated with quite the same rigor as before. In many firms in Châteauneuf, very traditional methods are still used despite much shorter times together with the mash. Large wooden barrels or even old concrete tanks for fermentation are, with the exception of estates such as Mont Redon, encountered far less often than barrels, except with whites, whose best representatives are fermented in small oak barrels.

Despite the stream of visitors to the former summer residence of the popes, Châteauneuf-du-Pape has retained an air of quiet and tranquillity. Its wine has recently re-established its former reputation.

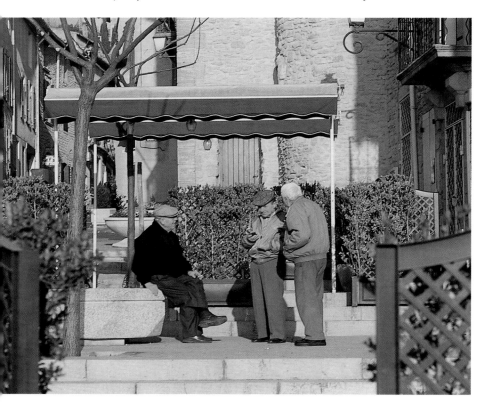

Select Producers of Châteauneuf-Du-Pape

Château de Beaucastel****—*****
Courthézon
247 acres (100 ha); 330,000 bottles • Wines:
→*Châteauneuf-du-Pape Blanc, Rouge; Roussane Vieilles Vignes, Côtes du Rhône Coudoulet de Beaucastel, La Vieille Ferme*
However unusual the vinification of the red Châteauneuf-du-Pape by forced heating of the mash may seem, the quality in good years is incontestable. However, the estate's top wine is the white Châteauneuf. The estate also sells good generic Côtes du Rhône and wines under the Perrin & Fils brand.

Château la Gardine***—****
Châteauneuf-du-Pape
124 acres (50 ha); 220,000 bottles • Wines include: Châteauneuf-du-Pape Blanc, Rouge: Tradition,
→*Cuvée Les Générations*
The Brunel family has turned La Gardine into one of the best examples of the modern, balanced Châteauneuf style with excellent barrel maturing.

Château Mont Redon***—****
Châteauneuf-du-Pape
358 acres (145 ha); 640,000 bottles • Wines:
→*Châteauneuf-du-Pape Blanc, Rouge; Côtes du Rhône: Blanc, Rosé, Rouge, Lirac*
Mont Redon is one of the largest and most consistent wine-growing estates of the *appellation*. The Abeille and Fabre families have in recent years replaced the old concrete tank and wooden barrels of the winery with a modern stainless steel system. The Lirac Château Cantegril has also belonged to the estate for some time.

Château la Nerthe****—*****
Châteauneuf-du-Pape
222 acres (90 ha); 175,000 bottles • Wines: Châteauneuf-du-Pape: Cuvée des Cadettes, →*Blanc Clos de Beauvenir*
La Nerthe was the place where the 13 grape varieties that became the foundation of Châteauneuf-du-Pape were first planted after the phylloxera disaster. The former Parisian tax consultant Alain Dugas took over the state in 1990, brought it right up to date technically, and systematically reduced the Grenache constituent of the vineyard in favor of Syrah and Mourvèdre.

Château Rayas****
Châteauneuf-du-Pape
63 acres (25.5 ha); bottles not recorded • Wines: Châteauneuf-du-Pape Blanc, Rouge, Cuvée Pignan
One of the most fashionable wines of the *appellation* comes from Rayas, whose owner also runs the Château des Tours and Château de Fonsalette in the Villages. Rayas is a high class, finely structured wine that ages superbly.

Clos du Mont-Olivet***—****
Châteauneuf-du-Pape
99 acres (40 ha); 200,000 bottles • Wines include: Châteauneuf-du-Pape: Blanc, Rouge, →*Cuvée du Papet; Côtes du Rhône*
As traditional as this estate are its wines, in which tertiary aromas of brushwood, fungus and leather can quickly be detected. The top wine is Cuvée du Papet.

Domaine de la Janasse****—*****
Courthézon
124 acres (50 ha); 150,000 bottles • Wines: Châteauneuf-du-Pape Blanc, Rouge, Tradition, →*Chaupin,* →*Vieilles Vignes, Côtes du Rhône:* →*Le Chastelet, Les Garrigues*
Since young Christophe Sabon took over the winery side of the estate, the quality of the wine has stabilized at a

spectacularly high level, both for the three Châteauneuf *cuvées* and for the selection of Côtes du Rhône. The white wines are also of the same high standard.

Domaine de Marcoux****
Orange
47 acres (19 ha); 40,000 bottles • Wines: Châteauneuf-du-Pape Blanc, →*Rouge; Côtes du Rhône*
Catherine and Sophie Armenier, two sisters, use biodynamic cultivation in their vineyards and harvest very elegant, deep reds with fine tannins.

Domaine de la Mordorée***—****
Lirac
136 acres (55 ha); 280,000 bottles • Wines include: Châteauneuf-du-Pape, →*Lirac Cuvée de la Reine des Bois, Lirac Blanc, Tavel, Côtes du Rhône Blanc, Rosé, Rouge*
Although the estate is outside the *appellation*, it has been among the best producers of Châteauneuf for some time. In terms of quality, however, the red Lirac *cuvée* is on the same level.

Domaine du Pegaü***—*****
Châteauneuf-du-Pape
52 acres (21 ha); 90,000 bottles • Wines: Châteauneuf-du-Pape: Cuvée Laurence, Da Capo, Cuvée Réservée
Father Paul and daughter Laurence jointly run the estate, which has been marketing its own wine only since 1989. The whites are fermented after a short time in used barrels, the reds in concrete. No clarification or filtration is undertaken. The style is classic, powerful and full of volume.

Domaine Pierre Usseglio****
Châteauneuf-du-Pape
52 acres (21 ha); 60,000 bottles • Wines: Châteauneuf-du-Pape: Blanc, →*Rouge,* →*Cuvée de Mon Aïeul*
In recent years, Jean-Pierre and Thierry Usseglio have given their wines more body, but also more polish. Outstanding quality.

Domaine Vieux Télégraphe****
Bédarrides
173 acres (70 ha); 220,000 bottles • Wines: Châteauneuf-du-Pape Blanc, Rouge; Vieux Mas des Papes
The Brunier bothers' estate stands somewhat apart from Châteauneuf—they also own the Domaine de la Roquette directly in the heart of the locality. The quality of their wines is founded on the top location at La Crau, one of the highest points in the locality. Wine-making is traditional and yields are low.

Domaine de Villeneuve****
Orange
20.7 acres (8.4 ha); 29,000 bottles • Wine: Châteauneuf-du-Pape
Philippe and Marie-Christine du Roy de Blicquey have been running the state since 1993, using biodynamic methods. With admirable reliability, they produce a single wine full of finesse and complexity.

Vielle Julienne***—*****
Orange
76.5 acres (31 ha); bottles not recorded • Wines: Châteauneuf-du-Pape: →*Vieilles Vignes, Blanc, Côtes du Rhône Villages Vieilles Vignes*
That the normal version and the Special Cuvée of the Châteauneuf are of virtually the same high standard and in any case far above most rivals is a rare phenomenon. This estate is hidden behind the façade of a small farmhouse and produces absolutely top class wines without exaggerated attention to technology.

THE WINES OF THE SAVOIE

The Alpine Region of eastern France, which consists of the departments of Savoie and Haut-Savoie, used to be an independent kingdom that stretched a long way into modern Italy. The bilingualism of the neighboring Aosta Vallay goes back to this time. The individuality and seclusion of the area have meant that its wines are only rarely seen outside regional borders. Vines are grown on about 3,950 acres (1,600 ha), two thirds with white varieties and mainly in the Rhône Valley between Lake Geneva and the Lac du Bourget and south thereof as far as Chambéry and the Isère Valley, supplemented by smaller enclaves in the north and northeast. Unlike most French areas of cultivation, which are laid out compactly over large areas, the vineyards of the narrow valleys make a patchwork quilt. Despite this, there is only one larger *appellation*, Vin de Savoie, which covers a whole series of grape-variety wines, and besides this a number of mini-districts such as Crépy or Seyssel, plus a special *appellation* for the Roussette grape and Prickler Mousseux and Pétillant de Savoie.

The most notable feature of the wines is the range of native grape varieties, which probably owe their existence to the special political position of the former kingdom. Apart from the white Jacquère grape, which alone covers 2,470 of the 3,950 acres (1,000 of the 1,600 ha), and is notable mainly for its high yield and neutral character, it is the red Mondeuse and white Roussette that carry the banner for quality, alongside which even the increasingly cultivated Gamay or Chardonnay have a hard time.

NATIVE VARIETIES WITH FLAIR

In particular, the wines from the Mondeuse grapes—dark, juicy, and with a light peppery overtone—come up with astonishing quality. The variety is possibly related or even identical to the Refosco grape of North Italy. Nowadays it is unfortunately only cultivated on about 494 acres (200 ha), Gamay (which is easier to grow) having replaced it in many vineyards. Its white equivalent is Roussette, also called Altesse, a late-ripening variety that is possibly related or identical to the Hungarian Furmint grape. Roussette wines with their pronounced acidity and high aging ability can be among the best white wines of France, and this special position is recognized by the legislation with a separate

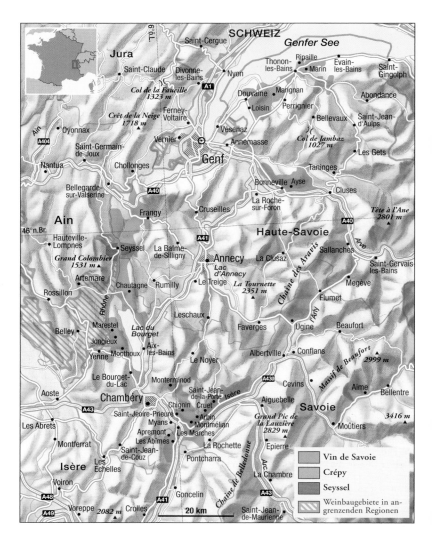

Opposite
Unusual grape varieties flourish in the alpine landscape that give Vin de Savoie quite a distinctive character.

appellation within the overall Vin de Savoie designation. Single-variety Roussette wines from low yields can also be marketed under the village name. If the latter is absent, the wines are made with up to 50 percent Chardonnay.

Chasselas, otherwise more popular in Switzerland and Alemannic areas, dominates not only the vineyards nearest Lake Geneva-where it has its own *appellation* in the Crépy mini-district, but is also the predominant variety in the Seyssel cultivation area north of the Lac du Bourget. In both areas, light, fruity, and sometimes fizzy wines are produced, though the fizzy and sparkling wines are generally sold as Mousseux and Pétillant de Savoie.

The larger part of the regional production reaches the market as Vin de Savoie, with the label also carrying the name of the commune in a number of cases. The red varieties allowed under this *appellation*, which are often single-variety, are Gamay, Mondeuse, Pinot Noir, Cabernet Franc, Cabernet Sauvignon and others, with a proportion of white grapes also being acceptable. Among the permitted white varieties are Aligoté, Roussette, the mass grape Jacquère, Chardonnay, and Mondeuse Blanche.

A similar range of varieties is found in Bugey, adjacent to western Savoie, even though it belongs neither administratively nor geographically to the departments of the former kingdom. The wines likewise show great affinities, apart from the absence of Chasselas. Here Montagnieu, Manicle, Machuraz, Virieu-le-Grand, and Cerdon have *villages* rights, and Cerdon even has a separate *appellation* for Mousseux and Pétillant.

Select Producers

PATRICK CHARLIN***–****
GROSLÉE
12 acres (5 ha); 40,000 bottles. Wines: Bugey: Montagnieu: → Brut and → Altesse, Pinot Noir, Pressurage de Novembre
Patrick Charlin has had great success with his sparkling wine and the Altesse from the vineyards on the slopes of Montagnieu. The Pinot is more unreliable, depending on location.

CHÂTEAU DE LA VIOLETTE**–***
LES MARCHES
20 acres (8 ha); 80,000 bottles • Wines: Abymes, Apremont, Roussette de Savoie, Vin de Savoie Rouge
The fact that the vineyards of Daniel Fustinoni contain two-thirds Jacquère does not necessarily make his drive for quality any easier. Nonetheless, he keeps coming up with good white wines of various *villages*.

DOMAINE DE MANICLE & VIRIEU**–***
MURS
25 acres (10 ha); 65,000 bottles • Wines: Roussette Virieu, Manicle Blanc, → Manicle Rouge, Mondeuse
Christian and Christiane Beaulieu are among the few winemakers of Bugey whose wines can hold their own in a national context. Their red Manicle in particular is worth noting.

DOMAINE DU PRIEURÉ SAINT-CHRISTOPHE***
FRÉTERIVE
16 acres (6.5 ha); Wines: Mondeuse Cuvée Prestige, Roussette de Savoie
As one of the pioneers of the Savoie *appellation*, Michel Grisard has specialized in the two native varieties, the red Mondeuse and white Roussette. His Roussette shows that the variety can stand aging in the barrel. The Mondeuse is not only of unusual density and intensity but also ageable.

LOUIS MAGNIN***–****
ARBIN
15 acres (6 ha); 35,000 bottles • Wines: Roussette de Savoie, → Arbin Mondeuse Vieilles Vignes, → Chignin-Bergeron
Béatrice and Louis Magnin have marketed their own wines since 1978. Their white Chignon-Bergeron from Roussette grapes and the red Arbin from old stocks are both convincing.

ANDRÉ & MICHEL QUÉNARD***–****
CHIGNIN
54 acres (22 ha); 150,000 bottles • Wines: Abymes, Chignin, → Chignin-Bergeron, Chignin-Gamay, → Chignin-Mondeuse
The strength of the Quénards father and son lies in their reds made from Gamay and Mondeuse, but the whites, especially the Chignin-Bergeron Les Terrasses, show consistently good quality.

RAYMOND QUÉNARD***
CHIGNIN
15 acres (6 ha); 50,000 bottles • Wines: Chignin Blanc, Chignin-Bergeron, Chignin Rouge, Chignon Gamay, Chignin Mondeuse
The ace up the sleeve of Raymond Quénard is the almost century-old stocks of his vineyards. Apart from Mondeuse, he has specialized mainly in white wines, which he develops into particularly soft and round wines by systematically converting the acidity.

CHARLES TROSSET***
ARBIN
8.5 acres (3.5 ha); 25,000 bottles • Wines: Arbin Mondeuse
Charles Trosset produces one of the strongest and most expressive Mondeuses of the Vin de Savoie *appellation*.

PROVENCE: THE SEA, THE SUN, AND MORE

Provence has a magic power of attraction. The name alone evokes a yearning for sunshine, azure blue skies, and rocky bays with clear blue water, umbrella pines and the intense scent of wild herbs such as thyme and lavender, leisure and carefree enjoyment. But only connoisseurs will appreciate that Provence is also an El Dorado for wine.

The first vine stocks were brought here in the 6th century BC by Phoenicians from the coast of the Levant and Phocaean Greeks from Asia Minor. After the Romans established their Provincia Romana in 154 BC, meritorious Roman veteran soldiers would be given, by way of a pension, a small estate here that they could develop to grow vines and other produce. In Fréjus, the launching point for Roman colonization, and Marseille, major potteries were established where amphorae were made to ship Provençal wine to the most distant imperial legionaries. In the Middle Ages, it was—like everywhere else—the monasteries that carried on the cultivation.

The first holiday guests—aristocrats from northern Europe—arrived in the 18th century. In the 19th century, the Côte d'Azur was defi-

Provence is one of the lushest fruit- and vegetable-growing areas of France, but also produces top wines.

Opposite
The intense aromas of herbs, flowers, and fruit are often found in the bouquet of the wines.

nitely a fashionable destination in winter for the rich and powerful. The year-round stream of tourists, which had a major effect on Provence in general and its wine industry in particular, began in 1936, when the Front Populaire government introduced paid holidays for everyone. After the Second World War, summer tourism exploded, plastering the whole coast with accommodation buildings of all kinds in order to absorb the hundreds of thousands of sun-seeking visitors. Holiday eating habits also assumed Provençal guise, consisting of *mesclun* (mixed green salad), tomatoes, ratatouille, grilled fish, lamb cutlets, and *aïoli* (garlic mayonnaise). Provence sold its most suitable accompaniment—ice-cooled rosé.

Following the succession of disasters (phylloxera, wars, and economic crises), and like most of their colleagues elsewhere, Provençal growers went over to mass production, and planted mainly Carignan, Cinsault, and Grenache vines for the *gros rouge*. The scratchy red was better suited to the world of the industrial cities of the north than to the summery Mediterranean atmosphere. But, pressed quickly or racked after only a short period on the mash, the lighter,

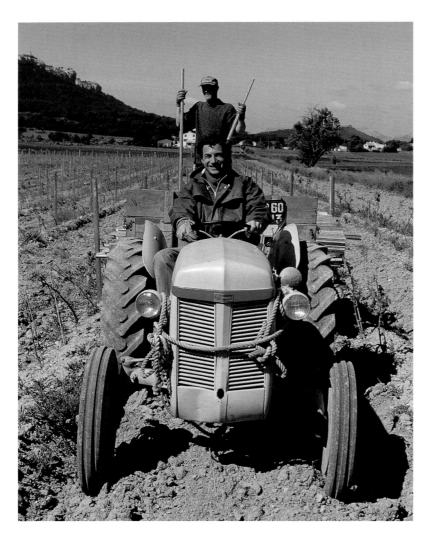

making red wines of much higher quality. White wines are made only in small quantities and are often of only average quality. The region has four small areas of cultivation that have long been famous and in the top rank: Bandol, Cassis, Bellet, and Palette. Their *terroirs* consistently produce convincing and fascinating wines of great expressiveness and quality.

NEWCOMERS THEN AND NOW

Two factors have exerted influence on the Provençal wine industry. The first was a stream of *pieds noirs*, Algerian French who left Algeria after 1962 and settled in Provence and the Midi mainly for climatic reasons. They put enormous effort into rebuilding their lives, not infrequently in the wine business. They often already had practical experience of growing wine in the dry heat of Algeria, and were therefore open to major innovations in matters such as temperature controls.

From around 1980, the wine estates also awoke the interest of other newcomers. Apart from the fascination of the landscape itself, it was the love of wine that they had in common, which had previously manifested itself generally in an enthusiasm for the great Bordeaux and Burgundies. On the basis of their expertise and often with the introduction of great financial resources, numerous *domaines* were completely renovated and restructured, laying the basis for the current explosion in quality. The newcomers hailed not just from other parts of France but also from other countries such as Germany, England, Scotland, Holland, Sweden, Denmark, Switzerland, and the U.S.A., often bringing with them great attention and devotion to natural winemaking that has shown up in the quality and expressiveness of the wines.

tannin-deficient rosés could be pressed from the same grapes and tossed down the throat—well chilled, of course.

Nothing has changed in this even today. Up to four-fifths of the total wine production of Provence is turned into rosé. What better outcome could there be for a grower than to have his product sold off a bare half year after the harvest and drunk before the following harvest? The cash till is quickly replenished, and work in the winery is gratifyingly minimal. Most estates and cooperatives are not reluctant to exploit the opportunity.

Quality, of course, often falls by the wayside in the process. It is no wonder, therefore, that rosé's image is that of a minor wine that need not be taken seriously. However, increasingly numerous excellent rosés are being produced, whether immediately pressed to make elegant pale wines or made by the alternative method into somewhat stronger raspberry-colored wines.

Moreover, along with the seasonal rosé there is another less obvious trend. Provence is developing no less rapidly than the other regions of southern France. More and more estates are

Raimond de Villeneuve has restored the Château de Roquefort estate with great zeal.

Tireless champions of Bandol—Comte Henri de Saint-Victor and his son Eric.

The extraordinarily broad range of grape varieties in Provence came in very handy for this upturn. Apart from the three varieties mentioned above there are Syrah, Mourvèdre, Cabernet plus Vermentino, Sémillon, Sauvignon, and Marsanne. Most businesses operate on a two-quality basis: simple, cleanly vinified, and cheap wines for everyday use and the general public, who often drive over from Marseille, Aix-en-Provence, and Nice to buy direct; and more ambitious and more expensive *cuvées* for connoisseurs and the many restaurants of the Côte d'Azur, that are only too happy to promote and give precedence to local growers. After

The quality of the wines of Château Simone is a match for the splendid appearance of the estate.

Provençal *restanques*—flat terraces shored up by stones.

locals, restaurants, and tourists have stocked up at cooperatives and estates, not much is left of the best wines of Provence and Corsica for export. If you want to get an impression of the best wines you are more or less obliged to visit them at home. The same is true in Corsica (see page 314), where the wines show an enchanting character of their own.

Coteaux d'Aix and Les Baux de Provence

On the chalk cliffs above the Étang de Berre are the ruins of one of the oldest settlements in Provence.

Coteaux d'Aix: A Mini-region with a Microclimate

Aix itself is not a wine-producing city, apart from the tiny Palette *appellation*, whose north-facing slopes overlook part of it. Things were different in the 18th century: the total area planted to vines covered 56,800 acres (23,000 ha), reaching right up to the city. Only 8,150 acres (3,300 ha) of this remain, keeping the city at a respectful distance and lying mainly southwest, west and north of it. In the east, the Montagne Sainte-Victoire marks the beginning of the Côtes de Provence region.

In the north, the Durance constitutes the boundary, establishing its course between the Montagne du Lubéron and the Chaîne de Trévarasse. The loamy, sandy soils of the valley here are covered with extensive vineyards. Eastward, there is an exceptional area between Jouques and Rians, which belongs to the Var department, as does the neighboring Artigues, while the other 47 localities of the *appellation* belong to Bouches-du-Rhône. At a height of over 1,000 feet (300 m), it has a special microclimate that is much cooler than one would expect in Provence. This delays the ripening of the grapes, involving greater risks for the grower, but does wonders for the structure and aroma of the wines. The first grower to show what could be done was Georges Brunet, former owner of

Aix-en-Provence has been able to buff up its reputation as a city of arts and literature only in recent decades. In the 15th century, it was a stronghold of the arts under René the Good, Count of Provence and "Last of the Troubadors," who granted the city privileges and popularized its wines. The French Revolution, 300 years later, brought hard times. Marseille ousted Aix, and the latter struggled to establish an identity. Today the university city shines once again, not least because of its famous festival, for which a special *cuvée* is bottled.

the 3ème Cru Classé La Lagune at Vignelaure. From the 1989 vintage, Californian-trained German grower Peter Fischer at Château Revelette spearheaded development in the mini-region with his Grand Vin assembled from Syrah and Cabernet, which has a good ten-year aging potential. The other reds in the region are generally allowed a life of three to five years.

A NEW GENERATION OF RED WINES

Syrah and Cabernet Sauvignon have become the basis of the red wines that are to be taken seriously in the Coteaux d'Aix. Bordeaux's superstar grape has a distinctly non-Atlantic character of its own in Provence, whether in the Coteaux d'Aix or the Côtes de Provence. Mostly the weather is just right for the late-ripening Cabernet, so that the green vegetal aromas and tannins are replaced by full-bodied blackberry fruit tones. When combined with Syrah, the aromas and fruit take on a distinctly southern quality, though in the Coteaux d'Aix they do not seem awkward or heavy.

Other zones in the *appellation*, such as the areas around Saint-Cannat and Lambesc, lie between 650 and 1,000 feet (200 and 300 m) above sea-level and thus retain a moderate Mediterranean climate with a later ripening date. The wines mostly manifest slight increased acidity, giving balance and freshness to the rosés, which even here make up over half the production and are often more than 50 percent Grenache Noir. The occasional whites, for which growers have a choice of Clairette, Ugni Blanc,

Peacocks are the mascots of Château Revelette.

The wines of Mas de la Dame are best sampled in the courtyard of the farmhouse.

Rolle, Sémillon, or Grenache Blanc, have a pleasant freshness that is generally lacking in hotter localities. However, all estates offer all three types, often with a choice of two levels of quality.

The areas planted to vine around the Étang de Berre enjoy a particularly mild climate with higher humidity, producing grapes that ripen early and yield round, harmonious wines. On the limestone cliffs near Lançon, which belong to the 2,470-acre (1,000-ha) estate of Château Calissane, the ruins of a fortified village can be discerned, built by the Ligurian Celts in the 4th century BC before the Romans conquered the area. Grapes grow here alongside olive trees and almonds, and depending on the yield, selection, and vinification, produce wines with fruity, aromatic charm or—most notably after aging in the bottle for four or five years—that emphasize the dense, complex expressiveness of the *terroir*.

LES BAUX DE PROVENCE

The Alpilles are undoubtedly one of the most captivating landscapes in Provence. The fissured chalk cliffs contrast with the azure blue of the sky. Pines and wild herbs dominate the flora and vine stocks. In the small district comprising only six villages south of Avignon and northeast of the Camargue, the climate is hotter and more humid than in the Coteaux d'Aix and thus earlier-ripening than in the Coteaux d'Aix, to which it used to belong. The number of sunshine hours per annum varies between 2,700 and 2,900, enough to guarantee best ripening. In

CÔTES DE PROVENCE AND COTEAUX VAROIS

Aix, Toulon, and Fréjus are the three points that roughly mark out the main cultivation area of Provençal wines. It is an enormous triangle in which over 51,900 acres (21,000 ha) are classed as A.C., not to mention the additional areas under vine that furnish various *vins de pays*. The ancient Provincia Romana offers excellent conditions for viticulture, which has been carried out here on a large scale since antiquity. In summer, the temperature can rise far above 86°F (30°C), especially in the interior, but the Mistral often provides a touch of freshness and keeps the vine stocks healthy, because fungal and other diseases can scarcely tolerate its dry draft. Precipitation is low, and most common in spring and autumn. Growers have mostly storms and hail to fear, which can destroy their work and the harvest in minutes. Climatic conditions are modified by the great diversity of the sites and their alignment, because several chains of hills give the landscape a variegated aspect.

Geologically speaking, two elements dominate: a crystalline rock base dating back to the Paleozoic and later chalk formations. When the Alps folded upward, the limestone was thrust westward, while the rock base was folded upward in the east, and still shows visible influences of volcanic activity. There it constitutes the major massifs of the Maures, Esterel, and Tanneron. In the west, limestone sediments characterize the Bandol and Cassis areas and also the Montagne Sainte-Victoire near Aix.

On the Domaine Richeaume at the foot of the Montagne Sainte-Victoire an integrated concept was put into practice.

Parade in pastel tones: tank test at the Domaine Sant-André, near La-Londe-des-Maures.

The Côtes de Provence A.C. has been an umbrella designation for the cultivated areas of the Var department since 1977, from which only the cooperative growers around Brignoles gained nothing at the time. Their *appellation* Coteaux Varois was obtained only in 1993. It includes 28 parishes with 4,450 acres (1,800 ha) under vine overall, with a good two thirds of the production being sold as rosé, a quarter as red and the rest as white wine. In the meantime, there are an increasing number of independent estates with a concern for quality.

In the sister *appellation* there has been much renewed discussion about sites, with a view to subdividing the almost 47,000 acres (19,000 ha) under vine into *terroirs*. A provisional classification exists that follows geography and is based on five zones.
• La Bordure Maritime: the coastal strip between Saint-Raphael and Hyères;
• Les Collines du Haut-Pays: the hilly region around Lorgues and Draguignan, rising towards the north;
• La Vallée Intérieure: the valley stretching from Vidauban to Toulon behind the Massif des Maures;
• Le Bassin du Beausset: the Beausset basin adjacent to the *appellations* of Cassis and Bandol;
• La Sainte-Victoire: the vineyards at the foot of the Montagne Sainte-Victoire in the north and the Monts Auréliens in the south. La Sainte-Victoire was the first of these areas to obtain an official recognition.

The name of the mountain which Paul Cézanne painted again and again, almost obsessively, is now synonymous with the most highly developed Côtes de Provence area—in terms of cohesion, image, and the quality of the wines produced.

WINE STYLES AND GRAPE VARIETIES

Rosé is an important economic factor for Provençal growers. The chief varieties used are Grenache Noir and Cinsault, the former making the fruitier style, the latter the floral, fuller-bodied style. If the rosé is vinified like a white wine by immediate pressing, the color turns out very pale and the aromas are discreet but elegant. With the rosé derived by the *saignée* process, the must remains on the skins until it reaches the color tone the vintner requires, after which it is bottled without pressing. In this case, it often displays a slight violet shimmer and gives off aromas of small red fruits. A specialty is the Tibouren variety, which produces inherently little color but has a lot of body and liveliness.

The Roman past and the proximity of Italy are also evident in the range of grape varieties. The Trebbiano, here called Ugni Blanc, is particularly common in Provence and is really not serviceable for more than pleasant whites or to add a touch of acidity to the traditional, slightly oxidizing Clairette. However, the Ligurian Vermentino or Rolle is attracting renewed interest on the basis of its fresh aromas and lively structure. Sémillon has long been

Côtes de Provence

- La Sainte-Victoire
- Le Bassin du Beausset
- Les Collines du Haut Pays
- La Vallée Intérieure
- La Bordure Maritime
- **Coteaux Varois**
- **Bandol**
- **Cassis**
- Wine-growing areas in neighboring regions

common, and can produce very elegant wines, especially if fermented in the barrel. Recently some growers have been trying the Sauvignon and Marsanne varieties.

The more interesting wines of Provence are the reds. They have a wide range of varieties to draw on, with Syrah and Mourvèdre setting the pace today, but also quite a lot of Cabernet Sauvignon, domesticated for over a century. Enrichment comes from Grenache Noir and occasionally old Carignan. Although modern expertise is applied, the predominant character of the red wines is linked with tradition in the best sense, and unfurls a many-layered bouquet only after some years. They keep on the whole for about five years, but the aging potential of the concentrated top *cuvées* is often twice as long.

Coteaux de Pierrevert

In the very north of Provence, the district around the towns of Manosque, Forcalquier, and Peyrus succeeded in gaining A.C. status for a cultivated area of 642 acres (260 ha) in 1999. At the foot of the Provençal Alps cooler climatic conditions prevail that are reflected in the freshness of the wines. Rosé is made, of course, plus some white wine, but here too the best wines are the reds, particularly when they contain a healthy dose of Syrah.

Bandol

Bandol is among the rare spots in the world where all conditions coincide to make a completely original wine. Its slopes face the sea and are protected from cold north winds, making it ideal for viticulture. This awoke the interest of the Phocaeans almost immediately after they had established a base in what is now Marseille. Bandol is among the very first areas on the European side of the Mediterranean where vines were planted from the 6th century BC However, what predestined the small area for viticulture so early on was the natural harbor at Bandol, which lent the wine in the interior its name.

The fame of Bandol depends on a single grape variety, the Mourvèdre. It comes from Catalonia, where there are towns called Murviedro near Valencia and Mataró near Barcelona, as the extremely late-ripening variety is often called internationally. It is widely distributed in southern Spain, without, however, having brought forth any really remarkable wines so far. Things are different in the south of France. Mourvèdre is here a component of Châteauneuf-du-Pape, where it is documented as long ago as the 17th century and from where it is thought to have spread through Provence. Before phylloxera destroyed the vineyards, it had become one of the leading varieties there, and had established a solid position especially in Bandol along with Grenache and Cinsault.

One quality of Mourvèdre in particular contributed to the rise of Bandol, namely its marked

Clos Sainte-Magdeleine, a dream of an estate at the foot of Cap Canaille, France's tallest cliff, produces one of the best-known Cassis.

A vineyard stands on this promontory extending into the Mediterranean. Small wonder that its Cassis should give off a delicate aroma of iodine from time to time.

but very fine tannins derived from the chalk-rich slopes. This gives the wines an aging potential that is extraordinary for the south. Because of this, it became one of the most in-demand export wines in the 18th century, and over 1.5 million gallons (60,000 hl) of wine—more than is produced today—was shipped abroad every year from Bandol in barrels marked with a large B.

Right from the start Bandol was lucky to have devoted growers who believed in their wines and their estates. No *grand cru* comes about anywhere without people of this kind. Starting over after the phylloxera catastrophe was slow and difficult, but the growers worked at it and got their *appellation* in 1941. They themselves set up a strict discipline, namely a minimum 50 percent of the difficult Mourvèdre and a maximum yield of 428 gallons per acre (40 hl per ha). In addition, grapes for red wine could come from young stocks only from the eighth harvest or later. As far as aging was concerned, 18 months in the barrel was prescribed. With these criteria, which are far more rigorous than all *appellations* granted later, they consciously established the basis for the future of red Bandol.

In order to ripen best on Bandol's *terroir*, Mourvèdre requires special treatment. It must be thinned out. Long before growers in other regions realized that this is a means to master the yields and improve quality, the practice was quite the usual thing in the wine-growing communities of Saint-Cyr-sur-Mer, La Cadière d'Azur, Le Castellet, Le Beausset, and their immediate neighbors. Despite almost record levels of sunshine (3,000 hours a year) and the sheltered sites, Mourvèdre would otherwise not ripen and reach a potential alcohol content of 12.5 abv, without which it possesses no quality.

Bandol has not escaped the rosé problem. A substantial proportion of the grapes from the 3,210-acre (1,300-ha) *appellation* is turned into rosé. But however much this product displays a style of its own and shows more strength and finish on the palate than some other rosés, it is still only a small lad compared with a mature red.

In the south of France, Mourvèdre is valued for its intense fruit, often reminiscent of blackberries. But these primary aromas, which in Bandol are often accompanied by overtones of pepper, spices and even meaty tones, give but a slight intimation of the actual character of the wine, which becomes evident generally only eight years after the harvest. Leather and underwood then become the keynotes, accompanied by complex overtones of ripe and cooked berries, licorice, herbs, and spices, though the wines continue to manifest an amazing elegance and harmony.

Thanks to self-discipline and commitment, the *appellation* shows an astonishingly high

Left
Jean-Pierre Gaussen and his family swear by Mourvèdre.

Right
Nature and animal lover Laurent Bunan samples the aromas of a Bandol.

Cassis is one of the rarest white wines of Provence, and goes excellently with Mediterranean fish dishes.

overall level across its 50 estates and five *caves coopératives*, with a whole series of wineries standing out. That you can find still more convincing wines in Bandol has—as elsewhere— to do with hard work in the vineyard and winery and the associated investment. Part of this is a rigorous selection of grapes from special sites and from particularly old vine stocks. Since the end of the 1980s, more and more winemakers have gone over either to greatly increasing the proportion of Mourvèdre in their red *cuvées* or producing a second *cuvée* (almost) solely from Mourvèdre using the best selected grapes. The resulting wines include some of supreme quality. The growers of Bandol have also shown much sensitivity in the use of aging in wood. Most still work with large old tuns, to avoid masking the lively natural tannins of their wines. As far as vintages are concerned, Bandol is a total exception. Though difficult weather conditions may prevail everywhere else, when the Mourvèdre is ripening here in October, the sun is mostly doing its work properly. In contrast, the very rare white wines remain a Mediterranean curiosity, with growers going wherever the mood takes them.

Cassis and Bellet

The small port and neat coastal town of Cap Canaille, in the shadow of the highest cliff in France, offers growers no less favorable conditions for viticulture on their 420 acres (170 ha) planted to vine than Bandol. However, in contrast to the latter, its growers have oriented themselves more to white wines, which now constitute three quarters of total output. They are based on Ugni Blanc, Clairette, Sémillon, and Marsanne. Bulky, characterful and dry, the wines often smell of

almonds, white flowers, peaches, apricots, or even exotic fruits such as lychees or mangoes, and occasionally toss in an overtone of iodine.

The vines thrive on terraces facing the sea. Intent focus on quality reaped the first A.C. for the growers in Provence back in 1936. The remaining quarter of the output is made up of very light (i.e. mostly directly pressed) rosés of Grenache, Cinsault, and Carignan, while reds are a rarity.

Bellet, Nice's own *cru*, is cultivated in the heights above the city and produces barely 100,000 bottles a year. However, the area now exceeds 99 acres (40 ha). The 11 independent estates and single cooperative make very aromatic whites from Rolle, small additions of other southern varieties and some Chardonnay. Thanks to Braquet and Fuella (or Folle Noire), two local varieties, assembled with Grenache and Cinsault, the reds acquire charm and finesse. The rosés are agreeable and lively.

Languedoc and Roussillon

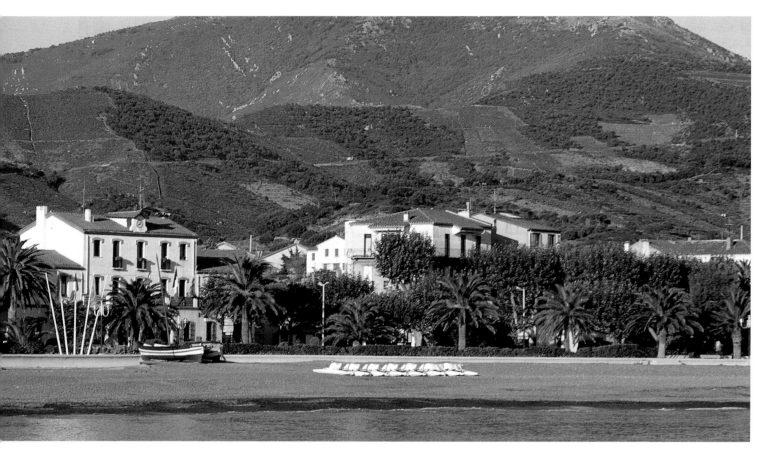

Revolution in the Midi

A wind of change has been blowing through the earthy vine-growing villages between the Rhône and the Spanish border. Instead of automatically tugging the forelock to the famous growths of Bordeaux and Burgundy, the growers of the Midi have rolled up their sleeves and got down to making their own superwines. These days, wine buffs around the world scramble to obtain the wines of the star growers of Languedoc and Roussillon. This did not happen by chance.

Ultimately it was no historical accident that France's viticulture outside Provence started 2,000 years ago at the gates of Narbonne. Barren slopes, a dry climate, and record annual hours of sunshine offer extraordinarily good natural conditions for healthy, aromatic, and concentrated wines.

Viticulture in the southernmost tip of France reached its first heyday under the Romans, when amphorae full of wine from Gallia Narbonensis enjoyed a good reputation even in Rome, and were exported as far as Germania.

Behind the bathing resort of Banyuls rise the steep foothills of the Pyrenees, where growers have worked for centuries to establish a unique vineyard architecture.

With the fall of the Roman Empire, viticulture lost its supra-regional importance. Though wine was grown by the numerous monasteries that sprang up from the 9th century, in the Middle Ages it was all drunk within the region. Only when the infrastructure was substantially improved at the end of the 17th century by the construction of a harbor at Sète, the Canal du Midi, and various cross-country roads was there an upturn in the wine industry. At that time there was great demand for eau-de-vie-brandy to fortify wine and conserve it. The result was that a major part of the local output was distilled. On the plains, this meant planting robust, high-yield varieties such as Aramon or Carignan. Growers in higher-placed villages went more for quality on their stony slopes and planted Grenache or Mourvèdre. The reputation of individual communities and vineyards dates from this period.

Rapid industrialization of the cities of northern France in the 19th century brought a decisive change in the market. A new class of consumer developed for whom wine had a firm place in providing nourishment and pleasure in an otherwise miserable working-class environment. Railways furnished the transport. The business was so lucrative that vines ousted all other crops from the Midi. With 1,140,000 acres (460,000 ha) planted to vines, Languedoc became the greatest wine-growing area in the world. This put paid to the better growths. Instead of being kept apart, their stronger, darker qualities only served to make thinner brews more tolerable. Through phylloxera, economic collapses, two World Wars, the growers of Languedoc persisted with mass production. Only the dramatic consequences of over-production brought a belated change of heart.

From 1970 on, the wine-growing region began to take on a new, very differentiated structure. On the plains, where irrigation was possible, more lucrative fruit and vegetable crops drove the vines out of the fields. However, wherever a long history of wine production had mastered sites that were good for particular quality and individual character, growers were rewarded with an A.C., the highest grade in the French vineyard classification system. To gain this accolade, however, the growers had to plant better varieties of vine and show that they took quality seriously. Thus, many aromatic varieties such as red Syrah, Mourvèdre, and Grenache Noir became domesticated on the schist, granite, or argillocitic soils; in the case of the whites, the main varieties were Roussanne,

Marsanne, Rolle, and Viognier. In deference to tradition, they are assembled with each other and with ancestral, less expressive varieties to produce complex, balanced wines.

VIN DE PAYS WITH CHARACTER

When another crisis hit the wine industry in the mid-1980s, a number of pioneers took the lead in establishing a growers' association (1987). They created a Vin de Pays d'Oc designation, with regional character and a guarantee of quality. They backed chiefly the internationally popular grape varieties and the more fertile vineyards classified as *vin de pays* on which higher but nonetheless restricted yields are permitted. Using modern winery techniques, especially temperature controls, they began to produce single-variety wines that matched market and consumer demand—and match it now even more. Initially the syndicate was launched with 200 members producing 5.2 million gallons (200,000 hl) of *vin de pays*. By the end of the millennium, it comprised over 1,000 firms who between them turned out over 68.7 million gallons (2.6 million hl), of which 80 percent is exported. And the trend is still upward. From a viticultural perspective, Languedoc-Roussillon has become one of the most attractive areas of cultivation worldwide, drawing investors from France and abroad to the Mediterranean coastal areas.

Apart from forests and wild herbs, only vines grow on the hot schist soils of Faugères—but what a wine they produce!

Though the present *appellations* gradually developed in Roussillon and Languedoc, in the early 1980s there were very few estates producing convincing wines. Top-ranking wines were not even a prospect. The region's main handicap was in the minds of its growers. The long history of mass production had left a deep sense of inferiority, and robbed the Midi of a proper wine culture. There was scarcely a grower who was familiar with the great Bordeaux and Burgundies, let alone the concept of what a great Midi wine might be like.

Red wine is unquestionably an essential feature of Mediterranean life. The *gobelet* (or goblet) profile of the vine stocks goes back to Roman times.

THE EMERGENCE OF GREAT WINES

Then the incomprehensible happened. At the beginning of the 1980s, a wine from Languedoc, called Mas de Daumas Gassac, pushed various Médoc *crus classés* off the rostrum. It was moreover just a *vin de pays* that had first come on the market in 1978. Aimé Guibert, a former leather manufacturer from Millau, was the very first to show the incredible potential of the region. Admittedly, he relied predominantly on the Bordelais Cabernet Sauvignon grape.

A more potent symbol of the revolution in attitudes and quality quickly followed—a whirlwind called Olivier Jullien, who hit the Midi in 1985. He might have seemed an unlikely candi-

In fact, a storm of inspiration suddenly blew out of nowhere that has not abated one jot since. On the contrary—initially only a few, but every year more and more growers have come to realize the opportunity offered them by the vineyards and their *terroirs*. They have caught on to how to make great wines, i.e. with the precisely the same great rigor that *grands crus* and *crus classés* require. At the same time they are lowering the yields, increasing the density of stocks on new plantations, and selecting the best plots. The first pioneers are going over to bottling their wines separately as well.

Since then, Languedoc and Roussillon have come up with outstanding wines of quite unique (i.e. Mediterranean) character. Even so, you have to know what you are looking for when you opt for wines from Languedoc or Roussillon. As a general rule, growers operate to different quality levels according to the age of the stocks, the grandeur of the *terroir*, and the varying levels of expense during vinification and aging. Just as car buyers accept that a car manufacturer can produce small, medium-sized family cars, and luxury vehicles, wine lovers have to get used to the idea that top growers here, whose super *cuvées* are the source of international wonder, also produce everyday tipple at reasonable prices. And that has its good side too.

Roses serve as warning indicators. Like vines, they are affected by mildew, but more quickly than the vines, giving the grower time to undertake preventive spraying in the vineyard.

date to show the world that Languedoc was in a position and mind to produce great wine. At the age of 20, when he was a first-year student of enology at Montpellier, the opportunity to lease vineyards came up. He acted quickly, and immediately set about building his winery himself. Olivier and the other pioneers of the first days had two things in common: enormous idealism and empty pockets. With healthy respect for the barren land and old vine stocks, the young grower of Mas Jullien produced *cuvées* of unheard-of density, spirit, and expressiveness. Others such as Michel Louison at the Château des Estanilles plumbed the potential especially of Syrah on very barren soils, with minimal yields, and using barrels for the aging.

Coteaux du Languedoc

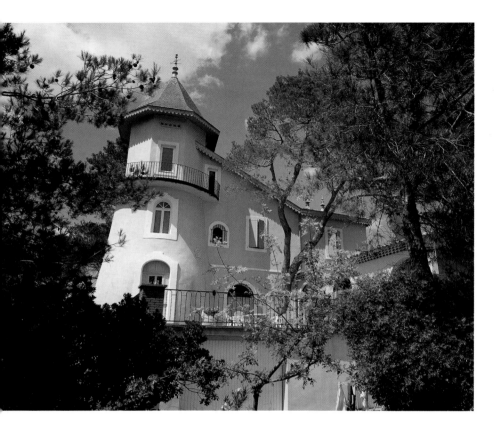

The success of the single-variety Syrah wines (they are often wholly Syrah, though this is not officially recognized) extends even to the *vin de pays*. At the same time, there has also been a growing regard for Grenache and Mourvèdre among the best producers. The latter is tricky to cultivate, and produces satisfactory results only in suitable localities that have still to be identified. Grenache Noir, notorious for its tendency to seepage and oxidation, has given growers something to ponder, chiefly because it has demonstrated its potential in Châteauneuf-du-Pape and Catalonia's Priorat.

Two attempts have been made to provide a suitable hierarchical classification for the geological and geographical diversity of the Coteaux du Languedoc. The older one (see map on opposite page) defines 12 *terroirs* that, regardless of size, manifest an identity of their own on the basis of their natural characteristics and earlier reputations. Eight of these *terroirs* lie mainly or predominantly on the terrain of a single commune. Among these, Picpoul-de-Pinet is the outsider, a white wine made from the Picpoul variety, which grows near the Bassin de Thau. Saint-Georges d'Orques, outside the gates of Montpellier and once a famous *cru*, is again attracting attention with concentrated, elegant red wines. Pic-Saint-Loup has leapt to the head of the *terroirs* thanks to its quality consciousness and solidarity of its growers; the smaller Montpeyroux is hot on its trail. La Clape, too, has produced convincing products of more reliable and sometimes even remarkable nature. The delightful ex-island near Narbonne was, like Pic and Pinet, classified with the *zones climatiques* encompassing larger territories, in order to allow more producers to look forward to possible upgrading to the benefits of an *appellation*.

Whether this system will match the reality in the glass, only the future can prove. The other zones are called Terre de Sommières, Terrasses du Larzac, Grès de Montpellier, and Terrasses de Béziers.

Clairette du Languedoc

Awarded in 1948, this A.C. acknowledged the grape variety of the same name, which has been cultivated for centuries in 11 villages between Pézénas and Clermont-l'Hérault, initially to produce a sherry-like Madeirized wine and subsequently the raw material for the vermouth

The islands of quality that its *appellations* represent still lie in an ocean of vines in the Languedoc, with around 741,000 acres (300,000 ha) under vine. The largest is the Coteaux du Languedoc, 20,800 acres (8,400 ha) in an area that begins south of Nîmes and ends in Narbonne. It stretches almost 80 miles (130 km) along the Mediterranean and extends 30 miles (50 km) into the interior, comprising 168 communes and a wide range of localities. Apart from history and political structure, sun, wind, and relative dryness, their common denominator is the red grape varieties. Hard action has been taken against Carignan. Though still the most widespread variety, its proportion in Coteaux du Languedoc has been restricted to 40 percent, while Pic Saint-Loup allows 10 percent, a qualitative maximum for the region. Among the three main varieties of Grenache, Mourvèdre, and Syrah, the latter has come to the fore. As an early ripening, high-colour, and aromatically complex variety, the grape acquires a fuller, warmer character on the barren upland sites, and to some extent even an extraordinarily dense structure with pronounced aromas of the *garrigue*, the Mediterranean moor.

Château Moulin de Ciffre is undergoing a renaissance under the management of Bordelais grower Jacques Lésinau.

industry. Only in recent years has modern winery technology brought out a wholly different aspect of the variety, which is cultivated on only 173 acres (70 ha), i.e. a fresh, fruity character with aromas of dried fruits, aniseed, and almonds.

FAUGÈRES

Faugères is a wild, thinly populated and thickly forested area that begins 10 miles (15 km) north of Béziers. Of the 12,400 acres (5,000 ha) that were included in the *appellation* in 1982, only 4,450 acres (1,800 ha) have been planted. Faugères is the only A.C. of Languedoc with homogeneous soils based on schist that are suited to high-quality red wines. Following the pioneering example of the Château des Estanilles, more estates have gone over to *cuvées* with high Syrah proportions aged in barrels, wines that are in demand for their complexity, concentration, and elegance. The fine fruit and often floral aromas of the rosés make them a popular choice for many restaurants.

SAINT-CHINIAN

Saint-Chinian lies between Minervois and Faugères, obtaining its A.C. status in the same year as the latter (1982). Center of the 7,410-acre (3,000-ha) *appellation* is the town of this name, which lies on a notable geological boundary. The area of cultivation is divided in two.

The southern zone possesses limey clay soils on which reds with body and much tannin prosper. The north stretches over the foothills of the Monts de l'Espinouse, and is made of schist. After a series of estates and the cooperatives of Berloup and Roquebrun had produced wines of reliable quality in the 1980s, from the mid-1990s a group of younger firms began to cause a stir with intensive, complex, and concentrated red wines. Some of the older estates have caught their enthusiasm. As in Faugères, only the rosé is also classified, whites being covered by the Coteaux du Languedoc *appellation*.

With his Château des Estanilles Michel Louson was the first to show the dimensions that Syrah can take on in Languedoc.

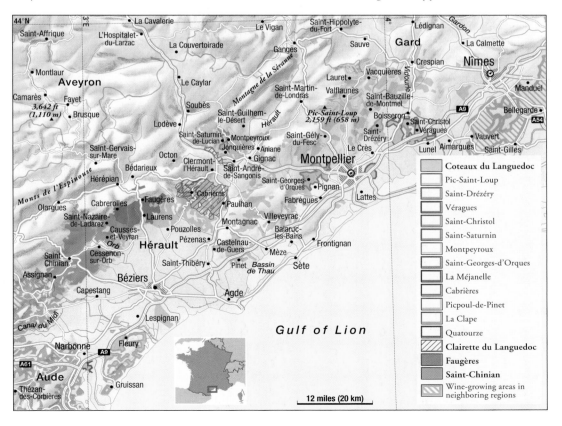

Coteaux du Languedoc
Pic-Saint-Loup
Saint-Drézéry
Vérargues
Saint-Christol
Saint-Saturnin
Montpeyroux
Saint-Georges-d'Orques
La Méjanelle
Cabrières
Picpoul-de-Pinet
La Clape
Quatourze
Clairette du Languedoc
Faugères
Saint-Chinian
Wine-growing areas in neighboring regions

12 miles (20 km)

Minervois

Minervois runs from the outcrops of the Montagne Noire to the Canal du Midi and from there down to the River Aude. In the south, the boundary runs between Narbonne and Carcassonne. Four rivers have created extensive, not very fertile terraces where mainly chalk, but also gravel, sand, and some slate form the soils. The area of cultivation, in which 11,100 acres (4,500 ha) furnish A.C. wines, is distributed among 45 communes of the Aude department and 16 of Hérault.

The center includes the stony terraces of the Argent Double, the Balcons de l'Aude with their brown marl, the great wine-growing community of Laure, and the hilly Petite Causse region with the famous wine locality of La Livinière. The latter was the first officially recognized *cru* of Minervois along with five neighboring parishes including Siran, in 1998. The barren *terroir* of the high plain gives the red wines a special full-bodied character. Toward the charming villages of Caunes schist and the famous pink marble are the determinative soil components. Here the climate manifests clear Atlantic influences and the wines display greater freshness. Around Minerve, the historic capital of the region, lie the Montagnes du Causse. Here the climate is dry but often cold, the soils are chalky, and the wines very individual.

To the east, where the vineyards stretch for 20 miles (35 km) toward Béziers, Mediterranean influences are most prominent. Often, an occasionally violent wind from the sea reaches right up to the Serres, Mourels, and the Terrasses de la Cesse, the hottest and driest area, where the wines turn out bulky and strong.

In 1990, the growers launched a quality initiative, which lowered yields to 481 gallons per acre (45 hl/ha) and limited the proportion of Carignan to 40 percent at most. Grenache Noir and Syrah dominate the *assemblage*. The traditional Cinsault also retains its place, giving the reds and rosés finesse. The Cinsault wines made from old vinestocks and vinified with *pigeage* are filigree from the soft *attaque* right up to the taste, but also have surprising finish.

Though some rosés and whites are vinified, including a number of delightful wines now made mainly with Marsanne and Roussanne, the forte of the district is its reds. More and more cooperatives and growers are coming up with well-structured growths that are matured in the barrel, often very spicy wines with fine ripe fruit and convincing body, that develop very advantageously.

Limoux

In the upper reaches of the Aude—16 miles (25 km) south of Carcassonne—sparkling wine was available as far back as 1544. The Benedictines of the abbey of Saint-Hilaire, who discovered

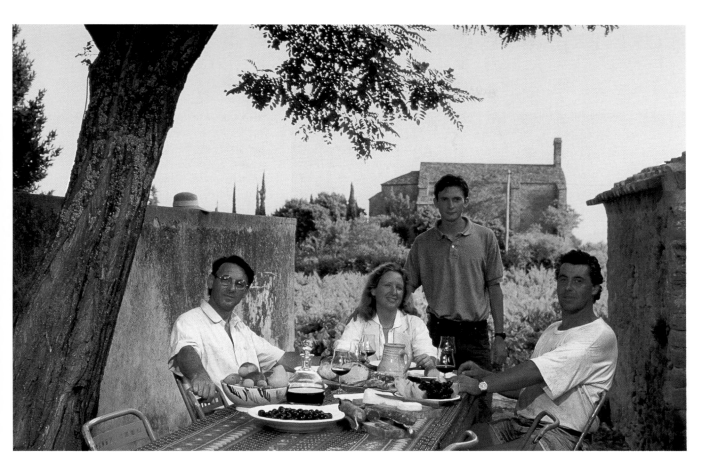

the *prise de mousse* in 1531, were 150 years ahead of Champagne. The native grape variety Blanquette, elsewhere called Mauzac, is what made it possible. It tends not to ferment the sugar completely. If the wine is drawn off into barrels or bottles, the yeast begins to revive in spring and convert the sugar residue into alcohol, producing carbonic acid. The *méthode ancestrale* following this process is still used, but since the end of the 19th century, Limoux has gone over to the *méthode champenoise* for sparkling wines.

Though Limoux gained its *appellation* for the sparkling wine back in 1938, its growers failed to gain the reputation it deserved. Since then, one or two things have happened, particularly to the grape varieties, where Chenin and Chardonnay have replaced the unsuitable Clairette. Since 1991 there has been a Crémant de Limoux, where the Chardonnay stands out. Several excellent wines exist under this *appellation* at a comparatively low price.

Meanwhile, Limoux means much more than this. With over 34,600 acres (14,000 ha) of vineyard, other products had to be made besides Blanquette, so bearing in mind the Atlantic aspects of their climate, the growers took to planting Bordelais varieties such as Sauvignon and others for the *vin de pays*. However, it is Chardonnay that has brought the

Midday meal at Clos Centeilles, where former bookseller Daniel Domergues (left) and his wife Patricia Boyer show what finesse Cinsault is capable of.

greatest success. The large cooperative, Les Caves du Sieur d'Arques, carried out an expensive *sélection* of the vineyard sites which culminated in the definition of four *terroirs* that reflect mainly different climatic conditions: Autan, Méditerranéen, Océanique, and Haute Vallée, with the latter featuring as *grand cru* and aging very well. The decidedly high quality of their wines gained the growers the *appellation* Limoux, reserved for dry white wines, for which Mauzac, Chenin, and Chardonnay are vinified and aged in the barrel.

Cabardès

Northwest of Carcassonne and adjacent to Minervois and therefore strongly exposed to Atlantic weather, the growers of this small region have the opportunity to combine Mediterranean and Bordelais grape varieties for their reds and rosés. Most prominent on the 988 or so acres (400 ha) planted to vines are Grenache and Syrah, Cabernet Sauvignon, and Merlot. Besides pleasing, fruity, substantial reds, the best *cuvées* show greater strength, structure, and interesting tannins. A tenth of the output is rosé.

Malepère

Situated on the hills southwest of Carcassonne and alongside the Limoux region, the 1,980-acre (800-ha) vineyards of Malepère are climatically exposed to the same wetter and cooler Atlantic climate, despite the southern position. Here, too, Mediterranean and Bordelais varieties thrive side by side, with Cabernet Franc being added to Cabernet Sauvignon and Merlot, plus Syrah, Grenache, and Cinsault. Its special strength lies in its fruity, aromatic, agreeable, and elegant reds and rosé wines.

Corbières and Fitou

Corbières forms an enormous rectangle covering 1,150 square miles (3,000 km²) south of a line from Narbonne to Carcassonne in the department of Aude. To the west, the hills rise to a height where it is too cold for vines. In the east, they thrust toward the lagoons of Leucate and Bages and the Mediterranean. In the south their realm ends in the rocky cliffs crowned by the Cathar castles of Quéribus and Peyrepertuse. The large area of cultivation—the A.C. covers 37,100 acres (15,000 ha)—is distinguished by a wealth of different soils and climates. Vine stocks grow on schist from the Primary, chalk and sandstone from the Secondary, layers of marls from the Tertiary and gravelly alluvium brought down in the Quaternary.

The proximity of the Mediterranean determines the climate, of course, but Atlantic influences are also perceptible depending on height and the degree of westerliness. In 1990, work was begun on a scheme to define 11 major areas that took account of these differing characteristics. They are the *terroirs* shown on the map (p. 155): Sigean, Durban, Quéribus, Termenès, Saint-Victor, Fontfroide, Lagrasse, Serviès, Montagne d'Alaric, Lézignan, and Boutenac.

The growers of Corbières have also replanted thousands of their acres with Grenache, Syrah, Mourvèdre and—to a much lesser extent—white varieties such as Grenache Blanc, Rolle, Marsanne, and Roussanne. But, above all, they have succeeded in mastering Carignan, much

A typical vineyard hut in Corbières, which provides shelter from weather.

Near Limoux, irises grow wild on the edge of many vineyards.

abused as a mass-wine grape. They kept vineyards with stocks where old Carignan furnished low yields but optimum quality, and developed a vinification method that suited it. From the mid-1960s, the general practice in Languedoc-Roussillon was to go over to vinifying Carignan by carbonic maceration.

In this, hand-selected grapes are put whole into a tank saturated in carbon dioxide, so that every berry is forced to ferment within its skin. The alcohol thus produced extracts the maximum possible content from the skins. If this fermentation is interrupted early by pressing after six to eight days, the wine has acquired color and aroma but loses structure and tannin. Carignan becomes more pleasant, i.e. commercial, but receives a typical, slightly animal overtone.

However, in Corbières many growers are able to extend the maceration period and achieve additional EXTRACTION in a grand finale, which gives the wine great strength and fine tannins. The Carignan thus becomes eminently keepable, acquires a spicy bouquet often reminiscent of wild herbs, and overtones of game and underwood which increase with age.

A preponderance of Carignan assembled with Grenache and Syrah, or more rarely Mourvèdre, produces a style of wine that gives Corbières a common denominator. By the end of the 1980s, Corbières growers were surpassing other Midi *appellations* with good, comparatively homogeneous quality. The feeling seemed to spread that they had cracked it. However, at the same time energy was expended in internecine strife within the association. And suddenly Corbières had been left behind. Inspired red wines with a hitherto unsuspected profile of fruit and zing sprang up in all corners of Languedoc—except here. This has changed in recent times, with *cuvées* that open up new, unsuspected dimensions.

The proportions of rosés and whites are 4 percent and 2 percent respectively. Cinsault is an important factor in the rosés, giving many wines their pale tones and rather floral nose. The dry white wines deserve notice. The Corbières growers were the first in Languedoc-Roussillon to take due note of interesting aspects of the Grenache Blanc, especially its Mediterranean character. Instead of vainly trying to imitate the acidity of northern wines, they went for equal amounts of taste and finish.

FITOU

Fitou has a story of its own, although all Fitous can be bottled as Corbières. In 1948, just by way of a hint to the winegrowers of Languedoc and Roussillon, the national wine institute I.N.A.O. awarded it an *appellation*, the first to a dry red wine of the region. The message was: "top honors await you beyond mass wines and sweet wines—but with low yields." However, such a red wine hardly existed in those days, because all the producers turned out Rivesaltes, the decidedly more lucrative sweet wine. When a crisis struck this at the beginning of the 1980s, Fitou pulled its finger out. Today, a mere 6,420 acres (2,600 ha) provide a good 13 million bottles of wine.

As an *appellation*, Fitou is nonetheless an oddball. It consists of two enclaves only six miles (10 km) apart within Corbières, under whose A.C. its growers bottle rosés and whites, and sometimes even reds. Fitou *maritime* stretches as far as the eastern foothills of the Corbières, on argillocitic, often stony and barren soils, and borders the Mediterranean. Moisture from the latter provides good ripening, and offers ideal conditions for the tricky but high-quality Mourvèdre. The A.C. belongs to the villages of Fitou, Caves, Treilles, La Palme, and Leucate. The other zone is called Fitou de Hautes-Corbières, as it lies right in the heart of Corbières. The classified vineyards of the villages of Cascatel, Villeneuve-les-Corbières, Tuchan, and Durban are the only cultivated spots in the wild, fissured, hilly landscape, where a diversity of Mediterranean herbs, bushes, and orchids prosper. The predominantly schist soils provide excellent conditions for Syrah vines. In the two zones, which together add up to 6,180 acres (2,500 ha) of vines, the summers are hot and rain is very rare. Though producers nowadays—who include seven wine-growing cooperatives and about 35 estates—are very keen on the newly introduced varieties, Fitou owes its character to old Carignan stocks and Grenache Noir.

The strong, rustic reds, which are aged for at least nine months but often much longer in large tuns, were popular in Britain, Belgium, and Denmark before 1982, in a period when Languedoc and Roussillon otherwise had little quality to offer. Since then, Fitou has undergone a cautious change. Carignan has been made more accessible by means of carbonic maceration, while the Syrah or Mourvèdre in the *assemblage* furnish finer tannins and spicier aromas. New small barrels give overtones of body and elegance. Meanwhile, competition to Fitou has grown up in all regions of the Midi, and the former huge commercial advantage has melted away.

The oldest sparkling wine in the world flows in long streams during the carnival of Limoux.

Unloved Carignan has found a refuge in the wild, dry landscape of Corbières, generating dense reds with good aging ability.

Select Producers in Languedoc

Abbaye Sylva Plana**–***
Alaignan du Vent
77 acres (31 ha); 130,000 bottles • Wines: Faugères: La Closerie, → Le Songe de l'Abbé.
Henri Ferdinand and Nicholas Bouchard, owners of the respected Domaine Deshenrys in the Côtes de Thongue, have taken over this former monastery estate near Laurens and, with the cooperation of Cédric Guy, are producing full-bodied, spicy reds.

Abbaye de Valmagne**–***
Villveyrac
161 acres (65 ha); 200,000 bottles • Wines: Vins de Pays d'Oc; Coteaux du Languedoc: Blanc, Rosé, Rouge
The imposing abbey has offered reliable wines for many years. It is now run using natural methods, and the Cuvée Turenne in particular has gained in concentration and depth.

Borie de la Vitarèle***–****
Causses et Veyran
32 acres (13 ha); 37,000 bottles • Wines include: Coteaux du Languedoc Les Terres Blanches; Saint-Chinian: Les Schistes, → Les Crés; → Vin de Pays La Combe; Lou Festéjaïre
Cathy Planès and Jean-François Izard have come a long way since founding their *domaine* in 1990. Their powerful reds are now differentiated according to *terroir* and have well-defined character.

Château Cazal Viel**–****
Cessenon-sur-Orb
205 acres (83 ha); 600,000 bottles • Wines include: Saint-Chinian: L'Antenne, → Cuvée des Fées, Larmes des Fées
The young, dynamic Laurent Miquel is currently giving this established estate a new impulse of quality. He also advises other wine-makers and offers an interesting collection of wines under his name.

Château des Estanilles****
Lenthéric
84 acres (34 ha); 200,000 bottles • Wines: → Coteaux du Languedoc Blanc; Faugères Rosé; Rouge: Tradition, Prestige, Château
Michel Louison is an example to today's young guard, he was the first to demonstrate what grandeur Syrah could achieve in the Midi. His white wine is also excellent.

Château Grès Saint-Paul**–***
Lunel
59 acres (24 ha); 130,000 bottles • Wines include: Muscat de Lunel; → Bohémienne; Coteau du Languedoc: Romanis, → Antonin, → Syrhus, Vins de Pays d'Oc
The old family estate near Lunel produces attractive dry and sweet Muscat wines and balanced, rounded reds with ripe tannins.

Château de Lascaux***
Vacquières
86.5 acres (35 ha); 150,000 bottles • Wines: Coteaux du Languedoc: Blanc, Rosé, Rouge; → Pic Saint-Loup
Syrah and Grenache dominate the vineyards of Jean-Benoît Cavalier, who has run the estate since 1984, and produces one of the most interesting whites in Languedoc from Viognier, Marsanne, Roussanne, and Rolle.

Château Mansenoble***–****
49.5 acres (20 ha); 110,000 bottles • Wines include: Vins de Pays, Corbières Rouge, → Réserve, → Cuvée Marie-Annick
The Flemish wine enthusiast Guido Janseger has shown in only a few years how to apply skill, nose, and enthusiasm to producing excellent red Corbières.

Château Moulin de Ciffre**–***
Autignac
74 acres (30 ha); 90,000 bottles • Wines: Coteau du Languedoc, Saint-Chinian, Faugères, Vin de Pays Val Tarou
Jacques and Bernadette Lésineau, growers in Pessac-Léognan, are bringing about a stylish renaissance with the three A.O.C.s at their outstandingly well restored estate. The Cuvée Eole shows first-class Bordelais barrel aging.

Château Saint-Auriol***
Lagrasse
124 acres (50 ha); 300,000 bottles • Wines: Corbières: Blanc, Rosé, Rouge
Claude Vialade and Jean-Paul Salvagnac are among the pioneers of quality in Corbières. Their whites and reds vinified and aged in the barrel offer consistently good quality.

Château Saint-Martin de la Garrigue***–****
Montagnac
148 acres (60 ha); 300,000 bottles • Wines include: Vins de Pays, Picpoul-de-Pinet, Coteaux du Languedoc, → Bronzinelle, Cuvée Réservée, → Saint-Martin
In the space of only a few years Umberto and Gregory Guida have made a byword of the imposing château and its large estate, both for their fresh and aromatic whites and the characterful reds with good aging ability.

Château la Voulte-Gasparets***–****
Boutenac
136 acres (55 ha); 230,000 bottles • Wines: Corbières: Cuvée Réservée, → Cuvée Romain Pauc
For many years the estate has been producing one of the most typical and best Corbières from its excellent *terroir*.

Les Chemins de Bassac***–****
Puimisson
35 acres (14 ha); 50,000 bottles • Wines: Vins de Pays des Côtes de Thongue: Blanc, Rosé, Rouge; Pierre Elie, → Cap de l'Homme, Camille Léonie
The Ducelliers and their friend Regis Abbal very aromatic, elegant, expressive wines with the best of vineyard techniques and controlled low yields.

Clos Bagatelle**–****
Saint-Chinian
136 acres (55 ha); 250,000 bottles • Wines include Vins de Pays; Saint-Chinain: Rosé, Rouge; Mathieu, → La Gloire de Mon Père, ; → Muscat de Saint Jean de Minervois
The Simon family has lived on the estate on the edge of the town of Saint-Chinian since 1623. In the last 40 years, its wines have always been among the most solid in the region, but the younger generation is now giving them fruit and structure.

Clos Centeilles****
Siran
35 acres (14 ha); 50,000 bottles • Wines include: Minervois Rouge: Capitelle, Campagne, Clos de Centeilles, Vin de Pays
No one understands how to give wines such subtlety and individual character—thanks to old stocks and a barren *terroir*—as well as Daniel and Patricia Boyer-Domergue.

Jean-Louis Denois***–****
Roquetaillade
17 acres (7 ha); 36,000 bottles • Wines include: Vin de Pays d'Oc: → Sainte-Marie, La Rivière, → Chloé; → Tradition Brut

Jean-Louis Denois from Champagne caused a stir in Limoux for his experiments with Riesling. He has now sold part of his Domaine de l'Aigle to Antonin Rodet and is making a convincing new start with new wines from old vines.

DOMAINE DES AIRES HAUTES**−****
SIRAN
59 acres (24 ha); 90,000 bottles • Wines include: Vins de Pays; →Minervois La Livinière, Minervois Domaine des Aires Hautes: Blanc, Rosé, Rouge
Gilles Chabbert offers consistent, velvety Minervois wines from the Domaine des Aires Hautes, but his Clos de l'Escandil in La Livinière always beats them in terms of body, structure, spice and finish.

DOMAINE JEAN-MICHEL ALQUIER****
FAUGÈRES
31 acres (12.5 ha); 40,000 bottles • Wines include: Faugères: Générique, Réserve: La Maison Jaune, →Les Bastides
Jean-Michel Alquier has produced excellent reds with *assemblages* of Grenache, Syrah and Mourvèdre and much more sensitive barrel aging. His white *vin de pays* made from Marsanne and Roussane is simply exquisite.

DOMAINE BAILLAT***−****
MONTLAUR
34.5 acres (14 ha); 50,000 bottles • Wines: Corbières: Rosé, Rouge; Domaine: →Clos de la Miro, →Cuvée Emilien Baillat
Both Austrian and Occitan wine-producing blood runs in Christian Baillat's veins. Steadfast in the search for perfection, he has graded his wines into three categories, with the top one being close to heaven. All the wines have a surprisingly enlivening character.

DOMAINE LEON BARRAL***−****
CABREROLLES
57 acres (23 ha); 95,000 bottles • Wines: Coteaux du Languedoc Blanc; Faugères
With conscientious work in the vineyard and winery, Didier Barral has taken the family estate into the select top ranks of Faugères. Outstanding white wine vinified in the barrel.

DOMAINE BORIE DE MAUREL***
FÉLINES MINERVOIS
66.5 acres (27 ha); 150,000 bottles • Wines include: Minervois Blanc, Rosé, Rouge; Belle de Nuits, Maxime, La Livinière, Sylla
An interesting range of red wines based on grape varieties of various degrees of dominance and always showing willingness to experiment. The best is Sylla, made wholly from Syrah.

DOMAINE CANET-VALETTE***−****
CESSENON-SUR-ORB
44.5 acres (18 ha); 80,000 bottles • Wines: Saint-Chinian Rouge: Domaine, →Le Vin Maghani
Marc Valette is one of the leading figures of the new guard in Saint-Chinian and produces concentrated reds full of spice, fruit, finish, and potential.

DOMAINE DE L'HORTUS***−****
VALFLAUNES
136 acres (55 ha); 310,000 bottles • Wines: Coteaux de Languedoc: Bergerie: Blanc, Rosé, Rouge; Domaine: Blanc, →Rouge, Grande Cuvée, Clos Prieur
Jean Orliac discovered his estate in 1980 while climbing Pic-Saint-Loup; he has since developed it through his own unique combination of natural methods and modern technology, making it one of the best of the Pic.

DOMAINE RAMBERT***−****
BERLOU
49 acres (20 ha); 90,000 bottles • Wines: Saint-Chinian: Le Travers de Marceau, →Mas au Schiste; Coteaux du Languedoc Blanc, Vin de Table: →Le Chant de Marjolaine, →Carignator 1er
Jean-Marie Rimbert founded his estate on the schist slopes of Berlou in 1996. Here he produces highly individual, extremely juicy, full-bodied, fruity wines, with two made only from Carignan.

DOMAINE JEAN-BAPTISTE SENAT**−****
TRAUSSE-MINERVOIS
39.5 acres (16 ha); 50,000 bottles • Wines: Minervois: La Line, Enclos de l'Ane, →Le Bois de Merveilles
Jean-Baptiste and Charlotte Senat abandoned the student life in Paris in 1996 and took over the family estate in the Minervois. With old vines, many of them Grenache, plenty of hard work and their own philosophy, they are on their way to working miracles.

MAS CHAMPART***
BRAMEFAN
39.5 acres (16 ha); 40,000 bottles • Wines include: Saint-Chinian: →Côte d'Arbo, →Causse du Bousquet; Coteaux du Languedoc
From 1976 onwards, Isabelle and Matthieu de Champart have been putting their estate together piece by piece. Replanting has been done, with mass removal of unsatisfactory vines. Their wines show plenty of fruit and harmony.

MAS DE DAUMAS-GASSAC****−*****
ANIANE
124 acres (50 ha); 200,000 bottles • Wines: Vin de Pays: Blanc, Rouge
Aimé Guibert was the first to demonstrate the unexploited potential of Languedoc with his 1978 vintage red wine. Since then his red has become ever finer, more polished, and profound, while the highly aromatic white wine is superb. Both wines age extremely well.

MAS JULLIEN****−*****
JONQUIÈRES
42 acres (17 ha); 60,000 bottles • Wines include: Les Etats d'âmes; Coteaux du Languedoc: Blanc, Rosé, Rouge
Olivier Jullien is a mild revolutionary and member of the awkward squad, who has probably done more than anybody to inspire his wine-growing colleagues—and continues to do so. His wines are classics of the new and up-and-coming Languedoc and beyond all fashion.

PRIEURÉ DE SAINT-JEAN DE BÉBIAN****
PÉZENAS
74 acres (30 ha); 88,000 bottles • Wines: Coteaux du Languedoc: Blanc, Rouge, Chapelle, Prieuré
Since 1994, this already legendary estate, which was producing superb, very Mediterranean red wines at the same time as Daumas-Gassac, has belonged to Chantal Lecouty and Jean-Claude Le Brun, who used to run the *Revue du Vin du France*. With great commitment, they have restored the vineyards and winery and deliberately modernized the general style of the wine. White and red wines reach high standards.

SOCIÉTE COOPÉRATIVE VINICOLE DE CASTELMAURE*−****
EMBRES-ET-CASTELMAURE
741 acres (300 ha); bottles not recorded • Wines include: Corbières: Blanc, Rosé, Rouge, →Envie de Raisin, →Cuvée Pompadour, →Grande Cuvée, →No. 3, Vin de Pays
In 20 years, president Patrick de Marien and director Bernard Pueyo have turned this small, remote cooperative into a flourishing, ground-breaking new company. The quality has been rising spectacularly for some years.

CÔTES DU ROUSSILLON AND VILLAGES

Few regions of Europe present such a fascinating variety of landscapes and such contrasts as Roussillon. It is just 30 miles (50 km) from the sandy beaches of the bathing resorts to the 9,133-foot (2,784-m) peak of Canigou. The upward folding of the Pyrenees in the Tertiary provided the variegated potpourri of schist, granite, gneiss, clay, chalk, gravel, and shingle. Only Alsace offers a comparable wealth of such diverse geological structures. Created at the same time was the impressive panorama from the slopes facing the Mediterranean. The vine stocks reach a height of 2,000 feet (600 m), but only where there is an unambiguously Mediterranean climate. The sun shines here more intensely, the average annual temperature is 59°F (15°C) and the northwest wind blows through the foliage of the vines on average every third day, doing wonders for their health.

Red varieties thrive best in these circumstances. Even in the 1960s, when Carignan reigned almost supreme, there was a far-sighted initiative to plant "improving" varieties such as the fruity, round Grenache Noir, the dark, complex Syrah, which is gaining ground enormously, and the ticklish but subtle Mourvèdre.

The winegrowers' commitment was acknowledged in 1977 by the award of the A.C., long before Corbières, Minervois, or Coteaux du Languedoc, which followed only in 1985. The Côtes du Roussillon A.C. comprises overall about 16,100 acres (6,500 ha) planted to vines, scattered over 125 parishes in the departments of the Pyrénées Orientales. In the particularly hilly north of the cultivation area, where schist, granite, and chalk predominate, the red wine was given a higher rating as Côtes du Roussillon Villages. The villages of Caramany and Latour-de-France and very recently Lesquerde and finally Tautavel were singled out as individual communal *appellations*. Since the mid-1990s, only Tautavel, which includes the neighboring

Côtes du Roussillon
Côtes du Roussillon Villages
Lesquerde
Caramany
Latour-de-France
Tautavel
Collioure
Wine-growing areas in neighboring regions

INSET MAP OF NATURALLY SWEET WINES (V.D.N.s)
Muscat de Rivesaltes and Grand Roussillon
Rivesaltes
Maury
Banyuls and Banyuls Grand Cru

parish of Vingrau, has produced wines that really prove how excellent their *terroir* is. In the other three communal *appellations* cooperatives run things, and only a fraction of their output meets the quality one could expect from the given specifications. The white and rosé wines are labeled Côtes du Roussillon even in the Villages.

In the more southerly part of Roussillon there are no common denominators in the soil conditions, and the vineyards are often flatter and more extensive. An interesting feature is the natural terraces of the Aspres consisting of large alluvial or worn slate pebbles. Devoted growers produce convincing wines even here, but it does not always work, and requires stricter selection of plots and grapes. The normal reds, still strongly Carignan in make-up, display rough tannins that take several years to acquire polish.

Red wine occupies the foreground in Roussillon, but rosé has also experienced an upturn in recent times. In the last two decades the wineries were brought in line with modern enological requirements, and temperature control in particular—a vital feature especially in the hot south—has become the norm.

As generally in the Midi—except in the few areas that specialize in it—white wine plays a subordinate role, and accounts for only 5 percent of the volume. While most of it is at best easy-drinking tipple lacking acidity, there are some delightful exceptions with very individual profiles. Instead of imitating northern freshness that they can never attain, they are based on concentrated grapes picked when ripe and fermented in the barrel. The result is wines of extraordinary strength and finish, which go extremely well with strongly seasoned Mediterranean or exotic cuisine.

Their secret—like that of all great wines—lies not least in selecting the right plots, i.e. identifying the *terroir*. This work is still at an early

Collioure and its light inspired Henri Matisse and the Fauvist painters. Nowadays its red wines excite the countless tourists.

stage in Roussillon, as in Languedoc. Although the first purely schist wine was bottled in 1984 and many estates and cooperatives have gone over to consciously planting particular sites with particular grape varieties, it is a lengthy enterprise, and only in recent times have individual growers had the courage to bottle and sell wines from specified *terroirs* separately.

Collioure

Collioure is the jewel among the coastal resorts of Roussillon. The medieval castle and picturesque fortified church have been immortalized countless times since Matisse and the Fauvistes first discovered and enthused about the legendary light of the former fishing township and port from 1905 onwards. Here at the French end of the Costa Brava, the slate core of the Pyrenees dips steeply into the Mediterranean. The Greeks were the first to hack out the slopes into terraces and cultivate vines. The *appellation* now covers 815 acres (330 ha) planted to vines.

Grenache ripens completely in this area and became famous as naturally sweet wine

under the name of neighboring Banyuls (see following two pages). The traditional dry, strong red gained its *appellation* only 32 years later, in 1971.

Made from vines growing on barren soil, smiled on by the sun and with a degree of moisture arising from the sea, the wines acquire particular fullness and structure on a maximum yield of 429 gallons per acres (40 hl/ha).

Though Collioure often used to be just a country tipple stored in great tuns, it has now developed into one of the most delightful *crus* of the Midi region. The most exciting Collioures still come from the vintages that favor Grenache Noir, but thanks to Syrah

and/or Mourvèdre, which have been permitted since 1982, there are deep red, spicy, polished, and yet clearly southern red wines that are nowadays often aged in the barrel. In addition, the three cooperatives and 20 or so estates produce a strong raspberry-colored rosé, which goes excellently with grilled fish.

The best white wines of the coast are made of immediately pressed Grenache Gris and Grenache Blanc and are (still) bottled as Vin de Pays de la Côte Vermeille.

Naturally Sweet Wines:
Banyuls, Maury, and Rivesaltes

The majestic peak of Canigou and its iron ore attracted Ligurians, Iberians, Greeks, and Romans even in antiquity. The Greeks, who reached the coast of Roussillon around 600 BC, introduced vine growing here. The schist terraces of the Côte Vermeille, the French end of the Costa Brava, were excellently suited to it, and produced strong, sugar-rich wines. The Romans were likewise very partial to them. In the 1st century AD Pliny enthused about the fiery tipple of Roussillon.

Wine production flourished again under the kingdom of Mallorca that Jaime the Conqueror had forged in 1276 out of the Balearics, Roussillon, and Montpellier for his youngest son, a man whose inclinations tended toward peace, the arts and crafts. Nine years later, the doctor and celebrated scholar Arnaldus of Villanova succeeded in distilling alcohol from wine at the estate of the Templars south of Perpignan, using an Arab recipe. Called *eau-de-vie* because of its exciting effects, he used this spirits of wine to carry out experiments. Thus he discovered that adding spirits of wine stopped fermentation, preserved part of the natural sugar in the wine and prevented it turning to vinegar. This was the birth of *vin doux naturel* (V.D.N.), naturally sweet wine. The method, called *mutage* or muting, ensured these durable wines a considerable success throughout the Middle Ages.

After he had finally gobbled up Roussillon in 1659, the French king Louis XIV introduced

Unusual wine specialties have been produced along the rocky coast between delightful Collioure and the Spanish Costa Brava since the Middle Ages.

Unusual wine specialties have been produced along the rocky coast between delightful Collioure and the Spanish Costa Brava since the Middle Ages.

the wines to his court in Versailles, and Voltaire became a great fan of Muscat de Rivesaltes.

Its long and fascinating history was turned to good advantage by Roussillon-born astronomer and politician François Aragon to get the special characteristics of *vin doux naturel* legally recognized in 1872. An *appellation* followed in 1936, when areas of cultivation, grape varieties, degrees of ripeness, yields, vinification, and minimum aging were specified. The driest and hottest slopes and terraces of Roussillon are reserved for V.D.N.s. The grapes must have developed a minimum 9 ounces (252 g) of sugar per quart (liter), corresponding to a potential alcohol content of 14.4 percent. Such a high degree of ripeness was attained not just by the sun, but also by limited yields of 321 gallons per acre (30 hl/ha) or less. After fermentation set in, the grower or vintner monitored conversion of sugar into alcohol. He chose the moment to add the pure and tasteless spirits of wine to the fermenting must, thus determining the character of the finished wine. The earlier he interrupted the fermentation, the higher the residual sugar content. The longer he waited, the drier the wine. The specifications say that the sugar residue value must be between 1.5 ounces and 4.5 ounces (50 g and 125 g) and the finished wine should have a total rating—alcohol + sugar residue—of 21.5 percent. The spirits of wine added thus varies between 5 percent and 10 percent by volume, the alcoholic strength between 16 percent and 18.5 percent. Roussillon produces 90 percent of French *vin doux naturels*.

Of the four varieties mainly permitted for them (Muscat, Macabeo, Malvoisie, and

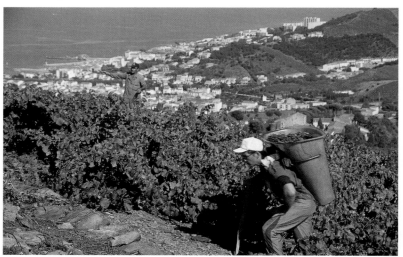

Grenache), the last-named, or to be more precise, Grenache Noir and not the likewise cultivated variants Grenache Blanc and Gris, has special status in that it gives the highest-quality Banyuls, Maury, and Rivesaltes their character. Whereas with simpler qualities, the spirits of wine is added to the must, with the best wines it is poured over the macerated grapes—which is called *mutage sur grains*—and macerated with them for several days, or often up to two to four weeks. During this period, the increased alcohol content releases pigments, aromatic substances, and tannins from the skins before pressing is carried out and part of the alcohol is thereby lost.

Traditional Banyuls, Maury, and Rivesaltes are aged in great tuns, in which they are intentionally exposed to oxidation.

To speed up the development of aromas, the wines are in part exposed to the high temperature contrasts between day and night, summer and winter by being placed outside in the open air in *demi-muids* (tuns holding 159 gallons (600 liters)) or even in demijohns, as at Mas Amiel. The bouquet and flavor of traditional V.D.N.s in the first phase of aging are reminiscent of stewed fruits, fresh figs, peaches, and candied cherries. There follows a phase in which dried fruits such as prunes, raisins, figs, and apricots dominate. Further aging—from around the seventh year—brings out roasting aromas such as rusks, roast nuts, and caramel. Then come cocoa, coffee, and later tobacco until finally, after 15 to 20 years, RANCIO tones, the same as one finds in very old cognacs, old dry sherries and *vins jaunes* from the Jura, reminiscent of the aroma of green walnut husks.

Since 1975 an additional type of sweet wine has been added to the range—Vintage, which is often called *Rimage* in Banyuls. These are usually dark red wines bottled early, and are highly juicy and thick. Their intense smell is principally that of fresh ripe cherries with overtones of berries, and the sweetness of the grape sugar hides the mostly very marked tannins. They age like great red wines, as the sweetness becomes steadily more discreet.

V.D.N.s are also made from white varieties (or a combination of them with Grenache Noir) that age beautifully. After ten or more years they often develop aromas of dried apricots, orange peel and—with some Muscat—a touch of pine resin. In their young days, Macabeo and Grenache Blanc remain rather reserved as sweet wines. In popularity and quality they are far outstripped by Muscat de Rivesaltes. This is based on Muscat of Alexandria with its large berries and Muscat Blanc à Petits Grains, which

Traditionally, Banyuls wines are aged in 159-gallon (600-liter) tuns in the open air. The radically forced oxidation thereby attained helps their complex aromas to unfurl.

has very small ripe golden berries. Vinified as a white wine at lower temperatures, in Roussillon it possesses very intensive fresh aromas of lemons or peaches, and occasional overtones of broom, fennel, and aniseed. A young Muscat should always have a very pale tone. In Languedoc, Muscat wines are also produced in St-Jean-de-Minervois, Frontignan, Lunel and Mireval, and at Beaumes-de-Venise in the Rhône area. The only dark V.D.N. outside Roussillon comes from Rasteau.

Chilled to 53–59°F (12–15°C), Banyuls, Maury, and Rivesaltes are pleasant aperitifs, and despite their intense aromas do not impair following wines. They are excellent with *foie gras* and duck dishes prepared with fruit, and go well with goat's cheeses and blue cheeses. As a dessert, they are served with cakes, and their association with chocolate desserts is legendary, the only wines that can easily cope with them, especially the young vintages or dry Banyuls. Once they develop ripe aromas, the connoisseur drinks them as a digestive and enjoys their stunning complexity.

ECKHARD SUPP, DUNJA ULBRICHT, STEFFEN MAUS

ITALY

The History of Italian Wine

Not only is Italy one of the most important wine-producing countries in Europe today, it is also one of the continent's oldest producers. Recent archeological finds have shown that the vine was first systematically cultivated in Italy by the Etruscans in the 8th century BC although viticulture did not arrive in France until the 6th century BC when the Greeks introduced it from their colony Massalia (Marseille). We can assume that efforts were made to cultivate the vine even earlier though clear proof of this has not yet been established. With the advent of the Roman Empire advanced skills and expertise in viticulture and winemaking spread throughout Western and Central Europe. The Romans were also responsible for the development of the wine trade into a very profitable economic activity. Pompeii, the port at the foot of Mount Vesuvius, evolved into the most important wine-trading city in the ancient world, and its destruction as a result of the volcanic eruption of AD 79 paved the way for the establishment of regional wine centers throughout the Roman Empire. The resulting rise of wine may have contributed to the fact that the total ban on the drunken revelry of the Bacchanalia (the Roman variant of the Greek cult of Dionysus), which was pronounced as early as 186 BC, was more honored in the breach than in the observance. With the rise of Christianity and up to its recognition as a state religion in the 4th century, the consumption of wine in the context of cult activities became more moderate.

No other Italian wine matures for so long and with such *grandezza* as Barolo, the great wine of Piedmont.

The city of Florence—renowned not only for culture and art but also for the wines of Tuscany, grown and produced on its doorstep.

Regional wine production figures		Source: Ismea, Istat 2003
Region	Vineyards in acres (ha) (2000)	Production in 1,000 gal (1,000 hl) (1997–2001)
Abruzzi	82,780 (33,500)	104,185 (3,959)
Apulia	210,030 (85,000)	202,235 (7,685)
Basilicata	19,025 (7,700)	13,158 (500)
Calabria	148,010 (59,900)	170,525 (6,480)
Campania	43,985 (17,800)	29,790 (1,132)
Emilia Romagna	33,360 (13,500)	21,050 (800)
Friuli-Venezia Giulia	71,900 (29,100)	53,235 (2,023)
Lazio	71,410 (28,900)	87,765 (3,335)
Liguria	7,410 (3,000)	3,945 (150)
Lombardy	54,360 (22,000)	38,155 (1,450)
Marches	48,925 (19,800)	45,235 (1,719)
Molise	14,580 (5,900)	9,210 (350)
Piedmont	129,970 (52,600)	84,765 (3,221)
Sardinia	63,255 (25,600)	24,370 (926)
Sicily	275,760 (111,600)	208,895 (7,938)
Trentino-Alto Adige	144,055 (58,300)	63,870 (2,427)
Tuscany	34,100 (13,800)	30,735 (1,168)
Umbria	35,090 (14,200)	23,685 (900)
Valle d'Aosta	1,235 (500)	790 (30)
Veneto	181,865 (73,600)	220,105 (8,364)
Total	1,671,114 (676,300)	1,282,703 (54,557)

The fall of the Western Roman Empire in AD 476 heralded a period of fundamental change in Italy, and the unrest arising from the migration of the peoples had a detrimental effect on all activities which require generations of peace and tranquillity. Wine growing and production, and particularly the creation of fine wines, declined. When a market for wine re-emerged with the rise of the trade centers of Genoa, Florence, and Venice, and the growth in the affluence enjoyed by their inhabitants, trade in wines from Bordeaux, Burgundy, the Rhine, and the Danube developed into a profitable business. Some of the names which are still well known in the world of wine today were established as early as the 13th and 14th centuries. These include the Antinoris, whose wealth was initially based on the silk trade, and the Frescobaldis, who financed the brisk trade in goods between Bordeaux and the English crown, and collected taxes in London on behalf of the popes.

While Italian bankers and traders made good profits from wine imports, vine cultivation in Italy itself survived only in the form of a subsistence activity among the—mainly extremely poor —rural population. In some regions of Italy, the wine-growing tradition only survived due to the work of the monasteries. This decline lasted into the 19th century when signs of a new beginning finally emerged in Piedmont and Tuscany. Vine varieties such as Barolo, Brunello, and Chianti were developed on the basis of the French models with the active involvement of French enologists. Within 150 years these wines were among the most popular and best in the world. The Italian schools of ENOLOGY, and wineries such as Gancia, Cinzano, and Bolla, which remain famous to the present day, were founded at this time.

In Italy, the ravages of PHYLLOXERA almost succeeded in bringing the aspiring wine culture to a standstill and the two world wars of the 20th century also played their part in blocking its development. During the difficult years in the aftermath of the Second World War, an approach which favored the planting of highly productive vineyards and the selection of high-yielding rather than qualitatively superior vine varieties became established. This trend was also supported by the French wine industry which provided a growing market for Italian "plonk" to mix with its own table wines, following the decline in supplies from its former colony Algeria.

THE NORTHWEST
Valle d'Aosta
Piedmont
Liguria
Lombardy

THE NORTHEAST
Trentino
Alto Adige (Southern Tyrol)
Friuli-Venezia Giulia
Veneto
Emilia Romagna

CENTRAL ITALY
Marches
Tuscany
Umbria
Lazio

SOUTHERN ITALY AND THE ISLANDS
Abruzzi
Molise
Apulia
Campania
Calabria
Basilicata
Sardinia
Sicily
Wine-growing areas in neighboring countries

60 miles (100 km)

Upturn and Obstacles

This trend toward increasingly high yields in Italy reflected the fact that during the food shortages of the post-war years, wine was not a luxury but considered to be an important source of calories. Consumer behavior did not begin to change in this regard until the 1960s when the annual per capita consumption of wine by the Italians initially decreased from 30 to 16 gallons (110 to 60 l).

At the same time, there was a radical shift in viticulture to an emphasis on quality, despite the scandal which shocked the entire country in the mid-1980s when it emerged that a group of irresponsible producers had sought to "improve" cheap wine through the addition of methanol.

Within a few weeks over 20 people died after drinking the contaminated wine.

The upturn in the fortunes of winemaking started in Tuscany where a completely new category of wines emerged: the Supertuscan table wines, which were made with the hitherto uncommon French vine varieties Cabernet Sauvignon, Merlot, Chardonnay, and Syrah and generally matured in small *barriques* made of new oak wood. Throughout the 1970s and 1980s, the new generations of winegrowers and producers looked to France and the New World for inspiration and tried to implement the new insights they gained there at home in Italy.

It was shortly after this that the equally radical process of the modernization of Barolo and Barbera started in Piedmont, with the aim of producing more intensely-colored, fruitier wines to satisfy the sophisticated tastes of the international market. While this development initially only affected winery practices, in the 1990s the focus shifted to the vineyards. Old and obsolete vineyards were cleared and replaced with modern more quality-oriented cultivation systems.

At the same time, Italian wine legislation was at least partly adapted to the new realities and requirements of the international markets. A new category of wine was created, that of the table wine with denomination of origin (*Indicazione Geografica Tipica*, I.G.T.), and thanks to changes in production regulations, a series of former table wines could be marketed as quality wines with denominated (and guar-anteed) origin (*Denominazione di Origine Controllata/ e Garantita*, D.O.C./D.O.C.G.).

Finally, Italian wine producers began to appreciate and exploit the country's vast but largely unused stock of indigenous vine varieties and took the first steps toward improving the stocks. This is where the most important challenge and opportunity for the future of winemaking in Italy lies, as the fashion for "international" grape varieties may well die and consumers will once again favor the specialties and unique characteristics of wines from individual countries.

The Nebbiolo grape matures to unique perfection on the slopes surrounding Barolo, the Piedmontese village which gave its name to Italy's most famous red wine.

HIERARCHY, ITALIAN STYLE

Although Cosimo III de'Medici first defined the Chianti area in 1716, and awarded the world's first binding *appellation* to Carmignano red wine, the legislation defining categories of wine and geographical provenance in Italy did not come into force until 1963. The principles of this law, which give legal protection to controlled production zones and wines, are still in place today. The law divided wine production into two classes in accordance with the European standard: table wines (*vini da tavola*) and quality or D.O.C. wines (DENOMINAZIONE DI ORIGINE CONTROLLATA) which were henceforth subject to precise regulations with respect to the vine varieties used in their production, the geographical provenance of the grapes, and vine cultivation and winery practices. The production statute for the first D.O.C. zone was developed for the Tuscan white wine Vernaccia di San Gimignano, three years after the passing of the new legislation. In subsequent years, over 300 of these D.O.C. denominations were established.

A MISSED OPPORTUNITY

The increase in the number of D.O.C. zones was accompanied by a growing criticism of the inadequacy of the options available to differentiate between the quality of individual *appellations*. While the market had long since created clear price-based distinctions, high-quality wines were otherwise deemed the equals of their basic mass-produced counterparts. Thus an additional classification was created at the top of the quality pyramid to designate wines whose quality was both controlled and guaranteed (DENOMINAZIONE DI ORIGINE CONTROLLATA E GARANTITA,

Morning mists in Carmignano, west of Florence.

D.O.C.G.). These wines were subject to more stringent production regulations, lower maximum yields, and longer aging. This mark of distinction was conferred on some of Italy's most prestigious wines, such as Barolo, Barbaresco, Brunello, Chianti, and Vino Nobile di Montalcino. However, when it was awarded to wines of less distinguished provenance, such as Albana di Romagna, Asti Spumante, and Vernaccia di San Gimignano, an important opportunity to establish a real quality hierarchy was missed.

Moreover, with their combination of bureaucratic detail and *laissez-faire* implementation, the production regulations were soon perceived by many top producers as a hindrance. Innovative growers realized that their efforts to improve their wines, for example through the introduction of changes in the composition of blends, were irreconcilable with the excessively precise regulations prescribed by the law. A winemaker who wanted to produce a Chianti Classico from 100 percent Sangiovese grapes, instead of the mandatory blend of red and white grapes, was just as far outside the legal framework as one who wanted to mature Barolo or Brunello in smaller new wooden barrels, or one wishing to process some of the indigenous Friulian vine varieties.

The most important Italian D.O.C.G. wines		
D.O.C.G. designation	Region	Main vine variety
Asti	Piedmont	Moscato
Barbaresco	Piedmont	Nebbiolo (single-varietal)
Barolo	Piedmont	Nebbiolo (single-varietal)
Brunello di Montalcino	Tuscany	Sangiovese (single-varietal)
Carmignano	Tuscany	Sangiovese, Cabernet
Chianti	Tuscany	Sangiovese
Chianti Classico	Tuscany	Sangiovese
Franciacorta	Lombardy	Chardonnay, Pinot Noir
Sagrantino di Montefalco	Umbria	Sagrantino
Taurasi	Campania	Aglianico (single-varietal)
Torgiano Rosso Riserva	Umbria	Sangiovese
Valtellina Superiore	Valtellina	Nebbiolo
Vernaccia di San Gimignano	Tuscany	Vernaccia
Vino Nobile di Montepulciano	Tuscany	Sangiovese

However, the Italian winegrowers were very resourceful. They simply defined their new wines as table wines, ignoring the fact that, for example, it was not possible to specify the year on the label. Thanks to their outstanding quality and some clever marketing, they quickly achieved prices which made most quality wines with protected *appellations* look like cheap mass-produced goods. Legislators were not pleased by the undermining of the quality hierarchy, and responded by revising the law in the 1990s. Under the new regulations, there is greater flexibility in the definition of the D.O.C.s and D.O.C.G.s and the ridiculously long cask-aging periods were reduced. Many of the super table wines were then marketed with an official denomination of origin and year, under the name *vini da tavola con indicazione geografica* or *Indicazione Geografica Tipica* (I.G.T.), while others were reclassified as D.O.C.s. Under the new hierarchy there are four categories:

• Table wines (*vini da tavola*) whose labels do not include information about the wine's geographical origin and year.
• I.G.T. wines whose labels include information about the geographical provenance, vine variety, specific vineyard, and year.
• D.O.C. wines (*Denominazione di Origine Controllata*).

Production volumes and regions of the main D.O.C. and D.O.C.G. wines		Source: Federdoc 2001
Designation of origin	Region	Volume 1,000 gal (1,000 hl)
Asti Spumante or Moscato d'Asti D.O.C.G.	Piedmont	20,000 (760)
Barbera d'Asti D.O.C.	Piemont	7,895 (300)
Oltrepò pavese D.O.C.	Lombardy	21,580 (820)
Bardolino D.O.C.	Veneto	7,630 (290)
Prosecco D.O.C.	Veneto	11,050 (420)
Soave D.O.C.	Veneto	18,420 (700)
Valpolicella D.O.C.	Veneto	13,945 (530)
Trentino D.O.C.	Trentino	12,105 (460)
Südtirol D.O.C.	Alto-Adige	9,210 (350)
Friaul Grave D.O.C.	Friuli	15,265 (580)
Colli Piacentini D.O.C.	Emilia Romagna	8,945 (340)
Lambrusco D.O.C.	Emilia Romagna	14,210 (540)
Sangiovese di Romagna D.O.C.	Emilia Romagna	7,370 (280)
Chianti Classico D.O.C.G.	Tuscany	8,685 (330)
Chianti D.O.C.G.	Tuscany	26,315 (1,000)
Verdicchio D.O.C.	Marche	7,630 (290)
Frascati D.O.C.	Lazio	6,840 (260)
Montepulciano d'Abruzzo D.O.C.	Abruzzi	21,840 (830)
Salice Salentino D.O.C.	Apulia	8,160 (310)

• D.O.C.G. quality wines (*Denominazione di Origine Controllata e Garantita*), with various additional labels, including RISERVA (longer cask aging); *superiore* (relating to alcohol content or maximum yield); *classico* (wine originating from the historical center of the cultivation area); and *vigna/vigneto* (single-vineyard bottling).

The towers of San Gimignano—symbols of the quest for power in medieval Italy.

Varieties for the Future

Italy's vineyards offer what is probably the largest resource of different types of the species *Vitis vinifera*. While the 12 most common varieties (see table on page 343) account for what is grown in more than half of the country's vineyards, dozens of other economically relevant varieties exist, in addition to probably hundreds of subspecies which survive hidden on a few acres of vineyard waiting to be rediscovered and transformed into quality wines.

Although the white varieties can easily compete with red in terms of quantity, Italy's truly great wines, with a few exceptions, are red. The prestige of all Italian viticulture rests on two grape varieties: Sangiovese and Nebbiolo (which is cultivated in less than one percent of Italian vineyards and is only really successful in a few locations).

Nebbiolo

Barolo and Barbaresco, Piedmont's top-quality wines, are pressed from Nebbiolo grapes. Nebbiolo is also the basis of other single-varietal and blended D.O.C. and D.O.C.G. wines, such as Gattinara, Ghemme, Roero, and the Lombardy *appellation*, Valtellina. This vine, which is also known as Spanna, Picutener, and Chiavennasca, is grown in cooler areas and is far less suited to excessive yields than other varieties. Its small fruit give a dark tannic wine. The distinctive features of the great Nebbiolo wines include

their dense, ruby-red, shimmering color and their aroma of tea leaves, spices, roses, and sometimes even a hint of tar. Extremely harsh and tannic when young, they age into outstanding, soft, alluring, and gratifying wines.

Sangiovese and its French Partners

Sangiovese, Italy's second top red variety, provides the basis for very famous wines, such as Brunello, Chianti, and Vino Nobile which are all produced in Tuscany. Torgiano and Montefalco, two other major representatives of the variety, are produced in Umbria. Romagna also has extensive tracts of Sangiovese. Here, however, in contrast to the fine, complex wines of Tuscany, it mainly yields rather light and sweet everyday wines, except for those produced from grapes harvested on the higher slopes.

The variety probably originated in Tuscany and is believed to have been known to the Etruscans. Its wines are characterized by a lively acidity and complex TANNIN structure which is why they lack the powerful and compact effect of Cabernet, for example. To compensate for this late-ripening variety's vulnerability in cooler weather conditions—causing high acidity and forcing the tannins to remain green and raw—it has generally been blended with other varieties to provide color, fruit, sweetness, and mildness. The traditional recipe for Chianti Classico, which actually used white grapes, is rarely used now, and single-varietal Sangiovese or blends with French varieties are more common—smooth and fruity Merlot has become a particular favorite in recent years.

As well as their use for blending with Sangiovese, the French Cabernet Sauvignon and Merlot varieties are well established in Italy in their own right. Introduced in the late 19th century, particularly in the north in response to the phylloxera disaster, up to the post-war years, Merlot was, in fact, Italy's most common variety. The advent of the Tuscan wine revolution brought these vines into focus once again. Sassicaia, the country's first major Cabernet Sauvignon wine, proved that this variety was suited to conditions in Italy. The Supertuscan table wines, which earned an international reputation for quality Italian winemaking, were based on this model. The fact that their Cabernet was almost impossible to distinguish

Hitherto, modern wine production tended to concentrate on only a dozen varieties. However, Italy's vineyards are host to a wealth of old, indigenous, and often unresearched varieties which are now attracting increasing interest among enologists and producers.

from French and Californian ones did not occur to critical Italian winemakers and producers until a very late stage.

In contrast, for many decades Merlot was merely used in the production of thin, acidic, mass-produced wines. It was not until the late 1980s and early 1990s that Tuscan and then Friulian Merlots came onto the market. These wines finally exploited the potential of this excellent variety to create intensely-colored, soft, full-bodied wines with a firm tannin structure and lovely fruit AROMAS. The fact that the two joint-venture companies in Tuscany, founded by the Californian Mondavi producers, have taken to blending Merlot with Sangiovese, is an indication of the potential of this early-maturing variety which, with its fruity wines, is perhaps more suitable than the originally favored Cabernet Sauvignon.

BARBERA AND UNDISCOVERED TREASURES

Since the 1980s, Italian producers have worked more intensively with other native varieties. The Piedmontese wine Barbera has enjoyed one of the most astonishing careers in European wine-making. Originally an acidic outsider, it developed to earn a reputation as a dense, spicy, modern, top-quality red. The major southern varieties, Aglianico, Negroamaro, Primitivo, Nero d'Avola, and Uva di Troia have also finally been enjoying a little of the attention they richly deserve. Northern Friuli is something of an exception. Here, the three outstanding red varieties, Refosco, Pignolo, and Schioppettino, survived and have been used to produce high-quality wines in recent decades. Finally, when Corvina—the basis for the great Amarone wine of the Veneto—is added to the list, Italy indeed emerges as a rich treasure-house which will continue to inspire great creativity in future decades.

WHITE VARIETIES

The story of the Italian white grape varieties couldn't be more different. Few areas in Italy are really suited to the production of great white wines. And while, for red wines, high-quality Sangiovese also leads the field in terms of quantity, the quantity league for whites is mainly led by grape varieties whose good wines are the exception rather than the rule. For example, Moscato Bianco—used in the production of the single-varietal Moscato d'Asti as well as the wonderful dessert wines of the island of Pantelleria—and Malvasia can give very interesting wines, but they are mostly used in mass

There can be no doubt the future lies with unique varieties like Sangiovese as opposed to the virtually ubiquitous international varieties. Sangiovese is the key to the outstanding character of the great Tuscan reds but it has yet to yield convincing results in other areas.

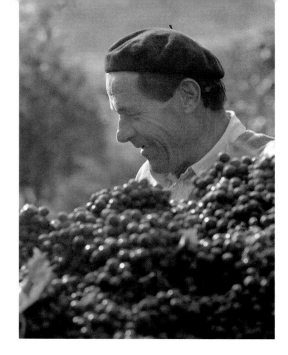

production where excessive yields are incompatible with high-quality production. Of the Trebbiano wines, none stands out in terms of complexity of taste; in France this variety is justifiably used in brandy distillation under the name "Ugni Blanc." The same applies to the Venetian Garganega variety, although it occasionally produces delightful sweet wines of the *appellation* Recioto di Soave. Along with the Tuscan white Vernaccia, the Piedmontese Arneis and Cortese, and Verdicchio from the Marches, it has failed to turn Italy into a country of white wines. Producers finally latched onto the French varieties Chardonnay and Sauvignon Blanc as part of the Italian wine revolution, but they have quickly discovered that these varieties are only really suited for cultivation in a few areas, such as Alto Adige (Southern Tyrol), eastern Friuli and a few upland areas in central and southern Italy. In addition, the enthusiasm of the international markets for these varieties, which are cultivated in vast quantities throughout the world, is threatening to wane in the not-too-distant future.

Varieties and their area of cultivation in 1,000s of acres (hectares)			*Source: Ismea, Istat 2003*
Rebsorte	1990	2000	Change
Sangiovese	213 (86.2)	172.2 (69.7)	–19%
Catarrato Bianco	160.6 (65)	106.7 (43.2)	–33%
Trebbiano Toscano	144.6 (58.5)	105 (42.5)	–27%
Montepulciano	76.6 (31)	73.6 (29.8)	–4%
Barbera	116.4 (47.1)	69.9 (28.3)	–40%
Merlot	78.8 (31.9)	63.2 (25.6)	–20%
Trebbiano Romagnolo	52.6 (21.3)	49.4 (20)	–6%
Negroamaro	77.6 (31.4)	41.5 (16.8)	–47%
Moscato Bianco	33.3 (13.5)	32.9 (13.3)	–2%
Chardonnay	15.3 (6.2)	29.1 (11.8)	+90%
Garganega	32.1 (13)	28.6 (11.6)	–11%
Nero d'Avola	35 (14.2)	28.1 (11.4)	–20%

THE NORTHWEST:
THE ALPS, THE APENNINES, AND THE PO

A view of Alberetto della Torre in Piedmont against the snow-capped Alps.

ticated red varieties positively thrive in its Alpine setting. It is surprisingly warm and dry here during the mid-year period, and the steep wine terraces benefit from every ray of sunlight. Similar conditions can be found in the Valtellina and Veltlin, on the Swiss border of Lombardy, where some of the most interesting results are obtained from Nebbiolo vines.

THE RIVIERA AND THE ADRIATIC COASTS

The situation in the rest of Lombardy, which opens out to the wide, misty plain of the Po toward the Adriatic Sea and is subject to its climatic influence, couldn't be more different. Even northern Italy can offer Mediterranean conditions in places where large expanses of water contribute to the regulation of the temperature, for example Lakes Iseo and Garda with their mineral-rich, gravelly, moraine soils. However, most Lombardian wines originate from the climatically less fortunate areas of Oltrepò Pavese on the northern foothills of the Ligurian Apennines, facing the Lombardy plain.

The vines that grow in elongated Liguria, the southernmost of the northwestern regions which extends along the southern edge of the Apennines, enjoy excesses of heat and sun. The sea-facing vineyards enjoy optimum conditions for quality production but, given the extremely difficult working conditions, they are rarely exploited to the full.

YOUNG GROWERS, NEW WINES

A fresh wind is blowing throughout the Northwest. The developments that have taken place over the past two decades, particularly in the Barolo area, can be described without hesitation as a revolution in winemaking. It all started with work on the vineyards. Inspired by experience gained in visits to France during the 1970s and 1980s, many young growers decided to reduce yields, mainly by means of radical crop-thinning in summer, to enable them to harvest fully ripe and extremely concentrated grapes in autumn.

The changes in winery practices were even more radical. Many producers replaced their stock of wooden casks—in which the Barolo was often stored, to its detriment, for excessive periods—with temperature-controlled stainless steel FERMENTATION tanks, and *barriques* for

Northwest Italy consists of four regions whose landscapes and climate vary considerably: Valle d'Aosta, Piedmont, Liguria, and Lombardy.

Piedmont lies sheltered by the western flank of the Alps which runs almost seamlessly into the Ligurian Apennines in the west and opens out onto the plain of the river Po. Its varied hilly landscape and soils are eminently suited to viticulture—the lime-rich marl of the Langhe hills in particular providing optimum conditions for top-quality wines. The region is the home of one of the world's best red varieties, Nebbiolo, and one of today's most popular sparkling wines, Asti or Asti Spumante.

A CONTINENTAL CLIMATE

Although Alba, Piedmont's most famous wine-producing area, is on the same latitude as Bordeaux, the two regions enjoy completely different climatic conditions. Unlike the Bordelais region, where the extremely mild sea climate is particularly suitable for vine cultivation, the seasons in Piedmont are dominated by a rather continental climate. With its short, dry summers, long and often foggy autumns, and very cold winters, the region does not conform to the stereotype of the Italian climate.

Viticulture is therefore only found in areas which are exposed to the alleviating influence of river valleys or on protected south-facing slopes where the heat of the sun can be exploited to the full. The Valle d'Aosta, for example, enjoys this combination of features, and sophis-

Modern wine production in *barriques* and stainless steel tanks at Rocche de Manzoni.

aging. While traditionalists were originally critical of the extremely brief fermentation and MACERATION periods, and the practice of aging the wines in new *barriques*, most were eventually spurred on to introduce one or more carefully considered innovations and often produced amazingly good wines in the 1980s and 1990s.

New Methods, all Varieties

The producers in Barbaresco and areas around Langhe, Roero, and Monferrato tentatively followed the example of the *Barolisti*. The results of the Barolo experiments also helped to improve the results obtained from other grape varieties: Barbera, which attained the status of a top international wine thanks of barrel-aging; Dolcetto, whose more clearly-defined fruit was greeted with enthusiasm; and, finally, Grignolino, Freisa, and the imported French varieties.

Even the white wines started to make progress but they failed to mirror the successes of the reds. Gavi and Arneis, from Roero, initially seemed to be capable of developing into fashionable wines, but their taste profile remained too neutral to withstand the competition from

Brachetto is a rare Piedmontese variety used to produce very unusual light red sparkling wines with an intense raspberry aroma.

French, German, and overseas whites. Asti only succeeded in meeting the increasing requirements of the international markets with its light, fruity variety, Moscato d'Asti, and, despite its elevation to D.O.C.G. status, still lost ground.

Progress in Lombardy

While the response to the new quality philosophy was tentative in Valle d'Aosta and Liguria, which mainly produce for the domestic market, the successes achieved in parts of Lombardy were almost as impressive as those of Piedmont. The Franciacorta area, in particular, distinguished itself. The producers from Lake Iseo achieved major successes in the quality of both bottle-fermented sparkling wines and still wines, which are usually based on blends of indigenous and international grape varieties.

Northwest Italy is, therefore, well armed for the future. The excessive price trends in the case of certain *appellations* is, however, casting a shadow. This is less true of the producers of the really top-quality wines than of those lower down the scale who sometimes demand top prices for wines which could not be described as top-quality.

Regional grape varieties in the Northwest

The Northwest is home to a wide variety of enological treasures in the form of indigenous vine varieties which have only been introduced to a wider audience in recent decades, particularly Dolcetto, which is popular in Piedmont and Liguria. This early-ripening, unproblematic variety yields fruity red wines which are low in acidity and have a characteristic cherry and pepper aroma. They should be drunk in their first two or three years.

The other Piedmontese red VARIETALS, such as Freisa which is often available in fizzy or semi-sparkling form, the light and intensely aromatic Grignolino, Pelaverga, Ruchè (Rouchet), Croatina, Bonarda, Vespolina, and the Muscat-like Brachetto, have hitherto been undervalued, even at regional level.

With its Petite Arvine, Premetta, and Petit Rouge, the Valle d'Aosta also has its indigenous red varieties whose sometimes very interesting wines receive no international attention. The same applies to Lombardy where, in addition to the native Groppello, varieties from the neighboring regions of Trentino, Veneto, and Emilia Romagna are also vinified: Schiava, Marzemino, Corvina, and Lambrusco.

Two exceptional regional white varieties can be found in Liguria: Vermentino, which is also cultivated in Sardinia, Tuscany, and France, and the indigenous Pigato, which yields pleasant fruity wines. The other whites tend to be more neutral in character and this is particularly true of the Piedmontese varieties Cortese (which is the base wine for Gavi), Arneis, and Favorita. The acidic Erbaluce is only suitable for the production of sparkling wine and sugary sweet wines. The Valle d'Aosta can add a Pinot Gris—known here as Malvasia—to the list, and the indigenous specialty of Blanc de Morgex. In Lombardy, Garganega, a variety from the neighboring region of the Veneto, deservedly attracts some attention.

Valle d'Aosta:
Specialties from the Foot of the Alps

Wine production reached this strategically important valley at the latest with the Roman legionaries. From their fortress of Augusta Praetoria, today known as Aosta, the Romans controlled the Alpine passes via the Great and Little St. Bernhard and also started to cultivate the land. The Aosta valley, which was a constant object of tension between France, Italy, and Switzerland right into modern times, is a unique viticultural world. The spectacular narrow vine terraces on the steep cliff walls are the highest in Europe and climb to heights of up to 4,265 feet (1,300 m). They lend the numerous indigenous vine varieties their distinctive character and the valley's most individual wines originate here.

The producers have benefited since time immemorial from the special climatic conditions along the Dora Baltea river. This horseshoe-shaped valley, framed by the Valais and French Alps, which are 13,120 feet (4,000 m) high, is one of Europe's most protected and driest areas. The climate is characterized by extreme winters and hot summers. Day and night temperatures differ significantly, which ensures ideal conditions for the formation of strong, fruity aromas during the growing season. While many of the high regions are suitable for growing white wine varieties with a good acidic balance, the south-facing terraces of the central valley—the best locations of all—are also suitable for the production of full-bodied reds.

After Roman times, wine production in this area was continued by Italian monks. The valley has the clergy to thank not only for planting the

Amphitheater of vines near Donnas (in the lower Valle d'Aosta).

terrace vineyards but also for their contribution to the preservation of this labor-intensive mountain viticulture right into the 20th century. Some of the monks made a name for themselves and their wines which spread beyond the region's borders, for example Don Augusto Pramontton, who produced a legendary Malvoisie de Nus from raisined Pinot Gris grapes. Although the area under cultivation continuously decreased in size over the 20th century, from around 7,410 to 1,235 acres (3,000 to 500 ha), it is now believed that a turning point has been reached in the valley. With financial aid from the state, the region's 2,400—mostly part-time—wine producers have rekindled their interest and ambitions for the business.

Varieties and Specialties

Around three quarters of the regional wineries have now regained D.O.C. status and are marketed under the D.O.C. *appellation* "Valle d'Aosta/Vallée d'Aoste" (the bilingualism is a legacy from the 9th century, when the Aosta valley belonged to the French kingdom of Savoie), with 27 types of wine and 22 authorized grape varieties defined in the regulations. Of these, the specialties produced from the indigenous vine varieties are particularly interesting.

Of the whites, the Petite Arvine—which is also cultivated in Valais in neighboring Switzerland—and the Blanc de Valdigne yield the most distinctive wines. The latter is used in the production of the well-known Blanc de Morgex et La Salle from the upper end of the valley. Its origin in Europe's highest mountain vineyards has earned it the nickname *Bianco dei ghiacciai*, "wine of the glaciers." Its producers, most of whom are members of the local cooperative, only work around 37 acres (15 ha) of vineyards and the vines are mainly cultivated on low pergolas. The Blanc de Valdigne, which is highly resistant to phylloxera, is one of the few European varieties which are not grafted onto American rootstocks but planted with its original roots. The climatic conditions of the steep terraces produce grapes which yield light-colored, spirited and often slightly fizzy wines with a citrus-like freshness and the aroma of mountain herbs.

Of the remaining white varieties, Moscato di Chambave stands out. This wine is produced in both a dry version and from raisined fruit for dessert wine (called PASSITO or Flétry in one of the local dialects). White wines are also produced from Müller-Thurgau, Pinot Blanc, Pinot Gris, Pinot Noir, and Chardonnay.

PETIT ROUGE—"THE LITTLE RED"

The indigenous Petit Rouge is used in the production of single-varietal and blended red wines which offer a unique embodiment of the raw, earthy character of the landscape. In Enfer d'Arvier, with its clear berry aroma, underlined with pepper and spice notes, it represents 85 percent of the total volume and is complemented by the native varieties Vien de Nus, Neyret, Gamay, and Pinot Noir. Torette, which originates from the Nus area and is cask-aged for six to eight months, consists of 70 percent Petit Rouge to which Fumin, Neyret, and Vien de Nus as well as Dolcetto, Gamay, and Pinot Noir are added.

The sensitive Nebbiolo matures on the central and lower reaches of the Dora Baltea valley. In high areas of up to 1,970 feet (600 m), above Pont-St-Martin, it is blended with small volumes

The Valle d'Aosta is enclosed by the Valais Alps, Mont Blanc, and the Graian Alps. One of the main trading routes near the region's most important vineyards was guarded from Fénis castle.

Grollo dell'amicizia — the wooden friendship drinking-vessel with six lips from Valle d'Aosta.

of Freisa, Neyret, or Vien de Nus to produce Donnas or Donnaz, a fruity and acidic, slightly rustic wine which is aged in wood for two years. Although it is lighter in structure than the famous Nebbiolo wines of Piedmont, after three to five years of bottle aging, Donnas can be an elegant and classy wine.

Needless to say, the advance of the international varieties did not halt at the high mountain backdrop of the Valle d'Aosta. Chardonnay, Cabernet, Merlot, and even Syrah can be found on numerous terraces. In some cases they yield interesting wines but in most, rather pedestrian products. Anyone wishing to become aquainted with the rare specialties of the Valle d'Aosta will find many treasures awaiting in the region's wineries and restaurants.

SELECT PRODUCERS OF THE VALLE D'AOSTA

COSTANTINO CHARRÈRE**–****
AYMAVILLES
27 acres (11 ha); bought-in grapes; 500,000 bottles
• *Wines include: Premetta, Vin de La Sabla, Les Fourches,*
→ *Le Crête di Costantino Charrère, Chardonnay Cuvée La Frissonière les Crêtes, Petite Arvine Champorette, Torrette Les Toules, La Tour: Fumin, Pinot Noir, Syrah*
In addition to the family estate which was established in 1955, Charrère also runs the Les Crêtes winery which is fitted out with the very latest equipment. With its almost full spectrum of Aosta D.O.C. varieties, this is one of the valley's few truly important producers.

COOPERATIVA CROTTA DI VEGNERON**
CHAMBAVE
74 acres (30 ha); 200,000 bottles • *Wines include: Chambave Moscato, Nus Malvoisie Passito, Nus Rosso, Müller-Thurgau, Pinot Noir, Gamay, Fumin*
The wines produced by this cooperative include some of the interesting types from the Valle d'Aosta. Its

Chambave Moscato and Müller-Thurgau are particularly consistent in terms of quality.

FONDAZIONE INSTITUT AGRICOLE RÉGIONAL***
AOSTA
17 acres (7 ha); 50,000 bottles • *Wines: Gamay, Pinot Noir, Petit Rouge, Müller-Thurgau, Pinot Gris, Trésor du Caveau, Sang des Salasses*
The red and white wines produced from the grapes grown in the institute's own vineyards are among the best of the Valle d'Aosta.

EZIO VOYAT**
CHAMBAVE
5 acres (2 ha); 15,000 bottles • *Wines: Rosso le Muraglie, Passito Le Muraglie, La Gazella*
Specialty: Moscato, Moscato Passito. The fourth generation of the Voyats appears to have missed the opportunity to become part of the new wave of quality Aosta wines.

PIEDMONT

Great past, great future—
top estate Elio Altare
(in La Morra).

Piedmont is mainly known as the home of two outstanding red wines: Barolo and Barbaresco. The former is often eulogized as the "wine of kings and king of wines," which suggests that it has enjoyed many centuries of tradition. However, neither of these cult wines was created until the second half of the 19th century, and the form in which they are known today did not emerge until the late 1970s. Nonetheless, Piedmont is a region with a long history of wine-making. The northwestern flank of the Alps, along with the Apennine mountain range, dictate climatic conditions which favor wine growing almost throughout the region, but above all in the provinces of Cuneo, Asti and Alessandria, Langhe, and Monferrato.

GREEKS OR ETRUSCANS?

It is not known whether the Greeks or Etruscans were responsible for introducing viticulture to this region. However, the long-established tradition of allowing the vines to be grown up trees or tall posts—*etrusco*—is at least a clue. The Romans did not value the wines of Piedmont very highly; Pliny the Elder does not include them in his list of the best Italian wines (although he mentions in his natural history an *"uvea spinea … quae sola alitur nebulis"* [a climbing vine … that is the only one which can withstand fog] which may refer to today's Nebbiolo). Following the fall of the Roman Empire, Piedmont became a passage area at the mercy of rival powers. During this period of economic insecurity, it was mainly the monks who engaged in wine production; it was not until the 13th century that Piedmont wine-making experienced a new lease of life. A reference to "Nibiol" appears in a document of 1268, from which it can be concluded that Nebbiolo is indeed an indigenous variety which

Grinzane Cavour—the birthplace of dry Nebbiolo.

is particularly well suited to the region's climate. A chronicle of the community of La Morra, on the northern periphery of today's Barolo area, contains a document dated 1512 which contains a reference to a "Nebiolum." In 1758 the town of Alba passed a decree prohibiting the import and use of wines from other wine-growing areas for blending, and specified a date for the start of harvesting. In addition to Nebbiolo, described at the time as being sweet and slightly fizzy, the main varieties cultivated in the area were Malvasia and Moscato.

The first dry Nebbiolo was created in the 19th century on the initiative of Camillo Cavour, the statesman who is renowned as the father of Italian unification. Around 1850 he employed the French enologist Louis Oudart to develop a dry red wine with good keeping properties, based on the Bordeaux model, for his own winery in Grinzane near Alba and for that of Marquise Giuletta Faletti von Barolo, a French-woman by birth. The result of Oudart's endeavors, a dry, full-bodied red wine which was given the name Barolo, enjoyed a privileged position from the beginning of its career. A successful politician with contacts in the royal house of Savoy and the aristocracy in the royal court in Turin, Cavour was well placed to launch his new wine. By 1896 it was one of Italy's best wines. Shortly before this, Domizio Cavazza had also succeeded in producing a dry Nebbiolo wine by fermenting all of the sugars. As the independent *appellation* Barbaresco, the latter at times enjoyed even greater appreciation than the more famous Barolo. Even phylloxera appears to have been impressed by this prestige, as Nebbiolo was spared when most of Piedmont's vines succumbed to its ravages in the late 19th century.

SMALL PRODUCERS VERSUS LARGE DOMAINS

Despite its prestige, the variety remained insignificant in terms of the quantity produced. Today barely three percent of Piedmontese wines are produced from this variety, a fact which is explained not least by its difficult requirements with respect to soil and climate. Instead, producers tended to favor the indigenous early-ripening Dolcetto and high-yielding Barbera, a choice largely dictated by economic factors.

In contrast to Tuscany, for example, ownership of the vineyards in Piedmont is extremely fragmented; for a long time many producers did not have sufficient capital to allow them to adopt a sophisticated quality-based approach. Unlike the rest of Italy, farmers here obtained relative freedom from the nobility at an early stage, but this brought no guarantees of economic independence as they still remained locked into a lease system. They were able to farm their smallholdings largely at their own discretion but the high taxes they were forced to pay ensured that they remained poor. Therefore, although viticulture had been part of the mixed-farming system since time immemorial, hardly any farmers had sufficient resources or enough land to sustain viable individual wine production. Even today, the region's largest estate, the Dogliani brothers' Batasiolo, has a mere 277 acres (112 ha) of vineyards. Consequently, the growers were forced to sell their products to a few wineries which, up to the 1980s, continued to exploit their position to obtain grapes, MUST, and even young wine at low prices.

The developments of recent decades, with quality wines yielding far better profits, has shifted the balance in favor of the individual producers. Whereas in the 19th century, only a few large landowners and affluent bourgeoisie established their own domains—including

Fog is a common phenomenon in the Langhe hills where some of the most popular wine regions are located, particularly near the river Tanaro which flows through the town of Alba.

Barale in Barolo (1870) and Pio Cesare in Alba (1881)—the upturn in recent decades afforded many others an opportunity to consolidate their holdings.

BAROLO LEADS THE WAY

Piedmont's success as a wine-producing region rests on Barolo. At one time known only to a select group of loyal followers, its more modern and accessible version, along with the Supertuscans, has become a symbol for the quality renaissance in Italian winemaking. Other wines also assumed a new revitalized allure in its wake: first the Barberas, whose vines occupy about half of the region's vineyard area, but also Dolcetto, Nebbiolo d'Alba, and Roero. Even the once famous, but subsequently almost forgotten, northern Piedmontese Gattinara and Ghemme attained new levels of quality and access to new markets.

With the exception of individual products from a handful of talented producers, the region's white wines fail to keep pace with the progress of the reds. This is true of the high-volume sparkling wine Asti as well as Gavi and Arneis, the blighted fashion wines whose celebrated career was limited to a single, fairly short and lukewarm season.

Northern Piedmont: Carema and Gattinara

The Nebbiolo vineyards of northern Piedmont are strung out like pearls on a necklace, along the Sesia river valley. Boca and Bramaterra are the northernmost D.O.C. zones situated on the foothills of the Monte Rosa massif. Bramaterra, Gattinara, Coste della Sesia, Lessona, Ghemme, Sizzano, Fara, and Colline Novaresi line the left and right banks of the Sesia downriver. The small vineyards in the narrow, mainly morainic hills, which roll gently down to the Lombardy plain in one direction and climb steeply to the protective main Alpine ridge in the other, are located at a height of between 660 and 980 feet (200 and 300 m). The orientation, height, and microclimatic conditions often vary significantly from one vineyard to the next, with damp and mist causing major problems in some areas. The soil composition also varies considerably and ranges from fine limestone gravel to volcanic porphyry.

Gattinara and Ghemme

Gattinara, the most famous wine-growing area in the foothills of the Piedmontese Alps, is the region's largest and it is mainly stocked with Spanna (Nebbiolo) vines. The widespread, fine, gravelly, volcanic soil yields well-structured wine with floral and fruit notes which is a serious rival to Barolo and can have similar aging qualities. The more interesting Gattinara wines are generally made from unblended Nebbiolo grapes, even if the D.O.C.G. regulations, which were defined in 1991, authorize the addition of ten percent Vespolina and Bonarda to soften the wine a little. In line with

Most of the northern Piedmontese D.O.C.s are concentrated around the fertile valley of the river Sesia, northwest of Novara, where vineyards, fields, and meadows alternate and vines are grown only in the most suitable sites.

the general trend for shorter aging periods, Gattinara need only age in wooden casks for one year, or two years for reserve quality.

Ghemme lies just a short distance away on the eastern side of the Sesia valley and belongs to the province of Novara. Its approximately 210 acres (85 ha) of vineyard slopes were awarded D.O.C.G. status in 1997. Up to 25 percent Vespolina and Uva Rara (the local variety of Bonarda) may be blended with the Nebbiolo. Good Ghemme is characterized by a silky bitter-sweet taste.

Varied Wines from Spanna Grapes

Four other D.O.C. zones with Spanna wines can be found not far from Gattinara, on the mountain range west of the Sesia and north of the town of Cossato. Bramaterra, which thrives on approximately 74 acres (30 ha) of volcanic soil, yields wines which are generally less full-bodied but develop an elegant aroma of violets and roses. The mandatory addition of 30 percent or more of Cratina, Bonarda, or Vespolina injects a fruity acidic character.

In the village of Lessona, with its mere 20 acres (8 ha) of vineyard, Spanna, which thrives on the very gravelly, lime-poor soils, can be produced as a single-varietal but it is generally blended with Vespolina and Bonarda to give robust, full-bodied, sometimes almost salty

SELECT PRODUCERS IN NORTHERN PIEDMONT

ANTONIOLO*—****
GATTINARA
49 acres (20 ha); 60,000 bottles • Wines include: Gattinara → Vigneto Osso San Grato, → Vigneto Castelle, → San Francesco; Coste della Sesia: Nebbiolo Juvenia, Bricco Lorella
Founded in 1949. The single-vineyard Gattinara Osso San Grato is one of the region's finest wines.

CIECK*
AGLIÉ–SAN GRATO
11 acres (4.5 ha); 25,000 bottles • Wines include: → Erbaluce di Caluso, Spumante, Caluso Passito Alladium Vigneto Runc, Canavese Rosso Neretto di San Giorgio
Lodovico Bardesono and Remo Falconieri's estate is one of the few reputable Caluso wineries. The Spumante is particularly good.

LUIGI FERRANDO & FIGLIO*—****
IVREA
11 acres (4.5 ha); 30,000 bottles • Wines include: Erbaluce di Caluso, Cariola, Caluso Passito, → Carema Etichetta Nera, Canavese Rosso Montodo, → Cariola Brut
Rich complex Nebbiolo and Erbaluce wines.

NERVI*
GATTINARA
74 acres (30 ha); 80,000 bottles • Wines include: → Gattinara Vigneto Mosino, Coste della Sesia Spanna, Amore
The Bocciolone family manages one of Gattinara's biggest wine estates. In addition to the outstanding single-vineyard Gattinara, they also produce a good Nebbiolo, Cabernet, and Merlot blend known as Amore.

PRODUTTORI NEBBIOLO DI CAREMA*—****
CAREMA
49 acres (20 ha); 70,000 bottles • Wines include: Carema, → Carema Carema
This cooperative was founded in 1959 and is financed using the members' own capital. Production is concentrated on two versions of red Carema.

TRAVAGLINI**
GATTINARA
74 acres (30 ha); 180,000 bottles • Wines include: Gattinara, Gattinara Riserva Numerata
Following the closure of the Le Colline estate, Travaglini assumed the top position for this *appellation*.

wines. Wines with a vigorous tannin structure and a BOUQUET which starts with violets and wild berries and is followed by notes of tea, spices, and rust thrive in the 37 acres (15 ha) of the Boca zone. The recently-created D.O.C., Coste della Sesia, allows the producers in these zones to make wines which lie outside previous D.O.C. boundaries and are dominated by Bonarda, Vespolina, and Croatina grapes.

In the neighboring province of Novara, this cross-boundary role is fulfilled by the D.O.C. *appellation* Connine Novaresi. In the D.O.C. zones of Sizzano (99 acres/40 ha) and Fara (54 acres/22 ha) which are located here, Nebbiolo represents merely 30 to 60 percent of the volumes harvested. This accounts for the less overtly tannic character of the wines produced here, which also develop more quickly.

The Erbaluce di Caluso zone is close to the Valle d'Aosta and the Alps. Snow is a common feature of winters here.

THE VETERAN OF MONTE ROSA

Nebbiolo changes its name once again at the entrance to the Aosta valley where it is known as Picutener. The steep terraces of moraine gravel soil, which climb to a height of up to 2,300 feet (700 m), go back to Roman times. Even then the yields were low; no other result is possible with such barren, stony soils and raw climate. The 99-acre (40-ha) D.O.C. region named after the mountain village of Carema produces original wines, whose aroma of wilting roses and tar, and hesitantly-unfolding flavor, are an impressive reflection of their unique *terroir*. This acidic wine needs at least five years' aging.

SWEET GOLD

Erbaluce, a light, acidic grape which only fully ripens in extremely sunny positions, can be found in the morainic lands of Canavese and the environs of the industrial town of Ivrea. Fully ripened, it makes wines with a straw-yellow color, an aroma of YEAST, bread, and hay, and a spicy finish. The natural acidity makes Erbaluce an ideal base wine for sparkling wine although its real strength lies in the dessert versions, Passito. The grapes for this wine must originate from the best locations and are not harvested until they are extremely ripe. Before pressing, they are dried for months in well-aired rooms and the wines are aged for years in small wooden casks. Then the refined sweet Erbaluce will finally develop its rich aroma of dried fruit, orange peel, and hazelnuts.

ASTI AND MONFERRATO

Monferrato and the more famous Langhe were once groups of islands in the Adriatic Sea which, in prehistoric times, covered the plain of the river Po. Both regions have the same geological formation, though their sediments differ in one respect which is important for wine growing: whereas the soils south of Alba are mainly lime and marl, the soils on the hills around the towns of Asti, Alessandria, and Acqui are more sandy.

A MODERN MASS-PRODUCED WINE

Alto Monferrato, the area including the southern part of the hill group and the town of Canelli, is synonymous with Asti Spumante. With an annual production level which is approaching 18,480,000 gallons (700,000 hl), it is the second most extensively produced Italian quality wine.

Moscato d'Asti—this has been a Muscat Mecca for five hundred years.

Legend:
- Barbera del Monferrato
- Barbera d'Asti
- Freisa d'Asti
- Malvasia di Castelnuovo Don Bosco
- Grignolino del Monferrato Casalese
- Grignolino d'Asti
- Ruchè di Castagnole Monferrato
- Piedmont
- Cortese dell'Alto Monferrato
- Brachetto d'Acqui
- Loazzolo
- Asti
- Dolcetto d'Alba
- Dolcetto d'Asti
- Dolcetto d'Acqui
- Dolcetto d'Ovada
- Gavi
- Wine-growing areas in neighboring regions

6 miles (10 km)

SELECT PRODUCERS OF ASTI AND MONFERRATO

CAUDRINA****
CASTIGLIONE TINELLA
62 acres (25 ha); 150,000 bottles • Wines: Asti La Selvatica, Moscato d'Asti La Caudrina, La Galeisa, →Barbera d'Asti La Solista, Montevenere, Piemonte Chardonnay Mej
Romano Dogliotti and his consultant Guilano Noè produce convincing Moscato and Barbera wines, which are among the best in Piedmont.

GUISEPPE CONTRATTO***–****
CANELLI
• Wines: Barolo Cerequio Tenuta Secolo, →Asti De Miranda, →Barbera d'Asti, Solus Ad, →Spumante Brut Riserva Guiseppe Contratto, Piemonte Chardonnay La Sabauda
This traditional winery was acquired by the Bocchino Grappa dynasty in 1994. The quality of the wines stabilized under the new owners; Contratto is once again one of the best names in Canelli.

FRATELLI GANCIA & C.**–***
CANELLI
6 acres (2.5 ha); some bought-in grapes; 23,000,000 bottles • Wines include: Barolo Mirafiore, →Asti, →Pinot di Pinot, Gancia dei Ganci Riserva Brut, Vermouth, Americano
Carlo Gancia founded his company in 1850 on completion of an apprenticeship in Champagne. Gancia is one of the leading Asti producers. Most famous wine: Pinot di Pinot.

PIERO GATTI***–****
SANTO STEFANO BELBO
18.5 acres (7.5 ha); 35,000 bottles • Wines: Piemonte Moscato, Moscato d'Asti, Langhe Freisa La Violetta

Pietro Gatti, one of the longest established Asti producers, is famous for his Moscato d'Asti. If it makes sense to bring harvesting forward, he simply labels the wine as Piemonte Moscato.

ELIO PERRONE***–****
CASTIGLIONE TINELLA
22 acres (9 ha); 60,000 bottles • Wines: Moscato d'Asti Clarté, Sourgal, Barbera d'Asti Grivò, Dolcetto d'Alba Guilin
For years, Stefano Perrone in Castiglione Tinella has been producing sparkling aromatic Moscato d'Asti wine.

PAOLO SARACCO****–*****
CASTIGLIONE TINELLA
33 acres (13.5 ha); 110,000 bottles • Wines include: Moscato d'Asti, Moscato d'Autunno, Langhe: Bianco Graffagno, Chardonnay Bianch del Luv and Prasuë
One of the best names for Moscato d'Asti, but the various Chardonnays have also long been among the most interesting of their kind in Piedmont.

LA SPINETTA-RIVETTI*****
CASTAGNOLE LANZE
79 acres (32 ha); 210,000 bottles • Wines include: Moscato d'Asti: Bricco Quaglia, Biancospina; Barbera d'Alba: Ca' di Pian, Vigneto Gallina; Monferrato Rosso Pin, Barbaresco Vursu Vigneto: Gallina, Starderi, Valeirano; Piemonte Chardonnay Lidia
The family attracted some attention in the mid-1980s with their single-vineyard Moscato, and—in red wines—with the Nebbiolo-Barbera-Cabernet blend Pin; in recent years also with their three outstanding single-vineyard Barbarescos and a Barolo.

This sparkling wine, which was surprisingly awarded D.O.C.G. status in 1994, is a single variety wine produced from Moscato Bianco, a descendant of the Muscat family. The D.O.C.G. regulations allow a maximum yield of 800 gallons per acre (75 hl/ha). To ensure survival against international competition, quantity is the sole priority.

When Spumante production was introduced in Piedmont in the mid-19th century, BOTTLE-FERMENTATION or the MÉTHODE CHAMPENOISE was used. Nowadays, the approximately 80 million bottles which flood the market annually are produced using the Charmat method whereby fermentation takes place in pressurized tanks. This eliminates the need to RIDDLE the bottles and makes it possible to prevent fermentation of almost one third of the grape sugar, ensuring that the wine remains sweet.

THE SCENT OF MUSCAT

Moscato d'Asti offers a newly fashionable alternative to Asti Spumante. It, too comes from Moscato Bianco and is fermented in pressurized tanks, but it differs from Asti Spumante in that it has more RESIDUAL SUGAR and is less alcoholic and fizzy. About two million bottles of Moscato d'Asti are

produced each year. Compared with Asti Spumante, the wine generally exudes a more aromatic complex bouquet, with notes of orange, elderberry, and pear, mainly due to the origin and quality of the grapes. Unlike the industrial producers, the wineries which have specialized in Moscato d'Asti can mostly work with their own grapes from good locations. Muscat was cultivated as early as 500 years ago around Santo Stefano Belbo, Castiglione Tinella, and between Canelli and Alba where the microclimate ensures a distinctive bouquet.

The Mecca of Muscat wines can be found in the Loazzolo D.O.C. zone. Here a few producers have concentrated on a Passito from late-harvested, partly dried grapes. Their dessert wine, with its complex aromas of roses, violets, melon, and mint, is as rare as it is expensive. Another still sweet wine from Moscato Bianco is produced in the Strevi area of the province of Alessandria. This is a rather light dessert wine which has a fine, appealing aroma, although it has not yet been awarded D.O.C. status. Brachetto, on the other hand, has had D.O.C.G. status since 1996 and is enjoying increasing popularity. The light red grape is currently grown on 148 acres (60 ha) of vineyard which produce approximately one million bottles per year.

Alba and Asti:
The Rise of Barbera and its Peers

Nebbiolo may be the driving force behind Piedmont's prestige as a wine-producing region but the locals have always drunk Barbera wines. Almost half of the vineyards in the region are stocked with this variety. For decades, it produced the highest yields and by far the worst wines. Barbera has probably been known in Monferrato since the 13th century, but its victorious march through the vineyards of Piedmont did not take place until after the phylloxera disaster, when it proved to be particularly adept at producing high yields on American rootstocks. It gave abundant harvests on almost all soil types at a time when quality was of necessity neglected by the crisis-shaken producers.

In the mid-1980s, Barbera found itself at the center of what became known as the methanol scandal. Criminal producers had "refined" the cheapest Barbera wines with methanol, killing over 20 people. At a time when the reputation of the grape could hardly sink any lower, a group of innovative and quality-oriented producers, notably Giacomo Bologna, had already started to work on this unjustly maligned variety. ACID adjustment and barrel aging were the magic formulae used to transform the robust acidic grapes into spicy, complex and longer-lived wines. Bologna's elegant Bricco dell'Uccellone was the first of the new Barberas produced in this way.

Concentrated elegance: Giacomo Bologna was the first to reveal the great qualities of Barbera with his Bricco dell'Uccellone.

Numerous small family wineries where the land and vineyards are farmed with basic implements can be found in the area surrounding the two rival towns. Many of them sell their grapes or wine to large producers or traditional *négociant* houses.

Another Nebbiolo Triumph

In the area around Alba, where producers were in the process of modernizing Barolo, they also started to experiment with the Barbera grapes which had been stocked in most of that area's vineyards for generations. The action of the *terroir*, combined with the experience gained in winery techniques by the *Barolisti*, could only have a positive outcome, and Barbera d'Alba became the prime D.O.C. of the new full-bodied, international-style reds. The Asti producers later made equally successful inroads with the new approach. Since the early 1990s, magnificent fruity and tannic wines, the best of which have sufficient structure to age for years, have been mainly produced from very old Barbera vines bearing concentrated grapes.

Freisa, Grignolino, and Ruchè

The two indigenous grape varieties, Freisa and Grignolino, survived phylloxera in the provinces of Asti and Monferrato. However, due to their sensitivity and low yields, they were not very popular with producers.

Light-colored, with a fresh and light taste, Grignolino wines once offered a welcome change to the heavy red wines of Langhe and were even popular at the royal court of Savoie. The best representatives of this variety, with their typical scent of roses, nuts, and white pepper and which, despite their lightness, are surprisingly tannic and full-bodied, thrive on the dry, loose soils of northern Monferrato.

In contrast, Freisa was never a very important variety. Although its presence in Piedmont can be traced back to 1799, the slightly fizzy, short-lived wines it produces have never enjoyed much popularity. The best of the remaining 4,920-acre (2,000-ha) Freisa sites can be found in the Asti region. Here, and in a small area east of Turin (D.O.C. Freisa di Chieri), particularly concentrated barrel-aged wines are now being produced from Freisa Piccola.

With their 247 acres (100 ha) of Ruchè or Rouchet, the producers in the area of Castagnole Monferrato have saved a red grape variety of unknown origin from decline and extinction. Ruchè wines have a balsamic aroma of roses and red fruit, a silky taste with good tannin structure, and hence the capacity to age for some years.

Select Producers of Barbera

Marchesi Alfieri****—*****
San Martino Alfieri
37 acres (15 ha); 60,000 bottles • Wines include: Barbera d'Asti: La Tota, →Alfiera; Monteferrato: Il Bianco dei Marchesi, Il Rosso dei Marchesi, Piemonte Grignolino Sansoero
Machesi Alfiera produce wonderful densely fruity Barberas.

Bava***—****
Cocconato
49 acres (20 ha); some bought-in grapes; 600,000 bottles • Wines include: Barbera d'Asti Stradivario, , Arbest and Piano Alto; Monferrato Bianco Alteserre, Giulio Cocchi Spumate Brut, Gavi Cor de Chasse, Malvasia di Castelnuovo Don Bosco, Moscato d'Asti Bass Tuba
The best wines produced by this well-known estate are the Barbera Stradivario and Piano Alto.

Bertelli****
Costogliole d'Asti
15 acres (6 ha); 25,000 bottles • Wines include: Barbera d'Asti: Montetusa, San Antonio, Cabernet 1 Fossareti
All the wines produced here are matured in *barriques*; the various Barberas are impressive.

Alfiero Boffa, Vigne Uniche****
San Marzano Oliveto
37 acres (15 ha); some bought-in grapes; 200,000 bottles • Wines include: Barbera d'Asti: →Collina della Vedova; Moscato d'Asti, Dolcetto, Spumante
Five single-vineyard Barberas prove that there are some remarkable *terroirs* between Nizza Monferrato and Costigliole d'Asti.

Braida di Giacomo Bologna***—*****
Rocchetta Tanaro
43 acres (17 ha); 200,000 bottles • Wines include: Barbera d'Asti: Bricco dell'Uccellone, →Ai Suma, →Bricco della Bigotta; Langhe Bianco Il Fiore di Serra dei Fiori, Pinot Nero del Monferrato Il Bacialé, Barbera La Monella, Moscato d'Asti Vigna Senza Nome
The single-vineyard Barberas are still top of the league in the Astigiano. An exemplary operation.

Cascina la Barbatella****
Nizza Monferrato
10 acres (4 ha); 15,000 bottles • Wines: Barbera d'Asti La Vigna dell'Angelo, Monferrato Bianco Noë, La Vigna di Sonvico
Low yields, careful treatment of the grapes and modern vinification ensure top wines such as Vigna di Sonvico (made from Cabernet and Barbera) are produced.

Cascina Castlet***
Costiglione d'Asti
25 acres (10 ha); 65,000 bottles • Wines include: Barbera d'Asti: →Passum and Policalpo; Moscato Passito Avié
A dry Barbera called Passum, matured as a dry, is produced here from partly dried grapes.

Andrea Oberto***—****
La Morra
20 acres (8 ha); 50,000 bottles • Wines include: Barolo: →Vigneto Rocche; Barbera d'Alba: Vigneto Boiolo, →Giada,; Dolcetto d'Alba: Vantrino Albarella, San Francesco, Langhe Rosso Fabio
The estate is actually in the Barolo area but its best wine is a Barbera d'Alba called Giada, followed by the Rocche vineyard Barolo Langhe Fabio and three Dolcetto versions.

Visitors to the Braida di Giacomo Bologna winery are greeted by a stylish interior with a view of the brand new *barriques*.

La Tenaglia**—****
Serralunga di Crea
32.5 acres (13 ha); 55,000 bottles • Wines: Chardonnay, Oltre, Grignolino del Monferrato, Barbera del Monferrato, Chiaro di Crea, Barbera d'Asti: Bricco Crea, Emozione, Giorgio Tenaglia
In Serralunga di Crea, somewhat removed from the center of Barbera production, La Tenaglia produces notable Barbera d'Asti selections and Chardonnay Oltre in good years.

Tenuta Garetto***—****
Agliano Terme
30 acres (12 ha); 70,000 bottles • Wines: Barbera d'Asti Superiore Favà, In Pectore, →Tra Neuit e Dì, Piemonte Chardonnay Diversamente
Alessandro Garetto took over the family business as a very young man, and has followed an unwavering and single-minded course to join the circle of the best Barbera d'Asti producers.

Villa Terlina*****
Agliano d'Asti
15 acres (6 ha); 25,000 bottles • Wines: Barbera d'Asti Gradale, →Barbera d'Asti Monsciuro
Paolo Alliata and Bettina Eickelberg produce wonderful dense and expressive wines from old vines on their unproductive soils.

Vinchia e Vaglio Serra**—****
Vinchio
320 ha; 150,000 bottles • Wines include: Barbera d'Asti: →Vigne Vecchie, →V.V. Bricco Laudana; Barbera del Monferrato Vivace, Cortese del Monferrato Dorato, Grignolino d'Asti, Chardonnay d'Asti
For a long time, the members of the Vinchio cooperative supplied the most famous wineries in the area with the raw materials for their top wines. However, since they began bottling and also marketing the Barbera d'Asti Vigne Vecchie, this has indisputably become one of the best wines of the region.

ALBA, LANGHE, AND ROERO

One of life's small pleasures
—a wine bar in Roero.

The hill landscape of Langhe covers an area of approximately 772 square miles (2,000 sq. km) enclosed by the plains of Turin and Cuneo, Monferrato and the Ligurian Maritime Alps. The unique geological formation of these hills emerged together with those of Monferrato and Roero during the tertiary period when the area now known as the Po plain was still flooded by the Adriatic Sea. The gray-white, limy, marl soils formed from the maritime deposits are rich in minerals and trace elements: iron, potassium, phosphorus, copper, manganese, and magnesium in varying volumes dictate the special character (*terroir*) of the vineyards here. Thanks to the exceptional potential of the Langhe soils, in 1881 King Umberto I founded an agricultural college in Alba, which was specially devoted to wine production.

ON THE LEFT BANK OF THE TANARO

Roero, the continuation of the Langhe hills on the west bank of the Tanaro northwest of Alba, may have been formed at the same time as the last wave of the Alpine massif. However, unlike the Langhe hills, its ranges run almost parallel to each other. Lime marl is rare here; the soils are based on Ice Age deposits which formed the deep valleys and steep slopes. Piedmont's most famous grape is indigenous here and the wine is marketed under the D.O.C. Nebbiolo d'Alba. Its cultivation area extends to the other side of the Tanaro. For almost too long, the local producers used the Nebbiolo grape to produce a sweet wine suitable only for drinking while young.

Finally, however, the modern age arrived with the introduction of restrictions on volume, controlled fermentation and barrel-aging. Wines from the better wineries now offer a serious alternative to Barolo, not quite as complex and long-lived as their model, but at least affordable.

In general, the wines from this *appellation* become lighter and less complex with the shift from south to north. The very sandy soils of the northern part of the zone yield very finely-structured wines which were popular in aristocratic circles in Turin as early as the 16th and 17th centuries. In 1985 a separate D.O.C. zone was created for Nebbiolo and Arneis in recognition of the individuality of the Roero wines.

MODEST DOLCETTO

To make use of the less blessed wine-growing sites, the Piedmontese producers have always

Map legend

- Barbera d'Alba
- Nebbiolo d'Alba
- Roero
- Dolcetto d'Alba
- Dolcetto di Diano d'Alba
- Barbaresco
- Barolo
- Asti
- Dolcetto di Dogliani
- Dolcetto delle Langhe Monregalesi
- Wine-growing areas in neighboring regions

planted Dolcetto on the cooler slopes. This low-acid variety ripens around four weeks before the sensitive Nebbiolo, which not only reduces the risk that it will be spoilt by fall rains but also has organizational advantages when it comes to harvesting. Having been ignored for many years, these mild, fruity, relatively light, everyday wines designed to be drunk when young, now enjoy seven individual D.O.C.s with more than half of production dedicated to Dolcetto d'Alba.

One of the most interesting Dolcetto wines is bottled by the producers in the area around Diano d'Alba. Here, the variety is not planted on the less favorable sites but instead is cultivated on the best south-facing slopes. This, combined with stringent production regulations—a maximum yield of 600 gallons per acre (56 hl/ha) and 12 percent minimum alcohol strength—brought the Diano producers the first official recognition of individual vineyard sites (*sori*) in Italy.

One of the most charming of red wines, Dolcetto can be drunk when young and has intense fruit aromas. The best Dolcettos, however, have considerable depth.

Another D.O.C. designation exists in Dogliani, which is probably the true home of Dolcetto. After above-average increases in quality, Dolcetto di Dogliani has developed into a relatively firm complex wine with fine fruit and lasting taste.

FRAGRANT RARITIES

The much respected Barbera is also cultivated in Roero and Langhe, and other regional specialties await discovery here, such as Pelaverga, an absolute rarity, which grows in the D.O.C. zones of Verduno and Colline Saluzzesi. It was one of the most popular varieties in the province of Cuneo between the 13th and 16th centuries. Its bright red wines with a color reminiscent of onion skins and the aroma of white pepper, are sometimes blended with Nebbiolo and Barbera. This undoubtedly does little to hamper their supposed aphrodisiac effects.

SELECT PRODUCERS IN AND AROUND ALBA

CLAUDIO ALARIO***–****
DIANO D'ALBA
15 acres (6 ha); 30,000 bottles • Wines: →Dolcetto di Diano d'Alba, →Barbera d'Alba Valletta, Nebbiolo d'Alba, Langhe
The best Diano Dolcettos as well as an excellent single-vineyard Barbera are produced here today.

CERETTO***–****
ALBA
247 acres (100 ha); 700,000 bottles • Wines include: Barbaresco Bricco Asili. Barolo Bricco Roche, Monsordo Langhe: Chardonnay, Cabernet, Pinot, Dolcetto d'Alba Rossana
The Cerettos manage three wineries from La Bernadina. Two produce single-vineyard Barolos and Barbarescos.

PIO CESARE***–*****
ALBA
74 acres (30 ha); some bought-in grapes; 320,000 bottles • Wines include: Barolo, →Barolo Ornato, →Barbaresco Il Bricco, Nebbiolo d'Alba, Dolcetto d'Alba, →Barbera d'Alba Fides, Moscato d'Asti, Il Nebbio, Gavi, Langhe Chardonnay Piodilei
A traditional winery in the center of Alba, its Barolo and Barbaresco are dense, modern, single-vineyard wines.

MATTEO CORREGIA****–*****
CANALE
45.5 acres (17 ha); 70,000 bottles • Wines include: →Barbera d'Alba Bricco Marun, →Nebbiolo d'Alba La Val del Preti, Roero, Roero Arneis
The Barberas are sensational, as is a Nebbiolo.

CARLO DELTETTO**–****
CANALE
25 acres (10 ha); 80,000 bottles • Wines include: Barbera d'Alba, Dolcetto d'Alba, Gavi, →Roero Madonna dei Boschi, →Roero Arneis San Michele
The Deltetto winery produces a top Arneis and has a good reputation for its Roero and Barbera d'Alba.

MALVIRÀ-FRATELLI DAMONTE***–****
CANALE
89 acres (36 ha); 70,000 bottles • Wines include Roero, →Roero Arneis Trinità, Langhe San Gugliemo Bianco and Rosso
This winery specializes in Arneis wine. Three of the five types of wine are fermented or matured in barrels.

PELISSERO****
TREISO
49 acres (20 ha); 90,000 bottles • Wines: Barbaresco, Barbaresco Vanotu, Barbera d'Alba Piani, Dolcetto d'Alba Augenta and Munfrina, Langhe Nebbiolo, →Langhe Long Now
Using Dolcetto and Barbera, Giorgio Pelissero produces modern wines characterized by barrel fermentation.

ALFREDO PRONUTTO***–****
ALBA
175 acres (70 ha); some bought-in grapes; 700,000 bottles • Wines include: Barolo: Bussia, Cannubi; Barbaresco: Montestefano, Rabajà; Barbera Pian Romualdo, Nebbiolo Occhetti
Barolo Bussia and Barbaresco Montestefano are the great wines of this winery, now part of the Florence-based Antinori empire.

PUNSET***–****
NEIVE
47 acres (30 ha); 50,000 bottles • Wines: Barbaresco, →Barbaresco Campo Quadro, Barbera d'Alba Superiore Vigneto Zocco, →Dolcetto d'Alba Campo Re, Langhe Rosso Dualis
On this organically managed estate run by Marina Marcarino, the selected harvests Campo Quadro and Campo Re are now among the top wines in Piedmont.

TENIMENTI DI BAROLO E FONTANAFREDDA*–****
SERRALUNGA D'ALBA
173 acres (70 ha); some bought-in grapes; 6,000,000 bottles • Wines include: →Barolo La Delizia, →Lazzarito, Barbaresco, Dolcetto d'Alba, Pinot Nero, Roero, Roero Arneis, Gavi, Spumante Brut Gattinera, Asti
This winery, owned by a Sienese bank, produces very good single-vineyard Barolos, matured by enologist Danilo Drocco.

BAROLO:
A UNIQUE COMBINATION

Probably the most reputable, if not the most popular, fine Italian wine, Barolo takes its name from a small town which lies around 9 miles (15 km) south of Alba in the Langhe hills. Even in this landscape which is dotted with numerous castles, the town's imposing *castello* and fortifications tower impressively over surrounding rooftops. On clear days, the sky-scraping Alpine peaks can be seen in the distance from the castle. In autumn, however, the fog, after which the region's best-known vine variety is named (*nebbia* means fog), rises from the Tanaro valley which separates the Langhe hills from Roero.

Barolo has Marquise Giulietta Faletti and her enologist Louis Oudart to thank for its prestige. They were the first to allow the must from the Nebbiolo grapes to ferment systematically and, with the resulting very powerful, dry but elegant wine, revealed the potential for quality concealed on the slopes and peaks around Alba. A difficult and demanding variety, which needs extremely high doses of summer sun, even in previous centuries Nebbiolo had conquered the best south-facing sites in the Barolo, Castiglione, Falletto, Serralunga, and Monteforte d'Alba areas which were generally accepted as its ideal *terroir*.

Nebbiolo is grown only in the southern zones of the Barolo township where it matures best. The calcareous marl ensures round and silky wines.

The special qualities of the variety, and the vineyards which enabled it to unfold to its maximum potential, have together created what is now acknowledged as one of Italy's greatest red wines.

FEW TERROIRS ARE CHOSEN

Nebbiolo vines mostly mature to their maximum potential on the calcareous marl soils of the Tortonian epoch. These top-quality sites are distributed among the south and southwest slopes of three high ridges which rise from Alba in a southerly direction. There are 11 townships in the Barolo area and together they have a mere 3,200 acres (1,300 ha) of vineyards—Bordeaux, by comparison, covers 250,000 acres (100,000 ha). However, the truly outstanding sites are concentrated around five core townships. The entire prestige of the *appellation* is concentrated in Barolo itself, La Morra, Castiglione Falletto, Serralunga d'Alba, and Monteforte d'Alba, while Verduno, Grinzane Cavour, Diano d'Alba, Cherasco, Novello, and Roddi have only small Barolo areas.

THE TORTONIAN AND HELVETIAN EPOCHS

Despite the shared history of their formation, the soils within the Barolo area vary significantly in type. To the west, at the level of La Morra, Barolo, and Novello, the calcareous marl is more compact, fresher, and more fertile than in the rest of the area and produces softer, fruitier, rounder wines. Geologists have defined this zone as Tortonian. In contrast, the eastern range of hills of Castiglione, Serralunga, and Monforte has been identified as originating in the Helvetian epoch and has a higher proportion of reddish weathered sandstone or contains quartziferous sand. These soils are, in general, less fertile and yield more intense, structured, tannic wines that mature more slowly.

Nebbiolo reacts very sensitively to all the soil variations and to the varying climatic conditions found in the different sites. There is a good reason why, even in the most prestigious Barolo vineyards, you are more likely to find Dolcetto vines than Nebbiolo on the lower slopes, as the latter simply would not ripen there. The varying chemical composition of the soils also influences the character of the wines. For example, the high manganese and magnesium content of the

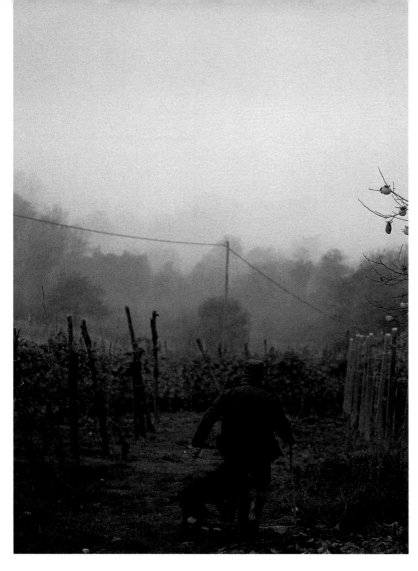

Historic and current top Barolo and Barbaresco vineyards	
BAROLO	
La Morra	Cerequio, Brunate, Rocche, Arborina, La Serra
Barolo	Cannubi
Serralunga d'Alba	Arione, Francia, Vigna Rionda, Ornato
Castiglione Falletto	Fiasco, Bussia, Monprivato, Rocche, Lazzarito
BARBARESCO	
Neive	Gallina, Santo Stefano
Barbaresco	Asili, Rabajà, Martinenga, San Lorenzo

producing areas. In the past, this repeatedly facilitated the misuse of the names of famous sites. On the other hand, in the case of Barolo, the highly varied character of the wines from the different sites prompted the development of the perfect Barolo, blended from grapes of different origins, taking their positive and negative characteristics into account. This was made easier by the fact that the area's vineyards are extremely fragmented in terms of ownership, and no individual producer would have been able to harvest sufficient volumes from a single site to produce estate or single-vineyard bottlings.

Furthermore, this situation very much suited the zone's major NÉGOCIANT houses which, in the past, processed most of the grapes and marketed the wine. The best known of these, companies like Prunotto and Bruno Giacosa, acquired such a detailed and intimate knowledge of the characteristics of the individual sites over time, and established such a solid base of suppliers of good grapes that, even today, their wines remain virtually untouchable in terms of high quality.

soils in La Morra lies behind the expressive bouquet and clear liquorice notes of the wines produced there. On the opposite hill chain, the higher levels of iron in the topsoil clearly intensify the youthful harshness of the wines produced in this area. While the wines from Serralunga and Monforte are among the area's top representatives in good warm years, under less advantageous conditions, the acidity combined with the tannins can yield bitter and unsatisfactory wines.

In addition to Barolo, the Langhe hills near Alba are home to the famous white truffle. In autumn, many winegrowers can be seen scouring the hills with their dogs in the hope of making a valuable find.

A gourmet's paradise— Barolo and truffles.

BLENDS AND ESTATE/ SINGLE-VINEYARD BOTTLINGS

Although it was always known that the quality of the Nebbiolo depended on conditions in the vineyard, it took almost a century to come to the conclusion that the wines from these estates and vineyards should be bottled separately. There were several reasons for this. First, unlike France and Germany, Italy never had an estate or vineyard definition policy. To the present day, there is no comprehensive register of vineyards with a precise and unambiguous definition of the best sites, even in the most reputable wine-

Barolo:
Past and Present

Classical Barolo is usually blended from a selection of musts produced in the area. In the 1960s, in an effort to achieve a more rounded and, if possible, reproducible taste, there was a move toward estate or single-vineyard bottling. Given that the quality of the grapes differs significantly in the different holdings in the Barolo and Barbaresco areas, the idea was that the best sources should be identified and receive the recognition they deserved. This development was pioneered by Alfredo Prunotto and his enologists, Beppe Colla and Renato Ratti, as well as the wine critic, Luigi Veronelli, a supporter of the French system of domain classification. Veronelli had in fact tried to persuade Prunotto and Colla to produce their wines as single-vineyard bottlings as early as the 1950s. The outstanding vintage of 1961 marked the birth of the estate/single-vineyard bottlings in Langhe. Renato Ratti, who had set up his winery in the former monastery, Abbazia dell'Annunziata near La Morra, soon followed suit and undertook extensive studies to identify the most suitable vineyard plots in the area. Ratti's research resulted in a map which is still the most comprehensive record available of the Barolo estates and their quality potential.

Mixing or Separating

Other wine producers and merchants such as Bruno Giacosa, the Ceretto brothers, Angelo Gaja, the Fontanafredda winery, and the

Wintry vineyards in Barolo where estate and single-vineyard bottlings are now the norm. Top producers try to reduce yields and achieve higher grape concentration through vigorous winter pruning.

Produttori di Barbaresco cooperative adopted this idea in the 1960s and over the following decades almost all the producers tried to win greater prestige and higher prices for their traditional wines. When the wave of estate bottlings spread to other Italian regions, such as Tuscany, the zone name was included as an official element of distinction in the D.O.C.G. legislation, and the option of higher-quality possibilities for individual estates was also created.

Today, some excellent Barolo is still blended using grapes from different zones in the area, but the best individual products are mostly bottled separately, while the rest are marketed with the generic D.O.C. label. It is admissable to drop the estate *appellation* for smaller vintages and this further increases the prestige of the estate and single-vineyard bottlings.

Downside

This development led to serious inflation in the price of estate and single-vineyard bottlings in the 1990s. The enormous commercial success prompted many producers to vinify the grapes separately, even if they had little potential to yield higher-quality wines. While most producers and consumers were still concentrating on the vineyard—known locally as *vigna* or *cru*—the innovative houses had already set to work on a new quality dimension. Strict limitations in yield were achieved through heavy winter pruning and radical summer thinning until the harvested yields matched those of the top French *crus* and lay well below the mandatory volumes prescribed in the legislation.

Revolution in the Wineries

The new viticultural practices were matched by changes in winery techniques. As was the practice almost everywhere in Piedmont, producers in the Barolo area traditionally allowed the must to stay in contact with the LEES for three, four, or more weeks to give the Nebbiolo sufficient structure, body, and, in particular, good aging capacity. Once racked, the wine was then left to the forces of nature and, when fully fermented, stored for years in large wooden barrels. Nebbiolo could only withstand this process in better years when its grapes were full, almost over-ripe, and correspondingly high in alcohol content.

In weaker years, generous tannins were released from the grape skins, pips, and stems, but the wines lacked the fruit to balance their harshness. By the time the tannins matured during the over-long cask-aging, the fruit had long faded and the presence of maturation acids rendered the wines bitter and aggressive.

What Happens if the Tannins are Heated?

A young generation of producers, led by Elio Altare from La Morra, followed the example of their colleagues in Bordeaux and Burgundy and radically reduced the fermentation period to between 48 and 72 hours, or at most eight to ten days. They learned that, if the fermenting mass is carefully heated, both the color achieved and tannin extracted during the first hours are completely adequate. The tannins extracted at the beginning of the fermentation process also have the major advantage of being sweet and round as opposed to bitter and harsh. The wines started in this revolutionary new way were then aged in *barriques* which in turn added pleasant tannins, spicy tastes, and aromas. It is occasionally rumored that the complex taste of modernist wines may also originate from varieties not defined in the D.O.C.G. rules, but this remains as yet unproven.

Elio Altare from La Morra is one of the most fervent and convincing of modernists: his Vigna Aborina has become legendary.

Bruno Giacosa is a traditionalist who as both a producer and *négociant* believes in long fermentation and maceration periods and has no interest in *barriques*.

Elio Altare is cautious with new wood and has not completely turned his back on the traditional, tried and trusted tuns.

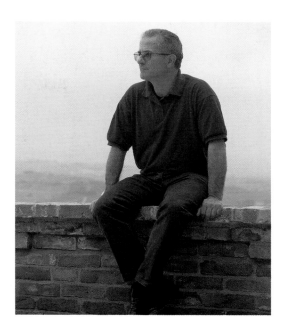

The Law and Success

The legal regulations governing the production of Barolo and Barbaresco have been updated in the meantime. The wines must still consist of 100 percent Nebbiolo—even the traditional addition of Barbera is no longer allowed—and yield is now restricted to $3^1/_2$ tons of grapes per acre (8 tonnes/ha). Quality-conscious producers still feel this is too much. The regulations prescribe two years of cask-aging for Barolo and one for Barbaresco, then both wines must mature in the bottle for one year before being put on the market. The traditionalists doubted the aging capacity of the modern wines, but now, 15 years on, the first vintages have proved that the new types of Barolo and Barbaresco have developed well and acquired more refined tastes with time.

The war over production techniques has petered out with no clear victor. Many excellent traditional wines can now stand alongside the "modern," top-quality products, as the traditionalists have also been making greater efforts with respect to quality. International success has vindicated all Barolo producers, traditionalists and modernists alike. In 1967 only 1,593 acres (645 ha) in the area were stocked with Nebbiolo vines, but by 1990 this had more than doubled to 3,228 acres (1,307 ha). Barolo and, to a lesser extent, Barbaresco, are now among Europe's most expensive wines, although the extension of the cultivation areas has also had a negative impact on quality. The threat of an unequal price-performance ratio, which has already resulted in economic turmoil in northern Piedmont in the recent past, should not be underestimated as a possible future scenario in the Northwest.

BARBARESCO

If Barbaresco was left in the shadow of Barolo up to the 1960s, this was a reflection not of its quality but of the class of its consumers: Barolo was to some extent produced for aristocratic and upper-class circles. The Barbaresco area, which stretches beyond the village of the same name and along neighboring townships of Treiso, Neive, and San Rocco Seno d'Elvio, had a major disadvantage to overcome: its producers included neither kings, aristocrats, nor government members who could give the wine the attention and inspiration it needed.

AN INDEPENDENT AREA

Castello di Neive, the castle in the village center, is an exception. Its owners commissioned Louis Oudart, the enologist responsible for the creation of dry Barolo, to work in its winery. In 1862 the Castello wines convinced a panel of experts in London, although at the time Neive did not belong to the Barbaresco area. Its sites were not in fact linked with those of the famous neighboring township until 1933.

The link with the development of Barolo was forged in the last decade of the 19th century by the enologist Domizio Cavazza, director of the Enological School of Alba, when he also produced dry red wines from the Nebbiolo grapes from Barbaresco. Cavazza carried out exemplary work in his role as director of the wine producers' cooperative founded in 1894, and his Produttori del Barbaresco are among the *appellation's* best producers to the present day.

The current boundaries of the area, which includes 1,250 acres (500 ha) of vineyards producing around three million bottles per year, were drawn in 1966. The fact that the new *appellation* was given the name Barbaresco is due mainly to the quality of the grapes in the best zones, such as Asili and Rabajà. At the same time, the wine began gradually to regain popularity, largely thanks to the efforts of Giovanni Gaja and the wine trader Bruno Giacosa. Almost two decades later, Giovanni's son, Angelo Gaja succeeded in bringing Barbaresco to the point of its international breakthrough.

In today's D.O.C.G. area, the best vineyards are located at a height of between 590 and 1,050 feet (180 and 320 m). This comparatively low altitude is the factor behind some of the differences between Barbaresco wines and Barolo. The warmer microclimate allows the grapes to ripen more quickly, which means that they ripen with lower levels of sugar than the Barolo. This is reflected in the legislation by a minimum alcoholic strength of 12.5 percent which is half a percent lower than Barolo. On the other hand, in difficult years the producers can often fully or at least partly harvest the grapes before the weather changes and thus avoid major differences between VINTAGES, which is a factor with Barolo. The homogenous calcareous marl soils of the Barbaresco area are similar to the Tortonian soils of the La Morra and Barolo townships. There are differences, however, in the mineral composition. Here, instead of manganese we find copper and zinc, which give rise to a different range of aromas in the wine.

In the 1960s, the Barbaresco producers also experimented with single-vineyard bottling and the debate between modernism and traditionalism also took place here, although it was less controversial than the Barolo version. The D.O.C. regulations were subsequently modified here, too, and the prescribed cask-aging period reduced by one year.

A wine-producing area with a bright future— Barbaresco.

Elegance versus Strength

Barbaresco is well able to compensate for what it sometimes seems to lack in structure and power with the balance of its alcoholic strength, tannins, and acidity as well as its intense aromatic qualities which initially evoke violets and fresh berries. At its best between ten and fifteen years old, it ages significantly less well than Barolo, and can reach optimum maturity at between five and ten years.

The wines from zones with above-average temperatures and a damp microclimate are particularly aromatic and elegant. They are mostly very small plots which open onto the river Tanaro, for example the Asili and Rabajà zones in the Barbaresco township, which manage to produce complex wines with fine fruit even in mediocre years. In contrast, the wines produced from the best vines in Neive have an excellent reputation for their outstanding power and structure. Their youthful rawness is often

Left
Angelo Gaja's old cellar full of wood casks.

Right
Wine shops like this one in Neive, one of the centers in the Barbaresco zone, offer great shopping opportunities for the region's numerous visitors as they mainly offer locally produced and traded wines. They often keep vintages which have long been sold out at the wineries themselves.

Angelo Nazionale, Italy's most unusual producer.

even reminiscent of Barolo, which is why their producers often describe themselves as *baroleg-giant*. They need longer cask- and bottle-aging to achieve their full potential. Gallina has the reputation of being the best site in Neive but other neighboring sites also now enjoy considerable prestige. Further south, in Treiso, where the soils are heavier and the wines more tannic, from among the small estates usually owned by individuals, only Pajorè has emerged as distinctive.

During Barolo's victory march, critics often accused the producers of Barbaresco of lacking concentration and paying insufficient attention to quality. However, in recent years, the situation has improved immensely. A small group of producers has emerged, making wines which have no problem measuring up to some Barolos. The future has just begun for Barbaresco.

Angelo Gaja, Barbaresco

"Angelo Nazionale," as people like to call him, is the master of winemaking in Piedmont, if not in all of Italy. His single-vineyard bottlings, Sorì San Lorenzo, Sorì Tildin, and Costa Russi, which are among the country's most expensive wines, have enabled Barbaresco to shine impressively. Since the 1996 vintage, they have, however, been produced under the Langhe D.O.C. *appellation* and as a registered trademark. Since then, Gaja has been fighting the multitude of increasingly futile single-vineyard bottlings and campaigning for the strengths of a general Barbaresco.

As a son of one of the region's first wine-producing families—his father Giovanni had acquired the zone's largest wine-growing estate as early as the 1950s and 1960s and converted it from mixed to monoculture—Angelo was predestined for his role as the

leading figure in the world of winemaking in his home town of Barbaresco. With his unerring instinct for innovations and unique marketing talents, he has established an outstanding international reputation in a very short time. He brought back new ideas from France: the quality-enhancing strategies of controlled fermentation temperatures, early biological acid conversion, and new *barriques* were among them, as well as rigorous yield restrictions; and the planting of Cabernet and Chardonnay vines in good Barbaresco vineyards, which led to considerable disputes with his father. However, success has vindicated him with the building of his wine-importing company, his acquisition of the Barbaresco Castello and the best Barbaresco vineyards, and his involvement in the vineyards of Chiesa di Santa Restituta in Montalcino and the Cá Marcanda estate in Maremma in Tuscany. Gaja's glory has faded somewhat with the international success of a whole raft of Piedmont producers in the 1990s.

Elio Altare*****
La Morra

20 acres (8 ha); 50,000 bottles • Wines include: Barolo: Vigneto Arborina; Barbera d'Alba, Dolcetto d'Alba, Langhe: →Vigna Larigi, →Vigna Arborina; →Langhe La Villa

Altare's Aborina proves that even less prestigious vineyards can produce top quality wines. The mash is left to stand for the shortest possible time and barrel maturing is as long as possible, resulting in plenty of fruit and perfectly ripe tannins.

Azelia—Luigi Scavino***–*****
Castiglione Falletto

20 acres (8 ha); 50,000 bottles • Wines: Barolo, →Barolo Bricco Fiasco, →Barbera d'Alba Bricco Punta, Dolcetto d'Alba Bricco Oriolo

Thanks to grape selection and barrel aging, the Dolcetto vineyard in Montelupo Albese and the Barolo sites in Fiasco provide the top quality Azelia wines.

Michele Chiarlo**–****
Calamandrana

250 acres (104 ha); some bought-in grapes; 1,100,000 bottles • Wines include: Barbaresco Rabajà, Barolo: →Cannubi, →Cerequio, →Rocche di Castiglione; Barbera d'Asti Valle del Sole, Dolcetto d'Alba, Gavi Fornaci di Tassarolo, Gavi di Gavi Rovereto, Barilot, Countacc

Recently this producer has been concentrating on fine Barolo, Barbaresco and Barbera wines.

Domenico Clerico*****
Monforte d'Alba

37 acres (15 ha); 65,000 bottles • Wines: Barbera d'Alba, Barolo: →Ciabot Menti Ginestra, Per Cristina, →Pajana, Briccotto Bussia; Langhe Arte Langhe Freisa La Ginestrina

This estate produces two of the best single-vineyard Barolos in the area and, with Arte, one of the most fascinating Nebbiolo and Barbera blends.

Aldo Conterno****–*****
Monforte d'Alba

59 acres (24 ha); 160,000 bottles • Wines include: Barolo: 'Vigna Colonello, Vigna Cicala, →Granbussia, →Bussia, Soprana, Romirasco; Barbera Conca Tre Pile, Langhe: Favot, Bianco Printanié, Chardonnay

Conterno combines the best of traditional and modern, and his single-vineyard Barolos are legendary.

Giacomo Conterno***–****
Monforte d'Alba

37 acres (15 ha); 65,000 bottles • Wines include: Barolo; →Cascina Francia, →Monfortino; Barbera d'Alba, Dolcetto d'Alba, Langhe Freisa

Giovanni Conterno is best known as the region's defender of tradition and Monfortino is his showpiece.

Paolo Conterno***–****
Monforte d'Alba

17 acres (7 ha); 40,000 bottles • Wines: Barolo Ginestra, Dolcetto d'Alba Ginestra, Barbera d'Alba Ginestra

With their balance of fruit and flavor, these wines are always among the most notable in the region.

Conterno-Fantino***–*****
Monforte d'Alba

32 acres (13 ha); 90,000 bottles • Wines: Barolo: Vigna del Gris, →Sori Ginestra; Barbera d'Albi Vignota, →Langhe Rosso Monprà, Langhe Chardonnay Bastia

Recommended: the Ginestra single-vineyard Barolo and the half-and-half Nebbiolo Barbera blend Monprà.

Barolo is famous for its longevity.

Giovanni Corrino****
La Morra

25 acres (10 ha); 20,000 bottles • Wines: Barolo: →Vigneto Rocche, →Vigna Giachini; Barbera d'Alba Vigna Pozzo, →Barbera d'Alba, Dolcetto d'Alba

Renato and Giuliano have attracted attention with their single-vineyard Barolos and excellent Barbera Pozzo.

Erbaluna—S. & A. Oberto**–***
La Morra

18.5 acres (7.5 ha); 40,000 bottles • Wines: Barbera d'Alba, Dolcetto d'Alba, Nebbiolo Langhe, Grignolino Langhe, Barolo Vigna Rocche

With its Rocche dell'Annunziata, Piedmont's best-known organic estate has one of the finest vineyards, and also produces a high quality Barolo.

Gaja*****
Barbaresco

238 acres (96 ha); 350,000 bottles • Wines include: Barbaresco: →Costa Russi, →Sorì San Lorenzo, Sorì Tildin; Barolo Sperss, →Langhe Darmagi, Barbera Sitorey, Dolcetto Langhe Cremes, Sito Moresco, →Langhe Chardonnay: Gaja & Rey and Rossj-Bass

The leading light of Italian wine production (see panel on preceding page).

Bruno Giacosa****–*****
Neive

37 acres (15 ha); some bought-in grapes; 550,000 bottles • Wines include: Barbaresco: →Santo Stefano, Gallina, Basarin; Barolo: →Falletto, Villero, →Collina Rionda, →Rocche di Castiglione Falletto; Nebbiolo d'Alba Valmaggiore, Roero Arneis, Spumante Giacosa

Every year, Giacosa sources the best grapes for his Barbaresco Santo Stefano and the traditional single-vineyard Barolos. The Spumante is one of the best in Italy.

Fratelli Giacosa***–****
Neive

49 acres (20 ha); some bought-in grapes; 500,000 bottles • Wines include: Barolo: Bussia, La Mandorla,; Barbaresco: →Rio Sordo, Roccalini; Barbera d'Alba: Bussia, Maria Gioana; Dolcetto San Rocco, Chardonnay, Roero Arneis

This négociant house moved out of the shadow of its famous namesake in the early 1990s, primarily because of its Barbaresco Rio Sordo and Barolo Bussia.

Elio Grasso****–*****
Monforte d'Alba

33 acres (13.4 ha); 50,000 bottles • Wines include: Barbera Langhe Vigna Martina, Barolo: →Ginestra Casa Matè, →Barolo Gavarini Vigna Chiniera, Dolcetto d'Alba Gavarini Vigna dei Grassi, Langhe Chardonnay

Grasso made the leap into the Piedmontese elite with his outstanding vintages of the late 1980s.

Silvio Grasso***–****
La Morra

17 acres (7 ha); 40,000 bottles • Wines: Barolo: →Bricco Luciani, →Ciabòt Manzoni, Langhe Nebbiolo, Barbera d'Alba Fontanile

This house has made tentative steps toward modernization.

Bartolo Mascarello***–****
Barolo

12 acres (5 ha); 35,000 bottles • Wines: Barolo, Dolcetto d'Alba, Barbera d'Alba Vigna San Lorenzo

Excellent traditional wines up till the 1980s, after which there was something of a decline. There are no single-vineyard wines.

GIUSEPPE MASCARELLO & FIGLIO**–****
MONCHIERO
124 acres (50 ha); 50,000 bottles • Wines include: Barolo: →Monprivato, Bricco, →Villero, Codana; Barbaresco Macarini, Barbera d'Alba, Dolcetto d'Alba: Bricco, Pian Romualdo; Nebbiolo d'Alba San Rocco
In good years, Monprivato is among the top group of traditionalist wines. The estate vineyards vary in quality.

VIGNA RIONDA—G. MASSOLINO & FIGLI***–****
SERRALUNGA D'ALBA
40 acres (16 ha); 90,000 bottles • Wines include: Barolo: Vigna Rionda, Parafada, Margheria; Barbera d'Alba, Dolcetto d'Alba Barilot, Piria, Moscato d'Asti, Chardonnay Langhe
Vigna Rionda is one of the best Barolo vineyards and its grapes yield the Massolinos' best wine.

MOCCAGATTA**–*****
BARBARESCO
27 acres (11 ha); 50,000 bottles • Wines include: Barbaresco: →Bric Balin,→Cole; Barbera d'Alba Vigneto Basarin' Dolcetto d'Alba Vigna Buschet, →Langhe Chardonnay Bric Buschet
This modern operation—the third generation of Minutos—has made a very good name for itself with single-vineyard Barbarescos and Chardonnay.

MONFALLETTO-CORDERO DI MONTEZEMOLO**–****
LA MORRA
67 acres (27 ha); 120,000 bottles • Wines: Barolo: →Monfalletto, →Enrico VI, Chardonnay Langhe Elioro, Barbera d'Alba, Dolcetto d'Alba, Pinot Nero
This traditional estate became famous for its Barolo Enrico VI. The current owners have also given the wine a more modern touch.

NADA***–****
TREISO
16 acres (6.5 ha); 20,000 bottles • Wines: Barbaresco, Dolcetto d'Alba, Langhe Rosso Seifile
With its Barbaresco and Nebbiolo blend, in good years, Nada is among the area's best, although it has no top quality Nebbiolo sites in Treiso.

FRATELLI ODDERO**–*****
LA MORRA
131 acres (53 ha); 250,000 bottles • Wines include: Barbaresco, Barolo: →Mondoca di Bussia, →Rocche di Castiglione, →Vigna Rionda; Langhe: Furesté, Chardonnay; Collaretto, Barbera d'Alba, Dolcetto d'Alba
The single-vineyard Barolos, particularly the Rionda, embody a good compromise between traditional and more modern styles.

ARMANDO PARUSSO***–*****
MONFORTE D'ALBA
20 acres (8 ha); 50,000 bottles • Wines include: Barolo: →Bussia Vigna Munie, →Bussia Vigna Rocche; Dolcetto d'Alba, Barbera d'Alba Ornati, Langhe Bricco Rovella Bianco, →Rosso
Marco and Tiziana Parusso are among the top group of modernists in the Langhe region. Of their wines, Barolo Bussia Rocche and the red Bricco Rovella are of particular high quality.

E. PIRA & FIGLI****–*****
BAROLO
9 acres (3.5 ha); 15,000 bottles • Wines: Barolo, →Barolo Cannubi
This estate is run by Chiara Boschis and is part of the Borgogno *négociant* company in Barolo. It has attracted attention with its very good single-vineyard Barolo Cannubi.

PODERI ROCCHE DEI MANZONI***–****
MONFORTE D'ALBA
148 acres (60 ha); 180,000 bottles • Wines include: Barolo: →Vigna d'la Roul, →Vigna Big; Bricco dei Manzoni
A convinced modernist, Valentino Migniori shines with his elegant single-vineyard Barolo, but also produces excellent sparkling wine fermented in the bottle.

PRINCIPIANO FERDINANDO***–****
MONFORTE D'ALBA
22 acres (9 ha); 25,000 bottles • Wines include: Barolo Boscareto, Barbera d'Alba Pian Romualdo, Dolcetto d'Alba
The abundantly fruity aroma and taste of the barrel-fermented, single-vineyard Barolo Boscareto is popular.

ALBINO ROCCA****–*****
BARBARESCO
22 acres (9 ha); 65,000 bottles • Wines: →Dolcetto d'Alba Vignalunga, Barbera d'Alba Gepin, Barbaresco: →Vigneto Loreto and Brich Ronchi; Langhe Bianco La Rocca
Angelo Rocca emerged from his cousin Bruno's shadow in the 1990s. The Loreto vineyard yields top class Barbaresco.

BRUNO ROCCA—RABAJ***–****
BARBARESCO
15 acres (6 ha); 30,000 bottles • Wines: Barbaresco: →Rabajà, Coparossa; Barbera d'Alba, Langhe Chardonnay Cadet, Dolcetto d'Alba Trifolé
One of Barbaresco's top estates of the 1980s, now a little tired, but still producing some very good wines.

LUCIANO SANDRONE****–*****
BAROLO
27 acres (11 ha); 40,000 bottles • Wines: →Barolo Cannubi Boschis, Barolo, Dolcetto d'Alba, →Barbera d'Alba, →Nebbiolo d'Alba Valmaggiore
Sandrone achieved world fame with his Cannubi Boschi single-vineyard Barolo and blotted out the memory of the difficult years in the early 1990s with his Barolo and Nebbiolo of 1995.

PAOLO SCAVINO*****
CASTIGLIONE FALLETTO
30 acres (12 ha); 65,000 bottles • Wines: Barolo: →Bric del Fiasc, →Cannubi, →Rocche dell'Annunzata; Barbera Carati
Enrico Scavoni's Barolo del Fiasco is legendary and he also sets standards with his barrel-aged Barbera.

SETIMO AURELIO***
LA MORRA
17 acres (7 ha); 40,000 bottles • Wines: Barolo, Barolo Vigneti Rocche, Dolcetto d'Alba, Langhe Nebbiolo
Tiziana Settimo is a woman who maintains the traditional style of Barolo. The single-vineyard Barolo Rocche is powerful and long-lasting.

MARO VEGLIO***–****
LA MORRA
25 acres (10 ha); 30,000 bottles • Wines: →Barolo Castelleto, Barolo Vigneto Arborina, Gattera, Rocche, →Barbera d'Alba Cascina Nuova, L'Insieme
Young Mauro and his wife Daniela have learned a lot from their neighbor Elio Altare, as is shown by the reliable quality of their barrel-aged wines.

ROBERTO VOERZIO*****
LA MORRA
25 acres (10 ha); 45,000 bottles • Wines: Barolo: La Serra, Cerequio, Brunate; Barbera d'Alba Vignasse, Vignaserra, Dolcetto d'Alba Priavino, Langhe Chardonnay Fossati e Roscaleto
Voerzio's best wines are Barolo La Serra and Cerequio, the Vignaserra and the Barbera Vignasse.

Piedmontese White Wines

Apart from Moscato, which is mainly made into sparkling wine, Cortese is the only vine variety from which large quantities of white wine are produced in Piedmont. It grows in the Monferrato hills, north and south of Alessandria, and in the mountains around Gavi, where it provides the basis for one of Italy's favorite white wines, Gavi or Cortesi di Gavi.

Cortese di Gavi

Vittorio Soldati, an ambitious amateur producer, was the first to demonstrate successfully, in the 1950s, that Gavi could be more than a very basic *trattoria* wine. He quickly recognized the relationship between the restriction of yields and the quality of the wine produced. After initial, very promising successes on the La Scolca estate, Soldati invested in a minimum of technology. In the winery, he concentrated on slow, controlled-temperature fermentation and reductive aging. In acknowledgment of the value of his wine, he called it Gavi di Gavi. International recognition was not long coming, and in 1998 the quality was legally prescribed and Cortese di Gavi, as it is now called, was awarded D.O.C.G. status.

A Little More, Perhaps?

The authorized yield is surprisingly generous: a maximum yield of 4.2 tons per acre (9.5 tonnes/ha) which corresponds to a must volume of almost 1,850 gallons (70 hl). If the 20 percent excess permitted in Italy, which winemakers almost always take advantage of, is added, this gives more than 850 gallons per acre (80 hl/ha). The 10.5 percent minimum alcohol content is probably an acknowledgment of the climatic conditions—because it is relatively cool in the vineyards, the must weight usually remains lower —and it is also an acknowledgment of the high vineyard yields, which at a minimum stock density of 1,340 vines per acre (3,300 vines/ha) translate into a yield of approximately seven pounds (3 kg) of grapes per vine or more. Top varieties generally yield less than two pounds (1 kg).

Quality-conscious producers try to compensate for the short growth period with vineyard work—denser planting, leaf work during the summer, and, above all, thinning the grapes to reduce the yield per vine, which brings the risk of a very late harvest. When its potential is

Arneis was groomed to become the white counterpart of the region's great reds. Despite its pleasant aromatic qualities, however, it lacks the pedigree and potential to become a truly great wine.

exploited to the full, Gavi is between straw yellow and golden yellow in color, its scent is based on exotic fruit notes as well as apricots and apple, and the taste is generally accompanied by a soft almond tone.

Some producers process their best grapes separately on a single-vineyard basis and age the wine partly in *barriques*. Wood-aging lends a fine, light, sweetish note to both the aroma and taste which balances the rather acidic Gavi well. However, most of what is produced from Cortese, under the original *appellation* Gavi, and in the D.O.C. areas Colli Tortonesi, Monferrato, and in the Piedmont area in general, remains little more than a light, fresh, pedestrian wine.

Arneis in Roero and Langhe

In the hills north of the Tanaro, the two regional white wine varieties, Arneis and Favorita, are arousing interest. For a long time they were used only for blending in red wines or as table grapes, and were threatened with complete neglect and extinction, until some innovative producers took up their cause. Today Arneis grows once again on around 1,235 acres (500 ha) of vineyard, a fact which is mainly due to the efforts of the Bruno Giacosa and Ceretto *négociant* houses. On the conical mountains of Roero, and in Langhe, the variety was even awarded D.O.C. status in 1989, but it yields very varied wines. Two types of Arneis wines have emerged, based on the production techniques used: the first displays a very one-dimensional fruit with a light almond taste and mild acid; the second is more complex, with an abundant aroma of blossoms, apples, peaches, or nuts.

Quality starts in the vineyard.

FAVORITA AND CHARDONNAY

The Favorita—another variety that is indigenous to Roero and Langhe—also seemed to have been completely forgotten and was almost forced to make way for Chardonnay. In all of Piedmont only 370 acres (150 ha) are planted with the variety. It is closely related (or even identical) to Ligurian Vermentino, whose taste characteristics it shares. Thirteen producers cultivate this variety and bottle fresh, fruity wines with a consistently good acid structure. When fermented in *barriques* they tend to have a sweeter bouquet and full, spicy taste.

Consumer popularity explains the unparalleled rise of Chardonnay. This popular grape was mainly grown in vineyards which had grown Dolcetto or indigenous white varieties.

Chardonnay is now usually part of the standard repertoire of the larger Piedmontese estates. Its wines enjoy D.O.C. status with the general *appellations* of Piedmont and Langhe. A prestigious wine, it is generally fermented and aged in small oak barrels, following the French and Californian models.

Finally, the dry, often bottle-fermented white sparkling wines deserve a mention. They do not have D.O.C. status in Piedmont and their existence depends entirely on the efforts of individual producers and wineries, but they often attain impressive levels of quality. The grapes are often purchased from neighboring Lombardy, vinification and bottle fermentation, however, are only carried out in Piedmontese wineries.

Pergola cultivation—as seen here in Carema—has only survived in areas close to the mountains where vines are threatened by frost.

SELECT PRODUCERS OF GAVI

CASTELLARI BERGAGLIO***–****
GAVI
25 acres (10 ha); 70,000 bottles • Wines: Gavi di Gavi Fornaci Rollona, →Gavi di Gavi Roverto Vigna Vecchia, Pilin
For years Marco Bergaglio has been committed to Gavi of outstanding quality, making him an exemplary winemaker. Bergaglio has broken ground in Gavi with his barrel-aged whites.

LA SCOLCA***
GAVI
111 acres (45 ha); 350,000 bottles • Wines include: Gavi Villa Scolca, Gavi di Gavi, Soldati La Scolca Spumante Brut

Vittorio Soldati started bottling Gavi as early as the 1950s, and with his Etichetta Nera in 1966 he created a model which had a stimulating effect on the entire region. He also produces notable sparkling wines.

TENUTA SAN PIETRO***
TASSAROLO
37 acres (15 ha); 100,000 bottles • Wines: Gavi: →San Pietro, Bricco del Mandorlo, Vigneto La Gorrina
Maria Rosa Gazzinga's estate in Tassarolo, only a few miles north of Gavi, is one of the historic founding estates in the Gavi region. The wines are light and harmonious but generally rather neutral in character.

LIGURIA

As well as Dolcetto, which is known as Ormeasco here, the varieties Vermentino, Pigato, and Rossese are cultivated near towns such as Triora in the mountainous hinterland of the western Riviera.

The orange and lemon blossoms are a real give-away: the climate in Liguria bears no resemblance to that of its neighboring regions. Its location on the Gulf of Genoa, nestled into the southern slopes of the western Maritime Alps, makes this half-moon stretch of coastline an almost tropical enclave in the predominantly cool regions of northern Italy. The Ligurian Alps, which climb to heights of over 8,120 feet (2,500 m), and the Ligurian Apennines, provide effective shelter from cold winds. The sea also stores and slowly releases the sun's heat so annual mean temperatures here are even higher than in Tuscany.

However, the topography of the region places significant obstacles in the way of agriculture. For even the most basic farming purposes, the Mediterranean *maquis* had to be cut back and terraces had to be dug into the steep slopes and

secured. As a result, a unique cultivated landscape has developed in Liguria over the centuries and has survived to the present day.

TRADITIONAL VITICULTURE

However, the survival of this landscape comes at a cost. Villages stand empty and terraces have fallen into decay. Wine production here has adhered to its traditions, or, to be more precise, winemaking is too unimportant in Liguria for anyone to have bothered to change it. Neither the quantitative euphoria of the 1960s nor the technological evangelism of the 1970s and 1980s made any impression here. However, with current yields at around 375 gallons per acre (35 hl/ha), it would appear that some quality-oriented producers are returning to Ligurian standards. Nowhere else in Italy have so many indigenous vine varieties managed to survive. At the last count, there were over 100, some merely covering a few acres. However, each abandoned vineyard means the potential loss of valuable varieties.

CINQUETERRE

The name of the steep coastal cliff on the Riviera del Levante, north of the town of La Spezia, is associated with a white wine produced from the local varieties of Bosco, Albarola, and Vermentino. When good, its slightly salty taste makes it an excellent accompaniment to the fish dishes which are a mainstay of the local cuisine.

Sciacchetrà, the dessert wine version produced from the same blend of grapes, was once well

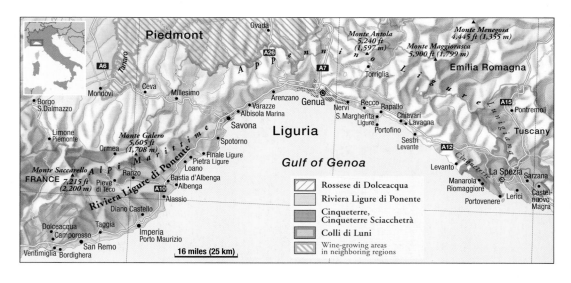

Select Producers in Liguria

Maria Donata Bianchi***–****
Diano Castello
6 acres (2.5 ha); 20,000 bottles • Wines: Riviera Ligure di Ponente: Vermentino, Pigato; →Eretico: Vermetino, Pigato
Emanuele Trevia, a pioneer of modern winery techniques in Liguria, produces powerful, structured whites.

Bruna***
Ranzo
13.6 acres (5.5 ha); 37,000 bottles • Wines: Riviera Ligure di Ponente: Pigato Le Russeghine, Pigato Villa Torrachetta, Rossese Le Russeghine, →Pigato U Baccan
Francesca Bruna's specialty is the Pigato grape and the very individual U Baccan from over-ripe selected grapes.

Cascina Feipu dei Massaretti***
Bastia d'Albenga
11 acres (4.5 ha); 45,000 bottles • Wines: Riviera di Ponente: Pigato, Rossese; Russu du Feipu, Due Anelli

The diligence of Agostino 'Pippo' Parodi turns the sensitive Pigato grape into high quality wines.

Tommaso e Angelo Lupi***–****
Pieve di Teco
34.5 acres (14 ha); 150,000 bottles • Wines: Riviera Ligure di Ponente: Pigato, Vermentino, Ormeasco; Vignamare
The very clean, pure wines are vinified in collaboration with Donato Lanati, considered the best enologist in Piedmont, who learned his skills from the Tuscan Giacomo Tachis.

Terre Rosse***
Finale Ligure
11 acres (4.5 ha); 25,000 bottles • Wines: Vermentino, Pigato, →L'Acerbina, Le Banche, →Solitario, Passito Terre Rosse
The minerals which give the vineyards soils their red color (*terre rosse*) are also found in the wines; there are vine varieties such as Lumassina, now considered extinct.

---

known far beyond the borders of Liguria but is now only produced in small quantities.

A Mediterranean Herb Garden

The few quality-oriented producers in Liguria have hitherto devoted all of their innovative energies to the white varieties of Vermentino and Pigato, the latter being one of the varieties exclusive to Liguria which was probably established here by the Ancient Greeks. This variety is mainly cultivated on around 490 acres (200 ha) in the Val d'Arroscia valley near Ranzo, and in the Albenga enclave.

As charming as towns like Triora look with their nooks and crannies, conditions for wine growing are difficult here and few producers succeed in providing more than simple table wines.

Pigato acquires its typical bouquet, with notes of wild herbs and wild flowers, on the sun-drenched terraces. The low yields and favorable climatic conditions ensure that even average years give structured wines with a high alcohol content. As a sweet dried-grape Passito—a kind of "straw wine" (vin de paille)—this variety exudes rich honey and apricot aromas.

Vermentino, Liguria's best-known white variety, has D.O.C. status in the Riviera Ligure di Ponente zone, between Genoa and the French border, and in Colli di Luni between La Spezia and Tuscany. Although less sophisticated than Pigato, this variety also has aromas of Mediterranean herbs and its soft taste has subtle lemon notes and pleasant spicy undertones.

Ligurian Red Wines

Rossese di Dolceaqua, from the mountains behind Ventimiglia, Bordighera, and San Remo, is a ruby-red wine of rustic simplicity. Just a few producers succeed in creating wines from Rossese grapes, which combine an aroma of dried roses and fruits of the forest with a subtle note of almonds. In the Albenga zone of the Savona province, where Rossese is bottled under the Riviera Ligure di Ponente D.O.C., it generally yields paler-colored and light-tasting everyday wine which is similar to the dry rosé from the indigenous Barbarossa grape.

Ormeasco is the name given here to the Piedmontese variety Dolcetto. When aged in wood, it can produce good, competitive wines. Finally, the best-known Tuscan variety, Sangiovese, also deserves a mention as it is occasionally found in the eastern part of Liguria under the Colli di Luni D.O.C.

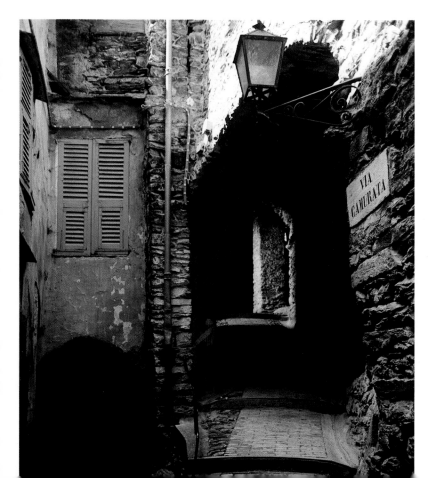

LOMBARDY

With its metropolis, Milan, Lombardy is the industrial heart of Italy and its most densely populated region. Its image as an agricultural region is dominated by the widespread cultivation of rice, maize, wheat, and vines. Vines can be seen growing everywhere in the region, from Veltlin in the narrow Alpine valley of the Adda, the west bank of Lake Garda, the plain of the river Po near Mantua, the hills to the south of Pavia and, finally, to the slopes near Bergamo and Brescia. A lot of wine is produced here but not much is of high quality. The enormous market for everyday and bulk wines in metropolitan Milan has hindered the development of a leading regional wine or even a uniform style of production. Local wines are in demand as a basis for sparkling wine production in other regions, and it is only in recent decades that smaller areas like Franciacorta have succeeded in establishing an independent image.

The climate is subject to continental Alpine and Mediterranean influences. With its hot summers and often very cold winters, high humidity levels, and fresh fertile soils, only a few parts of the Po plain are suitable for viticulture. However, the hill and mountain landscapes provide better locations for growing vines, thanks to their almost Mediterranean climate and the shelter of the Alps.

Left
Bottles are stored neck-down and shaken daily to move the yeast deposits to the neck of the bottle. This is done by hand at the Lorenzo Faccoli winery.

Right
Franciacorta is produced using the bottle-fermentation method. The Spumante is left lying on the lees for years. At the end of the storage period, the yeast deposit is removed by disgorgement.

A MODERN SPARKLING WINE

Today, Lombardy's most reputable individual zone is without doubt Franciacorta, where Italy's best dry sparkling wines have been produced for some years now, some of which enjoy D.O.C.G. status. In recent decades, a veritable Spumante industry, consisting of 80 wineries using the Champagne method, has established itself on the slopes around Lake Iseo. Since the changes in legislation, the area's still wines, some of which are truly excellent, also have their own D.O.C. designation, Terre di Franciacorta. At four million bottles, the total volume produced in the area is, however, too low to make an impact on the international market: by comparison, 270 million bottles are produced in Champagne each year.

Cellatico, a light red wine, is produced north of Brescia and is a blend of Schiava, Barbera, Marzemino, and Incrocio Terzi No. I, a hybrid of Cabernet Franc and Barbera, only cultivated in Italy. Cellatico, and the *appellations* Capriano del Colle and Botticino, are unknown outside the locality and the same applies for the D.O.C. wines of the Riviera del Garda Brescino, where Groppello is the main variety cultivated. The rather neutral white wine, Lugana, produced from Trebbiano grapes on the south bank of Lake Garda, is slightly better known.

Farmsteads nestled into the vineyard slopes in Valtellina.

■	Valtellina
■	Valcalepio
■	Franciacorta, Terre di Franciacorta
■	Cellatica
■	Capriano del Colle
◆	Botticino
■	Riviera del Garda Bresciano
□	Tocai di San Martino della Battaglia
◆	Lugana
■	Colli Morenici Mantovani del Garda
■	Lambrusco Mantovano
■	Oltrepò Pavese
▨	Wine-growing areas in neighboring regions

Mountain Nebbiolo

Previously, the Veltlin (known as Valtellina in Italian) region was mainly a supplier of bulk wine to the neighboring Swiss canton of Grisons. The main grape variety grown in Veltlin is Piedmontese Nebbiolo, known here as Chiavennasca; however, it does not always reach full maturity on the slopes of the narrow, steep Adda valley. Although the Rhaetian and Lepontine Alps deflect a lot of the rain and cold north winds, only the terraces on the southern slopes provide conditions that are adequate for vine cultivation.

Vines from these southern terraces, which develop a minimum alcohol content of 12 percent, have enjoyed D.O.C.G. status since 1998, and can bear the vineyard designations of Sassella, Grumello, Inferno, and Valgella, as can the D.O.C. Valtellina Superiore. As the Veltlin Nebbiolo generally produces rather bitter and acidic wines, the valley's producers

Franciacorta—the champagne of Italy

The name of the moraine landscape on the southern periphery of Lake Iseo between Bergamo and Brescia is probably derived from the "*francae curtes*," the tax exemption granted to the Benedictine Order in the area during the Middle Ages. Up to the mid-20th century, the area produced little more than ordinary wine for local consumption.

Franciacorta's rise to become the "Champagne of Italy" started in 1961 when Guido Berlucchi's enologist persuaded him to produce a sparkling wine. The success of the venture was so conclusive that in the 1970s Milanese industrialists started to invest in the area's growing Spumante industry. Following

Berlucchi's example—his winery produces over four million bottles annually from wines originating from Oltrepò and Trentino—local producers began to specialize in bottle-fermented sparkling wines produced using the Champagne method and based on Pinot and Chardonnay.

In 1995, Franciacorta was honored as Italy's first and (still) only bottle-fermented D.O.C.G. sparkling wine, and, unlike the other inglorious D.O.C.G. white wines, Albana di Romagna, Asti, and Vernaccia di San Gimignano, it actually deserved it.

The Franciacorta label may only be sported by wines produced from Chardonnay, Pinot Blanc, Pinot Noir, and a maximum of 15 percent of Pinot Gris, which mature on the

lees for at least 18 months, or 30 months in the case of vintage production.

The best Franciacorta Spumantes are BRUT. A sweetening dosage is not really necessary, as the temperatures enjoyed in the area are significantly higher than in the Champagne region of France. Body and aromatic richness, as well as additional subtleties of flavor, are provided by the storage of the basic wine in *barriques*. In addition to standard white sparkling wines, the area also produces rosé sparkling wines and the Franciacorta specialty, Satèn, which is aged for longer than normal sparkling wine and based on grapes originating from vineyards whose maximum official yield is around 20 percent lower than that allowed for the standard wines.

THE NORTHEAST:
BETWEEN THE HABSBURG EMPIRE AND VENICE

plain is characterized by Mediterranean influences. This balancing effect on temperatures extends right up to the west of the region—the shores of Lake Garda boast typical southern vegetation with cypress and palm trees. The higher locations on the edge of the Dolomites and the Alps experience a typical mountain climate, with significant differences between day and night temperatures. However, the peaks of up to 9,750 feet (3,000 m) provide shelter from the northern frosts and this significantly extends the growing season, particularly in spring. Thus, vine varieties which require relatively long growth and ripening periods can be cultivated in the higher locations in Friuli which are unlikely to be reached by the sea's temperate influence. Heavy storms, often with hail, which are capable of destroying entire harvests, are the main climatic problem on the southern edge of the Alps.

VARIETY IN THE VINEYARDS

The diversity of the region's soil and climate poses a real challenge to the range of indigenous and imported vine varieties cultivated there, and to the types of wine produced from them. International Merlot grows alongside local specialties such as Marzemino or Pignolo, and the weighty Amarone with its high alcohol content is produced along with fresh, light whites and delicate dessert wines. However, this diversity cannot be explained by the natural conditions alone. Just like the Tyroleans, Habsburgs, Venetians, and French of more recent periods, the Etruscans, Romans, Carelians, and Illyrians left their mark on this landscape. They all influenced viticulture, which to the present day remains partly based on old political boundaries or on wine growing in neighboring countries.

In the recent past also, developments in wine production in the various zones have followed anything but a simultaneous course. While in Alto Adige the emphasis on quality production started at a very early stage, thanks mainly to the efforts of the cooperatives and large wineries, in the neighboring province of Trentino, where wine growing was still largely in the hands of smaller operations, the quality movement did not really take hold until ten years later—one of the consequences of the area's traditional role as a supplier of base wine for the local and

The landscapes in this large region comprising Trentino, Alto Adige (Southern Tyrol), Friuli-Venezia Giulia, Veneto, and Emilia Romagna are formed by the Alps in the north, the Apennines in the south, the Po plain in the middle and the Adriatic coastal lands in the east. The soils available for viticulture vary as widely as these geological formations: the barren and highly porous soils of the deep Alpine valleys are composed of gravel and morainic scree with a high proportion of limestone; the soils found in floodplains of the Adige river valley are highly fertile; the barren dry soils of the morainic hills on the southern edge of the Alpine foothills are interspersed with glacial gravel; and the marine deposits of the coastal strips and the plain of the river Po, which was once almost completely flooded by the Adriatic Sea, are dominated by calcareous marl with sandstone inclusions. The foothills of the Apennines are less subject to erosion than those of the Alps, and their soils are dominated by lime gravel, sandstone, marl, and clay. The numerous rivers with their deposits create fertile soils in the valleys.

The climate in northeastern Italy varies as widely as its landscapes and soils. Although Trentino-Alto Adige enjoys a cool, Alpine-continental climate, the terraces of the Adige valley and its tributaries are blessed with around 2,000 hours of sun annually and an average temperature of 63°F (17°C), and are hence highly suited to viticulture. In contrast, the climate of the Po

With its Vinitaly trade fair, Verona becomes Italy's wine capital every April. However, there are many other wine-related events throughout the year and particularly in the Bottega del Vino, the city's best-known wine bar.

Silvio Jermann flouts Friulian tradition by creating his wines from blends of different varieties. He bottles them as table wines, gives them striking names, and lets their quality speak for itself.

international sparkling wine industry. In the 1980s, the producers in Friuli concentrated their energies on the production of fruity, light, modern white wines which were aimed at the gap in the Italian market which previously was only served successfully by Alto Adige. The developments of recent years indicate, however, that the main opportunities in the future could lie with the red or strongly structured white wines.

QUALITY OR QUANTITY?

Veneto, which is one of Italy's most prolific wine-producing regions and a traditional center of international wine trade with northern Europe, paints a contradictory picture. Winemaking in the areas around the city of Verona, for example Valpolicella, Soave, and Bardolino, yields both outstanding quality and anonymous mass-produced wines, as the vines here are cultivated not only on the slopes, which are best for quality, but also in the fertile flood plain of the river

Adige. The west of the region has established a good reputation in the past two decades, with products such as the heavy red wine Amarone and individual dessert wines.

In the east of Veneto, apart from the successful efforts of a minority of producers, a mass-production ideology still reigns. Prosecco —which can vary significantly in quality—is the only well-known wine produced here. As long as the region can find a secure market for its cheaper products, there will be little incentive to exploit the ideal conditions it enjoys for quality production. A change of heart with respect to quality can only be expected if the competition from other European or overseas countries becomes more acute.

This is even more true of Emilia Romagna, whose development has been blocked for decades by the huge volumes of basic Lambrusco produced there. The efforts of individual producers to improve quality are even more rare here, and all the more valuable.

Contrasting wine-growing landscapes in northern Italy: from Mezzolombardo, Trentino to Laimburg, Alto Adige.

Regional vine varieties

The international vine varieties have established a firmer foothold in the northeast than in any other part of Italy. Merlot (Friuli), Cabernet Sauvignon, Cabernet Franc, and Pinot Noir (Alto Adige) have been cultivated here since the phylloxera catastrophe of the late 19th century, and in some cases with very good results. Pinot Gris, or Pinot Grigio as it is known here, has become Italy's most popular wine. It is found together with Chardonnay in most of the region's newly established vineyards, while the only common Italian varieties are Sangiovese, Barbera, and Trebbiano (mainly in Emilia Romagna).

All of the other vines cultivated in the Northeast are regional varieties. The most popular is the Schiava or Vernatsch (called Trollinger in

Germany) in Trentino-Alto Adige which is mainly used in the production of the Lago di Caldaro (Kalterer See) D.O.C. Lagrein, Teroldego, and Marzemino are not very strongly represented in terms of volume, but there is currently a revived interest in their red wines.

Corvina, the main variety used in the production of Valpolicella, Bardolino, and Amarone, is widely planted in Veneto. The Po plain is stocked with sub-varieties of the Lambrusco family (Grasparossa, Marani, Maestri, Salamino, Monterico, di Sorbara). Other red varieties worthy of mention in this context include: Raboso (Veneto), Refosco Dal Peduncolo Rosso (Friuli), Pignolo (Friuli), Schioppettino (Friuli), and Tazzelenghe (Friuli).

With 32,000 acres (13,000 ha), the most widely-planted white variety in Veneto is Garganega, which is the main constituent of

Soave. White varieties from German-speaking areas, such as Riesling, Müller-Thurgau, Veltliner, Kerner, Silvaner, and Gewürztraminer, are common in Alto Adige, Trentino, and Friuli. In Trentino they are complemented by the indigenous Nosiola and Moscato Giallo/Rosa varieties. The indigenous variety Malvasia di Candia thrives in Emilia Romagna as does Albana, the first white wine variety to be awarded D.O.C.G. status. Albana can also be found in Friuli along with the other white varieties Tocai Friulano/Italico, Verduzzo, Ribolla Gialla, Picolit, and Vitovska.

In Italy, the Northeast is the region with the most interesting potential in terms of varieties. Their systematic improvement and use could inject badly-needed inspiration into a global market dominated by increasingly homogeneous wines.

TRENTINO

Trentino has the Etruscans, rather than the Romans, to thank for establishing viticulture in the region. It is even said that the Romans, who did much to spread wine growing within and outside of Italy, learned some of their vineyard and winery techniques, including the use of wooden casks as fermentation and storage containers, from the Etruscan cultures of northern Italy. As in the neighboring province of Alto Adige, wine production is mainly concentrated in and around the valley of the Adige river and its tributaries. Vines are cultivated on around 22,240 acres (9,000 ha)—partly in the fertile flood plain, and partly on the barren slopes whose soils mainly consist of moraine gravel. Seventy percent of the vines are distributed among five D.O.C. areas and four I.G.T. designations are available for the rest.

Artistically stacked bottles of Trento, a Spumante produced from Chardonnay and the Pinot varieties. This wine matures on the racks.

MARZEMINO AND TEROLDEGO

The wines of this province were first exposed to a wider public during the Counter-Reformation Council of Trent, the third session of which opened in Trent in 1545 and was completed, after repeated interruptions, in 1563. The participants may have focused their attention on the more delightful aspects of the sacrament of the mass after the actual council sessions, as some of the vine varieties used to produce the region's wines today were available at the time, for example Marzemino and Teroldego. Marzemino is one of the less well-known indigenous vine varieties of northern Italy. This late-ripening, resistant variety can produce full-bodied aromatic wines but it is often used as a high-volume base for lightly sparkling wines. Its

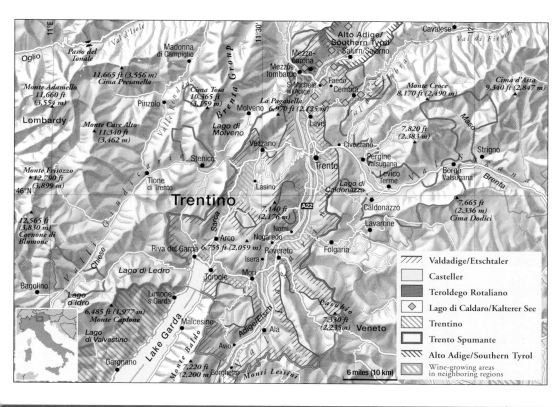

Trentino is a fascinating wine landscape located for the most part in the valley of the river Adige and framed by high mountains which protect it from inclement weather.

valley of lakes to the north of Riva del Garda—the range of vines cultivated here is dominated by international varieties. Chardonnay and Pinot Gris have had a major impact on the white wines, while interesting reds are being produced using Cabernet and Merlot.

MODERN WHITE AND RED WINES

The miles of wine-growing areas lining both sides of the Brenner expressway are dominated by high pergolas (a form of overhead vine training) which protect the grapes from excessive heat, decay, and disease. The disadvantage of this form of protection lies in the fact that it promotes excessive yields. This is reflected in the D.O.C. regulations, with their over-generous upper limits of up to 7 tons per acre (15 tonnes/ha) and the clear emphasis on quantity in Trentino viticulture. Individual producers have, meanwhile, proved that fresh, aromatic white wines can be yielded on the mountain slopes, despite their barren soils and significant variations between day and night temperatures. Most of the production, particularly from the major D.O.C. zone of Valdadige, can at best be described as "clean but inconsequential."

In addition to white varieties, large quantities of red grapes are also cultivated in this province.

potential can only fully unfold on suitable soils, for example the black basalt of the villages of Isera and Nomi in the Trentino D.O.C. zone. Isera Marzemino, an elegant wine with a subtle almond aroma, which was immortalized by Mozart in his opera *Don Giovanni*, can include the domain name in its designation.

Teroldego, the only Italian variety which thrives on flat ground as opposed to slopes, has even greater potential if cultivated in soils that are not too fertile. This vine variety, which is grown almost exclusively on the very gravelly flood plain of the Campo Rotaliano near Mezzocorona and Mezzolombardo in Trentino, yields deep-colored red wines with complex aromas. Its outstanding character won it the award of its own D.O.C., Teroldego Rotaliano. However, the D.O.C. regulations authorize yields of up to 1,335 gallons per acre (125 hl/ha) which is difficult to reconcile with modern quality standards. The best Teroldego producers in Campo Rotaliano limit themselves to yields of no more than 425–535 gallons per acre (40–50 hl/ha). The barrel-aged vintages, in particular, can display a depth and complexity of taste which is rarely found in the province. These wines have aromas of liquorice, plums, cherries, and violets, plenty of power and even some aging capacity.

In addition to the indigenous varieties, which also include red Schiava (called Vernatsch or Trollinger in Alto Adige) in its various variants, and white Nosiola—from which an interesting VIN SANTO is produced in Valle dei Laghi, the

Mezzolombardo against a mountain backdrop.

From *négociant* house to quality wine estate—Endrizzi in San Michele.

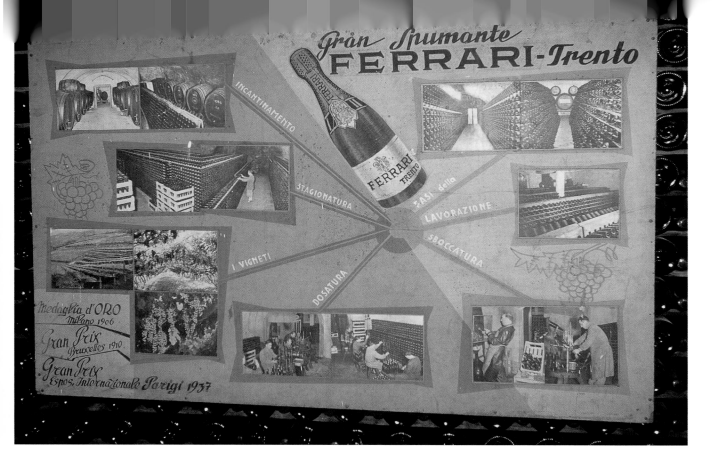

The top varieties include Merlot and Cabernet Franc, and to a lesser extent Cabernet Sauvignon, which are often bottled as single varietals. Some producers are experimenting with a Bordeaux blend which can yield successful, and powerful, wines. As with the whites, most of the Trentino reds bear the D.O.C. designation Trentino or Valdadige, of which the latter was mainly established for light, simple types of wine. The grassy notes often found in the Cabernet and Merlot wines and their blends can be explained by both the high yields and the restriction of ripening opportunities for the grapes growing under the shadows of the pergolas, which are not very suitable for use with these varieties.

Sparkling and Fruity

The School of Enology of San Michele all'Adige on the border of Alto Adige which, along with the Geisenheim School of Enology in Rheingau, Germany, and Davis University in Sacramento, California, is one of the best research institutes in the wine world, works in and for Trentino. The insights gained by the institute's scientists are often put directly into practice by the producers of the Adige valley in their vineyards and wineries.

A real quality movement did not emerge, however, until the 1990s, when the large cooperatives recognized the importance of high-quality premium wines, and some of the wineries, which had previously concentrated on the production of bulk wine for export, implemented successful measures to improve the quality of their products.

In economic terms, the sparkling wine industry is the most important sector of the Trentino wine industry. It produces five million bottles of sparkling wine each year, some of which is very high in quality. Most of it is produced using tank fermentation, known in Italy as the CHARMAT METHOD. However, some wineries produce sparkling wines using bottle-fermentation, a method introduced from Champagne in the early 20th century by the Ferrari winery. Some of these sparkling wines, which bear the Trento D.O.C. designation, are among Italy's best and are marketed internationally. A separate *appellation* also exists for bottle-fermented Trentino sparkling wines. However, unlike Franciacorta, they do not have D.O.C.G. status. Their name, "Trento D.O.C.," is easily confused with the still wine *appellation* "Trentino D.O.C." and, when combined with the brand name of the most important private alliance of sparkling wine producers, gives the rather unwieldy name of Trento Talento.

The old billboard in the Ferrari winery in Trento shows the different stages in the production of Spumante, from the vineyard, casks, and bottle fermentation to disgorgement and dosage, which in essence remain unchanged to the present day.

ALTO ADIGE

The Alto Adige (Southern Tyrol), a region which enjoys close historical and cultural links with the Austrian region of Northern Tyrol, has been part of Italy since the First World War and, together with Trentino, forms an autonomous region. Most of the vineyards in this most northerly province of Italy are located in the valley of the Adige (Etsch) river and its tributaries, in particular the Isarco (Eisach) which flows from Bolzano (Bozen) in the north.

The quality center in Alto Adige is located in the Überretsch area, a mountain terrace which lies above the Adige valley between Bolzano in the north and Ora (Auer) in the south. This is the most attractive section of the Alto Adige wine route. Smaller centers of quality can also be found in the area around Terlano (Terlan), Merano (Meran), and Santa Maddalena (Sankt Magdalen) as well as Mazzon and the left bank of the Adige.

The close links with German and Austrian models of viticulture, as well as its bilingualism,

An invitation to dine with Alto Adige red wine.

reflect the region's long association with Tyrol, and the German-speaking world. This starts with some of the 18 vine varieties cultivated here, which include typical German varieties, such as Riesling, Sylvaner, Müller-Thurgau, Gewürztraminer, Kerner, and Trollinger (also known as Schiava or Vernatsch), continues with the way in which zones are named, and extends to harvesting practices such as AUSLESE (selected harvest), which have been included in the D.O.C. regulations. Although 90 percent of wines produced in Alto Adige are legally defined as quality wines, this means as little here as it does in Germany. And yet, Alto Adige has emerged as one of Italy's most quality-conscious regions.

WINERIES AND COOPERATIVES

Unlike other regions, for example Piedmont, the quality initiative did not originate with the individual estates and small wineries but with the larger commercial wineries and cooperatives. Lageder and Hofstätter, and later also Niedermayer and a few others on the one hand, and Girlan, Schreckbichl, Terlan, and Cortaccia (Kurtatsch) on the other were the protagonists of the quality contest which radically changed vinification practices in Alto Adige from the mid-1980s. The cooperatives, which processed two thirds of the region's total grape harvest, assumed a central role in this process, as they were responsible for spreading the movement. Their payment of their member producers on a quality, as opposed to quantity, basis, their policy of separate vinification of wines from particularly suitable areas, in which yields were drastically reduced, and, not least, their delight in experimenting in the winery with steel tanks and *barriques*, became a model for producers throughout the province and beyond.

The withdrawal from the marketing of excessive volumes of cheap and simple Schiava (Vernatsch) wines (mainly sold as Lago di Caldero/Kalterer See, Colli di Bolzano/Bozner Leiten and Santa Maddalena/Sankt Magdalener) proved to be the making of the region. Taste was traditionally sacrificed for high volumes in the cultivation of the Schiava variety. However, its more careful treatment in recent decades allowed the astonishing qualities of the variety to come to the fore. Now it is often sold not as Lago di Caldero/Kalterer See, but under the variety *appellation*. Wines based on this variety are bright red in color, with an aroma of violets.

Alto Adige (Southern Tyrol)
Meranese Hills (Meraner Hügel)
Isarco Valley (Eisacktaler)
Bolzano Hills (Bozner Leiten)
Santa Maddalena (Sankt Magdalener)
Terlano (Terlaner)
Lake Caldaro (Kalterer See)
Valdadige (Etschtaler)
Wine-growing areas in neighboring regions

Varieties on the Move

The excessive planting of Schiava, in increasingly large and productive vineyards, resulted in the almost complete elimination of Gewürztraminer, which is one of the oldest known varieties in Italy. This grape, with its rich aroma, was present in the area now known as Alto Adige as early as the end of the first millennium. Like other varieties of German-Austrian origin, it managed to survive to the present day but now faces enormous competition. For, despite the fact that the varieties from German-speaking areas are still the most common in Alto Adige, the province's undisputed best wines are made from imported varieties such as Chardonnay, Sauvignon Blanc, Cabernet Sauvignon, and Pinot Noir.

The area's producers now enjoy a good international reputation, particularly for their clean, fresh, white wines. The trend toward firm-structured, dense white wines also prompted many wineries here to experiment with barrel-aging, although large wooden casks are also coming back into fashion when it comes to giving the wines maximum complexity while retaining their fruit.

In contrast, the red wines are more adversely affected by the consequences of the nonsensical policy of mass-production. In particular, the region's characteristic use of pergolas, and pruning for maximum yield, give rise to wines with strong herbaceous notes and high levels of acidity. However, in the best zones, and in those in which yields have been reduced, in good years Cabernet Sauvignon and Pinot Noir give results which undoubtedly stand comparison with the best wines in Italy—and perhaps even with those in France.

The province's most interesting red variety is the native Lagrein which has been experiencing something of a renaissance in recent years.

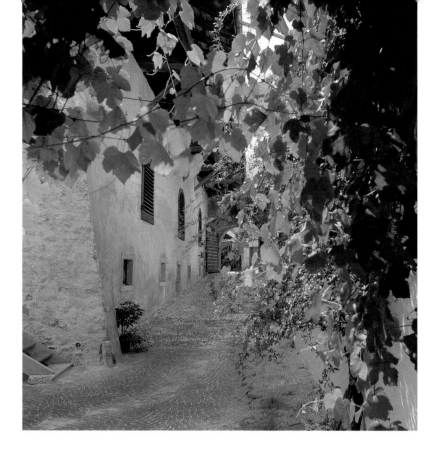

Behind the idyllic exterior of the Georg Baron Widmann estate in Cortaccia/Kurtatsch, a virtual revolution has been taking place in the vineyards and cellar. The estate now markets its own top-quality products.

An astonishing paradox: the ice which protects the vines from frost is produced by sprinkling.

Formerly used mainly in the production of an unprepossessing rosé known as Kretzer, over a very short period its wines have blossomed into powerful spicy wines that are valued for their color, tannins, and aging capacity. They now enjoy increasing popularity among wine connoisseurs. Of course, once again, strict limitation of volume is the key to quality. For a long time, it was believed that only the sandy, gravelly soils of Gris, a district of Bolzano where the best Lagrein vines thrive, could produce good wines. In the meantime, however, more and more producers in other locations have discovered that this belief is ill-founded and proved that it is possible to yield excellent Lagrein Scuro (Lagrein Dunkel) in other areas of Alto Adige.

Two Innovators on the Wine Lake

Just a few years ago, it was likely that someone talking about the Alto Adige wine lake was not referring to Lake Caldaro (Kalterer See) but rather to the enormous volume of the wine—of the same name and very questionable quality—which flooded the markets in countries bordering Alto Adige for decades. The fact that this is no longer the case is mainly thanks to the services of two winemaking protagonists in the Überretsch area, Alois Lageder, a winery owner, and Luis Raifer, the head of the Colterenzio/Schreckbichl cooperative winery.

The restored castle of Löwengang in Magré (Magreid) is the operative center of the Lageder winery, which was founded in 1855 and located, until a few years ago, on the outskirts of Bolzano. After four generations of exclusively buying in and vinifying grapes, the current owner of the company, Alois Lageder, did a radical turnabout and dedicated his efforts to acquiring the best wine-growing sites and traditional wineries. With Römigberg on Lake Caldaro and the Löwengang and Hirschprunn sites in Magré, Lageder is now the owner of the best domains in Alto Adige. Moreover, in addition to introducing modern, natural viticulture practices in his own vineyards, he also inspired his suppliers—most of his grape supplies are still bought in—to concentrate on maximum quality, rather than on quantity.

Traditional Methods and Modern Techniques

After the upgrading of the old winery in the 1970s and 1980s, the construction of a new winery behind the Löwengang estate triggered another significant shift toward modernization. With a capacity in excess of 790,000 gallons (30,000 hl) and production stages distributed on four levels, at a total height of 49 feet (15 m), so that the grapes and musts are transported almost exclusively by gravity and without pumps, the new winery is one of the most modern to be found in Alto Adige today. For example, the fermenting tanks are arranged in a circle so that all of the musts and wines cover the same path to reach the casks.

Of course, at Lageder many red wines are no longer pumped over, but, as in ancient times, the cap (i.e. layer of grape solids) is pressed down into the must automatically. The aging of better quality reds and whites in small or large

While his ancestors were mainly interested in the wine trade, Alois Lageder targeted his efforts on the expansion of his vineyards. Natural cultivation practices ensure that Löwengang is now one of the region's top vineyards.

wooden casks to enhance their complexity and structure is also standard practice at Lageder. Their Löwengang Chardonnay was one of the first in Alto Adige to be fermented in *barriques*.

This dynamic company's best asset remains, however, the many vineyards whose grapes Lageder transforms into a wide range of distinctive estate bottlings. Haberlehof, Tannhammerhof, Benefizium Porer, Lindenburg, and Oberingramhof were recently joined by the unequaled top-quality plot at Römigberg, where one of Italy's best Cabernet Sauvignons is grown.

The company's latest gem is the newly acquired wine estate of Hirschprunn, which was formerly used to house refugees fleeing Mussolini's fascist regime and then stood empty for many years. Its grapes are still processed at Löwengang with all of the other Lageder products, but it is planned to develop the estate into a separate domain with a "château character."

Stylishly renovated historic environment for the wines of the future.

The Cooperatives Hold their Own

The Colterenzio/Schreckbichl cooperative in Girlano (Girlan), the Cornelianum of Roman times, proved that the cooperatives were in a position to emulate the quality efforts of private producers and wineries, or even provide a model for them, during the very decade in which Lageder developed his new exemplary winery. Founded in 1960 by only 28 producers, within a few decades it became one of the leading forces in wine production in northern Italy. Today, its 350 members farm over 980 acres (400 ha) of vines in Girlano, Appiano (Eppan), and Salorno (Salurn).

Under the directorship of Luis Raifer, the winery is successfully run in accordance with the very latest principles. Above all, attention has been paid to work in the vineyards, something which is far from automatic in Italy's cooperatives. The almost complete elimination of chemical products, whose previously unrestricted use was replaced by a policy of maintaining beneficial insects, is as much a part of the Colterenzio/Schreckbichl philosophy today as the separate vinification and bottling of wines from the best locations.

Thanks to these new efforts in the area of quality, the Cornell series of wines—above all the red Cornelius, a blend of Cabernet Sauvignon and Merlot, and the barrel-fermented Chardonnay—and the excellent Praedium varietals from the Coreth, Puiten,

Lake Caldaro (Kalterer See) and its vineyards.

Left
Luis Raifer—visionary director of the region's foremost cooperative.

Right
Alois Lageder—a producer with foresight.

Prail, Siebeneich, Weißhaus, and Mantsch vineyards were created as early as the 1980s.

Equal virtuosity was shown with fruity wines reductively aged in steel tanks and with barrel-aged wines. Thanks to the rigid yield restrictions, which Raifer succeeded in motivating his producers to observe, the reds, in particular, show unusual density and complexity for wines from a northern climate zone.

Raifer has proved that his expertise in winery practices also extends to marketing in his own estate of Lafòa, whose Cabernet Sauvignon and Sauvignon Blanc grapes are now being separately bottled. Both products are among the Alto Adige wines which have successfully attained international standards and can even stand their ground in the face of heavy French competition.

The altitudes of the vineyards of Cortaccia/Kurtatsch in Alto Adige/Southern Tyrol vary between 800 and 1,600 feet (250 and 500 m) above sea level.

SELECT PRODUCERS IN TRENTINO AND ALTO ADIGE

TRENTINO

ENDRIZZI**–****
SAN MICHELE ALL'ADIGE
41 acres (16.5 ha); some bought-in grapes; 200,000 bottles • Wines include: Trento Masetto Brut; Trentino; Traminer Aromatico, Müller-Thurgau, →Chardonnay and →Cabernet Collezione, Pinot Grigio, →Teroldego Rotaliano, Dulcis in Fundo
This former *négociant* winery has been transformed into a quality-oriented estate under the management of Paolo and Christine Endrici. The best wines are marketed with artists' labels.

FERRARI—FRATELLI LUNELLI****
TRENTO
153 acres (62 ha); some bought-in grapes; 3,000,000 bottles • Wines include: Trento: Maximum Brut , Rosé, →Riserva del Fondatore
This sparkling wine house is not only the region's biggest, it also produces some of the best bottle-fermented products. In the last decade a mineral water label has also been acquired.

FORADORI****–*****
MEZZOLOMBARDO
37 acres (15 ha); 100,000 bottles • Wines include: →Granato, →Karanar, →Teroldego Rotaliano Vigneto Morei; Trentino: Pinot Bianco, Chardonnay, Myrto
Elisabetta Foradori has not only transformed the old family estate into Trentino's top winery, she has also begun to develop the potential of Sicilian winemaking through a joint venture. Her three Teroldego wines, particularly the Granato, are top class.

LA VIS***–****
LAVIS
1,976 acres (800 ha); 1,700,000 bottles • Wines include: Trentino Ritratti: Chardonnay, Cabernet Sauvignon, Pinot Nero, →Rosso Vigneti delle Dolomiti, Trentino Traminer Aromatico Maso Tratta, Mandolaia Vendemia Tardiva
Initially, this cooperative supplied the basic materials for some well-known Trentino wines, and today it very successfully bottles its own. Some of the wines, matured according to the individual vineyards, are among the best in the region.

POJER & SANDRI***–****
FAEDO
44.5 acres (18 ha); 200,000 bottles • Wines: Trentino: Müller-Thurgau, Nosiola, Sauvignon, →Rosso and Bianco Fayé, →Essenzia Vendemmia Tardiva, Spumante Cuvée Brut
The go-getting producers, Mario Pojer and Fiorentino Sandri, are known for their white and red wines, and also for their outstanding pomace brandies (*grappa*). Their Rosso Fayè is one of Trentino's best reds.

SAN LEONARDO***
BORGHETTO
40 acres (16 ha); 80,000 bottles • Wines: Trentino: Merlot, Cabernet, San Leonardo, Villa Gresti
The wines of the Bordelais region influence Carlo Guerrieri Gonzaga's San Leonardo, produced from Cabernet Sauvignon, Cabernet Franc and Merlot. It is a source of contention: some celebrate it as Trentino's greatest red, others consider it a soulless and lackluster drink.

ALTO ADIGE

ANSITZ ALTGRIES***
BOLZANO
12 acres (5 ha); 60,000 bottles • Wines include: Alto Adige: Cabernet Sauvignon, →Lagrein Dunkel Riserva, →Rosenmuskateller Passito, St. Magdalener Classico
A traditional estate, with origins in the 12th century, which also has a museum. In the old cellars there are now also *barriques* for Cabernet Sauvignon and Lagrein. The grapes for the luscious aromatic Rosenmuskateller are dried till February.

J. HOFSTÄTTER****
TRAMIN
111 acres (45 ha); some bought-in grapes • Wines include: Alto Adige: →Blauburgunder Barthenau, Lagrein Steinraffler, →Cabernet Sauvignon Yngram, Gewürztraminer Kolbenhof
In quality and quantity, this tradition-conscious winery is Alois Lageder's main rival. The grapes for the top wines of the Foradori family estate come from five different sites to the right and left of the Adige, growing at height of up to 2,000 feet (600 m). The Blauburgunder Barthenau Vigna S. Urbano sets standards.

KELLEREIGENOSSENSCHAFT BOZEN**–****
BOLZANO

741 acres (300 ha); 1,500,000 bottles • Wines include: Alto Adige: St. Magdalener Huck am Bach, →Lagrein Collection Baron Eyrl, Lagrein Perl, →Lagrein Taber, Blauburgunder Greel, Blauburgunder Sandlahner, Riesling Leitach, Gewürztraminer Kleinstein
The Kellerei Bozen was created in 2001, merging the Gries and St. Magdalena wineries. The average level of the three dozen different wines is remarkably high. The good reputation of the winery is primarily based on the Lagrein wines.

KELLEREIGENOSSENSCHAFT GIRLAN**–****
GIRLANO

667 acres (270 ha); 650,000 bottles • Wines: Südtiroler including Blauburgunder Trattmannhof, Vernatsch Fass Nr. 9, Weissburgunder Plattenriegl
Girlano's second cooperative demonstrated years ago that Schiava is not only suitable for the production of thin Lago di Caldaro (Kalterer See), but can also yield complex red wines suitable for aging. On the initiative of Hartmuth Spitaler, manager of the cooperative for many years, artists' labels were introduced at a very early stage.

KELLEREIGENOSSENSCHAFT KURTATSCH***–*****
CORTACCIO

544 acres (221 ha); 2,500,000 bottles • Wines include: Alto Adige: Cabernet Freienfeld, Merlot Brenntal, Cabernet/Merlot Soma, Blauburgunder Frotzenhof, Gewürztraminer Brenntal, →Chardonnay Eberlehof, Lagrein Fohrhof, Grauvenatsch Sonntaler
The 250 members of this winery own some of the best sites surrounding the historic wine-growing village of Cortaccio (Kurtatsch). The Soma is a *cuvée* produced on Bordelais lines.

ALOIS LAGEDER/ANSITZ HIRSCHPRUNN**–*****
MAGRÉ

119 acres (49 ha); some bought-in grapes; 950,000 bottles • Wines include: Südtiroler →Chardonnay and Cabernet Löwengang, →Cabernet C.O.R. Römigberg, Pinot Grigio Benefizium Porer, Pinot Bianco Haberlehof, Sauvignon Lehenhof, →Hirschprunn I.G.T. Mitterberg Bianco Contest, Etelle and Dronach, →Rosso Corolle
Alois Lageder is one of the main players in Alto Adige wine production, a role which he reinforced by acquiring the Hirschprunn estate and building the modern new winery in Magré.

MANINCOR***–*****
CALDARO

87 acres (35 ha); 100,000 bottles • Wines: Alto Adige: Terlaner Classico, Kalterer See Auslese, Moscato Giallo, Cuvée Sophie, Lieben Aich, Pinot Noir Mason di Mason, Merlot/Cabernet Sauvignon Cassiano
Michael Graf Enzenberg's spectacular new winery building generally produces decided individual wines, spontaneously fermented and matured for a long time on fine yeasts.

JOSEF NIEDERMAYR**–*****
GIRLANO

37 acres (15 ha); some bought-in grapes; 860,000 bottles • Wines: Südtiroler: →Sauvignon Naun Barrique, →Lagrein from Gries Blacedelle and Riserva, Gewürztraminer Doss; Kalterer See Auslese Ascherhof, Terlaner Hof zu Pramol, →Aureus, →Euforius
For a long time, Josef Niedermayr's winery stood in the shadow of its more famous counterparts, but thanks to the work of master winemaker Lorenz Martin, it has recently begun to shine with its Lagrein, Pinot Noir and Cabernet Sauvignon.

SCHRECKBICHL/COLTERNZIO****–*****
GIRLANO

790 acres (320 ha); 1,200,000 bottles • Wines: Alto Adige including Cabernet Sauvignon Lafòa, →Lagrein Cornell, →Cabernet/Merlot Cornelius, Pinot Nero Cornell Schwarzhaus Riserva, Gerwürztraminer Cornell, Sauvignon Praedium Prail, Chardonnay Praedium Pinay, →Pinot Nero Praedium St. Daniel
With strict control of grape quality of the cooperative, which numbers 310 members, Luis Raifer has made it into one of the leading wineries in Alto Adige. The wine comes in three quality levels, with the best wine being marketed under the brand of Cornell.

TIEFENBRUNNER CASTELL TURMHOF***–****
CORTACCIO

54 acres (22 ha); some bought-in grapes; 500,000 bottles • Wines include: →Müller-Thurgau Feldmarschal von Fenner, Alto Adige: Gewürztraminer, Lagrein, →Chardonnay Castel Turmhof, →Rosenmuskateller Linticlarus
Seldom has a Müller-Thurgau established such an international reputation as has Feldmarschall von Fenner. It grows at over 3,000 feet (1,000 m) on the Fennberg and produces a sophisticated wine reminiscent of Sauvignon. The best wines of the estate are sold under the brand name Linticlarus.

Careful handling of the grapes.

Down the slope, step by step.

Wine harvesting as in olden times.

Friuli-Venezia Giulia

Friuli-Venezia Giulia, known as Friuli for short, reflects more than most other regions of Italy the myriad contrasts and different ethnic, cultural, and political influences of the country's past. This strip of land was inhabited as early as the Stone Age, over 40,000 years ago, and, like Veneto, the Karst plateau, or Carso as it is known locally, was populated by highly-developed Bronze Age cultures. The area has long been a transitory region for different ethnic groups, some of which engaged in viticulture at least 3,000 years ago.

One particular political development in the 15th century was to have a significant effect on culture and viticulture in Friuli. In 1420, Venice conquered the western part of the region, with Udine as its center, while the Habsburg empire gained control of the eastern part around Gorizia. The border along the river Judrio today still separates the best cultivation areas of Friuli, Colli Orientali, and Collio. The division of the western zone into one with more red varieties and the eastern zone into one with a preponderance of white varieties, reflects the wine preferences of the two former powers. While the red varieties benefit from the many hours of sunshine and an annual mean temperature of 50°F (15°C), the constant movement of air between the Alps and the sea, which gives rise to significant variations between the day and night temperatures, is ideal for the white varieties and enhances their aromas.

The Marco Felluga family successfully combines a medieval legacy with modern winery practices on its prestigious Russiz Superiore estate where the winery is in a tunnel built into the slope.

In geological terms, Friuli is divided into two almost equally sized areas, the northernmost of which—the Alps and Alpine foothills—is unsuitable for vine cultivation. In contrast, the plains and hills of the southern area are dominated by soils which offer good conditions for viticulture: the morainic hills have dry, mineral-poor soils; the soils of the volcanic deposits are rich in minerals and trace elements; the alluvial plain has dry pebbly soil; and the soil in the coastal strip has sand, peat, and a high lime content. On the hills in the central area, the Cormòns *flysch*, a mix of marl and sandstone layers from the Eocene epoch, yields very lively complex wines.

Friuli's viticulture has a clearly identifiable structure. The region's eight viticulture zones line up, one next to the other, inside the protective arc of the Alps, and a specific range of vine varieties is authorized under each D.O.C. designation. The largest area is Grave del Friuli, which is located on the alluvial plain of the Tagliamento river. The coastal zones—Friuli Latisana, the newly-established Friuli Annia, and Friuli Aquileia—lie south of Grave del Friuli. With their excellent soils and ideal climate conditions, the hillside zones of Colli Orientali del Friuli and Collio (Collio Goriziano) yield wines which are the main source of the considerable prestige which the region has earned over the past two decades. Collio is bordered to the south by the Isonzo area, whose southeastern flank in turn borders the Carso, the Karst plateau which extends across the Slovenian border.

From Red to White to Red

Although Friuli is now best known as a white wine region, up to a few decades ago the region's winemaking was dominated by red varieties. In 1965, 80 percent of wines were based on dark grapes, mainly Merlot, the variety of preference following the ravages of phylloxera. It was only with the rise in consumer demand for clean white wines in the 1970s and 1980s that Friulian producers began to concentrate on Chardonnay, Pinot Gris, Sauvignon, and the indigenous variety Tocai Friulano. With the help of European Union subsidies, around 5,000 acres (2,000 ha) of mixed cultivation was transformed into specialized vineyards and many indigenous varieties eliminated in favor of popular international vines. Meanwhile, steel tanks and cooling machines for temperature-controlled reductive fermentation also arrived in the wineries, heralding a radical departure from the traditional style of production which tended to promote OXIDATION. The resulting success on national and international markets was impressive. The powerful aromatic white wines reflected contemporary tastes and quickly began to achieve astronomical prices.

In the 1990s, it was the turn of the red wines of Friuli to regain their prestige: initially Bordeaux blends, later single-varietal Merlot wines (whose name is all they have in common with the acidic sweet versions of the post-war period), and finally outstanding wines from indigenous varieties which had almost been allowed to die out.

If they can be used to produce expressive, individual wines which will stand out from the uniform products of other countries, these indigenous varieties represent the main opportunity available for future winemaking in Friuli. Great things are expected of the reds Refosco dal Peduncolo Rosso, Schioppettino, Pignolo, and Tazzelenghe, and the whites Tocai Friulano, Ribolla Gialla, Verduzzo, and Picolit.

Between Udine and Gorizia

The Colli Orientali hills, with their *flysch* soils, form a half-moon around the region's capital Udine and constitute the northwestern flank of the massif which includes Collio. They have great potential for red wines. High-quality Merlot, Cabernet, Schioppettino, Refosco, and Pignolo grapes thrive here, in particular on the southern slopes facing the Adriatic Sea. The single varietals and blends (often barrel-aged) produced from these grapes are powerful but elegant, combining a robust tannin structure

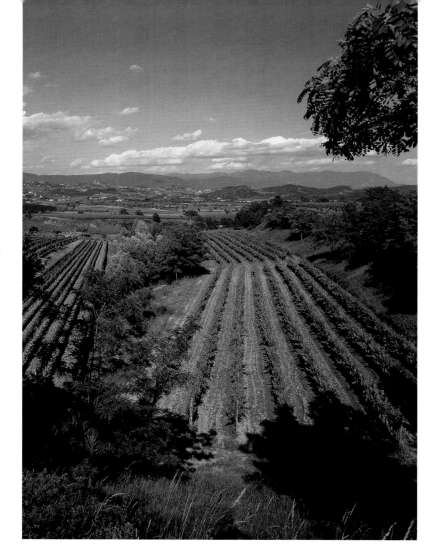

with abundant fruit. In good years, they are among the best red wines produced in Italy.

The climate on the northern slopes of these hills is significantly cooler, making them eminently suited to the production of particularly powerful, interesting white wines which have a good alcohol content and benefit from barrel-aging. The sweet white wine Picolit is a regional specialty which, in terms of quality, is often exceeded by the similarly indigenous but not always sweet Verduzzo. This is particularly true of the Verduzzo wines originating from the separate D.O.C. zone Ramandolo, on the northwest flank of the Colli Orientali.

The great individual reds and the best Friulian whites come from Collio. Many Collio producers have vineyards on Slovenian soil and, thanks to a special E.U. regulation, are allowed to market them with Collio labels. The specialties from Collio include Sauvignon Blanc and Chardonnay, complemented by the indigenous Ribolla Gialla. Thanks to their good acid content, the wines from this area—which represent 85 percent of the region's production—retain their freshness when aged in *barriques* and are among the few white wines Italy has to offer that can truly compete at international level.

The carefully cultivated vineyards in Capriva del Friuli near Gorizia bear witness to the ambition of the region's producers who cultivate impressive red varieties on the southern slopes and very pure white Collio on northern slopes.

THE FRIULIAN PLAINS
AND THE CARSO

While Collio and Colli Orientali enhanced the reputation of Friulian wine production, developments in the region's other zones followed quite a different course. Grave, Aquileia, Latisana, and Annia offer little more than well-made, pleasant, everyday reds. Some expressive varieties are grown in the Carso (Karst) area, but their wines are rather unusual for international tastes. Around a dozen of the Isonzo producers have succeeded in making the transition to the regional and, in some cases, national elite.

With more than 15,000 acres (6,000 ha) of vineyard, the Grave del Friuli zone represents only about one third of the total Friulian area, though it produces two thirds of the region's volume. The area starts in the west at the Livenza plain, and continues along the Tagliamento and Judrio rivers which form the border with Veneto, and across to the hills of Collio and Colli Orientali. The zone's name, Grave, is derived from the gravelly soils of the alluvial plain. While the fertile limy soils of the zone's south and western areas are only suited to industrial viniculture and the production of basic wines, the barren stony soils of the moraine landscape in the Tagliamento valley and the alluvial deposits produce rather appealing wines.

The Grave del Friuli whites of distinctive freshness and character are produced from the vines grown near the mountains on soils composed of glacier deposits.

ALONG THE COAST

The D.O.C. zones of Aquileia, Annia, and Latisana are located along the coast between the town of Grado and the Veneto border. The deep fertile soils of Aquileia, which lies furthest east and is named after the Roman garrison whose ruins can be visited there, yield light wines which must be drunk when young. There is little to report about Friuli Annia, the youngest D.O.C. area, as its establishment was the outcome of the granting of a political favor to one of Italy's largest private wineries. In the Latisana area, enormous volumes of grapes are ripened in vast vineyards for the production of uninteresting wines. The areas where the deep loamy soils are richer in minerals sometimes yield pleasant, light, everyday wines.

The situation in Isonzo, which lies south of Collio in the region of the same name, is somewhat better. This predominantly flat area, whose soils are heavy and calcareous, particularly in the south, was underestimated for a long time. The producers in northern Isonzo have meanwhile proved that the white and red wines they produced on sandy and gravelly soils could earn a place at the top of the Friulian league.

The Carso zone is located on a barren, elevated plateau with calcareous soil, an unusual site whose Bora vines are generally unprotected from the cold east winds. Despite the raw climate, wine has been produced here for centuries, with varieties such as Malvasia and Terrano—a Refosco variant—dominating. Terrano, with its hard tannins, is undrinkable when young and can only be appreciated by experienced palates. Few producers succeed in creating a pleasant wine with this variety. Finally, one last Carso rarity deserves a mention: white Vitovska, whose stringent aroma is unlikely to find appreciation outside of the region.

Picolit and Verduzzo

Friuli provides one of the best-known sweet wines of northern Italy, based on and named after the indigenous variety of Picolit. For a long time, Picolit was one of the most famous wines of the land; it was cultivated extensively in the late 18th century, and from the mid-19th century it was consumed in the royal courts of Austria, France, England, Russia, and Tuscany. However, the legendary reputation of this sweet wine, which was often compared with Château

d'Yquem, failed to last in the 20th century. The vine now survives on barely 500 acres (200 ha) and only around 100,000 bottles are produced each year. Picolit can develop a rich aroma of flowers, honey, and figs with notes of ripe apple and pears. Although the wines are much sought-after and expensive, their quality is, for the most part, questionable.

Verduzzo, the second of Friuli's sweet varieties, yields delightful and dense dessert wines,

particularly in Ramandolo. The vineyards climb to heights of 1,200 feet (370 m) along the ridges of Monte Bernadia where intensive daytime sun and a drastic reduction in temperatures at night ensure the development of its clear aromas. The yields are low and, following the drying of the grapes, the volumes seldom exceed 320 gallons per acre (30 hl/ha). Verduzzo does not enjoy the same prestige and reputation as Picolit and is hence less expensive.

SELECT PRODUCERS IN FRIULI-VENEZIA GIULIA

BORC DODÒN**–*****
VILLA VICENTINA UDINE
21 acres (8.5 ha); 8,500 bottles • Wines: →Cabernet Franc/Cabernet Sauvignon Uis Neris, Tocai/Sauvignon/ Verduzzo Uis Blàncis, →Refosco dal Pedunculo Rosso
Denis Montanar has been using biodynamic methods for years. The reds are among the finest in Friuli.

DORIGO**–*****
BUTTRIO
79 acres (32 ha); 180,000 bottles • Wines include C.O.F. Ronc di Jury: →Chardonnay, Sauvignon, Pinot Nero, →Pignolo; Picolit Vigneto Montsclapade; Refosco; Spumante Pinot Nero Pas Dosé
Modern vineyard practices with high stock density and low-growing vines were introduced in the 1980s.

IL CARPINO***
OSLAVIA
37 acres (15 ha); 60,000 bottles • Wines: Il Carpino Collio: Ribolla Gialla, →Sauvignon, Malvasia, Chardonnay, Cabernet Sauvignon-Merlot Rosso Carpino, Vigna Runc: Pinot Grigio, Chardonnay, Sauvignon
Half of the permitted maximum yields, thorough grape selection, and fermenting in wooden barrels give the Il Carpino white wines character and volume. Vigna Runc is produced by the estate's younger vines and is matured in steel tanks.

LIVIO FELLUGA*–*****
CORMÒNS
334 acres (135 ha); 650,000 Bottles • Wines: C.O.F.: Tocai Friulano, Pinot Grigio, Sauvignon, Refosco, Picolit; →Merlot Riserva Rosazzo Sossò, →Terre Alte
Merlot Sossò is one of Friuli's most lively whites.

MARCO FELLUGA/RUSSIZ SUPERIORE*–*****
GRADISCA/CAPRIVA
479 acres (194 ha); 850,000 bottles • Wines include: Collio: Chardonnay, Tocai Friulano, Pinot Bianco, Pinot Grigio, Sauvignon, →Molamatta, →Carantan; Russiz Superiore Collio: Pinot Bianco, →Rosso degli Orzoni
Apart from the winery in Gradisca, this house also owns estates in Capriva (Russiz Superiore), Buttrio and in the Chianti Classico region.

RONCO DEL GNEMIZ**–*****
SAN GIOVANNI AL NATISONE
26 acres (10.5 ha); 65,000 bottles • Wines include: C.O.F.: Ribolla Gialla, Sauvignon, Müller-Thurgau, Pinot Grigio, Tocai Friulano, →Chardonnay, Picolit, Verduzzo, →Rosso del Gnemiz, Schiopettino
Recommended: Chardonnay, Rosso del Gnemiz, Sauvignon, Pinot Grigio, Müller-Thurgau.

JOSKO GRAVNER*–*****
GORIZIA
43 acres (17.5 ha); 40,000 bottles • Wines: Ribolla Collio, →Breg, Rosso Gravner, →Ruino
Instead of *barriques*, this house now uses gigantic earthenware amphorae in its winery. The oxidized and concentrated wines do not really fit into the Friuli range of tastes, but are nonetheless among the greatest wines of Italy.

VINNAIOLI JERMANN*–*****
FARRA D'ISONZO
106 acres (43 ha); 28,000 bottles • Wines: Vinnae, →Vintage Tunina, →Where the Dreams have no End..., Sogno Terra Promessa..., Capo Martino, Chardonnay, Riesling Renano, Pinot Bianco, Moscato Rosa Vigna Bellina, Engelwhite, Cabernet, Traminer Aromatico, Pinot Grigio, Sauvignon, Tocai Italico
The wines from this house enjoy cult status.

LIVON*–*****
SAN GIOVANNI AL NATISONE
272 acres (110 ha); 450,000 bottles • Wines include: C.O.F. Pinot Grigio, Braide Grande, Refosco Riûl; Collio: Chardonnay Tre Clâs, Masarotte, Tocai Fruilano Ronc di Zorz, Sauvignon Gravalunga, Pinot Bianco Cavezzo, Plazate, →Tiareblù, Schioppettino Picotis, →Picolit Cumins, Moscato Giallo Planeces, Verduzzo Casali Godia
This estate has vineyards in the region's best locations.

MIANI–ENZO PONTONI***
BUTTRIO
28.5 acres (11.5 ha); 12,000 bottles • Wines: C.O.F.: Tocai Friulano, →Ribolla Gialla, Sauvignon, Merlot; →Miani Rosso, Miani Bianco
The old Merlot, Tocai and Refosco vines yield some of Friuli's best wines.

MARIO SCHIPETTO*–*****
CAPRIVA
74 acres (30 ha); 200,000 bottles • Wines: Collio: Tocai Friulano, Pinot Bianco, Pinot Grigio, Sauvignon, Malvasia Istriana; Merlot, Cabernet Franc; Rivarossa, Blanc des Rosis, Müller-Thurgau, Riesling Renano, Ribolla Gialla
Mario Schipetto has made sound investments in a modern winery and new vineyards in Collio and Colli Orientali.

BORGO DEL TIGLIO/NICOLA MAERRARI**–*****
CORMONS
20 acres (8 ha); 40,000 bottles • Wines: Collio including Tocai Friulano Ronco della Chiesa, Sauvignon, Chardonnay; Collio Bianco, Collio Rosso, →Rosso della Centa, →Studio
Recommended: Merlot Rosso della Centa. The quality of the white wines improved even more in the 1990s.

VIE DE ROMANS—S. GALLIO***
MARIANO DEL FRIULI
40 acres (16 ha); 100,000 bottles • Wines include: Isonzo: →Chardonnay Ciampagnis Vieris and Vie di Romans, Pinot Grigio Dessimis, Tocai Friulano, →Sauvignon Piere and Vieris, →Flors de Uis, Voos dai Ciamps
Sauvignon Vieris is one of the first Friulian quality wines to be produced from this variety.

LE VIGNE DI ZAMÒ*–*****
MANZANO
111 acres (45 ha); 250,000 bottles • Wines include: Series →Abazzia di Rosazzo, →Vigne dal Leon and Villa Belvedere
Estate bottled by three estates in Colli Orientali. The white Ronco delle Acacie, Cabernet Sauvignon, Pignolo and Refosco, plus the red Ronco dei Roseti blend, are among the best in Friuli.

VILLA RUSSIZ***
CAPRIVA
74 acres (30 ha); 130,000 bottles • Wines: Collio: Malvasia Istriana, Pinot Bianco, Pinot Grigio, Tocai Friulano, Sauvignon; →Sauvignon de la Tour, Merlot Collio; →Gräfin de la Tour, →Graf de la Tour
Top wines for a good cause: Villa Russiz also boasts a foundation for orphans.

ZIDARICH*–*****
DUINO-AURISINA
15 acres (6 ha); 13,000 bottles • Wines: Carso: Vitovska, →Malvasia, Terrano, Prulke
Benjamin Zidarich will have no truck with fashionable vines. In the vineyards which he took over from his father, he grows Terrano, Vitovska and Malvasia. In the winery, too, all up-to-date equipment is lacking, but instead there are large wooden barrels which are used for the fermentation and solid aging of the wines.

VENETO: THE WEST

Along with Sicily and Apulia, Veneto is one of Italy's most prolific winemaking regions. Around 211 million gallons (8 million hl) are produced from its approximately 40 cultivated vine varieties, a quarter of which enjoy D.O.C. status. This means that the region produces almost one fifth of Italian quality wines. However, a sharp west-east divide exists in terms of the reputation and quality of its wines. While the province of Verona in the west, with its Soave, Valpolicella, and Bardolino, produces some of the most popular Italian wines—and, with Amarone, one of the country's great reds—the wines of the Breganze, Colli Berici, and Colli Euganei, Pave, and Lison-Pramaggiore zones are virtually anonymous. Prosecco is the only wine produced in the east which has succeeded in establishing a strong D.O.C. designation and its quality varies considerably.

The region's wine-growing areas extend from Lake Garda along the Alpine foothills to the Adriatic lagoon at Venice and the borders of Friuli. The vineyards on the slopes are south-facing and are effectively sheltered from the cold north winds by the Alps. Soil types include morainic gravel at Lake Garda, mainly Dolomite residual gravel as well as fertile fields and alluvial deposits in the plains.

The predominant white vine variety cultivated in Veneto is the high-yielding Garganega which is the main constituent of Soave and Gambellara wines. Its aromatic potential can only fully unfold on particularly thin soils where it can

yield fragrant white wines with fine lemon and almond aromas. The red varieties cultivated in the region include Corvina Veronese, Corvinone, Rondinella, and Molinara. Corvina is also the base wine for Recioto, the sweet variant of Valpolicella. The ubiquitous international varieties Chardonnay, Cabernet, and Merlot are also cultivated in the vineyards of Veneto.

Soave is undoubtedly Veneto's best-known wine and its most important in terms of quantity. It is produced from Garganega supplemented with Chardonnay, Pinot Blanc, or Trebbiano and cultivated on around 16,000 acres (6,500 ha) of vineyard, most of which lie within the alluvial plain of the river Adige, whose fertile soils make it difficult to control the yields. The fresh, delicate wines, with fine, almond notes which lie behind Soave's widespread success only thrive on the volcanic soils of the Classico zone around Soave and Monteforte d'Alpone.

Valpolicella, the red counterpart of Soave, originates from the valleys to the north of Verona. As in the case of Soave, the Valpolicella zone is divided into two parts. The Classico zone around San Pietro in Cariano, Fumane, and Negrar produces very interesting, intense wines from grapes which ripen at heights between 490 and 1,500 feet (150 and 450 m). Meanwhile, the mass-consumption wines that line supermarket shelves throughout Europe are produced in the areas in the Adige valley, which were added to the zone in 1968.

Quintarelli

The estate on the hills above Negrar has almost 30 acres (12 ha) of vineyards, most of which belong to the Classico zone of Valpolicella. The barren soils consist of volcanic basalt. Good ventilation of the rows of vines prevents rotting and other diseases, largely avoiding the need for spraying.

Quintarelli started testing new varieties as early as the 1980s when Cabernet Franc and Sauvignon, Sangiovese, Nebbiolo, Croatina, Garganega, Saorin, and Trebbiano Toscano joined the traditional Valpolicella varieties Corvina, Rondinella, and Molinara. Some of them were used in the production of Valpolicella and a Cabernet table wine called Alzero was created, produced in a similar way to Amarone.

Perfect raisining, i.e. drying, is the key to Quintarelli winemaking. Unripe or rotting grapes are eliminated during harvesting which is carried out by hand. Following a second check, the grapes are spread out in flat slatted boxes. During the slow drying process, depending on the ventilation, humidity, and

Negrar, a wine-producing village in the Valpolicella zone.

temperature, BOTRYTIS CINEREA develops and Quintarelli has worked out exactly how to control the NOBLE ROT to prevent premature oxidation and ensure that the wines are perfectly matured.

In early February, when three quarters of the water has evaporated from the grapes, they are pressed and macerated. After around 20 days, alcoholic fermentation with the natural yeasts

begins. This takes 45 to 50 days. Recioto and Amarone age for seven years in Slovenian oak casks. Alzero spends 30 months in French *barriques* and the same period again in large Slovenian oak containers. The residual sugar results in further fermentation during cask maturation, which gives the wines their high alcohol content of 14 to 15 percent and particularly luxurious aromas. While Amarone and Alzero are mostly dry when bottled, only Recioto from the best years still has a high level of residual sugar. Amarone Riserva and Recioto Riserva are rare highlights: the best casks in the best years yield little more than 2,500 bottles of each.

At Quintarelli, normal Valpolicella also enjoys careful handling. Macerated, fermented on the skins for seven days and filled in tanks, it is then left waiting until April when the Amarone is racked off and it is then pumped onto the Amarone skins. The residual sugar triggers the second fermentation of the Valpolicella which gives it the strength it needs to ferment for six years in Slovenian oak casks without wasting away.

A proportion of the Valpolicella grapes—above all Corvina, Rondinella, and Molinara—has always been dried on timber racks after harvesting. The grapes were then pressed in December or January and their high sugar concentration prevented the musts from fermenting fully. The sweet wine yielded by this process was Recioto della Valpolicella. However, some of the zone's natural yeasts are capable of converting the high sugar content of raisined grapes into alcohol. Amarone, an opulent powerful red wine with a high alcohol content, was born when this phenomenon was systematically exploited for the first time in the 1950s. Its production has been perfected in the interim: the wines are now produced in accordance with modern enological methods and sometimes also aged in *barriques*, an innovation which has served them well. In the second half of the 1990s production of Amarone wines was more than doubled in response to growing demand, and prices rose as well. Many wine lovers now regard Amarone as one of the top Italian wines, comparable with Barolo and Brunello di Montalcino.

A third Valpolicella variant was created in the 1970s and 1980s when the producers reflected on the Ripasso technique and added fermented Valpolicella to the pressed skins of the fermented Recioto or Amarone to re-ferment it with the residual sugars and yeasts. These wines are often bottled under the D.O.C. designation Superiore or as table wines.

Bianco di Custoza dominates the large group of neutral white wines produced in Veneto. Its

zone extends from the southwest of Verona to Lake Garda. Its taste is characterized by the Soave grape Garganega as well as the "grape-of-all-trades," Trebbiano Toscano.

Custoza's next-door neighbor is red Bardolino. Although this is produced from the same grapes as Valpolicella, it is a lighter-tasting wine. The rosé version, Bardolino Chiaretto, is often more interesting than actual Bardolino.

Recioto and Amarone of astounding quality are bottled in the village of Garganago near Sant' Ambrogio di Valpolicella.

Veneto: The East

In Veneto, few quality wines are found outside of the province of Verona. Despite the fact that the eastern part of the region has extensive vineyards, high-quality production is a rarity. The few examples of quality production in the east are down to the efforts of individual maverick producers rather than the established characteristics of the region as a whole. The eastern zones start in the Gambarella area, the counterpart of Soave in the province of Vicenza—where, apart from a well-known large winery which has holdings and production centers in all of the important regions, only one single small producer occasionally attracts attention—and extend along two strips to the east, the first in a more southerly direction via Colli Berici and Colli Euganei toward the Po delta,

Does such a ripe firm Trebbiano grape justify the pride of the Soave producer?

and the second from Breganze along the edge of the Alps up to Conegliano and further east to the border of Friuli. It is difficult to understand why Colli Berici and Colli Euganei remain unknown to a wider public, as the morainic and volcanic soils of these hills, between the Alpine foothills and the Adriatic Sea, offer ideal conditions for the production of high-quality wines. This is borne out by a small group of producers who have been producing lively whites and dense reds for years. The international varieties Chardonnay, Pinot Blanc, Sauvignon, and Tocai are as common there as the red varieties Cabernet and Merlot. The Moscato wine, Fior d'Arancio, is a particular specialty of Colli Euganei. In its best guise as a Passito, it has a dense golden-yellow color and

Prosecco

The origin of the Prosecco grape, which yields a fresh neutral white wine suitable for sparkling production, is disputed. Some say it comes from the village of the same name near Udine and is similar to the indigenous Friulian variety Grela, others say it originates from Dalmatia.

The sparkling version of this wine can probably be explained by a quirk of nature. The fermentation of the late-ripening Prosecco grapes was sometimes interrupted by frost in the winter months so that the wine still has some carbon dioxide and residual sugar in spring. The history of the success of this wine started in the 19th century when Antonio Carpené and three partners founded a company with the intention of producing champagne. However, they did not produce champagne and instead, Prosecco di Conegliano-Valdobbiadene became a very popular and fashionable tipple. Nowadays, around 20 million bottles of Spumante are produced annually by means of secondary fermentation in pressurized tanks. If the product of this tank fermentation process is bottled after one month of storage with a bottle pressure of at least three atmospheres, it may legally be labeled *Spumante*, i.e. sparkling wine. If it does not reach this pressure, it must be labeled *Frizzante*, i.e. fizzy or semi-sparkling wine. Prosecco Spumante clearly yields higher prices than Frizzante; however, in qualitative terms the difference between the two is not always detectable. The Prosecco wines from the Cartizze zone, which generally have more residual sugar, are controversial. They are often more expensive but seldom better than Prosecco originating from the zone of the same name.

Prosecco needs a protective wire cap to prevent it from popping open.

Good Prosecco is also bottled in the Cartizze hills.

Prosecco develops its delicate bubbles in pressurized stainless steel tanks.

Select Producers in Veneto

Allegrini***–*****
Fumane
104 acres (42 ha); 370,000 bottles • Wines include: Valpolicella Classico: →Superiore La Grola, →Palazzo della Torre; →Amarone, Amarone Fieramonte, →Recioto Giovanni Allegrini, →La Poja
This house was behind the innovation in Valpolicella and produces noteworthy wines from the grapes of the La Grola vineyard in Sant'Ambrosio and from the highest plot, La Poja. These wines are among the most lively in the region.

Roberto Anselmi***–*****
Monteforte d'Alpone
111 acres (45 ha); 350,000 bottles • Wines include: Capitel Croce, Soave Classico Capitel Foscarino, Recioto I Capitelli, Cabernet Realda
With barrel aging, single-vineyard bottlings and an outstanding dessert wine, Ansemi in the 1980s served as an inspiration to the region's producers in more than one respect.

Ca'La Bionda***–*****
Marano dal Valpolicella
49 acres (20 ha); 110,000 bottles • Wines: Amarone della Valpolicella Vigneti di Ravazol, Recioto, →Valpolicella Classico Superiore
The Castellanis have been cultivating their hillside locations in the heart of Valpolicella for four generations. Since Allessandro took over running the winery, the estate has gone up in quality; the wines are amazingly mineral and cool.

Ca'Lustra***–****
Faedo di Cinto Euganio
52 acres (21 ha); 150,000 bottles • Wines: Cabernet Vigna Girapoggio, Chardonnay Vigna Marco, Sauvignon del Veneto, Spumante Fior d'Arancio
The single vineyard wines come from the best granite soils and provide a high degree of smooth, rounded drinking pleasure.

Romano dal Forno****–*****
Cellore d'Illasi
62 acres (25 ha); 26,000 bottles • Wines: Valpolicella superiore, →Amarone, Recioto
Extremely concentrated, dense, dark-colored wines. Despite long aging in new *barriques*, the wood does not dominate. The Amarone is of cult status and is usually sold out in advance.

Roccolo Grassi**–****
Mezzane di Sotto
30 acres (12 ha); 23,000 bottles • Wines: Soave Superiore La Broia, Valpolicella Superiore Roccolo Grassi, Amarone Roccolo Grassi, →Recioto Valpolicella, Recioto Soave
A young, modern operation with polished, elegant wines with a *barrique* note: the Roccolo Grassi vineyard is impressive, in particular the Recioto Valpolicella.

Maculan***–*****
Breganze
87 acres (35 ha); some bought-in grapes; 600,000 bottles • Wines include: Prato di Canzio; Breganze: di Breganze, Rosso Brentino and Marchesante, Cabernet, Cabernet Palazzotto, →Cabernet Fratta and Ferrata, →Chardonnay Ferrata, Sauvignon Ferrata, Torcolato, Acini Nobili
Part vineyard with revolutionary dense planting of vines, based on the French model, and part winery, Macula produces extraordinary wines. The specialty is the sweet Acini Nobili, which however does develop its noble rot in a climate-controlled room.

Masi/Boscaini**–****
Sant'Ambrogio
395 acres (160 ha); some bought-in grapes; 9,000,000 bottles • Wines include: Masi: Amarone: →Mazzano, →Campolongo di Torbe, →Vajo Amaron Serego Alighieri; Recioto Classico: Mezzanella, Casal dei Ronchi Serego Alighieri; Valpolicella Classico, Soave Classico, Bardolino Classico, I.G.T. Veronese: Brolo di Campofiorin, Rosso Osar, →Toar
In addtion to simple consumer wines, this house can offer all the region's top products, including the Ripasso wine Brolo di Campofiorin and Toar, which is mainly produced from almost extinct grape varieties.

Leonildo Pieropan****
Soave
79 acres (32 ha); 300,000 bottles • Wines: Soave Classico: Vigneto Calvarino and →Vigneto La Rocca, Recioto di Soave Le Colombare
The single-vineyard La Rocca (100% Garganega) and Calvarino (70% Garganega, 30% Trebbiano di Soave) wines are convincing due to their concentration, lush fruit and freshness. Good aging potential.

Giuseppe Quintarelli****
Negrar
38 acres (15.5 ha); 60,000 bottles • Wines: Amarone, Recioto Classico, Valpolicella Classico Superiore Monte Paletta (Rosso Ca' del Merlo), Alzero Cabernet Franc
The legend of the Valpolicella zone (see panel on preceding double page).

Serafini & Vidotto***–****
Nervesa della Battaglia
31 acres (12.5 ha); 65,000 bottles • Wines: Montello e Colli Asolani: Prosecco, Chardonnay, Cabernet, Merlot; Rosso dell' Abbazia, Pinot Nero
The Rosso d'Abbazia, a classic Bordeaux blend, is evidence that distinctive wines can also be produced in the eastern Veneto.

Fratelli Speri***–****
San Pietro in Cariano
148 acres (60 ha); 500,000 bottles • Wines: →Valpolicella Classico, →Amarone, Recioto
A large part of the harvest is sold to wine houses in the neighborhood, where they are used in the most famous *cuvées* of the Valpolicella region. But the product with the Speri label also belong to the elite.

Fratelli Tedeschi***–****
San Pietro in Cariano
52 acres (21 ha); some bought-in grapes; 400,000 bottles • Wines: Valpolicella Classico Superiore Capitel delle Lucchine, Amarone del la Fabriseria, →Capitel Monte Olmi, Recioto Classico Monte Fontana, →Vin de la Fabriseria San Rocco, Capitel San Rocco delle Lucchine, →Soave Classico Monte Tenda, Capitel San Rocco Bianco
The Amarone selections, Recioto, and the Ripasso wine Capitel Monte Olmi are among the best Valpolicella has to offer.

Villa dal Ferra***
San Germano dei Berici
15 acres (6.25 ha); 60,000 bottles • Wines: Colli Berici: Cabernet Le Rive Rosse, Merlot Campo del Lago, Pinot Bianco Bianco del Rocolo, Sauvignon Monte Cavallo, Tocai Costiera Granda; Pinot Nero Rosso del Rocolo, Riesling del Veneto Busa Calcara
The only Colli Berici house which produces distinctive quality wines. Donato Lanati, one of Italy's best enologists, is employed there. Radical new vineyard plantings ensure a good foundation for the future.

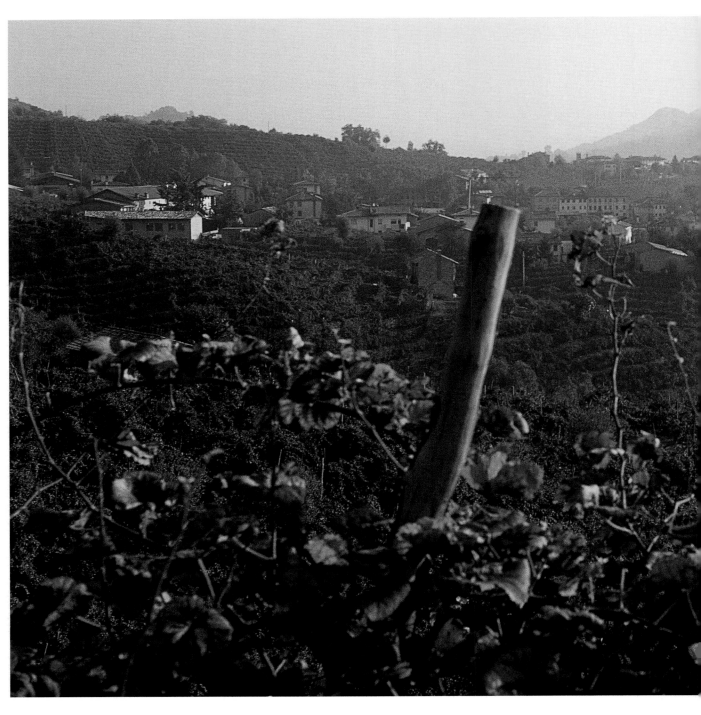

Not only indigenous varieties, such as Vespaiolo or Gropello, grow on the flat hills and gravelly soils near Breganze, but, thanks to the warm microclimate, Cabernet Sauvignon also matures well.

an aroma of honey and exotic fruit combined with a clear but successfully integrated sweetness. It is one of Veneto's most impressive dessert wines.

REVOLUTIONARY VINEYARDS

Breganze, the wine-growing area around the small town on the edge of the Alps, has the Maculan winery to thank for the prestige it now enjoys. In the late 1980s, Maculan initiated a modest revolution in its vineyards when it replaced its traditional, very high-yielding, tall cultivation systems with new vines planted in

the best French manner at a density of up to 4,000 vines per acre (10,000 vines/ha). The vines were pruned to unusually low heights in accordance with the Guyot system of cane pruning, which is named after the French scientist who was responsible for its promulgation in the 19th century. Unusual things also started to happen in the Maculan winery. After harvesting, the grapes were stored in a specially constructed, extremely humid, climate chamber until they developed the botrytis rot which they did not form naturally in the vineyard.

In the Montello e Colli Asolani zone, Serafini and Vitotto were responsible for the introduction of similarly revolutionary modern winemaking techniques and achieved results which left the Venegazzù estate of Conte Gasparini, who was the area's most prestigious producer in the 1970s, far behind.

The Prosecco zone starts on the far side of the Colli Asolani. Under the regulations defined for the D.O.C. Prosecco di Conegliano-Valdobbiadene, irrespective of where the grapes were actually grown, the wine may bear the name of either of the two townships as its designation of origin. This is intended to guarantee a certain level of quality, while offering the producers a degree of flexibility.

The wide Piave plain and the area bordering Friuli north of the Venetian lagoon complete the account of winemaking in this region. The extensive vineyards yield simple, mass-consumption wines which have no distinctive characteristics. Here, Ornella Molon, Conte Collalto, Rechsteiner, and some other producers have shown that with rigorous yield control and careful vinification it is possible to produce decent wines even on the fertile soils of Piave. Their Cabernet-Merlot blends were impressive but the influence of the wines made from the extremely acidic native Raboso variety has failed to penetrate beyond the immediate locality.

EMILIA ROMAGNA

Cozy wine bars are part of the national culture.

which are flushed out by the numerous rivers winding their way to the Adriatic Sea. As is the case all over the Po plain, the climate is very damp and precipitation often takes the form of dense fog. The summers are hot and humid while the winters are rainy and cold. The mountains and hills include the northern end of the Tuscan-Emilian Apennines. The soils here are more barren—depending on the zone, they consist of residual pebbles and red loam—and, thanks to the good air circulation, the climate is also less humid.

With an annual production volume in excess of 158 million gallons (six million hl), Emilia Romagna is Italy's fourth biggest wine producer after Sicily, Apulia, and Veneto. Most of the vines grow in heavy fertile soils on flat ground and, like the adjacent wheat and sugar beet crops, give particularly high yields. Depending on the year, only 12 to 15 percent of the total production is accounted for by quality wines.

IT DOESN'T ALWAYS HAVE TO BUBBLE

The belief that only fizzy semi-sparkling wines go well with the heavy local cuisine, with its fatty pork specialties, appears to be widely held in Parma, Modena, Reggio, and surroundings. Not only is Lambrusco bottled with varying degrees of fizz, but Barbera and other varieties also sparkle. Dry still wines are more a specialty of Romagna, the eastern part of the region which nestles into the Adriatic and borders the

If Lombardy and Milan are identified as Italy's head, Emilia Romagna can confidently be described as its stomach. This region, which ranges from the northern slopes of the Apennines to the southeast of the Po plain, mainly cultivates wheat and sugar beet on its 150,000 farms. Reflecting the advanced mechanization of agricultural processes and optimum use of agrichemicals, more crops are produced here per acre of agricultural land than in any other region in Italy.

In topographical terms, the region is divided into an extensive plain and the Apennine mountains. The lowlands consist of alluvial soils

Colli Piacentini
Colli di Parma
Lambrusco
Lambrusco Reggiano
Lambrusco di Sorbara
Lambrusco Graspa-rossa di Castelvetro
Colli Bolognesi

Trebbiano di Romagna
Sangiovese di Romagna
Albana di Romagna
Cagnina di Romagna
Pagadebit di Romagna

Wine-growing areas in neighboring regions

SELECT PRODUCERS IN EMILIA ROMAGNA

CASTELLUCCIO****
MODIGLIANA
47 acres (19 ha); 40,000 bottles • Wines: Ronco della Simia, →Ronco delle Ginestre, →Ronco dei Ciliegi, Le More, Lunaria
Standards are being maintained even in the wake of the departure of Gian Matteo Baldi, who was responsible for the development of the Sangiovese variants and blends.

UMBERTO CESARI**−****
CASTEL SAN PIETRO TERME
222 acres (90 ha); bought-in grapes; 1,400,000 bottles • Wines include: →Sangiovese Riserva, Liano, Albana Passita, Colle del Re, Trebbiano, Vigneto del Parolino
Recommended: Cabernet/Sangiovese Liano.

FATTORIA ZERBINA − GERMINIANI***−****
FAENZA
74 acres (30 ha); 190,000 bottles • Wines: Sangiovese di Romagna: Ceregio, Pietramora, Torre di Ceparano; →Albana di Romagna Scacco Matto, →Marzeno di Marzeno

This producer's top wine, the Albana Passito Scacco Matto, has attained D.O.C.G. status.

LA STOPPA****
RIVERGARO
59 acres (24 ha); 220,000 bottles • Wines: Bianco Ancarano, Sauvignon Colli Piacentini, Chardonnay Spumante Brut, Rosso Ancarano Frizzante; Colli Piacentini: Malvasia, Gutturnio, Barbera; →Macchiona, →Alfeo, →Stoppa, Buca delle Canne
Elena Pantaleone offers quality that is a rarity in this region, while maintaining regional flair.

LA TOSA − PIZZAMIGLIO***−****
VIGOLZONE
25 acres (10 ha); 60,000 bottles • Wines: Colli Piacentini: including Valnure, Sauvignon, Malvasia Sorriso di Cielo, Gutturnio Vignamorello, Cabernet; Luna Selvatica
This winery produces some of the best Emilian wines from the classical varieties of the Nure valley.

Marches. Albana di Romagna, the first Italian white wine to be awarded D.O.C.G. status, is produced here. This thriving variety, which needs abundant humidity, is extremely high-yielding as is reflected in the D.O.C.G. regulations which authorize a yield of 1,070 gallons per acre (100 hl/ha). Its sweet Passito version is, however, more interesting.

The other white varieties found in Romagna, Pagadebit and Trebbiano di Romagna, are

equally prone to excessive yields. The situation with respect to the red variety Sangiovese di Romagna is somewhat better, at least in parts of the region, although it does not achieve anything like the results yielded by its Tuscan cousin. The most that can be expected from this *appellation* is clean, drinkable wines. The wines from the other Emilia Romagna D.O.C. zones—Colli Bolognesi, Colli di Parma, and Colli Piacentini—are mostly light, semi-sparkling, and more or less sweet, and seldom display any interesting qualities.

The almost hopeless situation in winemaking in this region is down to the dominant position of the cooperatives. Almost all of the producers are cooperative members and the largest of these processes grapes from 67,000 acres (27,000 ha) of vineyards, which is more than one quarter of the area covered by Germany's vineyards. The cooperatives pursue a volume-oriented market policy and wield significant influence.

Legendary balsamic vinegar

Aceto Balsamico Tradizionale di Modena (traditional balsamic vinegar of Modena) and Aceto Balsamico Tradizionale di Reggio Emilia (traditional balsamic vinegar of Emilia Romagna) are the finest thing that can be made from Trebbiano grapes. The mean annual volumes produced do not exceed 795 gallons (3,000 l). Balsamic vinegar is made from concentrated Trebbiano must and aged for at least 12 years in a series of barrels that are usually made from a variety of woods. It is sold in bottles containing around 3 fluid ounces (100 ml) and, used sparingly by the drop, adds an exquisite taste to refined dishes.

Lambrusco

Like Prosecco, Lambrusco is first a grape variety, or more specifically a whole group of more than 40 different varieties. Traditional Lambrusco can be a wine of excellent quality which bears very little or no resemblance to the inferior product which has flooded the pizzerias of the world in recent decades. Unfortunately, the cooperatives have allowed this artisan wine to decline into a sticky sweet oddity and have even packaged their product in aluminum cans in order to create better marketing opportunities.

The qualities of traditional Lambrusco are, however, being rediscovered. Smaller producers are now offering wines under the Lambrusco di Sorbara, Lambrusco di Castelvetro, and Lambrusco di Salamino di Santa Croce *appellations* which are relatively dry with a bitter-fruity taste and which, in this—and only this!—guise, are truly a suitable accompaniment to the region's robust cuisine.

THE MARCHES

The Marches alternates between worlds, both geographically and in its wines. At its northern end, it is an extension of Romagna with its popular beaches, at its southern, the wilder landscape of Abruzzi. The Marches shares varieties, soils, and climate with almost all of the neighboring regions—and hence also its wine types—which is one of the reasons why, in the past, its reputation as a winemaking region was underdeveloped. Although its proximity to the popular resorts of Rimini and Riccione traditionally provided a captive market for its products, this factor also stifled efforts to establish quality winemaking. Why invest all that effort and money when it wasn't really necessary? For decades, white Verdicchio wine was the only product which succeeded in establishing a reputation beyond the region's borders, and the wine's amphora-shaped bottle—a stroke of genius of the Milanese marketing specialists—probably had more to do with its fame than the quality of the content.

And yet traditionally in the Marches, better quality-quantity balance was struck between white and red wines than in Umbria, where Orvieto prevails, or in the Sangiovese stronghold of Tuscany. In recent decades, the region's quality spectrum shifted from white to red wines based on the Montepulciano and Sangiovese varieties. Viticulture in the Marches covers large expanses of the hills in the hinterland of the Adriatic beaches and occasionally even extends right down to the coast, for example the cliff massifs south of the regional capital Ancona. The temperate influence of the sea, which reaches inland as far as the first hill ranges, contrasts with the climate of the Apennine and Abruzzian valleys which are buried deep in the region's interior. The cooler harsher climate here brings its own characteristics to the fore and appears to have a particularly good influence on the white wines, which are fresher and more lively than those produced from coastal vines.

RED WINE WITH A SEA VIEW

The Marches' best-known and best-quality red wine, Rosso Conero, grows almost directly by the sea in the coastal area around Ancona. Often a single variety made from Montepulciano grapes, the finesse of some of its representatives would suggest the occasional addition of small volumes of Sangiovese. A small group of Conero producers have been demonstrating the area's potential for some years now. Some of their barrel-aged wines can fully withstand comparison with top Tuscan wines. They have sought advice from Tuscany's most famous enologists, including the former chief Antinori enologist, Giacomo Tachis.

In the 1990s, Rosso Conero developed into a very interesting product which also represents

For a long time, quality was not a top priority in the Adriatic hinterland, which is also a fruit-growing area. However, this is gradually changing, and the Castelli di Jesi Verdicchio is a good example of the new trends.

Select Producers in the Marches

Fazi Battaglia*
Castelplanio
865 acres (350 ha); 3,000,000 bottles • Wines include: Verdicchio dei Castelli di Jesi: Le Moie, San Sisto
This winery in Castelplanio is owned by pharmaceuticals magnate Angelini (as are the Tuscan estates Val di Suga, San Leonino, and Trerose). Today the estate is once again one of the most consistent producers in the region.

Le Caniette**
Ripatransone
32 acres (13 ha); 50,000 bottles • Wines: Falerio Lucrezia, Veronica, →Rosso Piceno Morellone, Rosso Bello, →Rosso Piceno Riserva Nero di Vite, Sibilla Passerina
Raffaele Vagnoni is identified with the red wines Nero di Vite and Morellone, which are considered among the top Sangiovese-Montepulciano wines, not only in the Marches but throughout the whole of Italy.

Gioacchino garofoli−****
Loreto
62 acres (25 ha); some bought-in grapes; 1,300,000 bottles • Wines include: Verdicchio Castelli di Jesi: Serra del Conte, Macrina, →Serra Fiorese, →Podium; Rosso Conero: Piancarda, →Agontano; Kòmaros, Grillo, Guelfo Verde, Spumante
Both the Rosso Conero and the Verdicchio bottlings are impressive.

Cocci Grifoni*
Ripatransone
111 acres (45 ha); 130,000 bottles • Wines: Falerio Colli Asoclani San Basso, Rosso Piceno Superiore Le Torri, Vina Messieri, →Il Grifone, Poder Colle Vecchio Marche Bianco, Passerina Spumante Brut
The Cocci Grifoni family produces as range of good wines from native grape varieties. Il Grifone is the top red wine of the collection.

Lanari**
Varano
32 acres (13 ha); 40,000 bottles • Wines: Rosso Conero, →Rosso Conero Fibbio
Owner Luca Lanari and winemaker Giancarlo Soverchia make a good team, as is impressively demonstrated by the Fibbio, a red made from Montepulciano grapes.

Umani Ronchi*−*****
Osimo
360 acres (146 ha); some bought-in grapes; 4,500,000 bottles • Wines include: Verdicchio Castelli di Jesi: →Casal di Serra, Viall Bianchi; →Le Busche; Rosso Conero: Cùmaro, →San Lorenzo; Bianchello del Metauro, Rosso Piceno, Montepulciano d'Abruzzo, Maximo, Pelago, Tajano
Indisputably number one, thanks to Giacomo Tachis. This house also produces the top reds Cùmaro and San Lorenza, excellent Verdicchios, and a lovely, refined sweet wine.

good value for money. Rosso Piceno, its counterpart produced in the south of the region, is officially a Sangiovese-Montepulciano blend but fails to achieve the same power and complexity.

The New Face of Verdicchio

The white wines are dominated by Verdicchio from the two D.O.C. zones, Castelli di Jesi and Matelica, which together supply almost 80 percent of the total volume. This powerful rustic white often used to lack elegance, fruit, and freshness. Since the producers of the Marches stopped fermenting it on its skins and abandoned the *governo* technique—whereby dried grapes are added to the fermented wine to restart the fermentation—Verdicchio has evolved into a pleasantly fruity, light-to-medium-strength white wine. More powerful barrel-fermented wines have recently joined the fresh, light, original version.

The Bianchello del Metauro, Colli Maceratesi, Falerio dei Colli Scolani, Lacrima di Morro d'Alba, and Vernaccia di Serrapetrono *appellations* are not even familiar in Italy and are unlikely to attract attention beyond their localities in the future. Thus, the fate of winemaking in the Marches is in the hands of the producers of a small number of *appellations*. The fact that the region's most famous producers turned their backs on their native region decades ago may go

some way to explaining the current situation: the Mondavi family, which emigrated in the 1920s and has been making wine in the Napa Valley in California since the 1960s, is now one of the world's best-known producers.

Central Italy: The Region of Tuscany

Central Italy cannot be defined in terms of its geography alone. Whether the prosperous city of Bologna is still considered the north and Abruzzi the south, or whether they are both in the center of the country, is more a political, and most certainly a social, matter. Italy's poor south is everything that the rich north abhors—despite the fact that in the past the north not infrequently profited from the south and was even partly responsible for its poverty. The regions of the Marches, Tuscany, and Umbria are indisputably central Italian. The case of Lazio is less clear-cut; although its wines do exhibit strongly meridional traits, its classification in the center of the country can be justified by pointing to the example of Umbria, whose most important wine-growing region encroaches on the area around Rome. Abruzzi on the other hand is thought of as southern for historical and social reasons, although its topography, climate, and wines are not dissimilar to those of the Marches.

Ideal Growing Conditions

The natural conditions for growing top wines are ideal virtually throughout central Italy. Whether it is the eastern Adriatic foothills of the Apennines or their western slopes, or the mountainous volcanic landscapes of the Tyrrhenian coast from Siena southwards, the region's soils and climate favor powerful aromatic wines. The climate of the various growing regions is determined more by altitude than latitude: in the higher regions,

The vineyards of Nippozano are part of the Rufina area, which produces a wine which was long valued as a robust red before it was declared a Chianti.

such as Pomino between Florence and Arezzo, conditions are much cooler than in the more northern, populated area of the Po valley. The general tendency to grow grapes and olives on the slopes while cultivating grain and fruit on the plains is altogether beneficial for wine growing because it means the vineyards are situated on chalky, volcanic soils—conditions which are regarded as ideal for wine in Italy.

Grape Varieties and Types of Wine

Top-quality wines are more likely to be produced if the correct grape varieties are grown on these soils. The star among the local red varieties is the Sangiovese, a grape which forms the basis of Chianti Classico, Brunello di Montalcino, and Nobile di Montepulciano. Of the imported varieties Cabernet Sauvignon, Merlot, and, perhaps, Syrah do best. Together with other varieties such as Ciliegiolo or Montepulciano, the region has an enormous potential for red wines.

The range of white varieties still leaves something to be desired. Apart from some interesting grapes like Verdicchio or Vernaccia, along with the various successful applications of Chardonnay or Sauvignon, the spectrum is much too strongly dominated by the rather bland Trebbiano Toscano. There are even a number of critics who maintain that central Italy is simply not suited to growing high-quality white wines.

A White Past

While the wines of Tuscany have caused a sensation in the last two decades, the other central Italian regions have not been able to emerge from their neighbor's shadow despite ideal growing conditions and some excellent vines. Traditionally, Lazio, the Marches, and Umbria were—and still are—specialists in the production of precisely that type of white wine which finds no resonance on the international market. There are the beginnings of a new approach, however, and these have given cause for hope. In the Marches, the Rosso Conero has been especially impressive, while in Umbria, Torgiano and the heavy Sagrantino di Montefalco have provided a fresh stimulus to producers. In addition, the Antinori estate of Castello della Sala has inspired Orvieto producers to make good-quality whites.

The great success of Tuscan wines is largely due to an influx of enthusiastic amateurs and specialists who came from northern Italy and from abroad to seek a new start in Tuscany. Because they lacked experience themselves, they hired professional enologists to bring about a modernization of both vineyard practices and winery techniques.

THE TURN OF THE SOUTH

Together with the great wine merchants of Florence, who positioned themselves at the head of the movement for change, the new-comers revolutionized the region's most out-standing wine, Chianti. With their Supertuscans or *vini da tavola eccellenti* they created a new wine category which became a model for the entire country. These moves were sparked by general dissatisfaction with the rigid D.O.C.

Left
The real Tuscany—the estate of Vignamaggio in Greve.

Right
Traditional but always trendy—Cantinetta Antinori in Florence.

The ubiquitous Trebbiano.

definitions, which hindered quality work and stifled any attempts at experimentation with grape varieties and aging methods. Eventually the authorities accepted a *fait accompli* and retrospectively legalized Chianti Classico which has no white wine content. They also removed restrictions which compelled overly long cella-ring periods, and permitted aging in small *barri-ques* as well as the addition of international grape varieties. At the same time, the list of D.O.C. and D.O.C.G. names of origin was extended, and I.G.T. definitions were intro-duced under which the super table wines of approved origin could also be marketed—as had long been common practice in France, Spain, and Germany. In the past few years central Italian wine has increasingly turned to largely untapped but high-quality growing regions such as the Maremma and Morellino areas, as well as others in the Marches and Umbria.

Regional varieties

Central Italy has comparatively few grape varieties, but with the Sangiovese it can lay claim to one of the finest red varieties in the world. Known as Sangiovese in the Romagna and Chianti regions, the same grape is called Brunello in Montalcino, and Prugnolo Gentile in the growing areas of the Vino Nobile di Montepulciano—although it is still a matter of debate whether these types really do consti-tute independent clones or subspecies as has long been maintained.

In terms of quality and quantity, the Montepulciano of the Marches and Abruzzi takes second place among the red varieties; the round, soft, full wines may be pleasing and attractive but they never achieve the complexity and range of a really great Sangiovese. In the Chianti region, Canaiolo

Nero, Malvasia Nera, and Colorino are repre-sented in smaller quantities. Previously they were used to enrich the color, aroma or taste of Sangiovese, but have clearly forfeited this role with the rise of Cabernet Sauvignon and Merlot. The latter varieties—either on their own or as blends—have enhanced the spec-trum of Tuscan wines: Cabernet Sauvignon, especially in the shape of the cult wine Sassicaia, has even chalked up a number of triumphs in international competitions.

Trebbiano Toscano, the dominant white variety, is primarily used for distilling spirits in France (where it goes under the name Ugni Blanc)—a fact which can hardly be consid-ered a mark of quality. Light, neutral wines are the best one can hope to achieve with this variety. It was formerly used as a blend in Chianti to reduce the astringency and youthful aggression of the Sangiovese grape.

Since Trebbiano lost its main *raison d'être*, the Galestro wine made from it has probably been the most intelligent, if short-term, attempt to use the enormous quantities of wine avail-able. At the end of the 1980s and start of the 1990s Galestro even stood on the threshold of becoming a fashionable wine. The Verdicchio of the the Marches region is rarely able to exceed the quality of Trebbiano; and the growers of Vernaccia—the first Italian wine in San Gimignano to achieve D.O.C. honors and the first Italian white to gain D.O.C.G. status—have yet to outline a convincing concept for producing quality. Respectable white wines are occasionally made from Greco, Grechetto, Vermentino, and the various Malvasia varieties (Malvasia di Candia, Malvasia del Lazio, Malvasia del Chianti), but even in their growing regions in Umbria and Lazio it is quantity rather than quality that is emphasized.

TUSCANY AND ITS WINES

Tuscany is home to the most common Italian quality wine: Chianti. But Tuscany has more to offer than this popular red wine which is grown in the hills between Florence and Siena, Arezzo and Pisa. Around half of the harvest from Tuscany's 148,260 acres (60,000 ha) of vineyards is marketed as quality wine. In addition to Chianti, wines such as Brunello di Montalcino, Vino Nobile di Montepulciano, and Vernaccio di San Gimignano, along with other individual wines and brands, such as Tignanello or the famous Sassicaia, have made Tuscan wines renowned throughout the world.

Imitators have always been a problem: some of the Tuscan growing regions were so popular that their names had to be protected from forgers and those seeking to capitalize on their reputation. Designations of origin such as Carmignano, which was granted in 1716, are some of the oldest protected *appellations* in the world.

The variety of wines in the region is reflected in the variety of *terroirs*. The spectrum ranges from the great curve of the Apennines in the north and east to the hills of central Tuscany, and from the volcanic formations of the south to the coastal landscape of Livorno and Grosseto provinces. Hills and mountains cover more than two thirds of Tuscany, natural features which have provided ideal growing conditions for wine for thousands of years.

Roman art treasures still provide evidence of Florence's ancient glories. Wines from the surrounding hills include the reds Carmignano and Pomino.

Siena is the real capital of Tuscan wine. Vino Nobile, Brunello, and the majority of Chianti Classico wines are grown in the surrounding province.

The Etruscans brought viticulture and a wine industry to perfection, and their achievements established the model for Roman wine growing. In the Middle Ages it was mainly the Florentine nobility that was associated with wine, if more as merchants than growers. Names famous today, such as Antinori and Frescobaldi, have been linked to Tuscan wines since the 13th and 14th centuries.

THE BEGINNINGS OF WINE TOURISM

As the once powerful and wealthy patrons of Leonardo, Michelangelo, and other artists, the great Tuscan noble families are not only associated with wine but also with the region's art history. This artistic legacy, preserved in the historical cities studding one of Italy's most attractive landscapes, turned Tuscany into a popular tourist destination at an early stage. When wine tourism became fashionable in Tuscany, it was able to profit from a highly developed tourist infrastructure long before the advantages of the idea were recognized in the other wine-growing regions of Italy.

In spite of—or perhaps because of—its rich viticultural heritage, Tuscany, and indeed the whole of Italy, came close to completely losing contact with developments in other countries after the Second World War due to the disastrous effects on the wine industry of rural migration. Not until the 1970s did the great wine houses of Florence hesitantly begin to look for a new approach.

RIPE FOR THE VINEYARD

It was mainly wealthy city dwellers from the Italian north or abroad who were responsible for the turnaround; after settling in Tuscany to realize their long-cherished dreams of a quiet country life, they turned to wine growing either out of passion or as a means of realizing a return on their large investments. Most of them had absolutely no experience and so had to take advantage of the specialist skills of professional enologists. Quality was their mantra and they introduced essential elements from the vine-growing and wine-making practices of other countries to Tuscany, such as the use of French grape varieties, temperature-controlled fermentation and the technique of aging wines in

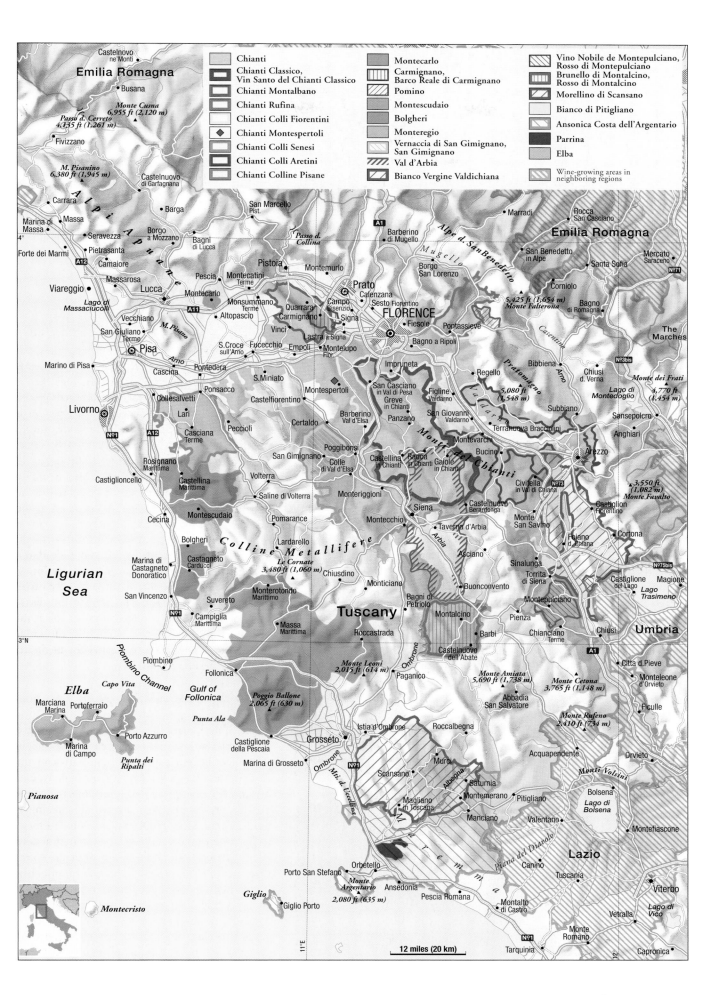

Chianti	Montecarlo
Chianti Classico, Vin Santo del Chianti Classico	Carmignano, Barco Reale di Carmignano
Chianti Montalbano	Pomino
Chianti Rufina	Montescudaio
Chianti Colli Fiorentini	Bolgheri
Chianti Montespertoli	Monteregio
Chianti Colli Senesi	Vernaccia di San Gimignano, San Gimignano
Chianti Colli Aretini	Val d'Arbia
Chianti Colline Pisane	Bianco Vergine Valdichiana

Vino Nobile de Montepulciano, Rosso di Montepulciano
Brunello di Montalcino, Rosso di Montalcino
Morellino di Scansano
Bianco di Pitigliano
Ansonica Costa dell'Argentario
Parrina
Elba
Wine-growing areas in neighboring regions

barriques. Uninhibited by history or tradition, they began to create a whole new generation of top class wines.

It was therefore unavoidable that these new wines, which were conceived according to international criteria, came into conflict with bureaucratic D.O.C. rules. Over the years these had fixed regulations for all sorts of irrelevant details: the recipes for blending varieties in a given wine were hopelessly out-of-date; barrel-aging often took several years; and the maximum yields allowed were wildly excessive. The "revolution" swept all the wine-growing areas of the region, beginning in the heart of the Chianti district, before spreading to the coastal vineyards near Bogheri and the Rufina hills at the foot of the Apennines and on up to Montalcino and Montepulciano, where two of the most famous regional red varieties—Brunello and Vino Nobile—grew in abundance. Not only did these new wines signal that a fresh wind was blowing through traditional designations of origin; the sense of change they inspired brought about entirely new designations. Many of the best products which had previously had to trade as table wines, because they contained Cabernet Sauvignon or because they had not undergone the requisite aging process, have now been legitimized through the allocation of new D.O.C. or I.G.T. names. Even the production restrictions on Chianti Classico were adjusted—varietals as well as wines with added Cabernet and Merlot have since been permitted—and Classico was granted a D.O.C.G. status separate from the other Chianti *appellations*.

But the Tuscan wine industry still has a major task ahead of it, namely the comprehensive over-

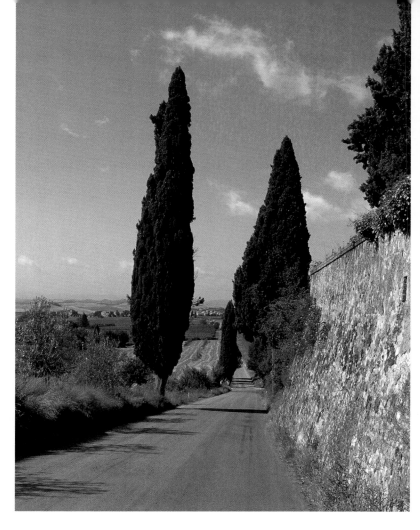

Cypress trees—the green symbol of Tuscany.

Opposite
Above vineyards at the Fattoria di Felsina estate in Castelnuovo Berardenga.

Arezzo—a Mecca for fans of antiques and bric-a-brac.

haul of most vineyards. The proportion of white varieties for which there is no longer any place in the modernized D.O.C. statutes is still too high, and there are still too many old and inferior vines even in the renowned vineyards. Many of the vineyards are so exhausted or riddled with viruses that one wonders how the growers are able to exploit their depleted stock to reach the maximum yield restrictions. The suspicion that some wines are purchased secretly from outside the region is today considered to be (more or less) an established fact.

In many areas, however, efforts have been undertaken to renovate vineyards and their vines. In the Chianti Classico area, for example, a far-reaching research program was initiated in the 1980s which is now beginning to bear the first fruits. In the past few years, the main centers of activity have shifted to the coast and southern Tuscany. Areas like Bolgheri, Montescudaio, or the region of Morellino di Scansano on the edge of the Maremma plain have, for some time now, been the targets of massive investment and new plantings by the greatest and most important houses of Tuscany.

Super Tuscans

Italian wine laws are like no others in Europe. Legislation has been devoted to the regulation of even the most trivial details, hindering the early efforts toward achieving quality in Tuscany and, later, in Piedmont.

Outdated prescriptions of the varieties allowed to make up a given wine or antiquated methods for pressing and aging did not, in the opinion of experts, allow for the development of the best quality. Winegrowers and producers preferred to experiment with French varieties such as Cabernet, Chardonnay, Syrah, and Merlot, as these types seemed to hold out the promise of greater success than that gained by the arduous, time-consuming propagation of superior Sangiovese or Trebbiano vines. Growers chose to expose their wines to the piquant effects of new wood, instead of allowing them to molder away for years in enormous, old wooden barrels. Ideas and processes developed in France and California seemed to make it a quicker and less complicated matter to endow wines with more body and concentration, greater elegance, a more pronounced longevity, and aromatic complexity.

Innovative growers in Italy who wanted to proceed in this direction were forced to downgrade the classification of their high-value wines and market them as simple table wines. The first examples of this new style came on the market at the start of the 1970s: these were Incisa's Sassicaia and Antinori's Tignanello. It was the Tignanello especially—a blend of Sangiovese and Cabernet in a ratio of 80:20—that paved the way for famous names such as Camartina, Vigorello, Grifi, I Sodi di San Nicolò, Siepi, Balifico, Cabero Il Borgo, Monte Vertine, and Convivio.

Gianni Nunziante, the owner of Vignamaggio in Greve.

Other wines were Sangiovese varietals such as San Martino, Solatio Basilica, Cappanelle, Cetinaia, Le Pergole Torte, Cepparello, Percarlo, and Flaccianello della Pieve; or they consisted mainly—if not entirely—of Cabernet Sauvignon, such as Campora, Solaia, Sammarco, Cortaccio, Nemo, Saffredi, Guado al Tasso, Maestro Raro, Il Pareto, Ornellaia, and Tassinaia. What the Italian authorities rejected with short shrift was speedily and enthusiastically embraced by the market. Within a short period of time supposedly simple wines began to win prizes and this caused a number of quality wine producers to begin reflecting on their own practices. In the mid-1980s the lessons learned had spread far beyond Tuscany and there was scarcely an estate without at least one of the new top-notch table wines, which American critics enthusiastically celebrated as Supertuscans.

A mere ten years later the controversy was no more: the authorities had established new D.O.C. areas in many of the regions, adjusted production regulations in line with existing practices, and assented to the category of *indicazione geografica*—the table wine with a geographical designation of origin. Many of the table wines that were previously considered so exceptional are today to be found under D.O.C. or I.G.T. names.

THE REINVENTION OF CHIANTI

In the 1970s and '80s the new ambitious estate owners in Tuscany had but one goal: to produce great, complex red wines which would improve on aging. Some of them pinned their hopes on French varieties and a broad range of wines while others perfected the native Sangiovese grape to produce a top-quality varietal. Two companies whose histories, strategies and quality are representative of the group are Castello di Ama, located several kilometers south of Gaiole in Chianti, and Fattoria di Felsina, situated in Castelnuovo Berardenga on the outermost edge of the Chianti Classico region.

THE ADVENTURE OF CHIANTI CLASSICO

In 1977 a group of Roman families decided to purchase a neglected estate above the hamlet of Monti, just south of Gaiole, in one of the best areas in the Chianti Classico region in order to pursue quality viticulture at the highest level. They had money but little in the way of wine-making skills to invest and so they hired, as their enologist, Marco Pallanti, a man who was to prove one of the most talented Italians in his field. Head of the operation was Silvano Formigli, an individual with a clear strategic concept as well as excellent contacts in the trade press.

Castello di Ama began by developing a series of single-vineyard variations on Chianti Classico which were later produced in three—then four—versions, each with its own blend and characteristics. Most made use of traditional Tuscan grape varieties—San Lorenzo with its mixture of Sangiovese and Canaiolo; Bellavista, which complemented these two

Left
Some of the oldest and most famous estates such as Badia a Coltibuono and Castello di Brolio are situated in Gaiolo, in the southwest of the Chianti Classico region.

Right
In spite of a rich wine-growing tradition, the Fattoria di Felsina in Castelnuovo Berardenga did not break into the elite group of Chianti Classicos until the end of the 1990s.

varieties with a dash of Malvasia; and the classic Chianti blend of Bertinga. Vigneto La Casuccia, however, was an innovative blend of Sangiovese with Canaiolo and the French grape, Merlot.

MERLOT MAKES A CAREER FOR ITSELF

It became clear that Merlot had fallen onto fertile soil here: 1985 saw the first vintage of a Merlot varietal, a table wine, from Vigna l'Apparita. Together with the 1987 vintage, it rose to become one of the very best Tuscan reds. In numerous tastings it outclassed all the most renowned Merlot wines from countries around the world including Petrus, Le Pin, and the Californian wines.

In France, Merlot—with few exceptions—is the variety responsible for the softer, fruitier components of the great Bordeaux wines. In Ama and on the other Tuscan estates which experimented with the variety, it was unusually high in tannins, exhibiting a complex, diverse nose and palate; Merlot was even able to absorb effortlessly the enormous boost in aroma and taste from the wooden casks used in the aging process.

Along with his top wines, Marco Pallanti presents an impressive range of good to very good wines to an astonished public every year. Whether it be Pinot Grigio from Vigna Bellaria, his two Chardonnays, the Pinot Nero Vigna Il Chiuso, the Sauvignon or the simple Colline di Ama from the classical white Chianti varieties—Pallanti's wines are almost always among the best in the region.

New Techniques

Pallanti caused a new sensation in the catastrophic year of 1992. At a time when the renowned firm of Antinori was unable to bottle a single one of its top wines and was only able to bring the high-volume Santa Cristina onto the market, Pallanti triumphed with another top vintage of Merlot l'Apparita, which bore comparisons with its legendary predecessor from 1988.

Rigorous selection and propagation in the vineyard, a meticulously supervised vinification process and the controlled, balanced aging of the wine had worked real wonders. These improvements were supported by the most modern cellaring technology, which included the somewhat controversial use of concentration equipment.

The Character of the Terroir

The wines of Fattoria di Felsina in Castelnuovo Berardenga, on the southern edge of the *appellation*, are more closely tied to the peculiarities of the *terroir* than at Ama, where the variety of vineyards has again been reduced. Felsina was purchased in 1966 by businessman Domenico Poggiali and systematically built up by his son-in-law, Giuseppe Mazzocolin, together with his friend, Franco Bernabei, a well-known enologist and also one of the most famous winemakers in Italy.

The vineyard is situated on the final gentle foothills of the Monti del Chianti as it runs down into the Ombrone Valley, and covers about 865 acres (350 ha) of land, of which only a seventh is given over to wine growing. The geological composition of the vineyards reflects this border location: there are blue-gray marlaceous soils—or *galestro*—rocky *albarese*, loamy and alluvial soils as well as marine sediments, and it is to this diversity that the wines of Felsina owe their extraordinary complexity and range.

Felsina is especially renowned for its Chianti Classico and even the normal version, supported by a clever mix of small and medium barrels in the aging process, makes an uncommonly rich and complex impression. The *riserva* is in fact a single vineyard wine from Rancia, Mazzocolin's favorite vineyard. The most mature vines on this quartzy, marlaceous soil with its strips of sand and loam are 35 years old. The stock has been carefully renewed and seedlings from the best vines have been propped up on existing plants in order to achieve a uniform improvement in the quality.

The cellar at Castello di Ama.

Sangiovese with Cabernet

In good years, the Vigneto Rancia is one the best wines in the entire growing region, but the real stars of Fattoria are two varietal table wines: Fontalloro from Sangiovese and Maestro Raro from Cabernet Sauvignon. They are aged in *barriques* and both perfectly harmonize structure and elegance, as well as fruity density and the ability to improve with age.

Mazzocolin and Bernabei have not ignored their white wines either. The barrel-fermented Chardonnay, I Sistri, initially suffered from a lack of structure and definition but by the 1991 vintage it had developed into one of the finest of its kind in Tuscany. When there is so much quality to be had, the cost-benefit relationship is particularly favorable for the more basic products.

Since the start of the 1990s, Mazzocolin has owned Castello di Farnetella in Sinalunga, outside the Chianti Classico area and close to the growing region of Nobile di Montepulciano. At the beginning of the 1980s the concentration of Sangiovese vines had been increased here and the vineyards cultivated according to modern methods. In addition, young Pinot Noir and Cabernet Sauvignon plants were propped up on older vines, and the wines improved with micro-vinification techniques to the point where, today, they are able to compete with produce from neighboring D.O.C.G. regions. The most interesting wines from the higher altitude vineyards are a Chianti Colli Senesi, in which a Merlot component reinforces the structure and fruit, and a very aromatic Sauvignon Blanc.

Italy's Most Popular Wines: The Chianti Family

The name "Chianti" has been in common usage since the 13th century when it was associated with the hills around Radda, Gaiole, and Castellina, and referred to as a white wine. It is only since the 1930s that the Chianti growing region has undergone continuous expansion, and it now covers a large part of Tuscany. Even the characteristic mixture of varieties that make up Chianti is comparatively recent. Before the 19th century Chianti—the name by then had come to mean a red wine—was made mainly from Canaiolo grapes, to which a Sangiovese or Malvasia component was added.

The Recipe

Bettino Ricasoli, Prime Minister of a newly united Italy from 1861, was the scion of an old Tuscan noble family and owner of the Ricasoli firm of wine merchants. He is also renowned for having developed the traditional Chianti recipe of 70 percent Sangiovese, 15 percent Canaiolo Nero, 10 percent white varieties—such as Trebbiano Toscano and Malvasia del Chianti—and five percent from other varieties. The addition of white wine was intended to take the edge off the harshness of the young, inaccessible Sangiovese and enable it to be consumed at an earlier date—a characteristic which was encouraged by the so-called *governo* process. This

The *gallo nero*, or black rooster, is the symbol of Chianti Classico. Its growing region was defined for the first time by Grand Duke Cosimo III de Medici in 1716.

Rufina is today the smallest of the seven Chianti zones. The region has enormous potential which is far from being fully exploited.

consisted of setting part of the grape harvest aside and drying it before adding it to the wine after fermentation had finished. Fermentation would then begin again, giving the wine not only a higher alcohol content, making it fuller and rounder, but also ensuring that the carbon dioxide remained in solution thus making it seem fresher and lighter. This type of blend, however, did not endow the wine with genuine quality.

The Growing Region

With production of around 26½ million gallons (one million hl) a year, Chianti has the largest volume of the officially recognized quality wines in Italy today. Behind the famous name, however, there lurks a contradictory reality. All wines with the name "Chianti" share a common basis in the robust Sangiovese variety. But because the extensive growing region provides such a variety of different *terroirs* and climatic conditions, the consumer is faced with a puzzling array of wines. For this reason eight different subregions have been instituted and these are stated on the label (although the designation "Chianti" without a geographical suffix is also permitted). The most important of these is the Classico region which has had its own D.O.C.G. statute since the mid-1980s and which is treated separately here. Around the central Classico area are distributed the growing regions of Chianti Rufina, Chianti Colli Fiorentini, Chianti Colli Aretini, Chianti Colli Senesi, Chianti Colline Pisane, Chianti Montalbano, and the most recent, Chianti Montespertoli.

Relatives both Rich and Poor

The most interesting wines, with the longest tradition of quality, are from the Chianti Rufina area. In some cases they have even surpassed many of the Classico wines. The growing region stretches across the slopes above the town of Pontassieve in the Arno valley and is part of the former Pomino region—a name which is also a designation of origin today, being reserved for the highest sites up to 2,950 feet (900 m). Most of the vineyards belong to the Frescobaldi and Giuntini Antinori families who also produce the best wines. The cool climate of the higher sites, together with their superb chalky, marl soils, provide the conditions for elegant, multifaceted wines.

Much simpler in structure and aromatic expression are the wines of the Colli Fiorentini, which come from the hills between the Arno valley and the Chianti Classico area. While it is undoubtedly true that this damp, cool growing region is less suited to producing high-grade wines, the continuing urban sprawl from Florence is also harming the area's grape crops.

The same can be said of the Chianti zones of Colli Aretini in the area around the city of Arezzo, as well as Colli Senesi, whose growing regions cover the eastern and central southern parts of Tuscany below Siena. The Colli Senesi also have to share their growing region with more famous wines like Brunello di Montalcino and Nobile di Montepulciano, which claim the best fruit from the top sites, leaving hardly anything for their poorer cousins.

Montalbano includes the small Carmignano region and is therefore fated to stand in the shadow of a superior wine—a position which it has to endure often enough as Carmignano's secondary wine in any case. The creation of Barco Reale has actually exacerbated the situation, as Carmignano itself—in spite of being awarded D.O.C.G.—has now been forced to contend with image problems.

Although its growing region undoubtedly has more potential, the Chianti Colline Pisane is the lightest member of the Chianti family.

Chianti history in the Frescobaldis' cellar.

In Chianti, wine and woods are neighbors.

With the exceptions of Classico—whose prestige and qualities seem to have consolidated—and the independent Chianti Rufina, the region offers little to impress the consumer. Growers on the edge of the area have sought to emphasize their connection with Classico in their use of the Chianti name, and Classico growers in turn demanded their own D.O.C.G. status at the end of the 1980s in order to distinguish themselves more clearly from these other regions. It is, in fact, high time that the definition of the Chianti family was given a thorough overhaul.

CLASSICAL CHIANTI AT THE PEAK

These were painful lessons. At the end of the 1970s the Chianti Classico region—one of the first regions in Italy to do so—began to take a more innovative tack. New, international grape varieties, more sophisticated aging techniques and modern marketing methods were already in full swing here when other regions were still intent on producing surpluses. These efforts at first bore fruit only in the table wines. At the time, Italy's rigid production regulations were intent on protecting quality wines, many of which had ceased to be as good as their reputations. The result was that some table wines were better than those which carried the region's prestigious designation of origin. Several years went by before it was ultimately decided to redefine the production regulations for Chianti Classico according to the quality criteria of the table wines. Furthermore, growers began to renew their interest in the local Sangiovese variety.

During the Middle Ages and shortly after, "Chianti" meant the communes of Radda, Gaiole, and Castellina, which formed a political and military whole in the *Lega del Chianti*. Grand Duke Cosimo III de' Medici (1670–1723) extended the area in his edict of 1716 to include the commune of Greve. After 1932 other areas were also added: parts of San Casciano Val di Pesa and Barberino Val d'Elsa—a group of villages close to Florence—as well as Castelnuovo Berardenga in the south. Even after the concept of "Chianti" was widened to include peripheral growing regions, the definition of its heartland remained unchanged. The countryside in Chianti is some of the most beautiful in Tuscany and it enjoys an excellent reputation not only through its wines—around a tenth of the total area is covered in vineyards—but also through its proximity to centers of art in Florence and Siena.

The silhouette of Greve, one of the oldest growing centers in the very heart of the Chianti Classico region.

VINEYARDS IN TRANSITION

In the 1960s and 1970s many of the vineyards were restocked, although in the course of this work less attention was paid to quality than to maximizing yields and rationalizing working methods. As it turned out, this approach was to demand a high price: samples taken from older Chianti vintages today clearly prove that wines from this era are less expressive than the Chiantis of earlier decades, or even those from more recent years, all of which have aged extremely well.

THE BEST TERROIR

Sangiovese is one of those varieties which needs a great deal of warmth and dry conditions in order to ripen, and the Chianti Classico area is exceptionally suited to these growing conditions. The large number of hillside vineyards allows an optimal orientation of the vines at an ideal height of between 820 and 1,640 feet (250 and 500 m) above sea level. The good drainage provided by the loose, blue-gray, chalky, marlaceous soils (*galestro*) or weathered sandstone (*albarese*) means that the vineyards rarely

⬛	**Chianti Classico**
⬜	San Casciano in Val di Pesa
⬜	Greve in Chianti
⬜	Tavarnelle Val di Pesa
⬜	Barberino Val d'Elsa
⬜	Poggibonsi
⬜	Castellina in Chianti
⬜	Radda in Chianti
⬜	Gaiole in Chianti
⬜	Castelnuovo Berardenga
⬜	**Chianti**
⬜	**Chianti Colli Fiorentini**
⬜	**Chianti Colli Senesi**
⬜	**Chianti Colli Aretini**

Nobility with red wine in its veins

In 1180 Ugo and Antinoro di Rinuccino were officially named owners of the Castello di Combiate. One hundred years later the family, which had in the meantime moved to Florence, was entered in the register of the silk trade corporation. In 1385 a certain Giovanni di Piero, son of a subsidiary line of the family, was apprenticed to the winemakers' guild. Since that date the wine-growing tradition of the Antinoris has proceeded without interruption, reaching a temporary peak in 1895 with the founding of the trading house of Marchesi Antinori. In 1898 the cellars in San Casciano Val di Pesa were built and today these function as the center of a diverse concern, with interests in all the important growing regions of Tuscany, Umbria, Piedmont, Apulia, and even California. This traditional firm owes much of its prestige to its former head enologist, Giacomo Tachis, who was responsible for such extraordinary wines as Sassicaia, Tignanello (largely made from Sangiovese), Solaia (mainly Cabernet), and many others. In addition, the enologist Renzo Cotarella created one of Italy's best Chardonnays on the Umbrian estate of Castello della Sala.

Piero Antinori, director of his family's estate, with more than 600 years of tradition.

The aristocratic banking family of Frescobaldi has been active in growing and trading wine since the 14th century. With estates in both the Classico and Rufina regions, a virtual monopoly in Pomino, large interests in Montalcino, and new vineyards in the Maremma region, the Frescobaldis are today

one of the biggest and best producers in Italy. Their best-known products are their Chianti Rufina wines, Pomino variants and the Luce della Vita. This latter wine is the result of a joint venture with the Californian firm of Mondavi.

Wine was thought to be an occupation suited to the upper classes, and other noble families also pursued the trade for this reason. Giuntini Antinori, distant relations of Marchesi Antinori, owned the Rufina estate of Selvapiana. In the 19th century they also owned the abbey of Badia a Coltibuono, which today belongs to another branch of their descendants, the banking family of Stucchi Prinetti. The Prinettis had formed an alliance with one of the most powerful Tuscan dynasties—the Medici—through the marriage of Piero Stucchi Prinetti to Lorenza de' Medici.

After a less than successful intermezzo in Australia, descendants of Baron Ricasoli, who developed the Chianti blend, are once again proud owners of the Castello di Brolio, which they manage together with another family with a long-standing tradition, the Mazzei from Castello di Fonterutoli. The Ricasoli name also resonates in the name of the proprietors of the Castello di Cacchiano, the Ricasoli Firidolfi family.

---

become too wet, even when there is heavy rainfall. Even the Bordeaux varieties of Cabernet Sauvignon and Merlot achieve good results on this *terroir*.

While in the past the acidity of Sangiovese often gave a sharp and immature impression—white grapes were added during fermentation to soften the tannins—modern Chianti Classico with a predominant or even exclusive Sangiovese component, forms a single, harmonious unit. As a young wine, its bouquet is floral and slightly spicy, taking on leather and tobacco notes as it ages; its tannins are elegantly structured and redolent of cinnamon, with a sophistication well supported by a slightly acidic tone. It is well-suited to most Tuscan dishes such as pasta, wild game, lamb, and beef.

The best wines of the Chianti Classico region come from medium altitude sites south of Greve and north of Radda and Castellina, as well as from the slopes stretching from Gaiole in the south into Castelnuovo, toward the Arbia valley. One of the very best *terroirs* is the Conco d'Oro at Panzano, part of the Greve commune.

GALLO NERO

Chianti, along with other Tuscan wines, was given a fresh lease of life by the traditional wine houses and the "newcomers" from the north and abroad, but developments in the last couple of decades have been dominated by the

The Castello di Brolio—long in the hands of the Ricasoli family—is thought to be the oldest vineyard in the world. It was here that Baron Bettino Ricasoli developed the recipe for Chianti in the 19th century.

sign of the black rooster, or *gallo nero* in Italian. This is the world-famous symbol of the Consorzio Chianti Classico, the region's federation of winegrowers, an organization to whom Chianti Classico owes its D.O.C.G. status. The federation also undertook the renovation of vineyards in the heart of Tuscany. Under the title "Chianti 2000," a long-term research project was instituted at the end of the 1980s to carry out research into the best varieties, clones, and systems of cultivation. Although many Chianti vineyards are still in need of an overhaul at the start of the new millennium, the knowledge gained from the project has already led to a series of new facilities being established.

SELECT PRODUCERS IN NORTHERN TUSCANY

AGRICOLA SAN FELICE**—****
CASTELNUOVO BERARDENGA
494 acres (200 ha); 1,200,000 bottles • Wines include: Chianti Classico: Riserva Il Grigio, Poggio Rosso, →I.G.T. Toscana Vigorello, Brunello di Montalcino Campogiovanni
This large estate in the southern Chianti Classico region belongs to the German Allianz group. The wines' quality is good to very good; the single-vineyard Chianti Poggio Rosso is ranked among the best in the region.

BADIA A COLTIBUONO**—****
GAIOLE
143 acres (58 ha); 330,000 bottles • Wines: Chianti Classico, Chianti Classico Riserva, →I.G.T. Toscana Sangioveto, Chianti Cetamura, Trapploine Bianco, Sella del Boscone, Chardonnay, Vin Santo del Chianti Classico
The Stucchi Prinettis' Sangioveto and Chianti Classico are among Tuscany's prize wines.

CAPANNELLE**—****
GAIOLE
15 acres (6 ha); 25,000 bottles • Wines: Capanelle: Riserva, →Barrique, Chardonnay, →50:50
Rosetti is considered a Sangiovese specialist. He set the standard with his 50:50, a Sangiovese-Merlot blend (the latter comes from Avignonesi vineyards in Montepulciano) and a red made from Syrah. Since 1997, the estate has been owned by J. Sherwood.

CASTELLO DI AMA***—****
GAIOLE
222 acres (90 ha); 300,000 bottles • Wines include: Chianti Classico: →Vigneto San Lorenzo, →Vigneto La Casuccia; I.G.T. Toscana: →Merlot, Chardonnay, Pinot Grigio, Pinot Nero, Vin Santo
This premium estate in the southern Chianti Classico region suffered severe competition in the 1980s.

CASTELLO DI FONTERUTOLI***—*****
CASTELLINA
171 acres (69 ha); 450,000 bottles • Wines: Chianti Classico Castello di Fonterutoli, , I.G.T. Toscana: →Siepi, →Poggio alla Badiola; Morellino di Scansano Belguardo
For years the Mazzeis' Sangiovese-Cabernet blend Concerto was one of the best of the Supertuscans, but production was terminated in favor of a Riserva Chianti. The new premier wine is the Merlot-Sangiovese blend Siepi. Castello di Fonterutoli also handles the wines of the neighboring estate of La Brancaia; until recently these underwent vinification in the Fonterutoli cellars.

CASTELLO DI MONSANTO***—*****
BARBERINO VAL D'ELSA
124 acres (50 ha); 270,000 bottles • Wines: Chianti Classico Riserva Il Poggio, →I.G.T. Toscana: Nemo, →Tinscvil, Chardonnay, Sangiovese, Vin Santo
Fabrizio Bianchi's Poggio was the first single-vineyard Chianti, and his Tincsvil the first really good successor to Tiganello. Nemo is a successful Cabernet.

CHIANTI RUFFINO AND TENUTA NOZZOLE**—****
PONTASSIEVE
1,483 acres (600 ha); some bought-in grapes; 16,000,000 bottles • Wines include: Brunello Riserva Greppone Mazzi, Chianti Classico: →Riserva Ducale Oro, →La Forra; Nero del Tondo, Nobile di Montepulciano, →Il Pareto, Le Bruniche
In the 1950s Ruffino was know for its bottles of Chianti in raffia baskets, but its Riserva Ducale was also a top quality wine. The best estate is Tenuta Nozzole in Greve, which produces outstanding Chianti and the great Cabernet Pareto.

LE CINCIOLE****
GREVE/PANZANO
27 acres (11 ha); 40,000 bottles • Wines: Chianti Classico, →Chinati Classico Riserva Il Petresco
Luca Orsini and Valeria Vigano rely on their splendid unadorned Sangiovese from the hills south of Florence.

COLLELUNGO****
CASTELLINA
27 acres (11 ha); 30,000 bottles • Wines: Chianti Classico, →Chianti Classico Riserva, Campocerchio
All of the wines display the special quality of the soil and location in the vineyard near Castellina. Wine-maker Alberto Antonini manages to transfer the quality of the grapes to the bottle in a convincing manner.

CORZANO & PATERNO****
SAN CASCIANO VAL DI PESA
27 acres (11 ha); 50,000 bottles • Wines: Chianti Terre di Corzano, Chianti Riserva Tre Borri, Il Corzano, Aglaia Chardonnay, Passito di Corzano
Under Alyosha Goldschmidt's management, the estate produces characterful wines typical of the region. The Passito di Corzano, made in Vin Santo fashion, is also impressive.

FATTORIA DI FELSINA***—*****
CASTELNUOVO BERARDENGA
128 acres (52 ha); 250,000 bottles • Wines: →Chinati Classico Vigneto Rancia; I.G.T. Toscana: →Fontalloro, →Maestro Raro, →I Sistri; Vin Santo
Fattoria's superb Chiantis, Chardonnays and Cabernets are made at the edge of the Chianti Classico region under the direction of Giuseppe Mazzocolin.

FATTORIA LA MASSA****—*****
GREVE
67 acres (27 ha); 90,000 bottles • Wines: Chianti Classico, Chianti Classico Giorgio Primo
Motta's' Chianti Classico variants, particularly the Giorgio Primo, have been among the greatest of Italian wines since the mid-1990s, with their fruity and cedary nose and wealth of essences on the palate.

FATTORIA SAN GIUSTO A RENTENNANO***—*****
GAIOLE
82 acres (33 ha); 60,000 bottles • Wines: Chianti Classico, I.G.T. Toscana: Percarlo, La Ricolma, Vin Santo del Chianti Classico
The fattoria run by Luca, Francesco and Elisabetta Martin di Cigala has for years been one of the best estates in the Chianti Classico region. The vintage Chianti has a very good price-to-performance ratio. Percarlo is a single-variety Sangiovese in a class of its own.

FATTORIA SELVAPIANA***—****
PONTASSIEVE
101 acres (41 ha); 100,000 bottles • Wines: Chianti Rufina: Riserva, →Vigneto Bucerchiale; Borro Lastricato, Vin Santo
Francesco Giuntini-Antinori owns some of the best vineyards in the region as well as a cellar whose bottles, some of them decades old, prove just how well a good Chianti Rufina ages.

FONTODI***—****
GREVE
116 acres (47 ha); 16,000 bottles • Wines: Chianti Classico, →Chianti Classico Vigna del Sorbo, →I.G.T. Toscana Flaccianello della Pieve, Pinot Bianco Meriggio, →Pinot Nero Casa Via, Syrah Casa Via, Vin Santo, Solstizio

In the 1980's Manetti's Flaccianello della Pieve, a single-variety Sangiovese, enjoyed great success, and in the 1990s experiments were undertaken with Syrah and Pinot Nero. Fontodi has almost completely restocked its vineyards.

ISOLE E OLENA***–*****
BARBERINO VAL D'ELSA
101 acres (41 ha); 200,000 bottles • Wines: Chianti Classico, →I.G.T. Toscana Ceparello, Collezione De Marchi: →Cabernet, →Syrah, Vin Santo
Paolo De Marchi was one of the first to modernize his vineyards systematically. The results of his efforts are internationally famous Sangiovese, Cabernet and even Syrah wines. The Vin Santo is impressive.

LIVERNANO****–*****
RADDA IN CHIANTI
30 acres (12 ha); 30,000 bottles • Wines: Anima Toscana Bianco, Livernano Rosso Toscana, Puro Sange Rosso Toscana
Marco Montanari bought the estate in 1990 and has replanted the vineyards. Today he produces three wines, two reds and a white, which are all excellent in quality.

MARCHESI ANTINORI***–****
FLORENCE
2,964 acres (1,200 ha); some bought-in grapes; 15,000,000 bottles • Wines include: Orvieto Classico Campogrande, Santa Cristina, Chianti Classico: Pèppoli, Badia a Passignana Riserva, →Tenute del Marchese; Vino Nobile di Montepulciano La Braccesca, Brunello di Montalcino Pian delle Vigne, →I.G.T. Toscana Tignanello and →Solaia, Bolgheri Guado al Tasso, Spumante
For decades this firm has been among the very best in the region.

MARCHESI FRESCOBALDI***–****
FLORENCE
2,125 acres (860 ha); some bought-in grapes; 8,000,000 bottles • Wines include: Chianti Rufina: →Castello di Nipozzano Riserva, →Montesodi; →I.G.T. Toscana Mormoreto and →Lamaione, Chianti Rémole, Ablaze, →Brunello di Montalcino Riserva Castelgiocondo, →Pomino Bianco Il Benefizio, Pomino Rosso, →Luce della Vita, Lucente, Dazante
The Frescobaldi produce one of the broadest ranges of wines in Tuscany, but no Chianti Classico.

MONTE VERTINE***–****
RADDA IN CHIANTI
22 acres (9 ha); 50,000 bottles • Wines: →Le Pergole Torte, →Montevertine, Il Sodaccio, M, Bianco di Montevertine, Pian del Ciampolo, Thea di Maggio
Sergio Mannetti, whose products rose to become cult wines in the 1980s, remained loyal to Sangiovese, complementing it only with the other local varieties Caniolo and Colorino.

PODERE IL PALAZZINO***–****
GAIOLE
30 acres (12 ha); 40,000 bottles • Wines: Chianti Classico, Chianti Classico Grosso Sanese, Rosso del Palazzino
The Sderci brought Rosso Sanese onto the market in the early 1980s, and it is still the firm's premier wine.

POGGERINO***–****
RADDA IN CHIANTI
17 acres (7 ha); 30,000 bottles • Wines: Chianti Classico, →Chianti Classico Riserva Bugialla, I.G.T. Toscana Primamateria, I.G.T. Rosato di Toscana Aurora

The Folonari family who took over the Chianti house of Ruffino in 1913 invested heavily in their own domains such as Santedame, Nozzole, Zano and Marzi (see below). They are among the best and most renowned producers of Chianti.

With the assistance of the enologist Nicolò d'Afflitto, the Lanzas developed their Chianti Riserva Bugialla into one of the region's most elegant wines.

RIECINE**–****
GAIOLE
10 acres (4 ha); 18,000 bottles • Wines: Chianti Classico Riserva, →I.G.T. Toscana La Gioia, Bianco di Riecine
La Gioia, a great Sangiovese wine, was created here with the help of enologist Sean O'Callaghan.

SAN VINCENTI****
GAIOLE
20 acres (8 ha); 30,000 bottles • Wines: Chianti Classico, Chianti Classico Riserva, →Stignano
Roberto Puccis owns unique, stony vineyard sites. Here, winegrower Carlo Ferrini produces mineral wines of outstanding quality.

TENUTA CAPEZZANA***–****
CARMIGNANO
235 acres (95 ha); 460,000 bottles • Wines: Carmignano: Villa di Capezzana, →Riserva; →Ghiaie della Furba, Barco Reale, Chianti Montalbano, Trebbiano di Toscana, Chardonnay, Tremisse, Vin Santo Riserva, Vin Ruspo
Apart from their two Carmignano versions, the top wine of the Contini Bonacossi is the Cabernet Merlot bled, Ghiaie della Furba.

VECCHIE TERRE DI MONTEFILI***–*****
GREVE
23 acres (9.5 ha); 45,000 bottles • Wines: Chianti Classico, Anfiteatro, Bruno di Rocca, Vigna Regis
Roccaldo Acuti and his enologist, Vittorio Fiore, produce premium quality wines, Including a Chianti Classico, the Sangiovese wine Anfiteatro, and the Cabernet-Sangiovese blend, Bruno di Rocca.

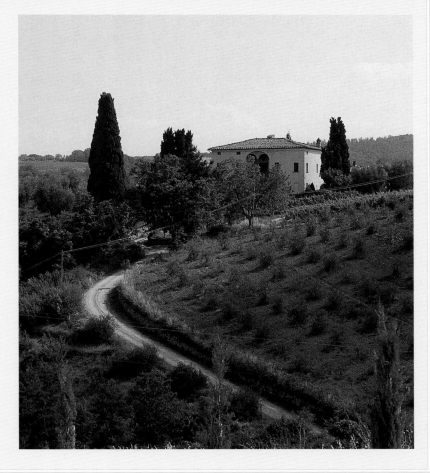

A Not So Holy Dessert Wine

Grapes hanging up to dry near Selvapiana in Rufina.

Vin Santo, holy wine, is the name given to Italy's famous sweet or sherry-like dessert wine. Its natural home is Tuscany but it is widely produced throughout central Italy and even in the northern region of Trentino. Normally Vin Santo is made from white grapes, especially Trebbiano Toscano and Malvasia which several decades ago were still cultivated in vast quantities in the Chianti region. Today, Sangiovese or other red varieties are only occasionally used, and in such cases the wine is often given the additional suffix of *occhio di pernice* (partridge eye). Vin Santo is processed in a similar manner to a "straw wine" (*vin de paille*), although today the fruit is no longer laid out to dry on straw matting but is instead hung up in well-ventilated rooms or placed on wooden grates. Not until the fruit has almost reached the raisin stage can it be pressed; the must which is produced is then so concentrated and sugary that the fermented wine achieves levels of 15 and 16 percent alcohol by volume while still containing residues of unfermented sugar.

A Second Fermentation in the Attic

After fermentation, barrels are half-filled with the young wine and then sealed. In the past these barrels were generally constructed from Italian chestnut but, since the 1980s, French oak, as elsewhere, has come into increasing use. The barrels are stored in the *Vinsantaia* which is normally the attic of the estate's buildings. Over a period of years the residual sugar undergoes fermentation again in the summer heat, due to the influence of yeast, and in time this seals up the staves of the barrel. The swings in temperature between the warmth of summer and the cold of winter give rise to the rich aromas of nuts, apricots, honey, spices, and flowers which are the mark of a good Vin Santo. The aging process is complete after between two and six years, the different periods of time producing different types of wine, all of which are defined by D.O.C. regulations. The range encompasses dry wines similar to a Fino sherry, as well as medium and sweet varieties.

Vernaccia di San Gimignano

Tuscany produces a small number of remarkable white wines including some interesting Chardonnays, and several good Montecarlo Biancos, as well as some Vermentino wines from the coast. The only really well-known white wine, however, comes from a small city to the northeast of Siena whose characteristic towers have made it one of the most popular tourist destinations in the region: San Gimignano. Vernaccia vines, particularly a white variant, have been grown here since the 13th century. The term "Vernaccia" refers to a large group of varieties—both white and red—which are not related to each other. These grapes can be found in a swathe stretching from the island of Sardinia and the far south to the far north and Alto Adige. Despite its name, it is thought that San Gimignano's Vernaccia is not related to any of the other varieties within the group, but is instead native to its region and a genuine local specialty.

In 1966 Vernaccia di San Gimignano was the first Italian quality wine to be given D.O.C. status—a measure which probably saved this rather unpopular variety from being permanently displaced by Trebbiano and Malvasia. The fortuitousness of its elevation to a D.O.C. wine was borne out by subsequent events when it became apparent that the wines of San Gimignano had far more interesting aroma and flavor traits than standard Tuscan blends of white wine. In spite of its undeniably unique character however, the wines were never really successful: national and international tastes increasingly turned to the red wines of Tuscany. Fermented in steel tanks, and often quite simply structured, these whites were only slowly accepted by the market. Even the awarding of D.O.C.G. status in the 1990s was unable to bring about a fundamental change.

The local designation of origin of San Gimignano, awarded simultaneously for rosés, red wines and Vin Santo, will have a more clearly defined impact on the local industry. It appears that the reds trading under this name—many of the Sangiovese varietals are similar to a moderately powerful Chianti—are achieving more interesting qualities with some growers than the more famous Vernaccia.

San Gimignano, the home of Vernaccia, and a popular tourist destination.

Each to his Own

Almost every D.O.C. region in Tuscany that takes itself seriously has its own definition for the local Vin Santo. Sometimes they are Canaiolo Bianco varietals (Bianco della Valdinievole), while in other places they are blends of Sangiovese and Malvasia Nera (Bianco dell'Empolese, Binaco Pisano di San Torpé, Bolgheri). Candia di Colli Apuani, Carmignano, Colli dell' Etruria Centrale have both white and red Vin Santo; Colline Lucchesi limits itself to red only; Elba, Montecarlo, and Monteregio have white and red varieties; Montescudaio is red; while Pomino, San Gimignano, and Val d'Arbia are white. Three of Tuscany's famous growing regions have created their own independent designation of origin for Vin Santo. These are Chianti, Chianti Classico, and Montepulciano where three, four or even more kinds are produced: *secco*, *amabile*, *occhio di pernice*, and *riserva*. Most of Tuscany's Vin Santo, however, is sold without a D.O.C. designation.

As with the wines, so it is with their quality—i.e. there is considerable variation. Almost every grower in Tuscany produces this traditional wine himself—irrespective of his grapes, *terroir*, or skill. Because the wines are aged for years in barrels of dubious quality and the proscription against moving the wine encourages the formation of short-lived acids, molds, and undesirable aromas, the production of Vin Santo is a demanding process and only a few are ever able to master it. Good Vin Santo, of the type made by around two dozen growers, stands comparison with any sweet or fortified wine from another country. For the most part, however, the Tuscan habit of dunking hard almond cookies into a glass of Vin Santo after a meal appears to be its only proper use.

Moscadello Montalcino

The Muscatel family has really only made a home for itself in the extreme north and south of Italy. The many variations on this grape variety—one of the most ancient in the world—produce both Asti and the sweet wines of Pantelleria. In Trentino (Alto Adige) they are noted for their delicate aromas, while in Loazzolo they excel in exotic fullness. It is only in the small commune of Montalcino, home of the Sangiovese classic Brunello, and Rosso di Montalcino, that Muscatel has been able to find a niche in central Italy, in the form of Moscadello. For years it was largely ignored until, at the end of the 1980s, several large and renowned Brunello producers took an interest in the grape, the result being a rather light, sweet wine.

The enormous commercial success of this wine contrasts with a small production volume of 39,600 gallons (1,500 hl) which is, in turn, shared among various different types of wine: there is a semi-sweet still Moscadello; a light, sweet, bubbly wine and a dense, sweet, alcoholic variety called Vendemmia Tardiva whose fruit is harvested late, and which is modeled closely on Vin Santo or the sweet wines of cooler wine-growing countries.

Vin Santo, the traditional Tuscan welcoming drink, is available in a wide range of styles, from those resembling liqueurs through to dry varieties. The best are aged for up to ten years before bottling and are fascinatingly complex.

THE OTHER SANGIOVESE

If Chianti is one of the most popular designations of origin in Italy today, then Brunello is without doubt one of the most prestigious. Its growing region is, for the most part, identical with the commune of Montalcino, a small town perched atop the northernmost salient of the 1,970-feet (600-m) high range running between the Ombrone and Arbia valleys, about 25 miles (40 km) south of Siena. With its steep, winding streets snaking between narrow medieval buildings, Montalcino has remained one of the best-preserved towns in Tuscany. However, in the last few years it has increasingly been opened up to tourism.

Like most red wines in Tuscany, Brunello di Montalcino is made with Sangiovese grapes, though in contrast to Chianti or Vino Nobile it is unblended. A good Brunello is an unmistakable wine. Remarkably robust throughout, the young wine is characterized by solid, though sometimes rough tannins. After aging for an appropriate period in a wooden barrel as well as in the bottle it develops a wonderful bouquet reminiscent of spices, game, and sweet tobacco.

Montalcino, south of Siena, did not become famous for its great Brunello until the 1960s; since then, the area devoted to wine growing has increased several times over.

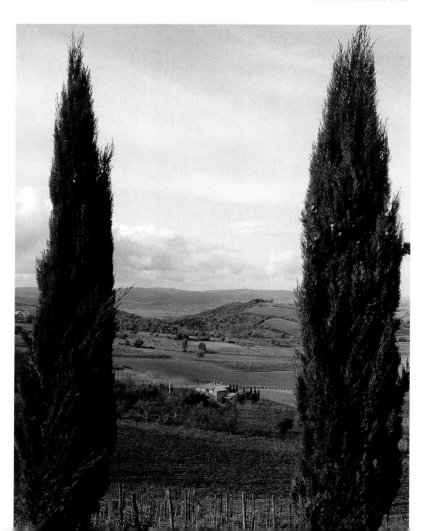

MULTIFACETED TERROIRS

The climate in Montalcino is dry and moderately Mediterranean. The massif of the 5,700-feet (1,738-m) high Monte Amiata in the south, which towers over the hilly countryside, shields the region from storms, while the high altitude means there is a clear contrast between daytime and night temperatures which encourages the development of a sophisticated bouquet. The higher vineyards in particular are characterized most years by the excellent quality of their fruit from which elegant wines with an overwhelming fullness of aroma are made. In difficult years, however, the thin-skinned Sangiovese has problems ripening and suffers from attacks of mold. In the southwest of Montalcino, on the other hand, and in Castelnuovo dell'Abate, it is somewhat warmer than in the northeast in the middle of the year and this explains why denser, more mineral wines are made here.

The soils, too, vary greatly and this influences the character of the wines. At the foot of the mountain of Montalcino clayey limestone alternates with stony, loamy soils, while the higher reaches are much sandier. As one approaches Monte Amiata deposits of volcanic tuff become more evident.

The sheer variety of natural conditions means that, in the past, wine was blended from fruit from several *terroirs*; by combining the grapes it was hoped that the advantages from some would compensate for the disadvantages of others. It was not until recently that the leading estates decided to attempt single-vineyard wines, though only the most exceptional of these have come to anything.

BRUNELLO THEN AND NOW

Wine growing can be traced back to the Romans and Etruscans here. The designation Brunello appeared for the first time at the end of the 14th century in documents from Montalcino but it is unclear what type of wine was meant. There is no evidence for a red wine based on Sangiovese—which was then still called Vermiglio—having been made before the 18th century, and Brunello in its present form only dates from the end of the 19th century. Brunello owes its existence to the work of Ferruccio Biondi-Santi (see page 417). Even after the war the name "Brunello" was only used by the Biondi-Santi family for the wines made on their Il Greppo estate.

Although a cooperative was formed in the 1930s, the name of the wine so familiar today did not catch on until the end of the 1950s and beginning of the 1960s. Even in 1970 Montalcino only had 161 acres (65 ha) of specialized vines; at that time Brunello's prestige was based on the fact that it was so rare. In 1980 Brunello was awarded the highest stamp of approval—the D.O.C.G.—from the Italian wine authorities. The legal provisions relating to its production, however, also proved too inflexible for Brunello. Winegrowers were compelled to age their Brunello for at least four years in wooden barrels—a year longer for the *riserva* wines—and were not allowed to sell it before January 1 in the fifth year. The more concentrated wines of previous years had easily coped with conditions which now proved disastrous for the much greater yields of destalked grapes, which were harvested earlier and left to stand as must for shorter periods. The result was thin wine which was only lent a certain

Left
Olives, the second crop for many producers in Tuscany.

Right
Castello Banfi—a wine empire in Montalcino.

freshness and fruitiness by the addition of younger wines. From the mid 1990s, therefore, regulations were modified. The total period of cellaring is now only two years; aging in *barriques* is permitted, and the wines may be sold at an earlier date.

In addition the simpler, second-class D.O.C. wine of Rosso di Montalcino was allowed to be made from Brunello grapes, using fruit taken from younger vines, cooler locations or suboptimal vintages. In the last few years, interest in this wine has grown much faster than in the more expensive Brunello. On average, around half the total production is bottled under the name Rosso and sold at an earlier date.

Worldwide demand has led to a great expansion in Brunello production. In the space of 30 years the area devoted to this variety grew from 247 to 3,706 acres (100 to 1,500 ha). At the same time the DOC Sant Antimo within the Montalcino district, which is still relatively young, is becoming increasingly popular for wines based on Cabernet-Sauvignon and Merlot.

A family and its wine

The history of Brunello is closely tied to that of the Biondi-Santi family. Some 150 years ago, Clemente Santi noticed that some of his vines grew more compact grapes, and he undertook the first experiments in the vineyards of his Il Greppo estate to isolate and propagate suitable Sangiovese rootstock. The berries from these vines were especially thick-skinned, and the resulting wine was more expressive than the rest of the estate's Sangiovese. In the following decades he perfected his propagation technique. His grandson, Ferruccio, was finally able to stock most of the vineyard with these selected vines and in 1888 the first wine to be called "Brunello" was bottled.

In those days Brunello was only bottled in exceptionally good years: the must was left to stand for a long period with its skins and stalks, making an acidic, tannic wine. There was a lower yield from these new vines, which made it more concentrated than today's equivalent. In order to make it more accessible and give it greater balance, Biondi-Santi left the wine to mature for several years in large barrels of Slovenian oak. The resulting wine aged well; it had the fine, ethereal scent of dried roses and a velvety but lively palate.

The estate's cellars still house rare bottles of the 1888 and 1891 vintages as well as bottles from the best years of the 20th century. These

rarities are regularly tested and recorked—a service provided for passionate Brunello collectors around the world.

Unfortunately the fame of Il Greppo has faded considerably in the last few years. The restocking of the vineyards, long an urgent necessity, has been put off, and the barrels used in the cellars are now simply too old. The concentration achieved by the older vintages has not been attained for some time. Nevertheless the reputation of Biondi-Santi Brunello continues to be high. For those consumers conscious of quality, however, Il Greppo wines cannot compete with today's top products from Montalcino.

A Noble Wine
from Montepulciano

From afar, this medieval town looks like something from a picture book: its historic buildings are in superb condition and many of them conceal a wealth of artistic treasures. It is no wonder, then, that Montepulciano is one of the most popular tourist destinations in southern Tuscany. The town is perched atop the extinct volcano of Monte Poliziano, from which it gets its name, and looks down over Lake Trasimeno and the Chiana valley, famed for its white cattle. In the Montepulciano region, Sangiovese is known as Prugnolo Gentile, and the local wine made from a blend similar to that of Chianti is called Vino Nobile di Montepulciano, or Nobile for short.

A D.O.C.G. wine since 1980, the growing area for Nobile is small. A mere 2,965 acres (1,200 ha), mostly in eastern and southeastern locations, are licensed for the production of Nobile. The soils here consist for the most part of yellow sand and clayey sandstone, while limestone formations, which produce the best wines in the Chianti Classico region, are completely absent because of the volcanic nature of the soil. As with Montalcino, the climate here is considerably warmer than in central Tuscany and the summers can occasionally be too hot. In dry years, therefore, it is mainly those vineyards facing Lake Trasimeno that provide the best results; in these locations, even a modicum of moisture is useful for promoting the growth and maturity of the grapes.

The hillside town of Montepulciano is famed for its stunning beauty and rich cultural history; it also has a long tradition of wine growing.

Vino Nobile, a wine based on the Sangiovese grape, began to be recognized for its quality in the 18th century long before its neighbor, Brunello. The newcomer, however, has since come to overshadow the reputation of Nobile.

Backing a Winner

The history of wine growing in Montepulciano dates back to the Middle Ages and is closely tied to the changing political and military fortunes of the commune. In the wars between Siena and Florence, Montepulciano—despite its geographical proximity to Siena—allied itself with the Medicis in Florence and it was they who, out of gratitude, later transformed the isolated hilltown into a center for the arts. Wine growing was a flourishing industry at that time and one from which the wealthy and noble families of the city profited. In the 16th century Popes Paul III and Sixtus V praised Nobile as Italy's "most perfect wine."

Whether the designation "Vino Nobile" derives from the involvement of the elite merchant class in the wine trade or from the harvest of the best fruit is unclear. In the 17th century the Nobile was still honored as the "King of Wines" but its reputation then began to diminish steadily.

It was not until the 20th century that it underwent a certain renaissance when Adamo Fanetti, the owner of an estate in Montepulciano, set out to make a high-quality wine on the model of Brunello, which he dubbed "Vino Nobile." Tancredi Biondi-Santi, one of the guardians of Brunello, assisted him with technical advice and provided ideas on how to market the new product.

Fanetti took the assortment of varieties which Ricasoli had established for Chianti Classico as the model for his new wine. Sangiovese provides the base, to which may be added 20 percent Canaiolo Nero, 20 percent from other red varieties, and 10 percent white wine. In spite of this, comparison between the two D.O.C.G. wines is not straightforward. As a rule, Vino Nobile has more body and a higher alcohol content than Chianti, which can largely be attributed to the more favorable climate of Montepulciano.

In spite of its strength, the Nobile consistently makes a relatively fruity impression and occasionally exhibits distinct floral aromas—connoisseurs speak of the scent of violets—and it has an unmistakable aftertaste somewhere between that of Chianti and Brunello. It is, of course, best suited to drinking as a hearty accompaniment to a juicy Chiana steak.

RESTING ON ITS LAURELS

Since 1989 Vino Nobile may be produced without the addition of white grapes, and this has had a beneficial effect on its quality. Today *riserva* wines are occasionally Sangiovese varietals, or a small amount of Cabernet Sauvignon may be added to lend the wine greater density and aromatic complexity. After obvious advances in recent decades, Nobile has been able to match the quality of the new styles of Chianti and Brunello. The maximum yield is restricted to 1,500 gallons (56 hl), as for Brunello, but the wines generated by a small group of top producers is now providing impressive proof that this limit is set at too generous a level to achieve quality.

For many years a second, pressing problem concerned the region's ancient wineries whose standards of hygiene often left much to be desired—though this is something that has recently begun to improve. D.O.C. guidelines had also laid down cellaring times which were simply too long: at least two years for Nobile and three years for *riserva* wines. Following the example of Brunello, however, this obligatory aging period was reduced by half. Including the prescribed final cellaring period in bottles, a Nobile today may be sold two years—the *riserva* three years—after the New Year following the harvest.

An increase in the minimum content of dried EXTRACTIONS, together with a lowering in the acid content of the wines, has done much to improve the average quality. Since the end of the 1980s a series of winegrowers has enthusiastically pursued new types of quality wines. It is hoped that careful selection of vines and a denser planting in the vineyards will lead to better fruit, while in the wineries there has been an emphasis on gentler pressing and pumping techniques, as well as on meticulous hygiene in the fermenting vats and wooden barrels.

A certain internationalization in the taste of the wine has also become apparent; this, it was supposed, would make it easier to sell wines at higher prices. Furthermore, the use of *barriques* and the internationally familiar varieties of Cabernet Sauvignon, Merlot, and Syrah would help many firms achieve greater success with their Nobile. The regional character of the wines and the specific qualities of the individual varieties, however, do not always appear to have been preserved in the process.

As with the system of secondary wines in Montalcino, simpler wines in Montepulciano may be declared Rosso di Montepulciano. This is a lighter, fresher wine, made primarily with the fruit of younger vineyards, which may be drunk earlier. The taste of Rosso can vary widely however. There are, for instance, Rosso di Montepulciano wines on the market which are the equal of Vino Nobile in their density and power, though they make a fresher and more vivacious impression because of their shorter aging period. Sometimes the Rosso even brings out the typical aroma and taste of Sangiovese better than some of the considerably more expensive Nobile brands. Nevertheless, the demand is almost entirely for Nobile wines, and an increasing number of vineyards are now producing a wine under their own label in addition to their Riserva wines.

Impressive Renaissance palaces frame the Piazza Grande in Montepulciano, which is the birthplace of the poet and humanist Poliziano. (His real name was Agnolo Ambrogini, but he adopted the old name of his native town, Politianus.) He was Chancellor under Lorenzo de' Medici.

Wine Growing on the Coast

For years the Tuscan coast between Livorno and Grosseto was considered a no man's land in terms of wine growing. There were only a few growers cultivating vines in the region and the wine they produced paled beside the reputation of the D.O.C. wines of central Tuscany. The area's climatic conditions are, in fact, extremely well-suited to growing good red wines. Apart from on the smaller islands, however, there was no wine-growing tradition to build on. The arable areas of the Arno delta and the coastal plain were already taken up with other types of agriculture, and the mountainsides were covered by forests and *maquis*, dense scrub vegetation common to the coasts of the Mediterranean.

The Gravel of Bolgheri

This area of Tuscany is dominated by sandy, loamy soils similar to the Colline Pisane area and the mountains of Montescudaio, so that grapes grown here produce both light, fruity wines and great reds which age well. In the region of Bolgheri, a small city in Livorno province, there are gravelly, chalky formations, known as Sassicaia, which provide conditions

Piermario Meletti Cavallari created the cult wine Grattamacco from Cabernet and Sangiovese. He has now stocked a new vineyard with Merlot.

ideally conducive to wine production. It is no coincidence, then, that the most famous wine in Italy today, the marchese Incisa della Roccheta's Sassicaia, was developed here after the Second World War. Made from Cabernet Sauvignon and a small amount of Cabernet Franc, and aged in French *barriques*, it became a model for Italian quality wine production in the 1980s.

Merlot and Sangiovese

Up to this time, the region had only produced the rather weak D.O.C. wine Rosé of Bolgheri, but word of its real potential quickly spread. The producers of the cult wine Sassicaia—the marchese Mario Incisa della Rocchetta, together with his cellarmaster Giacomo Tachis—quickly found that they had numerous imitators. Among them was one of the Antinori brothers, Lodovico, who, together with André Tchelistcheff, the famous enologist from Napa, developed a Californian-style estate close to San Guido. His Ornellaia and Masseto wines, which are based on Cabernet and Merlot, quickly won over an enthusiastic international audience.

Meanwhile in the small medieval town of Castagneto Carducci, near Bolgheri, Piermario Meletti Cavallari went about things rather more quietly. Cavallari, an urban refugee from Brescia, focused on Sangiovese; his red Grattamacco contains only a small portion of Cabernet Sauvignon to round off the aroma and taste. And the house of the Marchesi Antinori—which had neglected the region somewhat since their collaboration with Incisa —finally joined the ranks of the producers of excellent Tuscan coastal wines with a Cabernet called Guardo al Tasso.

In the 1990s this activity spread to the gentle slopes behind the coastal town of Cecina under whose red, compact, sandy soil there lay a stratum of gravel similar to that at Sassicaia. The region of Montescudaio in Cecina's hinterland is not as blessed by nature but is nevertheless capable of producing respectable, full-bodied red wines. Sea breezes here mean that the climate—as with all areas of the Tuscan coast—is mild and the differences between the seasons are far less marked than they are in many other regions, for example in Chianti Classico inland.

ON THE FRINGES

Sea breezes also regulate the climate on the island of Elba and in dry years they can even damage the grape harvest. As with the Tuscan mainland, wine has been grown here since the days of the Etruscans, although today only a few producers make good wines such as the sweet, red Aleatico which is the real specialty of the island.

In the northern part of the Tuscan coast, at the foot of the Alpi Apuane, as the Apennines are somewhat confusingly referred to here, lie the Colli di Luni, a continuation of a Ligurian range. This area's white Vermentino can be very fruity and well-balanced. The white Candia dei Colli Apuani, on the other hand, is almost unknown

Left
Ornellaia brought Californian concepts to Bolgheri and first caused a stir toward the end of the 1980s with its Merlot wine, Masseto.

Right
The horses of Sassicaia—winners on the racetracks of the world.

outside the region. The same applies to Colline Lucchesi, from the hills around the city of Lucca, where both white and red versions are made.

Probably the best and—at least among connoisseurs—best-known white wines in the region come from Montecarlo (not to be confused with the capital of Monaco), though they are native to a more inland area. Here, the neutral Trebbiano grape is enhanced by the addition of other interesting varieties which lend the wines a certain *terroir* character—a compliment that one is not able to pay to Bianco Pisano di San Torpé, whose only claim to fame seems to be that it was being made as long ago as the time of the Roman Empire.

Thoroughbred horses, thoroughbred wines

Sassicaia initiated the wave of Tuscan "super table wines." The process of aging the wine in *barriques*, and frequent addition of French varieties, enabled it to achieve a level of quality previously thought unattainable in the region. Although its name is closely tied to more recent developments in Italian wine growing, the origins of this red wine from Bolgheri reach further back than some of the most prestigious Italian D.O.C. wines.

The history of Sassicaia began after the Second World War when the marchese Mario Incisa della Rocchetta moved from Rome to his country estate of San Guido, in Bolgheri. He loved all things French, and, as the breeder of internationally successful racehorses, he was friendly with the Rothschilds, owners of some of the finest châteaux in the Bordeaux region. Francophilia and friendship therefore helped to transport Cabernet seedlings from the Gironde to Bolgheri.

During the 1960s, Incisa's nephew, Piero Antinori, his chief winemaker Giacomo Tachis, and the French enologist Emile Peynaud expressed an interest in this experiment. At

Marchese Incisa della Rocchetta, creator of Sassicaia.

their suggestion, a second vineyard was established; the first products to reach the market were 3,000 bottles from the 1968 vintage.

Around 1970—at about the same time as Antinori's Sangiovese table wine, Tignanello, was making waves—Sassicaia began to take off. Much of the wine's success was due to Giacomo Tachis, who had managed to perfect Sassicaia's

vinification and aging process to the point where it was able to compete with the most reputable of its Californian and French peers.

Production expanded under the direction of Mario's son, Nicolò. The original vineyard area of 4 acres (1.6 ha) was extended to around 74 acres (30 ha) and the annual yield increased to almost 200,000 bottles, making Sassicaia one of the highest volume, top-quality wines in Italy. The vineyards of Tenuta San Guido are today divided into four parcels: Sassicaia, Castiglioncello, Aia Nuova, and Quercione. Apart from the 1,150-feet (350-m) high Castiglioncello—a site which would be eminently suited to its own *cru*—none of the vineyards is higher than 320 feet (100 m) above sea level.

Since the 1980s Grattamacco, Ornellaia, Guado al Tasso and Tenuta Terriccio have also given proof of the potential for wine production offered by the Tuscan coast. And in the 2000 vintage the vineyard at last brought out a second wine. This wine is named Guido Alberto.

TUSCANY'S NEW EL DORADO

One of the most interesting areas under development in Tuscany—and perhaps in all Italy—is on the southern stretch of coast and its hinterland, which extends as far as the foothills of Monte Amiata and the Brunello area. This is the Maremma area, a landscape which has traditionally been more famous for its nature parks and cattle breeding than for its wines. Today its name has come to refer to all the wine-growing areas of southwest Tuscany.

In Maremma the red Sangiovese grape is dominant, and forms the basis of that most important *appellation*, the Morellino di Scansano, which is grown on the border between the coastal plain of Grosseto and the volcanic hills. Although little known to a wider public, this designation of origin has an undeniable potential, particularly when the vineyards are clayey and slaty soils stocked with mature Sangiovese vines.

Maremma stretches from the coast into the hinterland in the most southerly tip of Tuscany. It has considerable quality potential and has already attracted many investors.

AN ATTRACTIVE COMBINATION OF VARIETIES

The expressive character of Morellino wines is due both to the *terroir* and the unique composition of varieties to be found in many of the older vineyards. Apart from the dominant Sangiovese grape there are also Grenache—called Alicante here, a name which betrays its Spanish origins—Ciliegolo, Canaiolo, and Malvasia Nera, which provide aromatic complexity and a soft, full, fruity taste in some of the most interesting wines of the region. In addition, some of the estates have planted Cabernet Sauvignon, Merlot, or Chardonnay, though these are largely used for the high-quality table wines, the Supertuscans.

The unrealized potential of Maremma, especially the Morellino area, has been discovered by the more established estates and producers from northern Tuscany and the Chianti region. They have invested in new vineyards which have been organized according to the latest

The future of the Maremma region

The growing region of Morellino di Scansano, at the edge of Maremma, has become a magnet for investors in the past few years. The list of those who have either purchased new land for planting vines, or bought existing vineyards and established businesses, is quite extensive and encompasses a number of famous names from the Tuscan wine industry. They include large producers like Luigi Cecchi in Castellina and the Mazzei family, who own the famous Castello di Fonterutoli; Federico Carletti, the owner of the Poliziano estate in Montepulciano; and the Widmers, a Swiss couple whose Brancaia estate collaborates closely with Fonterutoli.

Even the Marchesi Frescobaldi have bought into the Maremma area. Their most recent company, Luce della Vita—a joint venture between the Tuscans and the Californian house of Robert Mondavi—includes new

Winegrowers were never interested before in the Morellino di Scansano region southeast of Grosseto, but today investors throng here.

vineyards, which the Frescobaldis had long had an eye on, inland from the Tuscan coast. Their 290 acres (120 ha) in the D.O.C. area of Morellino complement the 1,800 acres (740 ha) of vineyards the family already owns in central Tuscany and in the Brunello region; they are to be stocked with Sangiovese and Merlot at a density of 2,225 vines per acre (5,500 vines/ha).

Estates like those of Erik Banti, Le Pupille, or Moris Farms, which in the last few decades have produced good wines more or less anonymously, have undoubtedly played their part in this unusually hectic activity. Another motive for the decision to invest in Maremma was probably the sheer availability of cheap land suitable for viniculture that was not being fully exploited.

The tranquility and isolation of the region may soon be over forever: established producers in Chianti Classics and Montalcino have invested heavily in Maremma.

techniques and with an eye to the mistakes made by previous generations.

The reason for these investments is not hard to find. The success of Tuscan wine in the last 20 years has meant that the restricted area under cultivation has not been able to meet the demand for Chianti, Brunello, etc., especially as the vines themselves were older and yielded only limited harvests. The southern Tuscan areas offered a welcome opportunity for producing new wines with a Tuscan designation of origin—especially I.G.T. Toscana—without having to resort to less reputable Apulian or Sicilian *appellations*.

But even here the risks are not inconsiderable. Large areas have had to be freshly stocked and, on past experience, this means that top-quality wines cannot usually be expected for several years. On the other hand, only in exceptional cases do the sites of Maremma have a potential for quality which would put them on a level with central Tuscany: most of the vineyards are clearly inferior.

This problem of patchy vineyard quality is one that the growers of other designations of origin in southern Tuscany are having to come to terms with. As with southern Italy, it is often the case here that the list of wine types allowed by law is inversely proportional to the quality and reputation of the individual wines. On the slopes of the Massa Marittima, where the D.O.C. region of Monteregio has been established, there are at least still good Sangiovese, Cabernet, and Ciliegiolo wines. The same cannot be said of Parrina, whose whites, reds, and rosés from the Grosseto plain are virtually unknown, and the

Tradition and technology go hand in hand: on some estates the grapes are still brought in using baskets, and the wine is bottled in demijohns. In the surrounding area, however, there are also vast winemaking firms growing fashionable varieties and building hi-tech cellars.

Ansonica Costa dell'Argentario region is one of the new, highly productive regions which it might have been better not to have established in the first place.

The only white wine from southern Tuscany to enjoy a degree of popularity at the regional level is Bianco di Pitigliano, a Trebbiano blend with Greco and Malvasia, which finds a market in Rome. To claim that there is more than a mere handful of companies producing proper wines, however, would be an exaggeration—despite the fact that southern Tuscany has in recent years become the plaything of the large Chianti estates as well as other investors. If growers' achievements up until now are critically examined, one is forced to ask whether the optimism connected with all this hectic business activity has in fact been justified.

AVIGNONESI*−****
MONTEPULCIANO

208 acres (84 ha); 500,000 bottles • Wines: →Nobile di Montepulciano, Rosso di Montepulciano, Vignola, Marzocco, Pinot Nero, →Merlot, →Grifi, →50:50, Aleatico, Vin Santo, →Vin Santo Occhio di Pernice
The Falvo brothers created new trends for the region with their wines such as Grifi, a Sangiovese-Cabernet blend, the single-variety Merlot Desiderio, the internationally competitive sweet wine Vin Santo Occhio di Pernice, and the Chardonnay Marzocco.

CASTELLO BANFI*−****
MONTALCINO

1,730 acres (700 ha); some bought-in grapes; 5,000,000 bottles • Wines include: →Brunello di Montalcino Poggio all'Oro, Rosso di Montalcine Centine, →Summus Castello Banfi, Col di Sasso, Collalto, Pinot Nero Belnero, Merlot Mandrielle, Tavernelle, Chardonnay Fontanelle
The *castello* Poggio alla Mura, which belongs to Banfi, is well worth seeing. The range of wines from this American-owned winery has remained consistently high in quality for many years.

CIACCI PICCOLOMINI D'ARAGONA*−****
MONTALCINO

86 acres (35 ha); 90,000 bottles • Wines: →Brunello di Montalcino Vigna Pianrosso, Rosso di Montalcino Vigna della Fonte, →I.G.T. Toscana Ateo, →I.G.T. Sant'Animo Rosso Fabius
In recent years the estate has experienced an upturn in quality. The best vintages are bottled as single-vineyard wines. The Brunello and the table wine Ateo (which has 15% Cabernet Sauvignon) are around the same level of quality.

ANDREA COSTANTI**−*****
MONTALCINO

25 acres (10 ha); 40,000 bottles • Wines: →Brunello di Montalcino, Rosso di Montalcino, Vermiglio
Constanti's estate is one of the historical giants of Montalcino. The south-southwest orientation of the vineyards and the *galestro* soils of Eocene origin offer ideal conditions for Sangiovese. Constanti's wines are generally very elegant and fruity. The house olive oil is also outstanding.

CROCE DI MEZZO*−***
MONTALCINO

9 acres (3.5 ha); 15,000 bottles • Wines: Brunello di Montalcino, Rosso di Montalcino, Rosso della Croce
Paolo Nanetti and Fiorella Vannoni's estate has only recently begun producing above average quality wines.

FATTORIA DEI BARBI E DEL CASATO*−****
DONATELLA

133 acres (53 ha); 350,000 bottles • Wines: →Brunello di Montalcino Vigna del Fiore, Rosso di Montalcino, Vin Santo, →Bruscone dei Barbi, Brusco dei Barbi
Francesca Colombini-Cinelli's estate is a true farm, which raises sheep and pigs as well as producing wines. You can find its produce on the menu in the restaurant. The *fattoria* was one of the first to take up Biondi-Santi's idea of calling the local wine Brunello.

EREDI FULIGNI**−*****
MONTALCINO

20 acres (8 ha); 50,000 bottles • Wines: →Brunello di Montalcino Riserva Vigneti dei Cottimelli, Brunello di Montalcino, Rosso di Montalcino Ginestreto, Fuligni San Jacopo

The Fuligni family rely on maturing in big wooden barrels, and every year they produce one of the best wines within the Brunello di Montalcino boundaries.

GRATTAMACCO*−****
CASTAGNETO CARDUCCI

19 acres (7.5 ha); 50,000 bottles • Wines: Grattamacco Rosso, Grattamacco Bianco
The family of Paola and Piermario Meletti Cavallari has, since 2002, leased the estate for twelve years to Claudio Tipa.

GUALDO DEL RE**−*****
SUVERETO

35 acres (14 ha); 60,000 bottles • Wines: Val de Cornia Rosso Gualdo del Re, Val di Cornia Rossa and Bianco Esordio, →Federico Primo, →Rennero, →Strale Pinot Bianco, Vermentino Valentina
The owners, Nico Rossi and Maria Teresa Cabella, produce outstanding wines, with the aid of the wine-maker Barbara Tamburini. The single-variety Cabernet Sauvignon Federico Primo and the Merlot Rennero are among the top wines in Italy.

LISINI*−****
MONTALCINO

25 acres (10 ha); 50,000 bottles • Wines: →Brunello di Montalcino Ugolaia, Rosso di Montalcino
Wines have long been produced here under the guidance of the famous oenoligist Franco Bernabei; they are characterized by elegance and a fruity, floral bouquet.

MONTEPELOSO***
SUVERETO

15 acres (6 ha); 20,000 bottles • Wines: Val di Cornia Rosso, →Gabbro, →Nardo
Facio Chiarelotto is uncompromising in his pursuit of quality. The red Gabbro and Nardo wines, made from Sangiovese and Cabernet Sauvignon, are among the most concentrated wines in Italy.

CASANOVA DI NERI*−****
MONTALCINO

37 acres (15 ha); 70,000 bottles • Wines: →Brunello di Montalcino Cerretalto, →Tenuta Nuova, Rosso di Montalcino
Giacomo Neri's firm in Montalcino specializes in wines from selected vineyard sites. Neri is experimenting with aging in various kinds of wood and swears by the new *barriques*, which lend his complex, fruity wines a slight vanilla note, soft tannins and—most importantly—a long, powerful finish.

PODERI BOSCARELLI*−*****
MONTEPULCIANO

32 acres (13 ha); 60,000 bottles • Wines: Vino Nobile di Montepulciano, Rosso di Montepulciano
The Riserva del Nocio produced by Paolo di Ferrari Corradi and Sons is unanimously considered one of the best Nobiles. Also of consistent high quality are the Nobile and the Boscarelli I.G.T.

POGGIO ANTICO−****
MONTALCINO

49 acres (20 ha); 60,000 bottles • Wines: Brunello di Montalcino, Rosso di Montalcino, →Altero
This estate has superbly situated vineyards whose enormous potential has begun to be better exploited over the last few years. One of the very best Tuscan restaurants is also situated here.

POLIZIANO****–*****
MONTALCINO
297 acres (120 ha); 500,000 bottles • Wines: Nobile di Montepulciano: →Vigna Asinone and Caggiole; Rosso di Montepulciano, Chianti Colli Senesi, Bianco Valdichiana, →Elegia, Ambra, →Le Stanze, Vin Santo
With his Cabernet Le Stanze and Riserva Nobile Asinone, Federico Carletti is one of the very best wine producers in the Montepulciano region. Recently, a very good Morellino from the Lhosa estate has been added to the range. The wines are modern, but not too woody, and even the simpler quality wines attain a very high standard.

SALICUTTI****–*****
MONTALCINO
• Wines: →Brunello di Montalcino, Rosso di Montalcino
The organic grower Francesco Leanza surpassed all the elite wines in the region with his outstandingly excellent 1995 Brunello.

SAN GUIDO—INCISA DELLA ROCCHETTA****–*****
CASTAGNETO CARDUCCI—BOLGHERI
74 acres (30 ha); 200,000 bottles • Wines: →Sassicaia, →Guido Alberto
This estate is home to the cult wine Sassicaia.

SANTA RESTITUTA****–*****
MONTALCINO
37 acres (15 ha); 45,000 bottles • Wines: →Brunello di Montalcino Sugarile, Rosso di Montalcino, →Chiesa di Santa Restituta, Vin Santo
This famous Brunello estate was acquired some years ago by Angelo Gaia. The top Sangiovese, Chiesa di Santa Restituta, and the single-vineyard Brunello Sugarile are among the best wines in southern Tuscany.

VASCO SASSETTI***–****
CASTELNUOVO DELL'ABATE
• Wines: →Brunello di Montalcino, Rosso di Montalcino
Sassetti runs one of the up and coming estates in the region, along with a butcher's shop and the popular *trattoria-osteria* Bassomondo.

SASSOTONDO****–*****
SOVANA
27 acres (11 ha); 20,000 bottles • Wines: Franze Rosso Toscana, Sassotondo Rosso, San Lorenzo Rosso
Here in the most southerly corner of Tuscany, Carla Benigni Ventimiglia and her winemaker, Attilio Pagli, produce outstanding wines from the promising Ciliegiolo variety, as well as from Alicante and Sangiovese.

MICHELE SATTA****
CASTAGNETO CARDUCCI
74 acres (30 ha); 160,000 bottles • Wines: Bolgheri Bianco, Rosso Diambra, →Bolgherei Rosso Piastraia, I.G.T. Toscana Cavaliere Sangiovese, Costa di Giulia Bianco, Il Giovane Re Viognier
In the vineyard, Michele Satta relies on the natural balance of the vines. His wines express this close to nature philosophy.

TENUTA CAPARZO**–****
MONTALCINO
215 acres (87 ha); 420,000 bottles • Wines: Brunello di Montalcino, →Brunello di Montalcino La Casa, Rosso di Montalcino La Caduta, Chianti Classico, →I.G.T. Toscana Ca' del Pazzo, I.G.T. Sant'Animo Le Grance
Good vintages of the barrel-aged single-vineyard Brunello La Casa from Sante Turnone are considered among the best in the region. There is also a premium quality Cabernet-Sangiovese blend, Ca'del Pazzo.

Biondi Santi, originator of Brunelli, with his oldest wine.

TENUTA GHIZZANO***–****
PECCIOLI
40 acres (16 ha); 70,000 bottles • Wines: Chianti Colline Pisane, →Veneroso, →Nambrot, Vin Santo San Germano
The *tenuta* has been owned by the Venerosi Pasciolini family since the 14th century. The first Veneroso vintage garnered the highest praise. A high quality Merlot single variety, Nambrot, is produced.

TENUTA DELL'ORNELLAIA***–*****
CASTAGNETO CARDUCCI—BOLGHERI
148 acres (60 ha); 200,000 bottles • Wines: →Ornellaia, →Masseto, Poggio alle Gazze, Le Volte, Serre Nuove
Established by Ludovico Antinori with the assistance of the veteran Californian master, André Tchelistcheff. Largely focused on Merlot, the estate made a name for itself with a blend, Ornellaia, and a single variety Merlot called Masseto. It has since been bought by the Californian firm of Mondavi. Since 1997, the range has been extended by an interesting secondary wine, Serre Nuove, and the basic wine Le Volte.

TENUTA DI TERRICCIO***–****
CASTELLINA MARITTIMA
62 acres (25 ha); 50,000 bottles • Wines: Rondinaia, →Lupicaia, →Tassinaia, →Saluccio, Con Vento
The Luicaia, Tassinaia, Rondinaia, and Saluccio wines of the former showjumper Gain Annibale Rossi have fulfilled all expectations fueled by the ideal growing conditions of this estate.

VAL DI SUGA***–****
MONTALCINO
91 acres (37 ha); 180,000 bottles • Wines: →Brunello di Montalcino Vigna del Lago and →Spuntali, Rosso di Montalcino
Val di Suga, one of the best Brunello estates, was bought in the mid-1980s by the Angelini group, together with Tenuta Trerose in Montepulciano and San Leonino in the Chianti Classico region. The quality of all the wines has remained at the high level achieved.

UMBRIA

Despite its wine-growing potential, Umbria—like other central Italian regions—is overshadowed by its neighbor, Tuscany. In the green heart of Italy (as the tourist brochures call this part of the country), only Orvieto is familiar to a wider audience. Of the four and three quarter million gallons (180,000 hl) of quality wine produced in the region—a fifth of total Umbrian production—Orvieto accounts for two thirds.

Orvieto and Orvieto Classico are made from neutral local varieties such as Trebbiano

Sangiovese has a great future.

Toscano, Verdello, Grechetto, and Canaiolo Bianco, and are seldom more than merely drinkable, pleasant wines for everyday occasions. Previously the region preferred its wines sweet or medium-dry but today there are more intense tasting products—occasionally even barrel-fermented ones—which can provide a good accompaniment to strong-tasting dishes.

Although Orvieto production is largely in the hands of three cooperatives, a few small to medium-sized businesses have emerged since the 1980s with new ideas and remarkably good wines. One of these is the Chardonnay Cervaro from Antinori's Castello della Sala, an exceptional table wine which brilliantly exploits all the potential of modern Italian viticulture.

If Antinori's Umbrian wines at first profited from their association with this reputable Tuscan firm, they soon earned the industry's respect and established their own, independent image. This process was hastened along by a series of other companies in the Orvieto region who made similar efforts—including the largest cooperative in the area which produced some above-average, quality wines.

RED BEATS WHITE: TORGIANO

Although the dominance of Orvieto means that Umbria is mainly a white wine region, international acclaim was first achieved by a red wine. Torgiano, a wine with a Sangiovese base, was created virtually single-handed by Giorgio Lungarotti, and later awarded D.O.C. honors. In the 1970s Lungarotti ensured that the fame of this small commune *appellation*, close to the regional capital of Perugia, spread beyond Italy, and the Rubesco—especially the Riserva Monticchio—became a cult wine on the international wine scene.

The success of Torgiano was short-lived, however, in spite of the elevation of *riserva* wines to D.O.C.G. status in 1992. Lungarotti was practically the only producer of this designation of origin but he undermined the entire *appellation* by allowing the wines made by his company to stagnate in the 1990s. Nevertheless, Lungarotti's considerable achievements—he was also the initiator of the annual *Banco d'Assaggio dei Vini d'Italia*, one of the country's most important wine competitions, and the driving force behind a wine museum in Torgiano—provided an important stimulus to the Umbrian wine industry.

The Marches

4,460 ft
(1,414 m)
Monte
il Castello

Sansepolcro

Anghiari

43°30'

Arezzo

3,195 ft
(974 m)

3,550 ft
(1,082 m)
Monte Favalto

Città di
Castello

Castiglion
Fiorentino

**Colli
Altotiberini**

Tuscany

Cortona

Umbertide

Umbria

Gualdo
Tadino

Lago
Trasimeno

Magione

Castiglione
del Lago

Perugia

Chiascio

Nocera
Umbra

Lago di
Chiusi

Assisi

Monte Subasio
4,235 ft
(1,290 m)
Spello

Chiusi

**Colli del
Trasimeno**

Torgiano

**Colli
Perugini**

Bettona

Deruta

Tiber

Foligno

43°

Bevagna

A1

Città di Pieve

Marsciano

Montefalco

Trevi

Ficulle

Montefalco

Colli Martani

3,590 ft
(1,094 m)

Monti Martani

Monte Rufino
2,410 ft
Paglia
(734 m)

Orvieto

Todi

Lago di
Corbara

Spoleto

Castel Giorgio

Orvieto

Acquasparta

Monte Fionci
4,385 ft
(1,337 m)

Baschi

Monti Volsini

Ferentillo

Bolsena

Bagnoregio

Lago di
Alviano

San Gemini

3,675 ft
(1,121 m)

Lago di
Bolsena

Amelia

Terni

Piediluco

42°30'N

Montefiascone

Colli Amerini

Narni

Lago di
Piediluco

Lazio

Marta

Orte

Tuscania

Viterbo

Soriano
nel Cimino

3,455 ft
(1,053 m)

Velino

Nera

6 miles
(10 km)

	Colli Altotiberini
	Colli del Trasimeno
	Colli Perugini
	Torgiano / Torgiano Rosso Riserva
	Colli Martani
	Montefalco / Montefalco Sagrantino
	Orvieto
	Orvieto Classico
	Colli Amerini
	Wine-growing areas in neighboring regions

Umbria's North Gets Going

New designations of origin were created throughout the region, especially in the north at the upper reaches of the river Tiber and around Perugia. The commune of Montefalco, with its dry or sweet red wines from native Sagrantino and Sangiovese varieties, has been particularly impressive. The Sagrantino di Montefalco varietal, which has been promoted to a D.O.C.G. wine, shows a great deal of power and fullness accompanied by rich, spicy aromas. The sweet version, the Sagrantino di Montefalco Passito, is a specialty only found in this region. Good red and white wines from Sangiovese, Merlot, Cabernet Sauvignon, Trebbiano, Grechetto, and Chardonnay can be found here as Colli del Trasimeno and Colli Perugini. Even the more recent Umbrian designations of origin like Colli Martani and Colli Amerini—areas in the center and extreme south of the region which were defined in 1989 and 1990 respectively—have impressed in the wines made by several of the region's more interesting producers.

With the revived Orvieto (Classico), a powerful Montefalco, and a workhorse like Torgiano —providing the qualities of the latter stabilize— Umbria's future seems secure.

Left
In Orvieto more engaging white wines from traditional varieties are now being made, including a *barrique*-aged Classico from Tenuta Vellette.

Right
Visitors to Umbria and its wine-growing regions should include Assisi on their itinerary, a town famous for both its art and its religious history.

Select Producers in Umbria

Castello della Sala—Antinori**–****
Ficule
346 acres (140 ha); 300,000 bottles • Wines: Orvieto Classico, →Cervaro della Sala, →Muffato della Sala, →Pinot Nero Vigneto Consola
The Florentine house of Antinori was one of the first to invest outside its home region. Here, it produces one of the best Chardonnays in central Italy.

Giorgio Lungarotti***
Torgiano
692 acres (280 ha); 2,800,000 bottles • Wines include: San Giorgio, Torgiano: Torre di Giano Riserva Il Pino, Rubesco Riserva Vigna Monticchio; Chardonnay: Vigna I Palazzi, di Miralduolo; Caernet, Pinot Grigio, Buffaloro, Castel Grifone, Solleone, Metodo Classico Brut, Falò, Brezza, Pergoleto, Rondò, Vin Santo
In spite of a few new and sometimes insignificant wines, the backbone of this former leading vineyard is formed the red classics Rubesco Riserva Monticchio, which is only bottled in exceptional years, and San Giorgio, a 50:50 blend of Cabernet and the Tuscan varieties Sangiovese and Canaiolo.

Il Palazzone****
Orvieto
57 acres (23 ha); 45,000 bottles • Wines: I.G.T. Umbria Grechetto L'Ultima Speranza, Orvieto Classico: Terre Vineate, →Campo del Guardiano; →I.G.T. Umbria Rubbio

Giovanni Dubini has built up one of the few outstanding houses in the region. Strengths are the Orvieto variants and the Rubbio.

Tenuta Vellette***
Orvieto
247 acres (100 ha); 350,000 bottles • Wines include: Orvieto Classico: Velico, Amabile; Calanco, Rosso di Spicca, Monaldesco
The classic Orvieto of the Bottais is marked by density and expressive power. Since 1989, the estate has also added a barrel-fermented Orvieto Classico, Velico and the Sangiovese-Cabernet blend Calanco to its repertoire.

Val di Maggio—A. Caprai****–*****
Montefalco
116 acres (47 ha); 500,000 bottles • Wines include: →Sagrantino di Montefalco, Rosso di Montefalco
Marco Caprai has invested a great deal, and his wines are impressive, even in an international context. The top wine, Sagrantino "25 anni" is one of the great wines of Italy.

Vallesanta—L. A. Barberani***
Baschi
99 acres (40 ha); 300,000 bottles • Wines: Orvieto Classico: Secco Castagnolo, Amabile Pulicchio, Muffa Nobile; Calcaia, Pomaio, Foresco, Polvento, Grechetto, Pinot
Barberani and enologist Maurizio Castelli create an impressive palette of products. Painstaking work in the vineyard and winery yields cleaned-toned, good quality wines (with typical grape variety characteristics).

LAZIO

Few people know that a large area of the Eternal City is given over to vineyards. The names Frascati and Colli Albani are familiar, but they are not necessarily connected with Rome. However, with 74,130 acres (30,000 ha) under production the region is by no means insignificant. Lazio does not grow outstanding D.O.C.s to compare with other regions, and the few good Frascati wines (the biggest D.O.C. in Lazio) are outnumbered by the many mass products. But the region does have a growing number of quality-oriented producers who are offering reds that can certainly compete well.

In antiquity the farms surrounding the city served as both bread baskets and wine cellars to the state. The house wine of the Romans—Falernian, usually a red—was made from the native Aminea variety, though this is now probably extinct. The Roman writers Horace, Virgil, Martial, and Pliny the Elder recorded its popularity and variety. White Falernian was also made, and this family of wines could be anything from light to heavy, and from sweet to dry.

WHITE WINES PREDOMINATE

More than 85 percent of Lazio wines are white, mainly blended from Trebbiano Toscano and Malvasia. Vineyards in the south of Rome, which penetrate into the city itself, produce Frascati, one of Italy's best-loved quality wines. For a long time the producers of this generally sweet white wine trusted blindly in tradition and the loyalty of the consumer so that the shelves of European supermarkets became choked with Frascati, and its reputation degenerated into that of a cheap wine.

Another popular white wine in the region is Est! Est!! Est!!! di Montefiascone which is produced from Trebbiano and Malvasia grapes in Viterbo province, close to the Orvieto area. Its strange name is popularly explained by an anecdote which recounts how, whilst making a journey to Rome, a German bishop sent his priest ahead to find appropriate accommodation and seek out the best wines which were to be clearly marked with the word "Est!." The priest is said to have been so enthused by the white wines of Montefiascone that he wrote the expression three times—Est! Est!! Est!!! This wine was formerly highly thought of but it, too, has now found its way onto the supermarket shelves.

From around the end of the 1980s it was apparent that efforts were under way—especially on the Falesco estate—to produce real quality wines in the region again. The vineyards which face the banks of Lake Bolsena enjoy a mild climate which, together with the volcanic soil, provides excellent growing conditions for producing outstanding white wines.

Of the remaining areas in Lazio suited to quality vintages, the D.O.C. wines of Colli Albani, Colli Lanuvini, Marino, and Zagarolo, as well as the white variants from the regions of Castelli Romani, Cori, Velletri, and Cerveteri, all have similar characteristics to Frascati. Some growers are experimenting with imported vines such as Chardonnay or Sauvignon Blanc, but few have so far succeeded in producing wines capable of competing on the international or even national markets.

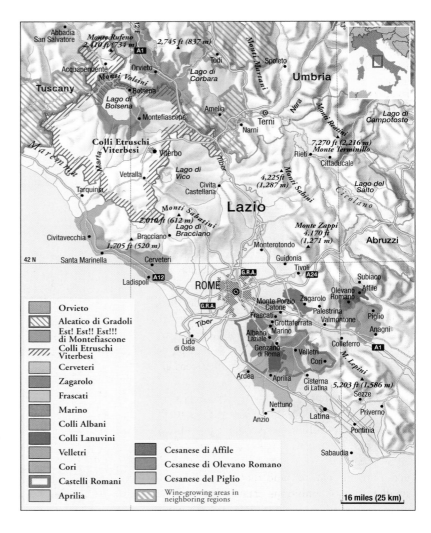

SELECT PRODUCERS OF LAZIO

COLACICCHI***−****
ANAGNI
12 acres (5 ha); 18,000 bottles • Wines: →Torre Ercolana, Romagnano Bianco, Romagnano Rosso
The family of wine merchant Trimani from Rome purchased this old estate in the 1980s and made great efforts to revive its potential. Under the direction of Giacomo Tachis and Attilio Scienza they produced one of Lazio's best red wines in the Ercolano, a Cabernet-Merlot blend with a small Cesanese component.

CASTEL DE PAOLIS—A. CROCE***−****
GROTTAFERRATA
25 acres (10 ha); 55,000 bottles • Wines: →Frascati: Vigna Adriana, →Selve Vecchio; Muffa Nobile, Moscato Rosa Rosathea, →I Quattro Mori
From the beginning of the 1990s Giulio Santarelli has been proving just how good a Frascati can be. His single vineyard Frascati, Vigna Ariana, is magnificent. Even more remarkable are the wines from his newly organized vineyards which grow Merlot, Cabernet, Syrah, Sauvignon, and Viognier grapes.

COLLE PICCHIONI – P. DI MAURO***−****
MARINO
23 acres (9.5 ha); bought-in grapes; 110,000 bottles • Wines: Marino Colle Picchioni Oro, →Colle Picchioni Rosso Vigna del Vassallo, Vignole
Paola di Mauro was one of the first to pursue quality wine growing in Lazio. The basis of her best red wines, such as the excellent Vigna del Vassallo, are French vines up to 60 years of age (which she discovered quite by chance on a newly purchased property). In good years the Colle Picchioni Oro is considered one of the best white wines in the entire region.

FALESCO****
MONTEFIASCONE
22 acres (9 ha); bought-in grapes; 220,000 bottles • Wines: →Est! Est!! Est!!! di Montefiascone, Poggio dei Gelsi, also Vendemmia Tardiva, →Montiano
Riccardo Cotarella (his brother is head enologist with the Marchesi Antinori) is not only one of the few producers of really good Est! Est!! Est!!!, but he also acts as a consultant to numerous Italian estates, and this work has provided him with many occasions on which to prove his talent. The estate's top wine is the red Montiano.

A GLIMMER OF HOPE FOR REDS

It is not by concentrating on long-established white wines that the region's future is likely to flourish, however; instead, in recent years, it has been the attempts made with imported red varieties such as Cabernet and Merlot which have produced impressive results. A few of these French varieties had already reached the region at the beginning of the 20th century; some vineyards in the Colli Romani have vines up to 70 years old which are the source of small quantities of exceptional wines. Merlot, Cabernet, and recently even Syrah have provided complex wines, capable of aging, which reveal the potential of the region for good red wines, in stark contrast to the traditional dominance of white wines.

Cesanese, the local standard red variety, seldom amounts to much, however. At their best, Cesanese wines are simple, harmless, fruity, and drinkable affairs for the everyday table. Even today, most growers are reducing the Cesanese proportion in their wines where this is allowed in the statutes of the various *appellations*. Instead, they are planting Sangiovese vines in order to profit from the great reputation of this premium Tuscan variety.

In contrast to neighboring Umbria, Lazio has not been able to stir itself into launching a really serious quality offensive at the turn of the millennium. While it is true that some of the large producers are bringing respectable products onto the market, and that there is even a small group of ambitious estates, the region's many cooperatives, who still control the wine-growing business according to their own whims, have yet to come up with a single competitive wine. Without real entrepreneurial initiative, the region's potential will remain unrealized in the future.

This grand gateway into a vineyard recalls the fame once possessed by wines grown to the south and east of Rome. Today, Lazio is known only for its mass-produced wines.

Southern Italy and the Islands: A Reawakening

According to one's perspective, southern Italy begins either in Rome or in Naples. From the point of view of wine growing, however, the border is marked by Abruzzi on the Adriatic, and Campania on the Tyrhennian coast of the Italian peninsula. The south then encompasses Molise, Apulia, Basilicata, and Calabria, as well as the large islands of Sicily and Sardinia.

A succession of cultures and dynasties have left their mark on southern Italy in the past: Greeks, Albanians, Arabs, Spaniards, Etruscans, and Romans, as well as the Vatican, and the great houses of the Hohenstaufens and Bourbons. In antiquity, wine growing owed much to the great contribution made by the Greeks. Later, the slopes of both Vesuvius and Etna, and the hills of Apulia and Campania, became the greatest suppliers of wine to Republican and Imperial Rome.

The southern latitudes of Italy are inevitably associated with heat and aridity, but it is surprising just how often the region is subject to very cold weather. Climatic conditions in this part of the country are marked by extremes, as are the soil types. From the fertile coastal strips of Apulia, with their maritime climate, to the bleak, rocky countryside of Basilicata and the Sicilian mountains, there is a diverse range of *terroirs* which provide the conditions for a wide spectrum of grape types, most of them local varieties. Several of these, for example the reds Aglianico, Nero d'Avola, and Montepulciano, are so promising that growers from the New World are starting to show an interest in them.

Rich and Poor Regions

Although there are hardly any of these varieties to be encountered in Abruzzi—Montepulciano and Trebbiano almost completely dominate the field—this northernmost region of the south has been able to build up a lucrative wine industry. Its good-value, easily drinkable wines are very much in demand, both at home and abroad.

The range on offer is sparser in Basilicata, where a single, superb variety—Aglianico—overshadows all others, though this has not helped the industry achieve even moderate prosperity. Calabria—the poorhouse of Italy—has few varieties with which it might cause a stir on the international scene, and its industry is the most archaic in the country.

In Calabria time seems to have stood still.

A magnificent view of Etna can be had from Taormina. At the foot of the volcano is a large wine-growing region which, despite its promising soils, has yet to produce anything of significant quality.

Such is not the case in Apulia, whose broad plains produce wine in industrial quantities, most of it being shipped abroad in tankers, or blended with inferior northern Italian wines; up until the 1970s the region's production ended up almost entirely as vermouth. In spite of this, efforts have been undertaken to match northern Italian standards for quality—standards which Calabria or Molise seem destined never to equal.

Enormous strides have been made toward producing quality wines on Sicily recently. For years the island produced nothing except sickly Marsalas, but since the start of the 1990s superb wines—barrel-aged Chardonnays, good local reds, opulent and exotic sweet wines from Pantelleria and the Eolian Islands—demonstrate that, in Sicily, too, a new age has dawned. In Apulia it was small and medium-sized wine companies that showed the courage to strive for quality, but in Sicily the avant-garde included large companies like the high-volume wine producer Corvo, which quickly recognized the possibility and even necessity of establishing a solid reputation with quality wines.

Signs of Change

The vinicultural methods and winery techniques of northern Italy may have established themselves in most regions of southern Italy, but the south has been slow to respond to the popular international varieties—mainly Cabernet and Chardonnay—which are so much in demand elsewhere. Only some of the top Sicilian wines are made from these grapes; most are still produced from local varieties.

This is especially the case in Campania and Sardinia, which have had no difficulty in finding a market, thanks to their healthy tourist industries. But on Sardinia, and in Basilicata and

Most of the vineyards in Abruzzi lie, like the countryside near Alba Adriatica, in the hilly hinterlands of the Adriatic where the climate is decidedly mild.

Calabria, time seems to have stood still in the last few years and there have been no enological advances. In Sicily the long-established ranks of the elite have at least been swelled by additional names.

The most positive picture is offered by the wine industry in Apulia where hitherto unknown firms have emerged with some astonishing wines. Apulia, Sicily, and perhaps also Campania and Abruzzi show that the conditions for achieving success on the national and international wine markets do exist, but growers must seize the initiative themselves. When this does finally happen, the prestige regions of northern and southern Italy will sit up and take notice.

Regional grape varieties

The great wealth of the vineyards of Apulia, Campania, and Sicily lies in largely undiscovered or untested grape varieties. Just how much might be slumbering away in these regions becomes clear when one realizes that a variety called Primitivo was leading a marginal existence in Apulia but became a superstar in California under the name of Zinfandel.

Even in southern Italy international varieties such as Chardonnay, Cabernet, and Merlot have taken root more or less successfully, as have national greats such as Barbera, Sangiovese, and Trebbiano. Of the red varieties, Montepulciano, Aglianico, Negroamaro, and Nero d'Avola dominate the quality wine scene. They share a vivid color, a relatively high alcohol content, and a neutral, aromatic base which makes them suitable for use in blending. What they might develop in terms of tannin structure and elegance, given the opportunity to grow in really good locations, has still not been sufficiently investigated.

Typical Trulli near Locorotondo in Apulia.

The red varieties also include Primitivo, Uva di Troia, and Piedirosso in Apulia, Gaglioppo in Calabria, and Nerello Mascalese and others in Sicily.

White varieties are no less interesting. Along with the international varieties already mentioned, Moscato and Malvasia also produce some interesting and complex sweet wines.

Probably the best white variety in the south is Fiano which is, unfortunately, cultivated on far too few vineyards in Campania. The more widespread Greco—not to be confused with the Umbrian Grechetto—is grown in only marginal quantities in Calabria, where it is used to make sweet wines.

The fruity, light wines which are made from Falanghina and Biancolella—two other white varieties from Campania—are familiar to whole armies of tourists. Less well known—but no less capable of producing quality wines—are the Sicilian varieties, Inzolia and Grecanico Dorato, and Sardinia's Vermentino.

The other indigenous white wine varieties in the south—such as Bombino, Forastera, Asprinio, Coda di Volpe, Monica, Cataratto, and Grillo—are generally processed into simple, rustic wines. Enormous efforts will still be required in both the vineyard and the cellar to reveal their true potential for the future.

ABRUZZI AND MOLISE

TREBBIANO AND MONTEPULCIANO

The spectrum of varieties grown here is one of the least diverse in Italy: for many years there was only one white variety, Trebbiano, and one red, Montepulciano. It is only in recent decades that varieties such as Ciliegiolo, Passerina, Merlot, Cabernet, and even Riesling have gained a tentative foothold here. White wines are dominated by Trebbiano d'Abruzzo, a variant of a widespread varietal group; wines of the same name with a D.O.C. designation are rarely suited for anything more than the daily table.

There are still a few growers who make expressive vintages from old vines, but their yields are now greatly reduced, and the distinctive aromas of the wines they produce are not to everyone's taste. The widespread cultivation of red Montepulciano d'Abruzzo grapes—not to be confused with the Sangiovese wine, Nobile di Montepulciano—which can produce wines with low acid and pleasant tannins, is more in line with international trends.

It is considered unlikely that Montepulciano is related to the Sangiovese of Tuscany, as its wines are markedly different from those of the great Tuscan red. Although they often share the same density, Montepulciano rarely attains the same elegance and longevity of its compatriot.

Abruzzi is one of the less well-known wine-growing regions in Italy, although it is home to the popular red wine, Montepulciano d'Abruzzo. One of the most productive regions in the country, it is bounded by Lazio to the west, Umbria and the Marches to the north and the small province of Molise to the south. Abruzzi also has the highest mountains in the Apennines, the Gran Sasso group, with peaks reaching 9,500 feet (2,912 m).

From a geographic and viticultural perspective Abruzzi is closely related to the neighboring, northern, province of the Marches which not only has a similar landscape and comparable climate but whose vineyards are also partly stocked with the red Montepulciano variety from Abruzzi.

Politically and socially, however, the region must be considered as belonging to the chronically underdeveloped south—which is why, in the past, wine growing had, and indeed still has, few chances of competing with northern and central Italian regions. At the foot of the mighty Apennine massif facing the Adriatic, slopes up to a height of 1,900 feet (600 m) are covered in vines. These hill sites, like the vineyards on the Adriatic, profit from an equable, almost mild climate despite their southern situation. This balance between sunshine and a cooler climate results in rich but not overly heavy wines.

Like a toy village: a huddle of houses in Scanno.

A good Montepulciano d'Abruzzo can, however, surprise with its unusual aromas and tannin structure, making it the ideal accompaniment to game dishes.

ALTERNATIVE TYPES OF WINE

Cerasuolo, the rosé variant of Montepulciano, is characterized by a pleasant fruitiness. Its often rather dark wines frequently have a high alcohol content, making them less suitable as light summer rosés.

The monotonous panorama of Abruzzi wine has recently been enriched. In the far north of the region, around the town of Controguerra on the borders with the Marches, a new D.O.C. region was established. Later, the hills to the south received the status of a sub-zone of D.O.C. Montepulciano d'Abruzzo as D.O.C. Colline Terre. As was the case in Tuscany and elsewhere in Italy, attempts were initially made to stem the tide of prestige table wines which were achieving better prices than D.O.C. vintages from the same areas. This was an especially risky strategy in Abruzzi; Montepulciano was able to build up a good position in that sector of the market which

Vineyards on the slopes produce the round, often tannic, Montepulciano d'Abruzzo, while flatter sites near the coast produce high yields and simpler wines.

Molise

Italy's second smallest region produces vast quantities of grapes but hardly any of these go into producing quality wines. Biferno and Pentro di Isernia, which were awarded D.O.C. designation in the 1980s, and the new I.G.T. names have achieved at best only a national reputation. This is not to say, however, that the region has no potential for top-ranking wines.

The climate in the hills, where wine is grown at up to 1,900 feet (600 m), is almost continental, and it is only on the slopes facing the coast that Mediterranean conditions prevail. The assortment of grape varieties is modeled on that of Abruzzi and there is an increasing experimentation with varieties from Campania such as Greco, Fiano, and Aglianico. Most wine is still made for domestic consumption and commercial wines are marketed almost exclusively by the cooperatives. Private estates have, to date, been very rare.

accounts for simple, well-balanced wines of origin because of its excellent value for money. In spite of all the efforts of individual growers, though, it has still not been possible to establish a prestigious reputation which would allow it to command a higher price. Thanks to new outside investment, a further upturn is to be expected.

SELECT PRODUCERS OF ABRUZZI

BARONE CORNACCHIA***
TORANO NUOVO
82 acres (33 ha); 450,000 bottles • Wines: Controguerra Cabernet Villa Torri, Montepulciano d'Abruzzo Poggio Varano and Vigna La Costa, Trebbiano d'Abruzzo
For years the Cornacchia family have been among the top producers in the Abruzzi, where they produce wines very typical of the area.

GIANNI MASCIARELLI****–*****
SAN MARTINO SULLA MARRUCINA (ABRUZZI)
• Wines: Montepulciano d'Abruzzo Villa Gemma, Chardonnay Marina Cvetic, Trebbiano d'Abruzzo Marina Cvetic, Villa Gemma Bianco
Produces some of the best wines for miles around, such as the single-vineyard Montepulciano and the barrel-fermented Chardonnay. The newly laid out vineyards, with up to 3,200 vines per acre (8,000 per hectare) are an intriguing development.

TENUTA CATALDI MADONNA***
OFENA (ABRUZZI)
47 acres (19 ha); 90,000 bottles • Wines: Montepulciano d'Abruzzo and →Cerasuolo Pié delle Vigne, Trebbiano d'Abruzzo, Malandrino, Pecorino, Vigna Cona Rosso
The estate's vineyards, which lie at about 1,400 feet (450 m) above sea level, produce especially fruity wines. The specialty is the rosé version of Montepulciano. The white wines have a simple but refreshing character.

LA VALENTINA***
SPOLTORE
74 acres (30 ha); 210,000 bottles • Wines: Montepulciano d'Abruzzo, →Montepulciano d'Abruzzo Spelt, Trebbiano d'Abruzzo
Sabatino di Properzio has invested heavily in the estate, and the results can be seen in the very good quality of the wines.

APULIA

Apulia is often referred to as the wine cellar of Italy. Its 210,000 acres (85,000 hectares) do indeed account for almost an eighth of the total grape-growing area in Italy, and with its 185 to 210 million gallons (7 to 8 million hl) it is, along with Sicily, the country's most productive region. Upon closer examination, however, Apulia's wine industry resembles a gigantic wine factory instead of a well-kept wine cellar. Yields are higher here than anywhere else in Italy. There are many vineyards which harvest up to 16 tons of grapes per acre (40 tons/ha)—four times the upper limit if wines are to be of moderate quality and retain the characteristics typical of their variety. It is not surprising therefore that only two percent of Apulian wines have D.O.C. status and that most of the production from the region is either distilled into industrial alcohol, converted to grape must concentrate, or sold in barrels to large northern Italian or French wine producers.

The small number of D.O.C. wines from the region are spread over 25 designations of origin, none of which commands a significant share of the market. In the case of most of these *appellations*, the quantities bottled and sold outside Apulia are negligible. Funds allocated by the European Union for clearing vineyards have only exacerbated the situation; instead of converting their large-scale industrial vineyards to other uses, Apulia's growers have abandoned their old, high-quality vines which were planted on awkward sites in the hills. And although more than 50,000 growers gave up their profession in the 1980s, Apulia's wine lake still refused to dry up. Conditions for quality wine growing in this region are almost ideal, in terms of both the climate and the intriguing local grape varieties. Even in Roman times the area was praised for its excellent wines and other agricultural products. In Rome's early days, the civilizing influence of Greek culture was particularly apparent here, and there are still traces of the Greek language in the region's dialect today.

In contrast to neighboring regions, which are dominated by the Apennines and characterized by desolate, stony soils, Apulia boasts broad, fertile, coastal plains with gentler hills in its interior. The fecundity of most its soil types, together with its relatively flat countryside, is a virtual utopia for highly productive industrial vineyards.

NATIVE TO APULIA?

As elsewhere in Italy, in Apulia the better wines are grown in bleaker locations with well-drained soils, such as the karst plateau of Le Murge, home to Castel del Monte. The region's indigenous varieties produce only a few great wines. The most widespread variety is Negro-amaro, which goes into making the D.O.C. wines Alezio, Brindisi, Leverano, and Salice Salentino. Wines of this variety are generally very dark and high in tannins—*negro amaro* means "bitter black"—and exhibit a powerful, occasionally rough, primitive taste.

Primitivo vines, a variety which produces a full-bodied red wine but seldom attains its best form in Apulia, cover a huge area. Primitivo is more renowned and of better quality in California, where it is known as Zinfandel; in the U.S. it produces a wine full of fruit which occasionally achieves great elegance and a capacity to age. It was previously—incorrectly—believed that Zinfandel was descended from Primitivo, but it has since been proved that the variety first appeared in Italy after it had already become firmly established in the northeast of the U.S. and later in California. In all probability, the vine originated in one of the Balkan lands and was taken to America before being reimported to the Old World.

Uva di Troia is Apulia's third premium grape variety. The name indicates the legacy left by

╲╲╲╲	Aleatico di Puglia
▢	San Severo
▢	Cacc'e Mmitte di Lucera
▨	Rosso Barletta
⁄⁄⁄⁄	Moscato di Trani
▢	Rosso Canosa
▨	Castel del Monte
▢	Gioia del Colle
▨	Martina Franca
■	Locorotondo
▨	Ostuni
▢	Brindisi
▢	Primitivo di Manduria
▨	Lizzano
▢	Salice Salentino
▨	Squinzano
▨	Copertino
◈	Leverano
■	Alezio
▨	Wine-growing areas in neighboring regions

The ancient city of Ostuni with its almost African ambience gave its name to a wine-growing region northwest of Brindisi in which southern grape varieties produce unusually dry, rather light wines.

Greek culture in the region. This grape makes the majority of red wines from Castel del Monte, a region in northern Apulia named after an octagonal castle built by the Hohenstaufen monarch, Frederick II, in the 13th century. The elite, D.O.C.-named wines of Castel del Monte include more than just this powerful red which ages well, however; they also embrace varieties such as Aglianico, Spätburgunder, Chardonnay, Pinot Blanc, and Sauvignon.

The wines with the best prospects for the future come from the far south and were previously bottled under one of the mini-D.O.C. desig-nations. Many of these *appellations*—such as Copertino, Brindisi, Salice Salentino, San Severo, and Alezio—are used for red as well as white wines. Occasionally, the *appellations* encompass a diverse array of other wine types—which, in the past, has been confusing for both growers and consumers.

Some of the best-known names in Italian wine—including the Marchesi Antinori from Florence and the Pasqua brothers in Verona—have recently begun to invest in Apulia, and this fact must surely confirm the region's potential for quality.

SELECT PRODUCERS IN APULIA

AGRICOLE VALLONE**–****
LECCE
336 acres (136 ha); 200,000 bottles • Wines: →Brindisi: Rosso Vigna Flaminio, Rosato Vigna Flaminio; →Graticciaia Rosso, Salice Salentino: Vereto, Rosso
The specialty is the Graticciaia, produced on the model of the Patriglione.

FRANCESCO CANDIDO***
SANDONACI BEI GUAGNANO
339 acres (137 ha); 900,000 bottles • Wines: Duca d'Aragona, →Cappello di Prete, Salice Salentino: Bianco Vigna Vinera, Rosso, Rosato Le Pozzelle; I.G.T. Salente Chardonnay Casina Cucci
The best products are generally made from Negroamaro; its aromas of tea and fruit and its full body, demonstrating the high potential of this Apulian variety.

CONTI LEONE DE CASTRIS**–****
SALICE SALENTINO
988 acres (400 ha); 4,000,000 bottles • Wines include: →Five Roses, Salice Salentino: →Rosso Donna Lisa, Bianco, Rosato and Rosso Maiana, Sauvignon Vigna Case Alte Bianco, Messapia Bianco, Aleatico Negrini
As well as its rosé, this estate is known for its excellent reds and good white wines.

FELLINE****
MANDURIA
• Wines: →Primitivo di Manduria, Salento Rosso Alberello, →Vigna del Feudo

The Perrucci make impressive red wines, including a very good Primitivo (known in California as Zinfandel).

ROSA DI GOLFO—D. CALÒ***
ALEZIO
99 acres (40 ha); 180,000 bottles • Wines: I.G.T. Salento: →Rosa del Golfo, Quarantale, →Portulano, Bianco Bolina
Known initially for remarkable rosés, but now has a good selection of whites and reds.

MASSERIA MONACI**–***
COPERTINO
40 acres (16 ha); 650,000 bottles • Wines: Copertino Rosso Eloquenzia, I Censi Salento Rosso, Sant Brigida Salento Bianco, Simposia Salento Rosso
Severino Garofano has brought to the family estate all the experience gained over decades as Apulia's most important wine consultant.

CONTI ZECCA****–*****
LEVERANO
791 acres (320 ha); 1,500,000 bottles • Wines: Leverano: →Malvasia Vigna del Saraceno, Rosato Vigna del Saraceno; Salice Salentino: Rosso Cantalupi, Rosato, Bianco; Cantalupi, I.G.T. Salento Donna Marzia Bianco / Rosato / Rosso
Three lines of wines—one from Leverano, one from Salice Salentino, and one sold under I.G.T. Salento, have for years been noted for their quality.

CAMPANIA

for a series of local white and red varieties, especially in the provinces of Avellino and Benevento. The most respected of these is Taurasi, whose *riserva* version has been awarded D.O.C.G. status. The best representatives of this powerful red, blended from Aglianico grapes and a small percentage of other varieties, age well and can easily stand comparison with the great red wines of northern and central Italy. The best known of the wines in Campania, Greco di Tufo and Fiano di Avellino, are also worthy of interest; the grape varieties which form their base were probably brought to Italy by the Greeks. They achieve their best form in the regions which bear their name: the Greco, with its scent of citrus fruit and almonds, from the village of Tufo (where it is generally blended with Falanghina and Biancolella), and Fiano from the region of Avellino.

FRUITY SUMMER WINES

In the area around Avellino a good Fiano, which the Romans praised as *vitis apianae*, has the potential to combine freshness and power with the scent of peaches and nuts. It therefore displays a greater complexity than the neutral whites of central and northern Italy, or the fruity but one-dimensional Biancolella and Falanghina summer wines made on the coast and the islands of Ischia and Capri.

Attempts to revive the once-famous wines of the region, such as Falerno, Lettere, Asprinio, and Lacryma Christi, should be seen as more archeo-

Campania stretches along the Tyrrhenian coast in the southwest of Italy. Its broad coastal plains are repeatedly broken by hills of sedimentary or volcanic origin, the most famous of these being Vesuvius, southeast of Naples. With around 74,000 acres (30,000 ha) of vines, Campania lies in ninth position nationally, just behind Sardinia. Of the approximately 53 million gallons (2 million hl) of wine produced here every year, less than six percent have D.O.C. status.

It was in the present-day province of Campania, however, that the Italian wine industry was born around 3,000 years ago. Greek settlers established their OINOTRIA ("Wineland") here. The later Latin expression *Enotria* came to be used as a synonym for all of Italy's wine-growing areas. The Greeks passed on much of their winemaking expertise to the native Etruscan inhabitants. The Romans later developed the region into the center of their wine trade. The eruption of Mount Vesuvius in AD 79, however, brought profound changes; the volcano's destruction of Pompeii meant that the Empire's greatest commercial harbor for wine was eliminated in a single blow, and Rome was compelled to develop the wine industry systematically in other parts of the Empire.

CHARACTER WINES

Campania's Mediterranean climate, in which the nearby sea and mountains prevent temperatures from becoming too hot, provides ideal conditions

	Falerno del Massico
	Solopaca
	Sant'Agata de' Goti
	Aglianico del Taburno
	Greco di Tufo
	Taurasi
	Fiano di Avellino
	Vesuvio
	Cilento
	Ischia
◇	Capri
	Wine-growing areas in neighboring regions

Aglianico—southern Italy's top variety

Aglianico produces full-bodied, intensely colored and aromatic wines, especially when grown on volcanic soils; a brilliant ruby red when young, it transforms on ageing into a mahogany hue. Good wines have a bouquet of maraschino cherry and violet notes, later becoming delicately spicy. The best-known wine made from Aglianico is Taurasi, from the mountains north of the town of Avellino in Campania. The *riserva* wines have even been awarded D.O.C.G. status. Aglianico del Vulture, from the slopes of the extinct volcano of the same name in the neighboring region of Basilicata, is almost as good. Recently, the region of Taburno has proved that it is also capable of growing superb wines. When used for blending, Aglianico enhances the final product—a role it performs in Falerno del Massico, Biferno, Castel del Monte, Cilento, Solopaca, Vesuvio, and Sant'Agata de'Goti.

Naples is the beating heart of an ancient land in which present-day winemakers are finding it difficult to achieve the fame of their antique forebears. Lacryma Christi, a wine once much in demand but now almost forgotten, is still made on the slopes of Vesuvius. This can be red, rosé or white, fortified or sparkling, but only occasionally is it anything other than mediocre.

logical than enological in nature. In spite of modern efforts, these varieties probably have little in common with their antique forebears.

The same is true for the red wines from the region of Lacryma Christi, which are sold as Vesuvio. The more interesting wines in recent years have come from one of the most beautiful coastlines in Europe, the Costa Amalfitana, where the vineyards have to be carved out of steep slopes, or in the Sant'Agata de'Goti and Solopaca *appellations*, between Caserta and Avellino in the north of the region.

Wine growing in Campania, as in other southern Italian regions, suffers from the general social and economic deprivation of the area, and an unnecessarily complex patchwork of *appellations*. As in Apulia, however, several producers have increased their efforts in the last few years and have been rewarded with some measure of success. By and large, the wine industry in Campania has not been active enough and the large investments that have had such a beneficial effect on Sicily and in Apulia tend to be rare in this region.

SELECT PRODUCERS OF CAMPANIA

CASA D'AMBRA VINI D'ISCHIA***–****
FORIO
17 acres (7 ha); some bought-in grapes; 320,000 bottles.
• *Wines include:* →*Biancolella Tenuta Frassitelli and Vigna di Piellero, I.G.T. Ischia: Per'e Palummo Tenuta Montecorvo, Forastera:* →*Cimentorosso Forastera, Arime*
Has earned an excellent reputation mainly for its fruity, fresh white wines made from Biancolella and Forastera. Also has a remarkable barrel-fermented white wine, Arime, made from local varieties.

FEUDI DI SAN GREGORIO***–*****
SORBO SERPICO
173 acres (70 ha); 2,500,000 bottles • *Wines:* →*Campanaro,* →*Taurasi,* →*Fiano di Avellino Pietracalda, Falanghina, Greco di Tufo Cutizzi, Serpico*
Probably Campania's best producer, this estate is still in the developing stage, but already has a series of excellent red and white wines.

MONTEVETRANO****
SAN CIPRIANO PICENTINO
10 acres (4 ha); 20,000 bottles • *Wines:* →*Montebetrano*
Silvia Imparato is the owner and Riccardo Cotarello makes the single wine.

OCONE—AGRICOLA DEL MONTE**–***
PONTE
114 acres (46 ha); 120,000 bottles • *Wines: Aglianico Del Taburno: Vigna Pezza la Corte and Diomede, Fanaghina del Taburno Vigna del Monaco; Calidonio*
Good to very good wines, of which the various Aglianico versions are the most impressive.

TERRADORA DI PAOLO***
MONTEFUSCO
371 acres (150 ha); 600,000 bottles • *Wines: Fiano di Avellino Terra di Dora, Campo Re, Greco di Tufo Loggioa della Serra, Terre degli Angheli,* →*Aglianico Irpinia, Falanghina Irpinia, Taurasi Fatica Contadina*
Paolo, Lucio, Walter and Daniela Mastroberardino have left the parent company. They are concentrating particularly on local grape varieties.

VILLA MATILDE**
CELLOLE
153 acres (62 ha); 200,000 bottles • *Wines include: Falerno del Massico: Bianco Vigna Caracci,* →*Rosso,* →*Vigna Camarato, Cecubo, Terre Cerase, Falanghina, Piedirosso*
Not only the red Falerno, but also the self-contained nature of the whole range of wines is impressive.

Calabria and Basilicata

The Aglianico del Vulture is only rarely aged in the grottoes of Barile, in the heart of its growing region; this greatest of the southern red wines is also slowly being modernized.

Together with the neighboring region of Basilicata, Calabria is structurally one of the weaker regions of Italy. It was the worst affected by the exodus of labor in the 1960s and 70s, and it was hardly able to develop a single sector of the economy with which to secure some measure of prosperity.

The wine industry shows little economic potential either, although with 32,120 acres (13,000 ha) Calabria has a considerable area given over to viticulture. Much of the fault for this must lie with the region's topography; its largely inaccessible mountains make it difficult to achieve any degree of agricultural efficiency. Nevertheless, the fundamental conditions for growing quality wines—as elsewhere in southern Italy—are more than favorable. In antiquity

Calabria's wines enjoyed the best of reputations, and it was no coincidence that the area belonged to *Oinotria*, the "Wineland" of the Greek settlers. In many parts of Calabria the heat of the southern climate is compensated for by the altitude of the vineyards, and the native varieties of grape also show great promise. Calabria is above all the home of Gaglioppo, also known as Montonico Nero, whose wines with their conspicuous tannins form the basis for most regional D.O.C. reds. The best known of these D.O.C. wines is Cirò, from the slopes of the Sila massif, which is said to have its origins in the wines of Kremissa—or Cremissa—fabled in antiquity for being presented to victors in the games at Olympia. A few producers have the skill necessary to make a well-balanced wine from this initially rather prickly, acidic product. Occasionally, it is matured in a *barrique* and exhibits a rich red color, a spicy palate, and even, given certain conditions, an ability to age well.

Origins Unknown

On the southern slopes of the Pollino mountains an eponymous D.O.C. wine is made from Gaglioppo and is marketed exclusively by the local cooperative. Savuto, from the other side of the Sila massif to Cirò, has a still greater potential. Here Gaglioppo is partly blended with Sangiovese which, given the altitude of the vineyards, leads to fine, expressive wines. The really interesting products in this area are sold by just a small group of growers. The other D.O.C. regions in Calabria like Lamezia, Sant'Anna di Isola Capo Rizzuto, and Melissa, on the other hand, have yet to come up with either appealing quality wines or regionally renowned products; they are among the numerous regions of origin in Italy which were set up simply to satisfy the ambitions of a political clientele.

Even Calabria's best dessert wine, the Greco di Bianco, makes virtually no impression on the market. It comes from Bianco, on the toe of the Italian "boot," where it is made from partially dried grapes. Under this name, dense, amber-colored wines with fine, fruity aromas and a marked spiciness are made by a small group of growers. The example of Greco di Bianco proves what can be achieved in Calabria—and makes one regret all the more the region's lack of real quality wines.

Pollino

Cirò

Melissa

Sant'Anna di Isola Capo Rizzuto

Donnici

Savuto

Lamezia

Greco di Bianco

Wine-growing areas in neighboring regions

The fruit-bearing shoots must be correctly tied in winter to allow the grapes to develop.

Young, flexible willow stems are used as ties, though these have largely been replaced by modern binding materials.

To avoid wind damage, the branches are tied to wire frames stretched between the vines.

Instead of the skillfully tied knots of former years, today's growers generally use mechanical binding.

At the end of April the young shoots appear from the buds of the year-old wood.

Pruning in winter is crucial for the healthy growth of the shoots.

Basilicata—volcanic wines

Basilicata's 19,765 acres (8,000 ha) of vineyards makes its wine-growing region twice as large as that of Trentino/Alto Adige, though only around 10 percent of this area produces quality wines. The almost completely landlocked and mountainous terrain of Basilicata, which only becomes flatter in the southeast on the coast, has a single designation of origin—the red Aglianico del Vulture. Most of the region's wine production is shipped in tankers to the north of the country and abroad. Unique to Italy are the region's underground cellars. In the area around Barile, the main town of the *appellation*, they can reach depths of more than 39 feet (12 m) in the loess soils of this rugged landscape. In the past they were used by growers for pressing grapes and storing their wines. Just as unique is the traditional method of training the vines on posts, which requires the plants to be bound together to form pyramids. According to experts, this method allows high-quality fruit to mature better than on modern, efficient wire frames.

Grown on the slopes of Monte Vulture, an extinct volcano in the north of the region, Aglianico is becoming one of the most popular southern Italian wines. Its dark color, strong aroma, and powerful, tannic accents make a good Aglianico del Vulture one of the best wines in Italy.

SELECT PRODUCERS IN CALABRIA AND BASILICATA

D'ANGELO**−***
RIONERO IN VULTURE (BASILICATA)
49 acres (20 ha); some bought-in grapes; 300,000 bottles • Wines include: Aglianico del Vulture: →*Riserva Vigna Caselle; I.G.T. Basilicata:* →*Rosso Canneto, Bianco Vigna dei Pini*
Canneto is harvested late and matured for 15 months in small oak barrels. With various Aglianico wines, Vigna dei Pini is an interesting Chardonnay-Pinot Bianco blend.

FATTORIA SAN FRANCESCO**−***
CIRÒ (CALABRIA)
173 acres (70 ha;) 120,000 bottles • Wines: Cirò Rosso Classico: →*Ronco dei Quattor Venti, Superiore Donna Madda, Superiore; Cirò Bianco*
The premium wine Quattro Venti was one of the earliest *barrique* versions of Cirò.

LIBRANDI***−****
CIRÒ MARINA (CALABRIA)
408 acres (165 ha); some bought-in grapes; 2,000,000 bottles • Wines: →*Gravello, Cirò Rosso Duca San Felice, Critone, Le Passule*

Top wines: Gravello, a Gaglioppo and Cabernet blend; Magno Megonio, made from Magliocco, and the white wine Mantonico.

ODOARDI**−***
COSENZA (CALABRIA)
124 acres (50 ha) • Wines: →*Savuto Superiore: Vigna Mortilla,* →*Vigna Vecchia;* →*Scavigna: Vigna Garrone, Pian del Corte;* →*Valeo*
The D.O.C. wines Savuto and Scavigna are still the only really excellent representatives of their respective designations of origin.

PATERNOSTER**−***
BARILE (BASILICATA)
16 acres (6.5 ha); some bought-in grapes; 130,000 bottles • Wines include: Aglianico del Vulture: Don Anselmo Riserva del Fondatore; Barigliott, Clivus, L'Antico, Il Moscato
A slightly bubbly wine called Barigliott is made from Aglianico, and there is even a red sparkling wines, L'Antico. Notable for its consistently high quality.

Sicily

Sicily is an island of contradictions. With Apulia it shares top place in Italy for the yield of its grape harvest and the amount of land dedicated to viticulture. On average, 211 million gallons (eight million hl) of wine are produced from 271,800 acres (110,000 ha) of vineyards. But more than any other region in southern Italy, Sicily has discovered its potential for creating really top-quality wines. The natural conditions for wine growing could not be better: long hours of sunshine, a warm climate and low rainfall provide optimal conditions for bringing the grapes to maturity. The island's barren soils result in expressive wines, while vineyards on highland slopes at up to 2,900 feet (900 m) produce particularly elegant, aromatic vintages.

Sicily was famed for its wines and agricultural produce even among the Greek settlers of antiquity. Vines were brought to the island by the Phoenicians, but the Greeks introduced new techniques and varieties such as Grecanico from their homeland—along with their native gods and mythology. The poetess, Sappho, who had been banished from her island home of Lesbos, is said to have cultivated wine here, and the Romans later thought Sicilian wine a welcome change from the famous Falernian.

Centuries later, under Arab rule, the island's viticulture did not suffer any real setbacks. The new rulers not only tolerated wine growing—despite the ban on alcohol in the Koran—they even introduced the technique of distillation. Throughout the entire Middle Ages it was mainly monks who distilled these mysterious "waters of life" with which they increased the wealth of their large estates. Sicily was therefore one of the few parts of Italy in which the traditions of wine growing were kept alive over centuries of social and political decline.

Marsala

Alcamo

Contessa Entellina

Menfi

Etna

Cerasuolo di Vittoria

Moscato di Noto

Malvasia delle Lipari

Moscato di Pantelleria, Moscato Passito di Pantelleria

A Crisis—In Spite of Marsala

It was only when Spanish viceroys ruled the island that Sicily's viticultural star began to wane. Under the Spaniards, grain was grown in preference to wine, and it was not until the end of the 18th century that an Englishman, John Woodhouse, began to revive Sicily's wine industry when he discovered Marsala, an alternative to the expensive commodity of sherry. Unfortunately, despite its isolated location, the island was not immune to the effects of phylloxera, and even the fame of Marsala began to fade. Today it is Trapani, in the west of the island, that is the largest wine-growing province on the island, with an annual production of 119 million gallons (4.5 million hl); this area is also home to the D.O.C. region of Marsala which is still the best known of the designations of origin. There is also a large continuous area of viticulture on both the southern and northern coasts, while in the east—with the exception of the area around Etna—mainly table grapes are grown.

Some of the most interesting Sicilian products are not grown on the main island but on the tiny Eolian islands to the northeast—including the volcanic island of Stromboli—and on Pantelleria, halfway between Sicily and Tunisia. A variety of dessert wines is made here, from Malvasia (on Lipari) and Zibibbo (on Pantelleria), also known as Muscat of Alexandria. All of these enjoy enormous popularity with Italian wine connoisseurs and they are even beginning to celebrate their first foreign successes.

The initial spark for this revival of older traditions was provided by Carlo Hauner, who had already caused a sensation in the 1980s with his Malvasia delle Lipari, and it was mainly the indigenous Malvasia and Corinto Nero varieties that were used. Hauner's example was not taken up by other producers, though this probably had more to do with the rather marginal nature of vineyards on Salina and its neighboring islands than with a lack of will on the part of the region's few growers.

Moscato di Pantelleria has since become more consistent and of better quality across a broad geographical area; several producers in the region around Marsala have now begun to invest in the wine. The sweet Passito and fortified Liquoroso versions are now numbered among the best sweet wines in the country.

Investing in Whites and Reds

The real revolution in the 1990s took place among the white and red wines. Apart from a

The Tasca d'Almerita bought the imposing estate of Regealeali in 1834. Today, it is one of the greatest and best-managed private domains in Italy.

Marsala—a sweet wine with a checkered history.

few successful attempts with Cabernet and Chardonnay wines, the protagonists of this new trend took advantage of the wide range of local varieties, some of which, in the course of time, proved they had greater potential than their previous incarnations as cheap, anonymous, mass-produced wines. Of the white wines, this role was played by Inzolia, alias Ansonica, the Cataratto grape, and possibly Grecanico Dorato. Grillo, on the other hand, is with few exceptions really only suited to producing Marsala.

Alcamo, a white wine from the largest D.O.C. region on the island (more than 49,000 acres/ 20,000 ha), demonstrates, however, that a limited harvest and careful cultivation of this traditionally high-volume variety can produce pleasant, full, dry whites.

Among red wines, the Nero d'Avola, alias Calabrese, has shown good potential, and the intensely colored, dense wines which it has produced since the mid-1980s exhibit at least the same levels of quality as those derived from Aglianico on the mainland. In the last few years some good wines made from Frappato and Nerello Mascalese grapes have come on the market: Frappato, in particular, which forms the basis for Cerasuolo di Vittoria on Sicily's southeastern corner, corresponds to the image of fruity and sunblessed red wine with its cherry-like, fruity aromas.

In contrast to Apulia or Campania, the drive to achieve quality did not occur through the initiative of the smaller producer (bearing in mind that, of the more than 100,000 producers in the region, only around 180 bottle and sell their own wines). Instead, the impetus came from large companies, including Settesoli, the biggest cooperative in Menfi on the south coast. This tendency has been reinforced by the recent investments by large Italian wine-producers such as Zonin or GIV in vineyards and production facilities, a development which expresses the confidence that Italy's wine industry has placed in what was once its sickest patient.

Sicilian Marsala

Sicily owes its greatest success in wine growing to Marsala, a fortified wine which was discovered almost by chance by a young Englishman. In 1770 John Woodhouse, a merchant's son from Liverpool, found himself in the harbor at Marshallà (present-day Marsala) where he was served a local wine which he thought equal to the Spanish sherries and Portuguese Madeiras so popular in Britain at the time. After long preparations and a three-year experimental phase, Woodhouse made his first shipment to England.

The real breakthrough came in 1800, when Admiral Nelson ordered a yearly delivery of 500 barrels to his fleet. Although grapes were, at first, in plentiful supply and cheaply priced, the wine's sudden success created problems in meeting the demand. Woodhouse therefore lent growers the necessary capital for new vineyards, receiving in return long-term price guarantees for both grapes and the base wines.

Woodhouse's example was, of course, not without its imitators. In 1812 Benjamin Ingham opened a new, larger, and technically superior operation close to Woodhouse in Marsala, and in 1833 businessman Vincenzo Florio became the first Sicilian to involve himself in this profitable trade. He purchased land between Woodhouse's and Ingham's cellars through a third party, establishing his own production site for a wine which the company's constitution described as "Madeira style."

For a century Sicily's wine industry basked in Marsala's success, but then came an inexorable, if slow, decline in the 20th century. The phylloxera disaster, new competition in the form of

Nets protect the slow-ripening Marsala grapes around Palermo against birds.

The Planeta estate in Sambuca is now ranked among Sicily's top producers, largely due to its French varietals.

Conte Tasca d'Almerita—specialist in Sicilian varieties.

mainly Australian wines (large areas of the hot, dry Australian interior had been given over to the production of fortified wines), and the usual spiral of overproduction and falling prices led to a deterioration in the quality of Marsala. Soon only the artificially scented versions of this once noble drink were available on the European market—including Marsala all'uovo which was mixed with an egg yolk—and customers simply lost interest.

It was not until the 1980s that there were again laborious and careful attempts by a few growers—such as Marco di Bartoli's Vecchio Samperi—to reconstruct the prestige of the old-style Marsala. Di Bartoli was unable to attract more than half a dozen followers, however, particularly as the interest of the wine world had shifted in the direction of the island's dry whites and reds. Today, high-quality Marsala is produced by a handful of companies in a variety of styles, and a cloud of forgetfulness has descended on the mistakes of the past. The most interesting products bear the designations *Fine*, *Superiore*, *Vergine*, and *Vergine Stravecchio*. These are wines with an alcohol level of 18 percent by volume, which are aged from four to ten years in a barrel before becoming available on the market. Good Marsala has an amber-yellow or brown color and generally develops rich honey aromas or the typical RANCIO of sherry. They are excellent as aperitifs or as an accompaniment to dessert. The very best exhibit an astonishing variety of aromas which makes Marsala's negative reputation seem all the more incomprehensible.

Select Producers of Sicily

Abbazia Sant'Anastasia****
Castelbuono
• *Wines: Santa Anastasia Rosso, Passomaggio, Baccante, Zurrica, →Litra*
This company, in Palermo province, produces impressive wines from local as well as French variants.

Marco de Bartoli—Vecchio Samperi***–****
Marsala
62 acres (25 ha); 60,000 bottles • Wines: Vecchio Samperi Riserva 20 Anni Solera, Moscato Passito di Pantelleria Bukkuram, Marsala Superiore: Oro Vigna La Miccia, Riserva 20 Anni Solera; Josephine Doré, Zibibbo, Vigna Verde, Grappoli del Grillo, Rosso di Marco
The Riserva Marsala Vecchio Samperi is exemplary: a non-fortified wine, its levels of alcohol and density are derived from over mature-grapes and a high degree of concentration, as well as up to 30 years of aging in the barrel.

Calatrasi—Terre di Ginestra*–***
San Cipirello
618 acres (250 ha); some bought-in grapes; 7,000,000 bottles • Wines: Terre di Ginestra: Bianco, Rosso; Calatrasi Terrale: Bianco, Rosso; Tenuta Calalbaio Olmobianco, Tenuta Calalbaio Rubilio, Pelavet di Ginestra, D'Istinto: Syrah, Cataratto / Chardonnay, Sangiovese /Merlot, Sangiovese
Maurizio Miccichè runs the successful winery. The Terre di Ginestra, Accademia del Sole 2001, and Distinto series offer a lot of wine for not much money. Miccichè also produces wine in Apulia and Tunisia.

Casa Vinicola Duca di Ginestra**–***
Casteldaccia
Some bought-in grapes; 9,500,000 bottles • Wines: Corvo: Bianco, Rosso, Glicine, Novello, Spumante Brut; Terre d'Agala, →Colomba Platino, Bianca di Valguarnera, →Duca Enrico, Portale d'Aspra
The red Duca Enrico was the first wine on the island to receive the highest praise. The winery has now returned to its old strengths.

COS***
Vittoria
35 acres (15 ha); 25,000 bottles • Wines: Cerasuolo di Vittoria, Frappato di Vittoria, Vignalunga, Ramingallo, Le Vigne di C.O.S.: Rosso, Bianco; Aestas Siciliae
The focus here is on the red wines from the Cerasuolo di Vittoria *appellation*: good Chardonnay and Cabernet.

Cusumano***–****
Partinico
124 acres (50 ha); 400,000 bottles • Wines: Alcamo Bianco Nandaria, Benuara Sicilia Rosso, Nadaria Inzolia Sicilia Bianco, →Nadaria Nero d'Avola, Nadaria Syrah, Noa Silicia Rosso, Sagana Rosso
The Cusumano brothers are young, ambitious producers, and they and their estate have rapidly risen to become one of the top operations in Sicily, thanks to very good wine quality and professional marketing.

Planeta****
Sambuca di Sicilia
• *Wines: La Segreta: Bianco, Rosso; Alastro, Chardonnay, Santa Cecilia, Merlot, Cabernet*
Single-variety wines made from French grape varieties, including one of the best Chardonnays in Sicily, and also balanced blends of local and French varieties.

Settesoli*–***
Menfi
18,530 acres (7,500 ha); 13,000,000 bottles • Wines: Settesoli: Bianco, Rosato, Rosso, Feudo del Fiori,

Bonera, Soltero Rosso, Chardonnay Sicilia, Nero d'Avola / Cabernet, Nero d'Avola / Merlot, Porto Palo Bianco
The largest cooperative and biggest bottler on the island makes plain, crisp products for everyday purposes as well as high quality varietals and blends.

Spadafora***–****
Palermo
222 acres (90 ha); 200,000 bottles • Wines: I.G.T. Sicilia: DiVino Bianco, Don Pietro Rosso, →Schietto Rosso, →Incanto, Vigna Virzi: Rosso, Bianco: Bianco d'Alcamo
An exemplary estate with consistent high quality; produces an outstanding red Schietto as well as Incanto, a sweet wine.

Conte Tasca d'Almerita—Regaleali***
Sciafani Bagni
988 acres (400 ha); 2,300,000 bottles • Wines: Cabernet, Chardonnay, Regaleali: Bainco, Rosso, Rosato, →Rosso del Conte, Nozze d'Oro, Villa Tasca, Conti d'Almerita Crèmant, Almerita Brut
The standard for native Sicilian varieties. Rosse del Conte, made from Nero d'Avola grapes, is a classic, as is the white Nozze d'Oro: both age exceptionally well. There is also excellent Cabernet and Chardonnay, both from recently established vineyards.

Tenuta di Donnafugata**–****
Marsala
420 acres (170 ha); 1,500,000 bottles • Wines: Contessa Entellina, I.G.T. Sicilia, Donnafugata: Bianco, Rosso, Rosato; Vigna di Gabri, →Chiarandà del Merlo, Tancredi, Damaskino, Moscato di Pantelleria, Lighea, Passito di Pantelleria Ben Ryé, Opera Unica, Milleunanotte
Mainly dry wines, with the focus on white varieties. The firm's best wine is the barrel-aged Chardonnay Chiarandà del Merlo.

Vinicola Italiana Florio***
Marsala
Bought-in grapes: 3,000,000 bottles • Wines: Marsala Superiore: Secco Ambra, Riserva Targa 1840, Baglio Florio, Vergine Terre Arse; Morsi di Luce
The traditional house of Marsala, owned by the Cinzano empire, is again producing clean, complex Marsala versions. The oenologist is Marco Rabino.

One of the best addresses for Marsala: Florio.

ECKHARD SUPP

GERMANY

WINEMAKING IN GERMANY

The Romans were the first to succeed in the systematic cultivation of vines along the rivers Mosel and Rhine. Diocletian had initially intended Trier to be a transit camp for the trade in Roman wines to the British provinces, but it soon became clear that production locally was more profitable. Probus, a successor of Diocletian, introduced the cultivation of grapes to the Mosel. Soon the slopes of the Rhine and Mosel, the hills of the Pfalz, the Bergstraße, and even Franconia and Württemberg were covered with vines. Around the year 800 Charlemagne began to encourage the selection of grape varieties of good quality, ensuring that the best sites for vineyards were identified, and passing laws to protect winemakers and wine traders.

The treasury of the monastery of Eberbach in the Rheingau.

Legend:
- Ahr
- Mittelrhein
- Mosel·Saar·Ruwer
- Rheingau
- Nahe
- Rheinhessen
- Hessische Bergstraße
- Pfalz
- Baden
- Württemberg
- Franconia
- Saale·Unstrut
- Saxony
- Wine-growing areas in neighboring countries

At the turn of the millennium, monasteries were the leading producers of wine. Cistercians from the Burgundian parent house of Cîteaux founded the monastery of Eberbach in the Rheingau in the 12th century, and it became Europe's largest and best known winemaking center. German wines were soon in demand all over Europe. In the 16th century, records show that vines were grown on an area of 740,000 acres (300,000 ha)—three times as large as the vine-growing area of Germany today—and that wine consumption per head was 32 gallons (120 liters) a year, almost five times the present quantity.

These record figures were followed by a crisis. Drastic deterioration in the climate of Central Europe, together with the wars that shook the continent, also destroyed the foundations of viticulture. It was not until toward the end of the 17th century that the economy began to revive.

While the Burgundian monks had at first grown the French Pinot Noir grape, here known as Spätburgunder, in German vineyards, a different, white grape variety soon conquered the banks of the Mosel and the Rhine-Riesling. With careful selection, it became the area's leading variety.

German winemaking suffered a severe setback in the second half of the 19th century when it was affected by the PHYLLOXERA louse from France. The devastating effects of phylloxera reduced the vine-growing area to a third of what it had once been. Two world wars and the economic crisis of the inter-war years prevented any real resurgence until the 1950s.

MASS PRODUCTION VERSUS QUALITY

In the 1960s, winemaking in the Federal Republic of the time saw perhaps its greatest period of expansion. By the beginning of the 1990s vines grew on over 245,000 acres (100,000 ha). Yields rose in the same period from 534 to over 1,070 gallons per acre (50 to 100 hl/ha): wine production had more than doubled in barely three decades.

This was the result of improved methods of vineyard cultivation, mechanization, and systematic pest control, and of the breeding of more resistant and higher-yielding grape varieties. The winemaking economy concentrated chiefly on its export trade, relying heavily on mass production: sweet or medium-sweet Liebfraumilch became synonymous with German wine in general in the British and American markets.

The German Wine Law, dating from 1971 but revised in the 1990s, did little to enhance the

Burg Rheinstein stands proudly above the vineyards opposite Assmannshausen. It was built around the year 900 for customs and excise purposes.

Bacchante on an ornamental panel from the Mosel.

reputation of German wines. Its refusal to adopt an estate classification system, and the legally equal standing of small top vineyards and *Großlagen* ("large sites," or groups of vineyards) without the potential to produce wines of high quality, denied consumers the opportunity to distinguish between the huge range of wines on offer. Leading viticulturists have called for the introduction of estate classification on the French model. However, the proposal is criticized by those winemakers who through their individual efforts make wines that are among the very best in their respective districts but who may not own vineyards in locations which would usually be considered worthy of classification.

The rise in quality during the 1990s was also the result of individual effort. Winemakers set about producing wines which took account of the public's higher expectations. Modern methods of vinification and concentration on the best grape varieties raised the international reputation of German white wines, both dry and sweet. The latest trend—toward the growing of black grapes, and the making of a number of intensely colored, complex, and powerful red wines—is also promising.

Vine-growing areas and quantities produced in winemaking regions				
2001 figures, source: DWI and Enzyklopädie des deutschen Weins (Eno-Verlag)				
Cultural region	Vine-growing area in acres (ha)		Average annual production for the 1990s in millions of gallons (hl)	
Ahr	1,282	(519)	1.15	(43,690)
Baden	39,204	(15,866)	31.6	(1,195,330)
Franconia	14,924	(6,040)	13.3	(503,420)
Hessische Bergstraße	1,126	(456)	.9	(37,660)
Mittelrhein	1,388	(562)	1.9	(72,830)
Mosel-Saar-Ruwer	25,678	(10,392)	40.0	(1,520,520)
Nahe	10,840	(4,387)	9.5	(362,520)
Pfalz	57,875	(23,422)	63.9	(2,420,710)
Rheingau	7,919	(3,205)	6.5	(246,130)
Rheinhessen	65,068	(26,333)	67.4	(2,552,790)
Saale-Unstrut	1,608	(651)	.4	(17,920)
Saxony	1,102	(446)	.3	(13,430)
Württemberg	28,010	(11,336)	29.4	(1,114,050)
Total	256,029	(103,615)	267.0	(10,101,000)

THE WINE LAW AND STYLES OF WINES

Classic and Selection

In the late 1990s two categories were added to the German legislation on wine, *Classic* and *Selection*. As additions to the existing quality range they were intended to make orientation and the choice of a wine easier for the consumer by providing a more precise definition of taste. *Classic* wines are defined as full-bodied (*gehaltvoll*) and dry, and they must be from varieties of grape that are typical of their area. Yields may not exceed 60 hl/ha. Between one and eight varieties whose wines may bear the new designation were established for each area of cultivation. The residual sugar content may not exceed 15 g/l or twice the acid content, and the alcohol content must be one volume percentage higher than required for the corresponding quality classification in that area. For *Selection* wines the range is narrower; the residual sugar content may not exceed 9 g/l or twice the acid content, with a limit of 12 g/l or one and a half times the acid content for Riesling.

German wines are divided by the Wine Law into four categories: *Tafelwein* (table wine), *Landwein* (country wine), QUALITÄTSWEIN *Bestimmer Anbaugebeite* (quality wine from defined regions), abbreviated to Q.b.A., and *Qualitätswein mit Prädikat* or *Prädikatswein* (wine with a distinction), Q.m.P. The majority of wines produced fall into the two last-named categories. Unlike the French wine law, its German equivalent does not classify wines on a geographical basis, but distinguishes between Q.b.A. only on the basis of the sugar content of the grape MUST. The "distinctions" are: KABINETT (cabinet), SPÄTLESE (late harvest), AUSLESE (select harvest), BEERENAUSLESE (select berry harvest), and TROCKENBEERENAUSLESE (T.B.A.) (select dried berry harvest), as well as the special case of EISWEIN (ice wine).

By German law, only *Tafelwein*, *Landwein*, and Q.b.A. wines can have extra sugar added. The minimum must weights for each grade of

Vinothèque wines from the Ratzenberger vineyard estate in the Mittelrhein. Old vintages were kept as a kind of reference library or archive.

The hydrometer or areometer used in determining the weight of the must measures its specific weight and thus its sugar content.

quality vary slightly, depending on where the vines are grown, and are expressed in degrees OECHSLE. As well as stating the minimum weight of the must, a finished wine must also have a minimum alcohol content. *Tafelwein* and *Landwein*, however, must not exceed a total alcohol content of 15 percent vol.

One of the prerequisites for describing the distinctions between categories of German wine was created by the Pforzheim physicist Ferdinand Oechsle (1774–1852) when he invented the hydrometer, also known as the areometer. This hollow glass instrument weighted with mercury (or lead) is marked with a scale and resembles a thermometer. If the hydrometer is placed in water (SPECIFIC GRAVITY 1) the weight of the amount displaced will be equal to the weight of the immersed instrument. If the density of the fluid is altered by the substances dissolved in the fluid of the must, the hydrometer will not sink so far in. It thus shows how many grams heavier a liter of

Lage, Großlage, Bereich

According to the definitions of the German Wine Law, the term *Lage* (site) or *Einzellage* (literally, single site) usually means a vineyard of at least 19 acres (8 ha) with a distinct name and a defined geographical extent and boundaries. The Wine Law states that the grapes from such a vineyard must produce wines of consistent flavor if it is to be granted the status of *Einzellage*.

Old rural place names were given to vineyards from the middle of the 19th century onward, although at first only the top wines bottled on the great estates—particularly *Spätlese* and *Auslese* wines—were identified in this way. After the passing of the 1971 Wine Law such vineyard descriptions became the general rule, since the Law drastically reduced the number of legally recognized names, and made it compulsory to state the geographical origin of a *Qualitätswein* on the label.

The Wine Law also defines the *Großlage* (literally "large site," a group made up of several *Einzellagen*) and the *Bereich* ("district," consisting of several *Großlagen*). But as these larger units cannot be distinguished from *Einzellagen* simply by the names on the label, the consumer cannot tell what kind of description of origin is conveyed. For a long time there has been criticism of the failure of the German Wine Law to classify geographical areas in terms of their potential for quality, as in France.

must is than a liter of water, and the difference in the sugar content can be calculated. Must with a specific weight of 1.050 is 50 degrees Oechsle (°Oe), corresponding to about 6 percent vol potential alcohol (1 oz = 28 g; 1 quart = 1 l).

In the 1970s German winegrowers and consumers alike favored *Spätlese* wines, and the market was positively flooded with cheap, so-called *Prädikat* wines, which could often be made drinkable only by the addition of "sweet reserve," unfermented grape juice.

Such wines were not to be confused with the great *edelsüß* (nobly sweet) wines made from over-ripe grapes affected by the BOTRYTIS CINEREA fungus. These fine wines have been made since the 18th century, and it is on them that the reputation of German wine, particularly the highly esteemed Rieslings from the Rheingau and Mosel, was at least partly founded until well into the first half of the 20th century. In contrast, the fashionably sweet wines of the 1960s and 1970s were to some extent the result of viticultural mass production, and the results, in the cool German climate, were bound to be thin and sour without an added dose of sugar.

Sweetness: Less is More

In the middle of the 1970s wines with a dry finish—first and foremost Edelzwicker wines from Alsace—became increasingly popular with wine lovers around the world, and German winemakers intent on quality began making their own wines dry and sometimes even "bone-dry": such wines could contain practically no residual sugar, and were no longer "improved" with sweet reserve, which did not always suit the acidic wines of the Mosel, Nahe, and Rheingau. Dry wines from more southerly vineyards were naturally better balanced and easier to drink than these German products.

It was not long before winemakers remembered the real criteria for wine of good quality: a full flavor and the right balance. A slight amount of RESIDUAL SUGAR is now tolerated, and the popularity of *edelsüß* wines is growing. Attempts were made to produce wines of a more "international" style. Burgundy vine varieties were more often grown, and even Chardonnay made its way into German vineyards. Experiments have also been made with *barrique* maturation and acidity conversion.

As a result of this development, the styles of wines made by leading German winemakers cover a broad range, with the makers' individual style now often determining the character of the wine more strongly than the idiosyncrasies of particular vineyards or regions. At the same time,

1. Logo and name of vineyard
2. Year
3. Grape variety
4. Nature of distinction in Q.m.P.
5. Indication of flavor
6. Designation of origin (*Bereich, Großlage, Einzellage, Gemeinde* (parish, community)
7. Identification as Q.m.P. (or Q.b.A., *Tafelwein*, or *Landwein*)
8. Region of cultivation of *Qualitätswein, Tafelwein,* or *Landwein*
9. Official inspection number for *Qualitätswein*
10. Name of firm bottling the wine (if estate-bottled, the winemaker's name and address)
11. Number of ecological inspection office
12. Volume contained in bottle
13. Alcohol percentage by volume (rounded to the nearest 0.5 percent)
14. Logo of winemaker(s)

the increasingly technological aspect of wine-making has ensured that the simpler wines in particular have become more uniform.

The range of German wines, then, has become wider, and can hold its own on the international market. Strong, dry, but well-balanced white wines, and expressive, rich, rounded red wines now stand side by side with the classic fruity Rieslings of the northern wine-growing regions, and their top quality *edelsüß* products.

The Label

Just as wine is the winemaker's creation, the design of the labels is often entrusted to experienced artists.

The labels of German wines have to provide certain facts, to which further information may be voluntarily added. It is compulsory to state the category of the wine (*Tafelwein, Landwein, Q.b.A.,* or *Q.m.P.*), and also the region of cultivation or origin of a *Tafelwein*. In addition, the names of the winemaker and the place where the wine was bottled must be given, as well as the volume in the bottle and the alcohol content. *Qualitätsweine* also have an official inspection number and a "lot number," allowing precise identification of the details of its bottling. In a *Prädikatswein* the "*Prädikat*" must be defined.

Optional information includes precise identification of the area of origin, the names of up to two grape varieties, the year the wine was made, an indication of whether the wine was bottled by the maker, the name of the vineyard, and a description of the flavor (dry, medium-dry, sweet, etc.).

Bottles with designer labels, perhaps mentioning only the name of the wine, the vineyard, and the year it was made, must carry an additional label, as specified by the Wine Law, giving the compulsory information.

THE MAIN VINE VARIETIES

Germany is first and foremost the land of the Riesling grape, but it is also a country of vine breeders. A great number of grape varieties developed here, for instance Müller-Thurgau and Scheurebe, spread to other countries during the 20th century. At the same time, such a wide range of varieties was introduced that today only Riesling and Müller-Thurgau can be said to occupy really large vineyard areas. Three other grape varieties have more than five percent of the share, while many of the rest are cultivated on less than one percent of the entire area on which vines are grown in Germany.

RIESLING AND RIESLING CROSSES

Riesling is probably descended from the wild vine *Vitis vinifera silvestris* growing in the forests on the Upper Rhine. There are records of grapes being grown here in the 11th century, but viticulture did not become really widespread until the 17th and 18th centuries. The best results with the Riesling grape are achieved when it is grown in temperate to cool climatic zones, providing conditions for as strong as possible a development of the AROMAS, and for a good balance of sugar and acidity. Together with Chardonnay, Riesling is regarded as having the most distinctive character of all white grape varieties. As a late-ripening grape, it produces wines suitable for drinking young and fresh, as well as growths capable of long maturing, and complex, concentrated dessert wines. Its ability to retain acidity as the grapes continue ripening makes it the ideal variety for *Spätlese* and *Auslese* wines.

More than almost any other variety, Riesling takes on the characteristics of the locality where it is grown, and brings them out in its wines. Riesling wines from the schist formations of the Mosel, the clay and loessial slopes of the Rheingau, the lower red sandstone strata of Rheinhessen, from Baden, Alsace, or the primary rocks of the Wachau district of Austria, can all be clearly distinguished from each other. Styles extend from wine with a mineral or fruity character, to a note of honey in a *Prädikat* wine. The wines are pale yellow with greenish reflections, or yellow to golden-yellow among the finest of the *Prädikat* wines. They have a fine fruitiness to the nose, with an aroma of apples, peaches, grapefruit, and other citrus fruits, or in the top quality *Prädikat* wines of honey and

The 12 most widely grown grape varieties (2001)		
Variety	Area of stocks in acres (ha)	% of grape-growing area
Riesling	53,160 (21,514)	20.8%
Müller-Thurgau	45,982 (18,609)	18.4%
Spätburgunder	23,736 (9,606)	9.5%
Silvaner	15,868 (6,422)	6.2%
Kerner	14,959 (6,054)	5.8%
Portugieser	13,664 (5,530)	5.3%
Bacchus	12,451 (5,039)	4.9%
Scheurebe	7,331 (2,967)	2.9%
Dornfelder	7,178 (2,905)	2.8%
Grauburgunder	6,654 (2,693)	2.6%
Trollinger	6,461 (2,615)	2.5%
Schwarzriesling	6,130 (2,481)	2.4%

exotic fruits. On the palate, fine Rieslings have a lively acidity and good body—a high concentration of EXTRACTIONS compensates for their sometimes low alcohol content—and their flavor is almost always intense.

In the last few decades there has been increasing cultivation of Riesling in the New World. California, Australia, New Zealand, and other countries have tried to imitate the winegrowers of the Rhine, the Mosel, and the Danube. The second largest Riesling-growing area in the world lies in the countries of the former Soviet Union, but although little is known of the vines grown there, the end products, with a few exceptions, are rather disappointing. The climate is too mild in general for the grapes to reach their potential: outside Central Europe wines made from the Riesling variety tend to be neutral and uninteresting in flavor. Quite often so-called Riesling wines are made without any Riesling grapes at all, for instance in Australia, where the well-known Hunter Riesling was previously made from Semillon grapes.

There is also some confusion in Europe, and not only because of the diversity of names given to "genuine," white Riesling, also called Rheinriesling in Austria. This confusion is caused by the so-called Welschriesling ("foreign" Riesling), known in Italy as Riesling Italico, which is in fact a completely independent grape variety and has nothing in common with the great Riesling grape.

At least as popular in Germany as Riesling is the Müller-Thurgau variety, a cross between Riesling and Gutedel, raised in 1882 by Hermann Müller of Thurgau in Geisenheim. This early-ripening variety needs fertile soil and produces a very high yield, and for that very reason its yield must be considerably restricted if it is to give good results. Usually wines made from Müller-Thurgau, with its mild acidity, are soft and rounded. The wines from grapes not yet fully ripe have a slightly aromatic, muscat note, which they lose as they mature further, often after two or three years.

The Kerner variety is the result of a cross between Trollinger and Riesling vines in 1969. This variety is regarded as robust, guaranteeing a good yield, and is therefore to be found in all German wine-growing areas today. Its wines resemble Rieslings, but cannot achieve the same high quality.

In terms of quantity, Silvaner was the major German grape variety grown in the 1950s, not least because it was the first to promise a really guaranteed yield. In time it was ousted in many regions by Riesling, Kerner, and Müller-Thurgau, but at present interest in Silvaner wines is increasing again. Their BOUQUET is rather restrained, they have moderate acidity, and are strong on the palate.

In 1916 Georg Scheu crossed Silvaner with Riesling to raise the Scheurebe variety (also known in Austria as Sämling 88). In the lower quality categories the wines made from this strong, lime-tolerant variety are often neutral, but it can produce fine, sweet *Auslese* wines.

The Bacchus grape was bred by crossing Silvaner, Riesling, and Müller-Thurgau. This variety has a high yield with good must weight, and its wines often have a slight muscat flavor, sometimes also showing a similarity to Riesling.

Particularly striking white wines—at their best they are rich in extracts, dense, and spicy—are made from Pinot Gris, known in Germany as Grauburgunder ("gray Burgundy") or Ruländer, and in Italy as Pinot Grigio. The grapes have skins of a grayish red color, and the variety is a direct descendant of Pinot Noir.

RED WINES IN SECOND PLACE

The most popular red wine variety grown in Germany is Spätburgunder (late Burgundy), known in Austria as Blauburgunder (blue Burgundy). In its native France, as Pinot Noir, it has one of the finest reputations of any red wine variety. The best wines made from Spätburgunder in Germany are those from grapes grown on the Ahr, in Baden, and in the Pfalz and Rheingau regions.

The Portugieser or Blaue Portugieser (blue Portuguese) variety came to Germany from Austria. Simple, straightforward wines are often made from this early-ripening variety, which has a reliable yield, but it can also produce dense,

powerful, fruity wines. The Portugieser variety is often used for Weißherbst wines (a kind of rosé).

Dornfelder is a cross between the Helfensteiner and Heroldrebe varieties, making wines notable for strong acidity and a spicy fruitiness. Originally it was bred to improve other varieties by intensifying their color. However, it has become established as a variety in itself and is now actually very fashionable. The grapes are also used to make Sekt, the German sparkling wine.

Trollinger, known as Schiava in Italy, and as Vernatsch in the South Tyrol, is the favorite variety of growers in Württemberg. The wines are light red and fruity, and are notable for their striking acidity. In other parts of Germany, Trollinger is not very often grown, because it ripens extremely late in the season.

Schwarzriesling (black Riesling) is not related to Riesling at all, but is one of the Burgundy varieties, and is known in France as Pinot Meunier. Despite its more intense color and stronger character it slightly resembles Spätburgunder, the Pinot Noir variety.

Grapes from old Riesling vines make concentrated wines expressing the character of their *terroir*, particularly when they are grown by biological methods.

MAKING WHITE WINES

293.—Wine-Press. (Cotton MS.)

This medieval print shows the three most important stages of winemaking: first harvesting the grapes, then treading with the feet and finally pressing in a table press.

It used to be so easy: the grapes were crushed in a vat at the vineyard itself, the must was put through a basket press in the PRESSING room, so that the YEASTS could then begin to work on it in the large and often ancient FERMENTATION tub, known as a *Fuder* on the Mosel. If the grapes were healthy, they produced a clear, clean must and a wonderful wine typical of its variety and locality. Unfortunately everything did not always go well, and countless ruses were devised to help the fermentation along quickly. Many of these techniques came from overseas, where research had long since revolutionized vineyard and winery work. These early successes led in time to an unlimited belief in the value of high-tech methods. Pumps and tubes, steel tanks for temperature-controlled fermentation, centrifuges, cross-flow filters, cultured yeasts, bacteria, enzymes, and finally concentrators working by evaporation or osmosis took over the wineries, while improved machines for pruning the vines, thinning the leaves, and finally for harvesting itself were introduced into the vineyards.

THE BLESSINGS OF TECHNOLOGY

The grape juice has to go through a lengthy process, particularly in large wineries. It is filtered in the separator, and may be pasteurized to ensure that no remains of wild or "ambient" yeast survive. Then it is fermented with exotic aromatic yeasts from Australia or America to emphasize the primary note of the fruit. Starter cultures of appropriate bacteria or enzymes set the conversion of acidity going, and the wine passes through a microfilter again before it is bottled under sterile conditions.

Such wines cannot really be faulted, but they have less and less individuality. Clean wines of neutral aroma and flavor are the inevitable outcome of wine made in this way.

RESPECTING THE GRAPES

In the early 1990s, when mechanization and the use of chemical aids, enzymes, and aromatic yeasts were being heavily promoted for purposes of mass production, leading winemakers put their minds to the real qualities of their wines. The guiding principle today is to treat the grapes as gently as possible, using only as much tech-

Battery of silvery stainless steel tanks, Brackenheim vineyard estate, Württemberg.

View of the winery of the Haarti vineyards in Piesport on the Mosel.

Barriques and fermentation casks at the Koehler-Ruprecht vineyard estate in the Pfalz.

Germany's viticultural areas are among the most northerly in the world. The average annual temperature is lower here than in Italy, Spain, or large parts of France, and there is less sunshine. While in the south musts and wines low in acidity usually have to be additionally acidified, German winemakers are more likely to have to counter excess acidity.

Modern winery technique follows two main methods of dealing with acidity in the must or the wine: de-acidification by the addition of calcium carbonate, and the biological conversion of acidity, a process in which the more aggressive malic acid, which with tartaric acid makes up most of the total acidic content, is split by enzymes and bacteria into lactic and carbon dioxide, a process known as MALO-LACTIC FERMENTATION.

A certain lively play of acidity is in fact one of the best qualities of German white wines: the correct amount and kinds of acids give it freshness and contribute to its ability to mature. The advantage of the biological conversion of ACID over chemical de-acidification is that only the malic acid is affected. Furthermore, any unwanted milky or buttery notes produced by the process, once a potential drawback to the biological conversion of acid, can now be avoided by the use of special enzymes.

But while large wineries use malolactic fermentation to give wines a more rounded or "international" character, leading German winemakers now abstain from either method. Since acid content is high as a result of early harvesting, in their view there is only one recipe for rich, rounded, wines: to leave the grapes on the vine until they have ripened fully.

nology as necessary; an example is the practice of pressing the whole grapes without previously removing the skins or crushing the berries. Even letting the must stand for a time to give the wines more structure and ability to mature is "permitted" again these days, and is no longer the sign of a hopelessly conservative attitude.

When wines are made with sweet reserve, the fermentation is interrupted (by pressure, or chilling and FILTRATION) so that the aromas typical of the variety are preserved. The major new development, however, is experimentation with *barrique* maturation for white as well as red wines—particularly those made from the Burgundy grape varieties. At the time of writing, German winemakers are in a forward-looking mood for which they deserve credit. The standard model of white winemaking in Germany is now definitely a thing of the past.

Picking grapes in steep hillside vineyards—as shown here in the Piesport on the Mosel—will still have to be done by hand in the future.

Mechanical concentrators

Attempts have always been made to concentrate the must, in particular its sugar content, which produces alcohol during fermentation. French winemakers have practiced *saignée* (bleeding), in which a little juice is drained from the crushed grapes for red wine in order to give a more intense color and richness to the rest of the must, which will then ferment on the grape skins.

In Austria and the Mediterranean countries wine is concentrated by leaving the grapes to dry for a certain time after harvesting—a procedure banned in Germany by the German Wine Law. The *vins de paille* (straw wines) thus produced are often very sweet, or like Italian Amarone, may be strongly alcoholic.

For more than ten years there have been experiments, particularly in France, with mechanical concentrators. Essentially, two procedures are involved: water is removed from the must in a vacuum evaporator at 77–86°F (25–30°C), or in a process known as REVERSE OSMOSIS the must is forced at high pressure against a membrane which holds back certain molecules, depending on the size of the pores. In this way fluid molecules as well as unwanted by-products of fermentation, such as volatile acids, are filtered out of the wine.

The advantage of this method is obvious. If, for instance, the year's weather was satisfactory until extensive rainfalls just before harvest, excess water can be removed from the must in this way. If the wine seems to be threatened by bacterial action, the damage can be rectified later. But there is no denying the disadvantages: first, the must or finished wine is subjected to violent treatment in clear contradiction to the gentler winemaking procedures which leading winemakers value so highly; and second, concentration of the must levels out differences between years and local origins. The wines become more and more uniform over time, and those from different vineyards or regions are more and more like each other.

Such procedures could seriously undermine the German Wine Law, which defines qualitative categories in terms of degrees Oechsle in the must. Instead of waiting for the grapes to reach the requisite ripeness on the vine, the winemaker can simply manufacture *Auslese* and *Beerenauslese* qualities in the winery.

THE CENTRAL MOSEL
AND THE TERRACED MOSEL

THE CENTRAL MOSEL

The Central Mosel, which in the latest changes to the definition of districts was classed with the Trier vineyards, is the best-known part of the Mosel region, and also the most popular with tourists. There are good reasons for this, since the narrow valley of the meandering river, bending sharply at Trittenheim, Piesport, Zeltingen, and Traben-Trarbach, offers increasingly impressive panoramas with miles of enclosed vineyard slopes, and these views have established the image of the Mosel worldwide.

The soils of gray and red schist here, together with the ideal south or southwest aspect of the slopes, give the Rieslings made in the Central Mosel an unusual amount of fullness and balance. The wines are more substantial than those of the Upper Mosel, and can sometimes be quite powerful. However, there are clear differences in the character of the wines made by the top vineyards of the Central Mosel. The Rieslings of the Trittenheimer Apotheke are both substantial and elegant. Even more powerful are those of the Piesporter Goldtröpfchen vineyard, although

it must be remembered that this vineyard was over-promoted by the Wine Law, and has been enlarged by the addition of less valuable plots of land. The Brauneberger Juffer-Sonnenuhr, one of the most famous of the vineyards, produces excellent wines from its predominantly very dry soil even in damp, cool years.

Almost as good as the wines of the Juffer-Sonnenuhr are those of the Kestener Paulinshofberger, although the potential of this vineyard has not really been fully exploited by winemakers. The most expensive vineyard in Germany—and surely one of the most expensive in the world—is the Bernkasteler Doctor, which makes wines of great elegance. The *Gemeinden* (communities) of Wehlen and Zeltingen divide the famous Sonnenuhr vineyard between them, with Wehlen clearly having the better part of the deal. It is no coincidence that an unusually large number of top winemakers have settled here. Different again are the wines from the vineyards of the Ürziger Würzgarten, with its red sandstone soil, and the Erdener Prälaten. Both vineyards make wines which unite strength and spiciness with the elegance of the Riesling grape.

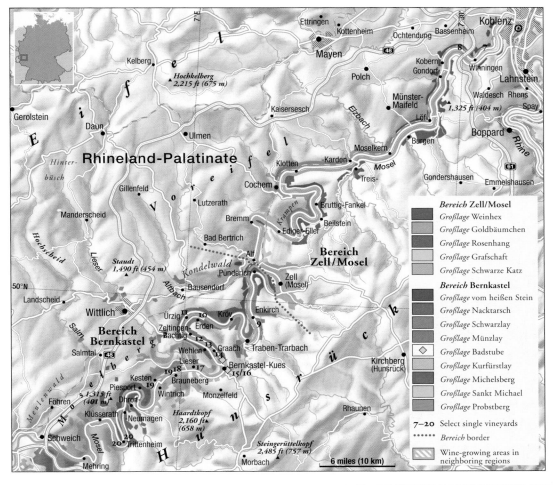

Select single vineyards

Even a glance at the steep vineyard slopes at Kröv shows their remarkable potential, although that has been somewhat impaired by the institution of the Kröver Nacktarsch Großlage.

Map legend

Bereich Zell/Mosel
Großlage Weinhex
Großlage Goldbäumchen
Großlage Rosenhang
Großlage Grafschaft
Großlage Schwarze Katz

Bereich Bernkastel
Großlage vom heißen Stein
Großlage Nacktarsch
Großlage Schwarzlay
Großlage Münzlay
Großlage Badstube
Großlage Kurfürstlay
Großlage Michelsberg
Großlage Sankt Michael
Großlage Probstberg

7–20 Select single vineyards
· · · · · *Bereich* border
Wine-growing areas in neighboring regions

6 miles (10 km)

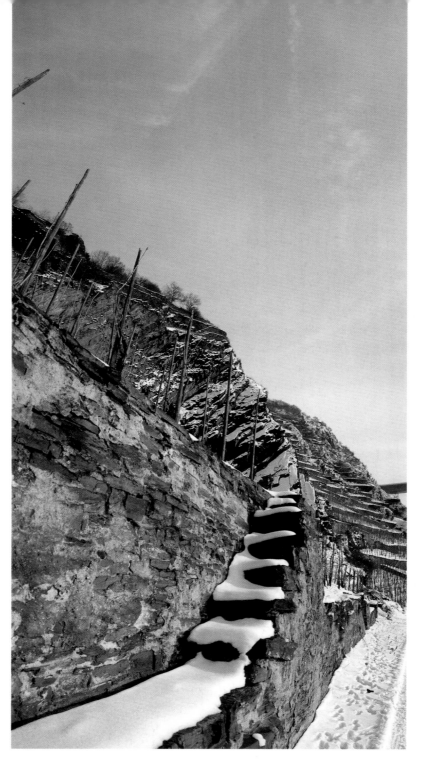

The Terraced Mosel

Before the Mosel turns to meet the Rhine it becomes truly spectacular once again. While the river here describes more of a straight line than on its course between Cochem, Zell, Bernkastel, and Piesport, the slopes on its banks become steeper, more rugged, and inaccessible, increasing the picturesque charm of its banks. The Bremmer Calmont in the border area between the Lower and Central Mosel is the steepest vineyard in Germany, although Kobern, and Uhlen and Röttgen in Winningen, do not lag far behind in this respect.

The leading Winninger Uhlen vineyard grows grapes which make several of the liveliest Rieslings along the Mosel, with a distinct mineral note.

Opposite
In vineyards on a steep gradient such as the Ürziger Würzgarten viticulturalists install tackle blocks to bring equipment up and take the grape harvest down.

This final section of the course of the river owes its name of the Terraced Mosel to the grayish brown, narrow stone terraces, which in winter can look very forbidding, and which seem to cover the landscape from this point on. Countless such terraces are crammed into a very narrow space, utilizing every patch of ground and leaving hardly any room for the vines themselves, so that the work of the winegrower is considerably more difficult.

Although more northerly than the vineyards of Brauneberg, Kasel, Trier, and Saarburg, the Terraced Mosel produces rounded wines with fewer acid notes. They are achieved not only by the perfect south-facing aspect of the terraces and the moderating influence of the river Mosel, a very broad expanse of water at this point, but also by the stony, poor soils, which demand all that the vines can give.

In order to keep up with the well-known and popular wine-producing areas of the Middle and Upper Mosel, the best winemakers and gastronomic experts of the area have joined together to form the "Terrassenmosel" association, which attracts tourists to the region in summer with culinary and cultural events.

A Return to High Quality

The Lower or Terraced Mosel with its steep vineyards—the steepest anywhere on the river—is the crown and conclusion of this unusual viticultural area. Despite its outstanding potential, in the 1970s the Mosel region stood for simple and usually sugary wines, which were especially popular in northern Germany and the English-speaking countries. Its image is still determined by the sweet wines it produces, yet 50 percent of the wines from the Mosel now on the market are dry, and another 30 percent medium-dry.

In addition, over the last ten years leading winemakers between Saarburg and Winningen have won over lovers of high-quality Rieslings. They began by making wines in the best vineyards of Wiltingen, Piesport, Bernkastel, and Ürzig, wines which were once again worthy of the fine Riesling grape variety and the region. The secret was in concentrating on winemaking methods producing only 430 or 530 gallons per acre (40 or 50 hl/ha), from vineyards which contain vines growing on their own roots and up to 100 years old, instead of the usual 1,068 or even 1,388 gallons (100/130 hl). This movement, promoted by growers on the Central Mosel in particular, is now being emulated everywhere in the region.

The Ahr

North Rhine-Westphalia

Hilberath

Kalenborn

Weidenhardt
1,285 ft (392 m)

Alteheck

Esch

Holzweiler

Ringener

Wald

Vettelhoven

Bölingen

Assbacherhof   Karweiler

Lantershofen

Ringen

Bengen

Bad Neuenahr

Kirchdaun

Auf
Plattborn

Köhlerhof

Gimmigen

Lohrs-
dorf

Heppingen

Dernau

Marienthal

Ahrweiler

Bachem

Bad Neuenahr-
Ahrweiler

Ahr

Heimersheim

Ehlingen

Mayschoß

Walporzheim

Steinthalskopf
1,370 ft (417 m)

Neuenahrer Berg
1,115 ft (340 m)

Neuenahrer

Rhineland-Palatinate

Schloss Vehn

Löhndorf

Altenahr

Rech

Ahrweiler

Wald

Kreuzberg

Hornberg
1,275 ft (388 m)

Häuschen
1,660 ft (506 m)

Wald

50°30'N

Hengstberg
1,440 ft (439 m)

Vischelbach

Ahr

Pützfeld

Steinerberg
1,740 ft (531 m)

Nollsrück

Ramersbach

Brück

Ahrbrück

Staffel

Kesseling

Kesselinger Bach

Hilgesberg
1,575 ft (480 m)

1.2 miles (2 km)

	Großlage **Klosterberg**		
	Altenahrer Eck		Walporzheimer Gärkammer
	Mayschoßer Laacherberg		Walporzheimer Kräuterberg
	Mayschoßer Mönchberg		Ahrweiler Silberberg
	Recher Herrenberg		Bachemer Karlskopf
	Dernauer Pfarrwingert		Neuenahrer Schieferlay
	Marienthaler Klostergarten		Neuenahrer Sonnenberg
	Ahrweiler Stiftsberg		Heppinger Burggarten

An Island of Red Wine

An island of red wine in northern Germany—
such is the description aptly given to the valley
of the Ahr, a river which makes its way between
Koblenz and Bonn on the left of the Rhine,
passing through the volcanic landscape of the
Eifel area. Wooded hillsides, pretty villages, and
little towns like historic Ahrweiler and romantic
Mayschoß, are the setting for one of Germany's
smallest wine-growing regions: it is only around
18 miles (30 km) long, and less than 1,200 acres
(500 ha) in total are devoted to the growing
of vines.

Vines were being grown on the schist and
basalt soils in the center of the Ahr valley and
the gravel soil of the Lower Ahr as early as the
8th century. French monks planted the black
grapes of their native country here, just as they
did on the Rhine, and in contrast to almost all
other German viticultural regions Pinot Noir,
otherwise Spätburgunder, managed to hold its
own against the Riesling grape on the Ahr.

Even today, by far the larger part of the area is
stocked with black grapes, and Spätburgunder
alone accounts for the vines in over half the
vineyards between Sinzig and Altenahr. The
overall picture of the black grape monopoly of
the Ahr valley is completed by the Portugieser
variety, although it produces amounts barely
worth mentioning here, and Frühburgunder,
which has become increasingly prominent in
recent years, while Riesling has to be content
with less than ten percent of the entire vineyard
area, and the heavy bearers of other viticultural
areas, such as Müller-Thurgau, are merely tolerated here.

The Most Northerly Red Wines
in the World

Because of its northerly situation, the Ahr is
among the most demanding and climatically
difficult vine-growing areas in the world. Why,
then, do black grapes in particular do so well
here, hungry for the sun as they are? The answer
lies in the ideal situation of the steep slopes with
their schist soils. The southern aspect of the vineyards catches all the sun available, and the schist
stores its warmth to pamper the sensitive vines.
At the same time, the narrow valley and wooded
hilltops ensure that warmth is built up over the

vineyards, greatly to their benefit, and they also give effective protection from cold winds.

Different as the Ahr is from the other German vine-growing landscapes, there is one point in which, until very recently, it fitted into the general philosophy of viticulture in Germany. Here too, only thin and pale wines were made over several decades, often either sweetly insipid or massively acid. Record yields were achieved, sometimes of over 1,068 gallons per acre (100 hl/ha) of vineyard area, but the quality of the wines was better left unmentioned.

Yet the region undoubtedly has great potential for producing wonderful wines. They may not be as rounded or as high in alcohol as those from more southerly vineyards, but their richness of aroma and fruity character will satisfy high requirements. This is particularly true of those velvety Spätburgunder wines matured to dryness, which can sometimes even benefit by a time spent aging in the *barrique*, a demanding method.

The prerequisite for making such wines is of course a carefully chosen situation (sites in the central valley of the Ahr between Bad Neuenahr and Altenahr are the best), a favorable climate and a good season, careful work in the vineyard

and winery, and rigorous limitation of yields, although it is still very difficult to convince most winemakers of this. A small group of producers willing to experiment, however, has shown more than once over the last decade how good the red burgundies of the Ahr can be. It is a pity, but understandable, that year after year the wines made by these producers sell out within a very short time.

STRIVING FOR QUALITY

Werner Näkel was one of the first to realize that an improvement in quality was essential. Even in the early 1980s Näkel, a native of Dernau, was dissatisfied with the thin, sweet, undistinguished wines which most of his local colleagues were content to make from the Portugieser or Spätburgunder varieties. He had learned his trade on the red wines of the 1970s, which all struck him as being made too simply and with too much technology, matured too fast, and with poor keeping qualities, let alone having any ability to age well. Above all, he did not like their flavor.

Yet there were countless examples of the way a good red wine ought to look and taste—after

The sensitive Spätburgunder variety growing in an ideal situation at Ahrweiler.

all, the Germans were already importing large quantities of fine foreign wines at this time. However, the search for the right path to take was not an easy one. As early as 1983 Näkel was experimenting with the *barrique* maturation of wine, but his inexperience and the paucity of literature on the subject led to a series of setbacks, since the wines still had nothing like the requisite structure to overcome the influence on their flavor of the new wood of the casks.

Fortunately Näkel was not alone in his endeavors. A few of his colleagues began following his example in the mid-1980s, and at the beginning of the 1990s efforts to achieve quality were being made by a good dozen winemakers in the Ahr valley.

The first revolution was in the vineyard: planting out many clones of different kinds, adapting the cultivation of the vines to new requirements, clearing the area around them to get healthy grapes and consequently a deeper

The spa of Bad Neuenahr-Ahrweiler is also the center of the best-known German red wine growing district.

color and cleaner-tasting wines, thinning out to at most ten or twelve bunches of grapes a vine, restricting yield to 530 or often even to only 430 or 320 gallons per acre (50, 40, or 30 hl/ha), and rigorous selection of the best grapes in up to three or four picking processes in the autumn—all these were soon part of the repertory of all really serious producers.

However, Näkel does not care for terms like "natural" and "biological," although to a great extent he works on the same principles as ecologically orientated winemakers. He is concerned primarily to cultivate the vineyard in such a way as to produce the best possible grapes with the minimum strain on the environment.

Methods of working have undergone radical alteration in the winery too. Instead of following the old practice of making what were really just red white wines, fermentation now takes place on the must (sometimes even on the whole grapes), the wines mature in new or used wooden casks, and as a general principle there is rather less use of modern winery techniques. "A coarse filter is enough to keep any particles from floating in red wine," today's innovators say, to explain their abstention from many of the new high-tech devices which are now part of the basic equipment elsewhere.

These tireless workers first showed that their new approach really could be successful with the vintages of 1988 and 1990, when the season's weather played a part. By now the new style has been largely accepted. Beside the Meyer-Näkel estate, Deutzerhof, Kreuzberg, Adeneuer, Nelles, Stodden, Sonnenberg, and several other vineyards have made themselves a solid reputation. Genuine red wine is being made again in the north of Germany.

Wine-tasting at the Meyer-Näkel winery in Dernau.

Werner Näkel of the Meyer-Näkel estate.

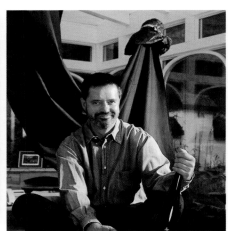

Wolfgang Hehle of Deutzerhof in Mayschoß.

Always good for a superior rating: the Deutzerhof estate in Mayschoß

Select Producers on the Ahr

J. J. Adeneuer***
Bad Neuenahr-Ahrweiler

22 acres (9 ha); 80,000 bottles • Wines: Spätburgunder and Frühburgunder, Portugieser, Dornfelder, from the Walporzheim →Gärkammer (a monopoly) and other vineyards

Since 1714 the miniature Gärkammer vineyard has been in the possession of the Adeneuer family estate, which has held a leading position in the region's winemaking trade since 1984. Thanks to reduced yields in its integrated viticulture the growths of this estate, which produces only red wine, have good concentration and a fine bouquet.

Deutzerhof—Cossmann-Hehle****–*****
Mayschoss

17 acres (7 ha); 50,000 bottles • Wines: Spätburgunder and Frühburgunder, Dornfelder, Portugieser, Riesling and Chardonnay from vineyards in Altenahr and Heimersheim, →Caspar C, →Grand Duc Select, Catharina C

After marrying into the Cossmann family estate Wolfgang Hehle, a former tax adviser, devoted himself entirely to its wines, introducing new momentum and innovative ideas. His Spätburgunder *barrique*-matured wines are now consistently among the best in the Ahr region. The *Trockenbeerenauslesen* and *Eiswein* made from the Riesling grape are also of top quality.

H. J. Kreuzberg***–****
Dernau

20 acres (8 ha); 45,000 bottles • Wines: →Spätburgunder and Frühburgunder, Portugieser, Dornfelder, Riesling from Dernau (→Pfarrwingert) and Bad Neuenahr (→Schieferlay, →Sonnenberg), →Spätburgunder Devon

The Kreuzberg brothers have made their estate one of the most famous in the Ahr region by virtue of skillful division of labor and a willingness to experiment in the winery. All their red wines are aged in wooden casks, and the best of them in the smaller *barrique*.

Meyer-Näkel****–*****
Dernau

32 acres (13 ha); 100,000 bottles • Wines: Spätburgunder and Frühburgunder, Dornfelder, Riesling from Dernau and Bad Neuenahr, →"S," →"G," Blauschiefer, →Illusion

A wide range of really top-quality wines, the best of them *barrique*-matured over a long period. Werner Näkel's methods include a natural approach to cultivation and strict selection in the vineyard. In the winery, Näkel is concerned to transfer the quality achieved in the vineyard to the bottle in as unadulterated a form as possible.

Nelles****
Heimersheim

12 acres (5 ha); 50,000 bottles • Wines: Spätburgunder and Frühburgunder, Portugieser, Domina, Riesling, Grauburgunder from vineyards in Heimersheim and Bad Neuenahr, the Triumvirat line: →Albus, →Clarus, →Ruber, →B, →Futura

The labels of this estate give prominence to the year of its first mention in the records, 1479, a date which illustrates the length of the family tradition. The estate's best wines today are matured in *barriques*, and both vineyard and winery work to avoid drastic methods. The top wines made by Nelles go under the overall name of Triumvirat.

Sonnenberg—Görres & Linden***
Bad Neuenahr-Ahrweiler

12 acres (5 ha); 50,000 bottles • Wines: Spätburgunder and Frühburgunder, Portugieser, Domina, Dornfelder, Riesling, Kerner from vineyards in Bad Neuenahr, →Schieferlay, →Sonnenberg and Ahrweiler, Tradition, Selection F.H.

Norbert Görres and Manfred Linden turned to viticulture only in 1980, but they soon acquired a high reputation beyond the Ahr region itself. Their wines are light and easy to drink, and they do not use *barriques* even to mature red wines.

The Mittelrhein

It was the Romans again who were responsible for planting the first vineyards at the foot of the Siebengebirge range. Much later the Franks extended these plantations. Many of the towns they founded have been connected with wine-making ever since, for instance Königswingert, now Königswinter, where grapes still grow near the ruins of Drachenfels, a popular tourist attraction. The vineyards of Oberdollendorf and Niederdollendorf were once cultivated by the Cistercians of the monastery of Heisterbach, now a ruin. The wines made here come from over 50 acres (24 ha) of land which have been reorganized and are part of the Petersberg Großlage group. Over a length of 30 miles (50 km) up the Rhine toward Koblenz, vine growing is successful only on the southern slopes of the right bank of the river. The best known winemaking villages here are Hammerstein and Leutesdorf. Vines are also grown at Ehrenbreitstein opposite the Deutsches Eck, and on the lower course of the Lahn, particularly in Weinähr and Oberndorf.

South of Koblenz and Lahnstein, not only does the Rhine display its full romantic beauty but the hillside vineyards here, some of them extremely steep, produce wines of better quality than those from further north. However, many of the old terraces cut into the slate slopes are very difficult to reach, and cultivating them is so cost-intensive that they have now been abandoned.

The largest vineyard of the Mittelrhein region is the Bopparder Hamm, running for four miles (6 km) down the left bank of the river, and with a full southern aspect. From the bend in the Rhine to St. Goarshausen there are steep vine-

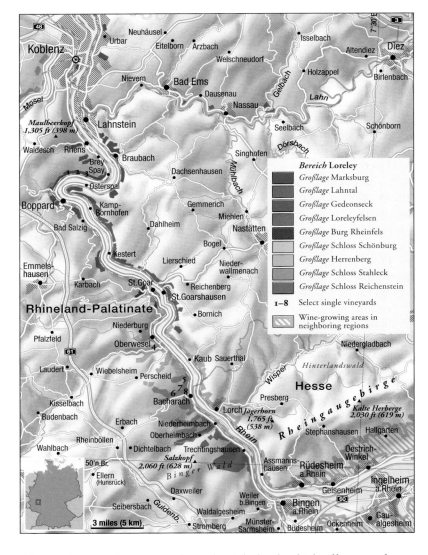

Bereich Loreley
- Großlage Marksburg
- Großlage Lahntal
- Großlage Gedeonseck
- Großlage Loreleyfelsen
- Großlage Burg Rheinfels
- Großlage Schloss Schönburg
- Großlage Herrenberg
- Großlage Schloss Stahleck
- Großlage Schloss Reichenstein

1–8 Select single vineyards

Wine-growing areas in neighboring regions

Select single vineyards
1 Mandelstein
2 Feuerley
3 Ohlenberg
4 Bernstein
5 Hahn
6 St. Jost
7 Wolfshöhle
8 Posten

yards on the right bank which offer more favorable conditions for the Riesling grape to ripen, while the best vineyards on the other bank lie opposite Kestert and at Burg Rheinfels. Only here does the left bank of the Rhine, with the valleys running off it, offer well-protected and sunny situations. The narrow, densely wooded valley of the Rhine and the broad surface of the river create the climatic prerequisites for vine growing in the Mittelrhein, but really outstanding wines can be produced only in the extreme south of the region.

The vineyards of the Mittelrhein and the Rheingau meet further along the right bank of the Rhine with its romantic castles, to the southeast; the first Rheingau vines grow at Lorchhausen, in sight of Bacharach, a place probably more visited by tourists than anywhere else in the Mittelrhein viticultural region, which on the left bank of the river extends to Bingerbrück.

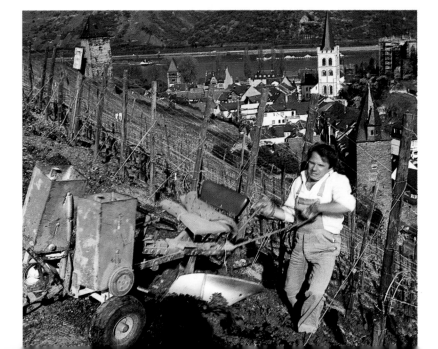

The Other Side of the Coin

Tourists visiting the border region between the Mittelrhein and Thurgau wine-growing areas are usually less interested in vineyards than in the fortresses, castles, romantic little towns, and the mysterious Lorelei, all of which have made this landscape a world-class tourist destination. Tourism may have brought benefits to the wine producers of the Mittelrhein (providing them with a guaranteed market for very little effort), but the other side of the coin is that the wine itself suffered: why go to the trouble of trying to make wines of high quality when tourists would drink anything on offer? But all that is in the past: today the producers of Sekt can buy their basic wines more cheaply in Italy and Spain, and consumers will no longer be fobbed off with poor wines of the kind made in the 1970s and 1980s.

About a dozen winemakers have seen the signs of the times. These viticulturalists have planted their vines with care on steep, south-facing vineyards in the bends of the Rhine and its lateral valleys, at Boppard, Oberwesel, Bacharach, and Steeg, and in the Kaub area on the right bank of the Rhine, and they make robust wines from the Riesling which covers three-quarters of the vineyard area.

Although the Mittelrhein used to be a much more important wine-growing region in past centuries—around 1900 there were still 4,940 acres (2000 ha) of vines under cultivation here, while today only 1,482 acres (600 ha) are cultivated—its wines are well on the way to making a fine name for themselves.

Rheinfels Castle high above St. Goar sponsored the organization of the *Großlage* vineyards on the left bank of the Rhine.

Opposite
Plowing steep vineyards like this one above Bacharach calls for skill and strength.

Select Producers of the Mittelrhein

Fritz Bastian****
Bacharach
23.5 acres (9.5 ha); 30,000 bottles • Wines: Riesling, Spätburgunder, Portugieser, Scheurebe from Bacharach vineyards (→Heyles'en Werth [a monopoly]), →Posten
The Bastians run the inn "Zum grünen Baum" (The Green Tree), and they also own the only island vineyard in Germany, the Heyles'en Werth. Their best wines are from the Posten vineyard.

Toni Jost, Hahnenhof***−****
Bacharach
30 acres (12 ha); 90,000 bottles • Wines: Riesling, Spätburgunder from Bacharach (→Hahn) and the Rheingau →(Wallufer Walkenberg)
Peter Jost also manages vineyards in the Rheingau producing grapes which are vinified in Bacharach. His wines in the *Spätlese* and *Auslese* ranges are full and strong, and the *edelsüß* variants are also excellent.

Martina & Dr. Randolf Kauer***−****
Bacharach
7 acres (3 ha); 20,000 bottles • Wines: Riesling from Bacharach (→Kloster Fürstental, Wolfshöhle) and Urbar (→Beulsberg)
Dry/medium-dry Rieslings made by biological methods.

Heinrich Müller***−****
Spay
15 acres (6 ha); 55,000 bottles • Wines: Riesling, Grauburgunder, Kerner, Spätburgunder from Boppard (Hamm, →Feuerlay, →Mandelstein)
One of the oldest wine-growing firms in Boppard.

TONI JOST
HAHNENHOF

2002
Wallufer Walkenberg
Riesling
Beerenauslese

ALC 9% RHEINGAU 375 ML
Gutsabfüllung Qualitätswein mit Prädikat 370190403
Weingut Toni Jost Hahnenhof D-55422 Bacharach

WEINGUT
DR. RANDOLF KAUER

2002
Riesling Kabinett Halbtrocken
Bacharacher Kloster Fürstental
Qualitätswein mit Prädikat · Erzeugerabfüllung
D-55422 Bacharach · Mainzer Straße 21
Öko-Kontrollstelle: DE-039
10.5% vol MITTELRHEIN 750 ml

WALTER PERLL

Qualitätswein mit Prädikat · A. P. Nr. 1671082-34-01
Erzeugerabfüllung
PRODUCE OF GERMANY
750 ml 10% vol

MITTELRHEIN
2000er
Bopparder Hamm Mandelstein
RIESLING SPÄTLESE
Halbtrocken
WEINGUT WALTER PERLL
D-56154 BOPPARD AM RHEIN
Ablass-Gasse 11
Telefon 06742/3671 · Fax 06742/3023

August Perll***−****
Bacharach
17 acres (7 ha); 90,000 bottles • Wines: Riesling, Spätburgunder from Boppard vineyards (→Feuerlay, →Mandelstein, Fässerlay, Ohlenberg)
The best Rieslings from Bopparder Hamm come from Lakes Mandelstein and Feuerlay.

Walter Perll***−****
Bacharach
15 acres (6 ha); 55,000 bottles • Wines: Riesling, Müller-Thurgau, Spätburgunder from the Bopparder Hamm (Mandelstein, →Fässerlay, Feuerlay, →Ohlenberg)
The best wines come from Fässerlay, where it is sometimes even possible to make *Beerenauslese* wines from Spätburgunder, and from Ohlenberg.

Ratzenberger****
Steeg
20 acres (8 ha); 55,000 bottles • Wines: Riesling, Spätburgunder, Müller-Thurgau from Bacharach (Wolfshöhle, Kloster Fürstental) and Steeg (→St. Jost)
Pressing the whole grapes, fermentation at a very cool temperature, and maturing in large wooden casks are processes producing clean, rich Rieslings.

Florian Weingart***−****
Spay
15 acres (6 ha); 85,000 bottles • Wines: Riesling, Müller-Thurgau, Grauburgunder from vineyards in Spay and Boppard (→Feuerlay, Ohlenberg, Engelstein)
One of the last three full-time viticulturalist families of Spay harvests some of the grapes for its Rieslings, which are clear as glass.

The Hotel Krone in picturesque Assmannshausen, where the Rheingau begins and where its best red wines are made.

Left
In the autumn of 1775 the grapes were harvested late at Schloss Johannisberg by mistake. According to the legend, this was the origin of Spätlese wines.

Right
The residential tower of Schloss Vollrads in Oestrich-Winkel. The estate, now under new management, is once again producing top-quality Rheingau wines.

Eberbach monastery, secularized in the Napoleonic period, is now part of the Hesse state vineyards managed from nearby Eltville, where the wines are also made. In addition, the red wine estate of Assmannshausen, where by common consent the best Spätburgunder grapes of the Rheingau are now pressed, the estate of Bensheim on the Bergstraße, and a winemaking business in Hochheim on the Main, are part of this small but nevertheless distinguished German wine empire.

JOHANNISBERG AND OTHER WINEMAKING CASTLES

It is to the Benedictines that Schloss Johannisberg, the other famous name of the Rheingau, owes its existence. The original monastery building, a foundation of the beginning of the 12th century, had only a moderate length of life. By 1716 it was in a state of dilapidation and was bought by

the princely abbey of Fulda, which demolished it and then replaced it with the present castle, visible from afar above the rows of vines in the single vineyard of the same name, both a landmark and the best-known architectural monument in the Rheingau.

Schloss Johannisberg was not only one of the first winemaking estates in the region, it was also here that the first pure-variety Riesling vineyard was planted in the early 18th century, amidst what had previously been the "red" or at least a predominantly mixed panorama of Rhenish vine growing. A century later, the estate's possessions were secularized under Napoleonic rule, and after the Vienna Congress of 1815 they passed into the hands of the Metternich family, whose descendants still live here. The landed property which used to belong to the castle is now owned by the firm of Oetker.

Together with the professional viticultural competence of the monks, the private interests of the old noble families formed the real backbone of the historical winemaking of the Rheingau. The lords of Schönborn, Vollrads, and Knyphausen, the princes of Hesse, and the princes of Prussia at Schloss Reinhartshausen worked at least as energetically as the monks to establish its reputation as a viticultural region.

Over a long period, the outstanding position of the Rheingau in German viticulture was also reflected in the progressive development of vineyard and winery technologies. The first wine filters were used here, it was here that *Spätlese* wines were "invented" and the selection of grapes with noble rot perfected, and one of the most famous schools of viticulture in the world—the Geisenheim research institute—indeed still is situated in the region.

Despite the famous past and the international renown of the wines of the Rheingau, which at the beginning of the 20th century were among the most expensive in Europe—even more expensive than claret, champagne, and burgundy—the decades after the Second World War saw this region of Germany, like others, suffering a deep identity crisis which affected the quality of its products. Even the famous monastic wine estates and those of the castles found it difficult to keep up with the rise in quality evident in other viticultural regions: the flagship of the Rheingau was close to foundering.

In recent years the situation has improved considerably, and Reinhartshausen, Vollrads, Schönborn, and Knyphausen may be well on the way to taking their place among the elite of the region again, and perhaps even among the top winemakers of Germany.

WINEGROWERS OF THE NOBILITY AND THE BOURGEOISIE

While in the 1920s the wines of the Rheingau could still fetch prices on the international market which made even the winemakers of Bordeaux and the great champagne houses green with envy, today that state of affairs is only a wistful memory. In the second half of the 20th century the history of the Rheingau, like that of almost all German wine-producing regions, was determined more by a policy of rationally managed mass production than by any concern for quality.

There has now been a return to something more like the higher standards of the past, at least in the making of *Qualität* wines, although that fact is not yet generally acknowledged. Obviously, expectations are particularly high in a viticultural region with such historic associations. Some uncertainty about the typical style of Rheingau Riesling still exists. First a flood of exaggeratedly dry wines with acid notes came on the market in reaction to the years of sweet wines, but at present stronger medium-dry wines are being made. This may be a logical development, but if residual sugar is to act as a

substitute for fullness and density it is as difficult as it ever was to judge the right balance. Winemakers almost find it easier to satisfy the rising demand for *edelsüß* growths with fine *Beerenauslese* and *Trockenbeerenauslese* wines, or even *Eiswein*.

Progress in the region today, however, is being made not so much by the old-established noble estates as by family-owned vineyards. Names like those of Gunter Künstler, Bernhard Breuer, Robert Weil, Diefenhardt, Querbach, Eser, Johannishof, Lang, and Ress have long denoted quality and have produced fine growths, something which can be said only with reservations of the Johannisberg, Knyphausen, Oetinger, Schönborn, Langwerth, and Löwenstein estates. It was also the bourgeoisie who strongly promoted discussion of the vineyard classification system, although the wines they have introduced as their "First Growths" in recent years have tended to prove quite disappointing in one way or another.

Heinrich Heine's pious wish was not a modest one, for in his time Schloss Johannisberg was at the height of its fame.

THE NAHE

The Nahe winemaking region appears at first glance to have more contradictions in it than the Mosel. At the beginning of the 20th century the wines from Bad Kreuznach, Schlossböckelheim, Niederhausen, and Dorsheim—for the viticultural region of the Nahe as it exists today was created only by the 1971 Wine Law—were at least as famous and sought after as those of the neighboring Rheingau. After the Second World War this region too concentrated almost entirely on mass production, doubled the area under cultivation by planting vines even in valleys and on level land which was not particularly suitable for them, and sought its salvation in the production of wines for blending to make the famous—or infamous—Liebfraumilch, and other popular and often even more dubious exports of German post-war viticulture.

As in the neighboring Rheinhessen area, a kind of mass hysteria quickly came to dominate the entire viticultural panorama of the region. It is no coincidence that its southern border merges so seamlessly with the vineyards of the Rheinhessen hinterland that the frontier is barely visible to the impartial eye. The result of this development is the fact, almost unique in Germany, that while individual estates on the Nahe may have a high

Traisen, southwest of Bad Kreuznach, little more than 74 acres (30 ha), is regarded as one of the best wine-making communities on the Nahe.

reputation, and some are even among the best in the country, the Nahe as an entire region, unlike the Mosel, Pfalz, Rheingau, or Franconia, is almost unknown to the general public, or at least seems to have little character.

Export Wines in Crisis

To meet consumer demand, over a long period only small quantities of dry or medium-dry wines were made here, although it is in that area that one of the strengths of the region could lie. The mild climate and the many different soil formations are ideal for growing and developing Reisling in particular—and Riesling accounts for over a quarter of the vineyard area, which amounts to a good 11,115 acres (4,500 ha). However, other varieties, for instance Müller-Thurgau, which covers only a slightly smaller area than Riesling, Silvaner, Kerner, Scheurebe, and Grauburgunder, have not yet been able to establish their own image, and are usually submerged in the anonymity of mass-market brand names.

As long as the tankers of Liebfraumilch and other popular "delicacies" were still driving all over the world at regular intervals, this lack of image and individuality could not do the viti-culture of the region much harm. Or such at least was the idea at the time, but the easy profits from the success of sweet wines did not pay off in the end. As other wine-producing

Select single vineyards
1. Pittermännchen
2. Goldloch
3. Brückes
4. Krötenpfuhl
5. Bastei
6. Hermannsberg
7. Hermannshöhle

Select Producers in the Nahe

CRUSIUS*—****
TRAISEN

31 acres (12.5 ha); 90,000 bottles • Wines: Riesling, Weißburgunder, Müller-Thurgau, Spätburgunder from vineyards in locations including Taisen, Schlossböckelheim, Niederhausen, Norheim
Although Peter Crusius largely converted his vinification procedures to the use of stainless steel tanks in the 1990s, the better Riesling qualities are still matured in wooden casks. His *edelsüß* qualities in particular are among the top wines of the Nahe.

HERMANN DÖNNHOFF**—*****
OBERHAUSEN

37 acres (15 ha); 100,000 bottles • Wines: Riesling, Grauburgunder and Weißburgunder from Oberhausen (→Brücke, Felsenberg, Leistenberg), Niederhausen (Hermannshöhle), Schlossböckelheim (Felsenberg), and Norheim, estate Riesling
Helmut Dönnhoff shows remarkable skill in bringing out the characteristics of the various *terroirs*—the family has owned plots in the best vineyards for generations. Dönnhoff restricts winery work to the minimum, treating the wines as gently as possible. They are matured in oak casks, without fining agents, and sweet reserve is used only for the simplest qualities. Only the *edelsüß* wines, in which Dönnhoff is regarded as a leading specialist, are fermented in small stainless steel vessels.

EMRICH-SCHÖNLEBER**
MONZINGEN

36 acres (14.5 ha); 110,000 bottles • Wines: Riesling, Grauburgunder and Weißburgunder, Kerner, Rivaner from estates in Monzingen
Because of its sheltered position, Monzingen has the benefit of a milder, drier climate than the rest of the Nahe, and Werner Schönleber exploits these natural conditions to make top-quality Rieslings.

HAHNMÜHLE*—****
MANNWEILER-CÖLLN

23 acres (9.5 ha); 60,000 bottles • Wines: Riesling, Traminer, Silvaner, Weißburgunder, Spätburgunder from vineyards in Oberndorf, Alsenz, Cölln, estate wines, →Silvaner Secco
Riesling and Traminer are probably the most unusual combination of vines grown on Martina and Peter Linxweiler's estate, particularly when they are planted together and ecologically cultivated and picked. Acidity in the wines made from them is generally very marked.

KRUGER-RUMPFF*—****
MÜNSTER-SARMSHEIM

49 acres (20 ha); 150,000 bottles • Wines include: Riesling, Silvaner, burgundy varieties from vineyards in Münster-Sarmsheim (→Dautenpflänzer, Pittersberg, Rheinberg, Kapellenberg)
Stefan and Cornelia Rumpf manage not only one of the best wine-growing estates in the Nahe region, but also a famous inn. The Rumpfs' wines, always straightforward, are particularly good in the higher *Prädikat* grades, where the typical rather rustic acidity is tempered by alcohol, sweet reserve, or extracts.

PRINZ ZU SALM-DALBERG*
WALLHAUSEN

28.5 acres (11.5 ha); 70,000 bottles • Wines include: Riesling, Grauburgunder, Spätburgunder from vineyards in Wallhausen and Roxheim, estate Riesling, Prinz Salm Qualitätsweine
Michael Prince of Salm-Salm is not only one of the famous winemakers of the Nahe, but also Federal German chairman of the V.D.P. and a politician. The range of wines produced at Schloss Wallhausen, where biological cultivation is practised, is of good quality and easy to survey. Vineyard details are given only on the labels of the best wines made by the firm.

SCHLOSSGUT DIEL*—*****
BURG LAYEN

42 acres (17 ha); 120,000 bottles • Wines: Riesling, Grauburgunder, Weißburgunder, Spätburgunder from vineyards in Dorsheim (Goldloch, →Pittermännchen, Burgberg), estate wine Diel de Diel, →Victor
The Rieslings made by the controversial winemaker and wine writer Armin Diel, particularly those from the Pittermännchen vineyard with its slatey soil, are model examples of wines from the Nahe.

BÜRGERMEISTER WILLI SCHWEINHARDT
NACHFAHREN—****
LANGENLONSHEIM

80 acres (32.5 ha); 180,000 bottles • Wines include: Riesling, Weißburgunder, Grauburgunder, Chardonnay, Spätburgunder, Portugieser from vineyards in Langenlonsheim, →Scala
One of the largest and at the same time best firms in the region (an unusual combination). As well as making white wines fermented in steel or plastic tanks, Schweinhardt is one of the few German producers to be experimenting with Cabernet Sauvignon.

Gutenberg on the Gräfenbach, with other viticultural villages, lies in a lateral valley of the Nahe running northwest.

The Bastei lies at the foot of the Roter Fels, a massive porphyry cliff near Traisen. It is the best vineyard in the community, and its grapes make remarkably complex Rieslings with a mineral note.

countries responded to the change in consumer taste, as well as competing in price with their now more popular product, these brands found that they were experiencing setbacks on the international markets. As a result, the Nahe seems to have suffered even more economic problems than other regions. Quite recently the largest winemakers' cooperative of the area was forced to give up its independence as it was subsumed under the roof of the Mosel cooperative, nor did the state viticultural estates in Niederhausen-Schlossböckelheim survive the crisis.

SOME OUTSTANDING WINES

The efforts and courage of a small group of leading winemakers within the regional V.D.P. association is all the more admirable. Once again they seek top quality in the wines they now produce, and they lead the way in the discussion of vineyard classification. Because for a long time the Wine Law did not allow them to put descriptions such as *erster Lage* or *grand cru* on their labels, they introduced through voluntary agreement among their members the principle that only well-established vineyard names classified within the area may appear on labels, while all other products must be marketed as simple estate wines. They dispense entirely with any mention of *Großlage* names for their wines, and indeed the practice of naming a *Großlage* has recently come under criticism.

The Nahe does have potential for the production of top quality wines, particularly because the wine styles of the three most important subdivisions of the region, the Upper Nahe, the area around Bad Kreuznach, and finally the Lower Nahe are clearly distinct from each other.

Steep, rocky hillsides leaving little space for vines are typical of the landscape along the course of the Nahe above Bad Kreuznach. The porphyry formations and the river are valuable here for the storage of warmth, and ensure the necessary conditions in which the grapes can ripen and give the wines their characteristically delicate fruity character. Viticultural centers acknowledged to have the best vineyards are Schlossböckelheim, Niederhausen, and Traisen, and the names of vineyards such as the Traisener Bastei, Niederhausener Herrmannshöhle and Hermannsberg, Oberhäuser Brücke, and Schlossböckelheimer Felsenberg are good references in themselves.

The natural conditions in and around Bad Kreuznach are very different. Here deep, heavy soil predominates, and the wines are denser and more powerful in style, making what is clearly a more southern general impression. The best vineyards are the Kreuznacher Brückes, Krötenpfuhl, and Kahlenberg, but unfortunately most of the once famous winemaking estates owned by the town of Kreuznach seem to have allowed the qualititative improvements of the region in recent years pass them by.

Viticulture does not become interesting again until we reach the Lower Nahe and its side valleys. The river, here flowing north and straight toward the Rhine, is accompanied on its eastern bank by the extensive vineyards of Rheinhessen, while the hillside vineyards of the Nahe region on the western bank are to some extent hidden behind hills, villages, and church towers.

The side valleys of the Nahe in particular, with their sunny south aspects, offer the Riesling grape optimum conditions, as the Dorsheim

vineyards of Pittermännchen and Goldloch, and the Münster vineyards of Pittersberg and Dautenpflänzer brilliantly show. Once again, however, there is an enormous range of diversity in the styles of wines made from vineyard to vineyard, and even from one winemaker to another, with Riesling sometimes tending toward the Mosel style, sometimes toward the neighboring Mittelrhein. The question of whether the wines of the Lower Nahe find their ideal expression in the dry, the medium-dry, or the very sweet range is much discussed by the leading winemakers of the region.

The fermentation tanks in the castle estate of Diehl in Burg Layen are artistically embellished. The estate's Auslese wines, made from Riesling grapes from the Dorsheimer Goldloch vineyard, are among the best on the Nahe.

Michael Prince of Salm-Salm, president of the V.D.P.

Helmut Dönnhoff, a leading viticulturist in Oberhausen on the Nahe.

RHEINHESSEN

Rheinhessen has a total vineyard area of over 64,000 acres (26,000 ha), divided into 24 *Großlagen* and an impressive 432 *Einzellagen*, and with yields per acre of only a little more than 1,068 gallons (100 hl/ha) (quite modest by comparison with the Mosel, Württemberg, and the Pfalz), it is indisputably the largest wine-producing region of Germany. Grapes and wine seem to be present everywhere, and there are only three communities in the entire region which do not have their own vineyards.

Rheinhessen is more firmly connected with Liebfraumilch than any other viticultural region, and indeed the vineyard which gives that famous mass-produced brand its name is on its territory: the Liebfrauenstift-Kirchenstück in Worms, a genuine *clos* within the walls of the collegiate church of the Virgin Mary. Large quantities of this blend of varieties and wines from different districts have continued to be produced in Rheinhessen in recent decades. It is the only such blend allowed by the German Wine Law to describe itself as a *Qualitätswein*.

Internationally, Liebfraumilch has become synonymous with German wine in general, and has undoubtedly contributed to the decline in

its reputation. That being so, it was almost a symbol of a radical new start in German viticulture when the vineyard, which had fallen into neglect, was put back into good order a few years ago by the energetic efforts of a famous Nierstein winemaking estate.

It was also in Rheinhessen that the unfortunate philosophy of the German Wine Law in grouping vineyards into *Großlagen* found its most notorious expression: the *Großlagen* of Oppenheimer Krötenbrunnen and the neighboring Niersteiner Gutes Domtal may stand today as perfect examples of a wrong-headed policy, which ultimately achieved nothing but to destroy any justification for the wines of these *Großlagen* to stake a claim to quality for almost two decades.

BEYOND LIEBFRAUMILCH

Fortunately Rheinhessen has much more to offer than Liebfraumilch, Krötenbrunnen, and Gutes Domtal. Today, outstanding wines are being made again, in particular on what is known as the Rhine Front, where the Rheinhessen plateau falls steeply to the left bank of the river between Nackenheim in the north and Alsheim in the south. Rieslings which can easily hold their own with the best products of the Rheingau, the Mosel, and the Pfalz grow on the red sandstone of Niersteim, a schist formation resulting from a geological rift which runs right through the Rhine valley. They combine the elegance of wines from the north with the power and spiciness of southern wines.

As a result the best vineyards of the region, such as the Rothenberg in Nackenheim, Pettenthal, Brudersberg, Hipping, Ölberg, and Orbel in Nierstein, have re-established themselves on a firm foundation in recent years. Oppenheim, too, has a consistently top-quality vineyard in the Sackträger, where the soils are no longer red sandstone schist formations, but consist of loess and calcareous marl.

Few people know what a wide spectrum of vines Rheinhessen grows. Most of the postwar crosses were raised at the Alzeyer vine-breeding institute, and varieties such as Scheurebe and Dornfelder, which attracted attention during the recent move toward making red wines, come from its trial grounds. Because of this extensive range of classic grape varieties and various crosses, no one variety can be said to dominate the viticulture of Rheinhessen. Müller-Thurgau grows on about 20 percent of the vineyard area, Silvaner occupies some 15 percent, but all the other varieties—Riesling, Kerner, Scheurebe, Bacchus, Portugieser, Faberrebe, Morio-Muskat, Spätburgunder, Huxelrebe, Ortega, and Siegerreber—occupy positions somewhere below the 10 percent mark.

Finally, it should not be forgotten that environmentally friendly and ecological viticulture was first introduced on German soil in Rheinhessen in the 1970s, and such methods have found many followers in the region since.

Select single vineyards
(see map opposite)

1	Pettenthal
2	Hipping
3	Ölberg
4	Sackträger
5	Geyersberg
6	Hubacker
7	Bürgel

Nierstein has some excellent sites on the Rhine, including the Brudersberg, Hipping, Pettenthal, and Ölberg vineyards, and a few leading winemakers are active there as well.

The Hessische Bergstraße (Hessian Mountain Road)

As a wine-growing area, the Bergstraße comprises the vineyard slopes on the borders of the Odenwald, between Darmstadt in the north and Weinheim in the south, where the soils and the climate are very suitable for viticulture.

The rugged terrain makes the steep vineyards difficult and cost-intensive to work, and there are many economic problems in cultivating them. Consequently almost 90 percent of winegrowers supply the largest of the regional cooperatives, in Heppenheim. If we remember also that the Bensheim estate alone cultivates around ten percent of the entire vineyard area, and that most of the wine produced stays in southern Hesse, it is obvious why wines made on the Bergstraße are almost unknown outside the region.

The strength of the Bergstraße lies in its Rieslings, which approach the quality of Rheingau Rieslings, and in its burgundy varieties. Although production here is restricted to two groups of varieties and kinds of wines, the great diversity of the local vineyards and soils is expressed in many different nuances. The Bergstraße Rieslings, most of which grow in the higher vineyards, have less acidity than in more northerly regions and generally have a more mineral character, which in turn varies between the granite and sandstone soils on which the vines grow. Burgundy

varieties ripen on lower-lying plots, some with very deep loessial soils, and differ from their cousins made in Baden chiefly in their lower alcohol content.

The fact that almost no winegrowers on the Bergstraße market their own products, and cooperatives dominate the scene, has done little to encourage the development of quality wines in the area. Over the years, only the state-run vineyards and one or two private winemakers have succeeded in producing wines which can claim to be of high quality.

STAATSWEINGUT BERGSTRASSE*–****
BENSHEIM**
94 acres (38 ha); 250,000 bottles
• *Wines: Riesling, Grauburgunder, Weißburgunder, Spätburgunder, Gewürztraminer from vineyards in Heppenheim (→Centgericht, Steinkopf), Schönberg, Bensheim (Kalkgasse, Streichling)*

SIMON-BÜRKLE*
ZWINGENBERG**
40 acres (16 ha); 80,000 bottles
• *Wines: Riesling, Weißburgunder, Grauburgunder, Silvaner, Spätburgunder, Lemberger, and Cabernet Sauvignon from the northern Bergstraße*

HESSISCHE BERGSTRAßE
Bereich **Starkenburg**

■ *Großlage* Rott
■ *Großlage* Wolfsmagen
□ *Großlage* Schlossberg
◆ Single vineyard not part of a *Großlage* group

BADISCHE BERGSTRAßE

1–2 Select single vineyards

Select single vineyards

1 Centgericht
2 Steinkopf

THE HEART OF THE AREA: NACKENHEIM TO DIENHEIM

No other viticultural region of Germany contains such great contrasts and differences of quality between its various districts as Rheinhessen. In the past it was notable almost exclusively for the mass production of wine and certain new strains of grapes, some of them of dubious quality and apparently bred with a view not so much to the quality of the wine as to at a kind of clinically clean production on an industrial scale. There are good reasons why the unspeakable Liebfraumilch is so firmly linked to the name of the region.

Nonetheless, a number of top winemakers producing wines of high quality have attracted attention in Rheinhessen in recent years. This trend begins on the excellent argillaceous slate soils of the Rhine Front, where some of the best vineyards in the region are found. On the steep slopes of the Rhine rift between Nackenheim and Dienheim such estates as Gunderloch, Heyl zu Herrnsheim, and Sankt Antony have shown for years that they are among the absolute elite of German viticulture, and houses like Schneider, Seebrich, and Kühling-Gillot consistently produce wines of high quality. Unfortunately, the poor image of Rheinhessen wines in general has so far made it difficult for the producers to market these products adequately, or to get suitable prices for them.

There are other remarkably good vineyards, for instance in the area between Bechtheim, Westhofen (particularly the Aulerde vineyard), and Flörsheim-Dalheim on the border with the Pfalz, where another group of leading wine producers has established itself, with names including Keller, Groebe, Schales, and Wittmann. It is true that in the hinterland of Rheinhessen top-quality wines are few and far between, but with a certain amount of effort good to very good wines can be made here, as they also can in the north, in the once-famous vineyards of Bingen and Ingelheim. Here, however, the policy of earning money quickly and easily from the tanker wine trade still predominates. It is an attitude which may also endanger future efforts to improve the image of Rheinhessen.

SELECT PRODUCERS IN RHEINHESSEN

BRÜDER DR. BECKER***—****
LUDWIGSHÖHE
28 acres (11.5 ha); 80,000 bottles • Wines include: Riesling, Silvaner, Scheurebe, burgundy varieties from vineyards in Dienheim and Ludwigshöhe
In the 1970s Helmut Pfeffer was one of the first Germany viticulturalists to practice biological winemaking, at the same time proving that such methods did not necessarily mean a lower quality of wine. His daughter Lotte is continuing his work with the same energy. Recently the estate has tended to return to making medium-dry wines.

K. F. GROEBE***
BIEBESHEIM
17 acres (7 ha); 50,000 bottles • Wines include: Riesling, Silvaner, Grauburgunder, Spätburgunder from vineyards in Westhofen (→Aulerde)
Although the Aulerde vineyard in Westhofen is not on the famous Rhine Front, its calcareous soil makes it an excellent site. Friedrich Groebe presses his best wines from its grapes. Grauburgunder and Spätburgunder wines of reliable good quality are marketed as *Tafelwein*.

GUNDERLOCH****
NACKENHEIM
31 acres (12.5 ha); 70,000 bottles • Wines include: Riesling, Silvaner from the →Nackenheimer Rothenberg vineyard, also from →Pettenthal and →Hipping in Nierstein, →Jean Baptiste
Since the middle of the 1980s Agnes and Fritz Hasselbach have brought their estate gradually into the top rank of

wine producers in Rheinhessen. Their success was founded on the possession of large areas in the leading vineyards of Rothenberg, Pettenthal, and Hipping. The Rothenberg site in particular, with its argillaceous slate soil, regularly produces excellent Rieslings with plenty of fruit, bouquet, and a firm, well-structured body. Their travels in other winemaking countries persuaded the Hasselbachs to modernize their vineyard work and winery techniques. One of their wines is called Jean Baptiste, in reference to Zuckmayer's play *Der fröhliche Weinberg* (The Merry Vineyard), which is a tribute to Carl Gunderloch, founder of the estate.

LOUIS GUNTRUM***
NIERSTEIN
49 acres (20 ha); 200,000 bottles • Wines include: Riesling, Müller-Thurgau, Silvaner, Scheurebe from many vineyards in Nierstein and Oppenheim, Guntrum Classic, Villa Guntrum, Louis Philipp
As a large-scale winery this old-established Nierstein firm did not enjoy a particularly good reputation for the quality of its wines. However, there has been a change since the estate began concentrating on the growths from its own vineyards—it is sole owner of a number of them. The Oppenheim wines in particular, including some made from Gewürztraminer and Silvaner, are of a good to very good standard.

FREIHERR HEYL ZU HERRNSHEIM***—****
NIERSTEIN
46 acres (18.5 ha); 180,000 bottles • Wines: Riesling, Silvaner, Müller-Thurgau, burgundy varieties from

vineyards in Nierstein (→Brudersberg, →Pettenthal, →Ölberg, Hipping, Orbel), →Liebfrauenstift Kirchenstück, →Arcadia

Peter von Weymarn made the Heyl estate not only one of the top winemaking estates in Rheinhessen, but one of the leading firms working with ecological methods in the whole of Germany. The best wines, which bear their vineyard names, are entirely fermented and matured in large wooden casks. Since the sale of the estate to the Ahr family, Markus Ahr and the estate manager Michael Burgdorf have continued to run the business in Weymarn's spirit.

KELLER****
FLÖRSHEIM-DALSHEIM
32 acres (13 ha); 120,000 bottles • Wines: Riesling, burgundy varieties, Huxelrebe from vineyards in Dalsheim (→Hubacker), Niederflörsheim, and Monsheim
The fact that the estate of Klaus and Hedwig Keller is among those to have won most awards in Germany might appear something of a paradox from the point of view of any classification of vineyards—which only goes to prove that the winemaker's feeling for quality counts for a great deal in viticulture. The Hubacker Rieslings are among the best of the estate's wines. The burgundy varieties are also remarkable.

KRUG'SCHER HOF***
GAU-ODERNHEIM
136 acres (55 ha); 250,000 bottles • Wines: Chardonnay, Weißburgunder, Spätburgunder, Riesling, Menger-Krug Sekt
The real center of the Menger-Krug business is the estate of Motzenbäcker at Deidenheim in the Pfalz, but the majority of its vineyards lie here in Rheinhessen, where most of the family's famous Sekts are also made. Since the middle of the 1980s Chardonnay has been grown for use in making Sekt and as a single-variety still wine—and the occasional *edelsüß* specimens are also remarkable.

KÜHLING-GILLOT****
BODENHEIM
22 acres (9 ha); 70,000 bottles • Wines: Riesling, Grauburgunder, Scheurebe, Portugieser, Spätburgunder and others, from vineyards in Oppenheim and Bodenheim, Sekt
The estate of Gabi and Roland Gillot dates from the 18th century. The Gillots' wines, particularly the *edelsüß* growths and the *barrique*-matured burgundies, are among the best in Rheinhessen, and the inn managed by Gabi Gillot makes its guests very comfortable.

MICHEL-PFANNEBECKER***
FLOMBORN
29 acres (11.8 ha); 70,000 bottles • Wines: Silvaner, Riesling, burgundy varieties, Müller-Thurgau from vineyards in Westhofen and Flomborn
This estate in Flomborn, where excellent Rieslings are made from the grapes of the Westhofener Steingrube, shows that the vineyards of Westhofen can make outstanding wines. The white burgundy varieties and the Chardonnay are also above average.

RAPPENHOF—DR. MUTH**−***
ALSHEIM
128.5 acres (52 ha); 300,000 bottles • Wines include: Riesling, burgundy varieties, Chardonnay, Kerner from vineyards in Alsheim, Diensheim, Guntersblum, Oppenheim and Nierstein
The estate of Reinhard Muth, formerly chairman of the German Winegrowers' Association, passed into the hands of his son Klaus some years ago. Muth was one of the pioneers of Chardonnay in Germany, using *barriques* for fermentation.

SANKT ANTONY***−*****
NIERSTEIN
54 acres (22 ha); 160,000 bottles • Wines: Riesling, Silvaner, etc., from vineyards in Nierstein (→Ölberg, →Hipping, →Pettental, →Orbel, Rosenberg, Heiligenbaum, Paterberg), Vom Rotliegenden
Alexander Michalsky makes delicately elegant wines with concentrated extracts on the estate originally founded by the Gutehoffnung works and now part of the M.A.N. company. With a wide range of Rieslings from the vineyards of the "Rotliegend" area, as it is called, Michalsky's business is one of the three best in Rheinhessen, and is among the elite viticultural estates of the whole of Germany.

SCHALES****
FLÖRSHEIM-DALHEIM
99 acres (40 ha); 400,000 bottles • Wines include: Riesling, Müller-Thurgau, Weißburgunder, Spätburgunder from vineyards in Dalsheim, →Trullo, Schales Selection
The Schales brothers are among the best winemakers in Rheinhessen. Their Trullo is a blend of Weißburgunder, Kerner, and Riesling grapes. Their *edelsüß* and *Eiswein* products are also good.

GEORG ALBRECHT SCHNEIDER***−****
NIERSTEIN
43 acres (17.5 ha); 90,000 bottles • Wines include: Riesling, Müller-Thurgau, Kerner, Silvaner from vineyards in Nierstein (→Orbel, →Hipping, →Ölberg, →Pettenthal and others)
When this traditional Nierstein estate moved to larger premises and changed its winery methods to fermentation in stainless steel tanks, its wines improved noticeably. Georg Schneider's Rieslings from the best vineyards of Nierstein, and his Grauburgunder from the Paterberg, are well above average in quality.

HEINRICH SEEBRICH***
NIERSTEIN
25 acres (10 ha); 80,000 bottles • Wines include: Riesling, Müller-Thurgau, Kerner, Silvaner, Dornfelder, Spätburgunder from vineyards in Nierstein (→Ölberg, →Hipping)
Heinrich Seebrich works with the same gentle methods in both vineyard and winery, and sets much store by the early bottling of his *Prädikat* wines, which will then mature in bottle before they are put on the market.

VILLA SACHSEN***
BINGEN
41 acres (16.5 ha); 130,000 bottles • Wines include: Riesling, Müller-Thurgau, Kerner, Silvaner from vineyards in Bingen (→Scharlachberg)
The Villa Sachsen estate was in deep trouble before Prince Salm, master of Schloss Wallhausen in the Nahe region, and his team took over its management and became co-owners. Today the firm is again doing well with its Rieslings from the once-famous vineyard of Scharlachberg in Bingen.

WITTMANN****
WESTHOFEN
62 acres (25 ha); 130,000 bottles • Wines include: Riesling, Müller-Thurgau, Silvaner, Huxelrebe, Spätburgunder from vineyards in Bechtheim and Westhofen (→Aulerde)
Although the estate has for some time been among the leading group of wine makers in Rheinhessen—and those using ecological methods—it was only recently accepted into the V.D.P. Its wines, particularly the Rieslings from vineyards in Westhofen, show that even beyond the Rhine Front the region has great potential for quality.

THE BIOLOGICAL HEYL ZU HERRNSHEIM ESTATE

The mediocre standards of winemaking in Rheinhessen during the 1970s may help to account for the fact that the movement toward ecological viticulture in Germany first developed in that area. Any producers who hoped to rise above the crowd making standard Liebfraumilch were obliged to draw attention to themselves, if only by adding new descriptions to the label. Another cause of this trend may have been that winemaking in Rheinhessen had gone too far in the use of technology and chemicals, and younger viticulturalists—inspired by the revolutionary ideas of environmentalists in the Rhine-Main area in general—thought they should make wines differently in response to the products of conventional vineyard and winery work. However that may be, the early stages of the ecological winemaking movement were motivated not so much by concern for the quality of the product as by general political and ideological concepts.

Nonetheless, the estate of Freiherr Heyl zu Herrnsheim in Nierstein has provided proof over many years that there are also other and far more personal reasons for turning to natural winemaking, reasons which can be reconciled with the idea of qualitatively excellent production. The motivation of Peter von Weymarn, who was then running the estate, was of a very personal nature. As a scientist, he had begun thinking about his own diet and making radical changes in it, and ultimately he could hardly avoid applying his own health-conscious attitude to the products and operating methods of his firm.

However, there are also other reasons why Heyl is an ecological vineyard of a kind not typical of German conditions, with its relatively large size and its established place among the best winemaking firms in Germany. From the first, the idea of quality played a dominant part. The wine was to be produced with ecological factors in mind to make it even better: it was to be a genuinely top-quality product.

Markus Ahr, the present head of the firm of Heyl, has a philosophy of quality which continues from Weymarn's ideas. It is a long way from the dogmatism of purely ecological doctrine. His version of natural viticulture rests mainly on three principles. He does not use synthetic fertilizers, only compost and green manure. As a substitute for herbicides, the soil is mechanically worked. His third principle is to refrain from using pesticides and fungicides—only Bordeaux mixture, a solution of copper sulfate, is permissible under the strict regulations of the European Union.

The young vineyard owner is of course also aware of the drawbacks of ecological viticulture, and in many respects has to agree with its critics. Growing vines by biological methods means driving machinery around the vineyards too often, and the tractors compact the ground. In addition, copper accumulates in the soil as time goes on, and—so the critics say—there is therefore still no sound ecological balance, particularly as frequent driving through the vineyards involves environmental pollution.

To Ahr, the biological arguments of recent years have been something of a distraction from truly relevant enological problems, allowing a series of dubious practices and such technological devices as concentrators, or the addition of enzymes and aromatic substances, to creep into the world of wine through the back door unnoticed. Nonetheless, he plans to continue with

Left
The interior of the estate, which dates back to the 16th century.

Right
The green manure, now often sown between the rows in certain regions by growers who prefer biological methods of viticulture, is cut with this mowing machine.

environmentally conscious methods at Heyl zu Herrnsheim. "Our estate has such a good name for the quality of its wines that on purely economic grounds I could have allowed myself to stop working with biological viticulture. But then I would probably have had to wave goodbye to some of my claims to quality as well!"

The Ahr family has now taken over the famous estate in Rheinhessen, but Markus Winfried Ahr and the estate manager Michael Burgdorf continue to practice methods of biological viticulture, and pursue a policy aiming for quality.

Ecological viticulture

Ecological viticulture, like biological agriculture in general, refrains from using chemical synthetic fertilizers, weedkillers, insecticides, fungicides, and acaricides. Instead it prefers a holistic approach involving the maintenance of soils and pure groundwater, the protection of species and the landscape, and ecological cultivation and waste disposal. The soil in the vineyard is at the root of everything. Ecological viticulturalists use organic materials to activate, encourage, and feed it. The principal role is played by compost, made from grapeskins (MARC), stable manure, chaff, straw, and vegetable matter. Often the vineyards have to bring in raw materials from outside, since only a very few concerns can build up a self-contained agricultural cycle of their own. However, some vineyards do keep pure-bred livestock so as to have valuable manure available.

In ecological viticulture sowing green plants among the vines is particularly important, and is the counterpart of the rotation of crops in biological agriculture. The dense root systems running through the soil have a positive long-term effect on the wealth of micro-organisms present. The various mixtures sown—leguminous plants, clovers, grain, grasses, and herbs, mown and used as mulch two or three times a year—serve as excellent green manure and help the formation of humus. The flowers bring insects back to the vineyards, and beneficial insects keep down the populations of red spider and vine moth. Green plants prevent erosion of the vineyards, and are a factor in maintaining the water balance. The practice must, however, be precisely adjusted to the conditions of the particular situation, and long-term green planting is not suitable everywhere.

In general the difference from conventional viticulture consists of a fundamental approach, not just to the cultivation of the soil but also to tending the vines and protecting them from disease. European viticulture has to face the constant threat of powdery mildew (*Oidium*) and downy mildew (*Plasmopara*). While winegrowers using traditional methods rely from the first on chemical substances, ecological winegrowers aim to reduce the risks of infection. To achieve this objective they begin with the selection:
• of suitable locations
• of the right variety of grapes
• of the correct distance between lines and rows, and
• of the best way of growing vines and continue by:
• reducing the number of shoots left during winter pruning
• breaking off shoots in spring to reduce the number of shoots per vine to the optimum
• carefully trimming the foliage to ensure good ventilation during the growing season
• thinning the bunches of grapes as needed.
These measures are not usually employed in conventional viticulture, the only exceptions usually being those estates which aim chiefly for top quality and are already to some extent adopting an ecological approach. The ecological viticulturalist finds it essential to avoid difficult sites and particularly vulnerable grape varieties. Liquid plant manure, plant preparations, ground minerals and so on can be used to strengthen the vines effectively.

The biological viticulturalist must also work considerably more carefully and thoughtfully than his conventional colleague. The result is that ecological vineyards, naturally enough, have lower yields than those of conventional concerns aiming for high quality. But successful ecological viticulture is reflected in fewer variations in yield and quality, and often in high must weights even in bad years.

As for the quality of the wine itself, viticulturalists are agreed that it is decided in the vineyard, so it is possible that ecological viticulture may point the way to the future.

A. Dominé

SEKT

Although the most famous of all sparkling wines comes from Champagne in France, and in recent years Italy has been very successful with its Prosecco and Spain with its Cava, the Germans have no equals in the production—and consumption—of their own sparkling wine, SEKT. While their average annual wine consumption per person, just over 5 gallons (20 liters), is not outstanding, when it comes to sparkling wine the Germans easily lead the field with almost 1.3 gallons (5 liters) per person.

This liking for sparkling wine pre-dates the Sekt industry of Germany itself. Several enterprising young Germans were attracted to the idea of making champagne in the early 19th century: Krug, Bollinger, Geldermann, Mumm, and Deutz went abroad to found the champagne-making firms whose products are still among the best and best known of brands.

The word Sekt was still unusual at this time, and is first recorded in Berlin around 1825. Its invention is usually ascribed to the actor Ludwig Devrient, and it is said to derive from either French *sec* (dry), or from "sack," in allusion to a kind of sherry popular in England.

The major German Sekt-making wineries, situated with only a few exceptions on the Rhine and Mosel, were founded in the second half of the 19th century, and the houses dating from that time—Kessler, Henkell, Söhnlein, Deinhard, Kupferberg, Kloss & Foerster, Schloss Vaux, and Faber—still have the largest turnover today, selling 30, 40, or 100 million or more bottles a year (by way of comparison, the annual production of French champagne is some 250–300 million bottles).

Such quantities cannot be made by the classic bottle fermentation process, and therefore German Sekt is usually made by tank or Charmat fermentation, with the second fermentation introduced in large pressurized containers from which the finished wine is filtered, still under pressure, and then bottled.

Many enologists prefer tank to bottle fermentation, since it has the advantage of maintaining

Amounts of sugar contained in different forms of Sekt	
naturherb, brut nature	under 3 g per liter
extra herb, extra brut	up to 6 g per liter
herb, brut	up to 15 g per liter
extra dry, *extra trocken*	12 to 20 g per liter
dry, *trocken, sec*	17 to 35 g per liter
medium dry, *halbtrocken, demi-sec*	33 to 50 g per liter
sweet, *mild, süß, doux*	over 50 g per liter

Various base wines are used to full the *cuvée*, and sugar and yeast are added.

For bottle fermentation, the bottle is closed with a crown cork and stored on slats.

In viticultural firms and small Sekt-making houses, *remuage* is still done by hand in the traditional way.

Remuage leaves the yeast sediment deposited in the neck of the bottle, and it must then be disgorged.

The bottle is topped up with the correct amount of wine, and is then finally corked.

The last step is to add the decorative bucket-shaped capsule typical of most Sekt bottles.

considerably more expensive, but German vineyards would very soon have reached the limits of their capacity. As a result, 90 percent of the base wines in the huge tanks of the Rhine and Mosel Sekt wineries come from Italy, Spain, or other parts of the European Union.

Together with the classic Sekt brands, a very interesting new category of product has made its mark in the last decade: Winzersekt, or winegrower's Sekt. It differs from the traditional branded products in that it may properly be regarded as an estate-bottled wine, although the actual second fermentation, with the *remuage* and *dégorgement* processes, is contracted out to other establishments, the best known of them being situated in the Sprendlingen area of Rheinhessen.

More and more viticulturalists have now begun fermenting their own wines to make Sekt, so that they can be sure of the quality of the finished wine. Only the finest grape varieties are used for the base wine: in the north the characteristic fruity Riesling of the area, in the south the burgundy varieties, which once they have undergone secondary fermentation are almost reminiscent of champagne with their winey, yeasty character.

While the Sekt market in general seems to have been stagnating for some time, Winzersekt is becoming increasingly popular: first with the viticulturalists themselves, since it offers the welcome opportunity of an interesting and profitable sideline, and second with consumers, who find them a change from the familiar Sekt brands and a pleasing alternative.

HENKELL, SÖHNLEIN, DEINHARD

The firm of Henkell did not intend to specialize in sparkling wine. When Adam Henkell founded his wine business in Mainz in 1832, he was thinking primarily of the export trade, in which good money could still be made at the time. The firm did not begin making Sekt until some 25 years later, still working from Mainz, where the family had set up a "champagne factory"—at this time there were no legal rulings prohibiting the use of the name.

Two generations after it was founded, the business had become a Sekt winery, production was moved to Henkellsfeld near Biebrich, and in 1898 the name Henkell Trocken was registered and patented as a trade mark. Today, a Sekt empire is run from the present suburb of Wiesbaden, and in many sectors of the field it has become the market leader. The original sternly neo-classical building of the time, its style softened by decorative elements of a more

a standard quality in every bottle. However, the yeast makes more contact with the wine in the smaller volume of a bottle than in a tank, where it sinks to the bottom. In addition, second fermentation in the bottle takes longer than the Wine Law will allow for the same process in a tank, and lengthy yeast contact is a crucial factor in the quality of the finished sparkling wine.

BOTTLE FERMENTATION AND WINZERSEKT

It is not surprising, then, that the great Sekt wineries use the more elaborate bottle fermentation process with its long maturing period for their top products, which are made either from Riesling or from the classic Burgundy grape varieties. Obviously this sector of the market will not produce quantities running into six-figure numbers, but the leading *cuvées* of the German Sekt wineries can compete with central Champagne itself in quality, quantity, and price.

While certain brands in this premium area are made entirely from German wines, the same, obviously, cannot be said for the great mass of German Sekt. If the huge quantities sold were to be made entirely from grapes grown in the country, not only would the final product be

Sekt made by the time-consuming traditional method of bottle fermentation is a complex sparkling wine with small bubbles and a delicate, attractive mousse.

SELECT GERMAN PRODUCERS OF SEKT

GELDERMANN***–****
BREISACH

2,900,000 bottles • Wines: Geldermann, Odeon, Cuvée Privée, Carte Blanche, Carte Rouge, Carte Noire
After leaving the champagne house of Deutz, René Lallier made his Sekt winery one of the most quality-conscious in Germany. However, a drastic fall in sales in 2003 led to a takeover by the Rotkäppchen-Mumm Sekt companies.

GODEFROY H. VON MUMM**–***
HOCHHEIM

• Wines: Mumm, Jules Mumm
This Sekt winery in Hochheim, which once formed part of the Seagram empire, was bought in 2002 by the Rotkäppchen company. The popular brand, MM, has been world-famous since 1850 and is protected by patents.

GÜNTER REH*–**
TRIER

200,000,000 bottles • Wines: Schloss Wachenheim, Faber, Feist, Schloss Böchingen, Rondel
The company of Reh is one of the largest winery groups in Europe. Originally best known for its Faber Sekt, the group has also expanded into the higher grades of Sekt and wines in the last decade, particularly with Schloss Wachenheim and the wine-growing estate of Reichsgraf von Kesselstatt.

ROTKÄPPCHEN-SEKTKELLEREI**–***
FREYBURG

92,000,000 bottles • Wines: Rotkäppchen Sekt, Riesling, Weißburgunder fom Saale-Unstrut
The Rotkäppchen winery is one of the large former East German businesses to have profited from reunification. Founded at the end of the 19th century, the firm was taken over by the state under the D.D.R. regime. Besides classic Sekts it makes still wines and aromatic, sweet sparkling wines.

RÜDESHEIMER SEKTKELLEREIEN KLOSS & FOERSTER UND OHLIG & CO.**–***
RÜDESHEIM

2,400,000 bottles • Wines: Riesling Sekts, E.G.-Cuvée, red and rosé Sekt
After the expropriation of the Rotkäppchen winery in Freyburg, its founding families made their new home in Rüdesheim and found a suitable partner in the Ohlig winery. Although the two brands retain their independence, their products are identical.

SEKTKELLEREIEN HENKELL & SÖHNLEIN***–****
WIESBADEN

234,000,000 bottles • Wines: Henkell Trocken, Fürst von Metternich, Adam Henkell, Söhnlein Rheingold, Söhnlein Brillant, Carstens S.C., Rüttgers Club, Deinhard, Lutter & Wegner
Some years ago what is easily the best known German Sekt winery took over the famous Sekt-making firm of Deinhard of Koblenz, and since then has been the market leader in every respect. The range includes such premium products as Adam Henkell and the Riesling Sekt Fürst von Metternich.

SEKTKELLEREI C. A. KUPFERBERG & CIE**–***
MAINZ

16,000,000 bottles • Wines: Kupferberg Gold
This Sekt winery in Mainz, rich in tradition and with old cellars well worth a visit, now belongs to the Racke G.m.b.H. empire.

SEKTKELLEREI SCHLOSS VAUX***
TRIER

5 acres (2 ha); 250,000 bottles • Wines: Riesling Sekts from leading Rheingau vineyards
This firm, originally founded in Berlin, has specialized in the production of Rheingau Riesling Sekts. It uses only *Qualitätswein* to make Sekt, and sometimes bottles the base wine as a still wine.

Baroque nature, contrasts with the down-to-earth working atmosphere of the four cubic, green winemaking halls adjoining the main building at the back, where almost two thirds of the wine and Sekt made by the present company of Henkell & Söhnlein are produced.

The success of Henkell, and later of Söhnlein too, was founded on a willingness to make large quantities of a branded product and market it with a great deal of publicity. To this day, over five percent of the firm's turnover is set aside for marketing purposes. Not for nothing is Henkell Trocken still the best known brand of Sekt in Germany.

The Henkell family itself retired from the actual running of the winery some time ago. In parallel to the career of the Henkells, Johann Jacob Söhnlein had founded a "Rheingau Sparkling Wine Factory" in nearby Schierstein. Contact with the Metternich family, which then owned Schloss Johannisberg, ensured a supply of the best base wines in Germany, and a right to use

Opposite
Kupferberg was founded in 1850 by Christian Adalbert Kupferberg, who created what is still the leading brand of Kupferberg Gold. The reception hall of the original building in Mainz was extended during the Jugendstil period.

one of the best-known trade names in the sector. Söhnlein was bought up by the industrialist Oetker family in 1958, and in 1987 they merged with Henkell, their keenest competitors in the field of branded Sekts. Investments in Hungary and Poland followed, and a decade after the merger another large company, Deinhard of Koblenz, was added to what is now the leading German Sekt empire. Today it produces over 100 million bottles of Sekt, and with its production of spirits, wines, and other drinks, output amounts to almost 240 million bottles a year.

The leader among the many brands made by the firm is Söhnlein Brillant, with a good 36 million bottles, followed by Henkell Trocken and Rüttgers Club. In addition, prestigious *cuvées* are made, for instance the single-variety Chardonnay Sekt Adam Henkell, a wine that can hold its own even on the international stage, or the Fürst Metternich Riesling Sekt, also a single-variety product, with all the base wine coming from the Rheingau.

THE PFALZ

The Pfalz (Palatinate), an area around 50 miles (80 km) in length, is the second largest wine-growing region in Germany, with around 57,820 acres (23,400 ha) under vines, and the beauty of its landscape makes it a popular tourist attraction. The region is also interesting in connection with the history of wine, for many winemaking cellars which lay buried beneath vineyards for centuries, and have only recently been discovered and restored, show that grapes were being grown on the slopes of the Palatine Forest as early as the Roman period.

The southern part of the region is the sunniest and warmest of German viticultural regions after Baden. In situations entirely sheltered from cold winds, for instance the low-lying valley of Birkweiler near Landau, the vegetation sometimes assumes an almost Mediterranean aspect. And the diversity of soil formations suits the expressive power of the wines. Sandstone, clay, marl, red marl, shelly limestone, porphyry, granite, and schist—practically every kind of soil on which vines will grow well is here in the Pfalz.

In accordance with the Wine Law, the Pfalz is divided into two regions, but we should really distinguish between three: the northern third, the Deutsche Weinstraße (German Wine Road), extends from the border with Rheinhessen

The Mittelhaardt area extends north and south of Bad Dürkheim. Almond trees thrive here, evidence of the mild climate which also grows an excellent fine and fruity Riesling.

at Worms to Grünstadt; the second, the Mittelhaardt area, runs to south of Neustadt; and finally the third, the Südliche Weinstraße (Southern Wine Road), extends to the Alsatian border at Wissembourg.

THE BEST VINEYARDS IN THE MITTELHAARDT AREA

The wine-growing district with the highest claims to quality, and with the greatest reputation as a tourist attraction, is the area between Herxheim and Neustadt known as the Mittelhaardt. Its aspects and its weathered sandstone soil are recognized as the best in the Pfalz. Vineyard names such as Ungeheuer and Reiterpfad are internationally famous, representating the high prestige of the wines of the Pfalz, especially its Rieslings.

Although the Pfalz, unlike the more northerly wine-growing regions, is not regarded as purely Riesling country, Riesling is still the variety most strongly represented here, accounting for rather more than one-fifth of the total vineyard area. Müller-Thurgau comes only a little way behind, while Kerner, Portugieser, Silvaner, and Scheurebe are of less importance.

The top vineyards of the Mittelhaardt would probably fall into the top group in any classification of German vineyards, along with those of the Mosel and the Rheingau. The estate registers of the 19th century, evaluating individual vineyards in accordance with their potential, show that such was already the case then. Rieslings from these leading vineyards are usually firmer in structure than their northern counterparts, with a higher alcohol content, and are matured to a drier finish.

THE RISE OF THE SOUTHERN PFALZ

The third part of the Pfalz, the Südliche Weinstraße, is unforunately still dominated by a kind of viticulture which seems to aim above all for production of the maximum amount of grapes to fill the large tank installations of the winemakers' cooperatives. The mania for quantity which infected many winemakers more than three decades ago led to the restocking of about 2,500 acres (1,000 ha) of vineyards between 1979 and 1982 alone—and they were of course planted with high-yielding varieties on level ground, where viticultural quality

Bereich Mittelhaardt/
Deutsche Weinstraße

- *Großlage* Schnepfenflug vom Zellertal
- *Großlage* Grafenstück
- *Großlage* Höllenpfad
- *Großlage* Schwarzerde
- *Großlage* Feuerberg
- *Großlage* Kobnert
- *Großlage* Rosenbühl
- *Großlage* Hochmess
- *Großlage* Honigsäckel
- *Großlage* Schenkenböhl
- *Großlage* Schnepfenflug an der Weinstraße
- *Großlage* Hofstück
- *Großlage* Mariengarten
- *Großlage* Meerspinne
- *Großlage* Rebstöckel
- *Großlage* Pfaffengrund

Bereich Südliche Weinstraße

- *Großlage* Mandelhöhe
- *Großlage* Schloss Ludwigshöhe
- *Großlage* Trappenberg
- *Großlage* Ordensgut
- *Großlage* Bischofskreuz
- *Großlage* Königsgärten
- *Großlage* Herrlich
- *Großlage* Kloster Liebfrauenberg
- *Großlage* Guttenberg

1–16 Select single vineyards

•••••• *Bereich* border

▨ Wine-growing areas in neighboring regions

Selected single vineyards

1 Spielberg
2 Michelsberg
3 Jesuitengarten
4 Kirchenstück
5 Ungeheuer
6 Kalkofen
7 Grainhübel
8 Klostergarten
9 Reiterpfad
10 Schäwer
11 Münzberg
12 Im Sonnenschein
13 Kastanienbusch
14 Mandelberg
15 Rosenberg
16 Sonnenberg

---

could hardly be achieved. Until recently, therefore, the southern Pfalz was active mainly in the sale of wine in casks. In 1971, when it was still permissible to blend wines of different areas, the sourest products of the Mosel were made drinkable by the addition of Pfalz wines, and later large quantities made their way into the wine trade as Liebfraumilch. To this day, about half the wines of the Pfalz are bottled outside the region.

Even in the southern Pfalz, however, there are some outstanding vineyards, for instance the Godramsteiner Münzberg, the Siebeldinger Im Sonnenschein, and the Kastanienbusch and Mandelberg vineyards in Birkweiler. The rather rich, deep soils, with their high lime content, are particularly suitable for the burgundy varieties. With the growing popularity of these burgundies, and their suitability as the ideal accompaniment to food—in contrast to Riesling, which today is often bottled and drunk much too early

to be much good for that—the southern Pfalz is to the forefront of present fashion.

While the famous large estates of the Mittelhaardt were still seeking some way out of the quality crisis they themselves had created, some dynamic young winegrowers emerged in the late 1980s in the southern Pfalz in particular, and were soon regarded as among the most innovative in the whole of Germany. With colleagues from other parts of the region, they modernized work in the winery, introducing steel tanks and wooden casks for the fermentation and VINIFICATION of their wines, making great efforts to limit yields, and even trying to make internationally acceptable red wines. Above all, they showed how the enormous potential for quality of the Pfalz vineyards could be fully exploited, following the tradition of the great estates of the Mittelhaardt which had been created as the result of secularization under Napoleon.

This attractive wayside shrine is the emblem of the Kirchenstück in Forst, one of the best Riesling vineyards in the Pfalz, situated in the Mittelhaardt not far from Deidesheim.

Red Wine in the Land of Riesling

The Pfalz is one of the most attractive wine-growing regions of Germany, and is notable for its hospitality. Burg Battenberg, southwest of Grünstadt, is surrounded by vines. Here visitors can enjoy a drink in a pleasant garden in good weather.

The Müller-Catoir vineyard in Haardt, near Neustadt, has been in existence for over 250 years, and is famous for its outstanding white wines. Its Spätburgunder wines are made with equal care.

Two or three centuries ago, the majority of vineyards in Germany were still stocked with black grape varieties—something that may seem impossible today in the land of Riesling, Silvaner, and Müller-Thurgau. Yet it is a fact that even on the Mosel and in the Rheingau, Riesling did not embark on its triumphal progress until modern times. Before that, and perhaps owing to the influence over several centuries of Burgundian monks such as the Cistercians, black burgundy grape varieties had dominated the range of vines grown.

From the 1970s onward, consumption of white wines in German households steadily fell, and in the last decade of the 20th century red wines were in such demand that German supply could not keep pace with it. The classic red wine regions such as Württemberg and the Ahr, not to mention the few vineyards stocked with black grape varieties in the west of the Rheingau, were severely overstretched; the people of Württemberg still drink almost all the red wine produced there themselves—even if they did not, the red wines of the region do not on the whole satisfy the new taste for red wine which has been formed by powerful wines from southern countries—and the area of vineyards in the Ahr and Rheingau growing black grape varieties is simply too small to meet demand.

Fortunately other regions were in a position to help. They included Franconia: while previously its merits had clearly lain in the area of dry white wines, it now filled this gap in the market with red burgundies from the vineyards of Burgstädt, and with the new Domina grape variety, a cross of Portugieser and Spätburgunder,

distinguished for its intensity of color and powerful fruit acidity.

It was an obvious move for southern Baden to be taken over by the making of red wines, if only because of its climate—amounts of sunlight and warmth reach top levels here—and in fact for the last few years several of the best *barrique*-matured Spätburgunder wines in Germany have been made here. Winegrowers such as Fritz Keller, Karl-Heinz Johner, Joachim Heger, and the Bercher brothers, as well as the cooperatives of Wasenweiler and Königschaffhausen, have now even seen their wines succeed outside the country.

The Dornfelder Grape

However, the Pfalz has a part of its own to play on the German red wine scene. The region has almost as good a climate as neighboring Baden, and consequently over the last few years many viticulturalists have enlarged the areas given over to varieties for making red wines. They not only plant the classic Spätburgunder grape, but are ready to risk experimenting with a whole range of varieties.

The best results have been achieved by the Sankt Laurent grape, possibly a descendant of Spätburgunder which originated in France in the and arrived in Austria by way of Germany, then to return to Germany from Austria again. If the good results achieved by Knipser and Messmer are emulated, then yet more may be expected of this variety in the country. The same may be said of the Dornfelder grape, a cross between Helfensteiner and Heroldrebe bred at the Weinsberg viticultural school, and already one of the three most widespread red wine varieties in Germany.

From the same breeding program come the new crosses based on Cabernet and only recently introduced to the public. They bear exotic names such as Cabernet Cubin and Cabernet Mitos, both of them crosses with Lemburger, and Cabernet Dorio and Cabernet Dorsa, where the Dornfelder variety was also involved in the breeding. In view of the poor results as yet achieved by German crosses in terms of quality, however, one may wonder whether the reliable old Cabernet Sauvignon very successfully grown by such viticulturalists as Knipser and Philippi in the Pfalz, and Männler and Keller in Baden, might not have served the purpose better.

FIVE FRIENDS

All used to be straightforward in the world of the Pfalz. A handful of vineyards with names well known to wine lovers existed in the Mittelhaardt area, and the wine-growing estates were dominated by the three Bs: Bassermann-Jordan, Reichsrat von Buhl, and Bürklin-Wolf, the first two located in Deidesheim and the last in Wachenheim. Almost no one else could compete with these distinguished names.

The three estates had been the outcome of secularization in the Napoleonic period. At the beginning of the 19th century, Andreas Jordan began to extend his parents' estate in Deidesheim and systematically enlarge the former ecclesiastical property. He planted Riesling and, unusually for the time, made single-variety wines from it. After Jordan's death the business was divided between his three children, laying the foundations of what were to become the estates of Reichsrat von Buhl and Dr. Deinhard. In neighboring Wachenheim the Bürkling-Wolf estate began to attract attention with its wines, and these two villages had a monopoly of quality that was soon known well beyond the region.

The crisis in the viticulture of the Pfalz did not leave the "three Bs" unaffected, for they had been unable to keep up their standards. In the mid-1980s, a group of younger and then little-known viticulturalists tried to turn the tide, and decided to coordinate their efforts. They soon found the formula that was to make them famous, and called themselves the Five Friends (though they were originally only four). Their names were Becker, Kessler, Rebholz, Siegrist, and Wehrheim. They all operated on the principle of team work, sharing their experience, and offering frank criticism within the group.

At first the Five merely held wine tastings together, but in 1991, they devised their first joint brochure and announced their first presentation of the year's wines. It was quickly evident that as a group they could attract greater public attention, and joint marketing activities had far more advantages than disadvantages, since they were not competing with each other on the market. They all sold mainly straight from the vineyard to private customers, supplying only small quantities to restaurants or the professional wine trade.

Most profitable of all, however, were their discussions among themselves. In order to increase their own expertise, the five organized visits together to Burgundy, Tuscany, Ribera del Duero, and Bordeaux, where they profited as viticulturalists and winemakers from their hosts' open-minded attitude.

To further the learning process, they organized a professional symposium in conjunction with the annual presentation of their wines. Subjects of discussion included the aging of red and white wines in *barrique*s, analysis of the influence of vineyard situations, and the importance of soil and climate.

For all their common interests, the Five do not try to bind themselves too closely together; theirs is a flexible cooperation. They deliberately encourage the individuality of their own styles of winemaking and the independent marketing of their products.

In many ways the tale of the Five Friends from the southern Pfalz symbolizes the modern viticulture of the region. It symbolizes the new atmosphere that has entered the business with the younger generation of winegrowers. The desire to achieve quality now infects even the former suppliers of cheap wines in casks, and there is greater self-confidence among winegrowers on the Südliche Weinstraße, who not so long ago were regarded as the outsiders of the Pfalz.

Nor will progress stop here, and the best evidence of that is the sudden changes in the estates of the "three Bs" over the last few years. It was as if they and other estates in the Mittelhaardt and Deutsche Weinstraße areas had woken from a long sleep; their wines suddenly regained their former quality. The future of the Pfalz looks bright.

The "Five Friends" wine-growing association was founded in 1991.

Burg Ortenberg stands proudly above its Schlossberg vineyard, one of the most outstanding sites in Baden, which makes excellent Traminer and Riesling wines.

DR. VON BASSERMANN-JORDAN****
DEIDESHEIM

104 acres (42 ha); 350,000 bottles • Wines: Riesling from vineyards in Forst (→Kirchenstück, Jesuitengarten), Ruppertsberg (→Reiterpfad, Nussbien), and Deidesheim (Hohenmorgen, →Kalkofen)
After Ulrich Mell joined this estate as cellarmaster, its wines rapidly improved. The potential of the estate's vineyards is one of the highest in the Pfalz.

FRIEDRICH BECKER***–****
SCHWEIGEN

35 acres (14 ha); 100,000 bottles • Wines include: Spätburgunder, Riesling, Chardonnay, Weißburgunder, Grauburgunder from the →Sonnenberg vineyard in Schweigen
Like the other members of the Five Friends, Friedrich Becker and his cellarmaster Stefan Dorst are among the innovative producers of the southern Pfalz. Their preference is for Pinot varieties, and French Burgundy is the example they emulate. Their program includes careful work in cultivating the vineyards by natural methods.

BERGDOLT–ST. LAMPRECHT***–*****
DUTTWEILER

45.5 acres (18.5 ha); 140,000 bottles • Wines include: Riesling, Weißburgunder, Spätburgunder, Dornfelder from vineyards in Kirweil (Mandelberg) and Duttweil (Mandelberg, Kalkberg, Kreuzberg)
The vineyards of thus monastic estate produce top-quality wines year after year. These wines—particularly those made from the Weißburgunder and Chardonnay grapes—are powerful, with good keeping quality.

JOSEF BIFFAR****
DEIDESHEIM

32 acres (13 ha); 80,000 bottles • Wines include: Riesling, Weißburgunder, Dornfelder from vineyards in Ruppertsberg (→Reiterpfad, Nussbien), Deidesheim (→Grainhubel, →Kalkofen, Kieselberg), and Wachenheim (Gerümpel, Goldbächel)
Under the management of Ulrich Mell, the Biffar estate was one of the most successful of the 1980s and 1990s, making a particular impression with its fresh, fragrant Rieslings. Time will show whether the new cellarmaster, Dirk Roth, can match his predecessor's achievements.

REICHSRAT VON BUHL****
DEIDESHEIM

124 acres (50 ha); 400,000 bottles • Wines: Riesling, Weißburgunder, Spätburgunder from vineyards in Forst (→Jesuitengarten, →Kirchenstück), Deidesheim (Leinhöhle, Kieselberg) and Ruppertsberg (Reiterpfad), →Buhl Classic, Riesling Sekt
Recently, and after a period of crisis lasting some time, the quality of the wines produced by the second largest of the "three Bs" of the Pfalz has again become evident, particularly in the *Auslese* and *edelsüß* area. The *Beerenauslese* wines from the Jesuitengarten are among the best in the region.

DR. BÜRKLIN-WOLF***–*****
WACHENHEIM

296 acres (120 ha); 670,000 bottles • Wines: Riesling, Weißburgunder and others from vineyards in Forst (→Kirchenstück, →Jesuitengarten, Pechstein, →Ungeheuer), Deidesheim (Hohenmorgen, Langenmorgen, →Kalkofen), Ruppertsberg (→Geisboehl), and Wachenheim (Gerümpel, Rechbächel, Goldbächel), Villa Eckel

Bettina Bürklin-Guradze and her husband Christian von Guradze have reduced their range of varieties to the essentials. Since the middle of the 1990s their wines have once again been among the best of the region, and 1996 was an outstanding vintage. Rieslings from the Forster Kirchenstück and Ruppertsberger Geisboehl vineyards are classified within the region as First Growths. The latter in particular are worthy of that status.

A. CHRISTMANN***–*****
GIMMELDINGEN

35 acres (14 ha); 100,000 bottles • Wines include: Riesling, Grauburgunder, Weißburgunder, Spätburgunder, Portugieser, St. Laurent from vineyards in Gimmeldingen (Meerspinne, →Mandelgarten), Königsbach (→Idig, Ölberg), Deidesheim (Hohenmorgen), and Ruppertsberg (→Reiterpfad, Linsenbusch, Nussbien), →Selektion "S."
The growths here are elegant, with fruity notes; Steffen Christmann does not make broad, heavy wines. Although the firm produces large quantities of red wines from the burgundy varieties, its leading products are still Rieslings from the Idig, Hohenmorgen, Mandelgarten, and Reiterpfad vineyards.

EYMANN***
GÖNNHEIM

42 acres (17 ha); 150,000 bottles • Wines: Riesling, Silvaner, Weißburgunder, Grauburgunder, Spätburgunder, Chardonnay, Gewürztraminer, Muskateller, Müller-Thurgau; St. Laurent, Portugieser, Dornfelder, Regent, Sekt from vineyards in Gönnheim
Rainer Eymann has been managing the family estate since 1983 by ecological methods, sowing green plants among the vines, using natural fertilizers and natural means of combating pests and disease, and reducing yields in order to increase the quality of the grapes. The estate now offers some very good wines, particularly in the Toreye-Selektion range, as well as *Auslese* wines made from Riesling, Muskateller wines, and Spätburgunder vinified as a white wine.

FITZ-RITTER****
BAD DÜRKHEIM

52 acres (21 ha); 160,000 bottles • Wines include: Riesling, Grauburgunder, Weißburgunder, Chardonnay, Gewürztraminer, Spätburgunder, Dornfelder from vineyards in Dürkheim and Ungstein, barrique wines, Ritterhof Sekts
The half-timbered house with its fine grounds belongs to one of the most beautiful wine-growing estates in Germany. Konrad Fitz and his cellarmaster Rolf Hanewald make Rieslings with a clean note, very good in the *edelsüß* area in particular, and also a delicate Gewürztraminer. The red wines of the estate are matured in *barriques*. The Sekt winery of Ritterhof, founded in 1837, is also part of the estate.

WINFRIED FREY U. SÖHNE***–****
ESSINGEN

25 acres (10 ha); 60,000 bottles • Wines: Riesling, burgundy varieties, Dornfelder, Portugieser, St. Laurent, from vineyards in Essingen
Winfried Frey and his sons use biological methods to cultivate vineyards in Essingen, aiming chiefly to produce *edelsüß* qualities. The broad spectrum of *edelsüß* wines and *Eiswein*, and the diversity of grape varieties grown, are evidence of the satisfaction the winemaker feels in being able to offer small quantities of as many products as possible.

KNIPSER****—*****
LAUMERSHEIM

62 acres (25 ha); 200,000 bottles • Wines include: Riesling from vineyards in Dirmstein, Großkarlbach, and Laumersheim

The Knipser brothers produce some remarkable wines: dense St. Laurents and Dornfelders with good maturing qualities, Cabernet Sauvignons which are unusually mature and strong for Germany, top-quality *edelsüß* wines made from the Scheurebe grape, and most of all dense, intensely flavored Chardonnays, Weißburgunder and Grauburgunder wines.

KOEHLER-RUPRECHT****—*****
KALLSTADT

35 acres (14 ha); 80,000 bottles • Wines include: Riesling, Weißburgunder, Grauburgunder, Chardonnay, Spätburgunder from vineyards in Kallstadt (→Saumagen, Steinacker, Kronenberg), →Philippi, Riesling "R.," Pinot Noir "R.R.," barrique-matured wines, Cuvée Elysium

Bernd Philippi is regarded as one of the best viticulturalists and winemakers in Germany. He shows as much virtuosity in making Rieslings (the best are from the Kallstadter Saumagen vineyard) as he does with wines from the Burgundy varieties. The best of his wines bear the selection mark "R." on the label, and an *edelsüß* cuvée is marketed under the evocative name Elysium. Philippi's methods are traditional—selective picking by hand, fermentation using natural yeasts—but the wines are unmistakably modern in character.

HERBERT MESSMER***—****
BURRWEILER

49.5 acres (20 ha); 190,000 bottles • Wines include: Riesling, Weißburgunder, Grauburgunder, Chardonnay, St. Laurent, Spätburgunder from vineyards in Burrweiler (→Schäwer) and Gleiswiler

Wines of excellent quality, not just in the special selection lines marketed but in the standard range too, are the trademarks of this estate. The *edelsüß* wines are top-quality products, and the estate's white wines are unusually fruity and delicate.

GEORG MOSBACHER****
FORST

35 acres (14 ha); 110,000 bottles • Wines include: Riesling from vineyards in Forst (Ungeheuer, Pechstein, Freundstück, Stift) and Deidesheim (Herrgottsacker)

The large amount of Rieslings is noticeable among the wines made by this estate, and they are surpassed only by a few leading winemaking firms. In the 1990s the Forst vineyard of Ungeheuer almost always produced some of the best wines in the area.

MÜLLER-CATOIR****
NEUSTADT-HAARDT

49.5 acres (20 ha); 140,000 bottles • Wines: Riesling, Rieslander, Weißburgunder, Grauburgunder, Scheurebe, Muskateller, Spätburgunder from Haardt (→Bürgergarten and Mandelring) and the →Mußbacher Eselshaut and →Gimmeldinger Schlössel vineyards (Trockenbeerenauslese)

Over the last 250 years, the firm has established a reputation as one of the best wine-growing estates in Germany. For 25 years, Jakob Heinrich Catoir and his excellent cellarmaster Hans-Günther Schwarz, now retired, have carried this banner. His successor, Martin Franzen, has continued the house tradition of refined style since 2002. As he continues to accumulate experience, he should continue to produce top quality *edelsüß* Rieslaners and spirited Rieslings.

MÜNZBERG – LOTHAR KESSLER & SÖHNE****
GODRAMSTEIN

27 acres (11 ha); 90,000 bottles • Wines include: Weißburgunder, Riesling, Spätburgunder, Dornfelder from the Münzberg vineyard in Godramstein

The dry *Spätlese* and *Auslese* wines made by the Kessler family from Weißburgunder are proof that this variety can sometimes be more interesting than the omnipresent Chardonnay. The close attention paid to *barrique* aging of the burgundy varieties is the great strength of the estate, which is a member of the Five Friends Society.

ÖKONOMIERAT REBHOLZ****
SIEBELDINGEN

32 acres (13 ha); 90,000 bottles • Wines include: Riesling, Weißburgunder, Grauburgunder, Chardonnay, Spätburgunder from Siebeldingen (→Im Sonnenschein, Rosenberg), Birkweiler (Kastanienberg), and Godramstein (→Münzburg), Hansjörg Rebholz "R."

Rebholz makes wines of unusual density and complexity for this region, particularly in the special selection lines. The motto of the house is the name of one of its *Trockenbeerenauslese* wines: *Zeit und Geduld* (Time and Patience).

THOMAS SIEGRIST***—****
LEINSWEILER

31 acres (12.5 ha); 80,000 bottles • Wines include: Riesling, Müller-Thurgau, Weissburgunder, Grauburgunder, Chardonnay, Silvaner, Spätburgunder, Dornfelder from vineyards in Leinswiler, Ilbesheim, and Wollmersheim, barrique-aged wines, Cuvée Johann Adam Hauck

Thomas Siegrist has made a name as one of the best producers of red wines in the southern Pfalz. Maturing in *barriques* has also become one of his specialties; the wood notes, which were very noticeable at first, have now been moderated, making way for a delicate fruitiness.

STIFTSWEINGUT FRANK MEYER**—***
KLINGENMÜNSTER

20 acres (8 ha); 70,000 bottles • Wines: Silvaner, Riesling, Weißburgunder, Grauburgunder and other white varieties, Sekt, Portugieser, Spätburgunder, new red crosses such as Cabernet Cubin

Meyer uses natural methods in cultivating vineyards with soils ranging from sandy gravel to calcareous clay, and picks by hand. His two dozen wines are dominated by dry *Spätlesen* made from Riesling and burgundy varieties, and his *barrique*-matured red wines made from Portugieser (!) and Spätburgunder are worth noting.

DR. WEHRHEIM***—****
BIRKWEILER

25 acres (10 ha); 80,000 bottles • Wines include: Riesling, Weißburgunder, Chardonnay, Spätburgunder from vineyards in Birkweiler (Kastanienbusch, Mandelberg, Rosenberg)

Wehrheim is almost unsurpassed in the Pfalz for Burgundy varieties and Chardonnay. The reason lies not only in the good vineyards, with soils of weathered sandstone or calcareous clay, but also in the professionalism shown in both vineyard and winery: sensible restriction of the yield is followed by gentle methods of cultivation and minimum filtration.

BADEN

With its 39,040 acres (15,800 ha) of vineyards, Baden is only the third largest viticultural area of Germany, but it is by far the most extensive. The region runs for nearly 300 miles (500 km) in an almost perfect north–south direction along the Upper Rhine, from the Rhine-Neckar area around Mannheim and Heidelberg to Basel. The larger part of the Baden viticultural region lies in the rift valley of the Rhine and the river's side valleys, with the exception of some small "islands" of vineyards on Lake Constance and the valley of the Tauber in Franconia.

The European wine-growing laws, which divide all vineyard districts on the Continent into various categories, place Baden in Zone B. This is not an arbitrary decision, since the upper valley of the Rhine is generally considered the warmest part of the whole Federal German Republic. While there can be considerable climatic differences in the various parts of Baden, the valley of the Rhine as a whole enjoys the protection of the Black Forest massif against rough east winds, while on the French side of the Rhine the Vosges Mountains successfully ward off rain. The Breisgau area near Freiburg can boast more hours of sunlight and thus higher average temperatures than any other German wine-growing district, and the Ihringer Winklerberg in the Kaiserstuhl area is considered to be the most reliably warm vineyard between the Lower Rhine and Lake Constance, and between Trier and Dresden.

A romantic vineyard castle, Ortenburg.

There are considerable differences between the constitution of the soil in the various vine-growing areas. Limestone, clay, and marl soils alternate, loess and volcanic rock predominate in the Kaiserstuhl, there is shelly limestone and red marl in the northeast, and the hills of Lake Constance consist of coarse moraine gravel.

SUCCESS WITH BURGUNDY VARIETIES

With all these climatic and geological differences, the various styles of wines made in the different parts of Baden sometimes display clearly marked individual characteristics.

White burgundy grape varieties do best along the Badische Bergstraße and in the Kraichgau, since they get sufficient sun there, while the climate provides the necessary fruit and elegance. In spite of high potential for quality and the efforts of individual viticulturalists, these areas have not yet managed to make a really distinctive name for themselves, which may be due partly to prejudices and ingrained ideas on the part of wine writers and consumers. In the

Bereich Tauberfranken, where the winegrowers have to expect frost and as a result vines are planted only on hillsides, the wines resemble those of neighboring Franconia. The favorite grape variety here is Müller-Thurgau, which covers two thirds of the area under vines.

Very different is the Ortenau, where vineyards thread their way through the Black Forest in the beautiful landscape of the valleys running off to the side of the Rhine. Riesling predominates here, and is also known in the area as Klingelberger, after the first vineyard in the Ortenau at Durbach, where it was originally planted as a single variety at the end of the 18th century. However, the little wine-growing village of Durbach shows that the Ortenau vineyards can be just as suitable for red wines made from the Spätburgunder grape.

The Spätburgunder is also the best and now the most widely grown variety in the warm, sunny Breisgau, with its calcareous soils. In the nearby Kaiserstuhl area and on the Tuniberg the range of varieties becomes more extensive again. Grauburgunder is used to make a dry wine fermented in wooden casks, invented here after the sweet, thick wines known by the variety's alternative name Ruländer fell out of fashion, and it does so well in this region that it can hold its own even with French growths. The same can be said of Spätburgunder and Müller-Thurgau; the latter is often labeled as Rivaner, and reaches a degree of ripeness which can give even this high-yielding grape an interesting structure or flavor.

Less impressive is the situation in the Markgräflerland, where viticulturalists have predominantly planted the Gutedel vine. This rather neutral grape variety has its charms, and can even achieve interesting quality, for instance in Switzerland and neighboring Alsace, where Gutedel is known as Chasselas. However, most of the Markgräfler viticulturalists seem to find realizing this potential in the bottle as hard as squaring the circle. The tourist attractions of the area, and consequently the absence of any problem in the marketing of wines, have probably tended to block motivation for making wines of really top quality.

AWARENESS OF QUALITY

The yields at harvest in particular, now almost a third less than the yields of the 1980s, show that some growers in Baden have taken the effort to achieve quality really seriously. At that earlier time Baden, like the other wine-growing regions of Germany, had its eye on the ideal of rationalized viticulture covering a large area,

Durbach is the unofficial capital of the Ortenau area. It has well-protected vineyards with favorable aspects, for instance the Schlossberg, Schloss Staufenberg, and Steinberg vineyards, and in good years the Rieslings grown there make wines of unique fullness.

Wine from Lake Constance

The vineyards around Lake Constance lie in two German states and three viticultural areas: Bavaria, Württemberg, and Baden. Baden, with around 988 acres (400 ha), is much the largest of the three.

The southern aspect here and the wide surface of the lake, which acts like a gigantic mirror and reflects back sunlight, are a guarantee of particularly mild climatic conditions, but as the vineyards are at a comparatively high altitude—up to 1,650 feet (500 m)—the wines made here are fruity in character as a rule, but not so concentrated and powerful as those of the Upper Rhine. High amounts of rainfall and rising mists are complicating factors.

Most of the wine from the Spätburgunder grape, which has been cultivated for over 200 years on the northern banks of the lake, is used to make Weißherbst wines. This pale rosé wine is the main product of the highly regarded state wine-growing estate of Meersburg, which with 148 acres (60 ha) is the largest estate on Lake Constance and grows Spätburgunder in half of its vineyards. Its Weißherbst is considered one of the best in Germany. With Spätburgunder, the main variety grown here is Müller-Thurgau. Vineyards on the Hohentwieler Olgaberg near Singen, the highest vineyard of Germany, at 1,840 feet (560 m), also belong to the state.

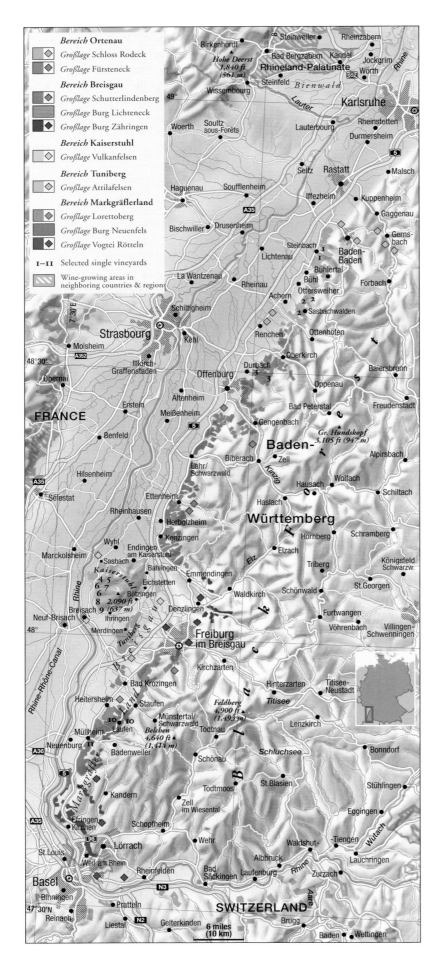

Bereich Ortenau
◇ *Großlage* Schloss Rodeck
◇ *Großlage* Fürsteneck

Bereich Breisgau
◇ *Großlage* Schutterlindenberg
◇ *Großlage* Burg Lichteneck
◇ *Großlage* Burg Zähringen

Bereich Kaiserstuhl
◇ *Großlage* Vulkanfelsen

Bereich Tuniberg
◇ *Großlage* Attilafelsen

Bereich Markgräflerland
◇ *Großlage* Lorettoberg
◇ *Großlage* Burg Neuenfels
◇ *Großlage* Vogtei Röttelen

I–II Selected single vineyards

Wine-growing areas in neighboring countries & regions

with the production of expressive wines of high quality taking only second place. The most notable example of this policy was the gigantic operation involved in the restructuring of land in the Kaiserstuhl area.

Baden is in fact organized by the Wine Law into very large wine-growing units: this extensive region is subdivided into no more than nine *Bereiche*, with only 16 *Großlagen* and 314 *Einzellagen*—obviously a more functional structure than prevails, for instance, in the comparatively small Mosel region with its 19 *Großlagen* and 500 *Einzellagen*. In addition, 85 percent of the vine-growing area is run by

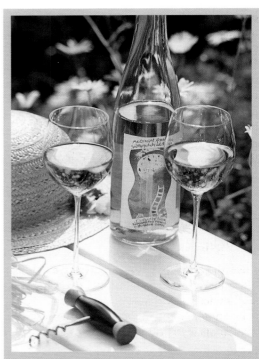

Weißherbst wine made from Spätburgunder

Weißherbst is a term introduced to describe German and Swiss rosé wines. Such wines are based on a single grape variety, which must be identified on the label. The variety most commonly used is Spätburgunder, vinified as white wine: that is to say, the grapes are pressed immediately they are delivered to the winery, so that the must can absorb only a few coloring substances from the skins, and this process gives Weißherbst its typical pale pink hue. Its charm resides in the freshness of its fruity and floral aromas, and it should always be drunk young and chilled. The Weißherbst wines of the Kaiserstuhl and Lake Constance are famous. Badisch-Rotgold, known as a "Rotling" and made of white or red grapes pressed together, is usually of lower quality. This rosé, which comes into the *Qualitätswein* category, is often made of mixed Ruländer (otherwise Grauburgunder) and Spätburgunder grapes. Rotling from Württemberg can be labelled as a "Schilcher" wine, a term also denoting that it is made from white and black grapes that have been mixed.

members of cooperatives, a ratio greater than any in Germany except for the small Hessische Bergstraße area and Franconia.

This has not prevented the growers of Baden from uniting their forces to promote quality in their products. Leading Baden wine-growing estates have combined not so much *with* one another—for the gulf between those who market their own products and the cooperatives is as great here as anywhere—but side by side with each other, in a minor viticultural revolution which has made a considerable difference to the styles and quality of the wines they produce.

Today, over half the wines of Baden are made dry, and another third are medium-dry. It is most obvious in the wine made from the Grauburgunder variety, alias Ruländer; with modern fermentation, and sometimes matured in *barriques*, it is no longer highly colored and sweet, and has become a modern, fruity wine. Unlike the wine made from its Italian counterpart Pinot Grigio, it is full-bodied. Spätburgunder and Weißburgunder wines also profit from concentration on the essentials, and even from *barrique*-maturing. This product of the burgundy varieties is certainly the most interesting wine that Baden has to offer.

THE RESTRUCTURING OF VINEYARDS

Since the 1950s, systematic efforts have been made in German viticulture to restructure the land under vines. These efforts began with the realization that the splintering of vineyards into small plots in many areas called for an econom-

Select single vineyards
(see map opposite)
1 Stich den Buben
2 Alde Gott
3 Plauelrain
4 Steinbuck
5 Enselberg
6 Henkenberg
7 Eichberg
8 Schlossberg
9 Winklerberg
10 Altenberg
11 Reggenhag

The Kaiserstuhl is an example of misconceived land restructuring; the vineyards here were artificially remodeled for purely economic reasons, and no account was taken of their original and natural qualities.

ically unjustifiable expenditure of labor, and was increasingly becoming an obstacle to any kind of rational viticulture. The reorganization of landed property not only created larger areas which were easier to cultivate, but also meant that drainage systems could be installed and suitable paths laid out to take machinery. The aim was to restock vineyards with higher-yielding cloned varieties—and all these measures were clearly likely to raise production.

Apart from the fact that such measures seldom increased quality, there were some undesirable side effects. On the Kaiserstuhl, for instance, the whole landscape of the loessial terraces of the volcanic hills was comprehensively remodeled, so that today, seen from the valley, it looks like a collection of huge slag heaps in an opencast mining landscape covered with the green of the vines. As a prime concern was to lay out the large terraces so that they would be suitable for machinery, there was a tendency to plant some of the vineyards inclining toward the slopes—with the unfortunate result that cold air cannot flow off but actually builds up in these vineyard valleys created by human hand, so that frost damage can now occur in regions once famous for their mild climate.

The restructuring of land was not wholly bad, and there are more successful examples in the Mosel and on the Rhine Front in Rheinhessen, where the appearance of the landscape was preserved and deteriorations in quality were on the whole kept within bounds.

Select Producers in Baden

Abril***—****
Bischoffingen
16 acres (6.5 ha); 40,000 bottles • Wines include: Grauburgunder, Weißburgunder, Müller-Thurgau, Silvaner, Riesling, Spätburgunder from vineyards in Bischoffingen and Schelingen, Weisse Linie, barrique-matured wines
The Bischoffingen vineyards seem particularly suitable for growing both red and white burgundy varieties. At least, it is from these grapes that Hans-Friedrich Abril makes the wines on which the good reputation of his little estate is founded. The *barrique*-matured whites are intense in color, and derive their aroma and flavor from the fact that the grapes are picked very ripe.

Affentaler W.G.**—***
Bühl-Eisental
612.5 acres (248 ha); 3,500,000 bottles • Wines include: Riesling, Spätburgunder, Müller-Thurgau from many vineyards around Bühl, Huber Althof, Orblie Secco
The Affental cooperative is one of the many such cooperatives in Baden working with a view to quality. In the past, nuns grew vines in what was then called Avetal, mainly to make wine for church use. Today the Affental cooperative has many outlets for its wines, including the top echelons of the restaurant trade.

Bercher***—*****
Burkheim
59 acres (24 ha); 170,000 bottles • Wines include: Riesling, Weißburgunder, Grauburgunder, Müller-Thurgau, Spätburgunder from Burkheim (→Feuerburg) and Sasbach
In the last decade Rainer and Eckhardt Bercher have made their estate one of the market leaders in Baden. The emphasis of their work is on the burgundy varieties, which do particularly well on the weathered volcanic soil of the Feuerberg, as their *barrique*-matured special selection wines and their dry Spätburgunder *Auslese* wines in particular show.

Duijn****
Bühl
20 acres (8 ha); 25,000 bottles • Wines: Spätburgunder from Bühlertal Engelsfelsen, Sterneberg, Laufen
Jakob Duijn is Baden's vertical take-off in Spätburgunder. Within a few years the Dutchman has established his reds among Baden's top quality wines.

Freiherr von Gleichenstein***—****
Oberrotweil
59 acres (24 ha); 150,000 bottles • Wines include: Spätburgunder, Weißburgunder, Grauburgunder, Müller-Thurgau from Oberrotweil (→Henkenberg), Amolten, and Achkarren (→Schlossberg)
Unlike many of his colleagues, Hans-Joachim von Gleichenstein, an opponent of *barrique*-maturing, seldom attracts much public attention. However, he quietly makes excellent Grauburgunder wines from the Henkenberg vineyard in Oberrotweil, and the time they spend maturing in new wooden casks does not detract in the least from their quality.

Dr. Heger***—*****
Ihringen
40 acres (16 ha); 120,000 bottles • Wines include: Riesling, Grauburgunder, Weißburgunder, Silvaner, Chardonnay, Spätburgunder from Ihringen (→Winklerberg), Achkarren (→Schlossberg), Merdingen (Bühl), and Freiburg (Schlossberg), →Spätburgunder Mimus

On entering the family firm, Joachim Heger found himself in possesion of some very good vineyards. The Winklerberg of Ihringen in particular, Germany's warmest vineyard, regularly produces outstanding grapes. Riesling, Silvaner, Muskateller, and the burgundy varieties all thrive here in harmony together. The Grauburgunder and Weißburgunder wines have much power, as well as attractive fruit.

Albert Heitlinger***—*****
Östringen-Tiefenbach
86 acres (35 ha); 210,000 bottles • Wines include: Riesling, Grauburgunder, Weißburgunder, Müller-Thurgau, Spätburgunder barrique-matured wines, Dialog, Grand Étage
Although it took Erhard Heitlinger a little longer than some other winegrowers to present his wines in the right light to appeal to a critical public, the reason lay less in their quality than in the position of his estate, which lies in a part of Baden not generally thought capable of anything but simple wines. Today, however, this energetic viticulturalist has made it abundantly clear that his is one of the elite estates of Baden, particularly with his Grauburgunders and other *barrique*-matured wines.

Reichsgraf und Marquis zu Hoensbroech****
Angelbachtal-Michelfeld
54 acres (22 ha); 120,000 bottles • Wines include: Weißburgunder, Grauburgunder, Riesling, Silvaner, Spätburgunder from vineyards in Michelfeld and Eichelberg
Rüdiger zu Hoensbroech founded his firm in 1968, and his wines soon attracted attention in following decades. He was one of the founding members of the V.D.P. in Baden. His Chardonnay and Weißburgunder from the Himmelberg vineyard in Michelfeld represent the best quality in his range.

Bernhard Huber***—****
Malterdingen
32 acres (13 ha); 80,000 bottles • Wines: Spätburgunder, Chardonnay, Weißburgunder, Grauburgunder, Müller-Thurgau, Riesling, from vineyards in Malterdingen and Hecklingen
Bernhard Huber was one of the first German viticulturalists to make an international impression with *barrique*-fermented Chardonnays. He is also regarded as a Spätburgunder specialist. His Weißburgunder and Grauburgunder wines from Malterdingen vineyards are above average too.

Karl H. Johner****—*****
Bischoffingen
33 acres (13.5 ha); 85,000 bottles • Wines: Spätburgunder, Grauburgunder, Weißburgunder, Chardonnay, Müller-Thurgau, "S.J."
After having spent years helping to develop English wines, Johner began building up his own estate in his native Kaiserstuhl at the end of the 1980s. In less than five years, the new winegrower had already become something of a superstar in German viticulture. He does not take much notice of the absurdities of the German Wine Law and the discussion of vineyard classifications—he simply bottles his products as *Tafelwein*, and they still fetch top prices. His Spätburgunder, Chardonnay, and Grauburgunder wines, and even the rather plain Müller-Thurgau which Johner sells as Rivaner, have a fullness of flavor which raises them well above the average.

FRANZ KELLER—SCHWARZER ADLER****–*****
OBERBERGEN
81.5 acres (33 ha); 200,000 bottles • Wines:
Grauburgunder, Weißburgunder, Müller-Thurgau,
Spätburgunder, from vineyards in Oberrotweil
(Kirchberg, Eichberg) and Oberbergen (Bassgeige,
Pulverbuck), Kellers Keller, barrique-matured wines,
Classik, special selection lines "A." and "S."
The Schwarze Adler in Oberbergen is much better
known as a top restaurant than for the wine-growing
estate which is part of the property. However, the
wines bottled under the management of Fritz Keller
are more than adequate to match the restaurant's
culinary achievements. This is true not only of classic
wines from the vineyards of Bassgeige and Pulverbuck,
but even more so of the *barrique*-matured special
selections which go under the unpretentious names
of "A." and "S." Wines made from Weißburgunder,
Grauburgunder, Spätburgunder, and Chardonnay
have reached a standard that can stand up to foreign
competition.

ANDREAS LAIBLE****
DURBACH
10 acres (4 ha); 35,000 bottles • Wines include:
Riesling, Traminer, Scheurebe, Spätburgunder
from the →Durbacher Plauelrein vineyard
The talented and ambitious Andreas Laible runs his
small estate on the outskirts of Durbach with exemplary
commitment. The secret of his dense, fruity, and spicy
Riesling, Scheurebe, and Weißburgunder wines lies in
choosing the best vineyard plots and aiming for
moderate yields.

LÄMMLIN-SCHINDLER***
SCHLIENGEN-MAUCHEN
47 acres (19 ha); 170,000 bottles • Wines include:
Spätburgunder, Weißburgunder, Grauburgunder,
Gutedel, Chardonnay from vineyards in Mauchen
Some wine lovers may be surprised to find that a
viticulturalist using biological methods, and with
vineyards in a remote Black Forest valley of the
Markgräflerland at that, can produce top quality wines,
but Gerhard Schindler really does make outstanding
white and red wines from the burgundy varieties and
Chardonnay.

HEINRICH MÄNNLE****
DURBACH
13.5 acres (5.5 ha); 40,000 bottles • Wines include:
Spätburgunder, Weißburgunder, Grauburgunder,
Scheurebe, Riesling, Traminer from the Kochberg
vineyard in Durbach
Unusually for Durbach, Heinrich Männle's vineyards
are mainly stocked with black grape varieties. Even
more unusual is the quality of the red wines he makes,
some of them matured in *barriques*. Recently Männle
has also been experimenting with Cabernet Sauvignon,
and has shown that this variety can produce good
results in Germany.

SALWEY***–****
OBERROTWEIL
49.5 acres (20 ha); 150,000 bottles • Wines include:
Spätburgunder, Grauburgunder, Weißburgunder,
Riesling, Silvaner from vineyards in Oberrotweil
and Glottertal (Eichberg)
Wolf-Dieter Salwey took over his parents' business
in 1964, and through the years has confirmed his
reputation as a fine viticulturalist and winemaker.
His Grauburgunder wines are among the very best
in Baden.

SEEGER****
LEIMEN
20 acres (8 ha); 40,000 bottles • Wines include:
Riesling, Weißburgunder, Grauburgunder,
Spätburgunder from the Heidelberger and Leimener
Herrenberg, barrique-matured wines
Thomas Seeger began maturing his red and white
burgundy varieties in the middle of the 1980s. He has
been one of the most unconventional viticulturalists
in Baden, but is also recognized as one of the best.
As well as his single variety growths, he shines with
an unusual Cuvée Anna, made from Spätburgunder,
Schwarzriesling, Lemberger, and Portugieser grapes.

MAX MARKGRAF VON BADEN
SCHLOSS STAUFENBERG**–****
DURBACH
66.5 acres (27 ha); 100,000 bottles • Wines include:
Riesling, Müller-Thurgau, Spätburgunder from
vineyards in Durbach (→Klingelberg)
Of the Margrave's two estates, Staufenberg and Salem,
this is easily the better, although the wines themselves
are vinified at Salem. The Riesling made here takes its
name, specifying its Ortenau origin, from the estate's
top vineyard, the Klingelberg. The Chardonnay and
Gewürztraminer wines are of top quality.

W.G. EHRENSTETTEN***
EHRENSTETTEN
350 acres (140 ha); 1,500,000 bottles • Wines include:
Gutedel, Müller-Thurgau, burgundy varieties from
vineyards in Ehrenstetten, Chasslie
This viticulturalists' cooperative in the Markgräfler
area, managed by Franz Herbster and his cellarmaster
Norbert Faller, has attracted attention in recent years
not only with its Chasslie, a Gutedel wine bottled *sur lie*,
but also with good Spätburgunder wines from the
Ölberg, marketed in modern designer bottles.

W.G. KÖNIGSCHAFFHAUSEN***–****
KÖNIGSCHAFFHAUSEN
889 acres (360 ha); 1,300,000 bottles • Wines include:
Spätburgunder, Müller-Thurgau, Weißburgunder,
Grauburgunder from vineyards in Königschaffhausen,
Regnum, "S.L."
The Königschaffhausen cooperative was one of the first in
Baden to aim its production deliberately at the market for
wines of top quality, and from the first it was also one of
the most successful. In particular, the *barrique*-matured
Spätburgunder wines from the Steingrüble—named
Regnum or "S.L."—have been widely appreciated.

W.G. OBERBERGEN**–***
OBERBERGEN
691 acres (280 ha); 2,800,000 bottles • Wines include:
Müller-Thurgau, Spätburgunder, Grauburgunder,
Silvaner from vineyards in Oberbergen (Baßgeige,
Pulverbuck), Frühlingsbote, Konrad
The majority of the wines are from the large single
vineyard of the Baßgeige in Oberbergen, and the
Grauburgunder and Spätburgunder wines are even
a little better than the rest of the excellent range.

W.G. WASENWEILER AM KAISERSTUHL**–****
WASENWEILER
222 acres (90 ha); 650,000 bottles • Wines include:
Spätburgunder, Müller-Thurgau, Silvaner, Weißburgunder,
Grauburgunder from vineyards in Wasenweiler, Die Neun
A German cooperative which succeeds in attracting
attention with its red wines in Italy is something out
of the ordinary. Johann Haberl, who manages the
cooperative in Wasenweiler, did just that, and brilliantly,
with his 1990 vintage. The best wines are from the
Kreuzhalde vineyard. Biologically made wines are
marketed under the name of "Die Neun."

WÜRTTEMBERG

As others see them, and indeed as they see themselves, the people of Württemberg are almost exclusively drinkers of red wine, most of it made from the black Trollinger grape. However, that idea is only partly accurate. It is true that the viticultural area of Württemberg—at about 27,920 acres (11,300 ha), this state is the fifth largest wine-growing region in Germany—is predominantly stocked with black grapes, but of the individual varieties Riesling in fact holds first place. Its lead over Trollinger is narrow but undeniable, however little this may suit the self-image of the Württembergers. As for the rest, the amount of black grape varieties planted does not necessarily mean that the red wines made

from them are actually drunk in Württemberg. On the whole the wines made from Trollinger, Lemberger, and Schwarzriesling grapes are still rather thin and colorless, and in the past they rightly attracted little critical attention outside the region.

Vines in Württemberg grow mainly in the valley of the Neckar and on the hills around it, but the outskirts of the region officially extend to the valley of the Tauber in the northeast and as far as Tübingen and Reutlingen in the south, with a small self-contained area of vineyards by Lake Constance, between Friedrichshafen and Lindau. The cool, continental climate, with only the surface of the river Neckar exerting

Select single vineyards
1 Zuckerle
2 Herzogenberg
3 Gips
4 Mönchberg

Opposite
If it weren't for the Neckar, pictured here at Mundelheim, and its influence on the temperature, the grapes would find it difficult to ripen in cool Württemberg.

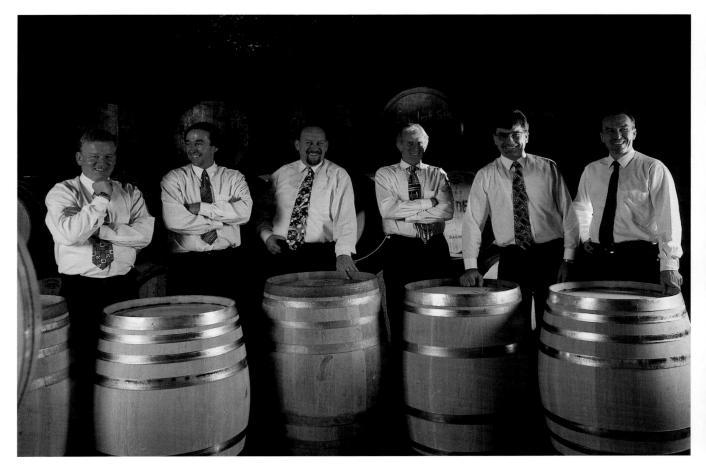

a moderating influence, can make viticulture a very arduous task, although it is perhaps less difficult to grow Riesling, which is the dominant variety in the south of the area around Stuttgart in particular, since such conditions suit the grape well. In more northerly vineyards the predominant variety is Lemberger, known in Austria as Blaufränkish. Similarly, the Trollinger grape is known as Vernatsch in its native South Tyrol.

FROM MERELY DRINKABLE TO BIG RED WINES

It seemed for a long time that the fate of Württemberg was to make red wines which were pleasing and drinkable, but seldom really interesting. The situation was not improved by the cooperatives' winery techniques, involving methods of what was almost the mass production of simple wines: ready to drink young, but without expressiveness or elegance. A favorite method was to heat the must briefly to a temperature of 185°F (85°C) to hasten color extraction, instead of achieving it by the classic process of must fermentation. As a result most of the so-called red wines supplied by these wineries were sadly lacking in both structure and character. Only around ten years ago did some of the Württemberg estates again start to make

These viticulturalists and cellarmasters are the outstanding proponents of *barrique* maturation in Württemberg: the initial letters of their names form the word HADES, the title of their association. They worked together to optimize methods of maturing in small oak casks, and have made an international reputation for themselves.

powerful, genuinely red wines with an intense flavor again, wines to which the increasingly popular practice of *barrique* maturation even lent a certain international character.

Some of the leading viticulturalists of Württemberg joined together in an association known as "Hades" in order to pool their experience of *barrique*-maturation. The name consists of the initial letters of the five member estates: Hohenlohe-Öhringen, Adelmann, Drautz-Able, Ellwanger, and the state-owned Weinsberg estate. The Hades group has succeeded in persuading even the most critical among wine writers of the potential of their vineyards.

In the future, much may be expected of Württemberg. A potential reservoir of quality, as yet unexploited but very promising, exists in the region's Riesling and also in its Lemberger, which is successful in Austria under the name of Blaufränkisch, and in Württemberg is also suitable for blending with other varieties. The first results are already making their mark, but longer and more intensive efforts will probably be needed before the merely drinkable wines of Württemberg become genuine, fully developed products of European stature.

SELECT PRODUCERS IN WÜRTTEMBERG

GRAF ADELMANN***–****
KLEINBOTTWAR

49 acres (20 ha); 120,000 bottles • Wines include: Riesling, Trollinger, Lemberger, Samtrot, Frühburgunder, Spätburgunder from solely owned vineyards in Kleinbottwar, Die Mauern von Schaubeck, Cuvée Vignette I, Brüssele'r Spitze

It seems natural to look in the field of red wine for the best wines made by one of the pioneers of the *barrique* maturation of red wines in Germany; they are marketed under the name of Brüssele'r Spitze. However, the estate's top Rieslings are also very good, and so is the red Cuvée Vignette I, made from Lemberger, Samtrot, and Spätburgunder grapes.

GERHARD ALDINGER***–****
FELLBACH

79 acres (32 ha); 160,000 bottles • Wines include: Trollinger, Spätburgunder, Riesling from the →Untertürkheimer Gips (a solely owned vineyard), and vineyards in Fellbach, Hanweiler, Uhlbach, and Rotenberg, Cuvée C., G.A. Weisswein, G.A. Rotwein

Gert Aldinger is the 15th generation of his family to run this estate. Its most valuable item of capital lies in its sole ownership of the Untertürkheimer Gips, an excellent vineyard for growing Riesling and Spätburgunder. Aldinger uses mainly traditional methods in the winery, but presents his wines in a very up-to-date style, in conical bottles with designer labels.

ERNST DAUTEL****
BÖNNIGHEIM

26 acres (10.5 ha); 80,000 bottles • Wines include: Riesling, Chardonnay, Trollinger, Lemberger, Schwarzriesling from vineyards in Bönnigheim, Besigheim, and Meimsheim, Kreation (white and red), Selektion "S.," Essenz

As a member of the German Barrique Forum, Ernst Dautel naturally pays special attention to his red and white wines matured in wooden casks, including those made not only from his experimental plantings of Cabernet Sauvignon and Merlot vines, but also from the Trollinger and Lemberger varieties traditionally grown in Württemberg. By sensibly restricting yields, he succeeds in making wines of great density and structure.

DRAUTZ-ABLE**–****
HEILBRONN

36 acres (14.5 ha); 150,000 bottles • Wines: many varieties from Leben in Neckarsulm, Heilbronn, Lauffen, and Erlenbach, →Jodokus, barrique-aged wines, Composition L., Häusles-Wein

Richard Drautz represents the letter D in the name of the Hades association which has attracted attention with its experiments in *barrique* maturing. The name of Jodokus given to his best red wines (made from the Dornfelder and Lemberger varieties) is that of an ancestor of the Drautz family.

KARL HAIDLE****
KERNEN-STETTEN

42 acres (17 ha) 150,000 bottles • Wines include: Riesling, Kerner, Trollinger, Spätburgunder from vineyards in Stetten and Schnait, Selektion "S."

Karl Haidle's estate was thoroughly modernized in 1992, and since then this viticulturalist has been among the best in the whole area around Stuttgart. He still likes to ferment his wines in wooden casks, and also works with *barriques*. His best *Einzellage* wines are his Riesling Pulvermächer and the Spätburgunder wines from the Burghalde. Some of his top wines are bottled without

any mention of the vineyard on the label, including Dornfelder, Lemberger, the Dornfelder-Lemberger "S.," and his Weißburgunder "S."

GRAF VON NEIPPERG**–****
SCHWAIGERN

78 acres (31.5 ha); 240,000 bottles • Wines include: Riesling, Lemberger, Schwarzriesling, Spätburgunder, Samtrot, Trollinger from vineyards in Neipperg (Schlossberg), Schwaigen (Ruthe), and Klingenburg (Schlossberg)

Besides its main seat in Neipperg, the family owns a series of famous wine-growing estates in Bordeaux. The castle accommodates the fermentation plant and storage cellars. The estate's Lembergers and Rieslings are in the top category of Württemberg wines.

SCHLOSSGUT HOHENBEILSTEIN***
BEILSTEIN

33 acres (13.5 ha); 100,000 bottles • Wines include: Riesling, Trollinger, Samtrot, Lemberger, Spätburgunder from the Beilsteiner Schlosswingert vineyard

Schloss Hohenbeilstein is only 100 years old, and has a modern wine-growing estate behind its handsome façade. The vineyards are cultivated by biological methods, and only the Spätburgunder wines may carry the vineyard name of Schlosswingert. The wines themselves are of consistently good to very good quality.

STAATSWEINGUT WEINSBERG***–****
WEINSBERG

99 acres (40 ha); 250,000 bottles • Wines include: Riesling, Lemberger, Trollinger, Spätburgunder, Samtrot from vineyards in Gundelsheim, Abstatt, and Weinsberg, "G.V."

The Weinsberg state-owned estate has long had a good reputation in the world of wine, and not just since its recent introduction of a number of new Cabernet crosses. It has been practicing biological methods of winemaking at Burg Wildeck for some time. An interesting wine is its blend of Kerner, Silvaner, and Burgundy varieties sold under the name of "G.V."

W.G. GRANTSCHEN**–***
GRANTSCHEN

346 acres (140 ha); 1,600,000 bottles • Wines include: Riesling, Trollinger, Lemberger, Schwarzriesling from vineyards in Grantschen, "S.M.," Grandor, Schwarze Serie

In contrast to Baden, where a whole series of cooperatives makes outstanding wines, the Grantschen cooperative is alone in Württemberg in producing wines of really top quality. Its Auslese made from Lemberger and called Grandor, and "S.M.," a blend of Dornfelder and Lemberger, reach a very high standard in good years.

ALBERT WÖHRWAG***–****
STUTTGART-UNTERTÜRKHEIM

45.5 acres (18.5 ha); 160,000 bottles • Wines: Riesling, Trollinger, Lemberger, Spätburgunder, etc., from the Untertürkheimer Herzogenberg vineyard, →Phillip

Hans-Peter Wöhrwag's estate has been known to lovers of wine for some time, and not just since the introduction of his magnificent Riesling *Eiswein* of 1994. He regularly makes outstanding wines from Riesling, Trollinger, and Spätburgunder grapes on his premises. The blend of Lemberger, Spätburgunder, and Dornfelder marketed under the name of Phillip is also very good.

FRANCONIA

Franconia is one of the most soundly established and popular viticultural regions of Germany. The vineyard slopes on the river Main and in the Steigerwald, their furthest outposts running to the Rhine-Main area in the west and the diocese of Bamberg in the east, have long attracted wine lovers from far and wide who appreciate the clear, straightforward style of the indigenous Franconian wines.

The focal point of the area is the old episcopal city of Würzburg, with its fortress of the Marienberg and the Renaissance and Rococo buildings in the city center: architectural jewels which were destroyed in the war but have been restored with loving care and admirable attention to detail. The city is dominated by the famous vineyard Am Stein, which seen from a distance appears to tower above the rooftops like a wall. A good mile long, and with a surface area of 227 acres (92 ha), it is the largest of all self-contained German hillside vineyards, and the best part of it, known as the Stein/Harfe vineyard, is in the sole ownership of the Bürgerspital.

For the rest, Franconia is dominated by a continental climate, with cold winters scarcely tempered by the river Main and its smaller tributaries, and warm, very dry summers, providing the grapes with optimum conditions in which to ripen. Franconia has few soil formations by comparison with the geological diversity of the Pfalz or Baden. The soils of the Mainviereck (the "square" of the Main), the eastern part of the region, are mainly of residual primary rock and red sandstone, and further to the east the

soils are clay, loess, and shelly limestone. Red marl dominates the Steigerwald area.

BACK TO THE ORIGINAL FRANCONIAN WINES

Monks began growing vines in Franconia as early as the 8th century, and in the Middle Ages the vineyard area of the region was enlarged to almost 247,000 acres (100,000 ha), as large as the entire area down to vines in Germany today. At the time Franconia was the largest viticultural area of the German Empire, with a vineyard area far exceeding that of the Mosel or the banks of the Rhine.

Today the situation has clearly changed: with little more than 14,800 acres (6,000 ha) under vines, Franconian viticulture comes only sixth among the German wine-growing regions. Less than ten percent of the viticulturalists active in this region (over 7,000 of them) market their own wines. The overwhelming majority deliver their grape harvest to the various cooperatives, which then supply must or wines for bottling and marketing, most of these supplies going to the large local winemakers' cooperative in Kitzingen.

In the past Franconia was known principally as the land of the Silvaner grape. This variety, low in acidity and of rather subdued character, did very well on the shelly limestone soil of the Maindreieck (the "triangle" of the Main), where it developed a strong style with a slightly earthy touch. Today, however, the picture is

Select single vineyards
1 Stein
2 Stein/Harfe
3 Innere Leiste
4 Teufelskeller
5 Pfülben
6 Sonnenstuhl
7 Ratsherr
8 Lump
9 Schwanleite
10 Küchenmeister
11 Julius-Echter-Berg
12 Kalb

FRANCONIA
Bereich **Mainviereck**
◆ *Großlage* Reuschberg
◇ *Großlage* Heiligenthal
Bereich **Maindreieck**
◈ *Großlage* Burg
◆ *Großlage* Rosstal
◆ *Großlage* Ravensburg
◆ *Großlage* Kirchberg
◆ *Großlage* Engelsberg
◇ *Großlage* Marienberg
◇ *Großlage* Honigberg
◆ *Großlage* Ewig Leben
◆ *Großlage* Hofrat
■ *Großlage* Teufelstor
◆ *Großlage* Ölspiel
□ *Großlage* Markgraf Babenberg
Bereich **Steigerwald**
◇ *Großlage* Kapellenberg
◇ *Großlage* Zabelstein
◆ *Großlage* Steige
◇ *Großlage* Schild
◇ *Großlage* Schlossberg
◆ *Großlage* Herrenberg
Großlage Burgweg
◇ *Großlage* Frankenberger Schlossstück
◆ *Großlage* Ipsheimer Burgberg
□ Single vineyards not belonging to any *Großlage*
BADEN
◆ *Bereich* **Tauberfranken**
•••••• *Bereich* border
1–12 Select single vineyards

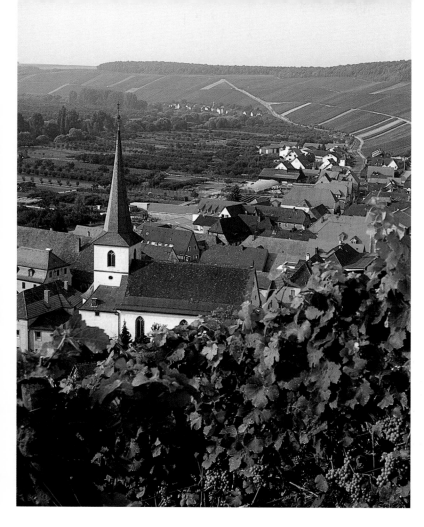

very different. Many viticulturalists decided that the variety was too difficult to grow, and consumers, out of ignorance, believed them. Today the old-established Silvaner grape has to be content with one-fifth of its original area, ceding the rest to Müller-Thurgau, which in some places even approaches the 50 percent mark. Luckily recent years have seen a reversal of the trend, and more and more consumers are re-discovering the superiority of the native and old-established Silvaner vine to the heavy-yielding Müller-Thurgau grape.

The region grows few other varieties. Only the white, densely-berried Bacchus variety with its faint muscat note occupies any amount of the entire vineyard area worth mentioning— about one-tenth—although Riesling and Rieslaner can produce excellent results, especially in the field of *edelsüß* wines. However, in contrast to almost all other winemaking areas of Germany, Franconia make no wines with any residual sugar worth mentioning. The majority of its products are dry, and the Franconians even use a special term to describe the flavor of their wines: if they have less than four grams of residual sugar they are called *Fränkisch trocken* (Franconian dry).

A good 95 percent of the vineyards of Franconia are planted with white grapes, but in

Escherndorf is a charming wine-growing village in an attractive area of country where the river Main describes a curve. It is well known for the Lump, its best vineyard.

The historic cellar with its barrels in the Bürgerspital in Würzburg.

recent years a small group of winemakers has shown that the region also has good potential for red wines. The Frühburgunder and Spätburgunder wines from Bürgstadt were known in the past for their good qualities, and for some time now good quality red wines have also been made from the Domina and Schwarzriesling varieties in the Randersacker and Nordheim area.

TEUFELSKELLER AND KÜCHENMEISTER

Although the region is divided into only three *Bereiche* (if we leave aside the Bavarian part of Lake Constance, which is of only minor viticultural importance), several centers of winemaking can be easily distinguished, each having its own independent wine typology. And one of the undisputed centers of Franconian winemaking lies at the geographical heart of the region, from Würzburg to Sommerhausen by way of Randersacker.

This area contains a large number of the really famous vineyards of Franconia, including the Würzburg Stein, Innere Leiste, and Abtsleite, and the vineyards of Pfülben, Teufelskeller (Devil's Cellar), and Sonnenstuhl around Randersack. Expressive Rieslings and spicy Silvaners are the local specialties, but even Müller-Thurgau can sometimes produce impressive *Spätlese* wines, and as mentioned above, experiments with red wines have been made near Randersack and the results promise well for the future.

Going upstream along the river and past the knee-shaped bend of the Main triangle, one comes to Sulzfeld and Kitzingen, where the region's large winemaking cooperative is located, and where, apart from a few undaunted viticulturalists, few people hope to make quality products. The situation is much more hopeful a few miles to the east, where a completely different viticultural landscape begins in the Steigerwald at Iphofen. Here the river no longer exerts any perceptible moderating influence, and but for the protection of the mountains to the east and north there could be little question of growing vines in this fundamentally bleak climate.

However, the major wine-growing areas of the Steigerwald at Iphofen include the world-famous Julius-Echter-Berg and Kalb vineyards, the nearby Rödelsee with the Küchenmeister

Left
Franconian wine with fish—a harmonious partnership of flavors.

Right
The cellarmasters still wear their traditional leather aprons for wine-tastings in the Hofkeller of Würzburg.

Drinking wine in comfort in the Juliusspital, Würzburg.

vineyard—the name means literally "kitchen-master," and one can only speculate on what it originally implied about the quality of its wines—the Schwanleite vineyard, and finally Castell, further to the northeast, with the Schlossberg. The vineyards at high altitude here produce excellent Riesling and Silvaner. The Franconian-bred Rieslaner and Kerner, Scheurebe, and burgundy varieties also do very well, sometimes producing outstanding *Beerenauslese* and *Trockenauslese* wines, as does the rare Huxelrebe grape.

The Heart of Red Wine

As the river Main continues its course northward from Kitzingen, it describes three huge loops; some of the most popular vineyards in Franconia stand on their banks. The leading vineyards of this *terroir* are the Escherndorfer Lump and Volkacher Ratsherr, to which the names of the Nordheimer Vögelein and the Dettelbacher Berg Rondell should perhaps be joined. Unfortunately, it must be said that the fame of the vineyards and the attractions of the picturesque towns and villages of the area are not always calculated to promote the quality of the wine. As elsewhere, meticulous care in vineyard and winery does not seem worth so much trouble when it is too easy to sell the wines which are the end product.

The last large viticultural center of the region is situated on the southern flank of the "square of the Main," between Bürgstadt in the west and Kreuzwertheim and Marktheidenfeld in the east, and some of the estates here also own vineyards in the neighboring Bavarian Tauber valley. This is the center of Franconian red winemaking. Bürgstadt, with its Centgrafenberg vineyard and its red sandstone soil, has always been known for this specialty, but the red burgundies produced in Erlenbach near Marktheidenfeld are also good, while classic Riesling and Silvaner varieties predominate again in the neighboring Homburger Kallmuth vineyard. This is one of the most remarkable hillside vineyards on shelly limestone soil in Franconia, and is even under a preservation order.

Silvaner and Domina Grapes

Hardly any other viticultural area of Germany grows as many different vine varieties as Franconia, and nowhere else is the policy of choosing which varieties to grow so strongly marked by tradition and progress alike. Today it seems scarcely credible that the vineyards of Franconia were once dominated by Silvaner, which until just three decades ago was grown even more widely than Riesling, not only here but in all the German wine-growing regions. At the time Franconia and Silvaner were synonymous with the indigenous spicy, full-bodied wines made between Würzburg and Iphofen, Volkach and Wertheim.

However, with the spread of such new crosses as Müller-Thurgau, Scheurebe, and Rieslaner, which guaranteed the winemaker musts with more weight, or greater ease of picking, or both, the Silvaner grape increasingly fell out of favor: it is not entirely straightforward to grow and does not produce above average yields. Now grown in just under one-fifth of the entire viticultural area of Franconia, it occupies only about half the space given over to Müller-Thurgau.

Nonetheless, the genuine white wines of Franconia can still be found. The best grapes for them grow on the Escherndorfer Lump, the Randersackerer Pfülben, the Iphofener Julius-Echter-Berg, the Homberger Kallmuth, and the Würzburger Stein, and have survived all the modernization of vineyard and winery work, still tasting as good as they did years ago: spicy, nutty, earthy, and smoky, powerful on the palate, and even with a faint suggestion of honey when the grapes are fully ripe.

Not so with Domina, the fashionable variety among the new crosses. When the local viticulturalists of Kitzingen took the name of the variety too literally and put the picture of a genuine dominatrix on their labels—along with her accessories and attributes—there was great indignation among puritans in the wine world. In fact the wines made from Domina deserve more respect, for this variety has given evidence of Franconia's potential to produce red wines even more convincing than Spätburgunder.

The powerful and intensely colored Domina, a Portugieser–Spätburgunder cross, has aromas of jam and berries, is very suitable for *barrique* aging, and with its astringent, rustic tannins benefits by being left to mature for some time. It is even possible to make *Beerenauslese* and *Trockenbeerenauslese* wines from Domina.

Going up the Main from Würzburg, the principal estates of this wine-growing district own large plots of land in the best of the Randersacker vineyards, for instance the Pfülben, Teufelskeller, Marsberg, and Sonnenstuhl.

THE BOCKSBEUTEL

In the 18th century there was concern among German viticulturalists over the increasing number of fakes then beginning to undermine the wine trade on an extensive scale. The famous Würzburger Stein in particular attracted the attention of the makers of adulterated wines, and at the time there was no wine law to ban imitations. To the Würzburgers of the time, the only proven method of giving some protection to the genuine Stein wines was a special bottle, sending the consumer an unmistakable signal that he had the genuine article before him and had not purchased a forgery. In 1718 the shape of bottle

known as the BOCKSBEUTEL was developed at the Bürgerspital in Würzburg, then the largest vineyard estate of the region. It is a squat flask, convex in front but flat when seen from the side, and it has become been the emblem of Franconian wine in general. Today the shape is protected by law, and elsewhere in Germany it can be used only for wines from the Ortenau area in Baden. Products from other countries can be marketed in bottles resembling the Bocksbeutel only when there is a proven tradition of that shape in their areas of origin, for instance in parts of Portugal.

SELECT PRODUCERS IN FRANCONIA

WALDEMAR BRAUN***–*****
NORDHEIM
15 acres (6 ha); 55,000 bottles • Wines include: Müller-Thurgau, Silvaner, Bacchus, Riesling, Chardonnay from vineyards in Nordheim (Vögelein, Kreuzberg) and Sommerach (Katzenkopf), barrique-matured wines
Braun ferments and matures his wines exclusively in steel tanks and new *barriques*. His reds are among the best in Franconia. Braun also sometimes produces such exotic wines as his Weißherbst *Beerenauslese* of 1994, made from Domina grapes.

BÜRGERSPITAL ZUM HEILIGEN GEIST**–****
WÜRZBURG
297 acres (120 ha); 900,000 bottles • Wines include: Riesling, Silvaner, Weißburgunder, Grauburgunder from vineyards in Würzburg (→Stein, →Stein/Harfe, Abtsleite, Pfaffenberg) Randersacker (→Teufelskeller, →Pfülben, Marsberg), Michelau, and Gössenheim
The smallest of the famous "Three Hospitals" owns not only the largest plot in the famous Stein vineyard of Würzburg, but also the heart of that vineyard, known as the Stein/Harfe. The range of varieties embraces the entire spectrum of Franconian wine growing, although with a rather disproportionate amount of white varieties.

FÜRSTLICH CASTELL'SCHES DOMÄNENAMT***
CASTELL
161 acres (65 ha); 400,000 bottles • Wines include: Silvaner, Müller-Thurgau, Rieslander, Riesling from vineyards in Castell (→Schlossberg, etc.), Sommer-Linie
This traditional estate on the slopes of the Steigerwald works its vineyards according to the guidelines of the Naturland association. Its Riesling and Rieslaner wines, its red wine *cuvée*, and its *edelsüß* wines are good to very good, although occasionally it does not seem to exploit its potential to the full.

RUDOLF FÜRST****
BÜRGSTADT
30 acres (12 ha); 100,000 bottles • Wines include: Spätburgunder, Frühburgunder, Riesling, Weißburgunder from the Bürgstadter →Centgrafenberg and Großheubacher Bischofsberg vineyards, →Parzival
Paul Fürst is the only winegrower of any great reputation in Bürgstadt, and has long been regarded

as one of the few German red wine specialists; his red wines grown on the weathered red sandstone soil of the Centgrafenberg are of top quality. His Frühburgunder wine is his great pride, but his Rieslings and occasional *edelsüß* wines are also outstanding.

GLASER—HIMMELSTOSS***
NORDHEIM
25 acres (10 ha); 100,000 bottles • Wines include: Müller-Thurgau, Silvaner, Bacchus, Kerner, Scheurebe, Spätburgunder from vineyards in Nordheim, Sommerach, Obervolkach, Dettelbach, and Neusses
The estate is in two parts, and the wines are made in the Nordheim buildings constructed in 1979. Modern winery techniques—the estate management, formerly opposed to *barrique*-maturing, has recently adopted the practice of aging the wines in small wooden casks—and moderate yields give straightforward, clean whites, and excellent sweet wines.

MARTIN GÖBEL***
RANDERSACKER
15 acres (6 ha); 55,000 bottles • Wines include: Silvaner, Müller-Thurgau, Riesling, Domina, Spätburgunder from vineyards in Randersacker (→Teufelskeller, →Pfülben, Sonnenstuhl, Marsberg, Lämmerberg)
Hubert Göbel cultivates 14 different grape varieties on his 15 acres (6 ha) of vineyards. This committed winemaker turns them into wines which are notable even in Randersacker, a place which is spoilt for choice. Especially good are his Rieslaner, Silvaner, and Domina wines, and his *edelsüß* growths.

JULIUSSPITAL***–****
WÜRZBURG
402 acres (163 ha); 1,000,000 bottles • Wines include: Silvaner, Müller-Thurgau, Riesling from many of the best vineyards in Franconia (→Würzburger Stein, Iphöfer Julius-Echter-Berg, Randersackerer Pfülben, Escherndorfer Lump, Rödelseer Küchenmeister)
The largest of the "Three Hospitals" of Würzburg is accommodated in the historic buildings of the Juliusspital, which can boast a spectacular cellar 273 yards (250 m) long containing wooden casks, as well as the oldest pharmacy still operating in Germany. Its wines have long placed it among the leading viticultural groups of Franconia.

FÜRST LÖWENSTEIN***—****
KREUZWERTHEIM

74 acres (30 ha); 150,000 bottles • Wines include: Silvaner, Müller-Thurgau, Riesling, Spätburgunder from vineyards in Franconia (→Homburger Kallmuth, → Richolzheimer Satzenberg) and Baden (in the Tauber valley), Fürst von Löwenstein in Hallgarten/Rheingau
This family estate owns the Homburger Kallmuth, one of the best vineyards on shelly limestone soil in Franconia. Recently the estate has also resumed operating its Rheingau vineyards.

JOHANN RUCK****—*****
IPHOFEN

27 acres (11 ha); 120,000 bottles • Wines include: Silvaner, Müller-Thurgau, Riesling, from vineyards in Iphöfen (→Julius-Echter-Berg, Kalb, Kronsberg, Burgweg) and Rödelsee →Schwanleite, (Küchenmeister), →Dolce Vita, Johann Rosé
Ruck has built a modern winemaking and storage plant behind the firm's traditional façade on the historic market place of Iphofen. The wines are among the best made in Franconia, with unusual size and elegance in the *Auslese* wines made from Huxelrebe and Rivaner in particular. Also to be recommended are wines made from the Kerner, Silvaner, Riesling, and Grauburgunder varieties.

EGON SCHÄFFER****
ESCHERNDORF

17 acres (7 ha); 30,000 bottles • Wines include: Silvaner, Müller-Thurgau, Riesling from vineyards in Escherndorf (Fürstenberg, Lump) and Untereisenheim (Sonnenberg)
Almost all of Egon Schäffer's few wines are sold to private customers—apart from certain quantities exported to Japan. The Silvaners in particular are well above average in quality.

RICHARD SCHMITT***—****
RANDERSACKER

27 acres (11 ha); 90,000 bottles • Wines include: Müller-Thurgau, Silvaner, Kerner, Riesling from vineyards in Randersacker (→Pfülben, →Teufelskeller, Sonnenstuhl)
Using gentle methods, Bernhard Schmitt gets the very best out of the grapes in his top vineyards. His method of working produces excellent results in his Riesling, Silvaner, and Rieslaner wines, as well as those made from the less usual Traminer.

TROCKENE SCHMITTS**—****
RANDERSACKER

31 acres (12.5 ha); 110,000 bottles • Wines include: Müller-Thurgau, Silvaner, Kerner, Riesling from vineyards in Randersacker (→Pfülben, Sonnenstuhl) and Würzburg (Abtsleite), table wines
Bruno Schmitt is the successor to his legendary uncle Robert, and makes mainly dry wines very much in the spirit of the founder of the business. His dry *Spätlese* and *Auslese* wines made from Riesling and Silvaner in particular are among the best in the region.

SCHMITT'S KINDER****
RANDERSACKER

32 acres (13 ha); 100,000 bottles • Wines: Silvaner, Müller-Thurgau, Bacchus, Riesling, etc., from vineyards in Randersacker (→Pfülben, Sonnenstuhl, Marsberg)
Since 1984 Karl Martin Schmitt has been working on old agricultural land outside the gates of Randersacker. Only the force of gravity will take the grapes here from one stage of vinification to the next, and it obviously does the wines good. Schmitt even succeeds in making excellent wines from the Müller-Thurgau variety, otherwise known as Rivaner, and in good years his Dominas are among the best red wines of the region.

SCHLOSS SOMMERHAUSEN***
SOMMERHAUSEN

49.5 acres (20 ha); 200,000 bottles • Wines: a full range of varieties from vineyards in Iphofen, Radnersacker, Eibelstadt, and Sommerhausen
The Steinmann family was better known in the past for its viticultural college than for the estate belonging to it. Today, the firm makes wine from an impressive number of different varieties, some as exotic as Blaue Silvaner, and bottles fine sweet wines made from the Scheurebe variety.

ZUR SCHWANE—JOSEF PFAFF****
VOLKACH

44 acres (18 ha); 150,000 bottles • Wines include: Silvaner, Riesling, Müller-Thurgau from vineyards in Volkach (→Ratsherr), Obereisenheim, Escherndorf (→Lump), Iphofen, and Wipfeld, →Schwanen
Modern vinification and modern marketing are very much part of the operation here, despite the wealth of tradition in the background. The firm's strength lies in soft Silvaners, delicate Rieslings, and rounded, well-balanced wines made from Spätburgunder grapes.

STAATLICHER HOFKELLER***—****
WÜRZBURG

297 acres (120 ha); 1,000,000 bottles • Wines include: Riesling, Silvaner, Müller-Thurgau, Rieslaner, Spätburgunder from many leading Franconian vineyards (the Würzburger Stein, Randersackerer Pfülblen, Hörsteiner Abtsberg), →Tiepolo
Although the Residence Palace in Würzburg was never devoted to the care of the sick, the Staatlicher Hofkeller here is counted as one of the "Three Hospitals." The estate saw its fortunes revive rapidly in the 1990s under the management of Rowald Hepp, who brought it back into the top group of Franconian winegrowers. The best results are obtained from the Würzburg and Randersacker vineyards. Hepp had made some truly spectacular wines here before moving on to the Rheingau estate of Schloss Vollrads in 1999.

JOSEF STÖRRLEIN***—****
RANDERSACKER

18.5 acres (7.5 ha); 75,000 bottles • Wines: Müller-Thurgau, Silvaner, Riesling, and red varieties from vineyards in Randersacker (Sonnenstuhl, Marsberg)
Armin Störrlein makes 80 percent of his wines dry, and does not make *edelsüß Auslese* wines, so that the very best grapes of his grapes can go into the basic range. Even better than his good Rieslings are the red wines he makes from Domina and the usually disregarded Schwarzriesling.

HANS WIRSCHING***—****
IPHOFEN

155 acres (63 ha); 500,000 bottles • Wines include: Silvaner, Riesling, Müller-Thurgau, Scheurebe from vineyards in Iphofen (→Julius-Echter-Berg, Kronsberg, Kalb) and Rödelsee (→Küchenmeister), Sommerweine, barrique-matured wines
This estate is one of the biggest and best in Germany, and produces mainly Franconian dry wines, which are carefully matured, keep their freshness for a long time, and are capable of aging well.

ZEHNTHOF—THEO LUCKERT***—****
SULZFELD

30 acres (12 ha); 70,000 bottles • Wines include: Silvaner, Müller-Thurgau, Weißburgunder, Riesling from vineyards in Sulzfeld, barrique-matured wines
The only estate in Sulzfeld which can claim to be really well known. Luckert's wines are dense on the palate, with a clean tone.

The Three Hospitals

There are really only two "hospitals," the Juliusspital and the Bürgerspital, but traditionally the number three has a good ring to it, and the Staatlicher Hofkeller belonging to the Residential Palace in Würzburg was associated with the two real hospitals, so that it is now customary to speak of the "Three Hospitals."

The Bürgerspital is the oldest of these three institutions, which have connections with other aspects of the daily life of Würzburg besides winemaking, although their vineyards are indisputably their most famous property. Founded in 1319 as a civic institution for the care of the aged, it acquired its first vineyards a few years later, and today has been growing wine for almost 700 years. The secular counterpart to the episcopal Juliusspital, which still fulfils its original medical purpose, it works some 415 acres (168 ha) of vineyards, and is thus the fourth largest winemaking estate in Germany. Its famous cellar containing old wooden casks is also the largest of its kind that remains fully functional.

The reputation of the Bürgerspital is founded chiefly on the Würzburger Stein/Harfe, a *clos* in the center of the famous Stein vineyard itself, solely owned by the foundation and recognized as one of the best vineyards in Franconia. The Rieslings from the other parts of the Bürgerspital's plots in the Stein and its Randersacker vineyards are also of outstanding quality, and remarkable white wines are even made from the burgundy varieties from the Würzburger Pfaffenberg, which cannot really be considered one of the very top vineyards of the region.

Tastings in the Department of Anatomy

While the strength of the Bürgerspital tends to lie in its sweet *Auslese* wines, it is with the dry or medium-dry *Qualität* and *Kabinett* wines that the neighboring Juliusspital excels. Fully integrated into the medical hospital which gives the institution its name, and which was completed in 1576 under Julius Echter of Mespelbrunn, after whom the famous Iphofen vineyard is named, the estate also enjoys the luxury of its historic setting, a jewel among the architectural monuments of Würzburg. The princely building itself—with its 820-foot (250-m) cellar containing wooden barrels, the beautiful Rococo pharmacy (the oldest still in use in Germany), and the old Department of Anatomy, a hall now used for wine tastings and other events—make a visit to it an unforgettable experience.

With its top vineyards in the Stein, Pfülben, Julius-Echter-Berg, Küchenmeister, and Lump, the Juliusspital can boast the most consistent production of high-quality wines of all three hospitals in recent decades. One might be tempted to regard the estate as a pure Silvaner specialist, but that would not do justice to its outstanding Rieslings, and even Müller-Thurgau and the rarely grown Traminer can sometimes be matured into very fine wines here.

The two hospital vineyard estates are complemented by the Staatlicher Hofkeller, located in the Würzburg Residence Palace. We need hardly say that all the plots owned by this institution

The three great Würzburg winemaking institutions: the oldest is the Bürgerspital, founded in 1319.

The Juliusspital was founded in 1576 and established itself as the second largest wine-growing estate in Germany.

The Staatlicher Hofkeller, part of the residence palace of Würzburg, can hold its own with the other two in the extent of the area its owns and the quality of the wines produced.

too, the largest wine-growing estate in Franconia with its 370 acre (150 ha) of vineyards, are in the best situations of the region, and that it is not unusual for grapes to be brought here after picking from 60 miles (100 km) away, to be vinified and matured in the great building in the city center of Würzburg.

Although the wines of the Hofkeller were neglected too long, that situation was to change fundamentally in the middle of the 1990s. Rowald Hepp, who had previously been managing the state-owned vineyards in the Rheingau, helped the estate to make a new start, and the results showed within a very short time. Modernized fermentation procedures and a new stock of barrels created the right conditions for vinifying the grapes from the estate's top vineyards to bring out their potential for quality effectively.

Würzburg, a winemaking metropolis combining a taste for good living with remarkable cultural achievements. The inner city is bounded to the north by the famous Stein vineyard.

The largest German vineyards and wineries

The largest businesses in the German wine economy are found not among the wine-growing estate owners, but in the big wineries and the cooperatives. However, it is difficult to find reliable statistics on the amounts produced. Among the cooperatives the leaders in the field are the Badischer Winzerkeller in Breisach (ca. 30 million bottles) and the Weingärtner-Zentralgenossenschaft of Möglingen in Württemberg (ca. 27 million bottles), closely followed by the Moselland-Kellerei in the Mosel region and the Franconian Gebietswinzergenossenschaft.

However, by comparison with the amounts produced in the large privately-owned wineries, these are very modest figures. The output of the Reh-Gruppe alone is estimated at 200 to 300 million bottles. The volume produced by the Sekt winery of Henkell-Söhnlein in Wiesbaden is similar (including Deinhard Sekts and products other than wines, the firm produces 234 million bottles a year). The winery of Peter Mertes in Bernkastel-Kues is usually estimated to produce 100 to 200 million bottles, Peter Herres in Trier markets about 70 million, and a group of other firms (Zimmermann-Graeff, Langguth Erben, Pieroth, Rheinberg-Edeka, Kupferberg-Racke, A. Oster, and Rotkäppchen) produce somewhere between 40 and 60 million bottles a year.

Assessment of wine-growing estates must take into account the total area under vines and the quantities of wines bottled. The list is headed by the state-owned estates of Hesse,

An enormous and impressive cellar for storing casks lies below the historic princely building of the Juliusspital.

cultivating just under 470 acres (190 ha) of vineyards and producing 1,250,000 bottles a year. Next come Franconian firms: the Juliusspital (415 acres/168 ha; 1,000,000 bottles), the Staatlicher Hofkeller (297 acres/120 ha; 1,000,000 bottles), and finally the Bürgerspital (297 acres/120 ha; 900,000 bottles).

The largest family estates are in the Pfalz: Heinrich Vollmer in Ellerstadt (311 acres/126 ha; 1,500,000 bottles), and Dr. Bürklin-Wolf in Wachenheim (297 acres/120 ha; 670,000 bottles). Only two other estates in Germany (if we leave aside the very heterogeneous property of the state of Baden-Württemberg) have more than 247 acres (100 ha) of vines under cultiva-

tion (for the fate of Schloss Wackerbarth in Saxony, with its 300 acres/121 ha of vineyards, seems to be sealed). They are the Margrave of Baden's estates of Salem and Schloss Staufenberg (279 acres/113 ha; 900,000 bottles), and the episcopal estates in Trier (254 acres/103 ha; 850,000 bottles).

In all 14 major vineyard estates cultivate between 125 and 247 acres (50 and 100 ha):

Schloss Reinhartshausen (Rheingau; 214 acres/87 ha; 550,000 bottles), the three Wegeler estates (Rheingau/Mosel/Pfalz; 175 acres/71 ha; 750,000 bottles), the two properties of the Menger-Krug family (Pfalz/Rheinhessen; 185 acres/75 ha; 500,000 bottles), the Fürstlich Castell'sche Domänenamt (Franconia; 173 acres/70 ha; 600,000 bottles), Paul Anheuser (Nahe; 160 acres/65 ha; 500,000 bottles), Hans Wirsching (Franconia; 170 acres/69 ha; 500,000 bottles), the state-owned Meersburg estate (Baden; 153 acres/62 ha; 450,000 bottles; however, the state-owned vineyards in Baden-Württemberg in all cultivate over 247 acres/100 ha), Reichsgraf von Kesselstatt (Mosel; 150 acres/61 ha; 400,000 bottles), the state-owned Kloster Pforta estate (Saale·Unstrut; 148 acres/60 ha; 300,000 bottles), Fritz Allendorf (Rheingau; 131 acres/53 ha; 700,000 bottles), the Rappenhof-Muth estate (Rheinhessen; 128 acres/52 ha; 300,000 bottles) and the Reichsrat von Buhl estate in Deidesheim (Pfalz; 124 acres/50 ha; 400,000 bottles).

SAALE-UNSTRUT AND SAXONY

Vines were already being grown in the Middle Ages in almost the whole of what are now the eastern states of the Federal Republic of Germany. At that time the vineyards extended to the Baltic coast, covering an area many times greater than they do today. The inexorable decline began during the Thirty Years' War, to which countless vineyards fell victim, and those spared by the mercenaries fell victim to phylloxera at the end of the 19th century. Viticulture in the east of the country today, therefore, is confined to small parcels of land in the states of Saxony and Saxony-Anhalt, more precisely in the valleys of the rivers Elbe, Saale, and Unstrut. Naturally, vines continued to be grown here during the years of the German Democratic Republic, but even more than in the west growers concentrated almost exclusively on the amounts that could be harvested, and the quality of the products took second place in the planned economy.

Although the move toward quality began in the west in the 1980s and 1990s, the comparable process in the east set in only very hesitantly after the reunification of the country. The economic difficulties facing most firms in former East Germany, and the absence of any structure of small and medium-sized wine-growing businesses, made the production of top quality wines almost impossible. In addition, viticulture in the

new wine-growing regions of Saale-Unstrut and Saxony had to be organized in difficult climatic conditions. These are the two most northerly wine-growing areas in Germany, and come up against the viticultural limit beyond which grapes cannot be expected to ripen regularly. As in Franconia and Württemberg, the climate is continental in nature, but here the mild summers are counteracted by even colder winters.

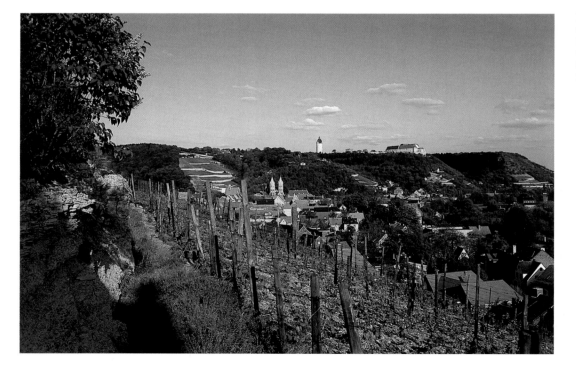

Freyburg on the Unstrut is the center of viticulture in the Saale-Unstrut region: there is little rain, the sun ripens the grapes well, and yields are naturally low.

SAALE-UNSTRUT

In the Saale and Unstrut region, vines have been cultivated for a thousand years. There are documentary records as early as 1066 showing that grapes were grown by the Cistercian monks of Kloster Pforta, today a state-owned vineyard. The grapes which ripen on the slopes rising above the banks of the rivers Saale, Unstrut, and Ilm and the lake called the Süßer See are mainly white. The most important factor in the favorable climate here is the slight amount of rainfall, only 19.5 inches (50 cm) a year.

The principal grape grown in the 20 single vineyards of the area is a rather insipid Müller-Thurgau, which accounts for a quarter of the bottles of wine here, although its stocks have been considerably reduced since 1991. Silvaner and Weißburgunder each occupy one-tenth of the cultivated vineyards, followed by Kerner, Riesling, and Traminer. Of the 235 acres (95 ha) stocked with black grape varieties, Portugieser is grown on 99 acres (40 ha). At the time of writing experiments are in progress with Zweigelt, Lemberger, and the cross known as Regent. The entire cultivated vineyard area is 1,284 acres (520 ha), of which 864 acres (350 ha) are part of the viticulturalists' association of Freyburg, comprising some 500 part-time winegrowers and six agrarian cooperatives. Of the 18 vineyard estates, ten are run by full-time viticulturalists.

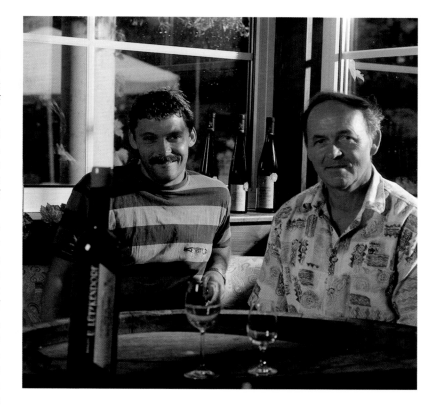

Uwe Lützkendorf and his father Udo make wines which give evidence of the potential of former East German wine-growing areas, particularly in wines from the Pfortenser Köppelberg, a vineyard laid out by the monks of the monastery of Pforta as early as 1154.

SAXONY

The smallest wine-growing area of Germany, in the valley of the Elbe between Dresden and Meissen is also dominated by Müller-Thurgau. However, through the extension of the cultivated vineyard area from about 495 acres (200 ha) in the days of the D.D.R. to over 865 acres (350 ha) at present, with the support of a reunification bonus from the European Union,

The Rotkäppchen Fairy Tale

Children are not aware of this, but their parents have suspected it for a long time and several tests have revealed that generations of parents, grandparents, brothers, and sisters have unwittingly spread a false fact. What the innocent granddaughter was given to take to her sick grandmother in the woods by her mother, was not any old wine, it was Sekt! And the name of a Sekt brand has become so linked to the fairytale character, that experts still believe the sparkling wine was named after this girl.

That may be a fairytale in itself, but what is true is the one success of the former East Germany's winemaking industry: the story of Rotkäppchen (Little Red Riding Hood) Sekt. The winery in Freyburg on the Unstrut, founded in 1856 by the families of Kloss and Foerster, had sold the brand name which they had used since 1894 (and which originally referred to the red foil caps on the bottles), to a Rüdesheim winery making Sekt founded in

The Rotkäppchenhaus—the scene of Sekt production.

1919. After reunification the name was sold back to Freyburg, and this incident marked the start of an astonishing rise in the firm's fortunes.

Although the Sekt market was in crisis, the winery, which had scarcely managed to sell 15 million bottles before reunification, was very soon marketing 25 million, then after the purchase of Mumm 92 million bottles a year, and Rotkäppchen became one of the most widely drunk German sparkling wines. Of course the base wines to make such quantities do not now come from East German vineyards, but are bought in from various European countries, as is the case with almost all German Sekt wineries. This success has been made possible by modern winemaking technology and exemplary management, and Rotkäppchen could perhaps motivate other viticulturalists and cellarmasters on the Elbe, Saale, and Unstrut to provide wine growing in the east with a future.

Riesling and above all Weißburgunder have increased in importance.

Viticulture can look back over a long history on the Elbe as well, as a document of 1161 shows. The vineyards of Pillnitz and Wachwitz where the kings of Saxony grew their own wine are famous. The vines here were planted on particularly steep slopes so that they would be less exposed to the frequent spring frosts. In many years, however, extremely low temperatures reduce yields considerably. But the small amount of rainfall, on average amounting to no more than 19.5 inches (50 cm) a year, also restricts the yield. Where harvests yield no more than 320 to 530 gallons per acre (30 to 50 hl/ha) the environmental conditions in themselves will ensure that the best wines have

This winemaker's sign in Roßbach near Naumburg illustrates the pride in viticulture felt in the East.

Opposite
One of the finest opera houses in the world—the Dresden Opera House, built by Gottfried Semper.

a good concentration, despite their northern origins.

By far the largest number of vineyards, most of them only a few acres in extent, are cultivated today by part-time winegrowers who have organized themselves into the Meissen viticultural cooperative. The grapes picked in about half the vineyard area of the state as a whole are processed by this cooperative.

The state of Saxony originally ran the estate of Schloss Wackerbarth near Radebeul, which once comprised 299 acres (121 ha), with considerable success, and its Sekt was famous. However, as most of the vineyards were only leased, and many of them have now had to be returned to their owners, the future of this estate is uncertain, since its economic infrastructure has been withdrawn. On the other hand, Schloss Proschwitz, under Georg Prinz zur Lippe, is seeing a period of revival, and viticulturalists such as Vincenz Richter, Walter Schuh, and Klaus Zimmerling, who cultivates his vines by biological methods, are already offering wines of good quality.

The wine-growing area of Saxony, like the Saale-Unstrut area, is a favorite tourist attraction. Neither region has any problem in disposing of its wines at the moment, and both sell most of their products at high prices to day trippers. The rest strike a regional note on the wine lists of East German hotels and restaurants.

SELECT PRODUCERS IN SAALE-UNSTRUT AND SAXONY

GÜNTER BORN***
HÖHNSTEDT
21 acres (8.5 ha); 30,000 bottles • Wines include Müller-Thurgau, Weißburgunder, Silvaner, Riesling from vineyards in Höhnstedt
The Born family have built up a good reputation for the dry, straightforward white wines made on their estate, one of the first new estates founded in former East Germany after reunification.

LANDESWEINGUT KLOSTER PFORTA**
BAD KÖSEN
148 acres (60 ha); 300,000 bottles • Wines include: Müller-Thurgau, Weißburgunder, Silvaner, Riesling from vineyards in Bad Kösen, Schulpforte and Goseck
Originally founded by the Prussian state, Kloster Pforta passed into the hands of the state of Saxe-Anhalt after reunification. Today it makes mainly dry, light wines, although most of them are matured only in stainless steel tanks.

LEHMANN***
SEUSSLITZ
5 acres (2 ha); 20,000 bottles • Wines include: Müller-Thurgau, Riesling, Weißburgunder, Traminer, Spätburgunder from the Heinrichsberg vineyard in Seusslitz
Joachim Lehmann was endeavoring to produce grapes of high quality even in the days of the D.D.R. His wines,

which he has made and marketed himself since reunification, are fresh, with a clean note. Most of his output is sold through the estate wine shop and the inn also attached to the winery.

LÜTZKENDORF***
BAD KÖSEN
27 acres (11 ha); 55,000 bottles • Wines include: Silvaner, Riesling, Weißburgunder, Portugieser, Spätburgunder from vineyards in Karsdorf and Freyburg
Uwe Lützkendorf is now one of the best (and best-known) winegrowers in the east German viticultural regions. With his father Udo, formerly the cellarmaster of a state-owned winery, he has made the estate one of the most important in the Saale-Unstrut region.

SCHLOSS PROSCHWITZ—PRINZ ZUR LIPPE***
MEISSEN
78 acres (31.5 ha); 95,000 bottles • Wines include: Müller-Thurgau, Grauburgunder, Riesling, Scheurebe, Spätburgunder
As the first V.D.P. member from former East Germany, the castle estate of Georg Prinz zur Lippe deservedly enjoys a high reputation. The Prince courageously built it up after being one of the first to have his former family property restored. His wines have a clean note, with a good bouquet, and are almost all dry.

ULRICH SAUTTER, ECKHARD SUPP, PATRICK FIÉVEZ, ANTHONY ROSE

WESTERN EUROPE

SWITZERLAND

Switzerland is world-famous for banks, watches, and cheese, but beyond its borders you rarely hear about Swiss wines. You might just be offered a few rather mediocre examples in the course of some quaint promotional event where fondue, cowbells, and alpenhorns will probably be featured as the essence of Swiss lifestyle.

And yet there are grapes aplenty thriving on the 37,000 acres (15,000 ha) of Swiss vineyards, and the wines produced from them speak for themselves. Not a few achieve international standards of quality these days, and yet they hardly receive the recognition they deserve. Even in areas close to the Swiss border the people are more likely to have tried New Zealand or Chilean wine than to know anything about the products of one of the oldest wine-growing regions in the heart of Europe.

A COMPLEX HISTORY

Switzerland is a federated state which unites people and regions of varying different cultural backgrounds. There are four official languages:

This vineyard with its vineyard hut in Beringen, not far from Rheinfelden in the northwestern corner of Switzerland, belongs to the widely scattered region of eastern Switzerland, stretching from Basel to Liechtenstein.

German, French, Italian, and Rhaeto-Romanic. The history of wine growing in Switzerland reflects this diversity of cultural influences and historical developments. There are probably several ways by which wine cultivation reached the lands of present-day Switzerland:

• From Massilia (Marseille), the ancient Greek entryway for central European wine growing,

up the Rhône valley to Lac Léman (Lake Geneva) and into the lower Valais;
• From the Rhône through the Doubs valley to the Burgundian Gate and from there by one route to the Swiss side of the Jura mountains, by another to the upper Rhine and Lake Constance;
• From Lombardy to Ticino and from there via the San Bernadino pass to the Rhine valley in Grisons;
• From the Aosta valley via the Great Saint Bernard pass to Valais.

The history of Swiss wine growing is generally traced back to the Roman era, although their records of viticulture are poor. In the 6th century, more numerous traces were left by the Burgundian monks. They not only founded the monastery of St. Maurice (near Aigle), but also brought to Lake Geneva the first rudimentary wine legislation. In the following years, viticulture grew along with the monasteries. There is evidence of wine growing at Mont Vully in the early 7th century. In the mid-8th century there is proof of vineyards in the Rhine valley in Chur and along Lake Constance. Finally, by the high Middle Ages, no part of the country was without vines. They even grew in the Bernese Oberland. However, despite the quantities produced, the domestic consumption of wine could only be satisfied, right up until the 16th century, by additional imports from Alsace and the southern Baden region.

The 19th century brought about events that were to develop into a crisis by the early 20th. When the states of Baden, Württemberg, and Bavaria joined the German Customs Union in 1835, the eastern Swiss border cantons lost a market which had been significant. Things were made worse by the opening of the Gotthard tunnel in 1882, which allowed for cheap imports from Italy. Between 1874 and 1907, the vine parasite PHYLLOXERA devastated all the major Swiss wine growing areas. The situation was further complicated by creeping outbreaks of mildew. The vast extent of cultivated vines, some 84,920 acres (34,380 ha) in 1884, had fallen to almost a third, 30,769 acres (12,457 ha), by 1932. Not until the 1970s did increasing internal demand boost the wine-growing economy once more. At present, Switzerland's 13 gallons (49 l) per person demonstrates a fairly high annual wine consumption. The wine-growing area today amounts to almost 37,000 acres (15,000 ha), with a relatively stable trend.

Geology, Topography, and Climate

Almost everywhere in Switzerland, the Alps and their foothills set the conditions for wine

Swiss wine economy in figures				
Areas of cultivation (in 2002)				
Eastern Switzerland	6,397 acres	(2,590 ha)	72% red	28% white
Ticino and Misox	2,548 acres	(1,031 ha)	94% red	6% white
Romandie	28,144 acres	(11,390 ha)	46% red	54% white
Total area	37,089 acres	(15,011 ha)	53% red	47% white

The most important wine cantons Areas of cultivation in acres (ha)		The most important varieties Areas of cultivation in acres (ha)		
			1998	2001
Valais	12,911 (5,225)	Chasselas	13,336 (5,399)	12,970 (5,249)
Vaud	9,577 (3,876)	Pinot Noir	11,320 (4,583)	11,389 (4,609)
Geneva	3,294 (1,333)	Gamay	4,925 (1,994)	4,687 (1,897)
Ticino	2,471 (1,000)	Merlot	2,038 (825)	2,165 (876)
Zürich	1,542 (624)	Müller-Thurgau	1,712 (693)	1,611 (652)
Neuchâtel	1,497 (606)	Chardonnay	541 (219)	625 (253)
Schaffhausen	1,189 (481)	Sylvaner	516 (209)	516 (209)
Grisons	1,021 (413)	Pinot Gris	358 (145)	410 (166)
Aargau	981 (397)	Gamaret	121 (49)	272 (110)
Thurgau	657 (266)	Red Hybrids	111 (45)	250 (101)

growing. Close to the Alps there are TERROIRS which were created as the mountains pushed upwards. In the Pre-Alpine valleys and along the lakes, most vines grow on glacial moraines. The climate conditions also depend on the direct proximity of the mountains. The Alpine foothills vary the height and steepness of the vineyards, the mountain ranges themselves

View over Epesses on Lake Geneva with its impressive vineyards.

The Maison Carré in Auvernier, by Lake of Neuchâtel, has some old tools and equipment as well as some equally traditional wines.

constantly provide rain shadow and often serve as wind tunnels.

The unique topographical and climatic qualities of the different regions of the country each have their own very special strengths. On the southern side of the Alps, the sun shines at an annual average of well over 2,000 hours. However, excellent red wines can be found both in dry Valais, with 16 inches (41 cm) of rain a year, and in Ticino, which, with its 71 inches (180 cm), is definitely heavy on precipitation. On the northern side of the Alps, Grisons, with its 1,700 hours of sunshine, brings a comparable expressiveness to a glassful. Here, the southern föhn wind, so picturesquely known as the "grape boiler," blows along the Rhine valley. Other areas, such as Neuchâtel at the foot of the Jura, profit from the marked differences in temperature between day and night. Steep slopes in the vicinity of water are also considered indicators of quality in Swiss viticulture.

QUESTIONABLE CLASSIFICATION

Switzerland has no national wine legislation. The Foodstuffs Act of 1909 regulates the basics as regards the protection of consumer health. Wine-growing policy is mainly a matter for the 26 cantons. The Federal Resolution on Viticulture passed in 1992 is an attempt to define a set of uniform conditions. However, the situation has not fundamentally changed. On the one hand, the generously set upper yield limits (for instance, 25 gallons per 120 square yards (96 l/100 sq. m) for top-quality red wine), formulated in this paper, make the avowed declaration to promote quality wines appear questionable. On the other hand, the definitions of the *appellations contrôlées* sketched out in the above-mentioned resolution are, in the end, still going to be a matter for the cantons. In the 1990s, several cantons did decide on A.O.C. statutes. However, the intended reliability of quality often suffered from political concessions, so much so that in the late 1990s some winegrowers of high standing in cantons with an A.O.C. statute preferred to label their wines as *vin de table* in protest.

Due to the unalterable topographical conditions and climatic risks, Swiss wine growing has to live with high operating costs, which means that the country's wines are only represented internationally in the top price groups. Switzerland as a wine country therefore faces the task of justifying the fact that most of its large vineyards are stocked with Chasselas—a grape that is seen in other countries as being more of a dessert fruit. Such justification would be made easier with a less half-hearted official quality policy. Indeed, in the best situations in the Romandie, the Chasselas grape achieves a high degree of expressive power, depending on the *terroir*. In addition, Switzerland also produces remarkable red wines. The Merlot of Ticino has already developed into a variety of international caliber.

But Switzerland is also, not least, a treasure house of Pinot Noir. Almost unnoticed by the international wine markets, there are Pinot Noir wines ripening in some regions of Switzerland which seem to approach considerably closer than many others in the world to the Burgundian ideal.

The Château d'Aigle in the midst of the vineyards of the Chablais by Lake Geneva, where the Chasselas grape rules. Pinot Noir, in particular, also gets interesting results here.

EASTERN SWITZERLAND

Eastern Switzerland, with 6,175 acres (2,500 ha), is a small and scattered wine-growing region. The largest single area is the Hallauer Berg in the canton of Schaffhausen, covering about 370 acres (150 ha). The geographical term "eastern Switzerland" is used simply to separate it from French-speaking "western Switzerland." The vineyards of central and northwestern Switzerland are thus also counted as part of the "east." A unifying factor for the eastern Swiss regions is the predominance of two varieties of grape. The dominant red wines are almost exclusively prepared from Pinot Noir. For the whites, the leading grape is Müller-Thurgau. More sophisticated white wines are, however, produced from Pinot Blanc and Pinot Gris, while the best vineyards also use Chardonnay and Sauvignon Blanc. There are, in addition, two interesting native white varieties: in Grisons, the oily and at the same time robust Completer, and the fine, delicate Räuschling along Lake Zürich.

Small-scale vineyards in this area tend to encourage the opinion that its wines are provincial. In the 1970s, some producers further fostered this assumption with bland *vins de pays*. Nowadays, however, many family concerns cultivate a great variety of local and regional varieties of wine to a high standard. The present active generation of growers and producers is highly qualified, has a broad viticultural horizon, and can avail itself, even in smaller companies, of high quality (and expensive) winery techniques. It is the Pinot Noir wines, from grapes of strongly limited yields, must-fermented and aged in wooden casks, which are raising the reputation here.

In the föhn wind tunnel of the Grisons Rhine valley, the Pinot Noir is heavy and well structured. These wines, because of their expressive power, are made as if for oak-cask aging. The southern autumn wind also favors the remaining vineyards along the Walensee and in the inner Swiss cantons. In both Appenzell half-cantons, vines grow up to an altitude of 2,130 feet (650 m). The northern Rhine valley in Sankt Gallen forms a stylistic and climatic bridge to the viticulture of Lake Constance.

As the Swiss shore of Lake Constance faces north, the best wines here are grown on moraine hills behind the lake, along the Thur and Seebach valleys, and at Stein am Rhein, where the Rhine leaves the lake. The local Pinots possess a fruity, robust quality. The Pinots Noirs from the low rainfall Klettgau region are as a rule softer and fleshier. This also applies to the area known as the "Zürich Wine Country" (Zürcher Weinland) which lies between Schaffhausen and Winterthur. Its lush Pinots Noirs are drunk, almost without exception, in the capital. Along the upper Rhine and its tributaries are the lowest lying wine-growing areas of Switzerland: 1,165 feet (355 m) above sea level at Eglisau, 1,116 feet (340 m) at Döttingen in Aargau, 1,024 feet (312 m) at Aesch in the Birs valley in the Basel-Land canton.

In the canton of Aargau, the regional style of the Pinot is decided mainly by winery techniques. The almost universally practiced blending of fermented MUST and warmed must parts allows for balanced, accessible wines. In the Limmat valley and along Lake Zürich you can find robust, firmly structured Pinots Noirs. It is from this area, from the village of Stäfa, that one of the Pinot Noir clones originates. The Mariafeld clone is widely distributed throughout eastern Switzerland and southern Germany.

Since 1998 Schaffhausen, Aargau, and Zurich have passed A.O.C. statutes. However, it is not yet apparent that this has had more than a symbolic significance. In addition, just as in Germany, the quality labels *Spätlese* and *Auslese* have always been used. However, in contrast to their use in that country, their use here is down solely to the judgment of the producer.

This picture is deceptive. The old traditions are today being kept up by the younger, excellently trained generation of winemakers.

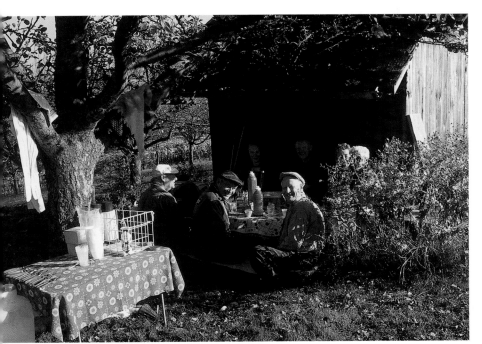

Select Producers in Switzerland

Bad Osterfingen★★★★
Osterfingen (Schaffhausen)
5 acres (2 ha); bought-in grapes; 20,000 bottles • Wines: Pinot Blanc; Pinot, → Pinot Badreben (Barrique)
From their gravelly, poor soil the Meyer family produce very stylish gastronomic wines. The vineyard also has a restaurant.

Georg Fromm★★★★
Malans (Graubünden)
10 acres (4 ha); 35,000 bottles • Wines: Riesling x Sylvaner, → Pinot Gris; → Pinot Noir Barrique, Merlot
Georg Fromm produces delicate but highly flavored wines. He has another vineyard in Blenheim, New Zealand, which has an international reputation.

Martha and Daniel Gantenbein★★★★
Fläsch (Graubünden)
12.4 acres (5 ha); 25,000 bottles • Wines: Chardonnay, Riesling, Pinot Blanc, → sweet wines; Pinot
The Gantenbeins have great versatility. Their Chardonnay has long been the peak of excellence in Switzerland, and the Pinot, aged in oak casks, is an independent interpretation of this variety, repeatedly discussed by wine critics. With the help of the föhn, here known as the "grape boiler," they have had repeated success in producing excellent sweet wines.

Hofkellerei des
Fürsten von Liechtenstein★★–★★★
Vaduz
5 acres (2 ha); 10,000 bottles • Wines: Chardonnay; Pinot
Recommended rarities from the enclosed vineyard of the Prince of Liechtenstein in the historic royal residence city of Vaduz. The princely house also owns vineyards in the Weinviertel area of Lower Austria, and it is from here that interesting tasting trips to the former Liechtenstein-owned estates in the Czech Republic are organized. The wines from the Austrian estates—the Merlot is especially worthy of mention—are in part marketed via Vaduz.

Toni Kilchsperger★★★
Flaach (Zürich)
9.4 acres (3.8 ha); 30,000 bottles • Wines: Riesling x Sylvaner, Räuschling, Chardonnay, Gewürztraminer, → Worrenberger Räuschling; Pinot
Very good white wines, clear as a bell. The complexity of the fruit is quite consciously placed in the foreground. A finely adjusted oak cask note in the Worrenberger Chardonnay.

Urs Pircher★★★★
Eglisau (Zürich)
13 acres (5.3 ha); 25,000 bottles • Wines include Riesling x Sylvaner, Pinot Gris, → Räuschling, Gewürztraminer; Pinot, Eglisauer Stadtberg Blauburgunder Barrique
Spectacularly situated vineyards along the upper Rhine, and wines that are just as exceptional: delicacy and body in great harmony.

Rebgut Bächi★★★
Truttikon (Zürich)
17.3 acres (7 ha); 50,000 bottles • Wines include: Riesling x Sylvaner, Pinot Blanc, Gewürztraminer; Pinot vineyard wines, Truttiker Pinot Spätlese Barrique
The Zahner family's Pinot Noir wines are immensely loaded with tannin and strongly woody—and they ripen to a warmth of Burgundy quality.

Schlossgut Bachtobel★★★★
Weinfelden (Thurgau)
13.6 acres (5.5 ha); 30,000 bottles • Wines: Riesling x Sylvaner, Pinot Gris, Weißriesling, Sauvignon Blanc; Pinot, Claret, → Blauburgunder Auslese No. 2
A perfectionist pace-setting concern with three different stylish varieties of Pinot Noir. Hans Ulrich Kesselring now also produces white specialties and the Bordeaux Cuvée Claret.

Hermann Schwarzenbach★★★
Meilen (Zürich)
16 acres (6.5 ha); 40,000 bottles • Wines include: Sauvignon, Chardonnay, Sémillon, Pinot Gris, Completer, Freisamer, → Meilener Riesling x Sylvaner Spätlese, Meilener Seehalden Räuschling; Pinot, Lemberger
If a vintner exists who can convince you that Müller-Thurgau is a high-quality grape, Hermann Schwarzenbach would be the man. The many different trial varieties are worthy of recognition.

Gian Battista von Tscharner★★★–★★★★
Reichenau (Graubünden)
15 acres (6 ha); 30,000 bottles • Wines include: Pinot Gris, Maienfelder Brisig, Sauvignon, → Jeninser Completer, Gewürztraminer, Traminer; Pinot, Z'blau Wunder us Jenins, Jeninser Blauburgunder Mariafeld, Churer Blauburgunder Barrique, Cuvée Anna
Gian Battista von Tscharner grows Blauburgunder grapes, from which he produces strong tannin reds which require aging; he also produces high profiled white wines.

Weinbau Scadena★★★★
Malans (Graubünden)
11 acres (4.5 ha); 20,000 bottles • Wines: Kerner, Completer, Aligoté; Pinot, → Blauburgunder Spätlese Barrique
Peter Wegelin's Pinots, aged in oak casks, have a fullness and intensity that make them stand out even among the best wines of Grisons.

Weingut Baumann★★★–★★★★
Oberhallau (Schaffhausen)
18 acres (7.3 ha); 50,000 bottles • Wines: Müller-Thurgau, Chardonnay; Pinot, 'Blauburgunder Trockenbeere
This family concern ages typical—in the best sense of the word—Klettgau wines. There is also a high-quality range of oak-aged wines.

Zum Ochsen★★★–★★★★
Malans (Graubünden)
12 acres (4.7 ha); bought-in grapes; 50,000 bottles • Wines include: → Chardonnay Malanser Selvenen, Pinot Gris and Blanc, Sauvignon, Completer; Cabernet, Pinot Malanser Spiger, Pi-Ca-Do
After a long period of training in the Domaine de la Romanée-Conti, Thomas Donatsch began aging wines in oak in 1974. Today he is an almost unrivaled expert in this method.

Zum Sternen★★★
Würenlingen (Aargau)
17.3 acres (7 ha); 60,000 bottles • Wines include: Pinot Gris, Sauvignon, Gewürztraminer; Pinot, Malbec, Garanoir, Regent, → Blauburgunder Barrique
The Meier family is famous for their impressively finely structured Blauburgunder, and for fat, Australian-style Sauvignon.

THE THREE LAKES

Auvernier is one of the most important wine-growing communities by the Lake of Neuchâtel. Here, a number of mainly smaller estates mostly produce the slightly sparkling Neuchâtel Blanc.

Above the wine village of Auvernier, the vineyards spread up the slopes and offer a far-reaching view over Lake Neuchâtel.

The Lake of Neuchâtel, the Lake of Biel and the Lake of Morat make a picturesque scene, forming a bridge between Alemannic influences and the lifestyle of the Romandie—and this also applies to wine growing. Pinot Noir and Chasselas, representatives of the eastern and western Swiss wine-growing areas, each have about a half share of the area devoted to vines. The wines here have an excellent reputation among initiates.

NEUCHÂTEL

The main wine-growing area, some 1,500 acres (606 ha), is on the Neuchâtel side of the Three Lakes area. It begins at the canton border near Vaumarcus, continuing above the northwestern shore, through the Béroche region toward Bevaix, Cortaillod, and Auvernier. Neuchâtel and its outlying areas also have magnificent vineyards, and wine growing continues through Cressier, through the region famous as Entre-deux-Lacs, to Le Landeron, on the Lake of Biel. White wine production is dominated by Chasselas, and the Neuchâtel Blanc is a light wine, extremely refreshing due to the residual carbon dioxide from fermentation. Pinot Noir is the only variety of red wine in the canton. Even the clones, with their reduced yield, are prescribed—Pinot Noir de Cortaillod supplies a delicate and yet well-structured Burgundy, and is given character by the climate and limy soil at the foot of the Jura. The Pinots aged in oak are particularly reminiscent of the Côtes de Nuits wines. Another specialty is the salmon-pink Œil de Perdrix—a fruity elegant rosé produced

without botrytis. Perdrix Blanche is a Pinot Noir vinified as a white. Chardonnay and Pinot Gris are also grown in small quantities.

Neuchâtel's discipline in matters of yield is proverbial in Switzerland. On an average taken over many years, the Pinot Noir produces just over 13 gallons per 120 square yards (just under 50 l/100 sq. m). For Chasselas, an upper limit of 2.2 pounds per 1.2 square yards (1 kg/sq. m) was set as early as 1990. An A.O.C. regulation finally came into existence in Neuchâtel in 1993.

LAKE OF BIEL/BERN

The wine-growing villages of the Bern region along the Lake of Biel lie tightly and idyllically enclosed by their vineyards. Chasselas wines here are less tangy and somewhat fuller. The Pinot Noir is brighter and lighter, but some of the Bern producers clearly demonstrate its potential with their more extract-rich wines. La Neuveville, Twann, Schernelz, Schafis, and Ligerz are the most important wine-growing communities. Erlach, on the southwest shore of the Lake of Biel, at the foot of the Jolimont mountain, also grows vines. The entire wine-growing area along the Lake of Biel covers 603 acres (244 ha). There has been an A.O.C. statute since 1996. The Bern canton also has about 35 acres (14 ha) of vines growing near Spiez and Oberhofen along the Lake of Thun.

LAKE OF MORAT/FRIBOURG

Mont Vully is a moraine hill with a slope falling steeply down toward the Lake of Morat. The microclimate on the terraces running across the slope above the villages of Môtier, Praz, and Sugiez is exceptionally favorable and produces some spectacular wines. The Chasselas is mostly soft and smooth, but the Pinot Noir, in contrast, is robust and dense. Specialties such as Traminer, Pinot Gris, and the Freisamer—cultivated here as Freiburger (Sylvaner x Ruländer)—are as a rule substantial and aromatic. As the entire CRU, including the part in Vaud, covers a mere 296 acres (120 ha), it has remained a connoisseur's secret.

In the Broye area on the southern shore of the Lake of Neuchâtel, just under 30 acres (12 ha) of vines grow and Fribourg canton has had an A.O.C. system since 1997.

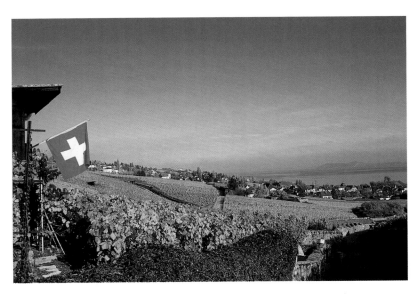

SELECT PRODUCERS OF THE THREE LAKES REGION

NEUCHÂTEL

CAVE DU PRIEURÉ**–***
CORMONDRÈCHE
111 acres (45 ha); 400,000 bottles • Wines: Chasselas: Perdrix Blanche; Œil de Perdrix; Pinot; →Domaine de Chambleau
Reliable cooperative with vineyards in Auvernier, Colombier and Cormondrèche.

CAVE DE LA VILLE DE NEUCHÂTEL***
NEUCHÂTEL
30 acres (12 ha); 100,000 bottles • Wines: Chasselas (Neuchâtel Blanc, →Cru de Champrevèyres), Pinot Gris, Chardonnay; Perdrix Blanche, Œil de Perdrix; Pinot
Very reliable production; the fruity, rounded Pinot Noir wines are very good.

CHÂTEAU D'AUVERNIER***–****
AUVERNIER
86.5 acres (35 ha); some bought-in grapes; 400,000 bottles • Wines: Chasselas (Neuchâtel Blanc, also Non Filtré) Pinot Gris, Chardonnay; Œil de Perdrix; Pinot Noir
A historic estate with wines to match; recommended standard quality →Château d'Auvernier Blanc, exemplary →Œil de Perdrix.

ENCAVAGE DE LA MAISON CARRÉ***
AUVERNIER
24 acres (9.5 ha); 50,000 bottles • Wines: Chasselas (Auvernier), Pinot Gris, Chardonnay; Perdrix Blanche, Œil de Perdrix; Pinot (Auvernier)
Wines produced with traditional equipment, sometimes rough, sometimes inspired; the →Pinot Noir is packed with body and oaky flavor.

ALAIN GERBER***–****
HAUTERIVE
17 acres (7 ha); 50,000 bottles • Wines: Chasselas (Neuchâtel Blanc, also Non Filtré), Pinot Gris, Chardonnay; Perdrix Blanche, Œil de Perdrix; Pinot
Particularly good are the extract-rich Pinot →Cru de Hauterive and the delicate, intense →Chardonnay made from old vines.

GRILLETTE—DOMAINE DE CRESSIER****
BOUDRY
49 acres (20 ha); 160,000 bottles • Wines: Chasselas, →Chardonnay "Premier," →Sauvignon Blanc "Premier," Viognier, →Pinot Noir "Graf Zeppelin"
Impressive, dynamic developments in quality in recent years: the wines have strength and elegance. Despite their international style, they don't deny their Neuchâtel origins.

OLIVIER LAVANCHY***
NEUCHÂTEL-LA-COURDRE
17 acres (7 ha); 50,000 bottles • Wines: Chasselas (Neuchâtel Blanc, Cru de Champrevèyres), Pinot Gris, Chardonnay; Perdrix Blanche, Œil de Perdrix; Pinot
Very clean, elegant wines and stylishly barrel-aged →Pinot.

A. PORRET & FILS***–****
CORTAILLOD
17 acres (7 ha); 60,000 bottles • Wines: Chasselas (Cortaillod, also Non Filtré) Pinot Gris, Chardonnay; Œil de Perdrix; Pinot
A concern with traditions, its own Pinot clone and a well-maturing prestige product, →Pinot Noir Cortaillod; in good years, there is a *non égrappé* version which is pressed.

VINS KELLER**–***
VAUMARCUS
32 acres (13 ha); some bought-in grapes; 100,000 bottles • Wines include: Chasselas "Cru des Terrasses" (Neuchâtel Blanc), Pinot Noir, Œil de Perdrix, Perdrix Blanche, Pinot Gris, Riesling x Sylvaner, Chardonnay, Garanoir, Gamaret
A well introduced traditional range and innovative wines, for instance the sweet →Lune de Mielle (Pinot Gris) and →Claire de Lune (Riesling x Sylvaner).

BERN

ERICH ANDREY***
LIGERZ
27 acres (11 ha); 70,000 bottles • Wines include: Chasselas, Sylvaner, Pinot Gris, Chardonnay; Œil de Perdrix, Pinot
Smooth, popular vineyard Chasselas, occasionally rounded off by a remnant of sugar; Schafiser, →Les Planches and →Marnin display mineral notes.

JOHANNITERKELLER MARTIN HUBACHER***
TWANN
12 acres (5 ha); 60,000 bottles • Wines include: Chasselas, Pinot Gris, Chardonnay, Sauvignon; Gamaret, Sankt Laurent, Pinot
Modern wines; clean, Twann Chasselas, typical, lightly wood-influenced →Chardonnay.

REBGUT DER STADT BERN**–***
LA NEUVEVILLE
52 acres (21 ha); 180,000 bottles • Wines: Chasselas, Pinot Gris, Pinot
Traditional, rarely exceptional but always reliable.

HEINZ TEUTSCH****
SCHAFIS
7.5 acres (3 ha); bought-in grapes; 70,000 bottles • Wines: Chasselas, Pinot Gris, Chardonnay, Blanc de Noirs; Œil de Perdrix; Pinot
A very reliable operation; even standard product →Gutedel Schlössliwy is of extraordinary stature.

FRIBOURG

CHÂTEAU DE PRAZ***
PRAZ
30 acres (12 ha); 75,000 bottles • Wines: Chasselas, →Pinot Gris, Pinot Blanc, Freiburger, →Traminer, Riesling x Sylvaner, Œil de Perdrix, Pinot
Powerful, mineral wines, which can be laid down.

ALBERT DERRON***
MÔTIER
12 acres (5 ha); bought-in grapes; 100,000 bottles • Wines include: Chasselas (Vully Bataille de Morat), Freiburger, Pinot Gris; Œil de Perdrix; Gamay, Pinot (Vully)
The Freiburger (new variety of Freisamer), a Sylvaner and Ruländer cross, is outstanding.

JURA

CENTRE AJOIE***
ALLE
12 acres (5 ha); 25,000 bottles • Wines: Riesling x Sylvaner, Pinot Gris; Garanoir, Pinot
In 1986 and 1992 a cooperative planted two areas of vineyards. This rare wine is seen in Switzerland as a symbol of a democratic federalism, and as such is held in high honor.

THE CANTONS OF VAUD AND GENEVA

VAUD

Some of the finest wine-growing areas are by Lake Geneva, in the Vaud canton. These vineyards cover a total area of 9,577 acres (3,876 ha), and are divided into the three areas of La Côte, Lavaux, and Chablais. Chasselas is the dominant vine. Red wines comprise only a fifth of the total, and of these the typical Vaud red wine of the A.O.C. Salvagnin is a blend of Gamay and Pinot Noir. An A.O.C. system has defined terms for regions and communities since 1995, though it seems dubious to allow not only the two historic crus of the Lavaux area, Dézaley and Calamin, to call themselves GRAND CRU, but all wines bear the description "*Château*," "*Clos*," *Abbaye*," or "*Domaine*."

On the moraine soil of La Côte, producers prepared to take a risk have raised the reputation of the previously average wines.

The steep vine-growing slopes of the Lavaux, especially the great vineyards of Dézaley and Calamin above Lake Geneva, are spectacular. Dézaley, inherited from Cistercian monks, produces fat, full-bodied Chasselas wines from granite soil. Its only problem is that its smoothness can overpower due to a lack of acidity. The particularly exquisite wine of the neighboring *cru* of Calamin is usually more classical. Wines of the surrounding communities also stand comparison. When the Alps arose, the tectonic displacement in the Lavaux region, exposed a great variety of geological strata. The diversity of the *terroirs* created is fascinating. Full, fruity red wines are also produced in the Lavaux in tiny quantities, usually *cuvées*, mostly from Pinot Noir. In Cully, there is also an interesting native red variety, Plant Robez.

The name Chablais is not a sad attempt at plagiarism; it derives from *caput laci*, head of the lake. The center of this region, known for Chasselas wines of great refinement, is Aigle, with its castle and museum of viticulture. Here, at the entrance to the Rhône valley, the northern föhn of Valais can already be felt. Typical for the region are shingly alluvial land and vineyards on landslip rubble. The soils also contain plenty of lime (Yvorne), magnesium (Aigle) or gypsum (Ollon and Bex). As far as body is concerned, the wines of Chablais lie between those of La Côte and Lavaux. Apart from Chasselas, Chablais also produces small quantities of red wine and some Pinot Gris.

The winemaker Dubois from Cully has plenty of reason to feel happy: around Lake Geneva, there are very interesting *terroirs* for vines, and there's no need to worry about demand.

The medieval castle of Vufflens le Château, to the west of Lausanne, lies in the midst of the best vineyard sites. From the tower, you can see Lake Geneva.

GENEVA

At 3,347 acres (1,355 ha), the Geneva canton is the third largest wine-growing canton. Only a small part of this area lies by the lake. The majority of production is in the Mandement, between the bank of the Rhône and the Swiss border. Here lies Satigny, at 1,205 acres (488 ha), the largest wine-growing community. The soils are rich in lime, clay and gravel.

Wine growing in the Geneva canton is highly mechanized, even using pick-up loader harvesting. The lower level of climate risk also sets wine growing in Geneva apart from that in other regions. The range of varieties is still dominated by Chasselas, and nearly a third of the area is given over to Gamay. Until the early 1980s, mainly plain wines sold by the liter were produced from both. The cooperative "Vin Union," which produced four-fifths of the wines in Geneva, failed to take advantage of new developments, and its operations were bought up in 1999 by the ecological vintner Jean-Daniel Schlaepfer, to shut them down for good. Today there are innovative vintners who sell their own products, creating interesting wines. However, the A.O.C. laws passed in 1988, which allow exaggerated upper yield limits and the adding of sugar at up to 9 pounds per 26 gallons (4 kg/hl), do still damage the area's reputation.

Select Producers of the Vaud and Geneva Cantons

Chablais
Henri Badoux**
Aigle
124 acres (50 ha); some bought-in grapes; 750,000 bottles • Wines include: Petit Vignoble Yvorne, →Aigle Les Murailles, Ollon Domaine Grange Volet, St. Saphorin, Pinot, Gamay
The company is famous mainly for its "lizard wine." High yields and an unclear branding policy have damage the reliability of the quality in recent years. These recent weaknesses have given rise to speculation as to whether all the grapes for the Aigle Les Murailles do in fact come from steep slope sites.

Cave de la Commune de Yvorne****
Yvorne
15 acres (6 ha); 45,000 bottles • Wines: Chasselas, Pinot
Wines which combine strength and refinement; the Chasselas →Trechene, which comes from a single, very low yield vineyard covering just under two and a half acres, is outstanding, as is the fruity Clos de l'Abbayé.

Domaine de la Pierre Latine***
Yvorne
22 acres (9 ha); 65,000 bottles • Wines: Chasselas, Pinot Gris, Gamay, →Pinot, Merlot, Gamaret, Garanoir, Diolnoir
The mayor of Yvorne is also a successful winegrower, producing harmonious and aromatic wines.

La Côte
Henri Cruchon****
Echichens
25 acres (10 ha); some bought-in grapes, 250,000 bottles. • Wines include: Chasselas, Pinot Blanc, Altesse, Viognier, Roquentin, →Sauvignon Barrique, Gamay, Pinot, Cabernet, Cabernet Franc, Merlot, Gamaret, Garanoir, Syrah
Because of his high quality and innovative experiments with different varieties, Henri Cruchon has become a pioneering figure in La Côte.

Domaine la Colombe***
Féchy
25 acres (10 ha); 75,000 bottles • Wines: →Chasselas, Chardonnay, Pinot Noir, Gamaret, Garanoir
Raymond Paccot is attempting, with great success, to rehabilitate the typical Chasselas places of origin of Féchy and Mont-sur-Rolle. Biodynamic cultivation and extract-rich, aromatic, clear wines.

Domaine Rolaz-Hammel**−***
Rolle
114 acres (46 ha); 300,000 bottles • Wines: Chasselas, Chardonnay, Viognier, Merlot, Syrah, Cabernet Sauvignon, Cabernet Franc, Pinot Noir, Gamay
A subsidiary of the mass producers Hammel, the company is experimenting with mainly international varieties. Of most interest are the *cuvées* of the →Domaine de Crochet.

Uvavins**−****
Tolochenaz
1,112 acres (450 ha); 2,000,000 bottles • Wines: a diverse range of product lines; varieties include Chasselas, Charmont, Aligoté, Sauvignon, Pinot Gris, Doral, Kerner, Pinot, Diolnoir, Gamaret, Garanoir, Cabernet, Merlot

A very good cooperative, which is working together with a renowned chef (of the same name) to produce the outstanding →Collection "Le vin vivant" de Bernard Ravet.

Geneva
Domaine des Balisiers***
Peney
62 acres (25 ha); 160,000 bottles • Wines include: Chardonnay, Sauvignon, Pinot Blanc and Gris, Chasselas, Aligoté, Cabernet Comte de Peney, Gamay Dame Noir, Gamaret
Jean Daniel Schlaepfer and his companion Gérard Pillon are important forces in the Geneva wine industry. Their vines are cultivated using the lyre system; the local hero Chasselas is being pushed ever further into the background in favor of more noble varieties. Red wine is prepared with a long standing time for the mash and partial barrel aging. Organic vines have been cultivated since 1980, and 66 percent of production today is red.

Domaine le Grand Clos****
Satigny
17 acres (7 ha); 35,000 bottles • Wines include: Chasselas, Chardonnay, Pinot Blanc and Gris, Sauvignon, Petite Arvine, Muscat, Gewürztraminer, Viognier, Petit Manseng, Pinot, Gamay, Syrah, Cabernet, Cabernet Franc, Merlot
The unconventional Jean Michel Novelle is Geneva's star winegrower and attracts attention every year with spectacular different *cuvées*.

Lavaux
Louis Bovard**−****
Cully
42 acres (17 ha); some bought-in grapes; 250,000 bottles • Wines include: Dézaley La Medinette, Epesses Terre à Boire, →Calamin Cuvée Speciale Collection Louis-Philippe Bovard, St. Saphorin, Sauvignon, →Dézaley Rouge, St. Saphiron Rouge Cuvée Louis
This house, rich in traditions, also values innovations such as the recent remarkable →Chasselas-Chenin *assemblage* from St. Saphorin.

Jean-François Chevalley***−****
Treytorrens
13.6 acres (5.5 ha); 30,000 bottles • Wine: Chasselas
A traditional family operation which manages to make the mineral qualities of Chasselas stand out. Particularly recommended are the two *grands crus* Dézaley "Es Embleyres" and →Calamin "Réserve du Margis."

Vincent & Blaise Duboux****
Epesses
6.2 acres (2.5 ha); 15,000 bottles • Wines: Chasselas: →Calamin Cuvée du Père Vincent, →Dézaley Haut de Pierre, Marsanne, Chardonnay, Pinot, Cabernet Franc, Syrah, Merlot
Duboux is one of the most distinguished family concerns in Lavaux, with small-scale but perfectionist production. The *grand cru* location brings a complex aroma profile previously considered almost impossible and a great elegance to the Dézaley Marsanne and Chardonnay.

Luc Massy***
Epesses
25 acres (10 ha); some bought-in grapes; 150,000 bottles • Wines include: Epesses Clos du Box, Dézaley Chemin de Fer, Dézaley Marsens, St. Saphorin Sous les Roces, Sauvignon Blanc de Epesses
Modern, very clean and smooth wines from the vineyards at the heart of the Lavaux region.

Valais

For many centuries wine growing in Valais satisfied only the canton's own requirements. Not until after the Second World War did commercialization produce yields that enabled wines to pass beyond the region's borders. The boom led to ill-advised speculation and excessive yields. Many vines were planted on the "wrong" bank of the Rhône, where there are no south-facing slopes for the vineyards. In the 1970s and 1980s, the Valais wine industry was in danger of losing its way in mass production.

Today, 50 different varieties of wine are cultivated in Valais. Some 22,000 owners share the wine-growing areas. However, over the past ten years Valais has succeeded in fixing and further refining its identity. The A.O.C. regulation of 1993, while establishing a few *grand crus*, has helped to achieve this. But even more important were the efforts of small- and medium-scale winegrowers, which have in turn influenced the cooperatives and wholesalers.

In the case of Fendant, the traditionally rather broad white Chasselas wine of Valais, biological ACID conversion (see page 125) is now no longer an irrefutable dogma. More and more, Fendant is bringing honor to its name by displaying the firm consistency of the flesh of the Chasselas clone in question, an indication of depth of AROMA and structure. The standard red wine, Dôle, produced from Pinot Noir and Gamay, and recently also from up to 20 percent of other varieties, was once a feeble imitation of the Bourgogne Passe-Tout-Grains. It has remained a juicy, easy-going wine, even though it could have gained in refinement—and has made room for alternative reds alongside it, such as the single-variety aged Pinot Noir. One specialty is the baroque Johannisberg, here a Sylvaner rather than a Riesling. The Malvoisie (Pinot Gris) is available in medium dry to sweet and fruity (*mi-flétri* or *flétri*) versions. Furthermore, highly successful wines are being created along the line of the Rhône, because varieties such as Marsanne (Ermitage) and Syrah thrive even on the banks of the northernmost section of the river.

In recent years the Valais winegrowers have rediscovered their great historic wealth of different native varieties. Humagne Rouge and Cornalin are striking, many-faceted red wine grapes, while Petite Arvine and Amigne are very, aromatic and also unusually independent white wine varieties.

With 12,911 acres (5,225 ha) of vines Valais is the largest of the Swiss wine-growing cantons. The valley rises from 1,509 feet (460 m) to 1,556 feet (630 m) over a distance of 31 miles (50 km). Some of the vineyards are even higher. There are gentle slopes where the vines spread out into the distance, and there are, as at Lake Geneva, spectacular terraces with vineyard walls many feet high. Despite the high altitude, the intense sunlight and the effects of the föhn create unique ripening conditions. As Valais is a very dry region, the winegrowers have to irrigate their vines in many places.

The region divides into three geographical zones. There is a small area in Lower Valais between Lake Geneva and the bend in the Rhône at Martigny. The heartland of Valais wine growing is spread out along the south-facing right-hand bank of the Rhône from Martigny to Leuk. This almost-enclosed wine-growing area has many different types of soil. In Fully and Martigny, the ground is poor in lime. In Leytron and Chamoson, the vines are grown on cones of volcanic debris. There are slate-based vineyards in the Sion area. As far as Salgesch and Leuk, the soils are poor in clay and rich in lime. Upper Valais is famous for the Visperterminen vineyard, which rises to a height of 3,609 feet (1,100 m). The oxidative "Glacier Wine," aged in the SOLERA manner (as with FINO sherry), is not from this area but from Val d'Anniviers near Sierre.

Visperterminen, in the Upper Valais, holds the altitude record for wine growing on the continent of Europe. The wine terraces rise to 3,610 feet (1,100 m), but the south-facing aspect and the warm föhn winds provide enough ripeness.

Vineyards in Sion— extremely steep and stony.

SELECT PRODUCERS IN VALAIS

GÉRALD BESSE****
MARTIGNY-COMBES
36 acres (14.5 ha); 100,000 bottles • Wines include: Fendant, Malvoisie Flétri, Petite Arvine, Ermitage, Johannisberg, Pinot Noir, → Gamay, Dôle, Syrah
A leading producer of the new, elegant Fendant. The Gamay (three different pressings from three communities) and Syrah are also remarkable.

CHARLES BONVIN***
SION
74 acres (30 ha); some bought-in grapes; 500,000 bottles • Wines include: Fendant, Petite Arvine, Amigne, Muscat, Ermitage, Pinot Blanc, → Dôle, Syrah Domaine Blûlefer, Humagne Rouge
Well-mannered, characteristic, accessible wines such as the very typical Dôle Clos du Château.

OSKAR CHANTON***
VISP
22 acres (9 ha); 60,000 bottles • Wines include: Gwäss, Lafnetscha, Himbertscha, Réze, Heida, Petite Arvine, Amigne, Humagne Blanche, Malvoisie, Hibou-Eyholzer Roter, Humagne Rouge, Cornalin
This pioneer of native varieties ages nearly 20 different single-variety wines.

MARIE-THÉRÈSE CHAPPAZ****
FULLY
17 acres (7 ha); 40,000 bottles • Wines include: Chasselas, Hermitage, Petite Arvine, Malvoisie, Rosé, Gamay, Dôle, Pinot, Cabernet, Cabernet Franc, Humagne Rouge
She is a specialist in sweet delicacies, but her other wines also display style and quality.

DOMAINE DU MONT D'OR***
PONT-DE-LA-MORGE
49 acres (20 ha); 200,000 bottles • Wines include: Riesling, Johannisberg, Fendant, → Petite Arvine "Sous l'Escalier," Malvoisie, Ermitage, Dôle, Syrah, Cornalin
This winery produces independent Rieslings, which sometimes take a little getting used to, from clayey calcareous schist soils; the acidity is low due to malolactic acid conversion.

BENOÎT DORSAZ***—****
FULLY
12 acres (5 ha); 30,000 bottles • Wines include: Chasselas, Petite Arvine, Pinot, Humagne Rouge, Cornalin
Benoît Dorsaz is one of the younger producers who concentrate mainly on the local varieties of Valais, and use modern winemaking methods and stylish barrel maturing to give them polish.

BON PÈRE GERMANIER***—****
VÈTROZ
27 acres (11 ha); 300,000 bottles • Wines include: Fendant Les Terrasses, → Amigne, → Mitis, Petite Arvine, Syrah, → Grand Cru Balavaud: Pinot and Dôle
Reliable medium-sized operation. The wines from the *grand cru* sites are to be recommended, as are the exemplary sweet Amigne Mitis and the exquisite oak-aged Syrah Cayas.

ROBERT GILLIARD S.A.**
SION
99 acres (40 ha); some bought-in grapes; 1,000,000 bottles • Wines include: Fendant Les Murettes, Ermitage, Amigne, Muscat, Humagne Rouge, Syrah, Cornalin, Diolnoir, Dôle, Antares
Fendant "Les Murettes" is the best known Fendant outside Switzerland. Robert Gilliard produces very good quality wines.

IMESCH VINS**—***
SIERRE
30 acres (12 ha); some bought-in grapes; 360,000 bottles • Wines include: Soleil de Sierre: Fendant, Johannisberg, Œil de Perdix, Dôle, Pinot; Nobles Cépages: Chardonnay, Marsanne, → Petite Arvine, Marsanne, Pinot, Humagne Rouge, → Cornalin, Syrah
This *négociant* company is over 100 years old and is now managed with great commitment by Yvon Roduit. From 120 contracted winegrowers, it only orders grapes cultivated according to principles of integrated viticulture.

DIDIER JORBIS****—*****
CHAMOSON
6.2 acres (2.5 ha); 10,000 bottles • Wines: Chardonnay, Savagnin, Pinot, Cabernet Sauvignon, Cabernet Franc, → Syrah
Didier Joris carries out his small-scale production using the techniques of his craft, aims for appropriate oxidizing in aging, and produces concentrated, stylish, top quality wines such as the deep, intense Syrah "Près de Pierre," which need fear no international comparison.

SIMON MAYE ET FILS***—****
ST. PIERRE-DE-CLAGES
27 acres (11 ha); 75,000 bottles • Wines include: Fendant Trémazières, Chasselas Cuvée Fauconnier, Petite Arvine, Pinot, → Syrah, → Humagne Rouge, → Païen
Simon Maye is on the small side as a producer, but always has very high-quality wines with a high proportion of specialties such as Syrah de Chamoson Vieilles Vignes, Humagne Rouge or the barrel-fermented Païen, rounded with residual sweetness.

DENIS MERCIER****—*****
SIERRE
14 acres (5.5 ha); 35,000 bottles • Wines: Fendant de Pradec, Johannisberg de Sierre, Pinot Blanc de Gouning, Petite Arvine de Pradec, Ermitage de Pradec, Dôle Blanche de Sierre, Pinot de Sierre, → Cornalin de Sierre, → Syrah de Pradec
Mercier is one of the most consistent, exceptionally perfectionist concerns in the region. The Syrah has cult status; the Cornalin's density and fineness are exemplary.

PROVINS VALAIS**—****
SION
3,112 acres (1,260 ha); 11,000,000 bottles • Wines include: Capsule Dorée series; Specialités series; → Sélection du Grand Métral series: Petite Ariven, Amigne, Marsanne, Pinot Blanc; Syrah, Païen; → Cuvée du Maître de Chais series: Fendant St.-Léonard, Johannisberg Chamoson, Sauvignon, Humagne Blanche, Petite Arvine Fully, Grains de Malice; Pinot Ardon. Cabernet, Syrah, Cornalin, Humagne Rouge
The cooperative, with its 5,250 members, processes a quarter of all the Valais wine harvest, and two thirds of this—mostly of good quality—is bottled by the cooperative itself. The premium ranges Sélection du Grand Métral and Cuvée du Maître de Chais (barrel-aged wines) are even among the top quality products in the region.

ROUVINEZ VINS***—****
SIERRE
109 acres (44 ha); some bought-in grapes; 1,200,000 bottles. Wines include: Fendant de Sierre, Dôle de Sierre, Muscat, Johannisberg, Ermitage, Malvoisie, Noble Contrée, Les Grains Nobles, → La Trémaille, Château Lichten Blanc and Rouge, Gamay, Pinot, → Le Tourmentin
This concern has taken on a leading role with ground-breaking *cuvée* wines. In the late 1990s the family took over the important dealer Cave Ostat.

Ticino

Ticino canton is considered the sun-terrace of Switzerland—and especially of its German-speaking regions. This opinion mixes truth and tourist legends into a long-lived clichée. Nowadays, Ticino is indeed one of the most interesting wine-growing regions in Switzerland. In the Merlot of Ticino, Switzerland has a wine which is a trend-setter even on an international scale.

In the mid-19th century, when mildew had destroyed the previously customary mixture of red European grapes such as Freisa and Barbera, the people of Ticino substituted more resistant American varieties. The wines from the hybrids may have been noticeably less tasty, but at least they ensured economic survival. The various trials with different varieties, carried out after 1900 by the canton's research station, must also be viewed with this aim in mind. The cultivation of Merlot has been encouraged since 1907. By the end of the Second World War, Merlot had made itself at home, although for a long time it was only used for unsophisticated, light-colored table wines. Hesitant attempts by larger wine dealers to expand their ranges with prestige wines largely met with no response. Only when a group of immigrants to Ticino from eastern Switzerland started to subscribe to the Bordeaux model in every detail did a movement toward improved quality begin, which has continued to the present day.

Geographically, Ticino is divided into the areas north and south of Monte Ceneri. In the Sopraceneri, on sandy alluvial soils in the Magadin plain and around Lake Locarno, light, fruity wines dominate. In the side valleys and

The vines grow on steep slopes high above Lake Lugano. Here, the preference is for planting Merlot of Ticino, which has acquired a good reputation thanks to a series of excellent winemakers.

The grapes cultivated all around the picturesque little town of Riva San Vitale are almost exclusively red varieties, as is the case everywhere in Ticino. In the Italian part of Switzerland, white wine is the outsider; white varieties cover barely a sixteenth of the area under vine.

along the Ticino river the soils are richer in granite and poorer in humus, and the local Merlot is correspondingly firmer and more substantial. The Misox—a mountain valley near Bellinzona, which politically speaking is part of Grisons—is also counted as part of the Sopraceneri. In the Sottoceneri, the rugged Malcantone produces robust, maturable wines, while the Mendrisiotto, with its moraine soils of lime and clay, is associated with particularly full-bodied, fiery wines. In the Lugano area, we find berry-rich, soft Merlots. Apart from Merlot, small quantities of Nostrani—rustic red wines made from a blend of mainly Piedmontese varieties—are produced all over Ticino. The Uva Americana, still cultivated here and there on trellises, is mainly used to make an aromatic grappa. The proportion of the total vine area of 2,471 acres (1,000 ha) given over to white varieties is at present a mere six percent.

A D.O.C. system has operated in Ticino since 1997. The upper yield limits of 2.2 pounds of grapes per 1.2 square yards (1 kg/sq. m), giving around 20 gallons per 120 square yards (75 l/100 sq. m) are so generously set that you can even find Merlots sold by the liter with D.O.C. On top of this, up to 10 percent of other wines (including foreign imports) may be blended with a D.O.C. wine. This regulation will, in 2005, come under pressure to be adjusted to the E.U. wine legislation. However, the Ticino D.O.C. statute has already resulted in a considerable loss of trust. Some growers (Kaufmann, Klausener, Stucki, Zündel) therefore prefer to market their wines as *vino da tavola della svizzera italiana*.

Select Producers in Ticino

Agriloro S.A.**–****
Arzo (Mendrisiotto)
18.5 acres (7.5 ha); 40,000 bottles • Wines: Chardonnay, Pinot Gris, Pinot Blanc; Sottibosco, →Merlot Riserva
The domaine white wines are overloaded with wood notes, but the velvety reds are impressive.

Cantina Kopp von der Crone***
Castel San Pietro
15 acres (6 ha); 19,000 bottles • Wines: Merlot "Gorla," →Merlot "Balino"
Anna Barbara von der Crone, like many of her colleagues, avoids the A.O.C., disputed because of their lax regulations, and markets her intensive Merlot as Vino di Tavola.

Chiodi S.A.***
Ascona (Locarnese)
7.4 acres (3 ha); some bought-in grapes; 20,000 bottles. • Wines: Merlot: Preludio (Bianco); Ria (Rosato), Tre Terre, →Rompidée
Rompidée, with its strong oak-aged character, has acquired a good reputation in recent years.

Gialdi S.A.***
Mendrisio (Mendrisiotto)
Bought-in grapes from 148 acres (60 ha); 400,000 bottles • Wines: Riserva Gionico, Sassi Grossi
A new dealership with great ambitions. The excellently structured barrel-aged Merlot →Sassi Grossi, partly produced from air-dried grapes, lives up to them.

Daniel Huber****
Monteggio (Malcantone)
16.8 acres (6.8 ha); 25,000 bottles • Wines: →Montagna Magica Ronco di Persico, Fusto 4
Pioneering family concern, very consistent in quality. The 1985 Ronco di Perrico gave the company the breakthrough into the top echelons of Swiss wine producers. Since then, wines have steadily been refined in quality. The Montagna Magica, produced from five varieties, can reliably be counted among the most delicate, most complex and most dense of Ticino wines.

Adriano Kaufmann***–****
Beride (Malcantone)
9.4 acres (3.8 ha); 18,000 bottles • Wines: Sauvignon, Vino de la Meditazione Sémillon; Pio della Rocca, Pio del Sabato, Rubino
Adriano Kaufmann produces powerful red wines based on Merlot and/or Cabernet. He also specializes in high quality white wine production, in part using cryoextraction (concentration by freezing) to emphasize the fruit.

Erick Klausener****
Purasca (Malcantone)
7.4 acres (3 ha); 15,000 bottles • Wines: Merlot: Trevano, →Gran Riserva di Trevano, Château de la Musique, →Rosso di Sera VdT
Extreme must fermentation here probably produces the most extract-rich Merlots in Ticino. It will be a long time before any final judgment can be made on some Gran Riserva di Trevano vintages.

Sergio Monti****
Cademario (Malcantone)
8.6 acres (3.5 ha); bought-in grapes from 2.5 acres (1 ha); 20,000 bottles • Wines: Bianco; Rovere, →Malcantone Rosso dei Ronchi

Sergio Monte runs an exceedingly experimental estate above Lake Lugano, and he makes extraordinarily velvety, deeply fruit barrel-aged wines.

Mauro Ortelli***–****
Corteglia (Mendrisiotto)
8.6 acres (3.5 ha); 20,000 bottles • Wines: Bianco: Corteglia, Novi dal Drunpa, I Trii Pin, Novi dal Drunpa
Ortelli's high-quality wines go their very own Ticino way. His extract-rich I Trii Pin, matured in steel tanks, skillfully questions the often rather uncritical use of *barriques*.

Werner Stucki****
Rivera (Monte Ceneri)
8.6 acres (3.5 ha); 15,000 bottles • Wines: Bianco: Temenos, Conte di Luna, →Tracce di Sassi
Werner Stucki is devoted to small, hand-finished production. His outstanding red wines—especially from the Merlot variety—are distinguished by tannins that gather softness and structure together, and at the same time the perfect proportions of fruit and wood are impressive. This innovative winegrower demonstrated his international commitment with the reorganization of La Brancaia in the Chianti Classico region.

Tamborini**–***
Lamone (Luganese)
124 acres (50 ha); 350,000 bottles • Wines: Merlot: Collivo Rosso, Collivo Riserva, Riserva San Zeno, Vegneto Comano, →Castello di Morcote
Old established dealers near Lugano. Over the last few years quality has been somewhat variable. Many of the red wines appear thin and over-extracted.

Tenuta Bally****
Breganzona (Luganese)
17 acres (7 ha); 35,000 bottles • Wines: Bianco, Cresperino, Riserva Crespera, Topazio
Most interesting here are the robust red wine *cuvées*; the premium ranges, matured in the barrel, have become better and better in recent years.

Valsangiacomo**
Chiasso (Mendrisiotto)
62 acres (25 ha); some bought-in grapes; 500,000 bottles • Wines include: Bianco: Il Mattirolo, Il Symposion, Ronco Grande; Il Forno di Pedrinate, Merlot: L'Ariete, Piccolo, Riserva di Bacco, Cuvée Speciale, Roncobello di Morbio Inferiore, Don Giovanni, Rubro, Dioniso
Valsangiacomo's by now admittedly somewhat dusty range of wines is due to be restructured.

Vinattiere***–****
Ligornetto (Mendrisiotto)
128 acres (52 ha); 200,000 bottles • Wines: Merlot: Castello Luigi, Vinatierri, Ligornetto
Luigi Zanini produces modern, accessible Merlots with body and strength. You could fairly easily mistake them for wines from Chile or California.

Christian Zündel****
Beride (Malcantone)
10 acres (4 ha); 15,000 bottles • Wines: Bianco: Velabona; Orizzonte, Terraferma
As well as his white Velabona, Christian Zündel from Beride produces wood-flavored, firmly structured and very elegant red wines, which are now among the most sought-after in Switzerland.

AUSTRIA

In some respects Austria is a newcomer to top-quality European wine growing, although it is one of the oldest wine-drinking cultures in central Europe. The Celts may or may not have grown vines along the banks of the Danube, but they were certainly familiar with the value of grapes. Systematic viticulture, however, was introduced by Romans to the Pannonia Superior province.

Austrian wine legislation is similar in many ways to the German and, as in Germany, in AD 280 Roman emperor Probus authorized the garrisons of the imperial provinces to cultivate wines to provide their legions with the desired mood enhancer. A few centuries later, Charlemagne allowed for further development with his selection of the best vines—which he called "Frankish," differentiating them from the

"Hunnish." He also saw to it that wine growing received a secure economic basis by granting the right of vintners to serve their own product.

The first written evidence of wine growing in Austria comes from Mautern in the Wachau. Here St. Severin carried out his charitable works in the 5th century. Krems, the famous viticultural town, is first mentioned in 995, and in the 11th, 12th and 13th centuries nearly all the major monasteries of the Austrian and Bavarian Pre-Alpine region had agricultural estates here, leading to the first blossoming of Austrian viticulture.

It was to be the late 18th century, however, before any more significant developments occurred. Emperor Joseph II, in 1784 confirmed the right of HEURIGER inns to serve wine, and brought new energy to the wine business. The tradition endures and even today, in Vienna, vintners can sell their wines direct from the vat in their own inns (see page 546). Emperor Joseph invested great efforts in the quest for growing quality wine that could be taken seriously. These efforts culminated, in the mid-19th century, in the foundation of the viticultural college of Klosterneuburg—one of the first such institutions in the world.

Not even the vine parasite, phylloxera, could slow down this progress, which early in the 20th century led to the cultivation of several different varieties such as Zweigelt, Blauburger, Goldburger, or Jubiläumsrebe, and, in the 1930s, to the development of high trellis growing by Professor Lenz Moser. In this method of cultivation, the vine stem is forced to grow very tall, and with an equally tall wall of foliage it allows more efficient working in the vineyard and guarantees a high number of healthy grapes.

Rapid expansion of the wine-growing area followed after the Second World War, as did the division of the country into particular areas. This steady growth continued until 1985. However, as in other European wine-growing nations, Austria was then ruled by the ill-fated idea of untrammeled mass production. The deep crisis into which a small group of adulterators threw the Austrian wine industry in 1985 when they brought *Spätlese* wines with added glycol onto the market was a nasty shock. The Austrian wine industry reacted quickly and forcefully, implementing a new wine law, the strictest in the world of European wine. With firm determination, the best winegrowers in the Wachau, Burgenland, and Styria began producing wines that were soon to draw attention to themselves for wholly positive reasons.

Since that time, at least, Austrian wines have counted among the very top quality products in dry white wines and sweet wines. And since then, Austrian winegrowers have been and still are inundated with national and international awards for their Rieslings, Veltliner, *Beerenauslese* or Ausbrüche. The focus on these varieties is due to the climate conditions in this Alpine republic, which favor the noble white wines, as these owe their delicacy but also their capacity for aging to such conditions. It is well known that Riesling produces wines of the very top quality in the Wachau region, but even Grüner Veltliner, often underestimated as a mass yield vine, can rise above itself in good vineyards with controlled yield. However, the real surprises are the wines produced in Burgenland or Styria from varieties such as Bouvier, Muscatel, or Welschriesling, conjuring up lush exotic character or the most delicate fruit according to VINTAGE and vineyard.

Through careful work in the vineyards, the introduction of oak casks in cellaring, and rigid control of yield, the winegrowers of the Burgenland in particular have succeeded in recent years in producing red wines of an almost Mediterranean quality. The fruit and the elegance of the wines, together with perfect VINIFICATION, have aroused a good deal of interest, even internationally. Austrian viticulture has, so to speak, three red aces up its sleeve: the native Blaufränkisch and the St. Laurent, introduced from France via Germany, from which the third ace, Zweigelt, was cultivated in the 1920s and 1930s. Individually or blended, these varieties have such potential that neither Cabernet Sauvignon nor Spätburgunder—despite their suitability for some of the warmer vineyard sites in the country—have really had a chance to develop. These aces could become trump cards, given that world wine production looks set to become more and more uniform in future.

Kapfenstein is in the southeast of Styria, near the Slovenian and Hungarian borders.

THE WINE REGIONS OF AUSTRIA

Austria's wine growing areas are, with the exception of a few acres of vines in the Vorarlberg, shaped like a crescent around the eastern half of the country and the capital Vienna, and they form a bridge from the cooler northern to the southern, warmer climate zones of Europe. Warmer climatic features are evident in the two main growing areas of Lower Austria and Burgenland, particularly in the meeting of the continental Waldviertel and the hot, Pannonian (southeast European) climate. The large areas of water provided by the Danube and the Neusiedler See also function as a buffer between extremes of climate. In cool weather, they provide reserves of warmth, but in the summer heat they lower the temperature. Under these conditions, the varieties that thrive are primarily those that are given body by the heat but which can obtain the necessary potential for aroma from the cool nights of late summer and autumn.

The coolest wine-growing areas of the country are those which are the furthest from the great Pannonian region and the Hungarian

plain. This applies particularly to the Wachau, Kremstal and Kamptal, and to the northwestern Weinviertel in Lower Austria and the southern and western parts of Styria. It is no accident that the finest and fruitiest white wines are produced here; Grüner Veltliner dominates above all in Lower Austria, and Riesling—although cultivated only on an insignificant percentage of the wine-growing area—here achieves some of its best wines in the world. In Styria, the white whites can be even more delicate, but sometimes a little thinner, and here, alongside the international varieties of Chardonnay and Sauvignon Blanc, the often somewhat pale and neutral-seeming Welschriesling produces surprisingly fine, fruity wines of good character.

A BRIDGE BETWEEN NORTH AND SOUTH

The situation is different in eastern parts of Lower Austria and in the Burgenland, especially around the Neusiedler See. Among the white varieties here the dominant ones are those which can stand a lot of warmth and which are suitable for producing rich, often sweet white wines. The red wine varieties, too, such as Blaufränkisch, Zweigelt, St. Laurent, Pinot Noir, even Cabernet Sauvignon, which all need more warmth and sun to ripen, have found their ideal TERROIR here. With the possible exception of Blaufränkisch, it is mainly blends of two or three of these varieties which have made news in recent years.

A healthy mixture of the two cooler areas and the hot, southeast European region is found in Vienna and the Thermenregion which adjoins it to the south. The white varieties may traditionally be the main grapes cultivated in Vienna, but some of the younger wine producers have, in the last few years, changed the wine world's mind with splendid red wines. In the Thermenregion, the division of red and white wines can even be set out geographically, with a line drawn between the slopes of the Vienna Woods and the lowlands toward the Neusiedler See, where conditions are already very similar to those in the easternmost areas of vine cultivation. Finally, mention should be made of Vorarlberg, the most westerly federal state in Austria, where small quantities of fine white wines are produced, which have, however, not been able to achieve any real commercial importance.

Weinviertel
Kamptal
Kremstal
Wachau
Traisental
Donauland
Vienna
Thermenregion
Carnuntum
Neusiedler See
Neusiedler See Hügelland
Central Burgenland
Southern Burgenland
Southeastern Styria
Western Styria
Southern Styria
Wine-growing areas in neighboring countries

Left
The most beautiful part of the Wachau: Dürnstein in the Danube valley.

Areas of cultivation and production quantities

Federal state area of cultivation	Vine-growing area in acres (hectares) in 1999		Ave. annual prod. in the 1990s in 1,000s gallons (hectoliters)	
Lower Austria	74,067	(29,975)	38,280	(1,450,000)
Wachau	3,435	(1,390)		
Kremstal	5,364	(2,171)		
Kamptal	9,555	(3,867)		
Danubelands	6,748	(2,731)		
Traisental	1,685	(682)		
Carnuntum	2,204	(892)		
Weinviertel	39,234	(15,878)		
Thermenregion	5,747	(2,326)		
Without wine-growing area	94	(38)		
Burgenland	35,925	(14,539)	20,460	(775,000)
Neusiedler See	20,521	(8,305)		
Neusiedlersee-Hügelland	9,664	(3,911)		
Central Burgenland	4,633	(1,875)		
Southern Burgenland	1,107	(448)		
Styria	8,112	(3,283)	3,828	(145,000)
Southern Styria	4,297	(1,739)		
Western Styria	1,067	(432)		
Southeastern Styria	2,743	(1,110)		
Without wine-growing area	5	(2)		
Vienna	1,675	(678)	581	(22,000)
Outside the areas under cultivation	52	(21)		n n
Total	119,832	(48,496)	63,360	(2,392,000)

Figures from 2002/1999. Source: Ö.W.M.

The weather in the famous wine village of Spielfeld in southern Styria is like the Mediterranean in summer, but snowy in winter.

New Wine Law

The Austrians are currently working on a new wine law. This is within the framework of the European Community, where the aim is to achieve uniform community wine regulations in every member state in the longer term. Following the controls on designation of the place of origin in France, Italy and Spain, Austria has also started to introduce the D.A.C. labelling for quality wines that are typical of their area. The classification *Districtus Austriae Controllatus* is being introduced on the basis of the present 16 wine-growing districts and their quality requirements. The growers will be able to decide themselves whether to adopt the marking, which will be applied through inter-professional committees. D.A.C. will replace the older commercial classifications *Qualitätswein* or *Prädikatswein* and the individual quality classes. The Weinviertel district has pioneered the application of D.A.C.

The Danube Lands

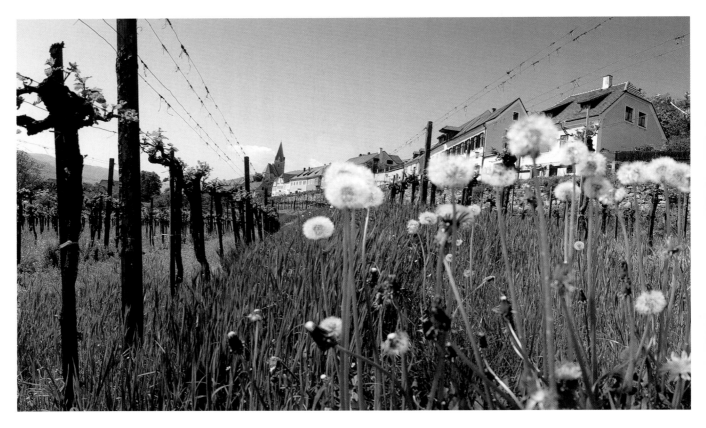

The best-known wine lands of Austria lie along the banks of the Danube, only about 60 miles (100 km) upriver from the capital of Vienna. Krems, the old wine city, is the center of a collection of wine-growing areas whose present shape has been determined only over the past two decades. The most famous of these areas, without a doubt, is the Wachau. Vines were grown here as early as the middle of the first millennium AD. The gently winding Danube valley between Melk and Mautern, with terraced vineyards growing on the slopes of the northern bank, rivals the most beautiful wine landscapes of Europe, and not least for that reason attracts and enchants hundreds of thousands of visitors every year.

The special climate conditions of the Danube valley arise from its particular position at the point where the southeast European climate region meets that of the Waldviertel, which is still Atlantic in type. Here there is a continuous exchange of warm and cold masses of air, which provides the grapes with the warmth to ripen and the nighttime coolness to develop their aroma.

As far as the ground is concerned, the vineyard hills of the Wachau—the Loibenberg,

In Austria, organic farming has become more widespread than in any other country. A "green" vineyard such as this one in the Wachau is no longer an unusual sight.

Dürnsteiner Kellerberg, Achleiten, Klaus, and the Spitzer Singerriedel are famous—are characterized by ancient rock formations of iron-rich gneiss, granite or slate, though in the lower-lying regions loess, sand, and alluvial gravel may predominate.

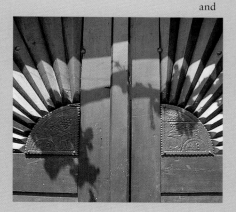
THE WACHAU

In the Wachau, Riesling reigns supreme. Indeed, many Austrians like to believe the grape originated here. However, because of the different types of soil, there is a wide range of vines grown here, each of which can find its own best environment. Apart from Riesling, Grüner Veltliner is the best known variety, which rarely develops a similar degree of aroma and flavor anywhere else. But even Sauvignon Blanc or Chardonnay (which the inhabitants of the Wachau, set on their claim to uniqueness, have tried to rename "Feinburgunder") may find their optimum *terroir* here, where they can develop all their delicacy.

Epitomizing the individuality, much prized by the people of the Wachau, is the "Vinea Wachau Nobilis Districtus" association, formed in the

On the road to the vineyard: everyday life in Loiben.

1980s and now highly respected. The association defined and named its own levels of quality and successfully fought for the right to use them officially as wine names. You will seek in vain for *Kabinett, Spätlese* or *Auslese* wines in the Wachau. Here they drink *Steinfeder, Federspiel,* or *Smaragd* instead.

KREMSTAL AND KAMPTAL

Much less well known than the Wachau, but with no less potential for quality, the two other wine-growing regions in the environs of the city of Krems are Kremstal and Kamptal. This is not surprising since the western vineyards of the Kremstal, on the Pfaffenberg and the Steinerne Hund, are geologically and climatically speaking still part of the Wachau, from which they were removed for purely political reasons.

Only a few hundred yards further on, where the Danube leaves the narrow valley of the Wachau and flows into the broad plain, there are noticeably stronger eastern European climate conditions, and the difference from the Wachau is also undeniable when it comes to soils. Mighty terraces of loess stretch out from the city to the northeast and form an outstanding *terroir* for Grüner Veltliner, which here sometimes produces wine more dense, but rarely more fine than in the Wachau. On the clay and conglomerate soils of the other parts of Kremstal and Kamptal, too, excellent Grüner Veltliner, Chardonnay, and even red varieties grow.

One of the few ancient rock formations of the Kamptal is the Heiligenstein, a monolithic crag towering above the villages of Zöbing and Langenlois. Its Rieslings are the absolute equals of any produced by the top Wachau vineyards, especially if they are pressed from grapes of old vines.

SELECT PRODUCERS IN WACHAU, KREMSTAL, AND KAMPTAL

LEO ALZINGER***—****
DÜRNSTEIN-UNTERLOIBEN
11 acres (4.5 ha); 36,000 bottles • Wines: Grüner Veltliner, Riesling, Chardonnay from Frauenweingarten, Mühlpoint, →Loibenberg, →Steinertal, Hollerin, Höhereck
Leo Alzinger's golden rule is to treat the grapes and the musts very carefully. The grapes are removed from the stalks, moved on without the use of pumps, fermented with their own yeasts and then matured in wooden casks or steel tanks. The resulting wines are always honest and complex, and of a convincing quality.

WILHELM. BRÜNDLMAYER/
SCHLOSS GOBELSBURG***—*****
LANGENLOIS/GOBELSBURG
203 acres (82 ha); 79 acres (32 ha); 350,000 bottles/ 350,000 bottles • Wines: Grüner Veltliner, →Riesling, →Chardonnay, Zweigelt, Blauer Burgunder, St. Laurent, Merlot and others from →Heiligenstein, →Spiegel, Loiserberg, →Berg Vogelsang, Dechant, Gaisberg, Hussen, →Lamm
In the late 1980s, Willi Bründelmayer was one of the first producers whose wines were successful abroad. His Chardonnay, in particular, attracted attention and often emerged favorably from comparisons with more famous vines. However, it is the Rieslings from Heiligenstein which are his best wines. Since 1996, Bründelmayer has also been managing the estate at Schloss Gobelsburg and has once more made its wines into what they should be, given the potential of their vineyard sites: top of the Kamptal range.

PETER DOLLE**—****
STRASS
74 acres (30 ha); 200,000 bottles • Wines: Grüner Veltliner, Riesling, Weißburgunder, St. Laurent and others from →Gaisberg, Brunngasse, Hasel, Sandgrube
While other wine producers in Lower Austria tried their hand at Chardonnay, Peter Dolle put his trust primarily in Weißburgunder. However, the highest position in current production is held by his Veltliner and Riesling.

LUDWIG EHN***—****
LANGENLOIS
35 acres (14 ha); 70,000 bottles • Wines: Grüner Veltliner, Riesling, Chardonnay, Sauvignon, Blauer Burgunder and others from →Seeberg, →Panzaun, →Heiligenstein, →Titan
Modern, fruity, rounded wines, where the sometimes clearly noticeable residual sweetness has a harmonious effect—these are the characteristic wines from Ludwig and Michael Ehn's estate in the center of Langenlois. The top wine is a Grüner Veltliner, aged in oak, called Titan.

FREIE WEINGÄRTNER WACHAU**—****
DÜRNSTEIN
1,610 acres (650 ha); 3,200,000 bottles • Wines: Grüner Veltliner, Riesling, Neuburger, Müller-Thurgau, Weißburgunder from Loibenberg, →Kellerberg, →Achleiten, Vorderseiber, →Singerriedel, Tausendeimerberg
The good value offered by this cooperative is astonishing. It can compete with the best wine producers in the Wachau as regards quality, but its pricing is not at all ambitious. Pressing is done in five houses, and the center of the operation is in Dürnstein, near the impressive little Baroque palace of the vintners, whose trump card, apart from a very high quality management team, is the large share they own of the top vineyard sites at Kellerberg.

GEYERHOF, FAMILIE MAIER**—****
FURTH/GOTTWEIG
41 acres (16.5 ha); 55,000 bottles • Wines: Grüner Veltliner, Weißburgunder, Riesling, Zweigelt and others from Richtern, Hoher Rain, Gaisberg, Rosensteig, →Sprintzenberg, 'Steinleithn
Outstanding red wines. However, the company's strengths lie in the Veltliner from the various different vineyards. Since the early 1990s, the company has been run on organic lines.

LUDWIG HIEDLER***—****
LANGENLOIS
57 acres (23 ha); 150,000 bottles • Wines: Grüner Veltliner, Weißburgunder, Riesling, Chardonnay and others from →Thal, 'Speigel, →Heiligenstein, Loiserberg, Kittmannsberg, →Liubisa
Hiedler has rigorously converted his winery to the most modern technology and methods. Liubisa, one of his best, is blended from Spätburgunder and Sangiovese and is one of Austria's most extravagant *cuvées*.

FRANZ HIRTZBERGER***—*****
SPITZ
27 acres (11 ha); 120,000 bottles • Wines: Grüner Veltliner, Riesling, Weißburgunder, Chardonnay and others from →Singerriedel, Hochrain, Rotes Tor, Steinporz, Donaugarten, →Grüner Veltliner Honivogl
The leader of the "Vinea Wachau" association not only owns large chunks of the absolute top quality vineyard site in the Wachau—the Singerriedel in Spitz—but is also an absolute perfectionist in the winery. His Rieslings are characterized by strength, elegance and structure, but the Honivogl and the Chardonnay are not far behind in quality.

JOSEF HÖGL***—*****
SPITZ
15 acres (6 ha); 35,000 bottles • Wines: Riesling, Grüner Veltliner, Sauvignon and others from →Bruck, →Schön, Birn, Riesling Terassengärten, Grüner Veltliner Gärten Loiben
Before taking over his father's business, Högl worked for several years with Franz Xaver Pichler and Franz Prager. His wines, especially the Veltliner from Schön and Riesling from Bruck, have been among the very top wines produced in the Wachau since the early 1990s, and in density and complexity, rival those of his teachers.

JAMEK*—****
WEISSENKIRCHEN
98 acres (25 ha); 195,000 bottles • Wines: Riesling, Grüner Veltliner, Chardonnay, Spätburgunder and others from →Klaus, →Achleiten, Zweikreuzgarten, Pichl, Stein am Rain, Marienfeld
In the 1990s, Jamek missed out somewhat on new developments, and his wines appeared tired and old-fashioned. His successor gives cause for hope.

EMMERICH KNOLL***—*****
DÜRNSTEIN-UNTERLOIBEN
23.5 acres (9.5 ha); 65,000 bottles • Wines: Grüner Veltliner, Riesling, Chardonnay and others from Loibenberg, Kreutles, →Schütt, Kellerberg, Pfaffenberg
Good vineyard sites such as Schütt, Kellerberg and Pfaffenberg form the foundation for Emmerich Knoll's excellent range of wines. In the vineyard, he works with the most natural methods possible; in the winery, he prefers using natural grape yeasts to pure yeast cultures, and his wines must be stored for six to nine months before they come onto the market.

KARL LAGLER**−****
SPITZ

20 acres (8 ha); 60,000 bottles • Wines, Grüner Veltliner, → Riesling and others from →Steinborz, Hartberg, Burgberg, Donaugarten, →Tausendeimerberg, Vorderseiber

Karl Lagler is one of the most famous winemakers in Spitz. His Rieslings from Steinborz and Tausendeimerberg are firm and spicy, at times really lush. From his winery, recently rebuilt in the midst of his vineyards, the family runs a comfortable hotel.

FRED LOIMER***−****
LANGENLOIS

39.5 acres (16 ha); 60,000 bottles • Wines: Grüner Veltliner, Chardonnay, Weißburgunder, Grauburgunder, Riesling and others from →Spiegel, Käferberg, Seeberg, Steinmassel, Ladner, Sachsenberg

Loimer's Grüner Veltliner from Spiegel, made from old vines, is consistently one of the best wines of this variety in the whole of Austria with an impressive dense fruit, complex bouquet, body, strength, and, occasionally, also harmoniously integrated residual sweetness.

GERALD MALAT***−****
FURTH/GÖTTWEIG

89 acres (36 ha); 200,000 bottles • Wines: Grüner Veltliner, Chardonnay, Riesling; Blauer Burgunder, Cabernet and others from Höhlgraben, Steinbühel, Hochrain, Pinot Blanc Sur Lie, → Das Beste vom Veltliner, →Das Beste vom Riesling.

Unlike many colleagues, Malat relies less on the selection of the vineyard than on *cuvées* for his top quality wines, with the label "*Das Beste von...*" (The Best of...). In his modern well-equipped winery, he also produces a convincingly good Chardonnay. Malat was one of the first to plant Cabernet Sauvignon.

MANTLERHOF***−****
BRUNN IM FELDE

39.5 acres (16 ha); 70,000 bottles • Wines: Grüner Veltliner, → Roter Veltliner, Riesling, Chardonnay and others from Weitgasse, →Spiegel, Tiefenthal, Wieland, →Reisenthal

Sepp Mantler is known as a specialist in a rare vine variety, the Roter Veltliner, from which, in good years, he produces intensive, substantial wines, often with residual sweetness. His Rieslings and Veltliner have also gained in expression and balance over recent years.

SEPP MOSER***−****
ROHRENDORF

128 acres (52 ha); 300,000 bottles • Wines: Grüner Veltliner, Chardonnay, Riesling, Zweigelt, Cabernet and others from →Gebling, Wolfsgraben, →Schnabel, Hedwigshof, Siebenhand, Hollabern, →Sauvignon Blanc Atriumweingärten

Moser, a member of the famous Rohrendorf wine dynasty, founded his wine-growing business at a late stage, but soon established himself as a top producer. He not only bottles outstanding Kremstal wines, but also owns excellent red wine vineyards.

NIKOLAIHOF, FAMILIE SAAHS***−*****
MAUTERN

39.5 acres (16 ha); 140,000 bottles • Wines: in Krems-Stein: Riesling, Grüner Veltliner, Weißburgunder, Neuburger and others from →Steiner Hund, →Im Weingebirge, →Vom Stein, Baumgarten, Burggarten, Süßenberg

Vines have been cultivated on the former estate of the archdiocese of Passau since 985. Klaus and Christine Saahs, the present owners, turned to organic wine growing early on and over the years they have demonstrated that top quality and organic methods of

cultivation and production certainly can go together. Their Rieslings and Veltliner from the Kremstal and Wachau vineyards have great capacity for aging.

FRANZ XAVER PICHLER****−*****
DÜRNSTEIN-OBERLOIBEN

18.5 acres (7.5 ha); 80,000 bottles • Wines: Grüner Veltliner, Riesling, Sauvignon and others from Loibenberg, Steinertal, →Kellerberg, →M.

The widely famed star of Wachau wine production almost places more trust in Veltliner than in Riesling. Franz Xaver Pichler produces monumental wines: dense, spicy, full of body (rather too much for some critics). The secret of his vines lies in the excellent vineyard plots, in the traditional methods of wine preparation—here, wine is still fermented with natural grape yeasts in wooden casks—and in rigid selection and limitation of yield. In good years the best casks are filled and designated "M.," no matter whether with Riesling or Veltliner.

RUDI PICHLER***−****
WEISSENKIRCHEN

22 acres (9 ha); 30,000 bottles • Wines: Grüner Veltliner, Riesling, Weißburgunder and others from →Achleiten, Kollmütz, →Hochrain, Hall, Kirchweg

Rudi Pichler has established himself over the last few years among the top echelons of the Wachau wine producers. His modern, extract-rich wines are fermented in steel tanks and then aged in wooden casks.

PRAGER**−****
WEISSENKIRCHEN

32 acres (13 ha); 85,000 bottles • Wines: Riesling, Grüner Veltliner, Chardonnay and others from →Achleiten, →Steinriegel, →Klaus, Hinter der Burg, Hollerin, Kaiserberg, Kollmitzberg

The company has been managed for over ten years by Prager's son-in-law Toni Bodenstein. A supporter of vineyard classification and author of a map of Wachau vineyards, he produces top quality wines in good years, but the levels of quality sometimes seem a little disjointed.

SCHLOSS GOBELSBURG****
LANGENLOIS

111 acres (45 ha); 180,000 bottles. • Wines: Riesling and Grüner Veltliner von Heiligenstein, Gaisberg, Grub, Renner, Lamm, Steinsetz, Spiegel and Alte Haide.

The old monastery vineyard of Schloss Gobelsberg transformed itself a few years ago. Under the direction of Michael Mossbrugger and with Willi Bründlmayer as adviser it has now secured itself a place among the top quality producers in Kamptal, chiefly with its outstanding Grüner Veltliner.

SONNHOF, FAMILIE JURTSCHITSCH**−****
LANGENLOIS

148 acres (60 ha); 360,000 bottles • Wines: Grüner Veltliner, Riesling, Chardonnay and others from →Loiserberg, →Steinhaus, Fahnberg, Spiegel, Ladner, Heiligenstein

Three brothers share the work on this exemplary Langenlois estate, which has made an outstanding name for itself, above all with its Grüner Veltliner wines.

UNDHOF, ERICH SALOMON**−****
KREMS-STEIN

49 acres (20 ha); 100,000 bottles • Wines: Grüner Veltliner, Riesling and others from Undhof-Wieden, Kögl, Wachtberg, Pfaffenberg, Hund

This traditional wine-growing estate in a monastery went through a crisis in the late 1980s, but after an all-round renewal of its stock of casks and modernization of wine production, it is once again among the elite of Kremstal. In Kögl and Pfaffenberg, it owns two of the best Riesling vineyards, while very good Veltliner grows directly behind the monastery.

THE WEINVIERTEL

The Weinviertel, or "wine quarter", is the largest and most productive wine-growing area in the country, and covers the whole northeastern part of Lower Austria. Here, around one-third of the total area of vines in Austria is cultivated, and individual wine-growing communities alone, such as Retz, can achieve similar quantities of production to the whole of the Wachau. However, for many years the reputation of this region's wines, with regard to quality, was questionable. This is by no means due to a lack of potential, but to the fact that here—perhaps thanks to the region's position at the edge of the former Iron Curtain—growers for too long limited themselves to supplying only basic wines.

The Weinviertel also lies on the border area of the Pannonian southeast European climate zone and therefore enjoys some of the best conditions for viticulture. Here thick layers of loess are to be found, suitable for Grüner Veltliner, but soil maps also register lime and silicate soils, clay,

The inner court of the Pfaffl vineyard in Stetten, only a short distance northeast of Vienna. The producers in this quiet retreat specialize in Grüner Veltliner and red wines.

sand, and even ancient rock formations such as are found in the Wachau, with the result that Pinot varieties, Traminer and even Riesling are at home here in certain vineyards.

The two wine-growing centers of this region are Retz in the west and Falkenstein in the northeast, both of which were independent regions in years gone by. Even if white wine dominates the Weinviertel, there are one or two definite "red wine islands" in the north along the border with the Czech Republic. In recent years these have shown interesting qualities which have attracted attention.

Along its southern edge, the western Weinviertel borders the Danube lands (Donauland). One of the youngest wine-growing regions of Austria, its present extent is made up of Carnuntum in the east, and the rather insignificant Traisental to the southwest. It stretches from the loess terraces of Kamptal to the foothills of the Vienna Woods at the gates of the capital. Most of its vineyards lie to the left of the Danube on the slopes of the Wagram; on the other side of the Danube, there are vines only at Klosterneuburg and on the northern slopes of the Kahlenberg.

Simple, fruity, full-bodied wines are produced here, from Grüner Veltliner and Müller-Thurgau; there is also a little Riesling, Roter and Frühroter Veltliner, Portugieser and Zweigelt.

Until around ten years ago, Carnuntum was part of the Danube lands. In the area of this old Roman garrison—which long before Vienna became the political and cultural center of Austria or rather of the then Roman province of Pannonia Superior—there are only around 2,470 acres (1,000 ha) stocked with vines. The vineyards on the foothills of the Thermenberge are particularly suited to the production of full-bodied white and red wines.

The mixture of thick strata of loess, gravel deposits from the Danube and occasional outcrops of loam provide an ideal *terroir*, above all for red wines. The young winegrowers and producers of Carnuntum have recognized this fact, and over the last few years they have caused quite a stir with their excellent products. The brand association "Rubin Carnuntum" has created publicity for them, and a few years ago they even successfully launched a white *primeur* wine called Primus Carnuntum.

SELECT PRODUCERS IN THE WEINVIERTEL

WALTER GLATZER ***–****
GÖTTLESBRUNN
22 acres (9 ha); 80,000 bottles • Wines: Grüner Veltliner, Welschriesling, Zweigelt, Blaufränkisch and others from Kräften, Heideacker, Schüttenberg, Aubühel, Zwiering
In recent years this company has switched to various red varieties. The Blaufränkisch, Zweigelt Dornenvogel and Cuvée Gotinsprun are excellent.

SCHLOSS WEINGUT GRAF HARDEGG **–****
SEEFELD-KADOLZ
102 acres (43 ha); 200,000 bottles • Wines: Grüner Veltliner, Riesling, Weißburgunder, Merlot, Zweigelt and others from Dreikreuzer, Lange Riede, Neuriß, Steinbügel, Sonnbergen, Zeiselberg, → Maximilian, → Merlot/Cabernet Max
Peter Veyder-Malberg is responsible for boost in quality, and for recent trials, including Rhône variety Viognier.

GERHARD MARKOWITSCH ***–****
GÖTTLESBRUNN
30 acres (10.5 ha); 70,000 bottles • Wines: Grüner Veltliner, Chardonnay, Riesling, Zweigelt, Blaufränkisch, Cabernet from → Rosenberg, Rubin Carnuntum, Redmont
Markowitsch is setting new standards for the region.

ROLAND MINKOWITSCH ***–****
MANNERSDORF
18.5 acres (7.5 ha); 30,000 bottles • Wines: Riesling, Welschriesling, Grüner Veltliner, Gewürztraminer and others from Zweifelhab, Kapellenfeld, Jäbelissen, Kohler
Traditional production in wooden casks and even an old log press. Wines are clear toned, at the same time complex.

BERNHARD OTT **–****
FEUERSBRUNN
25 acres (10 ha); 60,000 bottles • Wines: Grüner Veltliner, Riesling and others from → Rosenberg, Stiegl, Storz, → Brenner
Very good Veltliner, Sauvignon Blanc and even Riesling.

R. & A. PFAFFL ***–****
STETTEN/SCHLOSSGUT BOCKFLIESS
47 acres (19 ha); 150,000 bottles • Wines: Grüner Veltliner, Riesling, Weißburgunder, Chardonnay, St. Laurent, Zweigelt and others from Seiser am Eck, Sandlern, Zeiseneck, → Hundsleiten, Rossern, Haidviertel, Sandtal, Neuberg, Hochfeld, → Cabernet Excellent, Chardonnay Exclusive
The Grüner Veltliner wines are particularly successful.

FAMILIE PITNAUER ***–****
GÖTTLESBRUNN
23.5 acres (9.5 ha); 50,000 bottles • Wines: Grüner Veltliner, St. Laurent, Zweigelt, Cabernet and others from Kräften, Bärenreiser, Hagelsberg, Schüttenberg, Franz Josef, → Pegasos, Bienenfresser
Their latest creation, the 80 percent Syrah Pegasos, is most unusual in Austria.

ANTON WÖBER ***–****
ZIERSDORF
22 acres (9 ha); 40,000 bottles • Wines: Grüner Veltliner, → Roter Veltliner, Riesling and others from Katzensprung, → End des Berges, In der Schablau, Hirtenthal, Matinée
Wöber only took over the estate in 1993, but has acquired a solid reputation with very good Rieslings, Welschrieslings, Roter Veltliner and Grüner Veltliner.

Vienna and the Thermenregion

There are vines growing even in the neighborhood of the Schönbrunn palace, although most of the 1,730 acres (700 ha) of vines cultivated in the city area are in the north of Vienna.

It is possible that as early as pre-Roman times the Celts were growing vines on the slopes of the Vienna Woods, although systematic viticulture did not arrive until the legions of the Roman Empire introduced it. Even the famous Stephansdom (St. Stephen's Cathedral), the symbol of Vienna, to some extent owes its existence to wine—the Babenberg dynasty could not begin building the church until, in the 12th century, they had exchanged some of their vineyards in the Wachau for parish rights in Vienna.

Wine growing in Vienna is divided into two areas of approximately equal importance: the slopes of the Kahlenberg, with its shell limestone soils, in the northwest, and the Bisamberg, with its gravely loess and loam, in the northeast. The two areas also have considerable differences in climate, although the whole of Vienna is on the border of the half-oceanic climate of western Europe and the Pannonian climate of the southeast. While lighter, fruitier wines are produced on the cooler Kahlenberg, the grapes of the Bisamberg display a good deal more structure and complexity.

In earlier times, wine was grown even in the center of Vienna itself, and as late as 1547 there were vines quite close to the Hofburg. By the 1950s, wine growing in the city was markedly decreasing and only received a new boost in the second half of the 20th century. Today there are some 1,730 productive acres (700 ha) in the Vienna wine-growing region, worked by 400 winegrowers.

Although the *Gemischte Satz* (mixed blend), which formed the traditional *Heuriger* wine, is now only to be found on some 15 percent of the wine-growing areas, 85 percent of the wines are still produced from white varieties. In this region, too, pure varieties of Veltliner, Weißburgunder, Riesling, or Chardonnay have established themselves. The majority, even today, are served directly in the *Heuriger* pubs of the city, for production does not even cover the city's own needs.

The different companies often display great differences in quality. Where the customers are more or less uncritical, either because they are wedded to tradition or simply too comfortable, the vintner is also under no particular pressure, which is clearly to be seen in the wines served. On the other hand, there are an increasing number of wineries which over the last 15 years have made quite considerable efforts to establish their position among the elite of Austrian wine production.

THERMENREGION

In the past, the most famous wines from the area around Vienna have come from the southern continuation of the slopes of the Kahlenberg. Under the name "Gumpoldskirchen"—in those days, you could still call wine-growing regions

---

SELECT PRODUCERS IN VIENNA

KARL ALPHART ***−*****
TRAISKIRCHEN
35 acres (14 ha); 45,000 bottles • Wines: Riesling, Rotgipfler, Neuburger, Chardonnay, Zweigelt, Spätburgunder from Zistl, Rodauner, Hausberg, Mandl-Höh
Sparse, dry vineyards on the slopes of the Vienna Woods and rigid limitation of yield to a company average of no more than 11 gallons per 2.5 acres (40 hl per ha) are the secret behind the quality of the Alphart wines. The excellent Rotgipfler *Trockenbeerenauslese* wines are particularly remarkable. But the dry and medium-dry Zierfandler-Rotgipfler, Rieslings, and Chardonnays are also above average for this area.

MANFRED BIEGLER ***−****
GUMPOLDSKIRCHEN
20 acres (8 ha); 40,000 bottles • Wines: in Gumpoldskirchen: Riesling, Zierfandler, Rotgipfler and others—no vineyard origins
Manfred Biegler's company has long been among the best in the Thermenregion, but ever since his son Othmar started work in the winery, the level of wine quality has gone up still further. Rotgipfler wines, oak-aged or unoaked, are the specialty of the two Bieglers, who also produce successful Chardonnays and Rieslings. Their wines combine modern lushness with classical structure.

E. & C. FISCHER **−****
SOOSS
44 acres (18 ha); 80,000 bottles • Wines: Grüner Veltliner; Zweigelt, Portugieser, Cabernet, Spätburgunder and others from Paitzbreite, In den Robbingen, → Fasangarten, → Gradenthal, Aderhags, Steinhäufel, → Pinot Noir Barrique, Cabernet Barrique
Engelbert and Christian Fischer run a winery in one of the so-called *Urhäuser* (original houses) in Soos. Modern, cool fermented wines are produced here, but the best products are made from Zweigelt, Pinot Noir and Portugieser and aged in oak casks, with the vineyards of Fasangarten and Gradenthal offering the greatest potential.

JOHANNESHOF, J. & V. REINISCH **−****
TATTENDORF
99 acres (40 ha); 120,000 bottles • Wines: Chardonnay; → Cabernet, → Blauburgunder, St. Laurent and others from Dornfeld, Mitterfeld, Holzspur
Just outside the gates of Tattendorf, the Reinisch family has set up an almost Californian-style estate. Here, they produce excellent Cabernet Sauvignon, St. Laurent, Chardonnay and Pinot Noir. This modern winery not only has an inviting sales room, but it also accommodates a very commendable *Heuriger*, built over an ecological pond and now popular with the locals for excursions.

FAMILIE SCHWERTFÜHRER **−*****
70,000 bottles • Wines: Chardonnay; Zweigelt, Pinot, Cabernet, Portugieser and others, → Spada
The Schwertführers call their best wines, made from Zweigelt, Pinot Noir, St. Laurent and Cabernet Sauvignon, *Spada* or "sword." Although Chardonnay and Weißburgunder are good, the red varieties dominate in quality as in quantity: their harmonious unity makes them unparalleled over a wide area.

FRITZ WIENINGER ***−*****
VIENNA-STAMMERSDORF
32 acres (13 ha); 120,000 bottles • Wines: Grüner Veltliner, → Chardonnay, Riesling, → Blauer Burgunder and others from Jungenberg, Rothen, Gabrissen, Herrenholz, Wiethalen, Breiten, Wiener Trilogie, Select, → Grand Select
Wieninger is not only the star among Viennese wine producers, he is also one of the top winemakers in Austria. In his Chardonnay and Spätburgunder he has created two ranges of products which are unequaled far and wide, especially as far as the oak-aged wines Select and Grand Select are concerned. But Grüner Veltliner and Riesling, too, make lush and fruity wines here in most years. The Danubis blend and the Wiener Trilogie made from Zweigelt, Blauburgunder, Cabernet, and Merlot complete the outstanding range.

by place names, as was also the case with Rust and Retz—wines were produced which were famous and popular throughout Austria. The success of the region is mainly derived from its reputation as a much-visited excursion and vacation center for the Viennese. In the distant past, the Romans appreciated the spas between the present-day towns of Mödling and Bad Voslau, and, more recently, even Beethoven preferred to compose in Gumpoldskirchen. After 1985 however, the newly renamed region disappeared into anonymity for quite a considerable time.

This explains why today, many of the top wine producers of the region are better known than the Thermenregion, which, with over 5,683 acres (2,300 ha) of vines is by no means one of the smallest in the country. Around 60 percent of the vineyards are stocked with white varieties, among which are two unique specialties of the Thermenregion: Zierfandler and Rotgipfel. Both may be bottled together as a *cuvée* and are then put on the market under the name of Spätrot-Rotgipfler.

As far as climate is concerned, the Thermenregion belongs to the Pannonian region. With regard to soils, it is divided into two. In the northwest heavy clay and lime soils predominate, while the south, the plain of the Steinfeld, is characterized by alluvial gravel. Of course these different soils each bear different varieties: mainly white along the slopes of the Vienna Woods, red in the Steinfeld. The best wines of the Thermenregion are full-bodied, expressive, and even reasonably long-lived, which applies to both white and red wines. Here, too, many wine producers over the last few years have made strenuous efforts to make their wines nationally and internationally competitive.

GLASS MAKING

THE HISTORY OF THE WINE GLASS

The search for a specialized glass perfectly suited to the properties of wine is relatively recent. The great masters of early glass production were the 13th-century Venetians, who, through fear of catastrophic fires, exiled their glassblowers to the nearby island of Murano. Over the centuries, the costly works of the glassblower's art, sold primarily to royal courts throughout Europe and the Middle East by Venetian merchants, were considered the ultimate in drinking vessels. As artistic as they were, these are unsuited to enjoying wine, and apart from the thinness of the glass, they have few advantages over the plain beaker-like glasses used to serve wine in all Mediterranean countries in homes and simple restaurants. The main defect of these glasses is that they widen as they reach the top, and so instead of concentrating the BOUQUET they allow it to disperse rapidly.

The Bohemian glassblowers showed rather more feeling for the actual purpose of the wine glass, although they succumbed to a tendency for excessive decoration. This was expressed in cut glass, which is as artistically skilled as it is irritating.

In general, early glass shapes are exceedingly generous in the opening, but usually very sparing in the body. The most absurd example is the bowl-shaped champagne glass, a miniature

The Riedel family glassworks in Kufstein in Tyrol.

The composition of glass has not changed for 4,000 years.

The natural basic materials—quartz, lime and alkali—are melted at 2,120°F (1,000°C).

In this famous glass factory, the glassmakers still use traditional methods today.

bathtub on a stem, shaped so that if you want to balance your glass, you are obliged to hold the body, which quickly warms up cool sparkling wines.

Two classic forms have remained popular today, the balloon glass and the tulip. The simple French balloon glass, which you can buy in French supermarkets, often for very little more than decorated paper cups, does its job reasonably well as long as it is not filled too full. A variation of this basic form has been used in different countries and wine regions. In Alsace, the addition of a tall green stem and foot became the customary glass for white wine; on the Rhine, it had a thick, fluted green glass foot, and was called the *Römer*, to name only two of

the most common examples. Apart from being too wide at the top, and lacking a chimney for the full appreciation of the aroma, their major disadvantage is in their everyday use—they have become more of a unit of wine than a glass for enjoying your wine. The tulip glass, with its tall chimney, is generally more suitable, especially for white wines, but it has too little surface area to permit the best possible development of aroma.

Among the traditional glasses, the Andalusian and Manzanilla sherry drinkers deserve praise, for their COPITA is the original type of tasting glass, with a comparatively tall chimney that centers the aroma and guarantees full enjoyment.

The glassblower begins work on a still unformed lump, the "gob."

The glassmaker's pipe was used in a similar form 2,000 years ago in Rome.

The glass "gob" has little in common with the finished wine glass.

The work of art takes shape—in special molds for each type of glass.

BURGENLAND

With just under 35,829 acres (14,500 ha) devoted to vines and an annual production of 20,475,561 gallons (775,000 hl) the Burgenland is Austria's second largest wine growing area after Lower Austria. On the edge of the Hungarian plain, it profits from the hot Pannonian climate and is therefore better suited than any other region of the country to producing white wines from fully or over-ripe grapes, as well as for dense wines with the emphasis on fruit and tannin.

The major part of the vineyards lies close to or not very far away from the Neusiedler See, a body of water which has a decisive influence on the climate conditions of the region. While the land to the northeast is largely flat, on the western shore of the lake there are gentle rolling hills and steep slopes along the Leitha range. And, just as in the Bordeaux region, even slightly rising slopes may be of importance for the quality of the wine. In central and south Burgenland, on the other hand, the slopes are for the most part shallower. As far as viticulture

Reliable guests, the storks come back year after year to their nests on the rooftops of Rust.

The "Türkenturm" (Turk Tower) of Breitenbrunn can be seen from a great distance.

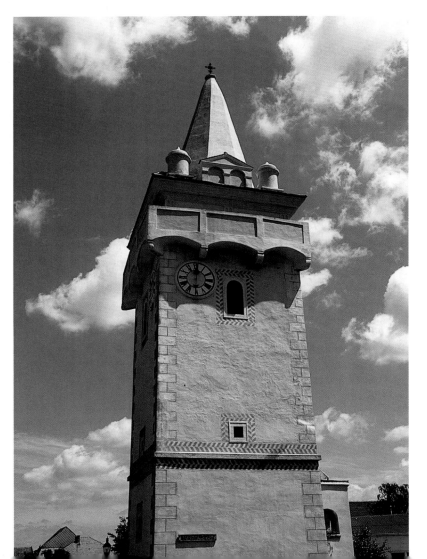

is concerned, the region is divided into four unequal areas, which for one thing have been rather unfortunately chosen, and to add to that they have been given unclear definitions, such as the awkward double-barreled name "Neusiedlersee-Hügelland" (Neusiedler Lake Hill Country). Many wine producers would therefore be grateful to see the whole of the Burgenland declared as a single wine region.

To the northeast lies the Neusiedlersee region, which is mainly known for its sweet wines. Full-bodied white wines are also made here, and among these are some of the best Chardonnays produced in the country. The red wines here are usually most successful as blends, either of various native varieties or native and international varieties. Particularly worthy of note are the wines from the "Pannobile" marketing cooperative, a small group of top producers who all age their wines in oak.

Along the northwest and west shores of the lake lies the region of Neusiedlersee-Hügelland. Here the variety of vineyard sites is much greater, as the lakeshore differs greatly from the neighboring hills on the one hand and slopes of the Leitha range on the other, not only in climate conditions but also in the composition of the soil. Apart from excellent Blaufränkisch and Zweigelt, outstanding white wines also thrive here, with not only Chardonnay, but even Sauvignon Blanc producing very good results. Even if the center of the area, the lakeside town of Rust, is mainly famous for its Ausbruch dessert wine, the actual strengths of the Neusiedler-Hügelland undoubtedly lie in the dry matured white and red wines, which have plenty of body and refinement.

To the south, the countryside becomes increasingly more hilly, but the range of varieties decreases. Especially in the central Burgenland, which borders the southern shore of the lake, the Blaufränkisch grape almost has a monopoly in the vineyards. Aged in a classic wooden cask, or in a BARRIQUE, it can produce magnificent results. The same variety is slightly less dominant, but nonetheless responsible for the best wines in the south Burgenland close to the borders of Styria. In what is perhaps the best-kept secret of the wine-growing areas of Europe, this is made into wonderfully fruity, spicy red wines, whose only real defect is the small quantities which arrive on the market.

STUDENTS OF WINE, HUNGRY FOR KNOWLEDGE

In the wine town of Rust—which is also worth seeing because of its protected historic old town—the Weinakademie Österreich (Austrian Wine Academy) represents a special center of wine knowledge. From introductory courses on the experience of wine and culinary weekends, as well as preparation for the much sought after title "Master of Wine," the institute offers a broad range of courses for development at many different levels.

Above
As in this vineyard on the Neusiedler See the growers in Burgenland often sow rape to loosen the soil and provide natural nutrients.

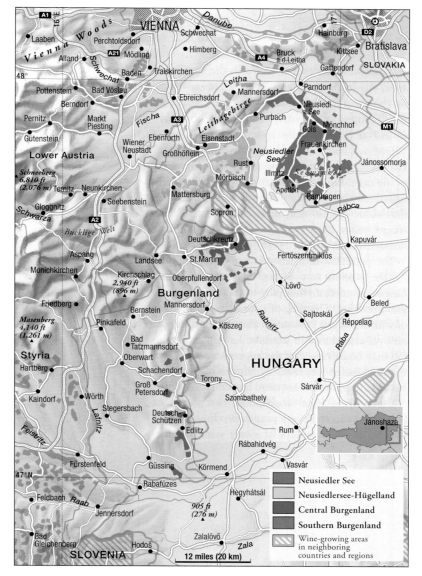

eury to improve the Zweigelt and the St. Laurent by giving them color, bouquet, structure, and the capacity for aging, the breakthrough had been made.

After a learning process that has lasted a decade, Austria's red wine producers have today achieved a respectable reputation. Their

Sweet Wines from Seewinkel and Ausbruch from Rust

nious combination of a high degree of sweetness with a rich fruit and extract content and a refreshing acidity.

the United Kingdom Vineyard Association recognizes six specific wine regions. Weald and Downland covers the vineyards of East and West Sussex and Kent and is relatively mild with clay and chalk soils. Wessex covers the more temperate climate counties on the south coast, of Dorset, Hampshire, Wiltshire, and the Isle of Wight. South West and Wales, which comprises the western tip of the British Isles, tends to be dominated by westerly winds blowing in off the Atlantic and with them, wet weather. Thames and Chiltern covers the Home Counties of Berkshire, Buckinghamshire, London West, and Oxfordshire and is the warmest of the regions. East Anglia comprises the flat, windy counties on the east coast, and, finally, Mercia, covers the Midlands and the North.

Not to be confused with British wine, which is made from imported grape concentrate, English wine is made from fresh grapes grown in England. Most of England's grape varieties are early ripeners, the most widely planted of which is Müller-Thurgau, which produces a fragrant floral, off-dry or medium dry. Müller-Thurgau is followed by Reichensteiner and then the hybrid Seyval Blanc, which suits the English climate and can be made in both unoaked and oaked

Denbies, the largest wine estate in England, in Surrey, southwest of London. Technically, it is state of the art. Harvesting here is done by machine.

The Hidden Spring Winery is not far from Hastings and the south coast. Apart from the fashionable red, their Seyval Blanc is of interest.

styles to produce, respectively, a Sauvignon-like or Burgundian-style dry white. It is controversial, however, in the sense that it has made it difficult for the English wine industry to gain recognition from the European Union whose Quality Wine Scheme excludes hybrid varieties. Aromatic whites are made from Huxelrebe, Schönburger, and Bacchus, while Madeleine Angevine is also a relatively popular white variety which can, on occasions, be characterful.

There are as many as 44 grape varieties grown to make wine in England and Wales, most of them hybrids or crossings of Germanic origin, although there are some premium varieties in the form of Chardonnay, Pinot Noir and even Cabernet Sauvignon. The Chardonnay and Pinot Noir is for the most part used to make sparkling wine with at least two estates, Nyetimber and Ridgeview, set up to make sparkling wine exclusively. Indeed there are those who believe that England's future, if it has one as a wine producer, lies in sparkling wines. Cabernet Sauvignon is grown with Merlot in polytunnels at Sharpham in Devon, where it is blended and aged in French oak to produce a light, cool-climate red table wine in the Loire Valley or New Zealand style.

Bill Darey from Denbies is happy with the ripeness of his Pinot grapes.

SELECT PRODUCERS IN ENGLAND

BREAKY BOTTOM***
RODMELL, EAST SUSSEX
5.5 acres (2.5 ha) • Wines: Müller-Thurgau, →Seyval Blanc, Cuvée Rémy Alexandre
Thanks to the dedication of its owner Peter Hall, this tiny vineyard in its lovely, isolated hollow of the southern Downs has become one of England's most sought-after addresses. Hall is celebrated because of the quality of his wines, which are based on low yields of the unfashionable hybrid Seyval Blanc. Some plots are having their stocks renewed with Chardonnay, Pinot Noir, and Pinot Meunier for sparkling wine.

CHAPEL DOWN**
TENTERDEN, KENT
27 acres (11 ha); some bought-in grapes • Wines include: Pinot Blanc, Bacchus, Schönburger, Reichensteiner, Pinot Noir
Britain's largest commercial winery produces a range of very interesting and also prize-winning wines, among them the Chapel Down sparkling wine, some remarkable reds, and aromatic dry whites under the Curious Grape label. The wines are made by Owen Elias, U.K. Winemaker of the Year in 2001 and 2002. Visitors' centers in the Tenterden and Lamberhurst vineyards are open daily.

DENBIES**
DORKING, SURREY
250 acres (101 ha) • Wines: 20 different grape varieties including Dornfelder and Pinot Noir; Brands: →Surrey Gold, →Special Late Harvest
With over 250 acres (100 ha) of wines, this company with its visitors' center and Napa-style winery in the hills near Dorking is England's biggest wine estate. It produces a variety of different styles of wine, including white and red table wines and sparkling wine. Surrey Gold was chosen for the House of Commons wine list.

NYETIMBER****
WEST CHILTINGTON, WEST SUSSEX
37 acres (15 ha) • Wines: Chardonnay, Pinot Meunier, Pinot Noir, Première Cuvée, Blanc de Blanc Brut, Classic Cuvée
This medieval estate, renovated by Stuart and Sandy Moss from Chicago, now belongs to the songwriter Andy Hill. Set in rolling downland near the south coast, it was the first estate in England to be planned and

planted so as to meet the exact requirements of the champagne method. The estate has gained recognition because of the excellent quality of its sparkling wine aged on the yeasts, and the most recently released vintages have won gold medals at the *Vinalies* in Paris and top awards in Britain.

RIDGE VIEW WINE ESTATE****
SUSSEX
16 acres (6.5 ha); some bought-in grapes; 30,000 bottles • Wines include: Blanc de Blancs, Blanc de Noirs
Mike Roberts has equipped his prize-winning estate to produce the best quality sparkling wines from classic champagne varieties. He uses traditional methods to create a series of five different wines. For the *assemblages*, he and his son, together with the assistant winemaker Simon, use a number of different grafts and clones.

SHARPHAM**
DART VALLEY, DEVON
10 acres (4 ha) • Wines include: Madeleine Angevine, Dart Valley Reserve, Sharpham Red, Beenleigh Red
Planted mainly to Madeleine Angevine, the estate produces, alongside cold-fermented, dry white wines, a barrel-fermented white. Pinot Noir, Cabernet, and Merlot are grown at nearby Beenleigh Manor. Sharpham's founder, the philanthropist Maurice Ash, died in 2003, but the partnership is continuing to develop estate activities such as wine growing, cheese-making, and organic milk production.

THREE CHOIRS **
NEWENT, GLOUCESTERSHIRE
74 acres (30 ha) • Wines include: Phoenix, Premium Selection; Classic Cuvée
Britain's second largest producer, which has invested a million pounds in a new winery, produces a series of commercial wines made from, among other varieties, Seyval Blanc, Schönburger, Bacchus, Huxelrebe, and Phoenix. It also makes a red and a white which are both barrel aged, a nouveau and a sparkling wine. The estate also operates an award-winning restaurant and hotel, and in 2003 it opened a small brewery.

David Schwarzwälder

SPAIN

Further to the southeast, you can take a walk through the history of Spanish wine. There are all sorts of sweet wines to taste, made from Muscatel, Monastrell (or Mourvèdre), and Malvasía grapes. Some of these wines are still produced in the same way that they were 300 years ago, when they were drunk in all the royal houses of Europe, together with the equivalent wines from Andalusia. The highlands of Valencia and Murcia produce a large quantity of red wine, which is traditionally sold for blending or in barrels as top-up wine. The large stocks of old vines have in the last few years prepared the soil for red wines of increasingly high quality. Jumilla has played a pioneering part in this development.

The region of La Mancha extends south of the mountain range that dissects Castile, and is famous for its good champagne base wines, which are mainly exported; light, clean white wines and sometimes earthy, soft, easy-drinking *tintos*. White grapes still clearly predominate, easily accounting for 70 percent of all grapes grown. The D.O. Valdepeñas lies like an enclave in the southern part of the D.O. La Mancha. It produces full-bodied and soft red wines that are sold fully aged in wooden casks in true Spanish style.

Andalusia has its own unique range of wines. The distinctive Finos, Manzanillas, and Olorosos, which occur here solely due to a vagary of nature, are indigenous to the province of Cádiz. Sea air, FLOR YEAST, the addition of wine spirits, and MATURING by a method of decanting vertically from one row of casks into another

Bill Darey from Denbies is happy with the ripeness of his Pinot grapes.

SELECT PRODUCERS IN ENGLAND

BREAKY BOTTOM***
RODMELL, EAST SUSSEX
5.5 acres (2.5 ha) • Wines: Müller-Thurgau, →Seyval Blanc, Cuvée Rémy Alexandre

Thanks to the dedication of its owner Peter Hall, this tiny vineyard in its lovely, isolated hollow of the southern Downs has become one of England's most sought-after addresses. Hall is celebrated because of the quality of his wines, which are based on low yields of the unfashionable hybrid Seyval Blanc. Some plots are having their stocks renewed with Chardonnay, Pinot Noir, and Pinot Meunier for sparkling wine.

CHAPEL DOWN**
TENTERDEN, KENT
27 acres (11 ha); some bought-in grapes • Wines include: Pinot Blanc, Bacchus, Schönburger, Reichensteiner, Pinot Noir

Britain's largest commercial winery produces a range of very interesting and also prize-winning wines, among them the Chapel Down sparkling wine, some remarkable reds, and aromatic dry whites under the Curious Grape label. The wines are made by Owen Elias, U.K. Winemaker of the Year in 2001 and 2002. Visitors' centers in the Tenterden and Lamberhurst vineyards are open daily.

DENBIES**
DORKING, SURREY
250 acres (101 ha) • Wines: 20 different grape varieties including Dornfelder and Pinot Noir; Brands: →Surrey Gold, →Special Late Harvest

With over 250 acres (100 ha) of wines, this company with its visitors' center and Napa-style winery in the hills near Dorking is England's biggest wine estate. It produces a variety of different styles of wine, including white and red table wines and sparkling wine. Surrey Gold was chosen for the House of Commons wine list.

NYETIMBER****
WEST CHILTINGTON, WEST SUSSEX
37 acres (15 ha) • Wines: Chardonnay, Pinot Meunier, Pinot Noir, Première Cuvée, Blanc de Blanc Brut, Classic Cuvée

This medieval estate, renovated by Stuart and Sandy Moss from Chicago, now belongs to the songwriter Andy Hill. Set in rolling downland near the south coast, it was the first estate in England to be planned and

planted so as to meet the exact requirements of the champagne method. The estate has gained recognition because of the excellent quality of its sparkling wine aged on the yeasts, and the most recently released vintages have won gold medals at the *Vinalies* in Paris and top awards in Britain.

RIDGE VIEW WINE ESTATE****
SUSSEX
16 acres (6.5 ha); some bought-in grapes; 30,000 bottles • Wines include: Blanc de Blancs, Blanc de Noirs

Mike Roberts has equipped his prize-winning estate to produce the best quality sparkling wines from classic champagne varieties. He uses traditional methods to create a series of five different wines. For the *assemblages*, he and his son, together with the assistant winemaker Simon, use a number of different grafts and clones.

SHARPHAM**
DART VALLEY, DEVON
10 acres (4 ha) • Wines include: Madeleine Angevine, Dart Valley Reserve, Sharpham Red, Beenleigh Red

Planted mainly to Madeleine Angevine, the estate produces, alongside cold-fermented, dry white wines, a barrel-fermented white. Pinot Noir, Cabernet, and Merlot are grown at nearby Beenleigh Manor. Sharpham's founder, the philanthropist Maurice Ash, died in 2003, but the partnership is continuing to develop estate activities such as wine growing, cheese-making, and organic milk production.

THREE CHOIRS **
NEWENT, GLOUCESTERSHIRE
74 acres (30 ha) • Wines include: Phoenix, Premium Selection; Classic Cuvée

Britain's second largest producer, which has invested a million pounds in a new winery, produces a series of commercial wines made from, among other varieties, Seyval Blanc, Schönburger, Bacchus, Huxelrebe, and Phoenix. It also makes a red and a white which are both barrel aged, a nouveau and a sparkling wine. The estate also operates an award-winning restaurant and hotel, and in 2003 it opened a small brewery.

David Schwarzwälder

SPAIN

Further to the southeast, you can take a walk through the history of Spanish wine. There are all sorts of sweet wines to taste, made from Muscatel, Monastrell (or Mourvèdre), and Malvasía grapes. Some of these wines are still produced in the same way that they were 300 years ago, when they were drunk in all the royal houses of Europe, together with the equivalent wines from Andalusia. The highlands of Valencia and Murcia produce a large quantity of red wine, which is traditionally sold for blending or in barrels as top-up wine. The large stocks of old vines have in the last few years prepared the soil for red wines of increasingly high quality. Jumilla has played a pioneering part in this development.

The region of La Mancha extends south of the mountain range that dissects Castile, and is

famous for its good champagne base wines, which are mainly exported; light, clean white wines and sometimes earthy, soft, easy-drinking *tintos*. White grapes still clearly predominate, easily accounting for 70 percent of all grapes grown. The D.O. Valdepeñas lies like an enclave in the southern part of the D.O. La Mancha. It produces full-bodied and soft red wines that are sold fully aged in wooden casks in true Spanish style.

Andalusia has its own unique range of wines. The distinctive Finos, Manzanillas, and Olorosos, which occur here solely due to a vagary of nature, are indigenous to the province of Cádiz. Sea air, FLOR YEAST, the addition of wine spirits, and MATURING by a method of decanting vertically from one row of casks into another produces wines worthy of a much more exalted status than mere aperitifs. Nor should we forget the respectable dessert wines from Málaga, which do not deserve the stigma of being cheap and mass-produced. Here, too, renewed efforts are being made to raise quality.

Extremadura in the Southwest is in a state of flux between modern and rustic wines. With only a few exceptions, the wines produced here are simple but smooth and rich, as you would expect Spanish wines to be. The range of grape varieties grown is as wide as the various soil conditions. Extremadura is both the underdog and the future of Spanish wine growing. This situation can also be applied to the islands in the Atlantic Ocean and Mediterranean Sea. The Balearic Islands, in particular Mallorca, offer the right climate and soil to produce original wines, but the range of varieties is an unknown quantity for many wine producers. The vintners there are beginning to exploit this potential. The classical Tintos, which now seem obsolete, are being replaced by modern qualities with greatly improved character. Some of the dessert wines produced on the Canary Islands are of excellent quality. Overall, the situation can be viewed in a positive light: the wines need to have a more consistent finish, and further research needs to be carried out into varieties. BARRIQUE wines are rare; young wines that can be quickly consumed are the order of the day. However, the potential is excellent.

Cádiz—the capital of the region of Andalusia, and the traditional home of sherry—still feels the effects of the raid led by Francis Drake. In 1587, he purloined 2,900 barrels of sack, as the sherry intended for export was known, from the harbor, loaded them onto ships he had seized, and dispatched them to England, where they received a very enthusiastic welcome.

SPANISH GRAPE VARIETIES

There is such a wide range of Spanish grape varieties that even experts find it bewildering. The picture becomes clearer only if you concentrate on the most important ones. Of the practically indeterminable number of grape varieties that grow in Spain—there are reputed to be approximately 600 varieties—about 15 principal varieties can be described as truly Spanish. These account for about 75 percent of the total wine-growing area. It is not only the names of some of these grapes that vary from region to region. The wines they produce also vary greatly due to the wide variations in climate and soil conditions.

At the top of the list are two black grapes that are Spanish grapes *par excellence*: the Tempranillo (called *Tinta del País* in Ribera del Duero, *Cencibel* in La Mancha and Valdepeñas, and *Ull de Llebre* in Catalonia) and the Garnacha.

To a great extent, Spanish winegrowers owe their top-quality wines to the blue-black-red Tempranillo, which develops magnificent fruit notes of cherry, raspberry, and blackberry and, because of its well-balanced tannin structure, ages excellently in oak. This most noble Spanish variety is the main black grape variety in the wine-growing regions of La Rioja, Ribera del Duera, Valdepeñas, and Penedès, and plays a prominent role in some smaller D.O.s.

Spain has several hundred grape varieties.

The Garnacha Tinta is the black variety most commonly grown in Spain. It is found practically everywhere. However, it plays a very important part in La Rioja, Navarra, Campo de Borja, Cariñena, Calatayud (Aragón), Madrid, and in the D.O.s of the province of Tarragona in Catalonia. Until recently, experts were rather dismissive of this grape because of its tendency to oxidize. It had a sound reputation only as a grape for producing *rosado*. Since the splendid wines of the D.O. Priorat brought it to fame overnight, it has aroused great interest. The Garnacha Tinta combines wonderful strawberry and raspberry fruit notes with strong spicy tones, giving it a very distinctive character. Some French wine enthusiasts know this grape, which originated in Spain, as Grenache, which produces spectacular results in Châteauneuf-du-Pape, for example.

Other important indigenous black varieties are Cariñena, Graciano, Tinta de Toro, Mencía, Monastrell, and Bobal. There is no doubt that the last three produce good wines, but like the Garnacha they tend to oxidize rapidly and so do not age well in oak casks. Wine producers counter this shortcoming by adding more stable varieties. The potential of these varieties has barely been explored, and undoubtedly in future it will be possible to produce wines that can be aged from them.

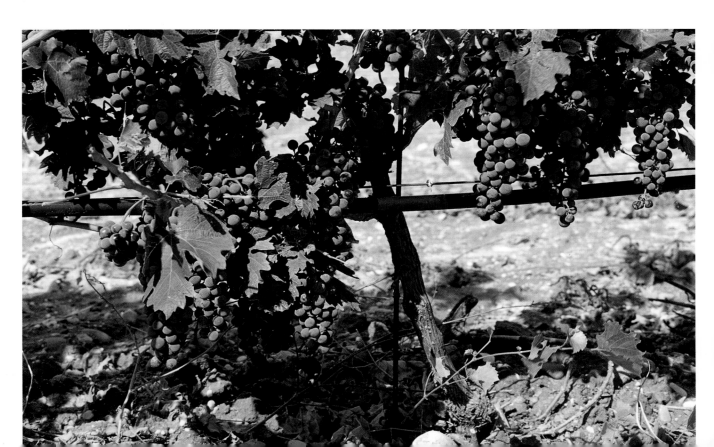

There are already examples of good Monastrell wines aged in oak. These require old vines that produce small quantities of grapes with a strong TANNIN structure, and Spain still has enough of these. Cabernet Sauvignon, Merlot, and Syrah, the three most important French red wine grapes, have acclimatized very successfully in many areas and have for many years now produced presentable results both as single-VARIETAL and blended wines. In Spain, the Cabernet matures to produce a soft wine. In the Mediterranean regions, this variety, with its marginally increased complexity due to its pronounced tannins, nearly always matures fully, but in the case of high yields it develops a roundness that lacks character. In areas where Cabernet is not grown in large quantities, it can produce excellent results. The best Spanish Cabernets are juicy, full-bodied, and extremely heavy.

The Syrah is worth a special look. It took Spanish wine producers a long time to recognize that this variety from the Middle East produces fantastic results in some areas, such as the Priorat region, the upland areas of Penedès, the highlands of the Levant (Jumilla), and Castile–La Mancha. At present, Syrah is grown in only very small areas, but it should have an important part to play among Spain's red wines in the future.

RARE AND MASS-PRODUCED WHITE WINES

The white varieties are led by two grapes, the Albariño from Galicia and the Verdejo from Rueda in Castile, both of which have only recently won the fame they deserve. They may not be widespread, but their potential and distinctive character place them at the top of the list of Spanish white wines. Verdejo produces expressive wines with good acidity, high glycerin content, and delicate citrus AROMAS. The strength of these wines does not lie in their fruitiness but in their mineral notes, coupled with slight hints of aniseed and a very typical, delicately spicy bitterness in the finish. This very unusual composition of BOUQUET and flavor gives Verdejo a character of its own among the white grapes of Europe. It is the main variety in the Castilian D.O. Rueda.

The Albariño, on the other hand, thrives on its impressive apricot, kiwi, and passionfruit notes. At home in the far northwest of the peninsula, it is the principle variety in the D.O. Rías Baixas of Galicia.

The most common white grape varieties are the Airén—indigenous to the largest consolidated wine-growing region in the world, La

Tempranillo or *Tinta del País* is the top-quality Spanish grape variety and is a defining feature of the best Rioja and Ribera del Duero wines.

The Albariño grape is Galicia's top variety and is responsible for making the Rías Baixas into a cult wine, blending freshness and strength to perfection.

Uva Palomino is really a very ordinary variety that does not reveal its true quality until the sherry *flor* yeast sets to work, when it develops its distinctive character.

Mancha, and the most frequently grown white wine grape in the world—and the Viura, also called Macabeo. It is no secret that the quality of the Airén bears no relation to its distribution. But with the help of modern technology, it can be used to make perfectly respectable, clean, if rather bland young wines.

The Viura, on the other hand, is a much classier grape altogether. It forms the basis for cavas and attractive white wines and is just as at home in La Rioja as it is in Navarra, the new D.O. Ribera del Guadiana in the southwest of the country, or in Costers del Segre in Lleida. In terms of distribution, it can be regarded as the counterpart of Garnacha Tinta. The wines it produces are accessible and have a floral, fresh fruit character with a pleasing acidity.

SWEET AND SPICY SPECIALTIES

The grape varieties used to produce wines from Jerez, Córdoba, Málaga, and Huelva merit special mention. Palomina is the grape that grows on the white *albariza* soils around Jerez de la Frontera in the province of Cádiz. Wines from the Montilla-Moriles region are produced mainly from the famous Pedro Ximénez grape, while the D.O. Málaga makes its astonishing wines partly by using sun-dried Moscatel grapes. Two varieties of Moscatel are at home in Spain. In the case of the large-berried Muscatel, which produces the famous sweet wines of the Levant area and Málaga, it is the popular Muscat of Alexandria grape, found throughout the world. Thanks to plenty of sun, its wines are extremely full-bodied and aromatic. The small-berried Muscatel, found in Navarra, is much more delicate and displays greater acidity, as can be seen from the fine, elegant Moscatel wines from this region.

This list of Spanish varieties is by no means exhaustive. Less common specialties can be found on the islands, but also in damp Galicia or in the hot Levant. They are nearly always used in *cuvée* wines or for blending, but definitely make their mark on the wines. These and other varieties will be discussed later, together with the more famous grape varieties.

The quality *barrique* cellar of the Bodegas Mont Marsal illustrates the fact that dry red and white wines are also a good bet in the Penedès region.

The cava *bodegas* now reserve the traditional, hand-operated vibrating racks solely for their prestige wines.

An Adventurous Choice of Varieties

Catalonia's wine regions offer an astounding range of varieties. In addition to the indigenous varieties, in particular some other native varieties that are needed to produce cava (see pages 584–5) and the Tempranillo, known here as Ull de Llebre, the Catalans were very forward-looking and quickly accepted high quality French grapes. Catalonia was the first place in Spain to produce the single-varietal Cabernet and the first successful vintages from indigenous and Bordelais grapes. The first such vineyards are now at least 20 years old and are able to produce deep and well-structured wines.

The cellarmen of Catalonia have been very resourceful. On the one hand, they have managed to keep up with fashion trends and produce some excellent barreled Chardonnay wines, for example, by being quick to make use of varieties that have now become international. On the other hand, they are aware of the astonishing wealth of native varieties that enables them to create wines with very individual styles. There is still great potential in this area, which enological grand masters such as Miguel Torres, José Luis Pérez (Mas Martinet), or the Albet y Noya brothers are only now beginning to exploit. Over 30 grape varieties that were under threat of extinction are now being grown again in trial plots belonging to major Catalan wineries and perfected by means of clone selection. A large part of the proceeds from wine production is invested in research in the field of enology, which is developing apace in this region.

Ecological Trends

In the last few years, the development of organically produced wines has caused a stir in Catalonia. With almost 50 recognized organic winegrowers, the region has more organic winegrowers than any other country. As a result of the ideal conditions for environmentally friendly cultivation (the dry and warm climate and the poor soils make it easy to do without chemical plant and grape treatments), winegrowers in Catalonia comply strictly with legislation, which pleases clients who are still mostly outside Spain.

Most of the estates are in the Penedès region, but there are also some in Tarragona. Top wine producers such as the Albet y Noya brothers or Antoni Capel (Masia Freixe), whose wines are mentioned in the same breath as the very best Catalonian vintages, insist that the wines produced by these organic winegrowers must be taken seriously. Low yields from the most carefully tended vineyards are another factor in attaining success.

UNDISCOVERED TRADITION

As in most regions that have gradually made a name for themselves with modern wines, the old styles of wine have by no means died out. In the small D.O.s, wines known as *vinos rancios* have a certain part to play in Spain's wine-growing history. These are dry wines made from Garnacha Blanca or Tinta, which are picked when very ripe and stored for many years in large tuns without the addition of any wine spirit. They are often stored in the open air, and occasionally glass containers are also used. The sweet *vino generoso* is another variety that a few producers continue to make. In its preparation, once FERMENTATION has begun, wine spirit is added to stop it, thereby retaining a considerable amount of RESIDUAL SUGAR. Unlike the southern Levant, Garnacha is the main predomi-

With its numerous restaurants, Barcelona is one of the most important buyers of its provincial wines, whether white, rosé, or red. But nothing tickles the Catalans' taste buds more than cava.

nant grape used to make the MUST, with Moscatel being used more rarely. Sweet Mistela grapes are also an old winegrowers' tradition. These are used to make unfermented sweet must, which is prevented from fermenting by adding wine spirit. Tasting these archaic wines is just like going back in time, but after a good meal, the dessert wines still prove that they have an important place.

Apart from the Penedès region and the Costers del Segre, the Garnacha and Tinta grape varieties account for a significant proportion of the vineyards in the Catalan *appellations*, a fact that is bemoaned by forward-thinking winegrowers. After the dramatic turn-around in the fortunes of wine in Priorat, whose new wines rely at least in part on musts from old Garnacha vines, people have come to recognize that the black Garnacha, if harvested in small quantities, can produce full-fruit and exceptionally rich wines. The problem facing the small D.O.s is how to break up the rigid, old structures, and to encourage winegrowers to allow new techniques to influence their wine-making methods. Priorat is not the same thing as Catalonia, but even the less well-known wine-growing areas of the region are still full of possibilities.

The History of La Rioja

The numerous Roman wine-fermenting vessels found cut into the rock in the region of La Rioja, and which can still be seen there, bear witness to the fact that the area was a wine-growing center way back in classical times. Later, it was the monasteries that encouraged wine growing and also supervised quality. A deed of donation, in which the king of Navarra transferred land and vineyards to the monastery of San Millán de la Cogolla, provides evidence that vines were also grown in the early medieval period. The pilgrims who went in their hundreds of thousands to Santiago de Compostela in distant Galicia to see the grave of James the Apostle were served the alcoholic grape juice in pilgrims' hostelries run by the monasteries. They spread the word about La Rioja wine far and wide.

Wine has always been very important for the region, and in 1560 the winegrowers formed an association and agreed on a standard brand mark for their barrels to guarantee the wine's origin. Even at that time, the wine from La Rioja enjoyed a certain reputation and its name was often wrongly applied, even though the region did not have any good transport routes to the distant coasts and large cities until the 19th century. The first wine companies—as we know them today with their huge cellars filled with thousands of BARRIQUES, or barrel, casks—did not come into being until the second half of the 20th century.

The Rise of Barrique Casks

The wine region took off only after the introduction of barrel production, which meant that the wine could be kept. Wines finished in small oak casks were unknown in La Rioja until 1862,

In the Middle Ages, when hundreds of thousands of St. James' pilgrims passed through La Rioja on their way to Santiago de Compostela, the region's towns and viticulture experienced the first major upturn in their economic fortunes. Many of their buildings date back to this period, including those located in Calahorra in the La Rioja Baja.

although as early as 1786 Manuel Esteban Quintano had experimented to some extent with oak casks after visiting the Bordeaux region. His wines passed the acid test of an ocean-crossing to the Latin-American colonies with flying colors, but he could not cash in on this new type of wine by charging a higher price, and Señor Quintano's pioneering enological experiment drifted back into oblivion. During his exile in London, Colonel Luciano de Murrieta acquired a taste for Bordeaux wines. Before returning to Spain to take over a *bodega* in La Rioja, he went to Bordeaux to study the wine preparation methods there. He had barrels brought from Bilbao, which he filled for the first time in 1850. Then he dispatched some of the 19-gallon (72-liter) barrels to Cuba, where he sold them for a good price. Encouraged by this success, he continued with barrel production. Around 1850, Camilo Hurtado de Amézaga, the Marqués de Riscal, also began to speculate on the future of La Rioja as a wine-growing region. He too had spent many years of his exile in Bordeaux, where he became a devotee of the wines of the Médoc. In

A century of viticultural history in the traditional winemaking firm of Tondonia in Haro.

1860, he had a *bodega*, based on the Bordeaux model, built at Elciego. In that same year, the Marqués had vines from Bordeaux planted on a quarter of his 494-acre (200-ha) estate.

When Bordeaux lost much of its harvest to a serious mildew epidemic and the phylloxera disaster, the region even took in wines from La Rioja. However, the traditional Rioja wines were often of poor quality and did not travel well, so on the advice of the Marqués the administration of the province of Álava decided to engage the services of a French expert by the name of Jean Pineau. He taught a select group of estate owners to appreciate the French method of mashing in large wooden barrels and then finishing the wines in small oak casks. This he did with no little success, for Monsieur Pineau was soon able to report to his patrons, "*que el año próximo casi todos los propietarios hagan el vino al estilo de Burdeos*" (that in the next year nearly all the proprietors should produce Bordeaux-style wines).

Despite the initial good results, however, most winegrowers fought shy, because finishing the wines in small oak casks seemed to them to be a nuisance and too costly. Pineau then entered the services of Riscal, and this *bodega* began to mature red Rioja wines in barrel casks in their cellar tunnels. Convincing other winemakers was a gradual process, and it was some time before some *bodegueros* adopted these techniques once more, impressed by the success of the wines at international wine exhibitions. Subsequently, many wine estates based on the French model grew up within a very short space of time. Many French people settled in La Rioja, and so began the history of a wine that now enjoys a widespread international reputation.

CASTILE–LEÓN

With its nine provinces, Castile–León is the largest regional entity in the European Union to have its own parliament. It is primarily agricultural, but with only 173,000 acres (70,000 ha) of vines, the area devoted to wine growing is relatively small in Spanish terms. So far, less than half of this area has D.O. status. There are currently five *Denominaciones de Origen*, but the district of Ribera de Arlanza in the province of Burgos will shortly be designated the sixth D.O.

In Castile, there is a long tradition of wine growing, which blossomed for the first time in the 16th and 17th centuries. The court in Madrid was the driving force, and the huge demand from the rapidly expanding new capital just had to be met. There was also great demand from abroad, which led to the wine-growing area spreading throughout the country. It is hard to calculate the precise extent of the total area in Castile–León at the end of the 19th century before the outbreak of the phylloxera disaster, but the small region of Rueda provides a starting point. It used to cover 222,400 acres (90,000 ha), but has now shrunk to less than a

Barren plateaus and a wide temperature range are features of the wine-growing regions in Castile-León. They ensure that the wines are balanced and expressive. Some of the region's best-known wines come from Pesquera del Duero in the Ribera del Duero area.

tenth of that figure. Despite massive replanting after the damage caused by the phylloxera outbreak, the wine-growing area has never regained its 19th-century proportions. Furthermore, in the 1950s when the national plan of the Franco regime turned large tracts of Castile over to cornfields, many vines had to give way to grain.

Castile has an excellent reputation among connoisseurs of Spanish wine, and this is not restricted to the Ribera del Duero. The wines are generally regarded as being full-bodied with character and intense fruit. There is no doubt that the soil and climatic conditions are responsible for much of the wines' profile. Castile–León has poor soils, extremes of hot and cold, and to a lesser extent, repeated periods of drought. El Bierzo in León provides an example of the low yield produced from the vines. This low yield is often further decimated by the inclement weather.

FIVE QUALITY WINE AREAS

Even as recently as the 1960s, the wine region of Castile was regarded as being antiquated. La Rioja was at its height of popularity. Today, however, many of the major Spanish wines are concentrated in this autonomous region. In addition to the Ribera del Duero, four more zones are classified as quality wine regions. El Bierzo, in the northwestern tip, produces the lightest wines, and Cigales, not far from Valladolid, supplies red- and rosé-lovers with robust wines. Together with the Catalan Priorats, Toro offers the most full-bodied wines of all Spain, which is not surprising, since Zamora has the third lowest rainfall of the country's provinces. Rueda deserves special quality that they have tempted famous wine-makers from La Rioja and Galicia, who believe they have found a distinctive new style of red wine here. The red wines from Valdevimbre-Los Oteros between Benavente and León are some of Spain's classic table wines.

Production of top-quality table wines has generally increased around the Duero basin. *Bodegas* such as Abadía Retuerta, Mauro, and Alta Pavina have basically reversed the sad reputation of table wines. Most of the country's famous table-wine producers are now concentrated in Castile.

To complete the picture, reference should be made to the wines right on the Portuguese border. The loops of the river Duero, where Castile's largest river becomes the border, are shared by the provinces of Salamanca and Zamora. *Rosados* and medium-bodied red wines are produced here, and after Ribera de Arlanza could possibly be regulated by a seventh D.O. in the region going by the name of Los Arribes.

In terms of winemaking technology, the region of Castile is definitely at the forefront. Yet the trend is leaning toward a controlled naturalness. The wine is not filtered so thoroughly, and the chemical treatment of vineyards is kept to a bare minimum. This is not particularly difficult in a region that is so bleak that its climate manages to make life miserable and difficult even for pests.

mention, because the change from oxidation-finished white wines to the fruity, delicate wines of today has been dramatic. Rueda could soon be giving Spain its first smooth white wines suitable for laying down, for the possibilities of the Verdejo grape variety have in no way been fully exploited.

However, the quality wine regions of Castile–León are not the only places to produce attractive wines. Cebreros in the province of Ávila produces robust and soft red wines of such

The rustic surroundings of the Bodega Monjardín in Navarra.

Toro, Spain's new viticultural heaven

When the wine-growing region around the small town of Toro, where monks grew wine as early as the 13th century, was finally recognized as a D.O., its wines immediately began to attract attention. But no one anticipated that only 11 years later some of Spain's most renowned enologists would rush to set up wineries in the D.O. Toro. The original area under cultivation has now been doubled to 14,826 acres (6,000 ha) and is still growing. Tinta de Toro is only native to this area; it is simply a clone of Tempranillo, created through the special climate conditions in Toro, and it provides 90 percent of the total harvest. Garnacha Tinta and the white

Malvasía and Verdejo grapes also play some part. The Tinta de Toro produces very dark red wines with high extract and tannin levels and is responsible for the fact that, alongside the Ribera del Duero and the Priorat, Toro is considered to be a new wine miracle. The young wines mostly contain a high proportion of Garnacha grapes, whereas the Tinta de Toro predominates in the barrel-aged quality wines. Most of the 30 winegrowers registered so far—the number of winegrowers selling their own wine should double shortly—produce the main variety as a single-varietal wine. The *appellation* regulations stipulate that a *crianza* wine should be aged in oak for at least six months. The white Malvasía provides soft wines that should be drunk when they are young.

Of the region's D.O.s, this area is the warmest and the driest. With 3,000 hours of sunshine each year, the grapes attain an enviable degree of ripeness. To avoid the development of an excessive alcohol content, the grapes are harvested here as early as the beginning of September. The Tinta de Toro with its 13.5 percent vol develops the best spicy-fruity character. Top wineries such as Vega Sicilia, Mauro, and Pesquera like the Tinta de Toro for its opulent fruit and soft tannins, which make this red wine smooth, yet profound, and give it considerable keeping potential. In the opinion of experienced winemakers, the Tinta de Toro is the only real alternative to Tempranillo. It is therefore assured a place in the Spanish wine Olympics.

Ribera del Duero

This wine-growing area extends for more than 68 miles (109 km) along both sides of the river Duero through parts of four provinces. Around 85 percent of the whole region lies within the province of Burgos, even though many of the *bodegas* are in the province of Valladolid. When, in 1982, the *Denominación de Origen* was first established, only a few wine producers existed alongside cooperatives. Today there are well over 150 *bodegas*, with more springing up. Scarcely any region growing quality wines has made such rapid progress as the Ribera del Duero, which has become a byword for excellence throughout the world.

The secret of this success lies in the region's red wines, which are exceptionally dark, superbly fruity, richly robust and remarkably well able to age. Apart from the main variety, Tinta del País, the following reds: Garnacha, Cabernet Sauvignon, Merlot, and Malbec, and the white, Albillo, are licensed.

The D.O. Ribera del Duero is best known for high-quality red wines aged in wood, which must contain at least three-quarters Tinta del País, as Tempranillo is called hereabouts. However, many top companies produce pure varietals from the best Castilian grapes. The continuing vast variation in styles and qualities is due largely to preparation methods and very variable harvests. The best vineyards are in the province of Burgos near the villages of Roa, La Horra, Gumiel, and Sotilla—these are also called the heartland of the

La Horra is one of the most famous wine areas in the Ribera del Duero.

Ribera. Nevertheless, we must avoid geographical classification, since the harvest from any area may circulate throughout the D.O. region. Styles are also determined by different oakwood, not only classic American oak but also French barrels are used.

The region has a greater variety of *terroirs* than is usual in Castile, and these mainly influence the personalities of small growers' wines. Thus, Ribera is not simply confined to Ribera. The 37,064 acres (15,000 ha) of vineyards, 80 percent stocked with the red main varietal, are sited not only on the Duero's banks, but also on surrounding hills. Most top-quality growing areas lie on south-facing, highly chalky slopes, which descend to the river from high ground. At several points the region reaches deep inland, up to nearly 22 miles (35 km). The extreme highland climate—many vineyards lie over 2,624 feet (800 m) up—often brings late frosts. These radically reduce harvests in a number of years, which explains the scarcity and consequent popularity of reds.

Cigales

Cigales, the smallest of the four D.O. regions in central Castile, lies on a tributary of the Duero, the Río Pisuerga. It is nearly 30 miles (48 km) long and 9 miles (15 km) wide. Currently the vineyards cover over 6,792 acres (2,750 ha), almost all sited in the north of Valladolid province. Only one district in the neighboring province, Palencia, is a D.O. area. Climatically, Cigales is somewhere between the warmish Toro region and the cooler Ribera del Duero, whose western edge lies only 15 miles (24 km) away. The landscape is generally flat, broken up by occasional tablemountains. Historically, the village after which the D.O. is named is a legendary center of Spanish winemaking.

From early mediaeval times the Claretes of Cigales, very full-bodied *rosados* (pinks), were considered the best in Spain. Juicy *rosados* are still trodden here, although recently sturdy but

In the twilight of an autumn day, the rich green vineyards stand out sharply against the burnt landscape of Castile–León.

palatable Tintos have found more favor. The permitted varieties are the whites Albillo, Verdejo and Viura, but they account for less than 10 percent of the total area under cultivation. The main varieties are Tinta del Pais and Garnacha. Ten years ago the red wines still

only accounted for just under 10 percent of the total wine output of this region; now their share has risen to 45 percent. Particularly the super-modern and largely unknown wine producers who have entered the market in recent years—the area now has around 20 bottling plants—are increasingly concentrating on pure Tinta del Pais wines, which age excellently in the small oak vats. The potential for high-quality Tintos is certainly there, but so far the Cigales Tintos have only in exceptional cases reached the heights of their neighbor's top quality products.

The expressive *rosados*, described on their back-label as "Cigales Nuevo," still account for most D.O. production. These wines are trodden from at least 60 percent Tinta del País, and released by the D.O. regulators as early as November. They have a fine freshness and an opulent bouquet.

Many wine drinkers will wonder how Riberas differ from Riojas, if the Tinta del País and Tempranillo are identical. In the Ribera region only a few wines are aged as long as traditional Riojas. Instead, they are often marketed soon after fermentation in small oak barrels. Thus, Ribera wines often have a relatively deeper color, sweeter tannins, and a darker fruitiness tending toward plum, while Riojas frequently exude stronger aromas of red berries. Recently, many new-generation Riojas, along with several Riberas, have acquired distinct vanilla and cinnamon aromas after fermenting in new wood.

RUEDA

The establishment of the first D.O. dedicated—at first—solely to white wine, Rueda, inaugurated the triumphal progress of a grape practically unknown before. The Verdejo grape is indigenous to this region, stocked with some 16,800 acres (6,800 ha) of vines, extending north of the Duero into Valladolid province and is also present in small areas of Ávila and Segovia. It constitutes nearly half the total vineyards. Alongside this main variety, Viura, Sauvignon Blanc, and Palomina are also licensed, though the latter must not be newly planted. The D.O. named after the small village of Rueda has one of the country's best wine cellar infrastructures and all of the 30 bottling plants have hyper-modern cellar facilities. The making of white wine, with temperature-controlled fermentation, is now standard practice, and cooling the harvested grapes before PRESSING, selection-tables, and cold maceration are no longer exceptional. Many old cave-cellars, with kilometer-long tunnels, have been redesigned into real showcases. Some store the sparkling wine: Rueda Espumoso, whose yeast needs at least nine months to mature, must contain up to 75 percent Verdejo. However, the region's stars are Rueda Verdejo, also with at least 75 percent Verdejo, and the intensely pure varietals of Sauvigon Blanc wines, which have developed a unique, robust structure on the bare high plains.

The strong point of Verdejo wine is its floral rather than distinctly fruity bouquet, underscored with a delicate bitterness and a strongly herbal taste. One of this varietal's outstanding features is its high extract-value, which can be seen from the substantial streaks in the glass. But this should cause no anxiety—far from indicating too much alcohol, it promises denseness and quality. The third variety is a straightforward Rueda, made with 50 percent Verdejo. Since 2000 the red varieties grown here, chief of which is Tinta del Pais, have also had D.O. protection. The red Ruedas are not as complex as the Riberas, but this could change in a few years.

EL BIERZO

Bordering on Galicia, El Bierzo D.O. definitely has the best balanced climate of any D.O. region in Castile–León. Atlantic rain and Castilian sun make El Bierzo's valleys one of the most productive of Spain's landscapes. Most vineyards lie on flat slopes in the valleys, scarcely over 1,641 feet (500 m) high. Sheltering mountain ranges ensure that late frosts rarely strike.

Main varieties are the whites Doña Blanca and Godello and the principal wine, the indigenous red, Mencía. All red wines must contain at least 75 percent of this grape. It has a delicate, red fruit aroma and produces fruity, subtle red wines with sturdy acidity and a characteristic mineral quality. If grown on old vines, blackberry notes predominate. Mencía wines are normally offered as *vino joven*, but the best producers prove that aging in barrels can add concentration and complexity.

The Prada a Tope vineyards with a taproom in Cacabelos independently produce red and white wines of the D.O. El Bierzo.

VEGA SICILIA, PESQUERA, AND PINGUS

The following three great vineyards have established, confirmed and constantly renewed the reputation of the Ribera region. Vega Sicilia, Bodega Alejandro Fernández-Tinto Pesquera, and Dominio de Pingus are not only some of Spain's best wines but also rank with the world's top labels.

VEGA SICILIA

Back in 1864, the first vines were planted in the western section of the present D.O. Ribera del Duero. However, only from 1915–17, under the Herrero family who gave the estate its current name, was a quality red wine produced that could be considered a forerunner of present-day varieties. Alongside viticulture, the house of Vega Sicilia has devoted most of its energy to a highly elaborate, sophisticated process of maturing wines—the key to the uniquely Baroque style of the Único, the estate's main *cuvée*. In good vintages the Único proves itself one of the world's most versatile reds, whilst its inimitably deep aromas evoke a unique character of fruit dried under southern sun. It also smells of dry fruit such as figs and plums, of forest berries, tobacco, coffee, and spices. In the mouth a very special velvety fullness develops, underscored by melting tannins.

The 445 acres (180 ha) of the estate's vineyards are dominated by the Tinta del País, which, in some of the oldest plots, is mixed with Cabernet Sauvignon vines. The hand-picked grapes are first taken in small crates to the cellar, where they are completely hulled and moved by conveyor-belt to the fermenting tanks. The best plots' harvest has already been pre-selected for the Único, and is fermented in wooden vats. The second-ranking wine, Valbuena, is stored in stainless steel tanks. After malolactic fermentation, which also takes place in large wooden tanks, the Único is first left to settle for six months in old barrels. Then all the wines are tasted and tested and their future decided. The second-rank wine, Valbuena, which is marketed after five years' fermentation, is now poured into pre-used barrels of French oak for 11 to 14 months. Then it is matured in bottles for at least 18 months more. What will become Único now proceeds on its complex way, by carefully selected steps, to ultimate perfection. Initially, the wine ferments for up to two years in new

Vega Sicilia, with its stately chapel and buildings around a courtyard, can be seen as the original core of the Ribera region that is so much in demand today.

French barrels, before maturing for five years or more in ever-older barrels, mainly American oak, until the day of bottling finally arrives.

The usual blending of the Único reflects the distribution of different wine varieties in the estate's vineyards. Tinta del País represents at least four-fifths, followed by Cabernet Sauvignon, Malbec, Merlot, and a drop of Albillo, the crowning glory. The Unico goes unfiltered into bottles, where it must mature for at least three years. The owner family, Álvarez, would leave an interval of at least 11 years before releasing it into the world of paying wine collectors and gourmets. In outstanding vintages like 1970 and 1981, the Tinto Fino often constitutes only two thirds of the *cuvée*, while the Cabernet Sauvignon rises to a fifth, reinforced by Merlot and Malbec. Then the Único will be commercially sold as a *reserva especial* only after several more years' aging.

The Vega Sicilia vine strips in the Duero valley extend between the river's left bank and the adjoining chain of hills in the western corner of the Ribera region.

Long before the Ribera del Duero had earned a reputation as a wine-growing region, Vega Sicilia was already legendary. It is reassuring for the wine world to know that this estate and its unique wines with their long tradition are still cared for so lovingly. This is at least partly due to the sensitivity with which innovations have been introduced. Yet Alión, the second estate which the Álvarez family stocked in 1992 only a few kilometers nearer Peñafiel, shows how carefully this legacy has been fostered. Here, on 124 acres (50 ha), only Tinta del País grapes were planted. When ripe, the grapes are selected with utmost care. They are generally macerated for three weeks at most, before the wine is matured in new French barrels for a maximum of 16 months. The result is a supremely smooth, fruity and spicy wine, which can stand comparison with any other modern Spanish red wine.

Pesquera

If Vega Sicilia is the Ribera region's grandfather, Alejandro Fernández is its father. He not only created the modern Ribera style, but also inaugurated a new kind of Spanish wine, combining the maturity of grapes grown under southern sun with full-bodied fruitiness and great finesse. Today this formula inspires great wines not only in the Ribera del Duero but all over Spain, especially in the region of La Rioja.

When he was young, Alejandro Fernández earned his living repairing and constructing agricultural machines of all kinds. Simultaneously, however, he managed several vine-

Left
The old wine cellars in Pesquera perforate the village hill. Only the acorn-like airshafts betray the fact that outstanding reds are slumbering here.

Right
Only when the vintage is exceptional will Alejandro Fernández bottle his Janus, which he produces by consciously conservative methods.

Tinto Pesquera consists exclusively of Tinta del País, as Tempranillo is called hereabouts.

yards in his home locality, Pesquera del Duero, which were left to him by his father. At that time grapes or young wines were still sold to those areas whose wines suffered from lack of color or body—for example, La Mancha. The more color a wine had, the more it cost. In 1972, angered by the contempt in which cooperatives held his excellent wines, Don Alejandro established his *bodega*. Without hulling his grapes, he fermented his harvest and pressed them in the old winepress that still stands near the estate. Initially, he kept his reds in champagne bottles with spring fasteners, and began marketing them throughout the region. Gradually, news of the quality of his wine

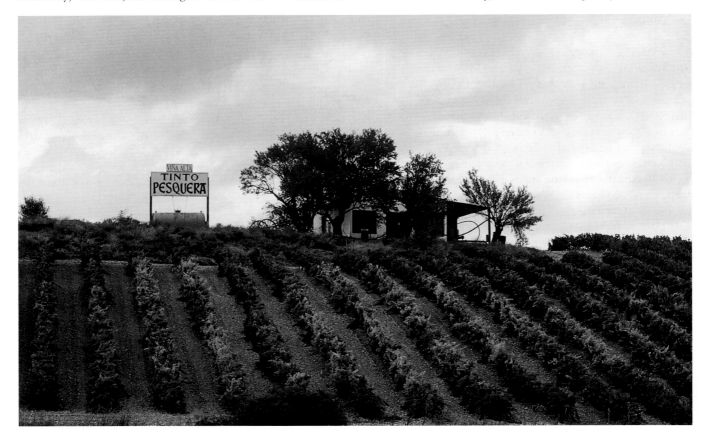

spread throughout Castile. An American importer helped him achieve his breakthrough. "Wine Pope" Robert Parker received a sample of Pesquera 1992 from Don Alejandro, and he christened this "the Petrus of Spain." World renown for Pesqueras and Alejandro Fernández were assured.

Pesquera wines always use pure-varietal Tinta del País grapes, which are harvested in deliberately limited quantities. After alcoholic fermentation, up to a fortnight of maceration generally follows. To mature the wines, and for the malolactic fermentation, barrels of American oak are selected—a technique that consciously upholds the region's tradition. The wines never become woody, yet age superbly. Different Pesquera qualities are manifested according to the age of the vines, the choice of grape, the age of the barrels used, and the duration of the aging in wood. Only the Janus Special Reserve, prepared in the most successful years, follows traditional methods of preparation, whereby the stems are also macerated with the juice, as if to remind people of the wines that have made Pesquera famous.

PINGUS

Pingus, at present Spain's most popular and dearest red wine, has given the Ribera region immediate renown. Since 1990 the young Dane, Peter Sisseck, has managed the estate, the Hacienda el Monasterio. He learned the craft of winemaking in Bordeaux and was inspired by Valandraud in Saint-Émilion. In the locality of la Horra he has also planted four plots of land with over nine acres (3.8 ha) of old Tinta del País—land which he used to rent in 1995 but has since purchased. With utmost care and following ecological principles, he still tends his vineyards, which lie in probably the best *terroirs* of the Ribera region, restricting his yields drastically. Then he waits patiently for the grapes' optimum ripeness, before they are hand-picked and taken 25 miles (40 km) in small crates by refrigerated truck to his wine cellar in distant Quintanilla de Onésimo. Here, ten women de-stalk the grapes by hand, before lightly crushing them underfoot in small stainless steel fermenting containers. By this time it is already early October and the nights are cool. The grapes lie in their own must for ten days before fermentation sets in; and this usually lasts another eight days. Generally, Peter Sissek lets the wine macerate for only a few days before he takes off the stems and pours the juice into new French barrels. In these, in the warmer spring weather, malolactic fermentation follows automatically. Then every single barrel is tasted and every wine, whose exceptionally strong nose suggests intense concentration, is further aged in another barrel—a process called "maturing in 200 percent new oak."

After nearly two years in a barrel, the Pingus is bottled. Since Robert Parker awarded the first vintage 98 out of 100 points in 1995, precipitating it into the small circle of the world's top wines, wine lovers all over the globe have been battling for one of the 7,000 bottles produced annually. This truly hand-made wine bewitches the nose with an intense aroma of fig, smoke, and tar, and the palate with its enormous body; here it develops similar aromas, and also dark chocolate, spices, and a prodigious length. It is altogether a dramatic wine with a thoroughbred backbone. Recently, Peter Sisseck has taken over other vineyards, which produce the more wood-oriented, less complex second-rank wine, Flor de Pingus.

By means of well-established vines and very sophisticated cellar work, the young Dane Peter Sisseck, called Pingus by friends and relatives, created the most expensive cult-wine in Spain—the Pingus.

Select Wine Producers in Castile–Léon

Bodegas Alejandro Fernández**
Pesquera de Duero (D.O. Ribera del Duero)
543 acres (220 ha); 850,000 bottles • Wines: Tinto Pesquera: Crianza, Reserva, Gran Reserva, Janus Reserva and Gran Reserva
Ribera owes its current prominence to Alejandro Fernández and his Pesquera wines. He also manages the excellent Condado de Haza estate near Roa de Duero.

Bodegas Arzuaga Navarra*–****
Quintanilla de Onésimo (D.O. Ribera del Duero)
346 acres (140 ha); some bought-in grapes: 450,000 bottles • Wines: Tinto Arzuaga Crianza, Tinto Arguaza Reserva, →Tinto Arzuaga Gran Reserva
The *bodega* belongs to the younger generation on the Duero. The vines are striking for their elegance and harmony. The better the quality (Reserva and Gran Reserva), the higher the proportion of Cabernet and French oak.

Bodegas de Crainza Castilla la Vieja*–****
Rueda (D.O. Rueda)
247 acres (100 ha); some bought-in grapes; 2,000,000 bottles • Wines: Palacio de Bornos: Rueda Superior, Fermentado en Barrica, →Sauvignon Blanc
Antonio Sanz and his son Ricardo are among Castile's most respected winegrowers. Alongside their very fruity Sauvignon and the crystal-clear Rueda Superior, the estate is experimenting with wood-aged Ruedas and white wines with residual sugar. The reds have no D.O.

Bodegas Emilio Moro*–*****
Pesquera de Duero (D.O. Ribera del Duero)
148 acres (60 ha); some bought-in grapes; 425,000 bottles • Wines: Finca Resalso, Emilio Moro, Malleolus, Malleolus de Valdemiro
The Moro family has gained in standing since 1991, when their first wine was bottled. Their selections from old vines, Malleolus and Malleolus de Valdemiro, have set the standards in the western Ribera region. Their style is lush and beefy with definite mineral notes.

Bodegas Hermanos Sastre*–****
La Horra (D.O. Ribera del Duero)
99 acres (40 ha); 140,000 bottles • Wines include: Via Sastre Crianza, Pago de Santa Cruz, Regina Vides, Pesus
Sastre is one of the top wine estates in Ribera del Duero. Production is small, and expensive specialties such as the single vineyard wine Pago de Santa Cruz or the wonderfully harmonious Regina Vides have character and great depth. The Merlot-dominated Pesus is one of the most exclusive wines in Spain.

Bodegas Hermanos del Villar*–****
Rueda (D.O. Rueda)
222 acres (90 ha); 300,000 bottles • Wines: Oro de Castila: Sauvignon Blanc, Fermentada en Barrica, →Rueda Superior
A serious *bodega* established in 1994. The estate, however, has old tunnel cellars. The wines are exceptionally fruity and soft, which gives them great charm. Pablo del Villar is one of the region's great hopes for the future.

Bodegas Ismael Arroyo**–*****
Sotillo de la Ribera (D.O. Ribera del Duero)
30 acres (12 ha); 360,000 bottles • Wines: Valsotillo: Crianza, Reserva, →Gran Reserva
The traditonial yet fruity and deep-colored style of the Arroyo brothers lifted the *bodega* to the peak of Spanish

winemaking. The single-variety wines are matured only in American oak and show great aging potential.

Bodegas Lezcano*
Trigueros del Valle (D.O. Cigales)
35 acres (14 ha); 120,000 bottles • Wines: Docetañidos, Lezcano Crianza, Lezcano Reserva
Young Félix Lezcano did not found his small wine estate until 1991. However, his still immature wines are in an excellent location. Alongside a fine *rosado*, he produces complex if slightly woody *tintos*, which are getting finer every year.

Bodegas Mauro**
Tudela de Duero (no D.O.)
Pedrosa del Rey (D.O. Toro)
136 acres (55 ha); 225,000 bottles • Wines: Mauro, Terreus, →Vendima Seleccionada
This *bodega* was among the first in Castile to produce an outstanding, non-D.O. red wine. Since 1997 there has been an additional red wine from Toro, of which some 40,000 bottles are produced under the brand name Viña San Román. All the brands, from Terreus through to Mauro and San Román, reveal a brilliant and noble structure.

Bodegas Peñalba López*–****
Aranda de Duero (D.O. Ribera del Duero)
500 acres (200 ha); 800,000 bottles • Wines: Torremilanos: Crianza, Reserva; Torre Albéniz Reserva
In recent years the *bodega* owned by Pablo Peñalba and Pilar Albéniz has risen to join the best companies in the D.O. The Torremilanos wines are single variety, prepared from Tempranillo; the Reserva Torre Albéniz contains a little Cabernet. The vines produce wine that is full-bodied and with finish, and has great aging potential. The *bodega's* own cask maker has switched all the barrels to French wood.

Bodega Pérez Pascuas**
Pedrosa de Duero (D.O. Ribera del Duero)
210 acres (85 ha); 350,000 bottles • Wines include: Viña Pedrosa: Reserva, Gran Reserva, Pérez Pascuas Gran Selección
The very complex, fine and acidic *tintos* of the Viña Pedros brand are intended to age, but can seem rather inaccessible in youth. The *bodega* has very old vineyards 2,625 feet (800 m) up. The Selección Pérez Pascuas is one of the D.O.'s supreme wines.

Bodegas Rodera*–****
Pedrosa de Duero (D.O. Ribera del Duero)
161 acres (65 ha); 200,000 bottles • Wines: Carmelo Rodero: Crianza, Reserva, →Gran Reserva
For years Camelo Rodero sent his grapes to Vega Sicilia; then he made himself self-sufficient. His *tintos* always have a robust consistency, underscored with plump tannins. He owns one of the best Cabernet vineyards in the Ribera region, a small percentage of whose grapes go into the *reservas* and *gran reservas*.

Bodegas Vega Sauco*
Morales de Toro (D.O. Toro)
30 acres (12 ha); 190,000 bottles • Wines: Vega Sauco Tinto, Vega Sauco Crianza, Vega Sauco Reserva, →Adoremus
The strength of Wenceslao Gil's wines lies in their exceptional color and intense taste. Although the enologist has prescribed long aging in American oak, the wood is not dominant, thanks to the concentration of Vega Saucos.

BODEGAS Y VIÑEDOS VEGA SICILIA*****
VALBUENA DE DUERO (D.O. RIBERA DEL DUERO)
445 acres (180 ha); 220,000 bottles • Wines: Unico Tinto: Gran Reserva, Reserva Especial, Valbuena Tinta Reserva

Since 1982, this has been owned by the Alvarez family, who keep this historic estate and its wines in top condition. They also own the nearby *bodega* Alión, where an impressive modern Ribera is produced from 124 acres (50 ha) of Tempranillo.

DOMINIO DE PINGUS****–*****
QUINTANILLA DE ONÉSIMO (RIBERA DEL DUERO)
12 acres (5 ha); 25 acres (10 ha) leased; 37,000 bottles • Wines: Pingus, Flor de Pingus

The Dane Peter Sissek succeeded in creating the Ribera's most sought-after cult wine. He cleverly exploited the success of his wine to give his estate a more extensive future base.

DOMINIO DE TARES***
SAN ROMÁN DE BEMBIBRE (D.O. BIERZO)
Bought-in grapes, 220,000 bottles • Wines: Domenico de Tares, Godello Fermentado en Barrica, Tinto Roble, Cepas Viejas

From the very beginning, this young company relied on grape varieties native to the region and uses the most modern technology in the production of both red and white wines. Even the grapes for the standard Roble come from old vineyards. Cepas Viejas comes from schist slope vineyards which are more than 60 years old.

DOS VICTORIAS***–****
SAN ROMÁN DE HORNIJA (D.O. TORO)
NAVA DEL REY (D.O. RUEDA)
20 acres (8 ha); some bought-in grapes; 25,000 bottles • Wines: Jose Pariente Rueda Superior, →Gran Elías Mora

In 1999 the two Victorias, both qualified enologists, followed two vintages of their white Rueda José Pariente with the first red table wine from the Toro region, where the two Castilian women are building a *bodega*. The 2000 vintage of their red wine, Elías Moroa, was the first to bear the Toro *appellation*. Both wines come from old vineyards and are outstandingly fruity and well-structured.

EXPLOTACIONES VALDUERO***–****
GUMIEL DEL MERCADO (D.O. RIBERA DEL DUERO)
494 acres (200 ha); 1,200,000 bottles • Wines: Valduero Crianza, Reserva, →Gran Reserva, Reserva Primium

This family business stands by long aging in wood, and always markets very mature wines, which seem well balanced, subtle, yet also dense. The reds are generally trodden as pure varietals from Tempranillo, and are among the most reliable and reasonably priced wines on the Duero.

HACIENDA MONASTERIO****
PESQUERA DE DUERO (D.O. RIBERA DEL DUERO)
173 acres (70 ha); 320,000 bottles • Wines: Hacienda Monasterio: Crianza, Reserva

A juicy Ribera type with an international profile, intensely fruity, with soft tannins. The hyper-modern estate and all its vines, working almost exclusively with French oak, was conceived by the Dane Peter Sisseck. Special emphasis is given to grape-selection and careful wine preparation. Nothing is filtered.

PAGO DE CARRAOVEJAS****
PEÑAFIEL (D.O. RIBERA DEL DUERO)
148 acres (60 ha); 320,000 bottles • Wines: Pago de Carraovejas: Crianza, Reserva

Highly aromatic wines of a very dark color are the *bodega's* specialty. The first vines were planted in the

late 1980s by chief enologist, Tomás Postigo—including a perfectly balanced Cabernet vine. All the *bodega's* wines contain 25 percent of the French grape.

VINOS BLANCOS DE CASTILLA***–****
RUEDA (D.O. RUEDA)
371 acres (150 ha); bought-in grapes; 1,500,800 bottles • Wines: Marqués de Riscal: Reserva Limousin, Sauvignon, →Rueda Superior

The undisputed pioneer of modern white wine preparation in Rueda uses the very latest techniques to tread his classic Marqués de Riscal Rueda Superior, made from Verdejo and a dash of Viura. The wine also exudes clean aromas of fruit and blossoms, and is a perfect balance between body and stylishness. The same applies to the Sauvignon Blanc.

VINOS SANZ***
RUEDA (D.O. RUEDA)
247 acres (100 ha); 350,000 bottles • Wines: Sanz Rueda Superior, Sanz Sauvignon, →Finca La Colina

The estate has the largest and oldest Sauvignon Blanc vineyard in the D.O. Rueda. So it is no surprise that the enologist Juan Carlos Ayala regularly treads one of the country's best Sauvignon Blancs.

Teófilo Reyes's extensive knowledge of the Ribera expresses itself in his wines' complex style.

Galicia

Galicia, a region where nature is wild and rampant, lies in the northwest of the Iberian Peninsula. Celtic traces remain not only in the language, Gallego, which is related to Portuguese, but also in a certain tendency toward mysticism. Pre-Christian and Christian elements mingle as in virtually no other area of Spain. Perhaps this also explains a recurring sense of reserve. That said, the switch from an almost medieval agrarian structure to avant-garde techniques in the modern cellars of Rías Baixas, home of the Albariño, has been so swift that it can hardly be said to be a transition.

Galicia produces roughly 26.5 million gallons (1 million hectoliters) of wine each year, and not so long ago there was the problem that no one knew where to put it all. Most of the wine-growing estates in Galicia are highly productive; the frequent rain and the temperate climate in the river valleys where most vines grow, do their work. On the one hand, the region of Galicia is plagued by excessive quantity and mediocrity, while on the other it can produce wines of such originality and quality that any enterprising wine lover will constantly find new surprises.

	Rías Baixas
	Ribeiro
	Ribeira Sacra
	Valdeorras
	Monterrei
	Wine-growing areas in neighboring regions

Opposite
Small land holdings, on which, in addition, livestock are kept and vegetables grown, share those areas of the Ribeira Sacra suitable for wine growing.

Even in the hinterland Galicia remains green and moist. In Ribeira Sacra many farmers cultivate only small terraces, which extend along south-facing slopes.

Ribeira Sacra

From an enological viewpoint, the Ribeira Sacra is certainly one of the most fascinating D.O. wines of recent years. Not least because in Galicia of northwestern Spain, a bastion of white wine production, it is the only region where reds exceed 75 percent of total winemaking. The quality varietal indigenous to this area is Mencía, and is probably derived from Cabernet Franc. The grape is only partially suitable for aging in wood and so it is marketed as a young wine. As a result, the region produces no *crianza*-quality wines.

The exquisite charm of these wines lies in their slender style and delicate fruitiness, which, according to vintage, can taste of licorice, plum, blackberry, or added fruit so that all Mencía wines from the Ribeira Sacra have undeniable

body. Climatic conditions are ideal: the combination of moderate rainfall with quasi-Mediterranean sunshine means that in the average temperature of 56.3°F (13.5°C) the grapes always mature fully. In Spain this varietal soon aroused attention, as its profile differs strikingly from the rounded, fully ripe red wine personalities which the country produces otherwise, and the prices for a red aged in the tank are almost disgracefully high. There are several reasons for this. First, 90 percent of the 2,965 acres (1,200 ha) of vineyards in the Ribeira Sacra (meaning "the holy bank" and referring to the numerous monasteries founded here in the 12th and 13th centuries) are on steep or very steep slopes. Over the millennia, viticulturalists have laboriously wrested an almost surreal-looking network of tiny terraces from these extremely unresponsive surfaces, on which any mechanical work is impossible. Prior to this, harvesters with full baskets were lowered on ropes to the river, where boats were waiting to take the grape harvest away. The slopes are so steep that it was often impossible to climb them with a full load of grapes.

NEW PATHWAYS ALONG THE HOLY BANK

The soil consists of residual shale and granite, which give the wines a very individual mineral note. As the gorge-like geography of the river valleys of the Sil and Miños and their tributaries offer no opportunity for extending the vineyards, other paths have to be trodden here. For the younger generation of winegrowers their only chance is to manage their companies in a competitive way, by eliminating inferior varieties and replacing them with quality grapes. At present, the top-quality varietal, Mencía, accounts for only 49 percent of the vineyards. Another 30 percent is occupied by weaker varieties such as Garnacha Tintoreta and others. At the moment astronomical sums are paid for 2.2 lb (1 kg) of Mencía grapes, because according to the 2004 Consejo Regulador's scheme for quality control in the D.O., at least 85 percent of this grape must grow in the Ribeira Sacra. By this date the vineyards' total transformation must be complete.

Even the whites that have been settled here are not exempt. The two white grapes planted here, Godello and Albariño produce excellent results on the slate soil. Their percentage share is due to increase from an unlikely 6 percent to at least 15 percent.

Monterrei

In the neighboring province, Ourense, is the small D.O. Monterrei, whose vines offer a mirror image. Here, white wines predominate, with the varieties Doña Blanca, Godello, and Treixadura, ahead of the reds Mencía and Bastardo. Yet here, too, the regulatory authorities must suffer grapes, including the white sherry grape Palomino Fino or the Garnacha Tintorera, which do not produce optimum results in a northern climate. Another drawback is that for the only varietal really characteristic of the region—the Blanca de Monterrei or even Monstruosa—only 99 acres (40 ha) remain free. Recently, however, vines have again become available, and reconstruction of the vineyards has begun, principally to increase the proportion of straw-colored Godello, with its stylish apple and lime aromas.

The whites produced by the ten registered *bodegas* include some good quality wines. Of the 7,410 acres (3,000 ha) of vineyard available in the Támega valley area only the best 650 are allocated to quality wine making. Here, whites with a high proportion of Godello and Treixadura predominate, as they display fruitiness, body, and superb acidity. Sampling the available D.O. wines, however, quickly shows that despite a clean, harmonious taste, many wines demand clear definition, which will undoubtedly come in time. The bottling plants have good technical standards, because sufficient investment has been made recently. Training new vines on wires, which allows better sanitary care for the fruit, will swiftly raise the white Monterrei wines' overall quality. Whether the reds will achieve importance outside the region in future is less certain.

The soil, which is very rich compared to the Ribeira Sacra, together with the temperate

climate, is not ideal for robust reds. Only extreme revenue-limitation, to maximize the Mencía's advantages, could help here.

Valdeorras

Also in Ourense, with some 3,705 acres (1,500 ha), is the D.O. Valdeorras. This regularly hits the headlines in the Spanish trade press, being the home of the recently re-discovered white Godello grape. Certainly, this cannot be compared with the aromatic opulence of a good Albariño, but produces middle-strength whites rich in extract and exuding fresh lemon, almonds, and very special earthy herbal aromas. Thanks to their distinctive personality the Godellos are slowly becoming a sought-after specialty. They are the pride of the D.O. and a bridge to the past, which threatened to disappear in the rather backward, rural Galician environment. Earlier, this role was taken by the main variety of white wine near the Sil. Looking at current varietals, it seems that the Garnacha, which normally needs limitless sun, is important. Nevertheless, most of the young wines are absorbed anonymously into table wine. Instead, *bodegas* in Valdeorras can turn to red Mencía, which has already been mentioned. This now forms the basis of some serious production of highly delicious, juicy red, but no longer very cheap young wines, which thanks to modern stainless steel techniques are trodden in many of the region's small cellars. The very limited quantities produced obviate distribution difficulties, especially as these wines are mostly consumed in Galicia itself.

Left
In Valdeorras one can often speak of vines that are literally trained by hand.

Right
The Río Sil region enjoys an especially temperate climate—ideal for wine—so that every well-situated terrace is used for wine growing. Recently more extensive vineyards, which are easier to cultivate, have been added.

Rías Baixas

Winemaking and fishing are the economic cornerstones of the Rías Baixas.

Only 20 years ago white wines from the D.O. Rías Baixas were completely unknown, and the vineyards covered less than a third of the present area of some 6,175 acres (2,500 ha). What is now celebrated as a Spanish white wine miracle then comprised a group of totally outmoded cooperative cellar owners. These accepted the harvest of thousands of part-purchase winegrowers and trod ungainly white wines, most of which soon became grassy and oxidated, ending up as barrel-fillers in large urban bottling plants. The farmers stored the only halfway pure vintage Albariño for themselves, and from April even this was hardly

drinkable. Once the Franco era had ended, there were a few enterprising individuals who invested in wine production, and proved that the despised Albariño grape could result in white wines that equaled any northern quality variety. Initially, winemakers wanted to create an exclusively Albariño *denominación*. However, since in the southwestern corner of Pontevedra province vines were traditional to certain areas, it was decided to uphold at least this tradition and include all long-established varietals in the arrangements. The provisional description, Albariño, was changed to Rías Baixas, which in Galician means the lower (southern) estuaries.

The D.O. divides into five sub-zones with different soil and climate conditions. As in other regions, producers can purchase harvests throughout the whole D.O. As a result, only a few ADEGAS—Galician for *bodegas*—can reckon on area-specific vines. The recent plethora of small vineyards will undoubtedly make *terroir* occupation more significant in future. Pure vintage Albariños are customary throughout the region. The center for this vine is the sub-zone El Salnés, with the appealing small town, Cambados, which has an annual festival celebrating this grape.

The Albariño is a very aromatic varietal, which has stylish fruit, an excellent extract, and subtle acidity. To be called Rías Baixas, a wine must contain at least 70 percent Albariño, and, depending on the region, the varieties Caiño, Loureira, Torrontés, or Treixadura. The production of red wines in this region is of little significance.

Ribeiro

The D.O. Ribeiro is the only region in Galicia to have always had a certain degree of renown. The reason is the myriad Galician taverns, which in all the largish towns serve this wine as a cheap tipple to wash down their particular specialties. Considering the cloudy, sour little wine that was produced in the past, wine drinkers must consider themselves very grateful to the winegrowers, cooperatives, and appropriate regulators for having improved Ribeiro wines beyond all recognition in recent years. The present-day quality rests mainly on the potential of the traditional white varieties, such as Treixadura, Loureira, and Torrontés, which are grown separately on

raised posts. These have proved themselves against negligible mass-market products such as Palomino. This particular grape was a typical relic of the post-phylloxera phase—planted for financial reasons, to recoup losses quickly. The old varietal whites prove fruity, light and pleasantly sparkly. The Ribeiros still stand for youth and freshness. Aging the wines in barrels is not usual. The wines have a substantial yet aggressive acidity. In their nose, dominant aromas are fruit and vegetable notes such as freshly mown grass and herbs. This region also produces reds—primarily from Caiño Tinto and Brancellano—that are simpler in character. The specialty

Vilariño: This picturesque village nestles among the Ribeiro vineyards.

of this region by the Río Miño is still young white wine.

ALBARIÑO AND SEAFOOD

In the north, near Santiago, lies the small sub-region of Val de Ulloa. Near the provincial capital of Pontevedra some 400 winegrowers in and around Soutomaior cultivate vineyards planted almost exclusively to Albariño. Further south, directly on the Portuguese frontier, the partial regions of O Rosal and Condado are sited. The Condado area has a most inclement climate, with late frosts. Otherwise the climate is very mild, with rainfall figures more reminiscent of northern Europe than the Iberian Peninsula.

Galicia is a land of Cockaigne for gourmets, and the Gallegos are famous in Spain for their tendency to eat a large amount of good food, especially seafood, which is uniquely plentiful in their estuaries. Rías-Baixas wines accompany this to perfection. Their superlative fruit, which often assumes exotic notes, and the slender but robust body, make these wines ideal accompaniments to meals. Almost all companies mature their wines in modern steel tanks. Some wines are marketed before Christmas, and these sparkle with fresh fruit. A good Rías Baixas is always highly aromatic. In recent years, however, the best wines have been left in the tank for longer—generally eight months—to achieve more complex fruit aromas and extra harmony. Nevertheless, all Galician white wines should be drunk, at the latest, two years after being harvested.

SELECT WINE PRODUCERS IN GALICIA

ADEGAS GALEGAS***–****
SALVATERRA DO MIÑO (D.O. RÍAS BAIXAS)
99 acres (40 ha); some bought-in grapes; 500,000 bottles • Wines include: Don Pedro de Soutomaior, Don Pedro de Soutomaior Neve, Tempo, Veigadares
With Don Pedro de Soutomaior, wine producer José Rodriguez succeeds year after year in creating a fine, clear, fruity but hard Albariño. Veigadares, due to the sensitive use of wood, holds a special place among the cask-fermented wines in the region.

ADEGAS MOURE***
ESCAIRÓN (D.O. RIBEIRA SCARA)
17 acres (7 ha); some bought-in grapes; 150,000 bottles. • Wines: Abadía da Cova, Albariño, Mencía
The two winemakers and owners of the small *adega* have taken enormous trouble to restore the old terraces on the steeps slopes of the Miño ravine. One famous wine is their extremely fruity young red from Mencía, and another is a *crianza* which is surprisingly fresh and delicate. In good years the Albariño, which is not actually typical of the region, displays a noticeably mineral, individual *terroir* character.

BODEGAS DEL PALACIO DE FEFIÑANES****
CAMBADOS (D.O. RÍAS BAIXAS)
Bought-in grapes; 50,000 bottles • Wines: Albariño de Fefiñanes, 1583 Albariño de Fefiñanes
In recent years this winery, housed in a medieval castle, has greatly improved its quality. The 1583, barrel-aged, powerful and with good finish, is a success, but it still takes second place to the brilliant, intense and complex wines not aged in wood.

BODEGAS TERRAS GAUDA***–****
AS EIRAS-O ROSAL (D.O. RÍAS BAIXAS)
173 acres (70 ha); 750,000 bottles • Wines: Abadía San Campio, Terras Gauda Etiqueta Negra, →Terras Gauda
In terms of size, the Terras Gauda is the most important *bodega* foundation in the recent history of the D.O. Rías Baixas. In an area which is noticeable for very small estates, the investors cleared an area of 148 acres (60 ha) of hill country to plant vines, thereby creating the largest connected vineyard in the D.O. In many years, Terras Gauda is one of Spain's five most aromatic dry white wines.

MARTÍN CÓDAX***–****
VILARIÑO-CAMBADOS (D.O. RÍAS BAIXAS)
371 acres (150 ha); some bought-in grapes: 1,250,000 bottles • Wines: Martín Códax, Burgáns, Gallaeca, Organistrum
Galicia's most popular Albariño is a byword for quality. This wine company started as a cooperative and has first-rate vineyards. Alongside Martín Códax, a juicy young wine, there is Gallaeca, a late harvest, plus Organistrum, a barrel fermented Albariño, and a wine with residual sweetness.

GODEVAL***
BARCO DE VALDEORRAS (D.O. VALDEORRAS)
42 acres (17 ha); some bought-in grapes; 200,000 bottles • Wines: Viña Godeval, Viña Godeval Fermentado en Barrica
Horacio Fernández is one of the fathers of the revival program that saved the Valdeorrs' white wine grape, Godello. The vineyards of the estate, some on barely accessible slopes, are cultivated with technical perfection, and produce a very flowery, clear Godello.

GRANJA FILLABOA****
SALVATERRA DO MIÑO (D.O. RÍAS BAIXAS)
371 acres (25 ha); 180,000 bottles • Wines: Fillaboa Fermentado en Barrica, →Fillaboa
This estate produces two wines: the young Fillaboa, which is striking for its fresh, stylish quality, and an exemplary cask-aged Albariño, which is produced only in small quantities.

PAZO DE SEÑORANS****–*****
MEIS (D.O. RÍAS BAIXAS)
25 acres (10 ha); some bought-in grapes; 180,000 bottles • Wines: Pazo de Señorans, Pazo de Señorans Selección de Añada
On this estate, owned by María Soleda Bueno, working together with the enologist Ana Quintela, harvesting is by vineyard, and some of the D.O.'s best structured Albariño is fermented separately in tanks. In outstanding years, a selection from the best vineyards is matured for eighteen months in steel tanks.

EMILIO ROJO***
ARNOIA-PONTE (D.O. RIBEIRO)
7 acres (3 ha); 11,000 bottles • Wines: Emilio Rojo
Emilio Rojo helped Lado make a comeback. His only wine, white Emilio Rojo, has power and fine flower notes.

CASTILE–LA MANCHA

The central region, as wine connoisseurs also call Castile–La Mancha (or New Castile), is the world's largest connected wine-growing region. It was a major talking point for the European Commissioners when, in 1986, Spain joined what was then the European Community. It was finally agreed that part of the vineyards would, for a compensation premium, be laid fallow. After almost a third of the vines have been removed, the region still has six D.O. areas: Méntrida, Mondéjar, La Mancha, Ribera del Júcar, Valdepeñas, and Almansa (east of Albacete, off the map). With these, and its impressive table wine area, the region still gathers half of Spain's annual wine harvest, which totals between 30 and 45 million gallons (15–20 million hectoliters), according to year.

La Mancha, as the whole region is laconically known, is not to be confused with the D.O. area of the same name, which only covers part of it. The region's problem is the predominance of one grape, the white Airén, the world's most frequently planted vine variety. Because of its resistance to climatic extremes, it was planted profusely as a rescue measure after the phylloxera devastation, though it produces only average-quality wine. Many conscientious winemakers marketed part of their produce as the basis of sparkling wines. Nevertheless, in La Mancha's D.O. regions and also in Valdepeñas and some other *appellations*, there are many

Left
To some extent in La Mancha wine is still fermented in these amphorae—called *tinajas*—which are as tall as a man.

Right
La Mancha, the largest wine region in Spain, extends across the broad, dry highlands of the Meseta.

good, even excellent producers. A few ambitious winemakers have accepted the challenge of creating first-rate wines of character outside the areas designated as quality-wine regions, partly by means of indigenous wines, partly by French varieties.

Discounting a few exceptions, the region's most remarkable wines are not whites, but made from red grapes, which cover only a quarter of over 1,235,500 acres (500,000 ha) of vineyards. In the D.O. La Mancha, the heart of New Castile, foremost among the reds are Cencibel or Tempranillo. The red *barrique* wines are generally soft, proverbially "spoilt" by the sun, fragrant, and often have a slightly earthy note. Modern, very fruity wines with a

Windmills are the landmarks of La Mancha. In Consuegra they stand beside the ruined fortress, towering above the endless fields and vineyards.

robust note of wood are also fermented and often blended with Cabernet Sauvignon. In Mondéjar and Méntrida good reds are still planted very thinly. The brand new, pure red D.O. Ribera del Júcar in the east of the region produces harmonious Tintos, mainly from Cencibel grown on stony ground 2,460 feet (750 m) above sea level. But Cabernet, Merlot, Syrah and the Bobal variety from the Levant are also permitted. Almansa primarily produces table wines from a grape of the Garnacha family, called Garnacha Tintorera, one of the world's very few grapes to have red fruit flesh. Mondéjar is also famous for deep-colored red wines. However, most of the 9,880 acres (4,000 ha) of vines are devoted to the white variety, Malvar.

D.O. Ribera del Guadiana

More for administrative reasons than because of shared characteristics, from 1997 this macro-D.O., consisting of some 17,290 acres (7,000 ha), brought together a small portion of the Extremadura vineyards in the southwest of the country. The wines vary enormously, for they originate from six different sub-regions, and are prepared on the basis of over 20 varieties, some of Portuguese origin. Definitive reds can be found in the sub-region of Tierra de Barros, around the city of Almendralejo. Here you also find some of the oldest wine cellars. The styles of the often very robust reds are scarcely comparable. Very

rustic and rounded wines rub shoulders with immaculately fruity, soft ones. The best reds are usually produced from Tempranillo blended with Garnacha, or even Cabernet. In good *bodegas*, aging in barrels is standard practice. In the other sub-zones there are also some very pleasant wines pressed. Up in the north, in the Sierra de Gata, in the Cañamero Mountains, near the monastery of Guadalupe, and in the far southwest on the Portuguese border, some wine producers have achieved success with clean, fruitily juicy reds that are nothing like the traditional, broad reds often encountered in more southerly parts.

Enormous *barrique* cellar with fine red wines in Almendralejo.

Select Wine Producers in Castile–La Mancha I

Bodegas Ayuso**–***
Villarrobledo (D.O. La Mancha)
Bought-in grapes; 5,500,000 bottles
• *Wines include: Armiño Viña Q. Estola Reserva*
Despite its large size, this is a totally reliable wine cellar, owned by the same family for over 50 years. Its best known wine is the velvety, appealing red, Estola. The pioneer of barrel-aging in La Mancha now has a *barrique* park of over 12,000 barrels.

Bodegas Centro Españolas***
Tomelloso (D.O. La Mancha)
543 acres (220 ha); bought-in grapes; 2,000,000 bottles
• *Wines include: Verdial; Allozo Crianza, Allozo Reserva*
One of the most spectacular *bodegas* of the last generation in La Mancha. Over three-quarters of the production comprises reds, for which almost all the vines had to be planted. With Allozo line reds, fruit and structural harmony are always more evident than oakiness. The young wines generally come out very aromatic and limpid.

Bodegas Alejandro Fernández***–****
Campo de Criptana, (D.O. La Mancha)
Bought-in grapes; 200,000 bottles • *Wine: El Vinculo*
In the late 1990s Alejandro Fernández, father of the famous Tinto Pesquera, bought an old *bodega* in the little windmill town of Campo de Criptana. Through contacts in La Mancha from the early Pesquera days, he was able to acquire excellent grapes and thus produce a wood-aged Cencibel and a Tempranillo. The wine is extremely concentrated, rich in tannins and powerful.

Bodegas Mariscal**
Mondéjar (D.O. Mondéjar)
247 acres (100 ha) • *Wines: Vega Tajuna, Blanco, Rosado: Tinto; Señorío de Mariscal Crianza*
Mariscal was the first wine cellar in Modéjar to age wines in oak, as it still does with the convincing Crianza. Nevertheless, its strength lies in the clean, fruity young wines. The Tinto is macerated carbonically.

Bodegas Piqueras**–****
Almansa (D.O. Almansa)
Bought-in grapes; 600,000 bottles • *Wines include: Marius, Crianza, Reserva; Castillo de Almansa; Blanco; Rosado; Crianza, Reserva, Gran Reserva*
This family firm, founded in 1915, has for years been the region's only plausible producer north of Yecla. The best reds often contain about three-quarters Cencibel and one quarter Monastrell. They are persuasively fruity and well balanced.

Bodegas Torres Filoso**–***
Villarrobledo (D.O. La Mancha)
99 acres (40 ha); 100,000 bottles • *Wines: Arboles de Castillejo, Torres Filoso, →Juan José*
Within a few years this hitherto large-scale producer has reduced his production of a million bottles by a tenth. His wines have great personality and—unusually for Mancha Tintos—need a lot of time. This is because they reveal a strong barrel oakiness, with an underlying subtle acidity; in time, they taste subtle, last well, and have limpid fruit.

Dehesa del Cabrizal****
Retuerta del Bullaque (Viña de Terra de Castillo)
37 acres (15 ha); 130,000 bottles • *Wine: Dehesa del Carrizal*
After an apprenticeship with Carlos Falcó, Ignacio de Miguel decided to create an equally sophisticated table wine in the neighboring province of Ciudad Real, in the heart of La Mancha. The resulting cask-aged Cabernet is wonderfully mature, yet fresh and marvelously well balanced.

Manuel Manzaneque***–****
El Bonillo (D.O. Finca Elez)
91 acres (37 ha); 300,000 bottles • *Wines: Manuel Manzaneque: Chardonnay, Crianza, Reserva, →Syrah; Finca Elez Crianza*
In the bleak mountainous landscape of Albacete province, theater producer Manuel Manzaneque has created a small wine paradise. At a height of 3,280 feet (1,000 m) his French winemaker produces very fruity yet well-structured and full-bodied wines—quite different from the norm in La Mancha. The *bodega* emphasizes strict selection of grapes in the vineyard and works only with French oak.

Marqués de Griñon****
Malpica de Tajo (D.O. Dominio de Valdepusa)
104 acres (42 ha); 330,000 bottles • *Wines: Marqués de Griñon: Cabernet Sauvignon, Eméritus, →Petit Verdot, Syrah*
The wines of the Marqués de Griñon, also known as Carlos Falcó, are a must among Spanish wines. In 1970 he risked planting French grapes at his family estate in the hot, dry climate of Toledo, using the most up-to-date viticultural methods. His single variety wines are elegant, fine and very complex. His top red *cuvée*, Eméritus, shows a great deal of volume and depth.

Mas Que Viños**–****
Dos Barrios (no D.O.)
25 acres (10 ha); some bought-in grapes; 125,000 grapes • *Wines: Ercavio: Joven, Roble, Reserva; La Plazuela*
The three enologists, Madrigal, Rodríguez and Schmedes, have been working since 1999 on a dense and fruity La Mancha type wine with soft, ripe tannins. The vines are in Toledo province, and the winery is being built. In 2003, they introduced the opulent and juicy elite Cencibel La Plazuela.

Viñedos y Bodegas El Barro***
Camarena (D.O. Méntrida)
247 acres (100 ha); 60,000 bottles • *Wines: Grand Vulture*
One of the few interesting producers in the D.O. Méntrida, south of the city of Toledo, which is dominated by wines aged in wood. The brand Grand Vulture sets a standard other *bodegas* will follow. The wine is soft, and the mature, sweet tannins give it class. Including this, El Barro shares some of the best vines in the D.O.

Vinícola de Tomelloso***
Tomelloso (D.O. La Mancha)
4,446 acres (1,800 ha); 1,000,000 bottles • *Wines: Añil, Torre de Gazate, Rosado, Crianza, →Reserva*
Everything that this company makes has quality—from white as a basis for sparkling wine to bottled wines. The *tintos*, especially the *reservas* of the brand Torre de Gazate, which are sometimes made from pure Cabernet varietal, sometimes blended with Cencibel, reveal respectable structure and depth. This is due to the strict selection of the harvest.

VALDEPEÑAS

The region of Valdepeñas, with its *Denominación de Origen*, covers 188 sq. miles (487 sq. km), and fits like an enclave into the southern section of the D.O. La Mancha. The city that has given the region its name lies in the center of a broad, very flat valley. On both sides rise small chains of hills, which bring some variation to the landscape and announce the first foothills of the Sierra Morena. *Val de peñas* is Castilian for "valley of rocks."

The glory days of the city and its wines go back to the mid-19th century. In those days the Madrid wine market had become so important that both cities were connected by rail. Every day the so-called "wine train" transported 2,500 skins of wine to the capital. Export trade also developed from Valencia's harbor. At this time a light red wine was produced, blended with 20 percent white. This fresh, light red—also

In summer it grows exceedingly hot in Valdepeñas. Only darkening the windows in good time offers any prospect of slight cooling.

called Clarete—achieved worldwide renown and was as sought-after in South America as in the Philippines. It still exists, though today white and red musts are blended, rather than finished wines. Although phylloxera attacked Valdepeñas 30 years late (La Mancha's extreme climate had delayed its incidence) the effects on the vineyards were just as devastating as in the rest of Europe. However, the city had such massive reserves in its cellars that trade in wine could continue.

Typical vessels for wine preparation and storage were *tinajas*, clay jugs, which from time immemorial had been covered with straw mats or wooden lids. Although *tinajas* are still in use in most *bodegas*, now they are mainly used for storage, rather than wine preparation. The colossal *tinajas* of the last generation are no longer made of clay, but cement, and fulfil the tasks of normal concrete tanks as found throughout Europe. In the age of modern fermentation tanks, only a few small-scale wine producers still ferment wine in classic *tinajas*. These small wine producers also press the earlier oxidating, but sometimes very expressive, Valdepeñas variety of wine. Nowadays, these wines are increasingly rare. The region's major *bodegas* started a full 20 years ago to make their wine production as modern as possible.

In the mid-1970s foundations were laid for the production of quality bottle wines. Modern cellar facilities, with stainless steel fermenting tanks that can be cooled down, stabilization casks, modern filters, and other equipment are now standard issue. Recently, almost all wine bottlers have started to use considerable quantities of

---

Madrid

Geographically, the small D.O. Madrid should be included in La Mancha. It sweeps round in a semicircle to the south of the capital, then extends into the wide plain of the central region. In earlier times, vineyards extended deep into the city. Madrid's main street, the Paseo de la Castellana, even had vines growing along it. The sub-region around Arganda comprises half of the 29,157 acres (11,800 ha) of vineyards. It produces mild, slightly nutty white wines from the Malvar grape, and by far the largest part of the *appellation's* Tinto-Fino (Tempranillo) reds. These represent the region's true potential, for the best Tinto Finos have a dark color, plenty of fruit, and robust

tannins. So far, unfortunately, there are only a few examples of this variety of red wine. Other sub-zones, around Navalcarnero and San Martín de Valdeiglesias, make up another 13,585 acres (5,500 ha). Neutral white cask-wines—as well as *rosados* and *tintos* from Garnacha—are produced here. An exception is wine from the white Albillo grape. Fermented by modern methods, these reveal a large amount of fruit and delicate acidity. After being totally dismissed in earlier years as oxidated, broad wines, these have recently experienced a quiet renaissance. Progress has also been made with red wines, and beside fresh Tintos we also find premium wines from the Tempranillo grape that should certainly be taken seriously.

Even in Madrid the best reds are aged from Tempranillo in barriques.

---

barrels, mostly of American wood, in which to mature the region's *crianzas*, *reservas*, and *gran reservas*.

These account for the region's comeback in wine production, for despite not insignificant white-wine production in Airén and Macabeo, today Valdepeñas is again known for reds. Cencibel grapes mature marvelously under the merciless sun of the southern Mancha and slide smoothly into oak casks. Thanks to the climate, all vintages achieve more or less consistent quality, and result in harmonious reds which are the ideal accompaniment to food. Often

Left
Near the town of Valdepeñas windmills indicate that the climate here is good for wine growing.

Right
Valdepeñas not only gave this wine region its name but also contains most of the well-known *bodegas*.

dismissed as cask-wine for the non-connoisseur, these rather light wines reveal a wealth of harmony, and are among Spain's export hits.

Select Producers In Castile-La Mancha II

Bodegas Los Llanos***
Valdepeñas (D.O. Valdepeñas)
865 acres (360 ha); bought-in grapes; 15,000,000 bottles • Wines: Armonioso Blanco; Loma de la Gloria, Señorío de los Llanos: Crianza, Reserva, Gran Reserva, Pata Negra Gran Reserva
A large-scale *bodega*, with a stock of 30,000 barrels, which produces an enormous quantity of good quality red wines aged in wood. Famous reds include the Señorío de los Llanos Reservas and Gran Reservas. These often reveal a mild, almost sweetish, fruit, in general superbly evocative of wood. A good record for winning prizes.

Bodegas Real***
Valdepeñas (D.O. Valdepeñas)
865 acres (350 ha); 1,000,000 bottles • Wines include: Viñaluz Blanco; Bonal Tinto, Vega Ibor Varietal, Palacío de Ibor Crianza
The owner Sergio Barroso swears by classic red wines not aged in wood, which he produces in a modern way, without oxidation. His *crianzas*, however, are noticeably underscored with wood.

Bodegas Orusco**–***
Valdilecha (D.O. Madrid)
30 acres (12 ha); bought-in grapes; 150,000 bottles • Wines: Viña Main: Rosado; Tinto, Crianza
This young family winery cultivates old vineyards. The red pure varietal Tempranillo-Crianza Viña Main could well be a classic, more subtle than ostentatious, more rotund than rigid, and is a pleasure to drink.

Bodegas Ricardo Benito***
Navalcarnero (D.O. Madrid)
198 acres (80 ha); bought-in grapes; 850,000 bottles • Wines include: Tapón de Oro: Maceración Carbonica, Crianza; Señorío de Medina Sindonia, Divo
The wine style of this old wine cellar is unexpectedly modern, especially regarding the reds. With young wines, the company has specialized in Beaujolais-like carbonic maceration. They have freshness, but also body. The Crianza Tapón de Oro offers a lot for a little money.

Casa de la Viña***
La Solana (D.O. Valdepeñas)
741 acres (300 ha); 1,000,000 bottles • Wines include: Casa de la Viña: Rosado; Crianza, Señorío del Val
Quite early on, the region's premier winery developed a gentle but well-structured style, which is regarded as setting the standard for present-day Valdepeñas wines. It belongs to the still-wine colossus, Bodegas y Bebidas, which invests enough money to ensure high quality.

Miguel Calatayud***
Valdepeñas (D.O. Valdepeñas)
124 acres (50 ha); 2,500,000 bottles; • Wines include: Vegaval Plata: Blanco; Tinto Crianza, Vegaval Tinto Reserva
Wines from this *bodega* have everything needed in a Valdepeñas: delicacy, maturity, a discreet note of wood, drinkability, and rounded fruit. The Vegaval Plata-Reserva offers the best quality that a varietal Cabernet or Cencibel can give.

in oak, as it tends to oxidate rapidly. Only top quality grapes allow pure Monastrell wines to age in barrels. Nowadays, the monopoly of this main varietal is limited primarily to the region's most important sub-zone, around Bullas and Caravaca de la Cruz, although more Tempranillo is being planted. Nevertheless, one cooperative ventured to mature a pure Monastrell 95-vintage Crianza in American oak. This example was soon followed, for other producers are starting to explore the potential of the many old Monastrell vines still available. Now as ever, this grape comprises 94 percent of all vines.

JUMILLA

With almost 99,000 acres (40,000 ha), extending more thinly across the New Castilian province of Albacete and parts of Murcia, Jumilla is now one of the country's leading *appellations*, not merely quantatively. Even though the underestimated Monastrell is also paramount here, some expert winemakers have joined the ranks of Spain's top producers. As in the Old Castilian Toro, the area's potential is rated very highly. As early as the late 1980s a group of famous French wine producers settled here, to entice superlative wines from the dry, chalky soil. Sure enough, notable successes were achieved with Monastrell, by bringing forward the harvest and producing more stylish, lighter reds with greater definition in their fruit—for the intense sunshine removes any concern about ripening.

However picturesquely the castles stand guard over Murcia and its wine regions, dryness and heat make conditions for wine growing very hard.

The red Syrah, which achieved fame mainly in the Rhône valley, develops its magnificently fruity, spicy character here on the slightly undulating high plateau, totally surrounded by precipitous, bare mountain chains. It is exploited by the small but enterprising avant-garde of the local *bodegueros* with remarkable success.

Cabernet and Merlot also produce small but qualitatively significant yields. Some of the finest *crianza* reds from the country's southern half are produced in Jumilla. Blended with Monastrell and those foreign varieties already mentioned, these show the region's immense potential.

Also worth specifying are those naturally sweet wines usually produced from Monastrell. After oxidating fermentation, these combine complex aromas like cocoa, coffee, and quasi-oriental spices in their intensive bouquet.

YECLA

Yecla is the only wine region in the whole of Spain comprising one single district. Overall, about 49,400 acres (20,000 ha) of vineyards surround the city, some of them planted with old grape varieties. Here, also, are ancient vineyards untouched by phylloxera. The very dry climate, the extremely bare soil, and the mountains that divide the region from the coast and the north, have halted the pest's advance. Even today, nearly half of all the vines have the original roots, which yield the characteristics of specific grapes better than grafted plants.

Upon its foundation, the D.O. Yecla decided to devote only 8,645 acres (3,500 ha) to quality wines, probably to remain competitive toward commerce in cask-wine. Logically, large areas of the vineyards were set aside for table-wine varieties like Garnacha-Tintorera or Forcallat. As in other inland areas of the Levant, the main varietal—with over 60 percent of the whole area—is Monastrell. There are also modest plantings of Cabernet Sauvignon, Merlot, and Tempranillo. The whites, Macabeo and Airén, are also found.

To produce reds that can also be drunk young, the Monastrell is often macerated carbonically—a process that eminently suits it. This method relies on the traditional regional cellar technique, whereby the grapes are fermented unpressed and without being hulled. Nonetheless, the leading local producer—only three companies bottle wines—produces excellent *crianza* reds from his harvests of old, tannin-rich Monastrell grapes. To increase complexity, blends of Cabernet Sauvignon, Tempranillo, and Monastrell are often prepared. These remain stable and, thanks to their proportion of Monastrell, are opulent and richly aromatic.

The men of the Castaño family can feel justly proud—their wines have become a byword for the quality of the D.O. Yecla.

The new vineyard planted by the Bodegas Castaño on a particularly stony slope is tended with loving care.

WINE IN ANDALUSIA

Andalusia is a world of wine in itself. Even within Spain it is known only superficially. Paradoxically, traditional wines from Jerez, Málaga, Huelva, and Córdoba are very unfamiliar. Nevertheless, they are unique in the world, and thus represent Spain's sole authentic contribution to the international history of wine. In Spain's most southerly autonomous region, wine growing is concentrated geograph-

The Bodega del Toro near Barbadillo in Sanlúcar de Barrameda.

ically in the area's western and central areas. Here, 3,000 years ago, the Phoenicians founded today's Cádiz, and planted the first vines. Presumably the Greeks, who introduced pruning, were the first to produce wine professionally. Each of the four *appellations* can look back on its own distinguished history. Only in the crisis years of the 20th century did the classic wines experience marketing problems, and these have persisted until today.

To contradict assumptions about sunny Spain, in winter and spring the coastal wine regions get heavy rain. Indeed, the Grazalema Mountains in Cádiz Province, which jut out near the sea, contain Spain's wettest area. Nonetheless, at 3,000 hours annually, the total hours of sunshine in Jerez and Sanlúcar de Barrameda are among the highest worldwide. Although the classic wine varieties in the four D.O. regions are not identical, they belong in the same category. They are all robust wines, which acquire a high alcohol content either by natural means or by having it added; for this reason they are often classified as aperitif or digestive wines. Yet several of these wines (the FINOS or Manzanillas, for instance) are agreeable accompaniments to food, ideal for Andalusian specialties such as air-dried ham, roast and fried seafood, or *tapas*.

FULL-BODIED WINES FROM THE SOUTH

By the High Middle Ages, at the latest, wines in Andalusia were systematically mixed with alcohol—the difference being that brandy, not pure ethyl alcohol was used. The industrialization of distillation had still not happened. Furthermore, the Arabs' advanced knowledge of this area (they used alcohol for medicinal purposes) had, like so much else, been forgotten. Adding alcohol helped make wines last longer. This way they could oxidate for longer in barrels and be transported halfway around the world without turning into vinegar. Most classic wine varieties from Jerez, Huelva, and Córdoba are prepared like this.

The famous sweet wines of Málaga, whose range and subtlety can give unique experiences to both tongue and nose, are also prepared in this particular way. In Andalusia—and more especially Huelva—in the last two decades of the 20th century, there was a switch toward producing table wines, as the market for fortified wines continued to shrink from year to year. Accordingly, the most western of Andalusia's quality wine D.O.s first obtained a license to register a non-fortified white wine in the D.O. The large cooperatives quickly adopted this new trend, and began pressing light, fresh whites, whose grapes were harvested very early to keep the alcohol content low. Nearly half the region's production is now devoted to this kind of wine. Unfortified wines are now also produced in the other D.O.

No work in the vineyards without protection from the sun.

regions, although compared to Huelva the quantity is negligible and the wines may not be accorded D.O. quality.

The recent boom in Spanish wine has led more than one winemaker from central Spain to look around in Andalusia, and seek out new sites for red-wine production. For some time now, the German Prinz von Hohenlohe has been cultivating vineyards he planted near Ronda, in the highlands of Málaga. Every year his *bodega* amply proves that it is perfectly possible to produce superior red vintages from Andalusian vineyards.

THE WINE REGIONS OF ANDALUSIA

D.O. MONTILLA-MORILES
This region's 24,700 acres (10,000 ha) of vineyards, sited in the south of Córdoba Province, are dominated by the variety Pedro Ximénez, which is well-suited to the heat. From their grapes it is largely aromatic, full-bodied Finos that are produced by the SOLERA method, though Amontillados, Olorosos, and Palo Cortados are also fermented. These grapes develop so much potential alcohol content on the stem that the wines do not need to be fortified. For the heavy, sweet, very complex dessert wines the grapes are left to dry in the sun before being pressed and muted by additional ethyl alcohol.

D.O. MÁLAGA Y SIERRAS DE MÁLAGA
The D.O. Málaga was already famous in the 13th century for its sweet wines, and sometimes outclassed wines from Jerez. The worldwide image problem for sweet wines in the second half of the 20th century led to a loss of interest in Málaga wines, with devastating results for the vineyards. Today 2,430 acres (950 ha) of vines are still designated a D.O. region, and the number of companies has dwindled to twelve. The main variety is Pero Ximén, as the Pedro Ximénez is called hereabouts, accompanied by Moscatel. The D.O. also covers red wines originating from the mountainous interior around Ronda.

D.O. JEREZ-XÉRÈS-SHERRY Y MANZANILLA DE SANLÚCAR DE BARRAMEDA
Between the cities of Jerez de la Frontera, Puerto de Santa María, and Sanlúcar de Barrameda lie this famous region's 24,700 or more acres (10,000 ha), highly praised by the Moorish geographer, Ibn Adbd al-Mun'im, 1,000 years ago. The white wine, Palomino Fino, which initially only yields neutral wines, comprises 96 percent of output. Remaining sweet wines are Ximénez and Moscatel. These are fermented by the *solera* method. A recent specialty is to offer old-vintage sherries. Some *bodegas* also produce fresh whites from Palomino grapes.

D.O. CONDADO DE HUELVA
Separated from the city of Seville and the Jerez wine region by the massive Gualadquivir Delta lies the D.O. region of Condado de Huelva. Here, the variety Zalema holds sway. Also matured by the *solera* method, this produces outstanding old Condados, which are similar to Olorosos. Recently most companies have switched to bottling dry, refreshing whites, although these are hardly known outside the region. After drastic cutbacks 18,525 acres (7,500 ha) are still cultivated.

Santa María are a touch darker and more robust. This is because in the east of the D.O. Jerez y Manzanilla de Sanlúcar de Barrameda the *flor* finds less favorable climatic conditions, and can therefore form no complete covering to the wine—though one side-effect is that a subtle scent of almonds can sometimes develop.

Manzanillas, however, only originate from Sanlúcar de Barrameda, the D.O.'s western region, near the Guadalquivir estuary. Here, a distinctly higher humidity level guarantees a constant yeast-covering, which protects the wine fully. Accordingly, the Manzanillas are paler, lighter, and harsher, often developing a uniquely distinctive note of iodine.

In the February after the grape-harvest, once a film of the all-important *flor* yeast has developed, the wines selected to mature into Olorosos are given two percent by volume of alcohol more than Finos. This kills the fungus. Subsequent maturing takes place solely by oxidation, without the help of the *flor*.

At the foot of the Alcázar of Jerez de la Frontera and near its cathedral, the cellar-halls of González Byass, the city's largest sherry *bodega*, stand side by side.

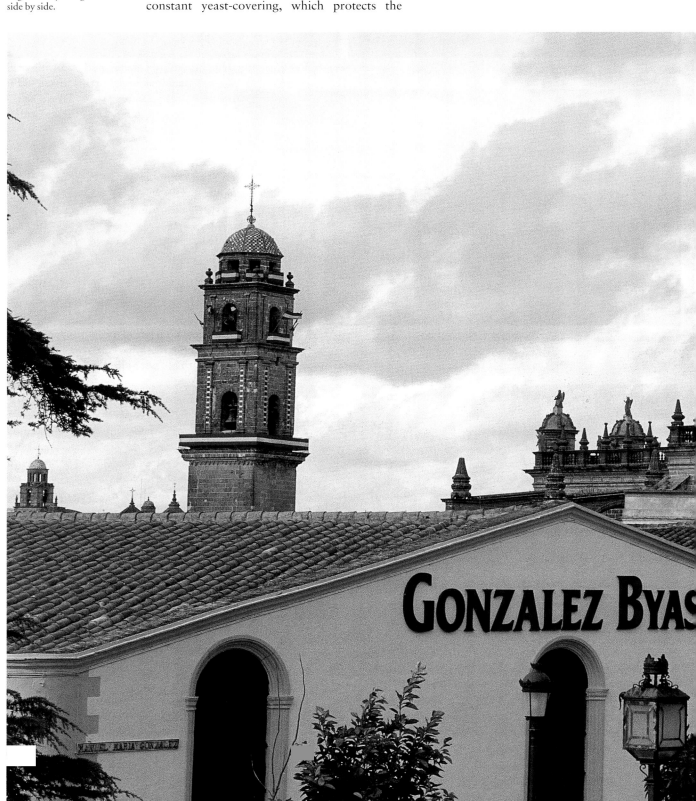

Varieties of Sherry

Almacenista-Sherry: Rarities from small, private producers

Amontillado: Aged, oxidated, and matured Finos of an exquisite amber color; dry top-range varieties are robust, multifaceted, with nutty aromas

Cream Sherry: Oloroso; a sherry to which sweet wine from Pedro Ximénez or Moscatel has been added; very full-bodied and round

Fino: Very dry, pale sherry, matured below *flor*, best drunk in the six months after being bottled; has aromas of yeast and almonds; consume well-chilled as an aperitif, with *tapas* or fish dishes; once opened will not last long

Manzanilla: An especially light, pale Fino from Sanlúcar de Barrameda, which has a subtle note of iodine

Manzanilla Pasada: Rare, exceptional Amontillado-variant from Sanlúcar; highly multifaceted and stylish

Oloroso: Fermented without any *flor*; slowly oxidated, full-bodied, complex wines with aromas of dried fruit and nuts

Palo Cortado:
A very rare, dry, subtle and complex sherry, also aged without any *flor*; lying between Amontillado and Oloroso, its aroma tends more toward Amontillado, whereas taste and nose incline more toward an Oloroso

Pedro Ximénez:
Rarely appears as a pure varietal; extremely sweet dessert wine, blended with Oloroso

THE SOLERA SYSTEM

From the 13th or 14th century at the latest, Jerez wines have been fortified, ensuring that they last a very long time. However, the *Solera* system dates from only the second half of the 19th century, when the English importers of sherry demanded that wine cellars in Jerez supply homogeneous wines of unvarying taste. Until then Jerez had been aged by a vintage-system, called *añada*. Nowadays old-vintage sherries are extremely rare.

We must imagine the *solera* system in principle as long rows of 110-gallon (500-liter) casks stacked one above the other. The chief cellarman draws out for bottling a certain quantity of sherry—never more than a third—from the lowest cask, called the *solera* (in Spanish *suelo* means floor). Then, from the cask above, the first *criadera*, he draws out the same

Left and right
With the help of a metal can the *capataz* fills the casks of a *solera*. Once he has drawn off wine from the lowest row, he fills the can from the next-youngest row of casks, to replace the drawn-off wine. He continues like this until he has reached the youngest *criadera*, to which he adds young wine.

Utensils like funnels, sieves, tubing, brushes, and spatulas are in constant use in *bodegas*.

quantity to top up the cask below. He continues like this until he reaches the top row of casks, where the missing quantity is replaced by wine from the vintage cellar. In this way, older wines add their character to the younger ones used to top them up. Through this step-by-step aging process, the *solera*, which retains the wines' specific character, imparts this to all the wines in the system. Thus, in time, all vintage-distinctions are erased, and the wine, which is still called *solera*, has a consistency that delights sherry-lovers.

The number of *criaderas* varies between sherries; with the higher-percentage (figuratively speaking) Olorosos and Amontillados, this total is less significant than with Finos or Manzanillas. Even after years of maturing, these latter two have a certain freshness and a subtle, slightly peppery note of yeast, which, sadly, disappears soon after bottling.

For practical reasons, *criaderas*—the different levels of a *solera* system—are no longer stacked one above the other, but lie separated, often even in different *bodegas*. After a topping-up operation, the missing quantity to come in from the next-youngest *criadera* is simply pumped in. Varying wine styles between one *bodega* and another also apply to Finos, which take longer to mature, and for which another row of *solera* casks is attached. If, after years of aging, a Fino's *flor* dies, the result is an Amontillado, which will be further fortified and matured in a separate *solera* system. Before bottling, many sherries undergo six or seven stages, while a complex *solera* system can pass through 12 to 14 stages.

Select Sherry Producers

A.R. Valdespino****
Jerez de la Frontera
741 acres (300 ha); bought-in grapes; 3,500,000 bottles
• *Wines include: Fino Innocente, →Amontillado Tío Diego, →Oloroso Solera 1842, →P.X. Solera Superior*
Valdespino is the oldest purely family firm in the city of Jerez. The company's sherries are among the D.O.'s best wines. Here you can still find wines immune to fashion.

Antonio Barbadillo****−*****
Sanlúcar de Barrameda
1,759 acres (712 ha); bought-in grapes; 10,000,000 bottles • *Wines: Manzanilla Eva, →Oloroso seco Cuco, →Manzanilla Solear, →Amontillado Principe, Oloroso Dulce San Rafael*
Sanlúcar's largest *bodega* has over 60,000 *botas* and produces legendary varieties such as the Oloroso seco Cuco. Best known is the Manzanilla Solear.

Croft***−****
Jerez de La Frontera
741 acres (300 ha); bought-in grapes; 6,750,000 bottles • *Wines: Fino Delicado, Amontillado Croft Classic, Dulce Croft Original, →Palo Cortado Croft*
This Spanish company dates from only 1970, after merging with a port wine producer. Yet still has a sufficient stock of old *soleras* with about 50,000 *botas* in total. The Fino Delicado is famous and extravagant in style; the Palo Cortado solid and subtle.

Garvey****
Jerez de la Frontera
124 acres (50 ha); bought-in grapes; 2,500,000 bottles • *Wines: Fino San Patricio, Oloroso Ochavico, →Amontillado Oñana, Oloroso Puerta Real, →Palo Cortado Jauna, →P.X. Gran Orden*
Garvey was among the first Irishmen to settle in the area (in 1756). Finos, like the superb San Patricio, comprise nearly three-quarters of production, but the exceptional Amontillados, Oñana and Palo Cortado Jauna, or the P.X. Gran Orden are top quality.

González Byass***−*****
Jerez de la Frontera
1,976 acres (800 ha); 14,500,000 bottles • *Wines: Fino Tío Pepe, Manzanilla El Rocio, Solera 1847 →Amontillado del Duque, Oloroso Matusalem, Dulce Noé*
The largest *bodega* in Jerez (founded in 1835), with 100,000 *botas*. The Fino, Tío Pepe, is named after an uncle of the founder: Manuel María González Ángel, and is the world's best-selling Fino and one of the most immaculate and reliable sherries ever. Sought-after rarities include Oloroso Matusalem, P.X. Noé, and Oloroso Vintage.

Herederos de Argüeso***−****
Sanlúcar de Barrameda
445 acres (180 ha); bought-in grapes; 2,000,000 • *Wines: Manzanilla: Las Medallas, →San Léon*
This wine cellar (founded in 1822) has specialized in high-quality Manzanillas. Supposedly, some of the company's *soleras* are 250 years old. Manzanilla San León is one of the D.O.'s best products.

Hijos de Rainera Pérez Marín****
Sanlúcar de Barrameda
445 acres (180 ha); bought-in grapes; 3,800,000 bottles • *Wines: Manzanilla La Guita*
This company, founded in 1865, produces only one wine, but this is the best-known Manzanilla worldwide, and one of the best quality.

Osborne***−*****
El Puerto de Santa María
543 acres (220 ha); 8,000,000 bottles • *Wines include: Fino Quinta, Amontillado La Honda, Oloroso Bailén, Solera India, →Amontillado Coquinero Dry, Palo Cortado P Triangulo P; P.X. 1827*
Thomas Osborne built his first *bodega* in Jerez in 1772. Until 1890 all wines were sold abroad under the name Duff Gordon. Their trademark is the bull, which still stands on 97 hills in Spain, though now without a signature. The best-known wines are the Fino Quinta and Coquinero. The series of Rare Sherries deserve special attention.

Emilio Lustau and Emilio Lustau Almacenista****−*****
Jerez de la Frontera
94 acres (200 ha); bought-in grapes; 2,750,000 bottles • *Wines include: Puerto Fino, Oloroso Don Nuño →Manzanilla Papirusa, Amontillado Escuadrilla, P.X. San Emilio*
This *bodega*, owned by Luis Caballero, exports nearly all its products. The firm was founded in 1886, and also functions as an *almacenista* outlet. From small producers, like Manuel Cuevas or Viuda de Antonio Borrego, Lustau buys a few sherries, and markets them as rarities. His own varieties are also famous.

Pedro Domecq***−*****
Jerez de la Frontera
1,976 acres (800 ha); bought-in grapes; 9,000,000 bottles • *Wines: Fino La Ina, Amontillado Río Viejo, Dulce Venerable, →Amontillado 51−1ª, Oloroso Sibarita, Palo Cortado Capuchino*
A firm rich in tradition which owns one of finest *bodegas* anywhere—the Mezquita. It also has wine cellars in La Rioja and South America. Domecq produces one of the region's most popular, stylish, and lively Finos in La Ina. Furthermore, real pearls are also bottled from ancient *soleras*.

Sanchez Romate****
Jerez de la Frontera
247 acres (100 ha); bought-in grapes; 1,250,000 bottles • *Wines: Fino Marismeño, Manzanilla Viva la Pepa, Amontillado Don José, Dulce Iberia, →Amontillado N.P.U.*
This winery has been producing *bodega*-classics in the heart of the city since 1871, and owns vineyards in the top sites, at San Julián and Espartina. The Amontillado N.P.U. and Fino Macharnudo offer superb value.

Sandeman**−****
Jerez de la Frontera
889 acres (360 ha); bought-in grapes • *Wines include: Don Fino; Oloroso: Armada, →Royal Ambrosante*
An innovative company, strong on exports, with highly valuable old specialties.

Vinicola Hidalgo***−****
Sanlúcar de Barrameda
494 acres (200 ha); bought-in grapes; • *Wines: Manzanilla La Gitana, Amontillado Viejo, Oloroso Napoleon and Viejo*
This very skillful, traditional, family-owned *bodega*, founded in 1792, produces one of the best-loved Manzanillas and stocks several outstanding old wines.

JOACHIM KRIEGER, WOLFGANG FASSBENDER

PORTUGAL

PORTUGAL: LAND OF EXPLORERS

Today, the direct descendants of Portugal's great seafarers and explorers are beginning to discover the value of their wine estates (QUINTAS), which date from Portugal's golden age. Thus they are closing the circle which began when Portugal's wine wealth created Europe's first nation and laid the foundations for a world power. With an amazing dynamism, and fueled by European development programs, the historically minded Portuguese are exploiting the potential of their vineyards, their grape varieties, and their long winemaking traditions to the full.

Toward the end of the millennium there was an explosion of new wines and new *quintas* coming onto the market which has exceeded anything imagined during the bloodless Carnation Revolution of April 25, 1974, with the subsequent dissolution of Salazar's long dictatorship and the opening up of the country to the community of European states.

No new estates were founded, but instead there was a return to the country's own wine-making tradition, a thoroughly reliable base to support a modern fairy tale of success.

Some winemakers, who in the past had been forced to produce old-fashioned and overpriced branded wines, found the courage and spirit of enterprise to demonstrate their almost forgotten skills and to put them to work. The wine

The imposing Quinta da Sanguinhal in Estremadura is an example of the adaptation of the estates to modern times.

The Casa de Sezim near Guimarães produces one of the finest Vinho Verdes. The interior of the house reflects the extraordinarily rich history of many of the wine families.

lover can visit their *quintas* and relive a little wine history with their wines.

Portuguese pride in their nation, and their wines, has often helped to revive the old, the great, and the traditional. This pride has a melancholy aspect, expressed in the Portuguese characteristic *saudade*, which means regret for the fading glory, the lost might and splendor of a great world empire which has declined, leaving Portugal an unimportant nation on the edge of Europe. This melancholy character finds its expression in *fado* music, the plaintive, emotional, and intense songs, which make their listeners weep and feel their own sorrow and pain.

UNDERDEVELOPMENT: A BLESSING IN DISGUISE

The time of Portugal's opening up and moving on was undoubtedly serendipitous; it occurred just as winemakers in other countries were looking to their traditions, and the cult of technology was no longer an end in itself. Well into the 1970s, the market for higher quality and standard wine was dominated by the large and medium-sized wineries, with the cooperatives serving only the cheaper sector, and only a handful of almost unknown *quintas* producing quality wine.

The production of port was still completely in the hands of the large and medium dealers in Vila Nova de Gaia, its story that of a monopoly which only allowed winemakers the role of suppliers, not of marketers and exporters. To the outside world, the image of Portuguese wine was formed by the most successful and innovative branded wine in the world, the medium-dry, slightly sparkling Mateus Rosé, and its great rival, Lancers Rosé, which was even more successful in America.

Some successful Vinho Verde brands had also arisen, copies, some sneered, of German Liebfraumilch. In fact, the slight fizz of the natural and traditional Verdes, their freshness, was the model for Lancers and Mateus, which were born in the 1940s. Verde, the true original, merely followed.

Vinho Verde which, up to that time, had been 90 percent red wine, was converted into the fashionable, slightly sparkling, white drink by continuous new plantings of white varieties in the 1960s and 1970s, driven by the hunger of those dealing in brand names.

These light wines are still on the market, and they are still successful, selling in millions. The Mateus Rosé bottle, very similar in shape to the German Bocksbeutel, is a permanent feature on the supermarket shelves in many European countries. But for some years now the other Portuguese wines have been attracting attention inside Portugal and on international markets. With evidently around 500 varieties of grape, numerous old stock, and highly committed vintners Portugal has a big future in the modern wine world. Since wine drinkers all over the world are increasingly looking for alternatives to the ever constant Chardonnays and Cabernets, Portugal's wines are certainly in tune with the times.

MICROCOSM OF THE WINE WORLD

Portugal is a microcosm of the wine world, uniting almost everything you could imagine. The diversity of viticultural tradition, nursed over centuries, may not run all the way back to the aboriginal Iberians, but it is certain that the Phoenicians, arriving in the first millennium BC, began the cultivation of vines in the Iberian Peninsula and that the Greeks and later the Romans further encouraged viticulture.

During the 19th century there was a flourishing of middle-class wine culture and the heyday of the great bottled wines. Portuguese wine writers described and analyzed the different characteristics of individual wine regions, and with their knowledge of wine areas and vineyard sites set out in old books, laid the foundations for a great wine culture, mastered in an unparalleled manner by the Portuguese wine producers.

In the standard work, *Memoria sobre os Processos de vinificação* (memories about the

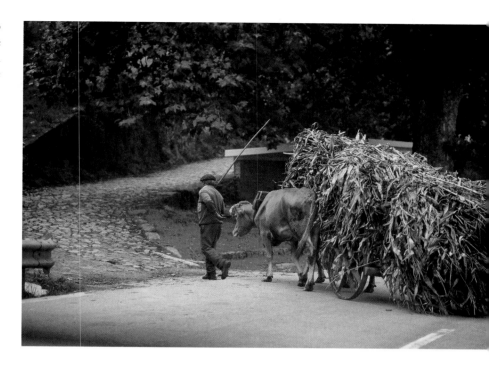

Portugal is a land of contrasts. Ox carts and sports cars use the same roads, and even in viticulture you can see both ancient hand skills and the most modern technology.

process of vinification), dating from 1867, details are researched and described down to the last village, always clearly differentiating between *vinhos de embarque* and *vinho do consumo*, the better wine suitable for export (bad wine could never be exported) and plain wine. Statistics are given about how much wine is consumed within the individual areas and how much is worthy of export.

This was somewhat different to Spain or Italy, where wineries had a stronger regional profile and sophisticated export houses such as those in Portugal (modelled on the early power of the port wine lodges) often simply did not exist.

Today Portugal offers a fascinating range from more than 40 wine-growing districts. Thirty-two are new, but many had already made a name among experts in the 19th century. A growing number of Portuguese reds can stand comparison with the best of Bordeaux or Burgundy—but they are certainly developing their own individuality in fruit, maturity, acidity and aging potential. The wines from the Douro, Bairrada, Alentejo or Dão regions are well set to become famous. But with all due praise for the reds, one should not forget the white wines. Really top growths are rare, but there are some.

Portuguese wine is becoming ever more up-to-date, both in equipment and content. The light, lively Vinho Verde was a forerunner of this development.

INTO THE MODERN AGE

In Portugal, tradition and modernity are not opposed to each other. Quite the contrary—the old traditional methods of wine production are more popular than ever. One of the pioneers of modern Portuguese wine has laid good foundations for the current respect in which ancestral methods of vinification are held. "Pick ripe grapes with ripe stalks," was the principle formulated by Ruis Alves, the great master of Barraida wine. And he went on to emphasize, "Fermented in the *lagar*, with natural stabilization and no artificial aids." The new young winemakers are also attracted by such consistent adherence to old traditions. And even if the more creative of Portuguese winemakers, or the big cooperatives looking for new markets, or foreign investors don't always follow Alves' ideas, tradition is definitely in fashion in Portuguese wine production.

After a long period of stagnation, more and more Portuguese producers have recognized the treasures they possess—unique *terroirs* and old vines with native grape varieties. Even many of the rapidly increasing number of innovative

In earlier times in the Douro valley, round masonry containers were built outside the cellars. Wine was stored in them until it was collected.

wine producers swear by local varieties and aging in a big wooden barrel. Which is not to say that *barriques* are not used—and international varieties such as Cabernet Sauvignon, Merlot, and Syrah do have their place in Portugal. However, nowhere as yet can producers be observed throwing out tradition just for the sake of short-term success—such excesses are very rare.

The move into the modern age has affected more than the old port wine region of Douro. Suddenly, from all corners of the country, exciting wines are appearing at prices that are still surprisingly low. Dão and Bairrada, Minho and Alentejo, Ribatejo and Palmela have become fashionable. If you want to mention a great Portuguese wine today, you are no longer limited to Vintage Port, Moscatel de Sétubal, or the great classic red wine Barca Velha. The competition among the *quintas*, wine estates which produce and market their own wines, is increasingly giving the large cooperatives and wine companies new ideas about wine. Wine dealerships are suddenly discovering such terms as "terroir" or "individuality," buying up *quintas* and bottling their wines as a separate line. Even the big companies, oriented more toward short-term success for balance sheet reasons, are following an amazing policy of quality, which is by no means a matter of course in other parts of the world. Even leading companies such as S.O.G.R.A.P.E. are managing exemplary wine estates in many parts of the country, supporting local varieties, and seeing no contradiction in having top quality wines in their range alongside mass produced ones.

For the consumer, the name of the wine producer is today more important than the traditional terms of maturity in the wine laws. Terms such as *Reserva* or *Garrafeira* have by no means disappeared from labels, but these definitions—referring to longer periods of aging in the barrel—have lost much of their original meaning. The "new winemakers" of Portugal often show little interest in the traditional legal terms.

Portugal's entry into the E.U. in 1986, the new markets, the subsidies—all of this has certainly contributed to the Portuguese wine miracle. However, the remarkable and exciting developments of the last few years were by no means a matter of course.

Today, the country has about 642,000 acres (260,000 ha) under vine, producing an average

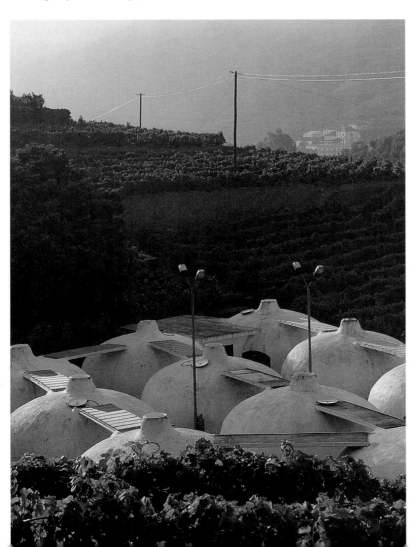

annual harvest of around 185 million gallons (7 million hl). That isn't much—the old vines and traditional Portuguese cultivation methods don't produce massive yields. This means that there are hardly any mass-produced wines. Apart from the not exactly sophisticated wines of the Mateus or Lancers brands, even standard Portuguese wines are often of remarkable quality. The marked differences between vintages in quantity and quality, along with the numerous unknown grape varieties, may not encourage the marketing of Portuguese wines abroad—but the considerable size of most estates, at 124 acres (50 ha) or more, can make up for these failings. The traditional dealership structures of the port business also have their advantages in making the new red and white wines of Portugal internationally known. Portugal could, at least in this regard, move "old world" European wines back into the foreground. True innovation in wine production is probably no longer limited to the New World (to the U.S.A., Chile, Australia, or South Africa). Given the developments in Alentejo or in the Douro valley, there is no reason to cast envious glances at the excellent New World wines and winegrowers. At some future time, Portugal could serve as an example of old traditions also being suitable—and perhaps particularly appropriate—for modern marketing.

For Vintage Port, the best results are achieved if the grapes are trodden by foot. As this is a very exhausting method, Peter Symington has devised a mechanical system which was used for the first time in 1998.

Conditions that elsewhere in Europe apply only to a few areas—Priorat in Spain, for example, or Languedoc-Roussillon in the south of France—are valid for the whole of Portugal. This vinicultural nation in the far west of Europe is a treasure trove for wine experts searching for the unusual. However, to be successful you do need to have detailed knowledge of what is on offer. Portugal is not really the place for impulse buying.

The garrafão culture

Wine containers like the Portuguese garrafão, bottles wrapped in straw or plastic containing 1½ gallons (5 liters), are to be found in many southern European countries, but nowhere are they such a country-wide feature as in Portugal, where they are used for wine and for mineral or table water. The Portuguese take them everywhere, originally mainly into the fields. Now, in today's more leisured society, they dominate every beach, picnic site, and natural beauty spot, for the Portuguese like eating in the open air. They take a piece of presunto (raw ham), a piece of pão (bread) and the unavoidable vinho, the people's drink, spoken more tenderly in this language than in any other. Only the young are increasingly doing without wine in the garrafão.

Portugal has long since lost its former first place among the wine-drinking countries for consumption per head, at over 34 gallons (130 liters). Now, at around 13 gallons (50 liters), the country has slipped below France and Italy, but is still well ahead of its neighbor Spain, which consumes less than 10.5 gallons (40 liters). However, the consumption of home-produced wine is unrecorded and this probably obscures the actual situation. The garrafão, which even today is still popular in

The 1.3 gallon (5 l) bottle: training for wine drinkers.

Portugal's former colonies, is an unloved object for many a serious winery, shamefully concealed behind the better-quality bottled wines. But it cannot be dispensed with, because that would amount to an insult to the people and their most enthusiastic representatives, the small and larger-scale dealers who would never give up selling wine by the garrafão, however small the profits.

Whether the garrafão is valued or despised, one factor has been completely overlooked; its secret contribution to the Portuguese taste in wine, to the surprisingly stable forces of tradition, which defend harsh, difficult, original wines, and despise the superficially more pleasant ones. It is, so to speak, a popular education, especially by the garrafão from Dão, which has always been available to the most ordinary worker as well as to the revolutionary intellectual.

Portuguese wines and regions, taken as a whole, are world leaders in wine styles, though this fact is not well enough known for the country to become a leader of world opinion. There is one reason for this. The former students and soldiers of the Revolution, that is to say the present day opinion leaders in the area of sought-after quality wines, schooled their palates with good garrafão or Alentejo liter wines, at home or in the bars. Someone used to such fare develops a distaste for pleasing, smooth, and polished wines and prefers the genuine, uncompromising drink, such as is common in Portugal today, popular with all people and not only in high society.

The old garrafão may, with a bit of luck, contain very good quality wine, perhaps not the most refined, but rarely thin. In certain circumstances, over the years, it can develop into a very fine wine indeed.

THE WINE REGIONS

Paradoxically, Portugal was the first country in the world to give wine-growing regions exact geographical boundaries and to classify the vineyards: the first in Porto e Douro in 1756 and the second in Vinho Verde in 1906 to 1911. Portugal also has perhaps the greatest tradition in Europe for anonymous wines, of which no more is known than that they originate in Portugal.

This game of hide and seek has long affected Mateus Rosé, for many years the most successful brand wine in the world, just as it did the famous Garrafeira wines or the legendary Barca Velha, which has only recently taken to printing its origins as a Douro wine on the label. Preparatory drafts of wine legislation lay for years in the files of the Salazar and other regimes. These bureaucracies favored monopolies and therefore had little interest in innovation. With the 1974 revolution, the opening out toward Europe, the entry into the E.C., everything was set in motion. Finally, regional wines were allowed onto the market with their names of origin.

Since the removal of restrictions, the Portuguese wine industry has undergone stormy developments, for example, in the case of Bairrada, which was demarcated as a region in 1979, swiftly followed by a partial withdrawal and redefinition of the region. However, there are now signs of consolidation. The Alentejo was one case in point, in which first of all individual regions acquired I.P.R. status (*Indicação de Proveniência Regulamentada*), then later D.O.C. (DENOMINAÇÃO DE ORIGEM CONTROLADA). Eight former regions have now been turned into sub-regions and the highly attractive wine, Alentejo, previously only permitted to be known as a Vinho Regional, has been designated D.O.C.

The upper course of the Douro, with its terraced vineyards, is one of the most spectacular wine-growing landscapes in the world. However, more profitable new sites are threatening this great heritage.

The same happened with D.O.C. Ribatejo in May 2000. Many of the wines on the market still carry the old terms, such as D.O.C. Borba. The six former I.P.R. regions became a new D.O.C. region at a stroke, and the wine-growing areas which had for some years acted as regions may now only appear as mere sub-regions.

As statistics show, the classic D.O.C. regions of Porto (1756) and Vinho Verde (1908) are still leaders of quality wine production, which is also in part due to their size. The third great classic region, Dão (1907), has over recent years dropped behind the highly dynamic Alentejo. Even the really extraordinary eagerness for innovation in the Douro region has come up with little that can really be compared to the classic Dão. The monopoly of port dominated this region for far too long and, apart

Vinho regional

Vinho regional (the Portuguese equivalent of *vin de pays*, often used in other countries only as a term for very plain wines), has an important part to play in Portugal.

First, many top-quality wine estates have been created on a TERROIR where wine growing has never been the center of attention, or has faded so far into the background that a wine region never properly developed. Second, for many Portuguese wineries, *vinho regional* is, to a certain extent, a substitute for their putting even their best brands onto the market with no indication of origin, and focusing on the house's

guarantee. While this is useful both to the consumer and the winery, it is a hindrance to the distinctive development of the regions. Even today there are still areas where you can buy excellent wines but the region itself knows little or nothing of its potential.

Vinho regional is linked to the tradition of freedom from the indication of origin. The brand name is considered more important than the more confining region. If a VINTAGE in a region turns out to be less good than usual, it is possible to use wine from a neighboring region instead. *Vinho regional* is also

important for the description of blended wines or CUVÉES which do not fit into the scheme of quality wine regions. The term is used only in a few regions by individual cooperatives and wine estates as a particular label for second- or third-class wines, i.e. to indicate a lower level of quality than the best D.O.C. wines. However, the opposite is also possible: *vinho regional* for the top quality, and D.O.C. for the plainer wines. There is therefore less of a golden rule here than in any other country—apart from one: respect the bottles containing *vinho regional*!

VINHO REGIONAL REGIONS

- Rios do Minho
- Trás-os-Montes
- Beiras
- Estremadura
- Ribatejo
- Terras do Sado
- Alentejo
- Algarve

D.O.C.-REGIONS

- Vinho Verde
- Porto e Douro
- Tavora-Varosa
- Barraida
- Dão
- Beira Interior
- Pinhel
- Castelo Rodrigo
- Cova da Beira
- Ribatejo
- Tomar
- Santarém
- Cartaxo
- Chamusca
- Almeirim
- Coruche
- Lourinhã
- Òbidos

- Alenquer
- Torres Vedras
- Arruda
- Bucelas
- Colares
- Carcavelos
- Palmela
- Setúbal
- Alentejo
- Lagos
- Portimão
- Lagoa
- Tavira

I.P.R.-REGIONS

- Chaves
- Valpaços
- Planalto Mirandês
- Encostas da Nave
- Lafões
- Encostas de Aire
- Alcobaça

- Madeira

Azores

- Biscoitos
- Pico
- Graciosa

- Wine-growing areas in neighboring countries

from legends such as Barca Velha, prevented the development of what is undoubtedly one of the best red wine regions in the world. Even some of the regional wine descriptions are now more important than Dão which, as far as exports are concerned, is still in third place behind Porto and Verde.

Of the other classics, Bucelas (1911) is experiencing a cracking revival at present, Carcavelos (1907) is struggling to survive, as is Colares (also 1907), which for many wine drinkers was long considered the best and most interesting red wine in Portugal. Both are in areas near the capital where building land is worth much more than the last few vineyards.

Some regions have not yet brought any quality wines onto the market because the companies concerned are not yet in a position to fulfill the required legal conditions, especially as regards the grape varieties, which in many ancient vineyards can hardly be determined with any accuracy.

PORTUGUESE WINE STYLES

There is a great deal to be said about styles of Portuguese wine, in particular about the white wines. Vinho Verde may be a highly individual wine because of its regional origin and its fresh, crisply accented acidity and lightness, but it is increasingly being produced by international methods. Things are no different for the other white wines of Portugal, which in many regions have extraordinary potential and which can, in their fruitiness, acidity, and refined quality, stand alongside the wines of other cooler European regions such as Burgundy, the Loire, and Germany. Cool FERMENTATION, careful processing of the grapes, and stainless steel tanks often bring out qualities in the wines unimaginable only a few years ago—clean and at the same time demonstrating the *terroir* and grape variety in their delicacy and expressiveness. All modern and traditional methods of white wine preparation are being used, such as stirring the YEASTS, and maturation in new wood barrels. However, the new wood is often used as a short-term additional procedure instead of a noble instrument of aging. Traditional wines from old wooden barrels are sadly becoming ever more rare, as they have brought too few good results.

New barrels are a contentious issue in Portugal, as for generations it has been the practice to use old ones. However, there are already some groundbreaking examples of their successful use.

Portugal is at present searching for the best grape varieties and the best styles for its wines and a clear structure and hierarchy can be seen in only a few companies. Producers with international experience seem, at the moment, to have an advantage. One could mention a number of examples: top of the list would be Esporão, partly managed by the Australian David Baverstock; J. P. Wines, previously developed by Australian Peter Bright, who now matures wines on his own behalf; and J. M. Fonseca, with their Californian-trained boss. Among the new famous names in the Alentejo are Cortes de Cima with the Dane Hans Kristian Jorgensen, and on the Douro the German wine producers Bernhard Breuer, Bernd Philippi, and Werner Näkel at the Quinta do Carvalhosa have attracted attention. And we mustn't forget Dirk van der Niepoort, whose ambition is big enough to tackle white and rosé wines.

However, apart from the great dessert wine specialties of port, Madeira, and Muscat from Setúbal, true originality is offered by red wine. Here a simply inexhaustible potential of good regions, vineyard sites, and grape varieties is pouring onto the market, dividing journalists and consumers into supporters of *estilo moderno* or *estilo classico*, sometimes also known as *estilo tradicional*. There is probably no other country in which this subject of style is so frequently, so passionately, and so systematically debated in periodicals and books, at the table, or during wine drinking and wine tasting. Basically, no journalist in Portugal can discuss wine without

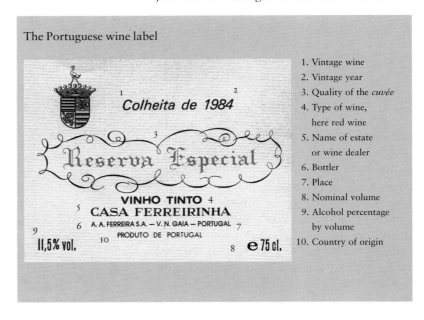

The Portuguese wine label

Colheita de 1984

Reserva Especial

VINHO TINTO 4
CASA FERREIRINHA
A. A. FERREIRA S.A. – V. N. GAIA – PORTUGAL 7
PRODUTO DE PORTUGAL
11,5% vol.
e 75 cl.

1. Vintage wine
2. Vintage year
3. Quality of the *cuvée*
4. Type of wine, here red wine
5. Name of estate or wine dealer
6. Bottler
7. Place
8. Nominal volume
9. Alcohol percentage by volume
10. Country of origin

Innovative energy on the banks of the Douro

"What varieties are my wines produced from?" Dirk van der Niepoort laughs mischievously and looks thoughtfully up at the sky. "Not such an easy question to answer." The name "Niepoort" crops up at some point whenever there is any discussion of the new style of Portuguese viticulture. Portuguese by choice, of Netherlandic ancestry, Dirk van der Niepoort promotes his cause most articulately in several languages. He is the founder of modern Douro wine and brought dry Portuguese wines to the world's attention.

The house of Niepoort has been famous for high quality port wine for a century and a half. But in the late 1980s Niepoort began to create wines without residual sugar or added alcohol, which became known outside the country in the 1990s. Sturdy independent products made from native varieties, the range of varieties used to make them differed from vintage to vintage. Together with his enologist, Jorge Serôdio Borges, Niepoort first created Redoma, a cask-aged red wine with class and elegance. The Douro valley wine producer is also interested in white and rosé wines. His Redoma Branca is considered one of the new classic whites, and the rare Redoma Rosé is far more than a by-product of red wine production.

Further projects are Niepoort's estate Quinta do Napoles and his new top red Batuta, but these are by no means the only

Portugal is a land with many different styles of wine—from plain everyday wines to full-bodied products, and truly royal Vintage Ports.

ones. Even classic port wines are benefiting from Niepoort's delight in experimentation. In Quinta do Passadouro, he has created a Single Quinta Port full of character, by no means to be considered a lesser variant of Vintage Ports. The new definition Single Quinta Vintage has also been shaped by Dirk van der Niepoort. This is a Vintage Port of very individual character, not just a secondary vintage from a big port house in poorer years. What could be more interesting than, in top

years, to taste the classic Niepoort Vintage alongside Passadouro?

And now there is yet a third Vintage Port on the market: Niepoort Secundum Vintage is intended to establish a different style, but not to form the "secondary, therefore lesser quality" port. More accessible, more favorably priced, uncomplicated: Vintage Port for beginners. This is no frivolity of Niepoort's, but an attempt to interest a younger public in the occasionally seemingly rather antiquated Vintage Ports. The high prices, unquestionably often justified by quality, do sometimes get in the way of this most noble of port wines, however.

Van der Niepoort was also one of the first producers in the Douro region to understand the important function of marketing. Wines of such a special nature as ports, or to an even greater extent dry reds, do not sell themselves. For this reason (and also because he enjoys it) you will often see Niepoort at trade fairs and wine events all over the world. He is then happy to explain on what occasions port wines are particularly enjoyable: not just with a cigar or chocolates, as most of the wine books insist "Try port wine with steak *au poivre*," is Niepoort's suggestion.

mentioning the subject of wine style. On the one hand are the wines with primary fruit aromas, with or without wood aroma (José Neva is a master of this area), on the other uncompromising wines aged in the old manner.

A focal point of these discussions is the *lagar*, the open basin of granite, slate, concrete, or even marble, in which the vineyard workers, singing, dancing, playing around, or stamping in military order, carry out the millennia-old work of treading the grapes. This is the only method in which not one pip or stalk is damaged and therefore the green, aggressive, bitter, and tannic ACID flavors, which can be tasted in countless wines, are avoided. Apart from *pisar a pé*, another topic of conversation, at all levels and not only for a few top wines, is the question of whether wine should be filtered, and made without any kind of prettification. Tradition is popular among the Portuguese, but even more decisive are the enticing density and rounded character of the tannins and the fruit you can taste in traditionally made wines. Despite the trends toward fruity wines for drinking while young, red wine in Portugal is still more of a stronghold of tradition than in any other country.

Vinho Verde is one of the most successful types of wine in Portugal, and has even been imitated abroad. This applies particularly to the Vinho Verde based on the Alvarinho variety.

At the moment there is a traditionalist movement, almost amounting to a dismissal of technology, as can be read on the back labels of wine bottles; *feito em lagares, pisar a pé*, or *estabiliazição natural, esta sujeito a criar depósito com o envelhecimento* (natural stabilization, intended to form a deposit with age), or *não foi tratado pelo frio* (not cold stabilized).

VINHO VERDE

The Vinho Verde region, in the extreme north-west of Portugal between Porto and the Spanish border, covers the same area as the Minho, the *vin de pays* named after the region. It is the largest D.O.C. region in Portugal and one of the biggest in the world. At around 86,450 acres (35,000 ha), the Vinho Verde region is the largest quality wine region in the country. Unofficial estimates assume even higher figures. On average, 21,000,000 gallons (800,000 hl) of wine and sparkling wine are produced—however, there are considerable variations from vintage to vintage. The proportion of wine exported is constantly rising.

In Minho, the former county of Portucale and the heartland of Portugal, Afonso Henriques of Guimarres once proclaimed the first Portuguese nation. The Minho contains only nine percent of the land area of Portugal, but 20 percent of the population. This has led to the creation of an intensive landscape of small farms in which the rampant growth of the vines is proof of the

Modern viticultural methods are advancing even into the north of Portugal. The vines in the new plantings near Cruzeta are growing on low trellises.

Opposite
The Quinta da Cerejeiras is decorated with magnificent blue tiles, the famous *azuelos*.

fertility of this area. It is the greenest region of Portugal, receiving 38 to 51 inches (150 to 200 cm) of rainfall a year. The vines shoot up the trees on the sides of the roads for 30 feet (9 m) or more, and this is not by accident, but to make harvesting easier. In meadows and pastureland where cattle graze, they are grown, intentionally, up trees, on poles, on wires strung on granite posts, or along wooden trellises. The pergola, already known to the Romans, is present everywhere and provides shade for small paths, tracks, and avenues, with grapes thriving at the top.

Despite the mainly unprolific sandy granite soils (only a few slate enclaves offer better conditions), often with only a few inches of topsoil, the Minho is one single green garden, which is probably the reason for the name of the wine. This miracle, in the Atlantic north of Portugal, has been created by the people of Minho in the smallest possible space, with their very own form of intensive cultivation, often based on an archaic system of self-sufficiency, which has only decreased in recent years due to the rise of numerous small textile and shoe factories. Once there was a great wine tradition here: wine from Monção is believed to be the first export wine of the Middle Ages, and many wealthy *quintas* all over the Minho are evidence of the profits to be made then. It was above all the strict legislation of Salazar which in 1930 interrupted this tradition by prohibiting the planting of vineyards and allowing vines only as hedging. While this encouraged the improvisation skills of the inhabitants, it also led to the division and break-up of their lands.

In a region where 100,000 farmers are registered, of which 90,000 consider themselves to be wine producers, it is a waste of time counting vineyards or even surveying them; some of the vineyards are simply borders to two or three

pieces of land and fill the occasional cask of wine. Here there is a unique mixture of intensive use of land with extensive growing of grapes. There are old vines with stems as thick as tree trunks and arm-thick twisted cords, which may spread for 240 or more square yards (200 sq.m) with the aid of supporting posts and wires. They may yield 22 to 44 pounds (10 to 20 kg) of little ripe grapes. These are made into the typical Verde which, unlike any other wine in Portugal or even in the world, often has difficulty in reaching the minimum alcohol content of 8.5 percent by volume. And yet this weakness is at the same time its strength. The acid red Verde, with its dry taste and its lightness, is the only proper red wine for summer; it even tastes good chilled. Unfortunately it is drunk almost exclusively within the country, because no one understands it as a red wine. In one of the typical little bars of the region, where the acid blackish-purplish red Vinho Verde, topped with white froth, is drunk from white porcelain bowls to quench the thirst, there is a lovingly framed piece of parchment. On it is a quote from the great professor of chemistry and wine expert António Augusto de Aguiar, dating from 1876, and it is a perfect description of Vinho Verde and its effects: "Vinho Verde is one of the most unusual of wines. It is original, young, refreshing, good for diets. It does not inebriate. That is the only reason I love it. It knows how to respect intelligence."

This judgment may have applied to red Vinho Verde, which at the time, and indeed up until a few years ago, dominated 90 percent of the country; it has since shrunk to around 50 percent. However, it does also apply to the core of the white Vinho Verde which, since the prohibition on planting vineyards was lifted, has had an unparalleled successful career as a lightly

Grape vines as natural boundaries between small fields are a typical sight in the Vinho Verde region.

Opposite
In the Vinho Verde area, the vines are trained on tall pergolas. This makes harvesting into a balancing act on ladders.

Spring pruning in the Vinho Verde region.

sparkling fashionable wine. It was the model for Mateus Rosé, for Verde sparkles naturally from the second fermentation which spontaneously occurs with rising temperatures in spring and in summer. This was perfected by the great brand-name wineries and bottled in quantity, today mostly with a little help from added carbon dioxide and some RESIDUAL SUGAR. Casal Garcia from Quinta da Aveleda, Gatão from Birges, and Gazela from S.O.G.R.A.P.E. are world brands today and sell several million bottles. Twenty-five other wineries are fighting for a market share of the highly drinkable light wine sector, ensuring that the last and smallest wine producer will have his *vinho* sold either by contract grape delivery or via a cooperative, in rounded, narrow-necked flagons, in Bordeaux-style or drumstick-shaped bottles, or in some other special form. The technical production standard of the bigger brands is quite high, the taste acceptable, if you are looking for an uncomplicated summer drink and not a sophisticated wine. Even in the cheap wine sector there are drinkable clean wines, though there are also coarse, thin, and over-frothy versions.

Some of the great wineries have concerned themselves with excellent dry Verdes as well as their mass-market brand names. Companies such as S.O.G.R.A.P.E., Quinta da Aveleda, and Solouro even bottle the rare and expensive specialty wine Alvarinho. However, the real revolution, in Vinho Verde as well, and earlier here than elsewhere in Portugal, consists in the rise of the *produtores-engarrafadores*—estates which bottle and sell their own wine. These prefer to produce a classic dry wine which contains less (and increasingly only natural) carbon dioxide. However, the picture is not a uniform one; there are also producers who make sweet and very fizzy carbon dioxide wines. In the late 1970s there were at most five of these *quintas*; a few years ago there were almost 200, with roots that can often be traced back to the Middle Ages. As *casas antigas*, they offer top-quality rooms to stay, and thus make an attractive stopover on a journey through this region, which is full of culture in every sense.

The driving force behind the increasing trend toward wine estates, higher quality and better marketing, was the A.P.E.V.V., the association of *produtores-engarrafadores*, founded in 1985. This association also contained the seeds of today's national marketing organization F.E.N.A.V.I. Many of the top *quintas* are members. There are at present 150 estates and these are constantly being joined by more. Many also give up, however, because sales are a problem for small unknown estates in a country dominated by large distributors; and marketing, following on the heels of the infant wine tourism industry, is still at an early stage. Too much optimism after planting, and certainly also the variable quality, have led many a producer to go back to vine growing.

The true Vinho Verde, a uniquely dry, steely wine which, like dry Saar or Mosel Rieslings, runs counter to popular taste, can still be found in the *quintas*, and it cannot be stressed often enough that those who like acidity should leave it well alone. Even the best, well made, ripe Verdes with alcohol volumes close to the upper limit of 11.5 percent by volume have an aftertaste that is more or less restrained in acidity. For lovers of seafood who want to quench their thirst, this is a positive, not a negative quality. Verde is not a wine to taste, sip and contemplate. It is a wine which definitely encourages the appetite.

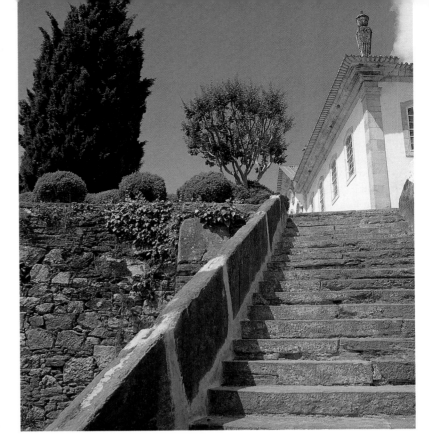

Lovers of Portuguese wines are impressed not only by Vinho Verde, but also by the architectural treasures of many estates such as the Quinta de Côtto in Mesão Frio.

All the sub-regions produce wines with similar characteristics: the finely aromatic Loureiro, which was the first to make a sensation, particularly in the Lima region, because of its fine expressiveness; or the recently discovered refinement of Azal, from the Basto or Amarante region. A higher alcohol content is not necessarily considered an advantage for the Verde connoisseur, but rather a weakness in style which deforms the otherwise very straight spine of the acidity.

However, there are two exceptions, and these regions should really be independent and not known as Verde, as some maintain. One of these is the area around Baião, down by the Douro, which is much warmer. Its wines should be placed between the very ripe Douro white wines and Verde. The other is Alvarinho, the king of Portuguese wines, a position held long before

Trás-os-Montes

The regional wine term for D.O.C. Douro is also the name for the barren, wild, deserted landscape north of the Douro, the isolated area toward the Spanish border.

It contains the I.P.R. Valpaços, from which, in the past, many a famous Garrafeira wine has drawn its red grapes. The I.P.R. Chaves, famous for its ham, is cooler and produces somewhat less full-bodied white and red wines. However, there are only a few producers.

The huge remaining areas of Trás-os-Montes offer scattered vineyards with one center,

among others, in the Macedo de Cavaleiros region, which is able to produce high-quality classic red wines.

The wine estate of Valle Pradinhos (with a large area planted with Cabernet Sauvignon vines) has frequently come to prominence with one of the best Portuguese red wines.

The opening up of the region by the new Porto–Bragança highway may make its vinological discovery possible. The geological conditions, with the finest eroded slate soils in many places, offer excellent opportunities for

further development of modern viticulture. There could soon be some interesting bottled wines starting to appear from this region apart from the good peasant wines to be found in bars and pubs. Besides red wines from the rougher highlands, some white wines with attractive acidity should now be possible.

the Spanish Albariño, beyond the Minho river, became fashionable and began its own brilliant career under the D.O.C. label Rías Baixas. In Portugal, wine from this thick-skinned, aromatic grape variety, whose alcohol content according to statute begins where Verde leaves off, is booming. The wine starts at 11.5 percent by volume and may rise to 13 percent.

Alvarinho does not taste like Verde. It is a specialty from the Monção region with opposing characteristics from the sub-zones of Monção and Melgaço. But the dryness and freshness—caused by the combination of unprolific granite soils (mixed in Monção with typical river gravels), a high volume of precipitation (here around 5¹/₂ inches/140 mm), together with high summer temperatures and cold September nights that encourage aroma —are combined in Alvarinho with elegant ripeness and an aroma with peach, lychee, pear, and citrus notes. Alvarinho—or medium-dry Verde—is the wine for lobster with a sweetish sauce, while the classic Verde Seco is the ideal wine for fish.

Alvarinho vines cover 1,730 acres (700 ha) in Monção, and nowadays the variety is even spreading as a minority vine beyond the borders of its home sub-region into other regions. There are 20 producers, including the market-domi-

nating cooperatives of Monção. It is a pity that, as with almost all Verdes, it is difficult to recommend estates: the quality of the vintages is so variable, depending on the weather, that it is almost impossible to make a judgment and praise an estate without systematically following up all its vintages. "Once it's drunk, it's drunk, once it's sold, it's sold" is a comment regularly made on Verde. And yet Alvarinhos cannot really bloom until they are five or six years old, and other Verdes also develop very fine notes in their maturity. Reliable selection, tasting, and evaluation of estates can therefore be made only in a few cases. The dominant wineries, which represent only two percent of the wine estates but sell 70 percent of the wines, have got a better grip on the variations between vintages. They do not name the vintage for brand name wines, even on their quality products, or, like Quinta da Aveleda, they simply leave out the vintage for their better grape variety wines if the year was not a success. This historic wine, which is only beginning to be discovered as an individual and not as a brand, has a long way to go before the consumer and the dealers have learned that a good Verde is really only able to demonstrate all its qualities when it's no longer quite young or fresh.

SELECT PRODUCERS FROM THE VINHO VERDE REGION

CASA DE SEZIM*−***
NESPEIRA, GUMARÃES
49 acres (20 ha); 100,000 bottles • Wines include: Colbeita Seleccionada Branco, Casa de Sezim Branco One of the finest Verdes of the region.

CASA DO VALLE***
CABECEIRAS DO BASTO
74 acres (30 ha); 150,000 bottles • Wines include: Branco, Azal, Casa do Valle Tinto Colonel Sousa Botelho's historic quinta produces one of the most brilliant Verdes of the region.

PALACIO DE BREJOEIRA**−***
PINHEIROS, MONÇÃO
42 acres (17 ha) • Wines: Alvarinho, Aguardente Vínica, Aguardente Bagaceira Dona Maria Herminia d'Oliveira Pães devised the first great modern Alvarinho estate, and has often demonstrated the richness of aroma that Alvarinho is capable of.

PROVAM, CABO-BARBEITA***
MONÇÃO
300,000 bottles • Wines: Alvarinho/Trajadura Varanda do Conde, Alvarinho Portal do Fidalgo, Alvarinho Vinha Antiga The Produtores de Vinho Alvarinho de Monção formed a company in 1992 and produce brilliant wine with great expertise in a modern winery.

QUINTA DA AVELEDA*−****
PENAFIEL
296 acres (120 ha); some bought-in grapes; 13,000,000 bottles • Wines include: Vinho Verde: Casal Garcia,

Quinta da Aveleda, Grinalda, Alvarinho; Beiras: Quinta d'Aguiera Chardonnay, Touriga Nacional/Cabernet Sauvingon; Estremadura; Tinto A beautiful estate with standard brands and red wine ambitions in other regions of Portugal.

QUINTA DA S. CLAUDIO***
CURVOS, ESPOSENDE
16 acres (6.5 ha); 15,000 bottles • Wine: Branco One of the few traditional quintas in Portugal which began bottling its own wines as early as 1960.

QUINTA DE COVELA**−***
S. TOMÉ DE COVELAS, BAIÃO
44.5 acres (18 ha); 60,000 bottles • Wines include: Covela, Quinta de Covela Nuno Cunha Araújo's ambitious quinta is an experimental area with many different grape varieties.

QUINTA DA LIXA**−***
LIXA
74 acres (30 ha); 100,000 bottles • Wines include: Quinta da Lixa, Trajadura, Terras do Minho Branco, Terras do Minho Tinto; Espumante Branco, Tinto Still a tip for those in the know. The Vinho Verdes, from various terroirs, have strong character. The sparkling wines, red or white, are more than just a curiosity.

SOALHEIRO (ANTONIO ESTEVES FERREIRA)***−****
MELGAÇO
25 acres (10 ha); 50, 000 bottles • Wines: Alvarinho, Soalheiro Espumante Brut Alvarinho João Antonio Cerdeira pioneered Alvarinho planting in 1974. His sparkling wine is masterful.

PORT WINE AND DOURO

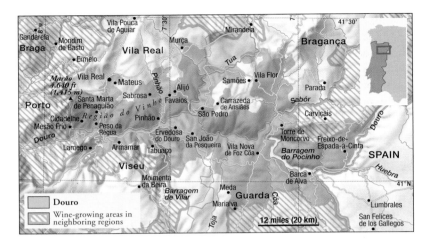

Port wine, otherwise simply known as port, *o vinho do Porto*, is a wine named not after its place of origin but after Porto, the harbor from which it is shipped (sometimes called Oporto). The Douro, its region of origin, begins some 60 miles (100 km) inland up the river of the same name, and stretches from around Régua, the first town worthy of the name, for about the same distance further into the interior, as far as the Spanish border.

It is the most imposing, the most intensive, and the wildest vine-growing landscape in the world; an isolated area, where donkeys and mules still provide the most valuable help and grapes still have to be carried on someone's back for a couple of miles until they reach a track suitable for wheeled transport. Even today, you can get an idea of the pioneering efforts of the first wine producers of the Douro and the first dealers.

If you look at the evidence of prehistoric times—preserved grape pips from the Bronze Age and charred vines in burial sites—you will get some idea of the great extent of viticulture even in these early times. During the Roman occupation, wine must have been produced in the Douro for export. It certainly cannot have been profitable to make wine for home consumption alone, given

The Quinta do Noval has an unusually high proportion of stone terraces.

the intensive labor needed to grow vines in this rough, wild, steep, and difficult country of slate and granite.

The twin towns of Porto (the harbor) and Vila Nova de Gaia, on the opposite side of the river, where the majority of port wines still lie today, maturing in the cellars on the cooler northern slopes, were always the dominant economic pulse of the region, due to the dynamism of the wine trade and the people who worked here.

To trace the origin of the name of this famous wine, we need to go back to the Middle Ages. Alfonso Henrique, Count of Portucale, first called himself king of Portugal in 1139 and thereby founded the first European nation, in the modern sense. This would have been unthinkable without the economic power and importance of his county and its outstanding harbor and trading place. This was the first great economic golden age for Portugal, thanks to the dynamism of the monastic orders (the Cistercian monks alone founded more than 100 monasteries in Portugal during the 12th century). Viticulture was the absolute summit of all profitable—and profitably exportable—cultivation. Since 1096, the Burgundian dynasty had ruled in Portugal, providing its kings from 1139 to 1385. This dynasty knew the finest wines of its time.

Perhaps the most important ruler was King Diniz I (1279–1325), who was, among other achievements, successful in implementing a national language throughout Portugal, which remains almost unchanged today. It was derived from the former Latin dialect of Porto.

Diniz had the nickname *rei lavrador* (the farmer king). He strongly encouraged land clearance and agriculture and, with the profits from agricultural production such as wine and olive oil, he built up an unequaled trading fleet —professional management by today's standards. He founded the University of Lisbon in 1290, which he moved a few years later to Coimbra, a city nearer to Porto and firmer in its faith. He also founded the Order of Christ in 1318, for which he bought up most of the resources of the Templars. In doing this he laid the foundations for Portugal's rise to become a world power, the nation of great explorers. Trade, export, and import were Portugal's great strengths which it used to secure its influence and its wealth. Only when you know this history does it become clear why port wine became the most widespread exported wine in the world and why, even today, export is still the identifying characteristic of Porto.

Today, it is not only the port wine trade that is flourishing. The demand for dry wines has dramatically increased. In two decades, the area under vine has almost doubled and now covers more than 98,800 acres (40,000 ha). Almost 40,000 winegrowers each cultivate plots of about two and a half acres (1 ha) each. The foundation for this renaissance, contrary to the development in most European regions, is not only to be found in successful sales, but also in the regulated, disciplined policies of the Instituto do Vinho do Porto, which annually forges agreement between the powerful export association and the equally powerful wine producers' organization Casa do Douro. It does this by determining exactly the amount of port wine that may be harvested on each vineyard plot, always basing it on the previous year's sales.

The character of the region is based on its infrastructure. It was the first and possibly most precisely recorded and classified region in the world. The creation of the *Companhia Goral da Agricultura das Vinhas do Alto Douro* (General Association of Viticulture on the Upper Douro) in 1756, pushed through by the absolutist prime

Once, the vine terraces above the Douro were laid out by hand and supported by dry-stone walls. Now bulldozers level the slopes for new plantings and the terrace walls are often too much work and too expensive for even the best producers.

Left
Work on the steep slopes is still largely carried out by hand.

Right
Picking grapes is hard work for those carrying the harvest. In order to provide top quality, the small modern grape boxes often have to be carried long distances on someone's shoulders.

minister later known as the Marquis de Pombal, may even today be seen as a model, in its consistency, of the protection of the reputation, market, and exports of a region. The project, known as the "Demarcation of the Hills," was probably undertaken by a Dominican monk named Father João de Mansilha. In its first articles of association, the organization stated that "the cultivation of wine is supported by the reputation of this wine, so that trade may profit by it, agriculture may be rewarded, and this all to be thus cleverly balanced that consumption should not be made impossible by high prices, nor yet cultivation by lowering of prices."

THE CAREER OF A REGION

Since the over-generous demarcation of borders of 1907 (corrected and made stricter in 1921), a policy of intensive brand protection for Porto had been implemented, but the prices were not high enough. In 1933, the organizations were formed which still protect the industry today: the Casa do Douro (Association of Wine Producers), the Grémio dos Exportadores do Vinho do Porto (Association of Port Wine Exporters) and the Instituto do Vinho do Porto (Port Wine Institute), an official institution responsible for the overall interests of the port wine industry. Among other bodies, the Câmara dos Provadores was set up to test port wine in the glass. However, the Casa do Douro's most important service was the provision of a new viticultural register of all wine producers and vineyard plots. This continues to the present day and has collected a wealth of data. Within the register, the most important information is the classification of all plots into six classes from A to F, devised by the agricultural engineer A. Moreira da Fonseca in 1947–8. Each vineyard is evaluated according to a points system to take account of all the factors affecting quality. This is still important today for the annual issue of *beneficio* (the right to produce a certain quantity of port wine). It also helps to decide the price when purchasing port.

Following the Marquis de Pombal's delimitation of the Douro region in 1756, the area was immediately extensively surveyed and divided into different price ranges. At a stroke, all imports of wine into the region were prohibited and the practice of blending wines to produce lower-priced products was stopped. Typically, the economic fate of a wine region is that, following a period of success, the wine producers, driven by the desire for profit, move toward bankruptcy because of unlimited increases in the quantity of wine produced, whether by extending the area under vine, or by blending or adulterating the wines. In the Douro, this process was reversed. Within 20 years, due to Pombal's authoritarian regime, not only was the protection of the wine area established, but prices even tripled. New port wine houses were founded, and the region flourished again, this time with organized and regulated quantities.

Demand was strong but cultivation was extended only in small stages, to prevent negative consequences. Only after increasing liberalization did the market become more unstable and crisis-prone. The final step toward stabilizing the market and securing the region which had contributed so much to Portuguese economic power and history was carried out during the Salazar dictatorship between the years 1930 through 1974.

More than 40,000 wine producers want a part in today's port wine boom.

The treasure-house of port wine begins near Regma.

If you also take into consideration the *Lei do Terço*, the rule that producers can sell only a third of their store of port wine a year, and that the port lodges are therefore forced every year to buy more wine if they want to keep selling, you

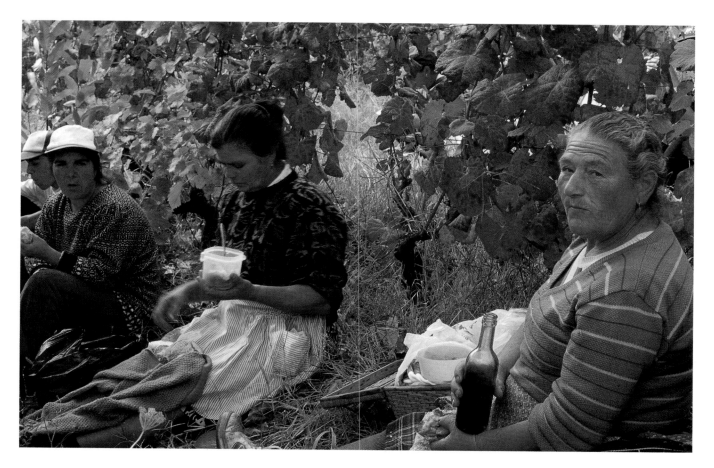

get an idea of the extent to which this cost-intensive business and this region are protected by a complicated system of rules. There was only one change as a result of Portugal's joining the E.C. in 1986: the monopoly of the port wine lodges in Vila Nova de Gaia to export port was broken. The Douro, a region previously protected but at the same time restricted, became free.

The development of the Douro and its vineyard sites marks a turning away from the exclusive production of fortified port wine. In 1982, the Douro was also officially declared a region for red and white wines (D.O.C.).

Sensational red wines come from the vineyards of the lower Corgo. In contrast, the Douro Superior often has temperatures over 130°F (45°C) and rainfall of 12 inches or less (30 cm). There are now test projects for root irrigation in progress. Barca Velha, and some of the other new top-quality red wines from Ferreira and Ramos Pinto, exploit this reservoir of the ripest grapes and tannins imaginable, although they mostly work with a blend which brings in acidity and freshness from grapes grown at a height of 1,600 to 2,000 feet (500 to 600 m). The upper Corgo, the region responsible for most of the better quality ports, lies in the heart of the Douro, not quite as dry and hot as the Douro Superior. Here you will also find the greatest number of high-quality port wine *quintas*.

Many families have been working for generations on the *quintas* in the Douro valley.

It is impossible, in the Douro region, to ignore the trend toward dry red wines—and the range on offer is vast. Compared to port wines, the unfortified wines previously amounted to no more than five percent. Now, apart from ambitious newcomers (for example, Quinta do Fojo), established producers (such as Niepoort's Quinta do Napoles) are also becoming more and more interested in this new branch of the wine trade. Traditional *quintas*, in earlier years interested only in sweet wines, are increasingly reacting to world-wide interest in Portuguese wine growing and in particular in dry reds. Modern technology, after all, has made possible what was in previous centuries hardly practicable: reductive production of non-fortified wines. There is as yet no distinctive style; native varieties are competing with international ones, and there is some enthusiastic experimenting with *barriques*. Traditionalists who will have pressing done only in *lagares* are competing with out-and-out modernists who are gathering experience from Spain and France. Red wine no longer plays a secondary role—indeed, the most far-reaching innovations are being made in this area.

PORTUGAL: LAND OF 500 GRAPE VARIETIES?

Portugal is often described as the country with the greatest variety of grapes in the world—according to frequently quoted estimates, there are supposed to be around 500 of them. But because no one has ever counted them all and distinguished genuine varieties from regional synonyms, there has to be some doubt about this figure. Wine experts assume, though, that there are 250 to 300 genuine grape varieties. Many have their origins in the early Middle Ages, and some may even be older. Over the centuries, they have often adapted perfectly to their individual *terroir*.

The climatic, geological, and topographical wealth on offer in Portugal is the principal reason for the development of such a great variety of grapes. The large wineries' tradition of blending wines, and taking no notice of the character of individual varieties, led to a situation which had lasted right up to the early 1980s, when research and registration was carried out for the purposes of joining the E.C. Before then, research into grape varieties and wines from single varieties was mainly a matter of accident, limited to a few initiatives such as that of the house of Ramos Pinto in the Douro region. Suddenly, decisions were needed as to which varieties were to be recom-

Pisar a pé (treading with the feet): this is the least damaging method of crushing grapes. However, it requires hours of rhythmical steady trampling. Not until the late evening does the bottle go round and people begin to enjoy themselves.

mended and authorized, to formalize the requirements for the quality wine regions. Single variety plantings are rare, except for a few regions which rely mainly on one variety, such as Baga in the Bairrada, or Periquita in Palmela. These decisions did not begin in any significant extent before the 1980s and continued into the 1990s.

Since these new plantations have started to bring in sufficient grapes, a positively meteoric fashion has arisen over the last few years of the last millennium for *vinhos varietais* or *vinhos estremes*, as the single-varietal wines are known. From a mixture of curiosity on the part of the wine producers and consumers, and hard work and good business sense on the part of the producers (who can thus sell specialty wines at higher prices), the range of these new wine varieties has increased enormously. Any sort of summing up is almost impossible. Some wine connoisseurs may be dubious that the aristocratic grape of the extreme north, the Alvarinho, has suddenly turned up in the south, and that there have been attempts to plant the Touriga Nacional, generally considered the noblest grape in Portugal (and possibly in the world), all over the place, wherever a producer's image needed a

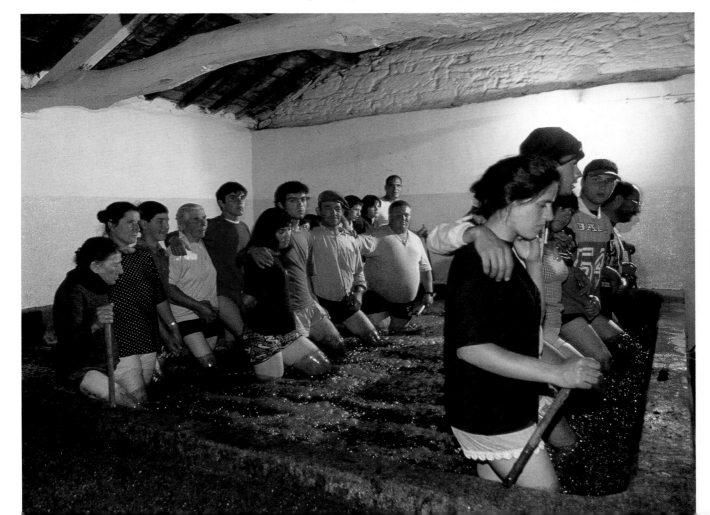

boost. But the fact that there are now many wines of all kinds coming onto the market is certainly more democratic and consumer-friendly than decisions taken in scientific experiments as to what grows best where. The overall picture of what varieties are to be recommended is changing with every new exciting wine that appears on the scene.

The danger exists, however, that if producers short-sightedly limit the varieties they grow to just a few, the diversity will soon become notice-ably less. But given their love of the peculiar, the typical Portuguese *bairrismo*, it is extremely likely that the unusual content of certain local specialties will continue.

It is important for the consumer to know that most of the single-VARIETAL wines come from new plantings. They cannot, therefore, ever have the concentrated expressiveness of older grape varieties. Some wines, though, do provide spec-

The traditional grape baskets in Portugal are tall woven baskets which may hold more than 100 lb (45 kg) of grapes.

tacular fruit and refinement. The *varietais* offer memorable, and often exciting, individual new wine experiences. Given the high prices, how-ever, it is worth asking whether, in some cases, cheaper wine from a blend of mixed-variety old vines would not have offered better value for money. The majority of leading dealers, such as the biggest Portuguese company S.O.G.R.A.P.E., are convinced that they should not invest every-thing in native or international grape varieties, and believe that blending varieties provides better, more complete wines. Many producers admit that the *vinhos estremes* are, at least for the moment, experimental, and they may perhaps go back completely or almost com-pletely to *cuvée* wines. And for those who dismiss *cuvées* of varieties because they cannot provide the traditional complexity of Portuguese wines, especially of port, we should point to the old traditional mixed blend of 10 or 20 varieties.

White grape varieties

• *Alvarinho*: A thick-skinned grape with only around 50 percent juice which combines body with a lot of freshness. It is the basis for Vinho Verde in the Monção sub-region. Often it is too smooth, and matured from vines which are too young; at the moment it is still sear-ching for a style.

• *Arinto*: This variety from Bucelas, praised by Shakespeare, is widespread in Portugal; it has unique piquancy and fine acidity and, though not related to Riesling, has a surpris-ingly similar flavor; it is traditionally also famed for fine sweet wines.

• *Azal*: A variety, underrated until now, from the Vinho Verde. In the Basto and Amarante sub-regions it can produce deliciously fresh, acid-accentuated, piquant aromatic wines.

• *Encruzado*: The best variety in Dão, with a low yield. Complex in aroma, it may, if aged in a *barrique*, approach the style of a good Burgundy.

• *Esgana Cão Sercial of Madeira*: Perhaps the finest and most stylish of all the varieties on Madeira. In Portugal itself it has impressively fine acidity, making it a rival of Arinto.

• *Loureiro*: The first grape variety developed in Verde after Alvarinho, this is extraordinarily fine and aromatic and reminiscent of Muscat; a slender delicate variety.

Red grape varieties

• *Aragonez (Tinta Roriz)*: The equivalent of the Spanish Tempranillo, with its deep blackish-red color, this is full of wild but fine fruit and intensive tannins. In the Douro, Dão, and other places it is also one of the top varieties if the yield is not too high.

• *Baga*: Small, thick-skinned grape which ripens late and has high acidity. It is vulnerable

Portugal's extraordinary wealth of native grape varieties is a treasure for the future.

to not ripening, and to rotting due to rain. In Bairrada it represents 90 percent of all vines and is mainly responsible for splendid wines with elegant fruit (blackcurrant) and tannin struc-ture, and also for characteristic table wines.

• *Bastardo*: Known in the French Jura as Trousseau, this is very rich in sugars and low in acidity, with a solid firmness but little refinement.

• *Castelão Nacional (Camarate)*: Because of its generous harvests, this is a popular variety in Estremadura, Ribatejo, and Bairrada. The first single-varietal wines have displayed com-plex fruit, class, and elegant, firm tannins.

• *Castelão Francês (Periquita)*: Probably the main variety in Portugal, particularly in the south and west. It has a very characteristic berry fruit; together with firm tannins, this can make great, maturable red wines in *terroirs* with low yield.

• *Tinta Barroca*: One of the five main port varieties, produces dark sweet grapes and a good yield. In northern sites the bite is missing.

• *Tinto Cão*: One of the top varieties in Douro, now also discovered in Dão. Low yields, herby flavors and sinewy acids; could rise to become a top wine.

• *Touriga Francês*: At 26.5 percent, this is the most frequently planted, stable-yield, late-ripening variety in the Douro region. Typically, it has fine fruit with plenty of black-berry and black cherry, and a herby note; very attractive red wines now also produced in the south, for example in Alequer.

• *Touriga Nacional*: The praises of this thick-skinned, small-berried, low-yield variety have been sung since the 13th century. In Dão, this grape is supposed to have provided 90 percent of all grapes until the phylloxera catastrophe in the 19th century. In Douro, it has always been praised as the Touriga Fina. Deep blackish-red opaque wines with complex aromas and no superficiality. The wine may vary from blackish to yellowish-red and contain flowery accents and herby notes. It is a miracle of complexity, ripeness, and tannins, but always astonishingly well balanced, and this applies to almost all Touriga Nacional wines that come onto the market. It is currently being discovered in Spain and could soon become one of the absolute top grape varieties in the world. Undoubtedly, it is one of the secrets of the great-ness of Vintage Port.

• *Trincadeira (Douro: Tinta Amarela)*: One of the leading Portuguese grape varieties, this produces herby, spicy wine with plummy, choc-olate fullness; in Ribatejo it often has excessive, sickly fruitiness. It can, however, depending on the vineyard site, produce good wines.

• *Vinhao (Douro: Sousao)*: This is the char-acteristic variety for the blackish-purplish-red Vinho Verde, but in the Douro it has pro-duced spectacular wines for laying down.

THE CULT OF
VINTAGE PORT

Vintage Port, the most interesting object of speculation among connoisseurs and collectors all over the world, was a cult wine long before the fine, fashionable wines of Italy, France, Spain, or the New World attracted the attention of wine enthusiasts. Port, in the past the standard drink in upper-class English society, was promoted to a popular status symbol for a new generation of American wine connoisseurs who liked particularly full-bodied wines. The development of port wine has been closely linked with British firms of shippers for several centuries, and the style of the wine has been formed by the demand from this export market. Many of today's port shipping firms, who still play a central role in the trade, show this legacy in their British names.

Vintage Port is not a liqueur, it is a wine. Only grapes, grown on a particular *terroir*, can produce such a wealth of aromatic substance, such an incomparable concentration of fruity sweetness, balanced by a restrained acidity and unrelentingly full, firm tannins. Anyone who has experienced the way in which slate soils can influence the elegance of many great white and red wines throughout the world will be able to discover the same inimitable delicacy and

The lines of the network of port production all meet up opposite Porto, in Vila Nova de Gaia. Here, nearly all the port houses keep their wineries, known as "Lodges."

subtlety in port wine, thanks to this type of rock, so common in Portugal and raised to exclusive status in the Douro valley (since 1756, grapes for port may be grown only on slate soils). No one would even think of producing port from grapes grown on granite soils. Granite can produce splendid dry red wines, as has been demonstrated in other regions, but never that degree of refinement in the sweetness of the fruit. Port wines from other regions, for example South Africa, Australia, or California, may be worthy of respect, but when it comes to the refinement and complexity of expression that distinguish a great Vintage Port,

The hour before midday

Eleven o'clock in the morning is the time for the daily wine tasting in Vila Nova de Gaia—the time for important decisions. With the greatest possible concentration, purchasing decisions are reached on samples from the Douro, or blends of wines in the cellars are devised and tasted. Such blends are necessary to keep up the stylistic continuity of a brand, but also to make delicate attempts at improvement, or to try out innovations.

Producing port wine is considered the most difficult task in any winery. All the classic improved wine-based drinks such as champagne, cognac, or sherry obtain their character from the master winemaker's work, and are creations made by experts, as different as they are difficult. But port, in all its diversity, its intensity, its delicacy, requires more than just a good master winemaker. The harmonious cooperation of sweetness, tannins, alcohol, and innumerable fruit notes in young port demands a genius. The port winemaker must always make the right decision among the many different sub-regions and vineyard sites, decide what should go in which corner of the cellar, whether the TAWNIES go into barrels for further maturing or

into the tank to support the character of the young fruit. He or she must subtly approach the desired nuance of color, find the balance between round, ripened and young, aggressive tannins, between the quiet maturity of age and energetic youthfulness. It is not an easy task. In many port lodges this gift, for it is a gift, has been handed down through the generations.

Probably the greatest of all port winemakers was the almost legendary Fernando Nicolai de Almeida, who not only formed a completely individual style of tawny for Ferreira, but also created, in Barca Velha, the most famous red wine in Portugal, and thereby began a development which today is being introduced to more and more port lodges.

In an age of technology, of academically qualified enologists with sober intellectual ideas about wine, in an age when marketing strategists and vintner-managers look on the grapes and wines of individual regions as the stuff of which entrepreneurial success is made, the respect shown in Gaia to styles of taste, as well as the serious discussion between modernism and tradition, may seem surprising. However, despite all the routine, in many lodges tasting is

a real process, and analysis is still decisive. It is interesting to note the way the taster, who is also in charge of the cellar, is able to express or convey his point of view to all the modern technicians and engineers, marketing experts, owners, and business managers, while in many other places it is the other way around. Long years of practical experience meet technical, chemical, and business knowledge, and all parties are bound to profit by it. Wine experts and business people create something together. Newly fashionable wine theories, such as those which dominate many regions today, making intrusive changes and influencing winemakers, thankfully do not yet have the last word in Gaia.

In the confrontation between wine theory and complex intuitive experience, gathered and increased over the years, the wines themselves are still the most convincing argument. How can such wines be produced in all their individuality and diversity according to a schedule based on dry facts? The last great port wine tasters, of whom only a few are left, are greatly superior to the wine experts, but the wine experts can learn about tasting from port wine—and they soon see that technology isn't everything.

the imitations cannot compete. Fortified sweet wines or "Port Wines" from other countries seldom achieve the complexity of a real Vintage Port. This guarantee is founded on the fact that the region was the first in the world to be demarcated, and then divided into levels of quality. As long as port wine was the monopoly of the port lodges and the estates were unable to export on their own behalf, Vintage Port was almost always made from A-sites, at worst from B-sites. The decisive factor for the unusually high standard, however, was the fierce competition in the narrow streets of the port of Vila Nova de Gaia, from which port wine was exclusively distributed until 1986. In addition, consumers could rely on the exporters' association, the Instituto do Vinho do Porto (I.V.P.), which would never have acknowledged a weak vintage in its sample testing. These quality-conscious guardians of a unique wine would never have tolerated any damage to the reputation of the most reliable economic power of the north, *vinho do Porto*, at least not in the top class. A certain readiness to compromise probably existed in the other categories.

The Douro river, which made wine history, is the lifeline of Porto.

This traditional system has started to change, due to the admission of the "Douro people," the estates and cooperatives in the region. With rather less in the way of experience and knowledge of winery techniques, but balanced by more confidence in producing good wines even from C-sites, some of them manage to do just that. Even if the reliability of the guarantee has suffered from these changes, it is still higher than for other wine categories, due to the tasting committee of the I.V.P., with their long experience and high standards. In the end, however, the strict selection of vintages decides the quality. Many houses produce Vintage Port only in really good years. In less favorable years the wine is sold as Single Quinta Vintage. But alongside these "second rank" Single Quinta Vintages, there are now a number of "first class" Single Quinta Ports, bottled both by new estates and the great port houses. Symington, for example, sells Quinta dos Malvedos as a so-called "off" port, but Quinta do Vesuvio is declared a Single Quinta Port even in top quality years.

Select Producers of Port Wine and Douro

The range offered by the port wine lodges comprises Ruby, Tawny, 10 Years, 20 Years, Vintage, Vintage Character, L.B.V. (Late Bottled Vintage). Colheita, 30 and 40 Years are rarities. There are also Single Quinta Vintages (S.Q.V.). To avoid repetition, the following section will refer only to dry, mainly red wines. Unless otherwise mentioned, the companies are based in Vila Nova de Gaia.

J. W. Burmester & CA***–*****
The new owners, the Amorims, have undertaken to keep up the high-quality stock of old Colheitas and Tawnies. The traditional Vintages and L.B.V.s display great structure, even in less good years.

Ferreira***–*****
• *Wines: Douro Tinto: includes Barca Velha, Reserva Especial, Callabriga, Quinta da Leda and Touriga Nacional, Vinha Grande*
The company, founded in 1751 and now taken over by S.O.G.R.A.P.E., is the market leader and synonymous with good port in Portugal. Excellent older Tawnies. Outstanding position in the red wine world with Barca Velha, the legendary and most expensive red wine in the country.

Niepoort S.A.***–*****
• *Wines include: Redoma Tinto, Batuta, Quinta do Passadouro, Secundum*
More than almost any other winemaker, Dirk van der Niepoort has created a furor in recent years with his excellent ports and complex dry wines. His Quinta do Napoles has become synonymous with a new generation of Douro wines.

Quinta dal Cavalhosa****
Santa Adrião
• *Wine: Campo Ardosa*
The German wine-producing trio Werner Näkel, Bernhard Breuer and Bernd Philippi brought their first wine onto the market in 2002. The Campo Ardos red, from their 20 acre (8 ha) estate, is produced solely from local grapes: Roriz, Touriga Francese, Touriga Nacional and Tinta Barocca.

Quinta de Covelos**–****
Peso du Régua
• *Wines: Tinto and Reserva, Calheiros Cruz Grande Escolha*
Until 1994, José Carlos Calheiros sold his wine to the big port houses. Together with the enologist Anselmo Mendes, he then began to produce Douro wines. His top quality wine thrives at a height of 1,500 feet (450 m).

Quinta do Côtto***–*****
Cidadelhe
• *Wines: Douro: Branco, Tinto, Grande Escolha Tinto, Vinho Regional Minho, Paço de Teixeiró*
As early as the 1970s, Miguel Champalimaud was one of the first to work on devising top quality red wines.

1   A.A. Cálem & Filho Lda
2   A.A. Ferreira S.A.
3   Adriano Ramos Pinto-Vinhos S.A.
4   Barros, Almeida & Cª Vinhos S.A.
5   C.N. Kopke & Cª VINHOS S.A.
6   C. da Silva (Vinhos) S.A.
7   Churchill Graham Lda
8   Cockburn Smithes & Cª S.A.
9   Croft & Cª Lda
10 Delaforce Sons & Cª Vinhos S.A.
11 Fonseca Guimaraens-Vinhos S.A.
12 Forrester & Cª S.A.
13 Gran Cruz Porto-Soc. Comercial de Vinhos Lda
14 Hunt Constantino-Vinhos S.A.
15 J. Carvalho Macedo Lda
16 J.H. Andresen, Sucrs. Lda
17 J.W. Burmester & Cª Lda
18 Manoel D. Poças Júnior-Vinhos S.A.
19 Martinez Gassiot & Co. Ltd
20 Niepoort (Vinhos) S.A.
21 Osborne (Vinhos de Portugal) & Cª Lda
22 Quarles Harris & Cª Lda
23 Quinta do Noval-Vinhos S.A.
24 Romariz-Vinhos S.A.
25 Rozés Lda
26 Sandeman & Cª S.A.
27 Silva & Cosens Lda
28 Smith Woodhouse & Cª Lda
29 Sociedade Agrícola e Comercial dos Vinhos Messias S.A.
30 Sociedade dos Vinhos Borges S.A.
31 Taylor, Fladgate & Yeatman-Vinhos S.A.
32 W. & J. Graham & Co.
33 Warre & Cª S.A.
34 Wiese & Krohn, Sucrs. Lda
35 Associação das Empresas de Vinho do Porto

Profiting from a mixed blend from many old vines, his plain Douro is often magnificent, while Grande Escolha, made only in top quality years, is a unique wine with a wild but fine expressiveness.

QUINTA DO FÓJO****
SABROSA
• *Wines: Fójo Tinto, Vinha do Fójo*
After supplying the most select Vintage brands for many years, Margarida Serôdio amazed the Portuguese wine world in 1996 with her first red wines.

QUINTA DA GAIVOSA***–****
SANTA MARTA DE PENAGUIÃO
• *Wines include: Branco, Tinto, Quinta das Caldas, Quinta do Vale da Raposa, Grande Escolha*
Domingos Alves e Sousa claimed their place as top Douro producers in 1992 with Gaivosa. An outstanding range of classic and red Douros.

QUINTA DO NOVAL***–*****
PINHÃO
This house produces excellent Vintages and fully fruited old Colheitas. The Nacional Vintage, from ungrafted vines, is legendary.

QUINTA DE LA ROSA**–****
PINHÃO
• *Wines: Tinto, Reserva, Vale da Clara Tinto*
One of the pioneers of port marketing. Even in weaker years, the Vintages are of a very high standard.

QUINTO DO VALE DE DONA MARIA***–****
PORTO
• *Wines: Tinto, Vintage*
This quinta on the Rio Torto has vines which are over 40 years old. Christiano van Zeller, previously the owner of the Quinta do Noval, produces both remarkable port and concentrated dry red wines.

For the latter, pressing in the *lagar* and aging in French *barriques* is a matter of course.

RAMOS PINTO***–****
• *Wines: Duas Quintas Tinto, Reserva*
A pioneer in the 1970s and 1980s of research on new types of cultivation and varieties, this company, still run by João Nicola de Almeida, now belongs to the champagne house of Louis Roederer. The red wines are among the best in the Duoro region.

REAL COMPANHIA VELHA**–****
• *Wines include: Douro Branco: Quinta do Sidrô Chardonnay; Douro Tinto: Porca de Murca Reserva, Evel Grande Escolha, Quinta dos Arciprestes*
The most important vineyard owner in the Douro can look back on a great past. The director of this family business, Pedro Silva Reis, is now bringing the house back to its origins in the Douro.

SYMINGTON GROUP: DOW'S**–*****/ W. & J. GRAHAM & CO.**–*****/ WARRE & CA. S.A. QUINTO DO VESUVIO****–*****
The fourth generation of the family is in charge of this company, which consists of seven houses (30 percent share of the market) and is mainly active in the higher quality sector. The Symingtons also own the *quintas* do Bomfin, da Cavadinha and dos Malvedos.

TAYLOR, FLADGATE & YEATMAN VINHOS S.A.***–***** / FONSECA ***–*****
Taylor, founded in 1692, was the first port house in 1744 to own vineyards, and has remained one of the most innovative today. One only needs to call to mind dry white port, S.Q.V., L.B.V., or the First Estate, a higher quality Ruby. With its sister house of Fonseca, it has become synonymous for top Vintages. Quinta de Vargellas is Taylor's most famous S.Q.V.

Port wine categories

• *Ruby*: The sweet, fruity and full-bodied wines are deep ruby red, usually aged without wood and two to three years old. Small houses often offer a better choice than the big brand producers.
• *Tawny*: This light-colored wine, about three years old, is today the standard aperitif in France. It is soft, harmonious, and uncomplicated. A noticeable maturity of wood, from aging in the barrel, and fine nut and caramel notes are displayed mainly by older Fine Tawnies.
• *New-Type Port*: This category, as yet without an official name, describes higher-quality port wines from the better vineyards, with a maturing period of four to six years. These are classified between the fruity Ruby type and Tawny.
• *Vintage Character*: These are concentrated, fruity, deep red port wines, rich in tannins, separated from Vintage only by the very last bit of finish and concentration.
• *L.B.V./Late Bottled Vintage*: A less expensive variation on Vintage Port, which does not need to be decanted as the wine has already spent four to six years in the barrel and/or in the tank. As with Vintage Character, it is a deep, almost blackish red, full-bodied and fruity, with an individual expression according to the vintage year, just as with the true Vintage. It also often possesses a specific refinement.
• *Port Wine with Age*: The age information refers to the average age of the blended wines. A reddish tone in the Tawny color indicates a share of younger wines, but it may provide attractive fruitiness. The increase in demand for truly old Tawnies has led to prices shooting upwards in recent years.
• *Colheita Port*: A port with a vintage year matured entirely in wooden casks, which has kept and concentrated its density of aroma and even its fruit notes. The argument as to whether Colheita is preferable to Vintage Port continues: it should be noted that the great Vintages of the 20th century were often in essence Colheita types, only being bottled after ten years or longer. Today, Colheita will be aged in the cask for at least eight years, but will not come onto (or back onto) the market for 50 or more years.
• *Vintage Port*: This is bottled after only two years. It is a reductively aged wine, which will keep its entire youthful fruit for the whole of its long bottled life. For good Vintage Ports, this may last many decades, whereas somewhat weaker Vintages reach their optimum level after 10 or 20 years. The most famous port wine lodges declare a vintage only in truly great years, at best three times in a decade. Over the last ten years Single Quinta Vintage Port has been produced. For these, the wine comes from a single *quinta* in the so-called off years, when quality and quantity are not worthy of a Vintage declaration, but the wine of the individual *quintas* has still been aged and bottled in the Vintage manner. Many new wine estates are bottling a Vintage every year, convinced that they can produce Vintage quality regularly. They are not wrong in this, as the great port houses are mainly concerned with sophistication and their exclusive reputation.
• *White Port*: A sweet alternative to red port, the white version is usually very plain and somewhat superficial by comparison, although there are a few very convincing examples which have been aged for longer periods in the cask. The dry (or *seco*) and extra dry (*extra-seco*) varieties are better known. Most are rather neutral, though some display a more intensive, nutty, finely matured style.

BAIRRADA

In the wine world it would be virtually impossible to find another region with such an unmistakably original and striking style, liable to split critics equally and irreconcilably into devotees and opponents. The Baga grape produces 90 to 100 percent of Bairrada red wine. This variety has a tendency to bear high yields and ripen late, which means that problems with the rain that slowly creeps up in October are often unavoidable. This wine is often accused of being too sour, too heavy in tannins, and sometimes also not intensive enough in color, that is to say that its deep red is not dark enough. All this may be true. Bairrada wine is not good in every year, and it is therefore unpopular among those who want to rely on as consistent a taste as possible for their marketing (or drinking) strategies, and who are not prepared to take on special qualities. The wine can change its character from a harsh, yet often amazingly hearty and drinkable wine to a highly concentrated, firm classic with many years of maturing potential. (The wines from the many old vines with low yields excel themselves particularly here.) Anyone who takes the trouble to judge the lesser wines together with the cuisine of the region, for instance in combination with *chanfana*, goat's meat marinated for a week in Bairrada and then slowly braised, will realize that no other wine suits it so well.

The weaknesses and the strengths of the Bairrada wines are reminiscent of Barolo, the Italian wine most highly estimated by connoisseurs. In bad years Barolo is not known by this name, but is leveled down to Nebbiolo d'Alba. Only the best producers in Bairrada do the same—bottling wine only in good or great years, and sometimes putting only *reservas* or

Coimbra, once the seat of the kings of Portugal, is better known as the oldest Portuguese university city than for its wine. But the quality of the surrounding red wine areas of Bairrada and Dão have made Coimbra into a popular place for wine connoisseurs.

garrafeiras (which means Private Reserve) onto the market. In general, however, this is not the case. "Little" Bairradas can be obtained from one of the six cooperatives, which produce quite worthy and occasionally even excellent wines, or you can go to one of the 30 or so wineries within the region (or to one of the 20 wineries outside—they mostly purchase their wine from cooperatives).

The "great" Bairradas are also reminiscent of the best traditional Barolos in their purity, but they are perhaps even more unwilling to compromise. Ruis Alves, who grew up in the Bairrada and has been a wine expert with practical experience for 35 years, runs a small laboratory, although he is no chemist. He represents the anachronistic fundamentalism of the region. Do not take the grapes off the stalks (or at most de-stem only part of them), ferment them all in cool *lagares*, which traditionally hold about 530 gallons (2,000 liters), do not improve, filter, or stabilize anything, age the wine in large wooden barrels holding many hundreds of gallons (as is done in Barolo) and allow it to clarify naturally over many years by RACKING.

On many estates today, wine is still made in exactly this manner. Some of these estates, led by those advised by Ruis Alves, are so consistent in following this line and their wines are so highly selected (late harvesting of grapes with ripe stalks is Alves' main tenet of belief), that a connoisseur of great wines would fall silent in awe at the effect on nose and tastebuds of such a 10-, 20-, or 30-year-old *garrafeira* or *reserva*. These wines are more drinkable, more elegant than a Barolo, sometimes close to Bordeaux and yet purer and wilder.

Acidity, tannin, and fruit, the three elements which characterize a great wine, are always present. Sugar comes from the late ripening process. This striking authentic style probably has its origins in history. Bairrada has been cultivated at least since antiquity, and it is believed that vines may have been grown here in prehistoric times. The region is close to the sea, there is sufficient rainfall (40 inches/100 cm), and the best vineyards, with their clay, marl, and chalk soils on rocks from the middle and upper Jurassic, lie along main roads. There has always been intensive trade, both within and outside the region, and successful exports can be made only with good quality, stable wines. Natural acidity, added to ripeness, originally made Bairrada an ideal blending partner for Douro wines.

In the Middle Ages, the powerful monasteries of Lorvão and Vacariça encouraged cultural

development in the region, as, to an even greater extent, did the church in Coimbra, promoting this third largest city in Portugal to be the religious center of the country, which it remained for centuries. The concentration of sacred knowledge was extended by the more profane variety (a small part of which may even have been viticultural knowledge) in 1307, when the University of Lisbon, founded in 1290, moved to Coimbra. In the 14th and 15th centuries, in the golden age of seafaring and trade, around 28 percent of the total area of the region is said to have been stocked with vines. Today, the wine-growing area is a modest 32,100 acres (13,000 ha), of which more than 80 percent is stocked with red varieties (primarily Baga). A few winegrowers are beginning to pay more attention to white varieties.

SELECT PRODUCERS IN BAIRRADA

CASA DO CANTO (ALEXANDRA TRINIDADE)**−****
ACAS, ANADIA
25 acres (10 ha) • *Wines: Tinto and Tinto Garrafeira*
This estate, dating from the 17th century, was in 1856 the largest *adega* in the entire region. Extraordinarily stern, classic, very pure red wines from the best *barrinhos* (mineral-rich clay) soils and old vines.

CASA DE SAIMA***−*****
SANGALHOS, ANADIA
49 acres (20 ha); 80,000 bottles • *Wines: Colheita Tinto, Tinto Reserva, Tinto Garrafeira, Branco*
The star of the region ever since the great Garrafeiras of 1985, 1987 and 1990. Even straightforward Colheita, the estate's only wine in weaker years, provides a classic red Barraida for not much money.

CAVES ALIANCA*−****
SANGALHOS, ANADIA
753.5 acres (305 ha); some bought-in grapes; 10,000,000 bottles • *Wines: Barraida: Geleria Bical, Tinto Reserva, Tinto Garrafeira; Dão: Reserva Tinto, Tinto Particular; Douro: Foral Reserva Tinto, Foral Grande Escolha Tinto; Alentejo: Alabastro Tinto, Quinta da Terrugem; Vinho Verde: Casal Mendes; Alenquer: Quinta da Cortezia Tinta Roriz*
The biggest winery in the Barraida is the third biggest name in the country after S.O.G.R.A.P.E. and J. Fonseca. Its range runs from simple branded products to some of the best wines. Alongside their outstanding in-house enologist, Franciso Antunes, the company has recently appointed the world-famous Michel Rolland as consultant.

CAVES SÃO JOÃO, AVELÃES DE CAMINHO**−****
ANADIA
62 acres (25 ha); some bought-in grapes; 1,300,000 bottles • *Wines include: Barraida: Frei João Tinto, Frei João Reserva Tinto, Reserva Tinto V.R. Poco do Lobo: Tinto, Arinto, Cabernet-Sauvingon; Dão: Porta dos Cavaleiros Branco, Tinto, Reserva Tinto, Espumante Branco Bruto, Espumante Tinto Bruto*
Luiz Costa and the Caves São João, which he manages with his brother Alberto, are an institution in the Barraida. Among the winery brands, the wines are the most reliable in the traditional style.

LUIS PATO*−****
ÓIS DE BAIRRO, ANADIA
173 acres (70 ha); 300,000 bottles • *Wines include: Quinta do Ribeirinho, João Pato Cabernet Sauvignon, Vinhas Velhas Branco, Tinto, Vinha Fromal Branco, Quinta do Moinho Tinto, Vinha Pan Tinto, Vinha Barrosa Tinto, Vinha Barrio Tinto, Baga pé Franco, Espumante Rosé Bruto, Baga Bruto*
As a protest against political in-fighting, the chemist Luis Pato, the best and most internationally renowned winemaker of the region, sells his wines as Vinho Regional Beiras. The wines are modeled on the style of Bordeaux.

QUINTA DAS BÁGHEIRAS
59 acres (24 ha); 90,000 bottles • *Wines: Tinto, Reserva, Garrafeira, Espumante Super Reserva Bruto Branca, Rosé Bruto, Tinto Bruto, Velha Reserva Bruto*
The young Màrio Sérgio Alves Nuno, a wine and sparkling wine enthusiast, produces some of the best sparkling wines in the region.

QUINTA DE BAIXO ****
CORDINHÃ, CASTANHEDE
25 acres (10 ha); 25,000 bottles • *Wines: Reserva Tinto, Garrafeira Tinto*
Traditional *lagar* winery with many old vines on excellent clay and limestone soils. The 1991 Garrafeira was the first great wine, and it has demonstrated consistency and class ever since.

QUINTA DA RIGODEIRA***−****
FOGUEIRA, ANADIA
37 acres (15 ha); 65,000 bottles • *Wines: Branco; Tinto: →Quinta da Dona Tinto, Espumante Branco Bruto*
Ataide Demedo produces the most classic and finest wines of all the "modern" winemakers. This is due to the best *terroir* and careful production.

SIDONIO DE SOUSA****−*****
LARGO DA VILA, SANGALHOS
25 acres (10 ha) • *Wines: Reserva and Garrafeira Tinto*
These wines have enjoyed cult status since the 1985 Garrafeira. The best are characterized by high tannin concentration but also by deep red fruit and elegance.

Dāo

Old Dāo wines are often still a pleasure today. Without new wood, indeed almost without wood at all, they display everything—apart from that final finishing touch of elegance—that makes a great wine, and is often missing in would-be great and high-priced ones: substance, character, hidden fruit, acidity, tense and delicate tannins, and an aging capacity of more than 10 or 20 years, together with a life span that can exceed this term considerably.

The secret of this quality is none other than the Dāo region itself, which is still dominated by vineyards 50 years old and more. These are scattered and hidden among the hilly landscape between thick forests of eucalyptus and pines, partly on terraces of granite which often have to be broken up or dynamited for new plantings. Few yields here exceed 530 gallons (20 hl). Of the 100,000 wine producers in Dāo, nine-tenths produce less than 1,320 gallons (5,000 liters) a year, and their production makes up 55 percent of the total for the region. A quarter of the 49,000 acres (20,000 ha) under vine is set out as hedging for other cultivation. Of the remaining three quarters, 19,026 plots are smaller than a half acre (0.25 ha), and 27,785 are even smaller than a quarter acre (0.1 ha).

In the summer heat, the grapes tend to be extraordinarily thick-skinned and thereby achieve a high concentration of color and tannins. High annual rainfall of over 40 inches

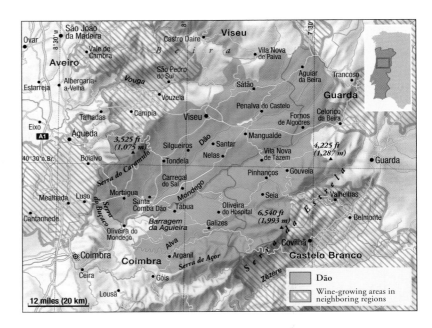

Apart from the numerous small producers, the hilly lands of the Dāo region also boast some larger estates, which plant and cultivate vines in a modern manner on the crumbly granite soils.

(100 cm), in places even over 47 inches (120 cm), also creates enough reserves of moisture somewhere in the granite and slate soils to do the old vines good. Other advantages of the region are the vineyard sites at a height of 2,600 feet (800 m), where the grapes are subject to distinct variations in temperature which help to conserve, in the best possible way, acidity, aromas, substance, and class. This means that natural qualities are developed in the grapes which in other places can be achieved only by the most cunning winemaking technology and aging in new oak casks. Dāo vintners still have to learn that a *barrique* does not add anything new, but merely intensifies what is there already. The exceptions are Senhores Costa and Alves, who have always maintained a healthy skepticism when it comes to the use of new wood.

One of the Dāo region's great disadvantages is, paradoxically, also a decided advantage and has secured it a reliable following. Its prices are in a class in which such compromise-free, solid, and even delicate wines are usually no longer to be found. In comparative tastings, it may show up worse in a class of wines costing less than 5–8 euros (US $6–10) than in a tasting of international quality wine costing 15, 20 or 25 euros (US $18, 25 or 31), according to how many true connoisseurs are present in each group. This has unfortunately led to many Dāo wines being made more pleasant, more rounded, and more stable, so that discovering their quality is not such hard work and they fit better into the under 5 euros (US $6) category. To save Dão wine's honor, it should be stressed that many wineries offer very reliable wines and most Dãos are well worth the money. At present, probably the most reputable and classic range is that offered by Maia Encosta from Borges, among the big brands (about a million bottles).

A good Dão, therefore, forms the taste of all levels of society, and Porta dos Cavaleiros is the evidence. It is a top-quality wine served in numerous small and simple *tascas* and bars. Often excellent Portuguese home cooking can be enjoyed together with this good, almost too great wine, and the landlord will enthuse about his wine because he treats himself to it on his few days off in the year. It is also the wine served every day at lunch, both in the works canteen and in the restaurant for the knowledgeable and experienced management of many famous port lodges. More's the pity that we can't get enough of it.

The wine has just the right strengths that characterize Dão as a whole, and have made it the greatest, most recognized, and first origin-demarcated red wine in the country. Luíz Costa, above all, is the man who has always tended these very strengths. He has never narrowly confined himself to his home ground—the Bairrada—but has considered the superior class of Dão and knows how to make use of it. All new developments in the Dão region, whether by the estates or the cooperatives, should always keep his long-term and consistent model in mind. The goal should be an improvement, a refinement of Costa's Porta dos Cavaleiros. Any divergence into aggressive new wood, to single-

In the Dão region, people are used to all too frequent rainfall, which even allows grass to spring up between the rows of vines. Quite surprisingly, the yields still remain minimal, but they produce wines of notable intensity.

Following page
Dão *garrafão*—the everyday wine of the inhabitants—is a basic commodity for the Portuguese population.

varietal wines, or toward young vines could take more class out of Dão than Porta already has. Its *reserva*, with the labelled cork, should long hold its place among the top wines of Dão. To better this wine in elegance and depth is a challenge which some have now risen to successfully.

Luíz Costa and Ruis Alves

It may seem surprising that Luíz Costa, the driving force behind Caves São João, the Bairrada, and indeed the whole Portuguese wine economy, should receive his well-deserved honors in this, the section on Dão. He is one of those responsible for the renaissance in the Bairrada and also the initiator and a co-founder of the Bairrada wine association, the Academy of Bairrada Wine, which has provided so many services after only two years. The list of Luíz Costa's great and remarkable services is a long one. He has inspired the whole wine world, devised a cork label and had it printed, opened the Portuguese market for the regular magnum bottle, supported the numbering of bottles, just as he does the regular indication of the vintage year even for his plain wines, not just for *reservas* and *garrafeiras*. At a time when Dão region is once more receiving praise from the critics, it is right and proper that we should honor the man who has been a constant advocate and champion of

Dão wine, even in times when (with a few exceptions) its reliability and continuity have been missing, and with them, the proof that Dão is always a vastly underrated wine, especially in the lower price categories.

In the 1960s, with his Dão brand Porta dos Cavaleiros, Luíz Costa created and nurtured a brand which perfectly expresses the greatest traditional strengths of the Portuguese wine trade up to the present day. These are the tracing and purchasing of good wines, in particular from good cooperatives, the care of these wines in his own winery, and their presentation to the market at the best possible time for the wine to have its full effect.

To be sure, Costa's Dão, from cultivation to aging, is not as finely formed as many of the Bordeaux wines which Costa considers as his models. Working within the established tradition of the great port wine houses, he demonstrates that a determined purchasing policy toward the raw material of the wine and its

origin from good vineyard sites can be used to create a quality standard, a brand which certainly approaches the great wines in purity and in character.

Wines nurtured since the 1970s by the Bairrada fundamentalist Ruis Alves display a style of aging which is otherwise only seen in top-quality grapes. These combine the classic Dão quality—a wine which may show greatness even as a peasant wine—with the greatest luxury and the eloquence of the wines of some cult wine producers. These are completely unsweetened, unimproved, unfiltered, unstabilized. They become ready for bottling and drinking only by repeated racking of the wine from barrel to barrel, or in this case mainly from tank to tank. While his João brand from the Bairrada is an excellent example of the success of this philosophy, an even better one is his plain Dão Porta dos Cavaleiros. (It goes without saying that the *reserva* is also an excellent wine.)

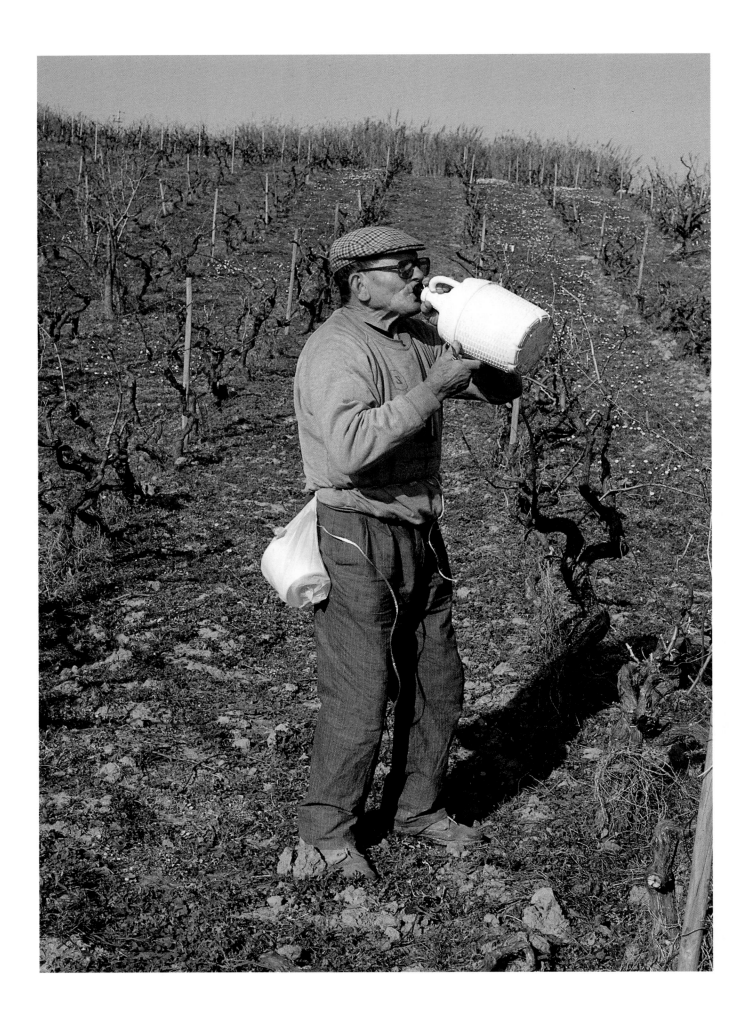

The undiscovered Beiras

As a Vinho Regional term, the Beiras extend across a great part of central Portugal and are divided into the sub-regions of Beira Litoral, to which the Bairrada and the areas extending beyond it belong, and the Beira Alta, the regional wine term for Dão. In the north, an additional part of the Beiras is the Lafoes I.P.R., producing its acidic fresh wine, both white and red, which is similar to Vinho Verde. In the interior of the country, just bordering on the Douro, is the D.O.C. region Tavora-Varosa which, until quite recently, consisted of the two separate I.P.R. regions of Varosa and Encosas da Nave.

Traditionally this region is the well-kept secret of wineries throughout Portugal, who see it as the source of base wines for their better-class sparkling and white wines. It was a deliberate move for the Sociedade Agrícola e Comercial do Varosa, also known as *Caves Murganheira*, to

settle in delightful Tarouca with its famous monastery. It is one of the oldest and biggest Portuguese sparkling wine producers, using the traditional method, and it is now also involved in producing red, white and rosé wine, although success has to date been variable.

The red wine potential of this region—of which 116,250 gallons (4,400 hl) have already been registered as D.O.C. in 1998—is excellent, as has been shown again and again by individual bottles. Slate soils like those in the Douro region, but combined with a higher altitude climate leading to more acidity and less alcohol, are guarantees of success.

Right in the east of Portugal, with a climate that is already clearly continental, the new D.O.C. Beira Interior has been formed from the I.P.R.s Castelo Rodrigo, Pinhel, and Cova da Beira. As in the rest of the region, the white wines here are interesting, while the red wine

potential has not yet been sufficiently exploited or is still hidden away and dormant.

The Quinta do Cardo in Figuera do Castelo Rodrigo is undoubtedly the most active company in the region at present. The exceptionally fruit-accented red wines, some of them single-varietal wines, are unfortunately aged for drinking young and do not make the most of their resources. The white wines, in their elegance and refinement, are already among the best that Portugal can offer, and demonstrate the potential excellence of the region.

If you look at the former greatness and fame of the Cistercian and Benedictine monasteries which existed in all the wine centers of the Beiras, and if in the vineyards you sample any of the grapes, which are outstanding even for Portugal, you can foresee a great future for interesting wines. However, for mass-produced wine, the region is much too barren, dry, and stony.

SELECT PRODUCERS IN DÃO

CASA DE SANTAR***–****
NELAS
296.5 acres (120 ha); 600,000 bottles • Wines: Tinto, Branco, Reserva Tinto, Castas de Santar Branco, Tinto, Touriga Nacional, Encruzado, Alfrocheiro Preto, Tinta Roriz
Casa de Santar is the oldest and biggest wine estate in the Dão area, but its rise to the top did not begin until 1991 with large-scale investment in its own production. Under the management of Pedro de Vasconcelos de Sousa, who studied enology in Montpellier, the wines have, over the last few years, increasingly shown the potential of the outstanding vineyard sites, which have granite soils partly mixed with slate.

MARIA DE FÁTIMA TEIXEIRA RIBEIRO SILVA***
22 acres (9 ha); 60,000 bottles • Wines: Tinto Reserva, Branco, Reserva, Tinto Garrafeira
On the south-facing granite soils, Maria de Fátima Teixeira Ribeiro Silva cultivates a classic mix of varieties. After fermentation in the traditional *lagar*, the wine is aged for two years in stainless steel and used French wood. Supple, relatively soft, and yet long-lasting Dão type.

QUINTA DA FONTE DE OURO***–****
MORTÁGUA
25 acres (10 ha); 70,000 bottles • Wines: Tinto, Touriga Nacional Vinho Regional: Quinta da Giesta Tinto, Branco
In 1991 Nuno Cancella Abreu, winemaker on the Quinta da Romeira in Bucelas, together with colleagues, decided to build up a new style of Dão wine *quinta* in his home region in Mortágua. With vineyards in Nelas and Mortágua (50 percent with the top-quality variety Touriga Nacional, the rest other classic Dão varieties), the aim is to create a premium Dão, to be sold only in good years, with careful aging. In other years, the Vinho Regional, to be drunk earlier, will be produced.

QUINTA DA PELLADA/QUINTA DE SÃES***–*****
PINHANCOS, SEIA
99 acres (40 ha); 100,000 bottles • Wines: Quinta de Sães: Branco, Tinto, Reserva Tinta Roriz, Quinta da

Pellada: Branco, Tinto, Tinta Roriz, Jaen, Jaen/Touriga Nacional, Tinta Roriz e Touriga Nacional. Touriga Nacional/Alfrocheiro, Touriga Nacional
Even if none of the new Dão *quintas* have yet come out of the stormy experimental phase, Alvaro de Castro has impressively demonstrated in recent years the great density and complexity, and the supple beguiling opulence that a great Dão can reveal.

QUINTA DOS ROQUES***–****
QUINTA DAS MAIAS
173 acres (70 ha); 150,000 bottles • Wines: Quinta dos Roques: Branco, Tinto, Reserva, Branco Encruzado, Alfrocheiro Preto, Tinta Roriz, Tinto Cão, Touriga Nacional; Quinta das Maias: Branco, Tinto, Malvasia Fina, Jaen
Manuel Lopes de Oliviera is a newcomer to the business with ideas. His recently planted vineyards are now coming into their "prime"; concentrated, spicy reds and surprising whites.

S.O.G.R.A.P.E.*–****
AVINTES
889 acres (360 ha); bought-in grapes; 35,000,000 bottles • Wines: Mateus Rosé, Branco, Vinho Verde Branco: Quinta de Azevedo, Morgadio da Torre, Gazela; Bairrada: Reserva Tinto, Branco; Dão: Grão Vasco Tinto, Branco, Sogrape Reserva Tinto, Quinta das Carvalhais →Tinto Reserva, →Touriga Nacional, Tinta Roriz, Alfrocheiro Preto, Duque de Viseu →Branco, →Tinto, Encruzado
The world's first great brand specialist today makes half its turnover with a diversified, in part very high-class, range. Gazela and Grão Vasco have been built up to sell millions. The most surprising thing about the company is that there are hardly any wines that are not worth the money; some, such as the Douro Reserva Tinto or the Duque de Viseu Branco and Tinto, are, especially in good years, excellent wines at an acceptable price. The Quinta da Carvalhais wines, especially the *reserva* (*cuvée*), and the Touriga Nacional in some years come close to the very peak of excellence of Portuguese wines.

ESTREMADURA

Estremadura, in the past known simply as "Oeste" (the West), today means the wine region formed by the 19-mile (30-km) wide coastal area from Lisbon to north of the town of Leira. Here an Atlantic-influenced climate provides freshness. In the past, Oeste was seen as a provider of cheap, light, mainly white wines. Hybrids, lower-quality grape varieties and mass yields were widespread. There were only a few quality products, such as the red wine from Obidos, one of the eight D.O.C. regions of today's Estremadura.

The old Oeste region, never precisely demarcated, was joined with the D.O.C. regions of Carcavelos, Colares, and Bucelas, making this region today the most complex creation of the new regional wine divisions. The classic Bucelas goes from strength to strength, and its Arinto, with its unbelievably attractive acidity, provides what is perhaps the most elegant and refined white wine in Portugal. Wines from the unfortunately almost moribund Colares region, with soils so sandy that PHYLLOXERA never had a chance there, can be magnificent and almost as capable of development as the legendary Colares red from Ramisco grapes, a wine of pure dune sand with powerful tannins and a distinct hint of salt.

Until recently no Syrah was grown in Portugal, but the new generation of wine producers are cosmopolitan.

It is a long time since red wine from the Ramisco grape has flowed as steadily as water from the fountain in Colares. Cultivation of this ungrafted variety in the dune sands is such hard work that it has been given up almost completely.

Carcavelos is an interesting nutty dessert and aperitif wine, not as sweet as port or Muscat from Setúbal. Together with port and Madeira, these form the quartet of famous Portuguese *appellations* and specialties in the fortified wine sector. Unfortunately the spread of villas and hotels in the environs of Lisbon has almost destroyed Carcavelos.

The greatest potential, apart from Bucelas, is held by the Alenquer region with more than 160 historic, often palatial *quintas*, some with medieval roots. In some, modern wine estates have been set up, using both native and international varieties to produce fruity red wines with great individuality which may, once the vines increase in age, compete with the best Portuguese wines. Chardonnay and Arinto also provide fine fruit aromas such as are hardly known in southern areas. In the Arruda and Torres Vedras regions there are also indications of better red and white wines.

The form of the young *appellations* and their producers is at present not yet decided, but it is progressing as dynamically as elsewhere. Divisions within the wine commission are hindering exchange and pollination of vines in this large region (150,000 acres/60,000 ha under vine) which is marked by a shortage of companies.

THE ORCHARD OF PORTUGAL

Ribatejo is the name of the region along the Tagus (Tejo) between the Atlantic-influenced Estremadura and the drier, hotter, less fertile northern Alentejo. In Ribatejo there are numerous huge estates covering many hundreds or even thousands of acres, with only a small part under vine. The region is not too dry, with 28 inches (70 cm) of rain a year, and all sorts of grain, fruit, and vegetables, from orchard fruit to rice, thrive here. For wine, however, the fertility of the region is something of a drawback, as far too much mass-produced wine has been cultivated in the flood plain along the Tagus. Nowadays the vineyards are retreating to the poorer soils in the hinterland, which are better for vines.

In recent years a comprehensive restructuring has taken place. As in Alentejo, six I.P.R. regions have been set up and in March 2000 they were turned into sub-regions. The whole region is now the D.O.C. Ribatejo, while the same area can also produce a *vinho regional*, Ribateja, which is more significant than the old I.P.R.

Vine varieties from abroad may be freely used here. It is no accident that the most famous and best Pinot Noirs and Syrahs in Portugal come from Ribatejo, which previously had no reputation as a wine region except for *vinho carrascão*. This is bottled in 1^1/$_3$-gallon (5-liter) flagons or sold directly from the cask in simple bars, especially in Lisbon. It can taste quite good as an accompaniment to typical dishes such as fried sardines, liver, or other meats cooked with lots of onions and garlic.

These traditional wines have occasionally created quite a stir, even among wine connoisseurs, as famous but anonymous *garrafeiras*. However, it is now well-known in Portugal that Ribatejo red wines, which are coming onto the market from seven cooperatives and more than 20 *quintas* (some of them huge), have now, after a rather weak start in the early 1990s, reached a remarkably good standard in some wine estates.

Almeirim and Cartaxo, previously I.P.R.s and now sub-regions, produce the most bottled wine by a large margin—a sector that is rapidly growing. Tomar, Santarém and Chamusca are

"Oeste," the West, was the earlier name of the wine-growing country in the coastal area of Lisbon.

lagging behind as regards wines and development. Coruche, right in the southeast on the borders with Alentejo, comprises only 8,650 acres (3,500 ha), but at the moment its light sandy soils show the best potential for finer red wines. The Ribatejo wine region cannot magically call up marble, slate, or the other geological advantages of the Alentejo vineyards, so it will remain interesting mainly for the relationship between price and quality.

Select Producers in Estremadura

Companhia das Vinhas de São Domingos**−***
Quinta da Boavista
Merceanan
321 acres (130 ha) • *Wines: Espiga Branco, Tinto, Setencostas Branco, Tinto, Palha-Canas Branco, Tinto, Touriz, Varietais Casa Santos Lima, Camarate Touriga Nacional, Touriga Franca, Tinta Minda, Tinta Roriz, Preto Martinho, Chardonnay*
José Luis Oliveira da Silva, formerly a baker, has made this historic estate into one of the model operations in the region, with passion and the help of wine expert José Neiva. He uses the various hill sites to produce what is perhaps the most exemplary range of grape varieties in Portugal. They are not classically aged, but matured for fruit, allowing the drinker the pleasure of getting to know the typical character of the varieties.

Quinta da Abrigada***
Alenquer
• *Wines include: Tinto, Branco, Vinha Nobre Tinto, V.R. Raizertinto*
This *quinta* at the foot of the Serra de Monganto today belongs to the ceramics manufacturer João Machada, who has been producing a respectable, classic red wine for decades. The Vinho Nobre, available only in great years, is a top-quality product with the length and firmness of a great red wine.

Quinta de Pancas**−***
Alenquer
198 acres (80 ha); 500,000 bottles • *Wines: Cabernet Sauvignon, C-S Spec. Selection, Touriga Nacional Spec. Selection, Quinta de Parrotes, Quinta D. Carlos Arinto, Chardonnay, Cabernet Sauvignon/Tinta Roriz*
With Pancas in the early 1990s, the Guimarães family was the first to show the great potential of Alenquer.

Pancas is the most ambitious of the three fellow *quintas*. However, the race to rise to the top group of red wines became too aggressive in the end with the investment in new vines. At present, the white wines appear to show the soil's class better than the red.

Quinta da Ponte Pedrinha***−****
Lagarinhos, Tazém
123 acres (50 ha); 50,000 bottles • *Wines: Tinto, Touriga Nacional*
This 618-acre (250-ha) estate has 74 acres (30 ha) of young and 49 acres (20 ha) of old vines, with an extension planned to 247 acres (100 ha). It is an absolute newcomer which, with the help of João Portugal Ramos, has been providing the market with very good, elegant, deep-red fruity wines from the beginning. The majority of this wine is sold in *garrafãos* and from the barrel. A marked development in a modern style, oriented more toward Bordeaux than toward traditional Dão, is becoming apparent.

Quinta da Romeira (Alcantara Agricola)**−***
Bucelas
190 acres (77 ha); bought-in grapes • *Wines: Arinto, Morgado de Santa Catherina, Calhandriz, Prova Regio Branco, Tinto, Perfumes da Romeira: Arinto, Chardonnay, Gewürztraminer, Rabo de Ovelha, Riesling, Sauvignon, Sercial, Espumante, Tradição; Beiras, Douro, Palmela, all Tinto*
Famous for centuries, this *quinta* was the starting point for the energetic revival of the white wines of Portugal. The unique delicate fruit of the Arinto grapes growing on the *caeiras* (a particular limestone) of Bucelas is very good when made in stainless steel and now also harmonizes with *barriques*. The respected wine expert Nuno Cancella Abreu is also involved with various reds from other regions and whites of single varieties.

Terras do Sado:
The Wealth of Setúbal and Palmela

The two D.O.C. regions of Palmela and Setúbal, together with a few other regions, are linked together as the Peninsula de Setúbal, after the peninsula which directly adjoins the capital city of Lisbon. The term for the regional wine is the more harmonious Terras do Sado, which is widely used for dry whites, for some medium-dry white wines, and even for a few sweet specialties, as well as some of the best red wines in Portugal. The great historic name of this region was defined as early as 1907 as a

This is where the successful history of the Fonseca family empire was made.

Opposite
Cheerful wine festival in Palmela, directly west of Lisbon on the Setúbal peninsula. Here, the Periquita variety is made into long-lived and full-bodied red wines.

quality wine-growing area and protected accordingly. The name Setúbal may be used on the labels for Muscat from Setúbal only, which acquires its fine aroma on the light, stony, limestone soils of the Serra da Arrabida, with their definite maritime influence. It is indisputably one of the great classics of the wine world, but because of the relatively low quantities produced (which have, however, now risen to about 264,000 gallons/more than a million liters), and because of the very slow revival of popular taste for sweet dessert wines, it is nowhere near as well known as it deserves to be today. In addition, the second largest wine-dealing and production company in Portugal, José Maria de Fonseca, a very traditional company, always—though surely unintentionally—seems to draw attention away from Muscat by its very extraordinary successes throughout the broad range of all its wines, both red and white.

However, it was the house of Fonseca who, in the middle of the 19th century, further perfected the production and aging of Muscat, which was famous as long ago as the 17th century. They soon acquired an increasing number of regular customers in three continents and the reputation that goes with such a customer list. João Ignacio Ferreira Lapa, in one of the great standard works on Portuguese wine published in 1867, describes the wine company's founder, who developed this style, not only as an experienced practitioner, but as a

A piece of Portuguese wine history

Ownership of more than 2,470 acres (1,000 ha) of vineyards, its traditions and innovative skills, and its numerous contacts to almost all the great wine producers, have combined to give the great house of J. M. da Fonseca a kind of monopoly, that has lasted for a long time, at least in the production of better-quality bottled wines. The enologist and vice-president of the company, Domingos Suares Franco, who trained at the Department of Viticulture and Enology of the University of California at Davis, is carrying on the family tradition, together with his brother António.

In the early 1980s, there was furious competition in the Setúbal peninsula, when António d'Avillez left the J. M. da Fonseca management and took his creative ideas to the João Pires winery. In the mid-1980s, the João Pires wine, medium-dry and at the time

displaying the finest fruit, was a sensational success. With the aid of the Australian enologist Peter Bright, d'Avillez demonstrated to the world the delicacy of the native Muscat grape in fresh white wines. From skillfully produced cheaper brands of a high standard, through to top wines from foreign grape varieties; from a Late Harvest Sauternes type to classics made from native varieties, the company, now re-named simply J. P., produced wines which showed how the Setúbal peninsula, with its mainly unprolific soils and maritime-influenced climate, is suitable for the most diverse styles of wine.

Nowadays other cooperatives and wine estates which previously sold to Fonseca and other dealers, are looking for their own niches to produce better-quality wines themselves. The first successes look very promising. How-

ever, for Moscatel de Setúbal, none of them is yet in the Fonseca class. The red wines of Palmela are among the most interesting, made from the Periquita grape, introduced to the region by José Maria da Fonseca about 160 years ago. Today this variety dominates the area at around 95 percent. But white wines, fresh, clean and in part finely adjusted with Muscat, are also on the increase. The Palmela area, at 32,000 acres (13,000 ha), contains about 70 percent of all the vines growing in the Terras do Sado, while Setúbal itself covers no more than around 2,800 acres (1,130 ha).

The sandy to clay soils of the Palmela bring out the characteristic fruit spectrum of the Castelão Frances grape (Periquita), in contrast to the grape's very individual soft and yet firm tannin, which gives the wine its excellent potential for laying down.

man familiar with the whole of contemporary wine literature who exchanged information with many wine experts of this time.

This dessert wine is fortified more lightly than port to only 17.5 percent by volume. A 20-year-old Moscatel de Setúbal (a blend in which the youngest wine included is 20 years old) contains RESIDUAL SUGARS of about seven ounces (200 g) and has almost double the sweetness of port. The very top-quality, even older, vintage wines are even more concentrated in their density of sugars and flavors. The secrets of producing the perfect Muscat wine are stopping fermentation at a residual sugar content of just over three ounces (90 g), and evaporation. As they age, the wines become thicker and sweeter. Wooden barrels, not completely filled, relatively warm storage (the old wines, of which a few still exist, were, like Madeira, shipped to India to be exposed to high temperatures), very clever OXIDIZATION, and evaporation turn the fresh and fruity, almost citrus-like Muscat grapes into dense, unforgettable wines, exotic and full of dried fruit aromas.

SELECT PRODUCERS OF TERRAS DO SADO

CO-OP. AGRICOLA DE SANTO ISIDRO DE PEGÕES**−***
PEGÕES VELHOS
2,223 acres (900 ha); 4,000,000 bottles • Wines: Fontinario de Pegões Branco, →Tinto, Fontanario de Pegões Garrafeira, Vale de Judia →Branco, Tinto
An exemplary cooperative, advised today by João Portugal Ramos. Fruity reds with a fine barrique note can be recommended, as can the delightful dry Muscat (Vale de Judia).

JOSÉ MARIA DA FONSECA*−*****
AZEITÃO
• Wines: Lancers Rosé, V.R. Albis Branco, Pasmados Branco, Tinto, Periquita Tinto, Tinto Classico; Quinta de Camarate Branco Seco, Branco Doce, Tinto; Primum Branco, Rosé, Tinto; Garrafeira C.O., R.A., T.E.; Alentejo: José de Sousa Tinto, D'Avillez Tinto, Tinto Garrafeira; Moscatel de Setúbal: Alambre Vintage, Alambre 20 Years, Superior 1962, and others, Trilogia
The top wine bottler in Portugal (excluding the port trade). This is a highly traditional family business which has had a decisive effect on viticulture in Setúbal, in Alentejo, and even in the Dão. Apart from its unique old Muscats, the house offers impressive wines in all price ranges, with constant and delightful new developments or new versions of traditional wines. A remarkable feature is their pioneering role in planting unusual grape varieties on the Setúbal peninsula: in earlier years, these tended to be more international, today they are national varieties, even Alvarinho.

SOC. AGR. DE PEGOS CLAROS***
PALMELA
198 acres (80 ha); 100,000 bottles • Wines: →Palmela Tinto, →Palmela Reserva Tinto

From the Periquita grape came the most notable red wine Periquita around 1850.

This country estate, founded in 1920, today owns 123.5 acres (50 ha) of old and 74 acres (30 ha) of new vineyards, exclusively planted with the Periquita grape. In the past, these were partly de-stalked and trodden by foot in lagares, and they are still treated in this very delicate way today. Consistent, classic, firm Periquita reds are produced here under the direction of João Portugal Ramos.

SOC. VINICOLA DA PALMELA (S.I.V.I.P.A.)**−***
PALMELA
988 acres (400 ha); bought-in grapes; 1,200,000 bottles • Wines: V.R.: Branco, Tinto, Veritas Palmela Tinto, Moscatel de Setúbal, Moscatel Roxo
A society founded in 1964 which over the last few years has produced ever improving wines at prices that are sometimes surprising, ranging from the characterful Veritas to the Muscat series, which are traditionally produced.

J. P. VINHOS*−****
PINHAL NOVO
1,111 acres (450 ha); bought-in grapes; 12,000,000 bottles • Wines include: J. P. Branco, Tinto, Loridos Espumante Bruto, Moscatel de Setúbal, Chardonnay Cova da Ursa, →Quinta da Bacalhoa Cabernet Sauvignon, →Má Partilha Merlot, Catarina Branco; Alentejo: →Tinto do Anfora
You could call J. P. Vinhos a wine factory in which mass-produced wines are skillfully created, as are better-quality wine brands from the company's own estates, and a few highly individual "hand-made" wines which are among the best wines in Portugal. In the range here you can find quite consciously undogmatic wines for everyone, even the elite. António d'Avillez has recently sold J. P. Vinhos after 20 years. However, thankfully for wine lovers everywhere, the good wine experts have stayed.

ALENTEJO

The Alentejo region is sometimes termed the California of Portugal. This is explained by the wine estates covering up to 1,500 acres (600 ha)—the biggest of all of them being the Herdade do Esporão—and the broad plains or only slightly rising slopes which are in marked contrast to the otherwise rather small-scale Portuguese agricultural and viticultural scene. Very efficient, sometimes even first-class cooperatives produce the bulk of the wine, but more and more committed wine estates are attracting attention with top class wines. Cortes de Cima is one of the most prominent companies. More than 40 wine estates and efficient regional organizations have succeeded in giving Alentejo an image of modernity and of generosity, which seems to suggest that success will result simply from the enjoyment of the right wine.

However, looking more closely, it is clear that history and tradition have played their part here too. It is still possible to find viticultural practices dating from Roman times in this otherwise very modern region: in some *lagares* grapes are still trodden by foot and in some estates great earthenware jars stand ready to age the wine. The principle of cooling by evaporation in earthenware amphorae is, after all, the oldest method of cooling fermentation in hot regions. The only place in Portugal that may possibly get hotter than Alentejo, where temperatures of 104°F (40°C) are often the rule in summer, is the Douro valley, the second great region for fashionable Portuguese wines. The heat—which often leads to picking taking place as early as August—has demanded considerable technical winery investment, which today makes it possible for some companies to produce elegant, fine, and structured white wines, even in a region generally estimated, and to an extent even celebrated, as a red wine area. Today, the Alentejo area once more has 47,000 acres (19,000 ha) under vine, about as much land as in the 19th century, before the region was turned into a grain-growing area. This is complemented by the biggest and best-quality cork oak plantations in the world, and by countless olive trees, whose oil is sold by some estates and cooperatives as single-variety specialties.

Of the 2,640,000 to 8,000,000 gallons (100,000 to 300,000 hl) of red wine produced in an average year (only years with frost can drastically reduce production), about half are classified as Vinho Regional Alentejano and D.O.C.

Alentejo. Alentejo red wine is very fashionable today in Portugal and especially in Lisbon, and is the wine of which there is most awareness in other countries, apart from Douro. This is probably due to its taste as well as its history.

The taste is immediately decisive, for a number of reasons, that affect both the vines and the cork oaks. One factor is the dry climate which here, in contrast to many other Portuguese regions, almost guarantees no rain at harvest time. Rotten grapes or corks damaged by damp are almost unheard of. Healthy, thick-skinned, blue-black grapes, however, guarantee a fruity wine with warm, ripe aromas.

The soils, the second factor, are equally positive in their effect on cork and wine. They tend to be unprolific and not suited to mass production. They often consist of slate, granite, and quartzite, with a proportion of other types of rock, among them the finest marble which, especially in the Estremoz and Borba areas, is quarried in great blocks. In addition, discipline and tradition, encouraged by an effective viticultural commission and technical advice, only permit vines on less fertile soil. The discipline for aging wine varieties

Alentejo has for centuries been the granary of Portugal. The number of old windmills are evidence of its past.

Opposite
Alentejo is a modern wine region with many newly created wine estates.

is also higher in Alentejo than elsewhere, which may be a result of the large-scale structures. Among the red varieties, Aragonês, known in the Douro as Tinta Roriz, and in Spain as Tinto Fino or Tempranillo, clearly excels in elegance and structure. Here it reaches its full ripeness.

The Trincadeira is valued equally highly, but is not necessarily better than Alfrocheiro or

SELECT PRODUCERS IN ALENTEJO

CO-OP. AGR. REGUENGOS DE MONSARAZ*−***
REGUENGOS DE MONSARAZ
8,398 acres (3,400 ha); bought-in grapes; 10,000,000 bottles • Wines include: Reserva Tinto, Garrafeira dos Sócios, Aragonez, Trincadeira, Monsaraz Tinto
The biggest cooperative in the Alentejo, with 576 members, advised by João Portugal Ramos, has made the leap from simple, average Alentejo wine to classic top-quality wine, the Garrafeira dos Sócios; also high-class red wines.

CORTES DE CIMA**−*****
VIDIGUEIRA
86.5 acres (35 ha) • Wines include: Courela, Cortes de Cima, Aragonez, Syrah, Incógnito, Reserva
The rising star among wine estates in the Alentejo region. The Dane Hans Kristian Jørgensen and his Australian consultant Richard Smart produce wines of character from local grapes (Aragonez) or international varieties (Syrah).

HERDADE DO ESPORÃO**−***
REGUENGOS DE MONSARAZ
1,383 acres (560 ha); 1,800,000 bottles • Wines: Alandra Tinto, Branco; Vinha da Defesa Tinto, →Branco; Esperão →Reserva, Tinto, Branco, Garrafeira Tinto; →Aragonês, Trincadeira, Touriga Nacional, Cabernet Sauvignon, →Arinto, →Roupeiro
This is the largest wine-bottling estate in Alentejo. The Australian David Baverstock is the director of enology. Especially at the simple or medium price level, the quality is very high.

HERDADE DO MOUCHÃO***−****
SOUSEL
57 acres (23 ha) • Wines: Mouchão Tinto, Tonel No 3–4, Dom Rafael

The red wines of Ann Reynolds and Emily Richardson are grown outside the demarcated region and are only *vinho regional*, but are sought-after classics. They are prepared in *lagares*, matured for three years in oak and chestnut casks, bottled with no improvement or FILTRATION.

QUINTA DO CARMO***−****
ESTREMOZ
235 acres (95 ha) • Wines: Quinta do Carmo Branco, Tinto, Tinto Reserva Dom Martinho Tinto V.R.
The Rothschilds acquired 50 percent of a "dream château" for a joint venture with the previous owner Julio Bastos.

JOÃO PORTUGAL RAMOS**−****
ESTREMOZ
Bought-in grapes; 500,000 bottles • Wines: Marquês de Borba Branco, Tinto, Tinto Reserva, Antão Vaz, Tinta Caida, Trincadeira, Aragonês, Vila Santa, Roupeiro, Syrah
Portugal's best-known wine expert superbly displays the potential of some varieties (using grapes from his own vineyards and from contracted growers). With the 1997 Marquês de Borba Reserva, Portugal Ramos brought out a new classic from Alentejo.

TAPADA DE COELHEIROS***−****
IGREJINHA, ARRAIOLOS
49 acres (20 ha) • Wines: Tapada de Coelheira Branco, →Tinto, →Tinto Garrafeira
With the aid of António Saramago, J. M. Fonseca's second enologist, Joaquim and Leonilde Silveira built up an exemplary wine estate in the 1980s, with red wines that are among the most structured and polished in Alentejo. The blend of Cabernet Sauvignon, Trincadeira, and Aragonês, aged in French oak, is unusual.

Periquita, which are also recommended. Some of the best wines are produced from the southern French mass variety Alicante Bouschet, and recently fashionable varieties such as Syrah or Cabernet Sauvignon have been introduced. Always fascinating in Alentejo wines is the combination of a high degree of pleasantness and character. Even the plainer wines possess, as well as charming ripe fruit, a certain tannin structure and a fineness determined by the soil, so clearly different from the jam-like fruitiness of the moister regions nearer to the coast. Despite early harvesting and the lack of harder acidity and tannins which may be so distinctive in Dão or Bairrada, despite the softness and character reminiscent of great Rhône wines, the wines are mostly well balanced, which is why the best wines are distinguished by great firmness and longevity. It is only a pity that this last

Today, both young and old have reason to be cheerful in Alentejo. The hard times under the dictator Salazar and the blind mass production which followed on the Carnation Revolution are almost forgotten. With quality-oriented wine and cork production, the future of the region is looking good.

Opposite
From their 25th year on, cork oaks are peeled every ninth year.

Quercus suber—the cork oak—has a major part to play in the Portuguese economy.

quality is rarely fully exploited and too rapid and reductive an aging process is used to maintain the strong emphasis on the charm of the young fruit. The danger of even high quality Alentejo wines being tailored to fast consumption in the near future probably cannot be entirely dismissed at the moment. With regard to complexity, however, a slower aging of the wine, and also the use of old vines, more closely planted, are important. The sub-regions of Portalegre and Granja-Amareleja, with their cooperatives of many small farmers, produce some quite outstanding classic wines in their more continental climate.

Another reason for the fashionable part played by the Alentejo, which has made it the most expensive wine, and the one most in demand, from the barrel, may have a historical explanation. After the end of Salazar's dictatorship, the communist party was the ruling party in Alentejo—as it is today in many towns and cities. Young people and students were enthusiastic about the wine of Alentejo and learned to treasure and love it. The cooperatives were already producing to quite a high standard in the 1970s, and Alentejo found popularity because it was the wine with the best symbolic red color, and was also nearly always the best and most reliable wine at an affordable price. The new *crus* don't have that much in common with these standard wines, which of course still exist. The new wines are most often produced using old native varieties but new methods of aging, and at peak quality will fetch prices of 30 euros (US $37) or more. Some of the new Alentejo reds are already on their way to cult status. But we shouldn't forget the white varieties because of the popularity of the red wines. White grapes may only cover ten percent of the cultivated vineyards, but they do have a very independent character, and the discovery is well worthwhile.

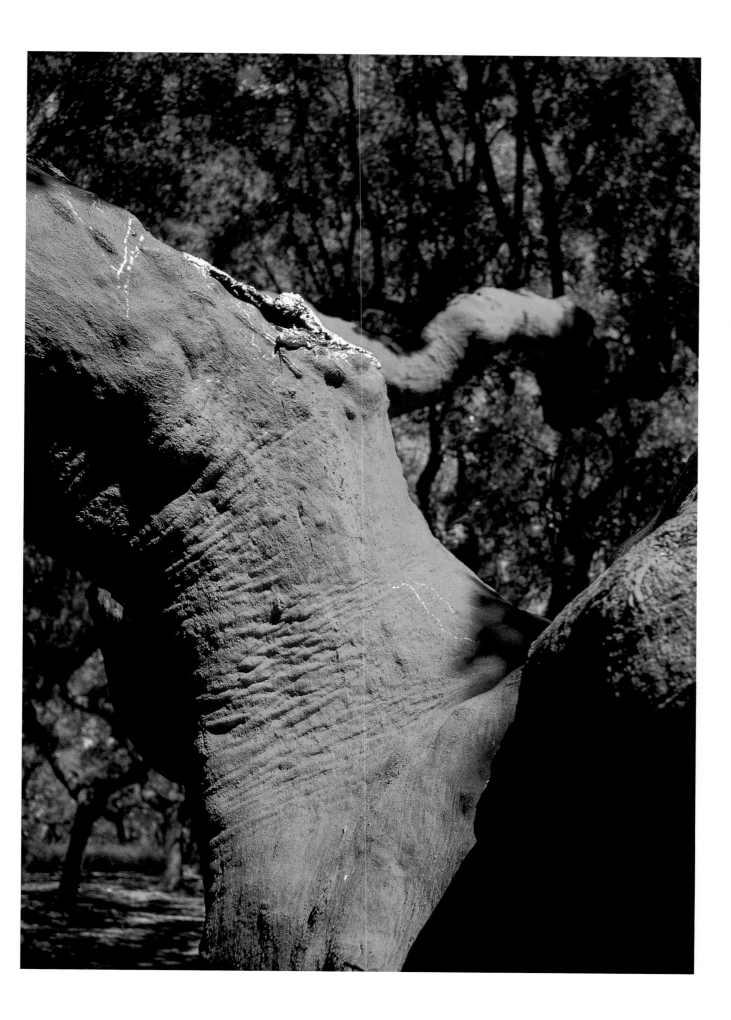

Cork Manufacture

The traditional bottle cork is cut from the bark of the cork oak (*Quercus suber*), a tree which grows mainly in Mediterranean countries. It grows very slowly and takes about 45 years to produce a cork layer thick enough to cut bottle corks. The harvest, also described as lifting or peeling, consists of removing the bark as carefully as possible from the tree. The cork layer should be as undamaged as possible to make it easy to work the material. Serious injury to the tree should also be avoided, as this will damage cork formation in the next growth cycle.

Cork oaks can first be peeled around their 25th year, and the bark is then lifted at regular nine-year intervals. The first harvests are used in construction, especially for soundproofing. The mats of bark are usually left in the forests for several months so that the tannins oxidize and the layer of tissue in direct contact with the trunk can dry out. Once the sheets have been delivered to the factory, they are first of all immersed for one or two hours in boiling water to kill off micro-organisms and insects, to dissolve tannins, and to increase the thickness and elasticity of the material in order to make the subsequent work easier.

After resting for one or two weeks, the cork may be boiled a second time. Afterwards the sheets are sorted according to quality and thickness and cut into strips, and then the corks are punched out, following the direction of the grain. This may be done by machine, but the results are not as good as with hand-operated or semi-automatic tools. Only a person working the machine can select the best place to punch.

The waste material is made into agglomerate from which pressed corks are manufactured.

After this, the corks are processed mechanically. The ends are cut to the desired size and the

The tree must not be damaged when the cork is peeled off.

body is smoothed. Any cork dust produced is also used in the manufacture of pressed corks.

Next, machines sort the bottle corks according to the number of bark pores visible on the surface. The corks are then disinfected in bleach. Few cork producers now use chlorine, because it may bring out an unpleasant taste in the wine. It is being replaced by peroxide. The dosage used and the time left to take effect depend partly on the color desired by the customer. Some countries prefer natural tones, others want very pale corks. Drying the corks once or twice gives a moisture content of six to nine percent. They are sorted one more time. The machines check the body of each cork, but not its ends.

The corks are then marked by branding or with ink; this may be a personalized mark with the name of the wine producer, the estate and/or

Left
After drying in the forest, the bark mats are transported to the factory.

Right
Selecting the best place to punch out the cork comes with lots of experience.

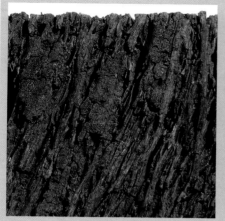
The outer surface of a piece of cork bark.

The structure of the inside of the bark.

The punching out is done by machines that are in part hand-operated.

Corks from Portugal

Portugal occupies first place among cork producers. With 1,655,000 acres (670,000 ha) of cork oak forest, it contains 31 percent of the cork-growing area in the world, more than Spain (24 percent), Algeria (19 percent), and Morocco (17 percent). At 190,000 tons a year, Portugal produces 51 percent of the corks used world-wide. In addition to its home productions, the country imports raw cork for further processing. Well behind Portugal is Spain in second place, with 26 percent of world production, in front of Italy at seven and Morocco at six percent. Corks are also manufactured in small quantities in northern countries, yet the best reputation for cork processing remains with Portugal. It is estimated that exported cork, in particular bottle corks, accounts for a turnover of about 610 million US dollars (500 million euros).

the *appellation*, and sometimes also the vintage, or it may be more general—it is left to the instructions from the customer. The higher the quality of the wine, the more precise is the marking of the cork. It should be possible to identify the wine by the information on the cork, which usually survives the label.

The final step is the treatment of the cork surface with silicon or paraffin. This allows the consumer to remove the cork without too much difficulty.

German top vintners reveal their cork secrets: the quality is good to very good all the way through, but length is deliberately limited.

Corking

Just like wine, cork is a natural living product. As a result, a certain quota of errors have to be reckoned with, and this can lead to your being confronted—despite all the cork manufacturer's efforts—with a corked bottle of wine. The wine smells very intensely of cork, a smell which usually increases on contact with the air. This has many causes, of which the two most common are improper storage of the corks or insufficient disinfection.

It may also happen that the wine, without displaying a definitely "CORKED" flavor, does not reach its usual standard or has an unpleasant note, reminiscent of wet dishcloths, mold, or something similar. In such cases it is not always easy to find the culprit, because the explanation may lie with the cork, with the adjustment of the corking machine, with hygiene problems in the winery, with storage conditions of the corks, or many other causes. Often one person will blame another, and the understandably disappointed consumer will usually blame the wine.

This is why some wine producers have decided to use non-cork stoppers for their bottles. In the face of this threat, European cork manufacturers have drawn up an international charter of cork manufacture. More and more of them voluntarily undergo quality controls which guarantee the quality of cork manufacture.

Natural wine cork
Quality: low
approx. 1 × 1 in (24 × 28 mm)

Pressed cork
Colored, in two sections
Quality: average
approx. 1 × 1½ in (23 × 44 mm)

Pressed cork
Colored, in two sections
Quality: low
approx. 1 × 1½ in (23 × 40 mm)

Natural wine cork
Quality: average
approx. 1 × 1 in (24 × 28 mm)

Natural wine cork
Quality: lower range
approx. 1 × 1½ in (24 × 45 mm)

Pressed cork
approx. 1 × 1½ in (22.5 × 38 mm)

Synthetic cork

Sparkling wine
cork
Quality: very good
approx. 1 × 2 in (30 × 48 mm)

Sparkling wine
cork
Quality: average
approx. 1 × 2 in (30.5 × 48 mm)

Bottle stoppers

The first bottles used in the 17th century were stoppered with a hemp-wrapped, tallow-drenched wooden bung. Corks were first used to close bottles securely by Dom Pérignon in Champagne. Since this time, cork has been the favored stopper for quality wines, and as a consequence several types of bottle cork have been devised.

There are many categories of natural corks, according to the number of pores in the bark, and their various lengths. The longer they are and the higher their quality is, the more expensive they become. The cheapest bottle corks, which are most often used for cheaper wines, are pressed corks, made of small particles of cork agglomerate glued together. An intermediate quality cork is made from cork dust and glue. This improves the appearance, but not the actual quality of the cork. Some producers resist using these corks because the wine will come into contact with the glue, and so cork manufacturers have devised a pressed cork with a slice of natural cork glued to each end.

For sparkling wines, the closures are made from glued and pressed cork. One or two thin discs of natural cork are glued onto one of the two ends of the cork. Natural corks with a plastic head are used for spirits such as cognac.

The range of products for closing bottles has been much expanded in recent years. For instance, a cork producer has developed a cork made of finest cork particles, less than 0.03 of an inch (1 mm) in size, held together by a synthetic tissue based on polyurethane. This product looks like a cork on the surface, but has, so it is claimed, none of its disadvantages.

The screw-top closure is at present undergoing surprising expansion in Swiss white wines, as it completely protects the wines from oxidization, which is particularly useful for the Chasselas variety. This system also has the advantage of allowing the bottle to be simply and effectively re-closed. However, many wine producers hesitate to introduce this form of closure, as it is claimed that consumers prefer the traditional cork. However, some experience has now been gained with wines under screw fastenings—and the results in regard to aging are positive.

The latest invention which is now spreading into continental Europe from California, Australia, and the big British wine companies, is the synthetic cork. These look just like natural corks; they can be used in bottling lines just as natural corks, and are removed from the bottle in the same way. These types of stoppers mean that the "corked" flavor is a thing of the past. They do not claim to replace natural cork but have been introduced as an alternative for lower priced wines in which otherwise only lower-quality corks would be used.

Natural wine cork
Quality: average
approx. 1 × 1½ in (24 × 45 mm)

Natural wine cork
Quality: very good
approx. 1 × 2 in (24 × 54 mm)

Cork from
Château d'Yquem,
1945

Often old wines can only be identified by means of the cork.

Madeira

In 1420, the Portuguese captain, João Gonçalves Zarco, in the service of Prince Henry the Navigator, landed on the legendary and cloud-surrounded shores of an island 370 miles (600 km) off the Moroccan coast. This mid-Atlantic mountain range rises to 6,100 feet (1,861 m) above sea-level, and was then thickly forested and uninhabited. Having cleared the island, Zarco planted sugar cane and Malvasia, the sweet grape variety known as Malmsey. After the discovery of America, Madeira gained in importance as a supply stop on the Atlantic route, as well as to Africa, and Asia. It was the only place that English ships were allowed to take on supplies.

Madeira wine began to be fortified with brandy, to allow it to survive these sea voyages without deteriorating. It was soon discovered that the wine improved astonishingly in the tropical climate. After 1750, British dealers, who took over the wine trade, began sending barrels of the fortified wine to India and the Far East to mature it. The last eight of 70 wine companies now recreate the tropical effect with

the original technology. They keep the wine in *estufas*, tanks warmed by heaters, for three to five months at a temperature of 112°F (45°C). There are two more elegant methods—they have now become rare, but are still practiced. In the luxury version of the *estufa*, the wine is put in pipes, typical barrels holding 160 gallons (600 liters), and developed in a room heated by steam. The second method is to store the pipes in a *canteiro* (attic) and thus expose them to extremes of temperature. The best wines are given 20, 30, or more years of aging in barrels. Only these are bottled with a vintage year, and often only in small quantities.

Of the 5,200 acres (2,100 ha) of vineyards on the island, which produce about 38 million gallons (10 million liters) per year, only a tenth are planted with the four noble varieties—Sercial, Verdelho, Boal, and Malmsey. Cultivation seems rather archaic. The vines of Madeira are mostly grown in low pergolas on terraces to allow the 4,000 wine producers to make the best possible use of the precious land. Picking is carried out crouching or kneeling. The harvest often has to be carried by hand 660–980 feet (220–300 m) uphill from the nearest road. The grapes are then crushed in simple continuous presses. Careful grape preparation is not necessary—the long aging process is all that matters.

Madeiras aged from the four noble varieties are unique specialties in the wine world. They have an incredible quality: they can age forever and seem steadily to improve, as some vintages still available from the 19th and early 20th centuries demonstrate. Unfortunately, the dominant grape grown on the island today is the Negra Mole, which growers and producers treat in a cavalier fashion, producing cheap Madeira for all sorts of tastes, and which now makes up 40 percent of the total production.

The vine terraces rise up the steep slopes beyond the fishing village of Câmara de Lobos. The most extensive wine-growing area on the island is located here on the south coast.

EXCELLENT MADEIRAS

• *Boal* or *Bual*: Medium-sweet Madeira is produced from this rare variety with small, astonishingly hairy leaves. It is planted on the south side of the island, as it needs more warmth, but does not produce more sugar. The wines develop, relatively early, with interesting aromas of dried apricots, raisins, nuts, caramel, and RANCIO, the typical Madeira note.

• *Malmsey*: Malvasia grapes, less often met with than Verdelho, need even more warmth than Boal, but they also develop a higher sugar content, making Malmsey the sweetest of the Madeira wines. The greater acidity of this variety, however, balances it out. It is very popular in Anglo-Saxon countries as a liqueur wine. It has great fullness and length and in age

Two birds with one stone: vegetables can be grown under the trellises where the vines are cultivated. This is a necessity of life for the farmers, who often only cultivate very small areas.

Madeiras seem to have the ability to age forever, and the very oldest vintages are among the rarest delicacies in the world.

it displays fine notes of cocoa and chocolate.

• *Sercial*: This variety prefers the north side of the island and cooler vineyards. It produces the driest and rarest Madeira which, after ten years, develops its exceedingly full and elegant BOUQUET, increasing in subtlety and refinement over further decades.

• *Terrantez*: There are a few very rare old wines of unbelievable refinement and longevity left from this legendary variety, almost exterminated by the phylloxera outbreak. The Barbeito Terrantez of 1795 became very famous.

• *Verdelho*: This widespread, early-ripening variety also likes the north side of the island. It produces a medium-dry Madeira with a restrained sweetness and fine acidity, which after long aging develops a highly individual smoky aroma with a tang of iodine.

Not all Madeira is the same

Not even the island in the Atlantic was safe from phylloxera, the vine louse. Here, too, the greedy pests did their work and destroyed the stock of high-quality vines. In replanting, many of the wine producers on the island took the cheaper option for economic reasons, and that meant either hybrids or Negra Mole. This is why there are only a few areas left today planted with high-quality varieties and producing high-quality wine. It is also why most Madeira is destined to be used for cooking, and is made by the *estufa* procedure in tanks.

Finest is the lowest level of drinkable Madeira and is three years old. Reserve is five years old, partly aged in the barrel. Special Reserve or 10 Years Old is mainly based on the top-quality grape varieties and is aged for at least 10 years in the barrel. After 15 years of aging, the label is marked 15 Years Old or, more rarely, Extra Reserve. Vintage Madeiras are the peak of quality, aged for at least 20 years in pipes and matured for a further two years in the bottle.

Patrick Fiévez

EASTERN EUROPE

Eastern Europe

Following the collapse of the former communist bloc in 1989, eastern Europe's wine-growing countries have now started to reorganize. The greatest challenge many of them faced, and indeed still face, is the need for a complete change of outlook. When the wine industry and prices were regulated by the state, the emphasis was on the size of yields, with quality very much a peripheral concern. Today, the wines have to be exported to the West, as the export markets in the East are no longer available to the same extent that they were before the political changes. This means that the managers of cooperatives and growers have to adapt to a completely new state of affairs. The need for reorientation will be even greater after these countries join the E.U.—in 2004 for Hungary and the Czech and Slovak Republics; Romania and Bulgaria should follow in 2007. Once they join, these countries will also be subject to E.U. regulations on wine production, not those of their own country. Competition with other countries is fierce, and wines from eastern Europe must measure up against products from everywhere in the world in order to win customers. Suddenly, the focus is on the quality of the wines, while the quantities produced have to be drastically reduced. Although great progress has been made the reorientation process is not yet complete.

Until 1990 there was a clear *status quo* in the European wine industry. On the one hand, there were the twelve member states of the European Community, as it was then, of which seven were wine producers (representing almost 50 percent of the world's wine-growing area, with 10 million acres or 4 million ha), and on the other hand the ten C.O.M.E.C.O.N. states with five wine-producing countries, Bulgaria, Romania, Hungary, Czechoslovakia, and the U.S.S.R. (representing around 20 percent of the world's wine-growing area with 5 million acres or 2 million ha). But while this second economic community no longer exists, many of the old structures persist, in terms both of people's attitudes and their everyday circumstances. Despite privatization, the vineyards of numerous cooperatives and estates in Hungary and Bulgaria remain in the hands of the state. In some countries, however, a new generation of wine producers is developing who have recognized how important a change of outlook is. They are open to advice from colleagues in other countries on matters such as cultivation, grape picking, and winemaking techniques, and their first efforts are already bearing fruit. In Slovenia and Hungary some excellent examples have been in existence for a few years now. These wines are well able to stand comparison with those produced by their international competitors. Croatia, too, is on the path to producing some genuinely good wines.

In order to attract consumers in the West, products from the past, such as basic branded wines, must be replaced with quality products. There is great ambition, a lot of potential in terms of soil types and climate, and a solid basis in the form of both indigenous and foreign grape varieties. Growers from the western wine-producing countries who have recognized this are investing a great deal of commitment into their attempts to exploit the change of circumstances in the East. Primarily in Hungary, but also in the other countries, first-class producers from Tuscany, major growers from Bordeaux, and German merchants and wine companies are joining forces with local growers to produce wines to international standards. In many cases, this is being done with grape varieties that have a worldwide reputation, such as Cabernet Sauvignon, and the remarkable results have already been unveiled at various trade fairs. Journalists traveling through the region have reported high levels of investment and great effort on the part of local figures in the wine business.

A number of producers are also now putting their faith in the quality of regional grapes such as Furmint, Rebola, and Plavac Mali in an attempt to capture the West's specialty wine market. When made using modern techniques, these wines are perfectly capable of taking up the position they deserve in the world of wine.

Left
Along with international varieties that have now become very widespread, native red wines can also be heartily recommended.

Right
In the case of white wines, these lesser-known regional grape varieties are a constant source of surprise.

Not only do Hungary's wine-growing regions have a glorious past, they also have a lot of potential for the future.

Hungary

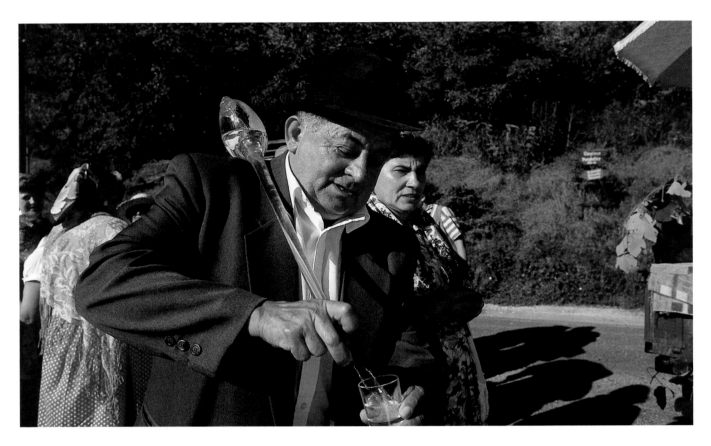

Of all the countries of eastern Europe, it is probably only Hungary that can boast a truly world-famous wine of exceptional quality. Tokaji Aszú has been a source of self-indulgent pleasure for lovers of rare wines for centuries.

Volcanic Subsoil

At one time the area we know today as Hungary was covered by the Pannonian Sea, and surrounded by the foothills of the Alps, the Carpathians, and the Dinaric Alps. The country's unique landscape is dominated by numerous small and long-extinct volcanoes, which created ideal soils for the cultivation of vines. The wine-growing area of Tokaj in the north of Hungary lies on the same degree of latitude as Colmar, in Alsace, while Hungary's most southern wine region, Villány, shares its latitude with that of Cognac, in southwest France.

In all likelihood it was the Romans who introduced wine and winemaking expertise to the area around the Danube, which at that time was part of their province of Pannonia. When the Magyars conquered the territory in the 9th

Wine from the previous year's harvest is poured at the wine festival in Badacsony, named after its box-shaped mountain.

Opposite
At the winegrowers' procession in Szigliget, in the Balaton region, grapes of the popular Szürkebarát variety, a type of Pinot Gris, are arranged into the shape of the traditional "wine bell."

century, they discovered thriving vineyards there. The Mongol invasion of 1241 caused such devastation to the vineyards that King Béla IV deemed it necessary to promote the replanting of vines, as Hungary's climate is so ideally suited to vine growing and a wide spectrum of grape varieties. These provide the basis for a range of wines, from dry and very aromatic whites to the famous Aszú, the sweet wine from the Tokaj region. In addition to these are many powerful reds made from both indigenous and international grape varieties.

The Hungarian wine industry faced enormous problems when the state put a stop to all subsidies in 1989. The area under vine cultivation shrank from 618,000 acres (250,000 ha) in the 1960s to 242,155 acres (98,000 ha) today. The areas that were closed down and cleared were, however, chiefly vineyards without *appellation*. Up to the time of the Soviet Union's collapse, Hungarian wine producers exported 50 percent of their production to the U.S.S.R. After its disintegration, export to countries in western Europe was made difficult by the high levels of competition. By the end of the 20th century, only 25 percent of production was being exported.

Hungarian Wine Laws

In July 1990 the old wine legislation, which dated back to 1970, was replaced by a stricter set of laws that took its cue from the regulations of the European Community, as it was known then. The classification system comprises five new grades of quality: table wines (*Asztali Bor*), regional wines or *vins de pays* (*Tajjelegü Asztali*), quality wines (*Minösegi Bor*), special quality wines (*Különleges Minösegi*), and finally wines made from overripe grapes and grapes affected by NOBLE ROT (*Aszú*), and VINTAGE wines (at least five years old).

Wine-growing Regions and Grape Varieties

Hungary has three large wine-growing areas, all of which are governed by a continental climate with hot, dry summers and very cold winters. Stretching down from Budapest to the south, between Hungary's two great rivers, the Danube and the Tisza, lies the Great Hungarian Plain, the Puszta, with its sandy soil. Growers in this region, also known as the Alföld, produce roughly half the output of the entire country, predominantly light red wines and medium-dry or sweet whites. The wines from Transdanubia, the area surrounding Lake Balaton, are primarily medium-dry and sweet whites. In north and northeastern Hungary are the Eger and Tokaj regions (Tokajhegyalja). The soil in Eger is dominated by black loam of volcanic origin. Mainly red varieties thrive here, although there are also some white wines worth mentioning. Tokaj is almost certainly the

Tokajhegyalja
Bükkalja
Eger
Mátraalja
Ászár-Neszmély
Pannonhalma-Sokoróalja
Sopron
Mór
Etyek-Buda
Somló
Balatonmelléke
Balatonfelvidék
Badacsony
Balatonfüred-Csopak
Dél-Balaton
Tolna
Kunság
Csongrád
Hajós-Baja
Szekszárd
Mecsekalja
Villány
Wine-growing areas in neighboring countries

country's oldest wine region. Its world-famous dry and sweet white wines are made from grapes grown on volcanic soil and loess-rich subsoil.

These main wine-producing areas are subdivided into a total of 22 smaller distinct regions, each with its own stock of grape varieties. Along with the popular varieties such as Cabernet Sauvignon, Cabernet Franc, Merlot, Pinot Noir, Sauvignon Blanc, Chardonnay, Riesling, Muscat Ottonel, and others, there are also indigenous varieties. These are Ezerjó, Furmint, Mézesfehér, Hárslevelü, Cirfandli, Leányka, and Szürkebarát for white wines and Kadarka and Kékfrankos for red.

Along with Tokaji, Hungary's best-known wine, light, dry and fruity whites, such as the Alföld wines with their frequently pronounced acidity, are also made almost exclusively by cooperatives. The wines made from the Chardonnay grape are often very well structured and light. In the Etyek-Buda region to the

Each individual bunch of grapes is carefully cut from the vine.

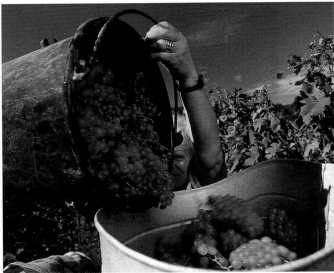

The grapes are emptied into tubs ready for transporting.

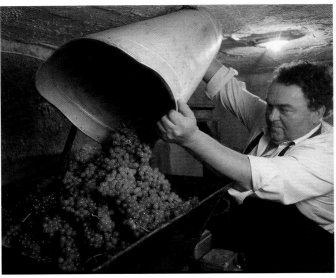

In the winery, the stalks are removed before PRESSING.

The grapes are pushed down into the pressing vat.

Even today, traditional wooden winepresses are used.

The fresh MUST flows out of the press.

west and southwest of the capital Budapest, the international grape varieties Chardonnay, Pinot Noir, Pinot Blanc, and Sauvignon Blanc are grown. Furmint, the grape from which Tokaji Aszú is made, is grown in the Somló region northwest of Lake Balaton, likewise in volcanic soil. In northern Transdanubia, north of Lake Balaton, central Europe's great white grapes, such as Riesling, Pinot Gris (Szürkebarát, meaning the "gray monk," after the Cistercians who brought it with them to these parts), Traminer, Muscat, and Müller-Thurgau are widespread. They make a fruity white wine with peach and apricot aromas. To the south of the lake, predominantly the Dél-Balaton region, Cabernet Sauvignon, and Pinot Noir (Nagyburgundi) grapes are also encountered; they sometimes turn out slightly sweet due to a certain amount of RESIDUAL SUGAR. The renowned and once sought-after indigenous Kadarka variety is still grown in the southern Transdanubia region of Szekszárd, on the eastern bank of the Danube, albeit in small quantities. It is virtually non-existent in the north, however, and is grown only on one well-known vineyard on the road leading from Budapest to the Tokaj region, where it was once widespread. In the Eger region, named after one of the most visited cities in Hungary, at the foot of the Bükk mountains, the soil is also volcanic.

This area is where Bull's Blood, the famous Hungarian red wine, is made, as well as Egri Bikaver, today a blend of Cabernet, Merlot, Kékoporto (Blauer Portugieser), and Kékfrankos (Blaufränkish or Lemberger) grapes.

ALFÖLD (THE GREAT PLAIN)

The largest single wine-growing area south of Budapest is also one of Hungary's youngest. The vines here were planted mainly after the PHYLLOXERA catastrophe, as the vine pests do not survive terribly well on sandy soil. This part of the country is characterized by hot summers and cold winters. In the spring there are frequent late frosts, which pose a danger to the young shoots, but in the summer the sandy subsoil heats up to such an extent that, on occasions, ground temperatures as high as 140°F (60°C) have been recorded.

In the remaining regions, mainly Olaszrizling (Welschriesling or Riesling Italico) and certain indigenous grape varieties are grown, as well as international grape varieties such as Cabernet Sauvignon, Merlot, and Pinot Noir. The wine producers make light red wines and whites that are low in acidity. The best red wines of this area originate in the Hajós-Baja region. Hungarovin, a Budapest-based wine company, is one of the major large producers here.

The end of grape-picking is celebrated with a large festival at which some lively dancing takes place.

THE WINE REGIONS AROUND LAKE BALATON

Sheltered vineyards and steep slopes with a sandy basalt base, assisted by a climate regulator in the form of Lake Balaton, provide perfect conditions for the cultivation of vines. This fact was recognized by the Romans, who planted more vineyards here than in any other part of their province of Pannonia.

The large wine-growing area of Transdanubia is split into two parts by Lake Balaton, each of which embraces a number of different regions, and stretches from Sopron in the northwest to Villány, the region around Siklós, in the south. The elongated shape of this large lake harmonizes the temperatures and provides the soils with a balanced source of water. In summer it lowers the heat and in winter it acts as a natural

store of warmth. The northern part of Transdanubia stretches down to the lake from the Austrian and Slovak borders. This side of the lake, in particular, has been of special significance to wine production in Hungary for centuries. A high proportion of the vineyards are on slopes made of volcanic loam soils. Predominantly white wines are made from the grapes grown here. The most widely grown grape is Olaszrisling, which produces a fresh, spicy wine.

In the northwesterly region of Sopron, on the other hand, exclusively red wines are made. In Somló, a small wine-growing area to the northwest of the lake, around 1,483 acres (600 ha) of vines grow on the slopes of the extinct volcano Mount Somló. The white wines from this region were once as highly prized as the famous Tokaji, and there was a very good reason for this: for centuries the wine was supplied to the Habsburg court. It was drunk on rulers' wedding nights in the belief that it would help them father male offspring. Presumably it was enjoyed on other occasions as well.

The area south of the lake, reaching down to the Croatian border, was planted with vineyards only a few years ago. Both red and white varieties thrive in the sandy, loess-rich subsoil. The other important areas are Villány, Szekszárd, and Mecsekalja. While mainly red grapes are grown in the mountains of Villány, growers around Siklós concentrate on making white wines. Some of this region's most ambitious and promising growers are Attila Gere, József Bock, and Kúria Malatinszky from Villány.

The most famous grape variety in Szekszárd is the Kadarka, which, given its long vegetation

SELECT PRODUCER

BALATONBOGLÁRI R.T.***
BALATONBOGLÁR
8,648 acres (3,500 ha); 24,000,000 bottles
• *Wines: Riesling, Chardonnay, Muscat, red wines*
This formerly state-owned enterprise, founded in 1952, is today one of the largest in the country and is now owned by a German firm, Henkell & Söhnlein. Most of the wines made here originate in the Lake Balaton region.

phase, is able to ripen fully here before being harvested. Among the best local producers are Ferenc and Csaba Vesztergombi. Powerful, spicy wines are made in Hungary's warmest region, the Mecsek mountains (also known as Mecsekalja). This is possible in spite of the long periods of very dry weather.

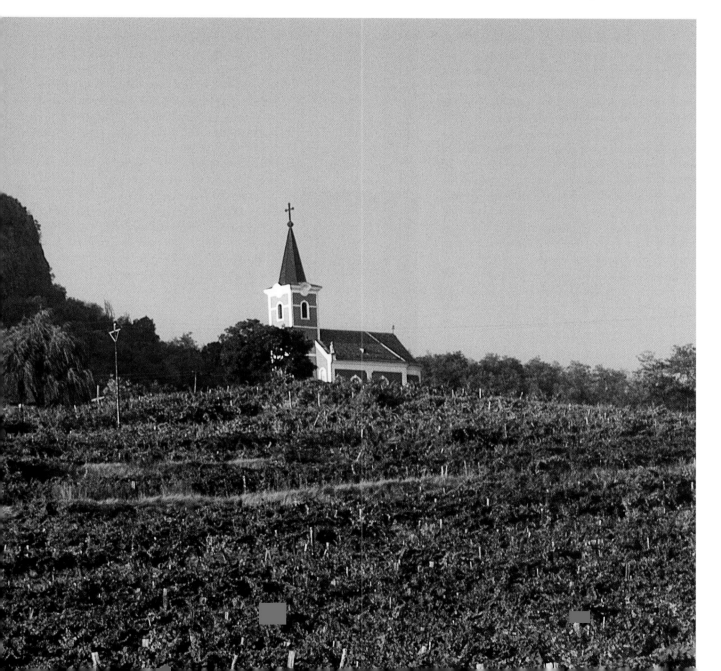

Extensive vineyards stretch back all the way around Lake Balaton, Europe's largest lake.

EGER

The old town of Eger is without doubt one of Hungary's most beautiful towns and is also one of the country's most important centers of wine trading. The most famous wine from the area of the same name is the red wine Egri Bikavér, or Bull's Blood. It has gone on to become the region's main brand-name wine and has made the region famous abroad too. The Kadarka grape, which was once the predominant variety in this blend, has now been replaced by Kékfrankos. The other grapes that go into Bull's Blood are Cabernet Sauvignon, Kékoporto, and Merlot. The name is taken from a legend that describes how, in the 16th century, the Eger fortress had to be defended against Turkish attackers. When the Magyars' strength abandoned them after five weeks of siege, the castle commander ordered the men to be given wine. After drinking it, their fighting spirit returned and their beards, dripping with wine, glistened red. At the sight of this, the Turks, who were superior in number, took flight, in the belief that their opponents had been drinking the blood of bulls.

Hungary's winegrowers are showing an impressive dynamic with these new plantings near Eger.

Opposite
The scenery around the old wine town of Eger is dominated by a patchwork of small vineyards.

Eger's "Bull's Blood" has a modern profile thanks to Cabernet and Merlot.

In its early years, Bull's Blood is a dark red, powerful wine and has very dominant TANNINS immediately after bottling. It is a legendary wine that recalls a time when wines were allowed to mature properly in the cellar. Today, western European palates demand wines with softer tannins that can be drunk young. When buying a bottle of Egri Bikáver, you should make sure it is sealed with an official state serial number. This guarantees that the wine really is from Eger, and protects the producers from counterfeiting.

The climate around the town of Eger is dry and very warm during the summer, although due to its long winters, the vegetation phase starts particularly late. In addition to the renowned Bull's Blood, interesting white wines are made from the Olaszrisling and Leányka varieties, with the latter producing the better examples. This grape is grown exclusively in the Eger region and, as a general rule, matures very early. The grapes have a high sugar content and the wines possess an intense honey AROMA.

Just as famous as its wines are the town's enormous wine cellars. With branches extending out from beneath the castle under large parts of the town, visitors are repeatedly fascinated by this extensive underground system. In earlier centuries, these cellars not only provided winemakers with storage space for their wines, they were also used as a place of refuge during times of war.

The wine industry in Eger remains in a state of transition. There is a new emphasis on quality and the wineries have started to modernize. Visiting the Egervin cooperative, it is difficult not to make a comparison with the cooperative wineries of southern France of around 25 to 30 years ago, with their large wooden barrels and old concrete vats. This winery, privatized in June 1993, was updated in 1997 to meet today's standards through the introduction of modern technology and equipment.

SELECT PRODUCERS IN EGER

G.I.A.***
EGER
Wine was first produced by this cooperative enterprise, formed by the Hungarian Tibor Gál (G), the Tuscan Marchese Incisa (I), and the German merchant Burkard Bovensiepen with his firm Alpina (A), in 1993. Since then, this winery has been responsible for some of Hungary's best wines, among them Chardonnay, Cabernet Sauvignon, and Kékfrankos.

HUNGAROVIN**
BUDAPEST
This enormous company makes wines from grapes grown throughout the whole of Hungary, but its Eger wine is worth mentioning in its own right. The enterprise has been owned by the German wine company Henkell & Söhnlein since the beginning of the 1990s and has switched since then from concentrating exclusively on quantity to placing a firm emphasis on quality.

TOKAJI

This famous wine, and the region it comes from, Tokajhegyalja, take their names from the town in the north of the country. The name of the wine has nothing to do with Tokay d'Alsace (the Alsace synonym for Pinot Gris), however, nor with Tocai Friulano, which is widespread in northern Italy. Tokaji, meaning "from (the town of) Tokaj"—has been a wine of renown since the 17th century, although it was hardly ever seen in western Europe following the collapse of the Austro-Hungarian Empire in 1918, and even less so after the communists came to power in 1949. The vineyards are situated just a few miles from the borders with Slovakia and the Ukraine, and cover 12,350 acres (5,000 ha) of mostly south-facing slopes. The Bodrog and Tisza rivers dominate the plain and create the specific climatic conditions which allow the indigenous grape varieties (Furmint and Hárslevelü) to concentrate their sugar content in the fall, either as a result of BOTRYTIS CINEREA (noble rot) or by allowing the grapes to dry out on the vine. These are the same conditions that are found in the Sauternes region. But the climatic conditions alone do not explain the exceptional properties of the best-

The exquisite sweet Eszencias and Aszús are once again delighting wine lovers. But extremely good dry Furmints as well as Hárslevelüs, benefiting from modern winemaking techniques, are also achieving considerable success.

Thanks to international joint ventures, the area around Tokaj is currently undergoing change on a large scale.

known of Tokaji wines produced from the overripe grapes known as *aszú*. The grape varieties, the volcanic soil, the classic VINIFICATION, and excellent storage conditions in tuff (volcanic detritus) caves with their rich microflora and walls thickly coated with mold—all these factors help make Tokaji what it is. The yield naturally depends on the crop and number of vines per acre. As a rule, the vineyards are planted with up to 10,000 vines, allowing the required quality to be achieved. But vineyards dating back to the communist era, with little more than 800 vines per acre

(2,000 per ha) produce outstanding results. Thanks to foreign investment from France, Spain and Britain, the vineyards in the northeast of the country are today experiencing a genuine renaissance. In the last few decades obsolete winemaking methods have affected quality and the producers could not keep pace with international developments. In addition to the high-quality sweet wines, dry white wines are also made in the Tokaj region, among them the well-known Tokaji Szamorodni Száraz.

OLDER THAN THE WINES OF SAUTERNES

Wine has been made in this region since before the invasion of the Magyars, who gave their name to the present-day inhabitants of the country. In the Middle Ages, winegrowers moved into the area around Tokaj from Italy, and also from Wallonia in the south of what is now Belgium. The wine's breakthrough did not come until the end of the 15th century, however, when the first Aszú sweet wines were made, predating the wines of Sauternes by about 200 years, and the first great wines from the Rhine valley by a century. Supposedly from the 16th century onwards, large quantities of the legendary Magyar wine were exported. Pope Pius IV was given some Tokaji Aszú as a gift by the Hungarian archbishop Draskovich at the Council of Trent in 1562. This could have marked the beginning of the wine's ascent. It should come as no surprise, therefore, that the world's prominent figures were initially astonished and then delighted by the unusual taste and character of Tokaji Aszú. It rapidly became the wine of kings and Czars, and for several centuries was a regular feature at the banquets of all the courts of Europe. "*vinum regorum, rex vinorum*" (the wine of kings and the king of wines) declared King Louis XIV of France, who prized the wine beyond measure. Writers such as Voltaire, Rabelais, and Goethe looked to this Hungarian wine for inspiration, valuing as they did its creative powers. During the course of the following centuries, numerous heads of European countries sang the wine's praises and helped it acquire its reputation. It is even extolled in the Hungarian national anthem.

Like countless others, the vineyards of Hungary were attacked and largely destroyed by phylloxera at the end of the 19th century. While they were being built up again, the country experienced major political upheavals, from the announcement of the republic at the end of the First World War to the agricultural reforms of 1945 and the end of the communist era in 1989.

These were decades that unfortunately did not serve Hungarian wine well in terms of quality. Since the fall of the Iron Curtain, however, the situation has started to change for the better, thanks to foreign investment and the long-overdue modernization of the wineries. Following some turbulent times, the great Tokaji Aszú has woken up again from its Sleeping Beauty-like slumber, as has the very aromatic and dry white wine made from the Furmint grape.

INTERNATIONAL INVESTMENT ENCOURAGES A NEW START

Following recovery from the phylloxera catastrophe, which was responsible for destroying a large part of the vineyards, and the replanting of vines, the wines of Tokaj became difficult to obtain in the west as a result of the isolationist policy of the communist bloc. The vineyards were nationalized in their entirety during the communist era and run by agricultural combines that were set up from 1949 onwards. Quality began to sink steadily: systematic pasteurization and OXIDIZATION, or even the

The wine of kings, the king of wines—but also now a treat for democrats.

Tokaji Aszú matures in cellars, some of which date from the 18th century. In the Tokaj wine museum the bottles filled with this nectar are stored with thick layers of mold growing on them, which heightens the impression that this place is truly ancient.

many others also produce wine in the Tokaj region. All these operations are striving to revive the original quality of the product.

VINIFICATION OF ASZÚ

Tokaji Aszú is made using a unique method. The overripe Furmint, Hárslevelü, and Muscat Lunel grapes, affected by the *Botrytis cinerea* mold, are individually picked and collected in small, 55-pound (25-kg) tubs (*puttonyos*) throughout October and November, according to strict selection criteria. Careful mashing of the grapes produces Aszú (meaning "dried") paste. Next, the desired number of *puttonyos* (between three and six) is added to 36 gallons (136 liters—the volume of the local barrel or *gönc* used) of fresh, white grape must. In contrast to previous methods, today's ambitious Tokaji vintners make sure this base wine is also of very good quality and has a certain amount of residual sugar. The number of *puttonyos* used determines the grade of sweetness under which the wine is later classified: the more *puttonyos* used, the sweeter the wine. The labels on the bottles indicate this level of sweetness. After mashing and pressing, the wine is matured in small wooden barrels for five to seven years and later bottled in the characteristic white, 17-fl oz (50-cl) bottles. Tasting a great Tokaji vintage is an unforgettable experience. The more *puttonyos* one uses, the more concentrated, rich, intense, and complex the wine becomes. As the high degree of sweetness fades it is met by a gentle acidity, providing balance and perfect harmony. The wines display an amazingly wide-ranging raisin, honey, plum, and apricot aroma. Sweet wine rarities such as this taste wonderful with warm apricot tart,

addition of alcohol to stop the FERMENTATION process, brought it to an all-time low. This mass-produced wine with its oxidized taste was exported (mainly in exchange for natural gas) primarily to the Soviet Union, its largest market in the period following the Second World War. From 1991, western European investors from France, Spain, and Britain took advantage of the Hungarian government's decision to dispose of 12,360 acres (5,000 ha) of vineyards. This resulted in the formation of a number of jointly owned companies, many of them involving the investment of French insurance companies. The management of Château Pajzos was entrusted to two Bordeaux enologists, Arcaute and Rolland. Today Jean-Louis Labarde owns the majority of the estate. The company that makes the most famous of all Spanish wines, Vega Sicilia (the Oremus winery), Cana (a cooperative from the Nantes region), G.M.F. (the Etzele estate), and

SELECT PRODUCERS OF TOKAJI

THE OLDEST A.O.C. IN THE WORLD?
As long ago as 1700, many years before the geographical limits were set for the fine Portuguese wines of the Douro valley, a list was drawn up of the best Tokaji vineyards, classifying the wines (in Latin) into three grades. The wines were placed in the first, second, or third categories according to characteristics that would still win A.O.C. plaudits today. Such a system was not introduced in France until 1935.

GRÓF DEGENFELD***
TARCEL
173 acres (70 ha) • *Wines: Furmint, Hárslevelü, Sárga Muskotály*
The former enologist with the Royal Tokaj Wine Company, Sarolta Bárdos, has already vinified her first top vintage with this estate that was newly established in 1996. The family of Count Degenfeld formerly owned two castles in the Tokaj region.

ISTVÁN SZEPSY***
MÁD
49 acres (20 ha)
István Szepsy is one of the great reformers of Tokaj. He has introduced a strict reduction in yields and gentle processing in the winery, which make his wines the very best of the region. With the backing of an American investor, he has also succeeded in resurrecting the Királyudvar winery. Since 1998 he's been president of the Tokaj Renaissance organization.

BODROG VÁRHEGY**
BODROG-KERESZÚR
37 acres + 370 acres (15 ha + 150 ha); bought-in grapes; 250,000 bottles • *Wines: Furmint, Hárslevelü, Muscat Lunel*
This enterprise buys in grapes from various contract growers and produces dry and white Szamorodni, both well worth trying, and an excellent Aszú, all of which are also exported to the West.

Behind the simple facades of the fermentation buildings in Tokajhegyalja extensive cellars stretch far back into the hill.

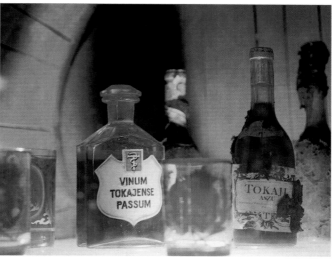

Tokaji enjoys its excellent reputation because it ages so well.

The Tokaj wine museum has typical cellar storage and a collection of legendary vintages.

Tokaji is still an exceptional wine today, although it is now available to a wider public.

hazelnut cake, duck with plums or orange, or endive leaves with Roquefort and green walnuts.

In very good years there is an even sweeter variety of Aszú, which is known as Eszencia. A particular type of YEAST is required for this. The wine can have residual sugar of up to 92 ounces per gallon (650 grams per liter) and matures for ten years in the barrel before being bottled. This Eszencia variety is really a viscous Tokaji with low levels of alcohol, which is made from the run-off must of the Aszú. Because of the high sugar content (up to 60 percent), fermentation requires several years.

Szamorodni (meaning "as grown") is also produced in Tokaj and is a simpler variety of the wine, made from common grapes widely grown in the region. The grapes used are only partly affected by botrytis, and are not selected individually. This wine displays varying levels of sweetness, depending on the quality of the harvest and the proportion of Aszú grapes it contains. In addition to sweet varieties of Szamorodni, there are also medium-dry and dry varieties. The grapes not affected by noble rot yield a pleasant-tasting white wine with a pronounced light fruit and a delicate aroma. To distinguish between the two types, Szamorodni is known as *száras* when it is dry, and *edes* when it is sweet.

THE CZECH REPUBLIC AND SLOVAKIA

At the beginning of the 1990s, the former Czechoslovakia was split into the Czech Republic and Slovakia. At this time the two countries had a total of 116,000 acres (47,000 ha) of vineyards, of which 89,000 acres (36,000 ha) were in production. Today the area is smaller. Most of the vineyards are in Slovakia, mainly in the south and southwest of the country, while in the Czech Republic, grapes are grown only in the southeast, in Moravia, and around the town of Melnik in Bohemia. Other than these Bohemian vineyards, the vine-growing areas border Austria directly, and those in Slovakian territory extend as far as the Hungarian Tokaji-producing region.

The vineyards of Slovakia cover around 49,419 acres (20,000 ha) of gentle slopes, a maximum of 800 feet (250 m) above sea level, and extend as far as the plain of the Danube basin. They are protected from cold northerly winds by high elevations. The climate is continental, with hot summers, cool winters, and moderate precipitation. The range of grapes grown is similar to that of Austria. The main white varieties are a tangy Riesling, Pinot Blanc, Ryzlink Vlassky (Welschriesling or Riesling Italico), a fresh Müller-Thurgau, peppery Grüner Veltliner (Veltlinské Zelené), a pleasant Sylvaner, and a spicy Irsay Oliver, a native variety resembling Muscadelle. Among the best reds are the full-bodied and fruity Blaufränkisch (Frankovka) and Saint Laurent (Vavrinecké or Svatovavrinecké), representing around 35 percent of the total. The best wines of Slovakia come from the area around the capital, Bratislava, and the extreme east of the country,

the Slovakian part of Tokaj. The estates of Milan Pavelka and the Matysák family in Pezinok, 12½ miles (20 km) from Bratislava, are currently two of the country's best-known wineries. Pavelka has been running the area's largest estate himself since 1995. The Matysák family is developing the estate to entice an increasing number of visitors interested in wine from Bratislava. They have built a restaurant on their estate and sell their best wines on the spot. The Ostrozovic estate, in Kosice in Slovakian Tokaj, has 17 acres (7 ha) of vineyards and concentrates on the production of superb Aszú wines. Very good dry varieties are produced here too.

As in the Czech and Slovak Republics, the number of privately-owned vineyards is also rapidly increasing in Slovenia, and they are producing more and more pleasing wines.

SLOVENIA

Slovenia, in 1991, was one of Yugoslavia's first republics to demand independence. Its wine-growing areas can be divided into three: Primorski, Podravski, and Posavski, with the first two of these having the largest share of the growing area (about 40 percent each). When Slovenia was part of the Austro-Hungarian Empire, its wines were much sought after. At that time, the vineyards covered around 124,000 acres (50,000 ha) of land; today they cover about 59,303 acres (24,000 ha).

Primorski lies on the country's eastern border with Italy, and the Italian wine-growing region of Collio was part of what is now Slovenia right up to the First World War. The soils are dominated by limestone and red clay. Podravski runs along the border with the Austrian region of southern Styria. Its vineyards are often situated on steep, sometimes terraced slopes with chalky or clay subsoil. The wines produced here are predominantly aromatic, fruity whites.

Among the grape varieties now offered by the Slovenian growers are Laski Riesling (Welschriesling), Gewürztraminer, Pinot Blanc, Riesling (Renski Rizling), Sauvignon Blanc, and the native Sipon variety (comparable to the Hungarian Furmint). A high plateau in the Primorski wine-growing area supports mainly red varieties, such as Refosco (Teran), Barbera, and Cabernet Sauvignon.

A large proportion of the wine is still produced by cooperative wineries, although the number of private estates is growing steadily. Techniques used in the cooperatives do not yet match the latest modern standards, as a rule. Indeed, many wines are still being sweetened and can be relatively characterless, but there are praiseworthy exceptions. More and more committed winemakers are recognizing the potential of their vineyards and are on the way to producing wines that will soon stand up well to comparison with those of neighboring Collio in Italy and Styria in Austria. A small number of producers also now enjoy international recognition.

SELECT SLOVENIAN PRODUCERS

MOVIA****
DOBROVO
44 acres (18 ha) • *Wines: Tokay, Rebula, Pinot Gris, Pinot Blanc, Chardonnay, Sauvignon Blanc, Merlot*
This winery is currently being run by the seventh generation of Ales Kristancic's family. He was the first winemaker in Yugoslavia, as it was then, to experiment with red wine matured in *barriques*—and with great success too, his aim being to preserve the characteristics of the grape without overloading the wine with wood. By increasing the density of the vines and radically reducing the quantities produced, he has managed to produce concentrated, characterful wines.

RADGONSKE GORICE***
GORNJA RADGONA
741 acres (300 ha); bought-in grapes; 2,500,000 bottles • *Wines: Welschriesling, Sipon, Riesling, Sauvignon Blanc, Traminer, Müller-Thurgau, Chardonnay, Ranina*
This combine and winery are backed up by 150 years of winemaking tradition. They are well-known for their sparkling wines, which have received numerous awards and won a degree of international recognition.

UNIVERZA V MARIBORU***
MARIBOR
44 acres (18 ha); 20,000 bottles
The wine estate belonging to the university of Maribor, founded in 1820, can look back on nearly 200 years of history.

VIPAVA***
VIPAVA
4,201 acres (1,700 ha) • *Wines: Zelen, Pinela, Rebula, Malvasia, Sauvignon Blanc, Chardonnay, Pinot Blanc, Welschriesling, Merlot, Cabernet Sauvignon, Barbera*
This winery, founded in 1894, is one of the most innovative cooperative associations in the country. It has its origins in the oldest peasants' cooperative winery in Slovenia, which had branches in Vienna, Prague, Graz, and Trier. Its wines, which are typical of the region, are popular abroad, and have won a number of awards. Those made from the local Zelen and Pinela grapes are an unusual feature.

BULGARIA

VINEYARDS IN THE LAND OF ROSES

Of all the countries belonging to the former eastern bloc, Bulgaria, which borders Romania to the north, Serbia and Macedonia to the west, the Black Sea to the east, and Turkey and Greece to the south, has benefited most from the new political and economic conditions. New export markets in many west European countries (notably Great Britain, Germany, and the Benelux countries) have been discovered for its red and white wines. Both the state-run and newly privatized wineries have thus been able to prepare for the future with new investment and, thanks to their exceptionally good value for money—a strong argument for buying Bulgarian wines—win a good market position for themselves.

The history of the kingdom of Bulgaria began in 680. Two hundred years later the nation experienced a golden age that brought important innovations to a wide area. The brothers St. Cyril and St. Methodius developed the Cyrillic alphabet which was to have a decisive influence on the whole of Slavic literature and culture. Numerous buildings, still standing or in ruins, bear witness today to the flourishing architectural activity and prosperity of this period and the centuries that followed. Until the end of the Second World War, which brought communist

Melnik, south of Sofia, has its own variety of grape, also known as Melnik. Another name for this is Bulgarian Syrah.

rule to the country, Bulgaria's wine industry had been almost exclusively in the hands of small growers who pressed their own wines. In 1944 the government took the decision to introduce a system of collectivization, which had been virtually unknown hitherto. New specialists were trained in winemaking schools, and numerous foreign grape varieties, for example Cabernet Sauvignon, Merlot, and Riesling were planted in addition to indigenous varieties such as Gamza and Mavrud.

Bulgaria's main wine exporter today has around 365,700 acres (148,000 ha) of vineyards, a smaller area than it had in the past. In fact, according to experts only around 247,100 acres (100,000 ha) are under cultivation. Bulgaria used to export a large amount of wine to the U.S.S.R. but, in the 1980s, as a result of a campaign against alcoholism in the Soviet Union, many Bulgarian vineyards were closed. Since the opening-up of western European markets, new vineyards are being planted again, mostly on sloping sites.

The climate is similar to that of Bulgaria's neighboring countries: hot summers and cold winters. Temperatures can climb to over 104°F (40°C) in the summer months and drop below −13°F (−25°C) in winter. The Black Sea in the north and the two big rivers, the Danube and the Maritsa, generally soften the effect of these extreme differences in temperature. Annual precipitation ranges roughly from $18^1/_2$ inches (47 cm) to $37^1/_2$ inches (95 cm).

THE MAIN WINE-GROWING AREAS

There are seven main wine-growing areas in Bulgaria, of which five have very well-defined borders: Dunavska Ravnina in the northwest, Thrakien in the south, Tsjernomorski Raion in the east, Dolinata na Struma in the southwest and Podbalkanski Raion in central Bulgaria.

In the north, in the Danube valley, and in the plains between the Danube and the Balkan Mountains, grapes grow both in the plains and in the mountains (up to 1,300 feet/400 m). The main varieties grown in the alluvial and loess plains are Cabernet Sauvignon, Merlot, Aligoté, Muscat Ottonel, Gamza (a Bulgarian grape with distinctive aromas, spicy and full-bodied while relatively young), and the white Misket grape, which is indigenous to the famous Valley of the Roses in central Bulgaria, and produces a flowery wine with overtones of Muscat.

Soil conditions in the south of the country are ideally suited to the Mavrud grape, from which a powerful wine is made, full-bodied in its early years and sometimes reminiscent of Mourvèdre.

The characterful white wines from the regions close to the Black Sea attain a real finesse: Riesling, Sauvignon, Chardonnay (aged in barrels made from young American oak), and some Gewürztraminer are the main ones. The coast in this area has a predominantly Mediterranean climate.

Another indigenous grape variety, Melnik, thrives in the warm climate of the Struma valley, to the south of the capital, Sofia. This grape, from the region that has given it its name, yields powerful wines with an intense BOUQUET and pronounced tannins. To a certain extent it can be seen as the Syrah of Bulgarian wines.

BULGARIAN WINE CLASSIFICATION

In 1978 regulations were introduced to classify Bulgarian wines. The standard-quality wines are known as *vins de table* and *vins de pays*. Wines with a geographical designation of origin (D.G.O., Declared Geographical Origin) carry the name of the *appellation*, region, district, and town or village. The top-quality wines are marketed under the name *controliran*, corresponding to the French A.O.C. designation (specific region of production, specific grape variety, prescribed quality), which has so far been awarded to 30 areas. In addition to these, there is a further category for fortified wines. The *kolektzione* quality designation is used for wines aged in wooden barrels, made of either native Bulgarian or American wood.

Yield levels—frequently too high—are a delicate subject, but Bulgarian growers deliver reasonable quality, in their export wines at least.

Average yields are 428 to 535 gallons per acre (40 to 50 hl/ha) for the D.G.O. wines and between 267 and 428 gallons per acre (25 and 40 hl/ha) for *controliran* wines.

PREPARING FOR THE FUTURE

Of all the countries of eastern Europe, Bulgaria is making the most determined efforts to ensure that the quality of its wines is directed toward the standards of its overseas sales markets. The fact that receipts are being invested in the re-equipping of the wineries is also having a positive effect. Around 70 percent of profits are reputedly flowing into the acquisition of new fermentation vats, presses, refrigeration plants, and *barriques*. The enologist Atanas Babaev is of the opinion that "the overall quality of Bulgarian wine has risen over the last few years thanks to this investment." He cites further reasons, for example the switch from large barrels made of Bulgarian oak to *barriques*, the mandatory de-stalking, and picking

DUNAVSKA RAVNINA
Novo Selo
Lozitza
Svishtov
Pavlikeni
Suhindol
Lyaskovetz

TSJERNOMORSKI RAION
Preslav
Chan Krum
Varna
Jujen Briag

PODBALKANSKI RAION
Sungurlare
Rozova Dolina

THRAKIEN
Oriachovitza
Asenovgrad
Stambolovo
Sakar

DOLINATA NA STRUMA
Harsovo

Wine-growing areas in neighboring countries

Left
The areas bordering Macedonia and Greece offers an ideal climate for good red wines.

Next double page
Although Bulgaria is now exporting modern consumer wines, many of its producers are still dependent on old implements and methods.

at higher levels of ripeness than before. CHAP-TALIZATION (enriching with sugar) is hardly necessary, he claims, but nevertheless allowed, depending on the sugar levels of the grapes that have been picked. Californian Chardonnay and Sauvignon Blanc clones are currently being tested at a special site, as the use of these two grape varieties is going to become increasingly widespread over the next few years.

Although many vineyards remain in the hands of the state, the privatization of a number of wineries has brought some beneficial changes to Bulgarian wine production. Once Bulgaria is a member of the E.U. the attitude of the wine-growers will certainly gradually change. The Suhindol winery, founded in 1909, one of the oldest in the country, is Bulgaria's showpiece winery and has been displaying a remarkable dynamism over recent years. So far 400,000 U.S. dollars have been invested in its modernization, and each year sees the creation of new top-class wines, some of which are aged in barrels made of French oak. In 1998 American investors also put money into the former state-owned producer Vinprom Russe. In 2001 it merged with the Boyar Domain to make the new Boyar Estate, which is now the biggest wine producer in Bulgaria.

BULGARIA'S FIRST PRIVATE WINE PRODUCER

BOYAR ESTATE**—***
65,000,000 bottles • Wines: Sauvignon, Chardonnay, Riesling, Cabernet, Merlot, Gamza, Varietals, Reserve
This organization (Bulgaria's first private wine-producing enterprise) is known throughout the country as a producer that can be relied upon for its quality. For a while now Domaine Boyar has been concentrating on the production of first-class wines, with the aim of creating a new style of Bulgarian wine by combining the best features of the old and new worlds. Examples are:
• Cabernet Sauvignon Premium Oak, Iambol Winery (wine production in an ultra-modern winery, aging in new oak barrels).
• Merlot Premium Cuvée, Shumen Winery (one of Europe's most modern wineries).
• Cabernet Sauvignon Premium Reserve, Iambol Winery.
In addition to these wines, which represent the new Bulgarian wine industry, the following wine deserves a special mention:
• Royal Reserve***, 20,000–30,000 bottles per year; this Cabernet Sauvignon special reserve wine is made by one of the best wineries in the country, that of Lovico Suhindol for Boyar Estate, and is matured for 36 months in barrels of American oak.

ROMANIA

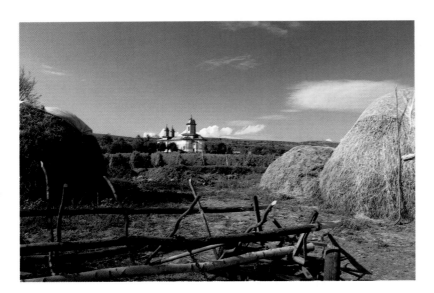

After 6,000 years of vine growing, Romania is now undergoing a fresh start with an emphasis on quality.

Romania, the result of the unification of Walachia and Moldavia in 1862, is one of eastern Europe's major wine-producing nations and one of the ten largest wine exporters in the world. Wine production in the area of present-day Romania has an ancient tradition going back over 6,000 years. The vineyards currently cover around 617,500 acres (250,000 ha), and 20 percent of these are given over to the production of table grapes. The climate is mainly continental.

THE MAJOR WINE-PRODUCING REGIONS

Of the total vineyard area, 79 percent is to be found in the Moldavia, Muntenia (Greater Walachia), and Oltenia (Little Walachia) regions. Moldavia, where winter temperatures can fall to –22°F (–30°C), is famous for Romania's best-known wine, Cotnari, which has been produced here for 600 years. This sweet, aromatic wine is made from the region's traditional grape varieties (Grasa, Feteasca Alba, Francusa, and Tamaioasa Romaneasca). Within the Muntenia and Oltenia regions are other areas similarly famous for their wines, for example Dealul Mare ("the big hill"). International red wine varieties such as Cabernet Sauvignon, Merlot, and Pinot Noir are grown here alongside the indigenous Feteasca Neagra. The white varieties are Welschriesling (Riesling Italico), Pinot Gris, Sauvignon Blanc, Muscat Ottonel, and Feteasca Alba.

The remaining wine-producing regions are centered around Transylvania, where the vineyards climb up the slopes to heights of 1,300 feet (400 m). In Tarnave, Alba, Sebes Apold, and Lechinia, mainly dry white wines, but also some pleasant sweet (some of them liqueur-like) white wines, are made from the Traminer, Sauvignon

In Buzau, in Greater Walachia, vintners are achieving success with international varieties like Cabernet Sauvignon.

Blanc, Muscat Ottonel, Pinot Gris, Feteasca Alba, and Welschriesling grapes.

Between 1991 and 1996, 76 percent of Romanian producers and properties passed into private ownership, which mainly took the form of joint ventures with foreign investors.

GRAPE VARIETIES AND APPELLATIONS

Romania possesses a wide range of imported grape varieties (for example Pinot Noir, which is very common in Dealul Mare) as well as numerous native grape varieties. The proportion of vineyards planted with local varieties is relatively large. Feteasca Regala is grown over an area of 42,500 acres (17,200 ha), mainly in Transylvania and on the slopes of Moldavia. It produces dry and sparkling wines. Feteasca Alba (57,000 acres/23,000 ha) is also found predominantly in these two regions. In good years this grape makes a substantial contribution to the success of sweet Cotnari wines. In terms of red varieties, Babeasca Neagra, 17,800 acres (7,200 ha) of which are planted in Moldavia, and Teteasca Neagra (over 2,800 acres/1,120 ha), a very old Romanian variety that has been indigenous to Muntenia for 1,500 to 2,000 years, are both widespread.

Romania introduced *appellations* in 1998 based on the models of other European wine-growing countries. Its wine laws created the following classification: everyday wines, superior quality wines (V.S.), superior quality wines with designation of origin (V.S.O.), and special quality wines with designation of origin (V.S.O.C.). This last category includes wines made with botrytized grapes (C.I.B.), two late-picked wines (C.M.D.), and two specialty wines (a liqueur wine and a sparkling wine). These legally binding regulations are set by the national wine authority.

MAJOR WINE PRODUCERS

Romanian producers can be divided into two groups: the private producers, who have no funds for the necessary investment and simply sell their wine in canisters, and the state wineries. The privatization of a small number of state wineries has been made possible with the injection of foreign investment.

The Vinvico winery is today Danish-owned. A majority share in producer Vinalcool Prahova, now trading as Prahova Winecellars, has been taken by a British company. Vinarte also now finds itself under foreign management. This firm, founded in 1998, is owned by Italians and is currently investing large sums of money in new winemaking technology. All these wineries have managed to raise the quality of their wines within a short space of time, albeit using international grape varieties. The indigenous varieties do not yet have a significant role to play in all of this, but at least a start has been made in establishing much-needed international relationships.

CROATIA AND THE WESTERN BALKANS

Veliki Tabor—monumental guardian of the vineyards.

Opposite
The wine village of Buje in western Istria.

CROATIA
- Istra
- Hrvatsko Primorje
- Sjeverna Dalmacija
- Dalmatinska Zagora
- Srednja i Južna Dalmacija
- Zagorje-Medimurje
- Prigorje-Bilogora
- Plešivica
- Pokuplje
- Moslavina
- Slavonija
- Podunavlje

BOSNIA HERZEGOVINA
- Hercegovina

SERBIA-MONTENEGRO
- Slibotičko-Horgoška Peščara
- Banat
- Sremski Karlovki/ Fruška Gora
- Belgrade
- Pocerina
- Sumadijsko-Velikomoravski
- Timočki
- Zahodnomoravski
- Nišavsko-Juznomoravski
- Crna Gora
- Kosovo

MACEDONIA
- Pčinsko Osogovski
- Povardarski
- Pelagonijsko-Pološki
- Wine-growing areas in neighboring countries

years before Christ, and this narrow strip of coast later experienced an unprecedented golden age under the Romans. Not only were magnificent buildings erected, such as the palace of Emperor Diocletian in Split, but the large-scale cultivation of wine and olives was also established. In the 11th century AD, the coastal region was conquered by Venice, which managed to maintain its influence despite the occupation of the whole of the Balkans by the Turks. The Yugoslav kingdom was created after the Balkan wars and the end of the First World War, and this became a people's republic in 1945. Under the communists the emphasis was less on the quality of the wines than on the quantities produced. Since the independence of Croatia in 1991, an increasing number of both private and cooperative winemakers have been concentrating on improving the quality of their products and modernizing their wineries.

Croatia's climate is varied, with both continental and Mediterranean influences. The wine-growing areas are divided into two regions, each in turn subdivided into different areas: Kontinentalna Hrvatska, inland, and Primorska Hrvatska, on the coast. The country has around

Not only in terms of wine growing, but also in a more general sense, Croatia can be divided into two main geographical regions: on the one hand there are the interior regions such as Slavonia and Krajina, and on the other there is the long, narrow strip of Adriatic coastline, comprising Istria and Dalmatia. The Greeks started to establish colonies on the Adriatic 700

148,000 acres (60,000 ha) of vineyards, many of which are planted mainly with indigenous varieties. The local grape, Plavac Mali Crni, forms the basis for some of the country's best reds, and also for some of its mass-produced wine. Among the best wines are those made by Mike Grgich, the top grower who emigrated to California in 1958 and travels back specially from the U.S.A. for the harvesting and bottling of his Plavac Mali. Other producers, such as Frano Milos, Ivo Skaramuca and the Domaine Zlatan Otok, also make top-flight wines with this strong-willed grape.

Croatia's winemakers have also concentrated on the Pinot Noir, Frankovka (Blaufränkisch), Merlot, Teran (Refosco), Blatina, Vranac, and Zweigelt varieties. Among the best-known white wines are Grasevina (Welschriesling), Zlahtina, Bogdanusa, Malvasija, Vugava, Posip, and international varieties such as Chardonnay, Pinot Blanc, Riesling, and Pinot Gris. One of the country's specialties is the sweet wine Prosek, which is made from a combination of white and red grapes. The best Grasevina wines come from the area around Kutjevo in northeast Croatia. They are graded from KABINETT through to

Trockenbeerenauslese in a classification system similar to the one that is used in Germany. Vlado Krauthaker and Ivan Enjingi are two of the major producers. Viticulture in Slovenia, which was also a part of the former Republic of Yugoslavia and became independent in 1991, was described at length previously.

RUMP STATE WITH A FUTURE IN WINE?

The Greeks and Romans also busied themselves with winemaking in the former Yugoslavia's other territories, i.e. the present-day state of Serbia-Montenegro, Kosovo, and Macedonia, which has been independent since 1991. The wines they produced enjoyed centuries of popularity, but under Turkish rule many vineyards were destroyed or fell victim to phylloxera. Today the larger part of the approximately 237,000 acres (96,000 ha) of vineyards is run by state-owned cooperatives.

The best red wines are made in the Kosovo region, along Montenegro's Adriatic coast, and in Macedonia. The other areas produce grapes that are mainly suited to making basic red and white wines.

Confederation of Independent States (C.I.S.)

The West as Primary Sales Market

The former Soviet Union was one of the biggest wine producers in the world. In 1985 it occupied third place behind Italy and France, even ahead of Spain. Large quantities of wine are still produced by the new southern republics of what was previously the world's largest state, around the Black Sea and Caspian Sea. What they lack is international recognition.

Before the collapse of the Soviet Union, most of the wine production of the present-day republics of Moldova, the Ukraine, Georgia, and Armenia was exported to Russia, usually in exchange for oil or natural gas, a system still in use in many areas today. In 1984 Mikhail Gorbachev, president of the Soviet Union at the time, declared war on alcoholism. Numerous vineyards were abandoned or closed down, a measure also carried through in friendly countries like Bulgaria. Today, attempts are being made, under a new set of conditions, to step up exports again, this time mainly to countries in western Europe.

Wine growing has a very long tradition in the southern republics of the former Soviet Union. But it was not until after the Second World War that anything resembling a proper wine industry developed, for two principal reasons: first, because countries such as the Republic of Moldova (Moldavia) became part of the Soviet Union; and second, because of attempts made by the authorities to replace consumption of vodka with wine drinking.

Moldova—Land of the Czars

The Republic of Moldova is one of the smallest member states of the Confederation of Independent States (C.I.S.), but has the largest acreage of vineyards, which are favored by a continental climate. In this emphatically agricultural country, around ten percent of the total area, or over 444,774 acres (180,000 ha), is planted with vines. The vineyards extend south toward the coast and also around the capital, Chisinau, which lies on the same latitude as Beaune in Burgundy. Archeological discoveries have revealed that wine production in this area of land, bordered by the Danube, the Dniester and the Black Sea, and once known as Bessarabia, has a history stretching back approximately 4,000 years.

Old wine cellars in the East are a treasure trove for wine globetrotters.

Until its annexation by the U.S.S.R. in August 1944, Moldova was officially part of Romania. Since gaining its independence in 1991, the Russian language and Cyrillic alphabet have no longer been stipulated by law. Moldavian, a Romance language that is also widespread in Romania, is spoken once again. The Republic of Moldavia used to be the largest wine producer in the Soviet Union, and its red and white wines were both extremely popular in Moscow.

The consequences of the collapse of the Soviet wine market are not as strongly felt here as in the other eastern bloc countries. Moldova's wines remain in demand. Since the political changes, various wine producers from abroad have either invested in or are advising Moldovan enterprises. But in spite of this support from western Europe (for example, by companies such as Wines of Moldova, an export company founded by the Dutchman Joop van de Kant), and the activities of well-known French enologists (such as Jacques Lurton), numerous problems still need to be overcome before the European market is opened up for Moldovan wine.

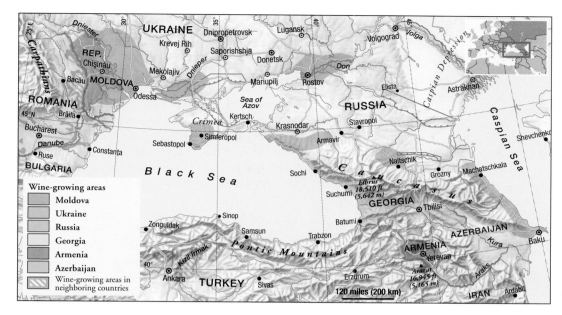

THE UNIQUE ROMANESTI

Following Moldova's entry into the Soviet Union after the end of the Second World War, Stalin created the first *sovchos*, after the Soviet model, on the estate of the Romanov family, the former Czars. Today, the estate's vineyards cover over 1,480 acres (600 ha) and are planted with Rkatsiteli, a local white variety, and the mainly French, Swiss, and German grape varieties introduced at the request of the Czars. But, as elsewhere throughout the country, international varieties such as Aligoté, Traminer, Pinot Noir (known here as Pinot Franc), Malbec, Merlot, and Cabernet Sauvignon are also grown. These last three join forces to make Romanesti de Moldova, Moldova's best-known, and without doubt also its best wine. This wine will certainly make a name for itself again, once its quality has been improved through the use of modern presses, better vinification, and good oak casks.

Before the outbreak of phylloxera, almost exclusively hybrid varieties grew on the Moldovon mountainsides. Following the reorganization of the vineyards, this was no longer the case, as it was considered desirable to replant with modern varieties. It was decided, however, that indigenous grapes such as Rkatsiteli and Feteasca (for white wine—the Dream of Maidens), and Saperavi (for reds) should be retained. A large number of sparkling wines are made in Moldova using traditional techniques, mostly with Riesling, Chardonnay, Aligoté, and Pinot Noir grapes. Wines with added alcohol are also produced with the SOLERA method, used in the production of fortified wines.

The old Soviet wine laws still apply, but Moldova has now also introduced an A.O.C. classification for some of its wines.

UKRAINE

The former "granary of the Soviet Union" has approximately 371,000 acres (150,000 ha) of vineyards, almost a tenth of the total growing area of the former Soviet Union. In ancient times the Greek colonists used to make wine on the Crimean Peninsula and along the whole of the southern coastal area. Ukraine's climate is predominantly continental, with hot summers and severe winters when temperatures can drop

Moldova has enormous potential, a fact that has already been recognized by several foreign investors. Hand-picking using the small crates shown here is reserved, however, for a very small number of top-quality wines.

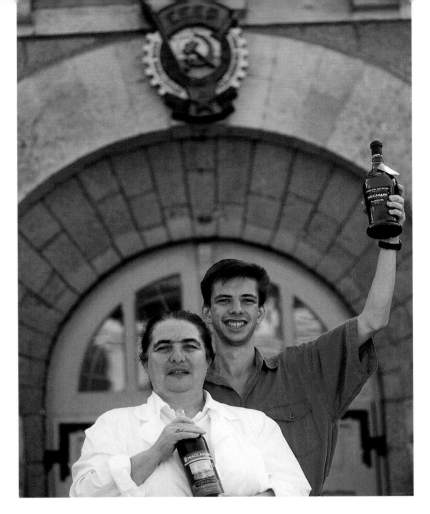

and held in storage on the Crimean Peninsula ever since, were sold at a wine auction. This winery, founded at the end of the 19th century, was one of the most modern operations of its time. Its wines were destined exclusively for the Czars' summer residence. The company still makes excellent dessert wines today.

The most famous enological teaching and testing institution in the C.I.S. was founded in 1828 and is also located on the Crimean Peninsula, in Yalta.

RUSSIA

Wine has been made in the south of the country, between the Black Sea and the Caspian Sea, for over 2,000 years. Following a period of decline under the Czars, the Russian wine economy experienced an upturn, in particular during the Napoleonic wars. But inevitably, Russian president Mikhail Gorbachev's campaign against alcohol in the 1980s had a serious effect on wine production here too.

The most important wine-growing regions are in the valleys and on the slopes of the northern Caucasus and, to a lesser extent, on steeper ground as well. They can be divided into five main areas: Rostov, in the estuary of the river Don surrounding the city of Rostov, Krasnodar, on the Black Sea south of the city of Krasnodar, Stavropol, Checheno-Ingush, and Dagestan at the eastern end of the Caucasus, on the Caspian Sea.

Many grape varieties are found among the 272,000 acres (110,000 ha) of vineyards, with Rkatsiteli among the most widespread. The climate is continental, and during the icy winters the vineyards in the least favorable positions need to be protected from the cold. Nearly 90 percent of the wine is still produced by the state cooperatives.

to −22°F (−30°C). The loess-rich soils are very fertile. Among the country's major grape varieties are Rkatsiteli, Aligoté, Cabernet Sauvignon, Saperavi, Riesling, Gewürztraminer, and indigenous varieties. Along with its production of still and sweet wines there is also a long tradition in Ukraine of making sparkling wine. Major producers have always appreciated the potential of these vineyards, and today around 50 million bottles a year are produced.

The wine world was amazed when, in 1990, some dessert wines made by the Massandra winery, once owned by the Russian royal family

Galina and Valentin proudly displaying some of their competitive products.

Opposite
The extensive vineyards are harvested by machine.

Left
Sparkling wines are among the best-known and most popular exports.

Right
Massandra, in the Crimea, has a reputation for producing outstanding dessert wines.

Patrick Fiévez, Sabine Rumrich, Klaus Feiten, Michael Ben-Joseph

THE MEDITERRANEAN COUNTRIES

GREECE

Wines was founded in Athens, and right up to their accession to the European Community in 1981 no laws were in force to regulate Greek wine production. This put Greece at a great disadvantage compared to other European wine producers, namely France, Portugal, Spain, and Italy. These countries had recognized at an earlier stage the need to guarantee the quality of wines (not least by rigorously limiting the yield) and to protect the *appellations*. For some 3,500 years the Greeks knew how to apply a range of pruning and training techniques appropriate to different soils and grape varieties, but they still had much to learn about wine laws. After joining the European Community (now the European Union), Greece rapidly set about introducing a legal framework for wine production in accordance with European regulations.

CULTIVATION AND CLIMATE

When viticulture began in Greece, most of the vineyards were in the coastal regions. From here they gradually spread into the interior, where the terrain, particularly on the border with Bulgaria to the north, becomes steeply mountainous. In some places vines are grown at altitudes of over 3,280 feet (1,000 m). Even in these locations the Mediterranean climate, with its hot summers and mild winters, and the limestone and volcanic soils provide ideal growing conditions. There are, however, great differences of climate between the various regions. While it is sometimes so cool in the mountains that the grapes cannot become fully ripe, down on the plains and on the islands the summers are so hot that harvesting has to begin very early. A majority of these vineyards, though, are situated close to the sea, where the constant wind provides some cooling. A major problem every year is the long dry period. Irrigation of the vine rows is prohibited except in newly planted vineyards, so that many of the vines suffer from an extreme shortage of water during the spring and summer months.

Ancient Greece, on which our Western civilization and culture are founded, led the way in winemaking too. Evidence of this can be found in written accounts of techniques of viticulture and wine production which sound quite modern. Today, in the Greek wine-growing districts—where half of the total of 370,500 acres (150,000 ha) is devoted to growing table grapes—great emphasis is still laid on maintaining the huge diversity of varieties. Even here, however, international grape varieties are gaining ground and threatening to oust the native varieties.

Greece's vine-growing regions extend from rugged mountains in the north to the coastal areas.

The history of Greece is inextricably linked with the history of its wine production, to which we owe a great deal. The Greeks saw wine as an invention given to them by the god Dionysus, whose cult was celebrated with rituals that were sometimes orgiastic in nature. Poets, philosophers, and artists sang the praises of wine, among them Homer in his *Iliad* and *Odyssey*, and Plato in many of his philosophical writings. During the period of the Ottoman Empire, Greek winemaking collapsed completely. Only when Greece gained independence in 1830 was wine once more considered to be an economic factor. It was not until 1937 that the Institute of

Roditis is one of the main grape varieties grown for white wine.

The Roman poet Virgil wrote of Greek wines that it was easier "to count all the grains of sand on the seashore than to name every variety of vine." By and large this still holds true today. About 300 different varieties are to be found in the vineyards. They are the sign of an ancient native tradition of winemaking, and the vintners take great pride in them. Of all this diversity,

MACEDONIA·
THRACE
Amynteon
Goumenissa
Naoussa
Côtes de Meliton

THESSALY
Anchialos
Rapsani

EPIRUS
Zitsa

PELOPONNESE
Mantinia
Nemea
Patras, Mavrodaphne
of Patras, Muscat
of Patras, Muscat
de Rio of Patras

IONIAN ISLANDS
Robola of Kefalonia,
Mavrodaphne of
Kefalonia,
Muscat of Kefalonia

CRETE
Archanes
Daphnes
Peza
Sitia

CYCLADES
Paros
Santorini

EASTERN
AEGEAN ISLANDS
Limnos,
Muscat of Limnos
Samos

DODECANESE
Rhodes,
Muscat of Rhodes

CENTRAL GREECE
Kantza

Wine-growing areas
in neighboring countries

The Cretans take minor
problems in their stride.

It was not until 1971 that a system of controlled *appellations* was introduced in Greece, and since the country's accession to the European Community (now the European Union) Greece has had laws regulating wine that comply with the European directive defining a "quality wine from a designated region." To this category belong 22 quality wines (O.P.A.P.) and 13 quality liqueur-wines (O.P.E.), including all the Muscat wines (Muscat of Samos, Patras, Rhodes, Lemnos, and Kefalonia). Besides these very aromatic wines, the most widely known ones are the *appellation* wines produced in Macedonia and Thrace (Naoussa, Côtes de Meliton) and the wines from the Peloponnese (Nemea), Crete (Peza), and the Cyclades (Paros, Santorini). The bottled wines are given a numbered label as proof of their origin. Some of the Greek quality wines are designated *réserve* and *grande réserve*. These terms indicate that the wines have been matured in wood for a certain minimum period. *Réserve* denotes maturation for at least two years (for white wines) or three years (for red wines). For *grande réserve*, a maturation period of at least three years is required for white wines and four for red.

Alongside the designation "quality wine," two other categories have been introduced: *vin de pays* (*topikos oinos*) and table wine (*epitrapezios oinos*). The designation *cava* is permitted for table wines that have been laid down to mature. They must mature, in the producer's own cellar, for a minimum of two years (for white wines) and three years (for red wines). As in France, the term *vin de pays* signifies a wine with a specified local origin and a limited yield.

most wine lovers are familiar only with retsina and with Muscat of Samos, the great aperitif and dessert wine that is prized as highly by the Greeks themselves as by visitors to their country.

THE PRINCIPAL WINES

About two dozen varieties of grape are of interest to the wine market, but even these are still relatively unknown internationally.

• Among the most important white wines are Assyrtiko (Santorini, Athos), Vilana (Crete), Robóla (Kefalonia), Roditis (Macedonia, Thrace, Peloponnese), and retsina wines, Muscat and Savatianó (Retsina).

• The most significant red wines are Xynómavro (chiefly in Macedonia and Thrace: Goumenissa, Naoussa), Agiorgitiko (in the Peloponnese, *appellations* from Nemea bear the name "Blood of Hercules"), Mavrodaphne (sweet wines: Patras, Kefalonia, Achaia), Mandelaria (Paros, Crete, Rhodes), and Limnio (a very ancient grape variety).

In addition, a large number of international grape varieties play a major part in the Greek wine industry. The red wines include Cabernet Sauvignon, Cabernet Franc (under the *appellation* Côtes de Meliton), as well as Grenache and Syrah. Of the white wines the most popular with growers is Chardonnay. All these varieties are used either to create one-grape wines or for blending with native grapes.

For the Greeks, wine is a gift from God and is the pride of even the smallest producer.

Opposite
Every year the harvest in Naoussa starts with a symbolic picking for which traditional costumes are worn.

Top of the range among red wines is Xynómavro.

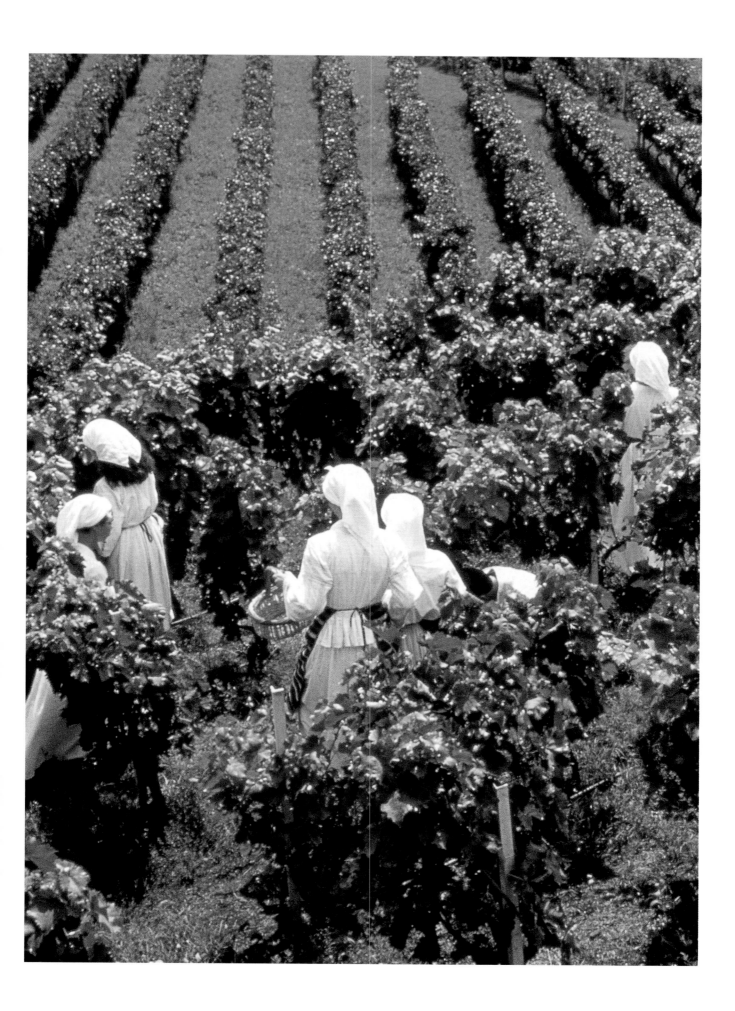

Retsina and Muscat

Greece's best-known wine is without a doubt retsina. Its origins can be traced back to antiquity, when it was found that the addition of pine resin during FERMENTATION not only improved the wine's keeping qualities but also gave it an agreeable tangy flavor. Retsina currently accounts for ten percent of the country's entire production of wine. The European Union has recognized it as a "traditional designation." Retsina is produced from dry white wine (table wine) made from Savatianó and Roditis grapes, flavored with Aleppo pine resin, most of which comes from the Attican Peninsula. Attica, Boetia, and Euboea (Evvoia) are the principal growing areas for this wine, which is as popular as it is characteristic. In cafés and restaurants it is enjoyed as an aperitif or as an accompaniment to the famous *meze*—starter courses with stuffed vine-leaves, *tarama*, *calamari*, and various salads. In recent years, an effort has been made to improve the image of this wine abroad by offering retsinas of higher quality. The wines are aged reductively and have a lower alcohol content than in the past, and the added resin is limited to 13.3 ounces per 375 gallons (100 g/hl).

The dry tang of retsina goes well with the local cuisine.

The soils of the Cycladic island of Santorini were produced by a volcano that is now extinct.

Apart from retsina, which every visitor to Greece ought to try, the best-known Greek wine is Muscat from the Aegean island of Samos. The vines grow on steep terraces, using a special method of production dating back to ancient times, and nowadays Samos is available in several styles. These include the Samos Doux liqueur-wine, Samos Doux Naturel (the fermentation of which is cut short), and Samos Nectar, which is prepared from sun-dried grapes and has an alcohol content of 15 percent by volume.

THE GREAT WINE-GROWING REGIONS OF GREECE

THE PELOPONNESE

Separated from the Greek mainland by the Corinth Canal, the islands of the Peloponnese have from time immemorial been the location of great vineyards producing both grapes for wine-making and grapes (for instance Sultanina and Korinthiaki) for the production of raisins.

There is great variation in the soils and the climate of the islands to the west of Athens. The lowland is at sea level and reaches to the very foot of the high mountains in the interior. The weather also differs markedly from one set of islands to another. In the west there is plentiful rain, while the east experiences dry conditions for most of the year. The great vineyards of this region—with the exception of Nemea and Mantinia—are located along the coast of the Gulf of Corinth and the Ionian Sea at altitudes rising to 1,476 feet (450 m).

The young Nemea wine called "Blood of Hercules" is produced from the Agiorgitiko (St. George) variety, which is found here between 820 and 2,600 feet (250–800 m) above sea level. The wines have a very strong color and keep well. The dry, light, and fruity Moschofílero variety is used for the white Mantinia wines and grows in hilly terrain up to 2,132 feet (650 m). The well-known Mavrodaphne from Patras, a wine with a good deal of RESIDUAL SUGAR, is a potent, oily wine with added alcohol. From the same locations close to Patras comes the white Muscat, another wine with high residual sugar and one that brings out this grape's extraordinarily aromatic quality. In the immediate vicinity of Patras, a dry and very light white wine is produced from the ancient and once very widespread Roditis grape.

CRETE

Historians believe that this southern Greek island was the location of the first vineyards in the Mediterranean region. For five months of the year the oppressive summer heat bears down on the island. One unusual aspect of growing vines here is that in the Cretan vineyards none of the vines are grafted onto American rootstock. Like Chile and Cyprus, Crete 215 miles long and 37 miles wide (350 km × 60 km) has up to now escaped the scourge of phylloxera, so that there has been no need for phylloxera-resistant rootstock. Of the local *appellations*, mention must be

made of Sitia, a vigorous red wine made from the Liatico variety, which thrives up to heights of 1,968 feet (600 m), and Daphnes. The latter is a liqueur wine containing a proportion of the Liatico variety, and it embodies the history of the legendary and mythic Malvasia, the "nectar of the gods" once produced in great butts in the palace of King Minos. The wines produced under the *appellations* Archanes and Peza are red wines blended from Kotsiphali grapes (with a strong BOUQUET) and Mandelaria (which is ruby-red when young). In Peza, the traditional Cretan grape variety Vilana is also used for producing white wines.

CENTRAL GREECE AND EUBOEA

Attica, Boetia, and the Aegean island Euboea constitute a unified wine region based on a single grape variety, Savatianó. In addition, these areas supply fresh MUST to inns and restaurants in Athens, which produce their own retsina from it. Light white, red, and rosé wines are also to be found in this part of Greece.

Some of the best Greek red wines are produced in the Côtes de Meliton, on one of the three peninsulas of Halkidiki, near Porto-Carras.

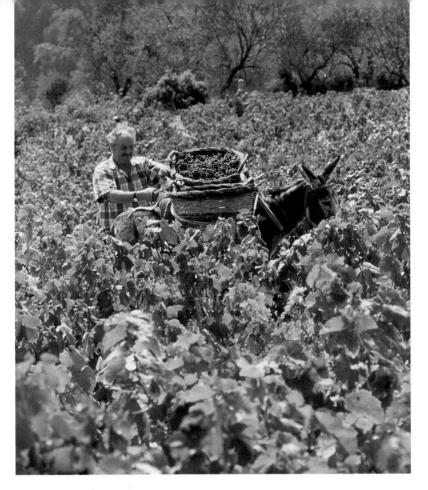

In Greece, as in many Mediterranean countries, an ancient tradition of winemaking by small growers still flourishes, using the simplest of methods.

MACEDONIA AND THRACE

The red wines of these two regions in north-eastern Greece have long been known for their outstanding quality, and include important *appellations* such as Naoussa and Côtes de Meliton. The climate in northern Greece is quite different from that of the rest of the country and the warmth of the sun on the south-facing slopes enables the large red grape variety of this area, the Xynómavro, to ripen superbly.

The Naoussa vineyards, situated at a height of about 1,148 feet (350 m), provide a good example of this celebrated red grape's potential for quality. The young wine has an intense color, and after a few years' aging in bottles it achieves an expressive bouquet with overtones of herbs, spices, and balsam, while the flavor contains restrained hints of TANNINS. Together with Negoska, the Xynómavro grape is used in the country's two most northerly *appellations*, Goumenissa and Amyndeo. However, these two reds do not have the body of the Naoussa wines.

Above the picturesque harbor of Porto-Carras on the Sithonian Peninsula, the middle one of the three fingers of Halkidiki, the Côtes de Meliton vineyards produce Cabernet Sauvignon and Cabernet Franc as A.O.C. wines. The Limnio grape is also found here. The white varieties Athiri, Assyrtiko, and Roditis give wines that are light and fresh.

EPIRUS

The vineyards of Metsovo in northwestern Greece, near the Albanian border, are situated in a mountainous region with very cold winters, and are often covered with snow for months at a time. After the phylloxera infestation the slopes were replanted with Cabernet Sauvignon (still rare in Greece), from which very vigorous red wines are produced. In the same area, the Debina variety, which is only found here—it grows in the Zitsa vineyards at around 1,968 feet (600 m)—gives a light, dry, semi-sparkling white wine with a delicate sweetness.

THE IONIAN ISLANDS

The western Greek islands, especially Corfu, are well known to tourists. The mild climate is ideally suited to wine growing, especially as there is adequate rainfall. The traditional *appellation* of these islands bears the name Verdea and is a white wine with a flavor reminiscent of RANCIO. The largest of the islands, Kefalonia, produces the light white wine made from the famous Robola grape, which thrives in the dry, mountainous terrain. Here, too, the Mavrodaphne and Muscat varieties give liqueur wines and wines with high residual sugar. Around Lafkáda on the island of Lefkas, Vertzami grapes grow on terraces reaching up to 2,624 feet (800 m) and give a red wine of individual character called Santa Mavra ("healthy black").

THESSALY

In Thessaly great quantities of grapes for table wines are grown. But here, as in many parts of Greece, there are also little-known and unique varieties, for instance the Noir de Messenikola and the white Batiki grape, which produce wines that are greatly prized in the region. On the coast of the central mainland, much frequented by tourists, the Savatianó and Roditis varieties are grown to produce Nea Anchalios and a range of good dry whites which are best drunk young. In the foothills of Mount Olympus, amid some of Greece's most striking scenery, are the vineyards of Rapsani. Here the Xynómavro, Krassato, and Stavroto varieties give a wine which, while young, has a deep red color.

THE ISLANDS OF THE EASTERN AEGEAN

The legendary islands of Samos, Limnos, Lesbos, and Chios are very well known. Samos has one of Greece's most renowned vineyard sites. Its

5,680 acres (2,300 ha) produce one of the best Muscat wines in the world. The vineyards stretch from the plains up to almost 985 feet (300 m) and so give grapes of greatly varying degrees of ripeness. The *appellation* Muscat of Samos may not be produced from anything other than Muscat Blanc à Petits Grains, to which 98 percent of the growing area is given over. The vineyards are often terraced, mostly planted with only two rows on each level.

The volcanic island of Limnos is less mountainous than Samos. According to legend, this was the home of Hephaistos, the god of fire and of blacksmiths, who was known to the Romans as Vulcan. The grape variety Limnio, also widely grown on the Greek mainland (Côtes de Meliton), was highly spoken of by Aristotle in his day and gives a very agreeable red wine. As on Samos, an outstanding Muscat is also produced, though on Limnos it is made from the Muscat of Alexandria variety; this is available both as a dry wine and a liqueur wine.

THE CYCLADES

On the islands of Paros and Santorini (site of the ancient city of Thera), the frequently strong winds oblige the growers to keep their vines very low in height. On Santorini the vine is trained into a kind of basket shape, an ingenious and unique way of protecting the grapes from violent gusts of wind. The soil of this wild volcanic island consists of slate and limestone. The vineyards defy the baking sun by storing the moisture that accumulates during the night. The island's characteristic microclimate enables excellent white wines to be made from the Greek Assyrtiko grape. The white Santorini wine, which used to have a very high alcohol content, is nowadays produced to suit a "modern" palate and has a good balance of fruit, alcohol, and acid. The island also produces a VIN DE PAILLE known as Liastos, a name derived from *helios*, the ancient Greek word for the sun. On Paros the Mandelaria variety is used to make a Mistelle from must fortified with alcohol. This variety is also highly prized by many vermouth producers around the world.

THE DODECANESE

On Rhodes, in the extreme southeast of this group of islands, the ancient traditions of wine-making have been faithfully preserved. It is thought that labeling of wine with its place of origin began here: amphorae of wine exported from Rhodes were always marked accordingly.

The island has two different types of terrain. One comprises mainly sandy soils, has little in the way of hills, and is exposed to the hot winds from North Africa; the other has high ground rising to more than 3,940 feet (1,200 m) and is the home of the white Athiri grape and the red Amorgiano, as the Mandelaria variety is known locally. It is to these grapes and this region that the *appellation* "Rhodes" refers. The white wines are generally fresh and dry, while the reds are slightly dry and supple. This is also where the celebrated sweet Muscat of Rhodes is produced.

Following page
The improving quality of present-day wines naturally does not go unnoticed among seasoned wine-drinkers.

The other face of wine production in Greece: large-scale modern vineyards growing international grape varieties.

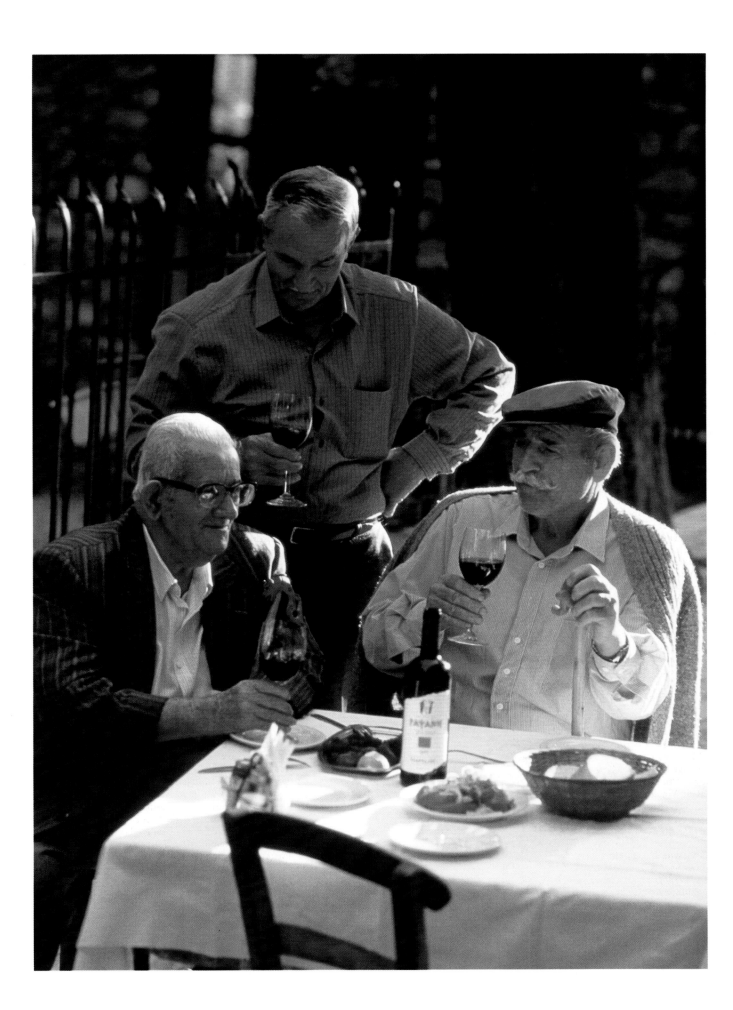

SELECT WINE PRODUCERS IN GREECE

BOUTARI**–***
THESSALONIKI

803 acres (325 ha); 1.2 million cases per year • Wines: white and red country wines, Nemea, Paros, Cava, Goumenissa, Naoussa; varietal selections of French and Greek grape varieties

The wine house of the Greek producer and merchant Boutari, with a history stretching back more than 100 years and beginning in Naoussa in Macedonia, offers both classic and more modern wines, and interesting one-grape wines or blends of two varieties ("varietal selections"). Also worthy of note are the Agiorgitiko, Greece's other great red wine grape (from the *appellation* Nemea), the Moschofilero (a white grape from the *appellation* Mantania on the Peloponnese), and blends of Roditis and Xynómavro (the white and red grape together give an interesting white wine) and of Merlot and Xynómavro, which are made in an ultra-modern fermenting tank on the island of Santorini.

DOMAINE CARRAS****
THESSALONIKI

1,110 acres (450 ha) • Wines: →Château Carras. Red and white quality wines from the Côtes de Meliton region (Vin de qualité produit dans une région déterminée); Athiri, Assyrtiko, Roditis, Sauvignon, Limnio, Cabernet Sauvignon, Cabernet Franc

Domaine Carras was created in 1960 by John Carras and has 1,110 acres (450 ha) of vines, grown on terraces, on an estate of 4,446 acres (1,800 ha) bordering the Aegean. On this huge estate several native varieties are grown (Limnio, Assyrtiko, Athiri, and Roditis), together with French varieties, chiefly ones that are common in the Rhône valley such as Syrah and Cinsault. On the terraces facing the sea the yields rarely exceed 425 gallons per acre (40hl/ha). Picking is done entirely by hand. The wine matures for 18–20 months in barrels of French oak and is nowadays blended with the three great Bordeaux varieties (Cabernet Sauvignon, Cabernet Franc, and Merlot) and with Limnio. Of the white wines, the estate's premium wine, the Melissanthi, is produced from Assyrtiko and Athiri grapes. This wine, introduced in 1990, is matured in barrels of French oak. So too is the red Limnio wine (for 6–12 months), which contains a small admixture of Cabernet Sauvignon. Domaine Carras has led the way in the development of modern Greek quality wines and still represents an undisputed standard of reference.

DOMAINE GEROVASSILIOU****
THESSALONIKI

99 acres (40 ha) • Wines: →red wine made from the varieties Grenache and Petite Sirah, Assyrtiko, Malagouzia, Chardonnay

This outstanding estate is owned by the agronomist and enologist Evangelos Gerovassiliou. His vineyards, located right next to the sea, are allowed to carry the label "Vin de Pays from Epanomi." He uses both Greek and French grape varieties and has established a modern winery, producing noteworthy red wine, which is among the best in Greece.

DOMAINE HATZIMICHALIS**–****
ATHENS

247 acres (100 ha) • Wines: →Cabernet Sauvignon. Exclusive table wines: white wines (Roditis, Robóla, Sauvignon, Chardonnay) and red wines (Cabernet Sauvignon, Xynómavro, Limnio)

On his estate close to Parnassus, Dimitris Hatzimichalis has planted traditional Greek and French varieties. The first Cabernet Hatzimichalis was launched in 1982 and was extremely successful. The grower is convinced of

the Greek origin of this variety, now grown worldwide and once known in Greece as *kapnias*. Excellent wines are also produced here from the major traditional Greek grape varieties.

DOMAINE COSTA LAZARIDI***
ADRIANI

494 acres (200 ha) • Wines: →Château Julia, red wine (Merlot) and white wine (Chardonnay); Vin de Pays from Dráma (white, rosé, and red wines); Sauvignon, Semillon, Assyrtiko, Cabernet

The Macedonian estate, with a growing area of about 494 acres (200 ha), offers two distinct lines. One bears the name Amethystos (white, rosé, and red wines) and comprises wines produced from native and French varieties; the other is called Château Julia and consists of one-grape wines—whites (Chardonnay, Sémillon, Assyrtiko) and reds (Merlot).

DOMAINE MERKOURI***
PELOPONNESE

123.5 acres (50 ha) • Wines: Vin de Pays from Letrinon (Refosco, Mavrodaphne)

Situated on the west coast of the Peloponnese, this estate produces an unusual red wine made from the Italian Refosco variety (85 percent). One year's aging in barrels.

DOMAINE SPIROPOULOS*–***
PELOPONNESE

124 acres (50 ha); 400,000 bottles • Wines include: Orino, Mantinia: Réserve, Fumé; Meliasto; Porfyros; Ode Panos (quality sparkling wine)

In 1993 this extensive estate on the eastern Peloponnese adopted organic principles, and planted—as well as the native varieties Moshofilero, Agiorgitiko, and Lagorthi—Cabernet, Merlot, Chardonnay, and Sauvignon. From these varieties it produces modern, clean-tasting, aromatic wines such as the white Orino or the fruity and spicy *barrique* red wine Porfyros.

SEMELI***
ATTICA

19 acres (7.5 ha) • Wines: →Château Semeli, Nemea, table wines in the form of white, rosé, and red wine (Agiorgitiko, Cabernet Sauvignon, Savatianó)

Anne and Georges Kokotos run this small family winery in Attica. Supreme among the wines they produce is the Château Semeli, usually a blend of 90 percent Cabernet Sauvignon with 10 percent Merlot. Two years' aging in new French oak barrels.

TSANTALIS**–***
CHALKIDIKE

617.5 acres (250 ha) • Wines: →Rapsani epilegmenos; a wide range of white and red quality wines and Vins de Pays; Assyrtiko, Sauvignon, Chardonnay, Athiri, Xynómavro, Syrah, Agiorgitiko, Merlot

As Greece's largest wine exporter, this firm deals in wines from almost all of the country's winemaking regions. Alongside its basic range, Tsantalis has also developed a premium selection which includes an interesting Rapsani epilegmenos *réserve*, which is matured for 12 months in French barrels and is produced using only native grape varieties.

Turkey

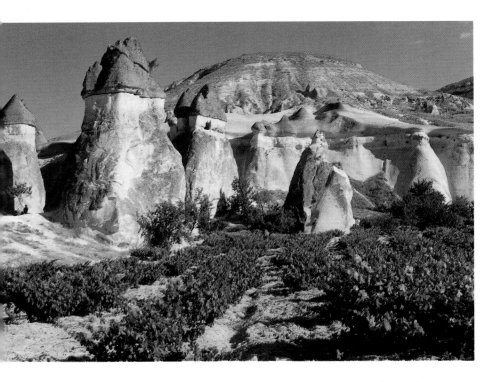

Vines—in this case the Emir variety—grow even among the strange rock formations of Cappadocia.

That wine growing originated in what is now Turkey is a matter of surmise. But scholars are fairly certain of a strong link between parts of Turkey and the earliest growing of the cultivated vine *Vitis vinifera*. Archeological finds from the time of the Hittites show that vines were cultivated in Anatolia as early as 4000 BC. Pictorial representations discovered during excavations of the city of Çatal Höyük, which was built in the 7th century BC, suggest that even at this early date wine was being made from berries, most probably from the Mediterranean nettle tree (*Celtis australis*). The tradition of winemaking, continued by the Greeks and Byzantines, was not developed further during the Seljuk and Ottoman Empires because of the Islamic prohibition on alcohol, but ethnic minorities continued to produce wine. Modern Turkish wine growing began in 1925 when, under the modernizing rule of Kemal Atatürk, the first technically advanced winery was established.

Nowadays Turkey's vineyards, at around 1,435,630 acres (581,000 ha), are the fourth largest in the world. However, only two to two-and-a-half percent of the average annual crop of 3.7 million tons/tonnes of grapes is made into wine. About three percent of the remainder is used for making Pekmez, a grape must thickened into a syrup, and some 20 percent for producing raisins—Turkey is second only to

California in the volume of raisins it produces. Around 75 percent of the crop is sold as table grapes, making Turkey the biggest producer of this commodity.

The earliest statistical evaluations of Turkish wine production date from 1928, when official figures record the production of 708,610 gallons (2,682,090 liters) of wine. Today the average figure is around 15 million gallons (60 million liters) of wine, about a quarter of which is used in the distillation of alcohol and the production of *rakı*, a brandy made with aniseed.

Alongside Tekel, the state alcohol and tobacco monopoly, which produces some 45 percent of all Turkish wine and which is about to be privatized, Turkey has a large number of private wineries, though only a small number of these are of real economic significance.

REGIONS AND VARIETIES

Turkey is one of the few agriculturally self-sufficient countries in the world. What is particularly striking is the difference in climate between the wet peripheral regions, which provide favorable conditions for farming, and the dry hinterland. In the north, the plateau is bounded by the

Pontic Mountains, on the northern slopes of which high rainfall and mild temperatures have led to the development of a zone of lush, damp deciduous forest. In the south are the Taurus mountain ranges, where mild sea breezes reach into the valleys and the vegetation on the slopes facing the Mediterranean has a subtropical character. Thrace, the region around the Sea of Marmara, and the Aegean coast enjoy a mild Mediterranean climate.

It has been estimated that recently between 500 and 1,000 different grape varieties are grown in Turkey; according to the Turkish wine expert Altay Yavuzeser 130 of these are properly described. About 60 varieties are cultivated and made into wine or sold as table grapes or raisins. For the production of wine no more than three dozen varieties are economically significant.

It is mainly in Thrace, in the Marmara region, and on the Aegean coast that international varieties are grown, though they still occupy only a very small part of the total growing area. The local varieties continue to be those that sustain the Turkish wine industry by providing a range of wines of original character.

• Thrace and the Marmara region: Traditionally it is chiefly Cinsault, Gamay, and the native Papazkarası grape that are grown here for red wines, and mainly Semillon for whites. Thrace and the Marmara region lead the way with 40 percent of Turkey's wine production, closely followed by central Anatolia and the

Doluca is a hill close to Mürefte on the Sea of Marmara, which gives its name to the region's traditional wine producer.

Aegean region. Of the 70 wine-producing concerns, six are under state control.

• The Aegean region: The predominant varieties here are those that are used as table grapes and for drying. Only 20 percent of Turkey's wine production is based in this region around Izmir. The white varieties cultivated are Semillon, Colombard, and to a very limited extent Chardonnay, as well as the native Bornova Misketi (a Muscatel grape) and Sultanye. The red varieties include the native Çalkaras as well as Cabernet Sauvignon, Carignan, Grenache, Merlot, and Alicante Bouchet. Of the 20 wine-producing firms three are state-controlled.

• Mediterranean coast: In the regions close to the Mediterranean coast the wine industry plays only a minor role. Among the varieties widely grown are Dökülgen (white), and Sergi

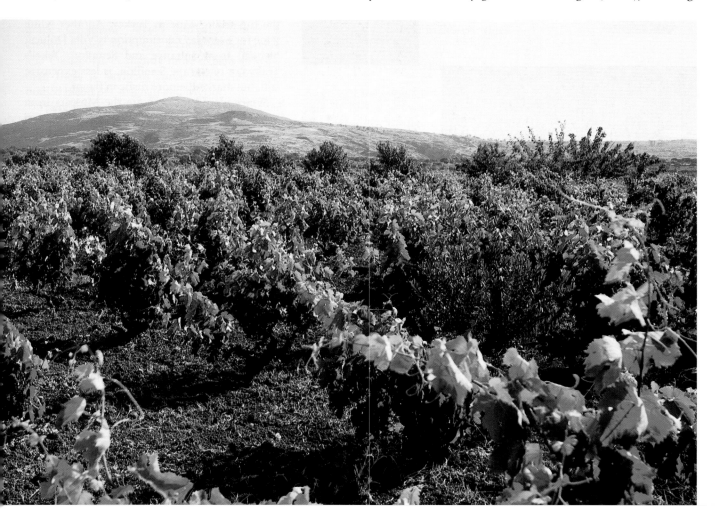

Israel

The Israel of Biblical times is regarded by historians and archeologists alike as the "cradle of vineyards and wines," the home of a wine industry that was also much admired by the Greeks and Romans. The word "wine" occurs in the Bible 207 times, "vine" 62 times, "vineyard" 92 times, and "winepress" 15 times, with images of grape growing and harvesting constantly being introduced to illustrate religious ideas. From time immemorial wine has been used by Jews for religious rituals, from celebrating a birth, bar mitzvah, marriage, the Sabbath and Pesach, the festivals of Purim and the New Year, to the mourning ritual following a burial, where the consolation cup consists of ten glasses of wine.

The first documented winery in modern times was established by Rabbi Shore in Jerusalem in 1848, and in 1870 the first Jewish agricultural college on the European model was founded at Miqve Israel to ease the way for the development of modern wine production. The decisive step, however, was taken in 1882 by "Hanadiv" (the benefactor) Baron Edmond de Rothschild, owner of the famous Château Lafitte estate in Bordeaux, France.

The history of the Carmel estate, which currently has an annual output in excess of 20 million bottles, is also the history of the Rothschild family's commitment to the land of Israel. The story begins in 1882 at Rishon-le-Zion, one of the early Jewish settlements in Palestine supported financially by Baron Edmond. Plans were drawn up for a winery and work began at once on its construction. There was not another building in the country of a similar scale. When it came to the ears of the Turkish Sultan that Rothschild was building a

Excavations constantly produce evidence of the ancient history of winemaking in this country.

Left and right
In 1882, with the help of Baron Rothschild a model winery was established.

"fortress" with the aim of liberating Palestine from the Turks, the work was immediately stopped. To this day it is not entirely clear what it was—a lavish bribe, or Rothschild's solemn promise not to attempt to conquer Palestine—that finally convinced the Sultan that the Baron's project was harmless.

Since the 1980s Israel's wine industry has moved from merely supplying simple, sweet wines for ritual use (Kiddush wines) to being a respected competitor on the international wine market. Growing and picking are nowadays carried out in accordance with the latest scientific knowledge. Stainless steel vats have replaced concrete tanks, and computer-controlled fermentation procedures have become the norm. The use of French and American oak barrels is steadily increasing. Finally, automated bottling allows more bottles to be filled more quickly.

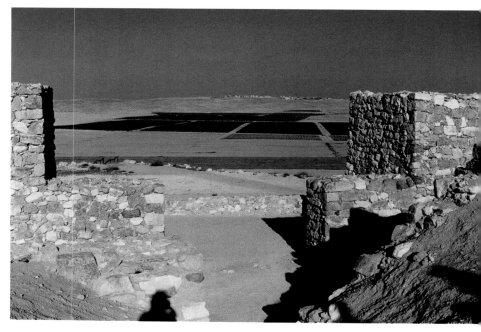

The citadel of Arad and the new plantings at Carmel well illustrate the coexistence of ancient and modern, the past and the future in the everyday life of Israel.

An ancient winemaking site: there are thousands like this all over present-day Israel, showing that wine has been produced between the Golan Heights and the Negev Desert since 3000 BC.

Galil
Shomron
Shimshon
Harey Yehuda
Negev
■ 1 Golan Heights Winery
■ 2 Dalton
■ 3 Carmel Zichron Yaakov
■ 4 Baron
■ 5 Binyamina
■ 6 Barkan
■ 7 Carmel Rishon-le-Zion
■ 8 Efrat
■ 9 Segal

HISTORY AND GEOGRAPHY

In ancient times, Israel lay on the "historic grape route" which later became the wine route from Mesopotamia to Egypt. A long navigable stretch of coast with easily accessible harbors enabled the wine trade to flourish. In addition to this, the region's relatively mild climate and unimpeded access to the sea both played a decisive role.

The Jews at first confined themselves to growing and producing wine, but later took to trading in it too. The areas suited to vine growing extend from the Golan Heights and the mountain ranges of Galilee in the north to Beersheba and Arad in the south. As an experiment, vineyards were planted some time ago

even further south, on the Mizpe Ramon plateau. In addition, vines are grown at Neot Samadar, a kibbutz located out in the desert, about 31 miles (50 km) north of Eilat.

Israel is blessed with a relatively mild climate with only two seasons: a long dry summer without a drop of rain, and a short wet winter with an average rainfall of about 20 inches (50 cm). Most of the rain falls in the northern half of the country. Ramot Naftaly, one of the best vineyards for Cabernet Sauvignon, receives as much as 35 inches (90 cm) of rain annually. Wine producers in the south have been able to exploit the special characteristics of the desert climate. The wide variation in temperature between day and night helps to maintain the acidity level in the grapes, while the dry conditions prevent the development of many diseases that might attack the vines and grapes in a damper climate. All the vineyards are equipped with the most up-to-date irrigation technology.

Malta

This small island republic with an area of 121 square miles (316 sq km) and population of 400,000 is situated 62 miles (91 km) to the south of Sicily, and in the course of its history, until it achieved independence in 1961, a succession of different cultures left their mark on it. It still possesses extraordinarily impressive megalithic monuments as well as both underground burial chambers and above-ground cult structures dating from the Neolithic and Bronze Ages.

Marsovin obtains a large proportion of its grapes from other Maltese producers or from Italy.

Exposure to Diverse Influences

It is known that winemaking here goes back to the days of the Phoenicians, who settled on the island from about 800 BC. The Roman occupation began in 218 BC, and the development of vine growing and winemaking was sustained without interruption until the 9th century AD. Then followed centuries of unrest, during which the importance of wine declined. It was the Knights of St. John (Knights of Malta), in whose possession the island remained from the 16th to the 18th century, who resumed the cultivation of vines, mainly in order to produce their Eucharist

Meridiana owns Malta's largest vineyard of 47 acres (19 ha) and uses only its own grapes.

wine. Finally, until its independence in 1961, Malta was under British rule.

Winemaking has been an integral part of the history of this multicultural island over the centuries, but the impetus for expansion of the industry always came from outside, since the islanders were not sufficiently interested in wine to initiate winemaking themselves. Currently vines are grown on some 791 acres (320 ha), distributed across the north and northwest of the two main islands, Malta and Gozo. In the spring the vineyards are often assailed by deluges of rain and in the summer they are exposed to extreme heat. Only two estates cultivate areas of any real size—Meridiana has 47 acres (19 ha) and Marsovin 21 acres (8.5 ha). The other winemaking firms use only extremely small areas, but precise figures are not known. Nor is there any precise record of the multiplicity of varieties grown. In recent years international varieties have been appearing more and more, but the small-scale growers still prefer the local varieties. These include Girgentina and Gennarua (both white grapes) and Gellewza (a red), and wine is also made from some table-grape varieties. Although the red and white wines rarely rise above the quality of table wine, Malta is known for its very sweet Muscat.

On average 2,642,000 gallons (100,000 hl) of wine are produced annually. Some growers have their own wineries and take the wine that they have bottled themselves to markets to sell, keeping back a proportion for their own consumption. Others sell all or part of the wine they produce to merchants.

Not all of the wine that is bottled in Malta comes from the island's own vineyards. The land available for wine growing is nowhere near sufficient to satisfy local demand. It is estimated that about 70 percent of wine is imported from Italy. The two biggest Maltese producers, Marsovin and Delicata, each achieve a volume of around 3.5 million bottles per year.

Marsovin harvests about 65 tons/tonnes of its own grapes each year, all of which are international varieties (Chardonnay, Merlot, Cabernet Sauvignon, and others). Some 400 tons/tonnes of grapes are bought in from local growers and about 4,000 tons/tonnes are imported from Italy. The Delicata firm has opted for a different solution. The winery does not have any vineyards of its own, but works with local producers: 53 local growers, whose area of vineyards amounts to about 62 acres (25 ha) in all, supply their grapes to Delicata, which imports the remainder from Italy.

Both companies generally try to process the Maltese and the Italian grapes separately, to ensure that the product of the Maltese grapes can be exported into the European Union as "Wine of Malta." Wines made from Italian grapes, on the other hand, are only allowed into the European internal market so long as they bear no information about origin, variety, VINTAGE, or producer. The label may only specify red or white wine. Under European regulations the "origin" of a wine denotes where the grapes are grown, not where the wine is made. On estimate, 90 percent of the wine produced in Malta is drunk on the island itself or is bought

by tourists to take home with them. In most wineries, therefore, only a small proportion of the wine produced is intended for export. But Malta is an E.U. membership candidate for 2004 and sooner or later will have to come into line with European regulations. Marsovin and Delicata intend to increase the proportion of local grapes they use so that the wines produced can be identified with Malta. In addition, the cost of transporting grapes from Italy would be avoided. However, the island is very small and because of urban growth agricultural land is at a premium. The wine merchants need to persuade the farmers to concentrate more effort on growing vines, and financial subsidies will need to be provided to ensure that only high-quality grapes are grown.

POSSIBLE WAYS FORWARD

An exceptional case in Malta's wine sector is the Meridiana estate, founded in the early 1990s. It uses production methods which, although untypical of Malta, are the norm in other wine-producing countries. Its aim is to grow grapes for top-quality wines in its own vineyards, so avoiding the need to buy in either grapes or wine. In 1994 and 1995, on the former British air force base near the ancient city of Medina, a total of 47 acres (19 ha) of vines were planted, giving Meridiana the largest single-site vineyard on the island. However, its annual production of 100,000 bottles still lags far behind that of its two big rivals.

When Meridiana embarked on its new planting program, the owners opted for the traditional international varieties (Chardonnay, Cabernet Sauvignon, Merlot, Syrah, and Petit Verdot), because they judged the local varieties unsuitable for top-quality wines. Other growers, however, believe that the native grapes are a part of the country's cultural identity and should continue to be grown. But these varieties, grown in the customary way without stakes or frames, need expensive, labor-intensive care if they are to reach the minimum must weight required for table wines in this region. It remains to be seen how Maltese wine production will develop from the present situation.

ANDRÉ DOMINÉ

SOUTH AFRICA

THE WINE LAND ON THE CAPE

For Europeans and North Americans wishing to escape their northern winter for at least a few days, South Africa—and especially the Cape of Good Hope—is an attractive destination. Fascinated by the dramatic landscape, where steep mountains sweep down almost to the sea, travelers coming here for the first time discover to their surprise that the country is actually quite European in character, and its climate Mediterranean.

A long, mostly sunny, summer with great intensity of light, and a mild but damp winter lasting from May to September, promise favorable conditions for wine growing. Where the oceans make their presence felt—and that can often be more than 60 miles (100 km) inland—thick banks of clouds build up with almost daily regularity, keeping the temperature down to reasonable limits, providing for relatively cool nights and adequately long ripening periods. Sometimes the so-called Cape Doctor puts in an appearance: a storm coming in from the southeast, which can cause great damage to the vineyards. But the climate of the best wine-growing regions, those near the coast, is changeable, and conditions are not always so ideal as winegrowers would wish. One consequence is that VINTAGES of South African wines are just as important as they are for those of Europe.

In 1652 a group of Dutch mercenaries went ashore at the Cape of Good Hope to establish a

Cape Town harbor is the starting point for South African wines on their journey to the world's export markets, where they are gaining steadily in importance.

provisioning base along the Spice Route on behalf of the Dutch East India Company. As the conditions for producing wine seemed good, Commander Jan van Riebeck, the Company's former ship's doctor, quickly had vines delivered from Europe—after all, wine was considered an effective antidote to scurvy. On February 2, 1659, the grapes from the first three vines were pressed. They are thought to have been Muscat de Frontignan (Muscat Blanc à Petits Grains) and Palomino; the Hanepoot (Muscat of Alexandria) was not yet ripe. The result was sufficiently encouraging for further vines to be planted, especially since new settlers were given the opportunity to set up their own farmsteads on allocated lands, as the growing demand on company ships could not be satisfied otherwise.

Produced without adequate experience, the wines of these "Boers" may well have left considerable room for improvement. This was to change with the new commander, Simon van der Stel. Very shortly after his arrival in 1679, he issued decrees which imposed heavy penalties on the winegrowers if they harvested their grapes before they were properly ripe, or fermented the juice in dirty barrels or cellars. He also advised them to plant six acres of grain for every acre of vines.

Although regulations forbade company employees to acquire colonial possessions or engage in trade on their own account, van der Stel succeeded in having an exception made for himself. Accordingly, in 1685 he was able to acquire, to the southeast of Cape Town, extensive estates which he named "Constantia." His well-managed vineyards were largely stocked with Muscat de Frontignan, since it produces decidedly finer wines than the Hanepoot. As early as 1692, a year after his appointment as first governor of the aspiring new colony, van der Stel succeeded in having his wines mentioned in the same breath as the most highly regarded European wines.

While Constantia underwent various divisions in the following years, and saw different owners come and go, the wines produced there rose to become an expensive and highly sought-after specialty in the courts of Europe. It was Napoleon's favorite wine—the largest quantity of Vin de Constance was supplied to him during the final years of his life while in exile on St. Helena —and right up to the middle of the 19th century it remained South Africa's enological showpiece.

A further decisive impulse for viticulture on the Cape came from the arrival, between 1688 and 1690, of some 200 French Huguenots, who were mostly settled in what is now called the Franschhoek Valley. Some of them already possessed wine-growing skills, and they established estates which soon developed a considerable reputation. Their descendants continue to play an important role in South African viticulture to this day.

During the 17th century, the colony supplied Great Britain for the most part with brandy and fortified wines in the port and sherry styles. Later, Cape wines profited from the Continental System, the blockade of the British Isles imposed by Napoleon in 1806, especially as it was in that same year that the British occupied the Cape for the second time. But this advantage turned out to be short-lived. Having neglected the quality of their wines, the Boers were hit by an ongoing sales crisis when France and Britain settled their differences once more. In the late 19th century, the mildew and phylloxera epidemics reached the Cape region too, forcing numerous winegrowers out of business. The start of the 20th century was a bad time for viticulture worldwide, and the export trade dried up almost completely. It was hoped that the establishment of the Kooperatieve Wijnbouwers Vereniging, a cooperative to which 95 percent of South Africa's winegrowers soon belonged, would improve matters. But it was not until 1924, when the government gave the K.W.V. powers to fix the price of the wine used for making brandy, that it was able to exercise any authority. But even this measure did not have the desired salutary effect on the market for fortified and dry table wines. As a result, in 1940 the government transferred the entire supervision of the wine sector to the K.W.V. From then on the organization determined not only prices but also permissible yields, varieties, planting rights, and production methods; it also controlled the disposal of surplus production, and the entire trade in wine and wine products. Not until 1992, when the quota system was abandoned, was new life injected into South African viticulture. As a result, old estates and merchants were able to develop and new ones were founded, while the K.W.V. and other cooperatives reoriented their activities.

For years, the boycott of South African produce by other countries in protest at the apartheid policy had meant that the South African wines were difficult to export, and with domestic consumption at only 2.37 gallons (9 liters) per person per year, there was little demand for quality wine. There was, however, a home market for brandy, where average consumption was 16 fl. oz (0.5 liters) per person. This situation was reflected in the small proportion of internationally popular varieties grown on the country's vineyards. For example, in 1981 only 3.3 percent of the area was devoted to Cabernet, Merlot, and Shiraz (the grape known in France as Syrah), while Chardonnay and Sauvignon accounted for just 0.4 percent of the total area. During the 1980s, however, interest in these varieties revived. In 1990 the red varieties had reached a share of more than 5.4 percent by area, and the whites 5.1 percent. In 2002 the three reds had reached more than 24 percent, while the two whites had almost 12 percent. The total area devoted to wine production had risen to about 266,860 acres (108,000 ha). The abolition of apartheid in 1991 resulted in a huge and sudden increase in demand from abroad, especially for inexpensive wines of good quality. Thus the winemakers also used naturalized varieties, in particular the dominant Steen (Chenin Blanc) and the Colombard, in order to supply internationally convincing wines. At the same time, the Pinotage, a variety obtained in 1925 by crossing Pinot Noir with Cinsault, also enjoyed a renaissance as an original red variety, and is being planted on a large scale. Today, about 4,350 winegrowers deliver their harvests to 66 winemaking cooperatives; 88 estates, 266 private cellars and 13 wholesalers bottle their wine themselves. Wine has become one of the Republic of South Africa's most important exports.

Top
Groot Constantia is where South African wine growing began.

Above
Cool humid breezes from False Bay outside Cape Town keep down the temperatures of the best-known wine regions: Constantia, Stellenbosch, and Paarl.

Dynamism and Fresh Thinking

If one traveled through the wine-growing regions of South Africa at the end of the 1990s one would have been assured by all the vintners and winemakers that their region was predestined for white wines. But since then there has been a change. In 1997 four-fifths of the vineyards were planted with white varieties, but today it is around three-fifths. A large proportion of the harvest is still used either for spirits or sweet wines, but with exports taking off in recent years the production of dry wines has increased. As with dry wines, the demand for red wines is far greater, which in South Africa has led to substantially more widespread planting of Cabernet, Merlot, Shiraz, and Pinotage. Careful observation of the various wine regions shows that where quality wines are concerned, red wines are now clearly ahead. The preference for white wine—which can still be found among Afrikaans-speaking winemakers—may be due to the fact that, not least for linguistic reasons, many received their training in Germany. Nowadays South African winegrowers and winemakers can be found in all of Europe's wine-growing regions, where they take advantage of the northern autumn to gather experience in the field of vinification for a second time in the year.

The modern cellar building at Rustenberg in Stellensbosch symbolizes South Africa's emergence. In the *barriques* high-quality whites are aged in new oak.

There is no overlooking the fact that, as a wine-producing country, South Africa is in a state of upheaval. Vines are being planted everywhere with great energy. The increased demand is only one of many reasons for this phenomenon. The actual cause is probably due to a more fundamental problem. The years of boycott, which the country suffered as a result of its apartheid policy, not only substantially restricted wine exports, but also, and more importantly, affected the vine stocks.

While in other wine-growing countries great progress had been made in respect of the resistance of clones to viruses and disease, and planting had been improved accordingly, the South Africans had to continue using and propagating their virus-infected material year after year. On infected vines the leaves rolled up so that the grapes rarely ripened evenly and well. The consequence, which can still be seen in red wines in particular, takes the form of vegetal tastes and unpleasantly green and dry TANNINS. Many reds from the 1990s still have that fault, but the situation has changed. First, the vine nurseries, particularly those in Wellington, have succeeded in supplying new and healthy plants by utilizing all their capacities, and second, new plants have also been imported. Major new plantings are now already yielding crops.

Easy Drinking Wines

There are already enough wines from healthy vines to show the extraordinary potential which South Africa enjoys as a wine-producing country. Whether this potential is exploited lies entirely in the hands of the producers. While the climatic conditions in general can be classified as Mediterranean, there is in reality a very broad spectrum, ranging from cooler locations such as Walker Bay to desert-like areas in Klein Karoo.

Although most of the regions in the vicinity of the coast receive sufficient rainfall, taking each year as a whole, providing a regular and adequate supply of water is a problem for all regions. Most vineyards have to be artificially irrigated, since in the often very hot and dry months from January to March the grapes would simply vegetate rather than ripen. And so the winegrowers' ponds form a characteristic element of the landscape, especially in Stellenbosch and Paarl. On some estates the water requirements of the vines are already

The wine-growing estates provide thousands of South Africans with employment.

constantly monitored and supply is managed electronically via a drip mechanism. This means the vines are subjected to less stress and produce higher yields. Until recently farmers, estate-owners, and winemakers saw themselves as an industry primarily oriented toward producing "easy-drinking wines." They are doing this with considerable success, producing good wines at surprisingly low prices. This industrial way of thinking is due not least to the structure of the operations. A typical estate consists of 370 acres (150 ha) or more. Fewer than 247 acres (100 ha) counts as small. In recent years, however, this has begun to change. On average, a new business is being set up every week. They include a growing number of small holdings aiming to produce high-quality wines. Many of the existing estates and private wineries have also added premium and super-premium wines to their range in recent years, and they certainly do not need to fear international comparison. The more moderate climate zones, in particular, are showing an astonishing potential for high-quality wines, and this development, which started rather hesitantly in the 1980s, is by no means complete.

GETTING THE CELLARS INTO TOP SHAPE

While the problems we have mentioned in relation to the vineyards can only be solved in the longer term, the South African winemakers are taking every opportunity to modernize by investing in efficient equipment. As long ago as the late 1920s the first experiments with temperature-controlled FERMENTATION began, with

the result that this method had come to be generally used by the 1950s. This allowed the hot temperatures of the harvest months and the resulting OXIDATION of the must to be countered, which unleashed a veritable revolution in white wine production in particular.

As a rule, white wines are vinified between 53°F and 59°F (12°C and 15°C), but the yeast that occurs naturally on the skin is not capable of multiplying in such low temperatures. As a result, winemakers were forced to develop purebred yeast which could work at these temperatures. The enological research department of the Nietvoorbij Wine Institute has achieved noteworthy progress in this area. The downside can be seen in the clear standardization of all wines, because low temperatures and the corresponding YEAST have a decisive influence on the aromatic spectrum. In addition, as it is entirely up to individual winemakers whether or not they acidify or de-acidify their must (the addition of sugar is prohibited), they have the enological means in their hands to produce clean, fresh, modern wines. At the same time, though, the character of the individual varieties, determined as it is by the TERROIR, is largely suppressed.

Leading winemakers realized this long ago, and are trying to do something about it. Noteworthy results have been achieved in particular by the red-wine specialists, who continue to use walled fermentation tanks that correspond to the *lagares* of the Douro Valley. The best port wines continue to be vinified in these to this day.

Georgio Dalla Cia, the Friulian enologist at Meerlust, is quite an individual.

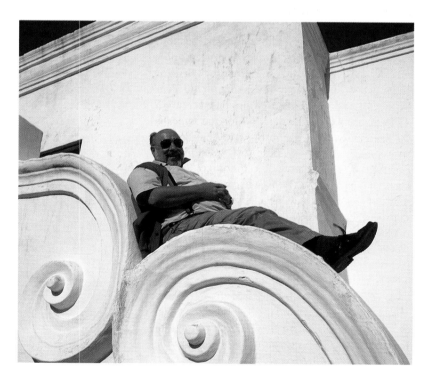

THE LEGENDARY CONSTANTIAS

The road to Constantia runs past the foot of famous Table Mountain. Like all the celebrities who honored the Cape with their presence in the past, modern-day tourists from home and abroad now make the pilgrimage to the peninsula, which juts out southwards into the Atlantic Ocean. And the object of all their veneration is the Groot Constantia estate. This is the cradle of South African wine: a neat-and-tidy château in the Cape Dutch style, a cellar that makes wines for every wallet, with a museum in the former cellar building. It is the most regularly visited attraction in Cape Town. Today, this former property of the first governor has become a desirable residential suburb, where real estate agents and winegrowers fight over every piece of ground. Sub-divided into five wine estates, this most renowned of all South African viticultural locations is currently enjoying a remarkable renaissance.

It owes its advantages primarily to the Atlantic Ocean. Toward the southeast, it faces False Bay, which is overlooked from the vineyards. But the Atlantic also stretches away to the west, behind the red hills. From there, gentle breezes waft over the vineyards, substantially reducing the temper-

This is where a great South African wine tradition began: Governor Simon van der Stel founded the Constantia Estate in 1685.

ature during the ripening period. The average temperature here during the South African summer is only 66°F (19°C). In winter it rains a great deal. Average rainfall is more than 39 inches (100 cm) a year, making irrigation unnecessary, especially as the red loam soil retains the water well. Depending on the location, the dominant rock in the fertile earth is either weathered granite or powdered sandstone from Table Mountain. Since some of the lower-lying vineyards have had to make way for elegant residential estates, new ones have been scrambling up the hillside, which may well result in better-quality wines.

Governor Simon van der Stel managed to make the sweet wine from Constantia well known. His

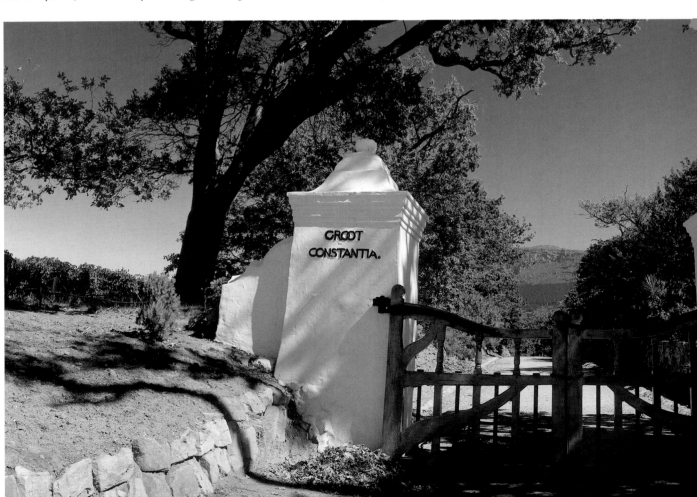

son, Wilhelm Adriaen, who succeeded his father both as governor and as owner of the estate, was altogether too selfish and too arrogant in the way he used his power, which led to his falling out of favor with the Dutch East India Company. As a result, he was banished from South Africa. Constantia was divided up into Buitenverwachting, Groot Constantia, and Klein Constantia, and the estates were sold off separately. The following 70 years saw a succession of owners, which had a negative effect on the wine. Finally, in 1778, the estates were bought by Hendrik Cloete, a descendant of German settlers and an experienced winegrower. In Stellenbosch and on his lands at Weltevrede and Zandvliet in Robertson, he was already growing vines successfully. The first thing he did was to put some order into the vineyards, and then he turned his attention to making wine. He allowed the small grapes of the Muscat de Frontignan variety to over-ripen, so that their natural sugar content may well have lain between 5–6 oz per pint (300–350 g per liter) or more. And so the wine fermented until its alcohol content reached 13 percent by volume, often retaining 2½ oz of residual sugar per pint (150 g per liter). Under Cloete's management, Groot Constantia and its Muscat wine reached the zenith of their fame, becoming—alongside Tokaji—one of the favorites of the royal and imperial courts of Europe and the first cult New World wine.

The newly erected cellars at Buitenverwachting blend harmoniously with the landscape.

It was the Dutch East India Company and the colonial government which profited most from this development, because each had a right to buy one-third of all the wine produced at a minimal price. In other words, only one-third could be traded on the free market. When the British took over the colony in 1795, Hendrik Cloete junior, who had meanwhile inherited the estates, hoped for an end to this restrictive imposition. His hopes were in vain: the new masters found the old agreements altogether in their interest. Even so, Hendrik Cloete junior managed to maintain the high quality of his wine. His son, Jacob Pieter Cloete, inherited the estates upon his father's death in 1818, but was granted little more than a decade in which to enjoy his inheritance. Wine growing in South Africa fell on hard times. In Europe, the Continental System (Napoleon's blockade of the British Isles) had been lifted and the British, having regained access to their old favorites, the wines of Bordeaux, lost interest in those of South Africa. And if that was not enough, the winegrowers on the Cape, like their counterparts in Europe, had to contend with the devastations of pests and disease. First, the vines were attacked by powdery mildew, which decimated the vineyards. Cloete died in poverty in 1875. Ten years later, when phylloxera reached South Africa, Groot Constantia was taken over by the government as an experimental and teaching estate. When it was forced to replace all the rootstocks with resistant American species, exclusively, dry wine varieties were selected marking the end of a great chapter in South African viticultural history.

In the early 1980s Constantia slowly roused itself from its long slumber. At this time, not only Klein Constantia but also Buitenverwachting were acquired by owners who realized the great potential of their estates. They began to renew and extend the vineyards and invested in new winemaking facilities. They also carefully restored the old stately homes and built model housing estates for their workers. This example by private growers was followed on the neighboring estate of Groot Constantia too. Today, the estate is independent and under the management of a trust.

The leading white varieties are Chardonnay and Sauvignon. The latter in particular develops a well-balanced and fresh expressivity in this temperate climate. The predominant AROMAS are reminiscent of fruits such as gooseberries and grapefruit, but in warmer years, stronger, exotic accents are present. Winemakers often prefer a vegetal character, with very green notes, reminiscent of grass and asparagus. A mineral quality is seen as especially characteristic. As a rule, winemakers go in for reductive low-temperature vinification, avoiding contact with the air, and for this reason the wines need either several months to mature in the bottle or else good ventilation, if they are to develop their BOUQUET. In the case of Chardonnay, there are unwooded versions, fermented in stainless steel tanks, and also wines fermented in barrels. In the case of Semillon, too, which is becoming increasingly popular with winemakers, fermentation in the wood is frequently employed. In addition, Groot Constantia also grows fresh Rieslings, as well as a certain amount of Pinot Gris, and of course Steen, as the almost ubiquitous Chenin Blanc is known here. White varieties considerably outnumber reds: the higher, south-facing slopes are particularly suited to them.

The example of Klein Constantia is especially noteworthy. Here, the Muscat de Frontignan has been replanted, and in 1986 the first new Vin de Constance was harvested and vinified in

THE FIVE CONSTANTIA ESTATES

BUITENVERWACHTING***−****
270 acres (110 ha); 900,000 bottles • Wines: Sauvignon, Chardonnay, Riesling, Buiten Blanc, Méthode Cap Classique, Christine, Cabernet Sauvignon
Lars Maack runs this exemplary family estate, which is known not just for wine but also for its gourmet restaurant. He grows well proven whites and more recently has achieved a marked rise in quality with his reds.

CONSTANTIA UITSIG***
79 acres (32 ha); 200,000 bottles • Wines: Chardonnay, →Chardonnay Reserve, Semillon, Sauvignon, Merlot, →Cabernet-Sauvignon-Merlot
An estate with a country lodge and two restaurants. Remarkable quality in the Chardonnay Reserve and the Cabernet-Merlot-Cuvée.

GROOT CONSTANTIA**−***
247 acres (100 ha); 560,000 bottles • Wines include: Sauvignon, Chardonnay, Riesling, Gourneurs Reserve, Cabernet Sauvignon, Shiraz, Pinotage, Port
The cradle of South African viticulture is constantly improving its quality. The Bordeaux-Cuvée (Cabernets and Merlot) is outstanding; the Pinotage is very good.

KLEIN CONSTANTIA**−****
182 acres (74 ha); 540,000 bottles • Wines include: Sauvignon, Chardonnay, Riesling, Semillon, Marlbrook, Cabernet Sauvignon, Shiraz, Vin de Constance
Under the Joostes and their winemaker Ross Gower, the estate is harking back to its legendary roots, in particular with its non-fortified Vin de Constance, made from Muscat de Frontignan. The dry wines don't reach the same level.

STEENBERG**
161 acres (65 ha); 400,000 bottles • Wines: Sauvignon, Chardonnay, Semillon, Cabernet Sauvignon, →Merlot; second label Motif, →Sauvignon Reserve
Complex investment project on Constantia's oldest farm, with a golf course, luxury hotel, restaurant, and wine-growing estate with hi-tech cellar; outstanding Sauvignon Reserve.

total accord with the old method. It is sold, after five years' maturation in the bottle, in bottles that are copies of those used in the 18th century. The 1997 vintage is amber-gold, a convincing wine with an intensive and complex bouquet, in which hints of orange and mandarin combine with honey and gingerbread. These aromas appear once more on the palate, enriched with toasted almonds. The oily texture and the sweetness are balanced by an elegant acidity. The example of Klein Constantia has inspired Groot Constantia to follow suit and plant its own Muscat grapes.

As there is so much to be said in favor of Constantia as a *terroir* for white wines, the quality of its reds is all the more surprising. Evidently Cabernet, Merlot, and Shiraz also like the red loam, and on the lower-lying locations they can produce outstanding results. Although many vines are still too young to deliver the required concentration, there are already some great *cuvées*. Groot Constantia bottles a wine known as Governor's Reserve, in which—as a rule—four-fifths Cabernet Sauvignon combines with one-fifth Cabernet Franc to produce a spicy, deep-red wine of medium structure with clear hints of eucalyptus.

Marlbrook, the top red wine from Klein Constantia, with its hints of toast and leather, is aged for a maximum of two years in French oak barrels. Klein Constantia's Shiraz Reserve is currently the subject of much discussion among the winemakers of Constantia. The dark wine, violet when young, has a very powerful bouquet in which the aromas of eucalyptus,

coffee, and smoke combine. Very rounded on the palate, with ripe fruit and a marked, albeit harmoniously integrated, spiciness derived from aging in American oak. It is the prime example of a modern red wine, which should set a precedent in South Africa too.

By contrast, Buitenverwachting's Cuvée Christine, which is aged in French *barriques*, is a classic. The clear emphasis of Cabernet Sauvignon, supported by a little Merlot and Cabernet Franc, leads to a dense wine characterized by black berries, damsons, undergrowth, eucalyptus, and spices. It achieves great harmony after several years in the bottle.

The wines from Buitenverwachting have made a decisive contribution to South Africa's image as a wine-producing country.

Opposite
Klein Constantia, one of the world's most attractive wine-making estates, also produces the highest quality wines of the five Constantia estates.

Constantia's vineyards seen from the air. The individual plots can easily be made out; recently they have been laid out on the slopes, too.

STELLENBOSCH

Stellenbosch, only 40 kilometers from Cape Town, is today the best-known wine region in South Africa. The town of the same name, with its famous university (founded in 1918), has succeeded in preserving much of its charm. This includes the numerous shade-giving oak trees, planted at the instigation of Simon van der Stel, who founded the township as the second European settlement on the Cape in 1679. The settlers built neat and tidy homes in the Cape-Dutch style, surrounded by gardens. These were joined later, in the immediate vicinity, by stately mansions built by the English in the Georgian and then Victorian styles.

In addition to the university, where most South African winemakers receive their viticultural and enological training, there is the highly regarded Elsenburg Agricultural College, and just outside the town, the Nietvoorbij Enological Institute. With its experimental vineyard and laboratory, Nietvoorbij is the center of South African wine research. This is also where control tastings take place for the recognition of a wine as a Wine of Origin.

Originally Stellenbosch was regarded as the stronghold of grain growing and cattle farming. The fertile flood meadows on the banks of the Eerste River produced much of the food needed by the ships of the Dutch East India Company. Even though wine, by dint of its non-perishable nature, was on the list of provisions at an early date, viticulture was of no great importance for the company, in spite of the decrees, mentioned above, which had been issued by its governor. The company's interests were not in the Cape, but in the huge profits to be made in India and

Like many of South Africa's estates, Meerlust looks after its Cape Dutch architecture. Its effect is enhanced further by the contrast with the spectacular Stellenbosch landscape.

the East Indies. For this reason it did nothing to market and publicize any wines other than Constantia. Nevertheless, viticulture developed spontaneously among the first, generally poor settlers who were allocated land in Stellenbosch. There was neither demand for, nor recognition of their wines, however, until the region came under British rule. In order to satisfy the demand for wine in England from 1812 to 1823, large quantities were exported. But this was the only period during the 19th century when farmers could make a living from wine. Not until the 20th century could Stellenbosch and Paarl create an image for themselves as viticultural centers.

From the point of view of landscape, Stellenbosch is one of the most beautiful wine regions in the world. In recent years, it has enjoyed a substantial boom, and now has the largest concentration of interesting winegrowers. Boland, with its well-equipped slopes and high-yield valleys, but especially its impressive hills, provides a wide variety of conditions, both in respect of climate and soil. This is reflected in the broad spectrum of wines produced here, ranging from the Cap Classique—

the South African version of champagne—to fruity, peppery Pinotages and noble, sweet Rieslings and fortified wines.

For red wine, the best *terroirs* are the hillside locations of weathered granite with acid soils. Some vineyards in the mountains lie at an altitude of nearly 2,000 feet (600 m) or more, and are characterized by a much sought-after temperate climate. To the west, the character of the soil is determined by the sandstone of Table Mountain, and produces convincing white wines. Altogether, Stellenbosch accounts for one-eighth of the country's total wine-producing area. Here, more often than elsewhere, there are dry farmed, in other words non-irrigated, vineyards. The yields are smaller, but the wines are well concentrated. Even so, the reservoirs are still a characteristic feature of the landscape.

Alongside various *cuvées* that are based on Cabernet Sauvignon, Merlot, and Cabernet

Left
Formerly an arable and cattle-farming region, Stellenbosch is now a stronghold of viticulture.

Right
Grape picking at Neethlingshof, one of the oldest and most important South African estates. In the background is the imposing Heldersberg.

Franc, impressive Shiraz wines are being produced on an ever-increasing scale. More and more winemakers are aging the wine in American oak, an unfamiliar taste for European palates at first, but with time a convincing combination with a typical hint of cinnamon. Stellenbosch is also the home of the best-quality Pinotages. Where white wines are concerned, the region produces not only good Sauvignons but also balanced (or in some cases very fruity) barrel-fermented Chardonnays with a hint of caramel. The Semillon, rich in finesse, is enjoying increasing popularity. And if these were not enough, the Noble Late Harvest Riesling from Neethlingshof, with its strong BOTRYTIS character, remains one of the region's most attractive wines.

Pinotage

Pinotage is without doubt an attractive red variety, with marked aromas of red berries, cherries, wild herbs, and often a discreet hint of banana peel. Its delights are quite different from those of the international standard varieties. Sometimes its fruit is reminiscent of stewed fruit, and its spiciness of pines and cinnamon. Occasionally it can smell of nail-varnish. While some producers praise this acetone note as typical, it points to grapes harvested too early and fermented at too low a temperature.

Pinotage is a variety first produced by Abraham Perold at Stellenbosch University in 1925. He crossed Pinot Noir with Cinsault, a widespread variety that thrives in a Mediterranean climate. Cinsault was known in South Africa at the time as Hermitage—quite unjustifiably, but that is how the new variety got its name. It was planted on the Kanonkop estate, for example, in 1941, and enjoyed its greatest historic success in 1959,

when it received first prize as a young wine from the Bellevue estate. There were few wine-makers who treated it as a major variety, producing such great wines as the 1973 Kanonkop, which turned out, after a quarter of a century, to be a highly complex red wine, by no means too old, and reminiscent of an old Pinot. However, badly vinified and over-produced, the Pinotage gave rise to unpleasant, coarse red wines, and its acceptance increased only slowly. When it was exposed to the criticism of British wine experts in 1976, it finally fell into disfavor, and it was planted less and less. Fortunately, however, winegrowers such as the Kriges at Kanonkop and their then winemaker Jan Boland Coetzee were not dismayed by the negative propaganda. While he later continued to make outstanding Pinotages on his own Vriesenhof estate, which he bottled as Paradyskloof, his successor at Kanonkop, Beyers Truter, succeeded in attracting attention once more to this idiosyncratic variety.

With a greater understanding of the natural preconditions which it requires, Pinotage has now embarked on a new career. At precisely the moment (1990) when it accounted for its smallest-ever proportion of South Africa's vines (1.9 percent), it started to attract interest again. It now accounts for 6.4 percent and is beginning to stabilize on that level.

Although the growers have now discovered how to make very pleasing, fruity wines from young Pinotage vines, the best results are from old, non-irrigated bush vines trained in the traditional Gobelet system. They yield some extraordinarily concentrated, highly individual wines. Recently Pinotage has been the focus of discussion as the essential component of the Cape Blend and a growing number of estates are blending it with Cabernet Sauvignon and Merlot. The results are often very convincing, and an unmistakeable and highly individual character has been achieved.

Brampton, is rather disappointing.

the blends.

Paarl

In Paarl, which with its 90,000 or so inhabitants is the second-largest town in the Cape region, you can still admire the numerous witnesses to Boer and British building styles, and stroll along the 7 miles (11 km) of the jacaranda-lined main street. The town, which dates from 1717, takes its name from the granite mountain at the foot of which it was established. When the sun shines on the mountain after a shower, it glitters like a pearl, or in Afrikaans, *paarl*. On the southeast slope is the Taal Monument, with its dazzling white columns of different heights, which is dedicated to Afrikaans, the language of the majority of the community in South Africa. Paarl Rock affords a magnificent view stretching to the Atlantic Ocean and even to Cape Town, 37 miles (60 km) away. From the summit you can also look down into the valley of Berg River, which makes possible the irrigation of the sandy soils on which the extensive vineyards are laid out. The Paarl region produces one-fifth of all the wine grown in South Africa.

On the slope above the town of Paarl is the Taal Monument, erected in 1875 in honor of the Afrikaans language.

In the past, the broad, flat vineyards were used almost exclusively for growing Chenin Blanc, Colombard, and Palomino (known as White French), which supplied the must for sherry production. After all, Paarl lies at the same latitude in the southern hemisphere as Jerez de la Frontera in the northern, and enjoys comparably favorable conditions for the SOLERA system of aging sherry. From about 1940, sherry and port dominated wine production in the region for a long time. But demand for fortified wines has declined dramatically in the meantime, while there has been a marked increase in the demand for dry white wines. Chardonnay and Sauvignon are gaining in popularity, but Chenin Blanc is now also used to produce attractive white wines.

The Paarl wine district is characterized by a decidedly Mediterranean climate, with hot, dry summers alternating with damp winters. The average temperature in the months from December to March (the decisive growing

Veenwouden—the red-wine refuge of a wine-obsessed opera singer.

period) is 72.5°F (22.5°C), two degrees higher than in Stellenbosch.

Maritime influences are of no great importance here. These natural conditions are reflected in the character of the wines, which often evince more volume and strength, and less frequently the elegance and delicate natural acidity of more temperate zones. The winemakers can be glad of South African legislation, which allows them to acidulate their wines. This is done at the pressing stage, and when done properly it provides for good balance; in other respects the wines always have a harmonious finish.

These days a broad spectrum of noteworthy white grape varieties can be found in Paarl. Besides those already mentioned, these include the White Riesling and Cape Riesling, Gewürztraminer and Bouquet, Hanepoot and Muscat de Frontignan (known here as Muscadel), Semillon, and Pinot Gris. The higher locations, including the neighborhood of the town where granite predominates (in contrast to the area

The Nederburg Auction

To the east of Paarl lies Nederburg, the best-known South African estate worldwide. It vinifies not only the produce of its own 247 acres (100 ha) of vineyards, but also the grapes from a further 1,358 acres (550 ha) belonging to three other estates. It maintains its own plantation to ensure the best clones and rootstocks.

The old-established property with its historic mansion enjoyed its first success under the German brewery director, Johann Georg Graue, who emigrated to South Africa in 1937 to get away from the Nazis. Graue planted first-class vines and was the first to conduct temperature-controlled vinification. After the death of his son Arnold, the winemaking was taken over by another German, Günther

Brözel, who created South Africa's first botrytis wine, Edelkeur.

In 1966 Nederburg was taken over by the Stellenbosch Farmers' Winery, and 1975 saw the first auction to be staged here. Every year since, in the spring, 120 to 150 different wines come under the hammer. Nederburg produces special wines for these occasions, but there is also a jury to select outstanding rare wines from other producers.

At this, which must surely be one of the most important enological and social events on the South African calendar, to which 1,600 guests are generally invited, the country demonstrates its top products to an amazed international public. Part of the proceeds goes to charity.

northeast of Malmesbury, which is characterized by a crumbly slate), are eminently suited to red wines. In general, the Bordeaux varieties are preferred, with Cabernet Sauvignon and Merlot often used for single-variety wines, or as a blend with or without Cabernet Franc. But here, too, there is increasing interest in Pinotage, which in line with tradition has hitherto been used for making port, often in combination with Tinta Barocca. Shiraz is also finding more and more devotees. The hot climate produces adequate ripeness and gentle tannins. Increasingly, ultramodern, electronically regulated irrigation techniques are being deployed. The DOSAGE is regulated by measuring stations, so that the vines get the right amount of moisture at the proper time.

The town of Paarl is the headquarters of the umbrella organization of wine-growing cooperatives, the Kooperatieve Wijnbouwers Vereniging founded in 1918. The cellars of the largest cooperative in the world cover an area of more than 47 acres (19 ha). The umbrella organization, with its various subsidiaries, is owned by the 4,000 wine-growing members. Beside the attractive facade of the head office building, La Concorde in Main Street, which was designed by the Spanish sculptor Florencio Quiran and provides K.W.V.'s logo, the Cathedral Cellar has become the company's trademark. Set up in 1930, the cellar contains huge oak vats with carved fronts illustrating the history of South African wine production.

The K.W.V. determined the course of history for all South Africa's wine industry for decades. From 1940 to 1992 the K.W.V. held unrestricted sway over it, and was able to prevent its

Cathedral Cellar in Paarl is the showpiece of the K.W.V., the winemaking cooperatives' umbrella organization. It serves as a cellar hall and gives its name to a series of wines. The carved ends of the barrels tell the story of South African viticulture.

collapse in times of crisis. The most powerful weapon of the K.W.V. was a quota system, which allowed it to fix, even for non-members, the quantity of surplus to be handed over to the organization free of charge for the purposes of distillation. At this time brandy and alcohol production—which still comprises two-thirds of its business—was very much at the focus of its interest. The repeal of this law and the sudden increase in demand from abroad not only transformed the situation of the independent producers but also forced the K.W.V. to reorient itself.

A major restructuring took place in 1995 when K.W.V. International was set up as an independent trading company. It now maintains branches in Great Britain, the Netherlands, Germany, and the United States, as well as the historical Laborie Estate in Paarl. Since January 1, 2003 it has been an independent joint stock company, with shares traded on the stock market. K.W.V. Limited and Wijngaard Ko-operative is an entirely separate entity, and it handles production. The conversion of K.W.V. into a group of companies, which was completed in 1997, can truly be described as revolutionary, for the wine division has been separately structured since that date. Investments in the millions, state-of-the-art vinification technology, and a barrel park of 14,000 units are the outward signs of this new orientation.

In terms of range, K.W.V. lays particular emphasis on slim lines, and it concentrates on a limited portfolio of well established brands. The most famous is Cathedral Cellar, named after the great cellar in Paarl, and it guarantees good to very good quality in whites and reds. At least as convincing are the other series like K.W.V., Roodeberg, Robert's Rock, and Perly Bay, if one considers that each name covers several million bottles. They are all cleanly made, very fruity and balanced wines. With Perold K.W.V. acquired a wine that achieved cult status. It was godfathered by Abraham Perold, the famous wine professor and grower of Pinotage. Made from the produce of a single vineyard near Paarl, this impressively intensive and complex Shiraz has only been made in great vintage years since 1996. K.W.V.'s own Laborie Estate, well known for its Cap Classique, has outstanding full-bodied reds and also offers the delicious Pineau de Laborie liqueur wine, made from Pinotage.

Franschhoek

The name means "French Corner," and it is developing into an autonomous growing region thanks to the cohesion of its 20 or so estates and the high quality of their products. Classed as a ward, it is officially part of the Paarl wine district. Located to the south of Paarl and the east of Stellenbosch, the area, however, has a character all of its own. From its source in the Franschhoek Mountains, the Berg River has found its way through the narrow valley, which is just 8 miles (14 km) long. This valley is not only closed off to the south by the mountains; but it is also sealed off to the east by a steep chain of cliffs. From this gorge, the only exit is by means of a road leading over a single pass, formerly the elephant trail. To the north, the valley is framed by the Drakenstein Mountains. Compared with Paarl, Franschhoek has a somewhat cooler, wetter climate, with annual rainfall of 46 inches (120 cm).

At the entrance to the valley lies the historic Boschendal Estate of almost 1,236 acres (500 ha) of vineyard; it now belongs to the Anglo-American Farms group. In 1685 Boschendal was transferred by Simon van der Stel to the

Huguenot Jean de Long. Between 1688 and 1690 the Governor encouraged the immigration of around 200 Huguenots forced to flee France after the Revocation of the Edict of Nantes. However, van der Stel forbade them to set up a village of their own and settled them among immigrants of Dutch and German origin. The allocation of land took place largely between

Well-tended wine estates are the symbol of Franschhoek.

Huguenots settled in Franschhoek in about 1690, and set up villages and well-tended estates, most of which bear French names to this day.

ELGIN AND WALKER BAY

Overberg is the name of the region, which comprises two up-and-coming wards. Elgin is a plateau to the east of False Bay, whose conditions make it a natural growing area for fruit. As can be seen from the newly laid out vineyards, more and more farmers are turning to grape production, and the first attempts are being made at bottling their own wine.

While Elgin still has to acquire a reputation in wine circles, Walker Bay is already a secret tip among *cognoscenti*. It is Africa's southernmost wine-growing area, and at the same time its coolest, lying as it does directly on the Atlantic, the water temperature of which rarely exceeds 59°F (15°C), because of strong Antarctic currents even in the summer.

Behind the hills which frame the charming little seaside resort of Hermanus, the former advertising manager Tim Hamilton Russell found excellent conditions for wine growing in Hemel-en-Aarde Tal ("Heaven and Earth

Hermanus is surely the most popular seaside resort in the Cape region and is always booked out at Christmas. Burgundy grape varieties thrive in its hinterland.

Peter Finlayson, director of the Bouchard-Finlayson joint venture.

Valley"). The climate is moderated by strong, humid Atlantic winds. The clay soil requires a hefty addition of lime, but the dominant slate promises great character and elegance. The first vines were planted in 1976. Three years later Peter Finlayson joined the operation, bringing with him substantial enological expertise gained in Burgundy. From the very first vintage, the pair aroused attention, and soon it was obvious that the future of the valley would be inseparable from Pinot Noir, Chardonnay, and Sauvignon.

In the 1980s Hamilton Russell's wines attracted international attention. They received numerous awards, and price-wise climbed to the top of the South African charts. While Tim Hamilton Russell sought to imitate Burgundy, his son, Anthony, has gone a step further. Everything is being done on the 160-acre (65-ha) estate to bring out the special flavor of the *terroir* and develop an individual style.

The first step was to subdivide the vineyards according to their natural character and different rootstocks. Separate harvesting and vinification then led, under the present winemaker Kevin Grant, to an internal classification of the various plots. Strenuous efforts were made to replace virus-infected stock. At the same time, the density of planting was substantially increased. Since 1993, the proportion of grapes from healthy vines has been steadily increased. In the great wine year of 1997, Hamilton Russell was finally able to vinify his Pinot Noir exclusively from totally healthy vines, enabling him to produce the best red wine made on the estate up until then. The Chardonnay is also top quality.

After 11 years of intensive work with Hamilton Russell, in 1990 Peter Finlayson finally succeeded in making his dream, of an estate of his own, come true. Together with Paul Bouchard from the Burgundy wine dynasty of that name, he acquired the neighboring estate of Hemel-en-Aarde. From the outset he stocked the vineyards with virus-free clones, planting 7,000 vines per hectare.

In the extensive, gently curving valley, which does not look at all African, irrigation ponds point to the fact that in this region you must still be prepared for periods of drought. Bouchard Finlayson grow Pinot Noir and Chardonnay in particular, with a small proportion of Pinot Blanc and Sauvignon. They have selected two locations: Galpin Peak for the reds, and Missionvale for the white varieties; they treat these as separate CRUS. From the outset they have produced—with the necessary investment in technology and winery equip-

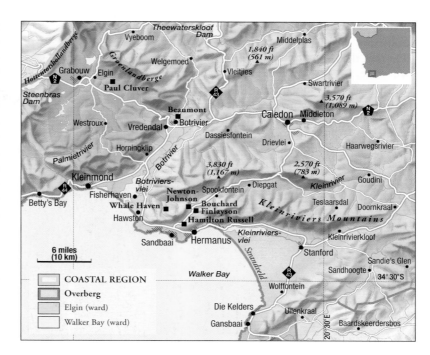

ment—top wines at top prices. They also succeeded in making outstanding wines, both Chardonnay and Pinot Noir, in 1997. If that vintage is still unsurpassed for Walker Bay Pinot Noir, the wines in the following good and great vintage years have gained in depth and richness as the vines have aged. The *terroir* is also gaining in character.

Walker Bay also includes Bot River, which lies a good bit closer to Cape Town than Hermanus. Raoul and Jayne Beaumont acquired the historic Compagnes Drift Farm in 1973. As it turned out, this former outpost of the Dutch East India Company also included about 123 acres (50 ha)

Hamilton-Russell is doing pioneering work with Pinot and Chardonnay.

ANTHONY ROSE

ASIA

Three factors are crucial to sake: the raw materials used, the method of brewing and the processing after brewing. The extent to which the rice has been "polished" is the first important factor. Basically, the more highly polished the rice, usually to between 50 and 55 percent of its original size, the finer the quality of the sake. Next the question arises whether it is a "pure rice" sake or whether it has had alcohol added. In a "pure rice" sake, the starch in the rice is first turned to sugar by obtaining a *koji*, or rice mold, which is added to rice, YEAST, and water, and FERMENTATION then takes place. This "pure rice" sake is known as *junmaishu*. A second type of sake, known as *honjozo*, has a limited amount of brewer's alcohol added, and tends to be lighter than a *junmaishu*, if not quite as delicate.

Above
Suntory is Japan's leading producer and distributor of alcoholic products.

Right
Grape harvest in Suntory's Yamanashi Winery, Japan's largest.

André Dominé

NORTH AMERICA

WINE IN NORTH AMERICA

Many of the European settlers who landed in the New World to seek their fortunes soon realized that there was something missing from their lives that had previously had a very firm place there: wine. However, as wild vines grow well in many areas of America, this did not appear to be an insuperable problem. The first wine was fermented from native grapes in 1607 in Jamestown, Virginia. Even so, it was to be another 200 years before reasonably drinkable wines began to be made on the East Coast, and only after 1960 was *Vitis vinifera*, the European vine species, cultivated successfully there. It was impossible to make acceptable wine from the wild American grape varieties, so innumerable experiments were undertaken with vines introduced from Europe, but none were successful. The European plants were unable to withstand the unsuitable climate or the unfamiliar diseases and pests.

It was not until the early-19th century that new hope dawned, when a white hybrid created by the spontaneous crossing of an American *Vitis labrusca* variety and a European *Vitis vinifera* variety was discovered. This grape was called Alexander, and it made wine that was, indeed, drinkable, though its rather foxy AROMA could hardly be described as attractive. Nevertheless, winemaking now spread in the eastern states as Alexander and other specially bred hybrids were planted.

After the Second World War there was an increasing concentration on French hybrids, which produced more palatable wines. Thanks

Buena Vista, one of the oldest wineries in California, in Sonoma Valley.

Sonoma City is a small town that has developed into a much visited wine center. Even the gas stations there sell "vintage" fuel.

to the development of chemical pesticides and insecticides, it also became possible to acclimatize European quality vines.

THE CALIFORNIAN MISSION

The conditions for winemaking were quite different in the south and west of the area that is now the United States. Thanks to the favorable climate, it was possible to cultivate vines imported from Europe in the Spanish colonies right from the beginning. Hernán Cortés had the first vines planted in Mexico in 1521, and the Spanish laid out vineyards in New Mexico and Texas about 100 years later. In 1769 the Spanish Crown began to send Franciscan monks to California in order to maintain Spanish claims in the region. The *padres* could not imagine life or work without wine, so they took the techniques of viticulture to California with them, introducing the appropriately named Mission grape variety.

Slowly the Franciscans moved up the *Camino Real* (Royal Road) to the north, establishing 21 mission stations, of which Sonoma (founded 1823) was the most northerly. Los Angeles was then an unimportant settlement, but it has now swallowed up San Gabriel, where the most extensive vineyards were planted, producing yields that went far beyond the missionaries' own requirements. Jean-Louis Vignes, who came from the Bordeaux area, founded his winery not far away in 1833, stocking it with French vines. Apart from this, ever more people were coming from the east to settle in Sonoma.

THE GOLD RUSH AND WINE FEVER

In 1848 an event took place that was to be decisive for Californian winemaking in general, and the wine-growing areas of the North Coast region in particular: gold was found at Sacramento. Hundreds of thousands of people were attracted to California, hoping to find riches overnight. Among them were many former winemakers from Europe, some of whom quickly saw their future in satisfying the gold diggers' thirst rather than digging for themselves. In consequence, viticulture experienced a completely unexpected boom in Sonoma, while in the neighboring Napa Valley cattle were still being grazed. However, wine fever soon spread there too, as well as to Livermore Valley and

Santa Clara Valley just south of San Francisco. The driving force behind this development was the Hungarian aristocrat and adventurer Agoston Haraszthy, who founded the Buena Vista vineyard in the Sonoma Valley. He went on a state-funded journey through the European winemaking countries, gathering information about cultivation methods and collecting cuttings of 300 vine varieties. America was beginning to take wine seriously.

Scientific research began to be conducted at Berkeley in 1880, and the results were put directly into practice. Viticulture had also been developing in the Central Valley from 1830, and the evident suitability of this area for the production of wine on a large scale was soon being exploited. The opening of the transcontinental railroad at about this time also caused demand to rise further.

The wine business was controlled by a small group of bottlers, who purchased wine by the barrel from about 800 wineries, and then mixed it to make blends with a wide range of different flavors to meet the requirements of the retail trade.

Business was flourishing when a catastrophic disaster struck the industry: the PHYLLOXERA (vine louse) epidemic. This rapacious insect originally came from the eastern United States, but around 1880 it began systematically to destroy all the crops planted on the West Coast. Almost all of California's vineyards fell victim in the two decades that followed. The winegrowers had hardly finished replanting their land with resistant rootstocks when the next blow hit them. Prohibition was introduced on January 17, 1920 and was not lifted until 1933. Though winegrowers and producers in Napa, Sonoma, Central Valley, and elsewhere managed to get round the restrictions by various ruses, such as producing communion wine or grapes for home

The Finnish captain Gustave Niebaum built this winery and château in 1887 with the aim of outdoing the wines of Bordeaux. Today the entire estate belongs to Francis Ford Coppola, the famous Hollywood director. He has restored the Niebaum-Coppola Estate to its former glory and made it a magnet for tourists.

The German Walter Schug built his winery in Carneros in the traditional style of his home, Assmannshausen am Rhein. His wines are equally European in style.

FERMENTATION, the real wine market collapsed, and with it the production of quality wines. Prohibition was followed by the Great Depression and the Second World War, and only 15 percent of California's wineries survived through to the end of the 1940s.

A NEW BEGINNING, NEW PROBLEMS

The remaining winemakers were confronted with the problem of having to maintain their position in the face of rising imports from Europe, so they marketed their own wines under foreign names. The most famous example was "Chablis," which denoted a relatively dry white wine, regardless of the kind of grape from which it was made. In Napa and Sonoma, wineries such as Beaulieu Vineyards, Inglenook, and Charles Krug re-established their former fame and quality, but it was only in the 1960s that greater investment became possible. Since 1970 there has been a growth of interest in wine among the American population, and this has been accompanied by an expansion of the areas under cultivation with vines and an increase in the number of wineries being launched (there are now well over 800).

In the 1990s, however, disaster struck yet again as the vine louse made a comeback. It became apparent that the rootstocks used when the vineyards were expanded in the 1980s were not actually resistant to phylloxera, and thousands of acres of vines were ravaged by a mutation of the insect. Farmers and wineries had to replant their vineyards, but in doing so they applied the latest techniques of quality wine production, establishing the foundations for an extremely promising future.

CANADA

Wine growing in Canada has a relatively short history. The first cautious steps in this field were taken in 1811 by Johann Schiller, a German officer who took part in several North American wars. After leaving the army, he retired to a plot of land near Toronto and undertook some very successful experiments with domesticated wild vines. After 35 years he sold his vineyard to a French aristocrat.

Canada is not the most ideal land for cultivating vines. Indeed, its winters are notorious for their harshness, and even in the most southerly regions that border the United States temperatures can easily drop to below 5°F (−15°C). But Canadian winemakers know how to make a virtue of necessity. Each year the Riesling and Vidal grapes freeze in the two most important wine-growing areas, Ontario and British Columbia, making this raw land the largest and most reliable producer of ice wines in the world. And the Vidal grape, which was bred by crossing Ugni Blanc and Seibel, is exceptional in being a hybrid with a touch of class.

The fact that ice wine has become one of the typical national specialties gives a clear indication of Canada's key characteristic as a wine-producing country: its cold climate. Although the main producing area, Ontario, where six sevenths of the roughly 20,300 acres (8,200 ha) of vines planted in the country are concentrated, is on the same latitude as the Midi region of France and also profits from the moderating influence of the Great Lakes, the outbreaks of cold weather in the spring and autumn restrict the period during which grapes can ripen. There are only a few wine-growing areas in Nova Scotia and Quebec, where each autumn the vines are protected from the frost with a covering of piled-up earth and then dug out again in the spring.

In view of the extremely difficult conditions prevalent in Canada, wine growing relied at

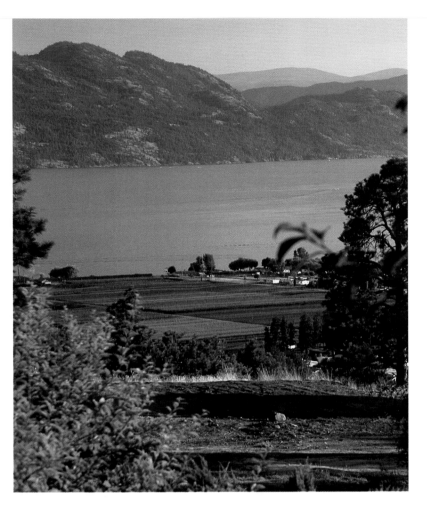

The Okanagan Valley is the most promising area in British Columbia.

first on resistant *labrusca* varieties, and subsequently on hybrids. The light red grapes of the indestructible Concord vine are still used for the production of sweet-sherry and port-wine imitations, while the Niagara variety is a popular choice for dry white wine. Nearly three-fifths of the vines grown in Canada are hybrids. Concord is the most common, followed by Elvira, De Chaunac, then—some way behind—Niagara, Seyval Blanc, Maréchal Foch, and Baco Noir. Vidal is the variety most often used for ice wine.

The modernization of the winemaking industry began in Canada after Inniskillin (not far from the Niagara Falls) was granted a license in 1975. It was the first private winery founded in Ontario. Since then, many winegrowers have succeeded in demonstrating that *Vitis*

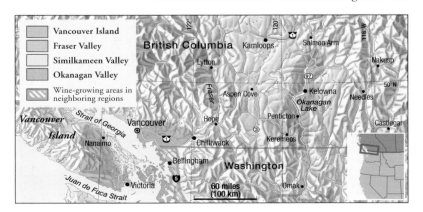

vinifera can flourish in Canada. At first they experimented mainly with German varieties, but Chardonnay and red French grapes are gaining more and more ground.

The increased awareness of quality issues led to the adoption of a wine-growing philosophy which resulted in the establishment of the Vintners Quality Alliance, an *appellation* system first introduced in Ontario in 1989, then, a year later, in British Columbia. Under this system, wines are defined by either the province or the wine-growing area where they originate (see page 792).

The Province of Ontario has three areas of *appellation*: Pelee Island, Lake Erie North Shore, and Niagara Peninsula.

On the whole, the Ontario climate is similar to that of Burgundy, and conditions are practically the same as in the nearby Finger Lakes region of New York State. With the exception of the ice wines, the area's most reliably successful products are Riesling and Chardonnay, which is often very reminiscent of Chablis. In warm years the region produces excellent, rounded Gamays and Pinot Noirs, and pleasant Cabernet Francs and Cabernet Sauvignons, while Merlot has recently begun to reach high standards as well. There are 45 wineries in Ontario, the best known being Cave Spring, Château des Charmes, Henry of Pelham, Hillebrand, Inniskillin, Konzelmann Winery, Pelee Island Winery, Reif Estate, Southbrook Farm, Stoney Ridge, and Vineland Estates.

Four geographical *appellations* are recognized in the Province of British Columbia: Vancouver Island, Fraser Valley, Similkameen Valley, and Okanagan Valley.

The most important region is the Okanagan Valley, a semi-arid area where there are extreme variations between night and day temperatures. As in the nearby Columbia Valley, heavy irrigation is needed to grow vines, though Okanagan Lake softens the climate. No hybrids are planted

The wine and souvenir shop of the Château des Charmes in Ontario: In a climate very similar to Burgundy the growers here produce very interesting Chardonnays.

The first real winery on Pelee Island in Lake Erie was founded in 1866. Pelee Island Vineyards continue the tradition.

in the Okanagan Valley, and most of the growers have chosen to cultivate German grape varieties, such as Bacchus and Ehrenfelser, as well as planting Chardonnay, while trials are being conducted with Pinot and Merlot. Mention should be made, above all, of Blue Mountain Vineyard, Calona Wines, Cedar Creek Estate, Gehringer Brothers, Gray Monk, Hainle Vineyards, Mission Hill, Quail's Gate, Sumac Ridge, and Summerhill.

There are two other wine-growing regions in Canada that do not meet the V.Q.A. requirements. Three producers are active in Nova Scotia, working 160 acres (65 ha) of vineyards where they cultivate hybrids and old Russian black grape varieties. And, whereas wine-growers in all of Canada's winemaking areas also offer guest rooms, in Quebec, where nine-tenths of the small yield is white wine, primarily Seyval Blanc, the industry is completely dependent on tourism.

make by blending Merlot and Cabernet in various proportions (see page 819). Merlot enjoys great popularity and is the leading black grape variety in Washington, ahead of Cabernet Sauvignon. Unfortunately, the Merlot harvest is sometimes poor, resulting in harsh, thin wines with vegetable notes. By contrast, the area's good Merlots are very full, silky, and ripe with berryish fruit and pleasant spices. The really convincing Cabernet Sauvignons in Washington have an intensive, juicy fruit, not infrequently reminiscent of black cherries and blackberries, but tend to taste of plums and stewed fruit when overripe. Newcomers to the trade often mature their wines with balance and finesse in barrels, but the notable winemakers of the pioneer generation are inclined to give their red wines excessively strong wood flavors.

In recent years Syrah and Sangiovese have received attention, though the fruity, rather light Lemberger remains something of a curiosity. Chardonnay is the leader among white varieties, but the best white wines are made from Semillon and Sauvignon Blanc. With their intense, fresh aromas of lemon, guava, and balm, highly nervous character, and elegant spiciness, the wines made with these grapes can be very exciting. Apart from this, the local Riesling, which is still the second most important grape variety, is sometimes highly vivacious.

SELECT PRODUCERS IN WASHINGTON

APEX—WASHINGTON HILL CELLARS**−***
SUNNYSIDE
Bought-in grapes; 1,200,000 bottles • Wines include: Chardonnay, Sauvignon Blanc, Semillon/Chardonnay; Lemberger, Merlot, Cabernet; →Apex Merlot
Apex is the prestige label of this winery, which produces good-value, often excellent wines in a former dairy.

CHÂTEAU STE MICHELLE*−****
WOODINVILLE
3,398 acres (1,375 ha) • Wines include: Columbia Valley Wines: 11 Sorten; Single Vineyard Wines, Reserve Wines; →Eroica, →Col Solare
A visitor center and white winery near Seattle; a red winery on the Canoe Ridge Estate on the Columbia River; three more grape farms. Like Columbia Crest, Ste Michelle belongs to Stimson Lane, the biggest wine enterprise in Washington. Eroica, a dry Riesling, is a highly successful joint venture with Dr. Ernst Loosen from the Mosel.

DELILLE CELLARS****
WOODINVILLE
Bought-in grapes; 40,000 bottles • Wines: one white wine, three red wines, all blends; →Chaleur Estate white and red, →Harrisson Hill
A boutique winery founded in 1992 by the DeLille family, who originally came from Karlovy Vary in the Czech Republic. Winemaker Chris Upchurch vinifies superb Bordeaux blends. Top of the range are the Chaleur Estate and the Harrisson Hill. The D2 is the second wine.

HEDGES CELLARS**−****
BENTON CITY
74 acres (30 ha); bought-in grapes; 700,000 bottles • Wines: Fumé-Chardonnay; Cabernet-Merlot; →Red Mountain Reserve Cabernet, →Three Vineyards
Tom and Anne-Marie Hedges began to plant red varieties on Red Mountain in 1987; the vineyard now has its own A.V.A. They also set up a château. They only produce four wines, and one, the rare Reserve, is top quality.

LEONETTI CELLAR**
WALLA WALLA
25 acres (10 ha); bought-in grapes; 55,000 bottles • Wines: Merlot, Cabernet, Sangiovese
Walla Walla's first winery, founded in 1978. Gary Figgins concentrates on the red wines matured in new barrels that have made him famous. Too much wood for some palates.

MATTHEW CELLARS***−****
WOODINVILLE
Bought-in grapes; 36,000 bottles • Wines: →Red, Yakima Valley
Matthew Loso is one of the most interesting young winemakers in Washington. This former restaurant manager certainly has a way with red wine, in which he specializes, composing blends of Cabernet Sauvignon, Cabernet Franc, and Merlot.

McCREA CELLARS***−****
LAKE STEVENS
Bought-in grapes; 36,000 bottles • Wines: Chardonnay, Viognier; Syrah, Grenache, →Tierra del Sol
Apart from his Chardonnays, Doug McCrea loves Rhône varieties. His Tierra del Sol is made of Syrah and Grenache, and tastes pleasantly fruity and herby. The Viognier is good, and the excellent Syrahs have a unique texture and fruit.

COLUMBIA*−****
BELLEVUE
Bought-in grapes; 1,500,000 bottles • Wines include: Gewürztraminer, Riesling, Pinot Gris, Semillon, Chardonnay; Sangiovese, Merlot, Cabernet Sauvignon, Cabernet Franc, Syrah; →Red Willow Merlot, Otis Cabernet
This enterprise was founded in 1962 by ten university lecturers and has been managed since 1979 by David Lake, a Master of Wine from Britain. The Otis and Red Willow lead his wide range.

COLUMBIA CREST*−***
PATERSON
2,471 acres (1,000 ha); bought-in grapes; approx. 14,000,000 bottles • Wines: Reihen: Columbia Valley, Grand Estates, Reserve: →Syrah
This winery opened in 1982 and it has grown to be the biggest wine producer in Washington. Under winemaker Doug Gore it has not only produced popular starter's wines but also several outstanding top quality wines, from Merlot and Syrah, for instance.

COVEY RUN*−***
ZILLAH
193 acres (78 ha); bought-in grapes; 840,000 bottles • Wines include: Riesling, Chardonnay, Sauvignon Blanc, Semillon; Merlot, Cabernet, Lemberger; →Riesling Icewine, Chardonnay Celilo, Chardonnay Reserve

The cozy tasting room of Woodward Canyon at Lowden in the Walla Walla area.

Formerly known as Quail Run, this winery is known for its pleasant, good-value white wines made by Dave Crippen.

KIONA**–****
BENTON CITY
32 acres (13 ha); bought-in grapes; 180,000 bottles • Wines include: Chardonnay, Chenin, Riesling; Cabernet Sauvignon, Merlot, Lemberger; →Red Mountain Reserve Cabernet, Late Harvest Riesling, Chenin Icewine
Two couples, the Holms and the Willimans, have been running this vineyard and winery together since 1979, selling some of their grapes to well-known vineyards. Kiona pioneered Lemberger in Washington.

L'ECOLE NO.41***–****
LOWDEN
More than 125 acres (50 ha); bought-in grapes; 240,000 bottles • Wines: Chardonnay, →Semillon; Merlot, Cabernet →Seven Hills Barrel Select Merlot, →Pepper Bridge Apogée
Marty Clubb, who is a partner in several important vineyards, has set standards for Merlot in Washington, but his barrel-fermented white wines are considered to be just as good. Apogée is a blend of Merlot and Cabernet Sauvignon.

NORTHSTAR****
WALLA WALLA
Bought-in grapes; 30,000 bottles • Wine: Merlot
This luxury brand, which was started in 1994 and also belongs to Stimson Lane, only markets a single wine, selecting the best Merlot and Cabernet grapes from the company's 8,649 acres (3,500 ha) of vines spread among 14 different plots of land. After five days in open fermentation vats the wine completes its fermentation in new *barriques*, where it lies for 19 months. Then follows the *assemblage* from 18 separate lots; the result is a grandiose wine, consisting of 80 percent Merlot and 20 percent Cabernet Sauvignon.

QUILCEDA CREEK*****
SNOHOMISH
Bought-in grapes; 30,000 bottles • Wine: →Cabernet Sauvignon
For many years Alex Golitzen only made one wine, Cabernet Sauvignon, which he and his son Paul compose with grapes from various areas, adding a hint of Merlot. Matured slowly in the finest oak, this wine is a monument. They now produce a second wine of the same quality.

SOOS CREEK****
RENTON
Bought-in grapes; approx. 6,000 bottles • Wine: Cabernet
Many producers in Washington began like Dave Larson and started making wine with bought grapes in their garage or a shed. Larson only makes Cabernet Sauvignon, which he matures for four years in the barrel. It is very voluminous, juicy, and silky: quite unique.

WALLA WALLA VINTNERS***–****
WALLA WALLA
Bought-in grapes; 50,000 bottles • Wines: →Merlot, →Cabernet Franc, Washington State Cuvée, Sangiovese
This winery is run by three wine lovers with fine palettes and a great deal of dedication. They make superb, finely crafted red wines, the best being their Cabernet Sauvignon.

ANDREW WILL****–*****
VASHON ISLAND
Bought-in grapes; 48,000 bottles • Wines: Chenin; →Merlot, Cabernet Sauvignon; Sangiovese Sorella
Chris Camarda only buys the best fruit from well-known vineyards, such as Ciel du Cheval, Pepper Bridge, Seven Hills, and Klipsun. The amazing texture he unlocks from these grapes is perfectly matched by the new French *barriques* he uses. His Sorella is astonishing.

WILRIDGE****
SEATTLE
Bought-in grapes; approx. 6,000 bottles • Wines: →Cabernet Franc, Cabernet Sauvignon, →Merlot
A lawyer making amazing wines with wild fruit, incredible structure, and real passion right in the middle of Seattle.

WOODWARD CANYON**–****
LOWDEN
27 acres (11 ha); bought-in grapes; 150,000 bottles • Wines: Chardonnay; Cabernet Sauvignon, Merlot; →Old Vine Cabernet Sauvignon
Rick Small founded the region's second winery in 1981 and is now planting vineyards above his vinification shed with Barbera, Nebbiolo, and Syrah. Well known for butterscotchy Chardonnay and powerful reds.

OREGON

	Willamette Valley
	Umpqua Valley
	Rogue Valley
	Columbia Valley
	Walla Walla Valley
	Wine-growing areas in neighboring regions

Cristom Vineyards in Salem are passionate defenders of a traditional approach to Pinot Noir.

The Coast Range runs along the 300 or so miles (500 km) of the Oregon seaboard, softening the influence of the Pacific on the winemaking areas of the Willamette, Umpqua, and Rogue Valleys that shelter behind the hills. In the east the Cascade Range, which rises to 11,240 feet (3,426 m) above sea level in Oregon, acts as a barrier that holds back the rain clouds from the Pacific. The few vineyards on the other side of the mountains therefore rely on intensive irrigation to cultivate their vines. The areas along the Columbia River, which forms the border with the state of Washington for more than 250 miles (400 km), are much better developed to the north of the river, but the section of the Walla Walla Valley that extends into Oregon is also seeing a boom now.

Oregon lies on the same latitude as the south of France, but the west of the state has a rather cool, damp climate. By contrast with California, where the winemaking regions that produce the best-quality wines are those in which the top temperatures are reduced by the influence of the Pacific during the summer and autumn, it is necessary to use the warmest, sunniest locations in Oregon's main wine-growing areas, as otherwise the grapes do not ripen sufficiently. Nature therefore presents the winemakers of Oregon with a unique set of difficulties. They cannot plant on the off chance or expand their vineyards on demand, but have to research their area very carefully in order to identify the few really suitable locations. Successful results are only achieved by committed winegrowers who bring prudence, a feel for the lie of the land, and real stamina to their work.

Wine growing in Oregon is a challenge. The region has none of the nonchalance, light-hearted entrepreneurial spirit, fashionable flair, or lively business sense common in California. Rather, the visitor will find friendly, open, but rugged individualists and philosopher winemakers. These are not people who have diversified into winemaking from show business. Nor is it the large wine companies or drinks multinationals that have made Oregon well known among wine lovers, but rather its Pinot Noir. The International Pinot Noir Convention draws passionate fans and producers of this grape from all over the world to the small town of McMinnville every year to exchange experiences and taste wines together.

THE RISE OF THE INDIVIDUALISTS

The first pioneers in Oregon began to produce wine in the second half of the 19th century. Winemaking also experienced a considerable boom in the state after Prohibition was repealed, but companies like the Honeywood Winery in Salem, which was founded in 1934, mainly produced fruit wines at this time. To the present day the favorable climate and fertile soils of Oregon ensure that there are rich harvests of berries, apples, pears, and stonefruit.

The pioneer of modern winemaking in the state was Richard Sommer. After studying at the University of California at Davis, he planted Riesling and other varieties in the Umpqua Valley, and launched the Hillcrest Winery there in 1963. The climate is comparatively dry and

The famous Burgundy wine house, Drouhin, have planted their own estate in Dundee, specializing exclusively in Pinot Noir and Chardonnay.

warm in the wine-growing area around Roseburg, with its low hills and wide valleys, so it is even possible to plant Cabernet Sauvignon, though varieties that are more resistant to low temperatures predominate, such as Riesling, Pinot, and Chardonnay. Pinot Noir and Pinot Gris dominate the scene closer to the Pacific in the Illinois Valley, while Oregon's best Cabernets and Merlots flourish in the warmer sub-A.V.A.s Applegate Valley and Rogue Valley, where vines are grown at higher altitudes.

Vineyards were being planted in the northern Willamette Valley as early as the 1960s, and 17 wineries had been founded there by the end of the 1970s. The majority concentrated on Pinot Noir and Chardonnay, varieties that were believed to be particularly promising on account of the area's climatic similarities with Burgundy. This confidence proved to be justified: the 1975 Pinot Noir from Eyrie Vineyards outclassed many a noted Burgundy at BLIND TASTING sessions. As a result, in about 1980 a succession of winemakers began to stream into the region, the majority of whom already had experience in California. There are now more than 220 wineries, mainly in the Willamette Valley. Most have their own vineyards, but still purchase grapes from specialized farms. The majority of these producers are small businesses that can be classed as boutique wineries. They concentrate on quality and seek to develop the individual character of their wines. Prices are correspondingly high.

A LOCAL SPECIALTY: PINOT NOIR

Pinot Noir has become a local specialty, and almost 50 percent of the approximately 12,100 acres (4,900 ha) of vineyard in the state are now planted with this demanding vine. After sunny, ripe vintages during the 1980s, the weather was more changeable and rainy in the 1990s, causing problems for the winegrowers as they had to harvest their grapes before they were fully ripe. Many of the new vineyards were planted without sufficient specialist input and have proved to be disappointing. They produce wines that have fresh aromas of red berries, but not infrequently need to be sweetened and de-acidified due to a lack of body and vegetable notes.

Most of the vineyards have been planted on slopes that face away from the sea wind and are cultivated without irrigation. The red earth of the Dundee Hills is famous, but aspect is more important than soil in this region. The higher locations are generally regarded as the best *terroirs* and do better in good years, but in poor years the grapes do not ripen there. Medium altitudes are the safest, while grapes that are planted in low situations often ripen too early. Winegrowers have to be as flexible as possible in reacting to weather conditions in a particular year, but most believe in "getting things right by doing them slowly," as Steve Doerner, the winemaker at Cristom, puts it.

Quality-conscious producers currently plant between 2,200 and 3,000 vines per acre (5,400–7,400 vines/ha) at new plantings, but 1,900 per acre (4,700/ha) is the norm at high locations, which is about twice as many as previously. Thanks to these higher vine densities, the grapes have a third less volume, which gives the wines a better texture and makes their flavors more concentrated. In general, Pinot Noir produces yields of 425 gallons per acre (40 hl/ha) or less. Picked grapes that have been affected by rot and would cause bad tones in the flavor are discarded before they leave the vineyard. Many winemakers rely on natural YEASTS, which work slowly but give the wine greater expressiveness. The VINIFICATION time of wines fermented in this way is about 15 to 21 days, after which the wine is usually matured for 12 to 15 months in small oak barrels.

July and August are usually very hot and dry in Oregon. The harvest then begins at the end of August and often goes on until well into October, with most of the picking being done by hand. The second most important grape is Chardonnay. In the Oregon climate it often develops a noticeable acidity and sour fruity aromas of lemon, gooseberry, and apple, which may be rounded off with buttery, nutty, and roasted notes, depending on its maturity and the vinification techniques used. Pinot Gris is now the third most popular grape and makes pleasing, pale, refreshing, fruity white wines. Riesling still has its supporters, but the interest in Gewürztraminer has faded. Bordeaux varieties ripen best in the south. If Cabernet Sauvignon is printed on the label, 75 percent of the wine must consist of the named variety, but all other varietal wines made in Oregon have to contain a prescribed minimum of 90 percent of the named variety.

REX HILL
NEWBERG
250 acres (100 ha); 480,000 bottles • Wines:
Chardonnay, Pinot Gris, Riesling, Gewürztraminer;
Pinot; →Pinot Reserve, →Adams Vineyard

Price Peak
2,204 ft (672 m)

Jefferson

Scio

Snow Peak
4,297 ft
(1,310 m)

12 miles (20 km)

Albany

Crabtree

WILLAMETTE VALLEY

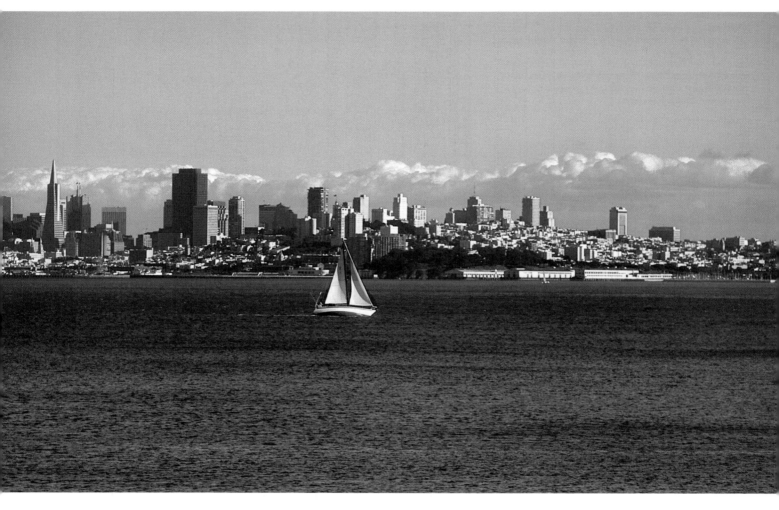

CALIFORNIA: LIFESTYLE, OPEN-MINDEDNESS, KNOW-HOW

CREATIVITY, OPEN-MINDEDNESS, KNOW-HOW

California radiates a unique flair and has an enduring appeal. The magnificent landscape, the extraordinarily fertile valleys, and a kind, sunny climate have rubbed off on the inhabitants, and they find expression in the natural cheerfulness that pervades this tolerant, multicultural society, with its openness to innovations of all kinds. For all their wealth of invention, all their business sense and all their productivity, Californians have not forgotten how to enjoy life—one of the things that most delights visitors. It is certainly no accident that both the hippy movement and the electronic revolution of Silicon Valley began here.

This open-mindedness and willingness to experiment, and the fusion of the most varied influences, are reflected in Californian cuisine, which draws inspiration from all hemispheres,

Top
San Francisco is just a stone's throw from Napa and Sonoma.

Opposite, top
The imaginative cuisine of Napa Valley makes use of culinary ideas from all round the world.

Opposite, bottom
Wine has been essential to the Californian lifestyle for many years, from refined dinners to informal garden parties.

combining very different sorts of food fearlessly and ingeniously in a surprising, but delightful fashion to create completely new flavors. The Mediterranean vines introduced by the Spanish *padres* found ideal conditions in California, and wine has become an essential part of the state's unconstrained, communicative, creative way of life. The Californian lifestyle began to develop in a completely new way after 1970, and the state's wine growing also gained a wholly new dimension at the same time. It suddenly became an expression of the art of living, and the Californians learned to see wine as something malleable, something that could be shaped artistically. The creativity of the newcomers to the business was unhindered by traditional wine-growing ideology. They traveled to the European wine-growing centers, helping out in vineyards and wineries, and gathering all the experience and information they could. Their pioneering work in the area of viticulture, as well as their willingness to share it, helped spread knowledge around the whole globe and fostered a completely new generation of cosmopolitan wine producers. Once they were back in Napa, Sonoma, Benito, and Santa Barbara, they put the knowledge they had gained into practice as soon as possible, but adapted it to local conditions and thinking. If something didn't work, they were quick to change and adapt it and they soon found out what really promoted quality.

In an atmosphere unbound by traditional customs and rigid regulations, there is nothing to hold back American winegrowers and winemakers. This situation, like that in the other wine-producing countries of the New World, is viewed with envy by their European colleagues from the classic, heavily-regulated wine-growing countries, and many have been inspired to look for lucrative opportunities in one of the New World wine-producing centers.

CALIFORNIAN WINEMAKING

Nine-tenths of all American wine is now produced in California, which has over 553,500 acres (224,000 ha) of vineyards. In the state with the largest population in the U.S.A., wine has been integrated more completely into the lifestyle than anywhere else in the country, except possibly New York. California is also the main purchaser of its own wines. By contrast with the wine industry on the East Coast, wine-growers in California consciously aimed to make wines with premium European grapes from the very beginning, and products from the Napa Valley were already being showered with high honors at European wine competitions at the end of the 19th century.

California's image—like that of the famous European wine regions—is based on the quality of a manageable number of excellent wines. The buying habits of American wine drinkers are also like those of their European counterparts, that is, they all want pleasing wines at the lowest possible prices. For seven out of ten bottles they spend less than eight dollars a bottle. Recently, wines selling for only two dollars have been a raging success. Two out of ten bottles cost up to twelve dollars, and only every tenth bottle may be more expensive. Mass-produced wines dominate the market. They are called "jug wines" and are often filled in boxes ("bag in a box" wines) and sold by the glass. "Blush wines," which are slightly sweet white or rosé wines made from dark grapes like White Zinfandel, are particularly popular. But although there are plenty of cheap blended table wines, varietal wines do predominate, and

It once used to be rare for Californian vineyards to be laid out as well as this planting on the Kunde Estate in Sonoma, but Californian winemaking went through a radical transformation during the 1990s.

Bien Nacido in Southern California's Santa Maria Valley is one of the most famous grape farms in the U.S.A. The special form of espalier cultivation used there gives the vines plenty of air.

in these at least 75 percent has to come from the variety of grape named on the label.

GRAPE FARMERS AND WINEMAKERS

In most Old World wine countries winemakers manage their own vineyards and vinify what they harvest or combine to set up wine-producing cooperatives. By contrast, in California, the majority of the grapes come from specialized farms. Wineries with their own vineyards are something of an exception. But the dynamism of the Californian wine world is not least a result of the fact that just about anyone can set up a winery, even if he or she does not own a single vine. All that's necessary is to find or construct a suitable building in which to make wine, and then try to purchase good grapes. This requires hardly any capital and makes it easy to get into the trade. Many winemakers first demonstrate their ability with large companies before taking the risk of going independent, while grape farmers can build strong reputations if talented winemakers make convincing wines with their fruit.

This has often resulted in cooperative arrangements, under which farmers have even been prepared to cultivate the varieties their wine-making clients requested. "In order to get good grapes, you first have to have good contacts, and they can only be built up over the years," says William Knuttler of Tria Winery. And a firm handshake still means a great deal more in this trade than meticulously negotiated contracts.

The "landless" wineries are now using their economic success and investing in vineyards so as to secure top-quality grapes for the future. Often, however, it is the other way round: winemakers with their own vineyards produce exciting wines, creating levels of demand that soon exceed their capacity, then buy in grapes in order to meet customers' requirements. Well-known producers have built up extensive ranges of wines in this way.

The division of labor between grape farming and winemaking allows the winemakers a great deal of scope for experimentation. Some of the most creative among them no longer use standard grapes like Cabernet Sauvignon, Pinot Noir, Chardonnay, and Sauvignon Blanc. Many have discovered a preference for Rhône varieties, such as Syrah, Mourvèdre, Viognier, and Roussanne, and now Italian varieties have come to their attention—not just Sangiovese, but Barbera, and even Teroldego as well. Borders and distances are no barrier, and the grapes can be transported for hundreds of miles in refrigerated trucks. As a result, it is possible to buy Pinot Noir from Oregon that has been fermented in Santa Barbara.

A BRIGHT FUTURE AHEAD

The number of excellent quality wines has risen markedly in recent years, although California has only just begun to exploit the huge potential of its terrain, for apart from a few exceptions in other growing regions, only in the Napa and Sonoma valleys have the best positions been recognized and carefully planted. The phylloxera disaster of the 1990s gave the growers the opportunity to put an end to the old method of planting, in which the fertile plains were covered with only a few vines per hectare, which were then amply fed with artificial fertiliser and irrigated until they grew into huge plants. This form of vine training, in which the individual canes put forth dozens of buds, is known as the TRUNK SYSTEM and made it possible to attain yields of up to 4,250 gallons per acre (400 hl/ha)! More serious producers worked with much lower yields, but even now people in California talk about 850 to 1,100 gallons per acre (80–100 hl/ha) as low yields, and maximum yields of 2,100 to 2,600 gallons per acre (200–240 hl/ha) are not uncommon in places that produce pleasant, average wines. By contrast, David Abreu, a winery consultant and top winemaker who lives in the Napa Valley and specializes in modern, natural winemaking, believes that just under 640 gallons per acre (60 hl/ha) is ideal. In this respect, some of the most outstanding wines hardly differ from their European counterparts, producing yields of less than 315, and certainly no more than 535 gallons per acre (30–50 hl/ha).

PHYLLOXERA: A BLESSING IN DISGUISE?

A great many new vineyards were planted in the 1970s when the renaissance of Californian wine was beginning to gain momentum. At this time the University of California at Davis was recommending the use of the high-yielding AxR 1 rootstock (a *rupestris-vinifera* hybrid). Only obstinate winegrowers insisted on the Saint George rootstock, which had proved itself to be resistant to phylloxera in practice. The majority chose AxR 1, so that eventually about three-quarters of all the vineyards in Sonoma and Napa were planted with it. However, it soon became apparent that this rootstock was susceptible to a mutation of the vine louse. In the meantime, the rapacious insect had destroyed almost all these vinestocks, wiping out vineyards that failed to meet the standards established by the latest research. Farmers, winemakers, and wineries have taken the opportunity to plant new vineyards, consciously taking steps to produce grapes of the highest quality. To this end, vine density has been increased decisively, and many vineyards have converted to natural-cultivation techniques.

It is possible to detect another new trend. In the past, winegrowers planted on the most convenient sites, such as valley bottoms and flat plains, where the subsequent costs of processing could be kept down, but a new generation of winemakers and wineries is consciously choosing to work on hillside *terroirs*, placing emphasis on the importance of aspect. Now that it has been established which types of vine do best in certain climates, scientists are also beginning to develop a better understanding of which soils are likely to achieve the most satisfactory result with particular grapes. As many of the Californian wines are already of high quality, there is every reason to expect great things in future.

The irony of fate: America supplied the world with resistant rootstocks, only to suffer its own phylloxera epidemic. More than three-quarters of the Californian vineyards were devastated by this rapacious insect during the last few decades of the 20th century.

THE BLESSINGS OF THE PACIFIC

California is a strip of land almost 1,250 miles (2,000 km) long on the western coast of North America. After Texas, it is the largest of the American states by area. Its most easterly part, which is dominated by the Sierra Nevada and the Mojave Desert, is hot, dry, and inhospitable. Between this area and the coastal region, we find the Central Valley, which is 55 miles (90 km) wide in some places. This is one of the most fertile regions in the world, and also one of the most intensively cultivated by fruit and vegetable growers. Thanks to highly refined irrigation systems, a great many agricultural products flourish here at high temperatures, under skies that are rarely overcast. Visitors to the area will understand why the Spanish called California *caliente fornalla*, or "hot oven," when they first arrived.

Thousands of acres are planted with vines, but most are the Thompson Seedless variety,

The hot climate in Napa and Sonoma would be far less favorable if it were not for the banks of fog that roll inland from the Pacific, moderating temperatures in the area.

and the grapes are sold as table grapes or made into raisins. Thanks to modern technology, appealing dry wines are now produced in Central Valley, but the high temperatures do not permit very high quality standards in this part of California.

The climate only becomes milder in the coastal areas, where ranges of hills run from north to south parallel to the sea. The water of the Pacific Ocean is comparatively cold, which is why banks of fog form along the coast during the summer and early autumn, extremely important times of the year for wine growing. Away from the coast, the air heats up and rises during the day, drawing moist air inland from the ocean. This helps the fog and cool sea winds to find their way into the interior wherever there is a gap in the mountains or they fall below a height of 2,000 feet (600 m) above sea level. The fog hides the sunshine, which has the direct consequence of reducing temperatures and, over the longer term, delays the ripening of the grapes. This is one of the basic conditions for the formation of intense, complex AROMAS, as long as it takes place within limits.

In places where the Pacific is able to exert its influence unhindered, including almost half of the Californian coast, the climate is too cold and wet for wine growing, though it is ideal for the redwood and other types of tree. The amount of protection from the Pacific afforded by the mountain ranges varies, and the temperature-reducing fogs and winds find their way inland at different speeds in different places, creating a large number of diverse microclimates. It is these variations that have ultimately been decisive in the delimitation of the region's A.V.A.s.

Climatic regions

The significance of climate for winemaking—temperature in particular—prompted Maynard Amerine and Albert Julius Winkler, two enologists at the University of California at Davis, to develop, in 1944, a regional classification method based on average daily temperatures during the growth period of the vine between April 1 and October 31.

According to the heat summation system they created for California, winemaking areas are defined and classified into five regions. The best dry wines come from Region I and Region II, which have the lowest heat sums, such as Sonoma and Napa Valley. Region III is

particularly suitable for red varieties that benefit from heat, but the hottest areas, Region IV and Region V, which include the Central Valley and the warmest parts of the San Joaquin Valley, usually produce wines of less convincing quality. The university also used this system as the basis for recommendations regarding the planting of particular grape varieties, but it proved not to be sufficiently sophisticated for this purpose. And that is not the only point of criticism: as the system is based on specifically Californian climatic conditions, it is transferable only to a limited extent.

Amerine and WINKLER calculated the number of "degree days" in various locations by taking the mean daily temperatures for all days during the chosen period on which the temperature exceeded 50°F (10°C) and adding up the sum of degrees Fahrenheit above this baseline.

Region	I	less than 2,500
Region	II	2,500 to 3,000
Region	III	3,001 to 3,500
Region	IV	3,501 to 4,000
Region	V	greater than 4,000

(To convert Fahrenheit to Celsius, subtract 32 and divide by 1.8.)

Medford
Upper
Klamath Lake
Oregon
Idaho

101

5
Mt. Shasta
14,162 ft
(4,317 m)
Klamath
Mountains

Eureka

Redding
Sierra

Elko
Humboldt

Utah

Great

40°

Mt. Linn
8,094 ft
(2,466 m)

Pyramid
Lake

101

Mendocino

1
Ukiah

99

Sacramento

Reno

Nevada

Basin

North
Coast

Yuba City

Lake Tahoe
Carson City

Napa

80

Sierra Foothills

Novato

Central

Mono Lake

San Francisco

Modesto

Valley

San Jose

Nevada

Santa Cruz
Monterey
Salinas

101

Fresno

Mt. Whitney
14,494 ft
(4,418 m)

Death Valley

Las Vegas

15

Central
Coast

San Joaquin Valley

99
Visalia

San Joaquin Range

Lake Mead

Pacific

San Simeon

California

Arizona

Ocean

35°N

San Luis Obispo

5

Bakersfield

Mojave

Barstow

Desert

40

Mt. Pinos
8,831 ft
(2,692 m)

15

Colorado

Santa Barbara

101

San Bernardino

Santa Cruz

North Coast

Santa Rosa

Los Angeles

5

Palm Springs

10
Blythe

Sierra Foothills

Salton Sea

Central Valley

Santa Catalina

South
Coast

Imperial
Valley

Central Coast

San Clemente

8

South Coast

San Diego

Wine-growing areas in
neighboring regions

120°W

60 miles (100 km)

Tijuana

MEXICO

Mendocino is a pretty
fishing village popular with
artists drawn by the rugged
beauty of the Mendocino
County coastline.

NORTH COAST

Carneros rises to the north of San Francisco Bay and enjoys a very mild climate that has proved to be ideal for Chardonnay and Pinot Noir.

If you leave San Francisco over the Golden Gate Bridge, you come first to Carneros, which is divided administratively between the counties of Sonoma and Napa, and forms what might be described as the gateway to the most famous wine-growing areas in the United States. The gently rolling foothills of the Macayamas Mountains rise covered in vineyards from the San Pablo Bay, the northern inlet of the San Francisco Bay. Apart from the fog coming off the Bay, these hills are also exposed to cool winds from the northwest. At the end of the 1960s the winemaking pioneers realized that, in combination with the area's generally poor soils, this mild, but dry climate was ideal for Chardonnay and Pinot Noir. Ten years later the area saw a second wave of wineries being established, including Saintsbury. During the 1980s it became ever more obvious what high-quality wines Carneros could produce, and a number of major wine companies drew the obvious conclusions and began to invest there, including Robert Mondavi. The winemakers of Carneros have cooperated with scientists from the University of California on a series of experiments, which first clearly defined the character of their Pinot Noir, and then of their Chardonnay, underpinning the area's status as an A.V.A. Its extraordinary Chardonnays and Pinot Noirs have also attracted the CAVA producers Freixenet (Gloria Ferrer) and Codorníu, as well as Taittinger, who built a Champagne château at their Domaine Carneros estate.

	NORTH COAST
	Mendocino
	Anderson Valley
◆	Cole Ranch
	Redwood Valley
	Potter Valley
◆	McDowell Valley
	Clear Lake
◆	Benmore Valley
	Guenoc Valley
	Sonoma Valley
	Napa Valley
◆	Wild Horse Valley
	Solano County Green Valley
	Suisun Valley
	Wine-growing areas in neighboring regions

There can be no question that the Napa Valley is the best-known wine-growing region in America. By far the majority of the great wines of the United States come from the Napa, and, with more than 220 wineries, the county also has the greatest concentration of producers in one place.

Sonoma extends from San Pablo Bay to Mendocino, and there are now ten different A.V.A.s in the county. Sonoma Valley is the place where Californian winemaking first began, and it is still the state's most important wine-growing area, as well as being the base for many outstanding wineries.

Anyone who drives from Sonoma to visit the attractive coastal town of Mendocino—where whales can occasionally be seen from the coast in spring—will probably take Highway 128, which runs directly through the Anderson Valley along the Navarro River. This route gives a vivid impression of one of the extremes of winemaking in Mendocino: the climate in this narrow valley, surrounded as it is by ranges of hills, is dominated by fog and moisture from the ocean, and its Chardonnay and Pinot Noir develop clearly northern characteristics. Anderson Valley grapes are made into high-quality sparkling wines by the Champagne houses Pommery, which has bought up the local wine company Scharffenberger, and Roederer. The smaller wineries in the valley mainly make white wines, including remarkable Gewürztraminer, as well as fruity Zinfandel. Further inland, about 35 miles (60 km) from the coast at Ukiah in the Redwood Valley, we find a growing area with extensive flat vineyards that

Codorníu Napa, the winery owned by the great Spanish cava producer, blends perfectly into the Carneros landscape. Nowadays, it concentrates mainly on the production of still wines.

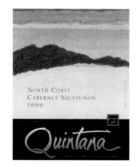

exemplifies another remarkable extreme: here the climate is warm and dry—according to Amerine and Winkler's heat-summation system (see page 812), the area is classed as Region III. The old Carignane grape can still be found here and there, but today most of the harvest is Cabernet Sauvignon, Petite Sirah, Zinfandel, Sauvignon Blanc, and Chardonnay. The largest wine company in the region is Fetzer, which now grows a proportion of its grapes by organic methods. Potter Valley to the north of Ukiah has become famous for white varieties and Pinot Noir, while the more southerly McDowell Valley is best known for its Syrah.

To the east of McDowell Valley is Lake County, which surrounds Clear Lake and has a mainly warm climate. The first estates were developed in the 1980s, and Kendall-Jackson is regarded as the best of the area's producers. The vineyards have expanded rapidly and now provide many companies with Cabernet Sauvignon, Zinfandel, Merlot, Chardonnay, and Sauvignon Blanc.

The Sierra Foothills, where the gold diggers once sought their fortunes—most of them in vain—lie to the east of Sacramento at the foot of the Sierra Nevada. The area's once defunct winemaking industry has been revived since 1970, principally in the districts of Amador and El Dorado. Depending on the altitude, which varies between 800 and 3,250 feet (250–1,000 m) above sea level, various varieties are cultivated there, but, as in the past, the Sierra Foothills' reputation is based on Zinfandel from the Shenandoah Valley and Fiddletown.

SONOMA

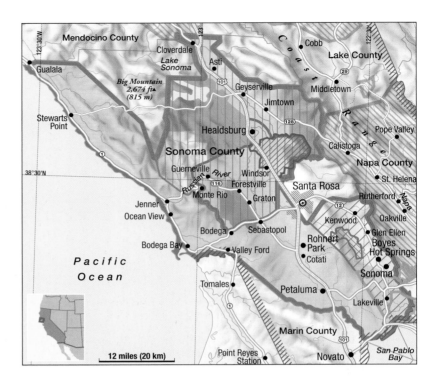

Visitors to the small town of Sonoma City can still admire the cradle of North Californian winemaking, the Mission Station, which was built in 1823 and carefully restored recently. Although winemaking spread from here to the rest of California in the middle of the 19th century, Sonoma Valley soon fell into the shadow of its neighbor Napa. On account of its dramatic topography, there are significantly fewer areas suitable for wine growing in this valley, and as a result, far fewer wineries were established here. To the present day there are still only about 30 of them cultivating approximately 6,900 acres (2,800 ha) of vineyards.

Cattle continue to be farmed in this attractive valley, parts of which are richly wooded. In general, it makes a more modest, more rural impression than its famous neighbor. Only in a few exceptional cases will you find magnificent buildings like the ones in Napa Valley at these wineries. The people of Sonoma are more modest, they build more conservatively, and, rather than professional bustle, the visitor is often met with hearty, unaffected hospitality.

Some wineries had made a good name for themselves before Prohibition, such as the pioneering Buena Vista estate or the company founded by Jakob Gundlach from Aschaffenburg in Germany that began selling wine in 1858. Even so, there was a dearth of outstanding winemaking personalities who might have been able to consolidate Sonoma Valley's reputation during the years of crisis.

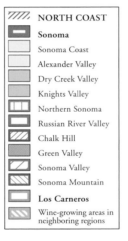

NORTH COAST

Sonoma
Sonoma Coast
Alexander Valley
Dry Creek Valley
Knights Valley
Northern Sonoma
Russian River Valley
Chalk Hill
Green Valley
Sonoma Valley
Sonoma Mountain
Los Carneros
Wine-growing areas in neighboring regions

The man who started the renaissance in Sonoma was former ambassador James D. Zellerbach, a lover and connoisseur of great Burgundies. In 1953 he started planting Chardonnay and Pinot Noir at Hanzell, his 200-acre (80-ha) farm north of Sonoma City, eventually devoting one-sixth of his land to grapes. He vinified his rich Chardonnay in small oak barrels, which he also used to slowly mature his Pinot Noir, demonstrating how Burgundy-style wines could be created with Californian grapes. It was not until the 1970s that more companies began to be founded and the quality of Sonoma's wine started to attract increasing attention in the world of wine.

Gallo

Anyone who happens to go to Modesto, a town of 30,000 in the Central Valley, will find that even on Yosemite Boulevard there is no indication that this is the headquarters of the largest wine company in the world, the E. & J. Gallo Winery. There is absolutely nothing about the imposing administrative building or its surrounding gardens to suggest wine production. But it is here that decisions are taken concerning the production of an estimated 720 million bottles of wine, and probably not much less than a million bottles of wine-based beverages and spirits. Effectively shielded from the gaze of visitors and passers-by, great rows of gigantic tanks stand ready to vinify grapes transported over long distances using the latest precision technology.

Despite its scale, Gallo remains a family firm. Ernest and Julio Gallo, who were born in the United States to a family of Italian immigrants from Piedmont, founded their winery in 1933, after Prohibition was repealed. Their presses, fermentation vats, and even their grapes were "borrowed," because the two self-taught winemakers had practically no capital and had to make their first 185,000 gallons (7,000 hl) of sweet wine on credit. But they had no problems selling it, and this wine remained their most important

Boxes full of Chardonnay grapes and a classy vehicle on the Frei Ranch.

product until 1967, when it was overtaken by standard American jug wines, before the varietal wines began to dominate the market in the 1980s. All this time, the brothers kept enlarging their empire, working constantly to keep their cultivation methods and winery technology at the cutting edge.

The brothers began purchasing grapes from the Frei Ranch at Sonoma in 1934 and eventually bought the farm in 1977 together with Laguna Ranch. Their first oak-matured Chardonnay came onto the market four years later. Since 1989 Gallo has pursued a careful policy of expansion, buying up another seven wine farms in Sonoma County so that the company now has over 3,954 acres (1,600 ha) of vines at its disposal there. A conscious decision was made in favor of Sonoma, with its diversity of distinctive growing zones, and they built an exquisite winery on the Frei Ranch in Dry Creek Valley, equipped with 2,000 barrels for MATURING the company's wines. Julio Gallo's granddaughter Gina is responsible for vinification there and produces some excellent premium wines. These are only sold under their estate names in the U.S.A., because the family has been associated with cheap wines for so long, but Gallo is conquering the European markets with Sonoma wines under its own brand. The good-value Turning Leaf is the most important product in terms of quantity, followed at some distance by Gallo Sonoma and the already excellent single-vineyard wines, while the Gallo estate wines form a rare, expensive group of select bottlings produced in quantities of 700 to 2,000 cases per wine.

SONOMA COUNTY

The situation in Napa is quite easy to survey, because the vineyards there have conquered the entire valley floor, but only extend to a few nearby hillside *terroirs* and small mountain valleys that are included in the Napa Valley *appellation*. Matters are quite different in Sonoma. Sonoma Valley, which includes the Sonoma Mountain sub-A.V.A., is only about 15 miles (25 km) long, but is the most famous growing area of this large county, which extends from San Pablo Bay to Mendocino and boasts a long, wild coastline and impressive redwoods. It now has a bigger wine-growing area than Napa—in all 48,926 acres (19,800 ha)—but it is divided into eleven clearly demarcated *appellations*. The area is divided into a number of clearly defined A.V.A.s, which differ very markedly from one another in their situations and climatic conditions. However, many producers prefer to market their wines using the better-known Sonoma County A.V.A.

The Russian River Valley extends to the west of Santa Rosa. It is surrounded by deep forests, and most of its soils are sandy and gravelly. This wide valley forms a significant gap in the Coastal Range, allowing low cloud to penetrate inland during the afternoon, and the area is well known for Gravensteiner apples, pears, and goat's cheese. Pinot Noir and Chardonnay

Opposite
Beginning in 1956, the Hanzell Winery created a Chardonnay style that has inspired countless Californian winemakers.

grow magnificently here, but its Sauvignon Blancs and Gewürztraminers are also satisfying, and the district's Zinfandel and Syrah produce particularly aromatic wines. More than 12,350 acres (5,000 ha) of land are now planted with vines, which makes this valley the largest growing area in Sonoma County.

Dry Creek Valley lies to the northwest of Healdsburg. It is 15 miles (25 km) from end to end and nearly two miles (3 km) across at its widest point. The winegrowers in the valley bottom concentrate mainly on white varieties and have a particular liking for Sauvignon Blanc, but the stony hillside *terroirs*, with their clayey, gravelly soils, also produce interesting red wines.

The wide, fertile Alexander Valley runs almost parallel with the Russian River Valley, but further to the east, and extends as far as the border with Mendocino County. It is significantly warmer and therefore perfectly suited for Cabernet Sauvignon and other red varieties. As a result, there has been feverish planting activity among the area's grape farmers in the last ten years. The Zinfandel grown in Geyserville has become especially famous.

To the south, bordering on the northern edges of the Napa Valley, the small Knights Valley A.V.A. offers conditions that particularly favor Cabernet Sauvignon. The quality of the grapes there has encouraged further planting.

The most important sub-A.V.A.s in the Napa Valley are:
• Rutherford: A river terrace with gravelly clay soils on the western edge of the valley. Famous as the Rutherford Bench, it produces balanced, vivacious, delicately spiced, dense, world-class Cabernet Sauvignon.
• Oakville: This A.V.A. encompasses part of the Rutherford Bench, though the climate here is slightly cooler and the soils more complex than in the Rutherford A.V.A. This district makes high-quality Cabernet Sauvignon with a great deal of finesse.
• Stag's Leap District: The red soils of Stag's Leap District lend Cabernet Sauvignon and Merlot particularly soft TANNINS, an attractive roundness, and emphatic, berryish fruit.

Left
Larry Turley works magic with Zinfandel.

Right
Cathy Corison—the Cabernet Queen.

Hordes of tourists flock to the Niebaum-Coppola Estate to taste its wines and see its film museum.

• Mount Veeder: The vineyards on this mountain between Sonoma and Napa rise to 2,500 feet (800 m) above sea level. Its volcanic soils produce low yields of fruity, wildly spicy, well-structured Cabernet Sauvignon and Chardonnay.
• Spring Mountain: Powerful Zinfandels, Petite Sirahs, Cabernet Sauvignons, and Merlots ripen here on the Macayamas Mountains to the west of St. Helena. Also attractive Chardonnays and Rieslings.
• Diamond Mountain: The steep slopes of this elevation in the Macayamas Mountains to the southwest of Calistoga get plenty of sun and produce ripe, full Cabernet Sauvignon with dark, berry fruit flavors and well-developed tannins.
• St. Helena: Chardonnay gains remarkable power on the valley *terroirs* around this charming wine town, while the Cabernet Sauvignon that is planted on the terraces at its western edge makes dense, full-bodied, tannin-rich wines with ripe cassis and raspberry fruit aromas.
• Calistoga: The warm climate of this Region III area is reflected in its powerful, well-rounded Cabernet Sauvignon and Zinfandel, and its very creamy Sauvignon Blanc.
• Howell Mountain: This mountainous, wooded district northeast of St. Helena has traditionally produced highly concentrated Zinfandels. But since the 1980s the district's growers have also enjoyed success with extraordinarily dense, fruity, rich Cabernet Sauvignons, which ripen at altitudes of over 1,400 feet (400 m) above sea level.

Conserving Napa's Future

The most famous wineries in the Napa Valley are found on Highway 29 between Oakville and St. Helena, and by the Silverado Trail that runs along the other side of the valley. The eccentric architecture of many of these wineries makes the pretensions of the confident Napa producers plain for all to see. As visitors are usually received in appropriately equipped tasting rooms with integrated souvenir shops, the valley is now the most visited destination in American wine tourism. Not everything that is served there is of fantastic quality, because most of the wineries buy in grapes from other regions in order to meet demand and offer wines that someone on a normal salary is able, or willing, to afford. Only a small percentage of the annual quarter of a million visitors is prepared to pay 50 dollars or more for a bottle of wine.

Some decades ago fears began to be expressed that this attractive valley, within commuting distance of San Francisco, might be designated a residential area. In response, far-sighted agricultural authorities set a process in motion that was intended to make the Napa Valley an Agricultural Preserve. Although things were hard economically for the farmers

Napa Valley has many sub-A.V.A.s that underline the clear differences between its various wines. The most famous districts are Rutherford and Stag's Leap.

in the valley at that time, the initiative was successful and resulted in the protection of a good 35 square miles (9,000 ha) from urbanization. The area covered by the Preserve has now grown to 47 square miles (12,000 ha).

Select Wineries

A large number of new wineries have been set up in Napa County just in recent years, and now the region has nearly 400. Wine consultants and experienced winemakers either run the wineries themselves or have been directly responsible for their quality. Only a very limited selection can be discussed in more detail here, but it will at least give an indication of the range of the Napa wineries, most of which are making wines of above-average quality. These operations tend to produce just a few hundred bottles, or at best a few thousand, which American collectors go to great lengths to lay their hands on. On the one hand, this has resulted in astronomical prices; on the other, it means that these wines are practically impossible to track down. We do not have space to discuss these star producers in detail here, but their ranks include David Abreu, Bacio Civino Cellars, Bryant, Colgin-Schrader Cellars, Grace Family, La Sirena, Screaming Eagle, Selene, and Vineyard 29.

Select Producers in the Napa Valley

Beringer Vineyards**−****
St. Helena

12,400 acres (5,000 ha) • Wines include: Beringer Wine Estates: Chardonnay; →Bancroft Ranch Merlot, →Cabernet Sauvignon Private Reserve, Zinfandel; Napa Ridge
Founded in 1876 by German immigrants. The Private Reserve is one of the most powerful Cabernet Sauvignons in the valley. In 1997 the company acquired the legendary Estrella Vineyards at Paso Robles, now marketed under the Meridian brand.

Cain Vineyard and Winery**−*****
St. Helena

87 acres (35 ha); bought-in grapes; 300,000 bottles • Wines include: Napa Valley: Cain Musqué; →Cain Five, →Cain Cuvée
Jim and Nancy Meadlock founded their estate in the hills above St. Helena in 1980 with the aim of producing a great Bordelais blend. Their Cain Five is one of the most elegant Napa wines.

Cakebread Cellars**−****
Rutherford

75 acres (30 ha); bought-in grapes; 780,000 bottles • Wines include: Napa Valley: Chardonnay, Sauvignon; →Cabernet Sauvignon Rutherford Reserve, Merlot, Zinfandel
This winery is a very active exporter and owns vineyards right next to the St. Helena Highway. The Cabernet Sauvignon Rutherford Reserve is one of the best.

Caymus Vineyards**−****
Rutherford

75 acres (30 ha); bought-in grapes; 720,000 bottles • Wines include: Napa Valley: Sauvignon Blanc Barrel Fermented, Conundrum White; Œil de Perdrix Pinot Noir; Cabernet Sauvignon Special Selection; Central Coast: Mer Soleil
Caymus is one of the icons of Napa and has been celebrated by the magazine *Wine Spectator* for years, but there are also many observers who criticize their wines as crude and extremely overpriced.

Chateau Montelena Winery***−****
Calistoga

220 acres (89 ha); 420,000 bottles • Wines include: Chateau Montelena; Silverado Cellars; Chardonnay, Riesling; Cabernet Sauvignon, Zinfandel
The estate became famous in 1976 when its Chardonnay outdid the best Burgundies. Its most important product is the costly Estate Cabernet.

Corison****
St. Helena

8 acres (3.2 ha); bought-in grapes; 36,000 bottles • Wines: Cabernet Sauvignon: Nappa valley, →Kronos Vineyard
Cathy Corison was winemaker at Chappellet before she finally started working for herself. Stylistically, her wines are very clear and fine. They also store extremely well.

Dominus Estate***−****
Yountville

104 acres (42 ha); 70,000 bottles • Wines: →Dominus Estate Napa
A joint venture led by Christian Moueix from the famous Bordeaux wine dynasty (Pétrus). In good years Dominus is a dense, firmly structured, very elegant wine.

Dunn Vineyards*****
Angwin

10 acres (4 ha); bought-in grapes; 60,000 bottles • Wines: →Howell Mountain Cabernet Sauvignon
Randy Dunn has worked on Howell Mountain since 1996. He only makes Cabernet Sauvignon, but has shown the potential power and elegance of Napa wines away from the overcultivated valley floor.

Forman****
St. Helena

124 acres (50 ha); 60,000 bottles • Wines: Napa Valley: Chardonnay; →Cabernet, →Merlot
Ric Forman makes low-yield, high-quality wines that he matures in the tunnels of his underground winery.

Franciscan Vineyards**−****
Rutherford

1,090 acres (440 ha); 4,200,000 bottles • Wines include: Napa Franciscan Oakville Estate: →Chardonnay Cuvée Sauvage; Cabernet, Meritage, Merlot; Pinot Noir Monterey Pinnacles, Estancia Estates, Mount Veeder Winery, Quintessa
The U.S.-based multinational Canandaigua recently bought Franciscan from the German firm Eckes. It also owns the very good Mount Veeder Winery.

Harlan Estate*****
Oakville

40 acres (16 ha); 18,000 bottles • Wines: Harlan Estate Red Wine
Real estate agent H. William Harlan produces one of the most eagerly sought-after cult wines in the United States, with the help of Michel Rolland and Bob Levy. The four Bordeaux varieties are used.

Havens Wine Cellars***−****
Napa

19 acres (7.6 ha); bought-in grapes; 165,000 bottles • Wines: Napa Valley: Merlot, Syrah, Carneros; Albarino, →Merlot Reserve, →Bourriquot, Hudson Vineyard "T" Syrah
Michael Havens, a former Professor of Literature, farms his own land and a further 36 acres (14.5 ha) of rented vines; his Merlots and Syrahs are fresh and refined.

The Hess Collection Winery***−*****
Napa

1,122 acres (454 ha) • Wines include: Collection, Select; Estate Napa Valley Cabernet Sauvignon
Swiss businessman Donald Hess has transformed the old Christian Brothers winery into a museum of winemaking and art. Its top product is the Cabernet Sauvignon made with the estate's own grapes. Wines from Monterey are also bottled under the Hess Selection label.

Robert Mondavi Winery*−*****
Napa

1,399 acres (566 ha); 3,200,000 bottles • Wines: Napa Valley, District, Reserve, Spotlight Wines
The winery now makes wines from its own estates in its state of the art cellars that were completed in 2001. The Cabernet Sauvignon Reserve is still the star (see following double page).

Niebaum–Coppola Estate**−****
Vineyards & Winery; Rutherford

299 acres (121 ha); bought-in grapes; 3,600,000 bottles • Wines include: Niebaum-Coppola, Rubicon, Francis Coppola Family Wines, Gustave Niebaum Collection, Edizione Pennino

In the 1970s Francis Ford Coppola purchased a share in the famous Niebaum estate and extended his holding over the years. In Chateau Inglenook, he owns one of the most spectacular winery buildings in the valley. The Cabernet Sauvignon marketed as Rubicon has become excellent under the enologist Scott McCleod.

JOSEPH PHELPS VINEYARDS**−*****
ST. HELENA
183 acres (74 ha); bought-in grapes; 1,200,000 bottles • Wines include: Insignia, Vin du Mistral, Backus
Insignia was the first outstanding non-varietal Bordeaux blend to be made in Napa in the 1970s and has remained consistently excellent. The most interesting wines in recent years have been made from Rhône varieties.

PINE RIDGE WINERY***−****
NAPA
222 acres (90 ha); bought-in grapes 1,000,000 bottles • Wines include: Chardonnay, La Petite Vigne; Merlot, Five Cabernet Sauvignons
This winery makes one of the best Cabernets in Napa in the Stag's Leap District, but the wines from its other estates, in Carneros, Oakville, Howell Mountain, Yountville and Oak Knoll are also of excellent quality.

ST. SUPERY VINEYARDS & WINERY***−****
RUTHERFORD
655 acres (265 ha) • Wines include: Sauvignon, Chardonnay; Cabernet Sauvignon, Merlot; →Meritage; Rutherford
The Skalli Group from the South of France produces very pleasing wines at the Dollarhide Ranch, the Rutherford Estate and the Hardester Ranch.

SAINTSBURY***−****
NAPA
55 acres (22 ha); bought-in grapes; 600,000 bottles • Wines include: Carneros: Chardonnay; Pinot Noir, →Pinot Noir Brown Ranch
David Graves and Dick Ward make fundamentally solid Chardonnays and Pinot Noirs with careful use of French oak and polished vinification. Excellent reserve wines.

SHAFER****−*****
NAPA
200 acres (81 ha); bought -in grapes; 384,000 bottles • Wines include: →Red Shoulder Ranch Chardonnay; Merlot, Firebreak, →Relentless, →Hillside Select Cabernet Sauvignon
John Shafer and his son Doug are two of the top winemakers in Napa and own the best *terroirs* in Stag's Leap, Oak Knoll, and Carneros. Their best wines are the Hillside Select Cabernet Sauvignon and the Chardonnay from Red Shoulder Ranch.

SPOTTSWOODE****
ST. HELENA
37 acres (15 ha); bought-in grapes; 70,000 bottles • Wines: Sauvignon Blanc; Cabernet Sauvignon
The Spottswoode estate was founded in 1882 and the Novaks acquired it in 1972. They renewed all the plantings and finally set up the winery in 1982. They have been working biologically since 1985. Only for their Sauvignon are grapes also bought in. Their wines are on a very high level.

SPRING MOUNTAIN VINEYARD****
ST. HELENA
225 acres (91 ha); 60,000 bottles • Wines: Sauvignon, Sirah, Cabernet Estate, Cabernet Reserve
A combination of three old estates, with impressive terraces on the eastern slopes of Spring Mountain. Their own wines are made from only the best grapes.

STAG'S LEAP WINE CELLARS***−*****
NAPA
371 acres (150 ha) • Wines include: Napa Valley: Chardonnay; Cabernet, →Cask 23, →S.L.V.; Hawk Crest
Warren Winiarski was a protagonist in the rapid rise of Stag's Leap District and has been making some of the best wines in the valley there since 1972. The company's top wines are the Cask 23 and S.L.V. Cabernet Sauvignons.

TURLEY WINE CELLARS****
ST. HELENA
99 acres (40 ha); approx. 80,000 bottles • Wines include: Viognier; various vineyard Zinfandels, →Hayne Vineyard Petite Sirah
Larry Turley and his winemaker Ehren Jordan have caused a sensation with their tremendously concentrated Zinfandels and Petite Sirahs. The Hayne is quite superb.

VIADER VINEYARDS****−*****
DEER PARK
42 acres (17 ha); 53,000 bottles • Wines: →Viader, V, Sirah
Delia Viaders' blend of the two Cabernets has now become a classic of Napa Valley. She also produces a blend in which Petit Verdot predominates, and a Sirah from a rocky site 1,640 ft (500 m) above sea level.

Petite Sirah

For a long time this variety was thought to be Durif, a low-quality grape from the Rhône region, though some believed it was a mutation of the real Syrah, but both theories have proved to be false. With a deep red color, plenty of volume and high tannin content, it came into its own as a blending wine in the 1970s, until it was uprooted or regrafted in the 1990s. Some winemakers use it to make stubborn, inky-black wines. The best places for Petite Sirah are old vineyards in Napa, particularly in Howell Mountain and Spring Mountain (York Creek).

ROBERT MONDAVI

In 1966, when Robert Mondavi founded his winery in Oakville with his son Michael, it was the first new wine company in the Napa Valley since the Prohibition era. The prominent buildings at their headquarters and visitor center are built in the style of the Spanish missions and have come to stand for the revival of the Californian wine industry, just as Robert Mondavi himself has become its most famous ambassador around the world. He was born in June 1913 in Virginia, Minnesota three years after his parents left their home in Italy. His father Cesare traded in fruit and grapes and established a business in Lodi in 1923. Cesare made his own wine for the family purely for pleasure, but eventually began to see it as a commercial proposition. After Robert had completed his studies at Stanford University in 1936, his family took over the Sunny St. Helena Winery in the Napa Valley.

The family only became serious about winemaking in 1943, when Cesare took over a vineyard with one of the richest traditions in the Napa, the Krug winery, which had been founded in 1861 by the Prussian emigrant Charles Krug. By the 1950s and 60s the Mondavis were gaining plenty of plaudits for their Cabernet Sauvignon, as well as achieving considerable success on the market with their C.K. brand of jug wines. Soon Robert took sole responsibility for marketing, while his younger brother Peter was in charge of the vineyards and winemaking. The Charles Krug Winery was the first to introduce temperature-controlled fermentation and created a sweetly

Robert Mondavi (left) presents the first case of Robert Mondavi wine to John Daniels Jr. from the Inglenook Winery, his supporter and friend of many years. Fred Holmes, Mondavi's partner during 1967–68, stands to the right.

Robert Mondavi—the grand old man of wine.

fruity Chenin that caused a stir throughout California.

After the death of their father in 1959, the two brothers began to argue with increasing bitterness. Finally, Robert Mondavi—who was deeply convinced of the Napa Valley's great potential—set up his own company in 1966. His first visit to Europe in 1962 had opened his eyes to what could be done by maturing wine in *barriques* (barrels). He diligently researched the method, and used it for his red and white wines. Robert Mondavi created his own style with the fully fermented, dry Sauvignon Blanc matured in oak barrels that he christened Fumé Blanc, a wine that was copied throughout California and helped to build respect for this grape variety. A readiness to experiment, and unceasing efforts to improve the company's vinification technology and raise standards in its vineyards, have been characteristic of the Mondavi Winery, from its foundation to the present. In addition to the harvest from Mondavi's three vineyards, which now cover a total area of 1,410 acres (570 ha) in Oakville, Stag's Leap District, and Carneros, grapes are purchased from various producers, who are rewarded for the quality of their fruit through a bonus system introduced by Robert Mondavi. In addition to the approximately 25 million bottles produced in the Napa Valley and Carneros, Mondavi makes about 60 million bottles of popular varietal wines at the Woodbridge Winery in Lodi that the company purchased in 1979. These wines are based on grapes bought in the Lodi, Central Valley, and North Coast areas, and are matured in a high-tech aging cellar accommodating 40,000 barrels. Of his joint ventures, the first, Opus One, which was launched in 1979 with Mouton Rothschild over the road from the main Mondavi winery, is still the most famous. Others include Luce, Lucente, and Caliterra.

All the members of the Mondavi family have taken an active role in the company's development since its foundation. Since 1993 it has been managed by Robert Mondavi's sons, Michael and Tim. The company bottles wines grown in the Oakville, Stag's Leap, and Carneros sub-A.V.A.s, as well as various Italian varieties branded as La Famiglia di Robert Mondavi. Mondavi also runs the Byron Vineyards in Santa Maria Valley, but in the crisis of recent years the company has greatly reduced its activities.

Left
The modern art at the Mondavi Winery is a reminder of the links between wine and culture.

Right
The hacienda-style Mondavi Winery attracts wine pilgrims from all over the world.

Satellite thermal imaging provides information about suitable sites for new plantings.

Natural wine growing

Since the 1970s natural wine growing has become a firm part of the Mondavi philosophy. Tim Mondavi, who graduated from the University of California at Davis in 1974 with a degree in ENOLOGY and winemaking, is responsible for the consistency with which this approach has been implemented.

Numerous research projects and experiments have been undertaken, and about two-thirds of the company's own vineyards are now managed using "natural" methods. These are based on the following principles:
• Use alternatives to chemicals, wherever possible.
• Replace the use of herbicides by mechanical cultivation techniques, such as hoe plowing.
• Counter insect attacks, powdery mildew and bunch rot by removing leaves.
• Use raw materials that are low in pollutants for soil building (e.g. composted pomace).

The motto is "natural." Meantime, vineyards are being planted and maintained on biological viticultural methods, like these new areas in Carneros.

• Use COVER CROPS and added organic matter in order to replenish the soil with nitrogen. Cover crops reduce the need to take action against phylloxera attacks and provide

varied, and therefore diverting food for a range of pests.

All the recently laid-out vineyards, such as the plantings in Carneros, are cultivated using organic methods. However, this does not mean that the Mondavis are slow to exploit the latest technology. As an example of this, satellite thermal imaging has been used to examine the heat conditions on the various slopes in Carneros in order to identify those sites where grapes will ripen uniformly and optimally.

Beyond its own vineyards, Mondavi takes part in more broadly based ecological projects that are intended to combat erosion and reduce water usage. As well as this, they promote the expansion of biotopes and woodland on their estates, and have reduced noise levels so as not to disturb nesting birds. Mitchell Klug, the company director responsible for Mondavi's vineyards in the Napa Valley, was chosen as Conservationist of the Year in 1991.

SELECT PRODUCERS IN THE CENTRAL COAST REGION

ALBAN VINEYARDS***—****
ARROYO GRANDE
374 acres (30 ha); 26,000 bottles • Wines: Arroyo Grande: Viognier; Grenache, Syrah
John Alban gained experience on the Rhône, then settled in Arroyo Grande in 1989. He produces excellent wines with the best Rhône varieties, which he grows in the highest vineyards in the area.

AU BON CLIMAT***—*****
SANTA MARIA
45 acres (18 ha); bought-in grapes; 360,000 bottles • Wines include: Chardonnay, Pinot Blanc; Pinot Noir; Il Podere dell'Olivos: Tocai Friulano, Arneis; Teroldego, Barbera, Sangiovese
Jim Clendenen uses the *barrique* with real mastery, and makes Chardonnays and Pinots of world class in a shed next to the Bien Nacido Ranch that he shares with Bob Lindquist of Qupé. His range includes amusing Italian wines and other agreeable bottlings under labels such as Vita Nova. He buys grapes from a wide variety of vineyards, including Alban, Talley, and Bien Nacido.

BABCOCK VINEYARDS***—****
LOMPOC
69 acres (28 ha); bought-in grapes; 180,000 bottles • Wines: Babcock, Riverbreak, Eleven Oaks, Fathom, Grand Cuvée, Cuvée Lestat
This estate is located directly next to the most strategically important air base in the U.S.A. It produces excellent Chardonnay, Pinot Noir, and even Gewürztraminer.

CALERA WINE COMPANY**—****
HOLLISTER
64 acres (26 ha); 300,000 bottles • Wines: Mount Harlan: Chardonnay, Viognier; Pinot Noir; Central Coast: Chardonnay; Pinot
Josh Jensen established one of the most remote wineries in San Benito after he discovered calceous soils suitable for Pinot Noir in the hills near Hollister. The wines from his own grapes are quite excellent.

CHALONE VINEYARD**—****
SOLEDAD
321 acres (130 ha); 420,000 bottles • Wines include: →Estate Chardonnay, Pinot Blanc; Estate Pinot Noir; Acacia; Echelon
The Chalone corporation also owns the small Acacia Winery in Carneros, Edna Valley Vineyard, and Canoe Ridge in Western Australia. Known for its well-structured Chardonnays and Pinots, but standards vary.

CLAIBORNE & CHURCHILL WINERY***
SAN LUIS OBISPO
3 acres (1.2 ha); bought-in grapes; 60,000 bottles • Wines: →California Edelzwicker, →Dry Gewürztraminer Alsatian Style, Edna Valley Chardonnay; San Luis Obispo County Cabernet Sauvignon
There is even an Edelzwicker in the selection produced by this small, friendly winery on the edge of Edna Valley. Almost all its wines are sold direct to the public on the estate.

DURNEY VINEYARDS***—****
CARMEL VALLEY
99 acres (40 ha); 250,000 bottles • Wines: Carmel Valley: Chardonnay, Chenin, Johannisberg Riesling Late Harvest; →Cabernet Sauvignon Private Reserve and Chachagua
Originally this winery was intended to be a cattle ranch, but there was a change of plan after the chance discovery of old vines. The best of just five wineries in this A.V.A.

on the hills above the picturesque Carmel Valley, Durney is now run by the Austrian company Schober.

EBERLE WINERY***—****
PASO ROBLES
38 acres (15.4 ha); bought-in grapes; 300,000 bottles • Wines include: Paso Robles: →Chardonnay; Counoise Rosé; →Cabernet Sauvignon, Cabernet/Syrah, →Côtes du Rôbles, →Syrah Fralich Vineyard, Zinfandel Steinbeck Vineyard
Gary Eberle made the Paso Robles district famous decades ago with his legendary Cabernet Sauvignons from the Estrella Vineyards. He produces very reliable, good-quality wines.

EDNA VALLEY VINEYARD**—***
SAN LUIS OBISPO
605 acres (245 ha); 1,100,000 bottles • Wines include: →Edna Valley Chardonnay, →Viognier Fralich Vineyard; Cellar Master's Selection: Sauvignon Blanc, Semillon, Muscat Canelli; Edna Valley Brut; Pinot Noir Paragon
This joint venture between Chalone and the enormous Paragon Vineyards surprises with fresh, almost light white wines, led by the Chardonnay.

FIRESTONE VINEYARDS***
LOS OLIVOS
593 acres (240 ha); bought-in grapes; 2,400,000 bottles • Wines include: California: Gewürztraminer, →Santa Ynez Valley: Chardonnay Barrel Fermented, Johannisberg Riesling Selected Harvest; Cabernet Franc, Firestone Reserve, Prosperity Red; Santa Ynez Valley Merlot, Carey Cellars
Bruce Firestone's winery was one of the first in this area of California to produce premium-quality wines. The barrel-fermented Chardonnay is the most impressive.

FOXEN**—****
SANTA MARIA
35 acres (14 ha); bought-in grapes; 150,000 bottles • Wines include: Chardonnay: Santa Maria, Bien Nacido, Tinaquaic; Pinot Noir: Santa Maria, Julia, Bien Nacido, Sanford & Benedict; Mourvèdre, Syrah, Cabernet Sauvignon, Cabernet Franc
Bill Wathen and Richard Doré offer a broad and original range of wines, including top-quality Chardonnay, Pinot Noir, Cabernet Sauvignon, and Cabernet Franc.

KATHRYN KENNEDY WINERY***—****
SARATOGA
7 acres (2.8 ha); bought-in grapes; 36,000 bottles • Wines: →Estate Cabernet Sauvignon Santa Cruz Mountains
After a few years of unreliability, this vineyard has found its equilibrium again with its famous Cabernet Sauvignon.

MORGAN WINERY***—****
SARATOGA
44 acres (18 ha); bought-in grapes; 480,000 bottles • Wines include: Classic series with Sauvignon, Chardonnay; Pinot, Cabernet; Single vineyard series: Chardonnay; Syrah, Pinot
Known for excellent Chardonnays and Sauvignons, Dan Lee is now aiming to produce highly complex wines from his own estate, using a big range of clones.

ANDREW MURRAY VINEYARDS***—****
LOS OLIVOS
35 acres (14 ha); 60,000 bottles • Wines: Santa Ynez Valley: Roussane, Viognier; Syrah
This 200-acre (80-ha) estate is located at 1,650 feet (500 m) above sea level. It was founded in 1990 and is

planted with 35 acres (14 ha) of Rhône varieties. After initially uneven results, the winery is now fulfilling its potential in ever more impressive style, especially with its Syrah and the rare Roussane.

OJAI VINEYARD★★★★
OAK VIEW
Bought-in grapes; 80,000 bottles • Wines: Chardonnay, Sauvignon Blanc, Viognier; Pinot Noir, Syrah, Mourvèdre
Adam Tolmach creates very individual, unusual wines with grapes from various contracted vineyards, such as Roll Ranch, Bien Nacido, and Stolpman Vineyard. Outstanding Syrah, silky Pinot Noir, and attractive Sauvignon Blanc.

QUPÉ★★★★
SANTA MARIA
Bought-in grapes; 240,000 bottles • Wines include: Chardonnay/Viognier, →Marsanne; →Syrah, Los Olivos Cuvée
Bob Lindquist works under the same tin roof as Au Bon Climat. He has specialized as one of the leading "Rhône rangers," and his Syrahs are among the best in the U.S.A.

RIDGE VINEYARDS★★★★★
CUPERTINO
242 acres (98 ha); 780,000 bottles • Wines: →Santa Cruz Mountains Chardonnay; Cabernet Sauvignon: →Montebello, Santa Cruz Mountains; California Zinfandel: Lytton Spring, Geyserville; California Mataro Evangelo Vineyard
Vineyards on the Santa Cruz Mountains high above San José provide the grapes for the high-quality Montebello, which was conceived as a Bordeaux-style wine. Paul Draper made the winery famous in the 1970s, and standards have not dropped in the slightest since then. The Zinfandels are outstanding.

SANFORD WINERY★★−★★★★
BUELLTON
Bought-in grapes; 600,000 bottles • Wines include: Chardonnay, Sauvignon Blanc; Pinot Noir: Central Coast, Santa Ynez Valley; Santa Barbara County Sanford & Benedict Vineyards
This estate is part of the historic El-Jabali Ranch and was founded by Richard and Thekla Sanford in 1981. The most famous Pinot Noir vineyard in southern California has now changed owners, but continues to be managed by Sanford, who is well known for his stylish Chardonnays and Pinots.

TALLEY VINEYARDS★★★
ARROYO GRANDE
140 acres (57 ha); 144,000 bottles • Wines: Chardonnay; Pinot Noir
Don, Rosemary, Brian, and Johnine Talley own two of the best vineyards in Arroyo Grande: Rosemary's and the Rincon Vineyard. Their outstanding grapes are made into some of the most sought-after wines in the U.S.A. by other winemakers.

LANE TANNER WINERY★★★
SANTA MARIA
Bought-in grapes; 27,000 bottles • Wines: San Luis Obispo County Syrah, Pinot Noir: Santa Maria Valley, Bien Nacido Vineyard, →Julia's Valley
Lane Tanner has been making innovative wines since 1989. She shares the storehouse in which her wines are made with other winemakers, who all use their barrels and equipment in common. Her grapes come from leased parcels.

VENTANA VINEYARDS WINERY★★★
MONTEREY
300 acres (120 ha); 500,000 bottles • Wines include: Chardonnay, Dry Riesling, Orange Muscat, Dry Rosado; Syrah, Sangiovese; J. Douglas

Doug Meador runs a recognized experimental vineyard in Monterey County that complies with the strict criteria of the University of California at Davis. He cultivates many varieties that are still rare in California. The vine density of about 2,000 per acre (5,000 per ha) is unusual, as are the finesse and aromatic richness of some of his wines. Great variations in output during the 1990s.

WENTE VINEYARDS★★−★★★
LIVERMORE
371 acres (150 ha); 4,800,000 bottles • Wines include: Wente, Family Selection, Murrieta's Well, Ivan Tamas, Concannon Vineyard, Vineyard Reserve, Brut Reserve, Ch. Wetmore Reserve, →Herman Wente Reserve, Blanc de Blancs, Johannisberg Riesling
The descendants of the German Karl Wente did good business in the 1960s with sweet Chenin Blanc and Gray Riesling, but also pioneered Chardonnay in California. Apart from Livermore, they own vineyards in Arroyo Seco and Monterey. Technically brilliant wines of impressive quality. The top of the range is the Herman Wente Chardonnay.

WILD HORSE WINERY & VINEYARDS★★−★★★★
TEMPLETON
37 acres (15 ha); bought-in grapes; 1,100,000 bottles • Wines include: →Central Coast: Chardonnay Unbridled, Arneis, Malvasia Bianca, →Pinot Blanc, →Cienega, Tocai Friulano, Roussane Late Harvest; Merlot, Pinot Noir, Negrette, Trousseau, Valley Old Vine Field Blend, Cabernet Sauvignon, Mourvèdre, Syrah, Cheval Sauvage, Santa Lucia, Equus
Ken Volk produces just about every grape variety he can find on this former horse farm. His wines are distinguished by their good fruit and firm structure. Many of the more exotic varieties are only sold in his tasting room.

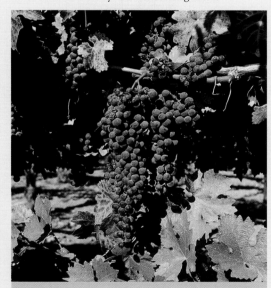

Zinfandel

Although it is really the southern Italian Primitivo, Zinfandel is regarded as a Californian star. Its career has known extreme heights and depths, but it has been consistently successful since the 1990s. Its showpiece role comes in good-quality red wines. Depending on the climate, it can be either cool and elegantly balanced, with fresh fruitiness and fine tannins, or baked, with overpowering fruit, spiciness, fullness, and almost staggering strength. California's best Zinfandels come from Dry Creek Valley, especially Geyserville and Lytton Springs, Howell Mountain, and Paso Robles.

CENTRAL VALLEY

Central Valley is the longest valley in California, running from Sacramento in the north to Bakersfield in the south. It is also one of the most intensively cultivated agricultural landscapes in the world. Not only do most types of fruits, nuts, and vegetables flourish here, but cotton and rice are also grown, and a large proportion of the table grapes and raisins consumed in the United States come from Central Valley vineyards. In the north of the valley, the Sacramento A.V.A., where the renowned University of California is based in Davis, is well-known for its excellent Chenin, and Rhône varieties have been planted there recently.

Well over half the acreage of vineyards in California is found in Central Valley, particularly in the San Joaquin Valley to the south. The region supplies more than two thirds of the state's wine production.

However, the American wine industry's main growing area is the San Joaquin Valley, which is 220 miles (350 km) long and more than 55 miles (90 km) wide in some places. This valley has a total of 120,000 acres (48,000 ha) of land under vines, and produces about 70 percent of Californian wine. The climate is hot and dry, and the growing areas are classified as Region IV and Region V (see page 812). The extensive grape fields require heavy irrigation, and there is always new planting or regrafting going on here so as to meet changing expectations and consumer tastes as flexibly as possible. Even cheap wines are having to meet higher quality standards, which is leading to considerable improvements in grape handling.

The wineries in this area are truly gigantic. They apply electronically controlled winemaking processes, using the latest technology to produce "easy drinking wines." Modesto is the headquarters of E. & J. Gallo, the biggest winery in the world, while Mondavi and Sebastiani own large plants at Lodi, and many famous wineries purchase the grapes for their basic brands from Central Valley. The local Colombard and Chenin were once prized for their acidity, but are increasingly being replaced by more popular varieties. At one time a large proportion of the Thompson Seedless harvest was fermented, but this leading table grape and raisin variety is hardly used for winemaking any more.

To the north of Stockton is Lodi A.V.A., which has a mild climate and rich soil, making it ideal for Zinfandel, Ruby Cabernet, and even Cabernet Sauvignon. The Clarksburg area to the south of Sacramento on the Sacramento River now produces various grape varieties, though its real strength, individual-

Texas

Texas is regarded as the cradle of U.S. winemaking, because the conquering Spanish planted the first vines there in the early-17th century. Of 25 wineries operating in the state in 1900, only one managed to survive until the repeal of Prohibition—the Val Verde Winery founded in 1883.

The 1970s saw a renaissance in Texan winemaking. The decisive stimuli were given by the 990-acre (400-ha) Sainte Genevieve Vineyard in Escondido Valley, a joint venture between the University of Texas and the famous Bordeaux

wine merchants Cordier that has achieved very satisfactory results over the years.

Interest in Texas has been growing of late, because its high *terroirs* offer very good, healthy conditions for wine growing, and there are now more wineries here than ever before. The six American Viticultural Areas (A.V.A.s) recognized so far in the state are the cool Texas High Plains, Escondido Valley to the north, Texas Hill County, with its sub-*appellations* Bell Mountain and Fredericksburg, and the westerly Melissa Valley, the state's most recent

A.V.A. A wide range of European varieties enjoy the conditions here, where the climate is dry and sunny with cool nights. Apart from Chardonnay, Sauvignon Blanc, and Cabernet Sauvignon, Merlot, Trebbiano, and Zinfandel are now being planted, while Chenin and Riesling are on the retreat. However, the first wines to demonstrate Texas's remarkable potential were a Carnelian—a cross based on Carignan, Cabernet Sauvignon, and Grenache —and a Colombard from Fall Creek Vineyards in Texas Hill County.

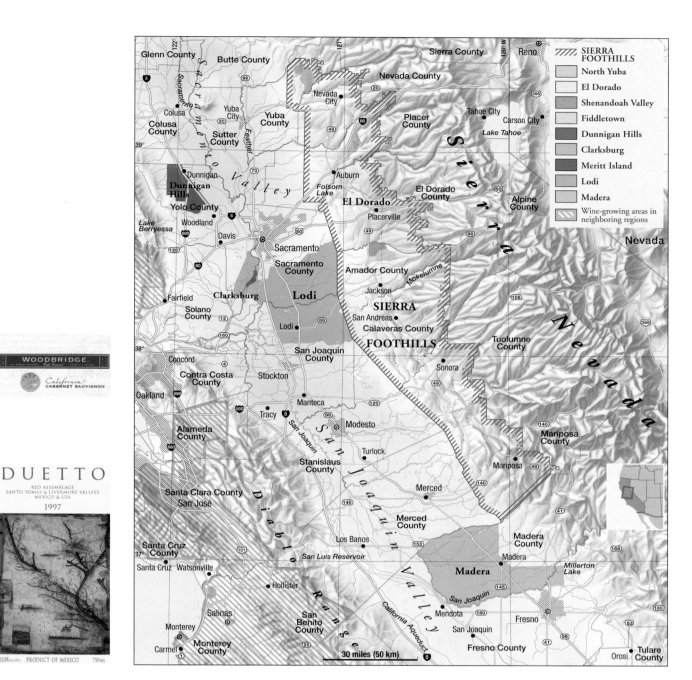

istic Chenin, is increasingly neglected. In the middle of the San Joaquin Valley the Madera A.V.A. produces popular mass-market wines and the dessert wines reminiscent of port wine or Muscat that used to be so common in California.

Mexico and Cuba

The first vines were cultivated in Mexico as early as 1522, making it the oldest winemaking country in the Americas, and 100,000 acres (40,000 ha) of vineyards were planted in the 1990s. However, although it can successfully claim to be the fourth-largest wine producer in Latin America after Argentina, Chile, and Brazil, only a small proportion of its grapes is used for wine. Most of the country's vineyards are found on the sandy soil in the north of the country in the state of Sonora, but their fruit is primarily used for brandy, table grapes, and raisin production. Quality wine is mainly produced in the heavily irrigated vineyards of Baja California, where some excellent Petite Sirah and Cabernet Sauvignon grapes are now being grown.

There are also vineyards further south on the high plains of Aguascalientes and Zacatecas, and in the new winemaking area of Querétaro. The historic Mission grape, which was probably introduced by the first Spanish settlers, continues to predominate, though modern vineyards are increasingly being planted with French varieties, such as Cabernet Sauvignon, Syrah, Merlot, and Malbec, together with varieties that are mainly cultivated in California, including Petite Sirah, Zinfandel, and Ruby Cabernet. Apart from Californian grape varieties, U.S. expertise is also reaching Mexico via the University of California at Davis.

Though it is more famous for cigars and rum, Cuba produces small quantities of wine. Thanks to a joint venture with an Italian producer, Chardonnay, Pinot Grigio, Tempranillo, and Cabernet Sauvignon have been planted in the region of Pinar del Río.

ANTHONY ROSE

SOUTH AMERICA

Wine Growing in South America

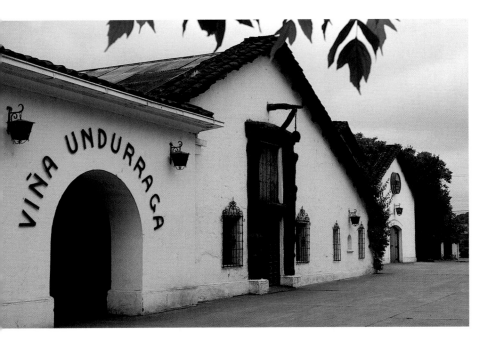

The development of wine production in South America is one of the most fascinating of wine stories. It is the Spanish and their great 16th-century voyages of discovery and conquest that we have to thank for the early dissemination of the vine and wine culture on the South American continent. As successive waves of settlers came to appreciate, South America's position, south of the Tropic of Capricorn, is well suited to viticulture. In particular, the slopes of the Andes provide the ideal terrain, complemented by ample sunshine, dry heat, cooling breezes, and irrigation waters from melted snow which feeds the many rivers flowing down the Andes to east and west. As a result, South America today is the second most important wine-producing continent after Europe. Argentina is the biggest producer by some way, followed by Chile and Brazil. Wine is also produced in Uruguay, Peru, and Bolivia, and even in Ecuador and Venezuela.

Mexico is the oldest wine producer on the American continent. In fact, records show Mexico to be the first New World country in which *vinifera* vines from Europe were planted. It was of the utmost importance to the conquistadors in the 16th century that there was an abundant supply of sacramental wine for religious purposes. Ships from Spain carried wine but supplies were limited. Hernán Cortés first sent for vine cuttings from Spain in 1522. He made *repartimiento* grants (of land and Indian slaves)

Like many other wine-growing estates, the Undurraga estate with its old barrel cellars was created in Chile's Maipo Valley in the 1880s.

Viña Santa Mónica in the Rapel Valley south of Santiago was created in 1976, partly by the acquisition of older vineyards. It has since become increasingly export-focused.

conditional on the planting of a quota of 1,000 of the best vines obtainable, for every hundred Indians. Criolla vines were most likely grafted onto native vines, and it seems quite possible that it was this measure that spared Mexico the disasters that befell those growers in North America who tried unsuccessfully to establish *Vitis vinifera* in the ubiquitous presence of PHYLLOXERA.

From Inca Gold to Gold Medals for Wine

Viticulture spread throughout South America, following the Jesuit missions, in the first phase of the conquest of the Incan empire of Tahuantinsuyu—Chile, Peru, Bolivia, Ecuador, and small parts of some other South American countries as they are now—which was completed in 1533. Peru and Chile were the first to be planted, simply because these were the most important parts of the Incan empire and rich in the right kind of mountain terraces, complete with irrigation channels, for the cultivation of the vine. The earliest record of the cultivation of the vine in Peru is 1550, based on the records of a Spanish settler, Bartolomé de Terrazas, who had received a *repartimiento* near Cuzco. Within 20 years, vineyards were flourishing in Chile.

Although it was the Jesuit missions which were initially responsible for the spread of viticulture, it seems likely that a gathering trend toward commercial production was fostered by secular and non-religious estates. The rate of viticultural expansion was considerable, despite the fact that the native Indians, who then grew grapes, regarded the vine as the very symbol of the white conquerors' power.

The first wide distribution of the vine throughout Peru, Chile, and Argentina was due mainly to Hernán de Montenegro, early in the 17th century. As the market for wine in South America grew, so did supply. From Chile, enthusiasm for wine spread to Argentina, but Madrid still had greater influence there and could, at first, keep production under control. Since the Spanish and Portuguese wanted to export their own wine in exchange for silver and gold, their governments soon became alarmed at the rapid rate of viticultural expansion in South America, and, in an echo of the Roman Emperor Domitian's ban on viticulture at the end of the 1st century AD, the king of Spain imposed a ban on vine planting and wine production in Peru and Chile. Later, a ban was laid on Argentina, with somewhat greater success. It appears, however, that the ban was generally ignored, and planting continued steadily. In 1767, Madrid again attempted to put a stop to it, but again it failed to keep expansion in check.

With the establishment of better transport links and trading opportunities with Europe, the foundations for the modern industries of South America were laid in the 19th century, when a number of pioneering enthusiasts started importing French vines and changing the fabric of the vineyards as well as modernising the wineries.

In Chile, the range of *vinifera* vines increased with the establishment of a nursery for the purpose in the early 1800s by a Frenchman, Claude Gay. With a direct shipping service between Valparaiso and Liverpool, and the fashion for all things French, in 1851 Bertrand Don Silvestre Ochagavía Echazareta began importing classic Bordeaux varieties from great French vineyards, a move which inspired a number of gentlemen farmers to follow suit. The new French vines made an invaluable contribution to the improvement of Chilean wines.

Argentina's viticultural revolution, based in Mendoza, did not really get under way until around 1870. The "grandfather" of the first new era of the Argentinian wine industry was Don Tiburcio Benegas, who was born in Rosario de Santa Fé in July 1844, and moved to Mendoza in 1865 following the devastating earthquake of 1861. He founded a bank and in 1870 he married Lubina Blanco, whose father published a pamphlet, *Viñas y vino en Mendoza*, in 1872. In 1883 he bought El Trapiche, and extended the existing 618 acres (250 ha) by planting French vines imported first from Chile and later from Europe. In 1886 he was elected governor of Mendoza. By 1910 many vineyards were planted with French varieties, known as *francescas*. Viticulture in Argentina was given a fresh boost by Leopoldo Suárez, who imported 600 varieties from every major viticultural region in Europe.

Left
One of the great Chilean wines on the international market—Santa Rita.

Right
Concha y Toro, founded in 1883, now exports to more than 75 countries worldwide.

Opposite
In Chile, vineyard workers habitually use horses to get around the huge vine plantations.

Criolla was the first grape variety introduced into South America. This ancient Argentine specimen has in the meantime grown into a tree.

With the maturation and bottling of the wines on the estate, the export trade flourished, aided by the fact that Chile managed to escape the scourge of phylloxera which devastated most of the world's vineyards in the latter part of the 19th century. In 1889 Chilean wine-growers were awarded a First Class Award at the Paris Exhibition and took six gold medals.

In contrast with North America, the avoidance of phylloxera damage ensured that the blueprint created by successive settlers over three centuries remained intact right up until the second half of the 20th century. By 1965 there were 272,000 acres (110,000 ha) under vine in Chile, most of it in smallholdings of less than 2½ acres (1 ha) and with only 250 growers owning more than 618 acres (250 ha). As domestic demand dried up, however, the industry went into decline and half of Chile's vineyards had to be pulled up. Only since the late 1970s and early 1980s has the industry reversed the decline and started to flourish.

Sadly, as late as the 1960s, a large part of the heritage of the main wine-producing countries was destroyed by systematic uprooting of vines in the wake of falling consumption and prices. Only with the arrival of the millennium have South America's two most important wine producers, Argentina and Chile, really started to regain the confidence, prosperity, and prestige that they once enjoyed.

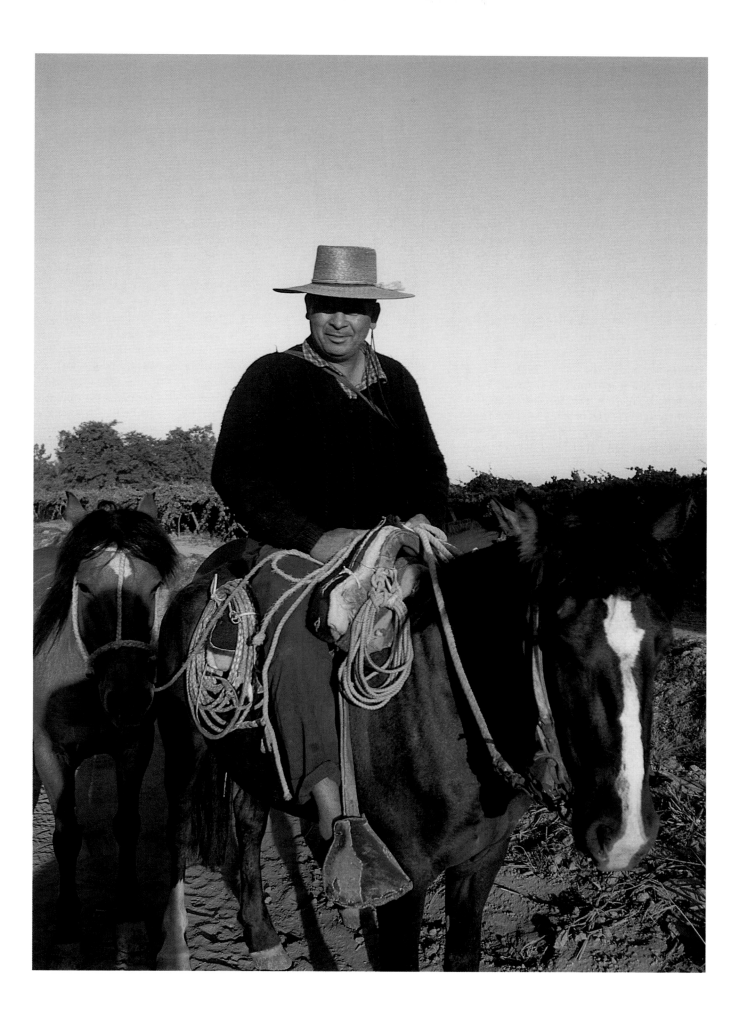

ARGENTINA

Argentina can lay claim to a wine culture stretching back to the early Spanish settlers in the 16th century, who found the foothills of the Andes ideal for the cultivation of the vine. *Vinifera* vines are believed to have entered Argentina via at least three different sources, namely from Spain in 1541, from Peru a year later, and from Chile in 1556. The first record of a vineyard was at Santiago del Estero in 1557, planted by the priest Juan Cidró a year or two earlier. Soon after, the city of Mendoza was founded. At the time, the important variety cultivated was a version of the Mission vine, or *criolla chica*, which itself laid the foundations of a vast wine industry based on Criolla, and Argentina's other workhorse variety, the Cereza.

Given Argentina's hot, dry climate, the early settlers established the beginnings of the modern industry by creating a series of dams and irrigation channels. A wave of European immigrants in the early part of the 18th century was followed by a second wave of settlers, mainly from Italy, Spain, and France, toward the end of the century, and the establishment of important railway networks from Mendoza and Patagonia to Buenos Aires. Bringing their European vines with them along with their winemaking expertise, these later settlers established a blueprint for the great diversity of wine styles to be found in Argentina today. At the same time, at the behest of the Governor of Cuyo, Domingo Faustino Sarmiento, the French

In old vineyards, the vines are trained on tall trellises, which are notoriously laborious to trim.

Spectacular landscape in Cafayate Valley.

agronomist, Miguel Aimé Pouget, brought the first Malbec vines to Argentina.

The upshot was that table wine consumption increased rapidly, becoming a significant part of Argentinian culture. Early prosperity under General Juan Domingo Perón came to an abrupt end in the mid 1950s, and for the next 30 years the fortunes of the Argentine wine industry, under a succession of corrupt military governments, declined. Wine consumption was extremely heavy at around 24 gallons (90 liters) per head in 1970, but it was for the most part large volumes of rotgut red and white made from the ubiquitous Criolla and Cereza grapes. A dramatic fall in domestic consumption combined with a period of prosperity under the new, democratic regime of President Menem has resulted in major changes in the Argentine wine industry in the 1990s. Investment in new plantings of premium varieties and wineries has brought a resurgence of natural confidence and a positive, outward-looking approach to winemaking which is now making itself felt in both the domestic and overseas markets.

The ten wine regions of Argentina are almost entirely concentrated in the narrow strip in the west of the country ranging from latitude 25° south in the Cafayate Valley down to 40° south in Patagonia. It is a unique environment of high, semi-desert ranging from between 980 and 5,250 feet (300 and 1,600 m) above sea level, traditionally irrigated by the waters that run off the Andes in a sophisticated system of man-made irrigation channels. Annual rainfall is low, at between 6 and 12 inches (15 and 30 cm), and so is humidity, while the air is clean and pollution-free. Sunlight is intense, and in most regions there are considerable differences between day and night-time temperatures. Although summers are for the most part hot, altitude and/or proximity to the Andes moderate the temperature in cooler regions such as Cafayate, upper Mendoza (Luján de Cuyo), Uco Valley (Tupungato), and Río Negro.

Irrigation is the lifeblood of Argentina's vineyards, which are mostly sandy and clay/loam soils over gravel, limestone, and clay. Traditionally, the system was based on flood and furrow irrigation, using a series of channels to bring water to the vineyard and flood it. This system is recognized as encouraging high yields and hence, in most modern vineyards, it has been replaced by drip irrigation, allowing the grower more control over the vine's vigorous growth. While flood irrigation is almost certainly responsible, along with Argentina's sandy soils, for keeping the destructive root louse, phylloxera, at bay, there are fears that drip irrigation may not be so effective in this regard. For this reason, most vineyards which have introduced drip irrigation have also introduced resistant American rootstocks.

With its summer heat and sunshine and plentiful water supply from irrigation, Argentina's vineyards have tended toward very high yields. In the 1970s, in particular, the trend was exacerbated by concentration on high-yielding grape varieties grown using the *parral cuyano* trellis system in place of the more traditional, lower-yielding *espaldera* system. Since producers began to take a renewed interest in producing quality wines, however, with the replacement of workhorse by noble grape varieties, there has also been a sea change in attitudes toward viticulture. Today, rigorous control of yields is the chief concern of the quality-conscious producer. It is achieved by plantings at higher densities, using noble vines, careful pruning, drip irrigation instead of flood irrigation, and generally looking for a better balance between fruit and foliage in the vineyard.

One of the most fascinating features of the Argentinian wine industry is the diversity of grape varieties planted, compared to many other countries of the New World. While the high-yielding Criolla and Cereza still account for the lion's share of the crop, their importance is rapidly diminishing as the consumer's increasing appetite for fine wines puts the focus on premium varieties. It is a paradox that Argentina's greatest red grape variety, the Malbec, is one that has failed to shine in its southwestern French homeland of Cahors. This is simply because it flourishes better in Argentina's semi-desert and warm, dry climate, where it produces a soft, mouth-filling, perfumed style of red.

Unfortunately, most of the old Malbec vines were pulled out in the white wine boom of the 1970s, but today there is upwards of 39,500 acres (16,000 ha) of Malbec and more is being planted. It is second only to Bonarda, a north Italian variety, which until recently has been regarded as suitable only for blending in Argentina's domestic product. Bonarda is a soft luscious variety, which, along with Tempranillo and, to a certain extent, Barbera and Sangiovese, has the potential to make good-value, everyday reds. Among new French premium varieties introduced, Cabernet Sauvignon shows good potential, along with Syrah and Merlot, but it

Michel Torino in Mendoza has a wide range of wines.

has yet to show that it can reach the peaks of good, old vine Malbec.

Argentina's most distinctive white wine style is made from the Torrontés grape, which is said to have come originally either from Galicia in Spain or from Muscat seeds brought to Argentina. There are three types, Torrontés Riojano (from La Rioja), Torrontés Mendocino (from Mendoza), and Torrontés Sanjuanino (from San Juan). It produces a uniquely perfumed, Muscat-like, dry white and does particularly well in the northern province of Salta. Argentina also has large quantities of Pedro Ximénez and Muscat of Alexandria, but it is, not surprisingly, Chardonnay, as yet for the most part undistinguished, which gives Argentinian white wine its best shot at achieving a respectable international range.

Traditionally, winemaking has been geared to volume production for an undiscriminating, brand-conscious domestic market. With demand for its wines overseas, however, winemaking is being adapted in order to produce superior quality wines from premium varieties. Temperature-controlled stainless steel FERMENTATION for whites, along with barrel fermentation for Chardonnay, is becoming the norm for export-orientated wineries. The aim with reds is to improve extraction by picking at optimum maturity, fermenting in smaller tanks, managing the cap of TANNINS with frequently longer macerations of up to three or four weeks, and better use of oak-cask maturation.

Argentina's Wine Regions

Mendoza

With its dramatic backdrop of the snow-capped Andes, Mendoza sits at the heart of the Argentine wine industry and is far and away the biggest and most significant of Argentina's wine areas, with its five distinct regions generating some two-thirds of the country's wines. Covering 356,000 acres (144,000 ha), they are: North Mendoza, the High Area of the Mendoza River, East Mendoza, Valle de Uco, and South Mendoza. The next biggest chunk is San Juan, immediately north of Mendoza, which accounts for upwards of 25 percent of Argentinian wine, depending on the vintage, followed by La Rioja, north of San Juan. Compared to these three regions, Salta, or Cafayate Valley, in the far north, and Río Negro in Patagonia, are comparatively minor producers, but because they both produce distinctively different, quality wines, the importance of these two regions outweighs the comparatively small area of their vineyards.

Mendoza is an attractive provincial city, low-rise due to the San Andreas fault, which creates a small earthquake every week or so. Plane and poplar trees line the long avenues, testimony to an era when growers had the foresight to protect weary laborers and animals from the glare of the midday sun. Along the tree-lined roads, monster

Tupungato and Uco valleys are developing rapidly. Lying at over 3,000 feet (900 m) above sea level, aromatic, balanced wines are guaranteed.

Mendoza is by far the most important area of cultivation in Argentina. The huge vine plantations stretch out along the foot of the Andes, which supply the region with the necessary water.

olive trees producing large Arauco olives run parallel to the vineyards, a vivid demonstration of the twin effects of solar energy and irrigation water. Looking at their oak-like trunks, it's easy to see how the vines are similarly affected. Three and a half percent of the surface area of Mendoza is cultivated. The rest is desert.

Irrigated by the Mendoza River, North Mendoza varies between 1,970 and 2,300 feet (600 and 700 m) in altitude and contains the sub-zones of Lavelle, Las Heras, Guaymallén, San Martín, and part of Maipú. Southwest of North Mendoza, the High Area of the River Mendoza ranges in altitude from 2,300 to 3,600 feet (700 to 1,100 m) and includes the important viticultural sub-zones of Luján de Cuyo and most of Maipú. The backdrop of the snow-capped peaks of the Cordón del Plata and the rounded peak of Tupungato makes these vineyards among the most picturesque in the world. This is Malbec country, with some of the best vineyard sites of old vine Malbec in Luján at Carrodillas, Las Compuertas, Vistalba, Perdriel, and Agrelo, and in Maipú, which is also well-known for quality Cabernet Sauvignon, at Cruz de Piedra, Barrancas, and Lunlunta. Many of Mendoza's most important wineries are here, among them Catena, Trapiche, and Norton.

The Valle de Uco, close to Tupungato, is becoming an increasingly important viticultural area due to its altitude of between 2,950 and 4,100 feet (900 and 1,250 m) and cool climate. Typically, it is a good area for aromatic white varieties and elegant Chardonnay as well as Semillon. The French winemaker, Jacques Lurton, has built a new winery at Vista Flores in this up-and-coming area close to the town of Tunuyan.

East of the Valle de Uco, East Mendoza is one of the biggest volume-producing areas and includes the sub-zones of Junin, Rivadavia, San Martín, and Santa Rosa. From the latter come many of La Agricola's best wines. South Mendoza includes General Alvear and San Rafael, where the family firm of Valentín Bianchi has its vineyards.

SAN JUAN AND LA RIOJA

North of Mendoza, San Juan is Argentina's second biggest wine region with 88,000 acres (35,600 ha). The climate is hotter than in Mendoza and, like Australia's Riverland, the region is best known for large quantities of cheap wine from undefined grape varieties. It has its moments, however, particularly in the sub-zones of Ullum, Calingasta, and Valle del Tullum, and, as wineries like Peñaflor and Santiago Graffigna have demonstrated, it is capable of producing good, robust, everyday red wines.

Further north still, La Rioja is much smaller, with 17,300 acres (7,000 ha). It is the oldest of the wine-producing provinces and produces attractive Torrontés.

CAFAYATE

Faraway Cafayate is best known in Argentina for its white wines. At 5,446 feet (1,660 m) above sea level, the vineyards of Cafayate are high, remote, and sunny. The Cafayate Valley sits in a delta formed by the Río Calchaquí and

Humberto Canale began producing wine in the extreme south of Argentina in 1913. The estate's museum preserves mementoes of those pioneering days.

The beaming faces of the harvesters cannot conceal the fact that the greater part of the output still fails to meet export standards.

Río Santa Maria, varying to as much as 12½ miles (20 km) from east to west and flanked on both sides by mountains. The föhn effect, as it is known, traps the clouds in the mountains, leaving the sunny, dry valley protected from cloud and rain. Its sandy, stony topsoils are covered in scrub and cactus. In summer the temperature rises to 100°F (38°C), dropping to between 54°F and 57°F (12°C and 14°C) at night. In winter the temperature can plummet as low as 21°F (–6°C). Irrigation, even more so than usual in Argentina, is the *sine qua non* of vine growth.

Representing a mere 1.5 percent of Argentina's production, with only 4,450 acres (1,800 ha) under vine, it makes a noise out of all proportion to its size. First, because of Torrontés, which produces a delicate, perfumed style here, and

Grower Vollmer almost at the peak of Mount Cabernet.

second, because of a gradual shift from white wines to reds, notably Cabernet Sauvignon, Tannat, and Malbec. Vines are grown on a combination of vertical trellises and pergola trellises, with new vineyards using vertical trellises. The big two wineries here are Etchart and Michel Torino, but there is also a handful of smaller operations, including Colomé, probably the highest vineyard in the world at 7,900 feet (2,400 m), and an experimental vineyard by Michel Rolland and Arnaldo Etchart with grapes at high altitude at San Pedro de Yacochuya.

RÍO NEGRO

Río Negro is named after the "black river" whose waters are the lifeblood of southern Argentina's fruit and wine industries. 5,440 acres (2,200 ha) of vines produce just three percent of Argentinian production, while 111,200 acres (45,000 ha) of orchards, producing mostly apples and pears, are the mainstay of the region's agricultural industry. Thanks to its dry heat and lack of rainfall, wide variations in temperature between day and night, and the remarkable topography, Río Negro is one of Argentina's most natural and potentially exciting regions.

Soils here are composed of alluvial sand and gravel, becoming lighter and sandier the closer the vineyards are to the river, and vice versa. The region was unaffected by the trend toward volume production in the 1960s and the wide-scale conversion of vineyards to the pergola trellising system. As a result, the traditional vertical cordon training system still holds sway.

The British pioneered Río Negro's irrigation system at the start of the 20th century by damming the Río Neuquén upriver from the Río Negro to create a fertile valley some 75 miles (120 km) long by five miles (8 km) wide. The first to plant vines on a commercial basis was Humberto Canale, who brought vines from Bordeaux. Today, Humberto Canale is Río Negro's major winery, with Merlot, Malbec, Cabernet Sauvignon, and Pinot Noir the principal red varieties, the main whites being Semillon, Sauvignon, Torrontés, Chardonnay, and Riesling. Canale has been joined by a number of Mendoza-based companies, notably Fabre Montmayou, with its Infinitus range, and the giant Catena group, which has purchased 740 acres (300 ha) of land south of the Río Negro. For some time, in the Patagonian province of Chubut further south, Weinert has been planting Pinot Noir, Merlot, Chardonnay, Riesling, and Gewürztraminer.

SELECT PRODUCERS IN ARGENTINA

ACHÁVAL FERRER*****
LUJÁN DE CUYO, MENDOZA
59 acres (24 ha); 60,000 bottles • Wines: Malbec-Cabernet Sauvignon-Merlot, Malbec-Merlot, →Finca Altamira Grand Malbec
Achával Ferrer is the creation of four friends, one of whom is the Italian enologist Roberto Cipresso. Old genuine-rooted vineyards set high on the hills, and with low yields provide the grapes from which the magnificent single terroir Malbecs and Malbec blends are made.

LA AGRICOLA**–***
MAIPÚ, MENDOZA
1,483 acres (600 ha); 10,000,000 bottles • Wines: various varieties; brands Santa Julia, Santa Rosa, →"Q"
José Alberto Zuccardi, a tireless innovator, is one of the most enthusiastic and most respected ambassadors for Argentinian wine. A true practitioner, he introduced biological methods and is experimenting with a range of new varieties on 37 acres (15 ha).

ALTA VISTA***–****
LUJÁN DE CUYO, MENDOZA
764 acres (309 ha) • Wines include: Cosecha, →Premium Torronte, Chardonnay; Malbec Grande Réserve, →Alto
The Aulan family from Bordeaux has restored the Bodega restaurant dating from 1890, and they own vineyards in famous locations on different heights. With advice from Michel Rollands they are succeeding in making quality wines that earn the respect this *terroir* deserves.

ALTOS LAS HORMINGAS***–****
LUJÁN DE CUYO, MENDOZA
99 acres (40 ha); bought-in grapes; 350,000 bottles • Wines: Altos la Hormigas Malbec, →Malbec Vina Hormigas
Six Italian friends and the Argentinian Carlos Vazquez started in 1995 with the aim of producing the best Argentinian Malbec from their excellent *terroir*. New cellar amidst the vineyards.

BODEGA LURTON**–***
ALTO VALLE DEL UCO, TUNUYÁN
371 acres (150 ha); 2,000,000 bottles • Wines include: →Pinot Gris, Chardonnay; Bonarda, →Malbec, Gran Lurton, Piedra Negra
The Lurton brothers were the first to plant in Vista Flores and they set up their *bodega* in 1997. Initially they produced low-cost brand name wines, but now they are also making high-quality reds.

BODEGA NORTON***
LUJÁN DE CUYO, MENDOZA
1,680 acres (680 ha); bought-in grapes; 7,500,000 bottles • Wines include: Torrontés; Barbera, Tannat, →Privada, Perdriel, →Lo Tengo Malbec
Norton is a winery in the Napa style and under its winemaker Jorge Riccitelli it is making white and red wines that are very good value. Its Malbec is particularly convincing thanks to the hard work put into the vineyard.

BODEGAS ESMERALDA**–****
MENDOZA
4,942 acres (2,000 ha); 20,000,000 bottles • Wines: wide variety of grapes and diverse brands
Nicolas Catena is one of the architects of the modern Argentinian wine industry. As well as the family winery Esmeralda, the Bodega Catena Zapata, built in the Inca-Maya style, produces 3,600,000 bottles of Alamos, Catena, →Catena Alta and →Nicolas Catena Zapata

from 1,050 acres (425 ha). The range also includes La Rural and Bodegas Escorihuela.

BODEGAS SALENTEIN***
ALTO VALLE DE UCO, TUNUYÁN
862 acres (349 ha); 1,200,000 bottles • Wines include: Chardonnay, Sauvignon, Cabernet, Malbec, Tempranillo, Pinot Noir
In the Uco Valley vines are grown on the highest slopes of the Fincas of Salentein. Winemaker Laureano Gomez combines traditional craftsmanship with progressive technology in his cruciform cellars.

BODEGAS TERRAZAS DE LOS ANDOS**–***
LUJÁN DE CUYO, MENDOZA
988 acres (400 ha) • Wines include: Chardonnay, Malbec Reserva, Gran Malbec, →Gran Cabernet
The premium winery of the Chandon Group owns vineyards in the best locations. Director Roberto de la Mota has developed a convincing range here.

BODEGAS Y CAVAS DE WEINERT***–****
MENDOZA
99 acres (40 ha); bought-in grapes; 1,600,000 bottles • Wines include: Chardonnay, Chenin; Malbec, Cabernet, →Carrascal, →Gran Vino
Founded in 1893, this traditional winery, with its spectacular brick-vaulted cellars, was renovated by Bernardo Weinert after his purchase in 1975. The reds age in big old vats but retain a remarkably clear fruit. New and promising investment in the cool Chubut in Southern Patagonia.

HUMBERTO CANALE***
RÍO NEGRO, PATAGONIA
371 acres (150 ha) • Wines include: brands Canale Black River, Diego Murillo
Father Guillermo Barzi, and son Humberto Canale run the first winery to be set up in Patagonia. It was established by the family in 1913 and is still Patagonia's foremost winery, exploiting the region's potential for wines of impressive concentration in color, aroma, and taste.

DOMAINE VISTALBA***
MENDOZA/RÍO NEGRO
581 acres (235 ha); 700,000 bottles • Wines: Chardonnay, Sémillon; Cabernet, Merlot, Malbec, Syrah
The Frenchman Hervé Joyaux-Fabre founded Fabre Montmayou near Mendoza and the Bodega Infinitus in Rio Negro. While the former makes fine Malbecs and a Bordeaux blend, the latter produces elegant white and red *cuvées* with a clear, fruity aroma.

FINCA LA ANITA****
AGRELO, MENDOZA
297 acres (120 ha) • Wines include: →Semillon, Syrah, →Malbec
The brothers Antonio and Manuel Mas tend their vineyards using natural methods and they follow their own ideas in their cellars as well. The result is highly individual white and red wines with a growing range of *cuvées* as well.

PEÑAFLOR**–***
MENDOZA
3,212 acres (1,300 ha); bought-in grapes; 150,000,000 bottles • Wines: various brands
This enterprise sells most of its wines in Argentina under the brand names Termidor, Tomba, and Finca La Escondida, and in Great Britain as Bright Brothers. The estate belongs to the DLJ, Donaldson, Luftkin, & Jenrette investment fund, which also owns Trapiche, Finca La Moras, Michel Torino, and Santa Ana.

Chile's Wine Regions

North of Santiago, the Aconcagua region contains the two sub-regions of the Casablanca Valley and the Aconcagua Valley itself. Cooled by Pacific morning fogs and breezes, the Casablanca Valley, which lies on the coastal plain about 18½ miles (30 km) southeast of Valparaíso, has become, in a short space of time, one of Chile's top regions for crisp, elegant whites made from Sauvignon and Chardonnay, at the same time producing flavorsome, minty reds from Merlot and Cabernet Sauvignon. With upwards of 7,400 acres (3,000 ha), this temperate sub-region was pioneered by Pablo Morande in 1982 and is now planted with vineyards owned by, among others, Concha y Toro, Santa Carolina, Viña Casablanca, Franciscan, Villard, and Santa Rita. The much higher Aconcagua Valley is also much smaller, with around 990 acres (400 ha), but in Errázuriz Estate's Don Maximiano, it includes one of Chile's top premium wines.

If any region can lay claim to the word "classic," it is the Maipo Valley to the west and south of Santiago. The Maipo Valley, which is sub-divided into six districts, comprises nearly 19,800 acres (8,000 ha) of vineyards, some of which overlook the city of Santiago, split evenly between red and white. The climate of Maipo, which is bisected by the river of the same name, is warm and temperate. Because of its proximity to Santiago, Maipo contains the head-

Cousiño Macul is well-known for red wines with aging ability.

Although San Pedro is one of the wine giants of Chile and has a highly modern winery, the grapes continue to be picked and brought in by hand.

quarters of many of Chile's oldest and biggest wineries, among them Concha y Toro, Santa Carolina, Santa Rita, and Valdivieso, and some of its most traditional in Cousiño Macul and Undurraga. Concha y Toro's Don Melchor, Santa Rita's Medalla Real, and Cousiño Macul's Antiguas Reservas are among Chile's best Bordeaux-style red wines, while Carmen is a modern winery to watch.

Further south, the Rapel Valley contains the two main sub-regions of the Cachapoal Valley and the Colchagua Valley, and comprises some 48,430 acres (19,600 ha) of vineyards planted on mainly alluvial soils at between 1,970 and 3,280 feet (600 and 1,000 m) above sea level. With Rancagua at the heart of the region, the Mediterranean climate is marginally wetter and windier than that of Maipo. It is a predominantly red wine region, with traditional wineries such as Bisquertt, Porta, Santa Emiliana, Santa Mónica, Torreón de Paredes, and Château Lafite's Los Vascos at Peralillo. There are a number of up-and-coming stars here, notably Viña Gracia, Luis Felipe Edwards, Casa Lapostolle, and MontGras, while Cono Sur is noted for its Cabernet Sauvignon and Pinot Noir.

There are approximately 36,000 acres (14,600 ha) planted in the Curicó Valley, which is subdivided into two smaller regions of the Teno and Lontue Valleys. Important wineries here include Viña Montes, San Pedro, and Torres. It is best known for the quality of its Chardonnay, although Valdivieso makes excellent value-for-money reds from Pinot Noir, Cabernet Sauvignon, Cabernet Franc, and Merlot.

With the coastal mountain range to the west and the Andes to the east, the Maule Valley contains three major sub-zones in the Claro, Loncomilla, and Tutuven Valleys, and comprises more than 56,830 acres (23,000 ha) of vineyard. With its volcanic soils and rolling hills, the climate here is Mediterranean, with relatively

Harvest workers having a break in the shadow of the vines. The wine-growing estates of Chile are among the country's biggest employers.

heavy winter rainfall, while its Pacific-influenced vineyards are often cooler than those of the regions immediately to the north. Notable producers here are Viña Calina, Carta Vieja, Bouchon, and Terra Noble, and reds are generally better than whites.

The southern region is subdivided into the Itata and Bío-Bío Valleys. Unlike regions further north, it is not sheltered by the coastal mountain range, so rainfall is much higher here, while average temperatures and sunshine hours are lower. Most of the wine from this unirrigated region is derived from the prolific País, or Mission vine, although there is also a significant amount of Muscat of Alexandria. Following research into this area's potential, new locations for premium-quality wines are sprouting up, notably Mulchen, which is well-suited to aromatic varieties such as Riesling and Gewürztraminer.

Pisco

The name of pisco, the national spirit of Chile, is derived from *piscu*, meaning "flying bird" in the language of the Incas, Quechua. It is made in the Pisco region of northern Chile around La Serena and Coquimbo, by distilling wine made mostly from Moscatel (Muscat) grapes. On May 16, 1931 it became the first alcoholic beverage to be protected by its own *denominación de origen*. There are some 14,800 acres (6,000 ha) of vineyard planted for the production of pisco, the main ones located in the Elqui and Limari Valleys. After fermentation and distillation in copper stills, the spirit is aged in large chestnut or oak casks for between four months and a year. The spirit is then diluted to one of four grades, varying between 30 percent (*selección*), 35 percent (*especial*), 40 percent (*reservado*), and 43 percent (*gran pisco*). It is a highly aromatic spirit, with characteristic aromas of prune, plum, bitter almond, and vanilla.

A typical pisco bar in Chile.

Pisco Sour

4 measures pisco
1 measure fresh lemon or lime juice
ice cubes
1 teaspoon egg white (optional)
sugar to taste

Combine in a cocktail shaker, shake vigorously and strain into glasses. The egg white gives the drink a foaming head.

Made with fresh lemon (or lime) juice, this is one of the great summer drinks.

ANTHONY ROSE

AUSTRALIA AND
NEW ZEALAND

FROM THE FIRST VINES TO AN INDUSTRY

On a condescending note, not untypical of the British toward the colonies, the English wine merchant T.G. Shaw wrote of Australia in the 1864 edition of *Wine, the Vine and the Cellar*: "So far as I can learn, Australia is not well adapted, either by soil or climate, for growing wine, and this opinion seems confirmed by the unsuccessful efforts of many years." Perhaps you cannot blame the man for being skeptical. The composition of Australia's climate and soil is so different from European standards that a man raised on claret, port, and champagne might well take a dim view of Australia's potential as a wine producer.

The first vines in Australia had already been planted back in 1788 on the site of the Intercontinental Hotel in Macquarie Street, Sydney, soon after Captain Arthur Phillip established Port Jackson as a convict settlement on January 26. From a few vines, an industry grew. It was the sheep-breeder, Captain John Macarthur, who laid the early foundations for Australia's 19th-century wine industry, bringing a wealth of vines back from France after investigating the French industry with his sons William and James. The explorer Gregory Blaxland, together with a young immigrant from

The imposing Yalumba Winery in the Barossa Valley was built at the end of the 19th century. The best-known wine of the family-owned firm is Angas sparkling wine.

At Penfolds, the pioneer George Fife Angas is commemorated on a barrel. From 1838, Angas brought refugee Lutheran Protestants to the Barossa Valley, and their role in developing viticulture was vital.

Edinburgh, James Busby, were major pioneering figures. Busby in particular, "the father of the Australian wine industry," brought a host of vines to Australia which he had collected on his travels in France and Spain, among them the Pineau Chardonnay (*sic*) and Pineau Noir (*sic*) from Clos Vougeot. In Western Australia, botanist Thomas Waters planted vines in 1829.

By the 1850s, Victoria's vineyards were spreading as the rush to the goldmines of Ballarat, Rutherglen, and Bendigo gathered pace. South Australia received a boost from the influx of Lutheran dissenters from Silesia, who were brought to Australia in the mid-1850s by, among others, the Smiths of Yalumba and the philanthropic Scotsman George Angas. By 1870, the author Anthony Trollope was able to report: "In all the Australian colonies, except Tasmania, wine is made plentifully." In that year, about 2.3 million gallons (8.7 million liters) were produced, and Australian wines started to win medals. At the 1873 Vienna Exhibition, a Victorian "Hermitage" was judged best of its type by an international jury, causing the French to walk out in disgust (they had assumed one of their wines would be picked).

Soon after, in 1877, the PHYLLOXERA louse struck. Discovered near Geelong in Victoria, it caused extensive damage in Victoria, but South Australia and New South Wales escaped. Nevertheless, the early promise faded, partly due to phylloxera but also because of changes in export markets and a developing local taste for stronger, sweeter wine.

Victoria was the pre-eminent wine state in the latter half of the 19th century, earning itself the nickname "John Bull's vineyard" for its exports to the United Kingdom. Then, in the first half of the 20th century, South Australia usurped the crown. Lutherans from Silesia had already established the Barossa Valley as a wine-growing center, and by 1930 South Australia, with the Barossa Valley at the hub, was producing three-quarters of all Australian wine. Many grapes were grown in the warm, irrigated area known as Riverland, and processed by the Teutonic winemaking families of the Barossa Valley. Between 1927 and 1939, when Australian trade benefited from the British imperial preference system, Australia exported a huge amount of wine to the United Kingdom, some with a high alcohol content, designed to strengthen thinner French wines, and some FORTIFIED WINES.

Delusions of Grandeur and Paradox

In the post-war era, immigrants who had a tradition of drinking wine with meals came to Australia. Technology brought stainless steel and with it the ability to make dry wines in volume. At the same time, big companies started to expand plantings in existing locations such as Riverina, Loxton, Berri, and Renmark, and plant new regions such as Padthaway and Drumborg. Regions with a developing reputation for fine wines continued to grow, among them Coonawarra, Clare Valley, McLaren Vale, and the Hunter Valley.

It was in 1951, following a visit to France, that Max Schubert of Penfolds created Grange Hermitage, based on the Shiraz grape. Now the most famous of all Australia's wines, Penfolds Grange was trashed by critics when it first appeared, being described as a dry port and worse. Schubert was ordered to cease production, but fortunately for Penfolds and Australian wine he had the foresight to disobey his master's orders and carry on. When the 1955 vintage was entered in the open claret class in the 1962 Royal Sydney Show, it duly struck gold and went on to win a total of 51 gold medals and 12 trophies.

In the 1960s, eating and drinking societies and wine clubs proliferated throughout Australia. Along with this movement, the demand for red wine accelerated so rapidly that Len Evans, one of Australia's most outspoken and influential proponents, wrote at the time: "The rapid acceleration in interest and consumption has caught the wine companies with their production pants down." He also pointed out that Shiraz was the variety best suited to Australia's soils and climate, a prescient point, which has been confirmed by the passage of time.

The red-wine boom coincided with plantings on unsuitable soils, overcropping in some instances and, as has so often happened in other countries in response to demand, a downturn in quality. Then, in the mid-1970s, the red-wine boom suddenly ended and there was a glut. For a while, demand switched from red to white wines, but now the wheel has turned full circle, with premium reds made from Shiraz and Cabernet Sauvignon once again in demand.

The Wine Barons

The robustness of Australia's reds has been matched by a number of equally forthright characters who, either in their winemaking or through their communication skills, have been influential in the development of Australian

Cyril Henschke made his Shiraz Hill of Grace one of Australia's most sought-after red wines. His son Stephen has succeeded in maintaining the quality.

Left
Grower and writer James Halliday.

Right
Peter Lehmann, the legendary Baron Barossa, a pioneer of German descent.

wines. Len Evans, who has been mentioned already, left England in 1958 for Sydney, where he began a lifelong mission to preach the joys of Australian wine as well as produce it. James Halliday, an equally forthright character, gave up a lucrative legal practice to make wine at Coldstream Hills in the Yarra Valley and communicate his enthusiasm for the grape in countless books and newspaper articles.

Each region in Australia has had its share of winemakers who have innovated, set standards, and articulated the pleasures of Australian wine with a quality and style that equals the wines they have produced. Along with Len Evans, both Max Lake and Murray Tyrrell were instrumental in putting the Hunter Valley on the map in the late 1960s. In Victoria, Mick Morris and the Campbells of Rutherglen honed the rich aromatic fortified Muscats and Tokays of northeast Victoria, while in Western Australia Jack Mann created Houghton's White Burgundy, which became one of Australia's best-selling white wines.

Among those who have been highly influential in the South Australian wine industry are Max Schubert at Penfolds, and Cyril Henschke with Hill of Grace, who set standards for Shiraz that others still strive to emulate. With his immaculate blending and barrel-aging of reds, Wolf Blass dominated the wine shows in the mid-1970s, winning three consecutive, coveted Jimmy Watson trophies for Wolf Blass Black Label in 1974, 1975, and 1976. In 1977, when the big companies stopped buying grapes from their growers because of the red wine glut, Peter Lehmann, the legendary "Bear of the Barossa," kept the flame alight by purchasing grapes and making wine himself. His robust attitude contributed in no small measure to the subsequent revival of Barossa Valley wines.

THE EMANCIPATION OF AUSTRALIAN WINES

Before varietal wines established themselves and Australia's growers pursued an individual path, attempts were made to sell wines imitating famous labels such as Chablis, Moselle, and even Lambrusco.

Australia's wine regions have established images of their own, and the number of premium wines on offer is rising sharply. This is very evident from the range of wines available in Australian wine stores.

"The traditional market in the U.K. will not grow greatly, and our top-quality wines will always suffer from the inborn, carefully perpetuated, and slightly supercilious snobbery that exists there." A generation after writing this fortuitously ill-fated pronouncement, the celebrated author and winemaker Len Evans is no doubt as delighted as anyone to have been forced to eat (and drink) his own words. For Australia is the success story of the modern era, coming from nowhere to become a significant player on the world stage.

While the modern Australian wine industry is founded on a diversity of styles, broadly based on the classic styles of Europe, the legacy of a century-old industry has given Australia a wealth of original wine styles. These range from the toasty Semillons of the Hunter Valley, the big, bold reds made from Barossa Valley Shiraz, to the sticky fortified Muscats and Tokays of northeast Victoria.

While many European countries have been busy uprooting unwanted vines, Australia has planted them. Where European countries have been casting around for importers, Australia has embarked on an aggressive export plan for the new millennium. It is a success story based on the confident will to succeed, together with an awareness of quality and appreciation of consumer tastes, whether for aromatic or dry table wines, sparkling or fortified. Today, Australia has about 1,500 wineries, from big concerns like Southcorp, Orlando, and Constellation Brands Thomas Hardy to committed one-man enterprises that are often run by a doctor or lawyer determined to give the Australian wine industry a little individuality.

Australia has gone through major changes since the late 1950s, when the modern wine industry was born. In that period, not much more than 98,400 tons/tonnes of basic grape varieties were crushed. Less than 10 percent of the total harvest was of premium varieties. By the mid-1980s, roughly 80 percent of Australian wine was sold in BAG IN A BOX or bulk with some five percent premium bottled wine. Since then, there has been a dramatic shift to premium varieties, notably Chardonnay, Semillon, and Riesling among the white varieties, and Shiraz and Cabernet Sauvignon among the reds. At the start of the new millennium, the total amount of grapes crushed was nearly one million tons, of which premium varieties represented well over 60 percent, and was increasing.

ENERGY FROM THE SUN AND COOLING TECHNOLOGY

As Australian wine producers have adopted and adapted the styles of the producers they most admire, they have come to realize that they can produce wines in a style that is uniquely Australian and, as such, much in demand. What is that style? In a nutshell, Australian wine is about intense fruitiness, abundance of flavor, and softness of texture, molded by exceptional sunshine and warmth. With fruit and flavor come cleanness of taste and the less appreciated, but no less discernible, texture. Typically, Australian wines have a lovely softness and rounded texture that makes them instantly accessible. These are not wines that have to be laid down forever in dark, damp cellars. Their appeal is not their longevity but their drinkability.

Technology (in particular, refrigeration), and subsequently night-harvesting and care in handling the grape juice, have played a crucial role in the modern evolution of Australian wine. The modern industry is founded on cold FERMENTATION, which enabled producers to move away from fortified wines to lighter table wines. The necessity for this is brought home by the author Oliver Mayo, who points out that while "in Europe grapes are grown on the warm fringes of a cold continent, in Australia they are grown on the cold margins of a hot continent." This means that, for the most part, Australia's viticultural regions are not in the hottest parts of the country and, with only a handful of exceptions, are never far from the ocean.

The Australian wine-show system has been instrumental in honing style and maintaining the quality of Australian wines. Australian wine producers submit their wines, almost without exception, to the local, regional or national show to be judged, like cows or sheep, for bronze, silver or gold medals, and trophies. Not only does this system have its marketing and promotional uses, but it also acts as a benchmark for winemakers.

Perhaps the most obvious difference between Australian and European wines is that the choice of Australian vineyards is not influenced by TERROIR in the way that traditional European vineyards are. In a hot country such as Australia, climate is considered to be of greater importance to producers than the composition of the soil, the slope of the hillside, and the altitude. Grapes are grown where it is most convenient to plant vines and so market the wines. It is no coincidence that the concentration of Australia's wine industry is around such major conurbations as Sydney, Melbourne, Adelaide, and Perth.

Thanks to this tradition, Australian wines are also blends that cut across regional or even state boundaries. The master winemaker in Australia is the master blender, the person who knows exactly what properties each region contributes to the final blend. Even Australia's greatest wine, Penfolds Grange Hermitage, is a regional blend of wines from various different vineyards within South Australia, blended to the proportion desired by the winemaker. For this reason, the winemaker has always been an important character on the Australian scene.

THE RISE OF REGIONAL IDENTITY?

Traditional attitudes are changing, however, as the focus turns towards the vineyard. Not content to settle for fruit and flavor, Australian producers have gone in search of some more elusive qualities, namely subtlety, structure, elegance, and complexity. Regional differences are becoming increasingly important as producers who previously supplied grapes to the big companies have set up on their own and started to win back some regional identity. At one time, the map of Australian vineyards showed little more than state boundaries. Today, vineyards such as McLaren Vale, Clare Valley, Mudgee, Mornington, and Eden Valley are staking their claim, while newer names, including Pemberton, Kuitpo, Robe, and Orange, are adding detail.

Australian producers have realized that to obtain elegance and structure they need to go in search of cooler locations, either up hillsides or in regions further south. And so Victoria, which lost out to South Australia in terms of importance, is now very much back on the map, with a host of small districts and regions under development. Tasmania is becoming more important, along with the southernmost parts of Western Australia. And in South Australia itself, huge vineyard sites have been planted on the Limestone Coast at Cuppacup, Robe, and Wrattonbully. Even New South Wales is coming up with cool climate areas such as Orange, and, for sparkling wines, the dramatically named Tumbarumba. The vineyards of the future have laid down the gauntlet to the vineyards of the present. The result is that by adapting to change, both can survive and prosper to increase the range of wine styles and improve the quality of Australian wines.

The breakdown of Australian wines (in %) of world-wide production, consumption, export, and import				
Year	Production	Consumption	Exports	Imports
1966–1970	0.8	0.7	0.3	0.0
1986–1990	1.4	1.4	0.7	0.2
1997	2.4	1.5	2.5	0.3
2000	3.1	1.6	4.5	0.2
2001	3.3	1.6	5.2	0.2

Australia has become a pioneer of modern enology and winery technology. Temperature-controlled, stainless steel fermentation tanks are standard equipment here.

Australian wine statistics	1997–1998	1998–1999	1999–2000	2000–2001	2001–2002
Wine producers	1,104	1,115	1,197	1,318	1,465
Area planted to vines in acres	243,571	303,719	345,592	366,383	391,880
Grape output in tons/tonnes	1,075,675	1,108,268	1,126,969	1,401,575	1,580,709
Wine output in million gallons	180	210	213	274	n.a.
Wine consumption in million gallons	96	99	105	105	n.a.
Wine exports in million gallons	51	57	76	90	110

For hectares × by 0.4
For liters × by 3.8

Clare Valley north of
Adelaide is a wine region
with one of the longest
histories in Australia. It was
formerly known for its
Rieslings, but nowadays
Cabernet Sauvignon and
other more fashionable
varieties are planted on
trellises and watered by drip
irrigation.

Left
The lush vegetation
indicates that it often rains
on the Margaret River.

Right
In cold Tasmania, vines are
trained on tall trellises to get
maximum benefit from
sunshine.

ries of the weather, the tendency to budburst and moderate temperatures during the final ripening months contributes to overall quality. There are few cold regions in Australia. Those considered to be cool are the Macedon Ranges, Ballarat, far southwest Victoria, and northern Tasmania, while southern Tasmania is positively chilly, with about the same H.D.D.s as Champagne in France.

SOIL CHARACTERISTICS

Generally speaking, Australia's soil varies so widely that it is impossible to characterize regions by specific soil type. The main soil types are so-called duplex soils, the most common of which have a red-brown subsoil overlain by a sandy loam surface. However, Coonawarra has become Australia's most famous region, not solely by virtue of the quality wines it produces, but because its boundaries are defined by the chocolate-brown (*terra rossa*) soils that sit on a limestone bedrock.

The emphasis of wine producing has shifted from the winemaker to the vineyard itself, in terms of density of vines, trellising systems and canopy management, and irrigation. In Australia, traditional density of between 1,500 and 3,000 vines per $2^{1}/_{2}$ acres (1 ha), to allow for mechanization, is considerably lower than the norm (between 4,000 and 8,000) in Europe. However, attention to yield and achieving a better balance between fruit and foliage has meant that many of the newer vineyards in cooler areas have been established with greater vine densities and more complex trellising systems. There has also been a move toward sustainable viticulture, which utilizes environmentally friendly ways of dealing with pests and diseases.

GRAPE VARIETIES ON DEMAND

Historically, premium grape varieties were brought in by pioneering growers in the first half of the last century. As tastes and commercial demands changed, the industry veered away from table wines toward sweeter, fortified wines. The kind of grape varieties best suited to Australia's so-called TAWNY ruby and vintage ports, are principally the Rhône grapes Shiraz, Grenache, and Mourvèdre (called Mataro in Australia). Shiraz was considered Australia's finest red grape for a long time, but as the more fashionable premium varieties, notably Cabernet Sauvignon, came into the frame, Shiraz became a "poor relation," along with its Rhône counterparts. Fortunately, visionary winemakers such as Max Schubert—and more recently small wineries such as Rockford and St. Hallett in the Barossa Valley—have kept the faith and tirelessly promoted Shiraz as Australia's best red variety.

SHIRAZ, CABERNET SAUVIGNON, AND MERLOT

Today, Shiraz is once again Australia's supreme red grape variety, its "trump card," which aligns it with the pedigree of France's great classic regions, yet differentiates its top premium reds from those of all other countries. With nearly 91,425 acres (37,000 ha), it is also Australia's most widely planted premium red variety. Stylistically, it changes considerably from region to region. So while its reputation is founded on the Barossa, where it produces richly concentrated, full-bodied reds, it becomes a more elegant creature in Victoria with wines of subtle fruitiness combined with mint, ginger, and spicy undertones. The Hunter Valley still produces traditional Shiraz, while Western Australia has examples that align themselves with the northern Rhône style.

Cabernet Sauvignon is a modern variety that barely existed in the 1950s. As a late-ripening, thick-skinned variety, it suited Australia's warm climate well, surging to prominence at the expense of Shiraz and staying there until the mid-1980s. Today there are nearly 72,900 acres (29,500 ha) of Cabernet Sauvignon, which is particularly suited for the soils in Coonawarra. Often blended with Shiraz, it is also mixed in perhaps the more classical style with the other Bordeaux varieties Merlot and Cabernet Franc. Thanks to its fashionable status in California, Merlot quickly became the most frequently planted premium grape in

High-quality varieties are not exactly a novelty in Australia. This Shiraz vine stock is a century old.

Down under, Shiraz turns out some very individual red wines that arouse much interest internationally.

Australia, and now covers 24,700 acres (10,000 ha). Mainly used in blends with Cabernet Sauvignon its future as an independent variety is already in view. Cabernet Franc only accounts for ten percent and is mostly used in Bordeaux blends.

GRENACHE, MOURVÈDRE, PINOT NOIR

Clinging to the coat-tails of Shiraz, Grenache and Mourvèdre have undergone a revival of sorts, particularly in areas of South Australia where old vines, typically bush-pruned in vineyards that have not been irrigated, are capable of producing concentrated, distinctive fruit. Although much Grenache and Mourvèdre was removed in the Vine Pull Scheme of the 1970s, fresh demand for these Mediterranean varieties has resulted in a modest increase in plantings, so that now they amount to some 9,266 acres (3,750 ha) in total. They do particularly well in the Barossa Valley and McLaren Vale and, as you might expect, blend well with Shiraz.

Pinot Noir, the grape of red Burgundy, is still the pimply adolescent of the Australian wine scene. Its recent successes, more than any other variety, reflect not only considerable dedication on the winemaker's part, but also a general move toward cool-climate viticulture. Tyrrells pioneered Pinot Noir in the warm Hunter Valley, but because it is acknowledged to grow best in a marginal climate, producers have actively sought out cooler areas like the Yarra Valley and other southern regions of Victoria, Adelaide Hills, Tasmania, and the cooler areas of Western Australia. As a result Pinot Noir, which covers more than 10,870 acres (4,400 ha), quickly yielded a wine of structure and complexity, pleasing to the senses.

CHARDONNAY & CO.

You might not guess it, but Australia is in fact more of a white- than a red-wine country. If this comes as a surprise, it is because much of Australia's white-wine production comes from bulk white varieties such as Sultana, Doradillo, Muscat Blanc, Palomino, and Trebbiano. Between bulk and premium, there is a significant amount of Chenin Blanc and Colombard, while Muscat Gordo Blanco is the variety that puts the flavor into cask wine. The four top premium varieties—Chardonnay, Semillon, Sauvignon Blanc, and Riesling—account for just over a quarter of Australian wine production, but their value to the industry and the consumer is much more important.

If Australia is the success story of the final two decades of the last millennium, Chardonnay takes the starring role in that story. It is far and away the most widely planted premium white variety, with in excess of 53,620 acres

Only nets are any use in keeping birds off, but of course they have to be removed before harvesting. They are then rolled up into large balls for re-use the following year, as here on the Margaret River.

(21,700 ha). When it first arrived on the scene in the mid to late 1980s, Chardonnay offered excitingly new, tropical fruit flavors along with the tremendously appealing taste of oak. Many of these early Chardonnays were one-glass wonders, which palled after the second or third glass. Australian winemakers responded rapidly by increasing the range of styles, and adding greater elegance and structure by taking grapes from cooler areas, using more sophisticated fermentation techniques and less heavy-handed oak treatment. More than any other grape, Chardonnay is the making of the modern Australian wine industry, because it has given the consumer exactly what he and she wants at an affordable price. Its versatility in the vineyard and cellar allows it to be grown in a style that not only reflects the climate but can also be molded to the particular style of the winemaker. It can be made as an affordable mass-market variety, such as Lindemans' hugely successful Bin 65, or, often using barrel-fermentation, turned into something more elegant, concentrated, and complex, such as Leeuwin Estate's world-class Art Series.

RIESLING AND SEMILLON

By adding a new string to its bow, Chardonnay has done for Australian white wine what Cabernet Sauvignon has done for its reds. Yet there are existing varieties, which, although less popular than Chardonnay, have nevertheless given Australian white wine an extra dimension. Thanks to its introduction by the Silesian settlers in the 19th century, Riesling has come into its own in the South Australian regions of Clare Valley, Eden Valley, and, of course, the Barossa Valley, along with parts of

Victoria and the lower part of Great Southern Region of Western Australia. Riesling produces full-flavored, lime-zesty, full-bodied dry wines of distinction and character, as well as some of Australia's best botrytized sweet wines.

The Semillon grape is another variety that produces wines of unique character in Australia, particularly in the Barossa Valley and parts of Margaret River, but most famously in the traditional region of the Hunter Valley, where, as an unoaked white, it develops haunting flavors of buttered toast and grilled nuts. It is often barrel-fermented in the Barossa Valley and also in Western Australia, where it is sometimes blended with Sauvignon Blanc in the Graves style. Sauvignon itself, rather like Pinot Noir, first began to gain recognition after being planted in cooler areas such as the Adelaide Hills, Frankland River, and Tasmania.

GRAPE VARIETIES AS BRAND NAMES

It is strange to think that a generation ago it was considered forthright to label an Australian wine by its grape variety. Varietal labeling began in California, but has become synonymous with wines from the New World. In Australia it is the key to a wine style and, once linked to the name of the producer and the region, becomes an integral part of the brand. As already mentioned, this is partly because Australia does not hold to the concept of *terroir* in the way that the French do. The Australian tradition is much more geared to blends of wine across district and regional boundaries.

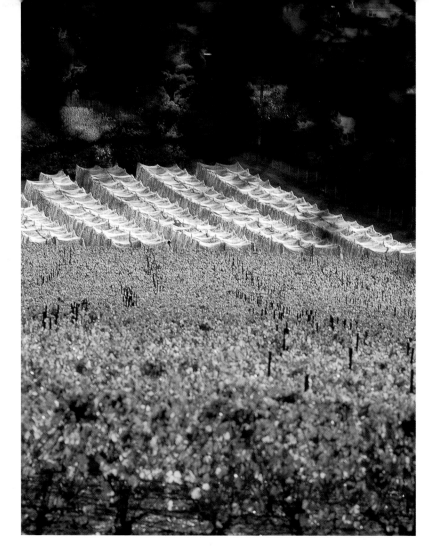

Nets are particularly essential for varieties that need longer ripening, as here in Tasmania.

AUSTRALIAN WINEMAKING

Rotation tanks and computer/temperature-controlled fermentation tanks at Haselgrove in McLaren Vale, where—as everywhere in Australia—the latest technology is the norm.

Cheap aging technique: oak shavings instead of a barrel.

The remarkable progress of Australian wine on the world stage has as much to do with the expertise of winemakers trained to deal with the continent's specific growing conditions as with the huge investment in winemaking equipment. In the well-equipped Australian winery, efficient overall quality control is the key, using up-to-date, hygienic equipment, in particular stainless steel for crushers, tanks, and presses, and caustic soda and citric acid solutions to keep equipment spotless. Cellars are also equipped with a laboratory for the analysis of sulfur, pH, acidity, sugar, and alcohol levels.

One of the keys to wine quality has been greater control over the maturity and soundness of the fruit as it arrives at the winery. Hence the importance of the liaison between winemaker and viticulturalist. With a tendency to pick on flavor rather than just sugar levels, the composition and soundness of the grapes is of vital importance, since this dictates the quality of the resulting wines. The yield, degree of TANNINS, and ripeness of the grapes at harvest depend on the style of wine to be made.

Above all, stylistic improvements have come about thanks to a gradual, systematic change in planting policy, from workhorse, wine-cask varieties such as Muscat Gordo Blanco, Sultana, and the unusually named Doradillo, to premium white grape varieties. This is especially the case in cooler parts of Australia, where the spread of Chardonnay, Sauvignon Blanc, Rhine Riesling,

and Semillon has resulted in more elegant wines. The same goes for red grapes, in particular the increase in plantings of Shiraz, Cabernet Sauvignon, Merlot, and Pinot Noir, at the expense of Grenache and Mourvèdre.

NO AIR FOR WHITE WINE

From the moment the grapes are harvested, the general modern approach is to employ reductive rather than oxidative winemaking. Reductive enology is centered on preventing air from oxidizing the MUST and wine by carrying out operations under inert gas, in clean conditions, and with effective temperature control. Keeping the grapes cool, preferably in the range of 45–60°F (8–16°C), is often best achieved by harvesting at night or the coolest part of the day. Another major factor in the process is the use of cooling during winemaking operations to conserve AROMA and flavor.

At harvest it used to be considered wise to add sulfur to prevent OXIDATION, although winemakers are increasingly conscious of reducing the levels of chemicals. The general aim is to limit sulfur dioxide levels to 50 parts per million (ppm) and free sulfur dioxide to 20 ppm. For careful control of pH, tartaric acid is usually added at the fermentation stage, while CHAPTAL-IZATION, or enrichment of the must, is not permitted. Closely monitoring the appearance of hydrogen sulfide by adding diammonium phosphate is important, and so is reductive treatment after fermentation by using inert gas and cooling to avoid unwanted YEASTS and bacteria.

Generally speaking, white winemaking avoids skin contact and aims for better-quality, free-run juice, and cooling during settling to allow wines to be clean with minimal PHENOLIC character. The use of enzymes and selected pure yeasts for white is widespread. Fermentation temperatures are normally relatively low, in the 54–60°F (12–16°C) range. MALOLACTIC FERMENTATION—the conversion of malic to lactic acid—is normally avoided in aromatic varieties to retain the natural crispness of the grape.

Although Australian winemakers normally aim for minimum handling of the must and wine, not all Australian winemaking follows the enology formula. A small percentage of premium wines, mainly Chardonnays, are produced by so-called "dirty winemaking" techniques, in which whole bunches are pressed, followed by barrel fermentation with LEES contact and stirring. Premium red wines, although normally fermented in stainless steel, may be run off before the fruit sugars are fermented out, and left to finish fermenting in small oak casks.

RED WINE ROTATED

Red wines are normally fermented in stainless steel tanks or, in the case of Pinot Noir, open-top fermenters, using selected yeast and tannins with control of pH. There is plenty of pumping over and widespread use of vinimatics, or rotofermenters, to achieve good color extraction and temperature control. Australian winemakers normally press off the skins as soon as they achieve the required color and tannin. In some instances, however, extended MACERATION may be used after fermentation, but this is done infrequently because it extracts tannins which then need to be softened by polymerization, a process that runs counter to standard Australian practice.

Malolactic fermentation immediately after fermentation is encouraged to achieve a more stable wine during winter. Racking the wine from barrels is handled in such a way as to avoid excessive oxygen. French oak is used for premium wines, both white and red, and particularly for Pinot Noir and Cabernet Sauvignon. American oak is widely used for Shiraz and Shiraz-Cabernet blends, although there is a move toward French or part-French oak for Shiraz, too. Oak chips, which Australian winemakers refer to as "microcasks," may be used for cheaper wines during or after fermentation to give some semblance of the effect of oak-cask maturation at a fraction of the cost. Inner staves are preferred because oak chips tend to have a coarse, almost resinous character.

To clarify the wines, many large wineries use centrifuges to reduce the chance of stripping flavor immediately after fermentation. After this, they employ diatomaceous earth FILTRATION, which doesn't take too much out of the wine. Pad filtration is used prior to bottling so that all yeast and bacteria are removed, avoiding any problems of spoilage in the bottle. Whites, particularly those containing RESIDUAL SUGAR, also go through a membrane filtration.

For sparkling wines, the links between Australian companies and Champagne houses have been vital to progress. Moët et Chandon's Green Point in the Yarra Valley has a direct input from its parent house in Épernay, and Croser in Adelaide Hills draws on the experience of Bollinger. The switch to champagne grape varieties and cooler areas for sourcing the raw material has had a tremendous impact on sparkling wine quality. And instead of picking the grapes for their acidity levels, winemakers are increasingly picking for flavor. Sparkling wines used to be made almost entirely by bulk fermentation or carbonation, but the transfer and champagne methods are on the increase.

The preliminary stage of making the wine is successfully completed.

Flying winemakers

The flying winemaker is essentially an Antipodean phenomenon. The term is credited to Tony Laithwaite, founder of Direct Wines in the U.K., who hired Australian Martin Shaw to work with a team of winemakers in French cooperatives in 1987. The aim was to tailor wines to the requirements of his customers by applying Australian technology and expertise to a relatively cheap source of grapes.

The practice works because Australian-trained winemakers can adapt to almost any situation. It is also possible because once vintage has finished in the southern hemisphere, Australians and New Zealanders are free to fly to Europe, where there is a demand for well-trained winemakers. This enables them to do two vintages in a year and gives them valuable experience to take back home.

The practice started in the south of France, a vast region full of cooperatives and outdated working methods. Flying winemakers were able to bring about instant improvements in other countries, too, through hard work and the application of standard hygiene and scientific practices. In the vineyard, the role of the flying winemaker has been to influence fruit quality by concentrating on flavor and picking riper fruit of the best quality.

Flying winemakers usually work in countries where the grape source is cheap and the potential for improvement considerable. The south of France, eastern Europe especially Hungary, southern Italy, parts of Spain and Portugal, Greece, South Africa, Chile, and Argentina have all seen improvements, thanks to the wholesale importation of Australian expertise and technology.

Some of the most successful flying winemakers have gone on to establish their own wineries. Others have gone on to employ teams of winemakers in various countries, with whom they communicate by telephone, fax, and e-mail.

New South Wales: An Excess of Sun

The first vines in Australia were planted in New South Wales. With Sydney as its capital, the state has always had a captive market for wine in its discriminating residents and numerous tourists. The early industry was based in the Hunter Valley, but in the absence of a gold rush, as in Victoria, or the influx of hard-working Lutheran immigrants to South Australia, New South Wales never experienced the rate of expansion of neighboring states. Nevertheless, through the Murrumbidgee Irrigation Scheme, established in 1914, a prolific state wine industry grew up around mass-market, mainly white-wine grapes, as well as some high-quality, BOTRYTIS-affected, sweet whites made from Semillon. More recently, Cowra, Mudgee, and Orange are gaining increasing recognition as quality regions in their own right.

Diversity in the Hunter Valley

At very first glance the viticulture landscape in the Hunter Valley region is remarkable for the large number of wineries, 64 on the relatively small area of around 10,870 acres (4,400 ha).

Although the climate in New South Wales is wet, irrigation is still necessary during the hot weather. At Lindeman's Winery in the Hunter Valley, water tanks take care of this.

Hunter has one of the hottest and wettest climates in Australia, with most of the rainfall coming in the summer months. With the varied soil, the difficult climate, and the big number of fiercely competing producers, it is not surprising that the region has produced a wide range of individual styles, especially in Shiraz and

S	**Western Plains**
T	**Northern Slopes**
U	**Hunter Valley**
	Hunter
V	**Northern Rivers**
	Hastings River
W	**Central Ranges**
	Mudgee
	Orange
	Cowra
X	**Big Rivers**
	Murray Darling
	Swan Hill
	Riverina
	Pericoota
Y	**Southern New South Wales**
	Hilltops
	Canberra District
	Tumbarumba
Z	**South Coast**
	Shoalhaven
	Wine-growing areas in neighboring regions

Semillon. Shiraz often provides a warm, heavy red wine that can age very well. Hunter Semillon (the grape variety behind the early Hunter River Chablis), is responsible for a unique style that develops a buttered-toast-and-lime-marmalade character with age. The Hunter Valley is the early home of Chardonnay too, introduced in 1971 by Murray Tyrrell, whose Pinot Noir was no less pioneering but not so successful. Meanwhile, Cabernet Sauvignon was reintroduced to the Hunter at Lake's Folly in 1963, by Dr. Max Lake, another of the region's great egos.

ACTIVE NEIGHBORS

With far fewer producers, the Upper Hunter Valley has almost as many acres/hectares of vines planted as the Lower Hunter, over half given over to Chardonnay and more than a quarter to Semillon. This is the home of Rosemount, one of Australia's richer, more complex styles of Chardonnay, produced at the Roxburgh vineyard. Cowra has long been a source of quality grapes for the Hunter's wineries, and in the 1990s it increased in both size and importance, with some 1,850 acres (750 ha) of vineyards, all producing grapes processed elsewhere. By contrast, Orange is a much smaller region, less than half the size of the Hunter Valley. Yet this fast-developing cool-climate region, which is best-known for its apples and pears, already has a number of wineries producing elegant Chardonnay, Sauvignon Blanc, Cabernet Sauvignon, and Shiraz. The small area of Hastings River is significant for its warm climate, its unirrigated vineyards and the fact that the relatively obscure Chambourcin is its main red grape variety.

On the other side (the inland western slopes) of the Great Dividing Range, Mudgee is a region which, despite a history stretching back to 1858, has had comparatively little recognition until recently. This is perhaps because, like other regions such as Langhorne Creek in South

Queensland's Granite Belt

Lying to the west of the Great Dividing Range, the distinguishing features of the Granite Belt are its relatively northerly latitude (28°S), its high altitude—2,650 feet (810 m) above sea level—and its lunar landscape of massive granite outcrops and boulders. The first vines were planted in Queensland's only quality wine-producing district in 1878, and it was only after 1965 that a modern industry of sorts was developed, with the city of Brisbane a natural captive market for wine. There are some 20-odd small wineries in the Granite Belt, but just over 1,458 acres (590 ha) of vines. Queensland's best wine is made from Shiraz, which produces a strong, spicy red. The aptly named Bald Mountain is the Granite Belt's most prominent winery.

Australia, it was traditionally a supplier of grapes, in this case to the Hunter Valley's bigger companies. Nevertheless, it has more than 22 small wineries of its own, mainly producing the typical New South Wales quartet of Shiraz and Cabernet Sauvignon, Chardonnay and Semillon. Mudgee was one of the first regions to introduce a rigidly controlled *appellation* scheme.

The unromantically named Murrumbidgee Irrigation Area, or Riverina, is New South Wales' answer to the irrigated Riverland of South Australia and Sunraysia of Victoria. Centered on Griffith, its hot dry climate produces nearly two-thirds of the state's entire wine crop, mainly from high-yielding, white grape varieties, the principal of which is Semillon. Reds are generally well made and based principally on Shiraz. Some 17,790 acres (7,200 ha) of Murray River vineyards, most of which fall on the Victorian side of the border, are situated in New South Wales. The Canberra district is home to 15 small wineries, many of which were established by academics or civil servants.

Despite the extreme continental heat they often succeed in producing interesting wines on their 618 acres (250 ha). Hastings River is an outsider, and with less than 494 acres (200 ha) under cultivation it is also one of Australia's small wine-growing regions. Close to the Pacific Ocean, far north of Sydney, it has a climate of high temperatures and high rainfall, actually anything but ideal conditions for wine. The first attempts to produce wine here were in the first half of the 19th century, but it is only since 1980 that viticulture has enjoyed a renaissance, thanks to the commitment of the Cassegrain family. The French hybrid Chambourcin has been the key factor. Resistant to downy mildew, this vine produces pleasant, fruity, very dark but lightly structured reds.

Tyrrell pioneered Pinot in the Hunter Valley.

VICTORIA: GOLD RUSH AND WINE

The distinctive "witch's hat" tower at Mitchelton Winery attracts many visitors to Goulburn Valley in Central Victoria.

De Bortoli, a family business with Italian roots, has established itself in the Yarra Valley.

If New South Wales is Australia's most historic wine region and South Australia the hub of the industry, Victoria, thanks to its diversity of styles and off-the-beaten-track districts, is in many ways the most fascinating. In sheer production terms, the vast, irrigated hinterland of Sunraysia produces the lion's share of Victorian wine. But it is the hundreds of small premium wineries north and south of Melbourne, which have sprouted up in a generation, that are setting the quality pace. The trend toward cool-climate viticulture in the last decade of the 20th century put the focus back on a state which, until the arrival of phylloxera and the shift to fortified wines a century ago, was Australia's most important wine producer.

Established by the Swiss in the mid-19th century, the picturesque Yarra Valley is one of Victoria's most historic wine regions and, thanks to the success of its Pinot Noir, probably its best-known today. As evidence of the Yarra Valley's claim to historic fame, there were already some 45 separate vineyards in the Yarra Valley by the end of the last century, including Yeringberg and St. Huberts. Today, there are some 44 wineries, but because of investments in new wineries by companies such as Moët et Chandon (Domaine Chandon), and acquisitions such as Mildara Blass (Yarra Ridge and St.Huberts), B.R.L. Hardy (Hoddles Creek), and Southcorp (Coldstream Hills), the area under vine has more than doubled the 2,470-odd acres (about 1,000 ha)

since the 1990s. Its relatively cool climate has been responsible for producing some of Australia's best Pinot Noir. Chardonnay in the elegant, melon-and-tropical-citrus-fruit style also does well here.

South of Melbourne, the Mornington Peninsula is a cool region with a maritime climate, strongly influenced by northerly winds and ocean breezes blowing across the Bass Strait. The region is a kaleidoscope of small, lifestyle wineries, many started up by city professionals with money to burn. Here you will find elegant, often complex, cool-climate Chardonnay, as well as some delicate Pinot Noir from producers such as Stoniers. In contrast to Mornington, Geelong, on Corio Bay, has never really recovered from its devastation by phylloxera, although Bannockburn, Scotchman's Hill, and Prince Albert all make creditable Pinot Noir.

The high altitude of the cool Macedon Ranges has made this one of the major new areas for the planting of Pinot Noir and Chardonnay grapes, destined for sparkling wines. Given the relatively small area under vine, there is also a surprising number—around 26—of small wineries, the best-known of which are Hanging Rock and Virgin Hills, the latter producing sulfur-free wines.

As a result of the gold rush, the mining towns of Ballarat and Bendigo gave rise to a significant wine industry in the 19th century. However, as in the case of Geelong, phylloxera put paid to the golden era, and it was not until 1969 in the case of Bendigo and 1971 in Ballarat that vines reappeared. Ballarat is the cooler of the two, more suited to sparkling wine production, while Bendigo has a number of wineries, among them Jasper Hill and Balgownie, making quality Shiraz. To the east, in central Victoria, lies the Goulburn Valley, where the ultra-traditional winery Château Tahbilk has set a trend, followed by Mitchelton, for the production of an unusual white made from Marsanne. It is also a good region for Riesling, Chardonnay, and powerful Shiraz. The Central Victorian High Country, formerly the Strathbogie Ranges, is well-suited to Riesling, a specialty of Delatite, elegant Bordeaux blends at Mount Helen, and the production of sparkling wine.

SWEET WINES AND DRY REDS

While much of the development of Victoria's wine reflects the trend toward cool-climate viticulture, there are two staunchly traditional districts, namely Rutherglen and Glenrowan in northeast Victoria, which resolutely stand out against the modern search for elegance. Steeped in history, this is an area that was established on the back of the 1850s gold rush. In terms of production, table wines account for about 2,300 acres (930 ha) of plantings, as opposed to only 170 acres (70 ha) of Muscat Blanc à Petits Grains and Muscadelle. They produce the fortified Muscats and Tokays that are known as "stickies." The grapes that make these rich and rare wines are allowed to shrivel on the vine. They are fortified during the winemaking process before being aged for years in small oak barrels to produce rich, sweet wines of intense aromatic power and concentration of fruit. The older the wine, the more complex it becomes, with flavors of rose petal and raisin (Muscat) as well as toffee, malt, and tea (Tokay).

The King Valley in northeast Victoria is perhaps best known as the home of Brown Brothers, a family company that has worked tirelessly to produce good-value table wines, particularly from Chardonnay, Riesling, and Cabernet Sauvignon. Next to it is the high Ovens Valley where Giaconda has established a reputation for exceptional Pinot Noir and Chardonnay. These are the two varieties that form the backbone of Gippsland, too—a sprawling, remote region on the undulating coastal plain of Victoria, capable of producing elegant Burgundian-style red and white wines.

REDEFINING THE WEST

West of Ballarat in the Western Victoria zone is the Pyrenees. Its soft, undulating landscape is wholly unlike the spectacular European mountain range from which it takes its name. This is mainly red-wine country. Grapes ripen later in the Grampians, formerly the Great Western, which became famous in the gold rush. The sparkling wine production of Seppelt Great Western, the best-known Australian brand, was set up with French technical help in the galleries abandoned by the miners. It is still made there, but the Grampians have in the meantime developed into a table-wine region that produces relatively small quantities of red and white wines.

Mass production is concentrated in an area of 437,360 acres (177,000 ha) in Victoria's river region. Agrarian technology allows a third of Australia's entire wine output to be produced here on flat, clay and sandy soil in a dry climate. A further 5,000 acres (2,000 ha) over the state frontier in New South Wales add their bit. Sultana and the aromatic Muscat Gordo Blanco go into the mass product here, while Chardonnay yields reasonably priced whites. However, this is also the home of Lindemans' very successful Bin 65 Chardonnay.

M	North West Victoria
	Murray Darling
	Swan Hill
N	Western Victoria
	Far South West Victoria
	Grampians
	Pyrenees
	Ballarat
O	Central Victoria
	Bendigo
	Goulburn Valley
	Central Victorian High Country
P	Port Phillip
	Geelong
	Macedon
	Sunbury
	Yarra Valley
	Mornington Peninsula
Q	North East Victoria
	Rutherglen
	Glenrowan
	King Valley
	Ovens Valley
R	Gippsland
	Gippsland
	Wine-growing areas in neighboring regions

NEW SOUTH WALES

BOTOBOLAR**
MUDGEE, MUDGEE
78,000 bottles • Wines include: Low Preservative Chardonnay, Marsanne, Preservative Free Dry Red, Shiraz, Cabernet, → The King
One of the few organic wineries in Australia, this was also one of the first, established by Gil Wahlquist in 1971. It has now been taken over by Kevin Karsyrom, who is continuing where Wahlquist left off, bringing organic practices to the winery with preservative-free wines.

BROKENWOOD***−****
POKOLBIN, LOWER HUNTER VALLEY
720,000 bottles • Wines include: → Cricket Pitch Unwooded Chardonnay, Sauvignon Blanc Semillon, → Graveyard Chardonnay; Shiraz, → Graveyard Shiraz
Established in 1970 with wine writer James Halliday as one of the leading lights, Brokenwood is now producing, under winemakers Iain Riggs and Dan Dineen, well-crafted, sought-after Semillon and Shiraz.

LINDEMANS**−****
KARADOC, COONAWARRA, PADTHAWAY, HUNTER VALLEY
Bought-in grapes; 40,000,000 bottles • Wines include: Coonawarra reds, notably Limestone Ridge, → St.George (Cabernet); varietals from Padthaway, from the historic Ben Ean winery in the Hunter Valley, Leo Buring brand, and various bin number varietals at the giant Karadoc facility
Part of the giant Southcorp group, in addition to the above Lindemans produces the fruit-driven, consistent, and inexpensive → Bin 65 Chardonnay, the biggest-selling Chardonnay brand in the world, blended by chief winemaker Philip John.

McWILLIAMS**−****
HANWOOD, RIVERINA
2,051 acres (830 ha); bought-in grapes; 2,000,000 bottles • Wines include: varietal wines from Riverina; Chardonnay, Shiraz, and Cabernet from Barwang at Hilltops, N.S.W., → Lovedale Semillon, → Eden Valley Riesling, and diverse fortified wines
Under winemakers Jim Brayne and Phillip Ryan, McWilliams' reputation for its fine Hunter Valley Semillon and fortified wines continues to grow, while table wines range from decent basic varietals to finer table wines.

ROSEMOUNT ESTATE**−***
DENMAN, UPPER HUNTER VALLEY
6,177 acres (2,500 ha); bought-in grapes; 36,000,000 bottles • Wines: a large range of varietal wines, including premium brands → Orange Chardonnay, → Roxburgh Chardonnay and wines from other regions
One of Australia's pioneering export companies, the rapidly expanding Rosemount, now under the umbrella of Southcorp, makes juicy, easy-drinking wines at the commercial end, appealing McLaren Vale Shiraz, and fine Chardonnay at the top end of the range.

ROTHBURY**−***
POKOLBIN, LOWER HUNTER VALLEY
455 acres (184 ha); bought-in grapes; 3,000,000 bottles • Wines: → Brokenback Shiraz, Cowra Chardonnay, → Rothbury Estate Chardonnay, Semillon, and Shiraz
Founded by Len "Mr. Wine Australia" Evans and taken over by the Beringer Blass group in 1996, Rothbury is producing pleasantly commercial wines from vineyards and contract growers in the Hunter Valley, Mudgee, and Cowra, following a major A \$2 million investment.

TYRRELL'S**−****
POKOLBIN, LOWER HUNTER VALLEY
803 acres (325 ha); bought-in grapes; 9,600,000 bottles • Wines include: varietal reds and whites; single vineyard wines including → Shee-Oak Chardonnay, → Lost Block Semillon, → Brokenback Shiraz, Vat 47 Chardonnay, → Vat 6 Pinot Noir
Murray Tirrell is celebrated for introducing Chardonnay and Pinot Noir to the Australian wine industry. His Long Flat label was sold to Cheviot Bridge; now this traditional family business concentrates on higher quality production. Vat 1 Hunter Semillon has joined the top wines; it can age for years.

VICTORIA

BAILEY'S OF GLENROWAN***
GLENROWAN
343 acres (139 ha); bought-in grapes • Wines include: Tokay, Muscat; Shiraz, Cabernet, Merlot, Touriga; 1904 Block Shiraz, → 1920s Block Shiraz; → Founder Muscat and Tokay
Bailey's continues to make well-structured reds with dark aromas, while the fortified "stickies" are of world class.

BANNOCKBURN VINEYARDS***−****
BANNOCKBURN, GEELONG
Bought-in grapes; 84,000 bottles • Wines: Riesling, Sauvignon Blanc, Chardonnay, Pinot, Noir, Shiraz
The pick of Geelong's small band of wineries, Bannockburn, under Gary Farr, has consistently produced high-quality whites from low-yielding vineyards. The rich, complex Pinot Noir benefits from Farr's experience of winemaking at Domaine Dujac in Burgundy with Jacques Seysses.

BEST'S****
GREAT WESTERN, THE GRAMPIANS
163 acres (66 ha); bought-in grapes; 360,000 bottles • Wines include: Chardonnay, Riesling, Pinot, Shiraz, Cabernet, and fortified wines
Best's is a more traditional winery of the Grampians region, producing wines from varieties which include Ondenc and golden Chasselas, and the northwest Italian red variety Dolcetto. Shiraz is probably its best wine.

BROWN BROTHERS**−***
MILAWA, KING VALLEY, NORTHEAST VICTORIA
1,502 acres (608 ha); bought-in grapes; 10,000,000 bottles • Wines include: Chardonnay, Riesling, Sauvignon, → Orange Muscat & Flora; Tarrango, Barbera, Tempranillo, Sangiovese, Shiraz, Cabernet, Graciano, and sparkling, fortified wines
The fifth generation of this family business are varietal specialists who experiment tirelessly, making good use of their "kindergarten winery," which is dedicated to research and development. But their broad range can be unreliable.

CAMPBELLS***
RUTHERGLEN, RUTHERGLEN
Bought-in grapes; 420,000 bottles • Wines include: Riesling, Semillon, → Bobbie Burn Chardonnay, Malbec, Cabernet, Muscat, and Tokay
Impressive, full table wines, notably the ginger and oak notes of Bobbie Burn's Shiraz. The real specialty is the range of aged, fortified Muscats and Tokays.

COLDSTREAM HILLS***−*****
COLDSTREAM, YARRA VALLEY
116 acres (47 ha); bought-in grapes; 420,000 bottles • Wines: Semillon, Sauvignon, Chardonnay, Pinot, Merlot, Cabernet

James Halliday founded this winery in 1985. It is particularly respected for its Chardonnays and Pinot Noir wines, especially the Reserve. Since it was taken over by Southcorp in 1996 production has been increased, but with Andrew Fleming as winemaker and Halliday's name unchanged at the top high standards are still being set.

DALWHINNIE****–*****
MOONAMBEL, PYRENEES
64 acres (26 ha); 54,000 bottles • Wines: Chardonnay and Pinot, Moonambel Shiraz, and Cabernet, Eagle Series
Situated in the Pyrenees, Dalwhinnie, owned by David and Jenny Jones, is making some of the greatest Chardonnay, Cabernet, and Shiraz to come out of Australia.

DE BORTOLI**–****
DIXON'S CREEK, YARRA VALLEY AND RIVERINA
Bought-in grapes; 3,500,000 bottles • Wines: varietal wines, Deen de Bortoli, → Noble Semillon in Riverina, Semillon, Chardonnay, Pinot, Shiraz, Cabernet, Cabernet-Merlot
Traditional family winery producing bread-and-butter varietals in quantity but a good, sweet white in Noble One, and in the Yarra Valley high-quality Pinot Noir.

DOMAINE CHANDON****
YARRA VALLEY
198 acres (80 ha); bought-in grapes; 1,500,000 bottles • Wines include: Marke Green Point, Chardonnay, Sauvignon-Semillon; Pinot Noir, Shiraz; sparkling wines under Green Point and Chandon labels
Founded in 1989 by Moët et Chandon, Green Point has acquired a reputation for its high-quality sparkling wines under the direction of Dr. Tony Jordan. It is also developing a range of equally high-quality still wines. Jordan has also been entrusted with the direction of Cape Mentelle, Cloudy Bay, and Mountadam by Veuve Clicquot.

MITCHELTON WINES***
NAGAMBIE, GOULBURN VALLEY
Bought-in grapes; 1,500,000 bottles • Wines include: brands: Thomas Mitchell; Mitchelton Airstrip with Marsanne, Roussanne, Viognier; Mitchelton Crescent with Shiraz, Mourvèdre, Grenache, → Mitchelton Print Shiraz
Under experienced winemaker Don Lewis, Mitchelton, the winery with the distinctive witch's hat tower, produces tasty wines typical of Central Victoria at reasonable prices.

MORRIS****
RUTHERGLEN, RUTHERGLEN
Bought-in grapes • Wines include: Shiraz, Durif, → Mick Morris Old Tawny Port, → Old Premium Liqueur Tokay and Muscat
Established in 1859, this northeast Victorian fortified wine producer carries on the family tradition of making "stickies" of high quality and style.

MOUNT LANGHI GHIRAN VINEYARDS***–*****
BUANGOR, THE GRAMPIANS
185 acres (75 ha); bought-in grapes; 1,200,000 bottles • Wines: Riesling, Chardonnay, Pinot Grigio, Shiraz, Cabernet, Merlot, → Billi Bill Creek Shiraz Cabernet
Trevor Mast makes distinctive, intense, cool-climate Shiraz with a twist of the pepper mill and plenty of spice, as a result of which Mount Langhi Ghiran Shiraz is in the top flight of Australian reds today.

MOUNT MARY****–*****
LILYDALE, YARRA VALLEY
• Wines: Chardonnay, Triolet (Sauvignon, Semillon, Muscadelle); Pinot, Cabernet, Quintet
Media-shy John Middleton has created a reputation for exclusive, high-quality reds made from Pinot Noir and

Cabernet, with Quintet in particular the only non-Shiraz blend to achieve "outstanding" status in Langton's classification of Australian wines.

SEPPELT**–****
GREAT WESTERN, THE GRAMPIANS
Bought-in grapes; 7,500,000 bottles • Wines: a wide range of varietal and sparkling wines, → Dorrien Cabernet, → Show Reserve Sparkling Shiraz, → Salinger
Owned by Southcorp, Seppelt is best-known for the sparkling wines it produces and ages in its historic subterranean cellars. It also produces excellent fortified wines from the Barossa Valley.

STONIER***–****
MORNINGTON PENINSULA
Bought-in grapes; 150,000 bottles • Wines: → Pinot Noir, → Chardonnay, and a Reserve range
Lying within sound of the surf beaches of the Bass Strait Stonier is a star of the cool climate of the Mornington Peninsula south of Melbourne. In its 20-year history the estate has earned an international reputation for exemplary Chardonnays and Pinot Noirs.

TAHBILK WINERY***–****
NAGAMBIE LAKES
452 acres (183 ha); 1,400,000 bottles • Wines: → Marsanne, Riesling, Chardonnay, Viognier, Shiraz, Cabernet Sauvignon
Founded in 1860 and still owned by the Prubrick family, Tahbilk produces a striking Marsanne and traditional reds, including small quantities from vines planted in 1860 and known to be the oldest Shiraz vines in the world

TARRAWARRA ESTATE***–****
YARRA GLEN, YARRA VALLEY
180 acres (73 ha); 180,000 bottles • Wines: Chardonnay; Pinot Noir, Shiraz, Merlot
Under winemaker Clare Halloran, this small winery makes easy-drinking styles under the Tunnel Hill label, which allows it to pursue a policy of making long-lived, complex, structured Chardonnay and Pinot Noir under the main winery label.

YARRA BURN***
YARRA JUNCTION, YARRA VALLEY
Wines include: Chardonnay, Sauvignon-Semillon, Cabernet Sauvignon, Shiraz, → Pinot Noir
This small winery also belongs to the big Hardy's Group. Under Steve Flamsteed it makes elegant Chardonnays and Pinot Noirs, mainly from two vineyards in Hoddles Creek and Bastard Hill.

YARRA RIDGE***
YARRA GLEN, YARRA VALLEY
304 acres (123 ha); 1,080,000 bottles • Wines: Semillon, Sauvignon, Chardonnay; Merlot, Shiraz, Pinot Noir, → Yarra Ridge Reserve Pinot Noir
Winemakers Nick Walker, Fiona Purnell, and Daniel Bettio are making increasingly good Burgundy-style whites and reds following the winery's purchase by Beringer Blass.

YARRA YERING****–*****
COLDSTREAM, YARRA VALLEY
49 acres (20 ha); 65,000 bottles • Wines: Dry White No. 1 (Sauvignon/Semillon), Chardonnay, Pinot Noir, Dry Red No. 1, Dry Red No. 2, Merlot, → Underhill Shiraz
Dr. Bailey Carrodus is one of the great eccentrics of the Australian wine industry, making intensely flavored, complex and much sought-after wines from low-yielding vineyards in wooden fermenting vats.

SOUTH AUSTRALIA: MASS PRODUCT AND RARITIES

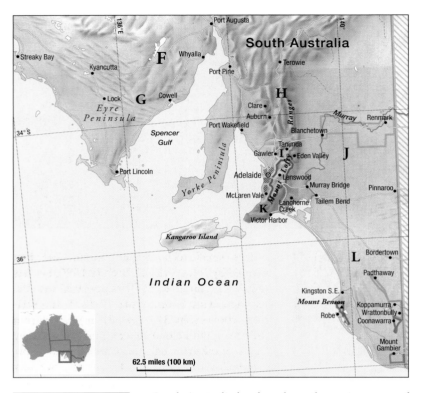

South Australia

Indian Ocean

62.5 miles (100 km)

F	**Far North**
G	**The Peninsulas**
	Port Lincoln
H	**Mount Lofty Ranges and Adelaide**
	Clare Valley
	Adelaide Plains
	Adelaide Hills
I	**Barossa**
	Barossa Valley
	Eden Valley
J	**Lower Murray**
	Riverland
K	**Fleurieu**
	McLaren Valley
	Langhorne Creek
L	**Limestone Coast**
	Padthaway
	Wrattonbully
	Coonawarra
	Mount Benson
	Robe
	Mount Gambier
	Wine-growing areas in neighboring regions

South Australia has long been the engine room of Australian wine production, thanks to the large volumes of wine made in the irrigated Murray Valley, which accounts for nearly 30 percent of Australia's total grape production. But the Barossa Valley was originally the heart and soul of South Australia's quality wine industry, largely due to the English who settled there in the first half of the 19th century and German immigrants who brought their wine culture with them. In the latter half of the 19th century, the wineries of Clare Valley, McLaren Vale, and Coonawarra were developed; Padthaway was not established until the 1960s. In addition to the Barossa Valley's revival, from the late 1980s new areas such as Adelaide Hills have come on line, together with the expansion of Langhorne Creek and the development of the Limestone Coast zone either side of Coonawarra and Padthaway.

The rolling green hills and transverse valleys, neat stone buildings, and Lutheran spires of the Barossa Valley make it one of Australia's prettiest wine regions. Its winery composition is varied and interesting, with large and small companies co-existing, for the most part, in peaceful harmony. Alongside industry giants such as Penfolds, Orlando, Beringer Blass, and Seppelt, sit a large number of smaller wineries which, with Peter Lehmann at the helm, have

contributed to the Barossa's reputation through a combination of commitment to quality, courage in the face of adversity, and imaginative marketing. Notable among these are St. Hallett, Rockford, Charles Melton, and Grant Burge.

The Barossa's warm climate makes it ideally suited to rich, chocolatey Shiraz, the base for Grange and the most widely planted grape in the district. Full-bodied styles of Riesling and Semillon, which both outnumber plantings of Cabernet Sauvignon, also do well here. In line with the trend toward cool-climate wines, Riesling, largely thanks to Yalumba, with Pewsey Vale and Heggies, is moving away from the warm valley floor to the cooler, hillier slopes of the East Barossa Ranges. The Barossa's revival has come about with the help of clever exploitation of the Valley's heritage of old, gnarled Shiraz BUSH VINES and, to a lesser extent, the old Grenache and Mourvèdre used to produce fortified wines prior to the table-wine boom. To the southeast of Barossa, the high country of Eden Valley is most famous for its elegant styles of Riesling, as well as Henschke's Hill of Grace and Mount Edelstone vineyards.

AN EL DORADO FOR SMALL WINERIES

North of Adelaide, the Clare Valley is one of South Australia's oldest and most traditional regions. Unlike Barossa, this beautiful region, with its stone-clad buildings, is covered with small wineries, many of which—notably Jim Barry, Tim Adams, Jeffrey Grosset, Petaluma, and Tim Knappstein—have gained a reputation for the quality of their perfumed, steely Rieslings, which develop a toastiness with age. Riesling is the dominant grape here, although Cabernet Sauvignon and Shiraz also perform well. A short drive east of Adelaide brings you to the high, wooded Adelaide Hills, a spectacular, cool-climate region which, in areas like Piccadilly and Lenswood, is rapidly gaining a reputation for elegant styles of Chardonnay and Sauvignon Blanc, as well as quality Pinot Noir. Just south of here, Kuitpo is a new sub-region, being developed by, among others, Rosemount Estate.

Until recently, McLaren Vale was one of the less well-known traditional regions of South Australia. To the south of Adelaide, it is an area of rolling hills and interesting small wineries, often called "the spiritual home of the small winery." Among the most notable wineries in this region are Wirra Wirra, Chapel Hill, d'Arenberg, Geoff Merrill, Clarendon Hills, Tatachilla, and Coriole. With its Mediterranean climate, it produces rich, smooth reds, with Shiraz and Cabernet Sauvignon the dominant red varieties, and Chardonnay far and away the major white grape. Still little known, Langhorne Creek is dominated by Cabernet Sauvignon and Shiraz, which supply much of the content of Orlando Jacob's Creek red.

Riverland comprises a series of sub-regions with a hot continental climate along the banks of the Murray River. It was originally developed by George and William Chaffey, who chose Renmark on the west bank of the Murray River as the site for their pioneering irrigation schemes. Not surprisingly, given its warm climate, there are significant plantings of Shiraz, Grenache, and Mourvèdre, used until recently for fortified and cask wines. There are also substantial plantings of Chardonnay, although the biggest category of grape here is generally described as "other," a term that covers the multitude of fruity Gordo, Doradillo, and Sultana varieties that go into the ubiquitous Australian wine cask.

RED EARTH AND RUBBER TREES

Almost certainly one of Australia's most haunting and mystical wine regions is Coonawarra. The reasons are simple. First, Coonawarra is Australia's first region to have its own *terroir*, in particular its famous chocolate-brown *terra rossa* soil, which sits on a bed of soft limestone. Second, the topography itself, the flat land surrounded by gum trees, is quite magical in a strangely peaceful way. And thirdly, Coonawarra has become synonymous with top-quality Cabernet Sauvignon and, perhaps to a lesser extent, Shiraz. Although overshadowed by reds, Chardonnay and Riesling also produce consistently good wines here on Coonawarra's black soils.

Top
Rosemount Estate proudly displays its award of Winemaker of the Year.

Above
The history of the wine giant Penfolds began near Adelaide in 1844. Its modern head office is now in Nuriootpa in the Barossa Valley.

Some of the best Shiraz wines in Australia grow in the Barossa Valley.

This small, cigar-shaped region was first planted by John Riddoch back in 1890, but has only really started to fulfill its potential with the red table-wine boom of the 1960s. It is a relatively cool region, 37 miles (60 km) inland from the ocean, with cloud cover contributing to the length of the growing season. Dominated by big companies such as Wynns, Lindemans, Beringer Blass, and Penfolds, there are nevertheless a significant number of smaller wineries in this region, among them Hollick and Bowen Estate, which produce wines of substance and quality. From Coonawarra, on the road to Adelaide, Padthaway is a giant expanse of vineyard almost entirely planted with premium grape varieties by the big companies: Seppelt, Lindemans, Hardys, and Wynns. Chardonnay is the most notable, but Padthaway Shiraz can be surprisingly good, even great. Along the Limestone Coast, a number of new grape-growing regions are emerging; among the best are Robe, Mount Benson, and Wrattonbully.

Western Australia: A Dream Country for Elegant Wines

While Western Australia is the country's biggest state, its wine regions are tucked away in the remote southwestern corner. Partly for that reason, and partly because there is no region like Riverland to drive volumes, the wine industry is on a smaller scale here than in Australia's three main wine-producing states—New South Wales, Victoria, and South Australia. Nevertheless, mirroring the trend towards the cool-climate viticulture of the other states—Victoria, in particular—Western Australia has become synonymous with premium-quality wines made in styles that are markedly different from their counterparts in the east of the country. In the Margaret River region, Cabernet Sauvignon produces one of the more European styles, and, around Mount Barker, Shiraz can have the elegant spicy and peppery quality of Syrah from the northern Rhône. Riesling, too, develops delicate flavors not encountered in many other parts of Australia.

Far Away in the Heat

The foundations of the Western Australian wine industry were laid in the first half of the 19th century, when both Thomas Waters and John Septimus Roe planted vineyards in the hot Swan Valley. It was, for a long time, the focus of Western Australian production. Subsequently, it was Yugoslav immigrants who turned the region into a significant wine-producing area. In the early days of the modern era, Swan Valley became known for Houghton's White Burgundy. Released in 1937 and made by the legendary Jack Mann, it was a wine of considerable rich-

Left
Morning mist is a common phenomenon in the Margaret River wine region.

Right
The direct vicinity of the Indian Ocean is the key factor tempering the climate of Margaret River.

Below
Nature looks its colorful best in the Margaret River region.

ness, thanks to the Swan Valley's hot climate—the hottest in Australia—and the fact that just about anything but Chardonnay (mainly Semillon with Muscadelle and Chenin Blanc) went into the blend. A short drive from Perth, there are a handful of wineries in the criss-cross valleys of the Perth Hills and spread out along the coast south of Perth. Geographe is a newly created region, with Bunbury at its center, which encompasses the coastal area around the Capel River, the Donnybrook area, and the Bunbury Hills. Chardonnay and Shiraz are the principal varieties here.

Margaret River

A stone's throw from the Indian Ocean, and 150 miles (240 km) south of Perth, Margaret River is a beautiful region of creeks and valleys, native trees, and wild flowers. It is characterized by surfing beaches, motels and restaurants, hardwood and pottery craft shops, and wineries, of which there are more than fifty. In its early inception, it was pioneered by doctors-turned-winemakers, but more recently it has been taken over by big companies. Southcorp Wines took over Devil's Lair and Brookland Valley, part of which now belongs to Thomas Hardy and so to Constellation Wines. The region is particularly good for Cabernet Sauvignon and Bordeaux blends, with Merlot producing ripe but elegant reds in the blackcurrant and redcurrant spectrum of fruit. Bordeaux blends apply to whites too, producing Sauvignon Blanc with Semillon in some highly successful wines; Chardonnay is also made into consistently excellent whites.

Leeuwin Estate has been credited with producing Australia's finest and perhaps longest-lived Chardonnay.

Also influenced by a maritime climate, the rambling Great Southern Region, with its spectacular jarrah, marri, and karri gum forests, is, for the most part, cooler than Margaret River, with a more continental climate inland. Its development is relatively recent, only beginning a decade or so after the Californian viticulturalist Harold Olmo reported its potential for good-quality wine to the Western Australian government in 1955. Riesling is as successful in Frankland River as in the Clare and Eden Valleys of South Australia, aging well with citrus undertones. Good Chardonnay is produced in the region, along with elegant styles of Cabernet Sauvignon and Shiraz. There appears to be considerable potential, too, for Pinot Noir in the cool-climate vineyards around Mount Barker and Albany. Climatically, Manjimup and Pemberton are respectively the Bordeaux and Burgundy of the region, with Chardonnay, Cabernet Sauvignon, and Pinot Noir the predominant varieties.

Left
The Voyager estate has some stunningly unusual architecture and full, spicy white wines.

Right
Vanya Cullen turns out high-class, stylish but individual wines on the family estate.

Select Producers in Western Australia

Alkoomi Wines***—****
Frankland River
198 acres (80 ha); bought-in grapes; 1,000,000 bottles
• Wines include: Riesling, Chardonnay, →Sauvignon, Shiraz, Cabernet Sauvignon, Blackbutt, →Jarrah Shiraz, Wandoo; Southlands range
Alkoomi, established by Merv and Judy Lange, is a family-run business that always produces fine wines. Apart from a small amount used in the Southlands range all the grapes are home-grown.

Cape Mentelle***—*****
Margaret River, Margaret River
321 acres (130 ha); bought-in grapes; 1,300,000 bottles
• Wines: Semillon Sauvignon, Chardonnay, Cabernet Merlot, Shiraz, →Zinfandel
Cape Mentelle, now owned by Veuve Clicquot, has developed into one of Western Australia's best quality wineries since it was set up under David Hohnen in 1970. Its winemaker John Durham is producing excellent whites and outstanding Cabernets and Shiraz wines, as well as Australia's best Zinfandel.

Capel Vale**—***
Capel, Geographe
395 acres (160 ha); bought-in grapes; 1,800,000 bottles
• Wines include: Chenin, Chardonnay, Verdelho; Merlot, Cabernet Sauvignon, Shiraz, Pinot Noir, Tawny, sparkling
This family-run winery owned by Dr. Peter and Elizabeth Pratten offers three series of wines: the CV range for day-to-day drinking, a white-labelled range for celebration meals, and a limited Reserve range of wines from individual plots, sold with a black label.

Cullen's*****
Cowaramup, Margaret River
79 acres (32 ha); 150,000 bottles • Wines: Chardonnay, Sauvignon, Semillon, →Cabernet Merlot, Pinot Noir
Established in 1971, Cullen was one of the pioneers of the Margaret River region. Now run by Vanya Cullen, Cullen's wines are made in an individual, full-flavored and intense style. Excellent blends.

Devil's Lair**—****
Forest Grove, Margaret River
110 acres (45 ha); bought-in grapes; 300,000 bottles
• Wines: Chardonnay, Pinot Noir, Cabernet Merlot; second label Fifth Leg
Bought by the giant Southcorp group in 1996, Devil's Lair continues to carve out a reputation for high-quality Chardonnay, in addition to good Burgundy and Bordeaux-style reds. A winery to watch.

Evans & Tate***
Margaret River
Bought-in grapes; 1,200,000 bottles • Wines: Semillon, Sauvignon, Chardonnay; Merlot, Shiraz, Cabernet, Gnangara Shiraz Cabernet, Barrique 61 Cabernet Merlot
Having moved its quality varietal wine operations to the Margaret River from Swan Valley, this winery continues to make easy-going whites and reds, although it does not scale the heights of the best that Margaret River can do.

Ferngrove Vineyards Estate**—***
Frankland River
704 acres (285 ha) • Wines include: Premium Orchid range with →Cossack Riesling; Chardonnay, Semillon-Sauvignon; Malbec, Cabernet-Merlot, Shiraz
Ferngrove's prize-winning wines are made from its own grapes, which ripen in a cool climate. The winery is run for the tourist market and affords magnificent views of the Stirnling Range.

HOUGHTON

Art Series
LEEUWIN ESTATE
2001
MARGARET RIVER
RIESLING
13.0% vol PRODUCE OF AUSTRALIA 750mL

Houghton**—****
Middle Swan, Perth
593 acres (240 ha); bought-in grapes; 3,600,000 bottles
• Wines: a broad range of varietals and blends, including Chardonnay, →Verdelho, Sauvignon, Merlot, Shiraz, Cabernet Sauvignon
In Hardy's Western Australia outpost Larry Cherubino creates a range of good, low-cost varietals and blends, and increasingly interesting wines from the Frankland Valley and Mount Barker. He also makes Hardy's Brookland Valley wines and the second label Verse I in Nannup.

Howard Park***—****
Denmark, Great Southern
74 acres (30 ha); bought-in grapes; 400,000 bottles
• Wines include: Riesling, Chardonnay, →Cabernet Merlot and second label Madfish Bay
Chief winemaker Michael Kerrigan is regarded as one of the best in Western Australia. His wines are made from carefully grown grapes from Margaret River and Great Southern. He also has a pleasing MadFish range.

Leeuwin Estate***—*****
Margaret River, Margaret River
346 acres (140 ha); 530,000 bottles • Wines: →Chardonnay, Riesling, Sauvignon; Pinot, Cabernet, →Art Series Chardonnay
Since 1974 Denis and Tricia Horgan's low-yielding vines from unirrigated vineyards have helped to create what is arguably Australia's most intense, finest Chardonnays in the Burgundian mold. Good Cabernet too from this estate, which has simultaneously developed a reputation for its high-profile, open-air concerts.

Moss Wood****—*****
Wilyabrup, Margaret River
20.6 acres (8.34 ha); 67,000 bottles • Wines: Semillon, Chardonnay; Cabernet, Pinot
Winemaker Keith Mugford has earned a reputation for finely crafted, barrel-fermented Semillon, as well as excellent Cabernet and Pinot Noir with finesse and structure.

Picardy***—****
Pemberton
20 acres (8.1 ha); 60,000 bottles • Wines include: Chardonnay, Pinot Noir, →Shiraz, Merlimont
Picardy is a boutique winery, founded in 1993, but it is one of the leading premium wineries in Western Australia, growing Chardonnay, Pinot Noir, Shiraz, and Bordeaux varieties. It belongs to Bill, Sandra, Dan, and Jodie Pannell, who run it. All the wines are made exclusively from estate-grown grapes.

Plantagenet***—****
Mount Barker, Great Southern
247 acres (100 ha); bought-in grapes; 1,200,000 bottles
• Wines: Riesling, Chardonnay; Pinot, Cabernet, Shiraz, →Omrak Chardonnay
Tony Smith's winery makes high-quality wines across the range with fine Cabernet; the Shiraz, in particular, most resembles a wine from northern Rhône.

Vasse Felix***—****
Wilyabrup, Margaret River
395 acres (160 ha); bought-in grapes; 1,000,000 bottles
• Wines: Semillon Sauvignon, Riesling, Semillon, Chardonnay; Shiraz, →Cabernet
The wines of Vasse Felix have been revitalized, thanks to a new winery and vineyard, which promises to bring continuing improvements. The winery suffered in the early 1990s, but their Cabernet in particular now appears to be back on form.

TASMANIA

As you might expect for an island some way south of the mainland, Tasmania is not like any other state in Australia. It has its own distinct topography, climate, culture and, not surprisingly, wine styles. Life is lived at a slower pace in Tasmania, one of Australia's natural beauty spots and, from a tourist's point of view, one of its most idyllic. More than half of Tasmania's wine is consumed by visitors to the island.

There was a small-scale wine industry in Tasmania in the 19th century, but it was not until Jean Miguet and Claudio Alcorso planted vineyards near Launceston and Hobart that the modern wine industry grew up. To speak of a wine industry in Tasmania would be an exaggeration, in view of the relatively small area of around 2,965 acres (1,200 ha) under cultivation and yielding grapes. On the other hand there is no lack of quality and individuality among the 50 wineries around Hobart in the south and in the sub-regions of Pipers River and Lamar Valley in the north.

Perhaps the best known is Pipers Brook, which was established by the pioneering Dr. Andrew Pirie, the driving force behind Tasmanian wine. With its closely-planted, European-style vineyards, Pipers Brook produces consummate Chardonnay and long-lived Riesling and, despite being one of the coolest regions in Australia, gets good results from both Cabernet Sauvignon and Pinot Noir—a veritable Bordeaux, Burgundy, and Alsace rolled into one.

With its cool climate, the coolest of all Australia's wine regions, the northern region around Pipers River is particularly suited to the production of sparkling wines, mostly made from the classic champagne grapes, Chardonnay and Pinot Noir. The aromatic Alsace varieties—

St. Matthias Vineyard in the Tamar Valley is known for Riesling and Pinot Noir.

Riesling, Gewürztraminer, and Pinot Gris—do well here, and to a lesser extent so does Pinot Noir. The picturesque Tamar Valley produces richer, fuller-bodied styles.

The southern pioneering winery is Moorilla, on the Derwent River near Hobart, planted by Claudio Alcorso. In addition to the Derwent River wineries, the region comprises the southernmost Huon Valley, the eastern zone with Freycinet Vineyards at Wine Glass Bay of particular note, as well as Domaine A in the Coal River Valley. Pinot Noir is the dominant grape variety in the south, and much of it, along with Chardonnay, is used for premium sparkling wine production.

SELECT PRODUCERS IN TASMANIA

PIPERS BROOK VINEYARD***–****
PIPERS BROOK, NORTHERN TASMANIA
494 acres (200 ha); bought-in grapes; 1,200,000 bottles • Wines: Pipers Brook Pinot Gris, Gewürztraminer, Riesling, Sauvignon Blanc/Chardonnnay; Pinot; reserve range and single-vineyard range, →Summit Chardonnay, →Pellion Pinot, Opimian, second label Ninth Island, →Pirie (sparkling)
This vineyard was set up in 1974 after a study identified the specifically "bio" climate of North Tasmania. The wines have maintained their quality although the founder Andrew Pirie has left, and they still have their intense, unique aromas and finesse.

PIPERS BROOK VINEYARD
1998 PELLION
Pinot Noir
Tasmania

MOORILLA ESTATE***
BERRIEDALE, SOUTHERN TASMANIA
Bought-in grapes; 106,000 bottles • Wines: Riesling, Chardonnay, Gewürztraminer, Pinot Noir, Cabernet, Cabernet Merlot, sparkling vintage brut
Founded by the Alcorso family in 1958, Moorilla pioneered intense, fruity white varietals. The future is less certain since its takeover, but this Derwent-River-based winery should continue to retain a captive market in Hobart, Tasmania's capital.

North Island

The early growth of Auckland as a wine-growing area owed much to the migration of Dalmatian settlers to work in the Kauri gum fields in the late 19th century. Auckland is still the headquarters of many of New Zealand's best-known wineries, including industry giant Montana and wineries whose names—Babich, Delegat, Selaks, Nobilo—testify to their European origins. However, Auckland's star has waned as regions further south have grown in importance. There has been a revival of sorts, with some excellent Chardonnay coming from both Kumeu River and Collards, while Stonyridge and Goldwater on Waiheke Island have the potential to produce spectacular reds in the Bordeaux style. Despite their humid summers, the far northern regions of Northland and Matakana also show potential for big, hearty reds. Immediately southeast of Auckland, the small region of Waikato and the Bay of Plenty is home to a handful of well-established wineries. Most of their grape sources come from Hawke's Bay and further south.

Red wines of the island—Goldwater Estate on Waiheke.

The Poor and the Classy Bays

On the east coast and at the northern tip of Poverty Bay, Gisborne has rather suffered by comparison with the more prestigious Hawke's Bay and Marlborough. In a decade, plantings here, along with production, have marginally declined. It's a rather remote region, with only a handful of wineries, of which Matawhero and the organic Millton stand out. Gisborne is white-wine country, with Chardonnay easily the most widely planted variety. Perhaps for

As everywhere in New Zealand, the presentation of wine in Auckland is a very straightforward, uncomplicated matter.

that reason, producers like to call it "the Chardonnay capital of New Zealand," but it has the dubious distinction of being best known for producing large volumes for the big companies, most of which goes into wine casks. Some premium Chardonnay is made here at Montana and Corbans.

South west of Gisborne on the east coast, Hawke's Bay is New Zealand's finest wine region for reds in the Bordeaux style and, arguably, for Chardonnay too. Plantings here have risen by a third in a decade, with Cabernet Sauvignon, Merlot, and Cabernet Franc together outstripping Chardonnay in vineyard area, even though Chardonnay is the most widely planted variety. It is a sunny region, but it is also prone to severe autumn rainfall, as occurred in 1988 and 1995. The terrain in the hinterland behind the town of Napier is diverse, with a mixture of fertile, coastal alluvial, and gravelly soils, and less productive, well-drained gravel soils not unlike the Médoc region of southwest France in parts. Hawke's Bay is home to more than 50 wineries, including Te Mata, C.J. Pask, Montana's McDonald Winery, Esk Valley, Te Awa Farm, Stonecroft, and Sacred Hill. Many of these produce notable Chardonnay and red wines of distinction.

Wairarapa and Pinot Noir

This cool, dry, small region to the east of Wellington, which includes the district of Martinborough, has emerged in the last decade as one of New Zealand's most exciting new wine areas. It is remote sheep-grazing country, in which a handful of small but highly determined growers have made their mark. Whether the gravelly Martinborough terraces are better suited to Pinot Noir or Cabernet Sauvignon is a moot point, but there is little doubt that many of New Zealand's top Pinot Noirs are from this region, notably those of Dry River, Ata Rangi, Martinborough Vineyard, and Palliser Estate. Pinot Noir is the most widely planted variety here. At the same time, the region produces fine Chardonnay and highly aromatic dry whites from Sauvignon Blanc, and in the Alsace mold from Riesling and Tokay Pinot Gris. With over 40 small wineries and plenty of restaurants, cafés, and hotels, it is one of the most attractive wine regions to visit.

SOUTH ISLAND

Of all New Zealand's wine regions, Marlborough has established the strongest reputation for itself, based on the quality and unique flavors of its Sauvignon Blanc. This is so much the case that it seems extraordinary that the region was not developed (by Montana) until 1973. Among the Sauvignon Blancs of the world, Marlborough Sauvignon stands out for its pungent aromas, ranging from asparagus and green bean to the more tropical flavors of citrus, mango, and passionfruit. Two-thirds of New Zealand's Sauvignon Blanc are planted in Marlborough, on the diverse, stony alluvial flats of the Wairau Valley. It is a cool region with a strong maritime influence, characterized by sunny days and cold nights, which keep acidity levels high.

In New Zealand's largest wine region, two wineries—Cloudy Bay and Montana—have blazed a trail for Sauvignon Blanc. Today, there are around 70 wineries producing consummate examples of the style, notably Hunter's, Jackson Estate, Wairau River, Vavasour, Villa Maria, and Seresin Estate. Marlborough also produces excellent Chardonnay and fine Riesling, as well as sparkling wines made from the champagne grapes Chardonnay and Pinot Noir. Fromm Estate is leading the way with table wines made from Pinot Noir, but Montana, Corbans, and Cloudy Bay, among others, are also producing good examples of the style.

DESPITE WET AND COLD

Closest of New Zealand's wine regions to the rainy west coast, Nelson is 46 miles (75 km) to the west of Marlborough. It is a small but rapidly expanding region of mainly white wines with a predominance of Chardonnay and Sauvignon Blanc produced at its 20 wineries. On soils not unlike Marlborough's alluvial flats, production has more than trebled in a decade here. Seifried is easily the biggest of Nelson's wineries, while Neudorf is not only its best, but one of New Zealand's best, particularly for its exceptional Chardonnay, which can be as sumptuous and complex as *premier cru* white Burgundy.

New Zealand's fourth-largest wine region, Canterbury, has vineyards concentrated in three zones: the flat plains surrounding the pretty city of Christchurch, the hills around Waipara, and the Banks Peninsula. Considered by many to be too cold for viticulture, the region was given a new lease of life when research carried out by

Thanks to its outstanding Sauvignon, Cloudy Bay in Marlborough has become the best-known New Zealand estate worldwide.

Rippon Vineyards by Lake Wanaka own one of the finest Pinot Noir vineyards in the world. It extends along the lake against a backdrop of New Zealand's Southern Alps and is run on biological principles.

Dr. David Jackson demonstrated its true potential. It is an extremely cool region, exposed to the ocean and consequently well suited to white grape varieties, in particular Chardonnay, Riesling, and Sauvignon Blanc. However, Pinot Noir is perhaps the best variety, creating wines of intense flavors in the elegant, red-berry spectrum. There are around 40 small wineries in the region, of which Giesen is the leader. There are also good wines from the Donaldson family's Pegasus Bay.

DRAMATIC VINEYARD SCENERY

If you want to see the most wildly beautiful vineyards in the world, you must travel to Central Otago and its capital Queenstown. Here, in the natural lakeland setting of southern New Zealand, you will find extremes of altitude, latitude (45° south), temperature, remoteness, and also dramatic beauty. The area is a tourist's paradise and a focus for exciting sports. Central Otago is the fastest growing wine region in New Zealand, with plantings of Chardonnay and Pinot Noir in more that 40 wineries now rivaling those of Canterbury. Although the Otago region defies conventional norms of suitable climate for viticulture, its long summer sunshine hours and relatively low rainfall suggest that grape-growing is not only possible here but, for certain styles, highly desirable. Chardonnay produces good, melon-and-citrus-style wines, while the potential of Pinot Noir's varietal character, from wineries such as Mount Edward, Mount Difficulty, Quartz Reef, Felton Road, and Rippon Vineyards, is starting to manifest itself.

Select Producers in New Zealand

North Island

Ata Rangi****
Martinborough, Martinborough
62 acres (25 ha); 66,000 bottles • Wines: Pinot Gris, →Craighall Chardonnay, Sauvignon; →Ata Rangi Pinot Noir, Célèbre, →Summer Rose
With low-yielding vines and meticulous attention to detail, Clive Paton and Oliver Masters make some of New Zealand's most intense Pinot Noir along with a concentrated, flagship Bordeaux blend in Célèbre.

Babich***
Henderson, Auckland
Bought-in grapes; 1,400,000 bottles • Wines include: Sauvignon, Chardonnay, Pinot Gris, Riesling; Syrah, Pinot; international renommee: Marlborough Sauvignon, Irongate Chardonnay, Cabernet Merlot
The winery is owned by Peter and Joe Babich, the two sons of pioneer Josip Babich, who founded the company in 1916. They produce consistent quality, premium varietal wines from the Hawke's Bay, Gisborne, and Marlborough regions.

C.J. Pask***–****
Hastings, Hawke's Bay
222 acres (90 ha); 600,000 bottles • Wines: Chardonnay, Sauvignon, Cabernet Merlot, Syrah, Merlot
High-profile winemaker Kate Radburnd makes equally high-profile wines, in particular fine Bordeaux-style reds, sourced from Pask's gravelly vineyard site at Gimblett Road, which many—including owner Chris Pask himself—claim to be New Zealand's best site for Cabernet-Merlot-based reds, and where Syrah is now gaining importance.

Craggy Range Winery***
Hawke's Bay and Martinborough
49 acres (20 ha); bought-in grapes; 300,000 bottles • Wines include: Sauvignon, Riesling, →Chardonnay, Merlot, →Syrah, Pinot Noir
Wines of great character from individual vineyards in Gimblett Gravels, Martinborough, and Marlborough. Very successful Sauvignon and highly-praised Prestige Collection, especially Les Beaux Cailloux Chardonnay, Sophie on a Merlot base and the Syrah Le sol.

Dry River*****
Martinborough, Martinborough
23 acres (9.5 ha); 30,000 bottles • Wines: Riesling, Pinot Gris, Chardonnay, Gewürztraminer, Sauvignon; Pinot Noir, Syrah
Neil McCallum's Dry River is one of the most extraordinary vineyards in the world, producing arguably the best Pinot Noir in the southern hemisphere.

Escarpement Vineyard***
Martinborough
59 acres (24 ha) • Wines include: Chardonnay, Pinot Blanc, Pinot Gris, Riesling, →Pinot Noir
Vineyards and winery, partnership between the McKennas—Larry took Martinborough Pinot Noir to international fame—and the Kirbys at the foot of the Aorangi Chain. The aim is clear—New World wines of complexity, texture, and structure.

Goldwater Estate***–****
Putiki Bay, Waiheke Island
35 acres (14 ha); bought-in grapes; 312,000 bottles • Wines: Chardonnay; Cabernet and Merlot from Waiheke Island, →Waiheke Island Esslin Merlot, Sauvignon and Chardonnay from Marlborough

The Goldwaters have turned a lifestyle choice into a thriving business, expanding production from picturesque Waiheke Island into Marlborough, where 86 acres (35 ha) under contract produce quality whites for them.

Kumeu River****
Kumeu, Auckland
64 acres (26 ha); bought-in grapes; 250,000 bottles • Wines: Chardonnay, →Mate's Vineyard Chardonnay, Pinot Gris, Melba, Pinot Noir
Michael Brajkovich makes finely honed, intense, Burgundian-style Chardonnay, which is a major achievement in Auckland's subtropical, humid climate.

Martinborough Vineyard****
Martinborough
90,000 bottles • Wines: Riesling, Pinot Gris, Sauvignon, Chardonnay; Pinot
Since Larry McKenna left in 1999 the estate has ceased to grow, and under Claire Mulholland it has devoted itself to a constant range of classical wines. The vines are now fully grown and their yields are reduced. They are pruned and trained by hand and the grapes are hand-picked. The winery is well known for classical, complex Pinot Noirs and elegant Chardonnays.

The Millton Vineyard***
Manutuke, Gisborne
49 acres (20 ha); 144,000 bottles • Wines: Chardonnay, Chenin, Riesling, Viognier, Malbec, Merlot Cabernet from Te Arai, Riverpoint and Opou vineyards, →Naboth's Chardonnay and Pinot
In 1984 James and Annie Millton, New Zealand's first commercial, fully certified organic winegrowers, established the Millton Vineyard, which rapidly gained a reputation for sweet, late-harvested Rieslings and Chenin. The distinctive wines are produced from estate-grown grapes employing biodynamic cultivation techniques.

Palliser Estate***–****
Martinborough, Martinborough
210 acres (85 ha); bought-in grapes; 480,000 bottles • Wines: Chardonnay, Riesling, Sauvignon, Pinot Gris, Noble Riesling, S.F.G.; Pinot
Winemaker Allan Johnson makes very intensive wines and a Sauvignon that puts many others from Marlborough in the shade.

Te Mata***–****
Havelock North, Hawke's Bay
321 acres (130 ha); 420,000 bottles • Wines include: Woodthorpe: Viognier, Chardonnay, Gamay; →Colerain Cabernet-Merlot, →Awatea Cabernet-Merlot, Bullnose Syrah
Under the stewardship of John Buck and winemaker Peter Cowley, Te Mata has become one of New Zealand's foremost premium New Zealand red wineries. It's noted in particular for fine Chardonnay and the Bordeaux-style finesse of its red blends.

Trinity Hill***–****
Hastings, Hawke's Bay
99 acres (40 ha); bought-in grapes; 420,000 bottles • Wines: Chardonnay, Sauvignon, Riesling, Pinot Gris; Cabernet/Cabernet Franc, Merlot/Syrah, Pinot
John Hancock produces two ranges under the Gimblett Road and Shepherds Croft labels. Warren Gibson is the winemaker at Trinity Hill, where Hancock's joint venture with London and Auckland partners is bearing fruit in the form of excellent Chardonnay and improving reds. He is also experimenting with Viognier and Montepulciano.

VILLA MARIA ESTATE**–****
MANGERE, AUCKLAND

*494 acres (200 ha); bought-in grapes; 6,000,000 bottles
• Wines include: Chardonnay, Sauvignon, Riesling,
Pinot Gris; Pinot, Cabernet/Merlot*
Founded in 1961, with the dynamic George Fistonich at
the helm and Michelle Richardson the winemaker, Villa
Maria has become New Zealand's third largest company
and consistently one of the best. It shines with excellent
Marlborough Sauvignons →Wairau Valley and
→Clifford Bay wines, with Botrytis Riesling, a fine reserve
Chardonnay, prize-winning Cabernet-Merlot blends
from Hawke's Bay, and Pinot Noirs from Marlborough.

SOUTH ISLAND
CLOUDY BAY***–****
BLENHEIM, MARLBOROUGH

*247 acres (100 ha); bought-in grapes; 800,000 bottles
• Wines: →Sauvignon, Te Koko, →Chardonnay, Pelorus
N.V. and Vintage Brut, Late Harvest Riesling,
Gewürztraminer; Bay Pinot Noir*
Chief winemaker and star photographer Kevin Judd
produces the best Sauvignon in the New World, but it
was recently outshone. However, his Chardonnay is also
good, and the Pinot Noir from this Veuve Clicquot Cape
Mentelle enterprise is very promising.

FELTON ROAD WINES****
BANNOCKBURN, CENTRAL OTAGO

*74 acres (30 ha); 120,000 bottles • Wines include:
Riesling, Chardonnay, Pinot Noir; →special bottlings
from individual blocks*
Since its first vintage in 1997 the winery on Felton
Road, near the little town of Bannockburn, which
tends its vines most carefully, has been giving the fruitiness and complexity of the vineyards of this region
full expression. The Pinot Noirs of Blocks 3 and 5 are
among the best in the southern hemisphere.

FROMM****
BLENHEIM, MARLBOROUGH

*10 acres (4 ha); bought-in grapes; 54,000 bottles
• Wines: Chardonnay; Pinot, Merlot*
Despite tiny production, Swiss George Fromm has made
an impact, thanks to his highly concentrated, complex
Pinot Noir from very low-yielding vines.

GIESEN**–***
BURNHAM, CANTERBURY

*86 acres (35 ha) (Canterbury), 165 acres (67 ha)
(Marlborough); bought-in grapes; 650,000 bottles
• Wines: Sauvignon, Chardonnay, Riesling, Late
Harvest and Botrytized Riesling, Reserves; Pinot*
Bringing German expertise with them, the three Giesen
brothers, together with winemaker Andrew Blake, have
worked assiduously to carve out a reputation for fine
Canterbury whites as well as a refined Pinot Noir.

HUNTER'S****
BLENHEIM, MARLBOROUGH

*222 acres (90 ha); bought-in grapes; 660,000 bottles
• Wines: Chardonnay, Sauvignon, Chardonnay Reserve,
Riesling, Gewürztraminer, Breidecker; Pinot, Merlot,
Estate Red; →Miru Miru*
With experienced winemaker Gary Duke, Jane Hunter
is responsible for making Hunter's one of
Marlborough's best estates, with fine Sauvignon and a
Graves-style, oak-aged blend as well as a finely crafted,
champagne-method fizz in Miru Miru.

ISABEL ESTATE****
RENWICK, MARLBOROUGH

*128 acres (52 ha); 180,000 bottles • Wines: Sauvignon,
Chardonnay, Riesling, Pinot Gris; Pinot Noir*
Winemaker Jeff Sinnott seems to make better wines
every year.

Purism in demand—a
tasting at Cloudy Bay.

New Zealand's wine giant
Montana maintains various
estates. The O from
Ormond Estate is an elegant
Chardonnay.

MONTANA**–****
BLENHEIM, MARLBOROUGH

*5,187 acres (2,100 ha); bought-in grapes; 27,000,000
bottles • Wines include: Sauvignon, Chardonnay,
Riesling, Gewürztraminer, Semillon, Müller-Thurgau;
Pinot, Merlot, Cabernet, Cabernet Franc*
In 1973 Montana decided to plant in Marlborough, and
today the region is world-famous for its Sauvignon.
Following substantial investment, Montana, under
senior winemaker Jeff Clarke, is now New Zealand's
largest producer.

MOUNT EDWARD****
GIBBSTON, CENTRAL OTAGO

*2.5 acres (1 ha); bought-in grapes; 20,400 bottles
• Wines: Riesling, →Pinot Noir*
Alan Brady was the first to plant vines in Gibbston in
1981. He set up Gibbston Valley Wines and ran the
company during the pioneer years from Central Otago.
In 1998 he built Mount Edward in order to specialize on
Pinot, signing exclusive contracts for three young Pinot
Noir plots of 17 acres (7 ha). The small winery
concentrates on quality and now exports 70 percent of
its hand-made wines to Europe.

NEUDORF VINEYARDS***–****
UPPER MOUTERE, NELSON

*60 acres (24 ha); bought-in grapes; 120,000 bottles
• Wines: →Moutere Chardonnay, Riesling, Pinot; plus
Nelson label varietals, Brightwater Riesling and
Sauvignon*
Tim and Judy Finn make some of New Zealand's finest
wines, in particular the Moutere Chardonnay, whose
occasional botrytis adds complexity to the power and
textural richness of the wines.

PEGASUS BAY***–****
WAIPARA, CANTERBURY

*69 acres (28 ha); bought-in grapes; 150,000–200,000
bottles • Wines: Chardonnay, Riesling, Sauvignon; Pinot
Noir, →Prima Donna, Cabernet Merlot, →Maestro
(Cabernet), second label called Main Divide*
Founded by Professor Ivan Donaldson Pegasus Bay is
now making most attractive wines under winemakers
Matthew Donaldson and Lynnette Hudson in its cellars
that are reminiscent of cathedrals.

QUARTZ REEF****
QUARTZ REEF, CENTRAL OTAGO

*37 acres (15 ha); bought-in grapes; 90,000 bottles
• Wines: Pinot Gris, →Chauvet Sparkling Wine,
→Pinot Noir*
Rudi Bauer, formerly winemaker with Rippon, has
specialized on sparkling wine and Pinot Noir. He is
arousing much attention with this small, quality-conscious winery.

RIPPON VINEYARDS****
WANAKA, OTAGO

*31 acres (12.6 ha); 72,000 bottles • Wines: Riesling,
Chardonnay, Sauvignon, Gewürztraminer, Osteiner,
→Emma Rippon; Pinot Noir, Merlot/Syrah*
Founded by Rolfe and Lois Mills, the tradition of
making elegant Pinot Noir at this wonderfully located
lakeside winery continues with winemaker Russell
Lake. They also produce varietals with exceptional
intensity of flavor.

SERESIN ESTATE***–****
RENWICK, MARLBOROUGH

*279 acres (113 ha); 180,000 bottles • Wines: Pinot
Noir, Pinot Gris, Sauvignon, Chardonnay, Riesling,
Noble Sauvignon, Noble Riesling, Moana (sparkling)*
Cinematographer Michael Seresin has had the vision
and energy to start Seresin Estate from scratch and turn
it into one of the top producers in Marlborough.

APPENDIX

Glossary

A.C.
Stands for *Appellation Contrôlée*. See also *Appellation d'Origine Contrôlée*.

ACID
A key component of wine, acid is present in all grapes, mainly in the form of tartaric acid. It gives wine freshness and long life, provided the acidity is in balance.

ADEGA (COOPERATIVA) (Portuguese)
Term for a grower's cooperative. Lit. "winery."

AMARONE
Dry Italian wine made from the must of air-dried berries.

AMONTILLADO
Designation for a mature dry Fino sherry aged naturally. Also a term for blended sweet sherries.

APPELLATION D'ORIGINE CONTRÔLÉE (A.O.C.)
The French system of defining wine by region, which has become the prototype in the wine world. Also prescribes yields and other viticultural practices.

AROMA
The scent of a wine that lends it its distinctive "nose" or "bouquet."

ASSEMBLAGE
Blending of high-value wines (*cuvée*), in contrast to *coupage*.

ASTRINGENT
Furry feeling on the tongue, often resulting from high tannin content.

AUSBRUCH
The famous wine style of Austria, a specialty of the town of Rust on the Neusiedler See.

AUSLESE
One of the *Prädikate* of the Q.m.P. category as defined by the German Wine Law, literally meaning "selected harvest." Sweet wines with a high must weight.

A.V.A. (American Viticultural Area)
The American version of France's *Appellation Contrôlée* system. It defines a wine by its geographic and climatic region but does not prescribe yields or grape varieties.

AZIENDA AGRICOLA
Italian term for an estate that makes wine exclusively from its own grapes, in contrast to an *azienda vinicola*.

BAG IN A BOX
Wine retailed in quantities of a liter or more. The box is furnished with a tap and often with a soda siphon that slows down the oxidation of the remaining wine.

BALLING
System used in South Africa to determine the concentration of the must. Roughly the same as the Brix scale used in the U.S.A.

BARRIQUE
Originally referred to the barrel type used in Bordeaux but now refers to the internationally used standard barrel in the wine trade containing 60 gallons (225 liters), used to age red wines and ferment and age white wines.

BASE STOCK
The base stock or root onto which another variety of vine is grafted.

BÂTONNAGE
The lees (deposit left after fermentation) are stirred periodically to ensure that the oxygen in the barrel is carried right to the bottom, preventing the development of any faults in the aroma of the finished wine.

BEERENAUSLESE
One of the *Prädikate* of the Q.m.P. category as defined by the German Wine Law, literally "selected berries." It should be made with botrytized grapes for an intense, sweet wine.

BENTONITE
A porous clay, rich in mineral and derived from volcanic rock. It is used to improve white wines.

BIODYNAMIC CULTIVATION (France)
An organic approach to viticulture, heavily influenced by the theories of Rudolf Steiner. It is the most ideological of the organic systems and includes elements of astronomy.

BIOLOGICAL ACID CONVERSION
See Malolactic acid conversion.

BLIND TASTING
A wine tasting term that means that wines are tasted with the labels hidden.

BLUSH WINE
American term for mostly light, sweetish white or rosé wines from dark grapes. The most popular is White Zinfandel.

BOCKSBEUTEL
Wide, rounded bottle used only by growers from Franconia and Portugal.

BÖCKSER
Sulfurous smell reminiscent of bad eggs arising during fermentation due to faulty processing.

BODEGA
Spanish term for a winery.

BODEGA COOPERATIVA
Spanish winegrowers' organization.

BOTRYTIS CINEREA
Noble rot, a fungus that attacks grapes and causes them to shrivel, thereby concentrating the flavors, sugar, and acid. It produces a complex and sweet wine, commonly referred to as "botrytized" wines: the most famous examples are Chateau d'Yquem from Sauternes, Sekt from Germany, and Tokaji from Hungary.

BOTTLE FERMENTATION
A method used in the production of sparkling wine, when the second fermentation takes place in the bottle. See also *Méthode champenoise*.

BOTTLE-MATURATION (also called Bottle-aging)
Maturing a wine in the bottle rather than a tank or barrel.

BOTTLE-READY
A term to describe a wine that has aged enough to be ready for bottling.

BOTTLING LIQUOR
In champagne production, the induction of the all-important second fermentation is achieved by the addition of a mixture called *liqueur d'expédition* or *liqueur de triage*. This bottling liquor consists of reserve wine, into which a small amount of cane sugar has been dissolved.

BOUQUET (NOSE)
The totality of aromas given off by a wine.

BOUTIQUE WINERY
Small winemaker producing wines with great care in small quantities, mostly at high prices. Contrasts with industrial-scale wineries.

BRIX
A system, used mainly in the U.S.A. and adapted from the sugar industry, to measure densities and by extension the density of must concentrates. See also Balling.

BRUT
Term for dry sparkling wines with less than $1/4$ oz/pint (15 g/l) residual sugar. Often used to denote a very dry sparkling wine.

BULK
Wine by the barrel.

BUSCHENSCHANK
Austrian term for →*Straußwirtschaft*, where home-grown wine is sold by the glass.

BUSH VINES
Bush-type vines found in some areas of Australia and South Africa that are not cultivated on wire frames (see also Cultivation systems), but have a short trunk on which the shoots are arranged in circles. Also called Gobelet-trained vines.

CARBON DIOXIDE
CO_2, carbonic acid; a natural gas, produced as a by-product during fermentation.

CARBONIC MACERATION
Process to soften and ferment grapes by means of carbonic acid. Used in the production of lighter, fruitier red wines that are to be drunk young. Uncrushed, undamaged berries are fermented in a container by adding carbonic acid. A small quantity of grape sugar (dextrose) is added to start fermentation.

CAVA
Term for a Spanish sparkling wine made by traditional fermentation procedure in the bottle. Literally "cellar."

CAVE
French term for "cellar."

CHAI
A term used in Southwest France for cellars, some of which are above ground.

CHAMBRER
French term meaning "allow to breathe," i.e. open a bottle of wine and leave in contact with the air to reach room temperature.

CHAMPAGNE METHOD
See *Méthode champenoise.*

CHAPTALIZATION
To add sugar before fermentation, to increase the alcohol content. Not permitted with every kind of wine.

CHARMAT METHOD
Tank fermentation process in the production of sparkling wine, where the second fermentation takes place in a pressure tank, not in the bottle.

CHÂTEAU-BOTTLED/ESTATE-BOTTLED
Term used on labels to show that a wine was grown, made and bottled in the same place. Also applies to cooperative-made wines but not to winery bottlings or bottlings of →bulk wines.

CLARET (CLAIRET)
Originally a medieval Norman English term for light red wines from the Haut Pays shipped through Bordeaux. In England the term later came to mean Bordeaux wines or wines in the Bordeaux style rather than Haut Pays (Bergerac or Gaillac). *Clairet* is now used in France again to designate light-colored Bordeaux wines.

CLARIFICATION
Clarification of wine, helping to stabilize it. A clarification agent is added to the wine that binds with cloudy substances and other unwanted particles and settles on the bottom with them as sediment.

CLASSICO
Precisely defined geographical zones in Italy from which the grapes of a *classico* wine must come.

CLIMAT
A term used in France, particularly in Burgundy, to describe a vineyard site by its climatic and geographical characteristics.

CLONE
Vine reproduced from a genetically identical parent plant.

CLOS
Term used in France to describe a vineyard enclosed by a wall or hedge.

COLD SOAK
Cold maceration, especially with Pinot Noir, when the grapes are left for some days in the tank at a cool temperature so that the pigment and aroma molecules are released in the juice before fermentation begins.

COOPERAGE
The place where coopers, those who make and repair barrels, work.

COPITA
A type of glass commonly used for sherry in Spain, but also used by wine tasters.

CORKED
Wine affected by a faulty cork, generally with an infiltration of 2.4.6 Trichloranisole, which is formed by mildew.

COSECHA
Spanish for "vintage," i.e. year of production.

COSECHERO
Spanish for "winegrower."

COUPAGE
Blending of simple wines, in contrast to →*assemblage.* (Hides bad qualities rather than bringing out good qualities.)

COVER CROPS
A crop other than vines planted in the vineyard to benefit the soil.

CRÉMANT
French sparkling wine produced according to traditional fermentation in the bottle but not from Champagne (→*Méthode champenoise*).

CRIANZA
Spanish wine that can only be sold after a certain period of aging in →*barriques.*

CRU
Literally, a "growth." By extension, an outstanding vineyard site or the wine from it.

CRYOEXTRACTION
The practice of artificially replicating the natural conditions necessary to produce sweet white Ice Wine.

CULTIVAR
Botanical term for cultivated varieties not widely used in the wine world except in South Africa.

CULTIVATION SYSTEMS
There are various methods of training and pruning vines, the choice depending on the variety, the location and how strongly the vine grows. Formerly the free standing bush varieties, or *Gobelets*, were widespread, but now most vines are trained on wire frames or stakes. The aim is to prevent the shoots and leaves from hanging down to the ground and give the plant enough air, to make it less vulnerable to disease. Vines yielding a full harvest have to be trained on wire frames. Beside Single Gobelet and Double Guyot the most important systems are Lenz-Moser, Cordon, Tendone, Lyr, and Scott-Henry.

CUVÉE
Blend of high-value wines →*assemblage*; in sparkling wine production, a term for the initial pressings from the wine press.

DECANT
To transfer wine slowly from a bottle into a carafe, either to add oxygen to it or to separate it from the → sediment.

DECANTING METHOD (TRANSVASER)
Method of producing sparkling wines, with the second fermentation taking place in the bottle, as with the *méthode champenoise.* In order to avoid the lengthy and expensive process of "degorging," the bottles are emptied into a pressure container, the wine is filtered and

subsequently bottled with the required *dosage* and the aid of a back-pressure bottling apparatus. In the shorter or longer term, more practical methods with yeast balls could well replace this technically expensive process.

DÉGORGER, DÉGORGEMENT
To remove the sediment from a sparkling wine, also called "disgorgement."

DÉGUSTATION
Wine-tasting.

DENOMINAÇÃO DE ORIGEM CONTROLADA (D.O.C.)
Guarantee of origin for Portuguese quality wines.

DENOMINACIÓN DE ORIGEN (D.O.)
Guarantee of origin for Spanish quality wines.

DENOMINAZIONE DI ORIGINE CONTROLLATA (D.O.C.)
Guarantee of origin for Italian quality wines.

DENOMINAZIONE DI ORIGINE CONTROLLATA E GARANTITA (D.O.C.G.)
Top guarantee of origin for Italian quality wines.

DISGORGEMENT
See *Dégorger.*

DOMAINE
French word for a wine-growing estate.

DOMÄNE
Term for a German estate that belongs to the state.

DOSAGE (DOSING)
French term for a mixture of wine and sugar or must that is added to sparkling wines. A distinction is made between full dosing (added before the second fermentation, by way of inducing it) and the final dosage given after the removal of the sediment, to add the right degree of sweetness.

DRINKING TEMPERATURE
The ideal temperature to serve a wine.

DRY
An adjective that refers to the lack of sweetness of a wine.

EISWEIN
A German and Austrian specialty with high sweetness and acidity. Produced with grapes that are picked and pressed at a temperature of 18°F/–7 °C or less.

ÉLEVAGE
A term used in France that has no direct English translation but refers to what a winemaker might do to his wines in the processes between fermentation and bottling.

EN VRAC
French term meaning "in bulk." Term for unbottled wine bought in volume, mainly by large shippers.

ENOLOGY
The science of wine production.

ENRICHMENT
The process of increasing the alcoholic strength of a wine, originally and still usually by chaptalization, i.e. adding sugar.

ESPUMANTE
Portuguese term for sparkling wine. Wines made by the traditional method (*metodo classico*) that have had 12 months maturing in the bottle are called *reserva*, from 24 months *super reserva* and from 36 months *velha* or *grande reserva*.

ESTATE-BOTTLED
See Château-bottled.

ETHANOL
Scientific name for ethyl alcohol, the intoxicating constituent of wine.

EXTRACT(ION)S
The totality of all non-volatile substances in the wine such as acidity, minerals, sugars, phenols, and glycerine.

FEDERSPIEL
Category introduced in the Wachau region of Austria to describe elegant wines of medium weight. See also *Steinfeder* and *Smaragd*.

FERMENTATION
Process in winemaking in which the sugar in the grape is turned into alcohol and carbonic acid, and must is turned into wine.

FILTRATION
The technique of quickly separating solids from the wine using filters. Its use for wines of high quality or high value is controversial, as it may lead to loss of color tone and remove valuable substances from the wine. A distinction is made between "membrane filtration" and "layer filtration" using a diatomite filter or other powder. See also Settlement, Deposit.

FINING
The process of removing unwanted particles from the wine. See also Clarification.

FINISH
The aftertaste of the wine retained on the tongue after you take a sip. It should last as long as possible.

FINO
Light, less alcoholic, and dry sherry.

FLOR YEAST
This is a naturally forming yeast called *flor*, which is derived from wild yeasts that are present in the atmosphere of the cellars. The *flor* protects the developing wine from the influence of too much oxygen, while imparting a characteristic nutty taste to classic Fino. Sometimes the *flor* breaks up and sinks to the bottom of the cask, thus allowing the wine more direct exposure to oxygen and causing it to darken. This style of sherry is known as Amontillado.

FLURBEREINIGUNG
A reorganization of the West German wine industry in the mid-20th century, affecting over half the total planted area. The vineyards were reparceled in order to make them easier to run.

FORTIFIED WINES
Port, sherry, madeira, malaga, marsala, Banyuls, Rivesaltes, etc.

FORTIFY
To add alcohol to the must to stop fermentation and increase the alcohol content of wi-

nes, especially with port, sherry, and madeira.

FOXY
Marked aroma reminiscent of the smell of wet fur that characterizes wines made from American hybrid vines. Most noticeable in the Concord grape cultivated in New York State.

FRIZZANTE
Italian sparkling wine.

GARRAFEIRA
Legendary term (lit. "bottle cellar") for Portuguese wines that are aged longer, i.e. at least two years in the barrel (red wines) or one year in the barrel and one in the bottle (white wines).

GOBELET
A method of training vines without using a wire construction frequently used in France. (→Cultivation systems); the vines remain low and their shape resembles a goblet.

GRAFT ROOTSTOCK/PROPFUNTERLAGE
Vine rootstock that is grafted with another variety in order to improve (refine) it.

GRAND CRU
Means "great growths" in French. Used generally for outstanding wines in Burgundy and Alsace, it refers to a specific group of superior vineyards.

GRAN RESERVA
Spanish classification. *Gran reserva* red wines have to be aged at least two years in small wooden barrels and then a further three in the tank or bottle before they are sold. Whites remain at least six months in the bottle and then four years in the tank or bottle.

GROWTH
A term for a particular wine or type of wine. A translation of →*cru*.

HEAT DEGREE DAYS
A system introduced by Amerine and Winkler in California to classify climate. Important in California and Australia. The system shows heat degree days for each month during the growing season, with the sum of daily average temperatures over 50°F/10°C being added up.

HECTARE
Metric unit of area, equivalent to 10,000 m² or 2.47 acres.

HECTOLITER
Metric unit of volume meaning 100 liters or 26 U.S. liquid gallons.

HERDADE
Portuguese term for a very large estate or vineyard, especially in the Ribatejo or Alentejo regions.

HEURIGER
The Austrian equivalent of the French *Nouveau*, which can be retailed from November 11 of the year in question to the end of the following year, mostly on a →*Straußwirtschaft* basis. *Heuriger* bars are called →*Buschenschänke* in Austria. See also *Nouveau, Novello*, and *Primeur*.

HOCK
Term for Rhine wine or German wines in general. Short for "hockamore," an anglicization of Hochheimer in a 17th-century English play (referring to wines from Hochheim in the Rheingau).

HYBRID VINES
The issues of two varieties of vine that do not belong to the same species. Also called "interspecies cross." The aim of hybridization (crossing) is to unite the positive qualities of various species in one variety.

ICE WINE
Made in exactly the same way as the German and Austrian *Eiswein*, from grapes that are left to overripen on the vine and then freeze as night-time temperatures start to fall with the onset of winter. Used particularly by Canadian producers making luscious, spicily exotic wines from the frozen grapes of varieties like Vidal.

INDICAZIONE GEOGRAFICA TIPICA (I.G.T.)
A category of Italian country wine. The designation was created in 1992, largely to give legal status to the good quality *Vino da Tavola* wines (table wines).

INTEGRATED WINE GROWING
The aim of this is to largely do without pesticides in order to protect beneficial insects and the environment.

JEROBOAM
Wine bottle with the capacity of four normal bottles, i.e. 112 fl oz (3 liters). Two →magnums.

JUG WINE
Wine sold over the counter by the jug in the U.S.A., i.e. open rather than bottled. Often sold in glass carafes.

KABINETT
The most basic of the *Prädikate* of the Q.m.P. category as defined by the German Wine Law.

KLOSTERNEUBURG MUST GAUGE
Unit of measurement for the specific density of a wine. 1°KMW = 10 g of natural sugar per kg of must.

LEES
Dead yeast cells or sediment remaining in tank after fermentation.

LIBRARY WINES
Older vintages offered for sale in small quantities.

LIQUOREUX
Literally, like liqueur. A term used for sweet wines, often made from grapes with *botrytis cinerea*.

LYRE (TRELLIS) SYSTEM
See Cultivation systems.

MACERATION
The steeping of the grape skins, seeds and stems in the fermentation process in order to increase the take-up of the phenolics.

MACÉRATION CARBONIQUE
Use of carbon dioxide in the mash to produce light, fruity red wines that are drunk young.

Perfectly whole, unpressed grapes are fermented in a vat to which carbon dioxide is added. This forces the grapes to ferment inside their skins, which release particularly strong aromas.

MADEIRIZATION
Term derived from Madeira wine and applied to greatly aged, or even too old wine.

MAGNUM
Wine bottle equal to two standard bottles, i.e. 56 fl oz (1.5 liters).

MALOLACTIC ACID CONVERSION
Conversion of malic acid into softer lactic acid by using lactobacilli, with the aim of reducing the (perceived) acid content of the wine. Also called biological acid reduction.

MARC
Solid residue left in the winepress after pressing (white wines) or fermentation (of red wines). Can also be distilled into brandy. See also Pomace.

MARC CAP/CAP OF SKINS
The layer of grape skins and other solid substances that collects at the top of a container during the fermentation of red wines. It has to be immersed and stirred up with the must. See also Punchdown.

MASH
The lightly pressed grapes that are put into the fermentation vats with the must; red wines are fermented on mash.

MASH HEATING
To soften and break up/ferment the grapes by steeping them in a liquid, possibly by heating. The mash is heated to around 158°F/70°C before fermentation, to release pigments from the skins. Rarely used with high-value wines.

MATURING (AFFINAGE)
Additional ripening in the bottle before a wine goes on sale.

MERITAGE
An invented term in the U.S.A. for a *cuvée* made from several varieties of grape, usually of the Bordeaux range (combines "merit" and "heritage").

MÉTHODE CHAMPENOISE
Method of producing sparkling wine (evolved in Champagne) whereby the second fermentation takes place in the bottle. See also Bottle-fermentation.

MÉTHODE TRADITIONELLE
Alternative term for *méthode champenoise*.

MICRO-ORGANISMS
A minute but continuous dose of oxygen introduced to wines in tanks even before the conversion of biological acidity, which is intended to replace part of the aging in wood. Widely used in many wine-growing estates in France.

MICRO-OXYGENATION
A method of wine-making developed by Patrick Ducourneau, an enologist and Madiran vintner. Very small and very carefully measured quantities of oxygen are blown into the tank or the vats.

MISCHSATZ
Austrian wine made from various grape varieties that all grow in the same vineyard, and are harvested and processed together.

MOELLEUX
French term for mellow wines (medium-sweet).

MOUTHFEEL
U.S. term to describe the overall impression of the wine on the palate.

MUST
Unfermented grape juice. (The raw material of wine after the first stage of processing.)

MUTAGE (MUTE)
The action of muting a must, i.e. stopping the fermentation by adding alcohol or sulfur dioxide.

NÉGOCIANT
A French wine merchant.

NOBLE ROT
See *Botrytis cinerea.*

NOSE
The general smell of a wine. Four noses can be distinguished.

NOUVEAU
Term for French wines that may be retailed soon after the harvest. See also *Heuriger, Novello,* and *Primeur.*

NOVELLO
Term for Italian wines that can be retailed soon after the harvest. See also *Heuriger, Nouveau,* and *Primeur.*

OECHSLE
A unit of measurement based on the specific weight of the must. The name comes from that of the physicist Ferdinand Oechsle. A must with a specific weight of 1.09 has 90° Oechsle. The term is used in Germany and Switzerland.

OENOLOGY
Alternative spelling of Enology.

OINOTRIA
When the Greeks popularized wine growing around the Mediterranean, this was the word for Italy, literally the "land of vine stocks attached to posts," more generally a wine paradise.

OLOROSO
A strong dry sherry with full body. A second basic type along with →*Fino.* Often used for sweet blends of simple sherry.

ORGANOLEPTIC
Refers to the process of tasting (wine).

OXIDATION
Chemical reaction when the wine comes into contact with excess oxygen. The wine loses freshness and changes color. The process can take place in the bottle, or even in the barrel or when still must.

PALO CORTADO
Rare dry sherry. In taste, it lies between Oloroso and Amontillado.

PARTHENOCARPY
In botany, parthenocarpy is the production of fruits without fertilization or seeds. Grapes can sometimes develop without pollination taking place; they are small, seedless and have a high sugar content when ripe.

PASSERILLÉ
(Grapes) left on the vine to dry out. (A feature of Béarnais winemaking.)

PASSITO
Italian method of making wine from dried grapes (raisins).

pH VALUE
Unit of measurement of a wine's acidity. The lower the pH value, the more acidic the wine tastes, pH7 is a neutral value (e.g. plain water).

PHENOLICS
Substances extracted from the skins of grapes that provide the coloring and texture for red wine.

PHYLLOXERA
The vine louse, the most dangerous enemy of the vine. It attacks the vine's roots and kills it. Imported from America to Europe in 1860. Most of the American varieties were resistant, the European ones were not and therefore succumbed, with devastating effects on European wine growing. Only by grafting European vines onto phylloxera-resistant American rootstocks could a remedy be provided. In the 1980s there was an epidemic in the U.S. due to non-resistant rootstocks being used.

PIGEAGE (PUNCHDOWN)
Breaking up and re-immersion of the cap of skins (marc) during the fermentation of red wine. Traditional with Pinot Noir and now many top wines.

POLYPHENOL
Chemical component of wine contained in pigments, tannins, and taste substances. Has a beneficial effect on the human body.

POMACE
The pulpy residue left in the press after the grapes are pressed. Originally a term reserved for apple pulp.

PREMIUM
A mark of top quality for grape varieties and the wines made from them in English-speaking and other wine-growing countries. The premium varieties include Chardonnay and Sauvignon, Cabernet Sauvignon, Merlot and Shiraz (Syrah).

PRESSING
Pressing takes place at different points in the winemaking process. There are a number of different techniques such as the horizontal press (which most producers use) where a press head forces the juice or wine through the perforated wall of a revolving cylinder. The latest stage in the development of horizontal presses is the pneumatic press. In the latter, an airbag inside the cylinder is inflated, squeezing the must against the walls.

PRIMEUR
Term for French wines that can be retailed soon after the harvest. See also *Heuriger, Nouveau,* and *Novello.*

PRÜFNUMMER

German term for the control number on the label of a *Qualitätswein* (= V.d.Q.) in Germany and Austria. Bestowed after the quality of a wine is checked.

PUNCHDOWN

American term for →*pigeage*.

PURE-YEASTING

Using cultured yeast for fermentation to convert the must in the wine. Its reactions are more predictable than the yeast in the grapes, whose fermentation can be difficult to control.

QUALITÄTSWEIN

General word for a higher-quality wine with a designation of origin, in contrast to a simple table wine. Roughly equivalent to *vin de qualité* in French and "fine wine" in English.

QUINTA

Portuguese estate or vineyard, comparable with *château* in viticultural French.

RACKING

Process by which the clear wine is pumped into an empty container to get rid of unwanted sediment.

RANCIO

Term for the aroma of very old fortified wines and brandies. It is reminiscent of walnut shells and is a sign of supreme quality.

REDUCTION (DEOXIDATION)

The opposite of oxidation. A chemical reaction in airtight conditions. Wines produced reductively are particularly fresh and aromatic.

REFRACTOMETER

Optical precision instrument used to measure the specific gravity of a wine so that its maturity can be assessed.

REMONTAGE

In the production of red wines, the grape juice is pumped over the cap of skins in order to keep the marc in the must so that as much pigment and aroma as possible is released from the skins. (In Australia, a system of rotating fermenters is used.)

RESERVA

A Spanish and Portuguese quality grade for the wines of a particular vintage that have to meet specific requirements—for Spanish reds, minimum aging of 36 months (12 of them in oak barrels), for whites 24 months (including 6 in the barrel). In Portugal, the alcohol content for these wines must be 0.5% above the prescribed minimum levels.

RESIDUAL SUGAR

The sugar not converted to alcohol during fermentation. Produces the natural sweetness of a wine.

REVERSE OSMOSIS

Reverse osmosis is the process of purifying water or other liquids such as fruit juices by passing them through a semi-permeable membrane that filters out unwanted substances. In winemaking, this is a filtering process whereby the must circulates along the filtration membrane, but does not penetrate it. A pressure differential allows only water to get through.

RIDDLING

Called *remuage* in French, it is the process in the → *méthode champenoise* whereby the sediment is shaken to the neck of the bottle for disgorgement.

RISERVA

An Italian quality grade comparable with Spanish → *reserva*.

SEDIMENT

Deposits of tannin and pigments in the bottle that can be separated from the wine by decanting. See also lees.

SEKT

German classified sparkling → *Qualitätswein* that carries an official control number (*Prüfnummer*). In Austria, applies to any sparkling wine. A sparkling *Qualitätswein* in Austria is called *Qualitätssekt*.

SÉLECTION MASSALE

The best vines of a vineyard are selected, in contrast to the cloned selection, where a single seedling is reproduced with genetically identical structure.

SETTLEMENT/DEPOSIT

Natural process that allows undesired solids present in the wine or must to settle slowly on the bottom of the container. See also Filtration.

SILICA (KIESELGUR)

Crystalline form of silicon dioxide [SiO_2] that is used to clarify the wine.

SKIN CONTACT

Macération pelliculaire or *macération préfermentaire*. A process of leaving the pressed grape juice in contact with the skins in the must in order to extract taste elements from the skin. This term is used more for white wines, while for reds the term *cold soak* is used.

SMARAGD (EMERALD)

A category introduced in the Wachau in Austria to designate mature, strong wines. See also *Steinfeder* and *Federspiel*.

SOLERA

System for making fortified wines, especially sherry and madeira, in order to obtain the same quality year after year. The basis is blending wines aged in the barrel. *Solera* is the lowest of a multi-grade series of barrels. The next up is *criadera*, the top one *sobretabla*. For every new sherry the *solera* is taken out and bottled, the bottles being topped up with *criadera* and finished with wines from the *sobretabla*, which are refilled with young wine.

SOMMELIER

French term for wine waiter.

SPARKLING WINE

General term for all carbonated wines, whether natural sparkling or not.

SPÄTLESE

One of the *Prädikate* of German Wine Law, literally "late picked."

SPECIFIC GRAVITY

Expresses the degree of ripeness of the berries. In Germany and Switzerland, it is measured on the Oechsle scale, in Austria on the Klosterneuburg Must Gauge (K.M.W.). In many countries the quality grade of a wine is calculated in terms of the prescribed minimum specific gravity of the must.

SPUMANTE

Italian term for sparkling wine.

STABILIZATION

A condition achieved when a wine has had all the undesired particles, suspension matter and cloudinesses removed, so that it looks clear in the bottle and no gas forms.

STALK SEPARATOR

The machine for plucking the stalks from the grapes before fermentation.

STEEN

South African term for Chenin Blanc, the most widespread grape variety. It serves as the basis for brandy and sherry production.

STEINFEDER

Category of wine in the Wachau region of Austria, designating light, tangy wines. See also *Federspiel* and *Smaragd*.

STRAUßWIRTSCHAFT

A bar in Baden, Franconia, Württemberg and Austria that sells home-grown wine during a defined period each year. A broom is displayed at the entrance to the estate to show when it is available. Light food can be served with the wine. See also *Heuriger*.

SULFUR

Used in winemaking in a variety of ways, e.g. to protect the vines, sterilize wooden barrels, or as a preservative.

SUR LIE (ON THE LEES)

French term used in connection with Muscadet and Gros Plant wines of the Loire. Refers to the practice of leaving the wine on the lees in the barrel over the winter and then bottling it without filtering. The process adds a touch of zest.

TANNIN

A vegetable element in wine that gives it its astringent effect. Important for the aging of red wines. It is especially prominent in young reds, but becomes less marked as the wine ages.

TARTRATES

Crystals deposited on the bottom of a wine bottle, created by the degeneration of the acid in the wine. Not a cause for complaint, as they do not affect the quality of the wine.

TAWNY

For port wines the word 'tawny' indicates that the wine has been aged in wood for several years. Simple tawny ports must spend an average of 7 years in pipes (long wooden vessels). Other categories of tawny include 10-, 20- and 30-year-old tawny port.

TENUTA

Italian term for a wine-growing estate.

TERROIR

In France, an agricultural region or area

whose soil and microclimatic characteristics give its produce its unique features.

TOASTING
A process in barrel-making which gives wine a "toasty" flavor.

TRANSVASIER METHOD
Method of producing sparkling wine in which, as in the traditional Champagne method (→*Méthode champenoise*) the second fermentation takes place inside the bottle. To avoid the ensuing costly and lengthy process to remove the sediment, the bottles are emptied into a pressurised container where the wine is filtered. It is then bottled with the desired dosage and with the help of a counter pressure plant.

TROCKENBEERENAUSLESE (T.B.A.)
One of the *Prädikate* of German Wine Law, literally "selected dried berries." This is the premium German and Austrian sweet wine.

TRUNK SYSTEM
Form of vine training whereby individual canes put forth dozens of buds. Vines are trained into enormous trunks. See also Cultivation systems.

TYPICITÉ (TYPICITY)
A wine tasting term that implies that a wine is typical of its type and *terroir*. It is the character given to it by the site in which it grows.

VARIETAL
Term used for a wine named after the dominant grape variety from which it is made.

V.D.Q.S.
In the French *appellation* system an interim classification between *vin de pays* and *appellation contrôlée*.

VEGETATIVE
A term for wines with unripe, green vegetable overtones, due to inadequate maturation.

VERAISON
A term applied to the intermediate stage of the ripening process where the grapes begin to change from their green state to their colored form.

VERBAND DEUTSCHER PRÄDIKATSWEINGÜTER (V.D.P.)
Registered and abbreviated name for the association of around 200 vintners in Germany known for the high quality of their produce.

VIN DE CALITATE SUPERIOARA CU DENUMIRE DE ORIGINE (V.S.O.)
Romanian designation for superior quality wines, also denoting origin.

VIN DE CALITATE SUPERIOARA CU DENUMIRE DE ORIGINE SI TREPTE DE CALITATE (V.S.O.C.)
Romanian designation for superior quality wines, their origin and degree of quality.

VIN DE GARAGE
A wine produced in only very small quantities but of supreme quality and often sold at top price. The first and most famous Vin de Garage is Château de Valandraud in Saint-Émilion.

VIN DE LIQUEUR
Official name for beverages made from grape must with the fermentation entirely prevented by adding sufficient amounts of ethyl alcohol.

VIN DE MASA/REGIUNE SUPERIOARA (V.S.)
Romanian designation for high quality wines.

VIN DE PAILLE
A strong, sweet white wine whose grapes are dried on straw mats.

VIN DE QUALITÉ PRODUIT DANS DES RÉGIONS DÉTERMINÉES (V.Q.P.R.D.)
General European name for *appellation* wines. In France it includes *Appellation d'Origine Contrôlée* (A.O.C.) and *Vin Délimité de Qualité Supérieure* (V.D.Q.S.).

VIN DE TABLE (V.D.T.)
The simplest category of French wine.

VIN DOUX NATUREL (V.D.N.)
Fortified wine from southern France.

VINE PRUNING
Drastically cutting back the shoots on the vine in order to promote growth and improve the quality.

VINIFICATION
The production of wine from the delivery of the grapes to the winery to the bottling.

VINO DE CALIDAD PRODUCIDO EN UNA REGIÓN DETERMINADA (V.C.P.R.D.)
Spanish term for wines of guaranteed origin (see also *Vin de Qualité Produit dans des Régions Déterminées*, V.Q.P.R.D.); includes *Denominación de Origen* (D.O.) and *Denominación de Origen Calificada* (D.O.Ca.).

VIN SANTO (HOLY WINE)
The classic dessert wine of Tuscany, made of dried grapes, aged oxidatively, dry or with various sugar residues.

VINS DE PLAISIR
Well-made, accessible, easy-drinking wines that do not claim to be high-value.

VINTAGE (MILLÉSIME)
Term for the year in which the grapes for a wine were grown, or more generally the qualities of a particular year relating to the weather and growth cycle of the grapes. Even more generally, as an adjective (millésimé) either refers to a wine for an exceptionally fine year (a vintage wine), or (in the case of champagne) old wine, though not necessarily from a particular year (vintage champagne).

VITIS
Vitis is the name of one of the 50 genera in the botanical family Vitaceae. The genus *Vitis* contains 22 species, including the vine *Vitis vinifera* from which around 8,000 cultivated varieties have been derived.

WATER SHOOT
A vigorous but unproductive shoot growing directly from the trunk.

WEIßHERBST (WHITE AUTUMN)
A rosé made from single grape variety in Germany. This is noted on the label.

WINERY
Used to mean both the winemaking facility and the wine-growing business or estate as a whole.

WINKLER SCALE
A system of viticultural climate classification for California, based on the average temperature. Growing zones are graded into five regions.

YEAST
Micro-organisms. Some of them are capable of making grape juice ferment. See also Pure-yeasting.

YIELD
The amount of wine produced from a grape harvest.

VINTAGES

Assessments of vintages are always only an approximation to the reality. The influence of climate on the varying grape varieties is too diverse, and the influence of microclimates in individual districts or sites too important.

The quality of the vintage is rated by means of stars.

*	poor vintage
**	moderate to good vintage
***	very good vintage
****	outstanding vintage

VINTAGES IN AUSTRALIA

2000**⁻***
High volumes (especially Cabernet Sauvignon and Shiraz), difficult weather conditions for Pinot Noir and white varieties).

1999***
Record volumes, very good quality (e.g. in Coonawarra).

1998***⁻****
Excellent Cabernet Sauvignons and Shiraz, but Chardonnays not always inspiring.

1997**⁻****
Varying from very good (Coonawarra, Barossa) to good (New South Wales).

1996***
Turned out very well particularly in the hotter areas of cultivation.

1995**⁻***
Low volumes but, with some exceptions, good quality.

1994**⁻****

1993**⁻***

1992*⁻***

1991****

1990***
Earlier very good and outstanding vintages: 1989, 1988, 1987, 1986, 1984, 1983, 1982, 1981, 1979, 1976, 1975, 1971, 1966, 1963, 1962.

VINTAGES IN CALIFORNIA

1999**⁻****
Low yield and very diverse qualities. The best Cabernets and Zinfandels have outstanding class.

1998**⁻***
Uneven vintage. Many Chardonnays and Pinot Noirs have potential.

1997**⁻****
High volumes, in part outstanding reds (Cabernet Sauvignon, Zinfandel).

1996**⁻***
Elegant red wines and noteworthy whites.

1995***
Remarkable whites and often very good red wines.

1994****
A great red wine year.

1993**

1992***

1991***⁻****

1990***⁻****

Earlier very good or outstanding vintages: 1987, 1986, 1985, 1984, 1981, 1979, 1978, 1975, 1974, 1971, 1970, 1968, 1966, 1958, 1951, 1946.

VINTAGES IN FRANCE

BORDEAUX

1999**⁻***
A good vintage (especially for Merlot), with some upwardly mobiles.

1998**⁻***
Successful especially in Saint-Émilion and Pomerol-another good Merlot vintage.

1997**
Tends toward early-ripening red wines.

1996***⁻****
Excellent particularly in the Médoc and for white wines.

1995***⁻****
In Saint-Émilion and Pomerol, but particularly good reds also in Pauillac or Graves; notable whites.

1994**⁻***
Good mainly on the right bank (Merlot), with the dry whites tending to the very good.

1993*⁻**
Almost a total write-off for sweet wines, while the red varieties are often only so-so.

1992*
Light wines with no great aging potential.

1991**
Very few interesting wines.

1990****
Great, long-lived wines and fabulous, concentrated Sauternes.

1989****

1988***⁻****

1987*⁻**

1986***⁻****

1985***⁻****

1984*

1983***⁻****

1982****

Earlier very good or outstanding vintages: 1979, 1978, 1975, 1971, 1970, 1967 (Sauternes) 1966, 1964, 1961 (!), 1959, 1955, 1953, 1952, 1949, 1947, 1945, 1937 (Sauternes) 1929, 1928, 1921 (Sauternes), 1900.

BURGUNDY

1999***
High volumes, generally considered very good, also in Beaujolais.

1998***
Consistently good wines.

1997**⁻***
Very good ripe Chardonnays, notable Beaujolais. The other reds tend to be early ripening.

1996****
A great year in every respect for red and white varieties.

1995**⁻****
Numerous very good white wines and mature reds.

1994**
High volumes, but rarely of impressive quality.

1993**⁻****
Slow-maturing, elegant reds. Whites at best good.

1992**⁻***
Early-ripening reds, some very good Chardonnays.

1991*⁻***
Good for Pinot Noirs of the Côte de Nuits, very good for Beaujolais, passable for white wines.

1990****
A great vintage in every respect.

1989***

1988**⁻***

1987*⁻***

1986**

1985***⁻****

1984*

1983 *⁻***

1982**

Earlier very good or outstanding vintages: 1978, 1971, 1969, 1964, 1962, 1961, 1959, 1955, 1953, 1952, 1949, 1948, 1947, 1945.

RHÔNE AND LANGUEDOC-ROUSSILLON

1999***
Good growers produced elegant wines to lay down. The vintage turned out particularly well in the southern Rhône.

1998***
Potentially great vintage, especially in the southern Rhône and Languedoc-Roussillon, but sometimes wines with excessive tannins.

1997**
A sometimes underrated vintage with some elegant reds and whites, especially of the early-ripening varieties.

1996**⁻***
Generally better in the northern Rhône than the south.

1995****
A warm wine year with very good, long-lived wines.

1994**⁻***
Rain during the harvest, but even so generally successful.

1993**⁻***
Very successful in the southern Rhône, and often very good in Languedoc-Roussillon. Not much luck for the northern Rhône.

1992*⁻**
Decent wines at best, and only in the northern Rhône.

1991*–*
Very good mainly in the northern Rhône, also in Languedoc-Roussillon, less so in the southern Rhône.

1990*–****
A great vintage on the Rhône, but not so impressive in Languedoc-Roussillon.

Earlier very good or outstanding vintages: 1989, 1988, 1985, 1983, 1982, 1981, 1979, 1978, 1970, 1967, 1966, 1961, 1959, 1953, 1949, 1945.

VINTAGES IN GERMANY

1999–***
Not the long-awaited vintage of the century, but a plentiful harvest and very successful in some regions (e.g. Saar, Ahr, Franconia).

1998–***
Very good wines in the Palatinate, but only so-so elsewhere (Baden, Württemberg, Franconia). Variable in Mosel-Saar-Ruwer.

1997*–****
A sunny wine year with many Spätlese wines and selections. Particularly successful in the Moselle region, on the Nahe and in the Palatinate, also the Ahr reds.

1996*
Fruity wines worth laying down, without exception.

1995–***
Many Spätlese and selections. Particularly successful in Rheingau and Mosel-Saar-Ruwer.

1994–***
Very good in many areas (Rheingau and Moselle), numerous botrytized wines.

1993*–****

1992–***

1991**

1990**

Earlier very good and outstanding vintages whose best representatives (mainly Riesling) may still be in good condition: 1989, 1988, 1986, 1985, 1983, 1981, 1979, 1976, 1975, 1971, 1964, 1959, 1953, 1949, 1945.

VINTAGES IN ITALY

PIEDMONT

1999*
Generally considered very good, especially for the late-ripening varieties (e.g. Nebbiolo).

1998**
Excellent particularly for red wines.

1997**
Fabulous, concentrated red wines, with very convincing Barolos and Barbarescos.

1996*–****
An excellent red wine vintage.

1995*–****
The first in a series of remarkable red wine vintages, with great Barberas and Nebbiolos.

1994*–
A disappointing vintage.

1993–***

1992*

1991**

1990**

Earlier very good and outstanding vintages: 1989, 1988, 1985, 1982, 1980, 1979, 1978, 1974, 1971, 1970, 1964, 1961, 1958, 1947.

TUSCANY

1999*–****
Very good, elegant red wines.

1998*
Good to very good red wines.

1997**
Outstanding, dense red wines in the top labels.

1996–***
Mostly successful, but few great Chiantis or Brunellos.

1995–****
Very variable quality due to autumn rain.

1994**
Brunello and Vino Nobile turned out better than Chianti.

1993*

1992**

1991**

1990**

Earlier very good to outstanding vintages: 1988, 1986, 1985, 1983, 1982, 1980, 1979, 1978, 1975, 1971, 1970, 1967, 1964, 1961, 1958, 1955, 1945.

VINTAGES IN PORTUGAL

1999–***
Generally considered good to very good.

1998–***
Some good red wines, but not an outstanding year for port.

1997**
The vintage ports look outstanding.

1996–***
Varying quality, with Dão reds turning out best.

1995**
Very good red wines in the Douro region.

1994*
Outstanding port and Madeira vintage.

1993*–

1992*

1991–***

1990**

Earlier very good or outstanding vintages for port: 1985, 1983, 1980, 1977 (!), 1970, 1966, 1963 (!), 1960, 1955, 1950, 1948, 1947, 1945, 1935, 1934, 1931, 1927, 1924, 1922, 1920, 1912, 1908, 1904, 1900.

VINTAGES IN SPAIN

RIOJA

1999–***
Varying qualities, but generally good to very good.

1998–***
Good yields and mostly equally good qualities.

1997**
Very variable, but rarely truly inspiring.

1996*–****
Late-harvesting growers produced great wines.

1995**
Relatively low yields, but excellent, long-lived wines.

1994**
A hot year produced superb wines.

1993–***

1992*

1991*

1990*

Earlier very good or outstanding vintages: 1989, 1988, 1987, 1985, 1982, 1981, 1978, 1976, 1975, 1973, 1970, 1968, 1964 (!), 1959, 1952.

RIBERA DEL DUERO

1999*
High volumes, very good quality.

1998*
Low volumes because of hail damage, but many good red wines.

1997**
Rarely inspiring, but notable wines do occur.

1996**
The third top-quality vintage in a row, producing mature, long-lived wines.

1995**
Great red wines from perhaps the best vintage of the century.

1994**
Many remarkable wines, and for many producers as good a year as 1995, presumably long-lived.

1993**

1992**

1991*–****

1990–***

Earlier very good or outstanding vintages: 1989, 1987, 1986, 1985, 1983, 1982, 1981, 1978, 1974, 1970, 1964.

VINTAGES IN SOUTH AFRICA

2000*
Despite the very dry weather, successful white and red wines.

1999*–*
A warm vintage with mature wines.

1998*–****
Excellent, long-maturing red wines.

1997–****
Fabulous red wines, but also less successful varieties. A vintage for the courageous grower.

1996
A cool year with heterogeneous quality.

1995**
Mature red wines to lay down.

1994*

1993*

1992*

1991**

1990–***

Earlier very good or outstanding vintages: 1989, 1988, 1987, 1986, 1984.

BIBLIOGRAPHY

ADAMS, L.
The Wines of America. New York 1990

AINSWORTH, JIM
The Mitchell Beazley Red Wine Guide. London 1999

ALLEN, MAX
Crush—The New Australian Wine Book. London 2000

ALLEN, MAX
New World of Wine. London 1999

AMERICAN EXPRESS TRAVEL GUIDES
San Francisco and the Wine Regions. London and New York 1992

ANDERSON, BURTON
The Wine Atlas of Italy. London and New York 1990

ASHLEY, MAUREEN
Touring in Wine Country: Tuscany;Touring in Wine Country: Northwest Italy. 1996

BECKETT, FIONA
Wine Uncorked. London 1999

BELFRAGE, N.
Barolo to Valpolicella-The Wines of Northern Italy. London and New York 1999

BERRY, E.
The Wine of Alsace: A Buyer's Guide. London 1989

BERRY, E.
The Wines of Languedoc-Roussillon. London 1992

BROADBENT, MICHAEL
Michael Broadbent's Wine Notes. London 1994

BROADBENT, MICHAEL
My Favourite Wines. London 1994

BROOK, STEPHEN
A Century of Wine: The Story of a Wine Revolution. London 2000

BROOK, STEPHEN
Sauternes and Other Sweet Wines of Bordeaux. London 1995

BROOK, STEPHEN
Sauvignon Blanc and Sémillon. London 1992

BROOK, STEPHEN
The Wines of Germany. London 2003

BURROUGHS, DAVID
Wine Regions of the World. London 1988; *The New Wine Companion*. London 1988

CASS, BRUCE/JANCIS ROBINSON (EDS.)
Oxford Companion to the Wines of North America. Oxford and New York 2000

CATHIE, KYLE
The Wine Experience. London 2000

CERNELLI, DANIELE/MARCO SABELLICO
A Complete Guide to Italian Wine. London 2000

CLARKE, OZ
Introducing Wine. Little Brown. New York 2000

CLARKE, OZ
Oz Clarke's Pocket Wine Guide 2004. London 2003

CLARKE, OZ
Oz Clarke's Wine Atlas. London 2002

CLARKE, OZ/RAND, MARGARET
Grapes & Wines. London 2001

COATES, CLIVE
An Encyclopedia of The Wines and Domaines of France. Berkeley and Los Angeles 2000

COATES, CLIVE
Cote d'Or: A Celebration of the Greatest Wines of Burgundy. Berkeley and Los Angeles 1997

COATES, CLIVE
Grands Vins. London 1994

COUVREUR, DOMINIQUE/A. GERBELLE
Vins et Vignobles en France. Paris 1998

COX, JILL
Australian Wine with Food. Ashbourne 1990

DUIJKER, H./M. BROADBENT
The Bordeaux Atlas. London 1997

DUIJKER, HUBRECHT
Touring in Wine Country: Alsace. London 1996; *Touring in Wine Country: Bordeaux*. London 1996; *Touring in Wine Country: Burgundy*. London 1996; *Touring in Wine Country: The Loire*. London 1997; *Touring in Wine Country: Provence*. London 1998

DUIJKER, HUBRECHT
The Wines of Rioja. London 1987

DUIJKER, HUBRECHT
The Wine Atlas of Spain. London 1992

FAITH, N.
The Winemasters. London 1998

FAITH, NICHOLAS
Australia's Liquid Gold. London 2002

FIELDEN, CHRISTOPHER
The Wines of Argentina, Chile and Latin America. London 2001

FLOWER, RAYMOND
Chianti: The Land, the People and the Wine. London 1988

FOULKES, CHRISTOPHER (HG.)
Larousse Encyclopedia of Wine. Paris 2001

FRIEDRICH, J.A.
Wine and Food Guide to the Loire. London and New York 1997

GAYOTT, A.
Guide to the Best Wineries of North America. New York 1993

GEORGE, ROSEMARY
Chianti and the Wines of Tuscany.London 1990

GEORGE, ROSEMARY
French Country Wines. London 1990

GLUCK, MALCOLM
The Sensational Liquid: A Guide to Wine Tasting. London 1999

GLUCKSTERN, WILLIE
The Wine Avenger. New York 1998

GOOLDEN, JILL
The Taste of Wine. London 1990

HALLIDAY, JAMES
Australian Wine Companion. London 2004

HALLIDAY, JAMES
An Introduction to Australian Wine. Pymble 1992

HALLIDAY, JAMES
Atlas of Australian and New Zealand Wine. Sydney 1998

HALLIDAY, JAMES
Classic Wines of Australia and New Zealand. Sydney 2002

HANSON, ANTHONY
Burgundy. London 2003

HUGHES, D./P. HANDS
Complete Book of South African Wine. Cape Town 1988

ILAND, PATRICK/GAGO, PETER
Australian Wine. Adelaide 2002

IRVINE, R./W. CLORE
The Wine Project. Vashon, Washington 1997

JAMIESON, IAN
German Wines. London 1991

JEFFS, JULIAN
Sherry. London 1992

JOHNSON, HUGH
Hugh Johnson's Modern Encyclopedia of Wine. Simon & Schuster Books, U.S.A. 1998

JOHNSON, HUGH
Hugh Johnson's Pocket Winebook 2004. London 2003

JOHNSON, HUGH
Hugh Johnson's Wine Companion. London 2003

JOHNSON, HUGH
The Story of Wine. London and New York 1989

JOHNSON, HUGH
Wine. London 1997

JOHNSON, HUGH
How to Enjoy Wine. London 1999

JOHNSON, HUGH
Tuscany and its Wines. London 2000

JOHNSON, HUGH/HALLIDAY, JAMES
The Art and Science of Wine. London and New York 1994

JOHNSON, HUGH/ROBINSON, JANCIS
The World Atlas of Wine. 5th edition, London 2001

JOSEPH, ROBERT
Sunday Telegraph Good Wine Guide. London 1999

JOSEPH, ROBERT
The Essential Guide to Good Wine. London 1990

JUKES, MATTHEW
Wine: Everything You Ever Wanted to Know About Wine But Were Afraid to Ask. London 1999

KING, ALICE
Atlas of Wine. London 1990; *Enjoying Wine.* London 1990

LAMBERT-GOCS, MILES
The Wines of Greece. London 1990

LAPSLEY, JAMES T.
Bottled Poetry: Napa Winemaking from Prohibition to the Modern Era. Berkeley, California 1996

LAROUSSE WINE
Dictionary of Vine and Wine. Paris 1999

LAUBE, JAMES
California Wine. Wine Spectator Press, New York 2000

LEITH, PRUE
Leith's Guide to Wine. London 1995

LIVINGSTONE-LEARMOUTH, J.
The Wines of the Rhône. London 1992

MATTHEWS, PATRICK
Real Wine. London 2000

MAYSON, R.
Portugal's Wines and Winemakers. San Francisco 1998

MCWHIRTER, KATHRYN/METCALFE, CHARLES
The Wine of Spain and Portugal. London 1988

MEREDITH, T.J.
Northwest Wine. Kirkland, Washington 1990

MO, YAN
The Republic of Wine. London 2000

MUSCATINE, D./M.A. AMERINE/ B. THOMPSON (EDS.)
The University of California/Sotheby Book of California Wine. Berkeley, California 1984

NORMAN, REMINGTON
The Great Domaines of Burgundy. London 1996

NORMAN, REMINGTON
Rhône Renaissance. London 1995

PARKER, ROBERT M. JR.
Bordeaux: A Comprehensive Guide to the Wines Produced from 1961–1997. New York 1998

PARKER, ROBERT M. JR.
A Consumer's Guide to the World's Finest Wines. New York 2003

PARKER, ROBERT M. JR.
Wines of Burgundy. New York 1990

PARKER, ROBERT M. JR.
Wines of the Rhone Valley. New York 1997

PARKER, ROBERT M. JR.
Parker's Wine Buyer's Guide. 6th edition, New York 2002

PENNING-ROWSELL, EDMUND C.
The Wines of Bordeaux. London 1989

PEPPERCORN, DAVID
Bordeaux. London 1991

PEYNAUD, ÉMILE
The Taste of Wine: The Art and Science of Wine Appreciation. New York 1996

PHILLIPS, ROD
A Short History of Wine. London 2000

PHILPOTT, DON
The Wine and Food of Bulgaria. London 1989

PIGOTT, STUART
The Mosel and Rheingau: Including the Ahr, Nahe and Pfalz. London 1997

PIGOTT, STUART
Riesling. London and New York 1991

PINNEY, THOMAS
A History of Wine in America from Beginnings to Prohibition. Berkeley, California 1989

PLATTER, JOHN
South African Wine Guide 1996. Antique Collectors Club, U.S.A. 1996

RADFORD, JOHN/STEPHEN BROOK
Aperitif and Dessert Wine. London 2000

READ, JAN
The Wine and Food of Spain. London 1987

RIBEREAU-GAYON, P. (ED.)
The Wines and Vineyards of France: A Complete Atlas and Guide. London and New York 1990

ROBINSON, JANCIS
Jancis Robinson's Guide to Wine Grapes. Oxford and New York 1996

ROBINSON, JANCIS
The Oxford Companion to Wine. Oxford 1999

ROBINSON, JANCIS
Vines, Grapes and Wines. London 1997

ROBINSON, JANCIS
Jancis Robinson's Wine Course. London 1999

ROSSO, GAMBERO
Guide to Italian Wine. London 2000

SCHOONMAKER, FRANK
Frank Schoonmaker's Encyclopedia of Wine. London 1979

SCHUSTER, MICHAEL
Understanding Wine. London 1989

SCHUSTER, MICHAEL
Essential Winetasting: The Complete Wine Tasting Course. London 2000

SKELTON, STEPHEN
The Wines of Britain and Ireland. London 2001

SLOAN, JOHN C.
The Surprising Wines of Switzerland: A Practical Guide to Switzerland's Best Kept Secret. London 1995

SPURRIER, STEVEN
Académie du Vin Wine Course. London 1994

STEIMAN, HARVEY
Essentials of Wine. Wine Spectator Press, New York 2000

STEVENSON, TOM
The New Sotheby's World Wine Encyclopedia. 1997

STEVENSON, TOM
Millennium Champagne and Sparkling Wine Guide 2000. London 1999

STEVENSON, TOM
The Wines of Alsace. London 1993

THOMPSON, BOB
Wine Atlas of California. London and New York 1993

VOSS, ROGER
Food and Wine of France. London 1993

WALDIN, MONTY
Wines of South America. London 2003

WALTON, STUART/ BRIAN GLOVER
The Ultimate Encyclopedia of Wine, Beer, Spirits and Liquers. London 1998

WATSON, JEREMY
The New & Classical Wines of Spain. Barcelona 2002

WHICH? WINE GUIDE
London 1981–

WILLIAMS, V.
The Penguin Good New Zealand Wine Guide. London, Auckland, New York 2000

WINE SPECTATOR
Wine Spectator's Pocket Guide to Wine. Wine Spectator Press, New York 2000

WINE SPECTATOR
Wine Spectator's Ultimate Guide to Buying Wine. 7th edition, New York 2000

WRIGHT, HILARY
Water into Wine: A Wine Lover's Cruise Through the Vineyards. London 1996

SUBJECT INDEX

Place Index

Château Calon-Ségur 244, 246
Château Cos d'Estournel 246
Château Grillet 291
Château-Chalon 177, 178, 179
Châteaubourg 288
Châteaugay 223
Châteaumeillant 223
Châteauneuf 294, 296, 297
Châteauneuf-du-Pape 155, 286, 288, 289, 290, 291, 296, 297, 310, 320
Châtillonais 182, 205
Chaudefonds-sur-Layon 226
Chaume 225, 226, 227
Chavanay 289
Chaves 658
Checheno-Ingush 718
Chénas 213, 214
Chenôvea 191
Cherasco 358
Chiana Valley 418
Chianti 337, 340, 341, 342, 400, 401, 402, 404, 405, 406, 407, 408, 409, 410, 411, 412, 413, 414, 415, 416, 418, 419, 420, 423, 424, 425
Chiasso 535
Chichée 189
Chignin 299
Chimbarongo 850
Chinon 217, 228, 229
Chios 731
Chiroubles 213, 215
Chisinau 716
Chiuro 373
Chodschand 783
Chorey-lès-Beaune 195, 202, 203
Christchurch 885
Chtauradas 741
Chusclan 291, 292
Cigales 604, 606, 612
Cinqueterre 368
Cintruénigo 601
Cirò 438, 439
Cirò Marina 439
Cirons 254, 259
Clare 857, 861, 864, 873, 874, 876, 877, 879
Clare Valley 857, 861, 864, 874, 876, 877, 879
Clarksburg 832
Claro 849, 850
Clear Lake 815
Clessé 209
Clos des Grives 289
Cluny 180
Coal River Valley 881
Cocconato 355
Cochem 462
Cocumont 280
Coimbra 661, 671
Colares 651, 676
Colchagua 849, 850, 851
Cold Creek 798, 800
Coldstream 857, 858, 873
Colli Asolani 395
Colli Berici 390, 392, 393
Colli di Luni 369, 421
Colli Euganei 390, 392, 393
Colli Orientali del Friuli 386
Colli Tortonesi 366
Colline Novaresi 350, 351
Colline Pisano 420
Collio 386, 387, 388, 389
Collio Goriziano 386
Collioure 329, 332, 333

Colmar 174
Colombier 529
Columbia River 798, 800, 802
Columbia Valley 795, 798, 799
Comblanchien 190
Conca d'Oro 411, 412
Conca de Barberá 587
Condado de Huelva 633, 635
Condrieu 286, 287, 288, 289, 291
Conegliano 392
Conne de Labarde 280
Conques 275
Constantia 752, 754, 758, 759, 760, 761, 762
Coonawarra 857, 861, 862, 863, 872, 874, 875, 876, 877
Copertino 435
Corbans 884, 885, 887
Corbières 324, 325, 326, 327, 328, 333
Cordinhã 671
Córdoba 572, 579, 632, 633, 634
Cordon del Plata 843
Corfu 730
Corgo 663
Corgoloin 190, 191
Corinth 729
Cormondrèche 529
Cormòns 386, 389
Cornas 288, 289, 291
Corsica 154, 155, 300, 314, 315
Cortaillod 528, 529
Cortefranca 372
Corteglia 535
Coruche 677
Corvino San Quirico 373
Cos d'Estournel 244, 246
Cosenza 439
Cossato 350
Costa Blanca 627
Costa Brava 586, 591
Coste della Sesia 350, 351
Costers del Segre 579, 583, 587, 590, 591
Costières du Gard 285
Costigliole d'Asti 355
Côte Chalonnaise 181, 182, 185, 204, 205, 208
Côte d'Azur 300, 303
Côte d'Or 154, 158, 180, 181, 182, 183, 197, 201, 204, 205, 206, 208, 210
Côte de Beaune 180, 182, 185, 187, 194, 196, 197, 198, 200, 201, 204
Côte de Brouilly 213, 215
Côte de Nuits 180, 182, 190, 191, 196, 197, 198, 201
Côte de Nuits-Villages 191
Côte de Sézanne 160
Côte des Bar 160
Côte des Blancs 160, 161
Côte Roannaise 218, 223
Côte Rôtie 284, 285, 287, 288, 289, 291
Coteaux d'Aix-en-Provence 304, 305, 306, 307
Coteaux d'Ancenis 220
Coteaux d'Utique 748
Coteaux de l'Aubance 224, 226, 227
Coteaux de la Loire 220
Coteaux de Mascara 749
Coteaux de Pierrevert 309
Coteaux de Tébourba 748
Coteaux de Tlemcem 749

Coteaux de Zaccar 749
Coteaux du Giennois 231
Coteaux du Languedoc 320, 321, 326, 327
Coteaux du Layon 218, 225, 226, 227
Coteaux du Lyonnais 213
Coteaux du Tricastin 285, 291, 295
Coteaux Varois 308, 313
Côtes d'Auvergne 218, 223
Côtes d'Auxerre 182, 189
Côtes de Bergerac 275, 276, 280
Côtes de Bordeaux Saint-Macaire 270
Côtes de Bourg 269
Côtes de Castillon 261, 265, 268, 269
Côtes de Forez 218
Côtes de Francs 261, 268, 269
Côtes de Millau 275
Côtes de Montravel 274, 276
Côtes de Nuits 182, 201
Côtes de Provence 304, 305, 306, 308, 309, 312, 313
Côtes du Brulhois 282
Côtes du Duras 274
Côtes du Jura 177, 178, 179
Côtes du Marmandais 276, 280
Côtes du Rhône 284, 285, 287, 288, 289, 290, 291, 292, 294, 295, 297
Côtes du Rhône Villages 287, 290, 291
Côtes du Roussillon 328, 332, 333
Côtes du Ventoux 285, 289, 294
Côtes Noires 322
Côtes-de-Bergerac 274
Côtes-de-Castillon 237
Côtes-de-Saint-Mont 275
Côte-Saint-Jacques 189
Couchey 191
Couchois 182
Courtenon 166
Courthézon 296, 297
Cova da Beira 675
Cowaramup 880
Cowra 861, 868, 869, 872
Cravant-les-Coteaux 229
Crèches-sur-Saône 215
Créon 270, 271
Crépy 298
Cressier 528
Crozes-Hermitage 285, 288, 291
Cru du Beaujolais 213
Cruz de Piedra 843, 845
Cruzille 209
Cuba 833
Cully 530, 531
Cuneo 348, 356, 357
Cupertino 831
Cuppacup 859
Curicó 846, 849, 850, 851
Curvos 659

Dafnes 729
Dagestan 718
Dahlenheim 173
Dahra 749
Dalmatia 714
Damazan 280
Dambach-la-Ville 173
Dão 647, 648, 650, 651, 652, 665, 671, 672, 673, 675, 677, 679, 682
Darmós 590
Dart Valley 569

Davayé 209
Davis 803, 811, 812, 818, 827, 831, 832, 833
Dayton 806
Dealul Mare 712, 713
Deccan-Plateau 782
Deer Park 825
Deidesheim 485, 492, 495, 496, 497, 515
Delaware River 797
Denman 872
Dentelles du Montmirail 290, 293
Dernau 467, 468, 469
Derwent River 881
Dettelbach 511, 512
Deutsch-Schützen 560, 561
Deutschkreutz 560
Devon 569
Devon Valley 764
Dezenzano del Garda 373
Diamond Mountain 822
Diano Castello 369
Diano d'Alba 357, 358
Dienheim 484
Dijon 180
Dinaric Alps 694
Diois 285, 291
Dnjestr 716
Dobrovo 707
Dogliani 349, 357
Dolomites 374
Donatella 424
Donau 536, 538, 540, 541, 545, 546, 547, 694, 695, 708, 716
Dora Baltea 346, 347
Dordogne 232, 236, 260, 261, 262, 264, 268, 270, 272, 276
Dorking 567, 569
Dorset 568
Dorsheim 478
Dos Barrios 623
Douglas River 773, 776
Douro 647, 648, 650, 652, 658, 660, 661, 662, 663, 665, 666, 668, 669, 671, 675, 677, 680, 681
Downland 568, 569
Draguignan 308
Dresden 498, 517
Drôme 287, 291, 292, 295
Drumborg 857
Dry Creek Valley 792, 817, 818, 819, 831
Du-Toitskloof-Berge 772, 773
Duero 605, 606, 607, 612, 613
Duhort-Bachen 280
Duino-Aurisina 389
Dunavksa Raunina 708
Dundee 804, 806, 807
Durance 304
Durbach 499, 503
Durban 325
Durbanville 773, 776
Dürnstein 542
Dürnstein-Oberloiben 543
Dürnstein-Unterloiben 542
Duttweiler 496

East Anglia 568
East Sussex 567, 568
Eberbach 449, 473, 475, 476, 477
Ebro 587, 589, 594, 595, 602
Echézeaux 192
Echichens 531
Echveronne 201

Index of Producers and Estates

Henri Maire 176
Henry of Pelham 795
Henschke 857, 874, 876
Herbert Meßmer 497
Herdade do Esporão 652, 680, 681
Herdade do Mouchão 681
Herederos de Argüeso 641
Hermann Dönnhoff 479
Hermann Schwarzenbach 527
Hermannshof 797
Heron Hill 796
Hessische Staatsweingüter 483, 515
Heymann-Löwenstein 464
Hijos de Rainera Perez Marin 641
Hillcrest Winery 803
Hillebrand 795
Hofkellerei des Fürsten von
  Liechtenstein 527
Honeywood Winery 803
Hospices de Beaune 180, 198, 199
Houghton 857, 878, 880
Howard Park 880
Huadong 783
Hugel 169, 171, 174
Humberto Canale 844, 845
Hungarovin 697, 700
Hunter's 877
Hupfeld 476

Il Carpino 389
Il Palazzone 427
Imesch Vins 533
Inglenook 791, 820, 826
Inniskillin 794, 795
Isabel Estate 887
Isole e Olena 413
István Szepsy 704
Itsasmendi 595

J. H. Hofstätter 380, 384
J. J. Adeneuer 469
J. M. Fonseca 652, 678
J. P. Vinhos 679
J. W. Burmester & Ca 668
J.P. Bredell 764
Jackson Estate 885
Jacobsdal Estate 764
Jacques Puffeney 179
Jacques Selosse 167
Jacques Tissot 179
Jacquesson 166
Jamek 542
Jean Durup 188
Jean León 590
Jean Macle 179
Jean-François Chevalley 531
Jean-Louis Chave 288
Jean-Louis Denois 327
Jean-Luc Colombo 288
Jean-Marc Brocard 188
Jean-Michel Gérin 289
Jean-Paul & Jean-Luc Jamet 289
Jean-Paul Droin 188
Jean-Paul Schmitt 175
Jim Barry 874, 876
João Portugal Ramos 677, 679,
  681
Joh. Jos. Prüm 464
Johann Ruck 513
Johanneshof, J. & V. Reinisch 549
Johanniterkeller Martin Hubacher
  529
Jordan 764
José Maria da Fonseca 678, 679
Josef Biffar 496
Josef Gager 560
Josef Högl 542
Josef Leberl 561
Josef Niedermayr 385

Josef Störrlein 513
Josep Anguera Beyme 591
Joseph Faiveley 195
Joseph Phelps Vineyards 825
Josh Jensens Calera Winery 828
Josko Gravner 389
Josmeyer 175
Julia Roch e Hijos 628
Juliusspital 512, 514, 515

K. F. Groebe 484
Kanonkop 763, 764, 765
Karl Alphart 549
Karl H. Johner 502
Karl Lagler 543
Karlsmühle 457, 464
Karthäuserhof 457, 464
Kathryn Kennedy Winery 830
Kavaklidere 738, 739
Kellerei Iambol 710
Kellerei Massandra 718
Kellerei Shumen 710
Kellerei Suhindol 710
Kellerei Vinvico 713
Kellerei Woodbridge 826
Kellereigenossenschaft Bozen 385
Kellereigenossenschaft Girlan 385
Kellereigenossenschaft Kurtatsch
  385
Ken Forrester 764
Kendall-Jackson 815, 828
Keo 735
Kiona 801
Kistler Vineyards 818
Klawer 773
Klein Constantia 760
Kloofzicht 773
Knapp 796
Knappstein 876
Knappstein Lenswood Vineyards
  876
Knipser 494, 497
Koehler-Ruprecht 497
Konzelmann Winery 795
Krug 157, 160, 163, 166, 167
Kruger-Rumpff 479
Krutzler 560
Ksara 741
Kühling-Gillot 484, 485
Kumeu River 884, 886
Kupferberg-Racke 515
Kutman 738, 739
Kyowa Hakko Kogyo 785

L. Mawby 797
L. Roederer 167
L'Avenir Estate 764
La Agricola 843, 845
La Caniette 399
La Chablisienne 188
La Mission Haut-Brion 252, 253
La Motte 770, 771
La Provence 770
La Réméjeanne 294
La Rioja Alta 599
La Scolca 366, 367
La Sirena 823
La Spinetta-Rivetti 353
La Stoppa 397
La Tenaglia 355
La Tosa – Pizzamiglio 397
La Valentina 433
La Vis 384
Lackner-Tinnacher 561
Lämmlin-Schindler 503
Lanari 399
Landesweingut Kloster Pforta 515,
  517, 518
Lane Tanner Winery 831

Langguth Erben 515
Lanson 166
Larios 635
Laurel Glen 818
Laurent & Dominique Courbis
  288
Laurent Martray 215
Laurent-Perrier 161, 166
Le Cinciole 412
L'Ecole No. 41 801
Le Vigne di Zamò 389
Leasingham 876
Leeuwin Estate 864, 879, 880
Lehmann 518
Lenz 796
Leo Alzinger 542
Leonetti Cellar 800
Leonildo Pieropan 393
Leopold Breyer 547
Les Bourgeois 797
Les Caves des Hautes-Côtes 201
Les Caves du Sieur d'Arques 323
Les Chemins de Bassac 326
Les Domaines de Vinsmoselle 564,
  565
Les Maîtres Vignerons de Saint-
  Tropez 313
L'Étoile 333
Les Vignerons Beaumes-de-Venise
  295
Les Vignerons du Buzet 280
Les Vignerons du Pays Basque 281
Les Vins de Vienne 289
Librandi 439
Limerick Lane 818
Lindemans 864, 871, 872, 875
Linton Park 773
Lisini 424
Livernano 413
Livio Felluga 389
Livon 389
Loel 735
López García 634
López Hermanos 634, 635
L'Ormarins 771
Louis Bovard 531
Louis Chèze 288
Louis Guntrum 484
Louis Jadot 201, 215
Louis M. Martini 820
Louis Magnin 299
Louis Roederer 166, 167
Louis Vuitton 157, 166
Louis Vuitton Moët Hennessy 157
Luc Massy 531
Luciano Sandrone 365
Ludwig Ehn 542
Ludwig Hiedler 542
Luigi Ferrando & Figlio 351
Luis Felipe Edwards 849
Luis Pato 671
Lützkendorf 517, 518
Lutzville 773

M. Chapoutier 288
Maculan 393, 394
Maison André Delorme 208
Maison Antonin Rodet 208
Maison Auvigne 209
Maison Bouchard Père & Fils 203
Maison Bouvet-Ladoubay 227
Maison Champy 203
Maison Chartron et Trébuchet
  203
Maison Joseph Drouhin 203
Maison Louis Jadot 203
Maison Olivier Leflaive 203
Maison Verget 209
Manfred Biegler 549

Manincor 385
Manns Wine 785
Mantlerhof 543
Manuel Manzaneque 623
Marc Kreydenweiss 175, 223
Marcassin 819
Marcel Deiss 174
Marcel Lapierre 215
Marchesi Alfieri 355
Marchesi Antinori 411, 413, 420,
  429, 435
Marchesi Frescobaldi 413, 423
Marco de Bartoli – Vecchio Sam-
  peri 445
Marco Polo Winery 781
Maria de Fátima Teixeira Ribeiro
  Silva 675
Maria Donata Bianchi 369
Marie-Thérèse Chappaz 533
Mario Schiopetto 389
Marne & Champagne 166
Marqués de Cacéres 599
Marqués de Griñon 623
Marsovin 747
Martha und Daniel Gantenbein
  527
Martín Códax 619
Martin Göbel 512
Martina & Dr. Randolf Kauer 471
Martinborough Vineyard 884, 886
Martini & Rossi 852
Marufuji 785
Mas Amiel 331, 333
Mas Champart 327
Mas de Daumas-Gassac 327
Mas de la Dame 307
Mas de Libian 295
Mas Estela 591
Mas Jullien 319, 327
Mas Martinet Viticultors 591
Mas Que Vinos 623
Mas Sainte-Berthe 307
Masi/Boscaini 393
Masseria Monaci 435
Mathias Bastian 565
Matteo Coreggia 357
Matthew Cellars 800
Mauro Ortelli 535
Mauro Veglio 365
Maximin Grünhaus 457, 464
McCrea Cellars 800
McDonald Winery 884
McWilliams 872
Meerendal 773
Meerlust 765
Melco-Kellerei 781
Menger-Krug 485, 515
Mercian Katsunuma Winery 785
Meridiana 747
Meyer-Fonné 175
Meyer-Näkel 468, 469
Miani – Enzo Pontoni 389
Michel Laroche 189
Michel Torino 844
Michel-Pfannebecker 485
Michele Chiarlo 364
Michele Satta 425
Miguel Calatayud 625
Miguel Torres 582, 591
Millbrook 796
Mission Hill 795
Mitchelton Wines 870, 873
Moccagatta 365, 367
Moët & Chandon 157, 161, 166,
  852, 853
Monfalletto-Cordero di Monte-
  zemolo 365
Mons Ruber 773
Mont du Toit 773, 777

PICTURE CREDITS

Acknowledgements

This book could never have been produced without the understanding and cooperation of growers, wine shippers and viticultural organizations in every wine-growing country. Our sincere gratitude is due to all of them.

We should also like to thank the following people, who have given advice and practical assistance in the production of the book: Erich Andrey, Lingerz; Javier Ausás, Penafiel; Marie-Pierre Bories, Villeneuve-de-la-Rivière; Jim Budd, London; Ray and Emiko Kaufman, Sonoma; Heinz Hebeisen, Madrid; Andreas Keller, Zürich; Martin Kössler, Nuremberg; Perta Mayer, Karlsruhe; Andreas März, Lamporecchio; Victor Rodríguez, Madrid; Alejandra Schmedes, Haro; Christina Tierno, Roa de Duero; Alexandre Wagner, Paris

Also Anne Marbot, C.I.V.C.; Hazel Murphy, Wine of Australia; Katharine O'Callaghan, New Zealand Wine; Françoise Peretti, Wine of Argentina; Sue Pike, Wines of Chile; Jean-Charles Servant, B.I.V.B.; Riette Steyn, Swasea; Julia Trustram-Eve, English Wine Producers; Laurent Overmans, our food stylists and Pamela Bober, Mareile Busse, Ina Kalvelage, Stefanie Rödiger and Claudia Voges for tireless commitment.